Lecture Notes in Computer Science 6247

Commenced Publication in 1973
Founding and Former Series Editors:
Gerhard Goos, Juris Hartmanis, and Jan van Leeuwen

Advanced Research in Computing and Software Science

Subline of Lectures Notes in Computer Science

Anuj Dawar   Helmut Veith (Eds.)

Computer Science Logic

24th International Workshop, CSL 2010
19th Annual Conference of the EACSL
Brno, Czech Republic, August 23-27, 2010
Proceedings

 Springer

Volume Editors

Anuj Dawar
University of Cambridge Computer Laboratory
15 J.J. Thomson Avenue, Cambridge, CB3 0FD, UK
E-mail: anuj.dawar@cl.cam.ac.uk

Helmut Veith
Vienna University of Technology
Formal Methods in Systems Engineering
Favoritenstr. 9-11, 1040 Vienna, Austria
E-mail: veith@forsyte.tuwien.ac.at

Library of Congress Control Number: 2010932191

CR Subject Classification (1998): F.3, F.4.1, D.3, D.2, F.4, F.1

LNCS Sublibrary: SL 1 – Theoretical Computer Science and General Issues

ISSN   0302-9743
ISBN-10   3-642-15204-X Springer Berlin Heidelberg New York
ISBN-13   978-3-642-15204-7 Springer Berlin Heidelberg New York

springer.com

© Springer-Verlag Berlin Heidelberg 2010
Printed in Germany

Typesetting: Camera-ready by author, data conversion by Scientific Publishing Services, Chennai, India
Printed on acid-free paper   06/3180   5 4 3 2 1 0

Preface

The annual conference of the European Association for Computer Science Logic (EACSL), CSL 2010, was held in Brno (Czech Republic), August 23–27, 2010. The conference started as a series of international workshops on Computer Science Logic, and then at its sixth meeting became the Annual Conference of the EACSL. This conference was the 24th meeting and 19th EACSL conference; it was organized at the Faculty of Informatics, Masaryk University, Brno.

In 2010, CSL and the 35th International Symposium on Mathematical Foundations of Computer Science (MFCS 2010) were federated and organized in parallel at the same place. The technical program and proceedings of MFCS 2010 and CSL 2010 were prepared independently. The federated MFCS and CSL 2010 conference had five common plenary sessions and common social events for all participants. The common plenary speakers were David Basin (Zürich), Herbert Edelsbrunner (Klosterneuburg), Erich Grädel (Aachen), Bojan Mohar (Burnaby, Ljubljana), and Joseph Sifakis (Grenoble). Invited papers by David Basin and Erich Grädel were included in the proceedings of CSL. In addition, CSL 2010 had five invited speakers, namely, Peter O'Hearn (London), Jan Krajicek (Prague), Andrei Krokhin (Durham), Andrey Rybalchenko (Munich), and Viktor Kuncak (Lausanne).

In response to the call for papers, a total of 122 abstracts were registered and 103 of these were followed by full papers submitted to CSL 2010. The Programme Committee selected 33 papers for presentation at the conference and publication in these proceedings. Each paper was reviewed by at least four members of the Programme Committee. In the call for papers, authors were encouraged to include a well written introduction. One of the four Programme Committee members for each paper was assigned as a "non-expert reviewer" whose main task was to assess accessibility of the introduction to the computer science logic community at large.

The federated MFCS and CSL 2010 symposium was accompanied by the following satellite workshops on more specialized topics:

- *Program Extraction and Constructive Proofs / Classical Logic and Computation: Joint Workshop in Honor of Helmut Schwichtenberg*, organized by Steffen van Bakel, Stefano Berardi, Ulrich Berger, Hannes Diener, Monika Seisenberger, and Peter Schuster
- *Randomized and Quantum Computation*, organized by Rūsiņš Freivalds
- *Workshop on Fixed Points in Computer Science (FICS)*, organized by Zoltán Ésik and Luigi Santocanale
- *Young Researchers Forum*, organized by Jan Strejček
- *Theory and Algorithmic Aspects of Graph Crossing Number*, organized by Drago Bokal, Petr Hliněný, and Gelasio Salazar
- *YuriFest: Symposium on Logic in Computer Science Celebrating Yuri Gurevich's 70th Birthday*, organized by Nachum Dershowitz

- *International Workshop on Reachability Problems*, organized by Igor Potapov and Antonín Kučera
- *Games and Probabilistic Models in Formal Verification*, organized by Tomáš Brázdil and Krishnendu Chatterjee
- *Mathematical Foundations of Fuzzy Logics*, organized by Agata Ciabattoni
- *International Workshop on Categorical Logic*, organized by Jiří Rosický
- *Logic, Combinatorics and Computation*, organized by Bruno Courcelle, Petr Hliněný, and Johann A. Makowsky
- *Parametrized Complexity of Computational Reasoning*, organized by Stefan Szeider

We sincerely thank the Programme Committee and all of the referees for their help in reviewing the papers. We also thank the local organizers for their help in the organization of the conference and the smooth collaboration with MFCS, in particular Tony Kucera and Jan Bouda. The conference received support from the *European Research Consortium in Informatics and Mathematics (ERCIM)* and the Czech national research center *Institute for Theoretical Computer Science (ITI)*. We are grateful to these institutions for their sponsorship.

August 2010   Anuj Dawar
                                                                             Helmut Veith

Conference Organization

Programme Committee

Isolde Adler
Armin Biere
Lars Birkedal
Nikolaj Bjørner
Manuel Bodirsky
Mikolaj Bojanczyk
Iliano Cervesato
Krishnendu Chatterjee
Agata Ciabattoni
Anuj Dawar (Co-chair)
Azadeh Farzan
Georg Gottlob

Martin Hofmann
Orna Kupferman
Christof Löding
Joao Marques-Silva
Tobias Nipkow
Prakash Panangaden
R. Ramanujam
Simona Ronchi della Rocca
Alex Simpson
Pascal Tesson
Helmut Veith (Co-chair)
Yde Venema

Organizing Committee

Jan Bouda (Chair)
Tomáš Brázdil
Libor Caha
Matj uhel
Jan Holeek
Dagmar Janoukov
Dana Komrkov
Zbynk Mayer

Matj Pivoluska
Adam Rambousek
Tom Rebok
Jan Staudek
Tom Staudek
imon Suchomel
Marek Trtk

External Reviewers

Andreas Abel
Piotr Achinger
Markus Aderhold
Fabio Alessi
Thorsten Altenkirch
Shunichi Amano
Takahito Aoto
Matthias Baaz
Michele Basaldella

Nick Benton
Stefano Berardi
Ulrich Berger
Dietmar Berwanger
Jasmin Christian Blanchette
Chad Brown
Véronique Bruyère
Guillaume Burel
Sam Buss

Arnaud Carayol
Felice Cardone
Balder ten Cate
Antonio Cau
Pavol Cerny
Peter Chapman
Arthur Charguéraud
Swarat Chaudhuri
Hubie Chen
Christian Choffrut
Alberto Ciaffaglione
Mihail Codescu
Thomas Colcombet
Thierry Coquand
Nadia Creignou
Marcello d'Agostino
Norman Danner
Ashish Darbari
Laurent Doyen
Arnaud Durand
Roy Dyckhoff
Jeff Egger
Constantin Enea
David Espionsa
Olivier Finkel
Guido Fiorino
Gaelle Fontaine
Dominik Freydenberger
Maja Frydrychowicz
Murdoch Gabbay
Marco Gaboardi
Didier Galmiche
Thomas Genet
Martin Giese
Rajeev Gore
Elsa Gunter
Petr Hajek
Peter Hancock
Daniel Hausmann
Olivier Hermant
Stefan Hetzl
Jan Hoffmann
Florian Horn
Joe Hurd
Tomasz Idziaszek

Bart Jacobs
Peter Jipsen
Jan Johannsen
Peter Jonsson
Łukasz Kaiser
Mamadou Kanté
Delia Kesner
Leszek Kolodziejczyk
Konstantin Korovin
Philipp Krause Klaus
Neelakantan Krishnaswami
Ralf Küsters
Oliver Kullmann
Clemens Kupke
Keiichirou Kusakari
Dominique Larchey-Wendling
Stephane Lengrand
Jerome Leroux
Xavier Leroy
Paul Levi Blein
Leonid Libkin
Dan Licata
Tadeusz Litak
Sylvain Lombardy
John Longley
Michael Ludwig
Thomas Lukasiewicz
Johann A. Makowsky
Moritz Müller
Damiano Mazza
Paul-André Melliès
Zoltan Miklos
Stefan Milius
Fabio Mogavero
Rasmus Møgelberg
J. Strother Moore
Barbara Morawska
Georg Moser
Leonardo de Moura
Koji Nakazawa
Aleksander Nanevski
Georg Neis
Dejan Nickovic
Vivek Nigam
Damian Niwinski

Carles Noguera
Michael Norrish
Timo von Oertzen
Albert Oliveras
Vincent van Oostrom
Nicolas Oury
Eric Pacuit
Michele Pagani
Erik Palmgren
Sungwoo Park
Madhusudan Parthasarathy
Marco Pedicini
Muino David Picado
Sophie Pichinat
Thomas Piecha
Tonian Pitassi
Andrew Pitts
Jan von Plato
Andre Platzer
Francesca Poggiolesi
Vinayak Prabhu
Riccardo Pucella
Jason Reed
Laurent Regnier
Wolfgang Reisig
Colin Riba
Dulma Rodriguez
Panos Rondogiannis
Sasha Rubin
David Sabel
Joshua Sack
Jeffrey Sarnat
Alexis Saurin

Ulrich Schöpp
Alksy Schubert
Carsten Schürmann
Klaus U. Schulz
Nicole Schweikardt
Jan Schwinghammer
Merlijn Sevenster
Viorica Sofronie-Stokkermans
Lutz Strassburger
Thomas Streicher
Aaron Stump
S.P. Suresh
Tony Tan
Paul Taylor
Kazushige Terui
Hayo Thielecke
Marc Thurley
Paolo Tranquilli
Nikos Tzevelekos
Jouko Väänänen
Viktor Vafeiadis
Femke van Raamsdonk
Carsten Varming
Barany Vince
Daria Walukiewicz–Chrząszcz
Mark Wheelhouse
Stefan Wölfl
Michael Wrona
Shaofa Yang
Anna Zamansky
Noam Zeilberger
Standa Zivny

Table of Contents

Invited Talks

Degrees of Security: Protocol Guarantees in the Face of Compromising
Adversaries 1
    David Basin and Cas Cremers

Definability in Games 19
    Erich Grädel

From Feasible Proofs to Feasible Computations 22
    Jan Krajíček

Tree Dualities for Constraint Satisfaction 32
    Andrei Krokhin

Ordered Sets in the Calculus of Data Structures 34
    Viktor Kuncak, Ruzica Piskac, and Philippe Suter

Abductive, Inductive and Deductive Reasoning about Resources 49
    Peter W. O'Hearn

Constraint Solving for Program Verification: Theory and Practice by
Example 51
    Andrey Rybalchenko

Contributed Papers

Tableau Calculi for $\mathcal{CSL}$ over Minspaces 52
    *Régis Alenda, Nicola Olivetti, Camilla Schwind, and
    Dmitry Tishkovsky*

A Resolution Mechanism for Prenex Gödel Logic 67
    Matthias Baaz and Christian G. Fermüller

Efficient Enumeration for Conjunctive Queries over X-underbar
Structures 80
    *Guillaume Bagan, Arnaud Durand, Emmanuel Filiot, and
    Olivier Gauwin*

A Formalisation of the Normal Forms of Context-Free Grammars in
HOL4 95
    Aditi Barthwal and Michael Norrish

Automata vs. Logics on Data Words 110
  Michael Benedikt, Clemens Ley, and Gabriele Puppis

Graded Computation Tree Logic with Binary Coding 125
  Alessandro Bianco, Fabio Mogavero, and Aniello Murano

Exact Exploration and Hanging Algorithms 140
  Andreas Blass, Nachum Dershowitz, and Yuri Gurevich

Embedding Deduction Modulo into a Prover 155
  Guillaume Burel

Exponentials with Infinite Multiplicities............................ 170
  Alberto Carraro, Thomas Ehrhard, and Antonino Salibra

Classical and Intuitionistic Subexponential Logics Are Equally
Expressive 185
  Kaustuv Chaudhuri

On Slicewise Monotone Parameterized Problems and Optimal Proof
Systems for TAUT 200
  Yijia Chen and Jörg Flum

A Logic of Sequentiality 215
  Martin Churchill and James Laird

Environment and Classical Channels in Categorical Quantum
Mechanics 230
  Bob Coecke and Simon Perdrix

Formal Theories for Linear Algebra 245
  Stephen Cook and Lila Fontes

Energy and Mean-Payoff Games with Imperfect Information 260
  Aldric Degorre, Laurent Doyen, Raffaella Gentilini,
  Jean-François Raskin, and Szymon Toruńczyk

Randomisation and Derandomisation in Descriptive Complexity
Theory 275
  Kord Eickmeyer and Martin Grohe

Towards a Canonical Classical Natural Deduction System 290
  José Espírito Santo

Coordination Logic.. 305
  Bernd Finkbeiner and Sven Schewe

Second-Order Equational Logic (Extended Abstract) 320
    Marcelo Fiore and Chung-Kil Hur

Fibrational Induction Rules for Initial Algebras 336
    Neil Ghani, Patricia Johann, and Clément Fumex

A Sequent Calculus with Implicit Term Representation 351
    Stefan Hetzl

New Algorithm for Weak Monadic Second-Order Logic on Inductive
Structures 366
    Tobias Ganzow and Lukasz Kaiser

The Structural λ-Calculus.. 381
    Beniamino Accattoli and Delia Kesner

The Isomorphism Problem for ω-Automatic Trees 396
    Dietrich Kuske, Jiamou Liu, and Markus Lohrey

Complexity Results for Modal Dependence Logic..................... 411
    Peter Lohmann and Heribert Vollmer

The Complexity of Positive First-Order Logic without Equality II: The
Four-Element Case 426
    Barnaby Martin and Jos Martin

On the Computability of Region-Based Euclidean Logics 439
    Yavor Nenov and Ian Pratt-Hartmann

Inductive-Inductive Definitions 454
    Fredrik Nordvall Forsberg and Anton Setzer

Quantified Differential Dynamic Logic for Distributed Hybrid
Systems 469
    André Platzer

Untyping Typed Algebraic Structures and Colouring Proof Nets of
Cyclic Linear Logic 484
    Damien Pous

Two-Variable Logic with Two Order Relations (Extended Abstract) 499
    Thomas Schwentick and Thomas Zeume

Signature Extensions Preserve Termination: An Alternative Proof via
Dependency Pairs... 514
    Christian Sternagel and René Thiemann

Coq Modulo Theory 529
    Pierre-Yves Strub

Ackermann Award

The Ackermann Award 2010 544
    Johann A. Makowsky and Damian Niwinski

Author Index 547

Degrees of Security: Protocol Guarantees in the Face of Compromising Adversaries

David Basin and Cas Cremers[*]

Department of Computer Science, ETH Zurich

Abstract. We present a symbolic framework, based on a modular operational semantics, for formalizing different notions of compromise relevant for the analysis of cryptographic protocols. The framework's rules can be combined in different ways to specify different adversary capabilities, capturing different practically-relevant notions of key and state compromise. We have extended an existing security-protocol analysis tool, Scyther, with our adversary models. This is the first tool that systematically supports notions such as weak perfect forward secrecy, key compromise impersonation, and adversaries capable of state-reveal queries. We also introduce the concept of a protocol-security hierarchy, which classifies the relative strength of protocols against different forms of compromise. In case studies, we use Scyther to automatically construct protocol-security hierarchies that refine and correct relationships between protocols previously reported in the cryptographic literature.

1 Introduction

Compromise is a fact of life! Keys are leaked or broken. Memory and disks may be read or subject to side-channel attacks. Hardware protection may fail. Security-protocol designers are well aware of this and many protocols are designed to work in the face of various forms of corruption. For example, Diffie-Hellman key agreement, which uses digital signatures to authenticate the exchanged half-keys, provides perfect-forward secrecy [1,2]: the resulting session key remains secret even when the long-term signature keys are later compromised by an adversary.

In this paper, we survey and extend recent results of ours [3] on a symbolic framework for modeling and reasoning about security protocols in the presence of adversaries with a wide range of compromise capabilities. Our framework is inspired by the models developed in the computational setting, e. g. [4,5,6,7,8], where principals may be selectively corrupted during protocol execution. We reinterpret these computational models in a uniform way, build tool support for analyzing protocols with respect to these models, and gain new insights on the relationships between different models and protocols.

Our starting point is an operational semantics for security protocols. We parameterize this semantics by a set of rules that formalize adversarial capabilities.

---
[*] This work was supported by ETH Research Grant ETH-30 09-3 and the Hasler Foundation, ManCom, Grant 2071.

A. Dawar and H. Veith (Eds.): CSL 2010, LNCS 6247, pp. 1–18, 2010.
© Springer-Verlag Berlin Heidelberg 2010

These rules capture three dimensions of compromise: *whose* data is compromised, *which* kind of data it is, and *when* the compromise occurs. These dimensions are fundamental and different rule combinations formalize symbolic analogs of different practically-relevant notions of key and state compromise from the computational setting. The operational semantics gives rise, in the standard way, to a notion of correctness with respect to state and trace-based security properties.

Symbolic and computational approaches have addressed the problem of formalizing adversary compromise to different degrees. Most symbolic formalisms are based on the Dolev-Yao model and offer only a limited view of compromise: either principals are honest from the start and always keep their secrets to themselves or they are completely malicious and always under adversarial control. In contrast, numerous computational models have been proposed that formalize different notions of adversary compromise in the setting of key-exchange protocols, e.g., the models of Canetti and Krawczyk [4,9], Shoup [6], Bellare et al. [10,11,12], Katz and Yung [13], LaMacchia et al. [5], and Bresson and Manulis [7], to name but a few. These models are usually incomparable due to (often minor) differences in their adversarial notions, the execution models, and security property specifics. Moreover, they are generally presented in a monolithic way, where all parts are intertwined and it is difficult to separate these notions.

Our framework has a number of advantages over alternative approaches, both symbolic and computational. First, it cleanly separates the basic operational semantics of protocols, the adversary rules, and the security properties. This makes it simple to tailor a model to the scenario at hand by selecting appropriate rules. For example, we can reason about the security guarantees provided when cryptographic protocol implementations mix the use of cryptographic co-processors for the secure storage of long-term secrets with the computation of intermediate results in less-secure main memory for efficiency reasons. Moreover, as we will see, it is easy to define new security properties in a modular way.

Second, our framework directly lends itself to protocol analysis and we have extended the Scyther tool [14] to support our framework. This is the first tool that systematically supports notions such as weak perfect forward secrecy, key compromise impersonation, and adversaries that can reveal agents' local state.

Finally, we introduce the concept of a protocol-security hierarchy, in which protocols are classified by their relative strength against different forms of adversary compromise. Protocol-security hierarchies can be automatically constructed by Scyther. As case studies, we construct protocol-security hierarchies that refine and correct relationships reported in the cryptographic literature. This shows that symbolic methods can be effectively used for analyses that were previously possible only using a manual computational analysis.

Organization. We present our framework in Section 2. In Section 3, we use it to construct protocol-security hierarchies. Afterwards, in Section 4, we prove general results relating models and properties, which aid the construction of such hierarchies. Finally, we draw conclusions in Section 5.

2   Compromising Adversary Model

We define an operational semantics that is modular with respect to the adversary's capabilities. Our framework is compatible with the majority of existing semantics for security protocols, including trace and strand-space semantics. We have kept our execution model minimal to focus on the adversary rules. However, it would be straightforward to incorporate a more elaborate execution model, e. g., with control-flow commands.

Notational preliminaries. Let f be a function. We write $dom(f)$ and $ran(f)$ to denote f's domain and range. We write $f[b \hookleftarrow a]$ to denote f's update, i. e., the function f' where $f'(x) = b$ when $x = a$ and $f'(x) = f(x)$ otherwise. We write $f : X \rightarrow Y$ to denote a partial function from X to Y. For any set S, $\mathcal{P}(S)$ denotes the power set of S and S^* denotes the set of finite sequences of elements from S. We write $\langle s_0, \ldots, s_n \rangle$ to denote the sequence of elements s_0 to s_n, and we omit brackets when no confusion can result. For s a sequence of length $|s|$ and $i < |s|$, s_i denotes the i-th element. We write $s\hat{\ }s'$ for the concatenation of the sequences s and s'. Abusing set notation, we write $e \in s$ iff $\exists i.s_i = e$, and write $set(s)$ for $\{x \mid x \in s\}$. We define $last(\langle\rangle) = \emptyset$ and $last(s\hat{\ }\langle e\rangle) = \{e\}$.

We write $[t_0, \ldots, t_n \ / \ x_0, \ldots, x_n] \in \mathcal{S}ub$ to denote the substitution of t_i for x_i, for $0 \leq i \leq n$. We extend the functions dom and ran to substitutions. We write $\sigma \cup \sigma'$ to denote the union of two substitutions, which is defined when $dom(\sigma) \cap dom(\sigma') = \emptyset$, and write $\sigma(t)$ for the application of the substitution σ to t. Finally, for R a binary relation, R^* denotes its reflexive transitive closure.

2.1   Terms and Events

We assume given the infinite sets *Agent*, *Role*, *Fresh*, *Var*, *Func*, and *TID* of agent names, roles, freshly generated terms (nonces, session keys, coin flips, etc.), variables, function names, and thread identifiers. We assume that *TID* contains two distinguished thread identifiers, *Test* and tid_A. These identifiers single out a distinguished "point of view" thread of an arbitrary agent and an adversary thread, respectively.

To bind local terms, such as freshly generated terms or local variables, to a protocol role instance (thread), we write $T\sharp tid$. This denotes that the term T is local to the protocol role instance identified by tid.

Definition 1. *Terms*

$$Term ::= Agent \mid Role \mid Fresh \mid Var \mid Fresh \sharp TID \mid Var \sharp TID$$
$$\mid (Term, Term) \mid pk(Term) \mid sk(Term) \mid k(Term, Term)$$
$$\mid \{\!| \ Term \ |\!\}^a_{Term} \mid \{\!| \ Term \ |\!\}^s_{Term} \mid Func(Term^*)$$

For each $X, Y \in Agent$, $sk(X)$ denotes the long-term private key, $pk(X)$ denotes the long-term public key, and $k(X, Y)$ denotes the long-term symmetric key shared between X and Y. Moreover, $\{\!| \ t_1 \ |\!\}^a_{t_2}$ denotes the asymmetric encryption (for public keys) or the digital signature (for signing keys) of the term t_1 with the key t_2, and $\{\!|\, t_1 \,|\!\}^{s}_{t_2}$ denotes symmetric encryption. The set *Func* is used to model other cryptographic functions, such as hash functions. Freshly generated terms and variables are assumed to be local to a thread (an instance of a role).

Depending on the protocol analyzed, we assume that symmetric or asymmetric long-term keys have been distributed prior to protocol execution. We assume the existence of an inverse function on terms, where t^{-1} denotes the inverse key of t. We have that $pk(X)^{-1} = sk(X)$ and $sk(X)^{-1} = pk(X)$ for all $X \in Agent$, and $t^{-1} = t$ for all other terms t.

We define a binary relation $\vdash$, where $M \vdash t$ denotes that the term t can be inferred from the set of terms M. Let $t_0, \ldots, t_n \in Term$ and let $f \in Func$. We define $\vdash$ as the smallest relation satisfying:

$$t \in M \Rightarrow M \vdash t \qquad M \vdash t_1 \wedge M \vdash t_2 \Leftrightarrow M \vdash (t_1, t_2)$$

$$M \vdash \{\!|\, t_1 \,|\!\}^{s}_{t_2} \wedge M \vdash t_2 \Rightarrow M \vdash t_1 \qquad M \vdash t_1 \wedge M \vdash t_2 \Rightarrow M \vdash \{\!|\, t_1 \,|\!\}^{s}_{t_2}$$

$$M \vdash \{\!|\, t_1 \,|\!\}^{a}_{t_2} \wedge M \vdash (t_2)^{-1} \Rightarrow M \vdash t_1 \qquad M \vdash t_1 \wedge M \vdash t_2 \Rightarrow M \vdash \{\!|\, t_1 \,|\!\}^{a}_{t_2}$$

$$\bigwedge_{0 \leq i \leq n} M \vdash t_i \Rightarrow M \vdash f(t_0, \ldots, t_n)$$

Subterms t of a term t', written $t \sqsubseteq t'$, are defined as the syntactic subterms of t', e.g., $t_1 \sqsubseteq \{\!|\, t_1 \,|\!\}^{s}_{t_2}$ and $t_2 \sqsubseteq \{\!|\, t_1 \,|\!\}^{s}_{t_2}$. We write $FV(t)$ for the free variables of t, where $FV(t) = \{t' \mid t' \sqsubseteq t\} \cap \big(Var \cup \{v \sharp tid \mid v \in Var \wedge tid \in TID\}\big)$.

Definition 2. *Events*

$$AgentEvent ::= \mathsf{create}(Role, Agent) \mid \mathsf{send}(Term) \mid \mathsf{recv}(Term)$$
$$\mid \mathsf{generate}(\mathcal{P}(Fresh)) \mid \mathsf{state}(\mathcal{P}(Term)) \mid \mathsf{sessionkeys}(\mathcal{P}(Term))$$
$$AdversaryEvent ::= \mathsf{LKR}(Agent) \mid \mathsf{SKR}(TID) \mid \mathsf{SR}(TID) \mid \mathsf{RNR}(TID)$$
$$Event ::= AgentEvent \mid AdversaryEvent$$

We explain the interpretation of the agent and adversary events shortly. Here we simply note that the first three agent events are standard: starting a thread, sending a message, and receiving a message. The message in the send and receive events does not include explicit sender or recipient fields although, if desired, they can be given as subterms of the message. The last three agent events tag state information, which can possibly be compromised by the adversary. The four adversary events specify which information the adversary compromises. These events can occur any time during protocol execution and correspond to different kinds of *adversary queries* from computational models. All adversary events are executed in the single adversary thread tid_A.

2.2   Protocols and Threads

A protocol is a partial function from role names to event sequences, i. e., *Protocol* : *Role* $\nrightarrow$ *AgentEvent**. We require that no thread identifiers occur as subterms of events in a protocol definition.

Example 1 (Simple protocol). Let $\{\mathrm{Init}, \mathrm{Resp}\} \subseteq Role$, $key \in Fresh$, and $x \in Var$. We define the simple protocol SP as follows.

$$\mathrm{SP}(\mathrm{Init}) = \langle \mathsf{generate}(\{key\}), \mathsf{state}(\{key, \{\!|\, \mathrm{Resp}, key \,|\!\}^a_{sk(\mathrm{Init})}\}),$$
$$\mathsf{send}(\mathrm{Init}, \mathrm{Resp}, \{\!|\, \{\!|\, \mathrm{Resp}, key \,|\!\}^a_{sk(\mathrm{Init})} \,|\!\}^a_{pk(\mathrm{Resp})}), \mathsf{sessionkeys}(\{key\})\rangle$$
$$\mathrm{SP}(\mathrm{Resp}) = \langle \mathsf{recv}(\mathrm{Init}, \mathrm{Resp}, \{\!|\, \{\!|\, \mathrm{Resp}, x \,|\!\}^a_{sk(\mathrm{Init})} \,|\!\}^a_{pk(\mathrm{Resp})}),$$
$$\mathsf{state}(\{x, \{\!|\, \mathrm{Resp}, x \,|\!\}^a_{sk(\mathrm{Init})}\}), \mathsf{sessionkeys}(\{x\})\rangle$$

Here, the initiator generates a key and sends it (together with the responder name) signed and encrypted, along with the initiator and responder names. The recipient expects to receive a message of this form. The additional events mark session keys and state information. The state information is implementation-dependent and marks which parts of the state are stored at a lower protection level than the long-term private keys. The state information in SP corresponds to, e. g., implementations that use a hardware security module for encryption and signing and perform all other computations in ordinary memory.

Protocols are executed by agents who execute roles, thereby instantiating role names with agent names. Agents may execute each role multiple times. Each instance of a role is called a *thread*. We distinguish between the fresh terms and variables of each thread by assigning them unique names, using the function $localize : TID \to Sub$, defined as $localize(tid) = \bigcup_{cv \in Fresh \cup Var}[cv \sharp tid / cv]$. Using $localize$, we define a function $thread : (AgentEvent^* \times TID \times Sub) \to AgentEvent^*$ that yields the sequence of agent events that may occur in a thread.

Definition 3 (Thread). *Let l be a sequence of events, $tid \in TID$, and let σ be a substitution. Then $thread(l, tid, \sigma) = \sigma(localize(tid)(l))$.*

Example 2. Let $\{A, B\} \subseteq Agent$. For a thread $t_1 \in TID$ performing the Init role from Example 1, we have $localize(t_1)(key) = key \sharp t_1$ and

$$thread(\mathrm{SP}(\mathrm{Init}), t_1, [A, B \,/\, \mathrm{Init}, \mathrm{Resp}]) =$$
$$\langle \mathsf{generate}(\{key \sharp t_1\}), \mathsf{state}(\{key \sharp t_1, \{\!|\, B, key \sharp t_1 \,|\!\}^a_{sk(A)}\}),$$
$$\mathsf{send}(A, B, \{\!|\, \{\!|\, B, key \sharp t_1 \,|\!\}^a_{sk(A)} \,|\!\}^a_{pk(B)}), \mathsf{sessionkeys}(\{key \sharp t_1\})\rangle .$$

Test thread. When verifying security properties, we will focus on a particular thread. In the computational setting, this is the thread where the adversary performs a so-called *test query*. In the same spirit, we call the thread under consideration the *test thread*, with the corresponding thread identifier *Test*. For the test thread, the substitution of role names by agent names, and all free variables by terms, is given by σ_{Test} and the role is given by R_{Test}. For example, if the test thread is performed by Alice in the role of the initiator, trying to talk to Bob, we have that $R_{Test} = \mathrm{Init}$ and $\sigma_{Test} = [\mathrm{Alice}, \mathrm{Bob} \,/\, \mathrm{Init}, \mathrm{Resp}]$.

2.3   Execution Model

We define the set *Trace* as $(TID \times Event)^*$, representing possible execution histories. The state of our system is a four-tuple $(tr, IK, th, \sigma_{Test}) \in Trace \times$

$\mathcal{P}(Term) \times (TID \nrightarrow Event^*) \times Sub$, whose components are (1) a trace tr, (2) the adversary's knowledge IK, (3) a partial function th mapping thread identifiers of initiated threads to sequences of events, and (4) the role to agent and variable assignments of the test thread. We include the trace as part of the state to facilitate defining the partner function later.

Definition 4 (TestSub$_P$). *Given a protocol P, we define the set of* test substitutions $TestSub_P$ *as the set of ground substitutions σ_{Test} such that $dom(\sigma_{Test}) = dom(P) \cup \{v \sharp Test \mid v \in Var\}$ and $\forall r \in dom(P).\ \sigma_{Test}(r) \in Agent$.*

For P a protocol, the set of initial system states $IS(P)$ is defined as

$$IS(P) = \bigcup_{\sigma_{Test} \in TestSub_P} \left\{ (\langle \rangle, Agent \cup \{pk(a) \mid a \in Agent\}, \emptyset, \sigma_{Test}) \right\}.$$

In contrast to Dolev-Yao models, the initial adversary knowledge does not include any long-term secret keys. The adversary may learn these from long-term key reveal (LKR) events.

The semantics of a protocol $P \in Protocol$ is defined by a transition system that combines the execution-model rules from Fig. 1 with a set of adversary rules from Fig. 2. We first present the execution-model rules.

The create rule starts a new instance of a protocol role R (a *thread*). A fresh thread identifier tid is assigned to the thread, thereby distinguishing it from existing threads, the adversary thread, and the test thread. The rule takes the protocol P as a parameter. The role names of P, which can occur in events associated with the role, are replaced by agent names by the substitution σ. Similarly, the createTest rule starts the test thread. However, instead of choosing an arbitrary role, it takes an additional parameter R_{Test}, which represents the test role and will be instantiated in the definition of the transition relation in Def. 7. Additionally, instead of choosing an arbitrary σ, the test substitution σ_{Test} is used.

The send rule sends a message m to the network. In contrast, the receive rule accepts messages from the network that match the pattern pt, where pt is a term that may contain free variables. The resulting substitution σ is applied to the remaining protocol steps l.

The last three rules support our adversary rules, given shortly. The generate rule marks the fresh terms that have been generated,[1] the state rule marks the current local state, and the sessionkeys rule marks a set of terms as session keys.

Auxiliary functions. We define the long-term secret keys of an agent a as

$$LongTermKeys(a) = \{sk(a)\} \cup \bigcup_{b \in Agent} \{k(a,b), k(b,a)\}.$$

---

[1] Note that this rule need not ensure that fresh terms are unique. The function *thread* maps freshly generated terms c to $c \sharp tid$ in the thread tid, ensuring uniqueness.

$$\frac{R \in dom(P) \quad dom(\sigma) = Role \quad ran(\sigma) \subseteq Agent \quad tid \notin (dom(th) \cup \{tid_A, Test\})}{(tr, IK, th, \sigma_{Test}) \longrightarrow (tr \hat{} \langle(tid, \mathsf{create}(R, \sigma(R)))\rangle, IK, th[thread(P(R), tid, \sigma) \leftarrow\! \shortmid tid], \sigma_{Test})} \, [\mathsf{create}]$$

$$\frac{a = \sigma_{Test}(R_{Test}) \quad Test \notin dom(th)}{(tr, IK, th, \sigma_{Test}) \longrightarrow (tr \hat{} \langle(Test, \mathsf{create}(R_{Test}, a))\rangle, IK, th[thread(P(R_{Test}), Test, \sigma_{Test}) \leftarrow\! \shortmid Test], \sigma_{Test})} \, [\mathsf{createTest}]$$

$$\frac{th(tid) = \langle \mathsf{send}(m)\rangle \hat{} l}{(tr, IK, th, \sigma_{Test}) \longrightarrow (tr \hat{} \langle(tid, \mathsf{send}(m))\rangle, IK \cup \{m\}, th[l \leftarrow\! \shortmid tid], \sigma_{Test})} \, [\mathsf{send}]$$

$$\frac{th(tid) = \langle \mathsf{recv}(pt)\rangle \hat{} l \quad IK \vdash \sigma(pt) \quad dom(\sigma) = FV(pt)}{(tr, IK, th, \sigma_{Test}) \longrightarrow (tr \hat{} \langle(tid, \mathsf{recv}(\sigma(pt)))\rangle, IK, th[\sigma(l) \leftarrow\! \shortmid tid], \sigma_{Test})} \, [\mathsf{recv}]$$

$$\frac{th(tid) = \langle \mathsf{generate}(M)\rangle \hat{} l}{(tr, IK, th, \sigma_{Test}) \longrightarrow (tr \hat{} \langle(tid, \mathsf{generate}(M))\rangle, IK, th[l \leftarrow\! \shortmid tid], \sigma_{Test})} \, [\mathsf{generate}]$$

$$\frac{th(tid) = \langle \mathsf{state}(M)\rangle \hat{} l}{(tr, IK, th, \sigma_{Test}) \longrightarrow (tr \hat{} \langle(tid, \mathsf{state}(M))\rangle, IK, th[l \leftarrow\! \shortmid tid], \sigma_{Test})} \, [\mathsf{state}]$$

$$\frac{th(tid) = \langle \mathsf{sessionkeys}(M)\rangle \hat{} l}{(tr, IK, th, \sigma_{Test}) \longrightarrow (tr \hat{} \langle(tid, \mathsf{sessionkeys}(M))\rangle, IK, th[l \leftarrow\! \shortmid tid], \sigma_{Test})} \, [\mathsf{sessionkeys}]$$

Fig. 1. Execution-model rules

For traces, we define an operator $\downarrow$ that projects traces on events belonging to a particular thread identifier. For all tid, tid', and tr, we define $\langle\rangle \downarrow tid = \langle\rangle$ and

$$(\langle(tid', e)\rangle \hat{} tr) \downarrow tid = \begin{cases} \langle e\rangle \hat{} (tr \downarrow tid) & \text{if } tid = tid', \text{ and} \\ tr \downarrow tid & \text{otherwise.} \end{cases}$$

Similarly, for event sequences, the operator $\upharpoonleft$ selects the contents of events of a particular type. For all $\mathsf{evtype} \in \{\mathsf{create}, \mathsf{send}, \mathsf{recv}, \mathsf{generate}, \mathsf{state}, \mathsf{sessionkeys}\}$, we define $\langle\rangle \upharpoonleft \mathsf{evtype} = \langle\rangle$ and

$$(\langle e\rangle \hat{} l) \upharpoonleft \mathsf{evtype} = \begin{cases} \langle m\rangle \hat{} (l \upharpoonleft \mathsf{evtype}) & \text{if } e = \mathsf{evtype}(m), \text{ and} \\ l \upharpoonleft \mathsf{evtype} & \text{otherwise.} \end{cases}$$

During protocol execution, the test thread may intentionally share some of its short-term secrets with other threads, such as a session key. Hence some adversary rules require distinguishing between the intended *partner threads* and other threads. There exist many notions of partnering in the literature. In general, we use partnering based on matching histories for protocols with two roles, as defined below.

Definition 5 (Matching histories). *For sequences of events l and l', we define* $\mathrm{MH}(l, l') \equiv (l \upharpoonleft \mathsf{recv} = l' \upharpoonleft \mathsf{send}) \wedge (l \upharpoonleft \mathsf{send} = l' \upharpoonleft \mathsf{recv})$.

Our partnering definition is parameterized over the protocol P, the test role R_{Test}, and the instantiation of variables in the test thread σ_{Test}. These parameters are later instantiated in the transition-system definition.

Definition 6 (Partnering). *Let R be the non-test role, i.e., $R \in dom(P)$ and $R \neq R_{Test}$. For tr a trace, $Partner(tr, \sigma_{Test}) = \{tid \mid tid \neq Test \wedge (\exists a.\mathsf{create}(R, a) \in tr \downarrow tid) \wedge \exists l \, . \, \mathrm{MH}(\sigma_{Test}(P(R_{Test})), (tr \downarrow tid) \hat{} l)\}$.*

A thread *tid* is a partner iff (1) *tid* is not *Test*, (2) *tid* performs the role different from *Test*'s role, and (3) *tid*'s history matches the *Test* thread (for $l = \langle\rangle$) or the thread may be completed to a matching one (for $l \neq \langle\rangle$).

2.4   Adversary-Compromise Rules

We define the adversary-compromise rules in Fig. 2. They factor the security definitions from the cryptographic protocol literature along three dimensions of adversarial compromise: *which* kind of data is compromised, *whose* data it is, and *when* the compromise occurs.

Compromise of long-term keys. The first four rules model the compromise of an agent a's long-term keys, represented by the long-term key reveal event $\mathsf{LKR}(a)$. In traditional Dolev-Yao models, this event occurs implicitly for dishonest agents before the honest agents start their threads.

The $\mathsf{LKR_{others}}$ rule formalizes the adversary capability used in the symbolic analysis of security protocols since Lowe's Needham-Schroeder attack [15]: the adversary can learn the long-term keys of any agent a that is not an intended partner of the test thread. Hence, if the test thread is performed by Alice, communicating with Bob, the adversary can learn, e.g., Charlie's long-term key.

The $\mathsf{LKR_{actor}}$ rule allows the adversary to learn the long-term key of the agent executing the test thread (also called the *actor*). The intuition is that a protocol may still function as long as the long-term keys of the other partners are not revealed. This rule allows the adversary to perform so-called Key Compromise Impersonation attacks [8]. The rule's second premise is required because our model allows agents to communicate with themselves.

The $\mathsf{LKR_{after}}$ and $\mathsf{LKR_{aftercorrect}}$ rules restrict when the compromise may occur. In particular, they allow the compromise of long-term keys only after the test thread has finished, captured by the premise $th(\mathit{Test}) = \langle\rangle$. This is the sole premise of $\mathsf{LKR_{after}}$. If a protocol satisfies secrecy properties with respect to an adversary that can use $\mathsf{LKR_{after}}$, it is said to satisfy Perfect Forward Secrecy (PFS) [1,2]. $\mathsf{LKR_{aftercorrect}}$ has the additional premise that a finished partner thread must exist for the test thread. This condition stems from [9] and excludes the adversary from both inserting fake messages during protocol execution and learning the key of the involved agents later. If a protocol satisfies secrecy properties with respect to an adversary that can use $\mathsf{LKR_{aftercorrect}}$, it is said to satisfy weak Perfect Forward Secrecy (wPFS). This property is motivated by a class of protocols given in [9] whose members fail to satisfy PFS, although some satisfy this weaker property.

Compromise of short-term data. The three remaining adversary rules correspond to the compromise of short-term data, that is, data local to a specific thread. Whereas we assumed a long-term key compromise reveals *all* long-term keys of an agent, we differentiate here between the different kinds of local data. Because we assume that local data does not exist before or after a session, we can ignore the temporal dimension. We differentiate between three kinds of local data: *randomness, session keys,* and *other local data* such as the results of intermediate

$$\frac{a \notin \{\sigma_{Test}(R) \mid R \in dom(P)\}}{(tr, IK, th, \sigma_{Test}) \longrightarrow (tr\,\hat{}\,\langle(tid_{\mathcal{A}}, \mathsf{LKR}(a))\rangle, IK \cup LongTermKeys(a), th, \sigma_{Test})} [\mathsf{LKR_{others}}]$$

$$\frac{a = \sigma_{Test}(R_{Test}) \qquad a \notin \{\sigma_{Test}(R) \mid R \in dom(P) \setminus \{R_{Test}\}\}}{(tr, IK, th, \sigma_{Test}) \longrightarrow (tr\,\hat{}\,\langle(tid_{\mathcal{A}}, \mathsf{LKR}(a))\rangle, IK \cup LongTermKeys(a), th, \sigma_{Test})} [\mathsf{LKR_{actor}}]$$

$$\frac{th(Test) = \langle\rangle}{(tr, IK, th, \sigma_{Test}) \longrightarrow (tr\,\hat{}\,\langle(tid_{\mathcal{A}}, \mathsf{LKR}(a))\rangle, IK \cup LongTermKeys(a), th, \sigma_{Test})} [\mathsf{LKR_{after}}]$$

$$\frac{th(Test) = \langle\rangle \qquad tid \in Partner(tr, \sigma_{Test}) \qquad th(tid) = \langle\rangle}{(tr, IK, th, \sigma_{Test}) \longrightarrow (tr\,\hat{}\,\langle(tid_{\mathcal{A}}, \mathsf{LKR}(a))\rangle, IK \cup LongTermKeys(a), th, \sigma_{Test})} [\mathsf{LKR_{aftercorrect}}]$$

$$\frac{tid \neq Test \qquad tid \notin Partner(tr, \sigma_{Test})}{(tr, IK, th, \sigma_{Test}) \longrightarrow (tr\,\hat{}\,\langle(tid_{\mathcal{A}}, \mathsf{SKR}(tid))\rangle, IK \cup set((tr \downarrow tid) \downharpoonleft \mathsf{sessionkeys}), th, \sigma_{Test})} [\mathsf{SKR}]$$

$$\frac{tid \neq Test \qquad tid \notin Partner(tr, \sigma_{Test}) \qquad th(tid) \neq \langle\rangle}{(tr, IK, th, \sigma_{Test}) \longrightarrow (tr\,\hat{}\,\langle(tid_{\mathcal{A}}, \mathsf{SR}(tid))\rangle, IK \cup last((tr \downarrow tid) \downharpoonleft \mathsf{state}), th, \sigma_{Test})} [\mathsf{SR}]$$

$$\frac{}{(tr, IK, th, \sigma_{Test}) \longrightarrow (tr\,\hat{}\,\langle(tid_{\mathcal{A}}, \mathsf{RNR}(tid))\rangle, IK \cup set((tr \downarrow tid) \downharpoonleft \mathsf{generate}), th, \sigma_{Test})} [\mathsf{RNR}]$$

Fig. 2. Adversary-compromise rules

computations. The notion that the adversary may learn the randomness used in a protocol stems from [5]. Considering adversaries that can reveal session keys, e. g., by cryptanalysis, is found in many works, such as [12]. An adversary capable of revealing the local state was described in [4].

In our adversary-compromise models, the session-key reveal event $\mathsf{SKR}(tid)$ and state reveal event $\mathsf{SR}(tid)$ indicate that the adversary gains access to the session key or, respectively, the local state of the thread tid. These are marked respectively by the **sessionkeys** and **state** events.

The contents of the state change over time and are erased when the thread ends. This is reflected in the SR rule by the *last* state marker for the state contents and the third premise requiring that the thread tid has not ended. The random number reveal event $\mathsf{RNR}(tid)$ indicates that the adversary learns the random numbers generated in the thread tid.

The rules SKR and SR allow for the compromise of session keys and the contents of a thread's local state. Their premise is that the compromised thread is not a partner thread. In contrast, the premise of the RNR rule allows for the compromise of all threads, including the partner threads. This rule stems from [5], where it is shown that it is possible to construct protocols that are correct in the presence of an adversary capable of RNR.

For protocols that establish a session key, we assume the session key is shared by all partners and should be secret: revealing it trivially violates the protocols' security. Hence the rules disallow the compromise of session keys of the test or partner threads. Similarly, our basic rule set does not contain a rule for the compromise of other local data of the partners. Including such a rule is straightforward. However it is unclear whether any protocol would be correct with respect to such an adversary.

We call each subset of the set of adversary rules from Fig. 2 an *adversary-compromise model*.

2.5   Transition Relation and Security Properties

Given a protocol and an adversary-compromise model, we define the possible protocol behaviors as a set of reachable states.

Definition 7 (Transition relation and reachable states). *Let P be a protocol, Adv an adversary-compromise model, and R_{Test} a role. We define a transition relation $\rightarrow_{P,Adv,R_{Test}}$ from the execution-model rules from Fig. 1 and the rules in Adv. The variables P, Adv, and R_{Test} in the adversary rules are instantiated by the corresponding parameters of the transition relation. For states s and s', $s \rightarrow_{P,Adv,R_{Test}} s'$ iff there exists a rule in either Adv or the execution-model rules with the premises $Q_1(s), \ldots, Q_n(s)$ and the conclusion $s \rightarrow s'$ such that all of the premises hold. We define the set of reachable states RS as*

$$\mathrm{RS}(P, Adv, R_{Test}) = \left\{ s \mid \exists s_0.\, s_0 \in IS(P) \wedge s_0 \rightarrow^*_{P,Adv,R_{Test}} s \right\}.$$

We now provide two examples of security property definitions. We give a symbolic definition of *session-key secrecy* which, when combined with different adversary models, gives rise to different notions of secrecy from the literature. We also define *aliveness*, which is one of the many forms of authentication [16,17]. Other security properties, such as secrecy of general terms, symbolic indistinguishability, or other variants of authentication, can be defined analogously.

Definition 8 (Session-key secrecy). *Let $(tr, IK, th, \sigma_{Test})$ be a state. We define the secrecy of the session keys in $(tr, IK, th, \sigma_{Test})$ as*

$$th(Test) = \langle\rangle \Rightarrow \forall k \in set((tr \downarrow Test) \mid \mathsf{sessionkeys}).\, IK \nvdash k\,.$$

Definition 9 (Aliveness for two-party protocols). *Let $(tr, IK, th, \sigma_{Test})$ be a state. We say that $(tr, IK, th, \sigma_{Test})$ satisfies aliveness if and only if*

$$th(Test) = \langle\rangle \Rightarrow \exists R_{Test}, R, tid, a.\, (Test, \mathsf{create}(R_{Test}, a)) \in tr$$
$$\wedge\, R \neq R_{Test} \wedge (tid, \mathsf{create}(R, \sigma_{Test}(R))) \in tr.$$

We denote the set of all state properties by Φ. For all protocols P, adversary models Adv, and state properties $\phi \in \Phi$, we write $sat(P, Adv, \phi)$ iff $\forall R.\, \forall s.\, s \in \mathrm{RS}(P, Adv, R) \Rightarrow \phi(s)$. In the context of a state property ϕ, we say a protocol is *resilient against* an adversary capability AC if and only if $sat(P, \{AC\}, \phi)$.

Finally, we define a partial order $\leq_A$ on adversary-compromise models based on inclusion of reachable states. For all adversary models Adv and Adv':

$$Adv \leq_A Adv' \equiv \forall P, R.\, \mathrm{RS}(P, Adv, R) \subseteq \mathrm{RS}(P, Adv', R).$$

We write $Adv =_A Adv'$ if and only if $Adv \leq_A Adv'$ and $Adv' \leq_A Adv$.

3 Protocol-Security Hierarchies

We introduce the notion of a *protocol-security hierarchy*. Such a hierarchy orders sets of security protocols with respect to the adversary models in which they satisfy their security properties. Protocol-security hierarchies can be used to select or design protocols based on implementation requirements and the worst-case expectations for adversaries in the application domain.

Because each combination of adversary rules from Figure 2 represents an adversary model, determining for which models a protocol satisfies its properties involves analyzing the protocol with respect to $2^7 = 128$ models. This is infeasible to do by hand and we therefore aim to use automatic analysis methods.

Automated analysis methods have the limitation that, in our models, even simple properties such as secrecy are undecidable. Fortunately, there exist semi-decision procedures that are successful in practice in establishing the existence of attacks. Moreover, some of these procedures can also successfully verify some protocols and properties. When analyzing the security properties of protocols with respect to an adversary model, we deal with undecidability by allowing the outcome of the analysis to be undefined, which we denote by $\bot$. The two other possible outcomes are F (falsified) or V (verified).

Definition 10 (Recursive approximation of *sat*). *We say that a function* $f \in Protocol \times A \times \Phi \to \{F, \bot, V\}$ *recursively approximates* sat *if and only if* f *is recursive and for all protocols* P, *adversary models* Adv, *and state properties* ϕ, *we have* $f(P, Adv, \phi) \neq \bot \Rightarrow \big(f(P, Adv, \phi) = V \Leftrightarrow sat(P, Adv, \phi)\big)$.

Given such a function f, we can define a protocol-security hierarchy.

Definition 11 (Protocol-security hierarchy). *Let* Π *be a set of protocols,* ϕ *a state property,* A *be a set of adversary models, and let* f *recursively approximate* sat. *The* protocol-security hierarchy *with respect to* Π, A, ϕ, *and* f *is a directed graph* $H = (N, \to)$ *that satisfies the following properties:*

1. *N is a partition of Π, i.e.,* $\bigcup_{\pi \in N} \pi = \Pi$ *and for all* $\pi, \pi' \in N$ *we have that* $\pi \neq \emptyset$ *and* $\pi \neq \pi' \Rightarrow \pi \cap \pi' = \emptyset$.
2. *The function f respects the partitions N in that for all $P, P' \in \Pi$ we have*

$$\big(\exists \pi \in N. \{P, P'\} \subseteq \pi\big) \Leftrightarrow \forall Adv \in A. f(P, Adv, \phi) = f(P', Adv, \phi).$$

3. *$\pi \to \pi'$ if and only if*

$$\forall P \in \pi. \forall P' \in \pi'. \forall Adv \in A.\ f(P, Adv, \phi) = V \Rightarrow f(P', Adv, \phi) = V \land$$
$$f(P', Adv, \phi) = F \Rightarrow f(P, Adv, \phi) = F.$$

Lemma 1. *Let* $H = (N, \to)$ *be a protocol-security hierarchy with respect to* Π, ϕ, A, *and* f. *Let* $\leq_H$ *be defined as follows: for all* $\pi, \pi' \in N$, $\pi \leq_H \pi'$ *iff* $\pi \to \pi'$. *Then* $\leq_H$ *is a partial order.*

Proof. First, $\rightarrow$ is reflexive by Property 3 and hence $\leq_H$ is also reflexive. Second, since $\rightarrow$ is transitive by Property 3, so is $\leq_H$. Finally, assume $\pi \leq_H \pi'$ and $\pi' \leq_H \pi$. Then $\pi \rightarrow \pi'$ and $\pi' \rightarrow \pi$. Hence, by Property 3, for all adversary models $Adv \in A$ and all protocols $P \in \pi, P' \in \pi'$, we have $f(P, Adv, \phi) = f(P', Adv, \phi)$. By Property 2, this implies that $\pi = \pi'$ and therefore $\leq_H$ is antisymmetric. Hence $\leq_H$ is a partial order.

3.1   Examples of Protocol-Security Hierarchies

In Fig. 3, we show the protocol-security hierarchy for the secrecy property of a set of protocols with respect to all possible sets of adversary rules from Fig. 2. In Fig. 4, we show a protocol-security hierarchy for authentication properties. We discuss the protocol sets in detail in Section 3.2.

Each node π in Fig. 3 and 4 corresponds to a set of protocols and is annotated with a set of adversary models. For each adversary model in the set, we require that no attacks are found in this or any weaker model, and also that attacks are found in all stronger models. Formally, each node π is annotated with all adversary models $a \in A$ for which

$$\forall a' \in A, P \in \pi.(a <_A a' \Rightarrow f(P, a', \phi) = F) \wedge (a' \leq_A a \Rightarrow f(P, a', \phi) \neq F).$$

The protocol-security hierarchies in Fig. 3 and 4 are automatically generated. We extended the symbolic security-protocol verification tool Scyther [14,18] with our adversary rules from Fig. 2. This tool recursively approximates *sat* and enables us to automatically analyze protocols with respect to any combination of adversary rules. Scyther produces an output from $\{F, \perp, V\}$, where F denotes that an attack was found, thereby falsifying the property, V denotes that the property was verified, and $\perp$ denotes that a timeout occurred. Using Scyther, the properties of each protocol are analyzed with respect to all adversary models. The graph is computed automatically by combining this data for each of the protocols with the order $\leq_A$ on the adversary models. The protocol description files, analysis tools, and graph generation scripts can all be downloaded from [19].

Ideally we would like to establish hierarchies based on *sat*. However, only the recursive approximation f is available, which may return $\perp$, thereby providing only partial information about *sat*. Consequently, some edges in the hierarchies (involving nodes where f yields $\perp$) are also based on this partial information. Roughly speaking, we say an edge is *strict* if an edge also occurs between the protocols when given complete information about *sat*. More formally:

Definition 12 (strictness of edges in a protocol security hierarchy). *We say an edge $\pi \rightarrow \pi'$ in a protocol-security hierarchy is* strict *if the following two properties hold.*

1. *The protocols in π' are at least as strong as those in π.*

$$\forall P \in \pi, P' \in \pi'. \forall Adv \in A. f(P, Adv, \phi) \neq F \Rightarrow f(P', Adv, \phi) = V$$

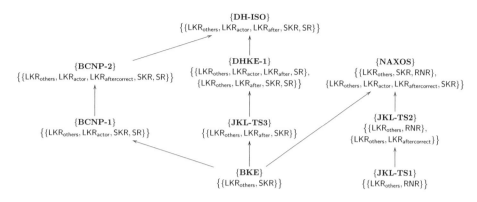

Fig. 3. Protocol-security hierarchy for secrecy

2. *The protocols in π are not equally strong as those in π'.*

$$\forall P \in \pi, P' \in \pi'. \, \exists Adv \in A. \, f(P, Adv, \phi) = F \wedge f(P', Adv, \phi) = V$$

All edges in the authentication hierarchy in Fig. 4 are strict. This reflects Scyther's success in either verifying or falsifying these protocols. In contrast, for the secrecy hierarchy in Fig. 3, most protocols contain Diffie-Hellman exponentiation, for which Scyther currently cannot provide verification. Therefore, the edges in Fig. 3 are only based on attacks. Because they are not strict, they might not occur in the corresponding hierarchy based on *sat*.

3.2 Analyzing Protocols Using Protocol-Security Hierarchies

Protocol-security hierarchies provide a novel way for choosing an optimal protocol for a given application domain, for example, exchanging a secret as illustrated here. We discuss below the protocols included in our two protocol-security hierarchies. We show how the resulting hierarchies facilitate fine-grained protocol comparisons that often refine or even contradict comparisons made in the literature. We start by discussing the hierarchy for secrecy in Fig. 3.

DH-ISO and DHKE-1. The original Diffie-Hellman protocol is only secure in the presence of a passive adversary since the messages sent are not authenticated. A simple fix is for agents to sign each message sent, along with the intended recipient, using the sender's long-term signature key. The resulting protocol family is referred to as *signed Diffie-Hellman*. We have analyzed the ISO variant of signed Diffie-Hellman as well as the DHKE-1 variant by Gupta and Shmatikov [20]. Scyther finds attacks on the Diffie-Hellman signed protocols for all models containing the RNR rule. This is consistent with the proof in [20], which does not consider this rule, as well as with the observation in [5] that RNR allows an attack on a signed Diffie-Hellman protocol.

JKL-TS1, JKL-TS2, and JKL-TS3. Jeong, Katz and Lee propose the protocols TS1, TS2, and TS3 [21]. TS1 is designed to satisfy *key independence* (keys of non-matching sessions may be revealed), whereas TS2 and TS3 should additionally satisfy *forward secrecy* (long-term keys of the agents may be revealed after the test session ends). They prove TS1 and TS2 correct in the random oracle model and TS3 in the standard model.

Our protocol-security hierarchy reveals the following. First, the TS3 protocol is incomparable to the other two. In contrast to TS2, TS3 additionally achieves resilience against $\mathsf{LKR}_{\mathsf{after}}$ and SKR, but it is not resilient against RNR. Second, the TS1 protocol is not resilient against SKR, which implies that the protocol does not satisfy key independence. Indeed, the missing identities in the session identifier of the protocol cause the protocol to be vulnerable to SKR. This is a flaw in the proof in [21]. Third, [21] suggests that the TS2 protocol satisfies forward secrecy. Our analysis shows that it only satisfies weak perfect forward secrecy, i.e., resilience against $\mathsf{LKR}_{\mathsf{aftercorrect}}$. The security model [21] requires the adversary to be passive when corrupting agents. This is in contrast to TS3, which does satisfy perfect forward secrecy. In this case, the authors have proven a weaker claim (weak perfect forward secrecy) whereas they might have been able to prove that TS3 satisfies a stronger property.

BKE. For the bilateral key-exchange (BKE) protocol [22], we find attacks in all models in our hierarchy except for adversaries capable of $\mathsf{LKR}_{\mathsf{others}}$ or SKR. BKE is therefore among the weakest protocols in our hierarchy. However, because it is resilient against SKR, it is not weaker than TS1 or TS2.

BCNP-1 and BCNP-2. Boyd, Cliff, Nieto, and Paterson propose two protocols [23], which we refer to as BCNP-1 and BCNP-2. When comparing their protocols to others, they focus on two properties, KCI resistance (resilience against $\mathsf{LKR}_{\mathsf{actor}}$) and weak forward secrecy (resilience against $\mathsf{LKR}_{\mathsf{aftercorrect}}$). Additionally, they claim that BCNP-2 provides more security that TS3 [21]. Our analysis allows for a more fine-grained comparison of the different protocols, confirming many remarks made in [23] but established by automatic instead of manual analysis. The hierarchy also explains why BCNP-2 does not provide more security than TS3. BCNP-2 is incomparable to TS3 because, unlike TS3, it is KCI-resilient (resilience against $\mathsf{LKR}_{\mathsf{actor}}$) but does not satisfy perfect forward secrecy (resilience against $\mathsf{LKR}_{\mathsf{after}}$). This disproves the claim in their paper.

NAXOS. LaMacchia, Lauter, and Mityagin propose the Naxos protocol [5] along with a new security model, claiming that this model is the strongest security model for AKE protocols. However, our hierarchy clearly reveals that NAXOS is not stronger than most other protocols in our set because it is vulnerable against SR and $\mathsf{LKR}_{\mathsf{after}}$. However, it is unique among the protocols we considered because it provides resilience against adversaries that are capable of both RNR and SKR.

Next, we discuss the hierarchy for authentication presented in Fig. 4. We verify the protocols with respect to a strong form of authentication called *synchronisation* [16]. Protocols that satisfy synchronisation also satisfy aliveness.

Needham-Schroeder. The Needham-Schroeder protocol [24] is resilient to adversaries capable of $\mathsf{LKR}_{\mathsf{after}}$ and SKR. As we will show in Theorem 1, all authentication properties of any protocol are resilient against $\mathsf{LKR}_{\mathsf{after}}$. The fact that

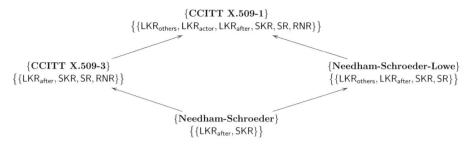

Fig. 4. Protocol-security hierarchy for authentication

the protocol is resilient against SKR is not surprising as the protocol does not contain any session keys.

Needham-Schroeder-Lowe. The original Needham-Schroeder protocol is vulnerable against a man-in-the-middle attack, which motivated Lowe's fix [15]. This attack requires precisely the $\mathsf{LKR_{others}}$ capability. Our hierarchy reveals that the Needham-Schroeder-Lowe protocol is resilient to adversaries capable of $\mathsf{LKR_{others}}$ and SR. The original Needham-Schroeder is not resilient against SR because the missing identity in the second message allows the adversary to exploit a non-matching session to decrypt this message, in which he uses SR to reveal the nonce of the first message.

CCITT X.509-1 and X.509-3. The CCITT X.509 standard [25] contains several protocol recommendations. Here we consider X.509-1 and X.509-3. X.509-1 satisfies its authentication properties with respect to the strongest possible adversary model, i. e., the adversary with all capabilities from Fig 2. The X.509-3 protocol is not resilient against $\mathsf{LKR_{others}}$ or $\mathsf{LKR_{actor}}$. However, unlike Needham-Schroeder(-Lowe), it is resilient against RNR.

4   Relations between Models and Properties

As previously noted, by classifying different basic adversarial capabilities from the literature, one quickly arrives at a large number of adversary models. Here we provide general results that aid in relating and reasoning with these models.

To begin with, our partial order on adversary models $\leq_A$ has implications for security protocol verification. Given a state property ϕ like those from Section 2.5, a protocol that satisfies ϕ in a model also satisfies ϕ in all weaker models. Equivalently, falsification in a model entails falsification in all stronger models. Formally, if $Adv \leq_A Adv'$, then for all protocols P and state properties ϕ, $sat(P, Adv', \phi) \Rightarrow sat(P, Adv, \phi)$ and, equivalently, $\neg sat(P, Adv, \phi) \Rightarrow \neg sat(P, Adv', \phi)$.

Since adding adversary rules only results in a larger transition relation and hence more reachable states, we have:

Lemma 2 (Adding rules only strengthens the adversary). *Let r be an adversary rule from Fig. 2 and Adv be an adversary model, i. e., a set of adversary rules. Then $Adv \leq_A Adv \cup \{r\}$.*

Most of our rules are independent in that they provide adversary capabilities not given by other rules. The following lemma formalizes this.

Lemma 3 (Rule independence). *Let Adv be an adversary model. Then we have for all adversary rules r from Fig. 2*

$$\left(r = \mathsf{LKR_{aftercorrect}} \wedge \mathsf{LKR_{after}} \in Adv\right) \Leftrightarrow \left(Adv \setminus \{r\} =_{\mathcal{A}} Adv \cup \{r\}\right).$$

Proof of ($\Rightarrow$): Let $r = \mathsf{LKR_{aftercorrect}}$ and $\mathsf{LKR_{after}} \in Adv$. Each transition using $\mathsf{LKR_{aftercorrect}}$ can be simulated using $\mathsf{LKR_{after}}$. Hence the sets of reachable states on both sides of the above equality are equal and thus $Adv \setminus \{r\} =_{\mathcal{A}} Adv \cup \{r\}$. Proof of ($\Leftarrow$): Let $Adv \setminus \{r\} =_{\mathcal{A}} Adv \cup \{r\}$. Suppose $r \neq \mathsf{LKR_{aftercorrect}}$. Then there are transitions enabled by r that are not enabled by the other rules. In particular, even if $\mathsf{LKR_{aftercorrect}} \in Adv$, there are protocols with roles that can be completed without matching sessions, whereby $\mathsf{LKR_{after}}$ enables transitions not enabled by $\mathsf{LKR_{aftercorrect}}$. Hence we have a contradiction and therefore $r = \mathsf{LKR_{aftercorrect}}$. Now suppose $\mathsf{LKR_{after}} \notin Adv$. Then some transitions enabled by r are not enabled by $Adv \setminus \{r\}$, contradicting $Adv \setminus \{r\} =_{\mathcal{A}} Adv \cup \{r\}$. Hence $r = \mathsf{LKR_{aftercorrect}}$ and $\mathsf{LKR_{after}} \in Adv$.

Corollary 1. *The rules in Fig. 2 give rise to $2^5 \times 3 = 96$ models with distinct sets of reachable states.*

This corollary follows from Lemmas 2 and 3.

Interestingly, to evaluate some properties it is only necessary to consider traces up to the end of the test session.

Definition 13 (post-test invariant properties). *We define the set Φ_{PTI} of post-test invariant properties as all state properties $\phi \in \Phi$ that satisfy*

$$\forall P, R, Adv. \forall (tr, IK, th, \sigma_{Test}) \in \mathrm{RS}(P, Adv, R). th(Test) = \langle\rangle \Rightarrow$$
$$\forall s.(tr, IK, th, \sigma_{Test}) \rightarrow^*_{P, Adv, R_{Test}} s \Rightarrow \left(\phi((tr, IK, th, \sigma_{Test})) \Leftrightarrow \phi(s)\right).$$

Aliveness, as defined earlier, is a post-test invariant property. Other authentication goals such as various forms of agreement [17] or synchronisation [16] are also post-test invariant properties. Secrecy however is not such a property.

Theorem 1 (post-test invariant properties are resilient against future capabilities). *Let r be an adversary rule from Fig. 2 and $\phi \in \Phi_{PTI}$ be a post-test invariant property. Then for all protocols P and adversary models Adv,*

$$r \in \{\mathsf{LKR_{aftercorrect}}, \mathsf{LKR_{after}}\} \wedge sat(P, Adv, \phi) \Rightarrow sat(P, Adv \cup \{r\}, \phi)$$

This theorem follows as $\mathsf{LKR_{aftercorrect}}$ and $\mathsf{LKR_{after}}$ only enable new transitions in those states where the test thread has ended. By definition, post-test invariant properties are invariant with respect to such transitions. As a result, we need only consider 32 (out of 96) models when analyzing a protocol with respect to post-test invariant properties.

5   Conclusions

We see our work as a first step in providing models and tool support for systematically modeling and analyzing security protocols with respect to adversaries endowed with different compromise capabilities. We presented applications to protocol analysis and constructing protocol-security hierarchies.

Our adversary capabilities generalize those from the computational setting and combine them with a symbolic model. In doing so, we unify and generalize a wide range of models from both settings. Exploring the exact nature of this generalization as well as mappings between the two settings remains as future work. Also interesting would be to develop methods for designing protocols optimized for different adversarial scenarios or strengthening existing protocols.

Finally, the concept of a protocol-security hierarchy can be naturally extended to any domain where security properties of systems can be evaluated with respect to a set of adversary models. This leads to the more general notion of a *security hierarchy*. For example, in the domain of access control, attackers could have different capabilities with respect to how policies are enforced. A hierarchy in this setting could help distinguish the degrees of security provided by different access-control mechanisms.

References

1. Günther, C.: An identity-based key-exchange protocol. In: Quisquater, J.-J., Vandewalle, J. (eds.) EUROCRYPT 1989. LNCS, vol. 434, pp. 29–37. Springer, Heidelberg (1990)
2. Menezes, A., van Oorschot, P., Vanstone, S.: Handbook of Applied Cryptography. CRC Press, Boca Raton (October 1996)
3. Basin, D., Cremers, C.: From Dolev-Yao to strong adaptive corruption: Analyzing security in the presence of compromising adversaries. Cryptology ePrint Archive, Report 2009/079 (2009), http://eprint.iacr.org/
4. Canetti, R., Krawczyk, H.: Analysis of key-exchange protocols and their use for building secure channels. In: Pfitzmann, B. (ed.) EUROCRYPT 2001. LNCS, vol. 2045, pp. 453–474. Springer, Heidelberg (2001)
5. LaMacchia, B., Lauter, K., Mityagin, A.: Stronger security of authenticated key exchange. In: Susilo, W., Liu, J.K., Mu, Y. (eds.) ProvSec 2007. LNCS, vol. 4784, pp. 1–16. Springer, Heidelberg (2007)
6. Shoup, V.: On formal models for secure key exchange (version 4) (November 1999); revision of IBM Research Report RZ 3120 (April 1999)
7. Bresson, E., Manulis, M.: Securing group key exchange against strong corruptions. In: ASIACCS, pp. 249–260. ACM, New York (2008)
8. Just, M., Vaudenay, S.: Authenticated multi-party key agreement. In: Kim, K.-c., Matsumoto, T. (eds.) ASIACRYPT 1996. LNCS, vol. 1163, pp. 36–49. Springer, Heidelberg (1996)
9. Krawczyk, H.: HMQV: A high-performance secure Diffie-Hellman protocol. Cryptology ePrint Archive, Report 2005/176 (2005), http://eprint.iacr.org/ (retrieved on April 14, 2009)
10. Bellare, M., Rogaway, P.: Provably secure session key distribution: the three party case. In: Proc. STOC 1995, pp. 57–66. ACM, New York (1995)

11. Bellare, M., Pointcheval, D., Rogaway, P.: Authenticated key exchange secure against dictionary attacks. In: Preneel, B. (ed.) EUROCRYPT 2000. LNCS, vol. 1807, pp. 139–155. Springer, Heidelberg (2000)
12. Bellare, M., Rogaway, P.: Entity authentication and key distribution. In: Stinson, D.R. (ed.) CRYPTO 1993. LNCS, vol. 773, pp. 232–249. Springer, Heidelberg (1994)
13. Katz, J., Yung, M.: Scalable protocols for authenticated group key exchange. In: Boneh, D. (ed.) CRYPTO 2003. LNCS, vol. 2729, pp. 110–125. Springer, Heidelberg (2003)
14. Cremers, C.: The Scyther Tool: Verification, falsification, and analysis of security protocols. In: Gupta, A., Malik, S. (eds.) CAV 2008. LNCS, vol. 5123, pp. 414–418. Springer, Heidelberg (2008)
15. Lowe, G.: Breaking and fixing the Needham-Schroeder public-key protocol using FDR. In: Margaria, T., Steffen, B. (eds.) TACAS 1996. LNCS, vol. 1055, pp. 147–166. Springer, Heidelberg (1996)
16. Cremers, C., Mauw, S., de Vink, E.: Injective synchronisation: an extension of the authentication hierarchy. Theoretical Computer Science, 139–161 (2006)
17. Lowe, G.: A hierarchy of authentication specifications. In: Proc. 10th IEEE Computer Security Foundations Workshop (CSFW), pp. 31–44. IEEE, Los Alamitos (1997)
18. Cremers, C.: Unbounded verification, falsification, and characterization of security protocols by pattern refinement. In: CCS 2008: Proc. of the 15th ACM conference on Computer and communications security, pp. 119–128. ACM, New York (2008)
19. Cremers, C.: Scyther tool with compromising adversaries extension Includes protocol description files and test scripts, http://people.inf.ethz.ch/cremersc/scyther/compromise/
20. Gupta, P., Shmatikov, V.: Towards computationally sound symbolic analysis of key exchange protocols. In: Proc. FMSE 2005, pp. 23–32. ACM, New York (2005)
21. Jeong, I.R., Katz, J., Lee, D.H.: One-round protocols for two-party authenticated key exchange. In: Jakobsson, M., Yung, M., Zhou, J. (eds.) ACNS 2004. LNCS, vol. 3089, pp. 220–232. Springer, Heidelberg (2004)
22. Clark, J., Jacob, J.: A survey of authentication protocol literature (1997), http://citeseer.ist.psu.edu/clark97survey.html
23. Boyd, C., Cliff, Y., Nieto, J.M.G., Paterson, K.G.: One-round key exchange in the standard model. IJACT 1(3), 181–199 (2009)
24. Needham, R., Schroeder, M.: Using encryption for authentication in large networks of computers. Communications of the ACM 21(12), 993–999 (1978)
25. CCITT: The directory authentification framework, Draft Recommendation X.509, Version 7 (1987)

Definability in Games

Erich Grädel

Mathematische Grundlagen der Informatik, RWTH Aachen University, Germany
graedel@logic.rwth-aachen.de

We shall present a survey on definability questions for graph games.

Infinite games on graphs, where two players move a token along the edges of a directed graph tracing out a finite or infinite path, are intimately connected with fundamental questions in logic and have numerous applications in different areas of mathematics and computer science. We consider here games with qualitative objectives: for each player, we have a winning condition, specified either by a logical formula on infinite paths (typically from monadic second-order logic S1S, first-order logic FO, or temporal logic LTL) or by automata-theoretic conditions such as Muller, Streett-Rabin, or parity conditions. For such a game $\mathcal{G}$, a position v and a player $\sigma = 0, 1$ the question we ask is whether Player σ has a winning strategy in $\mathcal{G}$ from position v.

To solve a game algorithmically thus means to compute *winning regions* and *winning strategies* for the two players. Here, the winning region of a player means the set of those positions from which the player has a winning strategy. While efficient algorithms exist for many classes of games, including those where the players have reachability, safety, recurrent reachability (Büchi) or eventual safety (Co-Büchi) objectives, the question whether the winning regions in *parity games* can be computed in polynomial time is one of the most important open problems in the field of infinite games. In parity games, one assigns to each position a natural number, called its priority, and the winner of an infinite play depends on whether the least priority occurring infinitely often is even or odd. Parity games are important because many games arising in practical applications, including all games with ω-regular winning conditions, can be reduced to parity games, because parity games arise as the model checking games for fixed-point logics, and because parity games are determined via memoryless winning strategies. It is known that the problem of solving parity games is in NP ∩ Co-NP, which is a direct consequence of the fact that parity games admit memoryless winning strategies. Much effort has also been put into identifying and classifying classes of parity games that admit efficient solutions. For instance, there are deterministic polynomial-time algorithms for any class of parity games with a bounded number of priorities, and for parity games with certain restrictions on the underlying game graph, such as bounded tree width, bounded DAG-width, and others.

In this talk we discuss the problems of the *definability* of winning regions and winning strategies, in logical systems such a mondic second-order logic, least fixed-point logic LFP, the modal μ-calculus and some of its fragments. Such a study of the *descriptive complexity of games*, of the logical ressources needed for specifying winning regions and winning strategies, may provide insights into

A. Dawar and H. Veith (Eds.): CSL 2010, LNCS 6247, pp. 19–21, 2010.

the structure of the associated algorithmic problems, and the sources of their algorithmic difficulty; on the other sides definability and non-definability results on games also have important applications on the structure and expressive power of logical systems.

Given a logic L and class $\mathcal{S}$ of games, presented as relational stuctures of some fixed vocabulary τ, we say that *winning regions on $\mathcal{S}$ are definable in L*, if there exist formulae $\psi_0(x)$ and $\psi_1(x)$ of $L(\tau)$ that define, on each game $\mathcal{G} \in \mathcal{S}$, the winning regions W_0 and W_1 for the two players. This means that, for each game $\mathcal{G} \in \mathcal{S}$ and each player $\sigma = 0, 1$

$$W_\sigma = \{v \in \mathcal{G} : \mathcal{G} \models \psi_\sigma(v)\}.$$

It is an obvious consequence of standard facts of finite model theory, such as Gaifman's Theorem on the locality of first-order logic, that FO is too weak for games, even for very simple objectives such as reachability and safety. On the other side, it can be shown that on any class $\mathcal{S}$ of games, on which the objectives of the two players can be uniformly described by formulae of S1S (which depend on a bounded vocabulary of monadic predicates), the winning regions for the two players are definable in LFP, in MSO, and also in the modal μ-calculus. This includes games with standard objectives such as reachability, safety, recurrent reachability and eventual safety, and indeed all parity, Streett-Rabin, and even Müller conditions with a bounded number of priorities.

Formulae defining winning regions in parity games with priorities $0, \ldots, d-1$, for any fixed d, have been essential for settling structural properties of fixed point logics. In the modal μ-calculus L_μ such formulae require d nested fixed points that alternate between least and greatest fixed points, and thus witness the strictness of the alternation hierarchy. It has been shown that such formulae can also be constructed in Parikh's Game Logic GL and in the two-variable fragment of the μ-calculus which proves that these fragments of L_μ intersect all levels of the alternation hierarchy. By a different use of games also the strictness of the variable hierarchy of the μ-calculus could be settled.

However, definability issues for classes of games where the objectives depend on an unbounded collection of local parameters (colours, priorities, atomic propositions etc.) are quite different. First of all games in such classes require a somewhat more complicated presentation as relational stuctures. Parity games, for instance, can be presented as game graphs with a pre-order on the positions, where $u \prec v$ means that u has a smaller (i.e. more relevant) priority than v. Definability issues of such classes of games also depend on whether only finite game graphs are considered, or also infinite ones. For instance, it is a consequence of the strictness of the alternation hierarchy for LFP on arithmetic, together with an interpretation argument for model checking games, that winning regions of parity games are, in general, not LFP-definable (even if we restrict attention to games on a countable graph and with finitely many priorities). On finite game graphs, however, this may well be different. Indeed the winning regions are LFP-definable if, and only if, they are computable in polynomial-time, despite the fact that, on unordered finite structures, LFP is weaker than PTIME.

We will also address the, much less understood, problem of defining *winning strategies* rather than just winning regions. Strategies can be viewed and presented in several different ways, and it is not always obvious what definability of strategies really means. However, for many of the games that we consider here, positional strategies suffice, and since we can identify a positional strategy with a set of edges in the game graph, definability questions for such games can be put very naturally.

While the two problems of defining winning regions and winning strategies are closely related, they are not always equivalent. Indeed one can construct games where winning regions can be determined trivially, but winning strategies are not even computable.

However, most algorithms that compute winning regions in games do so by revealing also winning strategies. Also from logical definitions of winning regions, one can often extract the underlying winning strategies. This is obvious in the case of a player with a safety objective who can win just by staying inside her winning region. For players with other objectives, such as reachability, natural LFP-definitions of winning regions associate with with each position a rank, and winning strategies progress by reducing the rank. In such a case, winning strategies may be LFP-definable by rank comparison.

From Feasible Proofs to Feasible Computations

Jan Krajíček*

Faculty of Mathematics and Physics, Charles University
Sokolovská 83, 186 75, Prague, Czech Republic

Abstract. We shall discuss several situations in which it is possible to extract from a proof, be it a proof in a first-order theory or a propositional proof, some feasible computational information about the theorem being proved. This includes extracting feasible algorithms, deterministic or interactive, for witnessing an existential quantifier, a uniform family of short propositional proofs of instances of a universal quantifier, or a feasible algorithm separating a pair of disjoint NP sets.

1 Universal Theories

Let L be a language that has a function symbol corresponding to every polynomial time algorithm, say as represented by clocked polynomial time Turing machines. We shall assume that polynomial time relations are represented by their characteristic functions and hence the only relation symbol is the equality, which we regard as a logical symbol.

Every function symbol from L has a canonical interpretation on the set of natural numbers $\mathbf{N}$ which we identify with the set of all binary words $\{0, 1\}^*$; the resulting L-structure will be called the standard model. Let T be the universal theory of the standard model.

Theory PV of Cook [7] can be thought of as a subtheory of T: its language has a symbol for every polynomial time algorithm as they are built in Cobham's theorem [6] by repeated composition and limited recursion on notation, and its axioms are universal statements codifying the equations defining this process (see also [5,8,13]).

1.1 Witnessing Existential Formulas

Assume

$$T \vdash \exists y A(x, y)$$

where A is an open formula. Herbrand's theorem implies that there are terms $t_1(x), \ldots, t_k(x)$ such that

$$T \vdash \bigvee_i A(x, t_i(x)) \ .$$

---

* Supported in part by grants IAA100190902, MSM0021620839, LC505 (Eduard Čech Center) and by a grant from the John Templeton Foundation. Also partially affiliated with the Institute of Mathematics of the Academy of Sciences and grant AV0Z10190503.

A. Dawar and H. Veith (Eds.): CSL 2010, LNCS 6247, pp. 22–31, 2010.

As the class of polynomial time functions is closed under definitions by cases distinguished by a polynomial time property, it follows that there is one term $t(x)$ such that

$$T \vdash A(x, t(x)) .$$

In particular, the polynomial time algorithm defined by $t(x)$ witnesses in the standard model the validity of the sentence $\forall x \exists y A(x, y)$.

Consequences of this simple witnessing are various independence results (conditioned upon complexity theoretic hypotheses). For example, let h be a one-way permutation (cf. [1]). As h must be surjective the sentence

$$\forall y \exists x \; h(x) = y$$

is valid. But it is not provable in T as the witnessing algorithm would compute the inverse function to h (which is supposed to be impossible).

Another example can be given by a hash function g that always outputs less bits than the input has. Then there must be a collision pair of any length:

$$\forall x \exists y_1, y_2 \; [\; y_1 \neq y_2 \wedge |x| = |y_1| = |y_2| \wedge g(y_1) = g(y_2) \;]$$

but this sentence cannot be provable in T as the witnessing algorithm would find a collision pair (which is supposed to be hard).

For the final example let P be a propositional proof system in the sense of Cook and Reckhow [9], i.e. a polynomial time function whose range is exactly the set of propositional tautologies. Any π such that $P(\pi) = \tau$ is called a P-proof of τ. The completeness of P can be stated as

$$\forall x \exists y \; [\; Fla(x) \rightarrow \; (\; SatNeg(x, y) \vee P(y) = x \;) \;]$$

where $Fla(x)$ and $SatNeg(x, y)$ are open L-formulas formalizing that x *is a propositional formula* and that y *is a truth assignment satisfying the negation of* x, respectively. Then unless P $=$ NP this is unprovable in T as a witnessing algorithm could be used to decide SAT.

1.2   Witnessing $\exists_2$-Formulas

Assume

$$T \vdash \exists y \forall z A(x, y, z)$$

where A is an open formula. Herbrand's theorem implies (see [22,13]) that there are terms $t_1(x), t_2(x, y_1), \ldots, t_k(x, z_1, \ldots, z_{k-1})$ such that

$$T \vdash \bigvee_i A(x, t_i(x, z_1, \ldots, z_{i-1}), z_i) . \tag{1}$$

This can be interpreted as an interactive algorithm witnessing the existential quantifier in the following way (cf. [21]). The computation is performed by a polynomial time Student and a Teacher of unlimited powers. Upon receiving an input x the Student computes his first candidate witness $y_1 := t_1(x)$ and sends it to the Teacher. If indeed $\forall z A(x, y_1, z)$ holds she will acknowledge it and the computation stops. Otherwise she will send to the Student a counter-example z_1: a string such that $\neg A(x, y_1, z_1)$. The Student then computes the next candidate witness $y_2 := t_2(x, y_1)$ and sends it to the Teacher, and so on.

The validity of the disjunction in (1) implies that the Student will find a valid witness in at most k rounds. In order to guarantee that the total time of the Student is polynomial in the length of x one needs to assume that the universal quantifier is bounded: $\forall z < s(x)$.

An interesting statement of this logical form is the following maximization principle. Let $R(x, y)$ be a polynomial time relation and assume

$$\forall x R(x, 0) \ \wedge \ \forall x, y \ (R(x, y) \to |y| \leq |x|) \ .$$

The principle says that for any x there is a solution y of maximal size:

$$\forall x \exists y \forall z \ [\ R(x, y) \wedge (R(x, z) \to |z| \leq |y|) \ ] \ .$$

For example, the principle implies the existence of a maximal clique in a graph. Krajíček, Pudlák and Takeuti [22] proved that there are polynomial time relations R for which the principle is not provable in T unless NP $\subseteq$ P/poly.

1.3   Universal Formulas

Assume

$$T \ \vdash \ A(x)$$

where A is an open formula. Herbrand's theorem implies that there are finitely many axioms $\forall y_1, \ldots, y_k \ B(y_1, \ldots, y_k)$ of T and for each of them finitely many k-tuples of terms $t_1(x), \ldots, t_k(x)$ such that $A(x)$ is provable already from all these finitely many instances

$$B(t_1, \ldots, t_k) \ .$$

To avoid an excessive notation we shall assume that instances of only one axiom $\forall y B(y)$ are used and that the open formula $B(y)$ has only one free variable y. Hence for some terms $s_1(x), \ldots, s_k(x)$

$$B(s_1) \wedge \ldots \wedge B(s_k) \ \vdash \ A(x) \ . \tag{2}$$

Formula $A(x)$ defines a polynomial time predicate and hence is computable by a (uniform) family of polynomial size circuits that we shall denote $||A(x)||^n$, and similarly $||B(s_i(x))||^n$ for the other formulas.

What we want to derive is a propositional implication

$$\bigwedge_i ||B(s_i(x))||^n \ \to \ ||A(x)||^n \ . \tag{3}$$

The qualification 'propositional' is not quite true as we use circuits rather than formulas. But one can either define a propositional calculus operating directly with circuits (cf. [10]) or replace circuits by formulas written using auxiliary variables used to define the circuit computations, as in the proof of the NP-completeness of SAT.

Implication (3) need not to be, in fact, a tautology as in the first-order derivation of (2) some equality axioms could have been used. Hence there is a finite set $\mathcal{E}$ of instances of equality axioms by terms in x such that

$$\bigwedge_{E \in \mathcal{E}} ||E||^n \wedge \bigwedge_{i} ||B(s_i(x))||^n \ \rightarrow \ ||A(x)||^n \ . \qquad (4)$$

Moreover, (4) is now valid as a propositional formula. This means that if we interpret atomic formulas as propositional atoms then the implication is valid under all truth assignments. Hence there is a template propositional derivation (in any proof system containing at least resolution) and proofs of (4) for specific $n \geq 1$ are obtained by replacing in the whole template derivation propositional atoms by translations $|| \dots ||^n$ of the atomic formulas from (2) (and of the equality axioms from $\mathcal{E}$).

The interesting thing on which a correspondence between theories and propositional proof systems rests is that for a subtheory S of T whose set of axioms is in NP one can define a proof system P_S that admits p-bounded proofs of all $|| \dots ||^n$-translations of term instances of all axioms of S (and of all equality axioms), and hence also of all $|| \dots ||^n$-translations of the universal consequences of S. Moreover, for natural S such a proof system is often defined quite naturally as well. For example, for Cook's PV [7] the corresponding proof system is the Extended Frege system (or, equivalently) the Extended Resolution. See [18,13] for details.

2 Theories of Bounded Induction

Let us recall first the concept of NP search problems.

2.1 NP Search Problems

A NP search problem is determined by a polynomial time relation $R(x,y)$ such that it holds

$$\forall x \exists y R(x,y) \ \wedge \ \forall x, y \ (R(x,y) \rightarrow |y| \leq |x|^{O(1)}) \ .$$

The task is: given x find a solution y such that $R(x,y)$. Note that the solution needs not to be unique, i.e. R is not necessarily a graph of a function.

The relative complexity of two NP search problems $R(x,y)$ and $S(u,v)$ can be compared by a *p-reduction*. A p-reduction of R to S is a pair of polynomial time functions $f(x)$ and $g(x,v)$ such that

$$S(f(x),v) \ \rightarrow \ R(x,g(x,v)) \ .$$

The interpretation of the reduction is this: if we want to find a solution y for x in R we take a solution v for $f(x)$ in S and compute from it $y := g(x,v)$.

There is a variety of classes of NP search problems that are p-equivalent (mutually p-reducible), often characterized by a problem with a transparent combinatorial meaning. A prominent example is the class PLS (polynomial local search), cf.[4,24]. It is given by a polynomial time relation $S(x,y)$ defining the set of possible solutions $\{y \mid S(x,y)\}$ for x (we assume it contains 0 and the size of any possible solution is polynomially bounded in $|x|$), an integer valued cost function $c(x,y)$ and a neighborhood function $N(x,y)$ such that

$$S(x,y) \;\rightarrow\; [\; S(x,N(x,y)) \wedge c(x,N(x,y)) \leq c(x,y)\; .\;]$$

Both functions $c(x,y)$ and $N(x,y)$ are polynomial time. The task is to find a locally optimal solution, i.e. a string y such that

$$S(x,y) \;\wedge c(x,N(x,y)) = c(x,y)\; .$$

2.2   NP Induction

Extend T by adding as new axioms formulas expressing induction

$$[\; B(0) \;\wedge\; \forall i < x\; (B(i) \rightarrow B(i+1)) \;]\;\;\rightarrow\;\; B(x) \qquad (5)$$

for all bounded existential formulas (the so called E_1-formulas) of the form

$$B(x) \;:=\; \exists y < s(x)\; C(x,y)$$

with C an open formula. Formula C can have other free variables (parameters). Every E_1-formula defines an NP predicate and vice versa, every NP predicate can be defined by such a formula. We shall call this extension of T as $NP-IND$.

  Assume

$$NP - IND \;\vdash\; \exists y A(x,y) \qquad (6)$$

A open. The witnessing can be analyzed using the Herbrand's theorem from Subsection 1.2 although other methods are available (cf.[3,13]). We shall explain the idea on a special case for which the easier form of Herbrand's theorem from Subsection 1.1 suffices.

  Assume that the formula in (6) is provable from T using just one induction axiom up to $t(x)$

$$[\; B(0) \;\wedge\; \forall i < t(x)\; (B(i) \rightarrow B(i+1)) \;]\;\;\rightarrow\;\; B(t(x))$$

for a formula B without any parameters (this is what allows us to use the simpler version of Herbrand's theorem). Assume also that $C(0,0)$ is valid, and that $C(x,y)$ implies $y < s(x)$ to ease the notation. Then (using the deduction lemma) T proves, in particular, the formula

$$[\; (i < t(x) \wedge C(i,z_i)) \rightarrow \exists z_{i+1}\; C(i+1,z_{i+1}) \;]\;\; \vee\;\; \exists y\; A(x,y)\; . \qquad (7)$$

and

$$\forall z \neg C(t(x),z)\;\; \vee\;\; \exists y\; A(x,y)\; . \qquad (8)$$

Using the witnessing from Subsection 1.1 to (7) we get a polynomial time algorithm $f(x, i, z_i)$ that either finds a witness y for $A(x, y)$ or a witness z_{i+1} for $C(i + 1, z_{i+1})$. Hence if we start from the triple $(x, 0, 0)$ and iterate f we either find suitable y or a witness z to $C(t(x), z)$. But in the latter case we apply a witnessing function for (8) to find y.

From this process we do not get a polynomial time witnessing algorithm. But it shows that the NP search problem defined by A is p-reducible to a PLS problem: interpret f as a neighborhood function and $t(x) - i$ as a cost function on a suitable set of possible solution (the triples above). See Buss and Krajíček [4] for details (and another proof).

2.3   NP Length Induction

One may extend T by a set of formulas expressing a weaker form of induction, the so called length induction (after Buss [3]):

$$[\, B(0) \, \wedge \, \forall i < |x| \, (B(i) \to B(i + 1)) \,] \; \to \; B(|x|)$$

again for all E_1-formulas, and denote the resulting theory $NP - LIND$.

By Krajíček, Pudlák and Takeuti [22] the theory $NP - LIND$ is stronger than T unless NP $\subseteq$ P/poly. On the other hand Buss [3] has proved that $NP - LIND$ is conservative over T w.r.t. existential formulas. Hence existential formulas provable in $NP - LIND$ can be witnessed by polynomial time algorithms.

2.4   Witnessing E_2-Formulas in NP-IND and NP-LIND

E_2-formulas are formulas of the form $\exists y < s(x) \forall z < t(x, y) \, A(x, y, z)$. E_2-formulas provable in $NP-IND$ can be witnessed by a polynomial time algorithm with an access to an NP oracle (cf.[3]). If an E_2-formula is proved using NP-LIND only it can be witnessed by a polynomial time algorithm which queries an NP oracle but only ($O(\log n)$ times (cf.[12]). It may be interesting to point out that the predicates in this class (i.e. 0/1-functions) are precisely those decidable in logarithmic space with an access to an NP oracle.

2.5   Induction for Predicates in PH

Predicates in Polynomial Hierarchy (PH) are defined by bounded formulas (no restriction on the quantifier complexity). Theory PH-IND augments T by adding the induction axiom for all bounded formulas. By [3] the same theory would be obtained if we added only PH-LIND: an IND axiom for a bounded formula with k quantifiers can be deduced from a LIND axiom for a formula with $k + 1$ quantifiers.

Analysis of witnessing of existential formulas provable in PH-IND is done using various classes of NP search problems. The original characterization of [19] used NP search problems related to the soundness of fragments of quantified propositional calculus. These characterizations have been greatly simplified and their combinatorial structure has been made more transparent using NP search problems defined in terms of games, cf. [26,23,27,28].

3   Propositional Proof Systems

A proof system for propositional logic (see Subsection 1.1) is p-bounded if there is a constant $c \geq 1$ such that any tautology τ has a P-proof of size at most $|\tau|^c$. Cook and Reckhow [9] noted that a p-bounded proof system exists iff NP is closed under complementation. It is thus expected that no such proof system exists and to prove this is the fundamental problem of proof complexity (cf. [15]).

Given a proof system P we would like to find an explicit infinite family of tautologies whose P-proofs cannot be polynomially bounded (such tautologies are called informally hard). For many proof systems explicit examples of hard tautologies are known but all these proof systems are weaker than the usual text-book propositional calculus based on a finite number of axioms schemes and inference rules (a Frege system in the terminology of [9]).

It is a very interesting problem to find such hard tautologies for Frege systems or even for stronger systems. In demonstrating the hardness of the formulas one would not hesitate to use a plausible hypothesis from the computational world, e.g. a hypothesis of the form that every circuit performing a specific task must be large. Several other fundamental problems of complexity theory were reduced to a hypothesis of this form. Examples include the conjectures that the classes P and NP differ, that a universal derandomization is possible or that a cryptographically strong pseudo-random generator exists (see [14] for a discussion).

3.1   Feasible Interpolation

Let $\alpha_n(x, y)$ and $\beta_n(x, z)$ be size $n^{O(1)}$ propositional formulas having common variables $x = (x_1, \ldots, x_n)$. Consider disjunctions

$$\neg \alpha_n(x, y) \vee \neg \beta_n(x, z) . \tag{9}$$

These disjunctions express the disjointness of sets

$$U := \bigcup_n \{x \in \{0, 1\}^n \mid \exists y \alpha_n(x, y)\}$$

and

$$V := \bigcup_n \{x \in \{0, 1\}^n \mid \exists z \beta_n(x, z)\} .$$

These sets are in NP/poly and in NP if the formulas are defined uniformly in n.

The idea of feasible interpolation is that having short proofs of the disjunctions (9) in a proof system P it ought to be possible to separate sets U and V by some feasible algorithm. The intended use is in the opposite direction: having a pair of disjoint NP sets hard to separate (such pairs are conjectured to exists in cryptography) allows to define formulas (the disjunctions above) hard for P.

This lower bound method is quite successful and applies to the most varied class of proof systems among all lower bound methods. Proof systems admitting some form of feasible interpolation include resolution, cutting planes proof system, algebraic and geometric proof systems, or the OBDD proof system. Most recent references (as well as some history) can be found in [16,25].

Feasible interpolation does not, however, work for strong proof systems. For example, assume $h(x)$ is a one-way permutation and $b(x)$ is its hard bit (cf. [1]). Assume in addition that there are polynomial size P-proofs of formulas expressing that h is injective; using the notation from Subsection 1.3 the formulas are

$$||x \neq y \rightarrow h(x) \neq h(y)||^n .$$

In such a case it is easy to see that the disjunctions expressing the disjointness of sets

$$U_i := \{y \in \{0,1\}^n \mid \exists x(h(x) = y \wedge b(x) = i\}, \text{ for } i = 0, 1$$

have short P-proofs as well. But an algorithm that would separate these sets would at the same time compute the hard bit, and that is (conjectured to be) impossible. This applies with $h = RSA$ to Extended Frege systems by [20], and there are similar constructions also for some weaker systems (cf.[2]).

3.2   Feasible Disjunction Property

A proof of feasible interpolation for a proof system P usually establishes a stronger property: There exists an algorithm that upon receiving a P-proof of a disjunction $\alpha \vee \beta$ of two formulas in disjoint sets of variables finds a P-proof of one of them.

Let us point out a property that can be assumed (for the purpose of proving lengths-of-proofs lower bounds) to hold for all proof systems. Following [17] we call it the *feasible disjunction property* (fdp).

A proof system P has fdp if there exists a constant $c \geq 1$ such that whenever a disjunction

$$\alpha_1 \vee \ldots \vee \alpha_k \tag{10}$$

of k formulas with no two having a variable in common has a P-proof of size s then one of α_i has a P-proof of size at most s^c.

A simple observation is that a proof system P that does not have fdp cannot be p-bounded. Assume for a simplicity that a P-proof of a formula is at least as long as the formula. Then all formulas α_i in (10) have size at most s, at least one of them must be a tautology but it does not have p-bounded proofs.

The feasible disjunction property appeared in a connection with the so called proof complexity generators. These are propositional tautologies of a certain specific form and they are proposed as candidate hard formulas for strong proof systems. The analysis of their hardness is quite related to various forms of witnessing theorems as above. It is consistent with the present knowledge that although feasible interpolation does not apply to strong proof systems, some of its features can be salvaged even in strong systems for these specific formulas, enough to deduce lengths-of-proofs lower bounds (see [17] for a background and references).

Acknowledgements. I thank N. Thapen (Prague) for comments on the draft of this paper.

References

1. Arora, S., Barak, B.: Computational Complexity: A Modern Approach. Cambridge University Press, Cambridge (2009)
2. Bonet, M.L., Pitassi, T., Raz, R.: On Interpolation and Automatization for Frege Proof Systems. SIAM J. of Computing 29(6), 1939–1967 (2000)
3. Buss, S.R.: Bounded Arithmetic. Naples, Bibliopolis (1986)
4. Buss, S.R., Krajíček, J.: An application of boolean complexity to separation problems in bounded arithmetic. Proceedings of the London Mathematical Society 69(3), 1–21 (1994)
5. Clote, P., Kranakis, E.: Boolean Functions and Models of Computation. Springer, Heidelberg (2002)
6. Cobham, A.: The intrinsic computational difficulty of functions. In: Bar-Hillel, Y. (ed.) Proc. Logic, Methodology and Philosophy of Science, pp. 24–30. North-Holland, Amsterdam (1965)
7. Cook, S.A.: Feasibly constructive proofs and the propositional calculus. In: Proc. 7th Annual ACM Symp. on Theory of Computing, pp. 83–97. ACM Press, New York (1975)
8. Cook, S.A., Nguyen, P.: Logical foundations of proof complexity. Cambridge U. Press, Cambridge (2009)
9. Cook, S.A., Reckhow: The relative efficiency of propositional proof systems. J. Symbolic Logic 44(1), 36–50 (1979)
10. Jeřábek, E.: Dual weak pigeonhole principle, Boolean complexity, and derandomization. Annals of Pure and Applied Logic 129, 1–37 (2004)
11. Kolodziejczyk, L., Nguyen, P., Thapen, N.: The provably total NP search problems of weak second order bounded arithmetic (2009) (preprint)
12. Krajíček, J.: Fragments of bounded arithmetic and bounded query classes. Transactions of the A.M.S. 338(2), 587–598 (1993)
13. Krajíček, J.: Bounded arithmetic, propositional logic, and complexity theory. Encyclopedia of Mathematics and Its Applications, vol. 60. Cambridge University Press, Cambridge (1995)
14. Krajíček, J.: Hardness assumptions in the foundations of theoretical computer science. Archive for Mathematical Logic 44(6), 667–675 (2005)
15. Krajíček, J.: Proof complexity. In: Laptev, A. (ed.) European congress of mathematics (ECM), Stockholm, Sweden, June 27-July 2, pp. 221–231. European Mathematical Society, Zurich (2005)
16. Krajíček, J.: A form of feasible interpolation for constant depth Frege systems. J. of Symbolic Logic 75(2), 774–784 (2010)
17. Krajíček, J.: On the proof complexity of the Nisan-Wigderson generator based on a hard NP ∩ coNP function (submitted, March 2010) (preprint); Preliminary version in Electronic Colloquium on Computational Complexity, Rep. No.54 (2010)

18. Krajíček, J., Pudlák, P.: Propositional proof systems, the consistency of first order theories and the complexity of computations. J. Symbolic Logic 54(3), 1063–1079 (1989)
19. Krajíček, J., Pudlák, P.: Quantified Propositional Calculi and Fragments of Bounded Arithmetic. Zeitschr. f. Mathematikal Logik u. Grundlagen d. Mathematik, Bd. 36(1), 29–46 (1990)
20. Krajíček, J., Pudlák, P.: Some consequences of cryptographical conjectures for S_2^1 and EF. Information and Computation 140(1), 82–94 (1998)
21. Krajíček, J., Pudlák, P., Sgall, J.: Interactive Computations of Optimal Solutions. In: Rovan, B. (ed.) MFCS 1990. LNCS, vol. 452, pp. 48–60. Springer, Heidelberg (1990)
22. Krajíček, J., Pudlák, P., Takeuti, G.: Bounded arithmetic and the polynomial hierarchy. Annals of Pure and Applied Logic 52, 143–153 (1991)
23. Krajíček, J., Skelley, A., Thapen, N.: NP search problems in low fragments of bounded arithmetic. J. of Symbolic Logic 72(2), 649–672 (2007)
24. Papadimitriou, C.: The Complexity of the Parity Argument and Other Inefficient proofs of Existence. J. of Computer and System Sciences 48(3), 498–532 (1994)
25. Pudlák, P.: The lengths of proofs. In: Buss, S.R. (ed.) Handbook of Proof Theory, pp. 547–637. Elsevier, Amsterdam (1998)
26. Pudlák, P.: Consistency and games - in search of new combinatorial principles. In: Stoltenberg-Hansen, V., Vaananen, J. (eds.) Proc. Logic Colloquium 2003, Helsinki. Assoc. for Symbolic Logic, pp. 244–281 (2006)
27. Pudlák, P.: Fragments of Bounded Arithmetic and the lengths of proofs. J. of Symbolic Logic 73(4), 1389–1406 (2008)
28. Skelley, A., Thapen, N.: The provably total search problems of bounded arithmetic (preprint 2007) (revised March 2010)

Tree Dualities for Constraint Satisfaction

Andrei Krokhin

School of Engineering and Computing Sciences
Durham University, Durham, DH1 3LE, UK
andrei.krokhin@durham.ac.uk

For a fixed relational vocabulary τ and a fixed finite τ-structure $\mathbf{B}$, the constraint satisfaction problem for $\mathbf{B}$, denoted CSP($\mathbf{B}$), is to decide whether there is a homomorphism from a given finite τ-structure $\mathbf{A}$ to $\mathbf{B}$ ($\mathbf{A} \to \mathbf{B}$, in symbols). The study of such problems has recently been a very active research area. One attractive feature of this line of research is that it uses, and often combines, many different mathematical approaches (e.g. combinatorics, logic, algebra). This feature is clearly seen in the study of CSP dualities (see survey [2]), where the non-existence of a homomorphism to $\mathbf{B}$ is explained by the presence of a "nice enough" obstruction. An excellent example of combining approaches is provided by the following theorem [6,5], which is classical in the area. In my talk, I will discuss the above mentioned approaches and some recent results, including [1,3,4], where conditions 1-6 of Theorem 1 are strengthened or relaxed.

Theorem 1. *For any τ-structure $\mathbf{B}$, the following conditions are equivalent:*

1. *The structure $\mathbf{B}$ has* tree duality,
   i.e. for each τ-structure $\mathbf{A}$ with $\mathbf{A} \not\to \mathbf{B}$, there is a tree obstruction: a tree τ-structure $\mathbf{T}$ such that $\mathbf{T} \to \mathbf{A}$, but $\mathbf{T} \not\to \mathbf{B}$.
2. *The class* co-CSP($\mathbf{B}$) = $\{\mathbf{A} \mid \mathbf{A} \not\to \mathbf{B}\}$ *is definable in* monadic Datalog, *where monadic Datalog is $\exists\wedge$-FO extended with recursion on unary predicates.*
3. *The problem CSP($\mathbf{B}$) can be solved by the* arc-consistency algorithm *which recursively reduces, until stable, the set of possible target values (in $\mathbf{B}$) for each element of an input structure $\mathbf{A}$ by inspecting one tuple in a relation in $\mathbf{A}$ at a time. The input is accepted whenever all the sets at the end of the run are non-empty.*
4. *We have $\mathbf{U}(\mathbf{B}) \to \mathbf{B}$, where $\mathbf{U}(\mathbf{B})$ is the τ-structure whose base set consists of all non-empty subsets of the base set of $\mathbf{B}$ and whose relations are formed as follows: for any (r-ary) relation symbol $R \in \tau$, we have $(A_1, \ldots, A_r) \in R^{\mathbf{U}(\mathbf{B})}$ if and only if, for each $j = 1, \ldots, r$ and each $a \in A_j$, there exists a tuple $(a_1, \ldots, a_r) \in R^{\mathbf{B}} \cap (A_1 \times \ldots \times A_r)$ such that $a_j = a$.*
5. *For each $n \geq 2$, $\mathbf{B}$ has an n-ary totally symmetric polymorphism, i.e. a homomorphism $f : \mathbf{B}^n \to \mathbf{B}$ such that $f(a_1, \ldots, a_n) = f(b_1, \ldots, b_n)$ whenever $\{a_1, \ldots, a_n\} = \{b_1, \ldots, b_n\}$. Here $\mathbf{B}^n$ denotes the n-th direct power of $\mathbf{B}$.*

A. Dawar and H. Veith (Eds.): CSL 2010, LNCS 6247, pp. 32–33, 2010.
© Springer-Verlag Berlin Heidelberg 2010

6. **B** *is homomorphically equivalent to a* τ-*structure* **C** *which has a* semilattice polymorphism,

> *i.e. we have both* **B** $\to$ **C** *and* **C** $\to$ **B**, *and there is a homomorphism* $g : \mathbf{C}^2 \to \mathbf{C}$ *with* g *being an associative, commutative, and idempotent binary operation.*

References

1. Barto, L., Kozik, M.: Constraint satisfaction problems of bounded width. In: FOCS 2009, pp. 595–603 (2009)
2. Bulatov, A., Krokhin, A., Larose, B.: Dualities for constraint satisfaction problems. In: Creignou, N., Kolaitis, P.G., Vollmer, H. (eds.) Complexity of Constraints. LNCS, vol. 5250, pp. 93–124. Springer, Heidelberg (2008)
3. Carvalho, C., Dalmau, V., Krokhin, A.: Caterpillar duality for constraint satisfaction problems. In: LICS 2008, pp. 307–316 (2008)
4. Carvalho, C., Dalmau, V., Krokhin, A.: CSP duality and trees of bounded pathwidth. Theoretical Computer Science (2010) (to appear)
5. Dalmau, V., Pearson, J.: Set functions and width 1 problems. In: Jaffar, J. (ed.) CP 1999. LNCS, vol. 1713, pp. 159–173. Springer, Heidelberg (1999)
6. Feder, T., Vardi, M.Y.: The computational structure of monotone monadic SNP and constraint satisfaction: A study through Datalog and group theory. SIAM Journal on Computing 28, 57–104 (1998)

Ordered Sets in the Calculus of Data Structures

Viktor Kuncak, Ruzica Piskac, and Philippe Suter*

Swiss Federal Institute of Technology Lausanne (EPFL)
`firstname.lastname@epfl.ch`

Abstract. Our goal is to identify families of relations that are useful
for reasoning about software. We describe such families using decidable
quantifier-free classes of logical constraints with a rich set of operations.
A key challenge is to define such classes of constraints in a modular
way, by combining multiple decidable classes. Working with quantifier-
free combinations of constraints makes the combination agenda more
realistic and the resulting logics more likely to be tractable than in the
presence of quantifiers.

Our approach to combination is based on reducing decidable fragments to a common class, Boolean Algebra with Presburger Arithmetic
(BAPA). This logic was introduced by Feferman and Vaught in 1959
and can express properties of uninterpreted sets of elements, with set
algebra operations and equicardinality relation (consequently, it can also
express Presburger arithmetic constraints on cardinalities of sets). Combination by reduction to BAPA allows us to obtain decidable quantifier-
free combinations of decidable logics that share BAPA operations. We
use the term *Calculus of Data Structures* to denote a family of decidable constraints that reduce to BAPA. This class includes, for example,
combinations of formulas in BAPA, weak monadic second-order logic
of k-successors, two-variable logic with counting, and term algebras with
certain homomorphisms. The approach of reduction to BAPA generalizes
the Nelson-Oppen combination that forms the foundation of constraint
solvers used in software verification. BAPA is convenient as a target for
reductions because it admits quantifier elimination and its quantifier-free
fragment is NP-complete.

We describe a new member of the Calculus of Data Structures: a
quantifier-free fragment that supports 1) boolean algebra of finite and
infinite sets of real numbers, 2) linear arithmetic over real numbers, 3)
formulas that can restrict chosen set or element variables to range over
integers (providing, among others, the power of mixed integer arithmetic
and sets of integers), 4) the cardinality operators, stating whether a
given set has a given finite cardinality or is infinite, 5) infimum and
supremum operators on sets. Among the applications of this logic are
reasoning about the externally observable behavior of data structures
such as sorted lists and priority queues, and specifying witness functions
for the BAPA synthesis problem. We describe an abstract reduction to
BAPA for our logic, proving that the satisfiability of the logic is in NP
and that it can be combined with the other fragments of the Calculus of
Data Structures.

---

* This research was supported in part by the Swiss NSF Grant #120433.

A. Dawar and H. Veith (Eds.): CSL 2010, LNCS 6247, pp. 34–48, 2010.
© Springer-Verlag Berlin Heidelberg 2010

1   Introduction

Many useful decidable constraints involve a notion of sets. To combine such constraints, we need a method that in addition to equality and propositional operations allows the constraints from different classes to have common operations on sets. Calculus of Data Structures [KPSW10] is an approach to combine multiple classes of constraints that allow sharing of set operations, by reducing each class to constraints of sets with a cardinality operation.

Constraints on sets arise in a variety of tasks, from software verification to interactive theorem proving. In addition to operators that combine collections into new ones (such as union or intersection), these formulas often involve the cardinality operator computing the number of elements in collections. Several decision procedures for sets and multisets with cardinality operator have been described recently [KNR06,KR07,PK08c,PK08a,PK08b]. Among these results is the NP-completeness of the theory of sets and multisets with the cardinality operator [PK08c]. In addition to their use in verification, these decision procedures can be used to synthesize code from specifications [KMPS10]. The applicability of these decision procedures can be increased by combining them with other decision procedures and theorem provers [KPSW10]. The existing decision procedures for collections with cardinality bounds do not consider operations that couple the collection operations with the operations on the elements.

In terms of quantified constraints, weak second-order theory of sets of totally ordered elements *without* cardinality operator is known to be decidable [Lae68], also as a consequence of S2S decidability [Rab69]. The restriction to quantification over finite sets is essential; the second-order theory of total order is undecidable, as is the theory with quantification over countable sets, or sets of rational or real numbers [She75].

The logic we consider is quantifier free. It tightly interconnects cardinalities, sets, and the underlying total order. Our operations of infimum and supremum only make sense when the underlying theory contains a complete lattice and are specific to theories that contain sets. Moreover, there is no natural way to e.g. remove the cardinality operator from a theory of sets without eliminating the notion of the set altogether. Therefore, previous general results on combinations of theories [RRZ05, SS07, Ghi05] do not appear to simplify the proofs that we present here, and have certainly not been used to show the present result.

We start from the NP-completeness result for sets with the cardinality operator [PK08c] and extend it to collections of totally ordered elements. The key challenge in considering such a logic is to avoid NEXPTIME hardness which easily arises in the presence of sets (see e.g. the addition of relation images to QFBAPA [YPK10]).

As a concrete and natural example of an ordered domain into which other orders can be embedded, we consider the set of real numbers (we do prove theorems that show that the automated reasoning can be performed in terms of rational numbers that denote bounds of certain intervals). To support discrete orders, we introduce the set of integers as a specific subset. Therefore, we can specify that a given set contains only integers, whenever this is desirable. Given a collection variable C, our formulas support computing the number of elements $|C|$, but also the minimum $\min(C)$ and the maximum $\max(C)$ of all elements of C (these operations are partial when the sets can be unbounded; our logic support appropriate predicates to check boundedness and finiteness). We can also define in our language the function $\mathsf{take}(k, C)$ that computes the least k elements from the collection C, where k is an integer variable. More generally, one can compute $\mathsf{lrange}(i, j, C)$ the collection of elements from position i to position j in the ordered collection, counting from the minimum element. A special case of this definable operation is extracting the ith smallest or i^{th} biggest element of a sorted collection.

There is a number of areas in which we believe our constraints are useful.

1. Our constraints can be used to model programs that manipulate data structures. Whereas previous decision procedures supported unsorted sets, our result allows us to additionally consider ordered sets. The presence of order means that we can define operations such as extracting the least element of a set, which gives us complete algebraic laws for the external behavior of priority queues and sorted lists or trees (without duplicates). Our language supports not only operations of insertion and removal but also merging and comparison of sets, as well as selecting subsets of given size and indexing elements.
2. We can define in our language a natural relationship $A < B$ on sets, denoting $\forall x \in A. \forall y \in B.\ x < y$, simply by $\max(A) < \min(B)$. This relationship is useful in specifying e.g. invariants of binary search trees and can be used to verify lookup operations on a binary search tree.
3. Using sets defined over total orders, we are able to remove non-determinism in program synthesis. In [KMPS10] we have developed a synthesizer that works for arbitrary QFBAPA formulas. The synthesizer invokes a quantifier elimination procedure and uses the test terms from quantifier elimination as the synthesized program. These test terms involve choosing k elements from a Venn region, where the value k is computed in the synthesized program. Despite many good closure properties of QFBAPA, we found no natural way to introduce such test terms as part of QFBAPA itself. With the addition of ordering, functions such as $\mathsf{take}(k, C)$ suffice to specify all test terms. The presence of ordering in the specification language means that the user of synthesis can write specifications that have a unique solution.

Our result is formulated as a BAPA reduction and can thus be combined with other logics using the non-disjoint combination framework of [WPK09].

2   Examples

2.1   Using Ordered Sets in Verification

As an example of the application of our decision procedure to program verification, consider first the program of Figure 1, which defines a functional binary search tree in the Scala programming language [OSV08] and introduces two functions. content computes the elements stored in the tree (and is used only for specification purposes). find checks whether a given element is contained in the tree and is a key data structure operation.

```
object BSTSet
  sealed abstract class Tree
  private case class Leaf() extends Tree
  private case class Node(left: Tree, value: Int, right: Tree) extends Tree
  @invariant(max(content(left)) < value && value < min(content(right)))

  def content(t: Tree): Set[Int] = t match {
    case Leaf() ⇒ ∅
    case Node(l,e,r) ⇒ content(l) ∪ { e } ∪ content(r) }

  def find(e: Int, t: Tree): Boolean = (t match
    case Leaf() ⇒ false
    case Node(l,v,r) ⇒
      if (e < v) find(e, l)
      else if (e == v) true
      else find(e, r)
  ) ensuring (res ⇒ (res == (e ∈ content(t)))))
```

Fig. 1. Looking up an element in a binary search tree

Verifying the property specified for find requires taking into account the invariant on the sortedness of trees. The difficult case is showing that if the procedure does *not* find an element, then the element is indeed not in the tree. The proof uses the fact that, for each node with value v, all elements L in the left subtree are less than v, and all elements in the right subtree are larger than v. We can express this condition as $\max(L) < v < \min(R)$. By applying standard techniques to reduce functional programs to formulas, we obtain verification conditions for find such as the following:

$$(\max(L) < v < \min(R) \wedge e < v) \rightarrow (e \in (L \cup \{v\} \cup R) \leftrightarrow e \in L)$$

Such a formula belongs to our decidable class, and can be handled using the decision procedure that we present in the sequel.

Figure 2 shows an example of lookup operation that finds the element of a given rank in a binary search tree. The verification condition formulas for this example can be expressed in our logic and proved using our decision procedure; one example verification condition is

$$C = L \cup \{v\} \cup R \wedge \max(L) < v < \min(R) \rightarrow \mathsf{lrange}(C, \mathsf{card}(L), \mathsf{card}(L)+1) = \{v\}.$$

Figure 3 shows a partitioning function such as the one used as part of the quicksort algorithm. The function splits an unordered collection into a collection

```
object BSTSet {
  sealed abstract class Tree
  private case class Leaf() extends Tree
  private case class Node(left: Tree, value: Int, right: Tree, size : Int) extends Tree {
    @invariant(content(this.left).max < this.value
          && this.value < content(this.right).min)
          && size = content(this).size }

  def lookup(index : Int, t: Tree): Int =
  require (0 <= index && index < t.size)
    t match {
    case Leaf() ⇒ error "out of bounds"
    case Node(l,v,r,_) ⇒
      if (index < l.size) lookup(index, l)
      else if (index == l.size) v
      else lookup(index − l.size − 1, r)
    }
  ensuring (v ⇒ (content(t).lrange(index,index+1))= {v}) }
```

Fig. 2. Finding an element of a given rank in a binary search tree

```
def partition(s: Set, pivot: Int): (Set,Set) =
  var remaining = s
  var below = {}
  var above = {}
  while (invariant below ∪ above ∪ remaining = s ∧
                  below = {} ∨ max(below) ≤ pivot ∧
                  above = {} ∨ pivot < min(above))
  (remaining != {}) {
    var e = chooseOne(remaining)
    remaining = remaining \ {e}
    if (e ≤ pivot)
      below = below ∪ {e}
    else
      above = above ∪ {e}
  }
}) ensuring ((below,above) ⇒ below ∪ above = s ∧
                  below = {} ∨ max(below) ≤ pivot ∧
                  above = {} ∨ pivot < min(above))
```

Fig. 3. Partitioning an unordered collection

of those elements that are less than equal to a given pivot element, and those elements that are greater than the pivot. Given the appropriate loop invariant (Figure 3), the following verification conditions can also be proved using our decision procedure:

$$(\text{above} = \emptyset \vee \text{pivot} < \min(\text{above})) \wedge \neg(e \leq \text{pivot}) \wedge \text{above}' = \text{above} \cup \{e\}$$
$$\rightarrow \text{pivot} < \min(\text{above}').$$

2.2 Using Ordered Sets in Program Synthesis

Synthesizing software from given specifications [MW80] should increase the productivity of a programmer and the chances of obtaining error-free software that entirely corresponds to its specification. The concept of ordering immediately yields a much larger number of definable functions, such as take and Irange. These functions are sufficient to express within the logic the Skolem functions of quantified formulas of BAPA. Consider, for example, the formula

$$\forall S. \forall k. \ \exists A. \exists B. \ (|S| = 2k \rightarrow S = A \cup B \wedge A \cap B = \emptyset \wedge |A| = |B|)$$

This formula has a witness function $f(S, k)$ computing the sets (A, B) by $f(S, k) = (\mathsf{take}(k/2, S), S \setminus \mathsf{take}(k/2, S))$, where $k/2$ denotes integer division by 2, which is definable in integer linear arithmetic. Using ordering on sets, we can define such a computable witness function for every valid BAPA formula with a $\forall^\star \exists^\star$ prefix, thus ensuring a stronger form of quantifier elimination. We have used such witness functions as an output of a synthesis procedure for BAPA [KMPS10]; there the underlying programming language implementation used an implicit ordering on elements to compute f. Without an ordering on elements in the logic it was not clear how to specify a particular subset of a set of a given size. Using the ordering of elements (and the induced partial order on the sets) make the specification more precise and thus improves the predictability of the synthesized code.

3 Unordered, Possibly Infinite Sets with Cardinalities

As a background for our main result on sets of *ordered* elements, we establish the complexity for the satisfiability problem for a logic of *unordered* sets, shown in Figure 4. (Therefore, in this section, the elements should not be assumed to range over real numbers or integers, but over some arbitrary infinite set.) The grammar symbol F ranges over formulas, T over terms denoting real numbers, and S over terms denoting sets. Note that we allow mixed linear constraints on the cardinalities of sets, but the cardinalities of sets themselves are integers or infinite (unlike [PK08b] where cardinalities could be fractional).

The decidability of a quantified version of the logic in Figure 4, based on quantifier elimination and without fractional constraints on cardinalities, goes back to [FV59]. The elementary complexity for the quantified case was shown in [KNR06] (see Section 8.1 for the case of possibly infinite sets). Using quantifier

$$F ::= F \wedge F \mid \neg F \mid S = S \mid T \leq T \mid \mathsf{card}(S) = T \mid \mathsf{card}(S) \geq \aleph_0 \mid T \in \mathbb{Z}$$
$$T ::= k \mid C \mid T + T \mid C * T$$
$$S ::= x \mid \emptyset \mid S \cap S \mid S^c$$

Fig. 4. The logic QFBAPA_∞ of sets with cardinalities. Here C denotes rational constants.

elimination for mixed linear arithmetic [Wei99], we can also obtain the decidability of the quantified language in Figure 4. In this paper, we are interested in efficient bounds for the quantifier-free fragment.

Using a sparse solution theorem for integer linear arithmetic [ES06] the NP membership (and, trivially, NP-hardness) for a simpler version of this logic was shown in [KR07]. However, previous statements of this complexity result considered interpretation where all sets are *finite*. The main claim of this section is that the NP membership remains even if we allow sets to be *infinite*, introduce a predicate to check finiteness, and allow the constraints on cardinalities to be embedded into constraints on linear real arithmetic.

As usual, by a Venn region over variables $x_1, \ldots, x_n$ we mean an intersection containing for each set x_i either x_i or its complement x_i^c. There are exactly 2^n Venn regions over n set variables.

Theorem 1. *Let F be a* QFBAPA$_\infty$ *formula (Figure 4) with free set variables $x_1, \ldots, x_n$ containing at most d atomic formulas ($d \geq 2$). Then F is satisfiable iff there exist*

- *at most $O(d \log(d))$ Venn regions $r_1, \ldots, r_N$ over variables $x_1, \ldots, x_n$ and*
- *non-negative integers $k_1, \ldots, k_N$ and $a_1, \ldots, a_N \in \{0,1\}$ whose number of bits is polynomial in the size of formula F*

such that F is true in some valuation in which for each i where $1 \leq i \leq N$ either $a_i = 0$ and card$(r_i) = k_i$*, or $a_i = 1$ and* card$(r_i) \geq \aleph_0$*, and such that the valuation of all Venn regions other than $r_1, \ldots, r_N$ is the empty set.*

The idea of the proof is to encode cardinalities of possibly infinite set with pairs of integer variables. We represent a finite set of size p by $(0, p)$. We represent an infinite set by pairs of the form $(1, p)$ where p is arbitrary. We then perform a similar but slightly more involved construction to the one in [KR07].

Proof of Theorem 1. Note that all set algebra equations can be encoded using cardinalities using the fact that $A = B$ iff card$((A \cap B^c) \cup (A^c \cap B)) = 0$. We can thus assume that set variables occur only in atomic formulas of the form card$(s) = t$ and card$(s) \geq \aleph_0$. For each set expression s_i in F introduce fresh variables p_i and q_i. Consider the formula

$$\bigwedge_i \left((q_i = 0 \wedge \text{card}(s_i) = p_i) \vee (q_i = 1 \wedge \text{card}(s_i) \geq \aleph_0) \right) \qquad (**)$$

Replace each card$(s_i) = t$ in F with $(q_i = 0 \wedge p_i = t)$ and replace each card$(s_i) \geq \aleph_0$ with $q_i = 1$. Then conjoin the result with $(**)$; we obtain a formula of the form $P \wedge (**)$ where P is a mixed linear arithmetic formula. The original input formula is equivalent to $\exists (p_i)_i (q_i)_i (P \wedge (**))$. Indeed, given the values of sets in the original formula, we assign $q_i = 0$ if s_i is finite and $q_i = 1$ if it is infinite. If s_i is finite, we assign p_i to its size, otherwise we assign p_i to 0. Then card$(s_i) = t$ and $(q_i = 0 \wedge p_i = t)$ evaluate to the same truth value, and so do card$(s_i) \geq \aleph_0$ and $q_i = 1$. Conversely, if $(**)$ holds then $q_i = 0$ if s_i is finite and $q_i = 1$ if s_i

is infinite, so the original and new atomic formulas again evaluate to the same truth values. Note that for s_i infinite, both $\mathsf{card}(s_i){=}p_i$ and $(q_i = 0 \wedge p_i = t)$ are false, regardless of the value of p_i. Thus, given an assignment for which $q_i = 1$, if we change the value of p_i the truth value of $(**)$ or P remains the same.

We next observe that $(**)$ is equisatisfiable with a formula in quantifier-free Presburger arithmetic, extending the construction for finite cardinalities of [KR07]. For each Venn region r_i over the set variables occurring in $(**)$, we introduce two fresh non-negative integer variables a_i and k_i, analogously to q_i and p_i. The intended interpretation is again

$$\bigwedge_j \left((a_j = 0 \wedge \mathsf{card}(r_j){=}k_j) \vee (a_j = 1 \wedge \mathsf{card}(r_j){\geq}\aleph_0) \right) \qquad (V)$$

We next use the property that the cardinality of a finite union of disjoint sets is the sum of the cardinalities of sets. We obtain the following linear integer constraint

$$\bigwedge_i \left(\sum_j \gamma_{ij} a_j \geq q_i \wedge \sum_j \gamma_{ij} k_j = p_i \right) \qquad (I)$$

where $\gamma_{i,j}$ equals 1 if $r_j \subseteq s_i$ is valid and 0 otherwise.

We claim that $(**)$ and (I) have equivalent sets of solution vectors for variables q_j, p_j. Two solutions $(q_j, p_j)_j$ and $(q'_j, p'_j)_j$ are equivalent if $q_j = q'_j$ and if $q_j = 0$ then $p_j = p'_j$.

$(\Rightarrow)$: In one direction, given the values of set variables such that $(**)$ holds, define a_j and k_j according to (V). Consider an arbitrary conjunct number i in the conjunction (I). Consider first the case when s_i is a finite set. Then all Venn regions contained in s_i are finite, so for all j for which $\gamma_{ij} = 1$ we have $a_j = 0$ and p_j denotes the size of the finite Venn region r_j. We also have $q_i = 0$ so $\sum_j \gamma_{ij} a_j \geq q_i$ reduces to $0 \geq 0$. The condition $\gamma_{ij} k_j = p_i$ holds because the size of a union of disjoint sets is equal to sums of the sizes of the sets. In the second case, s_i is infinite. Then $q_i = 1$. Because s_i is a finite union of Venn regions, there must be a Venn region r_j that is infinite. Therefore, there exists j such that $\gamma_{ij} = 1$ and $a_j = 1$. This ensures that $\sum_j \gamma_{ij} a_j \geq q_i$ holds. Given that $q_i = 1$, we can find an equivalent solution with arbitrary values of p'_j, so we can make $\sum_j \gamma_{ij} k_j = p_i$ hold as well.

$(\Leftarrow)$: In the other direction, suppose we have the values of variables a_i and k_i. We then define as Venn regions disjoint sets such that (V) holds. The proof that $(**)$ holds is straightforward.

This completes the proof of equisatisfiability of $(**)$ and (I). We are left with checking the satisfiability of $P \wedge (I)$. Transform P into disjunctive normal form $\bigvee_j D_j \cdot (\boldsymbol{k}, \boldsymbol{a}, \boldsymbol{v}) \geq e_j$, where each disjunct is a mixed linear programming problem and all coefficients in D_j are integers. The formula is satisfiable iff one of the disjuncts is satisfiable, so consider one disjunct $D_j \cdot (\boldsymbol{k}, \boldsymbol{a}, \boldsymbol{v}) \geq e_j$. As in [PK08b], let $\boldsymbol{v} = \boldsymbol{l} + \boldsymbol{f}$ where $\boldsymbol{l}$ are fresh integer variables, and $\boldsymbol{f}$ are real variables restricted to $[0, 1)$. Splitting D_j into two groups of columns $[D'_j, D''_j]$ we obtain a problem of the form $D''_j \boldsymbol{f} \geq b - D'_j \cdot (\boldsymbol{k}, \boldsymbol{a}) - D''_j \boldsymbol{l}$. Note that the right-hand side is integer so we can replace the left-hand side with g where $g = \lfloor D''_j \boldsymbol{f} \rfloor$. Because $\boldsymbol{f}$ has components from $[0, 1)$, the vector g is bounded by the norm of the matrix D''_j, and the values of g are representable by polynomially many bits. For each value of g, the original problem decomposes into one polynomial sized mixed linear programming problem $D''_j \boldsymbol{f} \geq g$, and one integer linear programming problem

$$(I) \ \wedge \ (g \geq b - D'_j \cdot (\boldsymbol{k}, \boldsymbol{a}) - D''_j \boldsymbol{l}) \tag{K}$$

Note that (I) is an integer linear programming problem with exponentially many variables (a_j, k_j). However, there are only polynomially many constraints in (I) (two for each expression s_i in the input formula) and therefore polynomially many in (K). Moreover, also the coefficients γ_{ij} are bounded. After introducing polynomially many slack variables for the inequations in (I), we obtain (K') that has the form arising in [KR07] from constraints over finite sets, and has sparse solutions with only $O(d \log d)$ variables a_i and k_i non-empty. The non-empty Venn regions $r_1, \ldots, r_N$ are precisely those Venn regions r_i for which $a_i \neq 0 \vee k_i \neq 0$.   □

If we know that sparse solutions exist, it is not necessary to generate an exponentially large integer linear programming problem; we can encode in quantifier-free Presburger arithmetic both the guessing of which regions are non-zero, and checking whether the constraints on sets are satisfiable for this guess. We therefore obtain the extension of the result in [KR07] to infinite sets and to mixed linear constraints on cardinalities.

Corollary 1. *Satisfiability for* QFBAPA$_\infty$ *(Figure 4) is NP-complete.*

4   Ordered, Possibly Infinite Sets with Cardinalities

Figure 5 shows the syntax of QFBAPA$_\infty^\leq$, our quantifier-free logic of sets of real numbers supporting integer sets and variables, linear arithmetic, the cardinality operator, infimum, and supremum. In this section we show our main result, which is a reduction of QFBAPA$_\infty^\leq$ to QFBAPA$_\infty$.

The predicates $T \in \mathbb{Z}$ and $A \subseteq \mathbb{Z}$ denote that T is an integer term and that A is a set containing only integers, respectively. $\mathsf{card}(A) \geq \aleph_0$ means that A is an infinite set. The predicate $\mathsf{card}(A) = T$ means that A is finite and its cardinality is the non-negative integer term T. The predicate $\mathsf{inf}(A) = -\infty$ means that A has no lower bound, whereas $\mathsf{inf}(A) = T$ means that the infimum of A is T. Analogously, $\mathsf{sup}(A) = \infty$ means that A has no upper bound, whereas $\mathsf{sup}(A) = T$

$$F ::= F \wedge F \mid \neg F \mid S = S \mid T \leq T \mid S < S \mid T \in S \mid S \subseteq \mathbb{Z} \mid T \in \mathbb{Z}$$
$$\qquad \mathsf{card}(S) \geq \aleph_0 \mid \mathsf{card}(S) = T \mid \mathsf{inf}(S) = -\infty \mid \mathsf{inf}(S) = T \mid \mathsf{sup}(S) = \infty \mid \mathsf{sup}(S) = T$$
$$T ::= k \mid C \mid T + T \mid C * T$$
$$S ::= x \mid \emptyset \mid S \cap S \mid S^c \mid \mathsf{take}(T, S) \mid \mathsf{lrange}(T, T, S)$$

Fig. 5. The logic QFBAPA$_\infty^\leq$ of ordered sets with cardinalities, infima and suprema. Here C denotes rational constants.

means that the supremum of A is T. As a special case, for finite non-empty sets the operations card, inf, sup correspond, respectively, to: the number of elements, the least element, and the greatest element. For the empty set, we define the infimum and supremum predicates to be false: we assume $\neg(\mathsf{inf}(\emptyset)=-\infty)$ and $\neg(\mathsf{sup}(\emptyset)=\infty)$, as well as $\neg(\mathsf{inf}(\emptyset)=v)$ and $\neg(\mathsf{sup}(\emptyset)=T)$ for every term T. Note that the logic can define arbitrary propositional operations, the subset relation ($A \subseteq B$ is $A \cap B = A$), and all set algebra operations (using $\cap$ and the complement S^c). We define the partial order on finite sets, denoted $A < B$ by $\mathsf{sup}(A)=k_A \wedge k_A < k_B \wedge \mathsf{inf}(B)=k_B$, where k_A and k_B are fresh integer variables. Define $\mathsf{take}(T, S) = A$ as $\mathsf{card}(A)=T \wedge A < (S \backslash A)$. We define $\mathsf{lrange}(T_1, T_2, S) = B$ as a shorthand for $B = A_2 \backslash A_1 \wedge A_2 = \mathsf{take}(T_2, S) \wedge A_1 = \mathsf{take}(T_1 - 1, S)$, where A_1, A_2 are fresh set variables.

4.1   A Decision Procedure for QFBAPA$^{\leq}_{\infty}$

We next describe our procedure for reducing QFBAPA$^{\leq}_{\infty}$ to BAPA. When we reduce fresh variables we assume that they are existentially quantified at the top level. The satisfiability of the resulting formula will thus reduce to satisfiability of a quantifier-free formula.

Rewritings. If k_f and A_f are fresh variables we replace $T \in S$ with

$$k_f = T \wedge \mathsf{card}(A_f)=1 \wedge \mathsf{inf}(A_f)=k_f \wedge \mathsf{sup}(A_f)=k_f \wedge A_f \subseteq S.$$

We also replace negative occurrences of the predicates $\mathsf{card}(S) \geq \aleph_0$, $\mathsf{card}(S)=T$, $\mathsf{inf}(S)=-\infty$, $\mathsf{inf}(S)=T$, $\mathsf{sup}(S)=\infty$, $\mathsf{sup}(S)=T$ with positive occurrences by introducing fresh variables and disjunctions. For example, we replace $\neg(\mathsf{inf}(S)=-\infty)$ with $(S = \emptyset \vee \mathsf{inf}(S)=k)$ for k fresh.

In the sequel we present an algorithm for *conjunctions* F of literals; formulas of arbitrary boolean structure can be handled by e.g. rewriting them into disjunctive normal form or using an approach analogous to DPLL(T) [GHN+04]. Some of the transformations below introduce new disjunctions by "guessing"; we assume that the process of selecting one disjunct is applied implicitly.

Decomposition into integers and non-integers sets. For each set variable A, we introduce two fresh variables $A^{\mathbb{Z}}$ and $A^{\mathbb{R} \backslash \mathbb{Z}}$, and add the constraints that $A = A^{\mathbb{Z}} \cup A^{\mathbb{R} \backslash \mathbb{Z}} \wedge A^{\mathbb{Z}} \cap A^{\mathbb{R} \backslash \mathbb{Z}} = \emptyset$. If the constraint $A \subseteq \mathbb{Z}$ appears in F, we replace it with $A^{\mathbb{R} \backslash \mathbb{Z}} = \emptyset$. This step effectively partitions every set variable into an integer and a non-integer part. In our reduction to QFBAPA$_{\infty}$, we will use this partitioning to encode the constraints on the integer and real parts of sets separately. In the following when we refer to "any set variable A", we refer to all set variables, including the ones introduced at this step.

Purification.   We flatten all arguments to the predicates $\mathsf{card}(S) \geq \aleph_0$, $\mathsf{card}(S)=T$, $\mathsf{inf}(S)=-\infty$, $\mathsf{inf}(S)=T$, $\mathsf{sup}(S)=\infty$, $\mathsf{sup}(S)=T$, $A \subseteq \mathbb{Z}$ and $T \in \mathbb{Z}$ by introducing fresh variables and new equalities when an argument is not already a variable. Then, for each set variable A such that $\mathsf{inf}(A)=-\infty$ or $\mathsf{sup}(A)=\infty$ appears in the formula, we add the constraint $\mathsf{card}(A) \geq \aleph_0$.

Guessing the empty and the infinite sets. For each set variable A, we guess whether A is empty, non-empty finite, or infinite. In each case, we add a constraint to F: If it is empty, we add the constraint $\mathsf{card}(A){=}0$. If it is infinite, we add the constraint $\mathsf{card}(A){\geq}\aleph_0$. If is it finite but non-empty, we add the constraint $\mathsf{card}(A){=}k_\mathsf{f} \wedge k_\mathsf{f} \geq 1$, where k_f is fresh.

Guessing the unbounded sets. For each set that we guessed was infinite, we now guess whether it admits an infimum and a supremum. Similarly to the previous step, we add the constraints $\mathsf{inf}(A){=}{-}\infty$, $\mathsf{sup}(A){=}\infty$, $\mathsf{inf}(A){=}k_\mathsf{f}$ and $\mathsf{sup}(A){=}k_\mathsf{f}$ to F as needed. We note that at the end of this step, there is a variable for the cardinality of each finite set appearing in the formula, as well as a variable for each bounded infimum and supremum, when they exist.

Guessing an ordering on bounds. We consider the set $\boldsymbol{B}$ of all numeric variables appearing in the predicates inf and sup as well as all integer and rational constants appearing in F. We guess an arrangement into (equality) equivalence classes of all variables and constants in $\boldsymbol{B}$. We then guess a total ordering between these equality classes. We number the classes in increasing order from 1 to n. We add to F equality constraints between members of the same equivalence class. For convenience, we also introduce a fresh variable b_i in each class. We finally add to F all constraints $b_i < b_{i+1}$.

Segmentation of the domain. For each of the equivalence classes, we create two fresh set variables $C_i^{\mathbb{Z}}$ and $C_i^{\mathbb{R}\backslash\mathbb{Z}}$. We then guess whether b_i is an integer or a non-integer value. In the first case, we add the constraint $b_i \in \mathbb{Z} \wedge \mathsf{card}(C_i^{\mathbb{Z}}){=}1 \wedge \mathsf{card}(C_i^{\mathbb{R}\backslash\mathbb{Z}}){=}0$ to F. Otherwise, we add the constraint $\mathsf{card}(C_i^{\mathbb{Z}}){=}0 \wedge \mathsf{card}(C_i^{\mathbb{R}\backslash\mathbb{Z}}){=}1$. We then create $2 \cdot (n+1)$ more fresh set variables $C_{n+1}^{\mathbb{Z}}$ to $C_{2n+1}^{\mathbb{Z}}$ and $C_{n+1}^{\mathbb{R}\backslash\mathbb{Z}}$ to $C_{2n+1}^{\mathbb{R}\backslash\mathbb{Z}}$. We make all the fresh set variables disjoint by adding to F the constraints $\mathsf{card}(C_i^{\star_1} \cap C_j^{\star_2}){=}0$ for $0 \leq i < j \leq 2n+1$ and $\star_1, \star_2 \in \{\mathbb{Z}, \mathbb{R} \backslash \mathbb{Z}\}$. In the following we interpret the fresh sets as points ($C_0^\star$ to $C_n^\star$) and intervals ($C_{n+1}^\star$ to $C_{2n+1}^\star$) on $\mathbb{R}$ (see Figure 6). As for our set variables previously, the points and intervals are split between integer and non-integer values. Note that in our interpretation, the introduced sets are all infinite, except for the sets of integers $C_{n+2}^{\mathbb{Z}}$ to $C_{2n}^{\mathbb{Z}}$. We therefore add to F the constraints

$$\mathsf{card}(C_i^{\mathbb{Z}}){=}k_\mathsf{f}^i \wedge k_\mathsf{f}^i = \lceil b_i - b_{i-1} \rceil - 1 \quad \text{for } n + 2 \leq i \leq 2n$$

$$\mathsf{card}(C_i^{\mathbb{Z}}){\geq}\aleph_0 \quad \text{for other values of } i$$

$$\mathsf{card}(C_i^{\mathbb{R}\backslash\mathbb{Z}}){\geq}\aleph_0 \quad \text{for all values of } i$$

where k_f^i are fresh integer variables. (Note that we can encode the first equality without $\lceil \ \rceil$ by using inequalities.) Following our interpretation, we express the

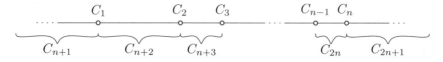

Fig. 6. Segmentation of $\mathbb{R}$. We use C_i here to denote $C_i^{\mathbb{Z}} \cup C_i^{\mathbb{R}\backslash\mathbb{Z}}$

set variables of F using the point and interval sets. For each non-empty set $A^\star$ ($\star \in \{\mathbb{Z}, \mathbb{Z} \setminus \mathbb{R}\}$), we introduce $2n + 1$ fresh variables $A_i^\star$ representing the intersection of $A^\star$ with $C_i^\star$. $A^\star$ can then be expressed as the (disjoint) union of all variables $A_i^\star$:

$$\bigwedge_{0 < i \leq 2n+1} A_i^\star = A^\star \cap C_i^\star \quad \wedge \quad A^\star = \bigcup_{0 < i \leq 2n+1} A_i^\star$$

We now need to express that some of these intersections are empty. If we guessed that $A^\star$ admitted an infimum in the equivalence class p we add the constraints $\bigwedge_{n+1 \leq i \leq n+p} A_i^\star \cap C_i^\star = \emptyset$, and similarly for sets that admit a supremum.

Solution of the QFBAPA$_\infty$ constraints. As a final step, we remove from F all occurrences of the predicates inf and sup. We observe that the resulting formula is in QFBAPA$_\infty$. We can use the results from Section 3 to determine its satisfiability. Our original formula is satisfiable if and only if F is satisfiable.

Theorem 2. *The decision procedure described above is sound and complete.*

Proof. **Soundness.** We first show that each of our reasoning steps results in a logically sound conclusion. The rewritings are correct by definition. Splitting each set into a partition is sound and the added constraints on the partition are consequences. The purification process introduces fresh variables that are constrained to be equal to the term they represent, so any model for the formula without the fresh variables can trivially be extended to the original variables. The constraints that we add after guesses are immediate consequences of these. It remains to show that when we introduce the fresh variables $C_i^{\prime\star}$ and $A_i^\star$ and the constraints on them, we do not exclude any solution for the existing variables. To show this, consider a model for all non-fresh variables, and consider the ordering of equivalence classes following from the values of the infima and suprema of these sets. For any set $A^\star$, we can build the sets $A_i^\star$ as in the construction by splitting $A^\star$ into subsets with bounds defined by the values in the equivalence classes. We can then construct the sets $C_i^\star$ by taking the union of all sets $A_i^\star$ (each time for a fixed i). Note that all the sets $C_i^\star$ are disjoint.

Completeness. To show completeness, we need to show that we can build a model for the original formula from a model for our formula in QFBAPA$_\infty$. The model for the reduced formula will contain values for all the bounds b_i as well as the cardinality of each set (and more generally of each Venn region), and we need to extend this model by populating the sets with elements from $\mathbb{R}$. We start by populating the singleton sets $C_i^\star$, for $0 < i \leq n$. If the value for b_i is an integer, we set in the extended model $C_i^{\mathbb{Z}} = \{b_i\}$, $C_i^{\mathbb{R} \setminus \mathbb{Z}} = \emptyset$, and the model for the case where b_i is not an integer is built similarly (note that the decision procedure will always return values that are in $\mathbb{Q}$). We then proceed to populate the sets C_{n+i}, for $0 < i \leq n+1$. We know the cardinality of each Venn region of such a set, and these regions are by definition disjoint. In the case of the integer sets $C_{n+i}^{\mathbb{Z}}$, we simply pick distinct integers for each Venn region. We know this is always possible because we encoded all the relevant cardinality constraints in the QFBAPA$_\infty$ formula. We can pick integers in any order, because our construction ensures that no ordering constraints concern elements *within* a set $C_{n+i}^{\mathbb{Z}}$. As a result, $C_{n+i}^{\mathbb{Z}}$ will always contain all integers from b_{i-1} to b_i. For the Venn regions of the non-integer sets $C_{n+i}^{\mathbb{R}\backslash\mathbb{Z}}$, the construction is slightly more involved. Because $C_{n+i}^{\mathbb{R}\backslash\mathbb{Z}}$ is infinite, we know that at least one of its Venn regions is infinite as well, and the model for the QFBAPA$_\infty$ formula will encode this. We name this region V_I. For a set $C_{n+i}^{\mathbb{R}\backslash\mathbb{Z}}$ with m distinct Venn regions, infimum b_{i-1} and supremum b_i, we can populate the jth Venn region V_j (with $V_j \neq V_I$) as follows. If V_j has finite cardinality k, we then define

$$V_j = \bigcup_{1 \leq l \leq \lceil \frac{k}{2} \rceil} \left\{ b_i + \frac{\varepsilon}{m \cdot l + j} \right\} \cup \bigcup_{1 \leq l \leq k - \lceil \frac{k}{2} \rceil} \left\{ b_{i+1} - \frac{\varepsilon}{m \cdot l + j} \right\}$$

If the cardinality of V_j is required to be infinite, we define V_j as the corresponding countable set $V_j = \bigcup_{l \in \mathbb{N}} \left\{ b_i + \frac{\varepsilon}{m \cdot l + j} \right\} \cup \bigcup_{l \in \mathbb{N}} \left\{ b_{i+1} - \frac{\varepsilon}{m \cdot l + j} \right\}$. In both cases, we define ε as $\frac{1}{2} \cdot \min(1, \min_{0 < i < n}(b_{i+1}, b_i))$ (ε is half the width of the smallest interval). Note that this generates distinct non-integer values for all the Venn regions because $m \cdot l + j \neq m \cdot l' + j'$ whenever $0 \leq j < j' < m$. For infinite sets, these values will converge to both ends of the interval represented by $C_i^{\mathbb{R}\backslash\mathbb{Z}}$. This means that constraints on infima and suprema outside of particular set will always be satisfied. We define the identified infinite region V_I to be $(b_{i-1}, b_i) \setminus \bigcup_{0 < j \leq k, j \neq I} V_j$ (i.e. the open interval corresponding to $C_{n+i}^{\mathbb{R}\backslash\mathbb{Z}}$ minus all other Venn regions). This set has uncountably many elements and is also dense towards its extreme points. The construction for the four intervals that are open either to the left or to the right is similar. This concludes the construction of the elements of the $C_i^\star$ sets. The construction for all the other sets follows then from their definitions in terms of the $C_i^\star$ sets.

Complexity. QFBAPA$_\infty$ is NP-hard because it subsumes propositional logic. The above reduction to QFBAPA$_\infty$ runs in NP-time. By Corollary 1, the satisfiability problem for QFBAPA$_\infty^{\leq}$ is NP-complete.

5   An Extension of the Calculus of Data Structures

We can now state an extension of Theorem 5 from [KPSW10] with the result on ordered collections.

Theorem 3. *There exist BAPA reductions for the following logics 1) WS2S [TW68], 2) two-variable logic with counting over finite models (C^2) [PH05, PST00], 3) Bernays-Schönfinkel-Ramsey over finite models [Ram30], 4) quantifier-free multisets with cardinality constraints [PK08a], 5) term algebras with the content function [SDK10], 6) the logic QFBAPA$_\infty^{\leq}$ in Figure 5. Thus, quantifier-free set-sharing combination of all these logics is decidable.*

6   Conclusions

We had previously identified a number of uses for constraints on sets and cardinality bounds and established their optimal complexity. In this paper we generalized these results to: a) infinite sets b) the case of a total, possibly dense, ordering relation on collection elements. In particular, we have looked at collections of numerical elements: in this context, constraints on cardinalities are naturally combined with constraints on minimal and maximal elements. In each case, we have shown that the NP-completeness complexity of the decision problem was preserved in the extension.

We have shown that these steps beyond uninterpreted elements provide important benefits: using this new expressive power, we were able to precisely specify the contracts of functions manipulating ordered data structures. We have also shown that the added expressiveness promises to make synthesis specifications more precise and the synthesized code more predictable. Finally, in addition to the uses of the presented decision procedure alone, the fact that the decision procedure works as a reduction to BAPA [WPK09] means that they can be naturally combined with a number of other logics such as WS1S [TW68] two-variable logic with counting [PST00], BAPA extensions [YPK10], and certain recursive functions over algebraic data types [SDK10]. Therefore, it presents another building block towards a rich decidable language useful in verification, synthesis, and automated reasoning.

Acknowledgements. We thank Yuri Gurevich for providing in 2008 helpful references on the decidability of the theories of total orders as well as the IJCAR and CSL reviewers for their feedback. We thank Robin Steiger and Utkarsh Upadhyay who have, in the meantime, implemented a decision procedure for finite sets of integers with the cardinality operator and made it more efficient.

References

[ES06]   Eisenbrand, F., Shmonin, G.: Carathéodory bounds for integer cones. Operations Research Letters 34(5), 564–568 (2006), http://dx.doi.org/10.1016/j.orl.2005.09.008

[FV59]   Feferman, S., Vaught, R.L.: The first order properties of products of algebraic systems. Fundamenta Mathematicae 47, 57–103 (1959)

[Ghi05]   Ghilardi, S.: Model theoretic methods in combined constraint satisfiability. Journal of Automated Reasoning 33(3-4), 221–249 (2005)

[GHN+04] Ganzinger, H., Hagen, G., Nieuwenhuis, R., Oliveras, A., Tinelli, C.: DPLL(T): Fast decision procedures. In: Alur, R., Peled, D.A. (eds.) CAV 2004. LNCS, vol. 3114, pp. 175–188. Springer, Heidelberg (2004)

[KMPS10] Kuncak, V., Mayer, M., Piskac, R., Suter, P.: Complete functional synthesis. In: PLDI (2010)

[KNR06]   Kuncak, V., Nguyen, H.H., Rinard, M.: Deciding Boolean Algebra with Presburger Arithmetic. J. of Automated Reasoning (2006)

[KPSW10] Kuncak, V., Piskac, R., Suter, P., Wies, T.: Building a calculus of data structures. In: Barthe, G., Hermenegildo, M. (eds.) VMCAI 2010. LNCS, vol. 5944, pp. 26–44. Springer, Heidelberg (2010)

[KR07]   Kuncak, V., Rinard, M.: Towards efficient satisfiability checking for Boolean Algebra with Presburger Arithmetic. In: Pfenning, F. (ed.) CADE 2007. LNCS (LNAI), vol. 4603, pp. 215–230. Springer, Heidelberg (2007)

[Lae68]   Laeuchli, H.: A decision procedure for the weak second order theory of linear order. Studies in Logic and the Foundat. of Math. 50, 189–197 (1968)

[MW80]   Manna, Z., Waldinger, R.: A deductive approach to program synthesis. ACM Trans. Program. Lang. Syst. 2(1), 90–121 (1980)

[OSV08]   Odersky, M., Spoon, L., Venners, B.: Programming in Scala: a comprehensive step-by-step guide. Artima Press (2008)

[PH05]   Pratt-Hartmann, I.: Complexity of the two-variable fragment with counting quantifiers. Journal of Logic, Language and Information 14(3), 369–395 (2005)

[PK08a]   Piskac, R., Kuncak, V.: Decision procedures for multisets with cardinality constraints. In: Logozzo, F., Peled, D.A., Zuck, L.D. (eds.) VMCAI 2008. LNCS, vol. 4905, pp. 218–232. Springer, Heidelberg (2008)

[PK08b]   Piskac, R., Kuncak, V.: Fractional collections with cardinality bounds. In: Kaminski, M., Martini, S. (eds.) CSL 2008. LNCS, vol. 5213, pp. 124–138. Springer, Heidelberg (2008)

[PK08c]   Piskac, R., Kuncak, V.: Linear arithmetic with stars. In: Gupta, A., Malik, S. (eds.) CAV 2008. LNCS, vol. 5123, pp. 268–280. Springer, Heidelberg (2008)

[PST00]   Pacholski, L., Szwast, W., Tendera, L.: Complexity results for first-order two-variable logic with counting. SIAM J. on Computing 29(4), 1083–1117 (2000)

[Rab69]   Rabin, M.O.: Decidability of second-order theories and automata on infinite trees. Trans. Amer. Math. Soc. 141, 1–35 (1969)

[Ram30]   Ramsey, F.P.: On a problem of formal logic. Proc. London Math. Soc. s2-30, 264–286 (1930), doi:10.1112/plms/s2-30.1.264

[RRZ05]   Ranise, S., Ringeissen, C., Zarba, C.G.: Combining data structures with nonstably infinite theories using many-sorted logic. In: Gramlich, B. (ed.) FroCos 2005. LNCS (LNAI), vol. 3717, pp. 48–64. Springer, Heidelberg (2005)

[SDK10]   Suter, P., Dotta, M., Kuncak, V.: Decision procedures for algebraic data types with abstractions. In: POPL (2010)

[She75]   Shelah, S.: The monadic theory of order. The Annals of Mathematics of Mathematics 102(3), 379–419 (1975)

[SS07]   Sofronie-Stokkermans, V.: Hierarchical and modular reasoning in complex theories: The case of local theory extensions. In: Konev, B., Wolter, F. (eds.) FroCos 2007. LNCS (LNAI), vol. 4720, pp. 47–71. Springer, Heidelberg (2007)

[TW68]   Thatcher, J.W., Wright, J.B.: Generalized finite automata theory with an application to a decision problem of second-order logic. Mathematical Systems Theory 2(1), 57–81 (1968)

[Wei99]   Weispfenning, V.: Mixed real-integer linear quantifier elimination. In: ISSAC, pp. 129–136 (1999)

[WPK09]   Wies, T., Piskac, R., Kuncak, V.: Combining theories with shared set operations. In: Frontiers in Combining Systems (2009)

[YPK10]   Yessenov, K., Piskac, R., Kuncak, V.: Collections, cardinalities, and relations. In: Barthe, G., Hermenegildo, M. (eds.) VMCAI 2010. LNCS, vol. 5944, pp. 380–395. Springer, Heidelberg (2010)

Abductive, Inductive and Deductive Reasoning about Resources

Peter W. O'Hearn

Queen Mary University of London

We describe a method for reasoning about programs that uses a mixture of abductive, inductive and deductive inference. It allows us to synthesize a pre/post spec for a program procedure, without requiring any information about the procedure's calling context. The method can be used to obtain partial specifications for portions of large code bases in the millions of lines of code.

The method begins by trying to deductively prove a procedure, with a precondition describing empty or no resources. If at some point we have insufficient information to perform an internal operation – perhaps a lock must be held, or a memory cell must be allocated – we perform abductive inference to infer what is missing, and hypothesize that this is part of the precondition that you need to describe the resources that the program requires. There is the possibility, though, that an unbounded number of abduced preconditions could be generated, if the procedure has a loop. To enable convergence of this process we apply an abstraction operation, which generalizes the more specific abduced facts that have been discovered. In this setup it is the job of abduction to discover descriptions of missing resource, where abstraction computes a generalization of the specific facts discovered by abduction: abstraction used in this way is a form of inductive generalization, rather than deductive reasoning about program behaviour.

Thus, our automated reasoning method involves a mixture of all three of the forms of reasoning – deductive, inductive, and abductive – that Charles Peirce identified in his analysis of the scientific process [5].

This talk presents a survey and further development of recent joint work with Cristiano Calcagno, Dino Distefano and Hongseok Yang on automatic program analysis [1,2,3]. Among other things, the current work automates ideas about local reasoning and footprints I put forward in a talk at the 2001 CSL conference [4]. In particular, our new inference technique attempts to *discover* assertions describing the footprint (the resources that a program component accesses), where previously the human was left to find them.

References

1. Calcagno, C., Distefano, D., O'Hearn, P.W., Yang, H.: Footprint analysis: A shape analysis that discovers preconditions. In: Riis Nielson, H., Filé, G. (eds.) SAS 2007. LNCS, vol. 4634, pp. 402–418. Springer, Heidelberg (2007)
2. Calcagno, C., Distefano, D., O'Hearn, P.W., Yang, H.: Compositional shape analysis by means of bi-abduction. In: 36th POPL, pp. 289–300 (2009)

A. Dawar and H. Veith (Eds.): CSL 2010, LNCS 6247, pp. 49–50, 2010.

3. Distefano, D.: Attacking large industrial code with bi-abductive inference. In: Alpuente, M. (ed.) FMICS 2009. LNCS, vol. 5825, pp. 1–8. Springer, Heidelberg (2009) (invited paper)
4. O'Hearn, P.W., Reynolds, J.C., Yang, H.: Local reasoning about programs that alter data structures. In: Fribourg, L. (ed.) CSL 2001 and EACSL 2001. LNCS, vol. 2142, pp. 1–19. Springer, Heidelberg (2001) (invited paper)
5. Peirce, C.S.: Collected papers of Charles Sanders Peirce. Harvard Univ. Press, Cambridge (1958)

Constraint Solving for Program Verification: Theory and Practice by Example

Andrey Rybalchenko

Technische Universität München

Abstract. Program verification relies on the construction of auxiliary assertions describing various aspects of program behaviour, e.g., inductive invariants, resource bounds, and interpolants for characterizing reachable program states, ranking functions for approximating number of execution steps until program termination, or recurrence sets for demonstrating non-termination. Recent advances in the development of constraint solving tools offer an unprecedented opportunity for the efficient automation of this task. This tutorial presents a series of examples illustrating algorithms for the automatic construction of such auxiliary assertions by utilizing constraint solvers as the basic computing machinery, and optimizations that make these constraint-based algorithms work well in practice.

A. Dawar and H. Veith (Eds.): CSL 2010, LNCS 6247, p. 51, 2010.

Tableau Calculi for $\mathcal{CSL}$ over minspaces

Régis Alenda[1], Nicola Olivetti[1], Camilla Schwind[2], and Dmitry Tishkovsky[3]

[1] LSIS - UMR CNRS 6168, Université de Provence – St-Jérôme, Marseille, France
regis.alenda@lsis.org, nicola.olivetti@univ-cezanne.fr
[2] LIF - UMR CNRS 6166, Université de la Méditerranée – Luminy, Marseille, France
camilla.schwind@lif.univ-mrs.fr
[3] School of Computer Science, The University of Manchester, Manchester, UK
dmitry@cs.man.ac.uk

Abstract. The logic of comparative concept similarity $\mathcal{CSL}$ has been introduced in 2005 by Shemeret, Tishkovsky, Zakharyashev and Wolter in order to express a kind of qualitative similarity reasoning about concepts in ontologies. The semantics of the logic is defined in terms of distance spaces; however it can be equivalently reformulated in terms of preferential structures, similar to those ones of conditional logics. In this paper we consider $\mathcal{CSL}$ interpreted over symmetric and non-symmetric distance models satisfying the limit assumption, the so-called minspace distance models. We contribute to automated deduction for $\mathcal{CSL}$ in two ways. First we prove by the finite filtration method that the logic has the effective finite model property with respect to its preferential semantics. Then we present a decision procedure in the form of a labeled tableau calculus for both cases of $\mathcal{CSL}$ interpreted over symmetric and non-symmetric minspace distance models. The termination of the calculus is obtained by imposing suitable blocking conditions.

1   Introduction

The logics of comparative concept similarity $\mathcal{CSL}$ has been introduced in [7] to capture a form of reasoning about qualitative comparison between concept instances. In these logics we can express assertions or judgments of the form: "Renault Clio is more similar to Peugeot 207 than to Ferrari 430". These logics may find an application in ontology languages, whose logical base is provided by Description Logics, allowing concept definitions based on proximity/similarity measures. For instance, the color "Reddish" may be defined as a color which is more similar to a prototypical "Red" than to any other color [7](in some color model as RGB). The aim is to dispose of a language where logical concept classification provided by standard DL is integrated with classification mechanisms based on calculation of proximity measures, typical for instance of domains like bio-informatics or linguistic. In this context, several languages comprising both absolute similarity measures and comparative similarity operator(s) have been considered [8]. In this paper we concentrate on the logic $\mathcal{CSL}$ which is obtained from the Boolean logic by adding one binary connective $\Leftarrow$ expressing comparative similarity to a propositional language. In this language the above examples can be encoded (using a description logic notation) by:

A. Dawar and H. Veith (Eds.): CSL 2010, LNCS 6247, pp. 52–66, 2010.

(1) Reddish $\equiv$ {Red} $\Leftarrow$ {Green, . . . , Black}
(2) Clio $\sqsubseteq$ (Peugeot207 $\Leftarrow$ Ferrari430)

Comparative similarity assertions such as (2) might not necessarily be the result of an objective numerical calculation of similarity measures, but they could be determined by the (integration of) subjective opinions of agents, answering, for instance, to questions like: "Is Clio more similar to Peugeot207 or to Ferrari 430?". In a more general setting, the language might contain several connectives $\Leftarrow_{\text{Feature}}$ corresponding to a specific distance function d_{Feature} measuring the similarity of objects with respect to each Feature (size, price, power, taste, color...).

The semantics of $\mathcal{CSL}$ is defined in terms of distance spaces, that is to say structures equipped by a distance function d, whose properties may vary according to the logic under consideration. In this setting, the evaluation of $A \Leftarrow B$ can be informally stated as follows: $x \in (A \Leftarrow B)$ iff $d(x, A) < d(x, B)$ meaning that the object x is an instance of the formula $A \Leftarrow B$ (i.e. it is more similar to A than to B) if x is strictly closer to A-objects than to B-objects according to the distance function d, where the distance of an object to a set of objects is defined as the *infimum* of the distances to each object in the set.

Properties of $\mathcal{CSL}$ with respect to different classes of models have been investigated in [7,4,8,9]. Moreover, $\mathcal{CSL}$ over arbitrary distance spaces can be seen as a fragment, indeed a powerful one (including for instance the logic $\mathbf{S4}_u$ of topological spaces), of a general logic for spatial reasoning comprising different modal operators defined by (bounded) quantified distance expressions (namely the logic $\mathcal{QML}$ [9]). The satisfiability problem for the $\mathcal{CSL}$ logic (and in particular in the case of symmetric minspaces) is EXPTIME-complete. Finally, when interpreted over subspaces of $\mathbb{N}^n$, $\mathbb{Z}^n$ or $\mathbb{R}^n$, it turns out that this logic is undecidable.

In this paper we consider the semantics of $\mathcal{CSL}$ induced by *minspaces*, that is to say distance spaces where the infimum of a set of distances is actually their *minimum* (the so-called limit assumption property). In this case, the logic $\mathcal{CSL}$ is naturally related to some conditional logics, whose semantics is often expressed in terms of preferential structures: that is to say possible-world structures equipped by a family of strict (pre)-orders $\prec_x$ indexed on objects/worlds [5].

Moreover, it has been shown that, under the limit assumption, $\mathcal{CSL}$ is able to distinguish between validity in symmetric and non-symmetric models[1] In this work we consider the logic $\mathcal{CSL}$ as defined over symmetric and respectively non-symmetric minspaces. The minspace property implies that the spaces have discrete distance functions. This requirement does not seem incompatible with the purpose of representing qualitative similarity comparisons, whereas it might not be reasonable for applications of $\mathcal{CSL}$ to spatial reasoning. The distinction between the symmetric and non-symmetric case is significant, for instance a kind of circular KB containing:

---

[1] In contrast, in the general case where limit assumption is not assumed the logic cannot distinguish between symmetric and non-symmetric models.

$$Clio \sqsubseteq (Golf \Leftarrow Ferrari430)$$
$$Golf \sqsubseteq (Ferrari430 \Leftarrow Clio)$$
$$Ferrari430 \sqsubseteq (Clio \Leftarrow Golf)$$

is satisfiable in non-symmetric minspace models with non-empty concepts Clio, Golf, Ferrari430, whereas it is not in symmetric minspace models [7].

In this paper we contribute to automated deduction of $\mathcal{CSL}$ over minspaces. We begin by showing that the semantics of $\mathcal{CSL}$ over minspaces can be equivalently restated in terms of preferential models satisfying some additional conditions, namely the modularity, centering, and limit assumption. For the symmetric case, preferential models involve a four-place relation, or more intuitively a relation between pairs of objects (Pair models). In the non-symmetric case, the corresponding preferential semantics is formulated in terms of a family of pre-orders (or a ternary relation) as described in [2].

We prove the effective finite model property of the logic with respect to the pair-model semantics. Any model of a formula gives rise to a *finite* model whose size is bounded by a computable function of the length of the formula. Decidability and ExpTime upper bound complexity of the logic are straightforward consequences of this result. The result is proved by a finite filtration method which is a standard method in modal logic. The filtration method proved to be very powerful for establishing decidability of many logics including logics outside the family of modal and description logics for which it was originally developed. Very recently the filtration technique has been shown strongly related to tableau blocking mechanisms used for detecting loops in tableau derivations, thereby obtaining termination of tableau algorithms [6].

Next we define a tableau calculus for checking satisfiability of $\mathcal{CSL}$ formulas in pair models. Our tableau procedure makes use of labeled formulas and of positive and negative preference relation. To the best of our knowledge it provides the first practically-implementable decision procedure for $\mathcal{CSL}$ logic over symmetric minspaces. The calculus makes use of blocking conditions to obtain termination. But the blocking conditions are not only an expedient to obtain termination, they have also a semantical meaning: they prevent the potential generation of infinite models violating the limit assumption. For this reason the soundness of the calculus under the termination restrictions is not a trivial consequence of the soundness of the tableau rules, as it discards some candidate models. The soundness argument relies on a partial filtration method, strongly related to the filtration method mentioned above. The whole argument has some similarity with the *unrestricted blocking* technique presented in [6].

We finally adapt our calculus to the simpler non-symmetric case. For this case, a tableau calculus was presented in [2], the calculus presented here is both significantly different and conceptually simpler.

2   Syntax and Semantics

$\mathcal{CSL}$ is defined as a propositional language. Formulas can be also be viewed as concepts expressions in a description logic notation that we like to adopt here. Propositional variables (or concept names) are denoted by $P_1, P_2, \ldots, P_n$ and the logical connectives are $\neg, \sqcup, \sqcap$, and $\Leftarrow$ (*comparative similarity operator*). *Formulas* are defined as follows:

$$C, D \stackrel{\text{def}}{=} P_i \mid \neg C \mid C \sqcup D \mid C \sqcap D \mid C \Leftarrow D.$$

Moreover we use the truth constants $\top \stackrel{\text{def}}{=} P \sqcup \neg P$ and $\bot \stackrel{\text{def}}{=} P \sqcap \neg P$, for some propositional variable P.

The original semantics of $\mathcal{CSL}$ [7] makes use of *distance spaces* to encode similarity measures between objects. In this paper, we restrict ourselves to symmetric distances spaces, which are presented below.

We say that a pair (Δ, d) where Δ is a non empty set and d is a function from Δ to $\mathbb{R}^{\geq 0}$ is a *symmetric distance space* if d satisfies the following conditions[2]:

(id) $d(x, y) = 0 \iff x = y$

(sym) $d(x, y) = d(y, x)$

We define $d(C, D) \stackrel{\text{def}}{=} \inf\{d(x, y) \mid x \in C, y \in D\}$, for all non-empty subsets[3] C, D of Δ. We call (Δ, d) a *symmetric minspace* if it additionally satisfies the following condition on the existence of a minimum of a set of distances:

(min) $C \neq \emptyset$ and $D \neq \emptyset \Rightarrow \exists x_0 \in C \, \exists y_0 \in D \; d(x_0, y_0) = d(C, D).$

$\mathcal{CSL}$-symmetric minspace models (or just minspace models, since we consider here only the symmetric ones) are then defined as Kripke models based on a minspace.

Definition 1 (Minspace model). *A minspace (distance) model $\mathcal{I}$ is a triple $\mathcal{I} = \langle \Delta^{\mathcal{I}}, d^{\mathcal{I}}, .^{\mathcal{I}} \rangle$ where:*
- $(\Delta^{\mathcal{I}}, d^{\mathcal{I}})$ *is a (symmetric distance) minspace.*
- $.^{\mathcal{I}}$ *is the evaluation function defined as usual on propositional variables and boolean connectives, and as follows for the concept similarity operator:*
$$(A \Leftarrow B)^{\mathcal{I}} \stackrel{\text{def}}{=} \{x \in \Delta^{\mathcal{I}} \mid d(x, A^{\mathcal{I}}) < d(x, B^{\mathcal{I}})\}.$$

$\mathcal{CSL}$ is a logic of pure qualitative comparisons, this motivates an alternative semantics where the distance function is replaced by preferential relations. In [2] it is shown that in non-symmetric minspaces the distance function can be replaced by a family of ternary relations. Although the same encoding can be also used for symmetric minspaces, we use here a binary relation on two-element multisets, which is more natural in this case and eases the formulation of both the semantics and the tableau calculus.

Given a non-empty set Δ, we denote by $\mathcal{MS}_2(\Delta)$ the set of two-element multisets over Δ; its elements are denoted by $\{a, b\}$ (abusing set-notation). Intuitively, each $\{a, b\}$ represents the distance from a to b. We define for all $X \subseteq \mathcal{MS}_2(\Delta)$, $x \in \Delta$ and $C \subseteq \Delta$:

---

[2] The case of the well known triangular inequality, which is not assumed here, is discussed in [7].

[3] If one of those sets is empty, the distance is by convention infinite.

$$\min_<(X) = \{\{x,y\}|\{x,y\} \in X \text{ and } \forall \{u,v\} \in X, \{u,v\} \not< \{x,y\}\},$$
$$\min_x(C) = \{a|\{x,a\} \in \min_<(\{\{x,a\}|a \in C\})\}.$$

As the relation $<$ represents distance comparisons, it is expected to satisfy some specific properties:

Definition 2. *Let Δ be a non empty set. We say that a relation $<$ defined on $\mathcal{MS}_2(\Delta)$ satisfies:*

pair-centering: *if $\forall x, y \in \Delta$: $\{x,x\} < \{x,y\}$ or $x = y$.*
modularity: *if $\forall x, y, z, u \in \Delta$:*
    $\{x,y\} < \{z,u\}$ implies $\forall v, w \in \Delta, \{x,y\} < \{v,w\}$ or $\{v,w\} < \{z,u\}$.
asymmetry: *if $\forall x, y, z, u \in \Delta$: $\{x,y\} \not< \{z,u\}$ or $\{z,u\} \not< \{x,y\}$.*
limit assumption: *if $\forall C, D \subseteq \Delta$: $C \neq \varnothing$ and $D \neq \varnothing$ implies*
    $\min_<\{\{x,y\}|x \in C, y \in D\} \neq \varnothing$.

In a few words, pair-centering corresponds to the property (id) of the distance function, asymmetry to the fact that the relation $<$ encode strict comparisons, the limit assumption to the minspace property (min), whereas modularity is related to the fact that distance values are linearly ordered. We can now restate the definition of a $\mathcal{CSL}$-model in terms of preferential structures of this kind:

Definition 3 (Pair Model). *A $\mathcal{CSL}$-pair-model $\mathcal{I}$ is a triple $\langle \Delta, <, .^{\mathcal{I}} \rangle$ where:*
 - *Δ is a non empty set.*
 - *$<$ is a transitive binary relation on $\mathcal{MS}_2(\Delta)$ satisfying asymmetry, pair-centering, modularity and limit assumption.*
 - *$.^{\mathcal{I}}$ is the evaluation function defined as usual on propositional variables and boolean connectives, and as follow for the concept similarity operator:*
    $$(A \Leftarrow B)^{\mathcal{I}} = \{x \in \Delta | \exists y \in A^{\mathcal{I}}, \forall z \in B^{\mathcal{I}}, \{x,y\} < \{x,z\}\}.$$

We can show that the pair semantics is equivalent to the distance semantics. We say that two models $\mathcal{I}$ and $\mathcal{J}$ are *equivalent* if they are based on the same set Δ and for all formula $A \in \mathcal{L}_{\mathcal{CSL}}$, $A^{\mathcal{I}} = A^{\mathcal{J}}$.

Theorem 4. *For every pair model there is an equivalent symmetric minspace model, and vice versa.*

3   Filtration

In this section we prove a filtration theorem for pair semantics of $\mathcal{CSL}$. As usual, for every formula C, let $\mathsf{sub}(C)$ denote the set of all sub-formulas of C. Clearly, the size of $\mathsf{sub}(C)$ does not exceed the length of C in symbols.

Let C be a fixed formula and $\mathcal{I}$ be a pair model satisfying the limit assumption. A *type* of an element x in a pair model $\mathcal{I}$ (with respect to C), denoted by $\tau^C(x)$, is the set of all formulas in $\mathsf{sub}(C)$ whose interpretations in $\mathcal{I}$ contain x, that is, $\tau^C(x) \stackrel{\text{def}}{=} \{D \in \mathsf{sub}(C) \mid x \in D^{\mathcal{I}}\}$. Let n be the length of C in symbols. Since every type is a subset of $\mathsf{sub}(C)$, the number of different types with respect to $\mathsf{sub}(C)$ does not exceed 2^n.

Let $\sim$ be an equivalence on $\Delta^{\mathcal{I}}$ which is defined by $x \sim y$ iff $\tau^C(x) = \tau^C(y)$ for every x and y from $\Delta^{\mathcal{I}}$. Based on a pair model $\mathcal{I}$, we will define a filtrated pair model $\overline{\mathcal{I}}$ as follows. For every element x of $\Delta^{\mathcal{I}}$, let $[x]$ be the equivalence class (with respect to $\sim$) of the representative x, that is $[x] \overset{\text{def}}{=} \{y \in \Delta^{\mathcal{I}} \mid x \sim y\}$. The domain of $\overline{\mathcal{I}}$ is defined as the set of all equivalence classes in $\Delta^{\mathcal{I}}$ (with respect to $\sim$), i.e. $\Delta^{\overline{\mathcal{I}}} \overset{\text{def}}{=} \{[x] \mid x \in \Delta^{\mathcal{I}}\}$. The relation $<^{\overline{\mathcal{I}}}$ on $\mathcal{MS}_2(\Delta^{\overline{\mathcal{I}}})$ is defined as follows. For all $[x_0], [y_0], [x_1], [y_1]$ from $\Delta^{\overline{\mathcal{I}}}$ we let

$$\{[x_0], [y_0]\} <^{\overline{\mathcal{I}}} \{[x_1], [y_1]\} \overset{\text{def}}{\Longleftrightarrow}$$
$$\exists x_0' \in [x_0] \exists y_0' \in [y_0] \forall x_1' \in [x_1] \forall y_1' \in [y_1] \; \{x_0', y_0'\} <^{\mathcal{I}} \{x_1', y_1'\}.$$

Finally, for every propositional variable P we define $P^{\overline{\mathcal{I}}} \overset{\text{def}}{=} \{[x] \mid x \in P^{\mathcal{I}}\}$. It is not difficult to see that the definition of $\overline{\mathcal{I}}$ does not depend on the choice of representatives of the equivalence classes, so that $\overline{\mathcal{I}}$ is defined correctly.

Lemma 5. $\overline{\mathcal{I}}$ *is a* $\mathcal{CSL}$ *pair model.*

Lemma 6 (Filtration Lemma). *Let* $\mathcal{I}$ *be a pair min-model. Then, for every formula* $D \in \mathsf{sub}(C)$ *and* $x \in \Delta^{\mathcal{I}}$, $x \in D^{\mathcal{I}}$ *iff* $[x] \in D^{\overline{\mathcal{I}}}$.

As a consequence, we obtain the following theorem.

Theorem 7 (Effective Finite Model Property). *A formula of a length* n *is satisfiable in a* $\mathcal{CSL}$ *pair model iff it is satisfiable in a finite* $\mathcal{CSL}$ *pair model where the number of elements of* Δ *does not exceed* 2^n.

4   A Tableau Calculus

In this section we present a decision procedure for $\mathcal{CSL}$ over symmetric minspaces based on a labeled tableau calculi. Tableau rules act on sets of tableau formulas, defined next. These sets of formulas are denoted by $\Gamma, \Delta, \ldots$, and are called *tableau sets*. As usual, we use the notation Γ, Δ for the set union $\Gamma \cup \Delta$. Given an enumerable set $\mathsf{Lab} = \{x_1, x_2, \ldots, x_n, \ldots\}$ of objects called *labels*, a tableau formula has the form i) $x : C$ where x is a label and C is a $\mathcal{CSL}$-formula. ii) $\{x, y\} < \{z, u\}$ or $\{x, y\} \not< \{z, u\}$ where $\{x, y\}, \{z, u\}$ denote two-element multisets of labels. iii) $x : f(y, C)$ where x, y are labels and C is a $\mathcal{CSL}$-formula.

As expected, labels represent the objects of the domain, so that i) states that $x \in C^{\mathcal{I}}$, and ii) encodes the preferential relation. Note that the calculus makes use of the dual relation $\not<$ (which can be seen as a non-strict relation $\geq$). The intuitive meaning of iii) is $x \in \min_y(C^{\mathcal{I}})$.

A tableau derivation (or simply a derivation) for C (the input formula) is a tree whose root node is the tableau set $\{x : C\}$, and where successors of any node are obtained by the application of a *tableau rule*. A tableau rule has the form $\Gamma[X]/\Gamma_1 \mid \cdots \mid \Gamma_m$, where $\Gamma, \Gamma_1, \ldots, \Gamma_m$ are tableau sets. The meaning is that, given a tableau set Γ in a derivation, if $X \subseteq \Gamma$, then we can apply the rule to it and create m successors $\Gamma_1, \ldots, \Gamma_m$. The denominator can be the empty set,

$(\neg\neg)$: $\dfrac{\Gamma[x : \neg\neg A]}{\Gamma,\; x : A}$

$(\sqcup)$: $\dfrac{\Gamma[x : A \sqcup B]}{\Gamma,\; x : A \mid \Gamma,\; x : B}$

$(\neg\sqcup)$: $\dfrac{\Gamma[x : \neg(A \sqcup B)]}{\Gamma,\; x : \neg A,\; x : \neg B}$

$(\sqcap)$: $\dfrac{\Gamma[x : A \sqcap B)]}{\Gamma,\; x : A,\; x : B}$

$(\neg\sqcap)$: $\dfrac{\Gamma[x : \neg(A \sqcap B)]}{\Gamma,\; x : \neg A \mid \Gamma,\; x : \neg B}$

$(T1\Leftarrow)$: $\dfrac{\Gamma[x : A \Leftarrow B,\; y : C]}{\Gamma,\; y : \neg B \mid \Gamma,\; y : B}$

$(F1\Leftarrow)$: $\dfrac{\Gamma[x : \neg(A \Leftarrow B),\; y : C]}{\Gamma,\; y : A \mid \Gamma,\; y : \neg A}$

$(T2\Leftarrow)$: $\dfrac{\Gamma[x : A \Leftarrow B]}{\Gamma,\; z : f(x, A),\; z : A}\,(*)$

$(F2\Leftarrow)$: $\dfrac{\Gamma[x : \neg(A \Leftarrow B),\; y : A]}{\Gamma,\; z : f(x, B),\; z : B}\,(*)$

$(T3\Leftarrow)$: $\dfrac{\Gamma[x : A \Leftarrow B,\; z : f(x, A),\; y : B]}{\Gamma,\; \{x, z\} < \{x, y\}}$

$(F3\Leftarrow)$: $\dfrac{\Gamma[x : \neg(A \Leftarrow B),\; z : f(x, B),\; y : A]}{\Gamma,\; \{x, y\} \not< \{x, z\}}$

(cnt): $\dfrac{\Gamma[x : A,\; y : B]}{\Gamma(y/x) \mid \Gamma,\; \{x, x\} < \{x, y\},\; \{y, y\} < \{y, x\}}$

(asm): $\dfrac{\Gamma[\{x, y\} < \{z, u\}]}{\Gamma,\; \{z, u\} \not< \{x, y\}}$

(mod): $\dfrac{\Gamma[\{x, y\} \not< \{v, w\},\; \{v, w\} \not< \{z, u\}]}{\Gamma,\; \{x, y\} \not< \{z, u\}}$

(tr): $\dfrac{\Gamma[\{x, y\} < \{v, w\},\; \{v, w\} < \{z, u\}]}{\Gamma,\; \{x, y\} < \{z, u\}}$

$(r\bot)$: $\dfrac{\Gamma[\{x, y\} < \{z, u\},\; \{x, y\} \not< \{z, u\}]}{\bot}$

$(\bot)$: $\dfrac{\Gamma[x : A,\; x : \neg A]}{\bot}$

(*) z is a new label not occurring in the current branch.

Fig. 1. Tableau calculus $T_{\mathcal{CSL}}$ for $\mathcal{CSL}$

in which case the rule is a *closure rule* and is usually written $\Gamma[X]/\bot$. Closure rules detect tableau sets which contain a contradiction. A tableau set to which a closure rule can be applied is said to be *closed*.

The rules for our calculus are given in Figure 1. The rules are grounded on the pair-model semantics. Observe that the rules for $\Leftarrow$ comprise a case analysis in the form of analytic cut. The semantic conditions for $(\neg)$ $\Leftarrow$ are captured by the rules $(T2\Leftarrow)$ and $(T3\Leftarrow)$ (resp. $(F2\Leftarrow)$ and $(F3\Leftarrow)$). For instance the rule $(F2\Leftarrow)$ introduces an element $z \in \min_x(B^{\mathcal{I}})$, whenever A is non-empty and the rule $(F3\Leftarrow)$ states that no A-element y can be closer to x than z. In the (cnt) rule, we denote by $\Gamma(y/x)$ the tableau set obtained by replacing y by x in every tableau formula of Γ.

A rule is *dynamic* if it introduces a new label, and *static* if it does not. In this calculus, the rules $(T2\Leftarrow)$ and $(F2\Leftarrow)$ are dynamic, all the others are static. We can note that, apart from the centering rule, no rule deletes any formula from tableau sets. The centering rule is special due to the substitution part. The first denominator of the rule identifies two labels. Thus it does not really suppress formulas. An alternative to the use of substitutions would be to make use of equality between labels, but this would lead to a more complex calculus.

This calculus does not provide a decision procedure, since the interplay between dynamic rules (introducing new labels) and static rules (adding new formulas to which the dynamic rules could be applied) can lead to infinite derivations. In order to make our calculus terminating, we introduce in Definition 8 some restrictions on the application of the rules.

Given a derivation branch **B** and two labels x and y occurring in it, we say that x is older than y if x has been introduced before y in the branch[4]. Note that this older relation is *well founded*. We also define Lab_Γ as the set of all labels occurring in a tableau set Γ, and $\Pi_\Gamma(x) = \{A | A \in \mathcal{L}_{\mathcal{CSL}} \text{ and } x : A \in \Gamma\}$.

Definition 8 (Termination restrictions).
Irredundancy restriction.   *1. Do not apply a static rule $\Gamma/\Gamma_1 | \ldots | \Gamma_n$ to a tableau set Γ if for some $1 \leq i \leq n$, $\Gamma_i = \Gamma$.*
   2. Do not apply the rule (T2$\Leftarrow$) to some formula $x : A \Leftarrow B$ in Γ if there exists some label u such that $u : f(x, A)$ and $u : A$ are in Γ.
   3. Do not apply the rule (F2$\Leftarrow$) to some formulas $x : \neg(A \Leftarrow B), y : C$ if there exists some label u such that $u : f(x, B)$ and $u : B$ are in Γ.
Subset blocking. *Do not apply the rule (T2$\Leftarrow$) to a formula $x : A \Leftarrow B \in \Gamma$, or the rule (F2$\Leftarrow$) to some formulas $x : \neg(A \Leftarrow B), y : C$ in Γ if there exists some label z older than x and such that $\Pi_\Gamma(x) \subseteq \Pi_\Gamma(z)$.*
Centering restriction. *Apply the rule (cnt) to $x : A, y : B$ in Γ only if x is strictly older than y.*

The purpose of the termination restrictions is to prevent unnecessary applications of the rules that could lead to infinite derivations, as we prove in the next section. The subset blocking condition is similar to dynamic blocking [3]. The centering rule in itself is similar to the unrestricted blocking rule [6]. Note that apart from the restrictions of Definition 8, we do not assume any strategy for the application of the rules.

A rule R is *applicable* to a tableau set Γ under termination restrictions if it respect all termination restrictions (Definition 8). A derivation is *under termination restrictions* if all rule applications respects the termination restrictions. From now on, we only consider derivations under termination restrictions.

Since termination restrictions prevent the application of some rules we have to define whenever a tableau is open or closed, thereby witnessing the satisfiability (or unsatisfiability) of the input formula.

Definition 9 (Finished / Bad / Good tableau sets, Finished / Closed/ Open derivation). *A tableau set is* finished *if it is closed or no rule is applicable to it.*

A tableau set Γ in a derivation is bad *if: (i) it is open. (ii) it is finished. (iii) there exist some labels x and y such that x is older than y and $\Pi_\Gamma(y) \subseteq \Pi_\Gamma(x)$.*

A tableau set is good *if it is open, finished, and not bad.*

A derivation is finished *if all its leaf nodes are finished, it is* closed *if all its leaf nodes are either closed or bad, and it is* open *if it contains a good tableau set.*

Here is an intuitive account of the above definitions. Finished tableau sets are leaf nodes in the derivation tree. Closed tableau sets contain a contradiction and thus they cannot provide a model for the input formula. Good tableau sets represent (partial) models of the input formula. Bad tableau sets are disregarded

---

[4] From a practical point of view, the order of introduction of the labels can be stored locally within a tableau set and does not require to inspect a whole derivation branch.

as potential models, for the reason explained below. An open tableau derivation provides a model of the input formula, whereas a closed tableau derivation shows that the input formula is unsatisfiable.

The status of a bad tableau set is unknown: it does not contain a contradiction, but we do not know whether it can provide a model or not. In any case, we disregard it, as it may potentially provide an infinite model which would violate the limit assumption property. To this regard, observe that the limit assumption property is not encoded by any rule of the calculus. It is the whole tableau construction that takes care to eliminate potential infinite models violating this condition, in accordance with the finite model property shown in the previous section. Disregarding bad tableau sets is essential in order to obtain a complete calculus, as the example below shows. Of course, since bad tableau sets may also provide correct models, we have to prove that ignoring *bad* tableau sets preserve the soundness of the calculus.

Example 10. We consider the example in the introduction of a 'cyclic' KB about cars. An inclusion $P \sqsubseteq Q$ is interpreted as $\square(P \rightarrow Q)$ where $\square$ is the **S5** modality. Observe that $\square A$ is encoded in $\mathcal{CSL}$ by $\neg(\neg A \Leftarrow \bot)$ [7]; thus $P \sqsubseteq Q$ is encoded by $\neg((P \sqcap \neg Q) \Leftarrow \bot)$, for which we get the derived rule $\frac{\Gamma[x:\neg((P \sqcap \neg Q) \Leftarrow \bot), y:R]}{\Gamma, y:\neg P \sqcup Q}$. We will also implicitly use the following facts: (a) If a tableau set contains a formula of the form $\{x, y\} < \{x, x\}$, then it will be closed by an application of (asm) followed by an application of (cnt). (b) If a tableau set contains $x : A \Leftarrow B$ and $x : B$, then it will be closed; an application of (T2$\Leftarrow$) will add some $y : f(x, A)$, and an application of (T3$\Leftarrow$) will add $\{x, y\} < \{x, x\}$ which is closed by (a).

Suppose now we initialize then the tableau by
$\Gamma = \{x_1 : G \sqsubseteq (F \Leftarrow C), x_1 : F \sqsubseteq (C \Leftarrow G), x_1 : C \sqsubseteq (G \Leftarrow F), x_1 : C\}$
Due to space limitations, we only show the generation of the tableau set built according to the termination restrictions that cannot be closed by simple rule applications. We apply obvious propositional simplifications (e.g. if a tableau set contains both A and $\neg A \sqcup B$, we only add B). A first set of applications of the rules add to Γ:
$x_1 : G \Leftarrow F, x_1 : \neg F \sqcup (C \Leftarrow G), x_1 : \neg G \sqcup (F \Leftarrow C), x_1 : \neg F, x_1 : \neg G$
To see the last two: by applying $(T1 \Leftarrow)$ to $x_1 : G \Leftarrow F$, the branch with $x_1 : F$ gives a closed tableau set; similarly, expanding $\neg G \sqcup (F \Leftarrow C)$, the tableau set with $x_1 : F \Leftarrow C$ will be closed because of $x_1 : C$. In the following we tacitly apply a similar pruning of the tableau derivation. We now apply $(T2 \Leftarrow)$ to $x_1 : G \Leftarrow F$ and then the same static rules as before, so that we add:
$z_1 : f(x_1, G), z_1 : G, z_1 : F \Leftarrow C, z_1 : \neg F \sqcup (C \Leftarrow G), z_1 : \neg C \sqcup (G \Leftarrow F), z_1 : \neg F, z_1 : \neg C.$
We continue by applying $(T2 \Leftarrow)$ to $z_1 : F \Leftarrow C$ we add:
$u_1 : f(z_1, F), u_1 : F, u_1 : C \Leftarrow G, u_1 : \neg F \sqcup (C \Leftarrow G), u_1 : \neg C \sqcup (G \Leftarrow F), u_1 : \neg C, u_1 : \neg G.$
We continue by applying $(T2 \Leftarrow)$ to $u_1 : C \Leftarrow G$ so that we add:
$x_2 : f(u_1, C), x_2 : C, x_2 : G \Leftarrow F, x_2 : \neg F \sqcup (C \Leftarrow G), x_2 : \neg G \sqcup (F \Leftarrow C), x_2 : \neg F, x_2 : \neg G$

Now we apply $(T3 \leftleftarrows)$ and then (tr) we add:
$\{x_1, z_1\} < \{x_1, u_1\}, \{z_1, u_1\} < \{z_1, x_2\}, \{z_1, u_1\} < \{z_1, x_1\}, \{u_1, x_2\} < \{u_1, z_1\},$
$\{z_1, u_1\} < \{x_1, u_1\}, \{u_1, x_2\} < \{z_1, x_1\}, \{u_1, x_2\} < \{u_1, x_1\}$
The last three are obtained by (tr). By (asm) and (mod) we add:
$\{x_1, u_1\} \not< \{x_1, z_1\}, \{z_1, x_2\} \not< \{z_1, u_1\}, \{z_1, x_1\} \not< \{z_1, u_1\}, \{u_1, z_1\} \not< \{u_1, x_2\},$
$\{x_1, u_1\} \not< \{z_1, u_1\}, \{z_1, x_1\} \not< \{u_1, x_2\}, \{u_1, x_1\} \not< \{u_1, x_2\}$
We now apply (cnt): for every pair of labels, except x_1 and x_2, the left tableau
set involving substitution will be closed, so that relations $\{x_1, x_1\} < \{x_1, u_1\},$
$\{z_1, z_1\} < \{x_1, u_1\} \ldots$ will be added. For x_1 and x_2, we get two tableau set
$\Gamma_1 = \Gamma[x_2/x_1]$ and $\Gamma_2 = \Gamma, \{x_1, x_1\} < \{x_1, x_2\}, \{x_2, x_2\} < \{x_1, x_2\}$. The former
Γ_1 is closed by (asm) and $(r\perp)$ since it contains $\{u_1, x_1\} < \{u_1, x_1\}$. The latter
Γ_2 is finished (and open): in particular we cannot apply $(T2 \leftleftarrows)$ to $x_2 : G \leftleftarrows F$
by the fact that $\Pi_{\Gamma_2}(x_2) \subseteq \Pi_{\Gamma_2}(x_1)$ and by the subset blocking restriction.
Thus Γ_2 is a *bad* tableau set and consequently it is disregarded. We can conclude
that the tableau for the input formula(s) is *closed*. Have we not applied subset
blocking restriction, the construction would have produced an infinite tableau
set with an infinite sequence of "closer" and "closer" pairs of labels (wrt. to
$<$). To this regard, observe that the initial formula is *satisfiable* in a symmetric
infinite model *which is not a minspace* [7].

5 Main Results

5.1 Termination

Theorem 11. *Any derivation of $T_{\mathcal{CSL}}$ under termination restrictions is finite.*

To prove the theorem we need some additional definitions. We define, for any
tableau derivation T, $\Pi(T)$ as the set of all $\mathcal{CSL}$-formulas occurring in T:

$$\Pi(T) \stackrel{\text{def}}{=} \{A \mid A \in \mathcal{L}_{\mathcal{CSL}} \text{ and } x : A \in \Gamma \text{ for some } \Gamma \text{ from } T\}.$$

Given a node Γ in a branch **B**, and x occurring in Γ or in any of its ancestors,
we define $\sigma^*(\Gamma, x) = x$ if x occurs in Γ, or $\sigma^*(\Gamma, x) = y$ where y is the label
which finally replaces x in Γ along a sequence of centering substitution applied
on the path between Γ and its closest ancestor in which x occurs. Observe that
this label y is unique, and is older than x (due to the centering restriction).

Proposition 12 (Monotonicity). *Let Γ be a tableau set in a derivation T,
and Γ' be any descendant of Γ in T. Let $x : A$ be in Γ. Then: (i) $\Pi_\Gamma(x) \subseteq$
$\Pi_{\Gamma'}(\sigma^*(\Gamma', x))$. (ii) if $x : A$ is blocked for a rule R in Γ by the irredundancy
restriction, then also $\sigma^*(\Gamma', x) : A$ is blocked in Γ' for the rule R by the irredundancy restriction.*

Proof (Theorem 11). Let T be a derivation for C. For a contradiction, suppose
that T contains an infinite branch $\mathbf{B} = (\Gamma_i)_{i \in \mathbb{N}}$. We can then prove the following:

FACT 13. There exists a dynamic formula $D = (\neg)(A \leftleftarrows B)$, a subsequence
$(\Theta_n)_{n \in \mathbb{N}}$ of **B**, and a sequence $(x_n)_{n \in \mathbb{N}}$ of labels such that: (i) For all n, x_n :
$D \in \Gamma_n$. (ii) For all n, Θ_n is a node corresponding to the application of the
corresponding dynamic rule to the formula $x_n : D$. (iii) There exists a label x^*
such that x^* occurs in each Γ_n and for all n, $\Pi_{\Theta_n}(x_n) \subseteq \Pi_{\Theta_n}(x^*)$

By the previous facts, we have that (i) for all n, x_n must be older than x^*, because if it were younger no dynamic rule could be applied to $x_n : D$, due to the subset blocking. (ii) for all n, m, if $n \neq m$ then $x_n \neq x_m$, because the irredundancy restriction prevents multiple application of the same rule to the same formulas, due to Proposition 12. Therefore we have an infinite sequence of labels, all different and older than x^*, which is impossible since the relation "older" is well founded.   □

We can estimate an upper bound of complexity of the tableau algorithm.

Proposition 14. *Let T be a tableau derivation for a formula C and n be the length of C in symbols. Then* $\mathsf{Card}\{\Pi_\Gamma(x) \mid \Gamma \text{ in } T \text{ and } x \text{ occurs in } \Gamma\} \leq 2^{2n-1}$.

By Proposition 14, the derivation T cannot produce more than 2^{2n-1} sets $\Pi_\Gamma(x)$ for different tableau sets Γ and labels x. Due to the subset blocking condition in Definition 8, we cannot have more than 2^{2n-1} labels in any branch of T. The number of $\mathcal{CSL}$ formulas associated with any label is less than $2n - 1$, also there are $2^{2n-1} \cdot (2n - 1)$ formulas of the kind $f(x, A)$ and furthermore any tableau set contains less than 2^{2n+1} preferential relations. Since the maximal number of premises in the tableau rules is 3 there can be no more than $3 \cdot (2^{2n-1} \cdot (2n - 1) + 2^{2n} \cdot (2n - 1) + 2^{2n+1}) = 3 \cdot 2^{2n-1} \cdot (6n + 1)$ rule application steps in any branch of the derivation.

Thus, the number of steps in any branch of a tableau derivation is at most exponential in the length of an input formula. This shows that the non-deterministic tableau algorithm runs in NExpTime.

5.2   Soundness

We first need the following definitions:

Definition 15 ($\mathcal{CSL}$-mapping). *Let Γ be a tableau set and $\mathcal{I}$ be a $\mathcal{CSL}$-pair model. A $\mathcal{CSL}$-mapping m from Γ to $\mathcal{I}$ is a function $m : \mathrm{Lab}_\Gamma \to \Delta^{\mathcal{I}}$ such that:*
- *if $\{x, y\} < \{z, u\} \in \Gamma$, then $\{m(x), m(y)\} <^{\mathcal{I}} \{m(z), m(u)\}$.*
- *if $\{x, y\} \not< \{z, u\} \in \Gamma$, then $\{m(x), m(y)\} \not<^{\mathcal{I}} \{m(z), m(u)\}$.*
We say that m is a min-mapping if it also satisfies the following property[5]:
if $z : f(x, A) \in \Gamma$, then $m(z) \in \min_{m(x)}(A^{\mathcal{I}})$.

Definition 16 (Satisfiability). *A tableau set Γ is satisfiable in a $\mathcal{CSL}$-pair model $\mathcal{I}$ under a $\mathcal{CSL}$-mapping m if $x : A \in \Gamma$ implies $m(x) \in A^{\mathcal{I}}$. A tableau set Γ is satisfiable if it is satisfiable in some model $\mathcal{I}$ under some mapping m.*

We then prove that, independently from the termination restrictions, the rules are sound, in the sense that they preserve satisfiability under a min-mapping.

Theorem 17 (Soundness of the rules). *Let Γ be a tableau set satisfiable under a min-mapping, and let $\Gamma/\Gamma_1 \mid \ldots \mid \Gamma_n$ be an instance of any rule. Then there is an i such that Γ_i is satisfiable under a min-mapping.*

---

[5] Note that any min-mapping is also a $\mathcal{CSL}$-mapping.

Corollary 18. *If C is satisfiable, then any tableau for C under termination restrictions contains a finished tableau set satisfiable under a min-mapping.*

We now show the soundness of the tableau calculus with the terminating conditions. The previous corollary does not suffice, as the satisfiable finished tableau set could be bad and thus discarded by the calculus.

Theorem 19 (Soundness of the calculus). *If C is satisfiable, then any finished derivation started by $x : C$ is open (that is it contains a good tableau set).*

To prove the theorem, we need the following definition:

Definition 20. *A tableau set Γ in a derivation is leftmost with respect to centering if (i) it is finished. (ii) for any labels x, y occurring in Γ (with x older than y) the following holds: if there exists an ancestor Δ of Γ to which (cnt)-rule has been applied with labels x and y, then $\Delta(y/x)$ is not satisfiable.*

Proposition 21. *Given a derivation, any leftmost tableau set satisfiable under a min-mapping is good.*

Proof (Proposition 21). Let Γ be a leftmost finished tableau set in a branch **B**, such that Γ is satisfiable in a model $\mathcal{I}$ under a min-mapping m. Suppose for a contradiction that Γ is bad. Then we can find two labels x and y in Γ such that: i) x is older than y. ii) x is the oldest label such that $\Pi_\Gamma(y) \subseteq \Pi_\Gamma(x)$. Notice that, being the oldest, x cannot be blocked in Γ by subset blocking.

FACT 22. There exists an ancestor Δ of Γ such that Δ is the node corresponding to an application of centering to x and y. Moreover, Δ is satisfiable in $\mathcal{I}$ under some min-mapping m'.

We now build a model $\mathcal{I}'$ by doing a "partial filtration[6]" of $\mathcal{I}$ in which we just identify the elements $m(x)$ and $m(y)$. To this purpose, we first define the relation $\sim_{x,y}$ as follows: i) $\forall u \in \Delta^\mathcal{I}$, $u \sim_{x,y} u$. ii) $m(x) \sim_{x,y} m(y)$ and $m(y) \sim_{x,y} m(x)$. It is easy to see that $\sim_{x,y}$ is an equivalence relation. For all $u \in \Delta^\mathcal{I}$, we note its equivalence class by $[u]$. We now build $\mathcal{I}'$ as follows:

- $\Delta^{\mathcal{I}'} = \{[u] | u \in \Delta^\mathcal{I}\}$.
- For all $[u], [v], [w], [z]$, we let $\{[u], [v]\} <^{\mathcal{I}'} \{[w], [z]\}$ iff
  $\exists u' \in [u], \exists v' \in [v]$, such that $\forall w' \in [w], \forall z' \in [z], \{u', v'\} <^\mathcal{I} \{w', z'\}$.
- For all propositional variables P and for all $u \neq m(y)$, $[u] \in P^{\mathcal{I}'}$ iff $u \in P^\mathcal{I}$. Since $[m(y)] = [m(x)]$, for all variables P, $[m(y)] \in P^{\mathcal{I}'}$ iff $m(x) \in P^\mathcal{I}$.

FACT 23. 1. $\mathcal{I}'$ is a $\mathcal{CSL}$-pair model. 2. $m'' : u \rightarrow [m'(u)]$ is min-mapping from $\Delta(y/x)$ to $\mathcal{I}'$. 3. $\Delta(y/x)$ is satisfiable in $\mathcal{I}'$ under m''.

By Fact 23, we conclude that Γ is not leftmost, and obtain the contradiction. $\square$

Proof (Theorem 19). Let C be a satisfiable $\mathcal{CSL}$-formula and let T be a derivation for C. By corollary 18, T contains a finished tableau set satisfiable under some min-mapping. Since T is finite, it also contains a leftmost tableau set which is satisfiable under some min-mapping. By Proposition 21, this tableau set is good, thus T is open. $\square$

---

[6] Observe that the filtration construction of Section 3 cannot be used as it does not preserve the relational formulas needed to find a min-mapping.

5.3   Completeness

Theorem 24. *If Γ is a good tableau set, then Γ is satisfiable.*

As usual, the completeness is proved by building a canonical model $\mathcal{I}_\Gamma$ from the good tableau set Γ. Observe that if Γ is a good tableau set, Γ is finite and contains no labels blocked by the subset blocking of Definition 8. Consequently Γ is saturated, where the notion of saturation is the usual one (closure under the rules). The main issue for building the canonical model is that the relation $<$ in Γ is not modular. We have to modularize it in order to define the model.

The relation $\not<$ in Γ can be seen as a partial relation $\geq$. From it we can define a binary relation $=_{\not<}$ as follow, for all $x, y, u, z \in \mathrm{Lab}_\Gamma$:
- $\{x, y\} =_{\not<} \{x, y\}$.
- if $\{x, y\} \not< \{u, v\}$ and $\{u, v\} \not< \{x, y\}$ are in Γ, then $\{x, y\} =_{\not<} \{u, v\}$.

It is easy to see that $=_{\not<}$ is an equivalence relation (transitivity comes from the rule (mod).). We denote by $[\{x, y\}]_{\not<}$ the equivalence class of $\{x, y\}$ modulo the relation $=_{\not<}$. Intuitively, if we see $\{x, y\}$ as the distance from x to y, then $\{x, y\} =_{\not<} \{u, v\}$ means that $d(x, y) = d(u, v)$.

The relation $\not<$ in Γ also induces a relation $<_e$ between the equivalence classes: we say that $[\{x, y\}]_{\not<} <_e [\{u, v\}]_{\not<}$ iff there exists $\{x', y'\} \in [\{x, y\}]_{\not<}$ and $\{u', v'\} \in [\{u, v\}]_{\not<}$ such that $\{u', v'\} \not< \{x', y'\} \in \Gamma$ and $\{x', y'\} \not< \{u', v'\} \notin \Gamma$.

FACT 25. The relation $<_e$ over the equivalence classes is a (strict) partial order.

We let $<^*$ be any linear extension of $<_e$ (by doing for instance a topological sort on $<_e$). We can now build the canonical model $\mathcal{I}_\Gamma = \langle \Delta^{\mathcal{I}_\Gamma}, <^{\mathcal{I}_\Gamma}, \cdot^{\mathcal{I}_\Gamma} \rangle$ as follow:
- $\Delta^{\mathcal{I}_\Gamma} = \mathrm{Lab}_\Gamma$.
- For all $x, y, u, v \in \Delta^{\mathcal{I}_\Gamma}$, $\{x, y\} <^{\mathcal{I}_\Gamma} \{u, v\}$ iff $[\{x, y\}]_{\not<} <^* [\{u, v\}]_{\not<}$.
- For all propositional variable P: $P^{\mathcal{I}_\Gamma} = \{x | x : P \in \Gamma\}$.

FACT 26. $\mathcal{I}_\Gamma$ is a $\mathcal{CSL}$-model, and Γ is satisfiable in it under the identity mapping $\mathrm{id} : x \to x$.

6   Non-symmetric Case

With minimal changes, we can also handle the non-symmetric case. In this case, the distance function of minspaces is not assumed to be symmetric. Minspace distance models are defined exactly as in section 2 and include obviously symmetric minspace models as a proper subclass. We still have a correspondence between non-symmetric minspace models, that is arbitrary minspace models, and pair preferential models where the preference relation is defined over ordered pairs $(x, y) < (x, z)$ of elements having the same first component. Let us call them *non-symmetric pair models*. In these models the preference relation over pairs $(x, y) < (x, z)$ can actually be replaced by a ternary relation $y <_x z$, as it is done for instance in [2].

Concerning the tableau calculus, the only thing to change is how we represent preferential relations: the two-element multisets $\{x, y\}$ now become *ordered pairs*.

$$(\text{T3}\Leftarrow): \frac{\Gamma[x : A \Leftarrow B, z : f(x, A), y : B]}{\Gamma, (x, z) < (x, y)}$$

$$(\text{F3}\Leftarrow): \frac{\Gamma[x : \neg(A \Leftarrow B), z : f(x, B), y : A]}{\Gamma, (x, y) \not< (x, z)}$$

$$(\text{cnt}): \frac{\Gamma[x : A, y : B]}{\Gamma(y/x) \mid \Gamma, (x, x) < (x, y), (y, y) \not< (y, x)}$$

$$(\text{asm}): \frac{\Gamma[(x, y) < (z, u)]}{\Gamma, (z, u) \not< (x, y)}$$

$$(\text{mod}): \frac{\Gamma[(x, y) \not< (v, w), (v, w) \not< (t, u)]}{\Gamma, (x, y) \not< (t, u)}$$

$$(\text{tr}): \frac{\Gamma[(x, y) < (v, w), (v, w) < (t, u)]}{\Gamma, (x, y) < (t, u)}$$

$$(\text{r}\bot): \frac{\Gamma[(x, y) < (z, u), (x, y) \not< (z, u)]}{\bot}$$

Fig. 2. Rules of $T_{\mathcal{CSL}\text{NS}}$

Thus in this setting $(x, y) \neq (y, x)$. Using this notation, we can reformulate the rules of $T_{\mathcal{CSL}}$ in figure 1 to obtain a calculus $T_{\mathcal{CSL}\text{NS}}$ for $\mathcal{CSL}$ over non-symmetric pair models, corresponding to non-symmetric (or arbitrary) minspace models. The reformulated rules are shown in figure 2 (the rules not mentioned in this figure are the same as in figure 1 with $\{x, y\}$ replaced by (x, y).). Termination, soundness and completeness proofs still holds for this case, as they are independent of the encoding of the pairs.

Theorem 27. *The calculus $T_{\mathcal{CSL}\text{NS}}$ gives a terminating, sound and complete decision procedure for $\mathcal{CSL}$ over non-symmetric minspaces.*

7 Conclusions and Related Works

In this work we have contributed to the study of automated deduction for the logic of comparative concept similarity $\mathcal{CSL}$ interpreted over symmetric (and non-symmetric) minspaces. Our first result is a proof of the finite model property with respect to the preferential semantics by means of a finite filtration method. Then we have presented a labeled tableau calculus which gives a practically implementable decision procedure for this logic. Termination of the calculus is obtained by imposing suitable restrictions reminiscent of dynamic blocking and unrestricted blocking known in the literature [3,6]. Our calculi give a NExp-Time decision procedure for deciding satisfiability of $\mathcal{CSL}$ formulas. However, it is not optimal in the light of the known ExpTime upper bound.

The original paper [7] for $\mathcal{CSL}$ reduces $\mathcal{CSL}$ satisfiability to checking emptiness of an automaton built from an input concept. This automaton based algorithm for checking $\mathcal{CSL}$ satisfiability runs in ExpTime. However, it requires a complex construction of a large automaton which turns in many simple cases to be excessive. Despite that the complexity of the proposed tableau algorithm is higher than the original automaton based algorithm, we expect that our tableau algorithm will perform better in practice. Moreover, known techniques (such as caching) could be employed to make the tableau calculus more efficient. In the future, a practical comparison of the two algorithms will be very interesting.

In [2] a labeled tableau calculus for $\mathcal{CSL}$ over non symmetric minspaces is presented; a theorem prover implementing the calculus is described in [1]. This calculus is similar to the one introduced here for the non-symmetric case, being based on the same preferential semantics. However, it makes use of a family of modalities indexed on labels and needs specific rules for handling them. The modal rules (similar to modal logic GL) force the limit-assumption property with respect to the ternary preference relation. Termination is obtained by imposing relatively complex blocking restrictions. In contrast the present calculus has only rules for $\mathcal{CSL}$-connectives and treats modularity more efficiently (by avoiding a branching rule) by means of a negative preference relation; by these features it is expectedly more efficient. Moreover, it is not obvious how to extend the approach of [2] to the symmetric case, in particular how to capture the limit assumption property by means of modal rules.

Finally the calculus may be extended to treat a wider language, more interesting for description-logic applications. For instance, we expect that we can easily treat individuals (nominals). Being a labeled tableau, handling individuals should not be too difficult. For this purpose, the calculus should integrate equality reasoning on individuals and the left conclusion of the (cnt) rule should make use of explicit equality rather than substitution.

References

1. Alenda, R., Olivetti, N., Pozatto, G.L.: Csl-lean: a prover for the logic of comparative similarity. In: Proceedings of M4M-6 (Methods for Modalities) (2009)
2. Alenda, R., Olivetti, N., Schwind, C.: Comparative concept similarity over minspaces: Axiomatisation and tableaux calculus. In: Giese, M., Waaler, A. (eds.) TABLEAUX 2009. LNCS, vol. 5607, pp. 17–31. Springer, Heidelberg (2009)
3. Horrocks, I., Sattler, U.: A description logic with transitive and inverse roles and role hierarchies. J. Logic Computation 9(3), 385–410 (1999)
4. Kurucz, A., Wolter, F., Zakharyaschev, M.: Modal logics for metric spaces: Open problems. In: Artëmov, S.N., Barringer, H., d'Avila Garcez, A.S., Lamb, L.C., Woods, J. (eds.) We Will Show Them! (2), pp. 193–108. College Publ. (2005)
5. Lewis, D.: Counterfactuals. Basil Blackwell Ltd. (1973)
6. Schmidt, R.A., Tishkovsky, D.: A general tableau method for deciding description logics, modal logics and related first-order fragments. In: Armando, A., Baumgartner, P., Dowek, G. (eds.) IJCAR 2008. LNCS (LNAI), vol. 5195, pp. 194–209. Springer, Heidelberg (2008)
7. Sheremet, M., Tishkovsky, D., Wolter, F., Zakharyaschev, M.: Comparative similarity, tree automata, and diophantine equations. In: Sutcliffe, G., Voronkov, A. (eds.) LPAR 2005. LNCS (LNAI), vol. 3835, pp. 651–665. Springer, Heidelberg (2005)
8. Sheremet, M., Tishkovsky, D., Wolter, F., Zakharyaschev, M.: A logic for concepts and similarity. J. Log. Comput. 17(3), 415–452 (2007)
9. Sheremet, M., Wolter, F., Zakharyaschev, M.: A modal logic framework for reasoning about comparative distances and topology. Annals of Pure and Applied Logic 161(4), 534–559 (2010)

A Resolution Mechanism for Prenex Gödel Logic

Matthias Baaz[*] and Christian G. Fermüller[**]

Technische Universität Wien, Vienna, Austria

Abstract. First order Gödel logic $\mathbf{G}_\infty^\triangle$, enriched with the projection operator $\triangle$—in contrast to other important t-norm based fuzzy logics, like Łukasiewicz and Product logic—is well known to be recursively axiomatizable. However, unlike in classical logic, testing (1-)unsatisfiability, i.e., checking whether a formula has no interpretation that assigns the designated truth value 1 to it, cannot be straightforwardly reduced to testing validity. We investigate the prenex fragment of $\mathbf{G}_\infty^\triangle$ and show that, although standard Skolemization does not preserve 1-satisfiability, a specific Skolem form for satisfiability can be computed nevertheless. In a further step an efficient translation to a particular structural clause form is introduced. Finally, an adaption of a chaining calculus is shown to provide a basis for efficient, resolution style theorem proving.

1 Introduction

Gödel logic is a prominent example of a t-norm based fuzzy logic [12], distinguished by the fact that validity and satisfiability depend only on the relative order of truth values of atomic formulas. It is sometimes also called intuitionistic fuzzy logic, following [18]. The importance of this logic is emphasized by the fact that one may arrive at it by different routes. Already Gödel [11] had introduced the truth tables for what is now called the family of propositional finite valued Gödel logics. Dummett [8] later generalized these to an infinite set of truth values and demonstrated that the set of corresponding tautologies is axiomatized by intuitionistic logic extended by the linearity axiom $(A \rightarrow B) \vee (B \rightarrow A)$; hence the alternative name Dummett's **LC** or Gödel-Dummett logic. On the first order level, different Gödel logics arise from differently ordered set of truth values (see, e.g., [2]). Here, we will deal with *standard first order Gödel logic* $\mathbf{G}_\infty$, where the truth values set is the real closed unit interval $[0, 1]$ in its natural order. In fact we will focus on the natural extension $\mathbf{G}_\infty^\triangle$ that arises from $\mathbf{G}_\infty$ by adding the unary propositional connective $\triangle$ that maps all formulas to 0 that do not receive the designated value 1. Unlike other important fuzzy logics defined over $[0, 1]$, including Łukasiewicz logic and Product logic (see, e.g., [12]), that are not recursively axiomatizable, validity for $\mathbf{G}_\infty$ and $\mathbf{G}_\infty^\triangle$ is Σ_1^0-complete.

While, besides Hilbert type systems, also cut-free Gentzen type systems are complete for $\mathbf{G}_\infty^\triangle$, none of these systems provides a suitable basis for automated

---

[*] Supported by FWF grant P22416.
[**] Supported by Eurocores-ESF/FWF grant 1143-G15 (LogICCC-LoMoReVI).

A. Dawar and H. Veith (Eds.): CSL 2010, LNCS 6247, pp. 67–79, 2010.

deduction. In [5] it has been shown that the *prenex fragment* of $\mathbf{G}_\infty^\triangle$ admits a Herbrand theorem and thus Skolemization. This in turn allows to translate prenex formulas of $\mathbf{G}_\infty^\triangle$ into a special clause form, based on the natural order relations $<$ and $\leq$. By adapting a so-called chaining calculus [7,6] an efficient resolution style mechanism for testing *validity* of prenex $\mathbf{G}_\infty^\triangle$-formulas is obtained. We call a formula A valid if $\|A\|_\mathcal{I} = 1$ for all interpretations $\mathcal{I}$. If $\|A\|_\mathcal{I} = 1$ for some interpretation $\mathcal{I}$ then A is satisfiable, or more precisely 1-satisfiable, otherwise A is called 1-unsatisfiable. It is important to keep in mind that, unlike in classical logic, *validity* and *satisfiability* are not dual to each other in most fuzzy logics. (Compare the case of monadic Łukasiwicz logic, for which the satisfiability problem is known to be Π_1^0-complete, but where the decidability of the validity is a well known open problem, see [16,17,15].) In fact, for Gödel logic *without* $\triangle$ satisfiability of a formula A *is* equivalent to the non-validity of $\neg A$ (see [13]). However for $\mathbf{G}_\infty^\triangle$ the duality vanishes: e.g., $\neg(B \wedge \neg\triangle B)$ is not valid, although $B \wedge \neg\triangle B$ is unsatisfiable. Therefore, if we are interested in testing whether a given formula A with occurrences of $\triangle$ has a model, we cannot rely on a mechanism for testing whether $\neg A$ is valid. Indeed, quite differently from classical logic, no direct and efficient reduction of the satisfiability problem to the validity problem, or *vice versa*, is known for $\mathbf{G}_\infty^\triangle$ and for other standard fuzzy logics.

We argue that it is in fact more important to be able to test whether a given specification expressed by a $\mathbf{G}_\infty^\triangle$-formula A is coherent in the sense of admitting a model, i.e., an interpretation that assigns 1 to A, than to have a procedure for testing whether $(\neg)A$ is valid. In this paper we address the former problem. Like in [5] we focus on the prenex fragment of $\mathbf{G}_\infty^\triangle$. It is shown in [5] that Skolemization preserves validity for prenex $\mathbf{G}_\infty^\triangle$-formulas. In contrast, we will observe that satisfiability is not preserved by standard Skolemization. We overcome this problem by defining a special alternative form of Skolemization that, in addition to Skolem terms, introduces a fresh monadic predicate symbol.

The central contribution of the paper consists in showing that any conjunction A of prenex formulas of $\mathbf{G}_\infty^\triangle$ can indeed be translated into a purely universal form A' that is equivalent to A with respect to 1-satisfiability. Similarly to [5] we then translate A' into a clausal form that is based on the underlying order relation. Once more we do not simply re-use results from [5], but rather present a more efficient version of a definitional clause form. The final part of the suggested deduction mechanism can then be directly transfered from [5]: a so-called chaining calculus can be straightforwardly adapted to test unsatisfiability. To achieve a self contained presentation, that does not rely on familiarity with Gödel logic or with chaining calculi we will explicitly specify all relevant schemes and inference rules.

The paper is organized as follows. After clarifying basic notions about Gödel logic in Section 2, a satisfiability preserving Skolemization operator is defined and investigated in Section 3. In Section 4 we present so-called chain normal forms. In particular we show how to translate arbitrary universal formulas into sets of clauses where the literals express basic order relations between atomic formulas. Section 5 describes a refutationally complete set of inference rules that can be applied to test unsatisfiability efficiently. Section 6 summarizes the results and indicates related problems.

2 Basic Notions and Facts

Kurt Gödel [11] has introduced the following truth functions for conjunction, disjunction, and implication

$$\|A \wedge B\|_{\mathcal{I}} = \min(\|A\|_{\mathcal{I}}, \|B\|_{\mathcal{I}}), \qquad \|A \vee B\|_{\mathcal{I}} = \max(\|A\|_{\mathcal{I}}, \|B\|_{\mathcal{I}}),$$

$$\|A \to B\|_{\mathcal{I}} = \begin{cases} 1 & \text{if } \|A\|_{\mathcal{I}} \le \|B\|_{\mathcal{I}} \\ \|B\|_{\mathcal{I}} & \text{otherwise.} \end{cases}$$

While Gödel referred to a finite set of values, we consider so-called standard Gödel logic $\mathbf{G}_\infty$ [13,14], where the set of truth values is the real unit interval $[0,1]$. The propositional constants $\bot$ and $\top$ are specified by $\|\bot\|_{\mathcal{I}} = 0$ and $\|\top\|_{\mathcal{I}} = 1$, respectively; $\neg A$ abbreviates $A \to \bot$ and $A \leftrightarrow B$ abbreviates $(A \to B) \wedge (B \to A)$. Therefore

$$\|\neg A\|_{\mathcal{I}} = \begin{cases} 1 & \text{if } \|A\|_{\mathcal{I}} = 0 \\ 0 & \text{otherwise} \end{cases} \quad \|A \leftrightarrow B\|_{\mathcal{I}} = \begin{cases} 1 & \text{if } \|A\|_{\mathcal{I}} = \|B\|_{\mathcal{I}} \\ \min(\|A\|_{\mathcal{I}}, \|B\|_{\mathcal{I}}) & \text{otherwise.} \end{cases}$$

Following [1] we enrich this set of connectives by adding the unary operator $\triangle$ with the following meaning:

$$\|\triangle A\|_{\mathcal{I}} = \begin{cases} 1 & \text{if } \|A\|_I = 1 \\ 0 & \text{otherwise.} \end{cases}$$

Note that $\triangle$ allows to embed classical logic immediately. For propositional logic a *(standard) interpretation* $\mathcal{I}$ is simply an assignment of values in $[0,1]$ to propositional variables. In first order logic atomic formulas (rather than $\top$ and $\bot$) are of the form $P(t_1, \ldots, t_n)$, where P is a predicate symbol and $t_1, \ldots, t_n$ are terms, where terms are built up from (object) variables and constant symbols using function symbols, as usual. An interpretation $\mathcal{I}$ now consists of a non-empty *domain D* and a *signature interpretation* $v_{\mathcal{I}}$ that maps constant symbols and object variables to elements of D, as well as every n-ary predicate symbol f to a function $v_{\mathcal{I}}(f)$ of type $D^n \mapsto D$. $v_{\mathcal{I}}$ homomorphically extends to arbitrary terms, as usual. Moreover, $v_{\mathcal{I}}$ maps every n-ary predicate symbol P to a function $v_{\mathcal{I}}(P)$ of type $D^n \mapsto V$. The truth value of an atomic formula $P(t_1, \ldots, t_n)$ is thus defined as

$$\|P(t_1, \ldots, t_n)\|_{\mathcal{I}} = v_{\mathcal{I}}(P)(v_{\mathcal{I}}(t_1), \ldots, v_{\mathcal{I}}(t_n)).$$

For quantification we define the *distribution* of a formula A with respect to a free variable x in an interpretation $\mathcal{I}$ as $\mathrm{distr}_{\mathcal{I}}(A(x)) = \{\|A(x)\|_{\mathcal{I}[d/x]} \mid d \in D\}$, where $\mathcal{I}[d/x]$ denotes the interpretation that is exactly as $\mathcal{I}$, except for insisting on $v_{\mathcal{I}[d/x]}(x) = d$. (Similarly we will use $\mathcal{I}[\overline{d}/\overline{x}]$ for the interpretation arising from $\mathcal{I}$ by assigning for all $1 \leq i \leq n$ the domain element d_i in $\overline{d} = d_1, \ldots, d_n$ to the variable x_i in $\overline{x} = x_1, \ldots, x_n$.) The universal and existential quantifiers correspond to the infimum and supremum, respectively, in the following sense:

$$\|\forall x A(x)\|_{\mathcal{I}} = \inf \mathrm{distr}_{\mathcal{I}}(A(x)) \qquad \|\exists x A(x)\|_{\mathcal{I}} = \sup \mathrm{distr}_{\mathcal{I}}(A(x)).$$

By $\mathbf{G}_\infty^\triangle$ we mean the just defined *(standard) first order Gödel logic with* $\triangle$. A $\mathbf{G}_\infty^\triangle$-formula A is *valid* if $\|A\|_{\mathcal{I}} = 1$ for all interpretations $\mathcal{I}$; A is *1-satisfiable* if there exists an interpretation $\mathcal{I}$ such that $\|A\|_{\mathcal{I}} = 1$. The set of all 1-satisfiable formulas will be denoted by 1SAT. As already mentioned in the introduction, 1-satisfiability is not dual to non-validity in $\mathbf{G}_\infty^\triangle$. But as for $\mathbf{G}_\infty$, both problems are Π_1^0-complete according to [13,14].

Like in intuitionistic logic, also in Gödel logic (with or without $\triangle$) quantifiers cannot be shifted arbitrarily. If x is not free in B we have

$- \models_{\mathbf{G}_\infty^\triangle} \exists x(A \to B) \to (\forall x A \to B)$ and
$- \models_{\mathbf{G}_\infty^\triangle} \exists x(B \to A) \to (B \to \exists x A),$

but the converse implications are not valid. As a consequence arbitrary formulas are not equivalent to prenex formulas, in general. Nevertheless the prenex fragment of $\mathbf{G}_\infty^\triangle$ is quite expressive. E.g., classical logic, where formulas can be reduced to prenex form without loss of generality, can straightforwardly be embedded into prenex $\mathbf{G}_\infty^\triangle$ using $\triangle$ as indicated above. We list a few further valid schemes of $\mathbf{G}_\infty^\triangle$ that will be used in later sections.

$- \models_{\mathbf{G}_\infty^\triangle} \triangle A \to A$
$- \models_{\mathbf{G}_\infty^\triangle} ((A \wedge B) \vee C) \leftrightarrow (A \vee C) \wedge (B \vee C))$
$- \models_{\mathbf{G}_\infty^\triangle} \triangle(A \to B) \vee \neg \triangle(A \to B)$
$- \models_{\mathbf{G}_\infty^\triangle} A(t) \to \exists x A(x)$, where x does not occur in $A(t)$
$- \models_{\mathbf{G}_\infty^\triangle} \triangle \forall x A \leftrightarrow \forall x \triangle A$

Since $\mathbf{G}_\infty^\triangle$ does not contain the identity predicate, the following version of the Löwenheim-Skolem theorem is straightforwardly obtained, just like for classical or intuitionistic logic.

Proposition 1. *Every 1-satisfiable formula of* $\mathbf{G}_\infty^\triangle$ *has a model with countably infinite domain.*

3   A Non-standard Form of Skolemization

In [5] it is shown that the prenex fragment of $\mathbf{G}_\infty^\triangle$ admits Skolemization *with respect to validity*: we have $\models_{\mathbf{G}_\infty^\triangle} A \Longleftrightarrow \models_{\mathbf{G}_\infty^\triangle} \mathrm{sko}(A)$, where the operator $\mathrm{sko}(\cdot)$ replaces universally quantified variables by Skolem terms in the usual manner. However, standard Skolemization for satisfiability (where existentially quantified variables are replaced by Skolem terms) does *not preserve 1-satisfiability*, as seen in the following simple example. A model $\mathcal{I}$ with domain $\{d_1, d_2, \ldots\}$ for $\exists x A(x) \wedge \forall x \neg \triangle A(x)$ is obtained by setting $\sup_{i \in \omega} \|A(x)\|_{\mathcal{I}[d_i/x]} = 1$, without admitting $\|A(x)\|_{\mathcal{I}[d_i/x]} = 1$ for any domain element d_i. But the Skolemized form $A(c) \wedge \forall x \neg \triangle A(x)$ is not 1-satisfiable. The example can obviously be made prenex by moving the second quantifier to the front. However, we will slightly widen our focus to *conjunctions* of prenex formulas, anyway.

We demonstrate that Skolem forms *with respect to satisfiability* can nevertheless be achieved by a nice trick, involving an additional monadic predicate symbol.

Definition 1. *Let E be a new monadic predicate symbol. The operator $\Psi_E(\cdot)$, to be applied to prenex formulas from outside to inside, is defined by*

- *$\Psi_E(\forall x A(x)) = \forall x \Psi_E(A(x))$;*
- *$\Psi_E(\exists x A(x)) = \forall x(E(x) \rightarrow \Psi_E(A(f(x, \overline{y}))))$, where f is a new (Skolem) function symbol and $\overline{y}$ are the free variables in $\exists x A(x)$;*
- *$\Psi_E(A) = A$, if A is quantifier free.*

The Skolem form $\mathrm{SKO}_E(A)$ of A is obtained by moving all (universal) quantifiers in $\Psi_E(A)$ to the front and inserting an occurrence of $\triangle$ immediately after the quantifiers. More precisely,

$$\mathrm{SKO}_E(A) = \forall \overline{x} \triangle (\Psi_E(A)^-)$$

where $\overline{x}$ are the variables in $\Psi_E(A)$ and $\Psi_E(A)^-$ denotes $\Psi_E(A)$ after removal of all quantifier occurrences.

Obviously $\mathrm{SKO}_E(\cdot)$ does not preserve logical equivalence. However it does preserve 1-satisfiability as shown in the following theorem.

Theorem 1. *Let $A_1, \ldots, A_m$ be prenex formulas. Then*

$$\Big(\bigwedge_{1 \leq i \leq m} A_i \Big) \in \mathrm{1SAT} \iff \Big(\exists x E(x) \wedge \bigwedge_{1 \leq i \leq m} \mathrm{SKO}_E(A_i) \Big) \in \mathrm{1SAT}$$

Proof. ($\Leftarrow$) We show that $\mathrm{SKO}_E(A_i)$ together with $\exists x E(x)$ implies A_i. Note that $\mathrm{SKO}_E(A_i)$ is of the form

$$\forall x_1 \ldots \forall x_n \triangle (E(x_1) \rightarrow \ldots (E(x_n) \rightarrow A_i^{sk}) \ldots)$$

where A_i^{sk} denotes the quantifier free part of A_i with all existentially bound variable replaced by Skolem terms, as specified in Definition 1. Since $\models_{\mathbf{G}_\infty^\triangle} \triangle \forall x B \leftrightarrow \forall x \triangle B$ and $\models_{\mathbf{G}_\infty^\triangle} \triangle B \rightarrow B$ for all formulas B, we can remove the indicated occurrence of $\triangle$ in $\mathrm{SKO}_E(A_i)$. Then we use $\models_{\mathbf{G}_\infty^\triangle} A(f(x, \overline{y})) \rightarrow \exists v A(v)$, where v is a new variable, to replace the Skolem terms by existentially quantified variables. Next we use $\models_{\mathbf{G}_\infty^\triangle} \forall x(E(x) \rightarrow \exists v A(v)) \rightarrow (\exists x E(x) \rightarrow \exists v A(v))$, where x does not occur in $\exists v A(v)$, to move existial quantifiers immediately in front of all occurrences of E. Finally we use the assumption that $\exists x E(x)$ to detach all these occurrences. The resulting formula is A_i, as required.

($\Rightarrow$) Suppose $\mathcal{I}$ satisfies A_i for $1 \leq i \leq m$. To obtain a model $\mathcal{J}$ of the formula at the right hand side we may augment $\mathcal{I}$ by a freely chosen interpretation of E and of the Skolem function symbols. In particular, to achieve $\|\exists x E(x)\|_{\mathcal{J}} = 1$ we use Proposition 1 and assign $v_{\mathcal{J}}(E)(d_i) = v_i$ for $d_i \in D_{\mathcal{J}}$ in such a manner that $\sup_i v_i = 1$, but $v_i \neq 1$ for all $i \in \omega$.

In interpreting the Skolem functions we have to make sure that

$$\|E(x) \to \Psi_E(A_i(f(x, \overline{y})))\|_{\mathcal{J}[d/x, \overline{e}/\overline{y}]} = 1,$$

for all $d \in D_{\mathcal{J}}$ and all $\overline{e} \in D_{\mathcal{J}}^n$, where n is the number of free variables in $\exists x A_i(x)$. To this aim we use the assumption that $\|\exists x A_i(x)\|_{\mathcal{I}[\overline{e}/\overline{y}]} = 1$. This means that for any $d \in D_{\mathcal{I}} = D_{\mathcal{J}}$ there is a further domain element d' such that $\|E(x)\|_{\mathcal{J}[d/x]} \leq \|A_i(x)\|_{\mathcal{I}[d'/x, \overline{e}/\overline{y}]}$. We assign $v_{\mathcal{J}}(f)(d, \overline{e}) = d'$. If there are no more existential quantifiers in A_i then we are done, since then $\Psi_E(A_i) = A_i$ and therefore $\|A_i(x)\|_{\mathcal{I}[d'/x, \overline{e}/\overline{y}]} = \|\Psi_E(A_i(f(x, \overline{y})))\|_{\mathcal{J}[d/x, \overline{e}/\overline{y}]}$. Otherwise we proceed by induction on the number of existential quantifiers replaced by applying Ψ_E, with (essentially) the presented argument as inductive step.   □

Remark 1. We have seen that only our alternative form of Skolemization is needed to preserve 1-satisfiability for prenex formulas A of $\mathbf{G}_\infty^\triangle$, in general. However standard Skolemization (where no additional predicate symbol is introduced) suffices if the quantifier free part of A is preceded by $\triangle$. This observation can be exploited to achieve more efficient translations. Those conjuncts of the formula in question that are of the form $\mathbf{Q}\overline{x}\triangle B$ can be Skolemized in the traditional manner, i.e., existentially quantified variables x are replaced by Skolem terms $f(\overline{y})$, where $\overline{y}$ denotes the variables bound by universal quantifiers in the scope of which x occurs. Only the remaining conjuncts will be treated using the fresh monadic predicate symbol E, as described above.

Note that the price we had to pay for preserving 1-satisfiability consists not only in the additional occurrences of the new predicate symbol E in the antecedents of universally quantified implications, but also in adding the conjunct $\exists x E(x)$. To obtain a purely universal formula that is ready for translation to chain normal form, we have to replace also $\exists x E(x)$ by a conjunction of universal formulas. To this aim we first introduce notation that will be useful also in defining chain normal forms in Section 4, below.

Definition 2. $A \trianglelefteq B \stackrel{\text{def}}{=} \triangle(A \to B)$ *and* $A \triangleleft B \stackrel{\text{def}}{=} \neg\triangle(B \to A)$.

It is straightforward to check that the suggestive symbols are justified by

$$\|A \trianglelefteq B\|_{\mathcal{I}} = \begin{cases} 1 & \text{if } \|A\|_{\mathcal{I}} \leq \|B\|_{\mathcal{I}} \\ 0 & \text{otherwise} \end{cases} \quad \text{and} \quad \|A \triangleleft B\|_{\mathcal{I}} = \begin{cases} 1 & \text{if } \|A\|_{\mathcal{I}} < \|B\|_{\mathcal{I}} \\ 0 & \text{otherwise.} \end{cases}$$

Definition 3. *Let* $P_1, \ldots, P_k$ *be the predicate symbols occurring in* $\mathrm{SKO}_E(A)$, *where* A *is a conjunction of prenex formulas. (Note that* $E \in \{P_1, \ldots, P_k\}$.)

$$\mathcal{H}_\exists(E, A) \stackrel{\text{def}}{=} \bigwedge_{1 \leq i \leq k} \forall \overline{y_i}(\top \trianglelefteq P_i(\overline{y_i}) \vee P_i(\overline{y_i}) \triangleleft E(f_{P_i}(\overline{y_i})),$$

where $\overline{y_i}$ is a sequence of fresh variables, according to the arity of P_i, and f_{P_i} is a fresh function symbol of corresponding arity.

Lemma 1. *Let $A = \bigwedge_{1 \leq i \leq m} A_i$ where for $1 \leq i \leq m$ A_i is of the form $\forall \overline{x_i} \triangle A_i^-$ for some is quantifier free formula A_i^-. Then*

$$\left(\exists x E(x) \wedge A \right) \in 1\text{SAT} \iff \left(\mathcal{H}_\exists(E, A) \wedge \bigwedge_{1 \leq i \leq m} \text{SKO}_E(A_i) \right) \in 1\text{SAT}$$

Proof. ($\Rightarrow$) Let $\mathcal{I}$ be a model of $\exists x E(x) \wedge A$. For every $\overline{d} \in D_\mathcal{I}^n$, where n is the arity of P_i the following holds. Either $\|P_i(\overline{y_i})\|_{\mathcal{I}[\overline{d}/\overline{y_i}]} = 1$, implying that the first disjunct $\top \trianglelefteq P_i(\overline{y_i})$ of the relevant conjunct in $\mathcal{H}_\exists(E, A)$ evaluates to 1. Otherwise, since we have $\|\exists x E(x)\|_\mathcal{I} = 1$, we can extend $\mathcal{I}$ by an interpretation of the new function symbols f_{P_i} in such a manner that $\|E(f_{P_i}(\overline{y_i}))\|_{\mathcal{I}[\overline{d}/\overline{y_i}]} > \|P_i(\overline{y_i})\|_{\mathcal{I}[\overline{d}/\overline{y_i}]}$ holds. But this implies that the second disjunct in $\mathcal{H}_\exists(E, A)$ is evaluated to 1.

($\Leftarrow$) Let $\mathcal{I}$ be a model of $\mathcal{H}_\exists(E, A) \wedge \bigwedge_{1 \leq i \leq m} \text{SKO}_E(A_i)$. If $\|E(x)\|_{\mathcal{I}[d/x]} = 1$ for some $d \in D_\mathcal{I}$ then nothing remains to prove. Otherwise remember that $E \in \{P_1, \ldots, P_k\}$, the set of predicate symbols occurring in $\text{SKO}_E(A)$. Therefore $\|\mathcal{H}_\exists(E, A)\|_\mathcal{I} = 1$ implies that for every $d \in D_\mathcal{I}$ we have $\|E(x)\|_{\mathcal{I}[x/d]} < \|E(f_E(x))\|_{\mathcal{I}[x/d]}$, since $\|\top \trianglelefteq E(x)\|_{\mathcal{I}[x/d]} < 1$. Consequently there must exist some $v < 1$ such that $\sup_{d \in D_\mathcal{I}} \|E(x)\|_{\mathcal{I}[x/d]} = v$, but $\|E(x)\|_{\mathcal{I}[x/d]} \neq v$ for all $d \in D_\mathcal{I}$. $\|\mathcal{H}_\exists(E, A)\|_\mathcal{I} = 1$ also implies that for every $\overline{d} \in D_\mathcal{I}^n$, where n is the arity of P_i, we have either $\|P_i(\overline{y_i})\|_{\mathcal{I}[\overline{d}/\overline{y_i}]} = 1$ or $\|P_i(\overline{y_i})\|_{\mathcal{I}[\overline{d}/\overline{y_i}]} < v$. In other words: no atomic formula is assigned a value in the interval $[v, 1)$ by $\mathcal{I}$. We may therefore define a new interpretation $\mathcal{J}$ over the same domain $D_\mathcal{I}$ by setting $\|P_i(\overline{y_i})\|_{\mathcal{J}[\overline{d}/\overline{y_i}]} = \|P_i(\overline{y_i})\|_{\mathcal{I}[\overline{d}/\overline{y_i}]} + (1 - v)$, whenever $\|P_i(\overline{y_i})\|_{\mathcal{I}[\overline{d}/\overline{y_i}]} \neq 1$. Otherwise the corresponding truth value remains 1.

It remains to show that $\mathcal{J}$ is a model of $\exists x E(x) \wedge A$. By definition of $\mathcal{J}$ we have $\sup_{d \in D_\mathcal{I}} \|E(x)\|_{\mathcal{J}[x/d]} = 1$. To complete the argument remember that A_i is the form $\forall \overline{x} \triangle A_i^-$ for $1 \leq i \leq m$. Therefore $\|A_i^-\|_{\mathcal{I}[\overline{d}/\overline{x}]} = 1$ for every appropriate tuple $\overline{d}$ of domain elements. This means that the evaluation essentially reduces to that of a propositional formula of $\mathbf{G}_\infty^\triangle$. But an inspection of the truth functions for the propositional connectives shows that whether a given interpretation $\mathcal{I}$ satisfies a formula only depends on the relative order of assigned truth values below 1, but not on their absolute values. Therefore, just like $\mathcal{I}$, also $\mathcal{J}$ is a model of A_i for $1 \leq i \leq m$. □

4 Chain Normal Form

The results of the last section imply that the satisfiability problem for prenex $\mathbf{G}_\infty^\triangle$ can be reduced to checking satisfiability of conjunctions of purely universal formulas. To define so-called chain normal forms [3,4] let us use, in addition to $\triangleleft$, also $A \triangleq B$ as an abbreviation for $\triangle(A \leftrightarrow B)$. Clearly $\|A \triangleq B\|_\mathcal{I} = 1$ iff $\|A\|_\mathcal{I} = \|B\|_\mathcal{I}$.

Definition 4. *Let F be a quantifier-free formula of $\mathbf{G}_\infty^\triangle$ and $A_1, \ldots, A_n$ the atoms occurring in F. A $\triangle$-chain over F is a formula of the form*

$$(\bot \bowtie_0 A_{\pi(1)}) \wedge (A_{\pi(1)} \bowtie_1 A_{\pi(2)}) \wedge \cdots \wedge (A_{\pi(n-1)} \bowtie_{n-1} A_{\pi(n)}) \wedge (A_{\pi(n)} \bowtie_n \top)$$

where π is a permutation of $\{1, \ldots, n\}$, $\bowtie_i$ is either $\lhd$ or $\trianglelefteq$, and at least one of the $\bowtie_i$'s stands for $\lhd$.

By Chains(F) *we denote the set of all $\triangle$-chains over F.*

The following follows immediately from Theorem 17 of [5].

Theorem 2. *Let F be of the form $\bigwedge_{1 \leq i \leq n} \forall \overline{x_i} \triangle F_i$, where F_i is quantifier free. Then there exist $\Gamma_i \subseteq$ Chains(F_i) for all $1 \leq i \leq n$ such that*

$$\models_{\mathbf{G}_\infty^\triangle} F \leftrightarrow \bigwedge_{1 \leq i \leq n} \bigvee_{C \in \Gamma_i} C.$$

While Theorem 2 can be used, in principle, to reduce Skolemized formulas to clausal form, the result might be exceedingly complex, since Chains(F) contains a super-exponential number of different elements (with respect to the length of F) in general. Therefore we present an alternative structural translation that results in clause forms of linear size.

Definition 5. *For any quantifier free formula F of form $F_1 \circ F_2$, where $\circ \in \{\wedge, \vee, \rightarrow\}$, let*

$$\mathrm{df}(F) \stackrel{\text{def}}{=} [p_F(\overline{x}) \trianglelefteq (p_{F_1}(\overline{x_1}) \circ p_{F_2}(\overline{x_2}))]$$

where p_F, p_{F_1}, p_{F_2} are new predicate symbols and $\overline{x}, \overline{x_1}, \overline{x_2}$ are the tuples of variables occurring in F, F_1, F_2, respectively. If F is of form $\triangle F_1$ then

$$\mathrm{df}(F) \stackrel{\text{def}}{=} [p_F(\overline{x}) \trianglelefteq \triangle p_{F_1}(\overline{x_1})].$$

If F is atomic then $p_F(\overline{x})$ is simply an alternative denotation for F.

For any quantifier free formula G the definitional normal form *is defined as*

$$\mathrm{DEF}(G) \stackrel{\text{def}}{=} \triangle p_G(\overline{x}) \wedge \Big(\bigwedge_{F \in \mathrm{nsf}(G)} \mathrm{df}(F) \Big)$$

where nsf(G) *is the set of all non-atomic subformulas of G, $\overline{x}$ is the tuple of variables occurring in G, and p_G is a new predicate symbol.*

The following is straightforwardly obtained from simple equivalences.

Proposition 2. *A quantifier free formula F is 1-satisfiable iff its definitional normal form* DEF(F) *is 1-satisfiable.*

Definition 6. *A* literal *is a formula of the form $A \lhd B$ or $A \trianglelefteq B$, where A and B are atomic formulas (including $\top$ and $\bot$). A* clause *is a finite set of literals, denoting a disjunction of its elements. A set of clauses is called satisfiable if the universal closure of the corresponding conjunction of disjunction of literals is 1-satisfiable in $\mathbf{G}_\infty^\triangle$.*

For the following it does not matter, whether we think of a clause as a disjunction of formulas built up using $\to$ and $\triangle$; or rather as 'logic free' syntax, where the semantics is fixed according to the indicated correspondence to $\mathbf{G}_\infty^\triangle$.

Definition 7. *Let A, B, and C be atomic formulas.*

$$\mathrm{cl}(C \triangleq (A \wedge B)) \stackrel{\mathrm{def}}{=} \{\{C \trianglelefteq A\}, \{C \trianglelefteq B\}, \{A \trianglelefteq C, B \trianglelefteq C\}\}$$

$$\mathrm{cl}(C \triangleq (A \vee B)) \stackrel{\mathrm{def}}{=} \{\{A \trianglelefteq C\}, \{B \trianglelefteq C\}, \{C \trianglelefteq A, C \trianglelefteq B\}\}$$

$$\mathrm{cl}(C \triangleq (A \to B)) \stackrel{\mathrm{def}}{=} \{\{A \trianglelefteq B, C \trianglelefteq B\}, \{\mathsf{I} \trianglelefteq C, B \triangleleft A\},$$
$$\{\top \trianglelefteq C, C \trianglelefteq B\}, \{B \trianglelefteq C\}\}$$

$$\mathrm{cl}(C \triangleq \triangle A) \quad \stackrel{\mathrm{def}}{=} \{\{C \triangleleft \top, \top \trianglelefteq A\}, \{\top \trianglelefteq C, A \triangleleft \top\}\}$$

For a quantifier free formula G the definitional clause form *is defined as*

$$\mathrm{CF}^{\mathrm{d}}(G) \stackrel{\mathrm{def}}{=} \{\{\top \trianglelefteq p_G(\overline{x})\}\} \cup \bigcup_{F \in \mathrm{nsf}(G)} \mathrm{cl}(\mathrm{df}(F)))$$

where $\mathrm{nsf}(G)$ denotes the set of all non-atomic subformulas of G, $\overline{x}$ is the tuple of variables occurring in G, and p_G is a new predicate symbol.

Theorem 3. *Let $A = \bigwedge_{1 \leq i \leq m} A_i$ where, for $1 \leq i \leq m$, A_i is a $\mathbf{G}_\infty^\triangle$-formula of the form $\forall \overline{x_i} \triangle A_i^-$ for some quantifier free formula A_i^-. Then A is 1-satisfiable iff $\mathrm{CF}^{\mathrm{d}}(A) = \bigcup_{1 \leq i \leq m} \mathrm{CF}^{\mathrm{d}}(A_i^-)$ is satisfiable.*

Proof. In light of Proposition 2 we only need to check that the clauses specified in Definition 7 are equivalent to the corresponding definitional forms. (Note that, by the way they involve $\triangle$, every interpretation $\mathcal{I}$ evaluates the clauses to either 0 or 1.)

$- C \triangleq (A \to B)$: We have

$$\|\triangle(C \leftrightarrow (A \to B))\|_{\mathcal{I}} = \|(A \trianglelefteq B \wedge \triangle C) \vee (B \triangleleft A \wedge C \trianglelefteq B \wedge B \trianglelefteq C)\|_{\mathcal{I}}.$$

By applying the law of distribution to the formula at the right hand side we obtain the conjunction of the following six formulas:

$$A \trianglelefteq B \ \vee \ B \triangleleft A \qquad (1)$$
$$A \trianglelefteq B \ \vee \ C \trianglelefteq B \qquad (2)$$
$$A \trianglelefteq B \ \vee \ B \trianglelefteq C \qquad (3)$$
$$\triangle C \ \vee \ B \triangleleft A \qquad (4)$$
$$\triangle C \ \vee \ C \trianglelefteq B \qquad (5)$$
$$\triangle C \ \vee \ B \trianglelefteq C \qquad (6)$$

Note that conjunct (1) is valid and that $B \trianglelefteq C$ is entailed by (6). $B \trianglelefteq C$ in turn entails conjuncts (3) and (6). Moreover we can express $\triangle C$ by the equivalent literal $\top \trianglelefteq C$. Thus we obtain the following four conjuncts that directly correspond to $\mathrm{cl}(C \triangleq (A \to B))$:

$$A \trianglelefteq B \ \vee \ C \trianglelefteq B$$
$$\top \trianglelefteq C \ \vee \ B \triangleleft A$$
$$\top \trianglelefteq C \ \vee \ C \trianglelefteq B$$
$$B \trianglelefteq C$$

– $C \triangleq (A \wedge B)$: $\triangle(C \leftrightarrow (A \wedge B))$ is easily seen to be equivalent to the conjunction of the three disjunctions

$$C \trianglelefteq A$$
$$C \trianglelefteq B$$
$$A \trianglelefteq C \ \vee \ B \trianglelefteq C$$

that directly correspond to $\mathrm{cl}(C \triangleq (A \wedge B))$.

– $C \triangleq (A \vee B)$: $\triangle(C \leftrightarrow (A \vee B))$ is to be equivalent to the conjunction of

$$A \trianglelefteq C$$
$$B \trianglelefteq C$$
$$C \trianglelefteq A \ \vee \ C \trianglelefteq B$$

that directly correspond to $\mathrm{cl}(C \triangleq (A \vee B))$.

– $C \triangleq \triangle A$: $\triangle(C \leftrightarrow \triangle A)$ is equivalent to the conjunctions of the following two disjunctions

$$C \vartriangleleft \top \ \vee \ \top \trianglelefteq A$$
$$\top \trianglelefteq C \ \vee \ A \vartriangleleft \top$$

that directly correspond to $\mathrm{cl}(C \triangleq \triangle A)$.   □

Remark 2. A somewhat different structural clause form has been described in [5]. The fact that the language there is directly referring to order claims relating terms instead of formulas is rather irrelevant. Also the context of testing validity is immaterial. But the definitional clauses in [5] contain redundancies that are eliminated here. Moreover the description of clauses is only indirect in [5], due to the fact that $\{A = B\} \cup E$ is used to represent the set containing the clauses $\{A \trianglelefteq B\} \cup E$ and $\{B \trianglelefteq A\} \cup E$. This has to be iterated for each occurrence of an identity to obtain, e.g., 6 clauses for conjunction as well as for disjunction where we need only 3 clauses in each case. Similarly only 4 instead of 5 clauses are needed here for implication.

5   Chaining Resolution

There are different methods to test the unsatisfiabilty of the sets of clauses $\mathrm{CF}^{\mathrm{d}}(A)$ obtained for a conjunction A of prenex $\mathbf{G}^{\triangle}_{\infty}$-formulas as described in the previous sections. In the following *literals* are understood to be of the form $s < t$ or $s \leq t$, for arbitrary first order terms s and t. This means that atomic formulas are considered as terms now and the order relation is directly expressed in the syntax, not indirectly using logical connectives. Note that by this final move we have reduced the 1-satisfiability problem for prenex $\mathbf{G}^{\triangle}_{\infty}$ to the satisfiability problem for sets of clauses referring to a dense total order with endpoints.

One possibility to proceed with $\mathrm{CF}^{\mathrm{d}}(A)$ is to add clausal forms of axioms $\mathcal{D}_<$ that express that $\vartriangleleft$ and $\trianglelefteq$ refer to a total denses order with endpoints $\bot$ and $\top$. The resulting set of clauses can be fed to any first order resolution theorem prover to $\mathrm{CF}^d(A)$ to check whether the empty clause, signaling unsatisfiability, can be derived.

Another, more efficient method, that has been presented in [5], is to employ a so-called chaining calculus [7,6] for this purpose. We will briefly describe this mechanism also here.

For the resulting *order clauses* we consider the following inference rules.

Irreflexivity Resolution:

$$\frac{C \cup \{s < t\}}{C\sigma}$$

where σ is the mgu of s and t

Factorized Chaining:

$$\frac{C \cup \{u_1 \lhd_1 s_1, \ldots, u_m \lhd_m s_m\} \quad D \cup \{t_1 \lhd'_1 v_1, \ldots, t_n \lhd'_n v_n\}}{C\sigma \cup D\sigma \cup \{u_i\sigma \lhd_{i,j} v_j\sigma \mid 1 \le i \le m, 1 \le n\}}$$

where σ is the mgu of $s_1, \ldots, s_m, t_1, \ldots, t_n$ and $\lhd_{i,j}$ is $<$ if and only if either $\lhd_i$ is $<$ or $\lhd'_j$ is $<$. Moreover, $t_1\sigma$ occurs in $D\sigma$ only in inequalities $v \lhd t_1\sigma$.

These two rules constitute a refutationally complete inference system for the theory of all total orders with endpoints $\bot$ and $\top$ in presence of set $\mathcal{E}q^{\mathbf{F}}$ of clauses

$$\{x_i < y_i, y_i < x_i \mid 1 \le i \le n\} \cup \{f(x_1, \ldots, x_n) \le f(y_1, \ldots, y_n)\}$$

where f ranges the set $\mathbf{F}$ of function symbols of the signature.

To achieve more efficient proof search, we impose the following conditions on the rules rules. These conditions refer to a complete reduction order $\succ$ (see [6]) declared on the set of terms. We write $s \not\succeq t$ if $\neg(s \succ t)$ and $s \ne t$.

Maximality Condition for Irreflexivity Resolution:
  - $s\sigma$ is a maximal term with respect to $\succ$ in $C\sigma$.

Maximality Condition for Chaining:
  - $u_i\sigma \not\succeq s_1\sigma$ for all $1 \le i \le n$,
  - $v_i\sigma \not\succeq t_1\sigma$ for all $1 \le i \le m$,
  - $u\sigma \not\succeq s_1\sigma$ for all terms u such that $u \lhd s \in C$ or $s \lhd u \in C$, and
  - $v\sigma \not\succeq t_1\sigma$ for all terms v such that $v \lhd s \in C$ or $s \lhd v \in C$.

It is convenient to view the resulting inference system $\mathrm{MC}_\succ$ as a set operator.

Definition 8. $\mathrm{MC}_\succ(\mathcal{C})$ *is the set of all conclusions of Irreflexivity Resolution and Maximal Chaining where the premises are (variants of) members of the set of clauses* $\mathcal{C}$*. Moreover,* $\mathrm{MC}^0_\succ(\mathcal{C}) = \mathcal{C}$*,* $\mathrm{MC}^{i+1}_\succ(\mathcal{C}) = \mathrm{MC}_\succ(\mathrm{MC}^i_\succ(\mathcal{C})) \cup \mathrm{MC}^i_\succ(\mathcal{C})$*, and* $\mathrm{MC}^*_\succ(\mathcal{C}) = \bigcup_{i \ge 0} \mathrm{MC}^i_\succ(\mathcal{C})$*.*

The set consisting of the three clauses $\{\bot \le x\}$, $\{x \le \top\}$, and $\{\bot < \top\}$, corresponding to the endpoint axioms, is called $\mathcal{E}p$. Let d be a fresh binary function symbol. The set $\{\{y \le x, d(x,y) < y\}, \{y \le x, x < d(x,y)\}\}$, corresponding to the density axiom, is called $\mathcal{D}o$.

The following completeness result follows directly from Theorem 2 of [6].

Theorem 4. *A set $\mathcal{C}$ of clauses has a dense total order with endpoints $\bot$ and $\top$ as a model iff $\mathrm{MC}^*_{\succ}(\mathcal{C} \cup \mathcal{E}q^{\mathbf{F}} \cup \mathcal{E}p \cup \mathcal{D}o)$ does not contain the empty clause.*

Remark 3. Yet more refined versions of chaining calculi are investigated in [6,7]. However, standard breadth-first proof search based on $\mathrm{MC}_{\succ}$ seems to be quite appropriate in our context; in particular, since the problem of "variable chaining" does not occur for the sets of clauses obtained using $\mathrm{CF}^{\mathrm{d}}(\cdot)$.

6 Conclusion

Remember that for testing whether a given specification expressed in fuzzy logic $\mathbf{G}^{\triangle}_{\infty}$ has a model we cannot rely on proof procedures for checking validity in $\mathbf{G}^{\triangle}_{\infty}$. As demonstrated in this paper, one can nevertheless apply a resolution style method for testing (1-)satisfiability for *prenex* $\mathbf{G}^{\triangle}_{\infty}$-formulas. While prenex $\mathbf{G}^{\triangle}_{\infty}$ admits Skolemization with respect to *validity* in a standard manner [5], this result does not transfer to *satisfiability*. However, we have shown that a new nonstandard form of Skolemization that involves the introduction of a fresh monadic predicate symbol preserves satisfiability. This in turn can be used to translate prenex $\mathbf{G}^{\triangle}_{\infty}$-formulas into a clausal form combining a definitional (structural) clause form translation with a generalized notion of literals that refers to the underlying order on the set of truth values $[0, 1]$. Finally efficient resolution style proof search, based on a so-called chaining calculus for the theory of dense total orders with endpoints, can be employed.

A number of related problems arise naturally. Can a similar method be found that covers full $\mathbf{G}^{\triangle}_{\infty}$, not only its prenex fragment? What about other t-norm based fuzzy logics, including other forms of Gödel logic? Instead of generalizing, it might also be interesting to go the other direction and focus on subclasses of prenex $\mathbf{G}^{\triangle}_{\infty}$. Of particular interest is the monadic class, where formulas contain only monadic predicate symbols. In fact, given the above results, it is straightforward to adapt the undecidability proof in [5] for the *validity* problem of the prenex monadic fragment of $\mathbf{G}^{\triangle}_{\infty}$ to the *1-satisfiability* problem for this class. Nevertheless it is likely that more refined proof search methods will allow to demonstrate the *decidability* of subclasses of $\mathbf{G}^{\triangle}_{\infty}$ in the style of, e.g., [9,10].

References

1. Baaz, M.: Infinite-valued Gödel logics with 0-1-projections and relativizations. In: Proceedings Gödel 1996. Kurt Gödel's Legacy. LNL, vol. 6, pp. 23–33. Springer, Heidelberg (1996)
2. Baaz, M., Preining, N., Zach, R.: First-order Gödel logics. Annals of Pure and Applied Logic 147(1-2), 23–47 (2007)
3. Baaz, M., Veith, H.: Quantifier Elimination in Fuzzy Logic. In: Gottlob, G., Grandjean, E., Seyr, K. (eds.) CSL 1998. LNCS, vol. 1584, pp. 399–414. Springer, Heidelberg (1999)
4. Baaz, M., Veith, H.: Interpolation in fuzzy logic. Arch. Math. Logic 38, 461–489 (1999)

5. Baaz, M., Ciabattoni, A., Fermüller, C.G.: Herbrand's Theorem for Prenex Gödel Logic and its Consequences for Theorem Proving. In: Nieuwenhuis, R., Voronkov, A. (eds.) LPAR 2001. LNCS (LNAI), vol. 2250, pp. 201–216. Springer, Heidelberg (2001)
6. Bachmair, L., Ganzinger, H.: Ordered Chaining for Total Orderings. In: Bundy, A. (ed.) CADE 1994. LNCS, vol. 814, pp. 435–450. Springer, Heidelberg (1994)
7. Bachmair, L., Ganzinger, H.: Ordered Chaining Calculi for First-Order Theories of Transitive Relations. J. ACM 45(6), 1007–1049 (1998)
8. Dummett, M.: A propositional calculus with denumerable matrix. J. of Symbolic Logic 24, 97–106 (1959)
9. Fermüller, C.G., Leitsch, A., Tammet, T., Zamov, N.: Resolution Methods for the Decision Problem. LNCS, vol. 679. Springer, Heidelberg (1993)
10. Fermüller, C.G., Leitsch, A., Hustadt, U., Tammet, T.: Resolution decision procedures. In: Robinson, J.A., Voronkov, A. (eds.) Handbook of Automated Reasoning, pp. 1791–1849. Elsevier/MIT Press (2001)
11. Gödel, K.: Zum intuitionistischen Aussagenkalkül. Anz. Akad. Wiss. Wien 69, 65–66 (1932)
12. Hájek, P.: Metamathematics of Fuzzy Logic. Kluwer, Dordrecht (1998)
13. Hájek, P.: Arithmetical complexity of fuzzy predicate logics – a survey. Soft Computing 9(12), 935–941 (2005)
14. Hájek, P.: Arithmetical complexity of fuzzy predicate logics – a survey II. Annals of Pure and Applied Logic 161(2), 212–219 (2009)
15. Hájek, P.: Monadic fuzzy predicate logics. Studia Logica 71(2), 165–175 (2002)
16. Ragaz, M.: Die Unentscheidbarkeit der einstelligen unendlichwertigen Prädikatenlogik. Arch. Math. Logik 23, 129–139 (1983)
17. Ragaz, M.: Arithmetische Klassifikation von Formelmengen der unendlichwertigen Logik. Dissertation ETH Zürich Nr. 6822 (1981)
18. Takeuti, G., Titani, T.: Intuitionistic fuzzy logic and intuitionistic fuzzy set theory. J. of Symbolic Logic 49, 851–866 (1984)

Efficient Enumeration for Conjunctive Queries over X-underbar Structures

Guillaume Bagan[1], Arnaud Durand[2], Emmanuel Filiot[3], and Olivier Gauwin[4]

[1] INRIA Lille – Mostrare
[2] ELM, CNRS FRE 3233 – Université Paris Diderot
[3] Université Libre de Bruxelles
[4] Université de Mons – UMONS

Abstract. We investigate efficient enumeration algorithms for conjunctive queries for databases over binary relations that satisfy the $\underline{X}$ property. Tree-like relations such as XPath axes or grids are natural examples of such relations. We first show that the result of an n-ary conjunctive query Q over an $\underline{X}$ structure S can be enumerated with a delay in $O(n \cdot |S| \cdot |Q|)$ between two consecutive n-tuples. Then, we consider acyclic conjunctive queries and show that such queries admit an enumeration algorithm with delay $O(|Q| \cdot |D|)$ and a preprocessing in $O(|Q| \cdot |S|)$ where D is the domain of S. The delay can even be improved to $O(n \cdot |D|)$ with a slightly more expensive preprocessing step. As an application of our method, we also show that any n-ary XPath acyclic conjunctive query Q over an unranked tree t can be enumerated with a preprocessing and delay $O(|Q| \cdot |t|)$. In the second part of the paper, we consider conjunctive queries with possible inequalities ($\neq$) between variables. In this case, we show that query evaluation is NP-hard and, unless P = NP, these queries do not admit enumeration algorithms with a combined polynomial time delay. However, we also show that hardness relies only on the number ℓ of variables that appear in inequalities. We propose efficient enumeration procedures for acyclic and general conjunctive queries whose delay is exponential in ℓ but polynomial (even quasi-linear) in $|Q|$ and $|S|$.

1 Introduction

Querying is a core task in database processing. Given a relational structure S, an n-ary query retrieves n-tuples of elements in the domain of S. For XML databases, the structure S is a tree modeling an XML document, and an n-ary query selects n-tuples of nodes of this tree.

Query computing can be seen as a generation process. In this case, one tries to output selected tuples one after the other, without duplicates, while minimizing the delay between successive answers. Good enumeration algorithms then carry additional information on the problem: it shows that the query is not only tractable but that the result can be obtained step by step in a very regular way. A nice feature is that enumeration permits to start a pipeline process, and thus allow tasks based on querying to start processing answers without waiting for the whole evaluation to be done.

More precisely, an enumeration algorithm is the process of generating one after the other the tuples of a given query $Q(S)$ for some given order $<$ [4]. In particular, the

A. Dawar and H. Veith (Eds.): CSL 2010, LNCS 6247, pp. 80–94, 2010.

enumeration process does not generate duplicates. The so-called *preprocessing* is a preliminary step performed before the enumeration phase. The *delay* of such an algorithm is the maximum between (i) the time to get the first tuple after preprocessing (ii) the maximal interval of time between the generation of two consecutive solutions for $<$.

In [13], a tractability frontier is established for conjunctive queries defined using XPath axes as predicates. This dichotomy relies on the $\underline{X}$ property (see Section 2 for a definition): if a structure S has the $\underline{X}$ property w.r.t. some total order $<$ on the domain D of the structure, then it can be checked in PTIME combined complexity whether the result of a conjunctive query Q over S is empty or not. If Q is an n-ary query, then the proof provides an evaluation algorithm with time complexity $O(|D|^n \cdot |S| \cdot |Q|)$. This holds for any conjunctive queries using unary and binary predicates, not only XPath expressions. For all conjunctive queries based on XPath axes combinations that do not have the $\underline{X}$ property, checking whether Q selects some tuples on S is NP-complete.

Based on the aforementioned dichotomy, we investigate enumeration of conjunctive queries over $\underline{X}$ structures, by providing enumeration algorithms (see Fig. 1) and hardness results. Enumeration complexity of query problems, in particular on tree structures and on tree-like queries, has deserved some attention recently [3,7,4]. However grids also have the $\underline{X}$ property, hence new tools are needed for such kind of structures.

Prior to this investigation, we show that deciding whether a structure S is $\underline{X}$ for some order on its domain is NP-hard when S contains two binary relations. If S contains only one binary relation, the problem is known to be in PTIME. [1]

Our first algorithm enumerates answers of an n-ary conjunctive query Q over an $\underline{X}$ structure S without preprocessing and with a delay in $O(n \cdot |S| \cdot |Q|)$. The method relies on the computation of maximal arc-consistent pre-valuations proposed in [13]. We then turn to *acyclic* n-ary conjunctive queries (ACQs) Q over $\underline{X}$ structures S, and propose an algorithm with preprocessing $O(|Q| \cdot |S|)$ and delay in $O(|Q| \cdot |D|)$, where D is the domain of S. We first reason on a conceptually simpler notion of tree-shaped queries, namely tree patterns. ACQs are then mapped to tree patterns. With a slightly more expensive preprocessing in $O(|Q| \cdot |D|^2)$, this delay can be reduced to $O(n \cdot |D|)$. This is to be compared with Yannakakis' algorithm [18] turned into an enumeration algorithm in [4], which computes all answers $Q(S)$ of an acyclic conjunctive query Q over an arbitrary structure S with delay $O(|Q| \cdot |S|)$, hence in total time $O(|Q| \cdot |S| \cdot |Q(S)|)$.

The set of XPath axes does not have the $\underline{X}$ property (only some combinations of them have it). However we show that the main ideas of the enumeration algorithm for ACQs over $\underline{X}$ can also be applied to ACQs over XPath axes. Given an unranked tree t and an ACQ Q over XPath axes, $Q(t)$ can be enumerated with a preprocessing and delay $O(|Q| \cdot |t|)$, where $|t|$ is the number of nodes. This is particularly relevant to XML processing as XPath has become one of the main query language for XML. Moreover, as XML documents can be very large in practice, even a square in the size of the tree for preprocessing and delay would not be feasible.

It is a natural question to ask whether the delay can be made polynomial in the size of the query only (and independent of the size of the $\underline{X}$ structure) in the case of conjunctive or even acyclic conjunctive queries. While this is still an open question, we obtain hardness results and tight algorithms when allowing inequalities in predicates.

---

[1] Personal communication with Pavol Hell and Arash Rafiey. To be published.

Source	Queries	Structures	Preprocessing	Delay
[13]	CQ	$\underline{X}$	$O(1)$	$O(|D|^n \cdot |Q| \cdot |S|)$
Section 3	CQ	$\underline{X}$	$O(1)$	$O(n \cdot |Q| \cdot |S|)$
Section 5	CQ($\neq$)	$\underline{X}$	$O(1)$	$O(\ell^{O(\ell)} \cdot |Q| \cdot n \cdot |S| \cdot \log |D|)$
[4]	ACQ	all	$O(1)$	$O(|Q| \cdot |S|)$
Section 4	ACQ	$\underline{X}$	$O(|Q| \cdot |S|)$	$O(|Q| \cdot |D|)$
Section 4	ACQ	$\underline{X}$	$O(|Q| \cdot |D|^2)$	$O(n \cdot |D|)$
Section 4	ACQ (XPath axes)	tree t	$O(|Q| \cdot |t|)$	$O(|Q| \cdot |t|)$
Section 5	ACQ ($\neq$)	$\underline{X}$	$O(|Q| \cdot |S|)$	$O(\ell^{O(\ell)} \cdot |Q| \cdot |D| \cdot \log |D|)$

Fig. 1. Enumeration algorithms for n-ary queries Q over structures S with domain D. ℓ is the number of variables used in inequalities, while $|t|$ denotes the number of nodes of the tree t.

For conjunctive queries with inequalities over $\underline{X}$ structures, satisfiability is NP-hard, even when the query restricted to $\underline{X}$ predicates is acyclic. As a consequence, these queries may not be enumerated with a polynomial delay, in terms of combined complexity. However, we propose an enumeration algorithm for such queries without preprocessing, and with a delay in $O(\ell^{O(\ell)} \cdot |Q| \cdot n \cdot |S| \cdot \log |D|)$ where the blowup is only in the number ℓ of distinct variables in inequalities. In the acyclic case, when allowing a preprocessing phase in $O(|Q| \cdot |S|)$, we obtain a delay in $O(\ell^{O(\ell)} \cdot |Q| \cdot |D| \cdot \log |D|)$.

Related work. Enumeration of acyclic conjunctive queries has been studied in [4]. It is shown that the result of such a query can be enumerated with a delay linear in $|S| \cdot |Q|$ (dependency on $|Q|$ is exponential when inequalities are allowed). They also formulate conditions on free variables to have a delay depending on $|Q|$ only. Monadic second order queries on structures of bounded treewidth are considered in [7,3] where enumeration algorithms are exhibited with a delay depending on $|Q|$ (non elementarily) and on the size of each tuple.

For acyclic conjunctive queries, Koch [16] provides an enumeration algorithm with preprocessing in $O(|S| \cdot |Q|)$ (for computing Θ) and delay $O(|D|)$, where $|D|$ is the domain size. For tree structures and tree-like queries over child/descendant axes, the delay can be improved to $O(1)$ with the algorithm *TwigStack* [5]. However in both works, all variables are considered as free. In our work, variables can be existentially quantified, so that it may be an exponential number of valuations (in the size of the domain) for a single answer tuple. However we can still achieve a polynomial delay between two successive tuples.

Conjunctive queries over child/descendant axes are considered in [6] for the class of graphs. No enumeration algorithms are provided, but query evaluation algorithms. In the case of tree-like queries over graphs the time complexity is $O(|Q| \cdot |D| \cdot |E| + |Q(S)|)$, where $|V|$ is the size of the domain and $|E|$ is the number of edges in the graph. However it is exponential in the number of variables in the case of graph queries. In [9], XPath dialects that can define n-ary queries are introduced. No enumeration algorithm is given, but a fragment that corresponds to union of ACQs over trees t is defined, for which evaluation is in time $O(n \cdot |Q| \cdot |t|^2 \cdot |Q(t)|)$.

2 $\underline{\textbf{X}}$ Structures

We consider relational structures over binary relational symbols only[2]. Formally let σ be a signature $\{R_1, \ldots, R_m\}$ of binary relational symbols R_i (equality $=$ is part of the language too). A (finite) σ-structure S consists of a finite domain D together with an interpretation of σ-symbols R_i as binary relations R_i^S on D (when it is clear from the context we do not distinguish a symbol from its interpretation). Let $\mathcal{R}$ be the set $\{R_1^S, \ldots, R_m^S\}$. The size $|D|$ of a domain D is its cardinality. The size of a σ-structure S over D, is $|S| = |D| + \sum_{R \in \mathcal{R}} |R|$, where $|R| = |\{(v, v') \in D \times D \mid R(v, v')\}|$ Given two binary relations R_1 and R_2 of $\mathcal{R}$, one defines the relations $R_1 \circ R_2$, $R_1 \cap R_2$, $R_1 \cup R_2$ and R_1^{-1} for the composition, intersection, union and inverse in the standard way. Given a set $A \subseteq D$, we denote by $R(A)$ the set $\{b \mid \exists a \in A. \ R(a, b)\}$.

The computation model used in this paper is a $\{+\}$-RAM with uniform cost measure as in [3,4]. It takes σ-structure as input (with each tuple in a distinct input register) and uses, during the computation, register contents and addresses always bounded by $O(D)$ (hence the correspondence with logarithmic cost is immediate).

The $\underline{X}$ property [14]. A binary relation R over D has the $\underline{X}$ property w.r.t. a total order $<$ on D iff for all elements v_0, v_1, v_2, v_3 of D the following holds:

$$(\underline{X} \text{ property}) \qquad R(v_0, v_1) \wedge R(v_2, v_3) \implies R(\min(v_0, v_2), \min(v_1, v_3))$$

A binary relation having the $\underline{X}$ property is also called an $\underline{X}$ *relation*. We say that a set of binary relations $\mathcal{R}$ over D has the $\underline{X}$ property if there is a total order $<$ on D such that all relations of $\mathcal{R}$ have the $\underline{X}$ property w.r.t. $<$. Similarly, a structure has the $\underline{X}$ property if its relations have the $\underline{X}$ property. We call it an $\underline{X}$ structure.

Example 1. Over tree structures, XPath axes define classical binary relations such as child, parent, descendant, ancestor, next-sibling, etc. There is no order $<$ on the set of nodes such that all XPath axes are $\underline{X}$ w.r.t. to the same $<$. However, such orders exist when considering some subsets of axes. For instance, $\{$child, next-sibling$\}$ are $\underline{X}$ for the order induced by a breadth-first left to right traversal of the tree. A complete list of subsets of tree relations (XPath axes) having the $\underline{X}$ property is established in [13].

Example 2. The $n \times n$-grid graph $G = (V, E)$ with $V = \{1, ..., n\}^2$ and for all $i, i', j, j' \in \{1, ..., n\}, ((i, j), (i', j')) \in E$ if and only if $\{|i - i'|, |j - j'|\} = \{0, 1\}$, is $\underline{X}$ for the lexicographic extension of the natural ordering $<$ on $\{1, ..., n\}$.

Lemma 1. *The class of $\underline{X}$ relations is closed by composition, intersection, and inverse (even for the same order). However, it is not closed by union and complement (even for different orders).*

Sorted representation of $\underline{X}$ relations. In this paper, for $\underline{X}$ structures, we assume that the order $<$ is given and that comparison can be done in $O(1)$. Relations are given by sets of pairs of elements and the domain D is given as a list of elements sorted according to $<$. To perform some operations more efficiently, we use the following so-called *sorted*

---

[2] To ease notations, we do not consider unary relation symbols, but all the results of the paper carry over to a signature with both binary and unary relation symbols.

Algorithm 1. Computing $R(A)$

---

   procedure IMAGE(R, A)
      sort A
      $S \leftarrow$ empty list; $max \leftarrow -\infty$
      for $v \in A$ w.r.t. $<$ increasing **do**
         for $w \in R(v)$ w.r.t. $<$ decreasing **do**
            if $w \leq max$ **then**
               exit inner for-loop
            S.append(w)
         $max \leftarrow \max(R(v))$
      sort S
      return S

---

representation for a relation structure S. Every element u of D is represented by an integer $i_u \in \{1, \ldots, |D|\}$. Moreover, we require that $i_u <_\mathbb{N} i_v$ iff $u < v$. Every relation R is represented by two arrays A and A^{-1} of size $|D|$ such that for all $i_u \in \{1, \ldots, |D|\}$, $A[u]$ is the sorted (increasing) list (for $<$) of successors of u in R, and $A^{-1}[u]$ is the increasing list of successors of u in R^{-1}. In other words, A is an adjacency list representation of R, viewed as a directed graph with vertex set D. We also require that the list is doubly-linked, so that we can traverse the list in both orders.

Lemma 2. *For every structure S with some total order $<$ on its domain D, whose domain and relations are represented by a sorted list and lists of pairs of elements respectively, one can compute a sorted representation of S in time $O(|S|)$.*

Given a subset $A \subseteq D$, we show that, for $\underline{X}$ structures, this representation allows us to compute $R(A)$ and $R^{-1}(A)$ efficiently.

Lemma 3. *For every $\underline{X}$ relation R over a set D in sorted representation, and every set $A \subseteq D$ given as a list, $R(A)$ and $R^{-1}(A)$ can be computed in time $O(|D|)$.*

Proof. See Algorithm 1. The set A can be sorted in $O(|D|)$ as we know that there are at most $|D|$ integers in A with maximal value $|D|$. The assumed orders on v and w elements ensure that each element $v \in A$ and $w \in R(A)$ is processed only once. The $\underline{X}$ property allows to skip w elements lower than w elements already processed. Note that the algorithm computes a sorted set. Since R^{-1} is also $\underline{X}$ for $<$, one can apply the same algorithm on the representation of R^{-1}. $\qquad\square$

Thanks to Lemma 3, we obtain the following proposition:

Proposition 1. *The composition of two binary relations over D can be computed in time $O(|D|^2)$, whenever one of them is $\underline{X}$. In other terms, the product of two $n \times n$ Boolean matrices is computable in linear time when one of them satisfies the $\underline{X}$ property.*

Finding $\underline{X}$ orders. In this part, one considers the problem of checking whether, for a given relation R, there exists an order for which R satisfies the $\underline{X}$ property. This problem has been considered under different angles in the CSP literature (see for example [15]).

$\underline{X}$-ENUMERATION(n)

Input: a finite domain D and $R_1, \ldots, R_n \subseteq D^2$

Question: does there exist a common $\underline{X}$-enumeration for $R_1, \ldots, R_n$ (*i.e.* a total order $<$ on D such that $R_1, \ldots, R_n$ are $\underline{X}$ for $<$)?

Deciding whether two relations are $\underline{X}$ for some total order is NP-complete. Hardness is proved by reduction from BETWEENNESS [17,11].

Proposition 2. *The problem* $\underline{X}$-ENUMERATION(2) *is* NP-*complete.*

For the case of one binary reflexive relation, it has been shown [8] that one can check in polynomial time whether R has an $\underline{X}$ enumeration. Recently, Hell and Rafiey (personal communication) proved that the problem $\underline{X}$-ENUMERATION(1) is in P.

3   Conjunctive Queries over $\underline{X}$ Structures

Queries. An n-ary *query* Q over a structure $S = (D, \mathcal{R})$ is a mapping from S to 2^{D^n}. The set $Q(S)$ is also called the *answer set* over S. Conjunctive queries are defined in the normal way [1]. In particular, an n-ary *conjunctive query* over S is a query defined by an existential first-order formula without negation nor disjunction, with n free variables and using relations from $\mathcal{R}$ as predicates. A 0-ary conjunctive query is called a *Boolean* conjunctive query. We recall that all the relations considered in this paper are binary. We write vars(Q) for the variables occurring in Q, and vars$_{\text{free}}$(Q) for the n free ones. We also write $R(x, y) \in Q$ if $R(x, y)$ appears in Q. Throughout this paper, we assume that formulas defining conjunctive queries are in prenex normal form. The *body* of Q is obtained from Q by removing its quantifiers. The *size* of a conjunctive query Q, denoted by $|Q|$, is the number of symbols of its first-order formula.

Pre-valuations and valuations. Given a conjunctive query Q over a structure $S = (D, \mathcal{R})$, we say that Θ is a *pre-valuation* for Q if it is a total function $\Theta : \text{vars}(Q) \to 2^D$ assigning a nonempty set of elements of D to each variable of Q. A pre-valuation Θ is *arc-consistent* on S iff for each binary predicate $R(x, y)$ of Q, for each $v \in \Theta(x)$, $R(v, w)$ is true for some $w \in \Theta(y)$, and for each $w \in \Theta(y)$, $R(v, w)$ is true for some $v \in \Theta(x)$.

A *valuation* θ is a total function $\theta : \text{vars}(Q) \to D$ assigning an element of D to each variable of Q. A valuation is *consistent* if it satisfies the body of Q. Conjunctive queries define n-ary queries in the following sense: $Q(S)$ is the set of tuples $(\theta(x_1), \ldots, \theta(x_n))$ such that θ satisfies Q and vars$_{\text{free}}$(Q) = $\{x_1, \ldots, x_n\}$. The *minimum* valuation θ in Θ w.r.t. some total order $<$ on D is written $\min_< \Theta$ and given by: $\theta(x) = \min_< \Theta(x)$ for all $x \in \text{vars}(Q)$. Valuations are ordered according to the lexicographical extension of $<$. The following properties will be the basis of our enumeration algorithm.

Lemma 4 (Gottlob, Koch, Schulz [13]). *Let S be a structure and Q a conjunctive query on S.*

1. the unique subset-maximal arc-consistent pre-valuation of Q on S can be computed in time $O(|S| \cdot |Q|)$.

2. *if all the relations in S are $\underline{X}$ w.r.t. the same order $<$, then for any arc-consistent pre-valuation of Q on S, the corresponding minimum valuation is consistent.*

This lemma provides a procedure to decide whether $Q(S) = \emptyset$ for every n-ary conjunctive query Q over an $\underline{X}$ structure S, in time $O(|S| \cdot |Q|)$. It suffices to compute the subset-maximal arc-consistent pre-valuation Θ of Q on S, and check that $\Theta(x) \neq \emptyset$ for all $x \in \mathrm{vars}_{\mathrm{free}}(Q)$. Equivalently, when Q has no free variable (*i.e.* $n = 0$), evaluating Q on S can be done in time $O(|S| \cdot |Q|)$.

In [13], a first evaluation algorithm is proposed for n-ary queries $Q(x_1, \ldots, x_n)$ over $\underline{X}$ structures. It consists in enumerating all tuples $(u_1, \ldots, u_n) \in D^n$, and for each of them, check the satisfiability of $Q(u_1, \ldots, u_n)$ where free variables are interpreted by $u_1, \ldots, u_n$ respectively. This algorithm outputs the answers of Q on S in time $O(|D|^n \cdot |S| \cdot |Q|)$. However the delay may be $O(|D|^n \cdot |S| \cdot |Q|)$.

In this section, we explain how to extend this algorithm into an enumeration algorithm without preprocessing, and a delay in $O(n \cdot |S| \cdot |Q|)$. The core idea is to consider distinct domains $D_1, \ldots, D_n$ for the free variables $x_1, \ldots, x_n$ of Q. This allows us to update these domains, in order to avoid duplicate answers and to ensure the enumeration of all answers in lexicographical order w.r.t. $<$.

In the sequel we will consider arc-consistent pre-valuations for S restricted to domains defined by $\overline{D} = (D_1, \ldots, D_n)$, with $D_i \subseteq D$ for all $1 \leq i \leq n$. To define this formally, we introduce fresh unary relation symbols $\widetilde{D}_i$, and consider the signature $\sigma' = \sigma \uplus \widetilde{D}_1 \uplus \ldots \uplus \widetilde{D}_n$. Consider the query $Q' = Q \wedge \widetilde{D}_1(x_1) \wedge \ldots \wedge \widetilde{D}_n(x_n)$ and the σ'-structure S' that is similar to S, but extends it by interpreting $\widetilde{D}_i$ in the following way: $\widetilde{D}_i^{S'} = D_i$. Then we define $pv_{max}(Q, S, \overline{D})$ as the unique subset-maximal arc-consistent pre-valuation for Q' over S', i.e. $pv_{max}(Q, S, \overline{D}) = pv_{max}(Q', S')$. The computation of $pv_{max}(Q, S, \overline{D})$ can still be performed in $O(|S| \cdot |Q|)$. The next lemma ensures that the subset-maximal arc-consistent pre-valuation on some domains $\overline{D}$ keeps all the answers in $D_1 \times \ldots \times D_n$. Let $ans_Q^S(\overline{D}) = (D_1 \times \ldots \times D_n) \cap Q(S)$ be the set of answers of Q on S using only values compatible with $\overline{D}$.

Lemma 5. *Let $\Theta = pv_{max}(Q, S, \overline{D})$. Then $ans_Q^S(\overline{D}) = ans_Q^S(\Theta(x_1) \times \ldots \times \Theta(x_n))$.*

We now present Algorithm 2, our enumeration algorithm. This algorithm outputs all elements of $Q(S)$ in lexicographical order w.r.t. $<$ (the order of $\underline{X}$ relations) for the chosen order on the free variables of Q.

We first use pv_{max} on the whole domain D for all free variables, and get a first answer $(v_1, \ldots, v_n)$ by taking the minimum valuation. Then we exclude v_n from the domain of x_n, and all smaller elements, by running pv_{max} on the domains $(\{v_1\}, \ldots, \{v_{n-1}\}, D_{v_n}^{>})$, where $D_{v_i}^{>} = \{v \in D \mid v > v_i\}$. If no answer is returned, we run pv_{max} on $(\{v_1\}, \ldots, \{v_{n-2}\}, D_{v_{n-1}}^{>}, D)$, and so on. Proposition 3 shows that the solution returned by the function $next$ is indeed the next answer in $Q(S)$ in lexicographical order. This proves the correctness of Algorithm 2.

Proposition 3. *For all tuples of elements $(v_1, ..., v_n) \in D^n$, the successor of $(v_1, ..., v_n)$ by $<_{lex}$, if it exists, is $\min_{0 \leq j < n} \min_{<} pv_{max}(Q, S, (\{v_1\}, \ldots, \{v_j\}, D_{v_{j+1}}^{>}, D, \ldots, D))$.*

Algorithm 2. Enumeration algorithm for conjunctive queries over $\underline{X}$ structures

> **procedure** MAIN$(Q, S, <)$
> 2: $(D, \mathcal{R}) \leftarrow S$; $\tau \leftarrow$ FIRST(D, Q)
>   **while** $\tau \neq \perp$ **do** output(τ); $\tau \leftarrow$ NEXT(τ, D, Q)
> 4: **function** FIRST(D, Q)
> $\Theta \leftarrow pv_{max}(Q, S, (D, \ldots, D))$
> 6:   **if** $\Theta \neq (\emptyset, \ldots, \emptyset)$ **then return** $\min_< \Theta$ **else return** $\perp$
>   **function** NEXT$((v_1, \ldots, v_n), D, Q)$
> 8: $j \leftarrow n - 1$
>   **repeat**
> 10: $\Theta \leftarrow pv_{max}(Q, S, (\{v_1\}, \ldots, \{v_j\}, D_{v_{j+1}}^>, D, \ldots, D))$; $j \leftarrow j - 1$
>   **until** $\Theta \neq (\emptyset, \ldots, \emptyset)$ or $j < 0$
> 12:   **if** $\Theta \neq (\emptyset, \ldots, \emptyset)$ **then return** $\min_< \Theta$ **else return** $\perp$

We call pv_{max} at most n times between two successive answers, *i.e.* Algorithm 2 has a delay in time $O(n \cdot |S| \cdot |Q|)$.

Theorem 1. *Let S be an $\underline{X}$ structure and Q an n-ary conjunctive query over S. Then $Q(S)$ can be enumerated without preprocessing, and with a delay in $O(n \cdot |S| \cdot |Q|)$ between two successive answers.*

4   Acyclic Conjunctive Queries over $\underline{X}$ Structures

A conjunctive query Q is *acyclic* if it admits a join-tree [1], or equivalently (for binary relations) if the following undirected graph G_Q is acyclic: $G_Q = (V_Q, E_Q)$ with $V_Q = $ vars(Q) and E_Q is the set of edges s.t. $\{x, y\} \in E_Q$ iff $R(x, y)$ occurs in Q for some R. In this section, we present an enumeration algorithm for ACQs over $\underline{X}$ relations (ACQs$(\underline{X})$). It works with a preprocessing $O(|Q| \cdot |S|)$ and a delay $O(|Q| \cdot |D|)$, where Q is the query and D the domain. Then we show that when paying a preprocessing in time $O(|D|^2 \cdot |Q|)$, one can reduce the delay to $O(n \cdot |D|)$, where n is the arity of the query. As the associated graph G_Q of an ACQ Q over a binary signature is nothing else than a forest, we define a notion of tree-like queries into which ACQs over a structure S can be naturally encoded (in linear-time), while preserving $\underline{X}$ properties of relations.

4.1   Tree Patterns

Definition 1. *A tree pattern over a binary signature σ and a countable set of variables V is an ordered binary tree whose nodes are labeled in $V \cup \sigma \cup \sigma \times \sigma$. It is inductively defined by terms generated by the following grammar:*

$$T ::= x \mid R(T') \mid (R, R')(T_1, T_2) \qquad \text{where } x \in V \text{ and } R, R' \in \sigma$$

Moreover, the variables occurring at the leaves are all pairwise distinct.

The semantics of tree patterns over σ is given by means of ACQs over σ. Intuitively, every inner-node corresponds to an existentially quantified variable, every leaf to a free variable, and every branching to a conjunction. Therefore to define the semantics in terms of ACQs, one needs to introduce a new bound variable for every inner-node. We denote by $\text{vars}_{\text{free}}(T)$ the variables occurring in T (necessarily at the leaves). For any variable x and fresh variables $y, z, x' \notin \text{vars}_{\text{free}}(T)$, we denote by $Q_{T,x}$ the CQ:

$$Q_{T,x} = \begin{cases} x = y & \text{if } T = y \\ \exists x'\ R(x, x') \wedge Q_{T',x'} & \text{if } T = R(T') \\ \exists y \exists z\ R(x, y) \wedge R'(x, z) \wedge Q_{T_1,y} \wedge Q_{T_2,z} & \text{if } T = (R, R')(T_1, T_2) \end{cases}$$

The ACQ Q_T associated with a tree pattern T is defined by $Q_T = \exists x \cdot Q_{T,x}$, for any variable $x \notin \text{vars}_{\text{free}}(T)$ (the choice of the variable does not matter as equivalence is preserved when choosing another variable). E.g. let $T = (R_1, R_2)((R_3, R_4)(x_1, x_2), x_3)$. Then $Q_T(x_1, x_2, x_3) = \exists x \exists y R_1(x, y) \wedge R_3(y, x_1) \wedge R_4(y, x_2) \wedge R_2(x, x_3)$, for some variables x, y. Since the variables of T are all distinct, Q_T is acyclic. We extend the notion of answer set to tree patterns naturally. For a structure S over σ, $T(S) = Q_T(S)$. The size of a tree pattern is its number of nodes.

We now show that for any tree pattern T and any $\underline{X}$ σ-structure S with domain D, $T(S)$ can be enumerated with a preprocessing $O(|S| + |D| \cdot |T|)$ and a delay $O(|D| \cdot |T|)$.

Let $x \notin \text{vars}_{\text{free}}(T)$, and consider the ACQ $Q_{T,x}$ as defined before. For all $a \in D$, we denote by $Q_{T,a}$ the ACQ $Q_{T,x}$ where each occurrence of x is replaced by a. We denote by $T(S, a)$ the answer set $Q_{T,a}(S)$. Clearly, $T(S, a) \subseteq T(S)$. Informally, $T(S, a)$ is the set of tuples that can be obtained by mapping the root of T to a.

We denote by $\text{Sub}(T)$ the set of subtrees (subterms) of T. The first step of the algorithm is to compute a mapping $\text{sat} : \text{Sub}(T) \to 2^D$ such that for all $T' \in \text{Sub}(T)$ and for all $a \in D$, $a \in \text{sat}(T')$ iff $T'(S, a) \neq \emptyset$. Informally, $\text{sat}(T')$ is the set of elements such that there exists a solution of T' in S that can be obtained when mapping the root of T' to a. This mapping can be computed efficiently in a bottom-up manner:

Lemma 6. *For every tree pattern T over σ and every $\underline{X}$ σ-structure S over a domain D given in sorted representation, sat can be computed in time $O(|D| \cdot |T|)$.*

Similar techniques have also been used to evaluate XPath (unary) queries [12]. Let T be a tree pattern over a binary signature σ, and let $x_1, \dots, x_n$ be the variables occurring at the leaves of T in left-to-right order (*i.e.* from the left-most leaf to the right-most leaf). Given an $\underline{X}$ σ-structure S for some total order $<$ on the domain D, we define an algorithm that enumerates $T(S)$ in lexicographic order with respect to $x_1, \dots, x_n$ and $<$. We denote by $<_{lex}$ this order. For all $A \subseteq D$, we let $T(S, A) = \bigcup_{a \in A} T(S, a)$. Let $T' \in \text{Sub}(T)$ and $\overline{u} \in T'(S)$. The tuple $\overline{u}$ defines the set $B(\overline{u}, T', S) = \{a \in D \mid \overline{u} \in T'(S, a)\}$. Informally, $B(\overline{u}, T', S)$ is the set of nodes from which we can obtain $\overline{u}$.

Lemma 7. *If $T = (R_1, R_2)(T_1, T_2)$, then for all $A \subseteq D$:*

$$T(S, A) = \bigcup_{\overline{u} \in T_1(S, R_1(A))} \{\overline{u}\} \times T_2(S, R_2(R_1^{-1}(B(\overline{u}, T_1, S)) \cap A))$$

Similar lemmas hold when T is a single variable node, or the root of T is branching-free. In particular, $T(S, A) = A$ if T is a variable. We now have the main ingredient of a recursive enumeration algorithm that we illustrate for the case $T = (R_1, R_2)(T_1, T_2)$:

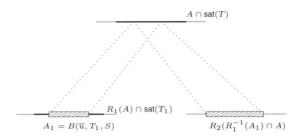

Fig. 2. Branching management for tree patterns enumeration

for each tuple $\overline{u} \in T_1(S, R_1(A))$ enumerated recursively in lexicographic order, we have to compute the set $A_1 = B(\overline{u}, T_1, S)$, and then the set $A_2 = R_2(R_1^{-1}(A_1) \cap A)$. Then we recursively enumerate the tuples $\overline{v}$ of $T_2(S, A_2)$ in lexicographic order. Instead of computing the set A_1 once $\overline{u}$ has been computed, A_1 can be computed recursively when applying the enumeration algorithm on T_1. This is because $B(\overline{w}, T, S) = R_1^{-1}(B(\overline{u}, T_1, S)) \cap R_2^{-1}(B(\overline{v}, T_2, S))$, where $\overline{w} = \overline{u}.\overline{v}$. The enumeration algorithm is therefore defined by a recursive procedure that outputs the next tuple $\overline{w}$ of $T(S, A)$ and outputs the set $B(\overline{w}, T, S)$. However it might be the case that A_2 is empty. In this case, one has to enumerate the tuples of $T_1(S, R_1(A))$ until there is a tuple $\overline{u}$ such that $R_2(R_1^{-1}(B(\overline{u}, T_1, S)) \cap A) \neq \emptyset$. This can lead to an unbounded delay between two consecutive tuples. Therefore we add one more constraint on the sets to ensure the following invariant: at each recursive call of the procedure, we must have $A \neq \emptyset$ and $A \subseteq \mathsf{sat}(T)$. Hence we are sure that there is at least one tuple in $T(S, A)$. If $A \subseteq \mathsf{sat}(T)$, when we call the procedure on T_1, instead of calling it on $T_1, S, R_1(A)$, we call it on $T_1, S, R_1(A) \cap \mathsf{sat}(T_1)$. Since $\emptyset \neq A$ and $A \subseteq \mathsf{sat}(T)$, $R_1(A) \cap \mathsf{sat}(T_1) \neq \emptyset$ and the invariant is satisfied. Similarly, for the right subtree, we call the procedure on $T_2, S, A_2 \cap \mathsf{sat}(T_2)$. This is depicted on Fig. 2.

If the root of T is branching-free, the enumeration works similarly. When T is reduced to a single node labeled by a variable x, the algorithm enumerates all elements a of A w.r.t. the order $<$ on D and for each element returns a and $\{a\}$ (*i.e.* $B(a, x, S)$).

The enumeration algorithm (Algorithm 3) is presented in a Python-like style, which allows us to write it in a very concise and readable way. In particular, we define an enumerator $\mathsf{ENUM}(T, A)$ that enumerates $T(S, A)$. The instruction *yield* passes its argument to the parent enumerator call, which outputs the yielded values and freezes the computation by storing the evaluation context. Therefore, when an instruction **for** $(\overline{u}, B) \in \mathsf{ENUM}(T, A)$ is executed, it passes through the loop each time $\mathsf{ENUM}(T, A)$ yields a new element. In other words, $\mathsf{ENUM}(T, A)$ is evaluated in a by-need lazy fashion. This comes without extra cost in time complexity.

Lemma 8 (Completeness and Soundness). *Given a tree pattern T and an $\underline{X}$ structure S for some total order $<$ on its domain D and a subset $A \subseteq D$, $\mathsf{ENUM}(T, A)$ enumerates all elements of $T(S, A)$ in lexicographic order, and only those tuples. Moreover for each enumerated tuple $\overline{u}$, it yields the set $B(\overline{u}, T, S)$.*

Algorithm 3. Enumeration algorithm for tree patterns over $\underline{X}$ structures

---

    function MAIN$(T, S, <)$ $\triangleright$ T:tree pattern, S:$\underline{X}$ structure for some order $<$ on its domain D

2:       compute a sorted representation for S

       compute the function sat

4:       **for** $(\overline{u}, B) \in$ ENUM$(T, \mathrm{sat}(T))$ **do**

          output $\overline{u}$

6: **function** ENUM(T, A)

       if $T = (R_1, R_2)(T_1, T_2)$ **then**

8:          **for** $(\overline{u}_1, B_1) \in$ ENUM$(T_1, R_1(A) \cap \mathrm{sat}(T_1))$ **do**

             for $(\overline{u}_2, B_2) \in$ ENUM$(T_2, R_2(R_1^{-1}(B_1) \cap A) \cap \mathrm{sat}(T_2))$ **do**

10:               yield $(\overline{u}_1.\overline{u}_2,\ R_1^{-1}(B_1) \cap R_2^{-1}(B_2))$

       if $T = R_1(T_1)$ **then**

12:          **for** $(\overline{u}_1, B_1) \in$ ENUM$(T_1, R_1(A) \cap \mathrm{sat}(T_1))$ **do**

             yield $(\overline{u}_1,\ R_1^{-1}(B_1))$

14:       **if** $T = x$ **then**

          for $a \in A$ w.r.t. $<$ **do**

16:             yield $(a,\ \{a\})$

Lemma 9. *Given a tree pattern T and an $\underline{X}$ structure S for some total order $<$ on its domain D and a set $A \subseteq D$ such that $A \neq \emptyset$ and $A \subseteq \mathrm{sat}(T)$, **ENUM**$(T, A)$ enumerates $T(S, A)$ with preprocessing in $O(|S| + |D| \cdot |T|)$ and delay in $O(|D| \cdot |T|)$.*

Therefore one obtains the following theorem:

Theorem 2. *For every tree pattern T and every $\underline{X}$-structure S for some total order $<$ on its domain D, $T(S)$ can be enumerated with preprocessing $O(|S| + |T| \cdot |D|)$ and delay in $O(|T| \cdot |D|)$.*

As a matter of fact, the delay mentioned in the previous theorem can be reduced to $O(n \cdot |D|)$, where n is the number of free variables, with the cost of a preprocessing in $O(|T| \cdot |D|^2)$. This is done by transforming the tree pattern in a full binary tree: the branching-free paths are replaced by a unique edge. The source of this edge is then labeled by a relational predicate interpreted by the composition of all the relations occurring along the path. Therefore one changes the pattern and the structure on which its relational symbols are interpreted. As we have to perform the composition of $\underline{X}$ relations, the time complexity of this reduction is $O(|T| \cdot |D|^2)$ (Prop. 1). The resulting tree pattern is a binary tree of size $O(n)$. Then we can apply Algorithm 3.

Theorem 3. *For every tree pattern T with n (free) variables and every $\underline{X}$-structure S, $T(S)$ can be enumerated with a preprocessing $O(|T| \cdot |D|^2)$ and a delay in $O(n \cdot |D|)$.*

Remark 1. Note that Algorithm 3 also works for any kind of structure over binary predicates (if we remove the computation of a sorted representation). The complexity of the preprocessing and delay depends on the following operations: computing $R(A)$ and $R^{-1}(A)$ for any relation R and subset A of the domain. In the general case of ACQs over an arbitrary structure where the (binary) relations are represented as pairs of elements, $R(A)$ and $R^{-1}(A)$ can be computed in $O(|R| + |A|) = O(|S|)$. This results in an enumeration algorithm with preprocessing and delay $O(|S| \cdot |T|)$.

4.2   From ACQs to Tree Patterns

Given an acyclic conjunctive query Q and an $\underline{X}$ structure S, one first transforms Q and S into a tree pattern T_Q and a structure S' with the same domain such that $|S'| = O(|Q| \cdot |S|)$ and $Q(S) = T_Q(S')$. Then we apply the enumeration algorithm for tree patterns. The transformation works on the labeled (directed) graph H_Q of Q defined by $H_Q = (V_Q, E_Q, \lambda)$ where $V_Q = \text{vars}(Q)$, $E_Q = \{(x, y) \mid R(x, y) \in Q$ for some $R\}$ and for all $(x, y) \in E_Q$, $\lambda(x, y) = \{R \mid R(x, y) \in Q\}$. Since Q is acyclic, this graph is acyclic as well (acyclicity in this case being defined without considering the orientation of edges). Therefore it is a forest, but it is not a tree pattern for one (or more) of the following reasons: (i) there might be several disconnected components, (ii) edges are labeled by several relational symbols, (iii) a vertex may have several incoming edges, (iv) a free variable may not be a leaf, (v) the branching is arbitrary.

It is technical but not difficult to transform an acyclic generalized graph into a tree pattern. It relies on the fact that $\underline{X}$ relations are closed under intersection and inverse. This allows to orient the relations to get a directed forest with a single label on edges. Then some filtering process is performed to eliminate the variables that are not free but are at the leaves. This is done by evaluating unary queries that filter the codomain of the binary relations that go to a subtree where all variables are bound. The complexity of this transformation depends on the complexity of intersection and inverse of relations, as well as evaluation of unary queries.

Lemma 10. *For every acyclic conjunctive query Q over an $\underline{X}$ σ-structure S, one can construct in time $O(|S| \cdot |Q|)$ a tree pattern T_Q over a signature σ' and an $\underline{X}$ σ'-structure S' with same domain such that $|T_Q| = O(|Q|)$, $|S'| = O(|S| \cdot |Q|)$ and $T_Q(S) = Q(S')$.*

As a corollary of Theorem 2, Theorem 3 and Lemma 10, we obtain

Theorem 4. *For every n-ary acyclic conjunctive query Q over an $\underline{X}$ σ-structure S, $Q(S)$ can be enumerated with a preprocessing $O(|S| \cdot |Q|)$ and a delay $O(|Q| \cdot |D|)$. This delay reduces to $O(n \cdot |D|)$ with a preprocessing in $O(|D|^2 \cdot |Q|)$.*

Remark 2. The translation of ACQs to tree patterns also works for the general case of ACQs over an arbitrary structure of binary relations. Its complexity depends on the time needed to compute intersection and inverse of relations, as well as the time to evaluate unary queries. The latter is known to be in $O(|S| \cdot |Q|)$ [18], the former remains the same as the case of $\underline{X}$. Therefore by Remark 1, we get an enumeration algorithm for general ACQs over a binary structure with a preprocessing $O(|S| \cdot |Q|)$ and a delay $O(|S| \cdot |Q|)$ (similar to that of [4]). Considering $\underline{X}$ relations, this delay reduces to $O(|D| \cdot |Q|)$.

4.3   Enumeration of Acyclic Conjunctive XPath n-ary Queries

In this section, we show that the ideas developed in the enumeration algorithm of ACQ $(\underline{X})$ can be adapted to an enumeration algorithm for ACQs over XPath axes interpreted on unranked trees. The case of XPath axes however differs in that the relations are not explicitly represented. *Unranked trees* is the widely accepted model of XML documents. In such trees, the nodes are labeled by elements of a finite alphabet Σ, sibling nodes are ordered, and a node may have an arbitrary number of children. We view

child	$= fc \circ ns^*$	parent	$= \text{child}^{-1}$
descendant	$= \text{child}^+$	ancestor	$= \text{descendant}^{-1}$
descendant-or-self	$= \text{descendant} \cup I_t$	ancestor-or-self	$= \text{descendant-or-self}^{-1}$
following-sibling	$= ns^+$	preceding-sibling	$= \text{following-sibling}^{-1}$
following	$= \text{ancestor-or-self} \circ ns^+ \circ$	preceding	$= \text{following}^{-1}$
	descendant-or-self		

Fig. 3. XPath axes

unranked trees as a structure over the signature $\sigma_{unr} = \{(lab_a)_{a \in \Sigma}, fc, ns\}$ where for all $a \in \Sigma$, lab_a is a unary predicate that denotes the nodes labeled a, fc is a binary predicate that relates a node and its *first-child*, and ns is a binary predicate that relates a node and its *next-sibling*. For any unranked tree t, we let $\text{Dom}(t)$ be its set of nodes and $|t| = |\text{Dom}(t)|$ its number of nodes.

XPath axes are listed in Fig. 3 together with their semantics by means of expressions over inverse, union, composition and iteration $.^*$ and $.^+$ of the relations fc, ns and I_t the identity relation on $\text{Dom}(t)$. XPath axes are not $\underline{X}$, and only some subsets of them are $\underline{X}$, as shown in [13]. However as we will show, ACQS over XPath axes still enjoy good enumeration properties, mainly because of the following fact:

Lemma 11 (Gottlob, Koch, Pichler [12]). *For all unranked trees t, all XPath axes χ, and all sets $A \subseteq \text{Dom}(t)$, $\chi(A)$ can be computed in time $O(|t|)$.*

In the context of XPath queries, it is important to consider the unary predicates lab_a that test the labels of the nodes. We can slightly extend the tree patterns with optional unary predicates lab_a attached to the nodes of the tree pattern. They just restrict the domain of the variables (bound and free) of the associated ACQ. As the unary predicates can be integrated into the binary relations, Algorithm 3 can also be used for tree patterns with both unary and binary predicates.

Consider now a tree pattern T over the XPath axes and the unary predicates lab_a, $a \in \Sigma$, and an unranked tree t (represented by a σ_{unr}-structure). We can choose an arbitrary total order on the nodes and apply Algorithm 3 directly on t (without considering line 2). In contrast to ACQ $(\underline{X})$ however, the predicates that appear in T are not explicitly represented in the σ_{unr}-structure t (otherwise its size would be $O(|t|^2)$). Thanks to Lemma 11 and the fact that XPath axes are closed under inverse, tree patterns over XPath axes can be enumerated with a preprocessing and delay $O(|T| \cdot |t|)$.

When going from ACQS to tree patterns over XPath axes, we apply the same construction as for ACQ $(\underline{X})$. As XPath axes are closed under intersection and inverse, the resulting tree pattern is a tree pattern over XPath axes. Therefore we do not need to precompute the interpretation of the axes and we can apply the enumeration algorithm as done for tree patterns over XPath axes. We obtain the following complexity:

Theorem 5. *For every ACQ Q over the XPath axes and the unary predicates $(lab_a)_{a \in \Sigma}$ and all unranked tree t represented as a structure over ns and fc, $Q(t)$ can be enumerated with a preprocessing and delay in $O(|Q| \cdot |t|)$.*

5 Conjunctive Queries with Inequalities

In this section, one considers conjunctive queries over $\underline{X}$ structures where in addition $\neq$ is allowed in the signature. Note that a conjunctive query with such inequalities is acyclic if the query obtained by ignoring inequalities is acyclic. In other words, inequalities play no role in defining acyclicity. We first show that even in the case of acyclic conjunctive queries, such queries are hard to evaluate for combined complexity. The proof is by reduction from POSITIVE 1-3 SAT [11].

Proposition 4. *The problem of checking whether a Boolean conjunctive query with inequalities is true on an $\underline{X}$ structure is* NP-*complete for combined complexity. The result remains true even if the query restricted to the $\underline{X}$ predicates is acyclic.*

In contrast with the preceding result, we show that the hardness only relies roughly on the number of variables involved in at least one inequality.

Theorem 6. *Let S be an $\underline{X}$ structure for some order $<$, let Q be an n-ary conjunctive (resp. acyclic conjunctive) query with inequalities with at most ℓ variables involved in at least one inequality. Then, $Q(S)$ can be enumerated with a delay $O(\ell^{O(\ell)} \cdot |Q| \cdot n \cdot |S| \cdot \log |D|)$ (resp. a delay $O(\ell^{O(\ell)} \cdot |Q| \cdot |D| \cdot \log |D|)$ and preprocessing cost in $O(|Q| \cdot |S|)$).*

Proof. The bound is obtained by partial application of techniques related to the color coding method of [2]. We will construct $h = O(\ell^{\ell} \cdot \log |D|)$ conjunctive (resp. acyclic conjunctive) queries Q_i, $i = 1, \ldots, h$, on some $\underline{X}$-structures S_i for order $<$ such that $Q(S) = \bigcup_{i \leq h} Q_i(S_i)$. Is it known (see for example [4]) that if each predicate of a union of size h can be enumerated by a bounded delay algorithm for some delay k and w.r.t. the same order, here $<_{lex}$, then the union can be enumerated by a bounded delay algorithm with delay $O(h \cdot k)$ for this same order. Hence the result will follow.

More precisely, the body of Q can be written as $Q^0 \wedge \bigwedge_{(i,j) \in I} x_i \neq x_j$ for some set of pairs I, where Q^0 is acyclic (if Q is acyclic) and free of inequalities. We write $\{x_1, \ldots, x_\ell\}$ for the variables appearing in inequalities (some of them may be free in Q), and $[\ell]$ for $\{1, \ldots, \ell\}$.

Let $\lambda : D \longrightarrow [\ell]$, be a proper ℓ coloring of D. Let (S, λ) be the extension of S by the coloring λ with each color i encoded by a new monadic predicate U_i. Obviously, if two elements have two different colors in a proper coloring then they are distinct. Let us consider query Q' whose body is: $Q^0 \wedge \bigwedge_{(i,j) \in I} \bigwedge_{k=1}^{\ell} \neg(U_k(x_i) \wedge U_k(x_j))$.

Claim. One can enumerate the elements of $Q'(S, \lambda)$ with delay $O(\ell^{\ell} |Q||S|)$. Moreover, if Q is acyclic then the delay can be improved to $O(\ell^{\ell} \cdot |Q| \cdot |D|)$.

Proof (of the claim). Since the interpretation is taken on a structure where the coloring is proper, then the number of possible colorings for $x_1, \ldots, x_\ell$ compatible with $\bigwedge_{(i,j) \in I} \bigwedge_{k=1}^{\ell} \neg(U_k(x_i) \wedge U_k(x_j))$ is bounded by ℓ^{ℓ}. The query Q' is equivalent to a disjunction of conjunctive queries Q_f of body $Q^0 \wedge U_{f(1)}(x_1) \wedge \cdots \wedge U_{f(\ell)}(x_\ell)$ for all functions $f : [\ell] \to [\ell]$ such that $f(i) \neq f(j)$ for all $(i, j) \in I$. Each Q_f is acyclic if Q^0 is acyclic. The result follows from Theorem 1 and 4.   □

It is known (see [2] and also [10]) that there exists an ℓ-perfect family Λ of size $2^{O(\ell)} \cdot \log |D|$ of hash functions from D to $[\ell]$, *i.e.* Λ is such that for every $C \subseteq D$ with $|C| = \ell$, there exists $\lambda \in \Lambda$ such that $\lambda(c) \neq \lambda(c')$ for all distinct $c, c' \in C$ (*i.e.* the restriction of λ to C is one-to-one). The following holds: $Q(S) = \bigcup_{\lambda \in \Lambda} Q'(S, \lambda)$. Clearly, if a tuple $\bar{a} = (a_1, \ldots, a_n) \in Q'(S, \lambda)$ for some $\lambda \in \Lambda$ then $\bar{a} \in Q(S)$. Conversely, let $\bar{a} \in Q(S)$

and A be a satisfying assignment of variables of Q such that the free variables of Q are assigned to $\bar{a}$. Let b_i be the assignment of x_i, $i = 1, ..., \ell$ in A. Then, it holds that $\bigwedge_{(i,j) \in I} b_i \neq b_j$. As λ is an ℓ-perfect family, there exists $\lambda \in \Lambda$ such that all distinct elements among $b_1, ..., b_\ell$ have distinct images (*i.e.* colors) by λ. Then $\bar{a} \in Q(S, \lambda)$. Then, the theorem follows by enumerating the union $\bigcup_{\lambda \in \Lambda} Q'(S, \lambda)$.   □

Conclusion. As a conclusion, we would like to address some further questions. First, we would like to characterise the complexity of the enumeration algorithms in terms of amortized delay, which we conjecture is smaller than the worst-case delay. Another question is to see whether the delays are tight. Finally, we will investigate the generalization to relations of arbitrary arity, as the $\underline{X}$ notion can be extended to n-ary relations.

Acknowledgments. We thank Joachim Niehren for fruitful discussions. This work was partially supported by the project ANR ENUM (ANR-07-BLAN-0327).

References

1. Abiteboul, S., Hull, R., Vianu, V.: Foundations of Databases. Addison-Wesley, Reading (1995)
2. Alon, N., Yuster, R., Zwick, U.: Color-coding. Journal of the ACM 42(4), 844–856 (1995)
3. Bagan, G.: MSO queries on tree decomposable structures are computable with linear delay. In: Duparc, J., Henzinger, T.A. (eds.) CSL 2007. LNCS, vol. 4646, pp. 208–222. Springer, Heidelberg (2007)
4. Bagan, G., Durand, A., Grandjean, E.: On acyclic conjunctive queries and constant delay enumeration. In: Duparc, J., Henzinger, T.A. (eds.) CSL 2007. LNCS, vol. 4646, pp. 208–222. Springer, Heidelberg (2007)
5. Bruno, N., Koudas, N., Srivastava, D.: Holistic twig joins: optimal XML pattern matching. In: Proceedings of the ACM SIGMOD, pp. 310–321 (2002)
6. Bry, F., Furche, T., Linse, B., Schröder, A.: Efficient evaluation of n-ary conjunctive queries over trees and graphs. In: Workshop on Web Information and Data Mining (2006)
7. Courcelle, B.: Linear delay enumeration and monadic second-order logic. Discrete Applied Mathematics (2007)
8. Feder, T., Hell, P., Huang, J., Rafiey, A.: Adjusted interval digraphs. Electronic Notes in Discrete Mathematics 32, 83–91 (2009)
9. Filiot, E., Niehren, J., Talbot, J.-M., Tison, S.: Polynomial time fragments of XPath with variables. In: ACM Symposium on Principles of Database Systems, pp. 205–214 (2007)
10. Flum, J., Grohe, M.: Parameterized Complexity Theory. In: Texts in Theoretical Computer Science. Springer, Heidelberg (2006)
11. Garey, M.R., Johnson, D.S.: Computers and Intractability, a Guide to the Theory of NP-Completness. W.H. Freeman and Co., San Francisco (1979)
12. Gottlob, G., Koch, C., Pichler, R.: Efficient algorithms for processing XPath queries. ACM Transactions on Database Systems 30(2), 444–491 (2005)
13. Gottlob, G., Koch, C., Schulz, K.U.: Conjunctive queries over trees. Journal of the ACM 53(2), 238–272 (2006)
14. Gutjahr, W., Welzl, E., Woeginger, G.: Polynomial graph-colorings. Discrete Applied Mathematics 35, 29–45 (1992)
15. Hell, P., Nešetřil, J.: Colouring, constraint satisfaction, and complexity. Computer Science Review 2(3), 143–163 (2008)
16. Koch, C.: Processing queries on tree-structured data efficiently. In: ACM Symposium on Principles of Database Systems, pp. 213–224 (2006)
17. Opatrny, J.: Total ordering problem. SIAM Journal on Computing 8(1), 111–114 (1979)
18. Yannakakis, M.: Algorithms for acyclic database schemes. In: Proceeding of VLDB, pp. 82–94. IEEE Computer Society, Los Alamitos (1981)

A Formalisation of the Normal Forms of Context-Free Grammars in HOL4

Aditi Barthwal[1] and Michael Norrish[2]

[1] Australian National University
Aditi.Barthwal@anu.edu.au
[2] Canberra Research Lab., NICTA
Michael.Norrish@nicta.com.au

Abstract. We describe the formalisation of the Chomsky and Greibach normal forms for context-free grammars (CFGs) using the HOL4 theorem prover. We discuss the varying degrees to which proofs that are straightforward on pen and paper, turn out to be much harder to mechanise. While both proofs are of similar length in their informal presentations, the mechanised proofs for Greibach normal form blow-up considerably.

1 Introduction

A context-free grammar (CFG) provides a concise mechanism for describing the methods by which phrases in languages are built from smaller blocks, capturing the "block structure" of sentences in a natural way. The simplicity of this formalism makes it amenable to rigorous mathematical study.

CFGs form the basis of parsing. We have already mechanised some of the theory of CFGs [1]. Grammars can be *normalised*, resulting in rules that are constrained to be of a particular shape. These simpler, more regular, rules can help in subsequent proofs or algorithms. For example, using a grammar in Chomsky Normal Form (CNF), one can decide the membership of a string in polynomial time. Using a grammar in Greibach Normal Form (GNF), one can prove a parse tree for any string in the language will have depth equal to the length of the string.

The Chomsky and Greibach normal form results were first presented in [3] and [4] respectively. Here, as part of a wider program, we work from the presentation in Hopcroft and Ullman [5], a standard textbook.

By mechanising these results, we gain extra confidence in their correctness. Because the results are so basic, this may not seem much of an achievement, but the mechanised proofs do provide a foundation for the development of yet more mechanised theory. For example, the proof in Hopcroft and Ullman of the standard result equating grammars and push-down-automata (mechanised in [2]), assumes that the grammar is in GNF. Moreover, simply assuming results such as these in order to pursue more complicated material defeats the motivation at the heart of mechanised mathematics.

A. Dawar and H. Veith (Eds.): CSL 2010, LNCS 6247, pp. 95–109, 2010.

Contributions

- The first mechanised proofs of termination and correctness for an algorithm that converts a CFG to Chomsky Normal Form (Section 3).
- The first mechanised proofs of termination and correctness for an algorithm that converts a CFG to Greibach Normal Form (Section 4).
- We also discuss the ways in which well-known, "classic" proofs can require considerable "reworking" when fully mechanised. Interestingly, though the proofs we mechanise here both expand dramatically from their length in Hopcroft and Ullman [5], the GNF proof expands a great deal more than the CNF proof.

All the assumptions and assertions in this paper have been mechanised and the HOL4 sources for the work are available at http://users.rsise.anu.edu.au/~aditi/.

2   Context-Free Grammars

A context-free grammar (CFG) is represented in HOL using the following type definitions:

```
('nts, 'ts) symbol = NTS of 'nts | TS of 'ts
('nts, 'ts) rule = rule of 'nts => ('nts, 'ts) symbol list
('nts, 'ts) grammar = G of ('nts, 'ts) rule list => 'nts
```

The => arrow indicates curried arguments to an algebraic type's constructor. Thus, the rule constructor is a curried function taking a value of type 'nts (the symbol at the head of the rule), a list of symbols (giving the rule's right-hand side), and returning an ('nts, 'ts) rule. The symbols are of two types, type 'nts used for non-terminals and type 'ts used for terminal symbols.

Thus, a rule pairs a value of type 'nts with a symbol list. Similarly, a grammar consists of a list of rules and a value giving the start symbol. Traditional presentations of grammars often include separate sets corresponding to the grammar's terminals and nonterminals. Our grammar type does not include these sets explicitly as it is easy to derive these sets from the grammar's rules and start symbol, so we shall occasionally write a grammar G as a tuple (V, T, P, S) in the proofs to come. Here, V is the list of nonterminals or variables, T is the list of terminals, P is the list of productions and S is the start symbol.

Definition 1. *A list of symbols (or* sentential form*) s derives t in a single step if s is of the form $\alpha A \gamma$, t is of the form $\alpha \beta \gamma$, and if $A \rightarrow \beta$ is one of the rules in the grammar. In HOL:*

```
derives g lsl rsl ⟺
∃ s₁ s₂ rhs lhs.
   (s₁ ++ [NTS lhs] ++ s₂ = lsl) ∧ (s₁ ++ rhs ++ s₂ = rsl) ∧
   rule lhs rhs ∈ rules g
```

(The infix ++ denotes list concatenation. The symbol ∈ denotes membership.)

We write $(\text{derives } g)^*$ sf_1 sf_2 to indicate that sf_2 is derived from sf_1 in zero or more steps, also written $sf_1 \Rightarrow^* sf_2$ (where the grammar g is assumed).

This is concretely represented using derivation lists. We write $R \vdash l \lhd x \to y$ to mean that the binary relation R holds between the successive pair of elements of l, which starts with x and end with y. Thus, $sf_1 \Rightarrow^* sf_2$ can be written as `derives` $g \vdash l \lhd sf_1 \to sf_2$ for some l. We also define the leftmost and the rightmost derivation relations, `lderives` $(\overset{l}{\Rightarrow})$ and `rderives` $(\overset{r}{\Rightarrow})$.

Definition 2. *The* language *of a grammar consists of all the words (lists of only terminal symbols) that can be derived from the start symbol.*

$$\text{L } g \; = \; \{\, tsl \mid (\text{derives } g)^* \; [\text{NTS } (\text{startSym } g)] \; tsl \wedge \text{isWord } tsl \,\}$$

(Predicate `isWord` is true of a sentential form if it consists of only terminal symbols.)

The choice of the derivation relation (`derives`, `lderives` or `rderives`) does not affect the language generated by a grammar. We say $x \overset{l}{\Rightarrow} y$ if y is obtained by expanding the leftmost non-terminal in x. Similarly, $x \overset{r}{\Rightarrow} y$ if y is obtained by the expansion of the rightmost non-terminal in x. We use this equivalence for the proof of normalisation to GNF. This equivalence forms a part of our background mechanisation.

3   Chomsky Normal Form

CFGs can be simplified by restricting the format of productions in the grammar without changing the language. Some such restrictions, which are shared by the normal forms we consider, are summarised below.

- Removing symbols that do not generate a terminal string or are not reachable from the start symbol of the grammar (useless symbols);
- Removing ϵ-productions (as long as ϵ is not in the language generated by the grammar);
- Removing unit productions, i.e. ones of the form $A \to B$ where B is a nonterminal symbol.

ϵ represents the empty word in the language of a grammar. An ϵ production is one with an empty right-hand side.

The proofs that these restrictions can always be made without changing the language are available in our online resources.

In this section we concentrate on Chomsky Normal Form, assuming the grammar has already gone through the above simplifications.

Theorem 1 (Chomsky Normal Form). *Any context-free language without ϵ is generated by a grammar in which all productions are of the form $A \to BC$ or $A \to a$. Here A, B, C are variables and a is a terminal.*

Proof. Let $g_1 = (V, T, P, S)$ be a context-free grammar. We can assume P contains no useless symbols, unit productions or ϵ-productions using the above simplifications. If a production has a single symbol on the right-hand side, that symbol must be a terminal. Thus, that production is already in an acceptable form. The remaining productions in g_1 are converted into CNF in two steps.

The first step is called trans1Tmnl, wherein a terminal occurring on the right side of a production gets replaced by a nonterminal in the following manner. We replace the productions of the form $l \rightarrow pts$ (p or s is nonempty and t is a terminal) with productions $A \rightarrow t$ and $l \rightarrow pAs$.

```
trans1Tmnl nt t g g′ ⟺
  ∃ℓ r p s.
    rule ℓ r ∈ rules g ∧ r = p ++ [t] ++ s ∧
    (p ≠ [] ∨ s ≠ []) ∧ isTmnlSym t ∧
    NTS nt ∉ nonTerminals g ∧
    rules g′ =
      delete (rule ℓ r) (rules g) ++
      [rule nt [t]; rule ℓ (p ++ [NTS nt] ++ s)] ∧
    startSym g′ = startSym g
```

(Function delete removes an element from a list. The ; is used to separate elements in a list.)

We prove that multiple applications of the above transformation preserve the language.

HOL Theorem 1

$\forall g\ g'.\ (\lambda x\ y.\ \exists A\ t.\ \texttt{trans1Tmnl}\ A\ t\ x\ y)^*\ g\ g' \Rightarrow (\text{L } g = \text{L } g')$

We want to obtain a grammar $g_2 = (V', T, P', S)$ which only contains productions of the form $A \rightarrow a$, where a is a terminal symbol or $A \rightarrow A_1...A_n$ where A_i is a nonterminal symbol. We prove that such a g_2 can be obtained by repeated applications of trans1Tmnl. The multiple applications are denoted by taking the reflexive transitive closure of trans1Tmnl.

We define the constant badTmnlsCount, which counts the terminals occurring in the RHSs of all productions in the grammar which have more than one terminal symbol present in the RHS.

```
badTmnlsCount g = SUM (MAP ruleTmnls (rules g))
```

(SUM adds the count over all the productions, MAP $f\ l$ applies f to each element in l.)

The auxiliary ruleTmnls is characterised:

```
ruleTmnls (rule ℓ r) = if |r| ≤ 1 then 0 else |FILTER isTmnlSym r|
```

($|r|$ denotes the length of a list r.)

Each application of the process should decrease the number of ruleTmnls unless there are none to change (*i.e.*, the grammar is already in the desired form). By induction on badTmnlsCount we prove that by a finite number of applications of trans1Tmnl we can get grammar g_2. This follows from the fact that the set of symbols in a grammar is finite.

HOL Theorem 2

```
INFINITE  𝒰(:α) ⇒
  ∃g′. (λx y. ∃nt t. trans1Tmnl nt t x y)* g g′ ∧
    badTmnlsCount g′ = 0
```

(Note the use of the assumption INFINITE $\mathcal{U}$. Here $\mathcal{U}$ represents the universal set for the type of nonterminals (α) in the grammar g and g'. The transformation process involves introducing a new nonterminal symbol. To be able to pick a fresh symbol, the set of nonterminals has to be infinite.)

The above process gives us a simplified grammar g_2 such that badTmnlsCount g_2 =0. By HOL Theorem 1 we have that $L(g_1) = L(g_2)$. We now apply another transformation on g_2 which gives us our final CNF. The final transformation is called trans2NT and works by replacing two adjacent nonterminals in the right-hand side of a rule by a single nonterminal symbol. Repeated application on g_2 gives us a grammar where all productions conform to the CNF criteria.

```
trans2NT nt nt₁ nt₂ g g'  ⟺
  ∃ℓ r p s.
     rule ℓ r ∈ rules g ∧ r = p ++ [nt₁; nt₂] ++ s ∧
     (p ≠ [] ∨ s ≠ []) ∧ isNonTmnlSym nt₁ ∧ isNonTmnlSym nt₂ ∧
     NTS nt ∉ nonTerminals g ∧
     rules g' =
        delete (rule ℓ r) (rules g) ++
        [rule nt [nt₁; nt₂]; rule ℓ (p ++ [NTS nt] ++ s)] ∧
     startSym g' = startSym g
```

We prove that the language remains the same after zero or more such transformations.

We follow a similar strategy as with trans1Tmnl to show that applications of trans2NT will result in grammar (g_3) where all rules with nonterminals on the RHS have exactly two nonterminals, *i.e.* rules are of the form $A \rightarrow A_1 A_2$.

To wrap up the proof we show two results. First, that applications of trans1Tmnl followed by applications of trans2NT, leaves the language of the grammar untouched, i.e. $L(g_1) = L(g_3)$. Second, that the transformation trans2NT does not introduce productions to change badTmnlsCount. We can then apply the two transformations to obtain our grammar in CNF where all rules are of the form $A \rightarrow a$ or $A \rightarrow A_1 A_2$ (asserted by the isCnf predicate). The HOL theorem corresponding to Theorem 1 is:

HOL Theorem 3

```
INFINITE  𝒰(:α) ∧ [] ∉ language g ⇒
∃g'. isCnf g' ∧ language g = language g'
```

4   Greibach Normal Form

If ϵ does not belong in the language of a grammar then it can be transformed into Greibach Normal Form. The existence of GNF for a grammar simplifies many proofs, such as the result that every context-free language can be accepted by a non-deterministic pushdown automata. Productions in GNF are of the form $A \rightarrow a\alpha$ where a is a terminal symbol and α is list (possibly empty) of nonterminals.

We assume an implicit ordering on the nonterminals of the grammar. The various stages in the conversion to GNF are summarised below.

Preprocessing. Remove useless symbols, ϵ and unit productions from the grammar and convert it into Chomsky Normal Form.

Stage 1. For each ordered nonterminal A_k do the following:
  Stage 1.1. Return rules of the form such that if $A_k \to A_j \alpha$ then $j \geq k$. This result
     is obtained using aProds lemma (Section 4.1).
  Stage 1.2. Convert left recursive rules in the grammar to right recursive rules. This
     is based on left2Right lemma (Section 4.2).
Stage 2. Eliminate the leftmost nonterminal from the RHS of all the rules to obtain a
  grammar in GNF.

In the discussion to follow we assume the grammar already satisfies the Preprocessing
requirements (following from the results already covered). We start at Stage 1 which is
implemented using relation r49 in Section 4.4. This is Phase 1 of the GNF algorithm.
Stage 1 depends on two crucial results, Stage 1.1 and Stage 1.2 which are established
separately. Stage 2 can be further subdivided into two parts covered in (Sections 4.5 and
4.6), the Phase 2 and Phase 3 of the algorithm, respectively.

All the stages preserve the language of the grammar. We devote much of our discussion to mechanising the more interesting stages for eliminating left recursion and
putting together Stage 1 and Stage 2 to get the GNF algorithm.

4.1 Eliminating the Leftmost Nonterminal

Let A-productions be those productions whose LHS is the nonterminal A. We define
the function aProdsRules A Bs $rset$ to transform the set of productions $rset$: the
result is a set where occurrences of non-terminals in the list Bs no longer occur in
leftmost position in A-productions. Instead, they have been replaced by their own right-
hand-sides.

HOL Definition 1

```
aProdsRules A l ru =
ru DIFF {rule A ([NTS B] ++ s) | (B,s) |
          B ∈ l ∧ rule A ([NTS B] ++ s) ∈ ru} ∪
{rule A (x ++ s) | (x,s) |
   ∃B. B ∈ l ∧ rule A ([NTS B] ++ s) ∈ ru ∧ rule B x ∈ ru}
```

*(The notation s_1 DIFF s_2 represents set-difference. Notation $|(p, B, s)|$ denotes that p,
B and s are the bound variables.)*

Lemma 1 ("aProds lemma"). *For all possible nonterminals A, and lists of nonterminals Bs, if* rules g' = aProdsRules A Bs (rules g) *and the start symbols
of g and g' are equal, then $L(g) = L(g')$.*

4.2 Replacing Left Recursion with Right Recursion

Left recursive rules may already be present in the grammar, or they may be introduced
by the elimination of leftmost nonterminals (using the aProds lemma). In order to deal
with such productions we transform them into right recursive rules. We show that this
transformation preserves the language equivalence.

Theorem 2 ("left2Right lemma"). *Let* $g = (V, T, P, S)$ *be a CFG. Let* $A \to A\alpha_1 \mid A\alpha_2 \mid \ldots \mid A\alpha_r$ *be the set of left recursive A-productions. Let* $A \to \beta_1 \mid \beta_2 \mid \ldots \mid \beta_s$ *be the remaining A-productions. Then we can construct* $g' = (V \cup \{B\}, T, P_1, S)$ *such that* $L(g) = L(g')$ *by replacing all the left recursive A-productions by the following productions:*

Rule 1. $A \to \beta_i$ *and* $A \to \beta_i B$ *for* $1 \le i \le s$
Rule 2. $B \to \alpha_i$ *and* $B \to \alpha_i B$ *for* $1 \le i \le r$

Here, B is a fresh nonterminal that does not belong in g. *This is our HOL Theorem 4.*

Relation left2Right A B g g' holds iff the rules in g' are obtained by replacing all left recursive A-productions with rules of the form given by Rule 1 and Rule 2 (implemented by the l2rRules function).

HOL Definition 2
```
left2Right A B g g' ⟺
    NTS B ∉ nonTerminals g ∧ startSym g = startSym g' ∧
    set (rules g') = l2rRules A B (set (rules g))
```

In the textbook it is observed that a sequence of productions of the form $A \to A\alpha_i$ will eventually end with a production $A \to \beta_j$. The sequence of replacements

$$A \Rightarrow A\alpha_{i_1} \Rightarrow A\alpha_{i_2}\alpha_{i_1} \Rightarrow \ldots \Rightarrow A\alpha_{i_p} \ldots \alpha_{i_1} \Rightarrow \beta_j\alpha_{i_p} \ldots \alpha_{i_1} \qquad (1)$$

in g can be replaced in g' by

$$A \Rightarrow \beta_j B \Rightarrow \beta_j\alpha_{i_p} B \Rightarrow \ldots \Rightarrow \beta_j\alpha_{i_p} \ldots \alpha_{i_2} B \Rightarrow \beta_j\alpha_{i_p} \ldots \alpha_{i_2}\alpha_{i_1} \qquad (2)$$

Since it is clear that the reverse transformation is also possible, it is concluded that $L(g) = L(g')$. This is illustrated graphically in Figure 1.

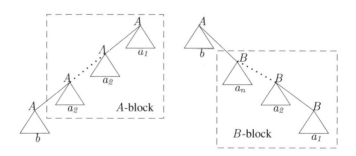

Fig. 1. A left recursive derivation $A \to Aa_1 \to Aa_2a_1 \to \cdots \to A_n \ldots a_2a_1 \to ba_n \ldots a_2a_1$ can be transformed into a right recursive derivation $A \to bB \to ba_n \to \cdots \to ba_n \ldots a_2 \to ba_n \ldots a_2a_1$. Here the RHS b does not start with an A.

HOL Theorem 4

```
∀g g'. left2Right A B g g' ⇒ (L g = L g')
```

This is a good example of a "proof" where the authors rely on "obvious" details to make their point: the proof in Hopcroft and Ullman consists of little more than equations (1) and (2), and a figure corresponding to our Figure 1. Unfortunately, a figure does not satisfy a theorem prover's notion of a proof; moreover it fails to suggest any strategies that might be used for rigorous treatment (such as automation) of the material.

In the following section, we describe the proof strategy used to mechanise this result in HOL4. For the purposes of discussion, we will assume that we are removing left recursions in A-productions in g, using the new nonterminal B, producing the new grammar g'.

Proof of the "if" direction. We use a leftmost derivation with concrete derivation lists to show that if $x \overset{l}{\Rightarrow}_g^* y$, where y is a word, then $x \Rightarrow_{g'}^* y$.

HOL Theorem 5

```
left2Right A B g g' ∧ lderives g ⊢ dl ◁ x → y ∧ isWord y ⇒
∃ dl'. derives g' ⊢ dl' ◁ x → y
```

The proof is by induction on the number of times A occurs as the leftmost symbol in the derivation dl. This is given by `ldNumNt A dl`.

Base Case. If there are no As in the leftmost position (*i.e.* `ldNumNt` $NTS\ A\ dl\ =\ 0$) then the derivation in g can also be done in g'.

Step Case. The step case revolves around the notion of a *block*. A block in a derivation is defined as a (nonempty) section of the derivation list where each expansion is done by using a left recursive rule of A. As such, the sentential forms in the block always have an A as their leftmost symbol. Figure 1 shows the A and B-blocks for leftmost and rightmost derivations.

If there is more than one instance of A in the leftmost position in a derivation, then we can divide it into three parts: dl_1 which does not have any leftmost As, dl_2 which is a block and dl_3 where the very first expansion is a result of one of the non-recursive rules of A. This is shown in Figure 2.

Fig. 2. We can split dl into dl_1, dl_2 and dl_3 such that dl_1 has no A-expansions, dl_2 consists of only A-expansions and dl_3 breaks the sequence of A-expansions so that the very first element in dl_3 is not a result of an A-expansion. The dashed lines are elements in the derivation list showing the leftmost nonterminals ($L_1 \ldots L_n, A, M_1$). $L_n \rightarrow Ay$ is the first A-expansion in dl and $A \rightarrow pM_1z$ (p is a word), breaks the sequence of the consecutive A-expansions in dl_2.

The division is given by HOL Theorem 6. The second $\exists$-clause of this theorem refers to the side conditions on the composition of the expansions shown in Figure 2.

In the absence of any leftmost As, a derivation is easily replicated in g'. Thus, the dl_1 portion can be done in g'. The derivation corresponding to dl_3 follows by our inductive hypothesis.

The proof falls through if derivation dl_2 can somehow be shown to have an equivalent in g'. This is shown by proving HOL Theorem 7. The theorem states that for a derivations in g of the form given by Equation (1), there is an equivalent derivation in g' in the form of Equation (2).

To show the remaining "only if" part, $(x \stackrel{r}{\Rightarrow}_{g'}^{*} y$, where y is a word, then $x \stackrel{r}{\Rightarrow}_{g}^{*} y)$, we mirror the leftmost derivation strategy. In this case we rely on the rightmost derivation and the notion of a B-block, wherein B is always the rightmost nonterminal. We omit the details due to the similarity with the proof of the if direction.

HOL Theorem 6

```
lderives g ⊢ dl ◁ x → y ∧ ldNumNt (NTS A) dl ≠ 0 ∧ |dl| > 1 ⇒
∃ dl₁ dl₂ dl₃ .
    dl = dl₁ ++ dl₂ ++ dl₃ ∧ ldNumNt (NTS A) dl₁ = 0 ∧
    (∀ e₁ e₂ p s. dl₂ = p ++ [e₁; e₂] ++ s ⇒ |e₂| ≥ |e₁|) ∧
    ∃ pfx .
        isWord pfx ∧
        (∀ e. e ∈ dl₂ ⇒ ∃ sfx. e = pfx ++ [NTS A] ++ sfx) ∧
        dl₂ ≠ [] ∧
        ( dl₃ ≠ [] ⇒
        |LAST dl₂| ≤ |HD dl₃| ⇒
        ¬(pfx ++ [NTS A]   HD dl₃))
```
(Here $x <<= y$ holds iff x is a prefix of y.)

4.3   Stitching the Pieces Together

Using the aProds lemma and eliminating of left recursive rules, it is clear that any grammar can be transformed into Greibach Normal Form. The textbook achieves this by providing a concrete algorithm for transforming rules in the grammar into an intermediate form where left recursion has been eliminated. This is Phase 1 of our HOL implementation. We model this transformation with a relation. From this point, multiple applications of the aProds lemma transform the grammar into GNF. These applications correspond to the Phase 2 and Phase 3. Each phase brings the grammar a step closer to GNF.

Let $g = (V, T, P, S)$ and $V = A_1 \ldots A_n$ be the ordered nonterminals in g. We will need at least n fresh Bs that are not in g when transforming the left recursive rules into right recursive rules. Let $B = B_1, \ldots, B_n$ be these distinct nonterminals. The three phases are applied in succession to the grammar and achieve the following results.

Phase 1. Transform the rules in g to give a new grammar $g_1 = (V_1, T, P_1, S)$ such that if $A_i \to A_j \alpha$ is a rule of g_1, then $j > i$. Since i not equal to j, we have removed the left recursive rules in g, introducing m new B non-terminals, where $m \leq n$. Thus, $V_1 \subseteq V \cup \{B_1, \ldots, B_n\}$. This is done using multiple applications of the aProds transformation followed by a single application of left2Right. This process is applied progressively to each of the nonterminals.

Phase 2. All the rules of the form $A_i \rightarrow A_j\beta$ in g_1 are replaced by $A_i \rightarrow a\alpha\beta$, where $A_j \rightarrow a\alpha$ to give a new grammar $g_2 = (V_1, T, P_2, S)$. This is done progressively for each of the nonterminals in V by using the aProds lemma.

Phase 3. All the rules of the form $B_k \rightarrow A_i\beta$ in g_2 are replaced with $B_k \rightarrow a\alpha\beta$, where $A_i \rightarrow a\alpha$ to give $g_3 = (V_1, T, P_3, S)$ such that g_3 is in Greibach Normal Form. Again, applying the aProds lemma progressively for each of the Bs gives us a grammar in GNF.

HOL Theorem 7

```
left2Right A B g g' ∧
lderives g ⊢ dl ◁ pfx ++ [NTS A] ++ sfx → y ∧
lderives g y y' ∧ isWord pfx ∧
(∀e. e ∈ dl ⇒ ∃sfx. e = pfx ++ [NTS A] ++ sfx) ∧
(∀e₁ e₂ p s. dl = p ++ [e₁; e₂] ++ s ⇒ |e₂| ≥ |e₁|) ∧
(|y| ≤ |y'| ⇒ ¬(pfx ++ [NTS A]   y')) ⇒
∃dl'. derives g' ⊢ dl' ◁ pfx ++ [NTS A] ++ sfx → y'
```

4.4   Phase 1—Ordering the A_i-productions

Phase 1 is represented by the HOL relation r49. This corresponds to Figure 4.9 in Hopcroft and Ullman showing the first step in the GNF algorithm. The r49 relation relates two states where the second state is the result of transforming rules for a single A_k.

HOL Definition 3

```
r49 (bs₀, nts₀, g₀, seen₀, ubs₀) (bs, nts, g, seen, ubs)  ⟺
∃ Aₖ b rules₀ rules₁.
    (nts₀ = Aₖ::nts) ∧ (bs₀ = b::bs) ∧ (ubs = ubs₀ ++ [b]) ∧
    (seen = seen₀ ++ [Aₖ]) ∧ (nts = TL nts₀) ∧
    (r49Elem Aₖ)* (seen₀,rules g₀,[]) ([],rules₀,seen₀) ∧
    (rules₁ = l2rRules Aₖ b (set rules₀)) ∧
    (startSym g = startSym g₀) ∧ (set (rules g) = rules₁)
```

(Here bs_0 consists of fresh B_is not in grammar g_0, nts_0 are the ordered nonterminals (increasing) in g_0, $seen_0$ holds the nonterminals and ubs_0 holds the B_is that have been already processed. The relation, r49, holds if the rules of g are obtained by transforming rules for a single nonterminal (A_k) and using up a fresh non-terminal b to eliminate (possible) left recursion for A_k. The b is used up irrespective of whether a left recursion elimination is required or not. This simplifies both the definition and reasoning for the relation.)

There are two parts to r49. The first part is the relation r49Elem. This works on a single nonterminal and progressively eliminates rules of the form $A_k \rightarrow A_j\gamma$ where j has a lower ranking than k and is in $seen_0$. We do this for each element of $seen_0$ starting from the lowest ranked. $seen_0$ consists of ordered nonterminals having a lower ranking than k.

HOL Definition 4

> r49Elem A_k ($seen_0$, ru_0, sl_0) ($seen$, ru, sl) $\iff$
> $\exists A_j$. ($seen_0$ = A_j :: $seen$) $\wedge$ (sl = sl_0 ++ [A_j]) $\wedge$
>   (set ru = aProdsRules A_k [A_j] (set ru_0))

Using the closure, r49Elem*, we can repeatedly do this transformation for all the elements in $seen_0$ to obtain the new set of rules $rules_0$ in the r49 definition. At the end of the above transformation, we have productions of the form $A_k \to A_j\gamma$, where $j \geq i$. In the second part (corresponding to l2rRules), we replace productions of the form $A_k \to A_k\alpha$ with their right recursive counterparts to obtain a new set of rules using the l2rRules function. The above process is repeated for each nonterminal in g by taking the closure of r49. Thus, if r49* ($B, V, g, [], []$) ($B_1, [], g_1, V, B_2$) holds then g_1 has successfully been transformed to satisfy the Phase 1 conditions. More explicitly, as mentioned in Hopcroft and Ullman, the rules in g_1 should now be of the form:

- **(C1) Ordered A_i rules** - if $A_i \to A_j\gamma$ is in rules of g, then $j > i$.
- **(C2) A_i rules in GNF** - $A_i \to a\gamma$, where a is T.
- **(C3) B_i rules** - $B_i \to \gamma$, where y is in $(V \cup B_1, B_2, \ldots, B_n)^*$.

Automating an algorithm. That Phase 1 has achieved these succinctly stated conditions is "obvious" to the human reader because of the ordering imposed on the nonterminals. A theorem prover, unfortunately, cannot make such deductive leaps. In an automated environment, the only assertions are the ones already present as part of the system or what one brings, *i.e.* verifies, as part of mechanising a theory. In particular, we need to define and prove invariant a number of conditions on the state of the system as it is transformed.

The composition of the rules from conditions **(C1)** and **(C2)** is asserted using the invariant rhsTlNonTms:

HOL Definition 5

> rhsTlNonTms ru $ntsl$ bs $\iff$
> $\forall e$. $e \in$ set $ntsl$ DIFF set bs $\Rightarrow$
> $\forall r$. rule e $r \in ru$ $\Rightarrow$
> $\exists h$ t. (r = h::t) $\wedge$ EVERY isNonTmnlSym t $\wedge$
> $\forall nt$. (h = NTS nt) $\Rightarrow$
> $nt \in$ set $ntsl$ DIFF set bs $\wedge$
> $\exists nt_1$ t_1. (t = NTS nt_1::t_1) $\wedge$ $nt_1 \in$ set $ntsl$ DIFF set bs

Invariant seenInv asserts the ordering ($j > i$) part of (C1):

HOL Definition 6

> seenInv ru s $\iff$
> $\forall i$. $i < |s|$ $\Rightarrow$
> $\forall nt$ $rest$. rule (EL i s) (NTS nt::$rest$) $\in ru$ $\Rightarrow$
> $\forall j$. $j \leq i$ $\Rightarrow$ EL j s $\neq nt$

(The notation EL i ℓ *denotes the ith element of ℓ.)*

The invariant rhsBNonTms ensures **(C3)**. This is stronger than what we need (at least at this stage of the process), since it also states that the very first nonterminal in the RHS has to be one of the A_is. This is observed in the textbook as part of later transformations (our own Phase 3), but actually needs to be proved at this stage.

HOL Definition 7

> rhsBNonTms *ru ubs* $\Longleftrightarrow$
> $\forall B$. $B \in ubs \Rightarrow \forall r$. rule B $r \in ru \Rightarrow$
> EVERY isNonTmnlSym $r \wedge r \neq$ [] $\wedge$
> $\exists nt$. (HD r = NTS nt) $\wedge \neg(nt \in ubs)$

(Function HD *returns the first element of a list.)*

Most of the reasoning in the textbook translates to providing such specific invariants. These assertions, easily and convincingly made in text, have hidden assumptions that need to be identified and proved before proceeding with the automation.

A straightforward example is one concerning the absence of ϵ-productions. From the construction, it is clear that there are no ϵ-rules in the grammar (because it is in CNF), and that the construction does not introduce any. One does not realise the need for such a trivial property to be established until its absence stops the proof midway during automation. There are ten invariants that had to be established as part of the proof. This has to be done both for the single step case and for the closure of the relation.

Proof of language equivalence. With all the required properties established, we can now go on to prove:

HOL Theorem 8

> r49* (bs_0, nts_0, g_0, $seen_0$, ubs_0) (bs, nts, g, $seen$, ubs) $\wedge$
> $|bs_0| \geq |nts_0| \wedge$ ALL_DISTINCT $bs_0 \wedge$ ALL_DISTINCT $nts_0 \wedge$
> (set (ntms g_0) $\cap$ set bs_0 = $\emptyset$) $\wedge$ (set bs_0 $\cap$ set ubs_0 = $\emptyset$) $\wedge$
> (set nts_0 $\cap$ set $seen_0$ = $\emptyset$) $\Rightarrow$
> (L g_0 = L g)

(The distinct nonterminals in a grammar g are given by ntms *g.)*

In order to reason about which nonterminals have already been handled, we maintain the seen nonterminals and the seen B_is as part of our states. Because of this, extra assertions about them have to provided. Once 'seen', a nonterminal or a B_i cannot be seen again (citing the uniqueness of the B_is and the nonterminals in g). These are reflected in the various conditions of the form $s_1 \cap s_2 = \emptyset$.

Proof. The proof is by induction on number of applications of r49.

The above proof becomes trivially true if relation r49 fails to hold. To counter this concern, we show that such a transformation does exist for any start state. This step is necessary because we have modelled transformations using relations (which can be partial) rather than by functions (which must be total in HOL).

HOL Theorem 9

$|bs_0| \geq |nts_0| \wedge$ ALL_DISTINCT $bs_0 \wedge$ ALL_DISTINCT $nts_0 \wedge$
(set $nts_0 \cap$ set $seen_0$ = $\emptyset$) $\wedge$ (set (ntms g_0) $\cap$ set bs_0 = $\emptyset$) $\wedge$
(set $bs_0 \cap$ set ubs_0 = $\emptyset$) $\Rightarrow$
$\exists g.$ r49* $(bs_0, nts_0, g_0, seen_0, ubs_0)$
(DROP $|nts_0|$ bs_0, [], $g, seen_0$ ++ nts_0, ubs_0 ++ TAKE $|nts_0|$ bs_0)

(Function DROP *n* ℓ *drops n elements from the front of l and* TAKE *n* ℓ *takes n elements from the front of l.)*

Proof. The proof is by induction on nts_0.

Note: Everywhere a relation such as r49, r49Elem is used we have provided proofs that the relation always holds.

4.5   Phase 2—Changing A_i-productions to GNF

We have already established that removing useless nonterminals does not affect the language of the grammar. The nonterminals in g_1 are ordered such that the RHS of a nonterminal cannot start with a nonterminal with lower index. Since g is in CNF and only has useful nonterminals, rule $A_n \rightarrow a$ is in g_1, where a is in T. A_n is the highest ranked nonterminal and as such cannot expand to any nonterminal.

Thus, if we transform nonterminals V using aProds, starting from the highest rank, we are bound to get rules of the form, $A_k \rightarrow a\alpha$, for a in T and α in V_1. This is done by repeated applications of fstNtm2Tm until all the nonterminals in V have been transformed.

HOL Definition 8

fstNtm2Tm $(ontms_0, g_0, seen_0)$ $(ontms, g, seen)$ $\iff$
$\exists A_k$ $rules_0.$ $(ontms_0 = ontms$ ++ $[A_k]) \wedge$ $(seen = A_k :: seen_0) \wedge$
(r49Elem A_k)* $(seen_0, $rules $g_0, [])$ $([], rules_0, seen_0)$
$\wedge$ (rules g = $rules_0) \wedge$ (startSym g = startSym g_0)

(Here $ontms_0$ are nonterminals with indices in decreasing order $(A_n, A_{n-1} \ldots A_1)$ and $seen_0$ contains the nonterminals that have already been processed.)

To prove that all the 'seen' nonterminals in V are in GNF, we establish that gnfInv invariant holds through the multiple applications of the relation.

HOL Definition 9

gnfInv ru s $\iff$
$\forall i.$ $i < |s| \Rightarrow$
$\forall r.$ rule (EL i s) $r \in ru \Rightarrow$ validGnfProd (rule (EL i s) r)

(Predicate validGnfProd *(rule ℓ r) holds iff $r = a\alpha$ for terminal a and (possibly empty) list of nonterminals α.)*

Multiple applications of this process result in g_2 satisfying the Phase 2 condition that all the rules for nonterminals in V are now in GNF.

4.6 Phase 3—Changing B_i-productions to GNF

The final phase is concerned with the rules corresponding to the B_is which are introduced as part of the left to right transformation. We follow a similar strategy to Phase 2 to convert all B_i-productions to GNF.

At the end of Phase 2, all rules involving nonterminals in V are of the form $A_i \rightarrow a\alpha$, for terminal a and list (possibly empty) of nonterminals α. From the invariant rhsBNonTms, we have that the B_i rules are of the form $B_i \rightarrow A_k\beta$ where β is a list (possibly empty) of nonterminals. The aProds lemma is now used to obtain rules of the form $B_i \rightarrow a\alpha\beta$ which satisfy GNF, done by establishing that gnfInv holds for seen B_is.

HOL Definition 10

> fstNtm2TmBrules $(ubs_0, ontms_0, g_0, seen_0)$ $(ubs, ontms, g, seen)$ $\Longleftrightarrow$
> $\exists b \; rules_0$.
> $(ubs_0 = b :: ubs) \land (ontms_0 = ontms) \land (seen = seen_0 ++ [b]) \land$
> $(rules_0 = $ aProdsRules $b \; ontms$ (set (rules g_0))) $\land$
>   (set (rules g) $= rules_0) \land$ (startSym g = startSym g_0)

($ubs0$ contains $B_1 \ldots B_n$, $ontms_0 = V$, the nonterminals in the original grammar g and $seen_0$ is used to keep a record of the B_is that have been handled.)

We show that the above transformation resulting in grammar g_3 preserves the language of the grammar.

Finally, the three phases can be combined to show that any grammar that can be transformed into Chomsky Normal Form can be subsequently transformed into a grammar in Greibach Normal Form.

This transformation resulting in grammar g_3 also preserves the language of the grammar and the invariant gnfInv over the seen B_is.

Finally, the three phases can be combined to show that any grammar that can be transformed into Chomsky Normal Form can be subsequently transformed into a grammar in Greibach Normal Form.

HOL Theorem 10

> INFINITE $\mathcal{U}(:\alpha) \land [] \notin$ language $g \land$ language $g \neq \emptyset \Rightarrow$
> $\exists g'$. isGnf $g' \land$ language $g =$ language g'

(The predicate isGnf *g holds iff predicate* gnfInv *is true for the rules and nonterminals of g.)*

5   Related Work and Conclusions

In the field of language theory, Nipkow [6] has provided a verified and executable lexical analyzer generator. This is the closest in nature to the mechanisation we have done.

The proof for CNF is ~1400 lines and GNF is ~6000, which is excluding proofs that are in the HOL library as well as the library maintained by us. Only parts of the proofs have been shown. The proof for CNF only covers half a page in the textbook. On the other hand, GNF covers almost three pages (including the two lemmas). This includes diagrams to assist explanation and an informal, high level reasoning. All of this is beyond the reach of automation in its current state. Issues such as finiteness and termination, which do not arise in a textual proof, become central when mechanising it. Similarly, choice of data structures and the form of definitions (relations vs functions) have a huge impact on the size of the proof as well as the ease of automation. These do not necessarily overlap. We have only presented the key theorems that are relevant to understanding and filling some of the deductive gaps in the textbook proofs. These theorems also cover the intermediate results needed because of the particular mechanisation technique. The size of these gaps also depends on the extent of detail in the text proof, which in our case is very sparse. It is hard to frame general techniques when the majority of the results require carefully combing the fine details in the text and making deductions about the omitted steps in the reasoning. From deducing and implementing the structure for induction for the left2Right lemma to establishing the numerous invariants for the final step of GNF algorithm, the problems for automation are quite diverse. Having extensive libraries is possibly the best way to tackle such highly domain specific problems. Like typical software development, the dream of libraries comprehensive enough to support all needed development fails as soon as one steps outside of the already conquered areas. The need for ever more libraries has never really gone away.

The simplification of CFGs (including CNF and GNF) is ~14000 lines. It took a year to complete the work which includes over 700 lemmas/theorems.

Acknowledgements. NICTA is funded by the Australian Government as represented by the Department of Broadband, Communications and the Digital Economy and the Australian Research Council through the ICT Centre of Excellence program.

References

1. Barthwal, A., Norrish, M.: Verified, executable parsing. In: Castagna, G. (ed.) ESOP 2009. LNCS, vol. 5502, pp. 160–174. Springer, Heidelberg (2009)
2. Barthwal, A., Norrish, M.: Mechanisation of pda and grammar equivalence for context-free languages. To appear in Proceedings of WoLLIC. Springer, Heidelberg (2010)
3. Chomsky, N.: On certain formal properties of grammars. Information and Control 2(2), 137–167 (1959)
4. Greibach, S.A.: A new normal-form theorem for context-free phrase structure grammars. J. ACM 12(1), 42–52 (1965)
5. Hopcroft, J.E., Ullman, J.D.: Introduction to Automata Theory, Languages and Computation. Addison-Wesley, Reading (1979)
6. Nipkow, T.: Verified lexical analysis. In: Grundy, J., Newey, M. (eds.) TPHOLs 1998. LNCS, vol. 1479, pp. 1–15. Springer, Heidelberg (1998)

Automata vs. Logics on Data Words

Michael Benedikt, Clemens Ley, and Gabriele Puppis

Oxford University Computing Laboratory - Parks Road, Oxford OX13QD UK

Abstract. The relationship between automata and logics has been investigated since the 1960s. In particular, it was shown how to determine,
given an automaton, whether or not it is definable in first-order logic
with label tests and the order relation, and for first-order logic with the
successor relation. In recent years, there has been much interest in languages over an infinite alphabet. Kaminski and Francez introduced a
class of automata called finite memory automata (FMA), that represent
a natural analog of finite state machines. A FMA can use, in addition to
its control state, a (bounded) number of registers to store and compare
values from the input word. The class of data languages recognized by
FMA is incomparable with the class of data languages defined by first-
order formulas with the order relation and an additional binary relation
for data equality.

   We first compare the expressive power of several variants of FMA with
several data word logics. Then we consider the corresponding decision
problem: given an automaton A and a logic, can the language recognized
by A be defined in the logic? We show that it is undecidable for several
variants of FMA, and then investigate the issue in detail for deterministic
FMA. We show the problem is decidable for first-order logic with local
data comparisons – an analog of first-order logic with successor. We also
show instances of the problem for richer classes of first-order logic that
are decidable.

Logics are natural ways of specifying decision problems on discrete structures,
while automata represent natural processing models. On finite words from a
fixed (finite) alphabet, Büchi [1] showed that monadic second-order logic has
the same expressiveness as deterministic finite state automata, while results of
Schützenberger and McNaughton and Papert showed that first-order logic with
the label and order predicates has the same expressiveness as counter-free automata [2, 3]. The latter theorem gives a decidable characterization of which
automata correspond to first-order sentences. Decidable characterizations have
also been given for first-order logic with the label and successor predicates [4].
These characterizations have been extended to many other contexts; for example
there are characterizations of the tree automata that correspond to sentences in
logics on trees [5].

   Automata processing finite words over infinite alphabets (so called *data words*)
are attracting significant interest from the database and verification communi-
ties, since they can be often used as low-level formalisms for representing and
reasoning about data streams, program traces, and serializations of structured

A. Dawar and H. Veith (Eds.): CSL 2010, LNCS 6247, pp. 110–124, 2010.

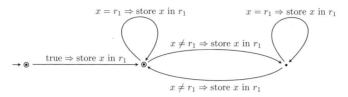

Fig. 1. A finite-memory automaton

documents. Moreover, properties specified using high-level formalisms (for instance, within suitable fragments of first-order logic) can be often translated
into equivalent automaton-based specifications, easing, in this way, the various
reasoning tasks.

Different models of automata which process words over infinite alphabets have
been proposed and studied in the literature (see, for instance, the surveys [6, 7]).
Pebble automata [8] use special markers to annotate *locations* in a data word. The
data automata of [9] parse data words in two phases, with one phase applying a
finite-state transducer to the input data word and another deciding acceptance
on the grounds of a classification of the maximal sub-sequences consisting of the
same data values. Of primary interest to us here will be a third category, the
finite memory automata [10], also called *register automata*, which make use of a
finite number of registers in order to store and eventually compare values in the
precessed data word.

It is known that the languages accepted by finite memory automata are strictly
contained in the languages definable in monadic second-order logic with the
successor relation and a binary relation to test data equality [8]. The first order
variant of this logic is incomparable in expressive power with deterministic finite
memory automata: The set of words of even length can be recognized by a finite
memory automaton but can not be defined in first-order logic; on the other hand
the set of words that have two positions with the same value can be expressed in
first-order logic, but it can not be recognized by any deterministic finite memory
automaton.

We will compare the expressive power of several restrictions of deterministic
finite memory automata with restrictions of MSO. We consider the class of finite
memory automata with a bounded number of registers as well as the class that
can only perform "local" data comparisons (within a fixed distance). We will
also look at several variants of first-order logic – we will look at logic where we
can use equality between any two symbols in the word, as well as logics where
one can only compare symbols "locally". We will look at logics where the word
ordering relation is present, as well as logics where only the successor relation
is available. We will also consider "non-uniform first-order definability" where a
different formula is used depending on the alphabet.

Our main goal is to find effective characterisations for these logics with respect
to the automata models described above. That is, we present algorithms that can
decide questions of the form: Given an automaton and a logic, can the language
of the automaton be defined in the logic?

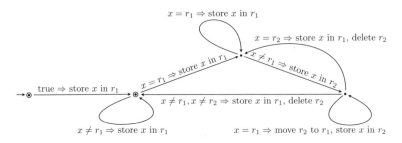

Fig. 2. A finite-memory automaton recognizing a first-order definable language

Example 1. Consider the automaton from Figure 1. We have had used an intuitive notation in the figure – a more precise syntax is given in Section 1. An edge is labeled with $g \Rightarrow a$ where, g is a guard (precondition) and a an action (postcondition); both g and a refer to the current symbol as x, and the ith register as r_i. This automaton accepts exactly the data words w such that there are an even number of places $n \le |w|$ with $w(n) \ne w(n-1)$. Our algorithms can check that this language is not definable in first-order logic with order and data equality, even in the non-uniform model. The automaton from Figure 2 accepts words such that for every n with $w(n) = w(n-1)$ there is $y > x$ such that $w(y) \ne w(y+1) \ne w(y+2)$ and $w(y) \ne w(y+2)$. Our techniques can determine that this language is first-order definable: in fact, definable using only local data comparisons.

We first show that one can not hope to characterize logical classes for many powerful classes of automata on infinite alphabets – for example, we show this for non-deterministic memory automata, and for two-way deterministic memory automata.

We thus focus on Deterministic Memory Automata (DMAs). We give a method for deciding non-uniform FO definability for two special classes of DMAs – 1-memory DMA and window automata (automata that can only make data comparisons locally). We then provide a decidable criterion for a DMA being expressible within the local variants of first-order logic. We then turn to non-local FO definability. The general question of decidability of non-local definability is open; however, we provide effective necessary and sufficient conditions for a subclass of DMA, the window automata, to be non-locally FO definable.

Organization: Section 1 explains the automata and logic formalisms that are the core topic of this paper, and their relationships. Section 2 gives undecidability results for several powerful models. Section 3 gives decidable criteria for non-uniform first order definability within certain classes of memory automata. Section 4 gives a decision procedure for first-order definability with only local data comparisons. Section 5 investigates the broader question of deciding first-order definability with unrestricted data comparisons. We do not resolve this question, but provide effective necessary conditions and effective sufficient criteria. Section 6 gives conclusions. All proofs can be found in [11].

1   Preliminaries

We fix an infinite alphabet D of $(data)$ $values$. A $(data)$ $word$ is a finite sequence of values from the infinite alphabet D. Two words u and v are said to be iso-morphic, and we denote it by $u \simeq v$, if $|u| = |v|$ and $u(i) = u(j)$ iff $v(i) = v(j)$ for all pairs of positions i, j in u. The $\simeq$-equivalence class of a word u, denoted by $[u]_{\simeq}$ or simply by $[u]$, is called the $\simeq$-$type$ of u. A $(data)$ $language$ is a set of data words. Given two words u and v, we write $u =_L v$ if either both u and v are in L, or both are not. From now on, we tacitly assume that any data language L is closed under $\simeq$-preserving morphisms, namely, $\simeq$ refines $=_L$.

1.1   Finite-Memory Automata

In this section, we introduce a variant of Kaminski's finite-memory automata [10] that recognize data languages over an infinite alphabet D. These automata process data words by storing a bounded number values into their memory and by comparing them with the incoming input values.

Definition 1. A k-memory automaton $(k$-$MA)$ is a tuple $A = (Q_0, \ldots, Q_k, q_I, F, T)$, where $Q_0, \ldots, Q_k$ are pairwise disjoint finite sets of states, $q_I \in Q_0$ is an initial state, and $F \subseteq Q_0 \cup \ldots \cup Q_k$ is a set of final states. T is a finite set of transitions of the form (p, α, E, q), where $p \in Q_i$ for some $i \le k$, α is the $\simeq$-type of a word of length $i + 1$, $E \subseteq \{1, \ldots, i+1\}$, and $q \in Q_j$ with $j = i + 1 - |E|$.

A $configuration$ of a k-MA A is a pair $(p, \bar{a})$ consisting of a state $p \in Q_i$, with $0 \le i \le k$, and a memory content $\bar{a} \in D^i$. The initial configuration is (q_I, ε), where ε denotes the empty memory content. The automaton can move from a configuration $(p, \bar{a})$ to a configuration $(q, \bar{b})$ by consuming an input symbol a iff there is a transition $(p, \alpha, E, q) \in T$ such that the word $\bar{a} \cdot a$ has $\simeq$-type α and $\bar{b}$ is obtained from $\bar{a} \cdot a$ by removing all positions in E.

We enforce the following sanity conditions to every transition (p, α, E, q) of a k-MA. First, we assume that E is non-empty whenever $q \in Q_k$ (this is in order to guarantee that the length of the target memory content $\bar{b}$ never exceeds k). Then, we assume that if the $\simeq$-type α is of the form $[\bar{a} \cdot a]$, with $\bar{a}(j) = a$ for some $1 \le j \le |\bar{a}|$, then E contains at least the index j (this is in order to guarantee that the target memory content $\bar{b}$ contains $pairwise$ $distinct$ elements).

A run of A is defined in the usual way. If u is a data word and A has a run on u from a configuration $(p, \bar{a})$ to a configuration $(q, \bar{b})$, then we denote this by writing either $u^A(p, \bar{a}) = (q, \bar{b})$ or $(p, \bar{a}) \xrightarrow{u}_{A} (q, \bar{b})$, depending on which is more convenient. The language recognized by A, denoted $L(A)$, is the set of all words u such that $u^A(q_I, \varepsilon) = (p, \bar{a})$, for some $p \in F$ and some $\bar{a} \in D^*$.

A finite-memory automaton $A = (Q_0, \ldots, Q_k, T, I, F)$ is $deterministic$ if for each pair of transitions $(p, \alpha, E, q), (p', \alpha', E', q') \in T$, if $p = p'$ and $\alpha = \alpha'$, then $E = E'$ and $q = q'$. Similarly, A is $complete$ if for every state $q \in Q_i$ and every $\simeq$-type α with $i+1$ variables, T contains a transition rule of the form (p, α, E, q). We abbreviate any $deterministic$ and $complete$ k-memory automaton by $(k$-$)DMA$.

Minimal deterministic finite-memory automata. Bouyer et. al. have given an algebraic characterization of the languages that are accepted by a generalization of DMA [12]. A Myhill-Neorde style characterization of the languages that are accepted by DMA was given by Francez and Kaminski in [13]. They state as an open question whether one can compute, given a DMA, a minimal DMA that accepts the same language. In [14] we gave a positive answer to this question. Precisely, we show that given a DMA that accepts a language L, one can compute a DMA A_L that has the minimum number of states and that stores the minimum number of data values for every consumed input word. A semantics-based definition of the set of values that need to be stored by any DMA A in order to recognize a given language L is as follows:

Definition 2. *Let L be a language. A value a is L-memorable in a word u if a occurs in u and there is a word v and a value $b \notin u \cdot v$ such that $u \cdot v \neq_L u \cdot v[a/b]$.*

We denote by $\mathsf{mem}_L(u)$ the sequence consisting of the L-memorable values of u in the order of their last appearance in u.

In [14], we showed that a language is DMA-recognizable iff the following equivalence relation has finite index:

Definition 3. *Given a language L, we define the equivalence $\equiv_L \subseteq D^* \times D^*$ such that $u \equiv_L v$ iff $\mathsf{mem}_L(u) \simeq \mathsf{mem}_L(v)$ and for all words $u', v' \in D^*$, if $\mathsf{mem}_L(u) \cdot u' \simeq \mathsf{mem}_L(v) \cdot v'$ then $u \cdot u' =_L v \cdot v'$.*

Let L be a language with equivalence $\equiv_L$ of finite index. We can define the *canonical automaton* for L as the k-memory automaton $A_L = (Q_0, \ldots, Q_k, q_I, F, T)$, where k is the maximum length of $\mathsf{mem}_L(u)$ over all words $u \in D^*$; Q_i, with $0 \leq i \leq k$, contains all $\equiv_L$-equivalence classes $[u]_{\equiv_L}$, with $u \in D^*$ and $|\mathsf{mem}_L(u)| = i$; q_I is the $\equiv_L$-equivalence class of the empty word; $F = \{[u]_{\equiv_L} \mid u \in L\}$; T contains all transitions of the form $([u]_{\equiv_L}, \alpha, E, [u \cdot a]_{\equiv_L})$, where $u \in D^*$, $a \in D$, α is the $\simeq$-type of $\mathsf{mem}_L(u) \cdot a$, and E is the set of positions in $\mathsf{mem}_L(u) \cdot a$ that have to be removed from $\mathsf{mem}_L(u) \cdot a$ to obtain $\mathsf{mem}_L(u \cdot a)$.

Theorem 1 ([14]). *Given a DMA A that recognizes L, the canonical automaton for L can be effectively computed from A.*

We will extensively exploit the following property of a canonical automaton A_L: after parsing an input word u, the automaton A_L stores exactly the sequence $\mathsf{mem}_L(u)$ of L-memorable values of u. It is also worth remarking that if two words lead to distinct states in the canonical automaton A_L, then they belong to distinct $\equiv_L$-equivalence classes.

Local finite-memory automata. A DMA A is *l-local* if for all configurations $(p, \bar{a})$ and all words u of length l, if $u^A(p, \bar{a}) = (q, \bar{b})$, then $\bar{b}$ contains only values that occur in u. We call *local* any DMA that is l-local for some $l \in \mathbb{N}$. The proof of the following Proposition can be found in [11].

Proposition 1. *The following problem is decidable: Given a DMA A, is A local? If A is local then we can compute the minimum number l for which A is l-local.*

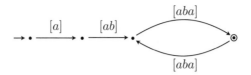

Fig. 3. A DWA that recognizes the language $L = \{aba \ldots ba \in D^* \mid a \neq b\}$

1.2   Window Automata

The class of languages recognized by local DMA can be equivalently defined using another model of automaton, which makes no use of memory:

Definition 4. *An l-window automaton (l-WA) is a tuple $A = (Q, q_I, F, T)$, where Q is a finite set of states, $q_I \in Q$ is an initial state, $F \subseteq Q$ is a set of final states, and T is a finite set of transitions of the form (p, α, q), where $p, q \in Q$ and α is the $\simeq$-type of a word of length at most l.*

An l-WA $A = (Q, q_I, F, T)$ processes an input word $u = a_1 \ldots a_n$ from left to right, starting form its initial state q_I, as follows. At each step of the computation, if A has consumed the first i symbols of the input word and has moved to state p, and if T contains a transition of the form (p, α, q), with $q \in Q$ and $\alpha = [a_{i+2-l} \ldots a_{i+1}]$, then A consumes the next symbol a_{i+1} of u and it moves to the target state q. The notions of successful run and recognized language are as usual.

   An l-WA is *deterministic* (denoted l-DWA) if for every pair of transitions $(p, \alpha, q), (p', \alpha', q') \in T$, if $p = p'$ and $\alpha = \alpha'$, then $q = q'$. Figure 3 shows an example of a 3-DWA.

   A *path* is a sequence of consecutive transitions in an automaton. A path ρ in a DWA is *realizable* if there is a word u that induces a run along ρ. For example, the path

$$p_0 \xrightarrow{[abc]} p_1 \xrightarrow{[aaa]} p_2$$

is not realizable: Assume that a window automaton uses the first transition to move from position i to $i + 1$ in the input word. This is only possible if the positions $i - 1, i, i + 1$ have pairwise different values. Then the next transition can not be used, as it requires that positions $i, i + 1, i + 2$ have the same value. A DWA A is *realizable* if all paths in A is realizable. Observe that an l-DWA is realizable iff for all transitions $(p, [a_1 \ldots a_n], q), (q, [b_1 \ldots b_m], r)$,

1. if $n \geq m - 1$, then $a_{n-m+2} \ldots a_n \simeq b_1 \ldots b_{m-1}$
2. if $n < m - 1$, then $a_1 \ldots a_n \simeq b_{m-n} \ldots b_{m-1}$.

Hence, it is decidable whether a DWA is realizable. In addition, for every DWA, there is an equivalent realizable DWA. Note that the DWA shown in Figure 3 is realizable.

Proposition 2. *For every l-local DMA, there is an equivalent l-DWA and, vice versa, for every l-DWA, there is an equivalent l-local (l-)DMA.*

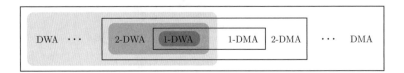

Fig. 4. The inclusions between DMA and DWA

In contrast to the above result, there is a non-local 1-DMA that recognizes the language $L = \{a_1 \dots a_n \in D^* \mid a_1 = a_n\}$, which is clearly not WA-recognizable.

Figure 4 shows the inclusions that hold between DMA and DWA.

1.3 Logics for Data Words

$\mathrm{MSO}(\sim, <)$ denotes monadic second-order logic with predicates $\sim$ and $<$, interpreted respectively by the data-equality relation and by the total order relation over the positions of a given data word. $\mathrm{FO}(\sim, <)$ is the restriction of $\mathrm{MSO}(\sim, <)$ that only uses quantification over first-order variables. An example of an $\mathrm{FO}(\sim, <)$ formula is $\forall x, y \ (x \sim y \rightarrow x = y)$, which requires all values in a data word to be distinct (observe that $=$ can be defined in terms of $<$). Note that the language defined by the above formula is not DMA-recognizable.

We also consider fragments of $\mathrm{FO}(\sim, <)$ where the predicates are replaced by local variants. For instance, $+1$ denotes the successor relation, which holds between two positions x and y (denoted $y = x + 1$) iff y is the immediate successor of x. We denote by $\mathrm{FO}(\sim, +1)$ the first-order logic where the total order $<$ has been replaced by the successor relation $+1$.

There is also a local variant of the data-equality relation: given $l \in \mathbb{N}$, $x \sim_l y$ can be viewed as a shorthand for the formula $y = x + l \wedge x \sim y$. We accordingly denote by $\mathrm{FO}(\sim_{\leq l}, <)$ the logic with the predicates $<$ and $\sim_i$, for all $i \leq l$. For example, the formula $\forall x, y \ \exists z \ (x \sim_5 y \rightarrow y \not\sim z)$ requires that if position y has the same value as its fifth neighbor x to the left, then there is a position z that has a different value than x and y.

It is easy to see that, for each number l, the language $L_l = \{a_1 \dots a_n \in D^* \mid n \geq l, \ a_1 = a_l\}$ can be defined in $\mathrm{FO}(\sim_{\leq l}, <)$, but not in $\mathrm{FO}(\sim_{\leq l-1}, <)$. Hence the family of logics $\mathrm{FO}(\sim_{\leq l}, <)$, where l ranges over $\mathbb{N}$, forms an infinite (strictly increasing) hierarchy. Note also that $\mathrm{FO}(\sim, +1)$ can express properties like "the first letter is equal to the last letter", which can not be expressed in $\mathrm{FO}(\sim_{\leq l}, <)$ for any $l \in \mathbb{N}$.

For each $n \in \mathbb{N}$, let D_n be a subset of D consisting of exactly n elements. We say that a language $L \subseteq D^*$ is definable in *non-uniform* $\mathrm{FO}(\sim, <)$, abbreviated $\mathrm{NUFO}(\sim, <)$, if for each $n \in \mathbb{N}$, the language $L_N = L \cap D_n^*$ can be defined in $\mathrm{FO}(\sim, <)$ (under the assumption that input words are over the finite alphabet D_n). Non-uniform variants of the other logics considered above are defined similarly.

Example 2. Consider the language $L_{2\times}$ of all words u whose length is two times the number of distinct values that occur in u. $L_{2\times}$ can not be defined in $\mathrm{FO}(\sim, <)$, but it is definable in $\mathrm{NUFO}(\sim, <)$ since $L_{2\times} \cap D_n^*$ is finite for every $n \in \mathbb{N}$.

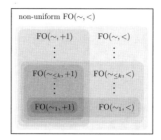

Fig. 5. An overview over some logics for data words

The above example shows that the non-uniform definability is much weaker than uniform definability (indeed, it can easily be shown that there are continuumly many non-uniformly definable languages for any of our signatures). Nonetheless, the following proposition shows that definability in the "local logic" $FO(\sim_{\leq k}, <)$ is equivalent to definability in $NUFO(\sim_{\leq k}, <)$, provided that we restrict to DMA-recognizable languages.

Proposition 3. *Let L be a language recognized by a DMA and let $l \in \mathbb{N}$. L can be defined in $NUFO(\sim_{\leq l}, <)$ iff it can be defined in $FO(\sim_{\leq l}, <)$. An analogous result holds when $<$ is replaced by $+1$.*

We do not know whether Proposition 3 holds also for the unrestricted logics $FO(\sim, <)$ and $FO(\sim, +1)$.

Figure 5 gives an overview over the logics considered so far.

1.4   DMA vs Logics

Recall that the class of languages recognized by (deterministic) finite-state automata strictly includes the class of languages over finite alphabets defined with first-order logic. This result does not extend to languages over infinite alphabets: the language of all words with pairwise distinct symbols can be defined in first-order logic with the (unrestricted) data-equality relation, but it can not be recognized by any DMA. As with languages over finite alphabets, the set of all (data) words of even length is clearly recognized by a 0-DMA, but it can not be defined in first-order logic. Hence, first-order logics and DMA are, in general, expressively incomparable.

For the restricted logics the situation is different. It follows from the next proposition that any language that is definable in $MSO(\sim_{\leq l}, +1)$ is recognized by an l-DMA. This also shows that local DMA are closed under the usual boolean operations, projection, concatenation, and Kleene star.

Proposition 4. *A language L can be defined in $MSO(\sim_{\leq l}, +1)$ iff it can be recognized by an l-local DMA.*

Figure 6 gives an overview over the relationships between logics and DMA.

FO($\sim$, +1)	MSO($\sim$, +1)	
$\bigcup_k$ FO($\sim_{\leq k}$, +1)	$\bigcup_k$ MSO($\sim_{\leq k}$, +1) = $\bigcup_k$ k-local DMA	$\bigcup_k$ k-DMA = DMA
$\vdots$	$\vdots$	$\vdots$
FO($\sim_{\leq k}$, +1)	MSO($\sim_{\leq k}$, +1) = k-local DMA	k-DMA
$\vdots$	$\vdots$	$\vdots$
FO($\sim_1$, +1)	MSO($\sim_1$, +1) = 1-local DMA	1-DMA

Fig. 6. Comparing the expressive power of automata with that of logics

Given that logics and automata are incomparable, we will focus on the problem of deciding *when an automaton-recognizable language is definable within a given logic*. The dual problem of determining when a logical sentence corresponds to a logic is not explored here – but it is easily shown to be undecidable for our most powerful logics, since the satisfiability problem for these logics is undecidable [8].

2   Undecidability Results

In this section we show that there is no hope for achieving effective characterizations of fragments of FO($\sim$, <) within several classes of languages recognized by automaton-based models stronger than DMA. We first consider the class of languages recognized by non-deterministic finite-memory automata (NMA):

Theorem 2. *Let $\mathcal{L}$ be a logic that is at most as expressive as FO($\sim$, <) and that can define the universal language D^*. The following problem is undecidable: Given an 3-NMA A, can L(A) be defined in $\mathcal{L}$?*

The proof (see [11]) is by reduction from the the Post Correspondence Problem (PCP) and it is along the same lines as the proof of Neven et al. that universality is undecidable for NMA [8].

Below, we show that similar negative results hold for two-way deterministic finite-memory automata DMA (2-way DMA) and for the weakest variant of pebble automata, namely, weak one-way pebble automata (weak 1-way DPA). We briefly sketch the distinctive features of these two models of automaton (see [8] for formal definitions). A 2-way DMA can revisit the same positions in a given input word several times, by moving its head in either direction. A pebble automaton, on the other hand, has the ability to mark a finite number of word positions by placing pebbles on them. The guards of the transitions of a 1-way DPA allow it to compare the current input value with the values of the positions marked by pebbles, but only the most recently placed pebble can be moved and only to the right. Moreover, in the *weak* variant of DPA, new pebbles are placed at the first position of the word. The proof of the following result is similar to that of Theorem 2 (and it can be found in [11]).

Theorem 3. *Let $\mathcal{L}$ be a logic that is at most as expressive as $FO(\sim,<)$ and that can define the universal language D^*. The following problem is undecidable: Given a 2-way 3-DMA A or a weak 1-way DPA A with 3 pebbles, can $L(A)$ be defined in $\mathcal{L}$?*

3   Characterizations of Non-Uniform FO

In this section we will look for effective characterizations of $\mathrm{NUFO}(\sim,<)$. Precisely, we will show that definability in $\mathrm{NUFO}(\sim,<)$ is decidable for languages recognized by local DMA and 1-memory DMA (these two models are incomparable in expressive power).

Theorem 4. *The following problem is decidable: Given a local DMA A, is $L(A)$ definable in $\mathrm{NUFO}(\sim,<)$?*

The idea of the proof is to show that $L = L(A)$ is definable in $\mathrm{NUFO}(\sim,<)$ iff $L_N = L \cap D_N$ is definable in $\mathrm{FO}(D_N,<)$, where N is a suitable number that depends only on A. The latter statement is decidable because L_N is a regular language over a finite alphabet and an effective characterization of regular language definable in $\mathrm{FO}(D_N,<)$ is known from [15]. One direction of this claim is straightforward: if L is definable in $\mathrm{NUFO}(\sim,<)$, then L_N is clearly definable in $\mathrm{FO}(D_N,<)$. For the opposite direction, we assume that L is not definable in $\mathrm{NUFO}(\sim,<)$. In this case, one can prove that there is a (potentially very big) number n such that $L_n = L \cap D_n$ can not be defined in $\mathrm{FO}(D_n,<)$. It follows from [15] that the minimal DFA A_n recognizing L_n has a counter. We then prove that there is a (potentially) much smaller alphabet D_N for which the minimal DFA A_N recognizing $L_N = L \cap D_N$ has a counter. Thus L_N can not be defined in $\mathrm{FO}(D_N,<)$. The full proof is in [11].

Below, we show that the analogous problem is decidable for 1-memory DMA. Observe that 1-DMA are incomparable with local DMA: On the one hand, the language of all words where the first value is equal to the last one is recognizable by 1-DMA, but not by local DMA. On the other hand, the language of all words where the third value is equal to either the first value or the second value is recognizable by local DMA, but not by 1-DMA.

Theorem 5. *The following problem is decidable: Given a 1-DMA A, is $L(A)$ definable in $\mathrm{NUFO}(\sim,<)$?*

The proof (see [11]) exploits, first, the fact that it is decidable whether a given DMA A is local. If A is local, then Theorem 4 can be applied and we are done. If A is not local, then A must contain certain 'non-local cycles'. By distinguishing several cases, depending on the way these cycles occur in A, it can be decided whether A is definable in $\mathrm{NUFO}(\sim,<)$.

4   Characterizations of Local FO

In this section we give effective characterizations for first-order logics with local predicates, namely, $FO(\sim_l, <)$ and $FO(\sim_l, +1)$. There are actually two variants of the definability problem for each of these logics. The first variant takes as input a DMA A and a number l and asks whether $L(A)$ is definable in $FO(\sim_l, <)$ (resp., $FO(\sim_l, +1)$). The second variant takes as input a DMA A and asks whether there is a number l such that A is definable in $FO(\sim_l, <)$ (resp., $FO(\sim_l, +1)$). The following theorem shows that both variants of the definability problems for $FO(\sim_l, <)$ and $FO(\sim_l, +1)$ are decidable.

Theorem 6. *The following problem is decidable: Given a DMA A, is there an l such that $L(A)$ is definable in $FO(\sim_{\leq l}, <)$? If such an l exists, then we can compute the minimal l_0 such that $L(A)$ is definable in $FO(\sim_{\leq l_0}, <)$. Analogous results hold when $<$ is replaced by $+1$.*

The proof exploits the fact that it is decidable whether a given (canonical) DMA A is local and, in such a case, one can compute the smallest l_0 such that A is l_0-local. We first show that if A is not local, then $L(A)$ is not definable in $FO(\sim_{\leq l}, <)$ (nor in $FO(\sim_{\leq l}, +1)$). Otherwise, if A is l-local, then we can reduce the $FO(\sim_{\leq l}, <)$ definability problem for L to a classical first-order definability problem for a regular language $\mathsf{abs}(L)$ over a finite alphabet, whose symbols are $\simeq$-types of words of length at most l. The argument for $FO(\sim_{\leq l}, +1)$ is similar. The full proof is in [11].

As an example, consider the 3-local DMA A equivalent to the 3-DWA depicted in Figure 3: if thought of as a DFA, such an automaton contains a counter over the $\simeq$-type $[aba]$, where $a \neq b$. It can then be proved that the data language $L(A)$ can not be defined in $FO(\sim_l, <)$, for any $l \in \mathbb{N}$.

The next corollary follows from Theorem 6 and Proposition 3.

Corollary 1. *The following problem is decidable: Given a DMA A, is there an l such that $L(A)$ is definable in $NUFO(\sim_{\leq l}, <)$? If such an l exists, then we can compute the minimal l_0 such that $L(A)$ is definable in $NUFO(\sim_{\leq l_0}, <)$. Analogous results hold when $<$ is replaced by $+1$.*

5   Necessary and Sufficient Conditions for $FO(\sim, <)$

The ultimate goal would be to decide, given a DMA, whether or not its language can be defined in the unrestricted first-order logic $FO(\sim, <)$. We present a partial decision procedure that classifies DWA (or, equivalently, local DMA) according to the $FO(\sim, <)$ definability of their recognized languages. For certain DWA, the algorithm answers correctly whether the recognized languages are definable in $FO(\sim, <)$ or not; for other DWA, the algorithm can only output "don't know".

Given a k-DWA A, we denote by $L^{\geq k}(A)$ the set of words in $L(A)$ that have length at least k. In the rest of this Section, we will only prove results about languages of the form $L^{\geq k}(A)$. This simplifies the presentation (for instance, we

Fig. 7. Two DWA. While $L(A_1)$ can be defined in $FO(\sim, <)$, $L(A_2)$ can not.

can assume that all $\simeq$-types in the transitions of a k-DWA have length exactly k) and or results easily generalize to arbitrary languages. As an example, the left DWA A_1 in Figure 7 recognizes language $\{u = aba \ldots ba \mid |u| \geq 3, a \neq b\}$, which is $L^{\geq 3}(A)$ where A is the DWA shown in Figure 3. Similarly, the right DWA A_2 recognizes the language of all constant words of odd length at least 3. Note that neither $L^{\geq 3}(A_1)$ nor $L^{\geq 3}(A_2)$ are definable in $FO(\sim_{\leq l}, <)$ for any l. On the other hand, $L^{\geq 3}(A_1)$ can be defined in $FO(\sim, <)$, while $L^{\geq 3}(A_2)$ can not. For the sake of simplicity, we will often write $L(A)$ instead of $L^{\geq k}(A)$.

To be able to effectively separate DWA recognizing languages in $FO(\sim, <)$ from DWA recognizing languages not in $FO(\sim, <)$, we extend DWA with some additional information. Precisely, we label the transitions with "parametrized types", which specify data-equalities between the local neighborhood of the current position and the local neighborhood of some other fixed position in the string (i.e., the parameter).

For $u \in D^k$ and $v \in D^l$, the k-*parametrized* l-*type* of (u, v) is the $\simeq$-type of $u \cdot v$, that is the set of words that are isomorphic to $u \cdot v$. We shortly denote this set by $[u; v]$. The set of all k-parametrized l-types is by $T_{k,l}$. To avoid confusion, we will refer to standard $\simeq$-types $[v]$ as *unparametrized* types through the rest of this section.

Definition 5. *A* parametrized k-window automaton *(k-PWA) is a tuple* $A = (Q, q_I, F, T)$, *where* Q *is a finite set of states,* $q_I \in Q$ *is an initial state,* $F \subseteq Q$ *is a set of final states, and* $T \subseteq Q \times T_{k-1,k} \times Q$ *is a finite set of transitions.*

The input to a k-PWA A is a pair of words $(u, w) \in D^{k-1} \times D^*$, called a *parametrized word*. A configuration of A is a pair (p, i), where p is a state of A and i ($\geq k$) is a position in w. The automaton A processes a parametrized word (u, w) in a single run, from left to right, starting from the initial configuration (q_I, k). At each step of the computation, A can move from a configuration (p, i) to a configuration $(q, i + 1)$ iff there is a transition of the form (p, α, q), with $u \cdot w[i - k + 2, i + 1] \in \alpha$. The notions of successful run and recognized (parametrized) language $L(A)$ are as usual. A k-PWA $A = (Q, q_I, f, T)$ is *deterministic* $(k$-DPWA$)$ if for every pair of transitions (p, α, q) and (p, α', q') in T, $\alpha = \alpha'$ implies $q = q'$. Note that a parametrized k-window automaton can be thought of as an window automaton that has k predicates for the first k symbols in the input string which it can evaluate when transitioning to a new state.

A path ρ in a PWA A is *realizable* if there is a parametrized word (u, w) that induces a run of A along it. A PWA A is *realizable* if all paths in it are realizable. It is easy to see that for any given k-PWA A, there is an equivalent realizable

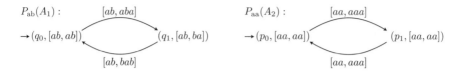

Fig. 8. The parametrized versions of the DWA of Figure 7

k-PWA A', which can be computed from A. Moreover, it can be decided whether a given PWA A is realizable or not (this test is similar to that for WA described in Section 1).

Definition 6. *Given a k-DWA $A = (Q, q_I, F, T)$ and a word u of length $k-1$, the u-parametrized version of A is the k-DPWA $P_u(A) = (\tilde{Q}, \tilde{q}_I, \tilde{F}, \tilde{T})$, where $\tilde{Q} = Q \times T_{k-1,k-1}$, $\tilde{q}_I = (q_I, [u; u])$, $\tilde{F} = \{(p, [v; w]) \in \tilde{Q} \mid p \in F\}$, and $\tilde{T}$ contains $(p, [u; a_1 \ldots a_{k-1}]) \xrightarrow{[u; a_1 \ldots a_k]} (q, [u; a_2 \ldots a_k])$ iff $(p, [a_1 \ldots a_k], q) \in T$.*

Figure 8 shows the ab-parametrized version of A_1 and the aa-parametrized version of A_2. Note that both are realizable.

We call *counter* of a DPWA B any cycle of transitions of the form

$$p_1 \xrightarrow{\bar{\alpha}} \ldots \xrightarrow{\bar{\alpha}} p_m \xrightarrow{\bar{\alpha}} p_1$$

where $m > 1$, $p_1, \ldots, p_m$ are pairwise distinct states of B and $\bar{\alpha}$ is a non-empty sequence of $(k-1)$-parametrized k-types.

The following result gives a sufficient condition for a language recognized by a DWA to be definable in $FO(\sim, <)$.

Proposition 5. *Let A be a DWA. If $P_u(A)$ is counter-free for all $u \in D^{k-1}$, then $L(A)$ is definable in $FO(\sim, <)$.*

The converse of the above proposition does not hold. Consider, for instance, the DWA A_3 in Figure 9: although $P_{ab}(A_3)$ has a counter (because $[ab, cdc] = [ab, dcd]$), $L(A_3)$ is still definable in $FO(\sim, <)$. We will thus distinguish between two kinds of counters, which we call "good" and "bad". We will show that if a DPWA contains a bad counter, then it recognizes a language that is not definable in $FO(\sim, <)$. In order to define bad counters, we need to consider a slightly modified (and more general) version of the automaton given in Definition 6.

Definition 7. *Let $A = (Q, q_I, F, T)$ be k-DWA and let $u, v \in D^{k-1}$. The (u, v)-parametrized version of A is the k-DPWA $P_{u,v}(A) = (\tilde{Q}, \tilde{q}_I, \tilde{F}, \tilde{T})$, where $\tilde{Q} = Q \times T_{k-1,k-1}$, $\tilde{q}_I = (q_I, [u; v])$, $\tilde{F} = \{(p, [v; w]) \in \tilde{Q} \mid p \in F\}$, and $\tilde{T}$ contains the transition $(p, [w; a_1 \ldots a_{k-1}]) \xrightarrow{[w; a_1 \ldots a_k]} (q, [w; a_2 \ldots a_k])$ iff $w \in D^{k-1}$ and $(p, [a_1 \ldots a_k], q) \in T$. We denote by $\mathcal{P}(A)$ the set $\{P_{u,v}(A) \mid u, v \in D^{k-1}\}$.*

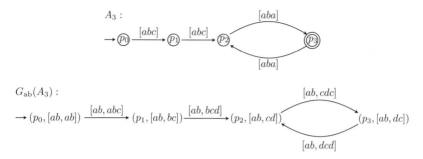

Fig. 9. A FO($\sim$, <) definable DWA and its parameterized version

Let A be a k-DWA and B be the (u, v)-parametrized version of A. A *bad counter* of B is a sequence of transitions

$$p_1 \xrightarrow{\bar{\alpha}_1} \ldots \xrightarrow{\bar{\alpha}_{n-1}} p_n \xrightarrow{\bar{\alpha}_n} p_{n+1} \xrightarrow{\bar{\alpha}} \ldots \xrightarrow{\bar{\alpha}} p_{n+m} \xrightarrow{\bar{\alpha}} p_{n+1}$$

such that

1. $n \geq 0$ and $m \geq 2$,
2. $p_1, \ldots, p_{n+m}$ are pairwise distinct states, and p_1 is of the form $(p, [u, u])$,
3. $\bar{\alpha}_1, \ldots, \bar{\alpha}_n, \bar{\alpha} \in T^l_{k-1,k}$ for some $l > 0$, and $\mathsf{loc}(\bar{\alpha}_1) = \ldots = \mathsf{loc}(\bar{\alpha}_n) = \mathsf{loc}(\bar{\alpha})$.

Here $\mathsf{loc} : T_{k-1,k} \to T_k$ is defined by $\mathsf{loc}([u, v]) = [v]$ and loc is extended to strings over $T_{k-1,k}$ in the usual way.

Similarly to a DWA, a DPWA A can be thought of as a deterministic finite-state automaton over the alphabet $T_{k-1,k}$ of $k - 1$-parametrized k-types. We say that A is *canonical* if A is minimal as a DFA. Clearly, a canonical DPWA contains only reachable states and for all pairs of states $p \neq q$, there is a $\bar{\alpha}$-labelled path that starts at p leads to an accepting state, while the $\bar{\alpha}$-labelled path that starts at q leads to a rejecting state. We can finally show that the absence of bad counters is a necessary condition for FO definability:

Proposition 6. *Let A be a canonical DWA. If there a DPWA $B \in \mathcal{P}(A)$ that contains a bad counter, then $L(A)$ is not definable in $FO(\sim, <)$.*

6   Conclusion

In this work we have studied a number of variants of first-order logic, and also introduced several natural subclasses of memory automata. We overviewed the relationships of the logics to one another, the relationships of the automata to one another, and the relationships of the logic and the automata. We then investigated the decidability of definability in logical classes within memory automata. We have shown that the problem is undecidable for natural extensions of deterministic memory automata, and decidable with certain restrictions on the

124   M. Benedikt, C. Ley, and G. Puppis

logics or the automata. Finally, we provide necessary and sufficient conditions
for determining when a memory automaton is definable within a logic.

The main question left open is an effective characterization of which deterministic memory automata are definable in first-order logic with unrestricted
data comparison. The conditions we give in Section 5 for window automata are
a step towards this. Another significant open question is the relationship between non-uniform and uniform (non-local) definability. Non-uniform first-order
definability is weaker then first-order definability for the vocabularies with unrestricted data equality, but we do not know if this separation is witnessed by
languages accepted by DMAs.

References

[1] Büchi, J.R.: Weak second-order logic and finite automata. S. Math. Logik Grun-
    lagen Math. 6, 66–92 (1960)
[2] Schützenberger, M.-P.: On finite monoids having only trivial subgroups. Informa-
    tion and Control 8, 190–194 (1965)
[3] McNaughton, R., Papert, S.A.: Counter-Free Automata. MIT, Cambridge (1971)
[4] Beauquier, D., Pin, J.-E.: Factors of words. In: Ronchi Della Rocca, S., Ausiello,
    G., Dezani-Ciancaglini, M. (eds.) ICALP 1989. LNCS, vol. 372. Springer, Heidel-
    berg (1989)
[5] Benedikt, M., Segoufin, L.: Regular Tree Languages Definable in FO and FOmod.
    TOCL 11 (2009)
[6] Segoufin, L.: Automata and logics for words and trees over an infinite alphabet.
    In: Ésik, Z. (ed.) CSL 2006. LNCS, vol. 4207, pp. 41–57. Springer, Heidelberg
    (2006)
[7] Schwentick, T.: Automata for XML - a survey. JCSS 73, 289–315 (2007)
[8] Neven, F., Schwentick, T., Vianu, V.: Finite state machines for strings over infinite
    alphabets. TOCL 5, 403–435 (2004)
[9] Bojanczyk, M., Muscholl, A., Schwentick, T., Segoufin, L., David, C.: Two-variable
    logic on words with data. In: LICS (2006)
[10] Kaminski, M., Francez, N.: Finite-memory automata. TCS 134 (1994)
[11] Benedikt, M., Ley, C., Puppis, G.: Automata vs. logics on data words (2010),
    http://www.comlab.ox.ac.uk/publications/publication3616-abstract.html
[12] Bouyer, P., Petit, A., Thérien, D.: An algebraic approach to data languages and
    timed languages. Inf. Comput. 182, 137–162 (2003)
[13] Francez, N., Kaminski, M.: An algebraic characterization of deterministic regular
    languages over infinite alphabets. TCS 306, 155–175 (2003)
[14] Benedikt, M., Ley, C., Puppis, G.: Minimal memory automata (2010),
    http://www.comlab.ox.ac.uk/michael.benedikt/papers/myhilldata.pdf
[15] Wilke, T.: Classifying discrete temporal properties. In: Meinel, C., Tison, S. (eds.)
    STACS 1999. LNCS, vol. 1563, p. 32. Springer, Heidelberg (1999)

Graded Computation Tree Logic with Binary Coding*

Alessandro Bianco, Fabio Mogavero, and Aniello Murano

Universitá degli Studi di Napoli "Federico II", via Cinthia, I-80126, Napoli, Italy
{alessandrobianco,mogavero,murano}@na.infn.it
http://people.na.infn.it/{alessandrobianco,mogavero,murano}

Abstract. *Graded path quantifiers* have been recently introduced and investigated as a useful framework for generalizing standard existential and universal path quantifiers in the branching-time temporal logic CTL (GCTL), in such a way that they can express statements about a minimal and conservative number of accessible paths. These quantifiers naturally extend to paths the concept of *graded world modalities*, which has been deeply investigated for the μ-CALCULUS (Gμ-CALCULUS) where it allows to express statements about a given number of immediately accessible worlds. As for the "non-graded" case, it has been shown that the satisfiability problem for GCTL and the Gμ-CALCULUS coincides and, in particular, it remains solvable in EXPTIME. However, GCTL has been only investigated w.r.t. graded numbers coded in unary, while Gμ-CALCULUS uses for this a binary coding, and it was left open the problem to decide whether the same result may or may not hold for binary GCTL. In this paper, by exploiting an automata theoretic-approach, which involves a model of alternating automata with satellites, we answer positively to this question. We further investigate the succinctness of binary GCTL and show that it is at least exponentially more succinct than Gμ-CALCULUS.

1 Introduction

Temporal logic is a suitable framework for reasoning about the correctness of concurrent programs [19, 20]. Depending on the view of the underlying nature of time, two types of temporal logics are mainly considered [14]. In *linear-time temporal logics*, such as LTL [19], time is treated as if each moment in time has a unique possible future. Conversely, in *branching-time temporal logics*, such as CTL [4] and CTL* [5], each moment in time may split into various possible futures and *existential* and *universal quantifiers* are used to express properties along one or all the possible futures. Recently in [2], *graded path modalities* have been introduced as a useful extension of these branching quantifiers in such a way that they can express statements about a *minimal* and *conservative* number of accessible paths. In particular, they allow to express properties such as "there are at least n minimal and conservative paths satisfying a formula ψ", by formally writing $E^{\geq n}\psi$, for suitable and well-formed concepts of minimality and conservativeness among paths. This generalization has been deeply investigated in [2] for the logic CTL, where the extended logic has been named GCTL. In particular, GCTL has been proved to be very powerful as it results in a logic more expressive

* Work partially supported by MIUR PRIN Project n.2007-9E5KM8.

A. Dawar and H. Veith (Eds.): CSL 2010, LNCS 6247, pp. 125–139, 2010.

than CTL where system specifications can be expressed in a very succinct way, without affecting the complexity of the logic. Indeed, the satisfiability problem for GCTL is EXPTIME-COMPLETE, as for CTL. There are several practical examples that show the usefulness of GCTL and we refer to [2, 6, 7] for a significant list.

Graded path modalities extend to paths the concept of *graded word modalities*, which has been investigated for several logics such as ALC, μ-CALCULUS, and the *first order logic* [3, 8, 10, 11, 22]. In particular, as for GCTL, the graded word modalities allow to extend the μ-CALCULUS (Gμ-CALCULUS, for short) in a very powerful logic, without increasing its computational complexity. Indeed, the satisfiability problem for the Gμ-CALCULUS remains solvable in EXPTIME. Despite its high expressive power, the Gμ-CALCULUS is considered in some sense a low-level logic (as this is intrinsic in the μ-CALCULUS), making it an "unfriendly" logic for users. On the contrary, although less expressive than the Gμ-CALCULUS, GCTL can easily and naturally express complex graded properties of computation trees. However, we recall that the logic introduced in [2] considers every number n appearing in a graded quantifier $E^{\geq n}\psi$ as coded in unary (*unary* GCTL), while the Gμ-CALCULUS, as it has been introduced and studied in [3, 11], considers these numbers as coded in binary[1]. In particular, the technique developed in [2] to solve the satisfiability problem for GCTL gives an exponential upper bound only in the unary case, while it gives a double-exponential upper bound if applied to the binary case. In [2], it was left as an open problem to check whether a single exponential upper bound may also hold for binary GCTL. We further remark that this problem was left open also in the case of "non-minimal" and "non-conservative" graded path quantifiers [7]. In this paper, we positively answer to this question. As for unary GCTL, we show an upper bound for the satisfiability of the binary GCTL, by exploiting an automata-theoretic approach [13, 23]. Before describing the technique we develop here, let us first recall the one we used in [2] for unary GCTL and discuss in detail the points that lead to a double-exponential upper bound when it is applied to binary GCTL. Then, we explain as we have managed these aspects for gaining the desired upper bound.

Recall that to develop a decision procedure automata-theoretic based for a logic with the tree model property, one first develops an appropriate notion of tree automata and studies their emptiness problem. Then, the satisfiability problem for the logic is reduced to the emptiness problem of the automata. To this aim, in [2], it has first shown that the tree model property for GCTL holds, by showing that each unary GCTL formula φ is satisfiable on a Kripke structure iff it has a tree model whose branching degree is polynomial in the size of φ. Then, a corresponding tree automaton model named *partitioning alternating Büchi tree automata* (PABT) has been introduced and shown that, for each unary GCTL formula φ, it is always possible to build in linear time a PABT accepting all tree models of φ. Then, by using a nontrivial extension of the Miyano and Hayashi technique [17] it has been shown an exponential translation of a PABT into a non-deterministic Büchi tree automata (NBT). Since the emptiness problem for NBT is solvable in polynomial time (in the size of the transition function that is polynomial in

---

[1] The Gμ-CALCULUS was first considered in the unary case [9] and it required much effort to be solved efficiently for the binary coding as well. This further gives an evidence that working with binary logics is rather than an easy task.

the number of states and exponential in the width of the tree in input) [24], we obtain that the satisfiability problem for unary GCTL is solvable in EXPTIME.

A detailed analysis on the above technique shows two points where it fails to give a single exponential-time algorithm when applied to binary GCTL. First, the tree model property shows for binary GCTL the necessity to consider also tree models with a branching degree exponential in the highest degree of the formula. Second, the number of states of the NBT derived from the PABT is double-exponential in the coding of the highest degree g of the formula. These two points reflect directly in the transition relation of the NBT, which turns to be double exponential in the coding of the degree g. To take care of the first point, we develop a sharp binary encoding of each tree model. In practice, for a given model $\mathcal{T}$ of φ we build a binary encoding $\mathcal{T}_D$ of $\mathcal{T}$, called *delayed generation tree*, such that, for each node x in $\mathcal{T}$ having $m+1$ children $x \cdot 0, \ldots, x \cdot m$, there is a corresponding node y of x in $\mathcal{T}_D$ and nodes $y \cdot 0^i$ having $x \cdot i$ as right child and $y \cdot 0^{(i+1)}$ as left child, for $0 \leq i \leq m$. To address the second point, we exploit a careful construction of the alternating automaton accepting all models of the formula, in a way that the graded numbers do not give any exponential blow-up in the translating of the automaton into an NBT.

We now describe the main idea behind the automata construction. Basically, we use alternating tree automata enriched with *satellites* (ATAS) as an extension of that introduced in [12]. In particular, we use the Büchi acceptance condition (ABTS). The satellite is a nondeterministic tree automaton and is used to ensure that the tree model satisfies some structural properties along its paths and it is kept apart from the main automaton. This separation, as it has been proved in [12], allows to solve the emptiness problem for Büchi automata in a time exponential in the number of states of the main automaton and polynomial in the number of states of the satellite. Then, we obtain the desired complexity by forcing the satellite to take care of the graded modalities and by noting that the main automaton is polynomial in the size of the formula.

The achieved result is even more appealing as we also show here that binary GCTL is much more succinct than Gμ-CALCULUS. We recall that some preliminary studies on this aspect were already carried out in [2], but only for the unary case. There, some examples in which unary GCTL is at least exponentially more succinct than binary Gμ-CALCULUS were also shown, but this does not hold in general as there are formulas from the latter that show the opposite[2]. In this paper, we show that binary GCTL is at least exponentially more succinct than binary Gμ-CALCULUS.

Finally, we report that in the full version we also discuss the application of the technique we have exploited for GCTL to the more expressive logic case of the binary *graded* CTL* (GCTL*, for short), i.e., CTL* augmented with graded path quantifiers. Clearly, we cannot simply use ABTS for GCTL*, as the Büchi acceptance condition is too weak already for CTL*. We use instead ATAS along with the hesitant condition (AHTS). Due to the particular semantics of the logic, based on minimality and conservativeness, we cannot use as automata states either formulas (as for GCTL) or atoms (i.e., consistent sets of formulas, as for CTL*). In fact, we need sets of atoms, instead. All these peculiarities lead to a 3EXPTIME satisfiability procedure for GCTL*.

---

[2] Note that in [2] it was erroneously stated that unary GCTL is in general exponentially more succinct than Gμ-CALCULUS.

Related work. Graded modalities along with CTL have been also studied in [6, 7], but under a different semantics. There, the authors consider overlapping paths (as we do) as well as disjoint paths, but they do not consider the concepts of minimality and conservativeness, which we deeply use in our logics, as it is well described and motivated in [2]. In [6] the model checking problem for non-minimal and non-conservative unary GCTL has been investigated. In particular, by opportunely extending the classical algorithm for CTL [4], they show that, in the case of overlapping paths, the model checking problem is PTIME-COMPLETE (thus not harder than CTL), while in the case of disjoint paths, it is in PSPACE and both NPTIME-HARD and CONPTIME-HARD. The work continues in [7], by showing a symbolic model checking algorithm for the binary coding and, limited to the unary case, a satisfiability procedure. Regarding the comparison between GCTL and graded CTL with overlapping paths studied in [6], it can be shown that they are equivalent by using an exponential reduction in both ways, whereas we do not know whether any of the two blow-up can be avoid. However, it is important to note that our technique can be also adapted to obtain an EXPTIME satisfiability procedure for the binary graded CTL under the semantics proposed in [6]. Indeed, it is needed only to slightly modify the transition function of the main automaton (w.r.t. until and release formulas), without changing the structure of the whole satellite. Moreover, it can be used to prove that, in the case of unary GCTL, the complexity of the satisfiability problem is only polynomial in the degree. Finally, our method can be also applied to the satisfiability of the Gμ-CALCULUS while the technique developed in [11] cannot be used for GCTL.

Due to space limitation, all proofs are omitted and reported in a full version of the paper. Preliminary materials on the subject can be found in [2].

2   Preliminaries

Given two *sets* X and Y of *objects*, we denote by $|X|$ the *size* of X, i.e., the number of its elements, by 2^X the *powerset* of X, i.e., the set of all its subsets, and by $Y^X \subseteq 2^{X \times Y}$ the set of *total functions* $f : X \mapsto Y$. By X^n we denote the set of all *n-tuples* of elements from X, by $X^* = \bigcup_{n=0}^{<\omega} X^n$ the set of *finite words* on the *alphabet* X, and by X^ω the set of *infinite words*, where as usual, ω is the *numerable infinity* and ε is the *empty word*. Moreover, by $|x|$ we denote the *length* of a word $x \in X^\infty = X^* \cup X^\omega$. As special sets, $\mathbb{N}$ is the sets of *natural numbers* and $[n]$ is its subset $\{k \in \mathbb{N} \mid k \leq n\}$, with $n \in \mathbb{N} \cup \{\omega\}$.

For a set Δ, we define a Δ-*tree* as a set $T \subseteq \Delta^*$ closed under *prefix*, i.e., if $w \cdot w' \in T$, with $w' \in \Delta$, then also $w \in T$, and we say that it is *full* iff it also holds that $w \cdot w'' \in T$, for all $w'' < w'$, where $< \subseteq \Delta \times \Delta$ is a strict order on the directions. The elements of T are called *nodes* and the empty word ε is the *root* of T. For every $w \in T$ and $w' \in \Delta$, the node $w \cdot w' \in T$ is a *successor* of w in T. For a finite set Σ, a Σ-*labeled* Δ-*tree* is a pair $\langle T, v \rangle$, where T is a Δ-tree and $v : T \mapsto \Sigma$ is a *labeling* function. When Δ and Σ are clear from the context, we call $\mathcal{T} = \langle T, v \rangle$ simply a (labeled) tree.

A *Kripke structure* (KRIPKE, for short) is a tuple $\mathcal{K} = \langle AP, W, R, L \rangle$, where AP is a finite non-empty set of *atomic propositions*, W is an enumerable non-empty set of *worlds*, $R \subseteq W \times W$ is a *transition* relation, and $L : W \mapsto 2^{AP}$ is a *labeling* function that maps each world to the set of atomic propositions true in that world. By $|\mathcal{K}| =$

$|R| \le |W|^2$ we denote the *size* of $\mathcal{K}$, which is also the size of the transition relation. A finite Kripke structure is a structure of finite size. A *path* of $\mathcal{K}$ is a finite or infinite sequence of worlds $\pi \in W^+ \cup W^\omega$ such that $(\pi_i, \pi_{i+1}) \in R$, for all $0 \le i < |\pi| - 1$. By $\mathrm{Pth}^\infty(w) \subseteq W^+ \cup W^\omega$ (resp., $\mathrm{Pth}(w) \subseteq W^+$) we denote the sets of all (resp., finite) paths starting at the world $w \in W$, i.e., $\pi \in \mathrm{Pth}^\infty(w)$ implies $\pi_0 = w$. Let π and π' be two paths. We say that π' is a *subpath* of π, in symbols $\pi' \le \pi$, iff π' is a non-necessarily proper prefix of π. Moreover, we say that π and π' are *comparable* iff *(i)* $\pi \le \pi'$ or *(ii)* $\pi' \le \pi$ holds, otherwise they are *incomparable*. For a set of paths X, we define the set of *minimal subpaths* (antichain) $\min(X)$ as the set consisting of the $\le$-*minimal* elements of X, i.e., it is the set containing all and only the paths $\pi \in X$ such that for all $\pi' \in X$, it holds that *(i)* $\pi \le \pi'$ or *(ii)* $\pi' \not\le \pi$. Note that all paths in $\min(X)$ are incomparable among them. A path π is *minimal* w.r.t. a set X (or simply minimal, when the context clarify the set X) iff $\pi \in \min(X)$. A set of paths X is minimal iff $X = \min(X)$.

The *unwinding* of a KRIPKE $\mathcal{K}$ starting at the world w is a 2^{AP}-labeled W-tree $\mathcal{T}_{\mathcal{K},w} = \langle T, v \rangle$ for which there exists a bijective function unw, called *unwinding function*, such that *(i)* $\mathrm{unw}(w) = \varepsilon$, *(ii)* $\mathrm{unw}(\pi) = \mathrm{unw}(\pi_0 \cdot \ldots \cdot \pi_{l-2}) \cdot \pi_{l-1}$, and *(iii)* $v(\mathrm{unw}(\pi_i)) = L(\pi_i)$, for all $\pi \in \mathrm{Pth}(w)$ and $0 \le i \le l = |\pi| > 1$. In this work, we also consider as unwindings of $\mathcal{K}$ also all 2^{AP}-labeled $\mathbb{N}$-tree that are isomorph to $\mathcal{T}_{\mathcal{K},w}$.

Finally, let $n \in \mathbb{N} \setminus \{0\}$. Then, we define $P(n)$ as the set of all *solutions* $\{p_i\}$ of the *linear Diophantine equation* $1 * p_1 + 2 * p_2 + \ldots + n * p_n = n$ and $C(n)$ as the set of all the *cumulative solutions* $\{c_i\}$ obtained by summing increasing sets of elements from $\{p_i\}$. Formally, $P(n) = \{\{p_i\} \in \mathbb{N}^n \mid \sum_{i=1}^n i * p_i = n\}$ and $C(n) = \{\{c_i\} \in \mathbb{N}^n \mid \exists \{p_i\} \in P(n). \forall 1 \le i \le n. c_i = \sum_{j=i}^n p_j\}$. Note that $|C(n)| = |P(n)|$ and, since for each solution $\{p_i\}$ of the above Diophantine equation there is exactly one *partition* of n, we have that $|C(n)| = p(n)$, where $p(n)$ is the number of partitions of n. By [1], it holds that $|C(n)| = \Theta(\frac{1}{n} \cdot 2^{k \cdot \sqrt{n}})$, with $k = \pi \cdot \log e \cdot \sqrt{2/3}$.

3   Full Graded Computation Tree Logic

We now define syntax and semantics of GCTL*.

Syntax. The *graded computation tree logic* (GCTL*) extends CTL* by using two special path quantifiers, the existential $E^{\ge g}$ and the universal $A^{<g}$, where g denotes the corresponding *degree*. As in CTL*, these quantifiers can prefix a linear-time formula composed of an arbitrary combination and nesting of the temporal operators X (*"effective next"*), $\tilde{X}$ (*"hypothetical next"*), U (*"until"*), and R (*"release"*). The quantifiers $A^{<g}$ and $E^{\ge g}$ can be respectively read as *"all but g minimal paths"* and *"there exist at least g minimal paths"*. The formal syntax of GCTL* follows.

Definition 1. (Syntax) *GCTL* state (φ) and path (ψ) formulas are built inductively from AP using the following context-free grammar, where $p \in \mathrm{AP}$ and $g \in \mathbb{N} \setminus \{0\}$:*

1. $\varphi ::= p \mid \neg\varphi \mid \varphi \wedge \varphi \mid \varphi \vee \varphi \mid E^{\ge g}\psi \mid A^{<g}\psi,$
2. $\psi ::= \varphi \mid \neg\psi \mid \psi \wedge \psi \mid \psi \vee \psi \mid X\psi \mid \tilde{X}\psi \mid \psi U \psi \mid \psi R \psi.$

The class of GCTL* formulas is the set of state formulas generated by the above grammar. In addition, the simpler class of GCTL formulas is obtained by forcing each *temporal operator, occurring in a formula, to be coupled with a path quantifier, as in the classical definition of* CTL.

For a state formula φ, we define the *degree* $\mathring{\varphi}$ of φ as the maximum natural number g occurring among the degrees of all its path quantifiers. We assume that all such degrees are coded in binary. The *length* of φ, denoted by $|\varphi|$, is defined as for CTL* and does not consider the degrees at all. Accordingly, the *size* of φ, denoted by $\|\varphi\|$, is defined in the same way that the length, by considering $\|E^{\geq g}\psi\|$ and $\|A^{<g}\psi\|$ to be equal to $\log(g+1) + \|\psi\|$. Clearly, it holds that $\log(\mathring{\varphi}) \leq \|\varphi\|$ and $|\varphi| \leq \|\varphi\|$. We use $cl(\varphi)$ to denote the classical Fischer-Ladner closure of φ augmented in a way that if $E^{\geq g}\varphi_1 R \varphi_2 \in cl(\varphi)$ (resp., $A^{<g}\varphi_1 U \varphi_2 \in cl(\varphi)$) then also $E^{\geq 1}\varphi_1 R \varphi_2 \in cl(\varphi)$ (resp., $A^{<\mathring{\varphi}}\varphi_1 U \varphi_2 \in cl(\varphi)$). Moreover, by $ecl(\varphi)$ (resp., $ecl(\varphi)^{\exists}$, $ecl(\varphi)^{\forall}$) we denote the set of all the (resp., existential, universal) quantification formulas in $cl(\varphi)$ deprived of the degree. Finally, by $rcl(\varphi)$ we denote the set of quantification formulas in $cl(\varphi) \cup ecl(\varphi)$ of the form $E^{\geq 1}\varphi_1 R \varphi_2$, $A^{<\mathring{\varphi}}\varphi_1 U \varphi_2$, and $A\varphi_1 R \varphi_2$.

Semantics. We now define the semantics of GCTL* w.r.t. a KRIPKE $\mathcal{K} = \langle AP, W, R, L \rangle$. For a world $w \in W$, we write $\mathcal{K}, w \models \varphi$ to indicate that a state formula φ holds at w, and, for a path $\pi \in Pth^{\infty}(w)$, we write $\mathcal{K}, \pi, k \models \psi$ to indicate that a path formula ψ holds on π at position $k \in [|\pi| - 1]$. Note that, the relation $\mathcal{K}, \pi, k \models \psi$ does not hold for any point $k \in \mathbb{N}$, with $k \geq |\pi|$. For a better readability, in the semantics definition of GCTL* we use the special set $P_A(\psi, w)$ and its dual $P_E(\psi, w)$, with the following meaning: $P_A(\psi, w)$ contains every path π starting in w such that all its extensions π' (including π) satisfy the path formula ψ. The semantics of GCTL* state formulas of the form $A^{<g}\psi$ and $E^{\geq g}\psi$ follows. The semantics of the remaining GCTL* state formulas and all GCTL* path formulas is defined as usual in CTL*.

Definition 2. (Semantics of $E^{\geq g}$ and $A^{<g}$) *Given a* KRIPKE $\mathcal{K} = \langle AP, W, R, L \rangle$, *a world* $w \in W$, *a natural number* $g \in \mathbb{N} \setminus \{0\}$, *and a* GCTL* *path formula* ψ, *we have:*

1. $\mathcal{K}, w \models E^{\geq g}\psi$ *iff* $|\min(P_A(\psi, w))| \geq g$;
2. $\mathcal{K}, w \models A^{<g}\psi$ *iff* $|\min(Pth^{\infty}(w) \setminus P_E(\psi, w))| < g$;

where $P_A(\psi, w) = \{\pi \in Pth^{\infty}(w) \mid \forall \pi' \in Pth^{\infty}(w).\pi \leq \pi' \implies \mathcal{K}, \pi', 0 \models \psi\}$ *and* $P_E(\psi, w) = \{\pi \in Pth^{\infty}(w) \mid \exists \pi' \in Pth^{\infty}(w) : \pi \leq \pi' \wedge \mathcal{K}, \pi', 0 \models \psi\}$.

Note that GCTL* formulas with degrees 1 are CTL* formulas. Moreover, the above definition of $P_A(\psi, w)$ and $P_E(\psi, w)$ formally states that they are dual of each other, i.e., $P_A(\psi, w) = Pth^{\infty}(w) \setminus P_E(\neg\psi, w)$.

In the rest of the paper, we only consider formulas in *positive normal form* (pnf, for short), i.e., the negation is applied only to atomic propositions. Under this assumption, we consider $\neg\varphi$ as the pnf formula equivalent to the negation of φ. Moreover, we only consider formulas that do not contain any subformula of the form $E^{\geq g}\tilde{X} \varphi$ or $A^{<g}X \varphi$. This can be done w.l.o.g. since each formula can be linearly translated into another formula not containing the above quantifications (see [2] for more). Finally, as abbreviation we use the boolean values t (*"true"*) and f (*"false"*).

We now give the formal definition of *conservativeness* and then, by means of two examples, we clarify the need of the concepts of minimality and conservativeness. A path π of $\mathcal{K}$ is conservative w.r.t. a path formula ψ iff, for all paths π' extending π, i.e., with $\pi \leq \pi'$, it holds that $\mathcal{K}, \pi', 0 \models \psi$. Note that this concept of conservativeness is automatically embedded in the definition of the set $P_A(\psi, w)$, since we consider only paths $\pi \in \text{Pth}^\infty(w)$ that, if extended, continue to satisfy the formula ψ. Now, for the minimality, consider a finite tree $\mathcal{T}$ having just three nodes all labeled by p, the root and two of its successors. Also, consider the formula $\varphi = E^{\geq 2}F\,p$. Because of the minimality, the two paths of length two that satisfy $F\,p$ collapse into the path containing just the root, hence $\mathcal{T} \not\models \varphi$. For the conservativeness, consider another tree $\mathcal{T}'$ equal to $\mathcal{T}$, but with one of the two root successors not labeled with p. Also, consider the formula $\varphi' = E^{\geq 2}G\,p$. At this point, by the conservativeness, we have that $\mathcal{T}' \not\models \varphi'$ even if there are two paths satisfying the formula $G\,p$, the root alone and its extension with one of the children, since the former is not conservative. Indeed, this path can be extended into a path that does not satisfy $G\,p$.

Let $\mathcal{K}$ be a Kripke structure and φ be a GCTL* formula. Then, $\mathcal{K}$ is a *model* for φ, denoted by $\mathcal{K} \models \varphi$, iff there is $w \in W$ such that $\mathcal{K}, w \models \varphi$. In this case, we also say that $\mathcal{K}$ is a model for φ on w. A GCTL* formula φ is said *satisfiable* iff there exists a model for it. For all state formulas φ_1 and φ_2 (resp., path formulas ψ_1 and ψ_2), we say that φ_1 is *equivalent* to φ_2, formally $\varphi_1 \equiv \varphi_2$, (resp., ψ_1 is *equivalent* to ψ_2, formally $\psi_1 \equiv \psi_2$) iff for all Kripke structures $\mathcal{K}$ and worlds $w \in W$ it holds that $\mathcal{K}, w \models \varphi_1$ iff $\mathcal{K}, w \models \varphi_2$ (resp., $\min(P_A(\psi_1, w)) = \min(P_A(\psi_2, w)))$.

The following lemma shows two exponential fixed point equivalences that extend to "graded" formulas the correspondign well-known result for "ungraded" formulas. These interesting equivalences among GCTL* formulas, are useful to describe important properties of the GCTL semantics.

Lemma 1 ([2]). *Let φ_1 and φ_2 be state formulas, $g > 1$, and $\text{ex}\langle \psi, g \rangle = \bigvee_{\{c_i\} \in C(g)}$ $\bigwedge_{i=1}^g E^{\geq c_i} X E^{\geq i} \psi$. Then, the following equivalences hold:*

1. $E\varphi_1 U \varphi_2 \equiv \varphi_2 \vee \varphi_1 \wedge \text{ex}\langle \varphi_1 U \varphi_2, 1 \rangle$
2. $E^{\geq g}\varphi_1 U \varphi_2 \equiv \neg\varphi_2 \wedge \varphi_1 \wedge \text{ex}\langle \varphi_1 U \varphi_2, g \rangle$
3. $E\varphi_1 R \varphi_2 \equiv \varphi_2 \wedge (\varphi_1 \vee E\tilde{X}\,f \vee \text{ex}\langle \varphi_1 R \varphi_2, 1 \rangle)$
4. $E^{\geq g}\varphi_1 R \varphi_2 \equiv \varphi_2 \wedge \neg\varphi_1 \wedge EXE\neg(\varphi_1 R \varphi_2) \wedge \text{ex}\langle \varphi_1 R \varphi_2, g \rangle$

Finally, by using a simple proof by induction, it is possible to show that GCTL* is invariant under the unwinding of a model. Hence, the next theorem follows.

Theorem 1. GCTL* *satisfies the tree model property.*

4 Succinctness

In this section, we show that binary GCTL is at least exponentially more succinct than binary Gμ-CALCULUS. We prove the statement by showing a class of GCTL formulas φ_g whose minimal equivalent Gμ-CALCULUS formulas χ_g needs to be in size exponentially bigger than (the size of) φ_g. Classical techniques ([15, 16, 25]) rely on the fact that in the more succinct logic there exists a formula having a *least finite model* whose size is double exponential in the size of the formula, while in the less succinct logic every formula has finite models of size at most exponential in its size. Unfortunately, in our case we cannot apply this idea, since, as far as we know, both GCTL and the

Gμ-CALCULUS satisfy the small model property, i.e., all their satisfiable formulas have always a model at most exponential in their size. To prove the succinctness of GCTL, hence, we explore a technique based on a characteristic property of our logic. Specifically, it is based on the fact that, using GCTL, we can write a set of formulas φ_g each one having a number of "characterizing models" that is exponential in the degree g of φ_g, while every Gμ-CALCULUS formula has at most a polynomial number of those models in its degree.

Consider the property "in a tree, there are exactly g grandchildren of the root labeled with p and having only one path leading from them, while all other nodes are not". Such a property can be easily described by the GCTL formula $\varphi_g = \varphi' \wedge \varphi''_g$, where $\varphi' = \neg p \wedge$ AX$(\neg p \wedge$ AX$(p \wedge$ AX AG$(\neg p \wedge A^{<2}\tilde{X}\, f)))$ and $\varphi''_g = E^{=g}F\, p$. Its size is $\Theta(\lceil \log(g+1)\rceil)$. We claim that a G$\mu$-CALCULUS formula χ_g requires exponential size to express the same property. More formally, our aim is to prove the following theorem.

Theorem 2. *Let* $\varphi_g = (E^{=g}F\, p) \wedge \varphi'$, *with* $g \in \mathbb{N}$ *and* $\varphi' = \neg p \wedge$ AX$(\neg p \wedge$ AX$(p \wedge$ AXAG$(\neg p$ $\wedge A^{<2}\tilde{X}f)))$. *Then, each* G$\mu$-CALCULUS *formula* χ_g *equivalent to* φ_g *has size* $\Omega(2^{\|\varphi_g\|})$.

The proof of this theorem proceeds directly by proving the following lemma and observing that, since $\|\varphi_g\| = \Theta(\lceil \log(g+1)\rceil)$, we can easily derive that $\|\chi_g\| = \Omega(2^{\|\varphi_g\|})$.

Lemma 2. *Every* Gμ-CALCULUS *formula* χ_g *equivalent to* φ_g *is of size* $\Omega(g)$.

5   GCTL Satisfiability

In this section, we describe the satisfiability procedure for GCTL. As we discussed in the introduction, we exploit an automata-theoretic approach by using satellites that are used to accept binary tree-encodings of tree models of a formula. So, we first introduce the automata model, then we discuss the binary tree encoding, and finally, we show how to build the automaton accepting all tree-model encodings of a given formula.

Tree automata with satellites. *Alternating tree automata* (ATA) [18] are a generalization of nondeterministic tree automata. Intuitively, on visiting a node of the input tree, while the latter sends exactly one copy of itself to each of the successors of the node, an ATA can send several copies of itself to the same successor. As a generalization of ATA, here we consider *alternating tree automata with satellites* (ATAS), in a similar way it has been done in [12], with the main difference that our satellites are nondeterministic and can work on trees and not only on words. The satellite is used to ensure that the input tree satisfies some structural properties and it is kept apart from the main automaton as it allows to show a tight complexity for the satisfiability problem. The formal definitions follow.

Definition 3. *An ATA is a tuple* $\mathcal{A} = \langle \Sigma, \Delta, Q, \delta, q_0, F \rangle$, *where* Σ, Δ, *and* Q *are nonempty finite sets of* input symbols, directions, *and* states, *respectively,* $q_0 \in Q$ *is an* initial state, F *is an* acceptance condition *to be defined later, and* $\delta : Q \times \Sigma \mapsto B^+(\Delta \times Q)$ *is an* alternating transition function *that maps a state and an input symbol to a positive boolean combination of moves in* $\Delta \times Q$.

Definition 4. *A run of an ATA $\mathcal{A}$ on a Σ-labeled Δ-Tree $\mathcal{T} = \langle T, v \rangle$ is a $(Q \times T)$-labeled $\mathbb{N}$-tree $\langle Tr, r \rangle$ such that (i) $r(\varepsilon) = (q_0, \varepsilon)$ and (ii) for all $y \in Tr$ with $r(y) = (q, x)$, there is a set $S \subseteq \Delta \times Q$ with $S \models \delta(q, v(x))$, such that, for all $(i, q') \in S$, there is a $j \in \mathbb{N}$ for which $r(y \cdot j) = (q', x \cdot i)$ holds.*

In the following, we consider ATA along with the *Büchi* acceptance condition $F \subseteq Q$ (ABT) (see [13] for more). By $L(\mathcal{A})$ we denote the language accepted by the automaton $\mathcal{A}$, i.e., the set of all trees $\mathcal{T}$ accepted by $\mathcal{A}$. Moreover, $\mathcal{A}$ is said to be *empty* if $L(\mathcal{A}) = \emptyset$. The emptiness problem for $\mathcal{A}$ is to decide whether $L(\mathcal{A}) = \emptyset$.

We now define automata with satellite.

Definition 5. *An ATAS is a tuple $\langle \mathcal{A}, S \rangle$, where $\mathcal{A} = \langle \Sigma \times P', \Delta, Q, \delta, q_0, F \rangle$ is an ATA and $S = \langle \Sigma, \Delta, P, \zeta, P_0 \rangle$ is a satellite, where $P = P' \times P''$ is a non-empty finite set of states, $P_0 \subseteq P$ is a set of initial states, and $\zeta : P \times \Sigma \mapsto 2^{P^{\Delta}}$ is a nondeterministic transition function that maps a state and an input symbol to a set of functions from directions to states.*

For the coming definition we need an extra notation. Given a $(\Sigma' \times \Sigma'')$-labeled Δ-tree $\mathcal{T} = \langle T, v \rangle$, we define the *projection* of $\mathcal{T}$ on Σ' as the Σ'-labeled Δ-tree $\mathcal{T}' = \langle T, v' \rangle$ such that, for all nodes $x \in T$, we have $v(x) = (v'(x), \sigma)$, for some $\sigma \in \Sigma''$.

Definition 6. *A tree $\mathcal{T}$ is accepted by an ATAS $\langle \mathcal{A}, S \rangle$, where $\mathcal{A} = \langle \Sigma \times P', \Delta, Q, \delta, q_0, F \rangle$, $S = \langle \Sigma, \Delta, P, \zeta, P_0 \rangle$, and $P = P' \times P''$, iff there exists a run $\mathcal{R}$ of S on $\mathcal{T}$, i.e., a $(\Sigma \times P)$-labeled Δ-tree, whose projection on $\Sigma \times P'$ is accepted by the ATA $\mathcal{A}$.*

In words, first the satellite S guesses and adds to the input tree $\mathcal{T}$ and additional labeling on the set P', thus returning the augumented tree $\mathcal{R}$. Then, the main automaton $\mathcal{A}$ computes a new run on $\mathcal{R}$ as input.

In the following, we also consider ATAS along with the Büchi condition (ABTS).

Note that satellites are just a convenient way to describe an ATA in which the state space can be partitioned into two components, one of which is nondeterministic and independent from the other, and has no influence on the acceptance. Indeed, it is just a matter of technicality to see that automata with satellites inherit all the closure properties of alternating automata. In particular, the following theorem, directly derived by the proof idea of [12], shows how the separation between $\mathcal{A}$ and S gives a tight analysis of the complexity of the relative emptiness problem.

Theorem 3. *The emptiness problem for an ABTS $\langle \mathcal{A}, S \rangle$, where $\mathcal{A}$ has n states and d directions and S has m states, can be decided in time $2^{O(n \cdot \log(m) \cdot d)}$.*

Binary tree model encoding. As first step, we define the infinite widening of a formula tree model $\mathcal{T}$, i.e., a transformation that, taken $\mathcal{T}$, returns a full infinite tree $\mathcal{T}_W$ having infinite branching degree and embedding $\mathcal{T}$. This transformation ensures that in $\mathcal{T}$ all nodes have the same branching degree and all branches are infinite. To this aim, we use a fresh label # as described in the following definition.

Definition 7 (Infinite Widening). *Let $\mathcal{T} = \langle T, v \rangle$ be a Σ-labeled Δ-tree, with $\Delta \subseteq \mathbb{N}$ and such that $\# \notin \Sigma$. Then, the infinite widening of $\mathcal{T}$ is the Σ_W-labeled $\mathbb{N}$-tree $\mathcal{T}_W = \langle \mathbb{N}^*, v_W \rangle$ such that (i) $\Sigma_W = \Sigma \cup \{\#\}$, (ii) for $x \in T$, $v_W(x) = v(x)$, and (iii) for $y \in \mathbb{N}^* \setminus T$, $v_W(y) = \#$.*

Now, we define a sharp transformation of $\mathcal{T}_W$ in a full binary tree $\mathcal{T}_D$. This is inspired but different from that used to embed the logic $S\omega S$ into $S2S$ [21]. Intuitively, the transformation allows to delay n decisions, to be take at a node y in $\mathcal{T}_W$ and corresponding to its successors $y \cdot i$, along some corresponding nodes $x, x \cdot 0, x \cdot 00, \ldots$ in $\mathcal{T}_D$. In particular, when we are on a node $x \cdot 0^i$, we are able to split the decision on $y \cdot i$ into an immediate action, which is sent to the right (effective) successor $x \cdot 0^i \cdot 1$, while the remaining actions are sent to its copy $x \cdot 0^{i+1}$. To differentiate the meaning of left and right successors we use the fresh symbol $\perp$.

Definition 8 (Delayed Generation). *Let* $\mathcal{T}_W = \langle \mathbb{N}^*, v_W \rangle$ *be the infinite widening of a Σ-labeled tree $\mathcal{T}$ such that $\perp \notin \Sigma$. Then, the* delayed generation *of $\mathcal{T}$ is the Σ_D-labeled $\{0,1\}$-tree $\mathcal{T}_D = \langle \{0,1\}^*, v_D \rangle$ such that (i) $\Sigma_D = \Sigma_W \cup \{\perp\}$ and (ii) there exists a surjective function $f : \{0,1\}^* \mapsto \mathbb{N}^*$, with $f(\varepsilon) = \varepsilon$, $f(x \cdot 0^i) = f(x)$, and $f(x \cdot 0^i \cdot 1) = f(x) \cdot i$, where $x \in \{0,1\}^*$ and $i \in \mathbb{N}$, such that (ii.i) $v_D(x) = v_W(f(x))$, for all $x \in \{\varepsilon\} \cup \{0,1\}^* \cdot \{1\}$, and (ii.ii) if $v_W(f(x)) \neq \#$, then either $v_D(x \cdot 0) = \perp$ and $v_D(x \cdot 1) \neq \#$ or $v_D(x \cdot 0) = v_D(x \cdot 1) = \#$, else $v_D(x \cdot 0) = \#$, for all $x \in \{0,1\}^*$.*

To complete the tree encoding, we have also to delay the degree associated to each node in the input tree model. We recall that, an original tree model of a graded formula may require a fixed number of paths satisfying the formula going through the same node. Such a number is the degree associated to that node and which we need to delay. To this aim, we enrich the label of a node with a function mapping a set of elements, named *bases*, into triples of numbers representing the splitting of the node degree into two components. The first is the delayed degree, while the second is the degree associated to one of the effective successors of the node. Such a splitting is the delayed action mentioned above customized to the need of having information on the degrees. This is formalized in the following four definitions.

Definition 9 ((Σ,B)-Enriched g-Degree Tree). *Let Σ and B be two sets, $g \in \mathbb{N}$, and $H(g) \subset \mathbb{N}^3$ be the set of triples (d, d_1, d_2) such that $d = d_1 + d_2 \leq g$. Then, a (Σ,B)-enriched g-degree tree is a $(\Sigma \times H(g)^B)$-labeled $\{0,1\}$-tree $\mathcal{T} = \langle \{0,1\}^*, v \rangle$.*

We now introduce (Σ_D, B)-enriched g-degree trees $\mathcal{T}_{D_{B,g}}$ as the extension of the delayed generation $\mathcal{T}_D$ of $\mathcal{T}$ with degree functions in its labeling. Intuitively, each function in a node represents how to distribute and propagate an information on the degrees along its successors.

Definition 10 (B-Based g-Degree Delayed Generation). *Let B be a set, $g \in \mathbb{N}$, and $\mathcal{T}_D = \langle \{0,1\}^*, v_D \rangle$ be the delayed generation of a Σ-labeled tree $\mathcal{T}$. Then, the B-based g-degree delayed generation of $\mathcal{T}$ is the (Σ_D, B)-enriched g-degree tree $\mathcal{T}_{D_{B,g}} = \langle \{0,1\}^*, v_{D_{B,g}} \rangle$ such that there is an $h \in H(g)^B$ with $v_{D_{B,g}}(x) = (v_D(x), h)$, for all $x \in \{0,1\}^*$.*

In order to have a sound construction for $\mathcal{T}_{D_{B,g}}$, we need to impose a coherence on the information between a node and its two successors. In particular, whenever we enter a node x labeled with $\#$ in its first part, as it represents that the node is fictitious, we have to take no splitting of the degree by sending to x the value 0. On the other nodes, we have to match the value of the first (resp., second) component of the splitting with the degree of the left (resp., right) successor.

Definition 11 (Sup/Inf Coherence). *Let* $\mathcal{T} = \langle \{0,1\}^*, \mathsf{v} \rangle$ *be a* $(\Sigma \cup \{\#\}, B)$*-enriched g-degree tree. Then,* $\mathcal{T}$ *is superiorly (resp., inferiorly) coherent w.r.t. a base* $b \in B$ *iff, for* $x \in \{0,1\}^*$ *and* $i \in \{0,1\}$ *with* $\mathsf{v}(x) = (\sigma, \mathsf{h})$, $\mathsf{h}(b) = (d, d_0, d_1)$, $\mathsf{v}(x \cdot i) = (\sigma_i, \mathsf{h}_i)$, *and* $\mathsf{h}_i(b) = (d^i, d_0^i, d_1^i)$, *it holds that (i) if* $\sigma_i = \#$ *then* $d_i = 0$ *and (ii)* $d_i \leq d^i$ *(resp.,* $d_i \geq d^i$).

Finally, with the following definition, we extend the local concept of sup/inf coherence of a particular base to a pair of sets of bases.

Definition 12 (Full Coherence). *A* $(\Sigma \cup \{\#\}, B)$*-enriched g-degree tree* $\mathcal{T}$ *is full coherent w.r.t. a pair* $(B_{\text{sup}}, B_{\text{inf}})$, *where* $B_{\text{sup}} \cup B_{\text{inf}} \subseteq B$ *iff it is superiorly (resp., inferiorly) coherent w.r.t. all bases* $b \in B_{\text{sup}}$ *(resp.,* $b \in B_{\text{inf}}$).

The coherent structure satellites. We now define the satellites we use to verify that the tree encoding the model of the formula has a correct shape w.r.t. the whole transformation described in the previous paragraph. In particular, we first introduce a satellite that checks if the "enriched degree tree" in input is the result of a "based degree delayed generation" of the model of the formula. Then, we show how to create the additional labeling of the tree that satisfies the coherence properties on the degrees required by the semantics of the logic. The following automaton checks if the $\#$ and $\bot$ labels of the input tree are correct w.r.t. Definitions 7 and 8.

Definition 13 (Structure Satellite). *The* structure satellite *is the binary satellite* $S^* = \langle \Sigma_D, \{0,1\}, \{\#, \bot, @\}, \zeta, \{@\} \rangle$, *where* ζ *is as follows: if* $p = \sigma = \#$ *then* $\zeta(p,\sigma) = \{(\#,\#)\}$ *else if either* $p = \sigma = \bot$ *or* $p = @$ *and* $\sigma \in \Sigma$ *then* $\zeta(p,\sigma) = \{(\bot,@),(\#,\#)\}$, *otherwise* $\zeta(p,\sigma) = \emptyset$.

The satellite S^* has constant size 3. Its transition function ζ is defined to directly represent the constraints on the $\#$ and $\bot$ labels, so the next lemma easily follows.

Lemma 3. *The satellite* S^* *accepts all and only the* Σ_D*-labeled* $\{0,1\}$*-trees* $\mathcal{T}_D$ *that can be obtained as delayed generation of* Σ*-labeled trees* $\mathcal{T}$.

The next satellite creates the additional labeling of the input tree of the main automaton in such a way that it is sup/inf coherent by using the properties *(i)* and *(ii)* of Definition 11. Precisely, if the satellite accepts the input tree, the additional labeling is given by its states.

Definition 14 (Sup/Inf Coherence Satellite). *The* b*-base* g*-degree sup (resp., inf) coherence satellite is the binary satellite* $S_{b,g}^{\Sigma} = \langle \Sigma \cup \{\#\}, \{0,1\}, H(g), \zeta, H(g) \rangle$, *where* ζ *is as follows: (i) if* $\sigma = \#$ *then* $\zeta(p,\sigma)$ *is set to* $\{(p,p)\}$ *if* $p = (0,0,0)$ *and to* $\emptyset$ *otherwise; (ii) if* $\sigma \neq \#$ *then* $\zeta(p,\sigma)$ *contains all and only the pairs of states* $(p_0, p_1) \in H(g)^{\{0,1\}}$ *with* $p_i = (d^i, d_0^i, d_1^i)$, *such that* $d_i \leq d^i$ *(resp.,* $d_i \geq d^i$), *for all* $i \in \{0,1\}$, *where* $p = (d, d_0, d_1)$.

Note that the satellite $S_{b,g}^{\Sigma}$ has size quadratic in its degree g.

Finally, we introduce the satellite that checks if the tree in input is coherent or not by merging the behavior of the two previous described satellites.

Definition 15 (Coherent Structure Satellite). *The g-degree structure $(B_{\sup}, B_{\inf})$-co-herent satellite is the binary satellite* $\mathcal{S}_g^{B_{\sup}, B_{\inf}} = \langle \Sigma_D, \{0,1\}, H(g)^{(B_{\sup} \cup B_{\inf})} \times \{\#, \bot, @\},$ $\zeta, H(g)^{(B_{\sup} \cup B_{\inf})} \times \{@\} \rangle$ *obtained as the product of the structure satellite $\mathcal{S}^*$ with all the b-base g-degree sup (resp., inf) coherence satellites* $\mathcal{S}_{b,g}^{\Sigma \cup \{\bot\}}$, *with $b \in B_{\sup}$ (resp., $b \in B_{\inf}$).*

Clearly, the size of $\mathcal{S}_g^{B_{\sup}, B_{\inf}}$ is polynomial in g and exponential in $|B_{\sup} \cup B_{\inf}|$, since its number of states is equal to $\frac{3}{2}((g+1)(g+2))^{|B_{\sup} \cup B_{\inf}|}$. Due to the product structure of the automaton, next result directly follows from Lemma 3, and Definitions 10 and 12.

Theorem 4. *The main automaton $\mathcal{A}$ of an ATAS $\langle \mathcal{A}, \mathcal{S}_g^{B_{\sup}, B_{\inf}} \rangle$ having satellite state space $P = P' \times P''$, with $P' = H(g)^B$ and $P'' = \{\#, \bot, @\}$, accepts only the B-based g-degree delayed generation $\mathcal{T}_{D_{B,g}}$ of Σ-labeled trees $\mathcal{T}$ that are coherent w.r.t. the pair $(B_{\sup}, B_{\inf})$, with $B = B_{\sup} \cup B_{\inf}$.*

The formula automaton. In this paragraph we introduce a Büchi tree automaton $\mathcal{A}_\varphi$ that checks whether a full bounded-width tree $\mathcal{T}$ satisfies a given formula φ by evaluating all B-based g-degree delayed generation trees $\mathcal{T}_{D_{B,g}}$ associated with $\mathcal{T}$, where $g = \mathring{\varphi}$ is the maximum degree of φ and $B = \text{ecl}(\varphi)$ is the extended closure of φ. The automaton works on any B-based g-degree generation tree, even those that are not associated to a full bounded-width tree. However, we make the assumptions that the trees in input are really associated to this kind of trees and that they are coherent with respect to $(B_{\sup}, B_{\inf})$, where $B_{\sup} = \text{ecl}(\varphi)^\exists$ and $B_{\inf} = \text{ecl}(\varphi)^\forall$. By Theorem 4, we are able to enforce such properties by using $\mathcal{A}_\varphi$ as a part of an ATAS having the g-degree structure $(B_{\sup}, B_{\inf})$-coherent satellite $\mathcal{S}_g^{B_{\sup}, B_{\inf}}$.

In order to understand how the formula automaton works, it is useful to gain more insights on the meaning of the tree $\mathcal{T}_{D_{B,g}}$ associated with $\mathcal{T}$. First of all, the widening operation has the purpose to make the tree complete by adding fake nodes labeled with #. Through this, we obtain the tree $\mathcal{T}_W$. Then, the delaying operation transforms $\mathcal{T}_W$ into a binary tree $\mathcal{T}_D$, such that at every level a node x associated to a node y in $\mathcal{T}$ generates only one of the successor of y in the direction 1, meanwhile it sends a duplicate of itself on the direction 0 labeled with $\bot$. The following duplicates have to generate the remaining successors in a recursive way. However, when there are no more successors to generate, the node x does not send in the direction 0 a duplicate of itself anymore, but just a fake node labeled with #. At this point, to obtain the tree $\mathcal{T}_{D_{B,g}}$, we enrich the labeling of the delayed generation tree, by adding a degree function $h : B \mapsto H(g)$. In the hypothesis that $\mathcal{T}$ satisfies φ, for every formula $\varphi' \in B$ and node $x \in \{0,1\}^*$ with $v_{D_{B,g}}(x) = (\sigma, h)$, we have that $h(\varphi') = (d, d_0, d_1)$ describes the degree with which the formula φ' is supposed to be satisfied on x. In particular d is the degree in the current node, and $d_0 + d_1$ explains how this degree is partitioned in the following nodes. More precisely d_1 represents the degree sent to the direction 1, which usually corresponds to a concrete node in $\mathcal{T}$, hence it is the degree sent to that node. Meanwhile, d_0 represents the degree sent to the direction 0, which usually corresponds to a duplicate of the previous node. Hence d_0 represents the degree that had yet to be partitioned among the remaining successors of the node y associated to x. To this aim, the coherence requirement asks:

(i) for an existential formula, the degree found in a successor node is not lower than the degree the father sent to that node (it may be higher as the node may satisfy the existence by finding more paths with a certain property, so it surely satisfies what the formula requires); *(ii)* for a universal formula, the degree found in a successor node is not greater than the degree the father sent to that node (it may be smaller as the node may satisfy the universality by finding less paths with a certain negated property, so it surely satisfies what the formula requires).

In the hypothesis of coherence, the formula automaton needs only to check that *(i)* the degree of every existential and universal formula is initiated correctly on the node in which the formula first appears in (e.g., for an existential formula it needs to check that the degree in the label of the node is not lower than the degree required by the formula), and *(ii)* that every node of the tree satisfies the existential or universal formula with the degree specified in the node labeling. To do this, the automaton has as state space $cl(\varphi) \cup ecl(\varphi) \cup rcl(\varphi)$: on one hand, the formulas in $ecl(\varphi)$ ask the automaton to verify them completely relying on the degree of the label, on the other hand, the existential and universal formulas in $cl(\varphi)$ ask the automaton even to check that the degree of them agrees with that contained in the label. Finally, states in $rcl(\varphi)$ are used for the Büchi acceptance condition.

Definition 16 (Formula Automaton). *The formula automaton for φ is the binary ABT $\mathcal{A}_\varphi = \langle \Sigma_\varphi \times P'_\varphi, \{0,1\}, Q_\varphi, \delta, \varphi, F_\varphi \rangle$, where $\Sigma_\varphi = 2^{AP} \cup \{\#, \bot\}$, $P'_\varphi = H(\mathring{\varphi})^{ecl(\varphi)}$, $Q_\varphi = cl(\varphi) \cup ecl(\varphi) \cup rcl(\varphi)$, $F_\varphi = rcl(\varphi)$, and $\delta : Q_\varphi \times (\Sigma_\varphi \times P'_\varphi) \mapsto B^+(\{0,1\} \times Q_\varphi)$ is described in the body of the article.*

We now describe the structure of the transition transition $\delta(q, (\sigma, h))$ through a case analysis on the state space.

As first thing, when $\sigma = \#$, the automaton is on a fake node $x = x' \cdot i$ of the the input tree $\mathcal{T}_{D_{B.g}}$, so every formula should be false on it. However, in the instant the automaton reaches such a node, by passing through its antecedent x', it is not asking to verify the formula represented by the state q. Indeed, we have that it is sent by another state q' on x' which corresponds to a universal formula. In that case, we are checking that the "core" of it is satisfied on all the successors (but a given number of them). Hence, since x does not exist in the original tree $\mathcal{T}$, we do not have to verify the property of q on it. Moreover, we are sure that q' does not represent any existential property. This is due to the fact that *(i)* the degree d_i related to the state q' in the labeling of x' needs to be 0 by the coherence requirements of Definition 11 and *(ii)* that, as we show later, the transition on existential formulas do not send any new state to a direction j having $d_j = 0$. For this reason, we set $\delta(q, (\sigma, h)) = t$. In the rest of this paragraph, we suppose $\sigma \neq \#$.

As we show later, the structure of the transition function does not allow to reach, at the same time, a state q belonging to the set $cl(\varphi) \cup rcl(\varphi)$ and a labeling $\sigma = \bot$. For this reason, w.l.o.g., we can set $\delta(q, (\sigma, h)) = f$.

Due to the lack of space, here we partially describe the transition function of $\mathcal{A}_\varphi$ (i.e., the cases EX and EU), and send the reader to the full version for the complete definition.

Let $h(EX \varphi) = (d, d_0, d_1)$. For a state of the form EX φ, we verify that this formula holds with degree d. Recall that in the input tree the degrees (d_0, d_1) describe the distribution of the nodes, which need to satisfy φ, among the successors of the current node.

Since the nodes on direction 1 are real successors of the node in the original input tree $\mathcal{T}$, we need that the state formula φ holds on them iff $d_1 = 1$. However, we cannot ask that a state formula holds more than one time, so, if $d_1 > 1$, the input tree cannot be accepted. Finally, on direction 0, we send the same state $\mathsf{EX}\,\varphi$ if $d_0 > 0$, in order to ask that the residual degree d_0 is distributed on the remaining successors. For a state of the form $\mathsf{E}^{\geq i}\mathsf{X}\,\varphi$ we have only to further verify that the degree i agrees with the value d, i.e., $d \geq i$. Hence, $\delta(\mathsf{E}^{\geq i}\mathsf{X}\varphi, (\sigma, \mathrm{h}))$ is set to f, if $d < i$, and to $\delta(\mathsf{EX}\varphi, (\sigma, h))$, otherwise.

Let now $\mathrm{h}(\mathsf{E}\varphi_1 \mathsf{U}\,\varphi_2) = (d, d_0, d_1)$. For a state of the form $\mathsf{E}\varphi_1 \mathsf{U}\,\varphi_2$ we check that this formula holds with degree d. If the node is not a duplicate of a previous node, i.e., $\sigma \neq \bot$, we check the formula that should hold in the current node by applying the one-step unfolding property derived by the semantics (see Lemma 1). If $d = 1$, then $\mathsf{E}\varphi_1 \mathsf{U}\varphi_2$ may be satisfied on the current node. Indeed, if φ_2 is true on it, we already have one and only one minimal path satisfying $\varphi_1 \mathsf{U}\varphi_2$. Otherwise, we need φ_1 to holds. If $d > 1$, we have to force $\varphi_1 \mathsf{U}\varphi_2$ to be not yet satisfied. So, we require $\neg\varphi_2$ to holds in the current node. These two cases, may also require $\mathsf{E}\varphi_1 \mathsf{U}\varphi_2$ to hold on some of the successors, so we may need to propagate the formula itself, by using the requirement $\gamma = (0, \mathsf{E}\varphi_1 \mathsf{U}\varphi_2) \wedge (1, \mathsf{E}\varphi_1 \mathsf{U}\varphi_2)$. In the case $d = 0$, we do not require anything, so we set the transition function to be t. On the other hand, if $\sigma = \bot$, we do not have to verify again what is check on a previous node, but only to propagate the formula on both the directions 0 and 1, by using the γ requirement. As for the EX case, for a state of the form $\mathsf{E}^{\geq i}\varphi_1 \mathsf{U}\varphi_2$ we have to do the same consideration on the relation between the degrees i and d. Moreover, we do not have to deal with the $\bot$ labeling, since the current state is never sent through the 0 direction. Hence, we do not consider it as a separate case.

We now briefly discuss the acceptance condition for the illustrated cases. In the full version we show that F_φ equals to $\mathrm{rcl}(\varphi)$. Here, we only show that the states EX and EU discussed above are not contained in F_φ. First note that states EX may generate themselves only along direction 0 but, in the hypothesis that $\mathcal{T}$ has bounded-width, this cannot occur infinitely often. Indeed, $\mathcal{T}_{D_{B,g}}$ can only have as many duplicates of a node x in the direction 0 labeled with $\bot$ as the number of successors of the related node in $\mathcal{T}$. Thus, along a direction 0, the automaton eventually meets a node labeled with # that does not allow the states to further propagate. For the same reason, also the states EU cannot progress infinitely often along direction 0. As concern direction 1, a state EU needs to follow the branches on $\mathcal{T}_{D_{B,g}}$ that satisfy the until. Since, on those branches, it needs to be satisfied within a finite path, we cannot allow it to progress infinitely often. Consequently, we do not add EU in the acceptance set F_φ.

Theorem 5. *Let φ be a GCTL formula, with $g = \mathring{\varphi}$, $B_{\mathrm{sup}} = \mathrm{ecl}(\varphi)^{\exists}$, and $B_{\mathrm{inf}} = \mathrm{ecl}(\varphi)^{\forall}$. Then, φ is satisfiable iff $\mathcal{L}(\langle \mathcal{A}_\varphi, S_g^{B_{\mathrm{sup}}, B_{\mathrm{inf}}}\rangle) \neq \emptyset$.*

By a matter of calculation, it holds that $|\mathcal{A}_\varphi| = O(|\varphi|)$ and $|S_g^{B_{\mathrm{sup}}, B_{\mathrm{inf}}}| = \mathring{\varphi}^{O(|\varphi|)}$. By Theorem 3, we obtain that the emptiness problem for $\langle \mathcal{A}_\varphi, S_g^{B_{\mathrm{sup}}, B_{\mathrm{inf}}}\rangle$ can be solved in time $2^{O(|\varphi|^2 \cdot \log(\mathring{\varphi}))} \leq 2^{O(\|\varphi\|^3)}$. Moreover, by recalling that GCTL subsumes CTL, the following result follows.

Theorem 6. *The satisfiability problem for GCTL with binary codings is* ExpTime-Complete.

References

[1] Apostol, T.M.: Introduction to Analytic Number Theory. Springer, Heidelberg (1976)
[2] Bianco, A., Mogavero, F., Murano, A.: Graded Computation Tree Logic. In: LICS 2009, pp. 342–351 (2009)
[3] Bonatti, P.A., Lutz, C., Murano, A., Vardi, M.Y.: The Complexity of Enriched μ-Calculi. LMCS 4(3:11), 1–27 (2008)
[4] Clarke, E.M., Emerson, E.A.: Design and Synthesis of Synchronization Skeletons Using Branching-Time Temporal Logic. In: Kozen, D. (ed.) Logic of Programs 1981. LNCS, vol. 131, pp. 52–71. Springer, Heidelberg (1982)
[5] Emerson, E.A., Halpern, J.Y.: "Sometimes" and "Not Never" Revisited: On Branching Versus Linear Time. JACM 33(1), 151–178 (1986)
[6] Ferrante, A., Napoli, M., Parente, M.: CTL Model-Checking with Graded Quantifiers. In: Cha, S(S.), Choi, J.-Y., Kim, M., Lee, I., Viswanathan, M. (eds.) ATVA 2008. LNCS, vol. 5311, pp. 18–32. Springer, Heidelberg (2008)
[7] Ferrante, A., Napoli, M., Parente, M.: Graded-CTL: Satisfiability and Symbolic Model Checking. In: Breitman, K., Cavalcanti, A. (eds.) ICFEM 2009. LNCS, vol. 5885, pp. 306–325. Springer, Heidelberg (2009)
[8] Fine, K.: In So Many Possible Worlds. NDJFL 13, 516–520 (1972)
[9] De Giacomo, G., Lenzerini, M.: Concept Language with Number Restrictions and Fixpoints, and its Relationship with Mu-calculus. In: ECAI 1994, pp. 411–415 (1994)
[10] Grädel, E.: On The Restraining Power of Guards. JSL 64(4), 1719–1742 (1999)
[11] Kupferman, O., Sattler, U., Vardi, M.Y.: The Complexity of the Graded μ-Calculus. In: Voronkov, A. (ed.) CADE 2002. LNCS (LNAI), vol. 2392, pp. 423–437. Springer, Heidelberg (2002)
[12] Kupferman, O., Vardi, M.Y.: Memoryful Branching-Time Logic. In: LICS 2006, pp. 265–274. IEEE Computer S., Los Alamitos (2006)
[13] Kupferman, O., Vardi, M.Y., Wolper, P.: An Automata Theoretic Approach to Branching-Time Model Checking. JACM 47(2), 312–360 (2000)
[14] Lamport, L.: "Sometime" is Sometimes "Not Never": On the Temporal Logic of Programs. In: POPL 1980, pp. 174–185 (1980)
[15] Lange, M.: A Purely Model-Theoretic Proof of the Exponential Succinctness Gap between CTL+ and CTL. IPL 108(5), 308–312 (2008)
[16] Lutz, C.: Complexity and Succinctness of Public Announcement Logic. In: AAMAS 2006, pp. 137–143 (2006)
[17] Miyano, S., Hayashi, T.: Alternating Finite Automata on ω-Words. TCS 32, 321–330 (1984)
[18] Muller, D.E., Schupp, P.E.: Alternating Automata on Infinite Trees. TCS 54(2-3), 267–276 (1987)
[19] Pnueli, A.: The Temporal Logic of Programs. In: FOCS 1977, pp. 46–57 (1977)
[20] Pnueli, A.: The Temporal Semantics of Concurrent Programs. TCS 13, 45–60 (1981)
[21] Rabin, M.O.: Decidability of Second-Order Theories and Automata on Infinite Trees. BAMS 74, 1025–1029 (1968)
[22] Tobies, S.: PSpace Reasoning for Graded Modal Logics. JLC 11(1), 85–106 (2001)
[23] Vardi, M.Y., Wolper, P.: An Automata-Theoretic Approach to Automatic Program Verification. In: LICS 1986, pp. 332–344 (1986)
[24] Vardi, M.Y., Wolper, P.: Automata-Theoretic Techniques for Modal Logics of Programs. JCSS 32(2), 183–221 (1986)
[25] Wilke, T.: CTL+ is Exponentially More Succinct than CTL. In: Pandu Rangan, C., Raman, V., Sarukkai, S. (eds.) FST TCS 1999. LNCS, vol. 1738, pp. 110–121. Springer, Heidelberg (1999)

Exact Exploration and Hanging Algorithms[*]

Andreas Blass[1], Nachum Dershowitz[2], and Yuri Gurevich[3]

[1] Mathematics Dept, University of Michigan, Ann Arbor, MI 48109, USA
[2] School of Computer Science, Tel Aviv University, Ramat Aviv 69978, Israel
[3] Microsoft Research, Redmond, WA 98052, USA

Abstract. Recent analysis of sequential algorithms resulted in their axiomatization and in a representation theorem stating that, for any sequential algorithm, there is an abstract state machine (ASM) with the
same states, initial states and state transitions. That analysis, however,
abstracted from details of intra-step computation, and the ASM, produced in the proof of the representation theorem, may and often does
explore parts of the state unexplored by the algorithm. We refine the
analysis, the axiomatization and the representation theorem. Emulating
a step of the given algorithm, the ASM, produced in the proof of the new
representation theorem, explores exactly the part of the state explored
by the algorithm. That frugality pays off when state exploration is costly.
The algorithm may be a high-level specification, and a simple function
call on the abstraction level of the algorithm may hide expensive interaction with the environment. Furthermore, the original analysis presumed
that state functions are total. Now we allow state functions, including
equality, to be partial so that a function call may cause the algorithm as
well as the ASM to hang. Since the emulating ASM does not make any
superfluous function calls, it hangs only if the algorithm does.

> *[T]he monotony of equality can only lead us to boredom.*
>
> —*Francis Picabia*

1 Introduction

According to Kolmogorov, "algorithms compute in steps of bounded complexity" [14]. We call such algorithms sequential; in the intervening years the notion
of algorithm was generalized to computations that may be vastly parallel, distributed, real-time. In the rest of this paper, algorithms are by default sequential
and deterministic. In particular, abstract state machines [12] will be by default
sequential and deterministic.

Abstract state machines (ASMs) constitute a most general model of (sequential deterministic) computation. They operate on any level of abstraction of data
structures and native operations. By virtue of the ASM Representaion Theorem

---

[*] Blass was partially supported by NSF grant DMS-0653696. Dershowitz was partially
supported by Israel Science Foundation grant 250/05. Part of the work reported here
was performed during visits of the first two authors to Microsoft.

A. Dawar and H. Veith (Eds.): CSL 2010, LNCS 6247, pp. 140–154, 2010.

of [13], any algorithm can be step-by-step emulated by an ASM. The theorem presupposes a precise notion of algorithm, and indeed algorithms are axiomatized by means of three "sequential postulates" in [13]. These postulates formalize the following intuitions:

(I) an algorithm is a state-transition system;
(II) state information determines (given the program of the algorithm) future transitions and may be captured by a logical structure;
(III) state transitions are governed by the values of a finite and input-independent set of ground terms.

All models of effective, sequential computation satisfy the postulates, as do idealized algorithms for computing with real numbers, or for geometric constructions with compass and straightedge. Careful analysis of the notion of algorithm [13] and an examination of the intent of the founders of the field of computability [9] have demonstrated that the sequential postulates are true of all sequential, deterministic algorithms, the only kind envisioned by the pioneers of the field. In Sects. 3 and 4, we explain the postulates, recall ASMs and formulate the ASM representation theorem.

The algorithms of the three sequential postulates will be called classical. The notion of behavioral equivalence for classical algorithms is rather strict: behaviorally equivalent algorithms have the same states, the same initial states and the same state transitions. The ASM representation theorem asserts that, for every classical algorithm, there is a behaviorally equivalent ASM. In various application domains, weaker notions of equivalence – e.g. bisimulation – may be useful, but the representation theorem remains valid for any weakening of the notion of behavioral equivalence.

Yet, from a certain point of view, the notion of behavioral equivalence is not strict enough. Equivalent algorithms may have different intra-state behavior. In particular the emulating ASM produced in the proof of the ASM representation theorem may and usually does explore parts of the state unexplored by the given algorithm. Superfluous evaluations do not prevent the ASM from arriving at the same transition as the algorithm it emulates but they waste resources. For example, an algorithm for removing duplicates from a file system may test equality of large files, but would first check to see that their recorded sizes are the same. The ASM produced by the proof of the ASM representation theorem would, however, always check both size and content, despite the overhead.

The universal construction of the emulating ASM was designed to simplify the proof of the ASM representation theorem. That construction was not designed to be used in applications. In fact, by the time of the publication of the ASM representation theorem, the ASM community had developed an art of efficient – and elegant – ASM emulation and had accumulated substantial evidence that efficient emulation of intra-step computations was always possible.

In the present paper, we prove that efficient emulation of intra-step computations is indeed always possible. In Sect. 5, we refine the axiomatization of algorithms. The algorithms of the new postulates are called exacting. And we strengthen the notion of behavioral equivalence. Two exacting algorithms are behaviorally equivalent if

(i) they have the same states, initial states and state transitions and
(ii) at each step they explore the same part of the state.

The new ASM representation theorem, in Sect. 7, asserts that, for every exacting algorithm, there is a behaviorally equivalent ASM. By eliminating unnecessary exploration, the emulating ASM, produced by the proof of the new representation theorem, is often simpler and shorter – with no need for human ingenuity to improve it.

Exact exploration allows us to handle faithfully algorithms that may hang. To this end, we liberalize the notion of algorithm's state. States of classical algorithms are (first-order) structures except that relations are viewed as Boolean-valued functions. Basic functions of the state (i.e. the interpretations of the function names in the vocabulary) are total. In the case of exacting algorithms, basic functions may be partial. That may sound like old news to ASM experts. Even though basic functions of classical ASMs are supposed to be total, partial functions are easily handled by means of various "error values", the most popular of which has been undef. The error values are elements of the state. For example, in a state with integer arithmetic, you may have that term $1/0$ evaluates to undef, equality term $1/0 = 7$ evaluates to false, and equality term $1/0 = $ undef evaluates to true. Here we are talking about a very different situation. A basic function f may have no value whatsoever at some tuple $\bar{a}$ of arguments. When $f(\bar{a})$ is called, the algorithm hangs (or stalls). This is very different from returning an error value. Hanging is more insidious – the computation gets stuck in a catatonic limbo, while an error value allows the algorithm to handle the situation as it sees fit.

Even equality can be partial in the states of an exacting algorithm. Why is that? Consider the following scenario. An algorithm works with genuine (infinite precision) real numbers. Internally, real numbers have finite representations, e.g. definite integrals. The problem of when two such expressions represent the same real number is undecidable of course. Accordingly, in algorithm's states, equality is partial. It need not be even transitive. It could be that a test $s = t$ yields false, whereas $t = u$ yields true, yet when the state asked about $s = u$, no answer is forthcoming, though the truth of the matter must be that $s \neq u$.

The possibility of hanging makes exact exploration crucial. Consider for example the Gaussian elimination procedure. It tests that a pivot element p is non-zero before evaluating expressions $a[i, j]/p$. In the case $p = 0$, it does not evaluate expressions $a[i, j]/p$, but the ASM, produced by the proof of the classical ASM representation theorem, does. In contrast, the ASM, produced by the proof of the new ASM representation theorem in Sect. 7, does not conduct such superfluous evaluations.

2   Related Work

Exact exploration that we preach here has been practiced by ASM experts for a long time, in various applications in academia and industry [1,7,25]. ASMs, sequential and otherwise, have been used to give high-level operational semantics to programming languages, protocol specifications, etc. In Microsoft, the ASM approach was used to develop Spec Explorer, a top tool for model-based testing.

The axiomatization of algorithms in [13], which is extended here to account for exact exploration, was extended to parallel algorithms and to interactive algorithms [6].

We are aiming for a model of computation that can faithfully support algorithms for which basic operations may have varying costs involved, and/or for which their domains of applicability may be unknown or uncomputable. The latter produces an ocean of related work.

First, constructive mathematics comes to mind [3,16]. Classical mathematics has no philosophical objections to working with various ideal elements that do not have finite representations. The BSS model of computation with real numbers reflects that attitude [4], and ASMs have been used in to emulate the BSS model [24]. On the other hand, constructive mathematics works only with objects that have finite representations. In their world, only computable reals exist, only computable reals-to-reals functions exist, etc. The question when two computable reals are equal is of course undecidable. Would ASMs be of any use to constructivists? We think so. Russian constructivists often used Markov's normal algorithms computation model [18] for programming. As a result some of their works are unnecessarily detailed and hard to read. Exacting ASMs would fit their purposes better.

You don't have to be a constructivist to be interested in computable mathematical analysis; you may be a recursion theorist [28]. One way to deal with partial-equality troubles is to avoid equality altogether [15,23]. Algebraic semantics has been used to tackle partial-functions difficulties in abstract data types and programming semantics; see [2,19] for interesting examples of that approach.

There exist a number of implementations of arithmetic with infinite-precision reals; see [11] for a survey. As far as we can determine, the most advanced and rapid implementations of exact real number arithmetic today are the iRRAM system of Norbert Müller [22] and the RealLib system by Branimir Lambov [17]. Let us mention also the xrc system (alluding to Exact Reals in C) of Keith Briggs [10] and a Common Lisp package Computable Real Numbers by Michael Stoll [26]. But there are other systems of interest.

One of our reviewers suggested that we "ought to engage with" Winskel's event structures [29] and noted a similarity between our Discrimination requirement in Sect. 5 and Winskel's coincidence-freeness of configurations. Well, the particular structure of exact exploration can be made to concur with a number of general frameworks including that of event structures. One may think of the exploration ordering as a partial ordering of term-evaluation events connected to an event structure associated to a given algorithm at a given state. And indeed there is some resemblance between Discrimination and coincidence-freeness. Discrimination asserts the existence of a partial order reflecting an intuition of causality, and coincidence-freeness can be cast in similar terms. But the resemblance is rather superficial; in most cases, the actual partial orderings differ.

The same reviewer also asked how our framework is related to Moschovakis's "abstract computation theories". Moschovakis has defined an abstract notion of recursor and has proposed that algorithms be identified with recursors; see for example [20,21]. For a discussion of this proposal in the light of ASMs, see [5]. We concentrate here on the aspect of Moschovakis's proposal connected with the main issue of the present paper, namely "What does an algorithm actually look at?" This issue arises implicitly in [20], but in a quite different context. Instead of being defined directly from explicit instructions in the algorithm, a set, which intuitively contains what the algorithm looks at, is obtained as the conclusion of a theorem for a specific example (see [20, Theorem 5.2]). The context there is estimating an algorithm's usage of a certain resource by checking how much of that resource it looks at. An important difference from our discussion is that in [20] the "looking" refers to an entire run of the algorithm, whereas our $\Gamma(X)$ refers to a single step. The latter can often be read off from a program (for example if the program is an ASM); the former, on the other hand, can generally be found only by running the program. Although the cited theorem in [20] provides an appropriate notion of "looking at" for the specific algorithm (mergesort) considered there, algorithms in general will not admit such explicit bounds on what they look at.

3   Axiomatization of Algorithms

Algorithms were axiomatized in [13]. Here we describe a slightly refined axiomatization that allows for a partial transition function.

3.1   Sequential Time

To begin with, algorithms are deterministic state-transition systems.

Postulate I (Sequential Time). An algorithm determines the following:

1. A nonempty set[1] $\mathcal{S}$ of *states* and a nonempty subset $\mathcal{I} \subseteq \mathcal{S}$ of *initial states*.
2. A partial *next state* transition function τ from $\mathcal{S}$ to $\mathcal{S}$.

Having τ depend only on the state means that states must store all the information needed to determine subsequent behavior. Prior history is unavailable unless stored in the current state. If $\tau(X)$ is undefined, we say that X is *terminal* and write $\tau(X) = \bot$.

---

[1] Or class; the distinction is irrelevant for our purposes and we shall ignore it.

3.2 Abstract State

Our notion of structure is that of first-order logic with equality except for the following modifications that are inessential but convenient for our purposes (and standard in the ASM literature).

- Propositional constants true and false are viewed as elements of the structure (and thus "live" inside the structure rather than outside).
- Relations are viewed as Boolean-valued functions.
- Standard Boolean connectives $\neg$, $\wedge$, $\vee$ are viewed as structures' basic functions. (The basic functions of a structure are the interpretations of the vocabulary's function names.)

The Boolean values, equality and the Boolean connectives are the *logic basic functions* of any structure; their names form the logic part of the structure's vocabulary, and they are interpreted as expected. As usual, constants are nullary functions.

All basic functions are total. A basic function may return an "error value", e.g. the value undef mentioned earlier, but error values denote elements of the structure. We write $\text{Dom}\, X$ for the base set of a structure X.

Postulate II (Abstract State). The states of an algorithm are structures over a finite vocabulary $\mathcal{F}$ such that the following conditions are satisfied.

1. If X is a state of the algorithm, then any structure Y isomorphic to X is also a state, and Y is initial or terminal if X is initial or terminal, respectively.
2. Transition τ preserves the base set; i.e. $\text{Dom}\, \tau(X) = \text{Dom}\, X$ for every non-terminal state X.
3. Transition τ respects isomorphisms, so, if $\zeta : X \cong Y$ is an isomorphism of non-terminal states X, Y, then $\zeta : \tau(X) \cong \tau(Y)$.

Closure under isomorphism ensures that the algorithm operates on the chosen level of abstraction; the states' internal representation of the data is invisible and immaterial to the program. Since a state X is a structure, it interprets function symbols in $\mathcal{F}$, assigning a value b from $\text{Dom}\, X$ to the "location" $f(a_1, \ldots, a_k)$ in X for every k-ary symbol $f \in \mathcal{F}$ and for every tuple $a_1, \ldots, a_k$ in $\text{Dom}\, X$. In this way, X assigns a value $[\![t]\!]_X$ in $\text{Dom}\, X$ to terms t over $\mathcal{F}$.

It is convenient to view each state as the union of the graphs of its operations, given in the form of a set of location-value pairs, each written conventionally as $f(\bar{a}) \mapsto b$. Define the *update set* $\Delta(X)$ of state X as the set $\tau(X) \setminus X$ of changed pairs where $\Delta(X) = \bot$ if $\tau(X) = \bot$. This Δ encapsulates the state-transition function τ by providing all the information necessary to update the current state. But to produce $\Delta(X)$, the algorithm needs to evaluate, with the help of the information stored in X, the values of some terms. Later, we will use $\Gamma(X)$ to refer to the set of these "exploration" terms.

3.3 Bounded Exploration

The third postulate simply states that there is a fixed, finite set of ground (variable-free) terms that determines the behavior of the algorithm. We say that states X and Y *agree* on a set T of terms, and we write $X =_T Y$, if $[\![t]\!]_X = [\![t]\!]_Y$ for all $t \in T$.

Postulate III (Bounded Exploration). For every algorithm, there is a finite set T of ground *critical terms* over the state vocabulary such that, for all states X and Y, if $X =_T Y$ then $\Delta(X) = \Delta(Y)$.

In what follows, we will presume that the set T of critical terms contains true, false and is closed under subterms. Algorithms satisfying Postulates I, II, and III will be called *classical*. It is argued in [13] that every (sequential deterministic) algorithm is classical in that sense.

If $\Delta(X) = \Delta(Y)$ and one of the two states is terminal then so is the other. It follows that states X and Y of a classical algorithm have the following property: if they agree on all critical terms then either both of them are terminal or else neither is terminal and the update sets $\Delta(X)$ and $\Delta(Y)$ coincide.

4 Abstract State Machines

4.1 ASM Programs

An *ASM program* P over a vocabulary $\mathcal{F}$ takes one of the following forms:

- an *assignment* statement $f(s_1, \ldots, s_n) := t$, where $f \in \mathcal{F}$ is a function symbol of arity n, $n \geq 0$, and s_i and t are ground terms over $\mathcal{F}$;
- a *parallel* statement $P_1 \parallel \cdots \parallel P_n$ $(n \geq 0)$, where each P_i is an ASM program over $\mathcal{F}$ (if $n = 0$, this is "do nothing" or "skip");
- a *conditional* statement **if** C **then** P, where C is a Boolean condition over $\mathcal{F}$, and P is an ASM program over $\mathcal{F}$.

Example 1. Here is a sorting program:

> **if** $j \neq n$ **then**
>   **if** $F(i) > F(j)$ **then** $F(i) := F(j) \parallel F(j) := F(i)$
> $j := j + 1$
> **if** $j = n \wedge i + 1 \neq n$ **then** $i := i + 1 \parallel j := i + 2$

where, as the indentation hints, the two statements given by lines 2 and 3 respectively are two components of a parallel combination, and similarly the two statements given by lines 1–3 and by line 4 respectively form a parallel combination. And $j \neq n$ is short for $\neg(j = n)$. The extra-logic part of program's vocabulary is $\{1, 2, +, >, F, n, i, j, \mathsf{undef}\}$.

Every state of the sorting program interprets the symbols $1, 2, +, >$ as usual. These are static; their interpretation will never be changed by the program. The semantics of statements is as expected. The program, as such, defines a single step, which is repeated forever or until it arrives to a terminal state. Fixed nullary functions 0 and n (programming "constants") serve as bounds of an array F, where F is a unary function. In addition, varying nullary functions i and j (programming "variables") are used as array indices. Initial states have

$n \geq 0$, $i = 0$, $j = 1$, integer values for $F(0), \ldots, F(n-1)$, and undef for all other points of F. The algorithm proceeds by modifying the values of i and j as well as of locations $F(0), \ldots, F(n-1)$. It always terminates successfully with $j = n = i + 1$ and with the first n elements of F sorted.

All terms in the sorting program are critical, and no other critical terms are needed. In general, the left-hand sides of assignments contribute only proper subterms to the set of critical terms but in this example the left sides are critical since they occur also elsewhere in the program.

4.2   ASM Updates

An ASM might "update" a location in a *trivial* way, giving it the value it already has. Also, an ASM might designate two conflicting updates for the same location, what is called a *clash*, in which case the ASM fails. To take these additional possibilities into account, a *proposed* update set $\Delta_P^+(X)$ for an ASM P at state X is defined as follows:

- $\Delta_{f(\ldots,s_i,\ldots):=t}^+(X) = \{ f(\ldots, [\![s_i]\!]_X, \ldots) \mapsto [\![t]\!]_X \}$;
- $\Delta_{[P_1 \parallel \cdots \parallel P_n]}^+(X) = \begin{cases} \Delta_{P_1}^+(X) \cup \cdots \cup \Delta_{P_n}^+(X) & \text{if there is no clash} \\ \bot & \text{otherwise}; \end{cases}$
- $\Delta_{\mathbf{if}\, C \,\mathbf{then}\, P}^+(X) = \Delta_P^+(X)$ if $X \models C$, and $\varnothing$ otherwise.

Here $X \models C$ means of course that C evaluates to true in X, and we stipulate that the union of $\bot$ with anything is $\bot$. If $\Delta_P^+(X) = \bot$ or $\Delta_P^+(X) = \varnothing$, X is a terminal state of P. Otherwise, the updates are applied to X to yield the next state, by replacing the values of all locations in X that are referred to in $\Delta_P^+(X)$. So, if the latter contains only trivial updates, P will loop forever. (As long as no confusion will arise, we are dropping the subscript P.)

ASMs clearly satisfy Postulates I–III, and thus the notion of update set $\Delta(X)$, defined after Postulate II, applies to any ASM P. Let $\Delta^0(X)$ denote the set $\{ f(\bar{a}) \mapsto [\![f(\bar{a})]\!]_X \mid \bar{a} \in \text{Dom}\, X \}$ of all possible trivial updates for state X. Thus X is terminal if $\Delta_P^+(X)$ is $\varnothing$ or $\bot$, and $\Delta_P(X) = \Delta_P^+(X) \setminus \Delta^0(X)$ otherwise. The update set for the sorting program, when in a state X such that $[\![j]\!]_X \neq [\![n]\!]_X$ and $[\![F(i)]\!]_X > [\![F(j)]\!]_X$, contains $F([\![i]\!]_X) \mapsto [\![F(j)]\!]_X$, $F([\![j]\!]_X) \mapsto [\![F(i)]\!]_X$, $j \mapsto [\![j]\!]_X + 1$.

4.3   Classical ASM Representation Theorem

Two classical algorithms are *behaviorally equivalent* if they have the same states, the same initial states and the same state transitions.

Theorem 1. *Every classical algorithm has a behaviorally equivalent ASM.*

The proof constructs an ASM that contains conditions involving equalities and disequalities between all critical terms. These conditions can be large. Given the critical terms for our sort algorithm, the ASM constructed by the proof in [13] would include statements like

$$\textbf{if } (F(i) > F(j)) = \textsf{true} \wedge j = n \wedge i+1 \neq n \textbf{ then } j := i+2.$$

This, despite the fact that the first conjunct of the conditional is irrelevant when the others hold.

5   Refined Axiomatization of Algorithms

The sequential-time Postulate I remains unchanged. We liberalize the abstract-state Postulate II to a new abstract-state Postulate II-lib, and replace the bounded-exploration Postulate III with an exact-exploration Postulate III-exact.

5.1   Liberalization of Abstract State Postulate

It is not uncommon in the logic literature to generalize the notion of structure so that basic non-logic functions may be partial. We do that. But we also do something that is not common: we allow equality to be partial. The reason for that was mentioned in the Introduction. Recall that scenario where an algorithm works with real numbers represented internally by expressions like definite integrals. In that scenario, the state may not know whether two reals are equal, i.e. whether their representations denote the same real number; the state may not know whether a real number equals zero. We insist, however, that true and false are defined (and thus total), and that the Boolean connectives are total; there is no reason to make these logic functions partial. And yes, equality remains true equality whenever it is defined. Thus equality is semi-logical: partial but correct when defined.

Postulate II-lib (Abstract State). The states of an algorithm are structures over a finite vocabulary $\mathcal{F}$, where equality and non-logic basic functions may be partial, such that the following conditions are satisfied.

1. If X is a state of the algorithm, then any structure Y isomorphic to X is also a state, and Y is initial or terminal if X is initial or terminal, respectively.
2. Transition τ preserves the base set; i.e. $\operatorname{Dom} \tau(X) = \operatorname{Dom} X$ for every non-terminal state X. And τ cannot change a value at any location $f(\bar{a})$ to no value.
3. Transition τ respects isomorphisms, so, if $\zeta : X \cong Y$ is an isomorphism of non-terminal states X, Y, then $\zeta : \tau(X) \cong \tau(Y)$.

Conditions 1 and 3 are exactly as in Postulate II. Only condition 2 is amended with a restriction on τ.

Thus some locations $f(\bar{a})$ may have no value whatsoever, not even an error value like undef; in such cases we write $f(\bar{a}) = \perp$. If an algorithm attempts, in some state X, to access a non-existent value, then it must hang. There will be no next state, yet the algorithm will get no indication of this failure. (Any such indication would be just an error value; as we said, error values can be treated as state elements.) If this situation occurs at any point during the evaluation of a term t, then t has no value in state X, symbolically $[\![t]\!]_X = \perp$. Thus $[\![t]\!]_X = \perp$ if $[\![t']\!]_X = \perp$ for any subterm t' of t.

Define the domain $\mathrm{Dom}\, f$ of a function f in state X to be the set of all tuples $\bar{a}$ such that the location $f(\bar{a})$ has a value in X, possibly an error value like undef. The restriction that we impose on the transition function τ says that $\mathrm{Dom}\, f$ can only grow.

5.2 Exact Exploration Postulate

Deciding which locations to explore is now part of the behavior we are interested in. If an algorithm acts differently on different states, either in the sense of exploring different terms or in the sense of performing different updates, then it must *first* find some term that distinguishes them. Furthermore, if the behaviors of the algorithm in two states differ, then that must be made evident from that part of the two states that is explored in both. Accordingly, what we should have is

$$X =_{\Gamma(X) \cap \Gamma(Y)} Y \longrightarrow \Gamma(X) = \Gamma(Y) \tag{1}$$

$$X =_{\Gamma(X) \cap \Gamma(Y)} Y \longrightarrow \Delta(X) = \Delta(Y) \tag{2}$$

In order to compute over a state X, the program evaluates – in some order – finitely many Boolean terms over X and learns their values. In order to produce updates, additional terms may be evaluated but the program does not need to know their values. The state may not determine the precise order of exploration, but some partial order is dictated by the possible behaviors. In general, if a conditional statement **if** C **then** P is executed and the test C is true, then the terms in C are explored before, or together with, those in P. One cannot, however, simply derive the exploration order from the conditionals in the program, making conditions in C precede any new terms in P. We might have an assignment **if** d **then if** b **then** $x := d$, in which case d needs to be explored before b, but when this assignment is placed in parallel with **if** b **then if** d **then** $x := c$, b and d can be explored at the same time. So, instead, we put all terms of the top-level conditions and assignments of components of a parallel statement at the bottom of the ordering, followed by contributions from the relevant cases of the conditionals. This order of exploration will be captured in what follows by a "causality" order $\prec_X$ on the explore terms $\Gamma(X)$ of states X. For example, the order for the sorting program, when $[\![j]\!]_X \neq [\![n]\!]_X$ and $[\![F(i)]\!]_X > [\![F(j)]\!]_X$ has the two conditions $j \neq n$ and $j = n \wedge i + 1 \neq n$ incomparable, with the first of these conditions being below both $F(i) > F(j)$ and $j + 1$.

Example 2. Consider this parallel combination of three ASM statements:

> **if** d **then if** c **then if** b **then** $s := x$
> **if** d **then if** $\neg c$ **then** $t := x$
> **if** d **then if** $\neg b$ **then** $s := y$.

Clearly, d must be explored first off, since nothing more transpires when $\neg d$, while further tests are necessary when d holds, in which case b and c must both be explored, though the order in which that occurs does not matter. Of course, x and/or y are only explored after it becomes clear that the relevant case holds.

Postulate III-exact (Exact Exploration). For every algorithm, there is a finite set T of ground *critical terms* over the state vocabulary such the following holds. For every state X, there is a finite *explore set* $\Gamma(X) \subseteq T$ satisfying the following two properties.

1. **Determination.** For every state $Y =_{\Gamma(X)} X$, $\Delta(Y) = \Delta(X)$.
2. **Discrimination.** There is a partial order $\prec_X$ of $\Gamma(X)$ such that, for every state Y and every $t \in \Gamma(X) \setminus \Gamma(Y)$, there is a Boolean term $s \prec_X t$ that takes on opposite truth values in X and Y.

The intention is that the explore set $\Gamma(X)$ consists of the terms that are actually explored by the algorithm at state X. We will assume that Γ contains true, false and all subterms of its members; the subterms of a term $f(t_1, \ldots, t_j)$ need to be evaluated before location $f(t_1, \ldots, t_j)$ can be accessed. An algorithm satisfying Postulates I, II-lib and III-exact will be called *exacting*.

5.3   Explore Terms of ASMs

The explore sets of ASMs are defined in the most natural way. If U is a set of terms, let $\bar{U}$ be the closure of $U \cup \{\text{true}, \text{false}\}$ under subterms. We have:

- $\Gamma_{f(s_1, \ldots, s_n) := t}(X) = \overline{\{s_1, \ldots, s_n, t\}}$;
- $\Gamma_{[P_1 \| \cdots \| P_n]}(X) = \Gamma_{P_1}(X) \cup \cdots \cup \Gamma_{P_n}(X)$; and
- $\Gamma_{\text{if } C \text{ then } P}(X) = \overline{\{C\}} \cup \Gamma_P(X)$ if $X \models C$ and just $\overline{\{C\}}$, otherwise.

Thus $\Gamma_P(X)$ contains all conditions that ASM P tests at state X, and all terms that occur in proposed updates.

Theorem 2. *Every ASM with explore sets as indicated is an exacting algorithm.*

Proof. Induction on ASM programs.   □

6   Exacting Algorithms

Theorem 3.

1. *Every exacting algorithm with no partial basic functions in its states is also classical.*
2. *Every classical algorithm can be equipped with explore sets so as to be exacting.*

Proof.
1. The claim is obvious.
2. Given a classical algorithm, define $\Gamma(X)$ to be the set of all critical terms (regardless of the state X).   □

A classical algorithm can often be equipped with explore sets in more than one way so as to be exacting. There is always a trivial way used in the proof above. But usually the algorithm will explore fewer terms than that in some (or even all) states, so a smaller $\Gamma(X)$ can be used.

A set V of states is *uniform* if all states in V have the same explore set, that is, if $\Gamma(X) = \Gamma(Y)$ for all $X, Y \in V$. For any set V of states, let $\Gamma(V)$ denote the *shared* explore terms $\bigcap_{X \in V} \Gamma(X)$. We say that V is *agreeable* if all states in V agree on the values of all their shared explore terms, that is, if $X =_{\Gamma(V)} Y$ for all $X, Y \in V$. It stands to reason that agreeable states engender uniform behavior, because the algorithm has no way of distinguishing between them.

Theorem 4. *For any exacting algorithm, agreeability of a set of states implies its uniformity.*

Proof. By contradiction, suppose that, despite V's agreeability, not all states in V have the same explore set. Without loss of generality, let $t \in \Gamma(X)$ be a minimal explore term for some $X \in V$ that is not also an explore term for all other states in V (minimal with respect to $\prec_X$), and let $Y \in V$ be a state such that $t \notin \Gamma(Y)$. By Discrimination, there is an $s \in \Gamma(X)$ such that $s \prec_X t$ and with different truth values in X and Y. By agreeability, $s \notin \Gamma(V)$. But then s must be a smaller choice of an explore term for X than is t, since perforce $s \notin \Gamma(Z)$ for some $Z \in V$. □

By Determination, we also have the following:

Corollary 1. *For any exacting algorithm, agreeability of a set V of states implies that $\Delta(X) = \Delta(Y)$ for all $X, Y \in V$.*

In a sense, the Discrimination requirement is equivalent to the requirement that "agreeability implies uniformity". The latter requirement does not involve any ordering of explore terms.

Theorem 5. *Consider an alternative definition of exacting algorithms where the Discrimination requirement is replaced with the requirement that every agreeable set of states is uniform. The alternative definition is equivalent to the original definition.*

Proof. One direction is proved in the previous theorem. It remains to prove that an arbitrary alternative exacting algorithm satisfies Discrimination. Let $\mathcal{S}$ be the set of states of the algorithm.

For each $X \in \mathcal{S}$, we define a partial order $\prec_X$ on $\Gamma(X)$. Explore terms that are shared by all states are smallest, because they are always needed. Next come those terms that are shared by all states that agree with X on the values of the lowest tier, $\Gamma(\mathcal{S})$, of terms. And so on. Thus, the ordering $\prec_X$, as a set of ordered pairs, is $L_X(\mathcal{S})$, where $L_X(V)$ is an ordering that discriminates X from other states in V. When V is uniform, $L_X(V) := \varnothing$; otherwise,

$$L_X(V) := (\Gamma(V) \times (\Gamma(X) \setminus \Gamma(V))) \cup L_X(\{Y \in V \mid Y =_{\Gamma(V)} X\}).$$

This recursion is bound to terminate, because $\Gamma(X) \setminus \Gamma(V)$ gets continually smaller. To see why, note that $X \in V$ always, so $\Gamma(V) \subseteq \Gamma(X)$. When V is not uniform, it cannot be agreeable, so there is an $s \in \Gamma(V)$ over which states in V disagree. But, by construction, all of V agrees on all terms in the previous $\Gamma(V)$.

Now consider any $t \in \Gamma(X) \setminus \Gamma(Y)$ for a $Y \in \mathcal{S}$. Initially, $t \notin \Gamma(V) = \Gamma(\mathcal{S})$, whereas $t \in \Gamma(V) = \Gamma(X)$ at the end of the recursion, so Y is not in the final argument V. At the point when Y is removed from V, there must be an $s \in \Gamma(V)$ that discriminates between X and Y. By construction, $s \prec_X t$.   □

Equation 1 gives an apparently weaker form of "agreeability implies uniformity". It turns out that it is strictly weaker and insufficient to replace Discrimination.

7   Exacting ASM Representation Theorem

Two exacting algorithms P and Q are *behaviorally equivalent* if they operate over the same states, have the same initial states, the same state transitions, and explore the same terms at every state. By Corollary 1, for all states X, we have also $\Delta_P(X) = \Delta_Q(X)$. Unless the order in which locations are explored affects what is actually explored in a given state, we do not care about the precise order of exploration, nor about the number of times a location is accessed.

Note that, if exacting algorithms P and Q are behaviorally equivalent and P hangs during the exploration of a state X, then so does Q, for the simple reason that they evaluate exactly the same terms. In the real world, a program may hang for various reasons, e.g. because the internet connection is poor. We abstract from such details in this theoretical study. An exacting algorithm hangs only because it attempts to evaluate an undefined term. Call a terminal state X of an exacting algorithm P *hanging* if P hangs at X. It follows that behaviorally equivalent exacting algorithms have exactly the same hanging states.

Theorem 6. *Every exacting algorithm has a behaviorally equivalent clash-free ASM.*

In the beginning, we mentioned Kolmogorov's posit: "Algorithms compute in steps of bounded complexity". How do you measure the complexity of a step? A most natural non-numerical measure is the set of terms actually explored during the step. Combined with the cost of function calls, it leads to a natural numerical measure. In both cases, ASMs preserve the step complexity.

And the theorem shows that abstract state machines are adequate to emulate algorithms that may hang.

8   Discussion

We have shown that every exacting algorithm can be step-by-step emulated by an abstract state machine that at no state attempts to apply equality or another function to more values than does the algorithm. This strengthens the thesis, propounded in [12], that abstract state machines faithfully model any and all sequential algorithms and bolsters the belief that the sequential postulates capture all sequential algorithms regardless of which model of computation they may be expressed in, including "continuous-space" algorithms.

"Continuous time" processes await further research. The easing of the requirements on fully-defined equality and other functions also lends strong support to the contention – put forth in [8,9] – that the Church-Turing Thesis is provably true from first principles. In addition to the sequential postulates, the arguments require that initial states contain only free constructors and functions that can be programmed from them (plus input). Our refinement of the ASM Representation Theorem strengthens those results by showing that the simulation of an algorithm, having no (unprogrammable) oracles, by an effective abstract state machine need not involve any operations not available to the original algorithm. It also follows from this work that there is no harm in incorporating partial operations in the initial states of effective algorithms, as long as they too can be computed effectively (whenever defined). Even with this relaxation of the limitations on initial states, it remains provable that no super-recursive function can be computed algorithmically.

Acknowledgment. We thank Olivier Bournez for his comments on an early draft and Ulrich Kohlenbach for information on computable reals.

References

1. ASM Michigan Webpage, http://www.eecs.umich.edu/gasm/, maintained by J. K. Huggins (Viewed June 4, 2010)
2. Bernot, G., Bidoit, M., Choppy, C.: Abstract data types with exception handling. Theoret. Comp. Sci. 46, 13–45 (1986)
3. Bishop, E.: Foundations of Constructive Analysis. McGraw-Hill, New York (1967)
4. Blum, L., Shub, M., Smale, S.: On a theory of computation and complexity over the real numbers. Bulletin of Amer. Math. Soc. (NS) 21, 1–46 (1989)
5. Blass, A., Gurevich, Y.: Algorithms vs. Machines. Bull. European Assoc. Theoret. Comp. Sci. 77, 96–118 (2002); Reprinted in Paun, G., et al. (eds.): Current Trends in Theoretical Computer Science: The Challenge of the New Century, vol. 2, pp. 215–236. World Scientific, Singapore (2004)
6. Blass, A., Gurevich, Y.: Algorithms: A Quest for Absolute Definitions. Bull. Euro. Assoc. for Theor. Computer Sci. 81, 195–225 (2003); Reprinted in Paun, G., et al. (eds.): Current Trends in Theoretical Computer Science, 283–311, World Scientific, Singapore (2004); Olszewski, A., et al. (eds.) Church's Thesis After 70 Years, 24–57, Ontos (2006)
7. Börger, E., Stärk, R.: Abstract State Machines. Springer, Heidelberg (2003)
8. Boker, U., Dershowitz, N.: The Church-Turing Thesis over arbitrary domains. In: Avron, A., Dershowitz, N., Rabinovich, A. (eds.) Pillars of Computer Science. LNCS, vol. 4800, pp. 199–229. Springer, Heidelberg (2008)
9. Dershowitz, N., Gurevich, Y.: A natural axiomatization of computability and proof of Church's Thesis. Bulletin of Symbolic Logic 14, 299–350 (2008)
10. xrc (exact reals in C), http://keithbriggs.info/xrc.html (viewed on June 4, 2010)

11. Gowland, P., Lester, D.: A survey of exact arithmetic implementations. In: Blanck, J., Brattka, V., Hertling, P. (eds.) CCA 2000. LNCS, vol. 2064, pp. 30–47. Springer, Heidelberg (2001)

12. Gurevich, Y.: Evolving algebras 1993: Lipari guide. In: Börger, E. (ed.) Specification and Validation Methods, pp. 9–36. Oxford University Press, Oxford (1995)

13. Gurevich, Y.: Sequential abstract state machines capture sequential algorithms. ACM Transactions on Computational Logic 1, 77–111 (2000)

14. Kolmogorov, A.N.: On the concept of algorithm. Uspekhi Matematicheskikh Nauk 8(4), 175–176 (1953) (in Russian); English version in [27, 18–19]

15. Korovina, M.: Gandy's theorem for abstract structures without the equality test. In: Vardi, M.Y., Voronkov, A. (eds.) LPAR 2003. LNCS, vol. 2850, pp. 290–301. Springer, Heidelberg (2003)

16. Kushner, B.A.: Lectures on Constructive Mathematical Analysis. Translations of Mathematical Monographs, vol. 60. American Mathematical Society, Providence (1984); The Russian original published by Nauka (1973)

17. Lambov, B.: The RealLib Project, http://www.brics.dk/~barnie/RealLib/ (viewed on June 4, 2010)

18. Markov, A.A.: The Theory of Algorithms. American Mathematical Society Translations 15(2), 1–14 (1960)

19. Meseguer, J., Roşu, G.: A total approach to partial algebraic specification. In: Widmayer, P., Triguero, F., Morales, R., Hennessy, M., Eidenbenz, S., Conejo, R. (eds.) ICALP 2002. LNCS, vol. 2380, pp. 572–584. Springer, Heidelberg (2002)

20. Moschovakis, Y.: On founding the theory of algorithms. In: Dales, H.G., Olivieri, G. (eds.) Truth in Mathematics, pp. 71–104. Clarendon Press, Oxford (1998)

21. Moschovakis, Y.: What is an algorithm? In: Engquist, B., Schmid, W. (eds.) Mathematics Unlimited – 2001 and Beyond, pp. 919–936. Springer, Heidelberg (2001)

22. Müller, N.: iRRAM - Exact Arithmetic in C++, http://www.informatik.uni-trier.de/iRRAM/ (viewed on June 4, 2010)

23. Naughton, T.J.: Continuous-space model of computation is Turing universal. Society of Photo-Optical Instrumentation Engineers (SPIE) Conference Series, vol. 4109, pp. 121–128 (2000)

24. Nowack, A.: Complexity theory via abstract state machines. Master's thesis, RWTH-Aachen (2000)

25. Spec. Explorer, http://msdn.microsoft.com/en-us/devlabs/ee692301.aspx (viewed on June 04, 2010)

26. Computable Real Numbers, http://www.haible.de/bruno/MichaelStoll/reals.html (viewed on June 4, 2010)

27. Uspensky, V.A., Semenov, A.L.: Algorithms: Main Ideas and Applications. Kluwer, Dordrecht (1993)

28. Weihrauch, K.: Computable Analysis – An introduction. Springer, Heidelberg (2000)

29. Winskel, G.: Event Structures – Lecture Notes for the Advanced Course on Petri Nets. Univ. of Cambridge Computer Lab. Tech. Report 95, UCAM-CL-TR-95 (1986)

Embedding Deduction Modulo into a Prover

Guillaume Burel

Max Planck Institute for Informatics
Saarland University, Saarbrücken, Germany
guillaume.burel@ens-lyon.org
http://www.mpi-inf.mpg.de/~burel/

Abstract. Deduction modulo consists in presenting a theory through rewrite rules to support automatic and interactive proof search. It induces proof search methods based on narrowing, such as the polarized resolution modulo. We show how to combine this method with more traditional ordering restrictions. Interestingly, no compatibility between the rewriting and the ordering is requested to ensure completeness. We also show that some simplification rules, such as strict subsumption eliminations and demodulations, preserve completeness. For this purpose, we use a new framework based on a proof ordering. These results show that polarized resolution modulo can be integrated into existing provers, where these restrictions and simplifications are present. We also discuss how this integration can actually be done by diverting the main algorithm of state-of-the-art provers.

Whatever their applications, proofs are rarely searched for without context: mathematical proofs rely on set theory, or Euclidean geometry, or arithmetic, etc.; proofs of program correctness are done using e.g. pointer arithmetic and/or theories defining data structures (chained lists, trees, ...); concerning security, theories are used for instance to model properties of encryption algorithms. It is therefore essential to have theoretical foundations and practical methods that handle theories conveniently and efficiently. For this purpose, there are two directions: to develop methods that are really specific to a particular theory; or to develop a generic framework that can handle all theories. The first option is appealing for efficiency reasons: for instance, combining a SAT solver with the Simplex method leads to very powerful SMT solvers for linear arithmetic. However, developing methods for new theories is hard. Even the combination of such specific methods is not trivial, although there have been a lot of interesting results in that direction in the recent years. In this paper, we are more interested in the second option: having a generic way to handle theories efficiently. A naive way to do so would be to use an axiomatization of the theory, but in general, this approach would be really inefficient for automated proving. Somehow, we need to present the theory so as to take advantage of its properties.

A first idea is to use the consistency of the theory. When proving a goal in a consistent theory by refutation, resolving the clauses of the theory is useless, since it will not bring out a contradiction. This idea defines the set-of-support strategy for resolution [19], where clauses generated by resolution must have

A. Dawar and H. Veith (Eds.): CSL 2010, LNCS 6247, pp. 155–169, 2010.
© Springer-Verlag Berlin Heidelberg 2010

at least one parent outside the theory. The completeness of this method can be proved provided the theory is consistent. However, unless the theory is saturated, this strategy is not compatible with other refinements of resolution, in particular ordering-based restrictions, in the sense that their combination is not complete. As state-of-the-art provers strongly rely on such restrictions to limit their search space, we cannot use the set-of-support strategy to integrate theories into them.

Another way to handle theories is deduction modulo [9]. In deduction modulo, the theory is presented by means of a congruence over propositions, the inference rules of existing proof systems being applied modulo this congruence. In practice, this congruence is often defined by a rewrite system that can rewrite not only terms into terms but also atomic propositions into general propositions. Corresponding proof search methods are then obtained by combining an existing method with narrowing[1]. Thus, there are proof-search procedures extending resolution, such as ENAR [9] or its more recent version called Polarized Resolution Modulo [7]; or extending tableaux methods. Examples of theories that can be used in deduction modulo include arithmetic [12], Zermelo's set theory [10], simple type theory (a.k.a. higher-order logic) [8], and there exists a procedure to present any first-order classical theory as a rewrite system usable in deduction modulo [4]. Depending on the rewrite system presenting the theory, proof search methods based on deduction modulo are not always complete. It can be proved that their completeness is equivalent to the admissibility of the cut rule in the sequent calculus modulo the rewrite system [15]. What can be seen as a drawback is in fact their strength. Indeed, the completeness of these methods implies the consistency of the theory represented by the rewrite system. Therefore, as a consequence of Gödel's incompleteness theorem (provided the theory is at least as strong as arithmetic), completeness cannot be proved in that theory itself. In particular, this shows that polarized resolution modulo is not an instance of known refinements of resolution [3], whose completeness can be proved in simple type theory. To prove the completeness of polarized resolution modulo, we therefore proceed in two steps: we first prove completeness w.r.t. the cut-free fragment of the sequent calculus modulo for any rewrite system. Then, for some particular rewrite system, we prove that cut admissibility holds, that is, the cut-free fragment corresponds to the whole. Due to Gödel's theorem, this proof has to be done in a stronger theory than the one defined by the rewrite system. A bunch of techniques exists to prove cut admissibility in deduction modulo [14,11,6] (in particular, they can be applied to the theories cited before, for which proof search methods modulo are therefore complete) and a completion procedure was designed to transform a rewrite system so that cut admissibility holds [4].

Instead of implementing polarized resolution modulo from scratch, we want to embed it into existing provers. Two points need to be overcome: First, existing provers are not based on general resolution, but on some refinement of it. We therefore need to check if narrowing is compatible with these refinements. In

---

[1] Meta-variables may need to be instantiated before being rewritten, hence the use of narrowing and not merely rewriting.

particular, we have to know if polarized resolution modulo with ordering-based restrictions (as in ordered resolution) is still complete. In this paper, we define Ordered Polarized Resolution Modulo, and we prove its completeness relatively to the cut-free fragment. Quite surprisingly, no compatibility between the rewrite system and the ordering is requested to ensure this completeness. We are also concerned with simplification rules, and we propose a general framework, based on a proof ordering, to show that some simplification rules preserve the completeness. We apply it to Strict Subsumption Elimination and Demodulation. Second, we need to see how to proceed from an implementation viewpoint. It turns out that seeing polarized resolution modulo as a combination of the set-of-support strategy and literal selection makes it easy to incorporate into provers based on a variant of the given-clause algorithm, as is the case for most of them.

The next section will present the minimal knowledge needed on deduction modulo to make the paper self-contained. In Section 2 we define the Ordered Polarized Resolution Modulo and prove its completeness. Section 3 introduces the ordering-based framework for completeness-preserving simplification rules, and applies it to Strict Subsumption Elimination and Demodulation. In Section 4, we discuss how the given-clause algorithm can be used to embed polarized resolution modulo into a prover.

1   Deduction Modulo

We use standard definitions for terms, predicates, propositions (with connectors $\neg, \Rightarrow, \wedge, \vee$ and quantifiers $\forall, \exists$), sequents, substitutions, term rewrite rules and term rewriting. $\mathcal{V}$ is the set of variables, the substitution of a variable x by a term t in a term or a proposition A is denoted by $\{t/x\}A$, and more generally the application of a substitution σ in a term or a proposition A by σA. To ensure the existence of ground terms (terms without free variable), we assume the existence of at least one constant. A term t can be narrowed into s using substitution σ at position $\mathfrak{p}$ ($t \overset{\mathfrak{p},\sigma}{\leadsto} s$) if σt can be rewritten to s using substitution σ at position $\mathfrak{p}$. A literal is an atomic proposition or the negation of an atomic proposition. A proposition is in clausal normal form if it is the universal quantification of a disjunction of literals $\forall x_1, \ldots, x_n.\ L_1 \vee \ldots \vee L_p$ where $x_1, \ldots, x_n$ are the free variables of $L_1, \ldots, L_p$. A multiset of propositions is in clausal normal form if all its elements are. In the following, we will often omit to write the quantifications, and we will identify propositions in clausal normal form with clauses (i.e. set of literals) as if $\vee$ was associative, commutative and idempotent. Justifications for this will be given later. $\square$ represents the empty clause. The polarity of a position in a proposition can be defined as follows: the root is positive, and the polarity switches when going under a $\neg$ or on the left of a $\Rightarrow$.

In deduction modulo, term rewriting and narrowing is extended to propositions by congruence on the proposition structure. In addition, there are also proposition rewrite rules whose left hand side is an atomic proposition and whose right hand side can be any proposition. Such rules can also be applied to non-atomic propositions by congruence on the proposition structure. It can be useful to distinguish whether a proposition rewrite rule can be applied at a positive or a negative position. To do so, proposition rewrite rules are tagged with a polarity; they are then called polarized rewrite rules. A proposition A is rewritten positively into a proposition B ($A \longrightarrow {}^+ B$) if it is rewritten by a positive rule at a positive position or by a negative rule at a negative position. It is rewritten negatively ($A \longrightarrow {}^- B$) if it is rewritten by a positive rule at a negative position or by a negative rule at a positive position. Term rewrite rules are considered as both positive and negative. $\xrightarrow{*}{}^{\pm}$ is the reflexive transitive closure of $\longrightarrow {}^{\pm}$.

In deduction modulo [9], the inference rules of an existing system such as the sequent calculus are applied modulo the congruence associated with the rewrite system (term rewrite rules and proposition rewrite rules). This leads for instance to the sequent calculus modulo. In polarized deduction modulo [5], polarities of rewrite rules are also taken into account. Some inference rules of the polarized sequent calculus modulo are presented in Figure 1. We write $\Gamma \vdash_{\mathcal{R}} \Delta$ if the sequent $\Gamma \vdash \Delta$ can be proved in the polarized sequent calculus modulo $\mathcal{R}$, and $\Gamma \vdash_{\mathcal{R}}^{cf} \Delta$ if it can be proved without the cut rule ($\subset$). In the original version of (polarized) deduction modulo, term rewrite rules are taken into account as an equational theory $\mathcal{E}$. In the extension of the resolution method based on deduction modulo, this is performed by using unification modulo $\mathcal{E}$ instead of syntactical unification, following the equational resolution [17] where unification constraints are used instead of substitutions. In addition to this **Resolution** rule, an **Extended Narrowing** rule permits to narrow propositions using the proposition rewrite rules. The Polarized Resolution Modulo is presented in Figure 2. Note that the polarized rewrite system $\mathcal{R}$ is assumed to be clausal, that is, the right hand side of negative rewrite rules is a proposition in clausal normal form, and the one of positive rules is the negation of a clausal normal form. This ensures that narrowed propositions stay in clausal normal form. To see some examples, in

$$\vdash \frac{}{\Gamma, A \vdash B, \Delta} \; A \xrightarrow{*}{}_{\mathcal{R}}{}^- C \; {}^+ \xrightarrow{*}{}_{\mathcal{R}} B \qquad \subset \frac{\Gamma, A \vdash \Delta \qquad \Gamma \vdash B, \Delta}{\Gamma \vdash \Delta} \; A \; {}^- \xrightarrow{*}{}_{\mathcal{R}} C \xrightarrow{*}{}_{\mathcal{R}}{}^+ B$$

$$\vee \vdash \frac{\Gamma, A \vdash \Delta \qquad \Gamma, B \vdash \Delta}{\Gamma, C \vdash \Delta} \; C \xrightarrow{*}{}_{\mathcal{R}}{}^- A \vee B \qquad \vdash \exists \frac{\Gamma \vdash \{t/x\}A, \Delta}{\Gamma \vdash B, \Delta} \; B \xrightarrow{*}{}_{\mathcal{R}}{}^+ \exists x.\, A$$

Fig. 1. Some inference rules of the Polarized Sequent Calculus Modulo $\mathcal{R}$

$$\text{Resolution} \; \frac{P_1 \vee \ldots \vee P_n \vee C \cdot [\mathfrak{C}_1] \qquad \neg Q_1 \vee \ldots \vee \neg Q_p \vee D \cdot [\mathfrak{C}_2]}{C \vee D \cdot [\mathfrak{C}_1 \cup \mathfrak{C}_2 \cup \{P_1 =_{\mathcal{E}}^? \cdots =_{\mathcal{E}}^? P_n =_{\mathcal{E}}^? Q_1 =_{\mathcal{E}}^? \cdots =_{\mathcal{E}}^? Q_p\}]}$$

$$\text{Ext. Narr.} \; \frac{P \vee C \cdot [\mathfrak{C}]}{D \vee C \cdot [\mathfrak{C} \cup \{P =_{\mathcal{E}}^? Q\}]} \; Q \to D \text{ is a negative rule in } \mathcal{R}$$

$$\text{Ext. Narr.} \; \frac{\neg P \vee C \cdot [\mathfrak{C}]}{D \vee C \cdot [\mathfrak{C} \cup \{P =_{\mathcal{E}}^? Q\}]} \; Q \to \neg D \text{ is a positive rule in } \mathcal{R}$$

Fig. 2. Inference rules of the Polarized Resolution Modulo $\mathcal{R}, \mathcal{E}$ (PRM$_{\mathcal{R},\mathcal{E}}$)

particular how higher-order logic is used in Polarized Resolution Modulo, see [7]. However, note that we do not rely on any result of [7] in this paper.

As far as the author knows, no efficient first-order theorem prover uses such constraints. It is indeed not trivial to implement them while avoiding clauses with unsatisfiable constraints. Instead, term indexing is used to reduce the number of clauses that are candidates for resolution. To get closer from the implementation, the idea would therefore be to adapt term indexing techniques to equational unification. However, as far as the author knows, no generic term indexing modulo exists, only term indexing for some particular theories such as AC or HOL. Instead, for want of a better solution, assuming that the equational theory is presented as a set of term rewrite rules, we will apply **Extended Narrowing** using these rules also:

$$\text{Ext. Narr. } \frac{L \vee C}{\sigma(L' \vee C)} \quad L \overset{\mathsf{p}, \sigma}{\underset{\varepsilon}{\rightsquigarrow}} L', \ L_{|\mathsf{p}} \notin \mathcal{V}$$

2 Refining Polarized Resolution Modulo

Literal selections in clauses permit to restrict the application of **Resolution**. In this section, we show that using an ordering-based literal selection preserves the completeness of $\text{PRM}_\mathcal{R}$. We use an ordering $\succ$ on literals which is well-founded and stable by substitution, and we assume that $\succ$ can be extended to an ordering $\succ_g$ that is total on ground literals. Note that it is more general than starting from an ordering on atoms and extending it to literals (furthermore, we do not require that $P \not\succ \neg P$ for all atoms P). Rules of the Ordered Polarized Resolution Modulo ($\text{OPRM}_\mathcal{R}^\succ$) are presented in Figure 3. To stay nearer from the existing implementations of resolution-based proved, we do not use constraints, **Resolution** only uses one literal per clause and there is therefore a **Factoring** rule. We write $\Gamma \mapsto_\mathcal{R}^\succ C$ when a clause C can be derived from the set of clauses Γ using finitely many inference rules of $\text{OPRM}_\mathcal{R}^\succ$.

We want to prove that any *cut-free* proof of the polarized sequent calculus modulo $\mathcal{R}$ can be transformed into a derivation of the empty clause in $\text{OPRM}_\mathcal{R}^\succ$. [9, Lemma 4.1] shows that transforming a formula into its clausal normal form does not change its refutability. The results from [15, Section 5] shows that the order of the quantifiers and of the disjunctions is not relevant w.r.t. refutability, so that we can consider propositions in clausal normal form as clauses. Therefore, we can restrict ourselves to proofs of sequents $\Gamma \vdash$ where Γ is in clausal normal form. The theorem we want to prove is then the following:

Theorem 1. *Given a set of clauses Γ, if $\Gamma \vdash_\mathcal{R}^{cf}$ then $\Gamma \mapsto_\mathcal{R}^\succ \square$.*

To get a less direct but more elegant proof, we use a couple of intermediary calculi. First, as in [9,7], we need an intermediary resolution calculus where the instantiations are separated from the resolution and extended narrowing rules. This calculus, which is essentially PEIR [7] but with ordering restrictions, is called $\text{OPEIR}_\mathcal{R}^\succ$ for Ordered Polarized Extended Identical Resolution and is presented in Figure 4. We write $\Gamma \hookrightarrow_\mathcal{R}^\succ C$ when a clause C can be derived from the set of clauses Γ using finitely many inference rules of $\text{OPEIR}_\mathcal{R}^\succ$.

$$\text{Resolution } \frac{P \vee C \qquad \neg Q \vee D}{\sigma(C \vee D)} \; ^{a,\,b,\,c} \qquad\qquad \text{Factoring } \frac{L \vee K \vee C}{\sigma(L \vee C)} \; ^{d}$$

$$\text{Ext. Narr.}^{-} \; \frac{P \vee C}{\sigma(D \vee C)} \; ^{a,\,b}, \; Q \rightarrow^{-} D \qquad \text{Ext. Narr.}^{+} \; \frac{\neg Q \vee D}{\sigma(C \vee D)} \; ^{a,\,c}, \; P \rightarrow^{+} \neg C$$

$$\text{Ext. Narr.}^{t} \; \frac{L \vee C}{\sigma(L' \vee C)} \; ^{e}, \; L \overset{\mathfrak{p},\sigma}{\rightsquigarrow} L' \text{ by a term rewrite rule, } L_{|\mathfrak{p}} \notin \mathcal{V}$$

---

^{a} $\sigma = mgu(P, Q)$
^{b} P maximal in $P \vee C$
^{c} $\neg Q$ maximal in $\neg Q \vee D$
^{d} L and K maximal in $L \vee K \vee C$, $\sigma = mgu(L, K)$
^{e} L maximal in $L \vee C$

Fig. 3. Inference rules of the OPRM$_{\mathcal{R}}^{\succ}$

$$\text{Identical Resolution } \frac{P \vee C \qquad \neg P \vee D}{C \vee D} \; ^{a} \qquad \text{Instantiation } \frac{C}{\{t/x\}C}$$

$$\text{Reduction}^{-} \; \frac{P \vee C}{D \vee C} \; ^{a}, \; P \longrightarrow^{-} D \qquad \text{Reduction}^{+} \; \frac{\neg P \vee D}{C \vee D} \; ^{a}, \; P \longrightarrow^{+} \neg C$$

$$\text{Reduction}^{t} \; \frac{L \vee C}{L' \vee C} \; ^{b}, \; L \longrightarrow L' \text{ by a term rewrite rule}$$

---

^{a} P maximal in $P \vee C$ (resp. $\neg P$ in $\neg P \vee D$)
^{b} L maximal in $L \vee C$

Fig. 4. Inference rules of the OPEIR$_{\mathcal{R}}^{\succ}$

We also need a sequent calculus modulo which is more adapted to our purpose. Following the ideas of [4], we introduce the one-sided polarized unfolding sequent calculus (short 1PUSC$_{\mathcal{R}}$) where all formulæ are put in the left-hand side of the sequents, instantiations are ground, rewrite steps are explicit, and rewriting and axioms can be applied to literals only. Its inference rules are presented in Figure 5. Note that there are no cut rule, so that 1PUSC$_{\mathcal{R}}$ is restricted to the cut-free fragment of deduction modulo $\mathcal{R}$. We write $\Gamma \vdash_{\mathcal{R}}$ when a sequent $\Gamma \vdash$ can be proved in 1PUSC$_{\mathcal{R}}$. To prove Theorem 1, we proceed as follows: a cut-free proof in the Polarized Sequent Calculus Modulo $\mathcal{R}$ is transformed into a proof in 1PUSC$_{\mathcal{R}}$, which is transformed into an OPEIR$_{\mathcal{R}}^{\succ}$ derivation, which is transformed into an OPRM$_{\mathcal{R}}^{\succ}$ derivation.

Proposition 2. *For all set of clauses* Γ*, if* $\Gamma \vdash_{\mathcal{R}}^{cf}$*, then* $\Gamma \vdash_{\mathcal{R}}$*.*

Proof. We need to prove that weakening is admissible, that we can make the rewriting explicits and that we can restrict $\frown$, $\uparrow^{-}\vdash$ and $\uparrow^{+}\vdash$ to literals. The

$$\widehat{\vdash}\ \frac{}{\Gamma, P, \neg P \vdash} \qquad\qquad {}^{\because}\vdash\ \frac{\Gamma, C, C \vdash}{\Gamma, C \vdash}$$

$$\vee\vdash\ \frac{\Gamma, C \vdash \qquad \Gamma, D \vdash}{\Gamma, C \vee D \vdash} \qquad\qquad \forall\vdash\ \frac{\Gamma, \{t/x\}C \vdash}{\Gamma, \forall x.\ C \vdash}\ t \text{ ground}$$

$$\uparrow^{-}\vdash\ \frac{\Gamma, C \vdash}{\Gamma, P \vdash}\ P \longrightarrow {}^{-}C \qquad\qquad \uparrow^{+}\vdash\ \frac{\Gamma, C \vdash}{\Gamma, \neg P \vdash}\ P \longrightarrow {}^{+}\neg C$$

Fig. 5. Inference rules of the $1\mathrm{PUSC}_{\mathcal{R}}$

proof is the same as for [4, Proposition 7], except that we are here in a one-sided sequent calculus, which is not problematic since all negations are put down on the literal level. We also need to prove that all instantiations can be ground. By induction on the proof structure. Recall that it is assumed that there exists some constant c, so that ground terms exist. If a $\forall\vdash$ in the Polarized Sequent Calculus Modulo instantiate a variable by a non-ground term t, then either the variables of this term are not instantiated in the proof above, in which case replacing them with c keeps the validity of the proof, or they are instantiated by some $\forall\vdash$. By induction hypothesis, they are instantiated by a ground term. One variable x may be instantiated by different ground terms $s_1^x, \ldots, s_n^x$ in the proof above, so we have to apply $\because\vdash$ before applying $\forall\vdash$ using each of the t where the variables x are instantiated by one of the s_i^x. $\square$

Lemma 3. *For all set of clauses Γ, for all ground clauses $C_1, \ldots, C_n$ and D such that the literals of D are smaller than or equal to the maximal literals of C_i for $\succ_g$, if $\Gamma, C_1, \ldots, C_n \hookrightarrow_{\mathcal{R}}^{\succ} \square$ and $\Gamma, D \hookrightarrow_{\mathcal{R}}^{\succ} \square$ then $\Gamma, C_1 \vee D, \ldots, C_n \vee D \hookrightarrow_{\mathcal{R}}^{\succ} \square$.*

Proof. By lexicographic induction on the multiset extension of $\succ_g$ applied on D and the number of derivation steps in $\Gamma, C_1, \ldots, C_n \hookrightarrow_{\mathcal{R}}^{\succ} \square$. We rely on the fact that $\succ_g$ is total on ground literals.

We try to reproduce the derivation $\Gamma, C_1, \ldots, C_n \hookrightarrow_{\mathcal{R}}^{\succ} \square$ but replacing the C_i by $C_i \vee D$. Let C be the first clause produced in that derivation. There are two cases:

- C is produced using other clauses than one of the C_i. We can therefore derive C in $\Gamma, C_1 \vee D, \ldots, C_n \vee D$.
  The derivation length of $\Gamma, C, C_1, \ldots, C_n \hookrightarrow_{\mathcal{R}}^{\succ} \square$ is strictly smaller than the derivation length of $\Gamma, C_1, \ldots, C_n \hookrightarrow_{\mathcal{R}}^{\succ} \square$. Of course $\Gamma, C, D \hookrightarrow_{\mathcal{R}}^{\succ} \square$. By induction hypothesis, we therefore have $\Gamma, C, C_1 \vee D, \ldots, C_n \vee D \hookrightarrow_{\mathcal{R}}^{\succ} \square$.
  Hence, $\Gamma, C_1 \vee D, \ldots, C_n \vee D \hookrightarrow_{\mathcal{R}}^{\succ} \square$.
- At least one of the parents of C is one C_i. As the literals of D are smaller than or equal to those of C_i for $\succ_g$, the maximal elements for $\succ$ of C_i are included in those of $C_i \vee D$. We can therefore derive $C \vee D$ in $\Gamma, C_1 \vee D, \ldots, C_n \vee D$.
  - If the literals of D are less than or equal to the maximal literals of C for $\succ_g$, as the derivation length of $\Gamma, C_1, \ldots, C_n, C \hookrightarrow_{\mathcal{R}}^{\succ} \square$ is strictly smaller than the one of $\Gamma, C_1, \ldots, C_n \hookrightarrow_{\mathcal{R}}^{\succ} \square$, we have by induction hypothesis $\Gamma, C_1 \vee D, \ldots, C_n \vee D, C \vee D \hookrightarrow_{\mathcal{R}}^{\succ} \square$. Hence $\Gamma, C_1 \vee D, \ldots, C_n \vee D \hookrightarrow_{\mathcal{R}}^{\succ} \square$.

- If at least one of the literals in D is strictly greater than one of the maximal literals of C, as $\succ_g$ is total on ground literals, the literals in C are strictly smaller than the maximal literals of D. The derivation length of $\Gamma, C, C_1, \ldots, C_n \hookrightarrow_{\mathcal{R}}^{\succ} \square$ is strictly smaller than the derivation length of $\Gamma, C_1, \ldots, C_n \hookrightarrow_{\mathcal{R}}^{\succ} \square$. Of course $\Gamma, C, D \hookrightarrow_{\mathcal{R}}^{\succ} \square$. By induction hypothesis, we therefore have $\Gamma, C, C_1 \vee D, \ldots, C_n \vee D \hookrightarrow_{\mathcal{R}}^{\succ} \square$. We have $\Gamma, C_1 \vee D, \ldots, C_n \vee D, D \hookrightarrow_{\mathcal{R}}^{\succ} \square$ and $\Gamma, C_1 \vee D, \ldots, C_n \vee D, C \hookrightarrow_{\mathcal{R}}^{\succ} \square$, and C is strictly less than D for the multiset extension of $\succ$, so that by induction hypothesis we have $\Gamma, C_1 \vee D, \ldots, C_n \vee D, D \vee C \hookrightarrow_{\mathcal{R}}^{\succ} \square$. Hence $\Gamma, C_1 \vee D, \ldots, C_n \vee D \hookrightarrow_{\mathcal{R}}^{\succ} \square$. $\square$

Note 4. The lemma does not use any compatibility between the polarized rewrite rules and the ordering $\succ$. Indeed, polarized rewrite rules may increase the maximal literals in the clauses, but this does not break the completeness.

Proposition 5. *A proof of $\Gamma \vdash$ in 1PUSC$_{\mathcal{R}}$ can be transformed into a derivation $\Gamma \hookrightarrow_{\mathcal{R}}^{\succ} \square$.*

Proof. By induction on the proof. If the last rule is $\vdash \overline{\Gamma, P, \neg P \vdash}$ then we apply Identical Resolution on P and $\neg P$ to derive the empty clause. If the last rule is $\therefore \vdash \dfrac{\Gamma, C, C \vdash}{\Gamma, C \vdash}$ then by induction hypothesis we have a derivation $\Gamma, C, C \hookrightarrow_{\mathcal{R}}^{\succ} \square$, which is also a derivation $\Gamma, C \hookrightarrow_{\mathcal{R}}^{\succ} \square$. If the last rule is $\vee \vdash \dfrac{\Gamma, C \vdash \quad \Gamma, D \vdash}{\Gamma, C \vee D \vdash}$ then by induction hypothesis we have $\Gamma, C \hookrightarrow_{\mathcal{R}}^{\succ} \square$ and $\Gamma, D \hookrightarrow_{\mathcal{R}}^{\succ} \square$. As variables are instantiated by ground terms, C and D are ground. Without loss of generality, we can assume that all the atoms in D are less than or equal to the maximal atoms in C for $\succ_g$ (else, exchange C and D since $\succ_g$ is total on ground literals), so that we can apply Lemma 3 to obtain a derivation of $\Gamma, C \vee D \hookrightarrow_{\mathcal{R}}^{\succ} \square$. If the last rule is $\forall \vdash \dfrac{\Gamma, \{t/x\}C \vdash}{\Gamma, \forall x.\ C \vdash}$ then by induction hypothesis we obtain a derivation $\Gamma, \{t/x\}C \hookrightarrow_{\mathcal{R}}^{\succ} \square$. Using Instantiation we can derive $\{t/x\}C$ from $\forall x.\ C$ (recall that we identify clauses and propositions in clausal normal form). We therefore have a derivation of $\Gamma, \forall x.\ C \hookrightarrow_{\mathcal{R}}^{\succ} \square$. If the last rule is $\uparrow^- \vdash \dfrac{\Gamma, C \vdash}{\Gamma, P \vdash} P \xrightarrow{-} C$ then by induction hypothesis we have a derivation $\Gamma, C \hookrightarrow_{\mathcal{R}}^{\succ} \square$. Using Reduction$^-$ or Reduction^t, we can derive C from P and get a derivation $\Gamma, P \hookrightarrow_{\mathcal{R}}^{\succ} \square$. The case of $\uparrow^+ \vdash$ is dual. $\square$

We now want to transform an OPEIR$_{\mathcal{R}}^{\succ}$ derivation into an OPRM$_{\mathcal{R}}^{\succ}$ one. The principal difficulty is that we may have instantiated literals too much before applying Identical Resolution, so that we cannot translate it directly into a Resolution with the appropriate mgu. Note that the Instantiations can be regrouped into a more general derived rule Instantiation $\dfrac{C}{\sigma C}$ for a substitution σ. We can also cut substitutions to transform Instantiation $\dfrac{C}{\sigma \theta C}$ into $\begin{array}{c} \text{Instantiation } \dfrac{C}{\theta C} \\ \text{Instantiation } \dfrac{}{\sigma \theta C} \end{array}$.

Proposition 6. *If $\Gamma \hookrightarrow_{\mathcal{R}}^{\succ} \square$ then $\Gamma \mapsto_{\mathcal{R}}^{\succ} \square$.*

Proof. We prove a stronger result: if $\Gamma \hookrightarrow_{\mathcal{R}}^{\succ} C$ then there exist a clause C' and a substitution θ such that $\Gamma \mapsto_{\mathcal{R}}^{\succ} C'$ and $C = \theta C'$.

By induction on the derivation $\Gamma \hookrightarrow_{\mathcal{R}}^{\succ} C$. If the last step is Instantiation, the result is immediate by induction hypothesis. If the last step is Reduction$^-$ $\dfrac{P \vee C}{D \vee C}$ where P is rewritten into D by the rule $Q \to^- E$ with substitution γ, then by induction hypothesis there exists C', $P'_1, \dots, P'_n$ and θ such that $C = \theta C'$, $P = \theta P'_i$ for all i, and $\Gamma \mapsto_{\mathcal{R}}^{\succ} P'_1 \vee \cdots \vee P'_n \vee C'$. As P is maximal in $P \vee C$ and $\succ$ is stable by substitution, all P'_i are maximal in $P'_1 \vee \cdots \vee P'_n \vee C'$. Let $\sigma_1 = mgu(P'_1, P'_2)$, we can apply Factoring to derive $\sigma_1(P'_1 \vee P'_3 \vee \cdots \vee C')$. Once again, $\sigma_1 P'_1$ is maximal in it. By repeating this process, we therefore obtain $\sigma P'_1 \vee \sigma C'$ with $\sigma = mgu(P'_1, \dots, P'_n)$. Since P is an instance of both $\sigma P'_1$ and Q, they are unifiable and there exists δ' such that $\gamma = \delta' \delta$ and $\theta = \delta' \delta \sigma$ with $\delta = mgu(\sigma P'_1, Q)$. Thus, we can apply Ext. Narr.$^-$ to derive $\delta(E \vee \sigma C')$, and $D \vee C = \gamma E \vee \theta C' = \delta'(\delta(E \vee \sigma C'))$. If the last step is Reduction$^+$ (resp. Reduction^t, resp. Identical Resolution), the proof is similar but using Ext. Narr.$^+$ (resp. Ext. Narr.^{t}, resp. Resolution) at the end. For Ext. Narr.^{t}, we just need to take care when the subterm that is narrowed is a variable, in which case we do not need narrowing and we can use instantiation instead. $\qquad\square$

Note 7. In [13], a syntactic proof of the completeness of several refinement of resolution, including ordered resolution, is given. This is done by seeing resolution derivations as proofs using only cuts, and by permuting cuts. Due to the incompleteness of Polarized Resolution Modulo when cuts cannot be eliminated, it is not clear whether this method could be extended to deal with Extended Narrowing. Furthermore, we prefer to show that a cut-free sequent calculus proof can be transformed directly into a derivation satisfying the ordering restrictions.

3   Clause Simplifications

Clause simplifications reduce the search space by eliminating redundancies or by putting clauses in some normal form. Not all simplifications preserving the completeness of ordered resolution can be used in OPRM$_{\mathcal{R}}^{\succ}$. For instance, the elimination of tautologies, i.e. clauses of the form $C \vee P \vee \neg P$, makes OPRM$_{\mathcal{R}}^{\succ}$ no longer complete.

Example 8. Consider the rewrite system $\mathcal{R} : P \to^+ \neg Q, P \to^- \neg Q$, and the ordering $\neg Q \succ Q \succ \neg P \succ P$. It can be proved that cut admissibility holds in the sequent calculus modulo $\mathcal{R}$. Hence OPRM$_{\mathcal{R}}^{\succ}$ is complete. In particular, the empty clause can be derived from the set of clauses $\neg Q \vee P, Q \vee \neg P$. However, the only clause that can be generated from these is $P \vee \neg P$, which is then narrowed into $P \vee Q$, but which would be eliminated as a tautology. OPRM$_{\mathcal{R}}^{\succ}$ with tautology deletion is therefore not complete.

3.1 $>$-Valid Simplification Rules

We give here a general framework, and we show that it can be applied to usual simplifications such as subsumption elimination or demodulation. A simplification rule is a schema of the form $\dfrac{C_1 \;\cdots\; C_n}{D_1 \;\cdots\; D_m}$ that must be interpreted by: If there are clauses of the form $C_1,\ldots,C_n$, they are replaced by the corresponding clauses $D_1,\ldots,D_m$. In other terms, a set of clauses $\Gamma,C_1,\ldots,C_n$ can be transformed don't-care non-deterministically into $\Gamma,D_1,\ldots,D_m$ in a derivation. To show that $\mathrm{OPEIR}_{\mathcal{R}}^{\succ}$ remains complete when adding some set of simplification rules, we will rely on some ordering on $1\mathrm{PUSC}_{\mathcal{R}}$ proofs:

Definition 9. *An ordering $>$ over $1PUSC_{\mathcal{R}}$ proofs preserves completeness*

- *if it is compatible with subproofs, i.e. if p is a subproof of q then $q > p$;*
- *and it is well-founded.*

A simplification rule $\dfrac{C_1 \;\cdots\; C_n}{D_1 \;\cdots\; D_m}$ *is said valid according to $>$ if for all its instances and for all set of clauses Γ,*

1. *if $\Gamma, D_1, \ldots, D_m \vdash_{\mathcal{R}}$ then $\Gamma, C_1, \ldots, C_n \vdash_{\mathcal{R}}$;*
2. *if $\Gamma, C_1, \ldots, C_n \vdash_{\mathcal{R}}$ then $\Gamma, D_1, \ldots, D_m \vdash_{\mathcal{R}}$ with a strictly smaller proof with respect to $>$;*
3. *the rule is stable by substitution, that is, for all θ, $\dfrac{\theta C_1 \;\cdots\; \theta C_n}{\theta D_1 \;\cdots\; \theta D_m}$ is also an instance.*

Condition 1 is needed to prove the soundness of the calculus with the simplification rules. Condition 2 implies its completeness. Condition 3 permits to extend completeness from $\mathrm{OPEIR}_{\mathcal{R}}^{\succ}$ to $\mathrm{OPRM}_{\mathcal{R}}^{\succ}$.

Proposition 10. *Given an ordering $>$ preserving completeness and a set of simplification rules valid according to this ordering, a proof of $\Gamma \vdash$ in $1PUSC_{\mathcal{R}}$ can be transformed into a derivation $\Gamma \hookrightarrow_{\mathcal{R}}^{\succ} \square$ using the simplification rules.*

Proof. We prove this by induction on $>$. If Γ can be simplified into Γ', then using Condition 2, we can find a smaller proof of $\Gamma' \vdash$ w.r.t. $>$, on which we can apply the induction hypothesis. If Γ cannot be simplified, we use the same arguments than in the proof of Proposition 5, relying on the fact that $>$ is compatible with subproofs. □

Proposition 11. *Given an ordering $>$ preserving completeness and a set of simplification rules valid according to this ordering, a derivation $\Gamma \hookrightarrow_{\mathcal{R}}^{\succ} \square$ using the simplification rules can be transformed into a derivation $\Gamma \mapsto_{\mathcal{R}}^{\succ} \square$ using the simplification rules.*

Proof. We use the same proof as for Proposition 6, with this supplementary argument: if a simplification rule can be applied to the clauses derived in $\mathrm{OPRM}_{\mathcal{R}}^{\succ}$, then stability by substitution (Condition 3) tells us that the simplification rule can be applied on the corresponding instances in $\mathrm{OPEIR}_{\mathcal{R}}^{\succ}$. □

3.2   Application

In this section, we assume that the term rewrite system that we are working modulo is terminating and confluent, and that polarized rewrite rules and term rewrite rules commute: if $P \longrightarrow^{\pm}(\neg)C$ in one step and $P \xrightarrow{*} Q$ with the term rewrite system, then there exists D such that $Q \longrightarrow^{\pm}(\neg)D$ in one step and $C \xrightarrow{*} D$ with the term rewrite system. The usual rewrite systems used in deduction modulo, such as the encoding of higher-order logic, have this property.

We want to prove that the following usual simplification rules are complete:

- Strict Subsumption Elimination: $\dfrac{C \qquad (\sigma C) \vee D}{C}$, D not empty;
- Demodulation: $\dfrac{C}{D}$ if $C \longrightarrow D$ by the term rewrite system.

Repetitively applying Demodulation permits to obtain the normal form w.r.t. the term rewrite system.

We use the following ordering over $1\text{PUSC}_{\mathcal{R}}$ proofs. The *skeleton* of a proof is the tree corresponding to the proof where nodes are couples of the inference rule and the principal formula. We define the following ordering $\rhd$ over inference rules: $\vee\vdash \rhd \forall\vdash \rhd \cdot\vdash$ and $\subset\hspace{-0.3em}\supset \rhd \uparrow^{\pm}\vdash \rhd \cdot\vdash$, and we order formulæ with the term rewrite system (which is assumed to be terminating). We define a precedence (also noted $\rhd$) as the lexical combination of this two orderings. This precedence is therefore well-founded. We define as $>$ the lexicographic combination of the RPO based on this precedence applied on the skeleton of the proof and of the subset relation applied to the conclusion of the proof.

Lemma 12. *The ordering $>$ preserves completeness.*

Proof. As the precedence is well-founded, so is the RPO, therefore $>$ is well-founded. Furthermore, since a RPO is a simplification ordering, subproofs are indeed smaller according to $>$.   □

Proposition 13. *Strict Subsumption Elimination and Clause Normalization are compatible with $>$.*

Proof. It is not hard to check that Condition 3 holds for these two rules.

Strict Subsumption Elimination: Condition 1 is a consequence of weakening. For Condition 2, we need to be more precise on the free variables of C and $(\sigma C) \vee D$. Let $x_1, \ldots, x_n$ be the free variables of C that are in the support of σ, and $z_1, \ldots, z_l$ the others free variables of C. Let $y_1, \ldots, y_m$ be the variables in the image of σ. Let $u_1, \ldots, u_k$ be the free variables of D not in $z_1, \ldots, z_l, y_1, \ldots, y_m$. A proof p of $\Gamma, \forall x_1 \ldots x_n, z_1 \ldots z_l. \ C, \forall y_1 \ldots y_m, z_1 \ldots z_l, u_1 \ldots u_k. \ \sigma(C \vee D) \vdash$ can be transformed into a smaller proof of $\Gamma, \forall x_1, \ldots, x_n, z_1, \ldots, z_l. \ C \vdash$: The idea is to follow the skeleton of p, except that we do not apply the instantiations of $y_1, \ldots, y_m$ and $u_1, \ldots, u_k$, and we replace the applications of $\vee\vdash$ such as

$$\vee\vdash \frac{\overset{\pi_1}{\Gamma', \theta\sigma C \vdash} \quad \overset{\pi_2}{\Gamma', \theta D \vdash}}{\Gamma', \theta\sigma C \vee \theta D \vdash} \quad \text{by} \quad \forall\vdash \frac{\overset{\pi_1}{\Gamma', \theta\sigma C \vdash}}{\Gamma', \theta C \vdash} \quad \text{where we instantiate the}$$

x_i by $\theta\sigma x_i$. A proof of $\Gamma, \forall x_1 \ldots x_n, z_1 \ldots z_l. \, C, \forall x_1 \ldots x_n, z_1 \ldots z_l. \, C \vdash$ is obtained this way, on which we apply $\because \vdash$. As $\vee\vdash \, \triangleright \, \forall\vdash \, \triangleright \, \because\vdash$ and $\uparrow^\pm\vdash \, \triangleright \, \because\vdash$, we can verify that the skeleton of the proof that we obtain is strictly smaller than the one of the original proof (or $(\sigma C) \vee D$ is not used, and there are less propositions in the conclusion).

Clause Normalization: For Condition 1, we need to add the term rewriting into the proof. Since $\uparrow^\pm\vdash$ can only be applied to literals, we have to postpone the rewriting to the places where we use literals, which is not problematic. For Condition 2, we prove the stronger result that if $C \xrightarrow{*} D$ with the term rewrite system and $\Gamma, C \vdash_\mathcal{R}$, then we can find a smaller proof of $\Gamma, D \vdash$. We proceed by induction on $\longrightarrow$ applied to C (recall that the term rewrite system is supposed terminating), and on the proof structure. The most interesting cases are for $\underset{\frown}{}$ and $\uparrow^\pm\vdash$. For $\underset{\frown}{}$, suppose that we have $\vdash \; \dfrac{}{\Gamma, \neg C, C \vdash}$. Then to get a proof of $\Gamma, \neg C, D \vdash$, we first need to apply (possibly several times) $\uparrow^+\vdash$ on $\neg C$ to obtain $\neg D$, which is possible since term rewrite rules have no polarity. After that we can apply $\underset{\frown}{}$. As $(\underset{\frown}{}, C) \triangleright (\underset{\frown}{}, D)$ and $\underset{\frown}{} \triangleright \uparrow^+\vdash$, we can check that the skeleton of the resulting proof is indeed smaller. For $\uparrow^\pm\vdash$, suppose that we have

$$\uparrow^-\vdash \dfrac{\overset{\pi}{\Gamma, E \vdash}}{\Gamma, C \vdash}$$

with $C \xrightarrow{-} D$. If it is a polarized rewrite rule that is used, we use the fact that polarized rules and term rewrite rules commute to obtain some F such that $D \longrightarrow {}^-F \xleftarrow{*} E$. By induction hypothesis, we can obtain a proof π' of $\Gamma, F \vdash$ smaller than π. Then, $\uparrow^-\vdash \dfrac{\overset{\pi'}{\Gamma, F \vdash}}{\Gamma, D \vdash}$ is smaller than the first proof. If it is a term rewrite rule that is used, we can proceed similarly using the confluence of the term rewrite system instead of the commutation. D may need several $\uparrow^-\vdash$ steps to be rewritten into F, but these steps will be smaller for $\triangleright$ than the step for $C \longrightarrow E$, therefore the resulting proof will be smaller.   □

Corollary 14. *OPRM$_\mathcal{R}^\succ$ with Strict Subsumption Elimination and Demodulation is complete, provided cut admissibility holds for $\mathcal{R}$.*

Note that we cannot hope to have completeness of full subsumption (i.e. with D possibly empty) in OPEIR$_\mathcal{R}^\succ$ since it would make **Instantiation** useless. It is not clear whether it is complete or not to eliminate full subsumptions in OPRM$_\mathcal{R}^\succ$.

Note 15. In [1], an ordering is also used to give a syntactic proof of the completeness of ordered resolution with some simplification rules. However, this ordering has to be defined on propositions and is then extended to proofs (which are in that case resolution derivations), and the same ordering is used for the literal selection and for the validity of the simplification rules. In our framework, $\succ$ and $>$ can be completely independent.

4   Implementation Issues

We have seen that polarized resolution modulo is compatible with the ordering restrictions and some simplification rules present in the calculi on which automated provers are based. In this section, we look at how, in practice, $\text{OPRM}_{\mathcal{R}}^{\succ}$ could be integrated in them.

The given-clause algorithm is used to organize which clauses must be used by inference rules in a automated prover. It is originally based on the set-of-support strategy for the resolution [19]. Depending on which clauses are simplified, there exists (at least) two variants of this algorithm, the Otter and the Discount loops, named after the prover in which they appeared. Most of today's automated provers are based on one of these variants. To keep it simple, we will only present the basic given-clause algorithm, without simplification rules. The proof space is separate into two sets of clauses: the first one contains the set-of-support clauses, also called passive clauses, also called unprocessed clauses; the other one in the set of usable clauses, also called active clauses. At each step of the loop, a clause, called the given clause, is extracted from the set of passive clauses and put into the set of active clauses. All inferences between the given clause and one of the active clauses (comprising the given clause itself) are performed, the generated clauses being put into the set of passive clauses. At the beginning, the set of active clauses is therefore empty, and the clauses we want to refute or prove satisfiable are put into the set of passive clauses. Given a fair choice of the given clause, completeness of such an algorithm is not hard to prove. This algorithm has been proved quite successful because the set of active clauses can be organized in order to restrict the clauses where to apply the inference rules. In particular, active clauses are put into a term index, often based on discrimination trees, to make the retrieval of clauses containing literals potentially unifiable with the complement of some literal more efficient.

When no literal selection is used and we know that some subset of the input clauses is consistent, we can put directly this subset of clauses into the set of active clauses. Completeness is ensured by the completeness of the set-of-support strategy. However, set of support is no longer complete when using literal selection, even for selection based on some ordering. Actually, it can be proved that the completeness of set of support with selection requires a stronger property than the consistency of the theory, namely the admissibility of the cut rule in the sequent calculus modulo the theory. Indeed, Dowek [7] has shown that polarized rewrite rules can be seen as special clauses, that he called one-way clauses, in which one literal only is selected, and which cannot be resolved one with the other. More precisely, a positive rule $P \rightarrow^{+} \neg C$ corresponds to the clause $\underline{P} \vee C$, and a negative rule $P \rightarrow^{-} C$ to the clause $\underline{\neg P} \vee C$ (selected literals are underlined). Then, using Resolution with one of these one-way clauses correspond exactly to using Extended Narrowing with the associated polarized rewrite rule, and one-way clauses are not resolved between themselves. To simulate Extended Narrowing into a prover, one can add the one-way clauses corresponding to the polarized rewrite rules directly into the set of active clauses, with their selected literal, and to put the input clauses as usual in the set of passive clauses. We have applied these ideas to integrate polarized resolution modulo into the resolution prover included in iprover [http://www.cs.man.ac.uk/~korovink/iprover/]. It would have been harder to integrate them into a prover based on superposition, because in these provers, selection is not symmetrical between positive and negative literals. We tested it using the encoding in deduction modulo of the problems of higher-order logic of the TPTP [18]. As can be expected, performances compared to the provers dedicated to higher-order logic such as TPS [http://gtps.math.cmu.edu/tps.html] is quite poor, but they are promising (about a third of the problems solved by TPS at the 22nd CASC can be solved by the modified iprover). We need to fine-tune the prover (for instance by choosing convenient orderings) to adapt it to HOL, and to look at other theories.

5 Conclusion and Discussion

We have shown how polarized deduction modulo can be embedded into an existing resolution-based prover and we have proved that ordered polarized resolution modulo with strict subsumption elimination and demodulation is complete. For this, we have defined an ordering-based criterion that ensures that simplification rules preserve completeness. Note that this criterion can also be used for standard resolution. These results are the first which lead to an actual and useful implementation of deduction modulo, and can be used to get automated theorem provers adapted to many theories, including arithmetic, Zermelo's set theory and higher-order logic. We are currently investigating whether using these refinements induces decision procedures for some classes of propositions, as it is the case for standard resolution [16].

Also, the treatment of equality in deduction modulo may be improved, because deduction modulo is originally based on proof systems without equality. Theoretically, this is not a problem, because the equality predicate can be encoded using a rewrite system representing Leibniz's axiom schema $x = y \Rightarrow A(x) \Rightarrow A(y)$. However, in practice, this encoding is not well suited, because the proposition A has to be guessed using narrowing steps. A solution would be to have a proof-search procedure modulo for first-order logic with equality, for instance by adding **Extended Narrowing** in the superposition calculus. It remains to be proved that the restrictions on the inference rules and the redundancy eliminations of superposition can be mixed with **Extended Narrowing** without breaking completeness. The usual proof of completeness of superposition relies on saturation up to redundancies w.r.t. $\succ$ [2]. If we want to adapt this proof directly, we have to require that the one-way clauses corresponding to the rewrite rules are saturated for $\succ$. On the contrary of what is done here, this creates a dependency between the rewrite system and $\succ$. It can be proved that this assumption implies the cut admissibility [14], which explains why we would have full completeness in that case. However, we would like to drop this assumption for at least two reasons: First, some rewrite systems are not compatible with any well-founded, stable by substitution ordering, although cut admissibility holds for them. We therefore conjecture that superposition modulo is fully complete for those systems too. Second, even if a rewrite system is compatible with some ordering, the results of this paper show that another ordering can be used while remaining complete, thus offering new perspectives on combining orderings.

References

1. Bachmair, L.: Proof normalization for resolution and paramodulation. In: Der-showitz, N. (ed.) RTA 1989. LNCS, vol. 355, pp. 15–28. Springer, Heidelberg (1989)
2. Bachmair, L., Ganzinger, H.: Rewrite-based equational theorem proving with selection and simplification. J. Log. Comput. 4(3), 217–247 (1994)
3. Burel, G., Dowek, G.: How can we prove that a proof search method is not an instance of another? In: LFMTP 2009. ACM International Conference Proceeding Series, pp. 84–87. ACM, New York (2009)
4. Burel, G., Kirchner, C.: Regaining cut admissibility in deduction modulo using abstract completion. Inform. Comput. 208, 140–164 (2010)
5. Dowek, G.: What is a theory? In: Alt, H., Ferreira, A. (eds.) STACS 2002. LNCS, vol. 2285, pp. 50–64. Springer, Heidelberg (2002)
6. Dowek, G.: Truth values algebras and proof normalization. In: Altenkirch, T., McBride, C. (eds.) TYPES 2006. LNCS, vol. 4502, pp. 110–124. Springer, Heidelberg (2007)
7. Dowek, G.: Polarized resolution modulo (2010) (to be presented at IFIP TCS)
8. Dowek, G., Hardin, T., Kirchner, C.: HOL-$\lambda\sigma$ an intentional first-order expression of higher-order logic. Mathematical Structures in Computer Science 11(1), 1–25 (2001)
9. Dowek, G., Hardin, T., Kirchner, C.: Theorem proving modulo. Journal of Automated Reasoning 31(1), 33–72 (2003)
10. Dowek, G., Miquel, A.: Cut elimination for Zermelo's set theory (2006), available on authors' web page
11. Dowek, G., Werner, B.: Proof normalization modulo. The Journal of Symbolic Logic 68(4), 1289–1316 (2003)
12. Dowek, G., Werner, B.: Arithmetic as a theory modulo. In: Giesl, J. (ed.) RTA 2005. LNCS, vol. 3467, pp. 423–437. Springer, Heidelberg (2005)
13. Goubault-Larrecq, J.: A note on the completeness of certain refinements of resolution. Research Report LSV-02-8, Laboratoire Spécification et Vérification, ENS Cachan, France (2002)
14. Hermant, O.: Méthodes Sémantiques en Déduction Modulo. Ph.D. thesis, École Polytechnique (2005)
15. Hermant, O.: Resolution is cut-free. Journal of Automated Reasoning 44(3), 245–276 (2009)
16. Joiner Jr., W.H.: Resolution strategies as decision procedures. J. ACM 23(3), 398–417 (1976)
17. Plotkin, G.: Building in equational theories. In: Meltzer, B., Michie, D. (eds.) Machine Intelligence, vol. 7, pp. 73–90. Edinburgh University Press, Edinburgh (1972)
18. Sutcliffe, G., Benzmüller, C., Brown, C.E., Theiss, F.: Progress in the development of automated theorem proving for higher-order logic. In: Schmidt, R.A. (ed.) Automated Deduction – CADE-22. LNCS, vol. 5663, pp. 116–130. Springer, Heidelberg (2009)
19. Wos, L., Robinson, G.A., Carson, D.F.: Efficiency and completeness of the set of support strategy in theorem proving. J. ACM 12(4), 536–541 (1965)

Exponentials with Infinite Multiplicities

Alberto Carraro[1,2], Thomas Ehrhard[2,*], and Antonino Salibra[1,**]

[1] Department of Computer Science, Ca' Foscari University, Venice
[2] Laboratory Preuves, Programmes & Systèmes, UMR 7126, University Paris Diderot, Paris 7 and CNRS

Abstract. Given a semi-ring with unit which satisfies some algebraic conditions, we define an exponential functor on the category of sets and relations which allows to define a denotational model of differential linear logic and of the lambda-calculus with resources. We show that, when the semi-ring has an element which is infinite in the sense that it is equal to its successor, this model does not validate the Taylor formula and that it is possible to build, in the associated Kleisli cartesian closed category, a model of the pure lambda-calculus which is not sensible. This is a quantitative analogue of the standard graph model construction in the category of Scott domains. We also provide examples of such semi-rings.

Keywords: lambda-calculus, linear logic, denotational semantics, differential lambda-calculus, resource lambda-calculus, non sensible models.

1 Introduction

The category of sets and relations is a quite standard denotational model of linear logic which underlies most denotational models of this system (coherence spaces, hypercoherence spaces, totality spaces, finiteness spaces...). In this completely elementary setting, a formula is interpreted as a set, and a proof of that formula is interpreted as a subset of the set interpreting the formula.

Logical connectives are interpreted very simply: tensor product, par and linear implication are interpreted as cartesian products whereas direct product (with) and direct sums (plus) are interpreted as disjoint union. The linear negation of a set is the same set: it is a remarkable feature of linear logic that it admits such a "degenerate" semantics of types, which is nonetheless non trivial in the sense that proofs are not identified.

Exponentials are traditionally interpreted by the operation which maps a set X to the set of all finite multisets of elements of X (the origin of this idea can be found in [Gir88]). One might be tempted to use finite sets instead of finite multisets since, in the coherence space semantics, the exponential can be interpreted by an operation which maps a coherence space to the sets of its finite cliques (with a suitable coherence). In the relational model however, such an interpretation of the exponentials based on finite sets is not possible as it leads to a dereliction which is not natural (in the categorical sense).

* Work partially funded by the ANR project CHOCO, ANR-07-BLAN-0324.
** Work partially funded by the MIUR project CONCERTO.

A. Dawar and H. Veith (Eds.): CSL 2010, LNCS 6247, pp. 170–184, 2010.

With this standard multiset-based interpretation of exponentials, the relational model interprets also the differential extensions of linear logic and of the lambda-calculus presented in [ER03, ER06b, EL10]. In the differential lambda-calculus, terms can be derived (differentiated): a term M of type $A \to B$ can be transformed into a term M' of type $A \to (A \to B)$ which is linear in its second parameter of type A (using a linear implication symbol " $\multimap$ ", the type of M' could be written $A \to (A \multimap B)$). The word "linear" can be taken here in its standard algebraic sense, or in its operational sense of "using its argument exactly once". This differentiation operation can be iterated, yielding a nth derivative $M^{(n)} : A \to (A^n \to B)$ which is n-linear in its n last arguments of type A, that is $M^{(n)} : A \to (A \otimes \cdots \otimes A \multimap B)$. The introduction of this new construction requires the possibility of freely adding terms of the same type: in the model **Rel**, this addition operation is interpreted as set union (remember that terms as interpreted as subsets of the interpretations of types). Also, each type has to contain a 0 element which, here, is the empty set.

This strongly suggests to consider the following "Taylor series", given a term M of type $A \to B$ and a term N of type A: $\sum_{n=0}^{\infty} \frac{1}{n!} M^{(n)}(0) \cdot (N, \ldots, N)$. In this formula, the map $N \mapsto \frac{1}{n!} M^{(n)}(0) \cdot (N, \ldots, N)$ is the approximation of degree n of the function M, that is the "part" of the function M which uses its argument exactly n times. For simplifying the setting and for dealing easily with untyped terms, it is suitable to consider a version of that formula where coefficients are all equal to one, and where addition of terms is an idempotent operation: terms form a complete lattice and the Taylor expansion of M can be written more simply $\bigvee_{n=0}^{\infty} M^{(n)}(0) \cdot (N, \ldots, N)$.

With Regnier, the second author studied this operation in [ER08, ER06a], introducing a *lambda-calculus with resources* which can be seen as the differential lambda-calculus where ordinary[1] application can be used only for applying a term to 0: this is the only ordinary application needed if we want to Taylor expand all the applications occurring in lambda-terms. In these two papers we proved in an untyped setting that, Taylor expanding completely a lambda-term M, one obtains a (generally infinite) linear combination of resource terms and that, if one normalizes each resource term occurring in that formal sum[2], one obtains the Taylor expansion of the Böhm tree of M.

This result implies that, in a denotational model which validates the Taylor expansion formula in the sense that the interpretation of a term M is equal to the interpretation of its Taylor expansion, the interpretation of an unsolvable lambda-term[3] is necessarily equal to 0. Since the multiset-based exponential of **Rel** validates the Taylor expansion formula, any model of the pure lambda-calculus in the

---

[1] In the differential lambda-calculus, there are two kinds of application: the ordinary application of a term to an argument, and the application of the nth derivative of a term to a n-tuple of terms. This latter application is n-linear in its arguments whereas the former is not linear.

[2] Resource terms are strongly normalizing, even if they are not typeable.

[3] We recall that a term is solvable iff its head reduction terminates, see [Kri93, Chapter 4].

corresponding cartesian closed category, such as the model presented in [BEM07, BEM09], seems to be bound to be sensible (at least if differential operations are interpreted in the standard way). This seems to be a serious limitation in the equational expressive power of this kind of semantics.

This problem arose during a general investigation undertaken by the authors, whose scope is to develop an algebraic setting for differential extensions of the lambda-calculus, in the spirit of [PS98, MS09].

Content. The present paper proposes a solution to this problem, by introducing new exponential operations on **Rel**. The idea is quite simple: we replace the set $\mathbb{N}$ of natural numbers (which are used for counting multiplicities of elements in multisets) with more general semi-rings which typically contain "infinite elements" ω such that $\omega+1 = \omega$. *Mutatis mutandis*, the various structures of the exponentials (functorial action, dereliction etc) are interpreted as with the ordinary multiset-based exponentials. For these structures to satisfy the required equations, some rather restrictive conditions have to be satisfied by the considered semi-ring: the semi-rings which satisfy these conditions are called "multiplicity semi-rings". We show that such a semi-ring must contain $\mathbb{N}$ and we exhibit multiplicity semi-rings with infinite elements.

In these models with infinite multiplicities, the differential constructions are available, but the Taylor formula does not hold. It is possible to find morphisms $f : A \rightarrow B$ (in the associated cartesian closed category) which are $\neq 0$ but are such that, for all n, the nth derivative $f^{(n)}(0) : A^n \rightarrow B$ is equal to 0. The Taylor expansion of such a function is the 0 map, and hence the function is different from its Taylor expansion. This is analogous to the well known smooth (C^∞) map $f : \mathbb{R} \rightarrow \mathbb{R}$ defined by $f(0) = 0$ and $f(x) = e^{-1/|x|}$ for $x \neq 0$: all the derivatives of f at 0 are equal to 0 and hence there is no neighborhood of 0 where f coincides with its Taylor expansion at 0. In some sense, f is infinitely flat at 0, and we obtain a similar effect with our infinite multiplicities.

For any multiplicity semi-ring which contains an infinite element, we build a model of the pure lambda-calculus, which is not sensible and, more precisely, where the term $\Omega = (\lambda x\,(x)\,x)\,\lambda x\,(x)\,x$ has a non-empty interpretation (we also exhibit a non solvable term whose interpretation is distinct from that of Ω). We use Krivine's notation for lambda-terms: the application of M to N is denoted as $(M)\,N$.

Warning. Most proofs are omitted and will be available in a longer version of this article.

2   The Relational Model of Linear Logic

Rel is the category whose objects are sets and with hom-sets $\mathbf{Rel}(X,Y) = \mathcal{P}(X \times Y)$. In this category, composition is the ordinary composition of relations: if $R \in \mathbf{Rel}(X,Y)$ and $S \in \mathbf{Rel}(Y,Z)$, then

$$S \cdot R = \{(a,c) \in X \times Z \mid \exists b \in Y\ (a,b) \in R \text{ and } (b,c) \in S\}.$$

and identities are the diagonal relations: $\mathsf{Id}_X = \{(a,a) \mid a \in X\}$.

This category has a well known symmetric monoidal structure (compact closed actually), with tensor product given on objects by $X_1 \otimes X_2 = X_1 \times X_2$ and on morphisms by

$$R_1 \otimes R_2 = \{((a_1, a_2), (b_1, b_2)) \mid (a_i, b_i) \in R_i \text{ for } i = 1, 2\}$$

for any $R_i \in \mathbf{Rel}(X_i, Y_i)$ ($i = 1, 2$). The associativity and symmetry isomorphisms are the obvious bijections, the neutral object of the tensor product is the singleton set $1 = \{*\}$.

This monoidal category is closed: the object of morphisms from X to Y is $X \multimap Y = X \times Y$, with evaluation morphism $\mathsf{ev} \in \mathbf{Rel}((X \multimap Y) \otimes X, Y)$ given by $\mathsf{ev} = \{(((a, b), a), b) \mid a \in X, b \in Y\}$. Given $R \in \mathbf{Rel}(Z \otimes X, Y)$, the linear curryfication of R is $\mathsf{cur}(R) \in \mathbf{Rel}(Z, X \multimap Y)$. This category is star-autonomous, with dualizing object $\bot = 1$.

The category $\mathbf{Rel}$ is also cartesian: the cartesian product of a family of objects $(X_i)_{i \in I}$ is $\prod_{i \in I} X_i = \bigcup_{i \in I}(\{i\} \times X_i)$. The binary cartesian product of X and Y is denoted as $X \& Y$ and the terminal object is $\top = \emptyset$. The projection $\pi_i \in \mathbf{Rel}(\prod_{i \in I} X_i, X_i)$ is $\pi_i = \{((i, a), a) \mid a \in X_i\}$ and, given a family $(R_i)_{i \in I}$ of morphisms $R_i \in \mathbf{Rel}(Y, X_i)$, the corresponding morphism $\langle R_i \rangle_{i \in I} \in \mathbf{Rel}(Y, \prod_{i \in I} X_i)$ is given by $\langle R_i \rangle_{i \in I} = \{(b, (i, a)) \mid i \in I \text{ and } (b, a) \in R_i\}$.

3   Exponentials

We present a way of building exponential functors, once a notion of multiplicity is given, as a semi-ring satisfying strong conditions.

3.1   Multiplicity Semi-rings

Notational convention for indices. We shall use quite often multiple indices, written as subscript as in "a_{ijk}" which has three indices i, j and k. When there are no ambiguities, these indices will not be separated by commas. We insert commas when we use multiplication on these indices, as in "$a_{i,2j,k}$" for instance.

A semi-ring M is a *multiplicity semi-ring* if it is commutative, has a multiplicative unit and satisfies

(MS1) $\forall n_1, n_2 \in M \quad n_1 + n_2 = 0 \Rightarrow n_1 = n_2 = 0$ (we say that M is *positive*)
(MS2) $\forall n_1, n_2 \in M \quad n_1 + n_2 = 1 \Rightarrow n_1 = 0$ or $n_2 = 0$ (we say that M is *discrete*)
(MS3) $\forall n_1, n_2, p_1, p_2 \in M \quad n_1 + n_2 = p_1 + p_2 \Rightarrow \exists r_{11}, r_{12}, r_{21}, r_{22} \in M \quad n_1 = r_{11} + r_{12}, \ n_2 = r_{21} + r_{22}, \ p_1 = r_{11} + r_{21}, \ p_2 = r_{12} + r_{22}$ (we say that M has the *additive splitting property*)
(MS4) $\forall m, p, n_1, n_2 \in M \quad pm = n_1 + n_2 \Rightarrow \exists p_1, p_2, m_{11}, m_{12}, m_{21}, m_{22} \in M \quad m_{11} + m_{21} = m_{12} + m_{22} = m, \ p_1 m_{11} + p_2 m_{12} = n_1, \ p_1 m_{21} + p_2 m_{22} = n_2$ and $p_1 + p_2 = p$ (we say that M has the *multiplicative splitting property*).

Remark 1. The motivation for Condition (MS4) is mainly technical: it is essential in the proof of Lemma 7. It has also an intuitive content, describing what happens when an element of M can be written both as a sum and as a product. The proof that this property holds in $\mathbb{N}$ is based on Euclidean division. We conjecture that this property is independent from Conditions (MS1), (MS2) and (MS3).

Generalized splitting properties. The splitting conditions are expressed in a binary way, we must generalize them to arbitrary arities. We first generalize Condition (MS3).

Lemma 1. *Let M be a semi-ring satisfying (MS1) and (MS3). Let $n_1, \ldots, n_l \in M$ and $p_1, \ldots, p_r \in M$ be such that $\sum_{i=1}^{l} n_i = \sum_{j=1}^{r} p_j$. Then there is a family $(s_{ij})_{i=1,j=1}^{l,r}$ of elements of M such that $\forall i \in \{1, \ldots, l\}$ $n_i = \sum_{j=1}^{r} s_{ij}$ and $\forall j \in \{1, \ldots, r\}$ $p_j = \sum_{i=1}^{l} s_{ij}$.*

Similarly, we generalize Condition (MS4).

Lemma 2. *Let M be a semi-ring satisfying (MS1), (MS3) and (MS4). Let $k \in \mathbb{N}$ with $k \neq 0$. Let $l = 2^{k-1}$. For all $n_1, \ldots, n_k, m, p \in M$, if $pm = n_1 + \cdots + n_k$, then there exist $(p_j)_{j=1}^{l} \in M$ and $(m_{ij})_{i=1,j=1}^{k,l}$ with*

- $p_1 + \cdots + p_l = p$
- $m_{1j} + \cdots + m_{kj} = m$ *for $j = 1, \ldots, l$*
- *and $p_1 m_{i1} + \cdots + p_l m_{il} = n_i$ for $i = 1, \ldots, k$.*

Proposition 1. *Any multiplicity semi-ring M contains an isomorphic copy of $\mathbb{N}$.*

We shall simply say that M contains $\mathbb{N}$, that is $\mathbb{N} \subseteq M$. In particular, a multiplicity semi-ring cannot be finite. An element m of a semi-ring will be said to be *infinite* if it satisfies $m = m + 1$.

Examples of multiplicity semi-rings. The elements of a multiplicity semi-ring should be considered as generalized natural numbers. We give here examples of such semi-rings.

Natural numbers. The most canonical example of multiplicity semi-ring is the set $\mathbb{N}$ of natural numbers, with the ordinary addition and multiplication. Of course, $\mathbb{N}$ has no infinite element.

Proposition 2. $\mathbb{N}$ *is a multiplicity semi-ring.*

Completed natural numbers. Let $\overline{\mathbb{N}} = \mathbb{N} \cup \{\omega\}$ be the "completed set of natural numbers". We extend addition to this set by $n + \omega = \omega + n = \omega$, and multiplication by $0\omega = \omega 0 = 0$ and $n\omega = \omega n = \omega$ for $n \neq 0$, so that $\overline{\mathbb{N}}$ has exactly one infinite element, namely ω.

Proposition 3. $\overline{\mathbb{N}}$ *is a multiplicity semi-ring.*

A semi-ring with infinite and non-idempotent elements. A more interesting example is $\mathbb{N}_2 = (\mathbb{N}^+ \times \mathbb{N}) \cup \{0\}$. The element (n, d) of this set (with $n \neq 0$) will be denoted as $n\omega^d$. We extend this notation to the case where $n = 0$, identifying $0\omega^d$ with 0, which is quite natural with these notations. Addition is defined as follows (0 being of course neutral for this operation)

$$n\omega^d + n'\omega^{d'} = \begin{cases} (n + n')\omega^d & \text{if } d = d' \\ n\omega^d & \text{if } n \neq 0 \text{ and } d' < d \\ n'\omega^{d'} & \text{if } n' \neq 0 \text{ and } d < d' \end{cases}$$

and multiplication is defined by $n\omega^d n'\omega^{d'} = nn'\omega^{d+d'}$. This semi-ring has infinitely many infinite elements: all the elements $n\omega^d$ of $\mathbb{N}_2$ with $n \neq 0$ and $d \neq 0$ are infinite.

Proposition 4. $\mathbb{N}_2$ *is a multiplicity semi-ring.*

From now on, $\mathbb{M}$ denotes a multiplicity semi-ring.

3.2   The Exponential Functor

Given a set X, we define $!_{\mathbb{M}}X$ as the free $\mathbb{M}$-module $\mathbb{M}\langle X \rangle$ generated by X, that is, as the set of all functions $\mu : X \to \mathbb{M}$ such that $\mathsf{supp}(\mu) = \{a \in X \mid \mu(a) \neq 0\}$ (the *support* of μ) is finite. These functions will be called $\mathbb{M}$-*multisets* (of elements of X).

Given $a \in X$, we denote as $[a] \in !_{\mathbb{M}}X$ the function given by $[a](b) = \delta_{a,b}$ (the Kronecker symbol which takes value $0 \in \mathbb{M}$ if $a \neq b$ and $1 \in \mathbb{M}$ if $a = b$). We use the standard algebraic notations for denoting the operations in the $\mathbb{M}$-module $!_{\mathbb{M}}X$. If $\mu \in !_{\mathbb{M}}X$, we define the *cardinality of* μ by $\#\mu = \sum_{a \in \mathsf{supp}(\mu)} \mu(a) \in \mathbb{M}$.

Given $R \in \mathbf{Rel}(X, Y)$, we define $!_{\mathbb{M}}R \in \mathbf{Rel}(!_{\mathbb{M}}X, !_{\mathbb{M}}Y)$ as the set of all pairs (μ, ν) such that one can find $\sigma \in \mathbb{M}\langle X \times Y \rangle$ with $\mathsf{supp}(\sigma) \subseteq R$ and

$$\forall a \in X \quad \mu(a) = \sum_{b \in Y} \sigma(a, b) \quad \text{and} \quad \nu(b) = \sum_{a \in X} \sigma(a, b).$$

We say then that σ is a *witness* of (μ, ν) for R. Observe that all these sums are finite because $\sigma \in \mathbb{M}\langle X \times Y \rangle$.

It is clear from this definition that $!_{\mathbb{M}} \mathsf{Id}_X = \mathsf{Id}_{!_{\mathbb{M}}X}$. Let $R \in \mathbf{Rel}(X, Y)$ and $S \in \mathbf{Rel}(Y, Z)$. We denote as $S \cdot R \in \mathbf{Rel}(X, Z)$ the relational composition of R and S.

Lemma 3. $!_{\mathbb{M}}(S \cdot R) = !_{\mathbb{M}}S \cdot !_{\mathbb{M}}R$.

Proof. This is essentially an application of Lemma 1. □

Lemma 4. *Let* $R \subseteq X \times Y$ *and let* $(\mu_i, \nu_i) \in !_{\mathbb{M}}R$ *and* $p_i \in \mathbb{M}$ *for* $i = 1, \ldots, n$. *Then* $(\sum_{i=1}^n p_i\mu_i, \sum_{i=1}^n p_i\nu_i) \in !_{\mathbb{M}}R$.

Proof. For each i, choose a witness σ_i of (μ_i, ν_i) for R. Then $\sum_{i=1}^n p_i \sigma_i$ is a witness of $(\sum_{i=1}^n p_i \mu_i, \sum_{i=1}^n p_i \nu_i)$ for R.   □

3.3   Comonad Structure of the Exponential

We introduce the fundamental comonadic structure of the exponential functor, which consists of two natural transformations usually called *dereliction* (the counit of the comonad) and *digging* (the comultiplication of the comonad).

Dereliction. We set $d_X = \{([a], a) \mid a \in X\} \in \mathbf{Rel}(!_{\mathbb{M}} X, X)$.

Lemma 5. d_X *is a natural transformation from* $!_{\mathbb{M}}$ *to* Id.

Proof. One applies Conditions (MS1) and (MS2).   □

Remark 2. One could consider taking $\mathbb{M} = \{0, 1\}$ with $1 + 1 = 1$, and then we would have $!_{\mathbb{M}} X = \mathcal{P}_{\text{fin}}(X)$, the set of all finite subsets of X. But this semi-ring does not satisfy Condition (MS2) and, indeed, dereliction is not natural as already mentioned in the Introduction.

Digging. This operation is more problematic and some preliminaries are required.

Lemma 6. *Let X and Y be sets and let $R \subseteq X \times Y$. Let $\nu_1, \nu_2 \in !_{\mathbb{M}} Y$ and $\mu \in !_{\mathbb{M}} X$. If $(\mu, \nu_1 + \nu_2) \in !_{\mathbb{M}} R$, then one can find $\mu_1, \mu_2 \in !_{\mathbb{M}} X$ such that $\mu_1 + \mu_2 = \mu$ and $(\mu_i, \nu_i) \in !_{\mathbb{M}} R$ for $i = 1, 2$.*

Proof. We use Lemma 1.   □

Given $M \in !_{\mathbb{M}} !_{\mathbb{M}} X$, we set

$$\Sigma(M) = \sum_{m \in !_{\mathbb{M}} X} M(m)m \in !_{\mathbb{M}} X.$$

Since M has a finite support, this sum is actually a finite sum (the linear combination, with coefficients $M(m) \in \mathbb{M}$, is taken in the module $!_{\mathbb{M}} X$).
We define $p_X \in \mathbf{Rel}(!_{\mathbb{M}} X, !_{\mathbb{M}} !_{\mathbb{M}} X)$ by

$$p_X = \{(\Sigma(M), M) \mid M \in !_{\mathbb{M}} !_{\mathbb{M}} X\}.$$

The next lemma is the main tool for proving the naturality of digging. It combines the two generalized splitting properties of $\mathbb{M}$.

Lemma 7. *Let X and Y be sets and let $R \subseteq X \times Y$ be finite. There exists $q(R) \in \mathbb{N}$ with the following property: for any $\mu \in !_{\mathbb{M}} X$, $\pi \in !_{\mathbb{M}} Y$ and $p \in \mathbb{M}$, if $(\mu, p\pi) \in !_{\mathbb{M}} R$, then one can find $p_1, \ldots, p_{q(R)} \in \mathbb{M}$ and $\mu_1, \ldots, \mu_{q(R)} \in !_{\mathbb{M}} X$ such that $\sum_{j=1}^{q(R)} p_j = p$, $\sum_{j=1}^{q(R)} p_j \mu_j = \mu$ and $(\mu_j, \pi) \in !_{\mathbb{M}} R$ for each $j = 1, \ldots, q(R)$.*

Proof. Let $I = \{a \in X \mid \exists b \in Y \ (a, b) \in R\}$ and $J = \{b \in Y \mid \exists a \in X \ (a, b) \in R\}$. Given $b \in J$, let $\deg_b(R) = \#\{a \in X \mid (a, b) \in R\} - 1 \in \mathbb{N}$ and let $\deg(R) = \sum_{b \in J} \deg_b(R)$. We prove the result by induction on $\deg(R)$.

Assume first that $\deg(R) = 0$, so that, for any $b \in J$, there is exactly one $a \in I$ such that $(a, b) \in R$, let us set $a = g(b)$: g is a surjective function from J to I whose graph coincides with R (in the sense that $R = \{(g(b), b) \mid b \in J\}$). Let σ be a witness of $(\mu, p\pi)$ for R. For all $b \in J$ we have $p\pi(b) = \sum_{a \in X} \sigma(a, b) = \sigma(g(b), b)$ and for all $a \in I$ we have $\mu(a) = \sum_{g(b)=a} \sigma(a, b) = p \sum_{g(b)=a} \pi(b)$. Let $\tau \in \mathbb{M}\langle X \times Y \rangle$ be defined by

$$\tau(a, b) = \begin{cases} \pi(b) & \text{if } g(b) = a \\ 0 & \text{otherwise.} \end{cases}$$

then clearly $\operatorname{supp}(\tau) \subseteq R$ and τ is a witness of (μ', π) for R, where $\mu' \in \,!_\mathbb{M} X$ is given by $\mu'(a) = \sum_{g(b)=a} \pi(a)$. Since $p\mu' = \mu$, we have obtained the required property (with $q(R) = 1$, $p_1 = p$ and $\mu_1 = \mu'$).

Assume now that $\deg(R) > 0$ and let us pick some $b \in J$ such that $k = \deg_b(R) + 1 > 1$. Let σ be a witness of $(\mu, p\pi)$ for R. Let $a_1, \ldots, a_k$ be a repetition-free enumeration of the elements a of I such that $(a, b) \in R$. We have

$$p\pi(b) = \sum_{i=1}^{k} \sigma(a_i, b).$$

Let $l = 2^{k-1}$. By Lemma 2, there exist $p_1, \ldots, p_l \in \mathbb{M}$ and $(m_{ij})_{i=1, j=1}^{k, l}$ elements of $\mathbb{M}$ with

- $p_1 + \cdots + p_l = p$
- $m_{1j} + \cdots + m_{kj} = \pi(b)$ for $j = 1, \ldots, l$
- and $p_1 m_{i1} + \cdots + p_l m_{il} = \sigma(a_i, b)$ for $i = 1, \ldots, k$.

Let $b_1, \ldots, b_k$ be pairwise distinct new elements, which do not belong to X nor to Y, and let $Y' = (Y \setminus \{b\}) \cup \{b_1, \ldots, b_k\}$. We define a new relation to which we shall be able to apply the inductive hypothesis as follows:

$$S = \{(a, b') \in R \mid b' \neq b\} \cup \{(a_i, b_i) \mid i = 1, \ldots, k\}.$$

Then we have $\deg(S) = \deg(R) - k + 1 < \deg(R)$. Let $\tau \in \mathbb{M}\langle X \times Y' \rangle$ be given by

$$\tau(a, c) = \begin{cases} \sigma(a, c) & \text{if } c \notin \{b_1, \ldots, b_k\} \\ \sigma(a_i, b) & \text{if } c = b_i \text{ and } a = a_i \\ 0 & \text{otherwise.} \end{cases}$$

It is clear that $\operatorname{supp}(\tau) \subseteq S$. Moreover, τ is a witness of $(\mu, \sum_{j=1}^{l} p_j \pi_j)$ for S, where $\pi_j \in \,!_\mathbb{M} Y'$ is given by

$$\pi_j(c) = \begin{cases} \pi(c) & \text{if } c \notin \{b_1, \ldots, b_k\} \\ m_{ij} & \text{if } c = b_i. \end{cases}$$

for each $j \in \{1, \ldots, l\}$. Indeed, for $a \in X$ we have

$$
\sum_{c \in Y'} \tau(a, c) = \sum_{c \in Y' \setminus \{b_1, \ldots, b_k\}} \tau(a, c) + \sum_{i=1}^{k} \tau(a, b_i)
$$

$$
= \sum_{c \in Y' \setminus \{b_1, \ldots, b_k\}} \sigma(a, c) + \sum_{i=1}^{k} \delta_{a, a_i} \sigma(a_i, b)
$$

$$
= \sum_{c \in Y' \setminus \{b_1, \ldots, b_k\}} \sigma(a, c) + \sigma(a, b) = \sum_{b \in Y} \sigma(a, b) = \mu(a)
$$

and for $c \in Y' \setminus \{b_1, \ldots, b_k\}$ we have

$$
\sum_{a \in X} \tau(a, c) = \sum_{a \in X} \sigma(a, c) = p\pi(c) = \sum_{j=1}^{l} p_j \pi_j(c) \quad \text{since} \quad \begin{cases} \forall j \; \pi_j(c) = \pi(c) \\ \sum_{j=1}^{l} p_j = p \end{cases}
$$

and last, for $c = b_i$ (with $i \in \{1, \ldots, k\}$), we have

$$
\sum_{a \in X} \tau(a, c) = \sigma(a_i, b) = \sum_{j=1}^{l} p_j m_{ij} = \sum_{j=1}^{l} p_j \pi_j(c) .
$$

By Lemma 6, since $\left(\mu, \sum_{j=1}^{l} p_j \pi_j \right) \in \, !_{\mathrm{M}} S$, we can find $\mu_1, \ldots, \mu_l \in \, !_{\mathrm{M}} X$ such that $\sum_{j=1}^{l} \mu_j = \mu$ and $(\mu_j, p_j \pi_j) \in \, !_{\mathrm{M}} S$ for each $j \in \bar{l} = \{1, \ldots, l\}$. Since $\deg(S) < \deg(R)$, we can apply the inductive hypothesis for each $j \in \bar{l}$. So we can find a family $(p_{js})_{j=1, s=1}^{l, q(S)}$ of elements of M such that $p_j = \sum_{s=1}^{q(S)} p_{js}$ and we can find a family $(\mu_{js})_{j=1, h=1}^{l, q(S)}$ of elements of $!_{\mathrm{M}} X$ such that $\sum_{s=1}^{q(S)} p_{js} \mu_{js} = \mu_j$, and moreover $(\mu_{js}, \pi_j) \in \, !_{\mathrm{M}} S$ for each $j \in \bar{l}$ and $s \in \overline{q(S)}$. We conclude the proof by showing that $(\mu_{js}, \pi) \in \, !_{\mathrm{M}} R$. Let $\tau_{js} \in \mathrm{M} \langle X \times Y' \rangle$ be a witness of (μ_{js}, π_j) for S. Let $\sigma_{js} \in \mathrm{M} \langle X \times Y \rangle$ be given by

$$
\sigma_{js}(a, b') = \begin{cases} \tau_{js}(a, b') & \text{if } b' \neq b \\ \sum_{i=1}^{k} \tau_{js}(a, b_i) & \text{if } b' = b. \end{cases}
$$

For $b' \in Y \setminus \{b\}$, we have $\sum_{a \in X} \sigma_{js}(a, b') = \sum_{a \in X} \tau_{js}(a, b') = \pi_j(b') = \pi(b')$. Next we have

$$
\sum_{a \in X} \sigma_{js}(a, b) = \sum_{a \in X} \sum_{i=1}^{k} \tau_{js}(a, b_i)
$$

$$
= \sum_{i=1}^{k} \sum_{a \in X} \tau_{js}(a, b_i)
$$

$$
= \sum_{i=1}^{k} \pi_j(b_i) = \sum_{i=1}^{k} m_{ij} = \pi(b) .
$$

On the other hand we have

$$\sum_{b' \in Y} \sigma_{js}(a, b') = \sum_{b' \in Y \setminus \{b\}} \sigma_{js}(a, b') + \sigma_{js}(a, b)$$

$$= \sum_{b' \in Y \setminus \{b\}} \tau_{js}(a, b') + \sum_{i=1}^{k} \tau_{js}(a, b_i)$$

$$= \sum_{c \in Y'} \tau_{js}(a, c) = \mu_{js}(a).$$

It remains to prove that $\mathsf{supp}(\sigma_{js}) \subseteq R$, but this results immediately from the definition of σ_{js} and from the fact that $\mathsf{supp}(\tau_{js}) \subseteq S$.

Observe that we can take $q(R) = lq(S)$, so that in general $q(R) = 2^{\deg(R)}$.

$\square$

Lemma 8. p_X *is a natural transformation from* $!_\mathsf{M}$ *to* $!_\mathsf{M}!_\mathsf{M}$.

Proof. This is essentially an application of Lemma 7. $\square$

Comonad equations. We prove that $\mathsf{d}_{!_\mathsf{M}X} \cdot \mathsf{p}_X = \mathsf{Id}_{!_\mathsf{M}X}$. Let $(\mu, \mu') \in !_\mathsf{M}X \times !_\mathsf{M}X$. Assume first that $(\mu, \mu') \in \mathsf{d}_{!_\mathsf{M}X} \cdot \mathsf{p}_X$. Then we can find $M \in !_\mathsf{M}!_\mathsf{M}X$ such that $(\mu, M) \in \mathsf{p}_X$ and $(M, \mu') \in \mathsf{d}_{!_\mathsf{M}X}$. This means that $M = [\mu']$ and hence $\Sigma(M) = \mu'$, hence $\mu = \mu'$. Conversely, for $\mu \in !_\mathsf{M}X$ we have $(\mu, [\mu]) \in \mathsf{p}_X$, therefore $(\mu, \mu) \in \mathsf{d}_{!_\mathsf{M}X} \cdot \mathsf{p}_X$.

Next we prove that $!_\mathsf{M}\mathsf{d}_X \cdot \mathsf{p}_X = \mathsf{Id}_{!_\mathsf{M}X}$. Let $(\mu, \mu') \in !_\mathsf{M}\mathsf{d}_X \cdot \mathsf{p}_X$. Let $M \in !_\mathsf{M}!_\mathsf{M}X$ be such that $(\mu, M) \in \mathsf{p}_X$, that is $\Sigma(M) = \mu$, and $(M, \mu') \in !_\mathsf{M}\mathsf{d}_X$. Let $\sigma \in \mathsf{M}\langle !_\mathsf{M}X \times X \rangle$ be a witness of (M, μ') for d_X. This means that $\mu'(a) = \sum_{\nu \in !_\mathsf{M}X} \sigma(\nu, a) = \sigma([a], a)$ since $\mathsf{supp}(\sigma) \subseteq \mathsf{d}_X$, and that $M(\nu) = \sigma([a], a)$ if $\nu = [a]$, and $M(\nu) = 0$ if $\#\nu \neq 1$. It follows that $\Sigma(M) = \sum_{\nu \in !_\mathsf{M}X} M(\nu)\nu = \sum_{a \in X} \sigma([a], a)[a] = \mu'$ and hence $\mu = \mu'$. Conversely, one has $(\mu, \mu) \in !_\mathsf{M}\mathsf{d}_X \cdot \mathsf{p}_X$, because $M \in !_\mathsf{M}!_\mathsf{M}X$ defined by $M(\nu) = \mu(a)$ if $\nu = [a]$ and $M(\nu) = 0$ if $\#\nu \neq 0$ satisfies $(\mu, M) \in \mathsf{p}_X$ and $(M, \mu) \in !_\mathsf{M}\mathsf{d}_X$.

Lemma 9. *Let* $\mathcal{M} \in !_\mathsf{M}!_\mathsf{M}!_\mathsf{M}X$. *Then* $\Sigma(\Sigma(\mathcal{M})) = \sum_{N \in !_\mathsf{M}!_\mathsf{M}X} \mathcal{M}(N)\Sigma(N)$.

Proof. We have

$$\Sigma(\Sigma(\mathcal{M})) = \sum_{\nu \in !_\mathsf{M}X} \Sigma(\mathcal{M})(\nu)\nu$$

$$= \sum_{\nu \in !_\mathsf{M}X} \left(\sum_{N \in !_\mathsf{M}!_\mathsf{M}X} \mathcal{M}(N)N(\nu) \right) \nu$$

$$= \sum_{N \in !_\mathsf{M}!_\mathsf{M}X} \mathcal{M}(N) \left(\sum_{\nu \in !_\mathsf{M}X} N(\nu)\nu \right)$$

and we are done. $\square$

Using Lemma 9, one proves the last comonad equation, namely $p_{!_M X} \cdot p_X = !_M\, p_X \cdot p_X$.

Fundamental isomorphism. One of the most important properties of the exponential is that it maps cartesian products to tensor products. Combined with the monoidal closure of **Rel**, this property leads to the cartesian closeness of the Kleisli category **Rel$_!$**.

Proposition 5. *Given two sets X_1 and X_2, there is an natural bijection $n_{X_1, X_2} : !_M X_1 \otimes !_M X_2 \to !_M(X_1 \,\&\, X_2)$ and a bijection $n_0 : 1 \to !_M\top$.*

Given $(\mu_1, \mu_2) \in !_M X_1 \otimes !_M X_2$, we define $\nu = n(\mu_1, \mu_2) \in !_M(X_1 \,\&\, X_2)$ by $\nu(i, a) = \mu_i(a)$ for $i = 1, 2$, and $n_0(*)$ is unique element of $!_M\top$ (the empty multiset).

Structural morphisms. They are used for interpreting the *structural rules* of linear logic, associated with the exponentials. The weakening morphism is $\mathsf{weak}_X : !_M X \to 1$ is $\mathsf{weak}_X = \{([], *)\}$. The contraction morphism is $\mathsf{contr}_X : !_M X \to !_M X \otimes !_M X$ is obtained by applying the $!_M$ functor to the diagonal map $X \to X \,\&\, X$, so that $\mathsf{contr}_X = \{(\lambda + \rho, (\lambda, \rho)) \mid \lambda, \rho \in !_M X\}$.

There are other equations to check for proving that we have defined a model of linear logic (see [Bie95]), the corresponding verifications are straightforward.

3.4   The Kleisli Cartesian Closed Category

The objects of the Kleisli category **Rel$_!$** of the comonad "$!_M$" are the sets, and **Rel$_!$**$(X, Y) = $ **Rel**$(!_M X, Y)$. Identity in this category is dereliction $d_X \in$ **Rel$_!$**(X, X) and composition is defined as follows: let $R \in$ **Rel$_!$**(X, Y) and $S \in$ **Rel$_!$**(Y, Z), then $S \circ R = S \cdot !_M R \cdot p_X$. We give a direct characterization of this composition law.

Proposition 6. *Let $(\mu, c) \in !_M X \times Z$, we have $(\mu, c) \in S \circ R$ iff there exist $b_1, \ldots, b_n \in Y$ (not necessarily distinct), $p_1, \ldots, p_n \in M$ and $\mu_1, \ldots, \mu_n \in !_M X$ such that*

$$\forall i \in \{1, \ldots, n\}\ (\mu_i, b_i) \in R, \quad \left(\sum_{i=1}^{n} p_i[b_i], c\right) \in S \quad and \quad \mu = \sum_{i=1}^{n} p_i \mu_i\,.$$

Proof. Assume first that $(\mu, c) \in S \circ R$. Let $M \in !_M !_M X$ such that $(\mu, M) \in p_X$ and let $\nu \in !_M Y$ be such that $(\nu, c) \in S$ and $(M, \nu) \in !_M R$. We have $\Sigma(M) = \mu$. Let $\sigma \in M\langle !_M X \times Y \rangle$ be a witness of (M, ν) for R, and let $(\mu_1, b_1), \ldots, (\mu_n, b_n)$ be a repetition-free enumeration of the set $\mathsf{supp}(\sigma) \subseteq R$. Taking $p_i = \sigma(\mu_i, b_i)$, we have $\sum_{i=1}^{n} p_i[b_i] = \nu$ and $\sum_{i=1}^{n} p_i[\mu_i] = M$, and therefore $\mu = \sum_{i=1}^{n} p_i \mu_i$.

Assume conversely that (μ, c) satisfies the conditions stated in the proposition. Then we take $\nu = \sum_{i=1}^{n} p_i[b_i]$ and $M = \sum_{i=1}^{n} p_i[\mu_i]$. We have $(\nu, c) \in S$ and $(\mu, M) \in p_X$ and we have just to check that $(M, \nu) \in !_M R$. We define $\sigma = \sum_{i=1}^{n} p_i[(\mu_i, b_i)]$; this is a witness of (M, ν) for R, as easily checked. $\square$

We recall that the cartesian product of X and Y in this category is X & Y, with projections obtained by composing π_1 and π_2 with $\mathsf{d}_{X\&Y}$ in **Rel**. The function space of X and Y is $!_{\mathbb{M}}X \multimap Y$. Evaluation $\mathsf{Ev} \in \mathbf{Rel}_!(X \; \& \; (!_{\mathbb{M}}X \multimap Y), Y) \simeq \mathbf{Rel}(!_{\mathbb{M}}X \otimes !_{\mathbb{M}}(!_{\mathbb{M}}X \multimap Y), Y)$ is

$$\mathsf{Ev} = \{((\mu, [(\mu, b)]), b) \mid \mu \in !_{\mathbb{M}}X \text{ and } b \in Y\}.$$

Curryfication is defined as follows: let $R \in \mathbf{Rel}_!(Z \; \& \; X, Y) \simeq \mathbf{Rel}(!_{\mathbb{M}}Z \otimes !_{\mathbb{M}}X, Y)$, then $\mathsf{Cur}(R) = \{(\pi, (\mu, b)) \mid ((\pi, \mu), b) \in R\} \in \mathbf{Rel}_!(Z, !_{\mathbb{M}}X \multimap Y)$.

Differential structure and the Taylor expansion. Without giving precise definitions, let us mention that the *differential structure* of this model, which consists of natural linear morphisms $\partial_X \in \mathbf{Rel}(X, !_{\mathbb{M}}X)$ (*codereliction*), $\mathsf{coweak}_X \in \mathbf{Rel}(1, !_{\mathbb{M}}X)$ (*coweakening*) and $\mathsf{cocontr}_X \in \mathbf{Rel}(!_{\mathbb{M}}X \otimes !_{\mathbb{M}}X, !_{\mathbb{M}}X)$ (*cocontraction*) allows to associate, with any morphism $R \in \mathbf{Rel}_!(X, Y)$, its Taylor expansion $R^* \in \mathbf{Rel}_!(X, Y)$. When $\mathbb{M} = \mathbb{N}$, one has $M^* = M$ but this equation does not hold anymore when $\mathbb{M}$ has an infinite element ω. In that case, if $R = \{(\omega[*], *)\} \in \mathbf{Rel}_!(1, 1)$, one has $R^* = \emptyset \neq R$.

4   Graph Models in Rel

Graph models [Bar84] have been isolated by Scott and Engeler in the continuous semantics. We develop here a similar construction, in the relational semantics. Let A be a non-empty set whose elements will be called atoms, and are not pairs. Let $\iota : A \to (!_{\mathbb{M}}A \multimap A)$ be a partial injective map.

We define a sequence $(D^\iota_n)_{n \in \mathbb{N}}$ of sets as follows: $D^\iota_0 = A$ and $D^\iota_{n+1} = D^\iota_n \cup ((!_{\mathbb{M}}D^\iota_n \multimap D^\iota_n) \setminus \iota(A))$. This sequence is monotone, and we set $D^\iota = \bigcup_{n \in \mathbb{N}} D^\iota_n$. We have $!_{\mathbb{M}}D^\iota \multimap D^\iota = \bigcup_{n \in \mathbb{N}} (!_{\mathbb{M}}D^\iota_n \multimap D^\iota_n)$.

We define a function $\varphi : D^\iota \to (!_{\mathbb{M}}D^\iota \multimap D^\iota)$ by

$$\varphi(\alpha) = \begin{cases} \iota(a) & \text{if } \alpha = a \in A \\ \alpha & \text{if } \alpha \notin A \end{cases}$$

and a function $\psi : (!_{\mathbb{M}}D^\iota \multimap D^\iota) \to D^\iota$ by

$$\psi(\mu, \alpha) = \begin{cases} a & \text{if } (\mu, \alpha) = \iota(a) \text{ where } a \in A \\ (\mu, \alpha) & \text{if } (\mu, \alpha) \notin \iota(A). \end{cases}$$

This definition makes sense because ι is injective, and because, if $(\mu, \alpha) \in (!_{\mathbb{M}}D^\iota_n \multimap D^\iota_n) \setminus \iota(A)$, then $(\mu, \alpha) \in D^\iota_{n+1} \subseteq D^\iota$. Let $(\mu, \alpha) \in !_{\mathbb{M}}D^\iota \multimap D^\iota$. If $(\mu, \alpha) \in \iota(A)$, let a be the unique element of A such that $\iota(a) = (\mu, \alpha)$. We have $\varphi(\psi(\mu, \alpha)) = \varphi(a) = \iota(a) = (\mu, \alpha)$. If $(\mu, \alpha) \notin \iota(A)$, we have $\varphi(\psi(\mu, \alpha)) = \varphi(\mu, \alpha) = (\mu, \alpha)$ because $(\mu, \alpha) \notin A$, since no element of A is a pair.

So we have $\varphi \circ \psi = \mathsf{Id}$. We define two morphisms $\mathsf{App} = \{([\alpha], \varphi(\alpha)) \mid \alpha \in D^\iota\} \in \mathbf{Rel}_!(D^\iota, !_{\mathbb{M}}D^\iota \multimap D^\iota)$ and $\mathsf{Lam} = \{([(\mu, \alpha)], \psi(\mu, \alpha)) \mid (\mu, \alpha) \in !_{\mathbb{M}}D^\iota \multimap D^\iota\} \in \mathbf{Rel}_!(!_{\mathbb{M}}D^\iota \multimap D^\iota, D^\iota)$. Then we have $\mathsf{App} \circ \mathsf{Lam} = \mathsf{Id}_{!_{\mathbb{M}}D^\iota \multimap D^\iota}$, so that D^ι is a reflexive object in $\mathbf{Rel}_!$, whatever be the choice of the multiplicity semi-ring $\mathbb{M}$.

4.1   Interpreting Terms

Given a lambda-term M and a repetition-free list of variables $\boldsymbol{x} = (x_1, \ldots, x_n)$ which contains all free variables of M, the interpretation $[M]_{\boldsymbol{x}} \in \mathbf{Rel}_!(D^{\iota n}, D^\iota)$ (where $D^{\iota n}$ is the cartesian product of D^ι with itself, n times) is defined by induction on M as follows

- $[x_i]_{\boldsymbol{x}} = \pi_i$ (the ith projection from $(D^\iota)^n$ to D^ι)
- $[\lambda x\, N]_{\boldsymbol{x}} = \mathsf{Lam} \circ \mathsf{Cur}([M]_{\boldsymbol{x},x})$, assuming that x does not occur in $\boldsymbol{x}$
- $[(N)\, P]_{\boldsymbol{x}} = \mathsf{Ev} \circ \langle \mathsf{App} \circ [N]_{\boldsymbol{x}}, [P]_{\boldsymbol{x}} \rangle$

Using the cartesian closeness of $\mathbf{Rel}_!$ and the fact that $\mathsf{App} \circ \mathsf{Lam} = \mathsf{Id}_{!_M D^\iota \multimap D^\iota}$, one proves that if M and M' are beta-equivalent, and $\boldsymbol{x}$ is a repetition-free list of variables which contain all the free variables of M and M', one has $[M]_{\boldsymbol{x}} = [M']_{\boldsymbol{x}}$. This requires to prove first a substitution lemma, see [AC98].

We present now this interpretation as a typing system (a variation of de Carvalho's system R [DC08]). A type is an element of D^ι. Given $\mu \in\, !_M D^\iota$ and $\alpha \in D^\iota$, we set $\mu \to \alpha = \psi(\mu, \alpha)$. A typing context is a finite partial function from variables to $!_M D^\iota$. If $\Gamma_1, \ldots, \Gamma_k$ are contexts with the same domain and $p_1, \ldots, p_k \in \mathbb{M}$, the sum $\sum_{i=1}^k p_i \Gamma_i$ is defined pointwise (using the addition of $!_M D^\iota$). The typing rules are

$$\frac{}{x_1 : [\,], \ldots, x_n : [\,], x : [\alpha] \vdash x : \alpha} \qquad \frac{\Gamma, x : \mu \vdash M : \alpha}{\Gamma \vdash \lambda x\, M : \mu \to \alpha}$$

$$\frac{\Gamma \vdash M : (\sum_{i=1}^n p_i [\beta_i]) \to \alpha \qquad \forall i \in \overline{n} \quad \Gamma_i \vdash N : \beta_i}{\Gamma + \sum_{i=1}^n p_i \Gamma_i \vdash (M)\, N : \alpha}$$

In the last rule, all contexts involved must have same domain, and the β_i's need not be distinct.

Proposition 7. *The judgment $\Gamma \vdash M : \alpha$ is derivable iff $(\Gamma(x_1), \ldots, \Gamma(x_n), \alpha) \in [M]_{\boldsymbol{x}}$ where $\boldsymbol{x} = (x_1, \ldots, x_n)$ is a repetition-free enumeration of the domain of Γ, which is assumed to contain all the free variables of M.*

Proof. Straightforward induction on the judgment, using Proposition 6. □

We take for $\mathbb{M}$ a multiplicity semi-ring which contains an infinite element ω (remember that this means that $\omega + 1 = \omega$). Let $A = \{a\}$, $\iota : A \to (!_M A \multimap A)$ be defined by $\iota(a) = (\omega[a], a)$, so that $(\omega[a] \to a) = a$. Let $\Omega = (\delta)\, \delta$ where $\delta = \lambda x\, (x)\, x$.

Proposition 8. *In the model D^ι, we have $[\Omega] = \{a\}$.*

Proof. We have the following deduction tree (we have inserted in this tree the equations between types or $\mathbb{M}$-multisets of types that we use)

$$\frac{\dfrac{x : [a] \vdash x : a = \omega[a] \to a \qquad x : [a] \vdash x : a}{\dfrac{x : [a] + \omega[a] = \omega[a] \vdash (x)\, x : a}{\vdash \lambda x\, (x)\, x : \omega[a] \to a}} \qquad \dfrac{\text{(same derivation)}}{\vdash \lambda x\, (x)\, x : \omega[a] \to a = a}}{\vdash (\lambda x\, (x)\, x)\, \lambda x\, (x)\, x : a}$$

Therefore $a \in [\Omega]$.

Conversely, let $\alpha \in D^\iota$ and assume that $\vdash \Omega : \alpha$. There must exist $\mu \in !_\mathsf{M} D^\iota$ such that $\vdash \delta : \mu \to \alpha$ and $\forall \beta \in \mathsf{supp}(\mu) \vdash \delta : \beta$. Form the first of these two judgments we get $x : \mu \vdash (x) x : \alpha$ and hence there must exist $\nu \in !_\mathsf{M} D^\iota$ such that $\mu = \nu + [\nu \to \alpha]$. From the second judgment we get $\vdash \delta : \nu \to \alpha$ and $\forall \beta \in \mathsf{supp}(\nu) \vdash \delta : \beta$. Iterating this process, we build a sequence $(\mu_i)_{i=1}^\infty$ of elements of $!_\mathsf{M} D^\iota$ such that $\vdash \delta : \mu_i \to \alpha$, $\forall \beta \in \mathsf{supp}(\mu_i) \vdash \delta : \beta$ and $\mu_i = \mu_{i+1} + [\mu_{i+1} \to \alpha]$ for all i. Let $\beta_i = \mu_i \to \alpha$, it follows that $\forall i\ \beta_i \in \mathsf{supp}(\mu_1)$ and since $\mathsf{supp}(\mu_1)$ is finite, we can find i and $n > 0$ such that $\beta_{i+n} = \beta_i$. We have $\beta_i = (\mu_i \to \alpha) = ((\mu_{i+1} + [\beta_{i+1}]) \to \alpha) = \cdots = ((\mu_{i+n} + [\beta_{i+1}] + \cdots + [\beta_{i+n}]) \to \alpha)$ and since $\beta_i = \beta_{i+n} = (\mu_{i+n} \to \alpha)$, we get $\mu_{i+n} = \mu_{i+n} + [\beta_{i+1}] + \cdots + [\beta_{i+n}]$ (because ψ is injective) and hence $\beta_{i+n} \in \mathsf{supp}(\mu_{i+n})$. But $\beta_{i+n} = (\mu_{i+n} \to \alpha)$ and hence we must have $\beta_{i+n} = a$. Indeed, if $\beta_{i+n} \notin A$ then by definition of ψ we have $\beta_{i+n} = (\mu_{i+n}, \alpha)$ and, if k is the least integer such that $\beta_{i+n} \in D^\iota_k$, we have $k > 0$ and $\beta \in D^\iota_{k-1}$ for all $\beta \in \mathsf{supp}(\mu_{i+n})$. This is impossible since $\beta_{i+n} \in \mathsf{supp}(\mu_{i+n})$. Since $(\mu_{i+n} \to \alpha) = a$, we have $\alpha = a$ and we are done.   □

Since $([] \to a) \in [\lambda y\, \Omega]$ and $a \neq ([] \to a)$, we have found two unsolvable terms (namely Ω and $\lambda y\, \Omega$) with distinct interpretations in D^ι and hence this model is not sensible.

5   Conclusion

We have introduced the algebraic concept of multiplicity semi-ring, which can be used for generalizing the standard exponential construction of the relational model of linear logic. Such a semi-ring must contain $\mathbb{N}$ as a sub-semi-ring but can also have infinite elements ω such that $\omega + 1 = \omega$. In that case, the corresponding model of linear logic is a model of the differential lambda-calculus which does not satisfy the Taylor formula, and it is possible to build non sensible models of the lambda-calculus in the corresponding Kleisli cartesian closed category. This shows that models of the pure differential lambda-calculus can have non sensible theories and provides a new way of building models of the pure lambda-calculus where non termination is taking into account in a quantitative way by means of these infinite multiplicities.

References

[AC98]   Amadio, R., Curien, P.-L.: Domains and lambda-calculi. Cambridge Tracts in Theoretical Computer Science, vol. 46. Cambridge University Press, Cambridge (1998)

[Bar84]   Barendregt, H.: The Lambda Calculus. Studies in Logic and the Foundations of Mathematics, vol. 103. North-Holland, Amsterdam (1984)

[BEM07]   Bucciarelli, A., Ehrhard, T., Manzonetto, G.: Not enough points is enough. In: Duparc, J., Henzinger, T.A. (eds.) CSL 2007. LNCS, vol. 4646. Springer, Heidelberg (2007)

[BEM09]   Bucciarelli, A., Ehrhard, T., Manzonetto, G.: A relational model of a parallel and non-deterministic lambda-calculus. In: Artëmov, S.N., Nerode, A. (eds.) LFCS 2009. LNCS, vol. 5407, pp. 107–121. Springer, Heidelberg (2008)

[Bie95]   Bierman, G.: What is a categorical model of intuitionistic linear logic? In: Dezani-Ciancaglini, M., Plotkin, G.D. (eds.) TLCA 1995. LNCS, vol. 902, pp. 73–93. Springer, Heidelberg (1995)

[DC08]   De Carvalho, D.: Execution Time of λ-Terms via Denotational Semantics and Intersection Types. Research Report RR-6638, INRIA (2008)

[EL10]   Ehrhard, T., Laurent, O.: Interpreting a finitary pi-calculus in differential interaction nets. Information and Computation 208(6) (2010); Special Issue: 18th International Conference on Concurrency Theory (CONCUR 2007)

[ER03]   Ehrhard, T., Regnier, L.: The differential lambda-calculus. Theoretical Computer Science 309(1-3), 1–41 (2003)

[ER06a]   Ehrhard, T., Regnier, L.: Böhm trees, Krivine machine and the Taylor expansion of ordinary lambda-terms. In: Beckmann, A., Berger, U., Löwe, B., Tucker, J.V. (eds.) CiE 2006. LNCS, vol. 3988, pp. 186–197. Springer, Heidelberg (2006)

[ER06b]   Ehrhard, T., Regnier, L.: Differential interaction nets. Theoretical Computer Science 364(2), 166–195 (2006)

[ER08]   Ehrhard, T., Regnier, L.: Uniformity and the Taylor expansion of ordinary lambda-terms. Theoretical Computer Science 403(2-3), 347–372 (2008)

[Gir88]   Girard, J.-Y.: Normal functors, power series and the λ-calculus. Annals of Pure and Applied Logic 37, 129–177 (1988)

[Kri93]   Krivine, J.-L.: Lambda-Calculus, Types and Models. Ellis Horwood Series in Computers and Their Applications. Ellis Horwood, Masson (1993) Translation by René Cori from French edition (1990)

[MS09]   Manzonetto, G., Salibra, A.: Applying universal algebra to lambda calculus. Journal of Logic and Computation (2009) (to appear)

[PS98]   Pigozzi, D., Salibra, A.: Lambda Abstraction Algebras: Coordinatizing Models of Lambda Calculus. Fundamenta Informaticae 33(2), 149–200 (1998)

Classical and Intuitionistic Subexponential Logics Are Equally Expressive

Kaustuv Chaudhuri

INRIA Saclay, France
kaustuv.chaudhuri@inria.fr

Abstract. It is standard to regard the intuitionistic restriction of a classical logic as increasing the expressivity of the logic because the classical logic can be adequately represented in the intuitionistic logic by double-negation, while the other direction has no truth-preserving propositional encodings. We show here that subexponential logic, which is a family of substructural refinements of classical logic, each parametric over a preorder over the subexponential connectives, does not suffer from this asymmetry if the preorder is systematically modified as part of the encoding. Precisely, we show a bijection between synthetic (i.e., focused) partial sequent derivations modulo a given encoding. Particular instances of our encoding for particular subexponential preorders give rise to both known and novel adequacy theorems for substructural logics.

1 Introduction

In [13], Miller writes:

> *"While there is some recognition that logic is a unifying and universal discipline underlying computer science, it is far more accurate to say that its universal character has been badly fractured . . . one wonders if there is any sense to insisting that there is a core notion of 'logic'."*

Possibly the oldest such split is along the classical/intuitionistic seam, and each side can be seen as more universal than the other. Classical logics, the domain of traditional mathematics, generally have an elegant symmetry in the connectives that can often be exploited to create sophisticated proof search and model checking algorithms. On the other hand, intuitionistic logics, which introduce an asymmetry between multiple hypotheses and single conclusions, can express the computational notion of *function* directly, making it the preferred choice for programming languages and logical frameworks. Can the rift between these two sides be bridged?

Miller proposes one approach: to use structural proof theory, particularly the proof theory of focused sequent calculi, as a unifying language for logical formalisms. There is an important proof theoretic difference between a given classical logic and its *intuitionistic restriction* (see defn. 8): the classical formulas can be encoded using the intuitionistic connectives in such a way that classical provability is preserved, *i.e.*, a formula is classically provable if and only if its encoding is intuitionistically provable. In the other direction, however, there are no such general encodings. The classical logic

A. Dawar and H. Veith (Eds.): CSL 2010, LNCS 6247, pp. 185–199, 2010.

will either have to be extended (for example, with terms and quantifiers) or refined with substructural or modal operators. For this reason, intuitionistic logics are sometimes considered to be *more expressive* than their classical counterparts.

In this paper, we compare logical calculi for "universality" using the specific technical apparatus of *adequate propositional encodings*. That is, given a formula in a source logic O, we must be able to encode it in a target logic M that must preserve the atomic predicates and must reuse the reasoning principles of M, particularly its notion of provability. An example of such an encoding would be ordinary classical logic encoded in ordinary intuitionistic logic where each classical formula A is encoded as the intuitionistic formula $\neg\neg A$. We can go further and also reuse the proofs of the target calculus; in fact, there are at least the following *levels* of adequacy:

Definition 1 (levels of adequacy). *An encoding of formulas (equiv. of sequents) from a source to a target calculus is*

- globally adequate *if a formula is true (equiv. a sequent is derivable) in the source calculus iff its encoding is true (equiv. the encoding of the sequent is derivable) in the target calculus;*
- adequate *if the proofs of a formula (equiv. a sequent) in the source calculus are in bijection with the proofs of the encoding of the formula (equiv. the sequent) in the target calculus; and*
- locally adequate *if open derivations (i.e., partial proofs with possibly unproved premises) of a formula (equiv. a sequent) in the source calculus are in bijection with the open derivations of the formula (equiv. the sequent) in the target calculus.*

Local adequacy is an ideal for encodings because it is a strong justification for seeing the target calculus as more universal: (partial) proofs in the source calculus can be recovered at any level of detail. However, it is unachievable except in trivial situations. Indeed, even adequacy is often difficult; for instance, the linear formula $!a \multimap !b \multimap !a$ has three sequent proofs, differing in the order in which the second $\multimap$ and the two $!$s are introduced, but there is only a single sequent proof of $a \supset b \supset a$.

It is nevertheless possible to define a kind of local adequacy that is more flexible: adequacy up to permutations of inference rules entirely inside one of the phases of *focusing*. A focused proof [1] is a proof that makes large *synthetic* rules that are maximal chains of positive or negative inference rules. An inference rule is positive, sometimes called synchronous, if it involves an essential choice, while it is negative or asynchronous if the choices it presents (if any) are inessential. The term "focus" describes the way positive inferences are chained to form synthetic steps: each inference is applied (read from conclusion to premises) to a single formula *under focus*, and the operands of this connective remain under focus in the premises.

Definition 2 (focal adequacy). *An encoding of sequents from a source to a target focused calculus is* focally adequate *if they have the same synthetic inference rules.*

Since focusing abstracts away the inessential permutations of inference rules, a focally adequate encoding can be used to compare logics for "essential universality". Surprisingly, there are very few known focal adequacy results (see [4,11] for practically all such known results). This paper fills in many of the gaps for existing (substructural) logics by proving a pair of general encodings (see theorems 12 and 17) about *subexponential logics* [8,15]. It is well known that the exponentials of linear logic are non-canonical. If a pre-order is imposed upon them with suitable conditions, then the resulting logic is well-behaved, satisfying identity, admitting cuts, and allowing focusing. Moreover, classical, intuitionistic, and linear logics can be seen as *instances* of subexponential logic for particular collections of subexponentials. Our encodings are *generic*, parametric on the *subexponential signature* of the source and target logics. As particular instances, we obtain focal adequacy results for: classical logic (CL) in intuitionistic logic (IL), IL in classical linear logic (CLL), CLL in intuitionistic linear logic (ILL), and an indefinite bidirectional chain between classical and intuitionistic subexponential logics, all of which are novel. Moreover, our encodings show that any analysis (such as cut-elimination) or algorithm (such as proof search) that is generic on the subexponential signature cannot (and *need not*) distinguish between classical and intuitionistic logics.

The rest of this paper is organized as follows: in sec. 2 classical subexponential logic is introduced, together with its focused sequent calculus and well known instances; in sec. 3 its intuitionistic restriction is presented; then in sec. 4 the bidirectional encoding between classical and intuitionistic subexponential logic is constructed. Details omitted here for space reasons can be found in the accompanying technical report [6].

2 Classical Subexponential Logic

Subexponential logic borrows most of its syntax from linear logic [9]. As we are comparing focused systems, we adopt a polarised syntax from the beginning. Polarised formulas will have exactly one of two polarities: *positive* $(P, Q, \ldots)$ constructed out of the positive atoms and connectives, and *negative* $(N, M, \ldots)$ constructed out of the negative atoms and connectives. These two classes of formulas are mutually recursive, mediated by the indexed subexponential operators $!_z$ and $?_z$.

Notation 3 (syntax). Positive formulas *(P, Q) and* negative formulas *(N, M) have the following grammar:*

$$P, Q ::= p \mid P \otimes Q \mid \mathbf{1} \mid P \oplus Q \mid \mathbf{0} \mid !_z N^+ \qquad \text{(positive)}$$

$$N, M ::= n \mid N \,\&\, M \mid \top \mid N \,\bindnasrepma\, M \mid \bot \mid P \multimap N \mid ?_z P^- \qquad \text{(negative)}$$

Atomic formulas are written in lower case $(a, b, \ldots)$, with p and q reserved for positive and n and m reserved for negative atomic formulas. P^- denotes either a positive formula or a negative atom, and likewise N^+ denotes a negative formula or a positive atom. We write $A, B, \ldots$ for any arbitrary formula (positive or negative).

Because we will eventually consider its intuitionistic restriction, we retain implication $\multimap$ as a primitive even though it is classically definable. However, we exclude the non-linear implication $(\supset)$ because the unrestricted zones are non-canonical; *i.e.*, there are many such implications, each defined using a suitable subexponential (or compositions thereof). The subscript z in exponential connectives denotes zones drawn from a *subexponential signature* (using the terminology of [15]).

Definition 4. *A subexponential signature Σ is a structure $\langle Z, \leq, \mathfrak{l}, U \rangle$ where:*

- *$\langle Z, \leq \rangle$ is a non-empty pre-ordered set (the "zones");*
- *$\mathfrak{l} \in Z$ is a "working" zone;*
- *$U \subseteq Z$ is a set of unrestricted zones that is $\leq$-closed, i.e., for every $z_1, z_2 \in Z$, if $z_1 \leq z_2$, then $z_1 \in U$ implies $z_2 \in U$. $Z \setminus U$ will be called the restricted zones.*

We use u, v, w to denote unrestricted zones and r, s, t to denote restricted zones.

Unrestricted zones admit both weakening and contraction, while restricted zones are linear. The logic is parametric on the signature. (Particular mentions of the signature will be omitted unless necessary to disambiguate, in which case they will be written in a subscript.) We use use a two-sided sequent calculus formulation of the logic in order to avoid appeals to De Morgan duality. This will not only simplify the definition of the intuitionistic restriction (sec. 3), but will also be crucial to the main adequacy result. Formulas in contexts are annotated with their subexponential zones as follows: $z : A$ will stand for A occurring in zone denoted by z, and $z : (A_1, \ldots, A_k)$ for $z : A_1, \ldots, z : A_k$. Sequents are of the following kinds:

$$\Gamma \vdash [P] \; ; \; \Delta \qquad \text{right focus on } P$$
$$\Gamma \; ; \; [N] \vdash \Delta \qquad \text{left focus on } N$$
$$\Gamma \; ; \; \Omega \vdash \Xi \; ; \; \Delta \qquad \text{active on } \Omega \text{ and } \Xi$$

The contexts in these sequents have the following restrictions:

- All elements of the *left passive* context Γ are of the form $z : N^+$.
- All elements of the *right passive* context Δ are of the form $z : P^-$.
- All elements of the *left active* context Ω are of the form P^-.
- All elements of the *right active* context Ξ are of the form N^+.

Notation 5. *We write Γ^u or Δ^u for those contexts containing only unrestricted elements, i.e., each element is of the form $u : A$ with $u \in U$. Likewise, we write Γ^r or Δ^r for contexts containing only restricted elements.*

The rules of the calculus are presented in fig. 1. Focused sequent calculi presented in this style, which is a stylistic variant of Andreoli's original formulation [1], have an intensional reading in terms of *phases*. At the boundaries of phases are sequents of the form $\Gamma \; ; \; \cdot \vdash \cdot \; ; \; \Delta$, which are known as *neutral sequents*. Proofs of neutral sequents proceed (reading from conclusion to premises) as follows:

1. *Decision*: a *focus* is selected from a neutral sequent, either from the left or the right context. This focused formula is moved to its corresponding focused zone using one of the rules RDR, UDR, RDL and UDL (U/R = "unrestricted"/"restricted", D = "decision", and R/L = "right"/"left"). These *decision* rules copy the focused formula iff it occurs in an unrestricted zone.

2. *Focused phase*: for a left or a right focused sequent, left or right focus rules are applied to the formula under focus. These focused rules are all non-invertible in the (unfocused) sequent calculus and therefore depend on essential choices made in the proof. In all cases except $!_zR$ and $?_zL$ the focus persists to the subformulas (if any) of the focused formula. For binary rules, the restricted portions of the contexts are separated and distributed to the two premises. This much should be familiar from focusing for linear logic [1,7].

(right focus)

$$\dfrac{}{\Gamma^{u}, z:p \vdash [p] \ ; \ \Delta^{u}} \text{PR} \qquad \dfrac{\Gamma^{u}, \Gamma_{1}^{r} \vdash [P] \ ; \ \Delta^{u}, \Delta_{1}^{r} \quad \Gamma^{u}, \Gamma_{2}^{r} \vdash [Q] \ ; \ \Delta^{u}, \Delta_{2}^{r}}{\Gamma^{u}, \Gamma_{1}^{r}, \Gamma_{2}^{r} \vdash [P \otimes Q] \ ; \ \Delta^{u}, \Delta_{1}^{r}, \Delta_{2}^{r}} \otimes \text{R} \qquad \dfrac{}{\Gamma^{u} \vdash [1] \ ; \ \Delta^{u}} \text{1R}$$

$$\dfrac{\Gamma \vdash [P_{i}] \ ; \ \Delta}{\Gamma \vdash [P_{1} \oplus P_{2}] \ ; \ \Delta} \oplus \text{R}_{i} \qquad \dfrac{\Gamma \ ; \ \cdot \vdash N^{+} \ ; \ \Delta \quad (\forall x:A \in \Gamma, \Delta.\, z \leq x)}{\Gamma \vdash [!_{z}N^{+}] \ ; \ \Delta} !_{z}\text{R}$$

(left focus)

$$\dfrac{}{\Gamma^{u} \ ; \ [n] \vdash \Delta^{u}, z:n} \text{NL} \qquad \dfrac{\Gamma \ ; \ [P_{i}] \vdash \Delta}{\Gamma \ ; \ [P_{1} \& P_{2}] \vdash \Delta} \& \text{L}_{i} \qquad \dfrac{\Gamma^{u}, \Gamma_{1}^{r} \ ; \ [N] \vdash \Delta^{u}, \Delta_{1}^{r} \quad \Gamma^{u}, \Gamma_{2}^{r} \ ; \ [M] \vdash \Delta^{u}, \Delta_{2}^{r}}{\Gamma^{u}, \Gamma_{1}^{r}, \Gamma_{2}^{r} \ ; \ [N \,\bindnasrepma\, M] \vdash \Delta^{u}, \Delta_{1}^{r}, \Delta_{2}^{r}} \bindnasrepma\text{L}$$

$$\dfrac{}{\Gamma^{u} \ ; \ [\bot] \vdash \Delta^{u}} \bot\text{L} \qquad \dfrac{\Gamma^{u}, \Gamma_{1}^{r} \vdash [P] \ ; \ \Delta^{u}, \Delta_{1}^{r} \quad \Gamma^{u}, \Gamma_{2}^{r} \ ; \ [M] \vdash \Delta^{u}, \Delta_{2}^{r}}{\Gamma^{u}, \Gamma_{1}^{r}, \Gamma_{2}^{r} \ ; \ [P \multimap M] \vdash \Delta^{u}, \Delta_{1}^{r}, \Delta_{2}^{r}} \multimap\text{L}$$

$$\dfrac{\Gamma \ ; \ P^{-} \vdash \cdot \ ; \ \Delta \quad (\forall x:A \in \Gamma, \Delta.\, z \leq x)}{\Gamma \ ; \ [?_{z}P^{-}] \vdash \Delta} ?_{z}\text{L}$$

(right active)

$$\dfrac{\Gamma \ ; \ \Omega \vdash \Xi \ ; \ \Delta, l:a}{\Gamma \ ; \ \Omega \vdash \Xi, a \ ; \ \Delta} \text{AR} \qquad \dfrac{\Gamma \ ; \ \Omega \vdash \Xi, N \ ; \ \Delta \quad \Gamma \ ; \ \Omega \vdash \Xi, M \ ; \ \Delta}{\Gamma \ ; \ \Omega \vdash \Xi, N \& M \ ; \ \Delta} \& \text{R} \qquad \dfrac{}{\Gamma \ ; \ \Omega \vdash \Xi, \top \ ; \ \Delta} \text{TR}$$

$$\dfrac{\Gamma \ ; \ \Omega \vdash \Xi, N, M \ ; \ \Delta}{\Gamma \ ; \ \Omega \vdash \Xi, N \,\bindnasrepma\, M \ ; \ \Delta} \bindnasrepma\text{R} \qquad \dfrac{\Gamma \ ; \ \Omega \vdash \Xi \ ; \ \Delta}{\Gamma \ ; \ \Omega \vdash \Xi, \bot \ ; \ \Delta} \bot\text{R} \qquad \dfrac{\Gamma \ ; \ \Omega, P \vdash \Xi, N \ ; \ \Delta}{\Gamma \ ; \ \Omega \vdash \Xi, P \multimap N \ ; \ \Delta} \multimap\text{R} \qquad \dfrac{\Gamma \ ; \ \Omega \vdash \Xi \ ; \ \Delta, z:P^{-}}{\Gamma \ ; \ \Omega \vdash \Xi, ?_{z}P^{-} \ ; \ \Delta} ?_{z}\text{R}$$

(left active)

$$\dfrac{\Gamma, l:a \ ; \ \Omega \vdash \Xi \ ; \ \Delta}{\Gamma \ ; \ \Omega, a \vdash \Xi \ ; \ \Delta} \text{AL} \qquad \dfrac{\Gamma \ ; \ \Omega, P, Q \vdash \Xi \ ; \ \Delta}{\Gamma \ ; \ \Omega, P \otimes Q \vdash \Xi \ ; \ \Delta} \otimes\text{L} \qquad \dfrac{\Gamma \ ; \ \Omega \vdash \Xi \ ; \ \Delta}{\Gamma \ ; \ \Omega, 1 \vdash \Xi \ ; \ \Delta} \text{1L}$$

$$\dfrac{\Gamma \ ; \ \Omega, P \vdash \Xi \ ; \ \Delta \quad \Gamma \ ; \ \Omega, Q \vdash \Xi \ ; \ \Delta}{\Gamma \ ; \ \Omega, P \oplus Q \vdash \Xi \ ; \ \Delta} \oplus\text{L} \qquad \dfrac{}{\Gamma \ ; \ \Omega, 0 \vdash \Xi \ ; \ \Delta} \text{0L} \qquad \dfrac{\Gamma, z:N^{+} \ ; \ \Omega \vdash \Xi \ ; \ \Delta}{\Gamma \ ; \ \Omega, !_{z}N^{+} \vdash \Xi \ ; \ \Delta} !_{z}\text{L}$$

(decision)

$$\dfrac{\Gamma \vdash [P] \ ; \ \Delta}{\Gamma \ ; \ \cdot \vdash \cdot \ ; \ \Delta, r:P} \text{RDR} \qquad \dfrac{\Gamma \vdash [P] \ ; \ \Delta, u:P}{\Gamma \ ; \ \cdot \vdash \cdot \ ; \ \Delta, u:P} \text{UDR} \qquad \dfrac{\Gamma \ ; \ [N] \vdash \Delta}{\Gamma, r:N \ ; \ \cdot \vdash \cdot \ ; \ \Delta} \text{RDL} \qquad \dfrac{\Gamma, u:N \ ; \ [N] \vdash \Delta}{\Gamma, u:N \ ; \ \cdot \vdash \cdot \ ; \ \Delta} \text{UDL}$$

Fig. 1. Focused sequent calculus for classical subexponential logic

The two unusual rules for subexponential logic are $!_{z}\text{R}$ and $?_{z}\text{L}$, which are generalizations of rules for the single exponential in ordinary linear logic. These rules have a side condition that no formulas in a strictly $\leq$-smaller zone may be present in the conclusion. If the working zone l is $\leq$-minimal (which is not necessarily the case), then this side condition is trivial and the rules amount to a pure change of polarities, similar to the $\uparrow$ and $\downarrow$ connectives of polarised linear logic [10]. For the other zones, this rule tests for the emptiness of some of the zones. It is this selective emptiness test that gives subexponential logic its expressive power [15,14].

3. *Active phase*: once the exponential rules $!_{z}\text{R}$ and $?_{z}\text{L}$ are applied, the sequents become active and left and right active rules are applied. The order of the active rules is immaterial as all orderings will produce the same list of neutral sequent premises. In Andreoli's system the irrelevant non-determinism in the order of these rules was

removed by treating the active contexts Ξ and Ω as ordered contexts; however, we do not fix any particular ordering.

In the traditional model of focusing, the above three steps repeat, in that order, in the entire proof. The focused system can therefore be seen as a system of *synthetic* inference rules (sometimes known as *bipoles*) for neutral sequents. It is possible to give a very general presentation of such synthetic inference systems, for which we can prove completeness and cut-elimination in a very general fashion [5]. It is also possible, with some non-trivial effort, to show completeness of the focused calculus without appealing to synthetic rules [7,11]. We do not delve into such proofs in this paper because this ground is well trodden. Indeed, a focused completeness theorem for a very similar (but more general) formulation of subexponential logic can be found in [14, chapter 6]. The synthetic soundness and completeness theorems are as follows, proof omitted:

Fact 6 (synthetic soundness and completeness). *Write* ⊪ *for the sequent arrow for an unfocused variant of the calculus of fig. 1, obtained by placing the focused and active formulas in the l zone and relaxing the focusing discipline.*[1]

 1. If Γ ; · ⊢ · ; Δ, then Γ ⊪ Δ (synthetic soundness).
 2. If $\Gamma, l:\Omega$ ⊪ $l:\Xi, \Delta$ then Γ ; Ω ⊢ Ξ ; Δ (synthetic completeness). □

Despite its somewhat esoteric formulation, it is easy to see how subexponential logic generalizes classical substructural logics.

Fact 7 (familiar instances)

- Polarised classical multiplicative additive linear logic *(MALL) is determined by* $\mathtt{mall} = \langle\{l\}, \cdot, l, \emptyset\rangle$. *The injections between the two polarised classes, sometimes known as* shifts, *are as follows:* $\downarrow = !_l$ *and* $\uparrow = ?_l$.
- Polarised classical linear logic *(CLL) is determined by* $\mathtt{ll} = \langle\{l, u\}, l \leq u, l, \{u\}\rangle$. *In addition to the injections of* $\mathtt{mall}$, *we also have the exponentials* $! = !_u$ *and* $? = ?_u$.
- Polarised classical logic *(CL) is given by the signature* $\mathtt{l} = \langle\{l\}, \cdot, l, \{l\}\rangle$. □

In addition to such instances produced by instantiating the subexponential signature, it is also possible to get the unpolarised versions of these logics by applying $!_l$ and $?_l$ to immediate negative (resp. positive) subformulas of positive (resp. negative) formulas.

3   Intuitionistic Subexponential Logic

One direct way of defining intuitionistic fragments of classical logics is as follows:

Definition 8 (intuitionistic restriction). *Given a two-sided sequent calculus, its intuitionistic restriction is that fragment where all inference rules are constrained to have exactly a single formula on the right hand sides of sequents.*

The practical import of this restriction is that the connectives $\⅋$ and $\bot$ disappear, because their right rules require two and zero conclusions, respectively. As a result, $\multimap$ becomes a primitive because its classical definition requires $\⅋$ (and De Morgan duals, which are also missing with the intuitioistic restriction). In a slight break from tradition [9,16,2], we retain $?_z$ in the intuitionistic syntax. The intuitionistic restriction produces the following kinds of sequents:

---

[1] This is basically Gentzen's LK in two-sided form for subexponential logic.

$$\Gamma \vdash [P] \qquad \text{right focus on } P$$
$$\Gamma \,;\, [N] \vdash z : Q^- \qquad \text{left focus on } N$$
$$\Gamma \,;\, \Omega \vdash N^+ \,;\, \cdot \qquad \text{active on } \Omega \text{ and } N^+$$
$$\Gamma \,;\, \Omega \vdash \cdot \,;\, z : Q^- \qquad \text{active on } \Omega$$

We shall use γ to stand for the right hand forms—either $N^+ \,;\, \cdot$ or $\cdot \,;\, z : Q^-$—for active sequents above. The full collection of rules is given in fig. 2. As before, we use Q^- (resp. N^+) to refer to a positive formula or negative atom (resp. negative formula or positive atom).

The nature of subexponential signatures does not change in moving from classical to intuitionistic logic. The decision rule UDR obviously cannot copy the right formula in the intuitionistic case. Thus, both the right decision rules collapse; $?_z$ takes on an additional modal aspect and is no longer the perfect dual of $!_z$. The standard explanation of this

(right focus)

$$\frac{}{\Gamma^u, z : p \vdash [p]}\text{PR} \qquad \frac{\Gamma^u, \Gamma_1^r \vdash [P] \quad \Gamma^u, \Gamma_2^r \vdash [Q]}{\Gamma^u, \Gamma_1^r, \Gamma_2^r \vdash [P \otimes Q]}\otimes\text{R} \qquad \frac{}{\Gamma^u \vdash [1]}\text{1R}$$

$$\frac{\Gamma \vdash [P_i]}{\Gamma \vdash [P_1 \oplus P_2]}\oplus\text{R}_i \qquad \frac{\Gamma \,;\, \cdot \vdash N^+ \,;\, \cdot \quad (\forall x : A \in \Gamma . z \leq x)}{\Gamma \vdash [!_z N^+]}\,!_z\text{R}$$

(left focus)

$$\frac{}{\Gamma^u \,;\, [n] \vdash z : n}\text{NL} \qquad \frac{\Gamma \,;\, [P_i] \vdash z : Q^-}{\Gamma \,;\, [P_1 \& P_2] \vdash z : Q^-}\&\text{L}_i \qquad \frac{\Gamma^u, \Gamma_1^r \vdash [P] \quad \Gamma^u, \Gamma_2^r \,;\, [M] \vdash z : Q^-}{\Gamma^u, \Gamma_1^r, \Gamma_2^r \,;\, [P \multimap M] \vdash z : Q^-}\multimap\text{L}$$

$$\frac{\Gamma \,;\, P^- \vdash \cdot \,;\, y : Q^- \quad (\forall x : A \in \Gamma, y : Q^- . z \leq x)}{\Gamma \,;\, [?_z P^-] \vdash y : Q^-}\,?_z\text{L}$$

right active

$$\frac{\Gamma \,;\, \Omega \vdash \cdot \,;\, l : a}{\Gamma \,;\, \Omega \vdash a \,;\, \cdot}\text{AR} \qquad \frac{\Gamma \,;\, \Omega \vdash N \,;\, \cdot \quad \Gamma \,;\, \Omega \vdash M \,;\, \cdot}{\Gamma \,;\, \Omega \vdash N \& M \,;\, \cdot}\&\text{R} \qquad \frac{}{\Gamma \,;\, \Omega \vdash T \,;\, \cdot}\text{TR}$$

$$\frac{\Gamma \,;\, \Omega, P \vdash N \,;\, \cdot}{\Gamma \,;\, \Omega \vdash P \multimap N \,;\, \cdot}\multimap\text{R} \qquad \frac{\Gamma \,;\, \Omega \vdash \cdot \,;\, z : P}{\Gamma \,;\, \Omega \vdash ?_z P \,;\, \cdot}\,?_z\text{R}$$

(left active)

$$\frac{\Gamma, l : a \,;\, \Omega \vdash \gamma}{\Gamma \,;\, \Omega, a \vdash \gamma}\text{AL} \qquad \frac{\Gamma \,;\, \Omega, P, Q \vdash \gamma}{\Gamma \,;\, \Omega, P \otimes Q \vdash \gamma}\otimes\text{L} \qquad \frac{\Gamma \,;\, \Omega \vdash \gamma}{\Gamma \,;\, \Omega, 1 \vdash \gamma}\text{1L}$$

$$\frac{\Gamma \,;\, \Omega, P \vdash \gamma \quad \Gamma \,;\, \Omega, Q \vdash \gamma}{\Gamma \,;\, \Omega, P \oplus Q \vdash \gamma}\oplus\text{L} \qquad \frac{}{\Gamma \,;\, \Omega, 0 \vdash \gamma}\text{0L} \qquad \frac{\Gamma, z : N \,;\, \Omega \vdash \gamma}{\Gamma \,;\, \Omega, !_z N \vdash \gamma}\,!_z\text{L}$$

(decision)

$$\frac{\Gamma \vdash [P]}{\Gamma \,;\, \cdot \vdash \cdot \,;\, z : P}\text{DR} \qquad \frac{\Gamma \,;\, [N] \vdash z : Q^-}{\Gamma, r : N \,;\, \cdot \vdash \cdot \,;\, z : Q^-}\text{RDL} \qquad \frac{\Gamma, u : N \,;\, [N] \vdash z : Q^-}{\Gamma, u : N \,;\, \cdot \vdash \cdot \,;\, z : Q^-}\text{UDL}$$

Fig. 2. Focused sequent calculus for intuitionstic subexponential logic loss of symmetry in the exponentials is the creation of a new *possibility* judgement that is weaker than linear truth; see [3] for such a reconstruction of the intuitionistic?.

The proof of completeness for focused intuitionistic subexponential logic has never been published. However, any similar proof for intuitionistic linear logic, such as [7,11], can be adapted. Again, we simply state the synthetic version of the theorems here without proof.

Fact 9 (synthetic soundness and completeness). *Write* ⊩ *for the sequent arrow for an unfocused variant of the calculus of fig. 2, obtained by placing the focused and active formulas in the* $\mathfrak{l}$ *zone and relaxing the focusing discipline.*

1. *If* Γ ; $\cdot \vdash \cdot$; $z : Q^-$, *then* $\Gamma \Vdash z : Q^-$.
2. *If* $\Gamma, \mathfrak{l} : \Omega \Vdash z : Q^-$ *then* Γ ; $\Omega \vdash \cdot$; $z : Q^-$.
3. *If* $\Gamma, \mathfrak{l} : \Omega \Vdash \mathfrak{l} : N$ *then* Γ ; $\Omega \vdash N$; $\cdot$.   □

The intuitionstic restrictions of the familiar instances from defn. 7 simply use the same subexponential signatures.

4   Focally Adequate Encodings

This section contains the main technical contribution of this paper: focally adequate encodings (defn. 2) that are generic on subexponential signatures. At the level of focal adequacy, therefore, the asymmetry in the expressive power of classical and intuitionistic logics disappears.

4.1   Classical in Intuitionistic

To introduce the mechanisms of encoding, we first look at the unsurprising direction: a classical logic in its own intuitionistic restriction. The well known double negation translation, if performed clumsily, can break even full adequacy. For example, if $N \bindnasrepma M$ is translated as $\neg(!_\mathfrak{l}\neg!_\mathfrak{l}N \otimes !_\mathfrak{l}\neg!_\mathfrak{l}M)$ where $\neg P \triangleq P \multimap k$ where k is some fixed negative atom that is not used in classical logic. In the rule $\bindnasrepma$R under this encoding, there are instances of $!_\mathfrak{l}$ that have no counterpart in the classical side. Indeed, there is no derived rule in the classical focused calculus that allows one to conclude Γ ; $\cdot \vdash N \bindnasrepma M$; $\cdot$ from Γ ; $\cdot \vdash \cdot$; $!_\mathfrak{l}N, !_\mathfrak{l}M$, which is what would result if the active phase could be suspended arbitrarily and the subformula property were discarded. Such a rule is certainly admissible, but admissibile rules do not preserve bijections between proofs, and are only definable for full proofs in any case.

How does one encode classical logic in its intuitionistic restriction such that polarities are respected? The above example suggests an obvious answer: when translating $N \bindnasrepma M$ as if it were right-active, do not also translate the subformulas M and N as if they were right-active, for they will be sent to the left. Instead, translate them as if they were *left*-active.[2]

Definition 10 (encoding classical formulas).

– *The encoding* $(-)^=$ *from classical positive (resp. negative) formulas to intuitionistic positive (resp. negative) formulas is as follows:*

---

[2] The astute reader might recall that this is the essence of Kuroda's encodings.

$$(p)^= = p \qquad (!_zN)^= = !_z(N)^= \qquad (P \otimes Q)^= = (P)^= \otimes (Q)^= \qquad (\mathbf{1})^= = \mathbf{1}$$

$$(P \oplus Q)^= = (P)^= \oplus (Q)^= \qquad (\mathbf{0})^= = \mathbf{0} \qquad (N)^= = \neg (N)^{\neq}$$

– *The encoding* $(-)^{\neq}$ *from classical negative (resp. positive) formulas to intuitionstic positive (resp. negative) formulas is as follows:*

$$(n)^{\neq} = n^{\perp} \qquad (?_zP)^{\neq} = !_z(P)^{\neq} \qquad (N \,\rotatebox[origin=c]{180}{\&}\, N)^{\neq} = (N)^{\neq} \otimes (M)^{\neq} \qquad (\perp)^{\neq} = \mathbf{1}$$

$$(N \,\&\, M)^{\neq} = (N)^{\neq} \oplus (M)^{\neq} \qquad (\top)^{\neq} = \mathbf{0} \qquad (P \multimap N)^{\neq} = (P)^= \otimes (N)^{\neq} \qquad (P)^{\neq} = \neg (P)^=$$

where for every negative atom n, *there is a positive atom* $n^{\perp}$ *in the encoding.*

Contexts are translated element-wise.

Definition 11 (encoding classical sequents). *The encoding* $(-)^{\perp\perp}$ *of classical sequents as intuitionistic sequents is as follows:*

$$(\Gamma \vdash [P] \;;\; \Delta)^{\perp\perp} = (\Gamma)^= , (\Delta)^{\neq} \vdash [(P)^=] \qquad (\Gamma \;;\; [N] \vdash \Delta)^{\perp\perp} = (\Gamma)^= , (\Delta)^{\neq} \vdash [(N)^{\neq}]$$

$$(\Gamma \;;\; \Omega \vdash \Xi \;;\; \Delta)^{\perp\perp} = (\Gamma)^= , (\Delta)^{\neq} \;;\; (\Omega)^= , (\Xi)^{\neq} \vdash \cdot \;;\; \mathrm{I}:k$$

In other words, focused sequents are translated to right-focused sequents, and active sequents to left-active sequents. The right contexts are dualised and sent to the left where the intuitionistic restriction does not apply, while the left focus on negative formulas is turned into a right focus because of the lack of a multiplicative left-focused rule (except $\multimap$L which would cause an inadvertent polarity switch).

Theorem 12. *The encoding of defn. 11 is focally adequate (defn. 2).*

Proof. We will inventory the classical rules in fig. 1, and in each case compute the intuitionistic synthetic derivations of the encoding of the conclusion of the classical rules. Here are the interesting[3] cases, with the double inference lines denoting (un)folding of defns. 10 and 11, and the rule names written with the prefix c/ or ɪ/ to distinguish between classical and intuitionistic respectively.

– *cases of* c/PR *and* c/!R :

$$\dfrac{\dfrac{\dfrac{\dfrac{\dfrac{(\Gamma \;;\; \cdot \vdash N \;;\; \Delta)^{\perp\perp}}{(\Gamma)^= , (\Delta)^{\neq} \;;\; (N)^{\neq} \vdash \cdot \;;\; \mathrm{I}:k}}{(\Gamma)^= , (\Delta)^{\neq} \;;\; (N)^{\neq} \vdash k \;;\; \cdot} \;\small\boxed{\text{ɪ/?}_{\mathrm{l}}\text{R}}}{(\Gamma)^= , (\Delta)^{\neq} \;;\; \cdot \vdash \neg (N)^{\neq} \;;\; \cdot} \;\small\text{ɪ/}\multimap\text{R}}{(\Gamma)^= , (\Delta)^{\neq} \vdash \left[!_z \neg (N)^{\neq}\right]} \;\small\text{ɪ/!}_z\text{R}}{\dfrac{(\Gamma)^= , (\Delta)^{\neq} \vdash [(!_zN)^=]}{(\Gamma \vdash [!_zN] \;;\; \Delta)^{\perp\perp}}}$$

$$\dfrac{\dfrac{(\Gamma^u)^= , z:p, (\Delta^u)^{\neq} \vdash [p]}{(\Gamma^u)^= , (z:p)^= , (\Delta^u)^{\neq} \vdash [p]} \;\small\text{ɪ/PR}}{(\Gamma^u, z:p \vdash [p] \;;\; \Delta^u)^{\perp\perp}}$$

All the logical rules used are invertible. The boxed instance of ɪ/?₁R requires some explanation: obviously a left active rule on $(N)^{\neq}$ can be applied before this rule. However, since they are both active rules, the choice of which to perform first is immaterial as they will produce the same neutral premises. If we want local—not focal—adequacy, we will have to impose a right-to-left ordering on the active rules. The case of c/NL and c/?L is similar.

---

[3] See [6] for the remaining cases.

– *case of* c/⅋R :

$$\frac{(\Gamma\;;\;\Omega\vdash\Xi,N,M\;;\;\Delta)^{\perp\perp}}{\dfrac{(\Gamma)^{=},(\Delta)^{\neq}\;;\;(\Omega)^{=},(\Xi)^{\neq},(N)^{\neq},(M)^{\neq}\vdash\cdot\;;\;\mathsf{l}:k}{\dfrac{(\Gamma)^{=},(\Delta)^{\neq}\;;\;(\Omega)^{=},(\Xi)^{\neq},(N)^{\neq}\otimes(M)^{\neq}\vdash\cdot\;;\;\mathsf{l}:k}{\dfrac{(\Gamma)^{=},(\Delta)^{\neq}\;;\;(\Omega)^{=},(\Xi)^{\neq},(N\,⅋\,M)^{\neq}\vdash\cdot\;;\;\mathsf{l}:k}{(\Gamma\;;\;\Omega\vdash\Xi,N\,⅋\,M\;;\;\Delta)^{\perp\perp}}}}}\;{\scriptstyle \mathsf{l}/\otimes\mathsf{L}}$$

The cases of c/⊥R, c/!$_z$L and c/?$_z$R are similar.

– *case of* c/RDR :

$$\frac{\left(\Gamma_1^{\mathsf{u}},\Gamma_2^{\mathsf{r}}\vdash[P]\;;\;\Delta_1^{\mathsf{u}},\Delta_2^{\mathsf{r}}\right)^{\perp\perp}}{\dfrac{\left(\Gamma_1^{\mathsf{u}},\Gamma_2^{\mathsf{r}}\right)^{=},\left(\Delta_1^{\mathsf{u}},\Delta_2^{\mathsf{r}}\right)^{\neq}\vdash[(P)^{=}]\quad\left(\Gamma_1^{\mathsf{u}}\right)^{=},\left(\Delta_1^{\mathsf{u}}\right)^{\neq}\;;\;[k]\vdash\mathsf{l}:k}{\dfrac{\left(\Gamma_1^{\mathsf{u}},\Gamma_2^{\mathsf{r}}\right)^{=},\left(\Delta_1^{\mathsf{u}},\Delta_2^{\mathsf{r}}\right)^{\neq}\;;\;[\neg(P)^{=}]\vdash\mathsf{l}:k}{\dfrac{\left(\Gamma_1^{\mathsf{u}},\Gamma_2^{\mathsf{r}}\right)^{=},\left(\Delta_1^{\mathsf{u}},\Delta_2^{\mathsf{r}}\right)^{\neq},r:\neg(P)^{=}\;;\;\cdot\vdash\cdot\;;\;\mathsf{l}:k}{\dfrac{\left(\Gamma_1^{\mathsf{u}},\Gamma_2^{\mathsf{r}}\right)^{=},\left(\Delta_1^{\mathsf{u}},\Delta_2^{\mathsf{r}}\right)^{\neq},(r:P)^{\neq}\;;\;\cdot\vdash\cdot\;;\;\mathsf{l}:k}{\left(\Gamma_1^{\mathsf{u}},\Gamma_2^{\mathsf{r}}\;;\;\cdot\vdash\cdot\;;\;\Delta_1^{\mathsf{u}},\Delta_2^{\mathsf{r}},r:P\right)^{\perp\perp}}}}}\begin{array}{l}{\scriptstyle \mathsf{l}/\mathsf{NL}}\\[10pt]{\scriptstyle \mathsf{l}/{-}\mathsf{oL}}\\[10pt]{\scriptstyle \mathsf{l}/\mathsf{RDL}}\end{array}$$

Note that the right premise is forced to terminate in the same phase. This would not be possible if, instead of k, we were to use some other negative formula such as $?_\mathsf{l}0$. In the presence of some unrestricted subexponential u, we might have used $?_u 0$ instead (note that, classically, $?_u 0 \equiv \perp$). $\qquad\square$

Corollary 13

- *There is a focally adequate encoding of classical MALL in intuitionistic MALL.*
- *There is a focally adequate encoding of CLL in ILL.*
- *There is a focally adequate encoding of CL in IL.*

Proof. Instantiate thm. 12 on the subexponential signatures from defn. 7. $\qquad\square$

These instances are all apparently novel, partly because focal adequacy of classical logics in their own intuitionistic restrictions has not been deeply investigated. In the work on LJF [11] there is a focally adequate encoding of classical logic in intuitionistic linear logic, which can be seen as a combination of the second and third of the above instances.

4.2   Intuitionistic in Classical

The previous subsection showed that the intuitionistic restriction of a classical logic can adequately encode the classical logic itself. This is not the case in the other direction without further modifications to the subexponential signature. It is easy to see this: consider just the MALL fragment and the problem of encoding the ɪ/−∘L rule. If −∘ is encoded as itself, then in the classical side we have the following derived rule (all the zones are ɪ, and elided):

$$\frac{\Gamma \vdash [P] \; ; \; Q^- \quad \Gamma \; ; \; [N] \vdash \cdot}{\Gamma \; ; \; [P \multimap N] \vdash Q^-}$$

This rule has no intuitionistic counterpart. Therefore, the encoding of $\multimap$ must prevent the right formula Q^- from being sent to the left branch, *i.e.*, to test that the rest of the right context in a right focus is empty. MALL itself cannot perform this test because it lacks any truly modal operators. Exactly the same problem exists for the encoding of IL in CL, which also lacks any true modal operators.

   Quite obviously, the encoding of $\multimap$ requires some means of testing the emptiness of contexts. CLL (defn. 7) has an additional zone ᴜ that is greater than ɪ, and therefore $!_\mathrm{u}$ can test for the absence of any ɪ-formulas. It turns out that this is enough to get a focally adequate encoding of IL as follows: the sole zone ɪ of IL is split into two, l_r (restricted) and l_u (unrestricted), and the right hand side of IL sequents is encoded with l_r. Then, whenever P is of the form $!_\mathrm{l}N$, the translation of it on the right is of the form $!_{\mathrm{l}_u}M$. In the rest of this subsection, we will systematically extend this observation to an arbitrary subexponential signature.

Definition 14 (signature splitting). *Let a subexponential signature $\Sigma = \langle Z, \leq, \mathrm{l}, U\rangle$ be given. Write:*

- $\hat{Z}$ *for the zone set $(Z \times \{\mathbf{l}\}) \cup (Z \times \{\mathbf{r}\})$, where $\mathbf{l}$ and $\mathbf{r}$ are distinct labels for the left and the right of the sequents, respectively, and $\times$ is the Cartesian product. $Z \times \{\mathbf{l}\}$ will be called the* left form *of $\hat{Z}$, and $Z \times \{\mathbf{r}\}$ will be called its* right form.
- $\hat{U}$ *for the unrestricted zone set $U \times \{\mathbf{l}\}$.*
- $\hat{\mathrm{l}}$ *for the working zone $(\mathrm{l}, \mathbf{l})$.*
- $\hat{\leq}$ *for the smallest relation on $\hat{Z} \times \hat{Z}$ for which:*
    - $(x, \mathbf{l}) \hat{\leq} (y, \mathbf{l})$ *if $x \leq y$;*
    - $(x, \mathbf{r}) \hat{\leq} (y, \mathbf{r})$ *if $x \leq y$; and*
    - $(x, \mathbf{r}) \hat{\leq} (x, \mathbf{l})$ *and $(x, \mathbf{l}) \hat{\not\leq} (x, \mathbf{r})$.*

The subexponential signature $\hat{\Sigma} = \left\langle \hat{Z}, \hat{\leq}, \hat{\mathrm{l}}, \hat{U}\right\rangle$ will be called the split form *of Σ.*

We intend to treat the right form specially. The zones in the right form are restricted, which encodes the linearity of the right hand side inherent in the intuitionistic restriction (defn. 8). Our encoding will guarantee that the right hand sides of sequents in the encoding contain no zones in the left form. Thus, when $!_{(z,1)}N$ is under right focus, the side condition on the $!$ʀ rule will ensure that there are no other formulas on the right hand side, because the right forms are made pointwise smaller than their left forms. Dually, on the left we shall use $?_{(z,\mathbf{r})}$ to encode $?_z$; since the right form zones are pointwise smaller than the left form zones, but retain the pre-split ordering inside their own zone, the side conditions enforce the same occurrences as in the source calculus.

Definition 15 (encoding intuitionistic contexts)

- *The left-passive context Γ is encoded pointwise using the translation $(-)^{\mathrm{lp}}$:*

$$(z:N^+)^{\mathrm{lp}} = (z,1):(N^+)^{\mathrm{lp}} \qquad (p)^{\mathrm{lp}} = p \qquad (N)^{\mathrm{lp}} = (N)^{\mathrm{lf}}$$

– *A left-focused formula N is encoded using the translation* $(-)^{\mathrm{lf}}$:

$$(n)^{\mathrm{lf}} = n \qquad (?_z P^-)^{\mathrm{lf}} = ?_{(z,\mathrm{r})} (P^-)^{\mathrm{la}} \qquad (N \,\&\, M)^{\mathrm{lf}} = (N)^{\mathrm{lf}} \,\&\, (M)^{\mathrm{lf}} \qquad (\top)^{\mathrm{lf}} = \top$$
$$(P \multimap N)^{\mathrm{lf}} = (P)^{\mathrm{rf}} \multimap (N)^{\mathrm{lf}}$$

– *A right-focused formula P is encoded using the translation* $(-)^{\mathrm{rf}}$:

$$(p)^{\mathrm{rf}} = p \qquad (!_z N^+)^{\mathrm{rf}} = !_{(z,1)} (N^+)^{\mathrm{ra}} \qquad (P \otimes Q)^{\mathrm{rf}} = (P)^{\mathrm{rf}} \otimes (Q)^{\mathrm{rf}} \qquad (1)^{\mathrm{rf}} = 1$$
$$(P \oplus Q)^{\mathrm{rf}} = (P)^{\mathrm{rf}} \oplus (Q)^{\mathrm{rf}} \qquad (0)^{\mathrm{rf}} = 0$$

– *A left-active context Ω is encoded pointwise using the translation* $(-)^{\mathrm{la}}$:

$$(a)^{\mathrm{la}} = !_{(1,1)} a \qquad (!_z N^+)^{\mathrm{la}} = !_{(z,1)} (N^+)^{\mathrm{lp}} \qquad (P \otimes Q)^{\mathrm{la}} = (P)^{\mathrm{la}} \otimes (Q)^{\mathrm{la}} \qquad (1)^{\mathrm{la}} = 1$$
$$(P \oplus Q)^{\mathrm{la}} = (P)^{\mathrm{la}} \oplus (Q)^{\mathrm{la}} \qquad (0)^{\mathrm{la}} = 0$$

– *A right-active formula N^+ is encoded using the translation* $(-)^{\mathrm{ra}}$:

$$(a)^{\mathrm{ra}} = !_{(1,\mathrm{r})} a \qquad (?_z P^-)^{\mathrm{ra}} = ?_{(z,\mathrm{r})} (P^-)^{\mathrm{rp}} \qquad (N \,\&\, M)^{\mathrm{ra}} = (N)^{\mathrm{ra}} \,\&\, (M)^{\mathrm{ra}} \qquad (\top)^{\mathrm{ra}} = \top$$
$$(P \multimap N)^{\mathrm{ra}} = (P)^{\mathrm{la}} \multimap (N)^{\mathrm{ra}}$$

– *A right-passive zoned formula $z : P^-$ is encoded using the translation* $(-)^{\mathrm{rp}}$:

$$(z : P^-)^{\mathrm{rp}} = (z, \mathrm{r}) : (P^-)^{\mathrm{rp}} \qquad\qquad (n)^{\mathrm{rp}} = n \qquad\qquad (P)^{\mathrm{rp}} = (P)^{\mathrm{rf}}$$

The cases for $(!_z N^+)^{\mathrm{rf}}$ and $(?_z P^-)^{\mathrm{lf}}$ will be crucial for the proof of thm. 17. Most of the remaining cases can be seen as an abstract interpretation of the focused rules (fig. 2) on the various contexts. The definition of the encoding of intuitionistic sequents is now completely systematic.

Definition 16 (encoding intuitionistic sequents). *The encoding $(-)^{?!}$ of intuitionistic sequents as classical sequents is as follows:*

$$(\Gamma \vdash [P])^{?!} = (\Gamma)^{\mathrm{lp}} \vdash \left[(P)^{\mathrm{rf}} \right] ; \cdot \qquad\qquad (\Gamma ; [N] \vdash z : Q^-)^{?!} = (\Gamma)^{\mathrm{lp}} ; \left[(N)^{\mathrm{lf}} \right] \vdash (z : Q^-)^{\mathrm{rp}}$$
$$(\Gamma ; \Omega \vdash N^+ ; \cdot)^{?!} = (\Gamma)^{\mathrm{lp}} ; (\Xi)^{\mathrm{la}} \vdash (N^+)^{\mathrm{ra}} ; \cdot \qquad (\Gamma ; \Omega \vdash \cdot ; z : Q^-)^{?!} = (\Gamma)^{\mathrm{lp}} ; (\Xi)^{\mathrm{la}} \vdash \cdot ; (z : Q^-)^{\mathrm{rp}}$$

Observe that the right hand sides of the encoding have the intuitionistic restriction (defn. 8). This restriction will be enforced at every transtion from a focused to an active phase, which is enough because the active rules cannot increase the size of the right contexts.

Theorem 17. *The encoding of defn. 16 is focally adequate (defn. 2).*

Proof. As before for thm. 12, we shall prove this by inventorying the intuitionistic rules of fig. 2, encode the conclusions of each of these rules, and observe whether the neutral premises of the derived inference rules are in bijection with those of the fig. 2. All but the following important cases are omitted here for space reasons.[4]

---

[4] See [6].

– *cases of* I/PR *and* I/!$_z$R :

$$
\cfrac{\cfrac{\left(\Gamma^{u}\right)^{\mathrm{lp}}, z:p \vdash [p]}{\left(\Gamma^{u}\right)^{\mathrm{lp}},(z:p)^{\mathrm{lp}} \vdash \left[(p)^{\mathrm{rf}}\right]}\ {}_{\text{C/PR}}}{\left(\Gamma^{u}, z:p \vdash [p]\right)^{?!}}
\qquad
\cfrac{\cfrac{\cfrac{\cfrac{\left(\Gamma ;\ \cdot \vdash N^{+} ;\ \cdot\right)^{?!}}{\left(\Gamma\right)^{\mathrm{lp}} ;\ \cdot \vdash (N^{+})^{\mathrm{la}} ;\ \cdot}}{\left(\Gamma\right)^{\mathrm{lp}} \vdash \left[!_{(z,1)}\,(N^{+})^{\mathrm{la}}\right] ;\ \cdot}\ \boxed{{}_{\text{C/!R}}}}{\left(\Gamma\right)^{\mathrm{lp}} \vdash \left[(!_{z}N^{+})^{\mathrm{rf}}\right] ;\ \cdot}}{\left(\Gamma \vdash [!_{z}N^{+}]\right)^{?!}}
$$

The boxed instance of C/!R is valid because all the zoned formulas in $(\Gamma)^{\mathrm{lp}}$ are in the left form zones, as is the zone of the ! itself, so the comparison $\hat{\le}$ is the same as $\le$ on the intuitionistic zones (defn. 14).

– *case of* I/$-$∘L :

$$
\cfrac{\cfrac{\cfrac{\left(\Gamma^{u},\Gamma^{\mathrm{r}}_{1} \vdash [P]\right)^{?!}}{\left(\Gamma^{u},\Gamma^{\mathrm{r}}_{1}\right)^{\mathrm{lp}} \vdash \left[(P)^{\mathrm{rf}}\right] ;\ \cdot}\qquad\cfrac{\left(\Gamma^{u},\Gamma^{\mathrm{r}}_{2} ;\ [N] \vdash z:Q^{-}\right)^{?!}}{\left(\Gamma^{u},\Gamma^{\mathrm{r}}_{2}\right)^{\mathrm{lp}} ;\ \left[(N)^{\mathrm{lf}}\right] \vdash (z:Q^{-})^{\mathrm{rp}}}}{\left(\Gamma^{u},\Gamma^{\mathrm{r}}_{1},\Gamma^{\mathrm{r}}_{2}\right)^{\mathrm{lp}} ;\ \left[(P)^{\mathrm{rf}} -\!\!\circ (N)^{\mathrm{lf}}\right] \vdash (z:Q^{-})^{\mathrm{rp}}}\ \boxed{{}_{\text{C/}-\!\circ\text{L}}}}{\cfrac{\left(\Gamma^{u},\Gamma^{\mathrm{r}}_{1},\Gamma^{\mathrm{r}}_{2}\right)^{\mathrm{lp}} ;\ \left[(P -\!\!\circ N)^{\mathrm{lf}}\right] \vdash (z:Q^{-})^{\mathrm{rp}}}{\left(\Gamma^{u},\Gamma^{\mathrm{r}}_{1},\Gamma^{\mathrm{r}}_{2} ;\ [P -\!\!\circ N] \vdash z:Q^{-}\right)^{?!}}}
$$

The boxed instance of C/$-$∘L contains the only split of the right context that can succeed in the same focused phase, *i.e.*, reach an initial sequent or a phase transition, becaue that $(P)^{\mathrm{rf}}$ eventually produces either a positive atom (which must finish the proof with C/PR and since right form zones are restricted $(z:Q^{-})^{\mathrm{rp}}$ cannot be present) or a $!_{(z,1)}$ which guarantees that the rest of the right context is empty.

– *cases of* I/?$_z$L *and* DR :

$$
\cfrac{\cfrac{\cfrac{\left(\Gamma ;\ P^{-} \vdash \cdot ;\ y:Q^{-}\right)^{?!}}{\left(\Gamma\right)^{\mathrm{lp}} ;\ (P^{-})^{\mathrm{la}} \vdash \cdot ;\ (y:Q^{-})^{\mathrm{rp}}}}{\left(\Gamma\right)^{\mathrm{lp}} ;\ \left[?_{(z,\mathrm{r})}\,(P^{-})^{\mathrm{la}}\right] \vdash (y:Q^{-})^{\mathrm{rp}}}\ \boxed{{}_{\text{C/?L}}}}{\cfrac{\left(\Gamma\right)^{\mathrm{lp}} ;\ \left[(?_{z}P^{-})^{\mathrm{lf}}\right] \vdash (y:Q^{-})^{\mathrm{rp}}}{\left(\Gamma ;\ [?_{z}P^{-}] \vdash y:Q^{-}\right)^{?!}}}
\qquad
\cfrac{\cfrac{\cfrac{\Gamma \vdash [P]}{\left(\Gamma\right)^{\mathrm{lp}} \vdash \left[(P)^{\mathrm{rf}}\right] ;\ \cdot}}{\left(\Gamma\right)^{\mathrm{lp}} ;\ \cdot \vdash \cdot ;\ (z,\mathrm{r}):(P)^{\mathrm{rf}}}\ \boxed{{}_{\text{C/RDR}}}}{\cfrac{\left(\Gamma\right)^{\mathrm{lp}} ;\ \cdot \vdash \cdot ;\ (z:P)^{\mathrm{rp}}}{\left(\Gamma ;\ \cdot \vdash \cdot ;\ z:P\right)^{?!}}}
$$

The boxed instance of C/?L is justified because the subscript zone (z,r) is of the right form (in order to compare with (y,r)) which is $\hat{\le}$-smaller than its corresponding left-form zone (defn. 14). Note that it is crucial for soundness to have (z,r) not be smaller than all left form zones. Since right form zones are restricted, there is no copying in the boxed instance of C/RDR. The other decision cases are similar.   □

We note one important direct corollary of thm. 17.

Corollary 18 (intuitionistic logic in classical linear logic). *There is a focally adequate encoding of intuitiontistic logic in classical linear logic.*

It is well known [9] that (classical) linear logic can encode the intuitionistic implication $\supset$ as follows: $A \supset B \triangleq !A \multimap B$. However, this encoding is only globally adequate [16]. It is possible to refine this encoding to obtain a fully adequate encoding [12] in an enriched classical linear logic which is not apparently an instance of classical subexponential logic. Corollary 18 further improves our undertanding of encodings of intuitionistic implicication by permuting ! into the antecedent of the implication until there is a phase change, which removes the bureaucratic polarity switch inherent in this implication.[5]

Proof (of cor. 18). The split of the signature 1 (defn. 7) is isomorphic to the signature 11, so apply thm. 17.   □

5   Conclusions

Section 4 shows that any given classical (resp. intuitionistic) subexponential logic can be encoded in a related intuitionistic (resp. classical) subexponential logic such that partial synthetic derivations are preserved. This is a technical result, with at least one of the directions of encoding being novel. It strongly suggests that one of the fractures in logic identified by Miller in [13]—the classical/intuitionistic divide—might be healed by analyses and algorithms that are generic on subexponential signatures. One might still favour "classical" or "intuitionistic" dialects for proofs, but neither format is more fundamental.

The results of this paper have two caveats. First, we only consider the "restricted" or the "unrestricted" flavours of subexponentials; in [8] there were also subexponentials of the "strict" and "affine" flavours for which our results here do not extend directly. Second, we do not consider encodings involving non-propositional kinds, such as terms or frames. Subexponentials are still useful for such stronger encodings, but *representational adequacy* may not be as straightforward.

References

1. Andreoli, J.-M.: Logic programming with focusing proofs in linear logic. J. of Logic and Computation 2(3), 297–347 (1992)
2. Barber, A., Plotkin, G.: Dual intuitionistic linear logic. Technical Report ECS-LFCS-96-347, University of Edinburgh (1996)
3. Chang, B.-Y.E., Chaudhuri, K., Pfenning, F.: A judgmental analysis of linear logic. Technical Report CMU-CS-03-131R, Carnegie Mellon University (December 2003)
4. Chaudhuri, K.: The Focused Inverse Method for Linear Logic. PhD thesis, Carnegie Mellon University, Technical report CMU-CS-06-162 (December 2006)
5. Chaudhuri, K.: Focusing strategies in the sequent calculus of synthetic connectives. In: Cervesato, I., Veith, H., Voronkov, A. (eds.) LPAR 2008. LNCS (LNAI), vol. 5330, pp. 467–481. Springer, Heidelberg (2008)
6. Chaudhuri, K.: Classical and intuitionistic subexponential logics are equally expressive. Technical report, INRIA (2010)
7. Chaudhuri, K., Pfenning, F., Price, G.: A logical characterization of forward and backward chaining in the inverse method. J. of Automated Reasoning 40(2-3), 133–177 (2008)

---

[5] Note that the polarised intuitionistic implication $P \multimap N$, if encoded using Girard's encoding, would be $!{\uparrow}P \multimap N$, which breaks the polarisation of the antecedent.

8. Danos, V., Joinet, J.-B., Schellinx, H.: The structure of exponentials: Uncovering the dynamics of linear logic proofs. In: Mundici, D., Gottlob, G., Leitsch, A. (eds.) KGC 1993. LNCS, vol. 713, pp. 159–171. Springer, Heidelberg (1993)
9. Girard, J.-Y.: Linear logic. Theoretical Computer Science 50, 1–102 (1987)
10. Laurent, O.: Etude de la polarisation en logique. Thèse de doctorat, Université Aix-Marseille II (March 2002)
11. Liang, C., Miller, D.: Focusing and polarization in linear, intuitionistic, and classical logics. Theoretical Computer Science 410(46), 4747–4768 (2009)
12. Liang, C., Miller, D.: A unified sequent calculus for focused proofs. In: LICS-24, pp. 355–364 (2009)
13. Miller, D.: Finding unity in computational logic. In: ACM-BCS-Visions (April 2010)
14. Nigam, V.: Exploiting non-canonicity in the sequent calculus. PhD thesis, Ecole Polytechnique (September 2009)
15. Nigam, V., Miller, D.: Algorithmic specifications in linear logic with subexponentials. In: PPDP, pp. 129–140 (2009)
16. Schellinx, H.: Some syntactical observations on linear logic. Journal of Logic and Computation 1(4), 537–559 (1991)

On Slicewise Monotone Parameterized Problems and Optimal Proof Systems for TAUT

Yijia Chen[1] and Jörg Flum[2]

[1] Shanghai Jiaotong University, China
yijia.chen@cs.sjtu.edu.cn
[2] Albert-Ludwigs-Universität Freiburg, Germany
joerg.flum@math.uni-freiburg.de

Abstract. For a reasonable sound and complete proof calculus for first-order logic consider the problem to decide, given a sentence φ of first-order logic and a natural number n, whether φ has no proof of length $\leq n$. We show that there is a nondeterministic algorithm accepting this problem which, for fixed φ, has running time bounded by a polynomial in n if and only if there is an optimal proof system for the set TAUT of tautologies of propositional logic. This equivalence is an instance of a general result linking the complexity of so-called slicewise monotone parameterized problems with the existence of an optimal proof system for TAUT.

1 Introduction

In this paper we relate the existence of optimal proof systems for the class TAUT of tautologies of propositional logic with the complexity of slicewise monotone parameterized problems. A *proof system* in the sense of Cook and Reckhow [4], say for the class TAUT, is a polynomial time computable function defined on $\{0,1\}^*$ and with TAUT as range. A proof system P is *optimal* if for any other proof system P' for TAUT there is a polynomial $p \in \mathbb{N}[X]$ such that for every tautology α, if α has a proof of length n in P', then α has a proof of length $\leq p(n)$ in P.[1] In their fundamental paper [9] Krajíček and Pudlák showed that an optimal proof system for TAUT exists if NE = co-NE and they derived a series of statements equivalent to the existence of such an optimal proof system; however they conjectured that there is no optimal proof system for TAUT.

On the other hand, Gödel in a letter to von Neumann of 1956 (see [6]) asked for the complexity of the problem to decide, given a sentence φ of first-order logic and a natural number n, whether φ has a proof of length $\leq n$. In our study [2] of this problem we introduced the parameterized problem

p-GÖDEL	*Input:*	A first-order sentence φ and $n \in \mathbb{N}$ in unary.
	Parameter:	$|\varphi|$.
	Question:	Does φ have a proof of length $\leq n$?

---

[1] All notions will be defined in a precise manner in later sections.

A. Dawar and H. Veith (Eds.): CSL 2010, LNCS 6247, pp. 200–214, 2010.

Here we refer to any reasonable sound and complete proof calculus for first-order logic. We do not allow proof calculi, which, for example, admit all first-order instances of propositional tautologies as axioms (as then it would be difficult to recognize correct proofs if $P \neq NP$).

In a different context, namely when trying to show that a certain logic $L_\le$ for PTIME (introduced in [7]) does not satisfy some effectivity condition, Nash et al. introduced implicitly [12] (and this was done explicitly in [1]) the *parameterized acceptance problem* p-$\mathrm{ACC}_\le$ *for nondeterministic Turing machines*:

p-$\mathrm{ACC}_\le$	*Input:*	A nondeterministic Turing machine $\mathbb{M}$ and $n \in \mathbb{N}$ in unary.
	Parameter:	$\|\mathbb{M}\|$, the size of $\mathbb{M}$.
	Question:	Does $\mathbb{M}$ accept the empty input tape in $\le n$ steps?

Both problems, p-GÖDEL and p-$\mathrm{ACC}_\le$, are *slicewise monotone*, that is, their instances have the form (x, n), where $x \in \{0, 1\}^*$ and $n \in \mathbb{N}$ is given in unary,[2] the parameter is $|x|$, and finally for all $x \in \{0, 1\}^*$ and $n, n' \in \mathbb{N}$ we have

if (x, n) is a positive instance and $n < n'$, then (x, n') is a positive instance.

A slicewise monotone problem is in the complexity class $\mathrm{XNP}_{\mathrm{uni}}$ if there is a nondeterministic algorithm that accepts it in time $n^{f(|x|)}$ for some function $f : \mathbb{N} \to \mathbb{N}$. And co-$\mathrm{XNP}_{\mathrm{uni}}$ contains the complements of problems in $\mathrm{XNP}_{\mathrm{uni}}$. We show:

Theorem 1. TAUT *has an optimal proof system if and only if every slicewise monotone problem in* NP *is in* co-$\mathrm{XNP}_{\mathrm{uni}}$.

There are trivial slicewise monotone problems which are fixed-parameter tractable. However, for the slicewise monotone problems mentioned above we can show:

Theorem 2. TAUT *has an optimal proof system* $\Longleftrightarrow p$-$\mathrm{ACC}_\le \in$ co-$\mathrm{XNP}_{\mathrm{uni}}$
$$\Longleftrightarrow p\text{-G\"ODEL} \in \text{co-}\mathrm{XNP}_{\mathrm{uni}}.$$

In [3] we showed that TAUT has a *p-optimal* proof system if and only if a certain logic $L_\le$ is a P-bounded logic for P (=PTIME). The equivalence in the first line of Theorem 2 is the nondeterministic version of this result; in fact, an immediate consequence of it states that TAUT has an optimal proof system if and only if $L_\le$ is an NP-bounded logic for P (a concept that we will introduce in Section 6). It turns out that a slight variant of $L_\le$ is an NP-bounded logic for P (without any assumption).

The content of the different sections is the following. In Section 2 and Section 3 we recall the concepts and results of parameterized complexity and on optimal proof systems, respectively, we need in Section 4 to derive the equivalence in the

---

[2] The requirement that n is given in unary notation ensures that the classical complexity of most slicewise monotone problems we consider is in NP.

first line of Theorem 2. Furthermore, in Section 3 we claim that every problem hard for EEXP under polynomial time reductions has no optimal proof system. In Section 5 we derive some basic properties of slicewise monotone problems, show that p-ACC$_\leq$ is of highest parameterized complexity among the slicewise monotone problems with classical complexity in NP, and finally show that all the slicewise monotone problems we consider in a certain sense have the same complexity (see Proposition 14 for the precise statement). This yields Theorem 1 and the remaining equivalence of Theorem 2. As already mentioned, in Section 6 we analyze the relationship of the existence of an optimal proof system for TAUT and the properties of the logic $L_\leq$.

2   Some Preliminaries

In this section we recall some basic definitions and concepts from parameterized complexity and introduce the concept of slicewise monotone parameterized problem.

We denote the alphabet $\{0, 1\}$ by Σ. The length of a string $x \in \Sigma^*$ is denoted by $|x|$. We identify problems with subsets Q of Σ^*. Clearly, as done mostly, we present concrete problems in a verbal, hence uncodified form or by using other alphabets. We denote by P the class of problems Q such that $x \in Q$ is solvable in time polynomial in $|x|$.

All deterministic and nondeterministic Turing machines have Σ as their alphabet. If necessary we will not distinguish between a Turing machine and its code, a string in Σ^*. If $\mathbb{M}$ is a Turing machine we denote by $\|\mathbb{M}\|$ the length of its code.

Sometimes statements containing a formulation like "there is a $d \in \mathbb{N}$ such that for all $x \in \Sigma^*$: ... $\leq |x|^d$" can be wrong for $x \in \Sigma^*$ with $|x| \leq 1$. We trust the reader's common sense to interpret such statements reasonably.

If $\mathbb{A}$ is any (deterministic or nondeterministic) algorithm and $\mathbb{A}$ accepts x, then we denote by $t_\mathbb{A}(x)$ the number of steps of a shortest accepting run of $\mathbb{A}$ on x; if $\mathbb{A}$ does not accept x, then $t_\mathbb{A}(x)$ is not defined.

2.1   Parameterized Complexity

We view *parameterized problems* as pairs (Q, κ) consisting of a classical problem $Q \subseteq \Sigma^*$ and a *parameterization* $\kappa : \Sigma^* \to \mathbb{N}$, which is required to be polynomial time computable. We will present parameterized problems in the form we did it for p-GÖDEL and p-ACC$_\leq$ in the Introduction.

A parameterized problem (Q, κ) is *fixed-parameter tractable* (or, in FPT) if $x \in Q$ is solvable by an *fpt-algorithm*, that is, by a deterministic algorithm running in time $f(\kappa(x)) \cdot |x|^{O(1)}$ for some computable $f : \mathbb{N} \to \mathbb{N}$.

Let C be a complexity class of classical complexity theory defined in terms of deterministic (nondeterministic) algorithms. A parameterized problem (Q, κ) is in the class XC$_{\mathrm{uni}}$ if there is a deterministic (nondeterministic) algorithm deciding (accepting) Q and witnessing for every $k \in \mathbb{N}$ that the classical problem

$$(Q, \kappa)_k := \{x \in Q \mid \kappa(x) = k\},$$

the kth *slice* of (Q, κ), is in C. For example, (Q, κ) is in the class $\mathrm{XP_{uni}}$ if there is a deterministic algorithm $\mathbb{A}$ deciding $x \in Q$ in time $|x|^{f(\kappa(x))}$ for some function $f : \mathbb{N} \to \mathbb{N}$. And (Q, κ) is in the class $\mathrm{XNP_{uni}}$ if there is a nondeterministic algorithm $\mathbb{A}$ accepting Q such that for some function $f : \mathbb{N} \to \mathbb{N}$ we have $t_{\mathbb{A}}(x) \leq |x|^{f(\kappa(x))}$ for all $x \in Q$. Finally, a parameterized problem (Q, κ) is in the class co-$\mathrm{XC_{uni}}$ if its complement $(\Sigma^* \setminus Q, \kappa)$ is in $\mathrm{XC_{uni}}$.

We have added the subscript "uni" to the names of these classes to emphasize that they are classes of the so-called uniform parameterized complexity theory. If in the definition of $\mathrm{XP_{uni}}$ and $\mathrm{XNP_{uni}}$ we require the function f to be computable, then we get the corresponding classes of the strongly uniform theory. For example, FPT is a class of this theory.

A parameterized problem (Q, κ) is *slicewise monotone* if its instances have the form (x, n), where $x \in \Sigma^*$ and $n \in \mathbb{N}$ is given in unary, if $\kappa((x, n)) = |x|$, and finally if the slices are monotone, that is, for all $x \in \Sigma^*$ and $n, n' \in \mathbb{N}$

$$(x, n) \in Q \text{ and } n < n' \text{ imply } (x, n') \in Q.$$

We already remarked that the problems p-GÖDEL and p-$\mathrm{ACC}_{\leq}$ are slicewise monotone.

Clearly, every parameterized problem (Q, κ) with $Q \in \mathrm{NP}$ is in $\mathrm{XNP_{uni}}$; thus we can replace co-$\mathrm{XNP_{uni}}$ by $\mathrm{XNP_{uni}} \cap \text{co-}\mathrm{XNP_{uni}}$ everywhere in Theorem 1 and Theorem 2.

3   Optimal Proof Systems

Let $Q \subseteq \Sigma^*$ be a problem. A *proof system for Q* is a surjective function $P : \Sigma^* \to Q$ computable in polynomial time. Then, if $P(w) = x$, we say that w is a P-*proof* of x. A proof system P for Q is *optimal* if for any other proof system P' for Q there is a polynomial $p \in \mathbb{N}[X]$ such that for every $x \in Q$, if x has a P'-proof of length n, then x has a P-proof of length $\leq p(n)$. Hence, any P'-proof can be translated into a P-proof by a nondeterministic polynomial time algorithm.

The corresponding deterministic concept is the notion of p-optimality. The proof system P for Q is *polynomially optimal* or *p-optimal* if for every proof system P' for Q there is a polynomial time computable $T : \Sigma^* \to \Sigma^*$ such that for all $w' \in \Sigma^*$

$$P(T(w')) = P'(w').$$

We list some known results. Part (1) and (2) are immediate from the definitions.

(1) Every p-optimal proof system is optimal.
(2) Every nonempty $Q \in \mathrm{PTIME}$ has a p-optimal proof system, every nonempty $Q \in \mathrm{NP}$ has an optimal proof system.
(3) ([8]) If Q is nonempty and $Q \leq^p Q'$ (that is, if Q is polynomial time reducible to Q') and Q' has a (p-)optimal proof system, then Q has a (p-)optimal proof system too.
(4) ([10]) Every Q hard for $\mathrm{EXP} = \mathrm{DTIME}\left(2^{n^{O(1)}}\right)$ under polynomial time reductions has no p-optimal proof system.

It is not known whether there is a problem $Q \notin P$ ($Q \notin NP$) with a p-optimal (an optimal) proof system. As mentioned in the Introduction, Krajíček and Pudlák [9] conjectured that there is no optimal proof system for the set TAUT of tautologies.

Concerning (4) we did not find a corresponding result for optimal proof systems in the literature. We can show:

Proposition 3. *Every Q hard for* $EEXP = DTIME\left(2^{2^{n^{O(1)}}}\right)$ *under polynomial time reductions has no optimal proof system.*

We do not need this result (and will prove it in the full version of the paper). However we state a consequence:

Corollary 4. *There is no optimal proof system for the set of valid sentences of first-order logic.*

3.1 Almost Optimal Algorithms and Enumerations of P-easy Subsets

Let $Q \subseteq \Sigma^*$ be a problem. A deterministic (nondeterministic) algorithm $\mathbb{A}$ accepting Q is *almost optimal* or *optimal on positive instances of Q* if for every deterministic (nondeterministic) algorithm $\mathbb{B}$ accepting Q there is a polynomial $p \in \mathbb{N}[X]$ such that for all $x \in Q$

$$t_{\mathbb{A}}(x) \le p(t_{\mathbb{B}}(x) + |x|).$$

By definition a subset Q' of Q is *P-easy* if $Q' \in P$. An *enumeration of the P-easy subsets of Q by P-machines (by NP-machines)* is a computable function $M : \mathbb{N} \to \Sigma^*$ such that

(i) for every $i \in \mathbb{N}$ the string $M(i)$ is a deterministic (nondeterministic) Turing machine deciding (accepting) a P-easy subset of Q in polynomial time;
(ii) for every P-easy subset Q' of Q there is an $i \in \mathbb{N}$ such that $M(i)$ decides (accepts) Q'.

If in the nondeterministic case instead of (i) we only require

(i') for every $i \in \mathbb{N}$ the string $M(i)$ is a nondeterministic Turing machine accepting a subset of Q in polynomial time,

we obtain the notion of a *weak enumeration of P-easy subsets of Q by NP-machines*.

We denote by TAUT the class of all tautologies of propositional logic. We need the following theorem:

Theorem 5. *(1) The following statements are equivalent:*
(a) TAUT has a p-optimal proof system.
(b) TAUT has an almost optimal deterministic algorithm.
(c) TAUT has an enumeration of the P-easy subsets by P-machines.

(2) The following statements are equivalent:
  (a) TAUT *has an optimal proof system.*
  (b) TAUT *has an almost optimal nondeterministic algorithm.*
  (c) TAUT *has a weak enumeration of the* P-*easy subsets by* NP-*machines.*
  (d) TAUT *has an enumeration of the* P-*easy subsets by* NP-*machines.*

The equivalence of (a) and (b) in (1) and (2) is due to [9], the equivalence to (c) to [13]. The equivalence in (2) to (d) will be a by-product of the proof of Theorem 8; the equivalence was already claimed in [13] but its author was so kind to point out to us that he did not realize the difference between (c) and (d): some machines $M(i)$ of a weak enumeration might accept subsets of Q which are not P-easy (but only in NP).

4   Linking Slicewise Monotone Problems and Optimal Proof Systems

The following result yields a uniform bound on the complexity of slicewise monotone problems whose complements have optimal proof systems.

Theorem 6. *Let (Q, κ) be a slicewise monotone parameterized problem with decidable Q.*
(1) If $\Sigma^* \setminus Q$ has a p-optimal proof system, then $(Q, \kappa) \in \mathrm{XP}_{\mathrm{uni}}$.
(2) If $\Sigma^* \setminus Q$ has an optimal proof system, then $(Q, \kappa) \in \mathrm{co\text{-}XNP}_{\mathrm{uni}}$.

As by (3) on page 203 every nonempty problem in co-NP has a (p-)optimal proof system if TAUT has one, we immediately get:

Corollary 7. *Let (Q, κ) be a slicewise monotone parameterized problem with Q in NP.*
(1) If TAUT has a p-optimal proof system, then $(Q, \kappa) \in \mathrm{XP}_{\mathrm{uni}}$.
(2) If TAUT has an optimal proof system, then $(Q, \kappa) \in \mathrm{co\text{-}XNP}_{\mathrm{uni}}$.

Concerning Theorem 6 (1) we should mention that Monroe [11] has shown that if the complement of (the classical problem underlying) $p\text{-}\mathrm{ACC}_{\leq}$ has an almost optimal algorithm (which by [9] holds if it has a p-optimal proof system), then $p\text{-}\mathrm{ACC}_{\leq} \in \mathrm{XP}_{\mathrm{uni}}$.

Proof of Theorem 6: We present the proof for (2), the proof for (1) is obtained by the obvious modifications. Let (Q, κ) be slicewise monotone and let $\mathbb{Q}$ be a deterministic algorithm deciding Q. Assume that $\Sigma^* \setminus Q$ has an optimal proof system. It is well-known [9] that then $\Sigma^* \setminus Q$ has an almost optimal nondeterministic algorithm $\mathbb{O}$. We have to show that $(Q, \kappa) \in \mathrm{co\text{-}XNP}_{\mathrm{uni}}$.

   Let $\mathbb{S}$ be the algorithm that, on $x \in \Sigma^*$, by systematically applying $\mathbb{Q}$ to the inputs $(x, 0), (x, 1), \dots$ computes

$$n(x) := \text{ the least } n \text{ such that } (x, n) \in Q.$$

If $(x, n) \notin Q$ for all $n \in \mathbb{N}$, then $n(x)$ is not defined and $\mathbb{S}$ does not stop. We show that the following algorithm $\mathbb{A}$ witnesses that $(\Sigma^* \setminus Q, \kappa) \in \mathrm{XNP}_{\mathrm{uni}}$.

$\mathbb{A}(x, n)$ // $x \in \Sigma^*$, $n \in \mathbb{N}$ in unary

1. In parallel simulate $\mathbb{S}$ on input x and $\mathbb{O}$ on input (x, n)
2.   if $\mathbb{O}$ accepts **then** accept
3.   if $\mathbb{S}$ stops, **then**
4.   if $n < n(x)$ **then** accept **else** reject.

By our assumptions on $\mathbb{O}$ and $\mathbb{S}$ and the slicewise monotonicity of Q, it should be clear that $\mathbb{A}$ accepts $\Sigma^* \setminus Q$. We have to show that $\mathbb{A}$ does it in the time required by $\mathrm{XNP}_{\mathrm{uni}}$. Hence, we have to determine the running time of $\mathbb{A}$ on inputs $(x, n) \notin Q$.

Case "$(x, \ell) \notin Q$ for all $\ell \in \mathbb{N}$": In this case $\mathbb{S}$ on input x does not stop. Hence, the running time of $\mathbb{A}$ on input (x, n) is determined by $\mathbb{O}$. The following algorithm $\mathbb{O}_x$ accepts $\Sigma^* \setminus Q$: on input (y, ℓ) the algorithm $\mathbb{O}_x$ checks whether $y = x$. If so, it accepts and otherwise it runs $\mathbb{O}$ on input (y, ℓ) and answers accordingly. Clearly, for all $\ell \in \mathbb{N}$

$$t_{\mathbb{O}_x}((x, \ell)) \leq O(|x|).$$

As $\mathbb{O}$ is almost optimal, we know that there is a constant $d_x \in \mathbb{N}$ (depending on x) such that for all $(y, \ell) \in \Sigma^* \setminus Q$

$$t_{\mathbb{O}}((y, \ell)) \leq \big(|(y, \ell)| + t_{\mathbb{O}_x}((y, \ell))\big)^{d_x}.$$

In particular, we have

$$t_{\mathbb{A}}((x, n)) = O(t_{\mathbb{O}}((x, n))) \leq O\Big(\big(|(x, n)| + O(|x|)\big)^{d_x}\Big) \leq n^{d'_x}$$

for some constant $d'_x \in \mathbb{N}$ (depending on x).

Case "$(x, \ell) \in Q$ for some $\ell \in \mathbb{N}$": Then $\mathbb{S}$ will stop on input x. Thus, in the worst case, $\mathbb{A}$ on input (x, n) has to wait till the simulation of $\mathbb{S}$ on x stops and then $\mathbb{A}$ must check whether the result $n(x)$ of the computation of $\mathbb{S}$ is bigger than n or not and answer according to Line 4. So in the worst case $\mathbb{A}$ takes time $O(t_{\mathbb{S}}(x) + O(n)) \leq n^{O(t_{\mathbb{S}}(x))}$.   □

We show the equivalence in the first line of Theorem 2:

Theorem 8. *(1)* TAUT *has a p-optimal proof system iff* $p\text{-}\mathrm{ACC}_{\leq} \in \mathrm{XP}_{\mathrm{uni}}$.
(2) TAUT *has an optimal proof system iff* $p\text{-}\mathrm{ACC}_{\leq} \in \mathrm{co\text{-}XNP}_{\mathrm{uni}}$.

Proof. Again we only prove (2) and by the previous corollary it suffices to show the corresponding implication from "right to left."

So assume that the complement of $p\text{-}\mathrm{ACC}_{\leq}$ is in $\mathrm{XNP}_{\mathrm{uni}}$ and let $\mathbb{A}$ be a nondeterministic algorithm witnessing it; in particular, $t_{\mathbb{A}}((\mathbb{M}, n)) \leq n^{f(\|\mathbb{M}\|)}$ for some function f and all $(\mathbb{M}, n) \notin p\text{-}\mathrm{ACC}_{\leq}$. We show that TAUT has an enumeration of the P-easy subsets by NP-machines (and this suffices by Theorem 5).

We fix a deterministic Turing machine $\mathbb{M}_0$ that given a propositional formula α and an assignment checks if this assignment satisfies α in time $|\alpha|^2$.

For a deterministic Turing machine $\mathbb{M}$ let $\mathbb{M}^*$ be the nondeterministic machine that on empty input tape

- first guesses a propositional formula α;
- then checks (by simulating $\mathbb{M}$) whether $\mathbb{M}$ accepts α and rejects if this is not the case;
- finally guesses an assignment and accepts if this assignment does not satisfy α (this is checked by simulating $\mathbb{M}_0$).

A deterministic Turing machine $\mathbb{M}$ is *clocked* if (the code of) $\mathbb{M}$ contains a natural number $\mathrm{time}(\mathbb{M})$ such that $n^{\mathrm{time}(\mathbb{M})}$ is a bound for the running time of $\mathbb{M}$ on inputs of length n (in particular, a clocked machine is a polynomial time one).

Finally, for a clocked Turing machine $\mathbb{M}$ let $\mathbb{M}^+$ be the nondeterministic Turing machine that on input α accepts if and only if (i) and (ii) hold:

(i) $\mathbb{M}$ accepts α;
(ii) $(\mathbb{M}^*, |\alpha|^{\mathrm{time}(\mathbb{M})+4}) \notin p\text{-}\mathrm{ACC}_{\leq}$.

The machine $\mathbb{M}^+$ checks (i) by simulating $\mathbb{M}$ and (ii) by simulating $\mathbb{A}$. Hence, if $\mathbb{M}^+$ accepts α, then

$$t_{\mathbb{M}^+}(\alpha) \leq O\left(|\alpha|^{\mathrm{time}(\mathbb{M})} + t_{\mathbb{A}}\left((\mathbb{M}^*, |\alpha|^{\mathrm{time}(\mathbb{M})+4})\right)\right),$$

and as $t_{\mathbb{A}}\left((\mathbb{M}^*, |\alpha|^{\mathrm{time}(\mathbb{M})+4})\right) \leq |\alpha|^{(\mathrm{time}(\mathbb{M})+4)\cdot f(\|\mathbb{M}^*\|)}$, the Turing machine $\mathbb{M}^+$ accepts in time polynomial in $|\alpha|$.

We show that $\mathbb{M}^+$, where $\mathbb{M}$ ranges over all clocked machines, yields an enumeration of all P-easy subsets of TAUT by NP-machines. First let $\mathbb{M}$ be a clocked machine. We prove that $\mathbb{M}^+$ accepts a P-easy subset of TAUT.

$\mathbb{M}^+$ *accepts a subset of* TAUT: If $\mathbb{M}^+$ accepts α, then, by (i), $\mathbb{M}$ accepts α and by (ii), $(\mathbb{M}^*, |\alpha|^{\mathrm{time}(\mathbb{M})+4}) \notin p\text{-}\mathrm{ACC}_{\leq}$. Therefore, by definition of $\mathbb{M}^*$, every assignment satisfies α and hence $\alpha \in$ TAUT.

$\mathbb{M}^+$ *accepts a P-easy set*: If $(\mathbb{M}^*, m) \in p\text{-}\mathrm{ACC}_{\leq}$ for some m, then, by slicewise monotonicity of $p\text{-}\mathrm{ACC}_{\leq}$, the machine $\mathbb{M}^+$ accepts a finite set and hence a P-easy set. If $(\mathbb{M}^*, m) \notin p\text{-}\mathrm{ACC}_{\leq}$ for all m, then $\mathbb{M}^+$ accepts exactly those α accepted by $\mathbb{M}$; as $\mathbb{M}$ is clocked, this is a set in P.

Now let $Q \subseteq$ TAUT be a P-easy subset of TAUT and let $\mathbb{M}$ be a clocked machine deciding Q. Then $\mathbb{M}^+$ accepts Q. □

5 Slicewise Monotone Parameterized Problems

In this section we observe that $p\text{-}\mathrm{ACC}_{\leq}$ is a complete problem in the class of slicewise monotone parameterized problems with underlying classical problem in NP. Furthermore, we shall see that in Theorem 8 we can replace the problem $p\text{-}\mathrm{ACC}_{\leq}$ by other slicewise monotone parameterized problems (among them $p\text{-}\mathrm{GÖDEL}$) by showing for them that they are in the class $\mathrm{XP}_{\mathrm{uni}}$ (co-$\mathrm{XNP}_{\mathrm{uni}}$) if and only if $p\text{-}\mathrm{ACC}_{\leq}$ is.

5.1   The Complexity of Slicewise Monotone Problems

We start with some remarks on the complexity of slicewise monotone problems. In [1,2] we have shown that $p\text{-}\mathrm{ACC}_{\leq}$ and $p\text{-}\mathrm{G\ddot{O}DEL}$ are not fixed-parameter tractable if "P $\neq$ NP holds for all time constructible and increasing functions," that is, if $\mathrm{DTIME}(h^{O(1)}) \neq \mathrm{NTIME}(h^{O(1)})$ for all time constructible and increasing functions $h : \mathbb{N} \to \mathbb{N}$. However:

Proposition 9. (1) ([2]) Let (Q, κ) be slicewise monotone. Then (Q, κ) is non-uniformly fixed-parameter tractable, that is, there is a $c \in \mathbb{N}$, a function $f : \mathbb{N} \to \mathbb{N}$, and for every k an algorithm deciding the slice $(Q, \kappa)_k$ in time $f(k) \cdot n^c$.
(2) Let (Q, κ) be slicewise monotone with enumerable Q. Then $(Q, \kappa) \in \mathrm{XNP}_{\mathrm{uni}}$.

Proof. (2) Let $\mathbb{Q}$ be an algorithm enumerating Q. The following algorithm shows that $(Q, \kappa) \in \mathrm{XNP}_{\mathrm{uni}}$: On input (x, n) it guesses $m \in \mathbb{N}$ and a string c. If c is the code of an initial segment of the run of $\mathbb{Q}$ enumerating (x, m), then it accepts if $m \leq n$. $\square$

We remark that there are slicewise monotone problems with underlying classical problem of arbitrarily high complexity that are fixed-parameter tractable. In fact, let $Q_0 \subseteq \Sigma^*$ be decidable. Then the slicewise monotone (Q, κ) with

$$Q := \{(x, n) \mid x \in Q_0,\ n \in \mathbb{N},\ \text{and}\ |x| \leq n\}$$

(and $\kappa((x, n)) := |x|$) is in FPT.

To compare the complexity of parameterized problems we use the standard notions of reduction that we recall first. Let (Q, κ) and (Q', κ') be parameterized problems. We write $(Q, \kappa) \leq^{\mathrm{fpt}} (Q', \kappa')$ if there is an *fpt-reduction* from (Q, κ) to (Q', κ'), that is, a mapping $R : \Sigma^* \to \Sigma^*$ with:

(1) For all $x \in \Sigma^*$ we have $(x \in Q \iff R(x) \in Q')$.
(2) $R(x)$ is computable in time $f(\kappa(x)) \cdot |x|^{O(1)}$ for some computable $f : \mathbb{N} \to \mathbb{N}$.
(3) There is a computable function $g : \mathbb{N} \to \mathbb{N}$ such that $\kappa'(R(x)) \leq g(\kappa(x))$ for all $x \in \Sigma^*$.

We write $(Q, \kappa) \leq^{\mathrm{xp}} (Q', \kappa')$ if there is an *xp-reduction* from (Q, κ) to (Q', κ'), which is defined as $(Q, \kappa) \leq^{\mathrm{fpt}} (Q', \kappa')$ except that instead of (2) it is only required that $R(x)$ is computable in time $|x|^{f(\kappa(x))}$ for some computable $f : \mathbb{N} \to \mathbb{N}$.

These are notions of reductions of the usual (strongly uniform) parameterized complexity theory. We get the corresponding notions $\leq^{\mathrm{fpt}}_{\mathrm{uni}}$ and $\leq^{\mathrm{xp}}_{\mathrm{uni}}$ by allowing the functions f and g to be arbitrary (and not necessarily computable).

We shall use the following simple observation.

Lemma 10. If $(Q, \kappa) \leq^{\mathrm{xp}}_{\mathrm{uni}} (Q', \kappa')$ and $(Q', \kappa') \in \mathrm{XP}_{\mathrm{uni}}$, then $(Q, \kappa) \in \mathrm{XP}_{\mathrm{uni}}$. The same holds for $\mathrm{XNP}_{\mathrm{uni}}$ instead of $\mathrm{XP}_{\mathrm{uni}}$.

We turn again to slicewise monotone problems. Among these problems with underlying classical problem in NP the problem $p\text{-}\mathrm{ACC}_{\leq}$ is of highest complexity.

Proposition 11. *Let (Q, κ) be slicewise monotone and $Q \in \mathrm{NP}$. Then*

$$(Q, \kappa) \leq^{\mathrm{fpt}} p\text{-}\mathrm{ACC}_{\leq}.$$

Note that this result together with Theorem 8 (2) yields Theorem 1.

Proof of Proposition 11: Let $\mathbb{M}$ be a nondeterministic Turing machine accepting Q. We may assume that for some $d \in \mathbb{N}$ the machine $\mathbb{M}$ on input (x, n) performs exactly $|(x, n)|^d$ steps. For $x \in \Sigma^*$ let $\mathbb{M}_x$ be the nondeterministic Turing machine that on empty input tape, first writes x on the tape, then guesses a natural number m, and finally simulates the computation of $\mathbb{M}$ on input (x, m). We can assume that there is a polynomial time computable function h such that $\mathbb{M}_x$ makes exactly $h(x, m) \in O(|x| + m + |(x, m)|^d)$ steps if it chooses the natural number m. Furthermore we can assume that $h(x, m) < h(x, m')$ for $m < m'$.

Then $(x, n) \mapsto \big(\mathbb{M}_x, h(x, n)\big)$ is an fpt-reduction from (Q, κ) to $p\text{-}\mathrm{ACC}_{\leq}$: Clearly, if $(x, n) \in Q$ then $\big(\mathbb{M}_x, h(x, n)\big) \in p\text{-}\mathrm{ACC}_{\leq}$ by construction of $\mathbb{M}_x$. Conversely, if $\big(\mathbb{M}_x, h(x, n)\big) \in p\text{-}\mathrm{ACC}_{\leq}$, then by the properties of h we see that $\mathbb{M}$ accepts (x, m) for some $m \leq n$. Thus, $(x, m) \in Q$ and therefore $(x, n) \in Q$ by slicewise monotonicity.   □

Later on we shall use the following related result.

Proposition 12. *Let (Q, κ) be slicewise monotone and assume that there is a nondeterministic algorithm $\mathbb{A}$ accepting Q such that $t_{\mathbb{A}}(x, n) \leq n^{f(|x|)}$ for some time constructible f and all $(x, n) \in Q$. Then*

$$(Q, \kappa) \leq^{\mathrm{xp}} p\text{-}\mathrm{ACC}_{\leq}.$$

Proof. Let (Q', κ') be the problem

Instance: $x \in \Sigma^*$ and $m \in \mathbb{N}$ in unary.
Parameter: $|x|$.
Question: Is there an $n \in \mathbb{N}$ such that $n^{f(|x|)} \leq m$ and $(x, n) \in Q$?

By the previous proposition we get our claim once we have shown:

(1) (Q', κ') is slicewise monotone and $Q' \in \mathrm{NP}$.
(2) $(Q, \kappa) \leq^{\mathrm{xp}} (Q', \kappa')$

To see (1) let $\mathbb{A}$ be as stated above and let $\mathbb{T}$ an algorithm witnessing the time constructibility of f; that is, $\mathbb{T}$ on input $k \in \mathbb{N}$ computes $f(k)$ in exactly $f(k)$ steps. An algorithm $\mathbb{B}$ witnessing that $Q' \in \mathrm{NP}$ runs as follows on input (x, m):

- $\mathbb{B}$ guesses $n \in \mathbb{N}$;
- if $n = 1$, the algorithm $\mathbb{B}$ rejects in case $m = 0$;
  if $n \geq 2$, the algorithm $\mathbb{B}$ simulates m steps of the computation of $\mathbb{T}$ on input $|x|$; if thereby $\mathbb{T}$ does not stop, $\mathbb{B}$ rejects; otherwise, the simulation yields $f(|x|)$ and $\mathbb{B}$ checks whether $n^{f(|x|)} > m$ (this can be detected in time $O(m)$); in the positive case $\mathbb{B}$ rejects;
- finally $\mathbb{B}$ simulates the computation of $\mathbb{A}$ on (x, n) and answers accordingly.

(2) Note that the mapping $(x, n) \mapsto \big(x, n^{f(|x|)}\big)$ is an xp-reduction.   □

5.2 Slicewise Monotone Problems Related to Logic

In the next section we will use some further slicewise monotone problems related to first-order logic and least fixed-point logic that we introduce now.

We assume familiarity with *first-order logic* FO and its extension *least fixed-point logic* LFP (e.g, see [5]). We denote by $FO[\tau]$ and $LFP[\tau]$ the set of sentences of vocabulary τ of FO and of LFP, respectively. In this paper all vocabularies are finite sets of relational symbols.

If the structure $\mathcal{A}$ is a model of the LFP-sentence φ we write $\mathcal{A} \models \varphi$. We only consider structures $\mathcal{A}$ with finite universe A. The size $\|\mathcal{A}\|$ of the structure $\mathcal{A}$ is the length of a reasonable encoding of $\mathcal{A}$ as string in Σ^*. An algorithm based on the inductive definition of the satisfaction relation for LFP shows (see [14]):

Proposition 13. *The model-checking problem $\mathcal{A} \models \varphi$ for structures $\mathcal{A}$ and LFP-sentences φ can be solved in time $\|\mathcal{A}\|^{O(|\varphi|)}$.*

Let $L = $ FO or $L = $ LFP. First we introduce the parameterized problem

p-L-MODEL	*Input:*	An L-sentence φ and $n \in \mathbb{N}$ in unary.
	Parameter: $|\varphi|$.	
	Question:	Is there a structure $\mathcal{A}$ with $\mathcal{A} \models \varphi$ and $|A| \leq n$?

Here, $|A|$ denotes the size of the universe A of $\mathcal{A}$. For every vocabulary τ we let $\tau_< := \tau \cup \{<\}$, where $<$ is a binary relation symbol not in τ. For $m \geq 1$ we say that an $L[\tau_<]$-sentence φ is $\leq m$-*invariant* if for all τ-structures $\mathcal{A}$ with $|A| \leq m$ we have

$$(\mathcal{A}, <_1) \models \varphi \iff (\mathcal{A}, <_2) \models \varphi$$

for all orderings $<_1$ and $<_2$ on A.

Finally we introduce the slicewise monotone parameterized problem

p-L-NOT-INV	*Input:*	A vocabulary τ, an $L[\tau_<]$-sentence φ and $m \geq 1$ in unary.
	Parameter: $|\varphi|$.	
	Question:	Is φ not $\leq m$-invariant?

5.3 Membership in XP$_{uni}$ and co-XNP$_{uni}$

Concerning membership in the classes XP$_{uni}$ and co-XNP$_{uni}$ all the slicewise monotone problems we have introduced behave in the same way:

Proposition 14. *Consider the parameterized problems*
    p-GÖDEL, p-FO-MODEL, p-LFP-MODEL, p-FO-NOT-INV, p-LFP-NOT-INV,
    and p-ACC$_\leq$.
If one of the problems is in XP$_{uni}$, *then all are; if one of the problems is in* co-XNP$_{uni}$, *then all are.*

By Theorem 8 this result yields Theorem 2. We prove it with Lemmas 15–18.

Lemma 15. ([2]) p-GÖDEL $\leq^{\mathrm{fpt}}$ p-FO-MODEL.

Lemma 16. Let $L =$ FO or $L =$ LFP. Then p-L-MODEL $\leq^{\mathrm{fpt}}$ p-L-NOT-INV.

Proof. Let φ be a sentence of vocabulary τ We set $\tau' := \tau \cup \{P\}$ with a new unary relation symbol P and consider the sentence of vocabulary $\tau'_<$

$$\psi(\varphi) := \varphi \wedge \text{ "}P\text{ holds for the first element of } <.\text{"}$$

Clearly, for every $n \geq 2$

$$(\varphi, n) \in p\text{-FO-MODEL} \iff \big(\psi(\varphi), n\big) \in p\text{-FO-NOT-INV}$$

and the same equivalence holds for p-LFP-MODEL and p-LFP-NOT-INV. Thus $(\varphi, n) \mapsto \big(\psi(\varphi), n\big)$ is the desired reduction in both cases. □

Lemma 17. p-LFP-NOT-INV $\leq^{\mathrm{xp}}$ p-ACC$_\leq$

Proof. Consider the algorithm $\mathbb{A}$ that on input (φ, m), where φ is an LFP-sentence and $m \geq 1$, guesses a structure $\mathcal{A}$ and two orderings $<_1$ and $<_2$ and accepts if $|A| \leq m$, $(\mathcal{A}, <_1) \models \varphi$, and $(\mathcal{A}, <_2) \models \neg\varphi$. Then, by Proposition 13, the algorithm $\mathbb{A}$ witnesses that p-LFP-NOT-INV satisfies the assumptions on (Q, κ) in Proposition 12. This yields the claim. □

Lemma 18. *(1)* If p-GÖDEL $\in$ XP$_{\mathrm{uni}}$, then p-ACC$_\leq$ $\in$ XP$_{\mathrm{uni}}$.
(2) If p-GÖDEL $\in$ co-XNP$_{\mathrm{uni}}$, then p-ACC$_\leq$ $\in$ co-XNP$_{\mathrm{uni}}$.

Proof. We give the proof of (2). By standard means we showed in [2, Lemma 7] that there exists a $d \in \mathbb{N}$ and a polynomial time algorithm that assigns to every nondeterministic Turing machine $\mathbb{M}$ a first-order sentence $\varphi_{\mathbb{M}}$ such that for $n \in \mathbb{N}$

$$(\mathbb{M}, n) \in p\text{-ACC}_\leq \implies (\varphi_{\mathbb{M}}, n^d) \in p\text{-GÖDEL}. \tag{1}$$

Moreover,

$$\varphi_{\mathbb{M}} \text{ has a proof} \implies \mathbb{M} \text{ accepts the empty input tape.} \tag{2}$$

Now assume that $\mathbb{A}$ is an algorithm that witnesses that the complement of p-GÖDEL is in XNP$_{\mathrm{uni}}$. We may assume that every run of $\mathbb{A}$ either accepts its input or is infinitely long. Let $d \in \mathbb{N}$ be as above. We present an algorithm $\mathbb{B}$ showing that the complement of p-ACC$_\leq$ is in XNP$_{\mathrm{uni}}$. On input $(\mathbb{M}, n)$ the algorithm $\mathbb{B}$ first computes $\varphi_{\mathbb{M}}$ and then runs two algorithms in parallel:

- a brute force algorithm that on input $\mathbb{M}$ searches for the least $n_{\mathbb{M}}$ such that $\mathbb{M}$ on empty input tape has an accepting run of length $n_{\mathbb{M}}$;
- the algorithm $\mathbb{A}$ on input $(\varphi_{\mathbb{M}}, n^d)$.

If the brute force algorithm halts first and outputs $n_{\mathbb{M}}$, then $\mathbb{B}$ checks whether $n_{\mathbb{M}} \leq n$ and answers accordingly.

Assume now that $\mathbb{A}$ halts first. Then $\mathbb{A}$ accepts $(\varphi_{\mathbb{M}}, n^d)$ and $\big((\varphi_{\mathbb{M}}, n^d) \notin p\text{-}\text{GÖDEL}$ and hence $(\mathbb{M}, n) \notin p\text{-}\text{ACC}_{\leq}$ by (1) and therefore$\big)$ $\mathbb{B}$ accepts.

The algorithm $\mathbb{B}$ accepts the complement of $p\text{-}\text{ACC}_{\leq}$; note that if no run of $\mathbb{A}$ accepts $(\varphi_{\mathbb{M}}, n^d)$, then $(\varphi_{\mathbb{M}}, n^d) \in p\text{-}\text{GÖDEL}$ and therefore $\mathbb{M}$ accepts the empty input tape by (2), so that in this case the computation of the brute force algorithm eventually will stop.

It remains to see that $\mathbb{B}$ accepts the complement of $p\text{-}\text{ACC}_{\leq}$ in the time required by XNP_{uni}. We consider two cases.

$\mathbb{M}$ *halts on empty input tape*: Then an upper bound for the running time is given by the time that the brute force algorithm needs to compute $n_{\mathbb{M}}$ (and the time for the check whether $n_{\mathbb{M}} \leq n$); hence we have an upper bound of the form $n^{c_{\mathbb{M}}}$.

$\mathbb{M}$ *does not halt on empty input tape*: Then, by (2), we have $(\varphi_{\mathbb{M}}, n^d) \notin p\text{-}\text{GÖDEL}$; hence an upper bound is given by the running time of $\mathbb{A}$ on input $(\varphi_{\mathbb{M}}, n^d)$. □

It should be clear that Lemmas 15–18 together with Lemma 10 yield a proof of Proposition 14.

6   Optimal Algorithms and the Logic $L_{\leq}$

In this section we interpret Theorem 2 in terms of the expressive power of a certain logic.

For our purposes a *logic L* consists

- for every vocabulary τ of a set $L[\tau]$ of strings, the set of *L-sentences of vocabulary* τ and of an algorithm that for every vocabulary τ and every string ξ decides whether $\xi \in L[\tau]$ (in particular, $L[\tau]$ is decidable for every τ);
- of a *satisfaction relation* $\models_L$; if $(\mathcal{A}, \varphi) \in \models_L$, written $\mathcal{A} \models_L \varphi$, then $\mathcal{A}$ is a τ-structure and $\varphi \in L[\tau]$ for some vocabulary τ; furthermore for each $\varphi \in L[\tau]$ the class $\text{Mod}_L(\varphi) := \{\mathcal{A} \mid \mathcal{A} \models_L \varphi\}$ of *models of* φ is closed under isomorphisms.

Definition 19. Let L be a logic.
(a) L *is a logic for* P if for all vocabularies τ and all classes C (of encodings) of τ-structures closed under isomorphisms we have

$$C \in \text{P} \iff C = \text{Mod}_L(\varphi) \text{ for some } \varphi \in L[\tau].$$

(b) L *is a* P*-bounded logic for* P if (a) holds and if there is an algorithm $\mathbb{A}$ deciding $\models_L$ (that is, for every structure $\mathcal{A}$ and L-sentence φ the algorithm $\mathbb{A}$ decides whether $\mathcal{A} \models_L \varphi$) and if moreover, for fixed φ the algorithm $\mathbb{A}$ runs in time polynomial in $\|\mathcal{A}\|$.

The relationship of these concepts with topics of this paper is already exemplified by the following simple observation.

Proposition 20. *Let L be a logic for* P *and define p-*$\models_L$ *by*

$p\text{-}\models_L$	*Input:*	A structure $\mathcal{A}$ and an *L*-sentence φ.
	Parameter:	$|\varphi|$.
	Question:	Is $\mathcal{A} \models_L \varphi$

Then L is a P*-bounded logic for* P *if and only if p-*$\models_L \in \mathrm{XP}_{\mathrm{uni}}$.

This relationship suggests the following definition.

Definition 21. *L is an* NP*-bounded logic for* P *if it is a logic for* P *and p-*$\models_L \in \mathrm{XNP}_{\mathrm{uni}}$.

We introduce the logic $L_\le$, a variant of LFP.[3] For every vocabulary τ we set

$$L_\le[\tau] = \mathrm{LFP}[\tau_<]$$

(recall that $\tau_< := \tau \cup \{<\}$, with a new binary $<$) and define the semantics by

$$\mathcal{A} \models_{L_\le} \varphi \iff \Big(\varphi \text{ is } \le |A|\text{-invariant and}$$

$$(\mathcal{A}, <) \models_{\mathrm{LFP}} \varphi \text{ for some ordering } < \text{ on } A \Big).$$

Hence, by the previous proposition and the definition of $\models_{L_\le}$, we get:

Proposition 22. *(1) The following statements are equivalent:*
- $L_\le$ *is a* P*-bounded logic for* P.
- *p-*$\models_{L_\le} \in \mathrm{XP}_{\mathrm{uni}}$.
- *p*-LFP-NOT-INV $\in \mathrm{XP}_{\mathrm{uni}}$.

(2) The following statements are equivalent:
- $L_\le$ *is an* NP*-bounded logic for* P.
- *p-*$\models_{L_\le} \in \mathrm{XNP}_{\mathrm{uni}}$.
- *p*-LFP-NOT-INV $\in$ co-$\mathrm{XNP}_{\mathrm{uni}}$.

By Theorem 2 and Proposition 14 we get:

Theorem 23. TAUT *has an optimal proof system if and only if* $L_\le$ *is an* NP*-bounded logic for* P.

Hence, if TAUT has an optimal proof system, then there is an NP-enumeration of P-easy classes of graphs closed under isomorphisms. We do not define the concept of NP-enumeration explicitly, however the enumeration obtained by applying the algorithm in $\mathrm{XNP}_{\mathrm{uni}}$ for *p-* $\models_{L_\le}$ to the classes $\mathrm{Mod}_{L_\le}(\varphi(\mathrm{GRAPH}) \wedge \psi)$, where $\varphi(\mathrm{GRAPH})$ axiomatizes the class of graphs and ψ ranges over all sentences of $L_\le$ in

---

[3] In this section, if the structure $\mathcal{B}$ is a model of an LFP-sentence φ we write $\mathcal{A} \models_{\mathrm{LFP}} \varphi$ instead of $\mathcal{A} \models \varphi$.

the language of graphs, is such an NP-enumeration. Note that even without the assumption that TAUT has an optimal proof system we know that there is such an NP-enumeration of P-easy classes of graphs closed under isomorphisms, as the following variant $L_\leq(\text{not})$ of $L_\leq$ is an NP-bounded logic for P. The logic $L_\leq(\text{not})$ has the same syntax as $L_\leq$ and the semantics is given by the following clause:

$$\mathcal{A} \models_{L_\leq(\text{not})} \varphi \iff \text{not } \mathcal{A} \models_{L_\leq} \varphi.$$

As the class P is closed under complements, $L_\leq(\text{not})$ is a logic for P. And $L_\leq(\text{not})$ is an NP-bounded logic for P, as p-LFP-NOT-INV $\in$ XNP$_{\text{uni}}$.

Acknowledgement. This research has been partially supported by the National Nature Science Foundation of China (60970011) and the Sino-German Center for Research Promotion (GZ400).

References

1. Chen, Y., Flum, J.: A logic for PTIME and a parameterized halting problem. In: Proceedings of the 24th IEEE Symposium on Logic in Computer Science (LICS 2009), pp. 397–406 (2009)
2. Chen, Y., Flum, J.: On the complexity of Gödel's proof predicate. The Journal of Symbolic Logic 75(1), 239–254 (2010)
3. Chen, Y., Flum, J.: On p-optimal proof systems and logics for PTIME. In: Gavoille, C. (ed.) ICALP 2010, Part II. LNCS, vol. 6199, pp. 321–332. Springer, Heidelberg (2010)
4. Cook, S., Reckhow, R.: The relative efficiency of propositional proof systems. The Journal of Symbolic Logic 44, 36–50 (1979)
5. Ebbinghaus, H.-D., Flum, J.: Finite Model Theory, 2nd edn. Springer, Heidelberg (1999)
6. Gödel, K.: Collected Works, vol. VI, pp. 372–376. Clarendon Press, Oxford (2003)
7. Gurevich, Y.: Logic and the challenge of computer science. In: Current Trends in Theoretical Computer Science, pp. 1–57. Computer Science Press, Rockville (1988)
8. Köbler, J., Messner, J.: Complete problems for promise classes by optimal proof systems for test sets. In: Proceedings of the 13th IEEE Conference on Computational Complexity (CCC 1998), pp. 132–140 (1998)
9. Krajíček, J., Pudlák, P.: Propositional proof systems, the consistency of first order theories and the complexity of computations. The Journal of Symbolic Logic 54, 1063–1088 (1989)
10. Messner, J.: On optimal algorithms and optimal proof systems. In: Meinel, C., Tison, S. (eds.) STACS 1999. LNCS, vol. 1563, pp. 361–372. Springer, Heidelberg (1999)
11. Monroe, H.: Speedup for natural problems. Electronic Colloquium on Computational Complexity, Report TR09-056 (2009)
12. Nash, A., Remmel, J., Vianu, V.: PTIME queries revisited. In: Eiter, T., Libkin, L. (eds.) ICDT 2005. LNCS, vol. 3363, pp. 274–288. Springer, Heidelberg (2004)
13. Sadowski, Z.: On an optimal propositional proof system and the structure of easy subsets. Theoretical Computer Science 288(1), 181–193 (2002)
14. Vardi, M.Y.: On the complexity of bounded-variable queries. In: Proceedings of the 14th ACM Symposium on Principles of Database Systems (PODS 1995), pp. 266–276 (1995)

A Logic of Sequentiality

Martin Churchill and James Laird

University of Bath, United Kingdom
{m.d.churchill,j.d.laird}@bath.ac.uk

Abstract. Game semantics has been used to interpret both proofs and functional programs: an important further development on the programming side has been to model higher-order programs with state by allowing strategies with "history-sensitive" behaviour. In this paper, we develop a detailed analysis of the structure of these strategies from a logical perspective by showing that they correspond to proofs in a new kind of affine logic.

We describe the semantics of our logic formally by giving a notion of categorical model and an instance based on a simple category of games. Using further categorical properties of this model, we prove a full completeness result: each total strategy is the semantics of a unique cut-free *core* proof in the system. We then use this result to derive an explicit cut-elimination procedure.

Keywords: Game semantics, sequentiality, full completeness.

1   Introduction

In recent years, it has proved fruitful to give semantics of proofs and programs using game models. A proposition is represented as a game, corresponding to a dialogue between a Proponent asserting the proposition and an Opponent attempting to refute it. The (winning) strategies for Proponent provide us with a syntax-independent meaning for proofs for the corresponding formulas. Inter estingly, there are typically winning strategies for dialogue games which do not correspond to any proof (see e.g [5]) whereas (viewed through the Curry-Howard correspondence) they are the denotations of programs in models of higher-order programming languages with imperative features. For such languages, a wealth of full abstraction and definability results have been established [4,1,13,15], with applications in verification.

Our work attempts to give a logical description of such strategies. We develop a logic where derivations correspond both to (winning) strategies on a natural, basic notion of game, *and* to finitary stateful programs. There is a good reason we achieve both in the same system: the simple game model we use contains fully abstract models of an object-oriented language [23] and a coroutine-based language [15].

Related work. Early game models give a computational meaning for formulas of first-order classical logic (Lorenzen) and Linear Logic [5]. One problem here

A. Dawar and H. Veith (Eds.): CSL 2010, LNCS 6247, pp. 215–229, 2010.

is that there are winning strategies which do not correspond to any proof — and even for formulas which are not provable, such as the MIX rule [5]. In [3] a games model of multiplicative linear logic was given where every (history-free, uniform) winning strategy is the denotation of some proof. In [18], a fully complete games model was given for Polarised Linear Logic, with a similar full completeness result with respect to a class of strategies with limited access to history (innocent strategies). In our work, we provide a logic which provides a full completeness result with respect to arbitrary history-sensitive strategies — further each strategy is the denotation of a *unique* proof of a certain kind. This is done by taking the (very natural, simple) games model itself as a starting point. Similarly motivated work includes independence-friendly logic [8], computational logic [12] and ludics [7].

It was first noted in [4] that history-sensitive game models have a notion of state "built in", and so they are well-suited to modelling imperative programs. Various extensions to this model have been proposed, including languages with expressive control operators [15] and higher-order store [1]. In [20], a fully abstract game model is given for an object-oriented language using a very simple class of game — games are just trees and strategies subtrees satisfying a determinacy condition. It is this notion of game we will consider here.

Contribution. We develop a core proof system where proofs are in bijective correspondence with history-sensitive strategies. This core proof system is focused — the rules that can be used to conclude a sequent (a list of formula) are determined by the outermost connective in the head of that sequent. We can extend this core proof system with rules such as cut, tensor and weakening. By giving semantics to these rules, we can show that they are admissible: we can explicitly eliminate them by calculating semantics and then computing the corresponding core proof.

As the games model in question can be used to model (finitary) imperative objects, so can this logic: cut corresponds to composition; tensor to aggregation of methods into a single object; and so on. We will explore this informally, with a particular example. More generally, we have a logic where the computational content of a proof is a *stateful* program.

The semantics of the proof system are given using categorical axioms. The requirements are based on a sequoid operator, and are a subset of those required to model a coroutine calculus in [15]. Categorical axioms for full completeness in the style of [2] are identified, and our game model satisfies these axioms.

2   Games and Strategies

2.1   Games

Our notion of game is essentially that introduced by [5], and similar to that of [3,16].

Definition 1. *A game is a tuple* $(M_A, \lambda_A, b_A, P_A)$ *where*

- M_A *is a set of moves*
- $\lambda_A : M_A \to \{O, P\}$
  - *We call* m *an* O-*move if* $\lambda_A(m) = O$ *and a* P-*move if* $\lambda_A(m) = P$.
- $b_A \in \{O, P\}$ *specifies a starting player*
  - *We call* $s \in M_A^*$ *alternating if* s *starts with a* b_A-*move and alternates between* O-*moves and* P-*moves. Write* $M_A^{\circledast}$ *for the set of such sequences.*
- $P_A \subseteq M_A^{\circledast}$ *is a nonempty prefix-closed set of valid plays.*

For example, the game **N** of natural numbers is $(q \cup \mathbb{N}, \{q \mapsto O, n \mapsto P\}, O, \{\epsilon, q\} \cup \{qn : n \in \mathbb{N}\})$ (where ϵ denotes the empty sequence). We write o, p for the "single move" games $(\{q\}, \{q \mapsto O\}, O, \{\epsilon, q\})$ and $(\{q\}, \{q \mapsto P\}, P, \{\epsilon, q\})$ respectively.

We will call a game A *negative* if $b_A = O$ and *positive* if $b_A = P$. We write $A, B, C, \ldots$ for arbitrary games; $L, M, N, \ldots$ for arbitrary negative games and $P, Q, R, \ldots$ for arbitrary positive games. Define $\neg : \{O, P\} \to \{O, P\}$ by $\neg(O) = P$ and $\neg(P) = O$.

2.2 Connectives

If X and Y are sets, let $X + Y = \{\mathsf{in}_1(x) : x \in X\} \cup \{\mathsf{in}_2 : y \in Y\}$. We use standard notation $[f, g]$ for copairing. If $s \in (X + Y)^*$ then $s|_i$ is the subsequence of s consisting of elements of the form $\mathsf{in}_i(z)$. If $X_1 \subseteq X^*$, $Y_1 \subseteq Y^*$ define:

- $X_1 \| Y_1 = \{s \in (X + Y)^* : s|_1 \in X_1 \wedge s|_2 \in Y_1\}$
- $X_1 \underline{\|} Y_1 = \{s \in X_1 \| Y_1 : \forall t \sqsubseteq s. t|_1 - \varepsilon \implies t|_2 = \varepsilon\}$
- $X_1 +^* Y_1 = \{s \in X_1 \| Y_1 : s|_1 = \epsilon \vee s|_2 = \epsilon\}$

We describe operators on games in Table 1 with abbreviations $M_{A+B} = M_A + M_B$, $\lambda_{A+B} = [\lambda_A, \lambda_B]$ and $P_A^{\circledast} = P \cap M_A^{\circledast}$. A play in $M \otimes N$ consists of an interleaving of a play in M and a play in N. A play in $M \oslash N$ is also such an interleaving, but with a further restriction: the first move must be in M. A play in $M \& N$ consists of a play in M or a play in N. The only play in **1** is the empty sequence. If M is a negative game, the positive game $\downarrow M = p \oslash M$ prefixes all plays with a single P-move. Each of these operators has a dual acting on positive games.

Table 1. Constructions on Games

$$N \otimes L = (M_{N+L}, \lambda_{N+L}, O, (P_N \| P_L)^{\circledast}_{N \otimes L}) \qquad Q \,\mathbin{\mathrm{\rotatebox[origin=c]{180}{\&}}}\, R = (M_{Q+R}, \lambda_{Q+R}, P, (P_Q \| P_R)^{\circledast}_{Q \mathbin{\mathrm{\rotatebox[origin=c]{180}{\&}}} R})$$

$$A \oslash N = (M_{A+N}, \lambda_{A+N}, b_A, (P_A \underline{\|} P_N)^{\circledast}_{A \oslash N}) \qquad A \lhd Q = (M_{A+Q}, \lambda_{A+Q}, b_A, (P_A \underline{\|} P_Q)^{\circledast}_{A \lhd Q})$$

$$N \& L = (M_{N+L}, \lambda_{N+L}, O, P_N +^* P_L) \qquad Q \oplus R = (M_{Q+R}, \lambda_{Q+R}, P, P_Q +^* P_R)$$

$$\uparrow Q = o \lhd Q \qquad \downarrow N = p \oslash N$$

$$\mathbf{1} = (\emptyset, \emptyset, O, \{\epsilon\}) \qquad \mathbf{0} = (\emptyset, \emptyset, P, \{\epsilon\})$$

We also have an operator $(-)^{\perp}$ inverting the role of Player and Opponent, with $A^{\perp} = (M_A, \neg \circ \lambda_A, \neg(b_A), P_A)$. Linear implication can then be derived, with $M \multimap N = N \lhd M^{\perp}$ (this agrees with the definition of $\multimap$ on negative games in [16,3] etc.).

2.3   Strategies

As usual we define the notion of strategy as a set of traces.

Definition 2. *A* strategy σ *for a game* $(M_A, \lambda_A, b_A, P_A)$ *is a subset of* P_A *satisfying:*

- *If* $\sigma = \varnothing$ *then* $b_A = P$, *and if* $\epsilon \in \sigma$ *then* $b_A = O$.
- *If* $sa \in \sigma$, *then* $\lambda_A(a) = P$.
- *If* $sab \in \sigma$, *then* $s \in \sigma$.
- *If* $sa, sb \in \sigma$, *then* $a = b$.

Definition 3. *A* strategy on a game A *is* total *if it is nonempty and whenever* $s \in \sigma$ *and* $so \in P_A$, *there is some* $p \in M_A$ *such that* $sop \in \sigma$.

2.4   Imperative Objects as Strategies

Semantics of a full object-oriented language can be given by interpreting types as games and programs as strategies [23]. As an example, we describe the interpretation of a imperative object as a strategy on an appropriate game. We will later see how this object can be represented as a proof in our system.

We shall consider a simple counter object with two methods: a void press() method and a nat read() method, returning the number of times the press method has previously been invoked. For simplicity here, we will allow the read method to be called only once, and thus its type may be represented by the game $\mathbf{N}$. The type of press — a command that may be repeated indefinitely — may be represented as a negative game Σ^* in which Opponent and Player alternately play q and a respectively. To combine these into an object, we use the operator $\otimes$.

The strategy count : $\Sigma^* \otimes \mathbf{N}$ representing this counter is $\{s \in P_{\Sigma^* \otimes \mathbf{N}} : \beta(s)\}$ where $\beta(s)$ holds if $s = \epsilon$ or $s = tq_1 a_1$ or $s = tq_2 m_2$ where s contains m occurrences of a_1. An example play in count is

$$\Sigma^* \otimes \mathbf{N}$$

q		O
a		P
q		O
a		P
	q	O
	2	P

By contrast with the *history-free* strategies which denote proofs of linear logic in the model of [3], this strategy is *history-sensitive* — the move prescribed by the strategy depends on the entire play so far. It is this property which allows the state of the object to described implicitly, as in e.g. [4].

3   The Logic WS

3.1   Proof System

We will now describe a proof system in which formulas represent (finite) games, and each proof of a formula represents a (total) strategy on the corresponding game. This logic is *polarised* — positive and negative formulas will represent positive and negative games, respectively.

The positive and negative formulas are defined as follows:

$$P := \mathbf{0} \mid \downarrow N \mid P \gamma Q \mid P \oplus Q \mid P \lhd Q \mid P \oslash N$$
$$N := \mathbf{1} \mid \uparrow P \mid N \otimes M \mid M \& N \mid N \oslash M \mid N \lhd P$$

Define an operation $-^\perp$ on formulas (inverting polarity) as follows:

$$
\begin{array}{llll}
\mathbf{0}^\perp & = \mathbf{1} & (P \gamma Q)^\perp = P^\perp \otimes Q^\perp & (P \lhd Q)^\perp = P^\perp \oslash Q^\perp \\
\mathbf{1}^\perp & = \mathbf{0} & (M \otimes N)^\perp = M^\perp \gamma N^\perp & (M \oslash N)^\perp = M^\perp \lhd N^\perp \\
(\downarrow N)^\perp = \uparrow N^\perp & & (P \oplus Q)^\perp = P^\perp \& Q^\perp & (P \oslash M)^\perp = P^\perp \lhd M^\perp \\
(\uparrow P)^\perp = \downarrow P^\perp & & (M \& N)^\perp = M^\perp \oplus N^\perp & (M \lhd P)^\perp = M^\perp \oslash P^\perp
\end{array}
$$

Linear implication is defined $M \multimap N = N \lhd M^\perp$.

A *sequent* of WS is a non-empty sequence of formulas $\vdash A_1, \ldots, A_n$. Semantically, the comma A, B will represent a left merge — $A \lhd B$ if B is positive or $A \oslash B$ if B is negative — and is therefore left-associative.

The proof rules for WS are defined in Table 2. Here M, N range over negative formulas, P, Q over positive formulas, Γ, Δ over lists of formulas, and Γ^p, Δ^p over lists of formulas with polarity p. The rules are partitioned into *core rules* and *admissible rules* — we will show that any proof is denotationally equivalent to one which uses only the core rules. Note that the core rules have a particular shape: none of them are multiplicative on sequents, all operate on the first (or head) formula of the sequent and the only connectives corresponding to a choice of introduction rule are γ and $\oplus$. Within this core, therefore, proof search is particularly simple.

The admissible rules include more familiar sequent-calculus style tensor and cut rules. These permit the embedding of multiplicative-additive linear logic by using the lifts to change polarities where necessary, as in [17,18,22]. Note that, whilst our notion of polarity differs from that of MALLP, the proof rules for the multiplicative connectives and lifts can be *derived* in WS (the roles of $\uparrow$ and $\downarrow$ are switched).

The non-core rules have also been chosen to facilitate representing finitary imperative objects in WS. For example, the $\mathsf{P_{cut}}$ corresponds to composition of functions, the $\mathsf{P_{mix}}$ to aggregating objects, and $\mathsf{P_{wk}}$ to hiding part of the object from the outside world.

3.2   Imperative Objects as Proofs in WS

We now show how a bounded version of our counter can be represented in WS.

Table 2. Proof rules for WS

Core rules:

$$\text{P1} \; \overline{\vdash 1, \Gamma} \qquad\qquad \text{P}\oslash \; \frac{\vdash A, N, \Gamma}{\vdash A \oslash N, \Gamma} \qquad \text{P}\lhd \; \frac{\vdash A, P, \Gamma}{\vdash A \lhd P, \Gamma}$$

$$\text{P}\otimes \; \frac{\vdash M, N, \Gamma \qquad \vdash N, M, \Gamma}{\vdash M \otimes N, \Gamma} \qquad \text{P}\otimes_1 \; \frac{\vdash P, Q, \Gamma}{\vdash P \otimes Q, \Gamma} \qquad \text{P}\otimes_2 \; \frac{\vdash Q, P, \Gamma}{\vdash P \otimes Q, \Gamma}$$

$$\text{P\&} \; \frac{\vdash M, \Gamma \qquad \vdash N, \Gamma}{\vdash M \& N, \Gamma} \qquad \text{P}\oplus_1 \; \frac{\vdash P, \Gamma}{\vdash P \oplus Q, \Gamma} \qquad \text{P}\oplus_2 \; \frac{\vdash Q, \Gamma}{\vdash P \oplus Q, \Gamma}$$

$$\text{P}{\uparrow}^+ \; \frac{\vdash\uparrow (P \otimes Q), \Gamma}{\vdash\uparrow P, Q, \Gamma} \qquad \text{P}{\uparrow}^- \; \frac{\vdash\uparrow (P \oslash N), \Gamma}{\vdash\uparrow P, N, \Gamma} \qquad \text{P}{\uparrow} \; \frac{\vdash P}{\vdash\uparrow P}$$

$$\text{P}{\downarrow}^- \; \frac{\vdash\downarrow (M \otimes N), \Gamma}{\vdash\downarrow M, N, \Gamma} \qquad \text{P}{\downarrow}^+ \; \frac{\vdash\downarrow (N \lhd P), \Gamma}{\vdash\downarrow N, P, \Gamma} \qquad \text{P}{\downarrow} \; \frac{\vdash N}{\vdash\downarrow N}$$

Other rules:

$$\text{P}_1^{\mathsf{T}} \; \frac{\vdash A, \Gamma, \Delta}{\vdash A, \Gamma, 1, \Delta} \quad \text{P}_0^{\mathsf{T}} \; \frac{\vdash A, \Gamma, \Delta}{\vdash A, \Gamma, 0, \Delta} \quad \text{P}_\otimes^{\mathsf{T}} \; \frac{\vdash A, \Gamma, M, N, \Delta}{\vdash A, \Gamma, M \otimes N, \Delta} \quad \text{P}_\otimes^{\mathsf{T}} \; \frac{\vdash A, \Gamma, P, Q, \Delta}{\vdash A, \Gamma, P \otimes Q, \Delta}$$

$$\text{P}_\perp \; \frac{\vdash\uparrow P, \Gamma}{\vdash\uparrow 0, P, \Gamma} \quad \text{P}_\top \; \frac{\vdash\downarrow N, \Gamma}{\vdash\downarrow 1, N, \Gamma} \quad \text{P}_{\text{sym}}^+ \; \frac{\vdash A, \Gamma, P, Q, \Delta}{\vdash A, \Gamma, Q, P, \Delta} \quad \text{P}_{\text{sym}}^- \; \frac{\vdash A, \Gamma, M, N, \Delta}{\vdash A, \Gamma, N, M, \Delta}$$

$$\text{P}_{\text{mix}} \; \frac{\vdash M, \Gamma, \Delta^+ \qquad \vdash N, \Delta_1^+}{\vdash M, \Gamma, N, \Delta^+, \Delta_1^+} \quad \text{P}_{\text{wk}} \; \frac{\vdash A, \Gamma, M, \Delta}{\vdash A, \Gamma, \Delta} \quad \text{P}_{\text{str}} \; \frac{\vdash A, \Gamma, \Delta}{\vdash A, \Gamma, P, \Delta}$$

$$\text{P}_{\text{cut}} \; \frac{\vdash A, \Gamma, N^\perp, \Gamma_1 \qquad \vdash N, \Delta^+}{\vdash A, \Gamma, \Delta^+, \Gamma_1} \quad \text{P}_{\text{id}} \; \overline{\vdash N, N^\perp} \quad \text{P}_{\oplus i}^{\mathsf{T}} \; \frac{\vdash \Gamma, P_i, \Delta}{\vdash \Gamma, P_1 \oplus P_2, \Delta}$$

Write $\top$ for $\downarrow 0$. If $\oplus_0 \top =_{df} \top$ and $\oplus_{n+1} =_{df} \top \oplus (\oplus_n \top)$ then $\mathbf{N}_n =\uparrow (\oplus_n \top)$ represents the type of numbers at most n. Similarly, if $!_0 A =_{df} \mathbf{1}$ and $!_{n+1} A =_{df} A \oslash !_n A$ then $!_n \Sigma$ represents a switch that can be pressed at most n times.

We may derive a proof $\text{count}_n \vdash !_n \Sigma \otimes \mathbf{N}_n$ for any n by induction. The crux of the proof is the concluding application of the $\text{P}\otimes$ rule: this partitions interactions in $!_n \Sigma \otimes \mathbf{N}_n$ into those that start in $!_n \Sigma$ (with a press) and those that start in $\mathbf{N}_n$ (with a read).

$$\text{P}\otimes \; \frac{\begin{array}{cc} \text{count}^1_{n,n} & \text{count}^2_{n,n} \\ \vdots & \vdots \\ \vdash !_n \Sigma, \mathbf{N}_n & \vdash \mathbf{N}_n, !_n \Sigma \end{array}}{\text{count}_n \vdash !_n \Sigma \otimes \mathbf{N}_n}$$

We first define $\text{count}^1_{n,m}$ for $m \geq n$ by induction on n. The base case is simple. For $\text{count}^1_{n+1,m}$, we have:

$$
\begin{array}{c}
\text{P}\otimes\ \cfrac{\text{P1}\ \dfrac{}{\vdash \mathbf{1}, !_n\Sigma, \mathbf{N}_m}}{}
\quad
\text{P}\otimes\ \cfrac{\text{P}^{\mathsf{T}}_1\ \dfrac{\begin{array}{c}\vdots\ {\scriptstyle\text{count}^1_{n,m}}\\ \vdash !_n\Sigma, \mathbf{N}_m\end{array}}{\vdash !_n\Sigma, \mathbf{1}, \mathbf{N}_m}}{\vdash (\mathbf{1}\otimes !_n\Sigma), \mathbf{N}_m}
\quad
\text{P}^{\mathsf{T}}_{\otimes}\ \cfrac{\text{P}^{\mathsf{T}}_1\ \dfrac{\begin{array}{c}\vdots\ {\scriptstyle\text{count}^2_{n,m}}\\ \vdash \mathbf{N}_m, !_n\Sigma\end{array}}{\vdash \mathbf{N}_m, \mathbf{1}, !_n\Sigma}}{\vdash \mathbf{N}_m, (\mathbf{1}\otimes !_n\Sigma)}
\end{array}
$$

$$
\begin{array}{c}
\text{P}\downarrow\ \cfrac{\vdash (\mathbf{1}\otimes !_n\Sigma)\otimes \mathbf{N}_m}{} \\
\text{P}\downarrow^-\ \cfrac{\vdash\ \downarrow((\mathbf{1}\otimes !_n\Sigma)\otimes \mathbf{N}_m)}{} \\
\text{P}\downarrow^-\ \cfrac{\vdash\ \downarrow(\mathbf{1}\otimes !_n\Sigma), \mathbf{N}_m}{} \\
\text{P}\oslash\ \cfrac{\vdash\ \downarrow \mathbf{1}, !_n\Sigma, \mathbf{N}_m}{} \\
\text{P}\oslash\ \cfrac{\vdash (\downarrow\mathbf{1}\otimes !_n\Sigma), \mathbf{N}_m}{} \\
\text{P}\uparrow\ \cfrac{\vdash (\downarrow\mathbf{1}\oslash !_n\Sigma)\oslash \mathbf{N}_m}{} \\
\text{P}\uparrow^-\ \cfrac{\vdash\uparrow((\downarrow\mathbf{1}\oslash !_n\Sigma)\oslash \mathbf{N}_m)}{} \\
\text{P}\uparrow^-\ \cfrac{\vdash\uparrow(\downarrow\mathbf{1}\oslash !_n\Sigma), \mathbf{N}_m}{} \\
\text{P}\oslash\ \cfrac{\vdash\uparrow\downarrow\mathbf{1}, !_n\Sigma, \mathbf{N}_m}{{\scriptstyle\text{count}^1_{n+1,m}}\ \vdash !_{n+1}\Sigma, \mathbf{N}_m}
\end{array}
$$

For $\text{count}^2_{n,m}\ \vdash\uparrow(\oplus_n\top), !_n\Sigma$, we first strip away the head $\uparrow$, requiring a proof $\text{count}^3_{n,m}\vdash \oplus_n\top, !_n\Sigma$. This proof uses the difference between m and n to determine the result of read.

$$
\text{P}\oplus_2\ \cfrac{\dfrac{\begin{array}{c}\vdots\ {\scriptstyle\text{count}^3_{n,n+a}}\\ \vdash \oplus_{n+a}\top, !_n\Sigma\end{array}}{}}{{\scriptstyle\text{count}^3_{n,n+a+1}}\ \vdash \top\oplus(\oplus_{n+a}\top), !_n\Sigma}
$$

$$
\begin{array}{c}
\text{P}\otimes\ \cfrac{\text{P1}\ \dfrac{}{\vdash \mathbf{1}, !_{n+1}\Sigma}\quad \text{P}^{\mathsf{T}}_1\ \dfrac{\begin{array}{c}\vdots\ {\scriptstyle !\text{com}_{n+1}}\\ \vdash !_{n+1}\Sigma\end{array}}{\vdash !_{n+1}\Sigma, \mathbf{1}}}{} \\
\text{P}\downarrow\ \cfrac{\vdash \mathbf{1}\otimes !_{n+1}\Sigma}{} \\
\text{P}\downarrow^-\ \cfrac{\vdash\ \downarrow(\mathbf{1}\otimes !_{n+1}\Sigma)}{} \\
\text{P}\oplus_1\ \cfrac{\vdash\ \downarrow\mathbf{1}, !_{n+1}\Sigma}{{\scriptstyle\text{count}^3_{n+1,n+1}}\ \vdash \top\oplus(\oplus_n\top), !_{n+1}\Sigma}
\end{array}
$$

We omit the simple proofs $\text{count}^3_{0,0}$ and $!\text{com}_n$.

4   Categorical Semantics for WS

We now describe a categorical model of WS, together with a principal, motivating example based on games and strategies. It will be based on the notion of *sequoidal category* [15]. We use notation $\eta : F \Rightarrow G : \mathcal{C} \to \mathcal{D}$ to mean η is a natural transformation from F to G with $F, G : \mathcal{C} \to \mathcal{D}$.

4.1   WS-Categories

Definition 4. *A* sequoidal category *consists of:*

- *A symmetric monoidal category* $(\mathcal{C}, I, \otimes)$ *(we will call the relevant isomorphisms* assoc, li, ri *and* sym)
- *A category* $\mathcal{C}_s$

- A right-action $\oslash$ of $\mathcal{C}$ on $\mathcal{C}_s$ (that is, a functor $\_\oslash\_ : \mathcal{C}_s \times \mathcal{C} \to \mathcal{C}_s$ with natural isomorphisms unit : $A \oslash I \cong A$ and pasc : $A \oslash (B \otimes C) \cong (A \oslash B) \oslash C$ satisfying some coherence conditions [11])
- A functor $J : \mathcal{C}_s \to \mathcal{C}$
- A natural transformation wk : $J(\_) \otimes \_ \Rightarrow J(\_ \oslash \_)$ satisfying some coherence conditions [13]

An inclusive sequoidal category is a sequoidal category in which $\mathcal{C}_s$ is a full-on-objects subcategory of $\mathcal{C}$ containing the monoidal isomorphisms and wk; and J is the inclusion functor.

We can identify this structure in a category of games, based on the constructions in Section 2. Let $\mathcal{G}$ be the category whose objects are negative games and an arrow $M \to N$ is a strategy on $M \multimap N$. Composition of strategies is by "parallel composition plus hiding", and identities are copycat strategies, as defined in [3]. In fact this category has been studied extensively in e.g. [16,6,20], and has equivalent presentations using graph games [10] and locally Boolean domains [14]. $\mathcal{G}$ can be enriched with symmetric monoidal structure based on the tensor $\otimes$ and unit I.

A strategy on $M \multimap N$ is strict if it responds to any first move in N with some move in M (if at all). Define $\mathcal{G}_s$ to be the subcategory of $\mathcal{G}$ consisting of only the strict strategies. Then we can extend the left-merge operator $\oslash$ to an action $\mathcal{G}_s \times \mathcal{G} \to \mathcal{G}_s$. There is a natural copycat strategy wk : $M \otimes N \to M \oslash N$ in $\mathcal{G}_s$ satisfying the required axioms [15], and we have our sequoidal structure.

Definition 5. An inclusive sequoidal category is Cartesian if $\mathcal{C}$ is Cartesian and $\mathcal{C}_s$ is a sub-Cartesian Category (we will write t_A for the unique map $A \to 1$.) It is decomposable if the natural transformations dec $= \langle \text{wk}, \text{wk} \circ \text{sym} \rangle : A \otimes B \Rightarrow (A \oslash B) \times (B \oslash A) : \mathcal{C}_s \times \mathcal{C}_s \to \mathcal{C}_s$ and $\text{dec}^0 = t_I : I \Rightarrow 1 : \mathcal{C}_s$ are isomorphisms (so, in particular, $(\mathcal{C}, \otimes, I)$ is an affine SMC).

A Cartesian sequoidal category is distributive if the natural transformations dist $= \langle \pi_1 \oslash \text{id}_C, \pi_2 \oslash \text{id}_C \rangle : (A \times B) \oslash C \Rightarrow (A \oslash C) \times (B \oslash C) : \mathcal{C}_s \times \mathcal{C}_s \times \mathcal{C} \to \mathcal{C}_s$ and $\text{dist}^0 = t_{1 \oslash C} : 1 \oslash C \Rightarrow 1 : \mathcal{C} \to \mathcal{C}_s$ are isomorphisms.

$M \& N$ is a product of M and N in our category of games, and the empty game I is a terminal object. In our sequoidal categories the decomposability and distributivity isomorphisms above exist as natural copycat morphisms [15].

Definition 6. A sequoidal closed category is an inclusive sequoidal category where $\mathcal{C}$ is symmetric monoidal closed and the map $f \mapsto \Lambda(f \circ \text{wk})$ defines a natural isomorphism $\Lambda_s : \mathcal{C}_s(B \oslash A, C) \Rightarrow \mathcal{C}_s(B, A \multimap C)$. Define $\text{app}_s : (A \multimap B) \oslash A \to B$ as $\Lambda_s^{-1}(\text{id})$.

In a symmetric monoidal closed category, if $f : A \to B$ let $\Lambda_I(f) : I \to A \multimap B$ denote the name of f, and Λ_I^{-1} the inverse operation. We can show that $\mathcal{G}$ is sequoidal closed, with the internal hom given by $\multimap$.

Proposition 1. In any sequoidal closed category, $\multimap$ restricts to a functor $\mathcal{C}^{op} \times \mathcal{C}_s \to \mathcal{C}_s$ with isomorphisms $\text{unit}_{\multimap} : I \multimap A \cong A$ and $\text{pasc}_{\multimap} : A \otimes B \multimap C \cong A \multimap (B \multimap C)$ in $\mathcal{C}_s$.

Proof. We need to show that if g is in $\mathcal{C}_s$ then $f \multimap g$ is in $\mathcal{C}_s$. This follows from the fact that $f \multimap g = \Lambda_s(g \circ \mathsf{app}_s \circ (\mathsf{id} \oslash f))$. We can define $\mathsf{unit}_{\multimap}$: $I \multimap A \cong A$ by $\mathsf{unit}_{\multimap} = \mathsf{app}_s \circ \mathsf{unit}^{-1}$ and $\mathsf{unit}_{\multimap}^{-1} = \Lambda_s(\mathsf{unit})$. We can define $\mathsf{pasc}_{\multimap} : A \otimes B \multimap C \cong A \multimap (B \multimap C)$ by $\Lambda_s \Lambda_s(\mathsf{app}_s \circ \mathsf{pasc}^{-1})$ and $\mathsf{pasc}_{\multimap}^{-1} = \Lambda_s(\mathsf{app}_s \circ (\mathsf{app}_s \oslash \mathsf{id}) \circ \mathsf{pasc})$. $\qquad\square$

We have yet to discuss representation of positive games in our categorical model. We will exploit the fact that a strategy on the positive game P is precisely a strategy on the negative game $P^\perp \multimap o$. The object o satisfies an additional special property: an internalised version of *linear functional extensionality* [2]. This property differentiates our model from that of Conway games and models without local alternation [13].

Definition 7. *An object o in a sequoidal closed category satisfies* linear functional extensionality *if the natural transformation* $\mathsf{lfe} : (B \multimap o) \oslash A \Rightarrow (A \multimap B) \multimap o : \mathcal{C} \times \mathcal{C} \to \mathcal{C}_s$ *given by* $\Lambda_s(\mathsf{app}_s \circ (\mathsf{id} \oslash \mathsf{app}) \circ \mathsf{pasc}^{-1})$ *is an isomorphism.*

Definition 8. *A WS-category is a distributive, decomposable sequoidal closed category with an object o satisfying linear functional extensionality.*

$\mathcal{G}$ is a WS-category. We can also consider the subcategory $\mathcal{G}_f$ of finite negative games and total strategies. The sequoidal structure on $\mathcal{G}$ and $\mathcal{G}_s$ restricts to $\mathcal{G}_f$ and its subcategory of strict and total strategies $\mathcal{G}_{f,s}$, providing another instance of a WS-category.

Proposition 2. $\mathcal{G}$ *and* $\mathcal{G}_f$ *both support the structure of a WS-category.*

Previous work of the second author [15] shows that if a WS-category has a well-behaved fixed point of $A \oslash \_$ for any A, then one can give a fully abstract model of a functional language with coroutines in that category.

4.2   Semantics of Formulas and Sequents

Let $\mathcal{C}$ be a WS-category. We give semantics of both positive and negative formulas as objects in $\mathcal{C}$ below. Note that in our semantics of formulas, $[\![A]\!] = [\![A^\perp]\!]$. However, the polarity of a formula will affect the type of proofs of that formula, as will be seen.

$$
\begin{array}{ll}
[\![0]\!] = I & [\![1]\!] = I \\
[\![\uparrow N]\!] = [\![N]\!] \multimap o & [\![\downarrow P]\!] = [\![P]\!] \multimap o \\
[\![M \otimes N]\!] = [\![M]\!] \otimes [\![N]\!] & [\![P \,\invamp\, Q]\!] = [\![P]\!] \otimes [\![Q]\!] \\
[\![M \& N]\!] = [\![M]\!] \times [\![N]\!] & [\![P \oplus Q]\!] = [\![P]\!] \times [\![Q]\!] \\
[\![M \oslash N]\!] = [\![M]\!] \oslash [\![N]\!] & [\![P \triangleleft Q]\!] = [\![P]\!] \oslash [\![Q]\!] \\
[\![M \triangleleft Q]\!] = [\![Q]\!] \multimap [\![M]\!] & [\![P \oslash N]\!] = [\![N]\!] \multimap [\![P]\!]
\end{array}
$$

We consider our list-connective comma to be a binary operator associating to the left. Then $[\![A, B]\!]$ is $[\![A]\!] \oslash [\![B]\!]$ if A and B are of the same polarity, and $[\![B]\!] \multimap [\![A]\!]$ otherwise.

4.3   Semantics of Contexts

A context is a nonempty list of formulas. If Γ is a context, we give semantics $[\![\Gamma]\!]^b$ for $b \in \{+, -\}$ as endofunctors on $\mathcal{C}_s$ below.

$$
\begin{aligned}
[\![\epsilon]\!]^+ &= \mathrm{id}_{\mathcal{C}_s} & [\![\epsilon]\!]^- &= \mathrm{id}_{\mathcal{C}_s}\\
[\![\Gamma, M]\!]^+ &= [\![M]\!] \multimap [\![\Gamma]\!]^+ & [\![\Gamma, P]\!]^- &= [\![P]\!] \multimap [\![\Gamma]\!]^-\\
[\![\Gamma, P]\!]^+ &= [\![\Gamma]\!]^+ \oslash [\![P]\!] & [\![\Gamma, M]\!]^- &= [\![\Gamma]\!]^- \oslash [\![M]\!]
\end{aligned}
$$

We have $[\![A, \Gamma]\!] = [\![\Gamma]\!]^b([\![A]\!])$ where b is the polarity of A. We can construct isomorphisms $\mathsf{dist}_{b,\Gamma} : [\![\Gamma]\!]^b(A \times B) \cong [\![\Gamma]\!]^b(A) \times [\![\Gamma]\!]^b(B)$ and $\mathsf{dist}^0_{b,\Gamma} : [\![\Gamma]\!]^b(\mathbf{1}) \cong \mathbf{1}$ by induction on Γ, with $[\![\Gamma]\!]^b(\pi_1) \circ \mathsf{dist}^{-1}_{b,\Gamma} = \pi_1$.

4.4   Semantics of Proofs

While the semantics of formulas are independent of polarity, semantics of proofs are not. If $p \vdash A, \Gamma$ is a proof, we define $[\![p \vdash A, \Gamma]\!]$ as an arrow $\mathcal{C}(I, [\![A, \Gamma]\!])$ in the case that A is negative, and as an arrow in $\mathcal{C}([\![A, \Gamma]\!], o)$ in the case that A is positive. Semantics of the core rules and $\mathsf{P}_{\mathsf{cut}}$ are given in Table 3 (interpretation of the remaining admissible rules in a WS-category is omitted for the sake of brevity).

In the semantics of $\mathsf{P}_{\mathsf{cut}}$ we use an additional construction. If $\tau : I \to [\![N, \Delta]\!]$ define (strict) $\tau^{\circ-}_{M,\Gamma} : [\![M, \Gamma, N^\perp]\!] \to [\![M, \Gamma, \Delta]\!]$ to be $\mathsf{unit}_{\multimap} \circ (\tau \multimap \mathrm{id}_{[\![M,\Gamma]\!]})$ if $|\Delta| = 0$ and $\mathsf{pasc}^n_{\multimap} \circ (\Lambda^{-n}\Lambda^{-1}_I \tau \multimap \mathrm{id}_{[\![M,\Gamma]\!]})$ if $|\Delta| = n+1$. Define (strict) $\tau^{\circ+}_{P,\Gamma} : [\![P, \Gamma, \Delta]\!] \to [\![P, \Gamma, N^\perp]\!]$ to be $(\mathrm{id}_{[\![P,\Gamma]\!]} \oslash \tau) \circ \mathsf{unit}^{-1}$ if $|\Delta| = 0$ and $(\mathrm{id} \oslash \Lambda^{-n}\Lambda^{-1}_I \tau) \circ ((\mathrm{id}_{[\![P,\Gamma]\!]} \oslash \mathsf{sym}) \circ \mathsf{pasc}^{-1})^n$ if $|\Delta| = n+1$.

5   Full Completeness

We now prove a *full completeness* result for the model of WS in $\mathcal{G}_f$: every total strategy on a game denoted by a formula is the denotation of a unique *core* proof of that formula (i.e. one which only uses the core rules). This exhibits a strong correspondence between syntax and semantics, and establishes admissibility of all non-core rules.

We first give categorical axioms in the style of [2], capturing the properties of a WS-category which enable us to prove full completeness and observe that they are satisfied by $\mathcal{G}_f$. Rather than identifying a class of categorical models with many or varied examples (precluded by the strength of the result itself), these axioms allow us to give a rigorous and abstract proof of full completeness using the structure of a WS-category.

Definition 9. *A complete WS-category is a WS-category such that:*

1a *The unique map $i : \varnothing \Rightarrow \mathcal{C}(I, o)$ is a bijection.*
1b *The map $\mathsf{d} = [\lambda f.f \circ \pi_1, \lambda g.f \circ \pi_2] : \mathcal{C}(M, o) + \mathcal{C}(N, o) \Rightarrow \mathcal{C}(M \times N, o)$ is a bijection. (π-atomicity [2]).*
2 *The map $\_ \multimap o : \mathcal{C}(I, M) \Rightarrow \mathcal{C}(M \multimap o, I \multimap o)$ is a bijection.*

Table 3. Categorical Semantics for WS (core rules, plus cut)

P1
$$\overline{[\![\Gamma]\!]^-(\mathsf{dec}^0)^{-1} \circ (\mathsf{dist}^0_{-,\Gamma})^{-1} \circ t : [\![\vdash 1, \Gamma]\!]}$$

P⊗
$$\frac{\sigma : [\![\vdash M, N, \Gamma]\!] \qquad \tau : [\![\vdash N, M, \Gamma]\!]}{[\![\Gamma]\!]^-(\mathsf{dec}^{-1}) \circ \mathsf{dist}^{-1}_{-,\Gamma} \circ \langle\sigma,\tau\rangle : [\![\vdash M \otimes N, \Gamma]\!]}$$

P&
$$\frac{\sigma : [\![\vdash M, \Gamma]\!] \qquad \tau : [\![\vdash N, \Gamma]\!]}{\mathsf{dist}^{-1}_{-,\Gamma} \circ \langle\sigma,\tau\rangle : [\![\vdash M\&N, \Gamma]\!]}$$

P⅋₂
$$\frac{\sigma : [\![\vdash Q, P, \Gamma]\!]}{\sigma \circ [\![\Gamma]\!]^+(\mathsf{wk}\circ\mathsf{sym}) : [\![\vdash P\,⅋\,Q, \Gamma]\!]}$$

P⅋₁
$$\frac{\sigma : [\![\vdash P, Q, \Gamma]\!]}{\sigma \circ [\![\Gamma]\!]^+(\mathsf{wk}) : [\![\vdash P\,⅋\,Q, \Gamma]\!]}$$

P⊕₁
$$\frac{\sigma : [\![\vdash P, \Delta]\!]}{\sigma \circ [\![\Delta]\!]^+(\pi_1) : [\![\vdash P \oplus Q, \Delta]\!]}$$

P⊕₂
$$\frac{\sigma : [\![\vdash Q, \Delta]\!]}{\sigma \circ [\![\Delta]\!]^+(\pi_2) : [\![\vdash P \oplus Q, \Delta]\!]}$$

P↑⁺
$$\frac{\sigma : [\![\vdash\uparrow (P\,⅋\,Q), \Gamma]\!]}{[\![\Gamma]\!]^-(\mathsf{pasc}_{-\!\circ} \circ (\mathsf{sym} -\!\circ \mathsf{id})) \circ \sigma : [\![\vdash\uparrow P, Q, \Gamma]\!]}$$

P↑
$$\frac{\sigma : [\![\vdash P]\!]}{\Lambda_I(\sigma) : [\![\vdash\uparrow P]\!]}$$

P↑⁻
$$\frac{\sigma : [\![\vdash\uparrow (P \oslash N), \Gamma]\!]}{[\![\Gamma]\!]^-(\mathsf{lfe}^{-1}) \circ \sigma : [\![\vdash\uparrow P, N, \Gamma]\!]}$$

P↓
$$\frac{\sigma : [\![\vdash N]\!]}{\mathsf{unit}_{-\!\circ} \circ (\sigma -\!\circ \mathsf{id}) : [\![\vdash\downarrow N]\!]}$$

P↓⁻
$$\frac{\sigma : [\![\vdash\downarrow (M \otimes N), \Gamma]\!]}{\sigma \circ [\![\Gamma]\!]^+((\mathsf{sym}-\!\circ\mathsf{id})\circ\mathsf{pasc}^{-1}_{-\!\circ}) : [\![\vdash\downarrow M, N, \Gamma]\!]}$$

P↓⁺
$$\frac{\sigma : [\![\vdash\downarrow (N \triangleleft P), \Gamma]\!]}{\sigma \circ [\![\Gamma]\!]^+(\mathsf{lfe}) : [\![\vdash\downarrow N, P, \Gamma]\!]}$$

P_cut
$$\frac{\sigma : [\![\vdash M, \Gamma, N^\perp, \Gamma_1]\!] \qquad \tau : [\![\vdash N, \Delta^+]\!]}{[\![\Gamma_1]\!]^-(\tau^{\circ-}_{M,\Gamma}) \circ \sigma : [\![\vdash M, \Gamma, \Delta^+, \Gamma_1]\!]}$$

P◁
$$\frac{\sigma : [\![\vdash A, P, \Gamma]\!]}{\sigma : [\![\vdash A \triangleleft P, \Gamma]\!]}$$

P_cut
$$\frac{\sigma : [\![\vdash P, \Gamma, N^\perp, \Gamma_1]\!] \qquad \tau : [\![\vdash N, \Delta^+]\!]}{\sigma \circ [\![\Gamma_1]\!]^+(\tau^{\circ+}_{P,\Gamma}) : [\![\vdash P, \Gamma, \Delta^+, \Gamma_1]\!]}$$

P⊘
$$\frac{\sigma : [\![\vdash A, N, \Gamma]\!]}{\sigma : [\![\vdash A \oslash N, \Gamma]\!]}$$

These axioms capture the properties of determinacy, totality and the object o — it is straightforward to show:

Proposition 3. $\mathcal{G}_f$ *is a complete WS-category.*

We can then prove the following full completeness result.

Theorem 1. *In any complete WS-category, if* $\sigma : [\![\vdash \Gamma]\!]$ *then* σ *is the denotation of a unique core proof* $\mathsf{reify}_\Gamma(\sigma) \vdash \Gamma$.

Informally, reify may be seen as a kind of semantics-guided proof search procedure: given a strategy σ, reify finds a proof which denotes it. It is defined by considering the outermost connective in the head formula of Γ, to which the core rule is always applied:

- If the head formula is a negative unit, then σ is the unique strategy on the terminal object. By axiom (1a) it cannot be a positive unit.
- If the outermost connective is $\otimes$ or $\&$, then we may reverse the associated rule (which corresponds to a bijection which holds for *any* WS-category) to decompose the head formula.
- If the outermost connective is $\oplus$ — i.e. $\Gamma = P_1 \oplus P_2, \Gamma'$ – then by axiom (1b), σ corresponds to a projection π_i (representing a unique choice of introduction

rule for ⊕) composed with a strategy on $[\![\vdash P_i, \Gamma']\!]$. If the outer connective in ⅋, then similar reasoning applies.

- If the outermost connective is a lift (↑ or ↓) then we may force it outwards through Γ using the rules $\uparrow^-, \uparrow^+, \downarrow^-, \downarrow^+$ (which correspond to isomorphisms in any WS-category) until we obtain a sequent consisting of a single, lifted formula. This lift may be "reversed" either by applying axiom (2) (for ↓) or by definition of the semantics (↑).

Formally, reify$_\Gamma$ is defined inductively in Table 4.

Table 4. Reification of Strategies as Core Proofs

$$
\begin{aligned}
\text{reify}_{\mathbf{1},\Gamma}(\sigma) &= \mathsf{P1} \\
\text{reify}_{\uparrow P}(\sigma) &= \mathsf{P} \uparrow (\text{reify}_P(\Lambda_I^{-1}(\sigma))) \\
\text{reify}_{\uparrow P,Q,\Gamma}(\sigma) &= \mathsf{P} \uparrow^+ (\text{reify}_{\uparrow(P⅋Q),\Gamma}([\![\Gamma]\!]^-((\mathsf{sym} \multimap \mathsf{id}) \circ \mathsf{pasc}_{\multimap}^{-1} \circ \sigma))) \\
\text{reify}_{\uparrow P,N,\Gamma}(\sigma) &= \mathsf{P} \uparrow^- (\text{reify}_{\uparrow(P⊘N),\Gamma}([\![\Gamma]\!]^-(\mathsf{lfe}))) \\
\text{reify}_{M\&N,\Gamma}(\sigma) &= \mathsf{P}\&(\text{reify}_{M,\Gamma}(\pi_1 \circ \mathsf{dist}_{-,\Gamma} \circ \sigma))(\text{reify}_{N,\Gamma}((\pi_2 \circ \mathsf{dist}_{-,\Gamma} \circ \sigma)) \\
\text{reify}_{M⊗N,\Gamma}(\sigma) &= \mathsf{P} \otimes (\text{reify}_{M,N,\Gamma}(\pi_1 \circ \sigma'), \text{reify}_{N,M,\Gamma}(\pi_2 \circ \sigma')) \\
&\quad \text{where } \sigma' = \mathsf{dist}_{-,\Gamma} \circ [\![\Gamma]\!]^-(\mathsf{dec}) \circ \sigma \\
\text{reify}_{A⊘N,\Gamma}(\sigma) &= \mathsf{P} \oslash (\text{reify}_{A,N,\Gamma}(\sigma)) \\
\text{reify}_{A◁P,\Gamma}(\sigma) &= \mathsf{P} \triangleleft (\text{reify}_{A,P,\Gamma}(\sigma)) \\
\text{reify}_{\downarrow N}(\sigma) &= \mathsf{P} \downarrow (\text{reify}_N((\_ \multimap o)^{-1}(\mathsf{unit}_{\multimap}^{-1} \circ \sigma))) \\
\text{reify}_{\downarrow N,M,\Gamma}(\sigma) &= \mathsf{P} \downarrow^- (\text{reify}_{\downarrow(N⊗M),\Gamma}(\sigma \circ [\![\Gamma]\!]^+(\mathsf{pasc}_{\multimap} \circ (\mathsf{sym} \multimap \mathsf{id})))) \\
\text{reify}_{\downarrow N,P,\Gamma}(\sigma) &= \mathsf{P} \downarrow^+ (\text{reify}_{\downarrow(N◁P),\Gamma}(\sigma \circ [\![\Gamma]\!]^+(\mathsf{lfe}^{-1}))) \\
\text{reify}_{P⊕Q,\Gamma}(\sigma) &= [\mathsf{P} \oplus_1 \text{oreify}_{P,\Gamma}, \mathsf{P} \oplus_2 \text{oreify}_{Q,\Gamma}] \circ d^{-1}(\sigma \circ \mathsf{dist}_{+,\Gamma}^{-1}) \\
\text{reify}_{P⅋Q,\Gamma}(\sigma) &= [\mathsf{P}⅋_1 \circ \text{reify}_{P,Q,\Gamma}, \mathsf{P}⅋_2 \circ \text{reify}_{Q,P,\Gamma}] \circ d^{-1}(\sigma \circ [\![\Gamma]\!]^+(\mathsf{dec}) \circ \mathsf{dist}_{+,\Gamma}^{-1})
\end{aligned}
$$

Proposition 4. reify$_\Gamma$ *is a well-defined, terminating procedure.*

Proof. We define a measure fd on formulas by

- $\mathsf{fd}(\mathbf{0}) = \mathsf{fd}(\mathbf{1}) = 2$
- $\mathsf{fd}(\uparrow A) = \mathsf{fd}(\downarrow A) = 2 + \mathsf{fd}(A)$
- $\mathsf{fd}(A \odot B) = (\mathsf{fd}(A) \times \mathsf{fd}(B)) + 1$ for $\odot \in \{\oplus, \&, \oslash, \triangleleft, \otimes, ⅋\}$

We extend this to sequents inductively with $\mathsf{fd}(\Gamma, A) = (\mathsf{fd}(\Gamma) \times \mathsf{fd}(A)) + 1$. We then define $\ell(A, \Gamma) = \langle \mathsf{fd}(A, \Gamma), |A| \rangle$ where $|A|$ is the size of A, and consider the well-founded lexicographical ordering on $\mathbb{N}^2$. Informally, reducing ℓ consists of (first priority) moving lifts outwards, and (second priority) simplifying the head formula. Then reify$_\Gamma$ is defined by induction on $\ell(\Gamma)$. It is routine to see in each case the call to the inductive hypothesis decreases the ℓ-measure (note that if M is a proper subformula of N then $\mathsf{fd}(M) < \mathsf{fd}(N)$ and $\_, \Gamma$ is monotonic with respect to fd). □

We can complete the proof of Theorem 1 by showing that reify$_\Gamma$ gives an inverse to $[\![-]\!]_\Gamma$:

Lemma 1. *1. For all $\sigma : [\![\vdash \Gamma]\!]$ we have $[\![\mathsf{reify}_\Gamma(\sigma)]\!] = \sigma$.*
2. For any core proof $p \vdash \Gamma$ we have $\mathsf{reify}_\Gamma([\![p]\!]) = p$.

Corollary 1. *In any complete WS-category, morphisms $\mathcal{C}([\![M]\!], [\![N]\!])$ correspond (bijectively) to core proofs of $\vdash N, M^\perp$.*

Proof. Such morphisms correspond to $\mathcal{C}(I, [\![M]\!] \multimap [\![N]\!]) = \mathcal{C}(I, [\![M, N^\perp]\!])$. □

Corollary 2. *All non-core proof rules are admissible.*

Proof. Let $p \vdash \Gamma$ be a proof. We can construct the proof $p' = \mathsf{reify}([\![p]\!]) \vdash \Gamma$ using only the core rules. By Lemma 1, we have $[\![p']\!] = [\![p]\!]$ (and p' is the unique such core proof). □

This yields reduction-free normalisation from proofs to core proofs.

6   Cut Elimination

We have shown that the non-core rules are admissible via a reduction-free evaluation with respect to a particular complete WS-category. However we do not know that such a procedure is sound with respect to any other WS-category. We will address this here in the case of (a restricted form of) cut elimination, by defining a corresponding syntactic procedure.

We describe a procedure to transform a core proof of $\vdash A, \Gamma, N^\perp$ and a core proof of $\vdash N, P$ into a core proof of $\vdash A, \Gamma, P$. We proceed by induction. The interesting cases are the lifts: if $A = \uparrow Q$ and $\Gamma = \epsilon$ then $\vdash \uparrow Q, N^\perp$ must have been concluded from $\vdash Q \mathbin{⅋} N^\perp$, i.e. $\vdash Q, N^\perp$ or $\vdash N^\perp, Q$. In the first case we can apply the inductive hypothesis, but in the second case we cannot. We need an auxiliary procedure cut_2 which turns core proofs of $\vdash N^\perp, Q$ and $\vdash N, P$ into a core proof of $\vdash Q \mathbin{⅋} P$ (from which we can deduce $\vdash \uparrow Q, P$ as required). If we think of this procedure as a representation of strategy composition, this corresponds to the situation when some player is set to play in N next and so the next observable move could be in Q or P.

Some cases of cut and cut_2 are given in Table 5 using a term notation based on the names of the core proof rules. All other cases just use the inductive hypothesis in an obvious way. We use a third trivial procedure $\mathsf{symP⅋}$ mapping core proofs of $\vdash P \mathbin{⅋} Q, \Gamma$ to core proofs of $\vdash Q \mathbin{⅋} P, \Gamma$.

Table 5. Cut Elimination for Core Rules (key cases)

A Γ cut $: \vdash A, \Gamma, N^\perp \times \vdash N, P$	$\to \vdash A, \Gamma, P$
$\uparrow$ _ ϵ $\mathsf{cut}(\mathsf{P} \uparrow^+ (\mathsf{P} \uparrow (\mathsf{P⅋}_1(y))), g)$	$= \mathsf{P} \uparrow^+ (\mathsf{P} \uparrow (\mathsf{P⅋}_1(\mathsf{cut}(y, g))))$
$\uparrow$ _ ϵ $\mathsf{cut}(\mathsf{P} \uparrow^+ (\mathsf{P} \uparrow (\mathsf{P⅋}_2(y))), g)$	$= \mathsf{P} \uparrow^+ (\mathsf{P} \uparrow (\mathsf{cut}_2(y, g)))$
$\downarrow$ _ ϵ $\mathsf{cut}(\mathsf{P} \downarrow^+ (\mathsf{P} \downarrow (\mathsf{P} \lhd (y))), g)$	$= \mathsf{P} \downarrow^+ (\mathsf{P} \downarrow (\mathsf{P} \lhd (\mathsf{cut}(y, g))))$
Q Γ $\mathsf{cut}_2 : \vdash Q, \Gamma, N^\perp \times \vdash Q^\perp, \Gamma^\perp, P$	$\to \vdash N^\perp \mathbin{⅋} P$
$\downarrow$ _ ϵ $\mathsf{cut}_2(\mathsf{P} \downarrow^+ (\mathsf{P} \downarrow (\mathsf{P} \lhd y)))(\mathsf{P} \uparrow^+ (\mathsf{P} \uparrow (\mathsf{P⅋}_1 y')))$	$= \mathsf{symP⅋}(\mathsf{cut}_2(y', y))$
$\downarrow$ _ ϵ $\mathsf{cut}_2(\mathsf{P} \downarrow^+ (\mathsf{P} \downarrow (\mathsf{P} \lhd y)))(\mathsf{P} \uparrow^+ (\mathsf{P} \uparrow (\mathsf{P⅋}_2 y')))$	$= \mathsf{P⅋}_2(\mathsf{cut}(y', y))$

Despite the fact that we are emulating the mechanics of strategy composition in WS, we can show that the procedure is sound with respect to any WS-category.

Proposition 5. *In any WS-category,* $[\![\mathsf{cut}(p_1, p_2)]\!] = [\![\mathsf{P_{cut}}(p_1, p_2)]\!].$

7   Further Directions

We first consider how exponentials can be introduced into WS. There are several different exponentials on games which one might wish to represent. As presented here all formulas represent finite games (total strategies on unbounded games do not compose, in general). The non-repetitive backtracking exponential of Lamarche [16,6] preserves finiteness, and the categorical properties characterising it can be used to give a variant of WS with exponentials, with a corresponding full completeness result and contraction as a non-core rule. It is possible to then embed full polarised linear logic [18] in such a system.

Other exponentials do not preserve finiteness of games, for example the least fixed point $!A \cong A \oslash !A$, which can be used to model stateful computation. In this case, totality can be retained by formulating a notion of an *exponential with variable bounds* including formulas such as $!_x A$ representing a family of (finite) games. In this system contraction would be represented by $\vdash !_x A \otimes !_y A \multimap !_{x+y} A$. Alternatively, we may abandon totality, and develop a type theory with fixed points, defining $!A = \mu X.A \oslash X$. Extending WS to infinite games via such fixed points (cf. [21]) is a future direction of this project. This will allow representation of imperative objects over infinite datatypes in WS, as well as methods that can be used arbitrarily many times. Thus, such an extension would be a natural setting for formal embedding of a programming language such as Lingay [19].

It is possible to extend WS with propositional variables, representing arbitrary games. In such an extension proofs represent total uniform history-sensitive strategies. Finally, we have formalised some of this work in the theorem prover Agda — including WS, its game semantics, and reification of strategies as proofs.

Acknowledgements. The authors would like to thank Guy McCusker for useful discussion and comments on earlier drafts; and Makoto Takeyama for the insights provided by jointly formalising this work in the theorem prover Agda.

References

1. Abramsky, S., Honda, K., McCusker, G.: A fully abstract game semantics for general references. In: LICS 1998: Proceedings of the 13th Annual IEEE Symposium on Logic in Computer Science, p. 334. IEEE Computer Society, Washington (1998)
2. Abramsky, S.: Axioms for definability and full completeness. In: Proof, language, and interaction: essays in honour of Robin Milner, pp. 55–75 (2000)
3. Abramsky, S., Jagadeesan, R.: Games and full completeness for multiplicative linear logic. J. Symb. Logic 59(2), 543–574 (1994)

4. Abramsky, S., McCusker, G.: Linearity, Sharing and State: a fully abstract game semantics for Idealized Algol with active expressions: Extended Abstract. Electronic Notes in Theoretical Computer Science 3, 2–14 (1996); Linear Logic 1996 Tokyo Meeting
5. Blass, A.: A game semantics for linear logic. Annals of Pure and Applied Logic 56(1-3), 183–220 (1992)
6. Curien, P.-L.: On the symmetry of sequentiality. In: Proceedings of the 9th International Conference on Mathematical Foundations of Programming Semantics, pp. 29–71. Springer, London (1994)
7. Girard, J.-Y.: Locus solum: From the rules of logic to the logic of rules. Mathematical Structures in Computer Science 11(03), 301–506 (2001)
8. Hintikka, J.: Hyperclassical logic (a.k.a. if logic) and its implications for logical theory. The Bulletin of Symbolic Logic 8(3), 404–423 (2002)
9. Hyland, J.M.E., Ong, C.-H.L.: On full abstraction for PCF: I, II, and III. Inf. Comput. 163(2), 285–408 (2000)
10. Hyland, M., Schalk, A.: Games on graphs and sequentially realizable functionals (extended abstract). In: Symposium on Logic in Computer Science, p. 257 (2002)
11. Janelidze, G., Kelly, G.M.: A note on actions of a monoidal category (2001)
12. Japaridze, G.: Introduction to computability logic. Annals of Pure and Applied Logic 123(1-3), 1–99 (2003)
13. Laird, J.: A categorical semantics of higher order store. In: Proceedings, 9th Conference on Category Theory and Computer Science, CTCS 2002. Electronic Notes in Theoretical Computer Science. Elsevier, Amsterdam (2002)
14. Laird, J.: Locally Boolean domains. Theoretical Computer Science 342(1), 132–148 (2005); Applied Semantics: Selected Topics
15. Laird, J.: Functional programs as coroutines: A semantic analysis. Logical Methods in Computer Science (to appear)
16. Lamarche, F.: Sequentiality, games and linear logic. In: Proceedings, CLICS workshop, Aarhus University. DAIMI-397–II (1992)
17. Lamarche, F.: Games semantics for full propositional linear logic. In: LICS, pp. 464–473 (1995)
18. Laurent, O.: Polarized games. In: Proceedings of 17th Annual IEEE Symposium on Logic in Computer Science, pp. 265–274 (2002)
19. Longley, J., Wolverson, N.: Eriskay: a programming language based on game semantics. In: Games for Logic and Programming Languages III Workshop (2008)
20. Longley, J.: Some programming languages suggested by game models (extended abstract). Electronic Notes in Theoretical Computer Science 249, 117–134 (2009); Proceedings of the 25th Conference on Mathematical Foundations of Programming Semantics (MFPS 2009)
21. McCusker, G.: Games and full abstraction for FPC. In: Proceedings of Eleventh Annual IEEE Symposium on Logic in Computer Science, LICS 1996, July 1996, pp. 174–183 (1996)
22. Melliès, P.-A., Tabareau, N.: Resource modalities in tensor logic. Annals of Pure and Applied Logic 161(5), 632–653 (2010); The Third workshop on Games for Logic and Programming Languages (GaLoP), Galop 2008
23. Wolverson, N.: Game Semantics for an object-orientated language. PhD thesis, University of Edinburgh (2008)

Environment and Classical Channels in Categorical Quantum Mechanics

Bob Coecke and Simon Perdrix*

Oxford University Computing Laboratory
CNRS, Laboratoire d'Informatique de Grenoble

Abstract. We present a both simple and comprehensive graphical calculus for quantum computing. We axiomatize the notion of an *environment*, which together with the axiomatic notion of classical structure enables us to define classical channels, quantum measurements and classical control. If we moreover adjoin the axiomatic notion of complementarity, we obtain sufficient structural power for constructive representation and correctness derivation of typical quantum informatic protocols.

1 Introduction

Categorical semantics for quantum protocols provides a new perspective on quantum information processing. Particularly appealing is the fact that the symmetric monoidal language comes with an intuitive Penrose-Joyal-Street graphical calculus [27,23]. Example applications are [11, QPL'09], [20, CiE'09] and [12,21, ICALP'10]. Meanwhile there exists a software tool with a graphical interface, called `quantomatic`, which (semi-)automates graphical reasoning [19].

Categorical quantum mechanics notions relevant for this paper are:

(A) Abramsky and Coecke proposed dagger compact categories as a means to axiomatize bipartite entangled states, map-state duality, bra-ket duality and unitary operations, by endowing compact categories [24] with an identity-on-objects involution, the dagger-functor [1, LiCS'04];

(B) Selinger proposed a construction which assigns to any dagger compact category **C** of pure states and operations another dagger compact category $CPM(\mathbf{C})$ of 'mixed states' and 'completely positive maps' [28, QPL'05]; Coecke axiomatized $CPM(\mathbf{C})$ as a dagger compact category with for every object A a privileged 'maximally mixed state' $\perp_A : \mathrm{I} \to A$ [9, QPL'06];

(C) Coecke and Pavlovic introduced 'classical structures' as certain Frobenius algebras [7], in order to handle classical data and control [16,17,15];

(D) Coecke and Duncan axiomatized 'complementary' classical structures and were able to construct from this basic quantum logic gates [10, ICALP'08].

The interaction of these concepts has not been subjected to a detailed study yet. Here, we distill the notion of *environment* out of **(B)**, and by blending it

* Work supported by EP/D072786/1, ONR N00014-09-1-0248 and EU FP6 STREP QICS. John Baez, Prakash Panangaden and Jamie Vicary provided useful feedback.

A. Dawar and H. Veith (Eds.): CSL 2010, LNCS 6247, pp. 230–244, 2010.

in an appropriate manner with **(C)** we define the notion of *classical channel*. These interact in a particularly nice manner with **(D)** and together they provide a simple and elegant graphical calculus to represent and prove correctness of typical quantum computational protocols e.g. teleportation (including classical control) [5], dense coding [6], and the BB84 and Ekert 91 QKD protocols [22].

Our main point is to show how with very little structural effort one straightforwardly reproduces these non-trivial quantum behaviors.

Section 2 outlines how we conceive the classical-quantum distinction. Section 3 recalls the notion of *classical structure*. Section 4 introduces the notion of *environment*, and Section 5 combines environment and classical structure to form a *classical channel*, a *measurement* and *control operations*, and studies the role of *complementarity*. In Section 6 we derive basic quantum informatic protocols.

While here we restrict ourselves to pure states and operations, all straightforwardly extends to mixed states and operations, as indicated in Section 7.

2   Classicality vs. Quantumness

The *no-broadcasting theorem* [3] states that only mixed states which share a basis in which they are jointly diagonal (i.e. those that can be simulated by classical probability distributions) can be broadcast by the same quantum operation. Broadcastability is a strictly weaker requirement than cloneability:

	pure classical	mixed classical	pure quantum	mixed quantum
broadcastable:	yes	<u>YES</u>	no	no
cloneable:	yes	<u>NO</u>	no	no

For us classicality means *broadcastability*. Equivalently, one can also conceive classicality as the result of *decoherence* [30]. Broadcasting and decoherence are indeed closely related: in the case of the first 'one copies into the environment', while in the case of the second 'one couples to the environment', and decoherent then means invariance under this coupling. Hence, in summary:

$$\boxed{\text{classical} := \text{broadcastable} \equiv \text{decoherent}}$$

Also, we take classicality to be a behavior, rather than a type. In other words, classicality refers to something that behaves as if it is classical (in the above discussed sense), rather than it physically being classical. Non-classicality is taken to be the default behavior. All this is best illustrated by the concept of a quantum measurement, which when applied to a quantum system changes the state of that quantum system and produces classical data. Since the resulting quantum state is an eigenstate for that measurement, hence broadcastable, it behaves precisely in the same manner as the classical data does. As a result, in the graphical calculus they won't be distinguishable if we omit their explicit type which tells us that physically they are either classical or quantum.

This seeming ambiguity about what is physically quantum and classical is a feature of the particular manner in which quantum and classical data interact, cf. that the creation of classical data renders the quantum state in an eigenstate.

3   Classical Structures

We will work in the graphical representation of symmetric monoidal categories, surveyed in [13,29]. Mac Lane's strictification theorem [26, p.257] allows us to take our symmetric monoidal categories to be strict, that is:

$$(A \otimes B) \otimes C = A \otimes (B \otimes C) \qquad \text{and} \qquad A \otimes I = A = I \otimes A.$$

Morphisms $f : A_1 \ldots A_n \to B_1 \ldots B_m$, which we interpret as processes are respectively represented as boxes where the input wires represent the objects $A_1 \ldots A_n$ and the output wires represent the objects $B_1 \ldots B_m$:

Other shapes may be used to emphasize extra structure. Elements $s : I \to A_1 \ldots A_n$, which in the graphical representation have no inputs, are interpret as 'states', and co-elements $e : B_1 \ldots B_m \to I$ with no outputs are interpreted as 'effects'. In standard quantum notation they would be kets $|\psi\rangle$ and bras $\langle\psi|$ respectively. Composition and tensoring are respectively represented as:

Theorem 1 (Joyal-Street 1991 [23,29]). *An equation follows from the axioms of symmetric monoidal categories if and only if it can be derived in the graphical language via isotopical rewrites.*

A *dagger functor* on a symmetric monoidal category [28] is an identity-on-objects contravariant involutive strict monoidal functor. It is graphically represented by flipping pictures upside-down, for instance:

Given such a dagger functor, a morphism $f : A \to B$ is an *isometry* if $f^\dagger \circ f = 1_A$, and it is *unitary* of both f and $f^\dagger$ are isometries.

   A *dagger compact category* [2] is a dagger symmetric monoidal category in which each object A comes with two morphisms $\eta_A : I \to A^* \otimes A$ and $\epsilon_A :$

$A \otimes A^* \to I$ which satisfy certain equations. In this paper we take all our objects to be *self-dual*, that is, $A = A^*$. Graphically, we represent η_A as:

$$A \qquad A \quad,$$

we take ϵ_A to be its dagger, and the equations that govern η_A and ϵ_A are:

Remark 1. The results in this paper can be extended to the case of non-self-dual compact structures, by relying on the results in [14]. This would, for example, be required when considering all three complementary measurements on a qubit.

Theorem 2 (Kelly-Laplaza 1980, Selinger 2007 [24,28]). *An equation follows from the axioms of (dagger) compact categories if and only if it can be derived in the corresponding graphical language via isotopical rewrites.*

Here, *classical structures* are internal commutative special dagger Frobenius algebras in a dagger compact category for which we also require 'compatibility with the compact structure' (see below). These classical structures admit an equivalent presentation in terms of 'spiders'. That is, any morphism

$$\Xi_n^m : \underbrace{A \otimes \ldots \otimes A}_{n} \to \underbrace{A \otimes \ldots \otimes A}_{m}$$

obtained by composing and tensoring the structural morphisms of a classical structure and the symmetric monoidal structure, and of which the diagrammatic representation is connected, only depends on n and m [25]; graphically we represent this unique morphism as:

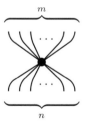

The axioms of classical structures tell us that these spiders are invariant under 'swapping legs', that $(\Xi_n^m)^\dagger = \Xi_m^n$, and that spiders 'compose' as follows:

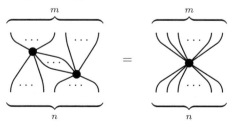

The axioms of a commutative special dagger Frobenius algebra all follow from this composition rule. Compatibility of the classical structure with the compact structure means that for a spider on A we have $\eta_A = \Xi_2^0$, and consequently that $\epsilon_A = \Xi_0^2$. In graphical terms, that is:

Definition 1. A *Hadamard* endomorphism $H : A \to A$ for a classical structure is a self-conjugate self-adjoint unitary endomorphism, i.e.

(self-adjointness is encoded in the symmetry of the small box depicting H), and which 'transforms a given classical structure into a complementary one', i.e.

$$\tag{1}$$

Remark 2. So rather than axiomatizing a pair of complementary classical structures as in [10], here we axiomatize a morphism which transforms a classical structure in the other one. The defining equation in [10] is obtained by precomposing both sides of eq. (1) with H, where $(H \otimes H) \circ \Xi_1^2 \circ H$ and $\Xi_1^0 \circ H$ then are the comultiplication and the counit of the complementary classical structure.

A *pure classical element* $e : I \to A$ for a classical structure satisfies:

$$\tag{2}$$

i.e. it is 'copied'. Below, by e we will denote pure classical elements only.

In the dagger compact category **FHilb** which has finite dimensional Hilbert spaces as objects, linear maps as morphisms, the tensor product as the monoidal structure, and adjoints as the dagger, classical structures are in bijective correspondence orthonormal bases [17], via this concept of pure classical elements.

Physically relevant, rather than **FHilb**, is the category $WP(\mathbf{FHilb})$ which is obtained by subjecting **FHilb** to the congruence which identifies those linear maps of the same type that are equal up to a complex phase, i.e.

$$f \sim g \iff \exists \theta \in [0, 2\pi[: f = e^{i\theta} \cdot g.$$

The reason is that vectors which are equal up to a complex phase represent the same state in quantum theory. The precise connection between classical structures in **FHilb** and those in $WP(\mathbf{FHilb})$ is studied in detail in [10]; roughly put, since this suffices for all practical purposes, classical structures are inherited.

4   Environment

Definition 2. An *environment* for a dagger compact category $\mathbf{C^{pure}}$ is an embedding of $\mathbf{C^{pure}}$ as a sub dagger compact category in another category $\mathbf{C}$, in which for all $A \in |\mathbf{C}|$ there is a morphism $\top_A : A \to I$ depicted as:

$$\top_A \;,$$

and these privileged coelements are such that for all $A, B \in |\mathbf{C}|$ we have

$$
\begin{array}{ccc}
\top_{A \otimes B} & = & \top_A \; \top_B
\end{array}
\qquad\qquad
A \;\bigcup\; = \; A \;\bot
\tag{3}
$$

and that for all $A, B \in |\mathbf{C}|$ and all $f, g \in \mathbf{C^{pure}}(A, B)$ we have

$$
\begin{array}{c}
\overset{A}{\underset{A}{\boxed{\substack{f \\ f}}}}
\end{array}
=
\begin{array}{c}
\overset{A}{\underset{A}{\boxed{\substack{g \\ g}}}}
\end{array}
\quad\Longleftrightarrow\quad
\underset{A}{\boxed{f}}
=
\underset{A}{\boxed{g}} \;.
\tag{4}
$$

Remark 3. Eq. (3) had already been introduced in [9], as part of an axiomatization of mixed states and completely positive maps, but it was never considered in relation to classicality, measurements, and complementarity thereof.

Example 1. [9] Let $CPM(\mathbf{FHilb})$ be the dagger compact category which has the same objects as $WP(\mathbf{FHilb})$ but of which the morphism are arbitrary (not necessarily normalized) completely positive maps [28]. When embedding $WP(\mathbf{FHilb})$ in $CPM(\mathbf{FHilb})$ and taking the usual trace on a Hilbert space to be the $\top$-morphisms we obtain such an environment. This example justifies the name 'environment', since tracing a system out in quantum theory is usually interpreted as considering this system as part of the environment. In $CPM(\mathbf{FHilb})$, the dagger to the $\top$-morphisms are the maximally mixed states.

Below we assume as given a dagger compact category with an environment. We set $\bot_A := \top_A^\dagger$. We call an element $\psi : I \to A$ *normalized* if $\top_A \circ \psi = 1_I$, and below we will assume that all elements depicted as triangles are normalized:

$$
\overset{}{\underset{\psi}{\triangledown}} \;=
\tag{5}
$$

where 1_I is graphically represented by an empty picture.

Proposition 1. [9] *A morphism $f \in \mathbf{C^{pure}}$ is an isometry iff $\top_B \circ f = \top_A$, and hence, it is unitary iff we moreover have that $f \circ \bot_A = \bot_B$.*

5   Classical Channels and Measurements

Definition 3. Let Ξ be a classical structure. The morphism:

$$C_\Xi = $$

is called the *classical channel of type Ξ*.

Given that we interpret the commultiplication of a classical structure as a copying operation (cf. [16,17]), in the light of the discussion in Section 2, this picture can indeed be interpreted as 'copying to the environment', that is, 'broadcasting'. Hence, our definition of classical channel enforces broadcastability of the data that it 'transmits'. Alternatively, taking the decoherence view, we can read it as the data 'being coupled to the environment'.

Example 2. In $CPM(\mathbf{FHilb})$ for $\Xi = (\mathcal{H}, \Xi_1^2 :: |i\rangle \mapsto |ii\rangle, \Xi_1^0 :: |i\rangle \mapsto 1)$ (cf. [15]) we have $C_\Xi(\rho) = tr(\Xi_1^2 \circ \rho \circ (\Xi_1^2)^\dagger)$ where tr is a partial trace on one of the two subsystems of $\mathcal{H} \otimes \mathcal{H}$. Then, $C_\Xi(-)$ sets all non-diagonal matrix entries to zero, and hence, $C_\Xi(\rho) = \rho$ if and only if ρ is diagonal in $\{|i\rangle\}$.

Remark 4. While physically all classical channels are of course the same, our classical channels in addition carry specification of how the classical data it transmits has been obtained, in terms of a dependency on the classical structure Ξ which specifies a particular quantum measurement. It is for this reason that we choose to axiomatize the H-morphism (cf. Remark 2), which enables us to restrict ourselves to a single classical structure.

The following proposition shows that a classical channel leaves its pure classical elements invariant, and that it is idempotent. We could define a more general *classical element $p : I \to A$* as one that satisfies $C_\Xi \circ p = p$.

Physically, this means that a classical channel 'transmits' its classical elements. Equivalently, classical elements are invariant under decoherence.

Proposition 2.

Proof. The first equality follows from eq. (2) and eq. (5). By eq. (4) we have

The last equality holds by the spider composition rule.   □

We can now construct a *measurement* as follows:

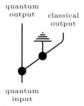

i.e. it copies the quantum data and specifies that one of the copies is classical. A *destructive measurement* is obtained by 'feeding the quantum output into the environment'. Proposition 2 then yields:

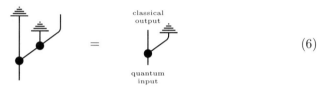

$$(6)$$

i.e. destructive measurements and classical channels are 'semantically equivalent'. Similarly, by the spider theorem we have:

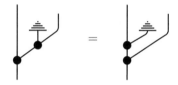

so the quantum output of a measurement is 'semantically equivalent' to its classical output, which captures change of the quantum state to an eigenstate. More generally, classicality 'spreads through a diagram' due to the spider theorem.

Note that by idempotence of C_Ξ it also follows that $\perp_A = \top_A^\dagger$ is a classical element, and in particular, that this does not depend on the choice of Ξ. We will call $\perp_A$ (unnormalized) *maximal mixedness*.

Example 3. In $CPM(\mathbf{FHilb})$ we indeed have that $\perp_{\mathcal{H}}$ is diagonal in any basis.

We call a morphism $f : A \to B$ *disconnected* if it factors along I, that is, if $f = \psi \circ \pi$ with $\psi : \mathrm{I} \to B$ and $\pi : A \to \mathrm{I}$. In the graphical representation we indeed obtain a disconnected picture in this case:

The topological disconnectedness physically stands for the fact that there is no dataflow from the input to the output.

If we introduce H between C_Ξ and itself, we obtain 'complementary behaviors'. The first equality of the following proposition implies that a measurement turns a pure classical element of a complementary measurement in maximal mixedness, i.e. any outcome is equally possible for that measurement (cf. 'unbi-asedness'). The second one implies that there is no dataflow from the input to the output when we compose complementary measurements.

Proposition 3.

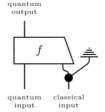

Proof. By eq. (4) we have

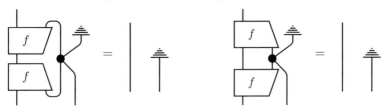

The first equation is derived from the second one and Proposition 2:

By a *controlled unitary* we mean an operation of the form:

which 'for all classical input values is unitary', that is:

Proposition 4. *The following morphism is a controlled unitary:*

$$(7)$$

Proof.

$$\text{(diagram equations)}$$

$\square$

Proposition 5. *The following morphism is unitary:*

$$CNOT \quad := \quad \text{(diagram)} \tag{8}$$

Proof. Follows again from eq. (1). $\square$

Proposition 6. *The following morphism is a destructive measurement:*

$$Bell\text{-}Meas \quad := \quad \text{(diagram)}$$

Proof. When transforming the classical structure canonically induced on $A \otimes A$ by means of $CNOT$, *Bell-Meas* arises as in eq. (6). $\square$

Example 4. These tables interpret basic graphical elements in $CPM(\mathbf{FHilb})$:

(pure) states & effects:

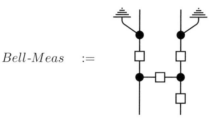

Notation:	(img)	(img)	(img)	(img)	(img)	(img)
FHilb:	$\sqrt{2} \cdot \lvert + \rangle$	$\sqrt{2} \cdot \langle + \rvert$	$\sqrt{2} \cdot \lvert 0 \rangle$	$\sqrt{2} \cdot \langle 0 \rvert$	$\lvert 00 \rangle + \lvert 11 \rangle$	$\langle 00 \rvert + \langle 11 \rvert$

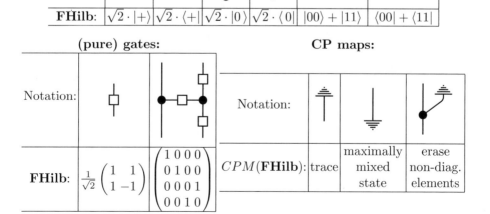

(pure) gates:

Notation:	(img)	(img)
FHilb:	$\frac{1}{\sqrt{2}} \begin{pmatrix} 1 & 1 \\ 1 & -1 \end{pmatrix}$	$\begin{pmatrix} 1 & 0 & 0 & 0 \\ 0 & 1 & 0 & 0 \\ 0 & 0 & 0 & 1 \\ 0 & 0 & 1 & 0 \end{pmatrix}$

CP maps:

Notation:	(img)	(img)	(img)
$CPM(\mathbf{FHilb})$:	trace	maximally mixed state	erase non-diag. elements

6   Example Protocols

In the statement of each proposition, we will specify protocols with explicit physical types, quantum channels being represented by full lines and classical channels being represented by dotted lines. We use the symbol ':≃' for the passage of this specification to the interpretation within the diagrammatic calculus.

First we show that the teleportation protocol, by means of a Bell state and two classical channels, realizes a (perfect) quantum channel.

Proposition 7 (correctness of teleportation)

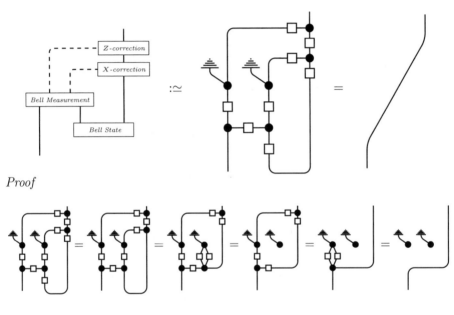

Proof

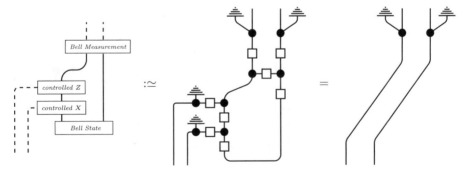

□

Now we show that the dense coding protocol, by means of a Bell state and a quantum channel, realizes two classical channels.

Proposition 8 (correctness of dense coding)

Proof

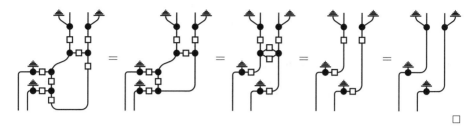

□

A diagrammatic presentation of key exchange protocols is in [18]. Here we provide a simplified presentation by relying on the notion of environment. We restrict ourselves to four representative cases.

Proposition 9 (correctness of BB84 and Ekert 91 key exchange)

– *Alice and Bob choose the same measurement in Ekert 91:*

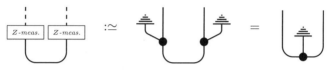

i.e. Alice and Bob share the same classical data.

– *Alice and Bob choose a different measurement in Ekert 91:*

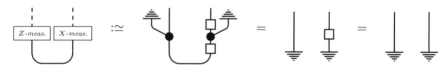

i.e. Alice's and Bob's data is not correlated.

– *Eve chooses the same measurement as Alice and Bob in BB84:*

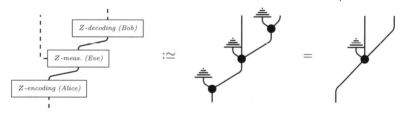

i.e. Alice, Bob and Eve share the same classical data.

– *Eve chooses a different measurement than Alice and Bob in BB84:*

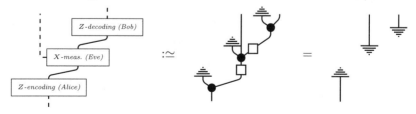

i.e. Alice's, Bob's and Eve's data is not correlated.

7   Connection to Selinger's CPM-Contruction

Here we briefly describe the connection of Definition 2 to Selinger's CPM-comstruction [28], which was established in [9].

Definition 4. An environment with *purification* $\mathbf{C^{pure}}$ is an environment as in Definition 2 for which we in addition have that, denoting morphisms in $\mathbf{C^{pure}}$ and more general morphisms in $\mathbf{C}$ respectively as

for all $A, B \in |\mathbf{C}|, F \in \mathbf{C}(A, B)$ there exists $f \in \mathbf{C^{pure}}(A, B \otimes C)$ such that

Theorem 3. [9] $CPM(\mathbf{C^{pure}}) = \mathbf{C}$.

The converse statement, that for any dagger compact category $\mathbf{C}$ the category $CPM(\mathbf{C})$ provides an environment with purification also holds, up to a minor and physically justified assumption related to the fact that vectors which are equal up to a complex phase represent the same state in quantum theory. Concretely, this axiom states the for all pure elements $\psi, \psi' : \mathrm{I} \to A$ we have:

$$\psi \circ \psi^\dagger = \psi' \circ \psi'^\dagger \;\Rightarrow\; \psi = \psi' \ .$$

This equation follows from eq. (4) when setting $f := \psi^\dagger$ and $g := \psi'^\dagger$.

Remark 5. The power of a purification axiom has recently been exploited in [8], although there, the authors also require certain uniqueness properties.

8   Conclusion

An axiomatization of the concept of environment resulted in a very simple comprehensive graphical calculus, which in particular enables one to reason about classical-quantum interaction in quantum informatic protocols.

  Several operationally distinct concepts turn out to have the same semantics within the graphical language (e.g. classical channel, measurement, preparation as in BB84). Consequently, all that one structurally truly needs are Propositions 2 and 3 on composition of classical channels and pure classical elements.

The examples given here are simple but representative. This work and the earlier contributions on which we relied together successfully addresses a challenge for the categorical quantum mechanics research program which was set at the very beginning: to have a very simple graphical description of all basic quantum informatic protocols, in particular including classical-quantum interaction.

The new graphical element 'environment' and the interaction rules for classical channels can now be integrated in the `quantomatic` software [19], so that it can now be used to (semi-)automate reasoning about full-blown quantum informatic protocols, including classical-quantum interaction.

Here we only considered two complementary observables. We meanwhile also have graphical calculi that are universal for quantum computing [10,12]. The next step of this research strand would be to extend the graphical calculus presented here to these calculi, which include, for example, phases and W-states.

This work could also be advanced in the direction of quantum information theory. In particular, one may want to study whether it would be possible to obtain a diagrammatic account on quantum informatic quantities. Some examples of diagrammatic quantum informatic quantities are in [9].

References

1. Abramsky, S., Coecke, B.: A categorical semantics of quantum protocols. IEEE-LiCS 2004 (2004), Revision: arXiv:quant-ph/0808.1023
2. Abramsky, S., Coecke, B.: Abstract physical traces. Theory and Applications of Categories 14, 111–124 (2005), arXiv:0910.3144
3. Barnum, H., Caves, C.M., Fuchs, C.A., Jozsa, R., Schumacher, B.: Noncommuting mixed states cannot be broadcast. Physical Review Letters 76, 2818–2821 (1996), arXiv:quant-ph/9511010
4. Bennett, C.H., Brassard, G.: Quantum cryptography: Public key distribution and coin tossing. IEEE-CSSP (1984)
5. Bennett, C.H., Brassard, G., Crépeau, C., Jozsa, R., Peres, A., Wooters, W.K.: Teleporting an unknown quantum state via dual classical and Einstein-Podolsky-Rosen channels. Physical Review Letters 70, 1895–1899 (1993)
6. Bennet, C.H., Wiesner, S.: Communication via one- and two-particle operators on Einstein-Podolsky-Rosen states. Physical Review Letters 69, 2881–2884 (1992)
7. Carboni, A., Walters, R.F.C.: Cartesian bicategories I. Journal of Pure and Applied Algebra 49, 11–32 (1987)
8. Chiribella, G., D'Ariano, G.M., Perinotti, P.: Probabilistic theories with purification (2009), arXiv:0908.1583
9. Coecke, B.: Axiomatic description of mixed states from Selinger's CPM-construction. Electronic Notes in Theoretical Computer Science 210, 3–13 (2008)
10. Coecke, B., Duncan, R.: Interacting quantum observables. In: Aceto, L., Damgård, I., Goldberg, L.A., Halldórsson, M.M., Ingólfsdóttir, A., Walukiewicz, I. (eds.) ICALP 2008, Part II. LNCS, vol. 5126, pp. 298–310. Springer, Heidelberg (2008); Extended version: arXiv:0906.4725
11. Coecke, B., Edwards, B., Spekkens, R.W.: Phase groups and the origin of non-locality for qubits. In: ENTCS-QPL 2009 (to appear, 2010), arXiv:1003.5005
12. Coecke, B., Kissinger, A.: The compositional structure of multipartite quantum entanglement. In: ICALP 2010 (2010), arXiv:1002.2540

13. Coecke, B., Paquette, E.O.: Categories for the practicing physicist. In: Coecke, B. (ed.) New Structures for Physics. Lecture Notes in Physics, pp. 167–271. Springer, Heidelberg (2009), arXiv:0905.3010

14. Coecke, B., Paquette, E.O., Perdrix, S.: Bases in diagrammatic quantum protocols. Electronic Notes in Theoretical Computer Science 218, 131–152 (2008)

15. Coecke, B., Paquette, E.O., Pavlovic, D.: Classical and quantum structuralism. In: Mackie, I., Gay, S. (eds.) Semantic Techniques for Quantum Computation, pp. 29–69. Cambridge University Press, Cambridge (2009), arXiv:0904.1997

16. Coecke, B., Pavlovic, D.: Quantum measurements without sums. In: Chen, G., Kauffman, L., Lamonaco, S. (eds.) Mathematics of Quantum Computing and Technology, pp. 567–604. Taylor and Francis, Abington (2007), arXiv:quant-ph/0608035

17. Coecke, B., Pavlovic, D., Vicary, J.: A new description of orthogonal bases (2008), arXiv:0810.0812

18. Coecke, B., Wang, B.-S., Wang, Q.-L., Wang, Y.-J., Zhang, Q.-Y.: Graphical calculus for quantum key distribution. In: ENTCS-QPL 2009 (to appear, 2010)

19. Dixon, L., Duncan, R., Kissinger, A.: quantomatic, http://dream.inf.ed.ac.uk/projects/quantomatic/

20. Duncan, R., Perdrix, S.: Graph states and the necessity of Euler decomposition. In: CiE 2009. LNCS, vol. 5635. Springer, Heidelberg (2009), arXiv:0902.0500

21. Duncan, R., Perdrix, S.: Rewriting measurement-based quantum computations with generalised flow. In: ICALP 2010 (2010)

22. Ekert, A.: Quantum cryptography based on Bell's theorem. Physical Review Letters 67, 661–663 (1991)

23. Joyal, A., Street, R.: The Geometry of tensor calculus I. Advances in Mathematics 88, 55–112 (1991)

24. Kelly, G.M., Laplaza, M.L.: Coherence for compact closed categories. Journal of Pure and Applied Algebra 19, 193–213 (1980)

25. Lack, S.: Composing PROPs. Theory and Applications of Categories 13, 147–163 (2004)

26. Mac Lane, S.: Categories for the Working Mathematician, 2nd edn. Springer, Heidelberg (2000)

27. Penrose, R.: Applications of negative dimensional tensors. In: Welsh, D. (ed.) Combinatorial Mathematics and its Applications, pp. 221–244. Academic Press, London (1971)

28. Selinger, P.: Dagger compact closed categories and completely positive maps. Electronic Notes in Theoretical Computer Science 170, 139–163 (2007)

29. Selinger, P.: A survey of graphical languages for monoidal categories. In: Coecke, B. (ed.) New Structures for Physics, pp. 275–337. Springer, Heidelberg (2009), arXiv:0908.3347

30. Zurek, W.H.: Decoherence and the Transition from Quantum to Classical. Physics Today 44, 36–44 (1991), arXiv:quant-ph/0306072

Formal Theories for Linear Algebra

Stephen Cook and Lila Fontes

Department of Computer Science, University of Toronto
{sacook,fontes}@cs.toronto.edu

Abstract. We introduce two-sorted theories in the style of [CN10] for the complexity classes $\oplus L$ and DET, whose complete problems include determinants over $\mathbb{Z}_2$ and $\mathbb{Z}$, respectively. We then describe interpretations of Soltys' linear algebra theory LAP over arbitrary integral domains, into each of our new theories. The result shows equivalences of standard theorems of linear algebra over $\mathbb{Z}_2$ and $\mathbb{Z}$ can be proved in the corresponding theory, but leaves open the interesting question of whether the theorems themselves can be proved.

1 Introduction

This paper introduces formal theories for the complexity classes $\oplus L$ (also called *ParityL*) and DET for reasoning about linear algebra over the rings $\mathbb{Z}_2$ and $\mathbb{Z}$, respectively. Complete problems for these classes include standard computational problems of linear algebra over their respective rings, such as computing determinants, matrix powers, and coefficients of the characteristic polynomial of a matrix [BDHM92]. (Recently [BKR09] proved that for each $k \geq 1$, computing the permanent mod 2^k of an integer matrix is in $\oplus L$, and hence complete.) Each theory allows induction over any relation in the associated complexity class $\oplus L$ or DET, and the functions definable in each theory are the functions in the class. Thus determinants and characteristic polynomials can be defined in the theories, but it is not clear that their standard properties can be proved without defining concepts outside the associated complexity classes. This remains an interesting open question [SK01, SC04].

The simplest way of defining the classes $\oplus L$ and DET is using uniform AC^0 reductions (see below). Thus $\oplus L = AC^0(det_2)$ and $DET = AC^0(det)$, where det_2 and det are the determinant functions for matrices over $\mathbb{Z}_2$ and $\mathbb{Z}$ respectively, and $AC^0(*)$ is the set of problems AC^0-reducible to $*$.

The usual definitions of these classes involve counting the number of accepting computations of nondeterministic log space Turing machines. Thus $\#L$ is the class of functions f such that for some nondeterministic log space Turing machine M, $f(x)$ is the number of accepting computations of M on input x. Then the sets in $\oplus L$ are those of the form $\{x \mid f(x) \bmod 2 = 1\}$ for some f in $\#L$. It turns out that $AC^0(det) = AC^0(\#L)$, and $AC^0(det_2) = AC^0(\oplus L) = \oplus L$. To get an idea of why det can be reduced to $\#L$, note that Berkowitz's algorithm reduces det to integer matrix powering. It is easy to see that powering $0-1$ matrices reduces to $\#L$ because the entry ij in the kth power of the adjacency

A. Dawar and H. Veith (Eds.): CSL 2010, LNCS 6247, pp. 245–259, 2010.

matrix for the configuration graph of a Turing machine is the number of computations of length k between configurations i and j. With a little creative thought this reduction can be generalized to binary integer matrices (see [Fon09, AO96]). Also $DET = \#LH = \bigcup_i \#LH_i$ (the $\#L$ hierarchy), where $\#LH_1 = \#L$ and $\#LH_{i+1} = \#L^{\#LH_i}$ (see [AO96]). (The exponent $\#LH_i$ indicates that a function from this class is allowed to be an oracle for the log space machine whose accepting computations are being counted.)

We should clarify that our definition of DET here differs from that in [Coo85], where DET is defined to be $NC^1(det)$, the closure of $\{det\}$ under the more general NC^1 reductions. Allender proved (see the Appendix to [All04]) that if $AC^0(det) = NC^1(det)$ then the $\#L$ hierarchy collapses to some finite level $\#LH_i$, something that is not known to be true. The present authors (now) believe that $AC^0(det) = \#LH$ is the more natural definition of DET, and makes the corresponding logical theory much easier to formulate.

The complexity classes satisfy the inclusions $L \subseteq \oplus L \subseteq DET \subseteq NC^2 \subseteq P$ and $L \subseteq NL \subseteq DET$ (ignoring the distinction between function and language classes) where L and NL are the problems accepted in deterministic and non-deterministic log space, respectively. It is not known whether $\oplus L$ and NL are comparable. (Of course we cannot disprove the unlikely possibility that all of the above classes could coincide.)

To construct formal theories for the classes $\oplus L$ and DET we follow the framework laid out in Chapter 9 of the monograph [CN10] of Cook and Nguyen for defining theories for complexity classes between AC^0 and P. All of these theories share a common two-sorted (number and string) vocabulary $\mathcal{L}_A^2$. The intention is that the number sort ranges over $\mathbb{N}$ and the string sort ranges over bit strings (more precisely, finite subsets of $\mathbb{N}$). The strings are intended to be inputs to the machine or circuit defining a member of the complexity class, and the numbers are used to index bits in the strings. Each theory VC for a class C extends the finitely-axiomatized base theory V^0 for AC^0 by addition of a single axiom stating the existence of a solution to a complete problem for C. General techniques are presented for defining a universally-axiomatized conservative extension $\overline{VC}$ of VC which has function symbols and defining axioms for each function in FC, and $\overline{VC}$ admits induction on open formulas in this enriched vocabulary. It follows from the Herbrand Theorem that the provably-total functions in $\overline{VC}$ (and hence in VC) are precisely the functions in FC.

Chapter 9 (with earlier chapters) of [CN10] explicitly defines theories for the following classes:

$$AC^0 \subset AC^0(2) \subset TC^0 \subseteq NC^1 \subseteq L \subseteq NL \subseteq NC \subseteq P \tag{1}$$

These classes are defined briefly as follows. A problem in AC^0 is solved by a uniform family of polynomial size constant depth Boolean circuits with unbounded fanin AND and OR gates. $AC^0(2)$ properly extends AC^0 by also allowing unbounded fanin parity gates (determining whether the inputs have an odd number of 1's) in its circuits. TC^0 allows majority gates rather than parity gates in its circuits (and has binary integer multiplication as a complete problem). NC^1 circuits restrict all Boolean gates to fanin two, but the circuits are allowed to have logarithmic depth. Problems in L and NL are solved respectively by deterministic and nondeterministic log space Turing machines. NC is defined like NC^1, but the circuits can have polylogarithmic depth (and polynomial size). Problems in P are solved by polynomial time Turing machines.

Our new theories $V \oplus L$ and $V \# L$ for $\oplus L$ and DET extend the base theory V^0 for AC^0 by adding an axiom stating the existence of powers A^k of matrices A over $\mathbb{Z}_2$ and $\mathbb{Z}$, respectively, where k is presented in unary. (Matrix powering is a complete problem for these classes [Fon09].) Here there is a technical difficulty of how to nicely state these axioms, since neither the parity function (needed to define matrix multiplication over $\mathbb{Z}_2$) nor integer product and multiple summation (needed to define matrix multiplication over $\mathbb{Z}$) is definable in the base theory V^0. We solve this by basing these theories on the theories $V^0(2)$ (for $AC^0(2)$) and VTC^0, and by using results from [CN10] to translate these axioms to the language of the base theory V^0. We then show that the resulting theories satisfy the requirements of Chapter 9 (existence of "aggregate functions") that allow the existence of the nice universal conservative extensions $\overline{V \oplus L}$ and $\overline{V \# L}$ of $V \oplus L$ and $V \# L$.

The new theories mesh nicely with the theories for the complexity classes in (1). In particular, we have

$$V^0 \subset V^0(2) \subset VNC^1 \subseteq VL \subseteq V \oplus L \subseteq V \# L \subseteq VNC \subseteq VP \qquad (2)$$

Next we study the question of which results from linear algebra can be proved in the theories. For this we take advantage of Soltys's theory LAP [SK01, SC04] for formalizing results from linear algebra over an arbitrary field or integral domain. We present two interpretations of LAP: one into $V \oplus L$ and one into $V \# L$. Both interpretations translate theorems of LAP to theorems in the corresponding theory, but the translations can alter the meaning of formulas by giving different interpretations of the ring elements.

LAP has three sorts: One for indices (natural numbers), one for field (or ring) elements, and one for matrices. When interpreting LAP into $V \oplus L$ our intention is that the field is $\mathbb{Z}_2$, so we interpret field elements as formulas, where true formulas represent 1 and false formulas represent 0. When interpreting LAP into $V \# L$ our intention is that the ring is $\mathbb{Z}$. In this case we interpret field elements as strings representing binary integers.

LAP defines matrix powering, and uses this and Berkowitz's algorithm [Ber84] to define several functions of matrices, including determinant, adjoint, and characteristic polynomial. The following standard principles of linear algebra are discussed:

(i) The Cayley-Hamilton Theorem (a matrix satisfies its characteristic polynomial).
(ii) The axiomatic definition of determinant (the function $det(A)$ is characterized by the properties that it is multilinear and alternating in the rows and columns of A, and $det(I) = 1$).
(iii) The co-factor expansion of the determinant.

Although it remains open whether LAP can prove any of these, a major result from [SK01, SC04] is that LAP proves their pairwise equivalence. As a result of this and our interpretations we have the following.

Theorem 1. $V \oplus L$ *proves the equivalence of (i), (ii), and (iii) over the ring* $\mathbb{Z}_2$, *and* $V \# L$ *proves their equivalence over* $\mathbb{Z}$.

An intriguing possibility (not yet realized) is that either $V \oplus L$ or $V \# L$ could use special properties of $\mathbb{Z}_2$ or $\mathbb{Z}$ to prove its version of the principles, while still leaving open whether LAP can prove them (for all integral domains or fields). For example there is a dynamic programming algorithm involving combinatorial graph properties (see the concluding Section 4) whose correctness for $\mathbb{Z}$ might be provable in $V \# L$ using combinatorial reasoning with concepts from $\# L$ which are not available in LAP.

[SK01, SC04] also present the so-called *hard matrix identities*, each equivalent to the implication

$$AB = I \rightarrow BA = I \tag{3}$$

where A, B are square matrices. Again it is open whether LAP proves these identities, but LAP does prove that they follow from any of the principles mentioned in Theorem 1 above. The next result follows from this and our interpretations.

Theorem 2. $V \oplus L$ *proves that (3) over the ring* $\mathbb{Z}_2$ *follows from any of the three principles mentioned in Theorem 1. The same is true for* $V \# L$ *over the ring* $\mathbb{Z}$.

[SK01, SC04] introduce an extension ∀LAP of LAP, which includes an induction rule that applies to formulas with bounded universally quantified matrix variables, and shows that the three principles mentioned in Theorem 1 and the four matrix identities are all provable in ∀LAP. The key idea in this proof uses induction on a polynomial time relation, and in fact this proof can be carried out in the theory VP for polynomial time defined in [CN10]. Since VP (see formula (2)) extends both $V \oplus L$ and $V \# L$ we have the following result (alluded to at the end of Section 6 in [SC04]).

Theorem 3. *The theory* VP *proves the three principles (i), (ii), (iii) and the matrix identity (3) for both the rings* $\mathbb{Z}_2$ *and* $\mathbb{Z}$.

2   Theories $V \oplus L$ and $V \# L$

We start by reviewing the two-sorted logic used here and in [CN10]. We have *number* variables $x, y, z, \ldots$ whose intended values are numbers (in $\mathbb{N}$), and *string* variables $X, Y, Z, \ldots$ whose intended values are finite sets of numbers. We think of the finite sets as binary strings giving the characteristic vectors of the sets. For example the string corresponding to the set $\{0, 3, 4\}$ is 10011.

All our two-sorted theories include the basic vocabulary $\mathcal{L}_A^2 = [0, 1, +, \cdot, | \ |; \in, \leq, =_1, =_2]$ which extends the first-order vocabulary of Peano Arithmetic. The symbols $0, 1, +, \cdot$ are intended to take their usual meanings on $\mathbb{N}$. Here $| \ |$ is a function from strings to numbers, and the intended meaning of $|X|$ is 1 plus the largest element of X, or 0 if X is empty. (If $X = \{0, 3, 4\}$ then $|X| = 5$.) The binary predicate $\in$ is intended to denote set membership. We often write $X(t)$ for $t \in X$ (think bit number t of the string X is 1). The equality predicates $=_1$ and $=_2$ are for numbers and strings, respectively. We will write $=$ for both, since the missing subscript will be clear from the context.

Number terms (such as $x + ((|X| + 1) \cdot |Y|)$) are built from variables and function symbols as usual. The only string terms based on $\mathcal{L}_A^2$ are string variables $X, Y, Z, \ldots$, but when we extend $\mathcal{L}_A^2$ by adding string-valued functions, other string terms will be built as usual. Formulas are built from atomic formulas (e.g. $t = u, t \leq u, X(t), X = Y$) using $\wedge, \vee, \neg$ and $\exists x, \forall x, \exists X, \forall X$.

Bounded quantifiers are defined as usual, except bounds on string quantifiers refer to the length of the string. For example $\exists X \leq t \varphi$ stands for $\exists X(|X| \leq t \wedge \varphi)$.

We define two important syntactic classes of formulas.

Definition 1. Σ_0^B *is the class of $\mathcal{L}_A^2$ formulas with no string quantifiers, and only bounded number quantifiers. Σ_1^B formulas are those of the form $\exists \boldsymbol{X} \leq \boldsymbol{t} \varphi$, where φ is in Σ_0^B and the prefix of bounded quantifiers may be empty.*

Notice our nonstandard requirement that the string quantifiers in Σ_1^B formulas must be in front.

We also consider two-sorted vocabularies $\mathcal{L} \supseteq \mathcal{L}_A^2$ which extend $\mathcal{L}_A^2$ by possibly adding predicate symbols $P, Q, R, \ldots$ and function symbols $f, g, h, \ldots$ and $F, G, H, \ldots$ Here $f, g, h, \ldots$ are *number functions* and are intended to take values in $\mathbb{N}$, and $F, G, H, \ldots$ are *string functions* and are intended to take string values. Each predicate or function symbol has a specified arity (n, m) indicating that it takes n number arguments and m string arguments. Number arguments are written before string arguments, as in

$$f(x_1, \ldots, x_n, X_1, \ldots, X_m) \qquad F(x_1, \ldots, x_n, X_1, \ldots, X_m) \qquad (4)$$

The formula classes $\Sigma_0^B(\mathcal{L})$ and $\Sigma_1^B(\mathcal{L})$ are defined in the same way as Σ_0^B and Σ_1^B, but allow function and relation symbols from $\mathcal{L}$ in addition to $\mathcal{L}_A^2$.

2.1   Two-Sorted Complexity Classes

In standard complexity theory an element of a complexity class is either a set of binary strings or a function $f : \{0,1\}^* \to \{0,1\}^*$. In our two-sorted point of view (Chapter 4 of [CN10]) it is convenient to replace a set of strings by a relation $P(\boldsymbol{x}, \boldsymbol{X})$ of any arity (n, m), and functions are generalized to allow both number functions and string functions as in (4). Each standard complexity class, including those in (1) and $\oplus L$ and $\#L$, is defined either in terms of Turing machines or circuit families. These definitions naturally extend to two-sorted versions by representing strings (as inputs to machines or circuits) in a straightforward way as binary strings, but by representing numbers using unary notation. This interpretation of numbers is a convenience, and is justified by our intention that numbers are 'small' and are used to index strings and measure their length. In particular, we have the following definition of two-sorted $\oplus L$.

Definition 2. $\oplus L$ *is the set of relations* $P(\boldsymbol{x}, \boldsymbol{X})$ *such that there is a nondeterministic log space Turing machine* M *such that* M *with input* $\boldsymbol{x}, \boldsymbol{X}$ *(represented as above) has an odd number of accepting computations iff* $P(\boldsymbol{x}, \boldsymbol{X})$ *holds.*

The class AC^0 can be defined in terms of uniform polynomial size constant depth circuit families, but it has a nice characterization as those sets recognized by an alternating Turing machine (ATM) in log time with a constant number of alternations. More useful for us, [Imm99] showed that an element of AC^0 can be described as an element of FO, namely the set of finite models of some first-order formula with a certain vocabulary. From this and the ATM definition of two-sorted AC^0, we have the following important results relating syntax and semantics (Theorems 4.18 and 4.19 of [CN10]).

Proposition 1 (Representation Theorems). *A relation* $P(\boldsymbol{x}, \boldsymbol{X})$ *is in* AC^0 *(respectively* NP*) iff it is represented by some* Σ_0^B*-formula (respectively* Σ_1^B*-formula)* $\varphi(\boldsymbol{x}, \boldsymbol{X})$.

For example the relation $PAL(X)$ (X is a palindrome) is an AC^0 relation because the Σ_0^B-formula $\forall x, y < |X|(x + y + 1 = |X| \supset (X(x) \leftrightarrow X(y)))$ represents it.

A number function $f(\boldsymbol{x}, \boldsymbol{X})$ (respectively string function $F(\boldsymbol{x}, \boldsymbol{X})$) is p-bounded if there is a polynomial $g(\boldsymbol{x}, \boldsymbol{y})$ such that $f(\boldsymbol{x}, \boldsymbol{X}) \leq g(\boldsymbol{x}, |\boldsymbol{X}|)$ (respectively $|F(\boldsymbol{x}, \boldsymbol{X})| \leq g(\boldsymbol{x}, |\boldsymbol{X}|)$). The *bit graph* of a string function F is the relation B_F defined by $B_F(i, \boldsymbol{x}, \boldsymbol{X}) \leftrightarrow F(\boldsymbol{x}, \boldsymbol{X})(i)$. (Recall that $Y(i)$ stands for $i \in Y$.)

Definition 3. *If* C *is a class of (two-sorted) relations then* FC *denotes the corresponding class of functions, where* f *(respectively* F*) is in* FC *iff it is* p-*bounded and its graph (respectively bit graph) is in* C.

We will consider two-sorted vocabularies $\mathcal{L}$ which extend $\mathcal{L}_A^2$, and in all cases each function and relation symbol in $\mathcal{L}$ has an intended interpretation in our standard two-sorted model (the two universes being $\mathbb{N}$ and the set of finite subsets of $\mathbb{N}$). Thus we can make sense of both syntactic and semantic statements about $\mathcal{L}$.

If $\mathcal{L}$ is a two-sorted vocabulary, then f (respectively F) is Σ_0^B-definable from $\mathcal{L}$ if it is p-bounded and its graph (respectively bit graph) is represented by a formula in $\Sigma_0^B(\mathcal{L})$.

$AC^0(\mathcal{L})$ (the AC^0 closure of $\mathcal{L}$) denotes the closure of $\mathcal{L}$ under Σ_0^B definability. To show a function is in $AC^0(\mathcal{L})$ requires giving a finite sequence of functions such that each is Σ_0^B-definable from the preceding ones. The relations in $AC^0(\mathcal{L})$ are those whose characteristic functions are in $AC^0(\mathcal{L})$.

2.2   Theories V^0, $V^0(2)$, and VTC^0

The theory V^0 for AC^0 is the basis for every two-sorted theory considered here and in [CN10]. It has the two-sorted vocabulary $\mathcal{L}_A^2$, and is axiomatized by the set 2-BASIC of axioms consisting of 15 Σ_0^B formulas expressing basic properties of the symbols of $\mathcal{L}_A^2$, together with the Σ_0^B comprehension scheme

$$\Sigma_0^B\text{-}\mathbf{COMP} : \quad \exists X \leq y \forall z < y (X(z) \leftrightarrow \varphi(z))$$

where $\varphi(z)$ is any Σ_0^B formula with no free occurrence of X.

V^0 has no explicit induction axiom, but nevertheless the induction scheme

$$\Sigma_0^B\text{-}\mathbf{IND} : \quad \big(\varphi(0) \wedge \forall x(\varphi(x) \supset \varphi(x+1))\big) \supset \forall z \varphi(z)$$

for Σ_0^B formulas $\varphi(x)$ is provable in V^0, using Σ_0^B-**COMP** and the fact that $|X|$ produces the maximum element of the set X.

Definition 4. *A string function $F(\boldsymbol{x}, \boldsymbol{X})$ is Σ_1^B-definable in a two-sorted theory $\mathcal{T}$ if there is a Σ_1^B formula $\varphi(\boldsymbol{x}, \boldsymbol{X}, Y)$ representing the graph $Y = F(\boldsymbol{x}, \boldsymbol{X})$ of F such that $\mathcal{T} \vdash \forall \boldsymbol{x} \forall \boldsymbol{X} \exists! Y \varphi(\boldsymbol{x}, \boldsymbol{X}, Y)$. Similarly for a number function $f(\boldsymbol{x}, \boldsymbol{X})$.*

It is shown in Chapter 5 of [CN10] that V^0 is finitely axiomatizable, and the Σ_1^B-definable functions in V^0 comprise the class FAC^0 (see Definition 3).

The definition in [CN10] of the theory $V^0(2)$ for the class $AC^0(2)$ is based on V^0 and an axiom showing the definability of the function $Parity(x, Y)$. If $Z = Parity(x, Y)$ then $Z(z)$ holds iff $1 \leq z \leq x$ and there is an odd number of ones in $Y(0)Y(1)\ldots Y(z \dot{-} 1)$. The graph of $Parity$ is defined by the Σ_0^B formula $\delta_{parity}(x, Y, Z)$, which is $\neg Z(0) \wedge \forall z < x(Z(z+1) \leftrightarrow (Z(z) \oplus Y(z)))$.

Definition 5. *[CN10] The theory $V^0(2)$ has vocabulary $\mathcal{L}_A^2$ and axioms those of V^0 and $\exists Z \leq x + 1 \; \delta_{parity}(x, Y, Z)$.*

The complexity class $FAC^0(2)$ is the AC^0 closure of the function $Parity(x, Y)$, and in fact the Σ_1^B-definable functions of $V^0(2)$ are precisely those in $FAC^0(2)$.

The theory VTC^0 for the counting class TC^0 is defined similarly to $V^0(2)$, but now the function $Parity(x, Y)$ is replaced by the function $numones(y, X)$, whose value is the number of elements (i.e. 'ones') of X that are less than y. The axiom for VTC^0 is based on a Σ_0^B formula $\delta_{NUM}(y, X, Z)$ defining the graph of a string function accumulating the values of $numones(y, X)$ as y increases.

The definition of $\delta_{NUM}(y, X, Z)$ uses the pairing function $\langle x, y \rangle$, which is the $\mathcal{L}_A^2$ term $(x+y)(x+y+1) + 2y$.

Definition 6. *[CN10] The theory VTC^0 has vocabulary $\mathcal{L}_A^2$ and axioms those of V^0 and $\exists Z \leq 1 + \langle y, y \rangle \delta_{NUM}(y, X, Z)$.*

The class FTC^0 is the AC^0 closure of the function $numones$, and in fact the Σ_1^B-definable functions of VTC^0 are precisely those in FTC^0.

In Chapters 5 and 9 of [CN10] it is shown that the theories $V^0, V^0(2), VTC^0$ have respective universally axiomatized conservative extensions $\overline{V^0}, \overline{V^0(2)}, \overline{VTC^0}$ obtained by introducing function symbols and their defining axioms for all string functions (and some number functions) in the corresponding complexity class. These have the following properties.

Proposition 2. *Let* $(FC, V, \overline{V})$ *be any of the triples* $(FAC^0, V^0, \overline{V^0})$ *or* $(FAC^0(2),$ $V^0(2), \overline{V^0(2)})$ *or* $(FTC^0, VTC^0, \overline{VTC^0})$, *and let* $\mathcal{L}$ *be the vocabulary of* $\overline{V}$. *Then (i)* $\overline{V}$ *is a universally axiomatized conservative extension of* V, *(ii) the* Σ_1^B*-definable functions of both* V *and* $\overline{V}$ *are those in* FC, *(iii) a string function (respectively number function) is in* FC *iff it has a function symbol (respectively term) in* $\mathcal{L}$, *(iv)* $\overline{V}$ *proves the* $\Sigma_0^B(\mathcal{L})$**-IND** *and* $\Sigma_0^B(\mathcal{L})$**-COMP** *schemes, and (v) for every* $\Sigma_1^B(\mathcal{L})$ *formula* φ^+ *there is a* Σ_1^B *formula* φ *such that* $\overline{V} \vdash \varphi^+ \leftrightarrow \varphi$.

2.3 New Theory $V \oplus L$

Recall (two-sorted) $\oplus L$ is given in Definition 2. It follows from results in [BDHM92] (see [Fon09]) that $\oplus L$ consists of the relations in the AC^0 closure of matrix powering over $\mathbb{Z}_2$. The theory $V \oplus L$ extends $V^0(2)$ by adding a Σ_1^B axiom for matrix powering over $\mathbb{Z}_2$.

Recall that the theory $\overline{V^0(2)}$ is a conservative extension of $V^0(2)$, and its vocabulary $\mathcal{L}_{FAC^0(2)}$ has function symbols or terms for every function in $FAC^0(2)$. We describe the Σ_1^B axiom for matrix powering as a $\Sigma_1^B(\mathcal{L}_{FAC^0(2)})$ formula and refer to part (v) of Proposition 2 to conclude that this formula is provably equivalent to a $\Sigma_1^B(\mathcal{L}_A^2)$ formula.

Hence we will freely use FAC^0 functions and the function $Parity(x, Y)$ (used to define the theory $V^0(2)$) when describing formulas which will help express the Σ_1^B axiom. In particular we will use the pairing function $\langle x, y \rangle$ and its inverses $left(z)$ and $right(z)$. Since the pairing function is not surjective, we use $Pair(z)$ to abbreviate the formula $z = \langle left(z), right(z) \rangle$ which asserts that z codes a pair.

We use the truth values $\{false, true\}$ to represent the elements $\{0, 1\}$ of $\mathbb{Z}_2$, and we represent a matrix over $\mathbb{Z}_2$ with a string X. Here $X(i, j)$ abbreviates $X(\langle i, j \rangle)$ and refers to the entry ij of the matrix. We number rows and columns starting with 0, so if X is an $n \times n$ matrix then $0 \le i, j < n$.

The function $Row(i, X)$ (written $X^{[i]}$) refers to row i of matrix X, and is defined by its bit graph $X^{[i]}(b) \leftrightarrow b < |X| \wedge X(i, b)$.

The string function $ID(n)$ codes the $n \times n$ identity matrix, and has a bit graph axiom $ID(n)(b) \leftrightarrow left(b) < n \wedge Pair(b) \wedge left(b) = right(b)$.

In order to define matrix product we start by defining the AC^0 string function $G(n, i, j, X, Y)$ equal to the string of pairwise bit products of row i of X and column j of Y. The bit graph axiom is $G(n, i, j, X, Y)(b) \leftrightarrow b < n \wedge X(i, b) \wedge Y(b, j)$.

Let $PAR(X)$ stand for the formula $Parity(|X|, X)(|X|)$. Thus $PAR(X)$ holds iff X has an odd number of ones. Let $Prod_2(n, X, Y)$ be the product of X and Y treated as $n \times n$ matrices over $\mathbb{Z}_2$. The bit graph axiom is

$$Prod_2(n, X, Y)(b) \leftrightarrow \tag{5}$$
$$Pair(b) \wedge left(b) < n \wedge right(b) < n \wedge PAR(G(n, left(b), right(b), X, Y))$$

Now we want to define the function $PowSeq_2(n, k, X)$ whose value is a string Y coding the sequence $I, X, X^2, \ldots, X^k$ of powers of the $n \times n$ matrix X. (Note that this function is complete for $F \oplus L$.) We do this by giving its graph, which is defined by the following $\Sigma_0^B(\mathcal{L}_{FAC^0(2)})$ formula $\delta_{PowSeq_2}(n, k, X, Y)$:

$$Y^{[0]} = ID(n) \wedge \forall i < k(Y^{[i+1]} = Prod_2(n, X, Y^{[i]})$$
$$\wedge \forall b < |Y|(Y(b) \supset (Pair(b) \wedge left(b) < n))$$

(The second line ensures that Y is uniquely defined.) Note that δ_{PowSeq_2} involves the function $Prod_2$ and hence is not equivalent to a Σ_0^B formula, but by part (v) of Proposition 2, $\overline{V^0(2)}$ proves it is equivalent to a Σ_1^B formula δ'_{PowSeq_2}.

Definition 7. *The theory $V \oplus L$ has vocabulary $\mathcal{L}_A^2$ and axioms those of $V^0(2)$ and the Σ_1^B formula $\exists Y \leq 1 + \langle k, \langle n, n \rangle \rangle \delta'_{PowSeq_2}(n, k, X, Y)$.*

Note that the function $PowSeq_2$ is Σ_1^B definable in $V \oplus L$. Since $\overline{V^0(2)}$ is a conservative extension of $V^0(2)$, it follows that the theory

$$\mathcal{T} = V \oplus L + \overline{V^0(2)} \tag{6}$$

is a conservative extension of $V \oplus L$, and this allows us to reason in $\mathcal{T}$ to make inferences about the power of $V \oplus L$.

Section 9B in [CN10] presents a general method for defining a universal conservative extension $\overline{VC}$ (satisfying the properties of Proposition 2) of a theory VC over $\mathcal{L}_A^2$, where VC is defined in a manner similar to $V^0(2)$ and VTC^0; namely by adding an axiom to V^0 stating the existence of a complete function for the complexity class C. Although our new theory $V \oplus L$ could be construed to fit this pattern, for the purpose of defining $\overline{V \oplus L}$ it is more naturally construed to be the result of adding the modified axiom of Definition 7 where δ' is replaced by the original formula δ, and the base theory is $\overline{V^0(2)}$ rather than V^0. Note that the resulting theory is the same as the conservative extension $\mathcal{T}$ (6) of $V \oplus L$ mentioned above. It turns out that the development in Section 9B easily generalizes to the case in which the base theory is an extension V of V^0 rather than just V^0, and the construction of $\overline{VC}$ works so that Proposition 2 holds, where now the complexity class C is the AC^0 closure of $\{\mathcal{L}, F\}$, where $\mathcal{L}$ is the vocabulary of V and F is the function whose existence follows from the axiom. In the present case, this allows us to define $\overline{V \oplus L}$ satisfying Proposition 2, where now the complexity class C is the AC^0 closure of $\{Parity, PowSeq_2\}$, which is same as the AC^0 closure of $\{PowSeq_2\}$, namely $\oplus L$.

There is a technical requirement for the new function F introduced in the above development in Section 9B, namely that the so-called aggregate F^* of F must be definable and its properties provable in the new theory VC. The aggregate satisfies $\forall i < b(F^*(X))^{[i]} = F(X^{[i]})$ in the simple case that F has a single argument X. In the case of $PowSeq_2$, the aggregate $PowSeq_2^*$ takes a sequence of matrices of various sizes as input and outputs a sequence of sequences of powers of the matrices. See [Fon09] to see how to define $PowSeq_2^*$ in $V \oplus L$.

2.4   New Theory $V \# L$

As explained in the introduction, our theory $V \# L$ is associated with the class DET, which is the AC^0 closure of det (determinant of integer matrices). It is interesting that integer matrix powering is complete for DET, even when restricted to 0-1 matrices, and yet it is still in DET when integers are represented in binary (see [Fon09]). Here we assume integers are represented in binary, and the axiom for $V\#L$ asserts integer matrix powers exist.

To define integer matrix product we must define integer multiplication and iterated integer summation. Both of these problems are complete for the complexity class TC^0, so we define $V\#L$ as an extension of the theory VTC^0 (Section 9C of [CN10]). We work in the conservative extension $\overline{VTC^0}$ of VTC^0. Functions for multiplication and iterated sum over $\mathbb{N}$ are defined in [CN10], and it is not hard to modify them to work for $\mathbb{Z}$. Integers are represented by strings, and matrices by arrays of strings. The entry ij of matrix X is the string $X^{[i][j]}$ obtained by two applications of the function Row. Now integer matrix product is the TC^0 function $Prod_{\mathbb{Z}}(n, X, Y)$ defined analogously to formula (5) for $Prod_2$, and the graph of iterated matrix product is defined by the $\Sigma_0^B(\mathcal{L}_{FTC^0})$ formula $\delta_{PowSeq_{\mathbb{Z}}}(n, k, X, Y)$ analogous to δ_{PowSeq_2}. By Theorem 2 $\overline{VTC^0}$ proves $\delta_{PowSeq_{\mathbb{Z}}}$ is equivalent to a Σ_1^B formula $\delta'_{PowSeq_{\mathbb{Z}}}$, which we use in an axiom for $V\#L$.

Definition 8. *The theory $V\#L$ has vocabulary $\mathcal{L}_A^2$ and axioms those of VTC^0 and the Σ_1^B formula $\exists Y \leq t\, \delta'_{PowSeq_{\mathbb{Z}}}(n, k, X, Y)$ for a suitable term t.*

The methods explained after Definition 7 can be used to construct the universal conservative extension $\overline{V\#L}$ satisfying the conditions of Proposition 2 (see [Fon09]).

The following summarizes properties of our new theories.

Theorem 4. *Proposition 2 holds when $(FC, V, \overline{V})$ is either of the triples $(F\oplus L, V\oplus L, \overline{V\oplus L})$ or $(FDET, V\#L, \overline{V\#L})$.*

3   Interpreting LAP

Soltys' theory LAP [SK01, SC04] (Linear Algebra with Powering) is a three-sorted quantifier-free theory based on Gentzen style sequents. The three sorts are indices i, j, k (intended to range over $\mathbb{N}$), field elements a, b, c (intended to range over some fixed field or integral domain $\mathbb{F}$), and matrices A, B, C (intended to range over matrices with entries in $\mathbb{F}$). The vocabulary of LAP has symbols $0, 1, +, -, *, \mathrm{div}, \mathrm{rem}$ (each with a subscript 'index') for indices, and symbols $0, 1, +, -, *, ^{-1}, \mathrm{r}, \mathrm{c}, \mathrm{e}, \sum$ (each with a subscript 'field') for field elements, and relations $\leq_{\text{index}}, =_{\text{index}}, =_{\text{field}}, =_{\text{matrix}}$, and functions $\mathrm{cond}_{\text{index}}, \mathrm{cond}_{\text{field}}, \mathrm{p}$.

The intended interpretations of $0, 1, +, *, ^{-1}$, and $-_{\text{field}}$ are obvious. The other intended interpretations are as follows. The symbol $-_{\text{index}}$ is cutoff subtraction; $\mathrm{div}(i, j)$ and $\mathrm{rem}(i, j)$ are the quotient and remainder functions; $\mathrm{r}(A)$ and $\mathrm{c}(A)$ return the number of rows and columns in A; $\mathrm{e}(A, i, j)$ is the $(i, j)^{\text{th}}$ entry of matrix A; $\sum(A)$ is the sum of all the entries of A; and for α a formula, $\mathrm{cond}_{\text{index}}(\alpha, i, j)$ is i if α is true and j otherwise (similarly for $\mathrm{cond}_{\text{field}}(\alpha, a, b)$). The function $\mathrm{p}(n, A) = A^n$.

Terms and quantifier-free formulas are mostly constructed in the usual way, respecting types. We use n, m for index terms, t, u for field terms, T, U for matrix terms, and α, β for (quantifier-free) formulas. The four kinds of atomic formulas are $m \leq_{\text{index}} n$, $m =_{\text{index}} n$, $t =_{\text{field}} u$, and $T =_{\text{matrix}} U$. Formulas are built from atomic formulas using $\wedge, \vee, \neg$. There are restrictions on terms beginning with cond: If α is a formula with atomic subformulas all of the form $m \leq_{\text{index}} n$ and $m =_{\text{index}} n$, then $\text{cond}_{\text{index}}(\alpha, m', n')$ is a term of type index and $\text{cond}_{\text{field}}(\alpha, t, u)$ is a term of type field.

Terms of type matrix also include the constructed term $\lambda_{ij}\langle m, n, t \rangle$ (with the restriction that i and j are not free in m and n). It defines an $m \times n$ matrix with $(i, j)^{\text{th}}$ entry given by $t(i, j)$. Many matrix functions such as multiplication, addition, transpose, can be defined using λ terms, avoiding the need for separately defined function symbols. For example $A^t = \lambda_{ij}\langle c(A), r(A), e(A, j, i)\rangle$ defines the transpose of A .

Lines in an LAP proof are Gentzen-style sequents $\alpha_1, \ldots, \alpha_k \rightarrow \beta_1, \ldots, \beta_\ell$ with the usual meaning $\bigwedge \alpha_i \supset \bigvee \beta_j$. The logical axioms and rules are those of Gentzen's system LK (minus the quantifier rules). The nonlogical axioms are numbered **A1** through **A36**. There are two nonlogical rules: one for induction (9) and one for matrix equality (10).

3.1   Interpreting LAP into $V \oplus L$

Here we interpret the field $\mathbb{F}$ in the semantics of LAP to be $\mathbb{Z}_2$. We will describe the interpretation so that each formula α of LAP is translated into a formula α^σ of $\overline{V \oplus L}$. Here α^σ is in $\Sigma_0^B(\mathcal{L}_{F \oplus L})$, so by Theorem 4 and part (v) of Proposition 2, α^σ is equivalent to a Σ_1^B formula $(\alpha^\sigma)'$ of $V \oplus L$. The translation preserves provability (sequent theorems are translated to sequent theorems) and it also preserves truth in our intended standard models: $(\mathbb{N}, \mathbb{Z}_2, \text{matrices over } \mathbb{Z}_2)$ for LAP and $(\mathbb{N}, \text{finite subsets of } \mathbb{N})$ for $V \oplus L$.

Each index term m (resp. matrix term T) of LAP is translated to a number term m^σ (resp. string term T^σ) of $\overline{V \oplus L}$. Since we represent elements of $\mathbb{Z}_2$ by Boolean values in $V \oplus L$, each field term t is translated to a $\Sigma_0^B(\mathcal{L}_{F \oplus L})$ formula t^σ. These translations are described in detail in [Fon].

The translation of terms involving matrices is complicated. Every matrix of LAP has three attributes: number of rows, number of columns, and matrix entries (field elements). Each matrix term is translated to a string term which codes all of these. Thus an $a \times b$ matrix A is interpreted as a string A^σ such that $A^\sigma(0, \langle a, b \rangle)$ is true, and for all i, j with $1 \leq i \leq a$ and $1 \leq j \leq b$ and $e(A, i, j) = A_{ij} = 1$, the bit $A^\sigma(i, j)$ is true. All other bits of A^σ are false.

We will use a Σ_0^B formula $isMatrix_2(X)$, which asserts that the string X properly encodes a matrix as above. We allow the number of rows and/or columns to be 0, but any entry out of bounds is 0 (a false bit).

The $\overline{V \oplus L}$ functions $f_r(X)$ and $f_c(X)$ extract the number of rows and columns of the matrix coded by X, and are used to translate the LAP terms $r(T)$ and $c(T)$. These have defining equations

$$f_r(X) = z \leftrightarrow (\neg isMatrix_2(X) \wedge z = 0) \vee \left(isMatrix_2(X) \wedge \exists y \leq |X| \, X(0, \langle z, y \rangle)\right)$$
$$f_c(X) = z \leftrightarrow (\neg isMatrix_2(X) \wedge z = 0) \vee \left(isMatrix_2(X) \wedge \exists y \leq |X| \, X(0, \langle y, z \rangle)\right)$$

The matrix term $\lambda_{ij}\langle m, n, t \rangle$ is interpreted by the $\overline{V \oplus L}$ term $F_{t^\sigma}(m^\sigma, n^\sigma)$. Here $F_{t^\sigma}(x, y)$ is a string function, which has additional arguments corresponding to any free variables in t^σ other than the distinguished variables i, j (we interpret $i^\sigma = i$ and $j^\sigma = j$). The bit defining formula for F_{t^σ} is

$$F_{t^\sigma}(x, y)(b) \leftrightarrow b = \langle 0, \langle x, y \rangle \rangle \vee \exists i \leq x \exists j \leq y (i > 0 \wedge j > 0 \wedge b = \langle i, j \rangle \wedge t^\sigma(i, j)) \tag{7}$$

where we have written $t^\sigma(i, j)$ to display the distinguished variables i, j. Then $isMatrix_2(F_{t^\sigma}(m^\sigma, n^\sigma))$ is always true.

A matrix power term $p(m, T)$ is translated $F_p(m^\sigma, T^\sigma)$ where $F_p(i, X)$ is a suitable version of a matrix powering function in $\overline{V \oplus L}$. It is related to the straightforward function $Pow_2(n, i, X) = X^i$ defined from $PowSeq_2$ in the defining axiom for $V \oplus L$, but complicated by the fact that the string A^σ translating an LAP matrix A codes row and column numbers along with matrix entries. See [Fon] for the definition of $F_p(i, X)$.

Atomic formulas involving $=$ and $\leq$ are translated in the obvious way, except $T =_{\text{matrix}} U$ translates into the formula

$$(\text{r}(T) = \text{r}(U))^\sigma \wedge (\text{c}(T) = \text{c}(U))^\sigma \wedge \forall i, j \leq (|T^\sigma| + |U^\sigma|) \, (\text{e}(i, j, T) = \text{e}(i, j, U))^\sigma \tag{8}$$

which asserts that the row number, column number, and entries of T and U are the same.

For general formulas, the connectives $\wedge, \vee, \neg$ translate to themselves, and sequents translate to formulas in the usual way.

It remains to show that theorems of LAP translate into theorems of $\overline{V \oplus L}$ (and hence further translate into theorems of $V \oplus L$). The underlying logic used by LAP is Gentzen's propositional sequent system, in which all axioms are valid sequents and for each rule, the bottom sequent is a logical consequence of the top sequents. Since formulas of LAP are quantifier free, and the connectives $\wedge, \vee, \neg$ translate to themselves, it follows that logical axioms translate to valid formulas, and the translated rules preserve logical consequence.

In addition to the logical axioms, LAP has 36 (nonlogical) axioms A1,A2,...,A36 and two nonlogical rules. The translation of each axiom is a theorem of $\overline{V \oplus L}$. This is easy to show for every axiom, with the exception of A32, A33, and A36. The first two of these help define $\sum(A)$ to be the sum of all entries of the matrix A (see below), and the third gives the recursive step in the definition of powering: $p(n + 1, A) = p(n, A) \times A$. Correctness proofs for the axioms are given in [Fon].

Axiom A33 gives the inductive step in the definition of $\sum(A)$. It is

$$1 < \text{r}(A), 1 < \text{c}(A) \rightarrow \sum(A) = \text{e}(A, 1, 1) + \sum(R(A)) + \sum(S(A)) + \sum(M(A))$$

where

$R(A) := \lambda_{ij}\langle 1, \text{c}(A) - 1, \text{e}(A, 1, i + 1) \rangle$
$S(A) := \lambda_{ij}\langle \text{r}(A) - 1, 1, \text{e}(A, i + 1, 1) \rangle$
$M(A) := \lambda_{ij}\langle \text{r}(A) - 1, \text{c}(A) - 1, \text{e}(A, i + 1, j + 1) \rangle$

e	R
S	M

This breaks the matrix A into four parts as indicated on the right, and sums them separately (a similar recursive step is used in Berkowitz's algorithm for computing the characteristic polynomial of a matrix). Correctness of the translation of this axiom involves proving in $\overline{V \oplus L}$ that the parity of the matrix is the sum (mod 2) of the four parities. This is done by considering a submatrix of A consisting of the first i rows together with the first j entries of row $i + 1$, and arguing by induction first on i and then on j. The second induction step uses the lemma stating that if two strings differ by exactly one bit, then they have opposite parities.

The first nonlogical rule is induction:

$$\frac{\Gamma, \alpha(i) \to \alpha(i+1), \Delta}{\Gamma, \alpha(0) \to \alpha(n), \Delta} \tag{9}$$

By Theorem 4 and part (iv) of Proposition 2 it follows that $\overline{V \oplus L}$ proves that the translation of the bottom follows from the translation of the top, as required.

The second rule is the Matrix Equality Rule:

$$\frac{S_1 \ \ S_2 \ \ S_3}{\Gamma \to \Delta, T =_{\text{matrix}} U} \quad \text{where} \quad \begin{array}{ll} S_1: & \Gamma \to \Delta, e(T, i, j) = e(U, i, j) \\ S_2: & \Gamma \to \Delta, r(T) = r(U) \\ S_3: & \Gamma \to \Delta, c(T) = c(U) \end{array} \tag{10}$$

It is immediate that the translation of the bottom follows from the translation of the top by the way $T =_{\text{matrix}} U$ is translated (8).

It follows that

Theorem 5. *Theorems of LAP translate to theorems of $V \oplus L$.*

3.2 Interpreting LAP into $V \# L$

Now we interpret the 'field' $\mathbb{F}$ in the semantics of LAP to be the ring $\mathbb{Z}$ of integers. Of course $\mathbb{Z}$ is not a field, so we cannot translate the axiom A21 $a \neq 0 \to a * (a^{-1}) = 1$ for field inverses. However according to the footnote on page 283 of [SC04], this axiom is not used except in the proof of Lemma 3.1 and Theorem 4.1. The latter theorem states that LAP proves that the Cayley-Hamilton theorem implies the hard matrix identities (3). However it is not hard to see that Theorem 4.1 does hold for integral domains, because the field inverse axiom can be replaced by the cancellation law $a \neq 0, a * b = a * c \to b = c$. Hence LAP with this axiom replacing A21 does prove that the Cayley-Hamilton theorem implies the hard matrix identities. It follows from our interpretation of LAP into $V \# L$ that $V \# L$ proves that the Cayley-Hamilton Theorem implies the hard matrix identities over $\mathbb{Z}$ (see Theorem 2).

The interpretation of LAP into $V \# L$ is similar to the interpretation into $V \oplus L$. We first translate LAP into $\overline{V \# L}$, and then into $V \# L$, using Theorem 4 and part (v) of Proposition 2. As before, terms of type index are translated into number terms. However elements of type field (integers) are translated into strings representing the integers in binary. Binary (rather than unary) notation for integers is chosen to match the axiom for matrix powering in $V\#L$ (see the end of the first paragraph in Section 2.4). Elements of type matrix are translated into strings representing arrays of binary integers. We define string functions $+_{\mathbb{Z}}$ and $\times_{\mathbb{Z}}$ in $\overline{VTC^0}$ representing integer plus and times, and $F_{\sum}(X)$ for iterated integer sum. See [Fon] for more details.

4   Conclusion

There are two general motivations for associating theories with complexity classes. The first is that of reverse mathematics: determining the complexity of concepts needed to prove various theorems, and in particular whether the correctness of an algorithm can be proved with concepts of complexity comparable to that of the algorithm. The second motivation comes from propositional proof complexity: determining the proof lengths of various tautology families in various proof systems.

Both of these motivations are relevant to the earlier open questions of whether LAP can prove properties of the determinant such as the Cayley-Hamilton theorem, and hence the hard matrix identities (3). Now we can refine these questions and apply them to the two complexity classes $\oplus L$ and DET. It is possible that $V \oplus L$ and $V\#L$ could prove these properties for their associated rings $\mathbb{Z}_2$ and $\mathbb{Z}$ by methods not available to LAP. For example $V \oplus L$ might take advantage of the simplicity of $\mathbb{Z}_2$, or $V\#L$ might be able use the algorithmic strength of integer matrix powering (as opposed to matrix powering over an unspecified field) to prove correctness of the dynamic programming algorithm for the determinant in [MV97]. This algorithm is based on a combinatorial characterization of $det(A)$ using clow (closed walk) sequences in the edge-labeled graph specified by the matrix A.

Over the field $\mathbb{Z}_2$ the hard matrix identities translate naturally to a family of propositional tautologies (and over $\mathbb{Z}$ they translate into another family of tautologies). The original motivation for studying these identities was to give further examples of tautology families (like those in [BBP94]) that might be hard for the class of propositional proof systems known as Frege systems. There is a close connection between the strength of a theory needed to prove these identities (or any Σ_0^B formula) and the strength of the propositional proof system required for their propositional translations to have polynomial size proofs. (Chapter 10 of [CN10] gives propositional proof systems corresponding in this way to five of the theories in (2).)

In particular, the fact that the hard matrix identities are provable in VP shows that their propositional translations have polynomial size proofs in Extended Frege systems. If the identities were provable in VNC^1 then the tautologies would have polynomial size Frege proofs. If the identities turn out to be provable in one of our new theories, then the tautologies would have polynomial size proofs in proof systems (yet to be defined) of strength intermediate between Frege and Extended Frege systems.

Finally, we point out a lesser open problem. The main axiom for our new theory $V\#L$ asserts that integer matrix powers exist, where integers are represented in binary. As explained at the beginning of Section 2.4, integer matrix powering is complete for the complexity class DET even when restricted to 0-1 matrices, because the binary case is AC^0-reducible to the 0-1 case. It would be interesting to investigate whether the nontrivial reduction (see [Fon09]) can be proved correct in the base theory VTC^0, so that $V\#L$ could equivalently be axiomatized by the axiom for the 0-1 case rather than the binary case.

References

[All04]   Allender, E.: Arithmetic Circuits and Counting Complexity Classes. In: Krajicek, J. (ed.) Complexity of computations and proofs, pp. 33–72. Quaderni di Matematica (2004)

[AO96]   Allender, E., Ogihara, M.: Relationships Among PL, $\#L$, and the Determinant. RAIRO - Theoretical Informatics and Applications 30, 1–21 (1996)

[BBP94]   Bonet, M.L., Buss, S.R., Pitassi, T.: Are there hard examples for frege systems? In: Clote, P., Remmel, J.B. (eds.) Feasible Mathematics II, pp. 30–56. Birkhauser, Basel (1994)

[BDHM92]   Buntrock, G., Damm, C., Hertrampf, U., Meinel, C.: Structure and Importance of Logspace-MOD Class. Mathematical Systems Theory 25, 223–237 (1992)

[Ber84]   Berkowitz, S.J.: On computing the determinant in small parallel time using a small number of processors. Information Processing Letters 18, 147–150 (1984)

[BKR09]   Braverman, M., Kulkarni, R., Roy, S.: Space-Efficient Counting in Graphs on Surfaces. Computational Complexity 18, 601–649 (2009)

[CN10]   Cook, S., Nguyen, P.: Logical Foundations of Proof Complexity. Cambridge University Press, Cambridge (2010),
            `http://www.cs.toronto.edu/~sacook`

[Coo85]   Cook, S.A.: A Taxonomy of Problems with Fast Parallel Algorithms. Information and Control 64, 2–22 (1985)

[Fon]   Fontes, L.: Interpreting LAp into V $\oplus$ L and V#L,
            `http://www.cs.toronto.edu/~fontes`

[Fon09]   Fontes, L.: Formal Theories for Logspace Counting. Master's thesis, University of Toronto (2009), `http://arxiv.org/abs/1001.1960`

[Imm99]   Immerman, N.: Descriptive Complexity. Springer, Heidelberg (1999)

[MV97]   Mahajan, M., Vinay, V.: Determinant: Combinatorics, Algorithms, and Complexity. Chicago Journal of Theoretical Computer Science 5 (1997)

[SC04]   Soltys, M., Cook, S.A.: The Proof Complexity of Linear Algebra. Annals of Pure and Applied Logic 130, 277–323 (2004)

[SK01]   Soltys-Kulinicz, M.: The Complexity of Derivations of Matrix Identities. PhD thesis, University of Toronto (2001)

Energy and Mean-Payoff Games
with Imperfect Information*

Aldric Degorre[1], Laurent Doyen[2], Raffaella Gentilini[3],
Jean-François Raskin[1], and Szymon Toruńczyk[2]

[1] Université Libre de Bruxelles (ULB), Belgium
[2] LSV, ENS Cachan & CNRS, France
[3] University of Perugia, Italy

Abstract. We consider two-player games with imperfect information and quantitative objective. The game is played on a weighted graph with a state space partitioned into classes of indistinguishable states, giving players partial knowledge of the state. In an energy game, the weights represent resource consumption and the objective of the game is to maintain the sum of weights always nonnegative. In a mean-payoff game, the objective is to optimize the limit-average usage of the resource. We show that the problem of determining if an energy game with imperfect information with *fixed* initial credit has a winning strategy is decidable, while the question of the existence of *some* initial credit such that the game has a winning strategy is undecidable. This undecidability result carries over to mean-payoff games with imperfect information. On the positive side, using a simple restriction on the game graph (namely, that the weights are visible), we show that these problems become EXPTIME-complete.

1 Introduction

Mean-payoff games (MPG) are two-player games of infinite duration played on (directed) weighted graphs. Two players move a pebble along the edges of the graph. The player owning the current state chooses an outgoing edge to a successor state, resulting in an infinite path in the graph called a play. The objective of Player 1 is to maximize the average weight of the edges traversed in the play, while Player 2 tries to minimize this value (hence, the game is zero-sum).

The algorithmics of MPG has been studied since the end of the seventies [12,24] and still attracts a large interest for several reasons. First, the problem of deciding the winner in MPG has a remarkable status: it is known to be in the intersection of the classes NP and coNP [12], yet no polynomial algorithm is known for solving it. This problem

* This research was supported by the projects: (*i*) Quasimodo: "Quantitative System Properties in Model-Driven-Design of Embedded Systems", http://www.quasimodo.aau.dk, (*ii*) Gasics: "Games for Analysis and Synthesis of Interactive Computational Systems", http://www.ulb.ac.be/di/gasics/, (*iii*) Moves: "Fundamental Issues in Modeling, Verification and Evolution of Software", http://moves.ulb.ac.be, a PAI program funded by the Federal Belgian Government, and (*iv*) GNCS-10, project of the Italian National Group for Scientific Computing (GNCS-INdAM).

A. Dawar and H. Veith (Eds.): CSL 2010, LNCS 6247, pp. 260–274, 2010.

has tight connection (through polynomial-time reductions) with important theoretical questions about logics and games, such as the μ-calculus model-checking, and solving parity games [13,14,17,18]. Second, quantitative objectives in general are gaining interest in the specification and design of reactive systems [8,5,11], where the weights represent resource usage (e.g., energy consumption or network usage); the problem of controller synthesis with resource constraints requires the solution of quantitative games [20,6,1,3]. Finally, mean-payoff games are log-space equivalent to energy games (EG) where the objective of Player 1 is to maintain the sum of the weight (called the energy level) positive, given a fixed initial credit of energy. This result leads to faster pseudo-polynomial time algorithms for solving mean-payoff games [4,10].

The previous works on MPG and EG make the assumption that the game is of *perfect information*: the players have complete knowledge of the history of the play up to the current state. However, for applications in controller synthesis, it is often more appropriate that the players have partial knowledge (e.g., because the private variables of other players are not visible, or because the sensors have poor accuracy). In this paper, we consider mean-payoff and energy games with *imperfect information*. The game graph is given with a coloring of the state space that defines equivalence classes of indistinguishable states called observations [23,7], and the strategies are observation-based (i.e., they rely on the past sequence of observations rather than states). Interestingly, we show that observation-based strategies may require infinite memory for mean-payoff games, while finite memory is sufficient for energy games, in contrast with games of perfect information where memoryless strategies suffice in both cases.

We consider the following decision problems on a weighted colored graph: (i) for MPG, given a threshold ν, decide if Player 1 has an observation-based strategy to ensure a mean-payoff value at least ν; for EG, (ii) given a *fixed* initial credit, decide if Player 1 has an observation-based strategy to maintain the energy level always positive; and (iii) if the initial credit is *unknown*, decide if there exists an initial credit such that Player 1 wins. Our results can be summarized as follows.

First, we show that energy games with fixed initial credit are decidable. The argument is based on the existence of a well quasi order on the infinite set of play prefixes, which gives a bound on the depth of unraveling of the game graph needed to decide the problem. The size of this bound gives non-primitive recursive complexity to our procedure. Beside establishing the existence of finite-memory strategies for energy games, this result also contrasts with the case of energy games with finite duration where the objective of Player 1 is to stop the game after finitely many steps with a positive energy level. There, even the fixed initial credit problem for blind games[1] is undecidable, using the note after Corollary 3.8 in [19].

Next, we show that for games with imperfect information (and even for blind games), both energy games with unknown initial credit, and mean-payoff games are undecidable, using reductions from the halting problem for two-counter machines. For energy games, since the problem with fixed initial credit is decidable, it shows that the problem with unknown initial credit is r.e. but not co-r.e. For mean-payoff games, we show that the problem is neither r.e. nor co-r.e. using a reduction from the complement

---

[1] Blind games have a single observation (i.e., all states have the same color). They correspond to solving universality questions on nondeterministic automata.

of the halting problem for two-counter machines. This second reduction however requires at least two observations (or two colors) in the game. This is the first example of a quantitative objective for which games with imperfect information are undecidable while games with perfect information are decidable. Note that this cannot happen for qualitative Borel objectives, because games of imperfect information then reduce to games with perfect information [7]. As a corollary of our results, we obtain the undecidability of universality and language inclusion for quantitative languages defined by mean-payoff conditions [6].

Finally, we identify a class of MPG and EG for which the decision problems are EXPTIME-complete. This class corresponds to the assumption that the weights are visible to the players, a reasonable restriction in the context of controller synthesis (if each process can observe its own energy level). The algorithmic solution of this class of games relies on a generalization of the classical subset construction that maintains the knowledge of Player 1 along the play [23,7]. On the way, we also obtain that exponential memory is sufficient to win, and we recover the nice property that MPG and EG with imperfect information and visible weights are log-space equivalent.

2   Definitions

Games. A *weighted game with imperfect information* (or simply a *game*) is a tuple $G = \langle Q, q_0, \Sigma, \Delta, w, \text{Obs} \rangle$, where Q is a finite set of states, $q_0 \in Q$ is the initial state, Σ is a finite alphabet, $\Delta \subseteq Q \times \Sigma \times Q$ is a labeled total transition relation, i.e. for all $q \in Q$ and $\sigma \in \Sigma$, there exists $q' \in Q$ such that $(q, \sigma, q') \in \Delta$; $w : \Delta \to \mathbb{Z}$ is a weight function, and Obs $\subseteq 2^Q$ is a set of observations that partition the state space. For each state $q \in L$, we denote by $\text{obs}(q)$ the unique observation $o \in \text{Obs}$ such that $q \in o$; and for $s \subseteq L$ and $\sigma \in \Sigma$, we denote by $\text{post}_\sigma^G(s) = \{q' \in Q \mid \exists q \in s : (q, \sigma, q') \in \Delta\}$ the set of σ-successors of s.

We consider the following special cases of interest. We say that the weights are *visible* if $w(q_1, \sigma, q_2) = w(q_1', \sigma', q_2')$ for all transitions $(q_1, \sigma, q_2), (q_1', \sigma', q_2') \in \Delta$ such that $\text{obs}(q_1) = \text{obs}(q_1')$, $\text{obs}(q_2) = \text{obs}(q_2')$, and $\sigma = \sigma'$. A game with *perfect information* is such that $\text{Obs} = \{\{q\} \mid q \in Q\}$, i.e. each state is observable, and a *blind* game is such that $\text{Obs} = \{Q\}$, i.e. all states are indistinguishable. We omit the set Obs in the definition of games of perfect information.

Games are played in rounds in which Player 1 chooses an action $\sigma \in \Sigma$, and Player 2 chooses a σ-successor of the current state. [2] The first round starts in the initial state q_0.

A *play* in G is an infinite sequence $\pi = q_0 \sigma_0 q_1 \sigma_1 \ldots$ such that $(q_i, \sigma_i, q_{i+1}) \in \Delta$ for all $i \geq 0$. The prefix up to q_n of the play π is denoted by $\pi(n)$, and its last element is $\text{Last}(\pi(n)) = q_n$. The set of plays in G is denoted $\text{Plays}(G)$ and the set of corresponding prefixes is written as $\text{Prefs}(G)$. The *observation sequence* of π is the sequence $\text{obs}(\pi) = \text{obs}(q_0)\sigma_0\text{obs}(q_1)\sigma_1 \ldots$ and the (finite) observation sequence $\text{obs}(\pi(n))$ of $\pi(n)$ is the prefix up to $\text{obs}(q_n)$ of $\text{obs}(\pi)$.

---

[2] For games of perfect information, this definition is equivalent to the classical setting where the state space is partitioned into Player 1 states and Player 2 states, and the player owning the current state chooses the successor.

The *energy level* of a play prefix $\rho = q_0\sigma_0 q_1 \ldots q_n$ is $\mathsf{EL}(\rho) = \sum_{i=0}^{n-1} w(q_i, \sigma_i, q_{i+1})$, and the *mean-payoff value* of a play π is either $\overline{\mathsf{MP}}(\pi) = \limsup_{n\to\infty} \frac{1}{n} \cdot \mathsf{EL}(\pi(n))$ or $\underline{\mathsf{MP}}(\pi) = \liminf_{n\to\infty} \frac{1}{n} \cdot \mathsf{EL}(\pi(n))$.

Strategies. A *strategy* (for Player 1) in G is a function $\alpha : \mathsf{Prefs}(G) \to \Sigma$. A strategy α for Player 1 is called *observation-based* if for all prefixes $\rho, \rho' \in \mathsf{Prefs}(G)$, if $\mathsf{obs}(\rho) = \mathsf{obs}(\rho')$, then $\alpha(\rho) = \alpha(\rho')$, and it is called *memoryless* if $\alpha(\rho \cdot q) = \alpha(\rho' \cdot q)$ for all $\rho, \rho' \in (Q\Sigma)^*$ and $q \in Q$. Memoryless strategies are best viewed as functions $\alpha : Q \to \Sigma$. A prefix $\rho = q_0\sigma_0 q_1 \ldots q_n \in \mathsf{Prefs}(G)$ is *consistent* with α if $\sigma_i = \alpha(\pi(i))$ for all $i \geq 0$. An *outcome* of α is a play whose all prefixes are consistent with α.

A strategy α has *finite-memory* if it can be encoded by a deterministic Moore machine $\langle M, m_0, \alpha_u, \alpha_n \rangle$ where M is a finite set of states (the memory of the strategy), $m_0 \in M$ is the initial state, $\alpha_u : M \times Q \to M$ is an update function, and $\alpha_n : M \to \Sigma$ is a next-action function. In state $m \in M$, the strategy plays the action $\alpha_n(m)$, and when Player 2 chooses the next state q of the game, the internal state is updated to $\alpha_u(m, q)$. Formally, the strategy α defined by $\langle M, m_0, \alpha_u, \alpha_n \rangle$ is such that $\alpha(\rho) = \alpha_n(\hat{\alpha}_u(m_0, q_0 \ldots q_n))$ for all $\rho = q_0\sigma_0 q_1 \ldots q_n \in \mathsf{Prefs}(G)$, where $\hat{\alpha}_u$ extends α_u to sequences of states as follows: $\hat{\alpha}_u(m, \epsilon) = m$ and $\hat{\alpha}_u(m, q_0 \ldots q_n) = \hat{\alpha}_u(\alpha_u(m, q_0), q_1 \ldots q_n)$ for all $m \in M$ and $q_1, \ldots, q_n \in Q$.

Objectives. An *objective* for G is a set ϕ of infinite sequences of states and actions, that is, $\phi \subseteq (Q \times \Sigma)^\omega$. A strategy α of Player 1 is winning for ϕ if $\pi \in \phi$ for all outcomes π of α. We consider the following objectives.

- *Safety objectives.* Given a set $\mathcal{T} \subseteq Q$ of safe states, the safety objective $\mathsf{Safe}_G(\mathcal{T}) = \{q_0\sigma_0 q_1\sigma_1 \ldots \in \mathsf{Plays}(G) \mid \forall n \geq 0 : q_n \in \mathcal{T}\}$ requires that only states in $\mathcal{T}$ be visited.
- *Energy objectives.* Given an initial credit $c_0 \in \mathbb{N}$, the energy objective $\mathsf{PosEnergy}_G(c_0) = \{\pi \in \mathsf{Plays}(G) \mid \forall n \geq 0 : c_0 + \mathsf{EL}(\pi(n)) \geq 0\}$ requires that the energy level be always positive.
- *Mean-payoff objectives.* Given a threshold $\nu \in \mathbb{Q}$, and $\sim \in \{>, \geq\}$, the mean-payoff objectives $\mathsf{MeanPayoffSup}_G^\sim(\nu) = \{\pi \in \mathsf{Plays}(G) \mid \overline{\mathsf{MP}}(\pi) \sim \nu\}$ and $\mathsf{MeanPayoffInf}_G^\sim(\nu) = \{\pi \in \mathsf{Plays}(G) \mid \underline{\mathsf{MP}}(\pi) \sim \nu\}$ require that the mean-payoff value be at least ν (resp., greater than ν).

When the game G is clear form the context, we omit the subscript in objective names. Mean-payoff objectives defined with $\sim \in \{<, \leq\}$ are obtained by duality since $\limsup_{i\to\infty} u_i = -\liminf_{i\to\infty} -u_i$.

We consider the following decision problems:

- The *fixed initial credit problem* asks, given an energy game G and an initial credit c_0, to decide whether there exists a winning observation-based strategy for the objective $\mathsf{PosEnergy}(c_0)$.
- The *unknown initial credit problem* asks, given an energy game G, to decide whether there exist an initial credit c_0 and a winning observation-based strategy for the objective $\mathsf{PosEnergy}(c_0)$.

– The *threshold problem* asks, given a mean-payoff game G, a threshold $\nu \in \mathbb{Q}$, and $\sim \in \{>, \geq\}$, to decide whether there exists a winning observation-based strategy for one of the mean-payoff objective $\mathsf{MeanPayoffSup}^{\sim}_G(\nu)$ or $\mathsf{MeanPayoffInf}^{\sim}_G(\nu)$.

Remark 1. The objectives $\mathsf{MeanPayoffSup}^{\sim}(\nu)$ and $\mathsf{MeanPayoffInf}^{\sim}(\nu)$ are equivalent for games with perfect information: Player 1 has a strategy to win according to $\mathsf{MeanPayoffSup}^{\sim}(\nu)$ if and only if he has a strategy to win according to $\mathsf{MeanPayoffInf}^{\sim}(\nu)$. However, the definitions are not equivalent for games with imperfect information.

As an example, consider the blind game of Fig. 1. All states are indistinguishable, and an initial nondeterministic choice determines the state q_1 or q_1' in which the game will loop forever.

We claim that Player 1 has an observation-based winning strategy for the objective $\mathsf{MeanPayoffSup}^{\geq}(0)$, but not for $\mathsf{MeanPayoffInf}^{\geq}(0)$. Note that in blind games, observation-based strategies can be viewed as infinite words. A winning strategy for the limsup version consists in playing sequences of a's and b's of increasing length in order to ensure a mean-payoff value $\overline{\mathsf{MP}}$ equal to 0 in both states q_1 and q_1'. For example, playing sequences of a's and b's such that the length of the i-th sequence is i times the length of the prefix played so far. This ensures that in q_1 and q_1', for all $i > 0$ there are infinitely many positions such that the average of the weights is greater than $-\frac{1}{i}$, showing that the limsup is 0 in all outcomes.

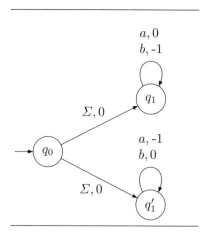

We show that for every word $w \in \{a,b\}^{\omega}$, the mean-payoff value according to $\underline{\mathsf{MP}}$ is at most $-\frac{1}{2}$. Let n_i and m_i be the numbers of a's and b's in the prefix of length i of w. Either $n_i \leq m_i$ for infinitely many i's, or $n_i \geq m_i$ for infinitely many i's. In the first case, the average of the weights (in state q_1) is infinitely often at most $-\frac{1}{2}$. The same holds in the second case using state q_1'. Therefore the lim inf of the weight averages is at most $-\frac{1}{2}$, and Player 1 has no winning strategy for the mean-payoff objective defined using lim inf and threshold 0.

Fig. 1. A blind mean-payoff game

Remark 2. Note that infinite memory is required to achieve mean-payoff value 0 (according to $\overline{\mathsf{MP}}$) in the game of Fig. 1. Indeed, for all finite-memory strategies (which can be viewed as ultimately periodic words), the mean-payoff value of an outcome is $\min\{-\frac{n}{n+m}, -\frac{m}{n+m}\} \leq -\frac{1}{2}$ where n and m are the numbers of a's and b's in the cycle of the strategy.

Note also that for finite-memory strategies, the mean-payoff objectives defined using $\overline{\mathsf{MP}}$ and $\underline{\mathsf{MP}}$ lead to equivalent games (see Theorem 6).

3   Energy Games with Imperfect Information

We present an algorithm for solving the fixed initial credit problem, and we show that the unknown initial credit problem is undecidable.

3.1   Fixed Initial Credit

Fix an energy game $G = \langle Q, q_0, \Sigma, \Delta, w, \text{Obs} \rangle$ and an initial credit $c_0 \in \mathbb{N}$. To solve this energy game, we construct an equivalent safety game of perfect information using the following definitions.

Let $\mathcal{F}$ be the set of functions $f : Q \to \mathbb{Z} \cup \{\bot\}$. The *support* of f is $\text{supp}(f) = \{q \in Q \mid f(q) \neq \bot\}$. A function $f \in \mathcal{F}$ stores the possible current states of the game G together with their energy level. We say that a function f is *nonnegative* if $f(q) \geq 0$ for all $q \in \text{supp}(f)$. Initially, we set $f_{c_0}(q_0) = c_0$ and $f_{c_0}(q) = \bot$ for all $q \neq q_0$. The set $\mathcal{F}$ is ordered by the relation $\preceq$ such that $f_1 \preceq f_2$ if $\text{supp}(f_1) = \text{supp}(f_2)$ and $f_1(q) \leq f_2(q)$ for all $q \in \text{supp}(f_1)$.

For $\sigma \in \Sigma$, we say that $f_2 \in \mathcal{F}$ is a σ-successor of $f_1 \in \mathcal{F}$ if there exists an observation $o \in \text{Obs}$ such that $\text{supp}(f_2) = \text{post}_\sigma^G(\text{supp}(f_1)) \cap o$ and $f_2(q) = \min\{f_1(q') + w(q', \sigma, q) \mid q' \in \text{supp}(f_1) \wedge (q', \sigma, q) \in \Delta\}$ for all $q \in \text{supp}(f_2)$. Given a sequence $x = f_0 \sigma_0 f_1 \sigma_1 \ldots f_n$, let $f_x = f_n$ be the last function in x. Define the safety game $H = \langle Q^H, f_{c_0}, \Sigma, \Delta^H \rangle$ where Q^H is the smallest subset of $(\mathcal{F} \cdot \Sigma)^* \cdot \mathcal{F}$ such that

1. $f_{c_0} \in Q^H$, and
2. for each sequence $x \in Q^H$, if (i) f_x is nonnegative, and (ii) there is no strict prefix y of x such that $f_y \preceq f_x$, then $x \cdot \sigma \cdot f_2 \in Q^H$ for all σ-successors f_2 of f_x.

The transition relation Δ^H contains the corresponding triples $(x, \sigma, x \cdot \sigma \cdot f_2)$, and the game is made total by adding self-loops (x, σ, x) to sequences x without outgoing transitions. We call such sequences the *leaves* of H. Note that the game H is acyclic, except for the self-loops on the leaves.

By Dickson's lemma [9], the relation $\preceq$ on nonnegative functions is a *well quasi order*, i.e., for all infinite sequences $f_1 f_2 \ldots$ of nonnegative functions, there exists k, l such that $k < l$ and $f_k \preceq f_l$. Hence the state space Q^H is finite.

Lemma 1. *The game H has a finite state space.*

Proof. By contradiction, assume that Q^H is infinite. By König's lemma, since the transition relation of H is finitely branching, there exists an infinite sequence $f_0 \sigma_0 f_1 \sigma_1 \ldots$ such that all its prefixes are in Q^H, and thus all f_i's are nonnegative and it is never the case that $f_k \preceq f_l$ for $k < l$. This is in contradiction with the fact that $\preceq$ is a well quasi order on nonnegative functions.   □

Define the set of safe states in H as $\mathcal{T} = \{x \in Q^H \mid f_x \text{ is nonnegative}\}$. Intuitively, a winning strategy in the safety game H can be extended to an observation-based winning strategy in the energy game G because whenever a leaf of H is reached, there exists a $\preceq$-smaller ancestor that Player 1 can use to go on in G using the strategy played from the ancestor in H. The correctness argument is based on the fact that if Player 1 is winning from state f in H, then he is also winning from all $f' \succeq f$.

Lemma 2. *Let G be an energy game with imperfect information, and let $c_0 \in \mathbb{N}$ be an initial credit. There exists a winning observation-based strategy in G for the objective $\mathsf{PosEnergy}(c_0)$ if and only if there exists a winning strategy in H for the objective $\mathsf{Safe}(\mathcal{T})$.*

Proof. First, assume that α^o is a winning observation-based strategy in the game G for $\mathsf{PosEnergy}(c_0)$. We construct a function $\alpha : (\mathcal{F} \cdot \Sigma)^* \cdot \mathcal{F} \to \Sigma$ as follows. Given $\rho^H = f_0 \sigma_0 f_1 \ldots f_n \in (\mathcal{F} \cdot \Sigma)^* \cdot \mathcal{F}$ such that $f_0 = f_{c_0}$ and f_{i+1} is a σ_i-successor of f_i for all $i \geq 0$, define the observation sequence $\mathsf{obs}(\rho^H) = o_0 \sigma_0 o_1 \ldots o_n$ such that $\mathsf{supp}(f_i) \subseteq o_i$ for all $i \geq 0$. It is easy to see that $o_0 = \mathsf{obs}(q_0)$ and that this sequence exists and is unique.

We define $\alpha(\rho^H) = \alpha^o(\rho)$, where $\rho \in \mathsf{Prefs}(G)$ is such that $\mathsf{obs}(\rho) = \mathsf{obs}(\rho^H)$. The function α is well defined because such a prefix ρ always exists, and α^o is observation-based.

Consider an infinite sequence $\pi^H = f_0 \sigma_0 f_1 \ldots$ consistent with α and such that $f_0 = f_{c_0}$ and f_{i+1} is a σ_i-successor of f_i for all $i \geq 0$. It is easy to show by induction on n that for all $q_n \in \mathsf{supp}(f_n)$, there exists a prefix $\rho = q_0 \sigma_0 q_1 \ldots q_n \in \mathsf{Prefs}(G)$ consistent with α^o such that $\mathsf{obs}(\rho) = \mathsf{obs}(\pi^H(n))$, and $c_0 + \mathsf{EL}(\rho) = f_n(q_n)$ for all such prefixes ρ. Since $c_0 + \mathsf{EL}(\rho) \geq 0$ for all prefixes ρ of all outcomes of α^o in G, the previous properties imply that all functions f_i are nonnegative. since $\preceq$ is a well quasi order in nonnegative functions, there exist two positions k, l such that $k < l$ and $f_k \preceq f_l$.

Hence, if we define the memoryless strategy α^H in H such that $\alpha^H(\rho^H) = \alpha(\mathsf{Last}(\rho^H))$ for all prefixes $\rho^H \in \mathsf{Prefs}(H)$ that contain no leaf of H, then α^H is winning for the objective $\mathsf{Safe}(\mathcal{T})$ in H.

Second, assume that α^H is a winning strategy in the safety game H. We can assume that α^H is memoryless because memoryless strategies suffice for safety objectives. We construct a winning observation-based strategy α^o in G as follows. Given $\rho = q_0 \sigma_0 q_1 \ldots q_n \in \mathsf{Prefs}(G)$, let $\rho^H = f_0 \sigma_0 f_1 \ldots f_n$ such that $f_0 = f_{c_0}$ and f_{i+1} is a σ_i-successor of f_i with $q_{i+1} \in \mathsf{supp}(f_{i+1})$ for all $i \geq 0$. The *stack-prefix* $[\rho^H]$ of ρ^H is obtained as follows. We push the elements of ρ^H onto a stack, and whenever we push a function f_l such that there exists f_k in the stack with $k < l$ and $f_k \preceq f_l$, we remove from the stack the sequence $\sigma_k f_{k+1} \ldots f_l$, and we replace the suffix of ρ^H after f_l by the sequence $\sigma_l f'_{l+1} \sigma_{l+1} \ldots f'_n$ such that $\mathsf{supp}(f'_{j+1}) = \mathsf{supp}(f_{j+1})$ and (assuming $f'_l = f_k$) f'_{j+1} is a σ_j-successor of f'_j for all $l \leq j < n$. Note that $f'_j \preceq f_j$ for all $l \leq j < n$. The sequence on the stack at the end of this process is the stack-prefix $[\rho^H]$ of ρ^H.

It is easy to show by induction that if ρ is consistent with α^o, then $[\rho^H]$ is consistent with α^H, that $c_0 + \mathsf{EL}(\rho) \geq f_{[\rho^H]}(q_n)$, and that if $\mathsf{obs}(\rho_2) = \mathsf{obs}(\rho)$, then $[\rho_2^H] = [\rho^H]$. Therefore, the strategy α^o in G such that $\alpha^o(\rho) = \alpha^H([\rho^H])$ is observation-based.

Towards a contradiction, assume that α^o is not winning for $\mathsf{PosEnergy}(c_0)$ in G. Then, there exists a finite prefix ρ of an outcome of α^o in G such that $c_0 + \mathsf{EL}(\rho) < 0$ (take the shortest such $\rho = q_0 \sigma_0 q_1 \ldots q_n$). Let $[\rho^H]$ be the stack-prefix obtained by the above construction. It is easy to see that $[\rho^H] = f_0 \sigma_0 f_1 \ldots f_n$ occurs in some outcome of α^H, and therefore $f_n(q_n) \leq c_0 + \mathsf{EL}(\rho) < 0$, i.e., $[\rho^H] \notin \mathcal{T}$ is not a safe state, contradicting that α^H is a winning strategy in the safety game H. $\square$

By Lemma 2, we get the decidability of the fixed initial credit problem, with non-primitive recursive upper bound since the size of the safety game H is bounded by the Ackermann function [22].

Theorem 1. *The fixed initial credit problem is decidable.*

Our algorithm for solving the initial credit problem has tight connections with the techniques used in the theory of well-structured transition systems [16]. In particular, the (finite) tree of reachable markings is used to decide the existence of an infinite execution in Petri nets from a fixed initial marking. This problem can be reduced to the initial credit problem (with initial credit 0) as follows. Given a Petri net, construct a blind energy game in which Player 1 wins only by playing an infinite sequence of transitions of the Petri net. The game initially chooses a place of the Petri to monitor, and gives weight equal to the value of the initial marking in the monitored place. The effect of each transition on the monitored place is encoded by two edges in the game with weights corresponding to a decrement for the input tokens, followed by an increment for the output tokens in the place. As the game is blind, Player 1 does not know which place is monitored, and therefore has to provide an infinite sequence of firable transitions (never letting the energy level go below zero in any place), ensuring that it corresponds to an infinite execution in the Petri net. This reduction gives EXPSPACE lower bound to the initial credit problem [15]. We do not know of any useful reduction of the initial credit problem to a decidable Petri net problem.

Note that from the proof of Lemma 2, it also follows that finite-memory strategies are sufficient to win energy games.

Corollary 1. *Finite-memory strategies are sufficient to win energy games with imperfect information.*

3.2   Unknown Initial Credit

We show that the unknown initial credit problem is undecidable by reducing to it the halting problem for deterministic 2-counter Minsky machines. A 2-*counter machine* M consists of a finite set of control states Q, an initial state $q_I \in Q$, a final state $q_F \in Q$, a set C of counters ($|C| = 2$) and a finite set δ_M of instructions manipulating two integer-valued counters. Instructions are of the form

$q: c := c + 1$ **goto** q'
$q:$ **if** $c = 0$ **then goto** q' **else** $c := c - 1$ **goto** q''.

Formally, instructions are tuples (q, α, c, q') where $q, q' \in Q$ are source and target states respectively, the action $\alpha \in \{inc, dec, 0?\}$ applies to the counter $c \in C$. We assume that M is deterministic: for every state $q \in Q$, either there is exactly one instruction $(q, \alpha, \cdot, \cdot) \in \delta_M$ and $\alpha = inc$, or there are two instructions $(q, dec, c, \cdot), (q, 0?, c, \cdot) \in \delta_M$.

A *configuration* of M is a pair (q, v) where $q \in Q$ and $v : C \to \mathbb{N}$ is a valuation of the counters. An *accepting run* of M is a finite sequence $\pi = (q_0, v_0)\delta_0(q_1, v_1)\delta_1 \ldots \delta_{n-1}(q_n, v_n)$ where $\delta_i = (q_i, \alpha_i, c_i, q_{i+1}) \in \delta_M$ are instructions and (q_i, v_i) are configurations of M such that $q_0 = q_I$, $v_0(c) = 0$ for all $c \in C$, $q_n = q_F$, and for

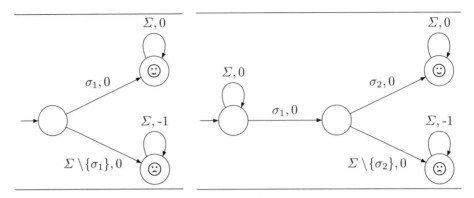

Fig. 2. Gadget to check that the first symbol is $\sigma_1 \in \Sigma$

Fig. 3. Gadget to check that every symbol $\sigma_1 \in \Sigma$ is followed by $\sigma_2 \in \Sigma$

all $0 \leq i < n$, we have $v_{i+1}(c) = v_i(c)$ for $c \neq c_i$, and (a) if $\alpha = inc$, then $v_{i+1}(c_i) = v_i(c_i) + 1$ (b) if $\alpha = dec$, then $v_i(c_i) \neq 0$ and $v_{i+1}(c_i) = v_i(c_i) - 1$, and (c) if $\alpha = 0$?, then $v_{i+1}(c_i) = v_i(c_i) = 0$. The corresponding *run trace* of π is the sequence of instructions $\bar{\pi} = \delta_0 \delta_1 \ldots \delta_{n-1}$.

The *halting problem* is to decide, given a 2-counter machine M, whether M has an accepting run. This problem is undecidable [21].

Theorem 2. *The unknown initial credit problem for energy games with imperfect information is undecidable, even for blind games.*

Proof. Given a (deterministic) 2-counter machine M, we construct a blind energy game, G_M, such that M has an accepting run if and only if there exists an initial credit $c_0 \in \mathbb{N}$ such that Player 1 has a winning strategy in G_M for PosEnergy(c_0). In particular, a strategy that plays a sequence $\#\bar{\pi}_0 \#\bar{\pi}_1 \ldots$ (where $\bar{\pi}_i$'s are run traces of M) is winning in G_M if and only if all but finitely many π_i's are accepting runs of M.

The alphabet of G_M is $\Sigma = \delta_M \cup \{\#\}$. The game G_M consists of an initial non-deterministic choice between several gadgets described below. Each gadget checks one property of the sequence of actions played in order to ensure that a trace of an accepting run in M is eventually played. Since the game is blind, it is not possible to see which gadget is executed, and therefore the strategy has to fulfill all properties simultaneously.

The gadget in Fig. 2 with $\sigma_1 = \#$ checks that the first symbol is a $\#$. If the first symbol is not $\#$, then the energy level drops below 0 no matter the initial credit. The gadget in Fig. 3 checks that a certain symbol σ_1 is always followed by a symbol σ_2, and it is used to ensure that $\#$ is followed by an instruction $(q_I, \cdot, \cdot, \cdot)$, and that every instruction $(q, \cdot, \cdot, q')$ is followed by an instruction $(q', \cdot, \cdot, q'')$, or by $\#$ if $q' = q_F$. The gadget in Fig. 4 ensures that $\#$ is played infinitely often. Otherwise, the gadget can guess the last $\#$ and jump to the middle state where no initial credit would allow to survive.

Finally, we use the gadget in Fig. 5 to check that the tests on counter c are correctly executed. It can accumulate in the energy level the increments and decrements of a counter c between the start of a run (i.e., when $\#$ occurs) and a zero test on c. A *positive*

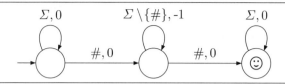

Fig. 4. Gadget to check that $\#$ is played infinitely often

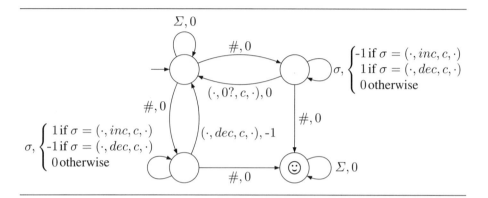

Fig. 5. Gadget to check the zero tests on counter c (assuming σ ranges over $\Sigma \setminus \{\#\}$)

cheat occurs when $(\cdot, 0?, c, \cdot)$ is played while the counter c has positive value. Likewise, a *negative cheat* occurs when $(\cdot, dec, c, \cdot)$ is played while the counter c has value 0. On reading the symbol $\#$, the gadget can guess that there will be a positive or negative cheat by respectively moving to the upper or lower state. In the upper state, the energy level simulates the operations on the counter c with opposite effect, i.e. accumulating the opposite of its value changes. When a positive cheat occurs, the gadget returns to the initial state, thus decrementing the energy level. The lower state of the gadget is symmetric. A negative cheat costs one unit of energy. Note that the gadget has to go back to its initial state before the next $\#$, as otherwise Player 1 wins.

The game G_M has such gadgets for each counter. Thus, a strategy in G_M which cheats infinitely often on a counter would not survive no matter the value of the initial credit.

The correctness of this construction is established as follows. First, assume that M has an accepting run π with trace $\bar{\pi}$. Then, the strategy playing $(\#\bar{\pi})^\omega$ is winning for PosEnergy($|\bar{\pi}|$) because an initial credit $|\bar{\pi}|$ is sufficient to survive in the "∞-many $\#$" gadget of Fig. 4, as well as in the zero-test gadget of Fig. 5 because all zero tests are correct in π and the counter values are bounded by $|\bar{\pi}|$. Second, if there exists a winning strategy in G_M with some finite initial credit, then the sequence played by this strategy can be decomposed into run traces separated by $\#$, and since the strategy survived in the gadget of Fig. 5, there must be a point where all run traces played correspond to faithful simulation of M with respect to counter values, thus M has an accepting run. $\qquad\square$

4   Mean-Payoff Games with Imperfect Information

In this section we consider games with imperfect information and mean-payoff objective. First, we recall that winning strategies may require infinite memory (see Remark 1 and Remark 2).

Theorem 3. *Finite-memory strategies are not sufficient in general to win mean-payoff games with imperfect information.*

We show that mean-payoff games with imperfect information are undecidable, which also shows that language inclusion and universality are undecidable for quantitative languages defined by mean-payoff functions [6].

Theorem 4. *The threshold problem for mean-payoff games with imperfect information and objective* MeanPayoffSup$^>$(0) *(or* MeanPayoffInf$^>$(0)) *is undecidable (it is not co-r.e.), even for blind games.*

Proof. We give a reduction from the halting problem for two-counter machines which is similar to the proof of Theorem 2. We adapt the gadgets as follows. We increment by 1 the weights of the gadgets in Fig. 2, 3 and 4. This way, faithful simulations of the machine get mean-payoff value 1, while wrong simulations get value 0. In the gadget of Fig. 5, the symbol $\#$ gets always weight 1, thus rewarding finite run traces. The rest of the gadget is left unchanged.

We claim that Player 1 has a winning strategy if and only if the machine M halts. Indeed, if the machine halts and π is the accepting run, then playing $(\#\pi)^\omega$ is a winning strategy for Player 1: there is no cheat, so the zero-test gadget either stays in the initial state and performs an increment whenever it sees a $\#$ (i.e., every $|\pi|$ steps), or it tries to detect a cheat and would end up in the sink state. Therefore, this gadget gives a mean-payoff value at least $1/|\pi|$. The modified gadgets in Fig. 2, 3 and 4 also cannot punish Player 1 in any way and thus they give mean-payoff value 1.

To prove the other direction, assume that the machine M does not halt. The sequence played by Player 1 can be decomposed as a word $w = \#\bar{\pi}_1\#\bar{\pi}_2\#\bar{\pi}_3\ldots$ If one of the words $\bar{\pi}_i$ is wrong with respect to the state transitions of the machine, or if there are finitely many $\#$'s, then Player 2 uses one of the modified gadgets in Fig. 2, 3 or 4 to ensure mean-payoff value 0. Thus, we can assume that each word $\bar{\pi}_i$ is finite and respects the state transitions. Since M does not halt, in each of the sequences π_i there must be a cheat, so Player 2 can guess it and choose a run in the gadget of Fig. 5 with negative payoff that cancels out the positive payoff for $\#$. Therefore, the outcome of the game cannot have positive mean-payoff value.   □

The proof of Theorem 4 shows that the threshold problem for mean-payoff games is not co-r.e. We show that the problem is neither r.e. using a reduction from the complement of the halting problem for deterministic two-counter machines. However, the reduction requires at least two observations in the game, and it crucially relies on using non-strict inequality in the objective and on the mean-payoff value being defined using lim sup. The cases of lim inf and blind games remain open.

Theorem 5. *The threshold problem for mean-payoff games with imperfect information and objective* MeanPayoffSup$^\geq$(0) *is undecidable (it is not r.e.).*

Proof sketch: We prove this theorem by using another reduction from two-counter machines. The main difference is that Player 1 wins in the constructed game if and only if the machine *does not* halt. Also, in contrary to the previous constructions, this one requires two different observations for Player 1.

We show that the result of Theorem 4 does not depend on the fact that winning observation-based strategies may require infinite memory: the question of the existence of a finite-memory winning strategy in MPG is also undecidable (but obviously r.e.).

Theorem 6. *Let G be a weighted game with imperfect information. A finite-memory strategy α is winning in G for* MeanPayoffSup$^{\geq}(0)$ *(and also for* MeanPayoffInf$^{\geq}(0)$*) if and only if there exists $c_0 \in \mathbb{N}$ such that α is winning in G for* PosEnergy(c_0).

Proof. ($\Leftarrow$) Let α be a finite-memory winning strategy in G defined by the Moore machine $\langle M, m_0, \alpha_u, \alpha_n \rangle$. Consider the graph G_α obtained as the product of G with M, where $(\langle m, q \rangle, \sigma, \langle m', q' \rangle)$ is a transition in G_α if $m' = \alpha_u(m, q)$, $\sigma = \alpha_n(m')$, and (q, σ, q') is a transition in G. All infinite paths in G_α from $\langle m_0, q_0 \rangle$ are outcomes of α in G (if we project out the m-component) and therefore all cycles in G_α reachable from $\langle m_0, q_0 \rangle$ have nonnegative sum of weights. Therefore, this ensures that an initial credit $c_0 = |M| \cdot |Q| \cdot W$ sufficient to win in G for PosEnergy(c_0), where W is the largest weight in G (in absolute value).

($\Rightarrow$) Let α be a finite-memory winning strategy in G for PosEnergy(c_0). Then $c_0 + \mathsf{EL}(\pi(n)) \geq 0$ for all outcomes π of α and all $n \geq 0$. This immediately entails that $\overline{\mathsf{MP}}(\pi) \geq 0$ (and $\underline{\mathsf{MP}}(\pi) \geq 0$). $\qquad\square$

Corollary 2. *The problem of determining if there exists a finite-memory winning strategy in mean-payoff games with imperfect information is undecidable (it is not co-r.e.), even for blind games.*

5 Games with Visible Weights

In this section, we show that energy games with visible weights are decidable using a reduction to energy games of perfect information. The reduction is based on the subset construction used to solve imperfect information games with ω-regular objectives [7]. Intuitively, the subset construction monitors the knowledge of player 1 about the current state of the play. Because weights are visible, this knowledge is sufficient to define a weight function on the subset construction.

Given a game $G = \langle Q, q_0, \Sigma, \Delta, w, \mathsf{Obs} \rangle$ with visible weights, the *weighted subset construction* of G is the game structure $G^{\mathsf{K}} = \langle Q^{\mathsf{K}}, q_0^{\mathsf{K}}, \Sigma, \Delta^{\mathsf{K}}, w^{\mathsf{K}} \rangle$ with perfect information, such that:

- $Q^{\mathsf{K}} = \{s \subseteq Q \mid s \neq \emptyset \wedge \exists o \in \mathsf{Obs} : s \subseteq o\}$;
- $q_0^{\mathsf{K}} = \{q_0\}$;
- Δ^{K} contains the transitions (s_1, σ, s_2) such that $s_2 = \mathsf{post}_\sigma^G(s_1) \cap o \neq \emptyset$ for some observation $o \in \mathsf{Obs}$;

- w^K is such that $w^K(s_1, \sigma, s_2) = w(q_1, \sigma, q_2)$ for all (s_1, σ, s_2) $\in \Delta^K$ and $(q_1, \sigma, q_2) \in \Delta$ such that $q_1 \in s_1$ and $q_2 \in s_2$. This definition is meaningful because weights are visible.

The correctness of the weighted subset construction for solving energy games is justified by the following lemma.

Lemma 3. *Let G be an energy game with imperfect information and visible weights, and let $c_0 \in \mathbb{N}$ be an initial credit. There exists a winning observation-based strategy in G for the objective $\mathsf{PosEnergy}(c_0)$ if and only if there exists a winning strategy in G^K for the objective $\mathsf{PosEnergy}(c_0)$.*

It follows from Lemma 3 that energy games with visible weights can be solved in EX-PTIME, using a pseudo-polynomial algorithm for energy games of perfect information [4,10]. Such an algorithm is polynomial in the size of the game and in the value of largest weight. The EXPTIME upper bound follows from the fact that the size of G^K is exponential in the size of G, and the largest weight in G^K and G coincide. A matching lower bound can be obtained using a reduction from safety games. Deciding the winner of a safety game with imperfect information is EXPTIME-hard, even if the set of safe sates is a union of observations [2]. The reduction to energy games assigns weight 0 to all transitions, and adds self-loops on non-safe states labeled by every action of the alphabet with weight -1. It is easy to see that a strategy is winning in the safety game if and only if it is winning in the energy game with initial credit 0.

Theorem 7. *The fixed initial credit problem and the unknown initial credit problem for energy games with visible weights are EXPTIME-complete.*

The result of Lemma 3 can be generalized to any objective which depends only on the sequence of weights in the outcomes. In fact, the proof of Lemma 3 shows that there exist mappings from the set of observation-based strategies in G to the set of strategies in G^K (from α^o we construct α^K), and back (from α^K we construct α^o), such that the set of sequences of weights in the outcomes is the same for the two strategies. Therefore, the subset construction can also be used to solve mean-payoff games and we get the following result.

Theorem 8. *The threshold problem for mean-payoff games with visible weights is EXPTIME-complete.*

6 Conclusion

Energy and mean-payoff games are important classes of games that are already well-studied under the hypothesis of perfect information. This paper studies extensions of those games with imperfect information. We have shown that the picture is much more complex under that hypothesis. We have established that, although energy games with known initial credit and imperfect information remain decidable, but EXPSPACE-hard, energy games with unknown credit and mean-payoff games, even restricted to finite memory strategies, are undecidable. To regain decidability, we have shown that weights have to be visible. For this subclass the problems are EXPTIME-complete, furthermore energy games and mean-payoff games are log-space equivalent as in the simpler case of perfect information.

To complete the picture about different versions of mean-payoff games with imperfect information, an open question is the decidability of the threshold problem for the objective $\mathsf{MeanPayoffInf}^{\geq}(0)$.

In games with imperfect information, randomized strategies are sometimes more powerful than pure strategies. For example, reachability objectives may be won with probability 1 (almost-sure winning) while no pure strategy is (surely) winning. Decision problems of interest include the threshold problem for mean-payoff games with imperfect information under almost-sure and positive winning conditions. Note that in the case of energy games, randomized strategies are not more powerful than pure strategies for almost-sure winning because the energy objectives define closed sets in the Cantor topology, and it is known that almost-sure winning coincides with sure winning for closed objectives (such as safety objectives).

References

1. Alur, R., Degorre, A., Maler, O., Weiss, G.: On omega-languages defined by mean-payoff conditions. In: de Alfaro, L. (ed.) FOSSACS 2009. LNCS, vol. 5504, pp. 333–347. Springer, Heidelberg (2009)
2. Berwanger, D., Doyen, L.: On the power of imperfect information. In: Proc. of FSTTCS. Dagstuhl Seminar Proceedings 08004. IBFI (2008)
3. Bloem, R., Chatterjee, K., Henzinger, T.A., Jobstmann, B.: Better quality in synthesis through quantitative objectives. In: Bouajjani, A., Maler, O. (eds.) CAV 2009. LNCS, vol. 5643, pp. 140–156. Springer, Heidelberg (2009)
4. Chaloupka, J., Brim, L.: Faster algorithm for mean-payoff games. In: Proc. of MEMICS: Math. and Engineering Methods in Comp. Science, pp. 45–53. Nov Press (2009)
5. Chatterjee, K., de Alfaro, L., Faella, M., Henzinger, T.A., Majumdar, R., Stoelinga, M.: Compositional quantitative reasoning. In: Proc. of QEST: Quantitative Evaluaiton of Systems, pp. 179–188. IEEE Computer Society, Los Alamitos (2006)
6. Chatterjee, K., Doyen, L., Henzinger, T.A.: Quantitative languages. In: Kaminski, M., Martini, S. (eds.) CSL 2008. LNCS, vol. 5213, pp. 385–400. Springer, Heidelberg (2008)
7. Chatterjee, K., Doyen, L., Henzinger, T.A., Raskin, J.-F.: Algorithms for omega-regular games of incomplete information. Logical Methods in Computer Science 3(3:4) (2007)
8. de Alfaro, L.: How to specify and verify the long-run average behavior of probabilistic systems. In: Proc. of LICS: Logic in Computer Science, pp. 454–465. IEEE Comp. Soc., Los Alamitos (1998)
9. Dickson, L.E.: Finiteness of the odd perfect and primitive abundant numbers with n distinct prime factors. Am. J. of Mathematics 35(4), 413–422 (1913)
10. Doyen, L., Gentilini, R., Raskin, J.-F.: Faster pseudopolynomial algorithms for meanpayoff games. Technical Report 2009.120, Université Libre de Bruxelles (ULB), Belgium (2009)
11. Droste, M., Gastin, P.: Weighted automata and weighted logics. Th. C. Sci. 380(1-2), 69–86 (2007)
12. Ehrenfeucht, A., Mycielski, J.: International journal of game theory. Positional Strategies for Mean-Payoff Games 8, 109–113 (1979)
13. Emerson, E.A., Jutla, C.: Tree automata, mu-calculus and determinacy. In: Proc. of FOCS, pp. 368–377. IEEE, Los Alamitos (1991)

14. Emerson, E.A., Jutla, C.S., Sistla, A.P.: On model-checking for fragments of μ-calculus. In: Courcoubetis, C. (ed.) CAV 1993. LNCS, vol. 697, pp. 385–396. Springer, Heidelberg (1993)
15. Esparza, J.: Decidability and complexity of Petri net problems - An introduction. In: Reisig, W., Rozenberg, G. (eds.) APN 1998. LNCS, vol. 1491, pp. 374–428. Springer, Heidelberg (1998)
16. Finkel, A., Schnoebelen, P.: Well-structured transition systems everywhere! Th. Comp. Sc. 256(1-2), 63–92 (2001)
17. Grädel, E., Thomas, W., Wilke, T. (eds.): Automata, Logics, and Infinite Games: A Guide to Current Research. LNCS, vol. 2500. Springer, Heidelberg (2002)
18. Gurevich, Y., Harrington, L.: Trees, automata, and games. In: Proc. of STOC, pp. 60–65. ACM Press, New York (1982)
19. Krob, D.: The equality problem for rational series with multiplicities in the tropical semiring is undecidable. In: Kuich, W. (ed.) ICALP 1992. LNCS, vol. 623, pp. 101–112. Springer, Heidelberg (1992)
20. Kupferman, O., Lustig, Y.: Lattice automata. In: Cook, B., Podelski, A. (eds.) VMCAI 2007. LNCS, vol. 4349, pp. 199–213. Springer, Heidelberg (2007)
21. Minsky, N.M.: Finite and Infinite Machines. Prentice-Hall, Englewood Cliffs (1967)
22. Rackoff, C.: The covering and boundedness problems for vector addition systems. Th. Comp. Sc. 6, 223–231 (1978)
23. Reif, J.H.: The complexity of two-player games of incomplete information. Journal of Computer and System Sciences 29(2), 274–301 (1984)
24. Zwick, U., Paterson, M.: The complexity of mean payoff games on graphs. Th. Comp. Sc. 158, 343–359 (1996)

Randomisation and Derandomisation in Descriptive Complexity Theory

Kord Eickmeyer and Martin Grohe

Humboldt-Universität zu Berlin, Institut für Informatik, Logik in der Informatik
Unter den Linden 6, 10099 Berlin, Germany
{eickmeye,grohe}@informatik.hu-berlin.de

Abstract. We study probabilistic complexity classes and questions of derandomisation from a logical point of view. For each logic L we introduce a new logic BPL, *bounded error probabilistic* L, which is defined from L in a similar way as the complexity class BPP, bounded error probabilistic polynomial time, is defined from P.

Our main focus lies on questions of derandomisation, and we prove that there is a query which is definable in BPFO, the probabilistic version of first-order logic, but not in $C_{\infty\omega}^{\omega}$, finite variable infinitary logic with counting. This implies that many of the standard logics of finite model theory, like transitive closure logic and fixed-point logic, both with and without counting, cannot be derandomised. We prove similar results for ordered structures and structures with an addition relation, showing that certain uniform variants of AC^0 (bounded-depth polynomial sized circuits) cannot be derandomised. These results are in contrast to the general belief that most standard complexity classes can be derandomised.

Finally, we note that BPIFP+C, the probabilistic version of fixed-point logic with counting, captures the complexity class BPP, even on unordered structures.

1 Introduction

The relation between different modes of computation — deterministic, nondeterministic, randomised — is a central topic of computational complexity theory. The P vs. NP problem falls under this topic, and so does a second very important problem, the relation between randomised and deterministic polynomial time. In technical terms, this is the question of whether P = BPP, where BPP is the class of all problems that can be solved by a randomised polynomial time algorithm with two-sided errors and bounded error probability. This question differs from the question of whether P = NP in that most complexity theorists seem to believe that the classes P and BPP are indeed equal. This belief is supported by deep results due to Nisan and Wigderson [1] and Impagliazzo and Wigderson [2], which link the derandomisation question to the existence of one-way functions and to circuit lower bounds. Similar derandomisation questions are studied for other complexity classes such as logarithmic space, and it is believed that derandomisation is possible for these classes as well.

A. Dawar and H. Veith (Eds.): CSL 2010, LNCS 6247, pp. 275–289, 2010.

Descriptive complexity theory gives logical descriptions of complexity classes and thus enables us to translate complexity theoretic questions into the realm of logic. While logical descriptions are known for most natural deterministic and nondeterministic time and space complexity classes, probabilistic classes such as BPP have received very little attention in descriptive complexity theory yet. In this paper, we study probabilistic complexity classes and questions of derandomisation from a logical point of view. For each logic L we introduce a new logic BPL, *bounded error probabilistic* L, which is defined from L in a similar way as BPP is defined from P. The randomness is introduced to the logic by letting formulas of vocabulary τ speak about *random expansions* of τ-structures to a richer vocabulary $\tau \cup \rho$. We also introduce variants RL, co-RL with one-sided bounded error and PL with unbounded error, corresponding to other well known complexity classes, but focus on BPL in this conference paper.

Our main technical results are concerned with questions of derandomisation. By this we mean upper bounds on the expressive power of randomised logics in terms of classical logics. Trivially, BPL is at least as expressive as L, and if this upper bound is tight we call BPL *derandomisable*. We prove that there is a query that is definable in BPFO, the probabilistic version of first-order logic, but not in $C^{\omega}_{\infty\omega}$, finite variable infinitary logic with counting. This implies that many of the standard logics of finite model theory, like transitive closure logic and fixed-point logic, both with and without counting, cannot be derandomised. Note that these results are in sharp contrast to the general belief that most standard complexity classes can be derandomised.

We then investigate whether BPFO can be derandomised on classes of structures with built-in relations, such as ordered structures. Behle and Lange [3] showed that the expressive power of FO on classes of ordered structures with certain predefined relation symbols corresponds to uniform subclasses of AC^0, the class of circuit families of bounded depth, unbounded fan-in and polynomial size. In fact, for a set $\mathcal{R}$ of relation symbols whose interpretation is prescribed (such as linear orders, addition and multiplication relations) they show that $FO[\mathcal{R}]$ captures $FO[\mathcal{R}]$-uniform AC^0. We show that on additive structures, BPFO can not be derandomised, and on ordered structures it is not even contained in MSO.

Arguably the most intensively studied uniformity condition on AC^0 is *dlogtime-uniform* AC^0, which corresponds to $FO[+, \times]$ by Barrington et al. [4]. The question of whether dlogtime-uniform $BPAC^0$ can be derandomised is still open, but there is a conditional derandomisation by Viola [5]. There are less uniform variants of $BPAC^0$ that can be proved to be derandomisable by standard arguments in the style of Adleman [6]. We prove the more uniform $FO[+]$-uniform AC^0 to be non-derandomisable. This raises the question of how weak uniformity must be for derandomisation to be possible.

In the last section of this paper, we turn to more standard questions of descriptive complexity theory. We prove that BPIFP+C, the probabilistic version of fixed-point logic with counting, captures the complexity class BPP, even on unordered structures. For ordered structures, this result is a direct consequence of the Immerman-Vardi Theorem [7,8], and for arbitrary structures it follows from the observation that we can define a random order with high probability in BPIFP+C. Still, the result is surprising at first sight because of its similarity with the open question of whether there is a logic capturing P, and because it is believed that P = BPP. The caveat is that the logic BPIFP+C does not have an effective syntax and thus is not a "logic" according to Gurevich's [9] definition underlying the question for a logic that captures P. Nevertheless, we believe that BPIFP+C gives a completely adequate description of the complexity class BPP, because the definition of BPP is inherently ineffective as well (as opposed to the definition of P in terms of the decidable set of polynomially clocked Turing machines). We obtain similar descriptions of other probabilistic complexity classes. For example, randomised logspace is captured by the randomised version of deterministic transitive closure logic with counting.

Related work

As mentioned earlier, probabilistic complexity classes such as BPP have received very little attention in descriptive complexity theory. There is an unpublished paper due to Kaye [10] that gives a logical characterisation of BPP on ordered structures. Müller [11] and Montoya (unpublished) study a logical BP-operator in the context of parameterised complexity theory. What comes closest to our work "in spirit" and also in some technical aspects is Hella, Kolaitis, and Luosto's work on *almost everywhere equivalence* [12], which may be viewed as a logical account of average case complexity in a similar sense that our work gives a logical account of randomised complexity. There is a another logical approach to computational complexity, known as implicit computational complexity, which is quite different from descriptive complexity theory. Mitchell, Mitchell, and Scedrov [13] give a logical characterisation of BPP by a higher-order typed programming language in this context.

Outside of descriptive complexity theory and finite model theory, probabilistic logics have received wide attention in mathematical logic and computer science, particularly in artificial intelligence and also in database theory. However, all this work has little in common with ours, both on a conceptual and technical level. A few pointers to the literature are [14,15,16,17].

Let us emphasise that the main purpose of this paper is not the definition of new probabilistic logics, but an investigation of these logics in a complexity theoretic context.

2   Preliminaries

2.1   Structures and Queries

A *vocabulary* is a finite set τ of relation symbols of fixed arities. A τ-*structure A* consists of a set $V(A)$, the *universe* of the structure, and, for all $R \in \tau$, a relation $R(A)$ on A whose arity matches that of R. Thus we only consider *finite* and *relational* structures. Let σ, τ be vocabularies with $\sigma \subseteq \tau$. Then the σ-*restriction* of a τ-structure B is the σ-structure $B|_\sigma$ with universe $V(B|_\sigma) := V(B)$ and relations $R(B|_\sigma) := R(B)$ for all $R \in \sigma$. A τ-*expansion* of a σ-structure A is a

τ-structure B such that $B|_\sigma = A$. For every class $\mathcal{C}$ of structures, $\mathcal{C}[\tau]$ denotes the class of all τ-structures in $\mathcal{C}$. A *renaming* of a vocabulary τ is a bijective mapping r from τ to a vocabulary τ' such that for all $R \in \tau$ the relation symbol $r(R) \in \tau'$ has the same arity as R. If $r : \tau \to \tau'$ is a renaming and A is a τ-structure then A^r is the τ'-structure with $V(A^r) := V(A)$ and $r(R)(A^r) := R(A)$ for all $R \in \tau$.

We let $\leqslant$, $+$ and $\times$ be distinguished relation symbols of arity two, three and three. Whenever any of these relations symbols appear in a vocabulary τ, we demand that they be interpreted by a linear order and ternary addition and multiplication relations, respectively, in all τ-structures. To be precise, let $[n]$ be the set $\{0, 1, \ldots, n\}$ for $n \geq 0$, and denote by $\mathcal{N}_n$ the $\{\leqslant, +, \times\}$-structure with

$$V(\mathcal{N}_n) = [n], \qquad \leqslant(\mathcal{N}_n) = \{(a, b) \mid a \leqslant b\} \text{ and}$$
$$+(\mathcal{N}_n) = \{(a, b, c) \mid a + b = c\}, \qquad \times(\mathcal{N}_n) = \{(a, b, c) \mid a \cdot b = c\},$$

and demand $A|_{\{\leqslant,+,\times\}\cap\tau} \cong (\mathcal{N}_{|A|-1})|_{\{\leqslant,+,\times\}\cap\tau}$ for all τ-structures A. We call structures whose vocabulary contains any of these relation symbols *ordered*, *additive* and *multiplicative*, respectively.

A *k-ary τ-global relation* is a mapping $\mathcal{R}$ that associates a k-ary relation $\mathcal{R}(A)$ with each τ-structure A. A 0-ary τ-global relation is usually called a *Boolean τ-global relation*. We identify the two 0-ary relations $\emptyset$ and $\{()\}$, where $()$ denotes the empty tuple, with the truth values **false** and **true**, respectively, and we identify the Boolean τ-global relation $\mathcal{R}$ with the class of all τ-structures A with $\mathcal{R}(A) =$ **true**. A *k-ary τ-query* is a k-ary τ-global relation $\mathcal{Q}$ preserved under isomorphism, that is, if f is an isomorphism from a τ-structure A to a τ-structure B then for all $\boldsymbol{a} \in V(A)^k$ it holds that $\boldsymbol{a} \in \mathcal{Q}(A) \iff f(\boldsymbol{a}) \in \mathcal{Q}(B)$.

2.2 Logics

A *logic* L has a *syntax* that assigns a set $\mathsf{L}[\tau]$ of L-*formulas of vocabulary* τ with each vocabulary τ and a *semantics* that associates a τ-global relation $\mathcal{Q}_\varphi^{\mathsf{L}[\tau]}$ with every formula $\varphi \in \mathsf{L}[\tau]$ such that for all vocabularies σ, τ, τ' the following three conditions are satisfied:

(i) For all $\varphi \in \mathsf{L}[\tau]$ the global relation $\mathcal{Q}_\varphi^{\mathsf{L}[\tau]}$ is a τ-query.

(ii) If $\sigma \subseteq \tau$ then $\mathsf{L}[\sigma] \subseteq \mathsf{L}[\tau]$, and for all formulas $\varphi \in \mathsf{L}[\sigma]$ and all τ-structures A it holds that $\mathcal{Q}_\varphi^{\mathsf{L}[\sigma]}(A|_\sigma) = \mathcal{Q}_\varphi^{\mathsf{L}[\tau]}(A)$.

(iii) If $r : \tau \to \tau'$ is a renaming, then for every formula $\varphi \in \mathsf{L}[\tau]$ there is a formula $\varphi^r \in \mathsf{L}[\tau']$ such that for all τ-structures A it holds that $\mathcal{Q}_\varphi^{\mathsf{L}[\tau]}(A) = \mathcal{Q}_{\varphi^r}^{\mathsf{L}[\tau']}(A^r)$.

Condition (ii) justifies dropping the vocabulary τ in the notation for the queries and just write $\mathcal{Q}_\varphi^{\mathsf{L}}$. For a τ-structure A and a tuple $\boldsymbol{a}$ whose length matches the arity of $\mathcal{Q}_\varphi$, we usually write $A \models_{\mathsf{L}} \varphi[\boldsymbol{a}]$ instead of $\boldsymbol{a} \in \mathcal{Q}_\varphi^{\mathsf{L}}(A)$. If $\mathcal{Q}_\varphi^{\mathsf{L}}$ is a k-ary query, then we call φ a *k-ary formula*, and if $\mathcal{Q}_\varphi^{\mathsf{L}}$ is Boolean, then we call φ a *sentence*. Instead of $A \models_{\mathsf{L}} \varphi[()]$ we just write $A \models_{\mathsf{L}} \varphi$ and say that A *satisfies* φ. We omit the index L if L is clear from the context.

A query $\mathcal{Q}$ is *definable* in a logic L if there is an L-formula φ such that $\mathcal{Q} = \mathcal{Q}_\varphi$. Two formulas $\varphi_1, \varphi_2 \in \mathsf{L}[\tau]$ are *equivalent* (we write $\varphi_1 \equiv \varphi_2$) if they define the same query. We say that a logic L_1 is *weaker* than a logic L_2 (we write $\mathsf{L}_1 \leq \mathsf{L}_2$) if every query definable in L_1 is also definable in L_2. Similarly, we define it for L_1 and L_2 to be *equivalent* (we write $\mathsf{L}_1 \equiv \mathsf{L}_2$) and for L_1 to be *strictly weaker* than L_2 (we write $\mathsf{L}_1 \lneq \mathsf{L}_2$). The logics L_1 and L_2 are *incomparable* if neither $\mathsf{L}_1 \leq \mathsf{L}_2$ nor $\mathsf{L}_2 \leq \mathsf{L}_1$.

Remark 1. Our notion of logic is very minimalistic, usually logics are required to meet additional conditions (see [18] for a thorough discussion). In particular, we do not require the syntax of a logic to be effective. Indeed, the main logics studied in this paper have an undecidable syntax. Our definition is in the tradition of abstract model theory (cf. [19]); proof theorists tend to have a different view on what constitutes a logic.

We assume that the reader has heard of the standard logics studied in finite model theory, specifically *first-order logic* FO, *second-order logic* SO and its fragments Σ_k^1, *monadic second-order logic* MSO, *transitive closure logic* TC and its *deterministic* variant DTC, *least, inflationary,* and *partial fixed-point logic* LFP, IFP, and PFP, and *finite variable infinitary logic* $\mathsf{L}_{\infty\omega}^\omega$. For all these logics except LFP there are also *counting versions*, which we denote by $\mathsf{FO+C}$, $\mathsf{TC+C}$, ..., $\mathsf{PFP+C}$ and $\mathsf{C}_{\infty\omega}^\omega$, respectively. Only familiarity with first-order logic is required to follow most of the technical arguments in this paper. The other logics are more or less treated as "black boxes". We will say a bit more about some of them when they occur later. The following diagram shows how the logics compare in expressive power:

$$\begin{array}{ccccccccccc}
\mathsf{FO} & \lneq & \mathsf{DTC} & \lneq & \mathsf{TC} & \lneq & \mathsf{LFP} & \equiv & \mathsf{IFP} & \lneq & \mathsf{PFP} & \lneq & \mathsf{L}_{\infty\omega}^\omega \\
\text{\rotatebox{90}{$\lneq$}} & & \text{\rotatebox{90}{$\lneq$}} & & \text{\rotatebox{90}{$\lneq$}} & & & \text{\rotatebox{90}{$\lneq$}} & & & \text{\rotatebox{90}{$\lneq$}} & & \text{\rotatebox{90}{$\lneq$}} \\
\mathsf{FO+C} & \lneq & \mathsf{DTC+C} & \lneq & \mathsf{TC+C} & \lneq & & \mathsf{IFP+C} & & \lneq & \mathsf{PFP+C} & \lneq & \mathsf{C}_{\infty\omega}^\omega.
\end{array} \qquad (1)$$

Furthermore, MSO is strictly stronger than FO and incomparable with all other logics displayed in (1).

2.3 Complexity Theory

We assume that the reader is familiar with the basics of computational complexity theory and in particular the standard complexity classes such as P and NP. Let us briefly review the class BPP, *bounded error probabilistic polynomial time*, and other probabilistic complexity classes: A language $L \subseteq \Sigma^*$ is in BPP if there is a polynomial time algorithm M, expecting as input a string $x \in \Sigma^*$ and a string $r \in \{0,1\}^*$ of "random bits", and a polynomial p such that for every $x \in \Sigma^*$ the following two conditions are satisfied:

(i) If $x \in L$, then $\Pr_{r \in \{0,1\}^{p(|x|)}} \left(M \text{ accepts } (x,r) \right) \geq \frac{2}{3}$.
(ii) If $x \notin L$, then $\Pr_{r \in \{0,1\}^{p(|x|)}} \left(M \text{ accepts } (x,r) \right) \leq \frac{1}{3}$.

In both conditions, the probabilities range over strings $r \in \{0,1\}^{p(|x|)}$ chosen uniformly at random. The choice of the error bounds $1/3$ and $2/3$ in (i) and

280   K. Eickmeyer and M. Grohe

(ii) is somewhat arbitrary, they can be replaced by any constants α, β with $0 < \alpha < \beta < 1$ without changing the complexity class. (To reduce the error probability of an algorithm we simply repeat it several times with independently chosen random bits r.)

Hence BPP is the class of all problems that can be solved by a randomised polynomial time algorithm with bounded error probabilities. RP is the class of all problems that can be solved by a randomised polynomial time algorithm with bounded one-sided error on the positive side (the bound $1/3$ in (ii) is replaced by 0), and co-RP is the class of all problems that can be solved by a randomised polynomial time algorithm with bounded one-sided error on the negative side (the bound $2/3$ in (i) is replaced by 1). Finally, PP is the class we obtain if we replace the lower bound $\geq 2/3$ in (i) by $> 1/2$ and the upper bound $\leq 1/3$ in (ii) by $\leq 1/2$. Note that PP is not a realistic model of "efficient randomised computation", because there is no easy way of deciding whether an algorithm accepts or rejects its input. Indeed, by Toda's Theorem [20], the class P^{PP} contains the full polynomial hierarchy. By the Sipser-Gács Theorem (see [21]), BPP is contained in the second level of the polynomial hierarchy. More precisely, $\mathsf{BPP} \subseteq \Sigma_2^p \cap \Pi_2^p$. It is an open question whether $\mathsf{BPP} \subseteq \mathsf{NP}$. However, as pointed out in the introduction, there are good reasons to believe that $\mathsf{BPP} = \mathsf{P}$.

2.4   Descriptive Complexity

It is common in descriptive complexity theory to view complexity classes as classes of Boolean queries, rather than classes of formal languages. This allows it to compare logics with complexity classes. The translation between queries and languages is carried out as follows: Let τ be a vocabulary, and assume that $\leqslant \notin \tau$. With each ordered $(\tau \cup \{\leqslant\})$-structure B we can associate a binary string $s(B) \in \{0,1\}^*$ in a canonical way. Then with each class $\mathcal{C} \subseteq \mathcal{O}[\tau \cup \{\leqslant\}]$ of ordered τ structures we associate the language $L(\mathcal{C}) := \{s(B) \mid B \in \mathcal{C}\} \subseteq \{0,1\}^*$. For a Boolean τ-query $\mathcal{Q}$, let $\mathcal{Q}_\leqslant := \{B \in \mathcal{O}[\tau \cup \leqslant] \mid B|_\tau \in \mathcal{Q}\}$ be the class of all ordered $(\tau \cup \{\leqslant\})$-expansions of structures in $\mathcal{Q}$. We say that $\mathcal{Q}$ is *decidable* in a complexity class K if the language $L(\mathcal{Q}_\leqslant)$ is contained in K. We say that a logic L *captures* K if for all Boolean queries $\mathcal{Q}$ it holds that $\mathcal{Q}$ is definable in L if and only if $\mathcal{Q}$ is decidable in K. We say that L is *contained* in K if all Boolean queries definable in L are decidable in K.

Remark 2. Just like our notion of "logic", our notion of a logic "capturing" a complexity class is very minimalistic, but completely sufficient for our purposes. For a deeper discussion of logics capturing complexity classes we refer the reader to one of the textbooks [22,23,24,25].

3   Randomised Logics

Throughout this section, let τ and ρ be disjoint vocabularies. Relations over ρ will be "random", and we will reserve the letter R for relation symbols from ρ. We are interested in *random* $(\tau \cup \rho)$-*expansions* of τ-structures. For a τ-structure A, by $\mathcal{X}(A, \rho)$ we denote the class of all $(\tau \cup \rho)$-expansions of A. We view $\mathcal{X}(A, \rho)$ as a probability space with the uniform distribution. Note that we can "construct" a random $X \in \mathcal{X}(A, \rho)$ by deciding independently for all k-ary $R \in \rho$ and all tuples $\boldsymbol{a} \in V(A)^k$ with probability $1/2$ whether $\boldsymbol{a} \in R(X)$. We are mainly interested in the probabilities

$$\Pr_{X \in \mathcal{X}(A, \rho)} (X \models \varphi)$$

that a random $(\tau \cup \rho)$-expansion of a τ-structure A satisfies a sentence φ of vocabulary $\tau \cup \rho$ of some logic.

Definition 1. *Let* L *be a logic and* $0 \leq \alpha \leq \beta \leq 1$.

1. *A formula* $\varphi \in \mathsf{L}[\tau \cup \rho]$ *that defines a k-ary query has an (α, β)-gap if for all τ-structures A and all $\boldsymbol{a} \in V(A)^k$ it holds that*

$$\Pr_{X \in \mathcal{X}(A, \rho)} (X \models \varphi[\boldsymbol{a}]) \leq \alpha \qquad or \qquad \Pr_{X \in \mathcal{X}(A, \rho)} (X \models \varphi[\boldsymbol{a}]) > \beta.$$

2. *The logic* $\mathsf{P}_{(\alpha, \beta)}\mathsf{L}$ *is defined as follows: For each vocabulary τ,*

$$\mathsf{P}_{(\alpha, \beta)}\mathsf{L}[\tau] := \bigcup_{\rho} \{\varphi \in \mathsf{L}[\tau \cup \rho] \mid \varphi \text{ has an } (\alpha, \beta)\text{-gap}\},$$

where the union ranges over all vocabularies ρ disjoint from τ. To define the semantics, let $\varphi \in \mathsf{P}_{(\alpha, \beta)}\mathsf{L}[\tau]$. Let k, ρ such that $\varphi \in \mathsf{L}[\tau \cup \rho]$ and φ is k-ary. Then for all τ-structures A,

$$Q_\varphi^{\mathsf{P}_{(\alpha, \beta)}\mathsf{L}}(A) := \{\boldsymbol{a} \in V(A)^k \mid \Pr_{X \in \mathcal{X}(A, \rho)} (X \models_\mathsf{L} \varphi[\boldsymbol{a}]) > \beta\}.$$

It is easy to see that for every logic L and all α, β with $0 \leq \alpha \leq \beta \leq 1$ the logic $\mathsf{P}_{(\alpha, \beta)}\mathsf{L}$ satisfies conditions (i)–(iii) from Subsection 2.2 and hence is indeed a well-defined logic. We let

$$\mathsf{PL} := \mathsf{P}_{(1/2, 1/2)}\mathsf{L} \quad \text{and} \quad \mathsf{RL} := \mathsf{P}_{(0, 2/3)}\mathsf{L} \quad \text{and} \quad \mathsf{BPL} := \mathsf{P}_{(1/3, 2/3)}\mathsf{L}.$$

We can also define a logic $\mathsf{P}_{[\alpha, \beta)}\mathsf{L}$ and let co-$\mathsf{RL} := \mathsf{P}_{[1/3, 1)}\mathsf{L}$. The following lemma shows that for reasonable L the strength of the logic $\mathsf{P}_{(\alpha, \beta)}\mathsf{L}$ does not depend on the exact choice of the parameters α, β. This justifies the arbitrary choice of the constants $1/3, 2/3$ in the definitions of RL and BPL.

Lemma 1. *Let* L *be a logic that is closed under conjunctions and disjunctions. Then for all α, β with $0 < \alpha < \beta < 1$ it holds that $\mathsf{P}_{(0, \beta)}\mathsf{L} \equiv \mathsf{RL}$ and $\mathsf{P}_{(\alpha, \beta)}\mathsf{L} \equiv$ BPL.*

We omit the straightforward proof.

Remark 3. For the rest of this conference paper, we focus entirely on logics BPL with two-sided bounded error. Many of our results have a version for logics RL with one-sided error as well. The logics PL are considerably more expressive and behave quite differently. For example, PFO contains the existential fragment Σ_1^1 of second-order logic. on all structures with at least one definable element (like the minimal element of a linear order). More results about the logics RL and PL will appear in the full version of this paper.

3.1   First Observations

We start by observing that the syntax of BPFO and thus of most other logics BPL is undecidable. This follows easily from Trakhtenbrot's Theorem (see [22] for similar undecidability proofs):

Observation 1. *For all α, β with $0 \leq \alpha < \beta < 1$ and all vocabularies τ containing at least one at least binary relation symbol, the set $\mathsf{BP}_{(\alpha,\beta)}\mathsf{FO}[\tau]$ is undecidable.*

For each n, let S_n be the $\emptyset$-structure with universe $V(S_n) := \{1, \ldots, n\}$. Recall the 0-1-law for first order logic [26,27]. In our terminology, it says that for each vocabulary ρ and each sentence $\varphi \in \mathsf{FO}[\rho]$ it holds that

$$\lim_{n \to \infty} \Pr_{X \in \mathcal{X}(S_n,\rho)} (X \models \varphi) \in \{0,1\}$$

(in particular, this limit exists). There is also an appropriate asymptotic law for formulas with free variables. This implies that on structures with empty vocabulary, BPFO has the same expressive power as FO. As there is also a 0-1-law for the logic $\mathsf{L}^{\omega}_{\infty\omega}$ [28], we actually get the following stronger statement:

Observation 2. *Every formula $\varphi \in \mathsf{BPL}^{\omega}_{\infty\omega}[\emptyset]$ is equivalent to a formula $\varphi' \in \mathsf{FO}[\emptyset]$.*

As FO+C is strictly stronger than FO even on structures of empty vocabulary, this observation implies that there are queries definable in FO+C, but not in $\mathsf{BPL}^{\omega}_{\infty\omega}$.

Finally, we note that the Sipser-Gács theorem [21] that $\mathsf{BPP} \subseteq \Sigma^p_2 \cap \Pi^p_2$, the fact that the fragment Σ^1_2 of second-order logic captures Σ^p_2 [29,30], and the observation that $\mathsf{BPFO} \leq \mathsf{BPP}$ imply the following:

Observation 3. $\mathsf{BPFO} \leq \Sigma^1_2$.

4   Separation Results for BPFO

In this section we study the expressive power of the randomised logic BPFO. Our main results are the following:

 - BPFO is not contained in $\mathsf{C}^{\omega}_{\infty\omega}$
 - BPFO is not contained in MSO on ordered structures
 - BPFO is stronger than FO on additive structures

It turns out that we need three rather different queries to get these separation results. For the first two queries this is immediate by the fact that *any* query on ordered structures is axiomatisable in $\mathsf{C}^{\omega}_{\infty\omega}$. The third query (on additive structures) is readily seen to be axiomatisable in MSO.

In fact, any BPFO-axiomatisable query on additive structures can be axiomatised in MSO. To see this, we first use Nisan's pseudorandom generator for constant depth circuits [31] to reduce the number of random bits to $m := \mathrm{polylog}(n)$, where n is the size of the input structure. We then use an expander random walk to generate $\sqrt{n}$ many blocks of m pseudorandom bits each, using a seed of only $s := m + O(\sqrt{n})$ bits, see [32]. Taking a majority vote over the $\sqrt{n}$ many trials, for large enough n, the error drops down to below $2^{-s/3}$, and we use an argument similar to that by Goldreich and Zuckerman [33]. Note that these pseudorandom generators are expressible in MSO on additive structures, essentially because we can quantify over binary relations on the first $\sqrt{n}$ numbers of the structure. Details of this proof will appear in the full version of this paper.

4.1   BPFO Is Not Contained in $\mathsf{C}^{\omega}_{\infty\omega}$

Formulas of the logic $\mathsf{C}^{\omega}_{\infty\omega}$ may contain arbitrary (not necessarily finite) conjunctions and disjunctions, but only finitely many variables, and counting quantifiers of the form $\exists^{\geq n} x \, \varphi$ ("there exists at least n x such that φ"). For example, the class of finite structures of even cardinality can be axiomatised in this logic by the sentence

$$\bigvee_{k \geq 0} \left(\exists^{\geq 2k} x . x \dot{=} x \right) \wedge \neg \left(\exists^{\geq 2k+1} x . x \dot{=} x \right).$$

Theorem 1. *There is a class $\mathcal{TCFI}$ of structures that is definable in BPFO, but not in $\mathsf{C}^{\omega}_{\infty\omega}$.*

Recall that by Observation 2 there also is a class of structures definable in FO+C $\leq \mathsf{C}^{\omega}_{\infty\omega}$, but not in BPFO.

Our proof of Theorem 1 is based on a well-known construction due to Cai, Fürer, and Immerman [34], who gave an example of a Boolean query in P that is not definable in $\mathsf{C}^{\omega}_{\infty\omega}$. We modify their construction in a way reminiscent to proofs by Dawar, Hella, and Kolaitis [35] for results on implicit definability in first-order logic, and obtain a query $\mathcal{TCFI}$ definable in BPFO, but not in $\mathsf{C}^{\omega}_{\infty\omega}$. Just like in Cai, Fürer and Immerman's original proof, the reason why $\mathsf{C}^{\omega}_{\infty\omega}$ can not axiomatise our query $\mathcal{TCFI}$ is its inability to choose one out of a pair of two elements. Using a random binary relation this can – with high probability – be done in FO. For details we refer to the full version of this paper.

4.2   BPFO on Ordered Structures Is Not Contained in MSO

In the presence of a linear order, *any* query becomes axiomatisable in $\mathsf{L}^{\omega}_{\infty\omega}$, and the query $\mathcal{TCFI}$ becomes axiomatisable even in FO. However, randomisation adds expressive power to FO also on ordered structures:

Theorem 2. *There is a class $\mathcal{B}$ of ordered structures that is definable in BPFO, but not in MSO.*

Remember that monadic second-order logic MSO is the the fragment of second-order logic that allows quantification over individual elements and sets of elements.

Let $\sigma_{EP\leq} := \{\leq, E, P\}$, with binary relations $\leq$ and E, and a unary predicate P. We define two classes $\mathcal{B}'$, $\mathcal{B}$ of $\sigma_{EP\leq}$-structures:

$\mathcal{B}'$ is the class of all $\sigma_{EP\leq}$-structures A for which

1. E defines a perfect matching on the set $M := P(A)$
2. the set $N := V(A) \setminus P(A)$ forms a Boolean algebra with the relation E and
3. no $x \in N$ and $y \in M$ are E-related
4. $\leq$ defines a linear order on the whole structure, which puts the M before the N and orders M in such a way that matched elements are always successive.

It is easy to see that the class $\mathcal{B}'$ is definable in FO. $\mathcal{B}$ is the subclass of $\mathcal{B}'$ whose elements satisfy the additional condition

$$2^{|M|} \geq |N|^2 . \tag{2}$$

We will prove that $\mathcal{B}$ is definable in BPFO, but not in MSO. To prove that $\mathcal{B}$ is definable in BPFO, we will use the following lemma:

Lemma 2 (Birthday Paradoxon). *Let $m, n \geq 1$ and let $F : [n] \to [m]$ be a random function drawn uniformly from the set of all such functions.*

1. *For any $\epsilon_1 > 0$ and $c > 2 \ln \frac{1}{\epsilon_1}$ there is an $n_c \geq 1$ such that if $n > n_c$ and $m \leq \frac{n^2}{c}$ we have*
$$\Pr(F \text{ is injective}) \leq \epsilon_1$$

2. *For any $\epsilon_2 > 0$, if $m \geq \frac{n^2}{2\epsilon_2}$, then*
$$\Pr(F \text{ is injective}) \geq 1 - \epsilon_2$$

Proof. For the first part, we note that

$$\Pr(F \text{ injective}) = \prod_{i=0}^{n-1} \left(1 - \frac{i}{m}\right) \leq \prod_{i=0}^{n-1} \exp\left(-\frac{i}{m}\right) = \exp\left(-\frac{n(n-1)}{2m}\right).$$

For the second part, note that

$$\Pr(F \text{ not injective}) = \Pr\left(\bigcup_{1 \leq i < j \leq n} \{F(i) = F(j)\}\right) \leq \sum_{i<j} \frac{1}{m} \leq \frac{n^2}{2m}. \qquad \square$$

Proof (Theorem 2). To see that $\mathcal{B}$ is not definable in MSO, we use two simple and well-known facts about MSO. The first is that for every $q \geq 0$ there are natural numbers p, m such that for all $k \geq 0$, a plain linear order of length m is indistinguishable from the linear order of length $m + k \cdot p$ by MSO-sentences of quantifier rank at most q. The same fact also holds for linear orders with a perfect matching on successive elements, because such a matching is definable in MSO anyway. The second fact we use is a version of the Feferman-Vaught Theorem. Suppose that we have a linearly ordered structure of the form $A \cup B$, and the two parts A, B are disjoint and not related except by the linear order, which puts A completely before B. Let $q \geq 0$ and A' another linearly ordered structure that is indistinguishable from A by all MSO-sentences of quantifier rank at most q. Then the structure $A' \cup B$ is indistinguishable from $A \cup B$ by all MSO-sentences of quantifier rank at most q. If we put these two facts together, we see that for every $q \geq 0$ there are p, m such that for all k, n the structure $A \in \mathcal{B}$ with parts M, N of sizes m, n, respectively, is indistinguishable from the structure A' with parts of sizes $m + k \cdot p$ and n. We can easily choose k, n in such a way that $A \notin \mathcal{B}$ and $A' \in \mathcal{B}$.

It remains to prove that $\mathcal{B}$ is definable in BPFO. Consider the sentence

$$\varphi_{\mathrm{inj}} := \forall x \forall y \Big(x \dot{=} y \vee Px \vee Py \vee \exists z \big(Pz \wedge \neg (Rxz \leftrightarrow Ryz) \big) \Big),$$

which states that the random binary relation R, considered as a function

$$f : N \to \mathrm{Pow}(M), \quad x \mapsto \{ y \in M \mid Rxy \}$$

from N to subsets of M, is injective. By the definition of R, the function f is drawn uniformly from the set of all such functions. If we fix $|N|$, the probability for f to be injective increases monotonically with $|M|$. Furthermore, for every structure in $\mathcal{B}'$, the size of N and M are a power of two and an even number, respectively. Thus either

$$2^{|M|} \leq \frac{1}{4} |N|^2 \quad \text{or} \quad 2^{|M|} \geq |N|^2,$$

and this factor of 4 translates into a probability gap for φ_{inj} in all sufficiently large structures in $\mathcal{B}'$, by lemma 2 with $\epsilon_1 = 0.2$, $\epsilon_2 = 0.5$ and $c = 4$. The remaining finitely many structures in $\mathcal{B}'$ can be dealt with separately.   □

4.3   BPFO Is Stronger Than FO on Additive Structures

Recall that an additive structure is one whose vocabulary contains a ternary relation $+$, such that $A|_+$ is isomorphic to $([|A| - 1], \{(a, b, c) \mid a + b = c\})$.

Theorem 3. *There is a class $\mathcal{A}$ of additive structures that is definable in BPFO, but not in FO.*

Our proof uses the following result:

Theorem 4 (Lynch [36]). *For every $k \in \mathbb{N}$ there is an infinite set $A_k \subseteq \mathbb{N}$ and a $d_k \in \mathbb{N}$ such that for all finite $Q_0, Q_1 \subseteq A_k$ with $|Q_0| = |Q_1|$ or $|Q_0|, |Q_1| > d_k$ the structures $(\mathbb{N}, +, Q_0)$ and $(\mathbb{N}, +, Q_1)$ satisfy exactly the same FO-sentences of quantifier rank at most k.*

Here $(\mathbb{N}, +, Q_i)$ denotes a $\{+, P\}$-structure with ternary $+$ and unary P, where $+$ is interpreted as above and P is interpreted by Q_i. For a finite set $M \subseteq \mathbb{N}$ we denote by $\max M$ the maximum element of M. By relativising quantifiers to the maximum element satisfying P, we immediately get the following corollary:

Corollary 1. *Let k, A_k, d_k, Q_0 and Q_1 be as above. Then the (finite) structures $([\max Q_0], +, Q_0)$ and $([\max Q_1], +, Q_1)$ satisfy exactly the same FO-sentences of quantifier rank at most k.*

We call a set $Q \subset \mathbb{N}$ *sparse* if $|Q \cap \{n, \dots, 3n\}| \le 1$ for all $n \ge 0$. Note that if Q is sparse and finite, then $|Q| \le \log_3(\max Q) + 1$. It is easy to see that there is an $\mathsf{FO}[\{+, P\}]$-sentence $\varphi_{\mathrm{sparse}}$ such that

$$([\max Q], +, Q) \models \varphi_{\mathrm{sparse}} \quad \Leftrightarrow \quad Q \text{ is sparse}$$

for all finite $Q \subseteq \mathbb{N}$.

Proof (Proof of Theorem 3). We define the following class of additive $\{+, P\}$-structures:

$$\mathcal{A} = \{([\max Q], +, Q) \mid Q \text{ is finite, sparse and } |Q| \text{ is even}\},$$

with $+$ defined as usual. It follows immediately from Corollary 1 that $\mathcal{A}$ is not definable in FO.

It remains to prove that $\mathcal{A}$ is definable in BPFO. We consider a binary random relation R on $\mathcal{Q} = ([\max Q], +, Q)$ for some finite $Q \subseteq \mathbb{N}$.

Each element $a \in [\max Q]$ defines a subset of Q, namely the set of $b \in Q$ for which $(a, b) \in R(\mathcal{Q})$ holds. If Q is a sparse set, it has

$$2^{|Q|} \le 2^{\log_3(\max Q) + 1} \le \frac{\max Q}{2 \ln(\max Q)}$$

many subsets, and by standard estimates on the coupon collector's problem (see, e.g., [37]; or use a union-bound argument), if $\max Q$ is large enough, every subset of Q is defined by some element of $[\max Q]$. Thus we may quantify over subsets of Q. Since we can define a linear order on the structure $\mathcal{Q}$ from the addition, we can now easily express evenness of Q in FO.   □

5 A Logic Capturing BPP

In this section, we prove that the logic $\mathsf{BPIFP+C}$ captures the complexity class BPP. Technically, the results of this section are closely related to results in [12].

Counting logics like $\mathsf{FO+C}$ and $\mathsf{IFP+C}$ are usually defined via two-sorted structures, which are equipped with an initial segment of the natural numbers of appropriate length. The expressive power of the resulting logic turns out to be rather robust under changes in the exact definition, see [38] for a detailed survey of this. However, we will only need the limited counting ability provided by the *Rescher quantifier*, which goes back to a unary majority quantifier defined in [39], see [38].

We let $\mathsf{FO}(\mathcal{J})$ be the logic obtained from first-order logic by adjoining a generalised quantifier $\mathcal{J}$, the *Rescher quantifier*. For any two formulas $\varphi_1(\boldsymbol{x})$ and $\varphi_2(\boldsymbol{x})$, where $\boldsymbol{x}$ is a k-tuple of variables, we form a new formula

$$\mathcal{J}\boldsymbol{x}.\varphi_1(\boldsymbol{x})\varphi_2(\boldsymbol{x}).$$

Its semantics is defined by

$A \models \mathcal{J}\boldsymbol{x}.\varphi_1(\boldsymbol{x})\varphi_2(\boldsymbol{x}) \quad$ iff

$$\left|\{\boldsymbol{a} \in V(A)^k \mid A \models \varphi_1[\boldsymbol{a}]\}\right| \le \left|\{\boldsymbol{a} \in V(A)^k \mid A \models \varphi_2[\boldsymbol{a}]\}\right|. \quad (3)$$

The logic $\mathsf{IFP}(\mathcal{J})$ is defined similarly.

Lemma 3. *Let R be a 6-ary relation symbol. There is a formula $\varphi_{\leq}(x,y) \in$ FO$(\mathcal{J})[\{R\}]$ such that*

$$\lim_{n\to\infty} \Pr_{A \in X(S_n, \{R\})} \Big(\{(a,b) \mid A \models \varphi_{\leq}[a,b]\} \text{ is a linear order of } V(A) \Big) = 1.$$

(Recall that S_n is the $\emptyset$-structure with universe $\{1, \ldots, n\}$. Thus $X(S_n, \{R\})$ just denotes the set of all $\{R\}$-structures with universe $\{1, \ldots, n\}$.)

Proof. We let

$$\varphi_{\leq}(x,y) := \mathcal{J}x_1 \ldots x_5.Rxx_1 \ldots x_5\, Ryx_1 \ldots x_5.$$

To see that $\varphi_{\leq}(x,y)$ defines an order with high probability, let A be a structure with universe $V(A) = \{1, \ldots, n\}$. For each $a \in V(A)$, let

$$X_a := \big| \{ \boldsymbol{a} \in V(A)^5 \mid A \models Ra\boldsymbol{a}. \} \big|$$

Then $A \models \varphi_{\leq}(a,b)$ iff $X_a \leq X_b$, and $\varphi_{\leq}$ linearly orders A iff the X_a are pairwise distinct. But for $a \neq b \in V(A)$, the random variables X_a and X_b are independent and each is binomially distributed with parameters $p = 1/2$ and $m = n^5$, and thus

$$\Pr(X_a = X_b) = \sum_{k=0}^{m} \left(\frac{1}{2^m} \binom{m}{k} \right)^2 = \frac{1}{2^{2m}} \sum \binom{m}{k}^2$$

$$= \frac{1}{2^{2m}} \sum \binom{m}{k} \binom{m}{m-k} = \frac{1}{2^{2m}} \binom{2m}{m} = \Theta\left(\frac{1}{\sqrt{m}} \right),$$

where the final approximation can be found, for example, in [40]. The second part now follows by a union bound over the $\binom{n}{2} = \Theta(m^{2/5})$ pairs $a \neq b$. □

Theorem 5. *The logic BPIFP$(\mathcal{J})$ captures BPP.*

Proof. BPIFP$(\mathcal{J})$ is contained in BPP, because a randomised polynomial time algorithm can interpret the random relations by using its random bits.

For the other direction, let $\mathcal{Q}$ be a Boolean query in BPP. This means that there is a randomised polynomial time algorithm M that decides the query $\mathcal{Q}_{\leq}$ of ordered expansions of structures in $\mathcal{Q}$. We may view the (polynomially many) random bits used by M as part of the input. Then it follows from the Immerman-Vardi Theorem that there is a BPIFP-sentence ψ_M defining $\mathcal{Q}_{\leq}$. Note that, by the definition of $\mathcal{Q}_{\leq}$, this sentence is order-invariant. We replace every occurrence of $\leq$ in ψ_M by the formula $\varphi_{\leq}(x,y)$ of Lemma 3, which with high probability defines a linear order on the universe. □

It is easy to see that BPIFP+C is also contained in BPP and that IFP$(\mathcal{J}) \leq$ IFP+C. Thus we get the following corollary.

Corollary 2. BPIFP+C = BPIFP$(\mathcal{J})$, *and both capture* BPP.

Remark 4. By similar arguments, we obtain logical characterisations of other randomised complexity classes. For example, BPL = BPDTC$(\mathcal{J})$ = BPDTC+C. (Here L does not denote a generic logic, but the complexity class logspace.)

Furthermore, it also follows from Lemma 3 that BPL$^{\omega}_{\infty\omega}(\mathcal{J})$ = BPC$^{\omega}_{\infty\omega}$. Actually, it follows that all queries are definable in BPL$^{\omega}_{\infty\omega}(\mathcal{J})$.

Acknowledgements

We would like to thank Nicole Schweikardt and Dieter van Melkebeek for helpful comments on an earlier version of this paper.

References

1. Nisan, N., Wigderson, A.: Hardness vs randomness. Journal of Computer and System Sciences 49, 149–167 (1994)
2. Impagliazzo, R., Wigderson, A.: P = BPP if E requires exponential circuits: Derandomizing the xor lemma. In: Proceedings of the 29th ACM Symposium on Theory of Computing, pp. 220–229 (1997)
3. Behle, C., Lange, K.J.: FO[<]-uniformity. In: IEEE Conference on Computational Complexity, pp. 183–189 (2006)
4. Barrington, D.A.M., Immerman, N., Straubing, H.: On uniformity within NC^1. J. Comput. Syst. Sci. 41(3), 274–306 (1990)
5. Viola, E.: The complexity of constructing pseudorandom generators from hard functions. Electronic Colloquium on Computational Complexity (ECCC) (020) (2004)
6. Adleman, L.M.: Two theorems on random polynomial time. In: FOCS, pp. 75–83 (1978)
7. Immerman, N.: Relational queries computable in polynomial time. Information and Control 68, 86–104 (1986)
8. Vardi, M.: The complexity of relational query languages. In: Proceedings of the 14th ACM Symposium on Theory of Computing, pp. 137–146 (1982)
9. Gurevich, Y.: Logic and the challenge of computer science. In: Börger, E. (ed.) Current trends in theoretical computer science, pp. 1–57. Computer Science Press, Rockville (1988)
10. Kaye, P.: A logical characterisation of the computational complexity class BPP. Technical report, University of Waterloo (2002)
11. Müller, M.: Valiant-vazirani lemmata for various logics. Electronic Colloquium on Computational Complexity (ECCC) 15(063) (2008)
12. Hella, L., Kolaitis, P., Luosto, K.: Almost everywhere equivalence of logics in finite model theory. The Bulletin of Symbolic Logic 2(4), 422–443 (1996)
13. Mitchell, J., Mitchell, M., Scedrov, A.: A linguistic characterization of bounded oracle computation and probabilistic polynomial time. In: Proceedings of the 39th Annual IEEE Symposium on Foundations of Computer Science, pp. 725–733 (1998)
14. Bacchus, F.: Representing and Reasoning with Probabilistic Knowledge. MIT Press, Cambridge (1990)
15. Dalvi, N., Ré, C., Suciu, D.: Probabilistic databases: diamonds in the dirt. Commununications of the ACM 52(7), 86–94 (2009)
16. Fagin, R., Halpern, J., Megiddo, N.: A logic for reasoning about probabilities. Information and Computation 87(1/2), 78–128 (1990)
17. Keisler, H.: Probability quantifiers. In: Barwise, J., Feferman, S. (eds.) Model–Theoretic Logics, pp. 509–556. Springer, Heidelberg (1985)
18. Ebbinghaus, H.D.: Extended logics: The general framework. In: Barwise, J., Feferman, S. (eds.) Model–Theoretic Logics, pp. 25–76. Springer, Heidelberg (1985)
19. Barwise, J., Feferman, S. (eds.): Model Theoretic Logics. Perspectives in Mathematical Logic. Springer, Heidelberg (1985)
20. Toda, S.: PP is as hard as the polynomial-time hierarchy. SIAM Journal on Computing 20(5), 865–877 (1991)

21. Lautemann, C.: BPP and the polynomial hierarchy. Information Processing Letters 17(4), 215–217 (1983)
22. Ebbinghaus, H.D., Flum, J.: Finite Model Theory. In: Perspectives in Mathematical Logic, 2nd edn. Springer, Heidelberg (1999)
23. Grädel, E., Kolaitis, P., Libkin, L., Marx, M., Spencer, J., Vardi, M., Venema, Y., Weinstein, S.: Finite Model Theory and Its Applications. Texts in Theoretical Computer Science. Springer, Heidelberg (2007)
24. Immerman, N.: Descriptive Complexity Theory. Graduate Texts in Computer Science. Springer, Heidelberg (1999)
25. Libkin, L.: Elements of Finite Model Theory. Texts in Theoretical Computer Science. Springer, Heidelberg (2004)
26. Fagin, R.: Probabilities on finite models. Journal of Symbolic Logic 41, 50–58 (1976)
27. Glebskiĭ, Y., Kogan, D., Liogon'kiĭ, M., Talanov, V.: Range and degree of realizability of formulas in the restricted predicate calculus. Kibernetika 2, 17–28 (1969); Englisch translation, Cybernetics 5, 142–154 (1969)
28. Kolaitis, P.G., Vardi, M.Y.: Infinitary logic and 0-1 laws. Information and Computation 98, 258–294 (1992)
29. Fagin, R.: Generalized first-order spectra and polynomial-time recognizable sets. In: Karp, R.M. (ed.) Complexity of Computation. SIAM-AMS Proceedings, vol. 7, pp. 43–73 (1974)
30. Stockmeyer, L.: The polynomial hierarchy. Theoretical Computer Science 3, 1–22 (1977)
31. Nisan, N.: Pseudorandom bits for constant depth circuits. Combinatorica 11(1), 63–70 (1991)
32. Zuckerman, D.: Simulating BPP using a general weak random source. Algorithmica 16(4/5), 367–391 (1996)
33. Goldreich, O., Zuckerman, D.: Another proof that BPP subseteq PH (and more). Electronic Colloquium on Computational Complexity (ECCC) 4(45) (1997)
34. Cai, J.Y., Fürer, M., Immerman, N.: An optimal lower bound on the number of variables for graph identifications. Combinatorica 12(4), 389–410 (1992)
35. Dawar, A., Hella, L., Kolaitis, P.G.: Implicit definability and infinitary logic in finite model theory. In: Fülöp, Z., Gecseg, F. (eds.) ICALP 1995. LNCS, vol. 944, pp. 624–635. Springer, Heidelberg (1995)
36. Lynch, J.: On sets of relations definable by addition. Journal of Symbolic Logic 47(3), 659–668 (1982)
37. Motwani, R., Raghavan, P.: Randomized Algorithms. Cambridge University Press, Cambridge (1995)
38. Otto, M.: Bounded Variable Logics and Counting. Lecture Notes in Logic. Springer, Heidelberg (1996)
39. Rescher, N.: Plurality quantification. Journal of Symbolic Logic 27(3), 373–374 (1962)
40. Feller, W.: An Introduction to Probability Theory and Its Aplications, vol. 1. John Wiley & Sons, Chichester (1957)

Towards a Canonical Classical Natural Deduction System

José Espírito Santo

Centro de Matemática
Universidade do Minho
Portugal
jes@math.uminho.pt

Abstract. This paper studies a new classical natural deduction system, presented as a typed calculus named $\lambda\mu$let. It is designed to be isomorphic to Curien-Herbelin's $\overline{\lambda}\mu\tilde{\mu}$-calculus, both at the level of proofs and reduction, and the isomorphism is based on the correct correspondence between cut (resp. left-introduction) in sequent calculus, and substitution (resp. elimination) in natural deduction. It is a combination of Parigot's $\lambda\mu$-calculus with the idea of "coercion calculus" due to Cervesato-Pfenning, accommodating let-expressions in a surprising way: they expand Parigot's syntactic class of named terms.

This calculus aims to be the simultaneous answer to three problems. The first problem is the lack of a canonical natural deduction system for classical logic. $\lambda\mu$let is not yet another classical calculus, but rather a canonical reflection in natural deduction of the impeccable treatment of classical logic by sequent calculus. The second problem is the lack of a formalization of the usual semantics of $\overline{\lambda}\mu\tilde{\mu}$-calculus, that explains co-terms and cuts as, respectively, contexts and hole-filling instructions. The mentioned isomorphism is the required formalization, based on the precise notions of context and hole-expression offered by $\lambda\mu$let. The third problem is the lack of a robust process of "read-back" into natural deduction syntax of calculi in the sequent calculus format, that affects mainly the recent proof-theoretic efforts of derivation of λ-calculi for call-by-value. An isomorphic counterpart to the Q-subsystem of $\overline{\lambda}\mu\tilde{\mu}$-calculus is derived, obtaining a new λ-calculus for call-by-value, combining control and let-expressions.

1 Introduction

In the early days of proof theory, Gentzen [9] refined the de Morgan duality between conjunction and disjunction by defining the sequent calculus LK, a symmetric proof system for classical logic exhibiting a duality, at the level of proofs, between hypothesis and conclusion. Recently Curien and Herbelin [3] extended the Curry-Howard correspondence to LK and showed, by means of the $\overline{\lambda}\mu\tilde{\mu}$-calculus, that classical logic also contains a duality, at the level of cut elimination, between call-by-name (CBN) and call-by-value (CBV) computation.

$\overline{\lambda}\mu\tilde{\mu}$ is remarkably elegant and simple, but not self-sufficient. For several reasons, it would be desirable to have a complementary systems for natural

A. Dawar and H. Veith (Eds.): CSL 2010, LNCS 6247, pp. 290–304, 2010.

deduction. First, because the computational intuitions about $\overline{\lambda}\mu\tilde{\mu}$ are expressed in terms of a never-formalized natural deduction notation. Co-terms and cuts (="commands") of $\overline{\lambda}\mu\tilde{\mu}$ are interpreted, respectively, as "contexts" and (the instruction of? the result of?) "hole filling", where "contexts" are expressions with a hole from a never-specified language. Second, because $\overline{\lambda}\mu\tilde{\mu}$ dispenses with functional application, but it is rather natural and useful to "read back" to a notation where such construction is available [3,12].

However, classical natural deduction suffers from several problems of *design* and *dimension*. First, classical natural deduction is often defined as an intuitionistic natural deduction system supplemented with some classical inference principle. Prawitz [20] admits that *"this is perhaps not the most natural procedure from the classical logic point of view"*, as it does not reflect the de Morgan symmetry at the level of proofs; and already Gentzen observed that there is no canonical choice as to what inference principle to add. Computationally, and speaking now about the implicational fragment, this means that the λ-calculus may be extended with a variety of control operators: for instance $\mathcal{C}$, Δ, or $\mathtt{call - cc}$, corresponding to the principles double-negation elimination, *reductio ad absurdum*, and Peirce's law, respectively [8,10,21].

Second, the problem of dimension is that, in retrospect, the standard natural deduction systems are CBN, and all attempts to define classical CBV systems in natural deduction style [16,3,22,11,12] do not show an explanation of the proof-theoretical issues involved, and a rationale for the hidden CBV side of natural deduction. For instance, let-expressions are unavoidable in CBV λ-calculi, but no proof-theoretical understanding of them is offered. Naively, it is often thought that let-expressions form terms and are typed with the cut rule (of sequent calculus).

In this paper we introduce a new natural deduction system $\underline{\lambda}\mu\mathsf{let}$ for classical logic, presented as an extension of Parigot's $\lambda\mu$-calculus [17], and equipped with let-expressions. Like $\lambda\mu$, $\underline{\lambda}\mu\mathsf{let}$ does not depart from some intuitionistic system, but instead manipulates multiple conclusions. But the main design principle, of course not shared by $\lambda\mu$, is to obtain a system *isomorphic* to $\overline{\lambda}\mu\tilde{\mu}$, in order to have, in the natural deduction side, a system as faithful as LK to the dualities of classical logic. So, $\underline{\lambda}\mu\mathsf{let}$ comes with a sound bijection $\Theta : \overline{\lambda}\mu\tilde{\mu} \rightarrow \underline{\lambda}\mu\mathsf{let}$ at the level of the sets of proofs, that is also an isomorphism at the level of normalisation relations; and this isomorphism ensures that $\underline{\lambda}\mu\mathsf{let}$ is not yet another calculus, but rather a canonical classical natural deduction system.

As a proof system, $\underline{\lambda}\mu\mathsf{let}$ has an inference rule named *primitive substitution*, which is the typing rule for let-expressions. Primitive substitution is different from cut because its left premiss can be the conclusion of an elimination. When this is not the case, the primitive substitution is a mere *explicit substitution*[1][1].

---

[1] At the level of expressions, the corresponding particular case of let-expressions is called explicit substitution too. So we have the Curry-Howard pair (primitive substitution/let-expression), with particular case (explicit substitution/explicit substitution). To avoid confusion, we refer to any meta-*operation* of substitution as "meta-substitution".

This is the proof-theoretical understanding of let-expressions put forward by this paper.

$\lambda\mu$let is a "coercion calculus" [2,6,7], with its syntax carefully organized into syntactic classes. It has a class of *statements*, extending Parigot's named terms. Surprisingly, this is where let-expressions live. $\lambda\mu$let also has a class of *hole expression*, where applications live, suitable to be filled in the hole of *contexts*. These are a derived syntactic class, as usual in natural deduction, and consist of statements with a hole in the left end.

Such ingredients allow us to give a formalization, via Θ, of the usual semantics of $\overline{\lambda}\mu\tilde{\mu}$. We derive yet another syntactic notion in $\lambda\mu$let, that of *contextual*. Contextuals stand to contexts as numerals 0, $s(0)$, $s(s(0))$, etc. stand to numbers, and are therefore *instructions* for building contexts; and they are manipulated formally in $\overline{\lambda}\mu\tilde{\mu}$ as co-terms. Similarly, "commands" of $\overline{\lambda}\mu\tilde{\mu}$ are *instructions* of hole-filling, but the *result* of those instructions are the statements of $\lambda\mu$let. The isomorphism $\Theta : \overline{\lambda}\mu\tilde{\mu} \to \lambda\mu$let boils down to the execution of such instructions.

Θ is also the tool for doing "read-back" into natural deduction systematically. We use it to reflect in natural deduction the simple and elegant treatment of CBN and CBV computation offered by $\overline{\lambda}\mu\tilde{\mu}$ [3]. That is, we find in $\lambda\mu$let the right definitions of CBN and CBV reductions or subsystems when the appropriate restrictions of Θ from the known counterparts in $\overline{\lambda}\mu\tilde{\mu}$ can be established. In particular, we find new CBV λ-calculi in natural deduction syntax by reflecting, through Θ, the known CBV fragments of $\overline{\lambda}\mu\tilde{\mu}$. Surprisingly, the resulting calculi have escaped the recent efforts in the literature [3,22,11,12] for obtaining through similar proof-theoretical means λ-calculi for CBV combining control operators and let-expressions in a logically founded way.

Structure of the paper. The paper is organized as follows. Section 2 recalls $\overline{\lambda}\mu\tilde{\mu}$. Section 3 presents $\lambda\mu$let. Section 4 proves the isomorphism $\overline{\lambda}\mu\tilde{\mu} \cong \lambda\mu$let and explains the semantics of $\overline{\lambda}\mu\tilde{\mu}$ and the proof-theoretical foundation of let-expressions, explicit substitutions, and named expressions. Section 5 investigates CBN and CBV in $\lambda\mu$let, as well as "read-back" into natural deduction. Section 6 summarizes the paper, reviews the literature, and suggests future work.

2   Background

In this section we fix notation and recall Curien-Herbelin's $\overline{\lambda}\mu\tilde{\mu}$ [3].

Notations. In λ-calculi for classical logic, like $\lambda\mu$ or $\overline{\lambda}\mu\tilde{\mu}$, there are variables and co-variables. Variables (resp. co-variables) are always ranged by x, y, z (resp. a, b, c). Meta-substitution is denoted with square brackets $[\_/x]\_$. Similarly for other forms of meta-substitution used in λ-calculi for classical logic, like "structural" substitution. Explicit substitution is denoted with angle brackets $\langle\_/x\rangle\_$. All calculi in this paper assume Barendregt's variable convention (in particular we take renaming of bound variables or co-variables and avoidance of capture for granted).

$$\overline{\Gamma|a:A \vdash a:A, \Delta} \; LAx \qquad \overline{\Gamma, x:A \vdash x:A|\Delta} \; RAx$$

$$\frac{\Gamma \vdash u:A|\Delta \quad \Gamma|e:B \vdash \Delta}{\Gamma|u::e:A \supset B \vdash \Delta} \; LIntro \qquad \frac{\Gamma, x:A \vdash t:B|\Delta}{\Gamma \vdash \lambda x.t:A \supset B|\Delta} \; RIntro$$

$$\frac{c:(\Gamma, x:A \vdash \Delta)}{\Gamma|\tilde{\mu}x.c:A \vdash \Delta} \; LSel \qquad \frac{c:(\Gamma \vdash a:A, \Delta)}{\Gamma \vdash \mu a.c:A|\Delta} \; RSel$$

$$\frac{\Gamma \vdash t:A|\Delta \quad \Gamma|e:A \vdash \Delta}{\langle t|e\rangle:(\Gamma \vdash \Delta)} \; Cut$$

Fig. 1. Typing rules for $\overline{\lambda}\mu\tilde{\mu}$

A *value* is a variable or λ-abstraction, and usually is denoted V or W. If $\boldsymbol{N} = N_1, \cdots, N_m \, (m \geq 0)$, then $M\boldsymbol{N}$ denotes $MN_1 \cdots N_m$, that is, $(\cdots (MN_1) \cdots N_m))$, and $\boldsymbol{N} :: e$ denotes $N_1 :: \cdots :: N_m :: e$, that is, $(N_1 :: \cdots :: (N_m :: e) \cdots))$.

Types (=formulas) are ranged over by A, B, C and generated from type variables using the "arrow" (=implication), written $A \supset B$.

$\overline{\lambda}\mu\tilde{\mu}$**-calculus.** Expressions are either terms, co-terms or commands, and are defined by the following grammar:

$$t, u ::= x \mid \lambda x.t \mid \mu a.c \qquad e ::= a \mid u :: e \mid \tilde{\mu}x.c \qquad c ::= \langle t|e\rangle$$

There is one kind of sequent per each syntactic class $\Gamma \vdash t:A|\Delta$, $\Gamma|e:A \vdash \Delta$, and $c:(\Gamma \vdash \Delta)$. In the first two kinds, the displayed formula A is *selected*. Typing rules are given in Figure 1. A typable term is a term t such that $\Gamma \vdash t:A|\Delta$ is derivable, for some Γ, Δ, A. Similarly for co-terms e and commands c.

In addition to three ordinary substitution operators, there are three *co-substitution* operators $[e/a]c$, $[e/a]u$, and $[e/a]e'$. We use the abbreviations

$$\langle t/x\rangle c := \langle t|\tilde{\mu}x.c\rangle \qquad \langle e/a\rangle c := \langle \mu a.c|e\rangle \qquad (1)$$

called *explicit substitution* and *explicit co-substitution*, respectively.[2]

We consider 5 reduction rules:

$(\beta) \quad \langle \lambda x.t|u::e\rangle \rightarrow \langle u/x\rangle \langle t|e\rangle$

$(\sigma) \quad \langle t/x\rangle c \rightarrow [t/x]c \qquad (\eta_{\tilde{\mu}}) \; \tilde{\mu}x.\langle x|e\rangle \rightarrow e, \; \text{if } x \notin e$

$(\pi) \quad \langle e/a\rangle c \rightarrow [e/a]c \qquad (\eta_{\mu}) \; \mu a.\langle t|a\rangle \rightarrow t, \; \text{if } a \notin t$

The reduction rules usually named $\tilde{\mu}$ and μ are here renamed σ and π, respectively, and written with the (co)substitution abbreviations. The rules η_{μ} and $\eta_{\tilde{\mu}}$ are considered *e.g.* in [19][3]. There is a critical pair, called the *CBN-CBV dilemma*:

---

[2] It is useful to recall that Parigot's named terms are derived in $\overline{\lambda}\mu\tilde{\mu}$ as $a(t) := \langle t|a\rangle$.

[3] Curiously, if we omit the η-like rules, we do not see any of μ or $\tilde{\mu}$ in the reduction rules, when the (co-)substitution abbreviations (1) are used. The notation (1) emphasizes that β, σ, and π are about generation and execution of explicit (co-)substitution. The execution itself, by σ or π, is in one go, by calling meta-operations.

294   J. Espírito Santo

$$[\mu a.c/x]c' \xleftarrow{\quad \sigma \quad} \langle \mu a.c | \tilde{\mu} x.c' \rangle \xrightarrow{\quad \pi \quad} [\tilde{\mu} x.c'/a]c$$

According to [3], avoiding this dilemma is the principle for the definition of the CBN and CBV fragments of $\overline{\lambda}\mu\tilde{\mu}$. See section 5 for more on this.

3 The Natural Deduction System $\underline{\lambda}\mu$let

As we present $\underline{\lambda}\mu$let, we compare informally with Parigot's $\lambda\mu$ [17].

Primitive syntax. Expressions of $\underline{\lambda}\mu$let are defined by the following grammar:

(Terms)	$M, N, P ::= x \mid \lambda x.M \mid \mu a.S$
(Hole Expressions)	$H ::= \mathsf{h}(M) \mid HN$
(Statements)	$S ::= a(H) \mid \mathsf{let}\, x = H \,\mathsf{in}\, S$

Terms are either variables, λ-abstractions $\lambda x.M$, or μ-abstractions $\mu a.S$ whose body is a statement S. *Statements* are either *named expressions* of the form $a(H)$, or *let-expressions* $\mathsf{let}\, x = H \,\mathsf{in}\, S$. Hole expressions H are either *coercions* $\mathsf{h}(M)$, or *applications* HN^4. Informally, every statement has one of two forms $a((\mathsf{h}(M)N_1 \cdots N_m))$ or $\mathsf{let}\, x = (\mathsf{h}(M)N_1 \cdots N_m) \,\mathsf{in}\, S$, with $m \geq 0$. So, not only $\mathsf{h}(M)$ means M coerced to a hole expression, but it also signals the *head* term of a statement. In $\lambda\mu$ there are neither hole expressions, nor let-expressions. Applications are terms and statements are just named terms $a(M)$.

Typing system. The typing system of $\underline{\lambda}\mu$let, given in Fig. 2, derives three kinds of sequents, one for each syntactic class:

$$\Gamma \vdash M : A|\Delta \qquad \Gamma \rhd H : A|\Delta \qquad S : (\Gamma \vdash \Delta) \ .$$

The first and third kinds (*term sequents* and *statement sequents*, resp.) are familiar from $\lambda\mu$. If we disregard the distinction between the first two kinds of sequents, then the first five typing rules in Fig. 2 are exactly those of $\lambda\mu$, and the coercion rule is a trivial repetition rule. So, up to the substitution rule, we have a refinement of the typing system of $\lambda\mu$, that is, a classical natural deduction system where sequents have to be chosen of the appropriate kind, and containing an extra-rule for coercing between two different kinds of sequents.

The final rule, called primitive substitution, or just substitution, is also standard, apart from the fact that sequents have to be chosen of the appropriate kind. The connection and the difference relatively to sequent calculus' cut rule will become clear after the proof of $\overline{\lambda}\mu\tilde{\mu} \cong \underline{\lambda}\mu$let.

A *typable* term is a term M such that $\Gamma \vdash M : A|\Delta$ is derivable, for some Γ, Δ, A. Similarly for hole expressions H and statements S.

---

[4] Hole expressions are indeed expressions that go into the hole of contexts: see below. Ordinary application between two terms is derivable: $MN := \mu a.\mathsf{a}(\mathsf{h}(M)N)$; so are Parigot's named terms: $a(M) := a(\mathsf{h}(M))$

$$\frac{}{\Gamma, x : A \vdash x : A | \Delta} \; Assumption \qquad \frac{\Gamma \vdash M : A | \Delta}{\Gamma \triangleright \mathsf{h}(M) : A | \Delta} \; Coercion$$

$$\frac{\Gamma \triangleright H : A \supset B | \Delta \quad \Gamma \vdash N : A | \Delta}{\Gamma \triangleright HN : B | \Delta} \; Elim \qquad \frac{\Gamma, x : A \vdash M : B | \Delta}{\Gamma \vdash \lambda x.M : A \supset B | \Delta} \; Intro$$

$$\frac{\Gamma \triangleright H : A | \Delta, a : A}{a(H) : (\Gamma \vdash \Delta, a : A)} \; Pass \qquad \frac{S : (\Gamma \vdash \Delta, a : A)}{\Gamma \vdash \mu a.S : A | \Delta} \; Act$$

$$\frac{\Gamma \triangleright H : A | \Delta \quad S : (\Gamma, x : A \vdash \Delta)}{\mathsf{let}\, x = H \,\mathsf{in}\, S : (\Gamma \vdash \Delta)} \; Subst$$

Fig. 2. Typing rules for $\lambda\mu$let

Derived syntax. *Explicit substitution* in $\lambda\mu$let is the following abbreviation:

$$\langle N/x \rangle S := \mathsf{let}\, x = \mathsf{h}(N) \,\mathsf{in}\, S$$

Another *derived* syntactical concept of $\lambda\mu$let, crucial for the definition of reduction rules and for the comparison with $\overline{\lambda}\mu\tilde{\mu}$, is that of *context*[5]. A context is an expression of the two possible forms ($m \geq 0$):

$$a(([\,]N_1 \cdots N_m)) \qquad \mathsf{let}\, x = ([\,]N_1 \cdots N_m) \,\mathsf{in}\, S \qquad (2)$$

So, a context is a statement with a "hole" $[\,]$ in a position where a hole expression H is expected. Let $\mathcal{E}[\,]$ range over contexts, and $\mathcal{E}[H]$ denote the statement obtained by filling the hole of $\mathcal{E}[\,]$ with H. Such expressions are generated by the following algebra $\mathbb{E}$: two constants $a([\,])$ and $\mathsf{let}\, x = [\,] \,\mathsf{in}\, S$ and an operation that sends $\mathcal{E}[\,]$ to $\mathcal{E}[[\,]N]$. We introduce the signature of this algebra:

$$\begin{array}{cc} a([\,]) & a \\ \mathsf{let}\, x = [\,] \,\mathsf{in}\, S & \tilde{\mu}x.S \\ \mathcal{E}[\,] \mapsto \mathcal{E}[[\,]N] & N :: \_ \end{array}$$

The closed terms of the free algebra with the same signature are called *contextuals* and defined by the following grammar[6]:

$$\text{(Contextuals)} \quad \mathcal{E} ::= a \mid \tilde{\mu}x.S \mid N :: \mathcal{E}$$

In the same way as the numeral $s(s(0))$ denotes the number 2, the contextual $N ::$ $N' :: a$ (resp. $N :: \tilde{\mu}x.S$) denotes the context $a(([\,]NN'))$ (resp. $\mathsf{let}\, x = [\,]N \,\mathsf{in}\, S$).

---

[5] Rocheteau [22] *extends* $\lambda\mu$ with certain contexts. We follow the style of the natural deduction systems of [7], where contexts are not primitive.

[6] The notation is of course chosen to match that of $\overline{\lambda}\mu\tilde{\mu}$, but while in $\overline{\lambda}\mu\tilde{\mu}$ "contexts" (that is, co-terms) belong to the primitive syntax, context(ual)s in $\lambda\mu$let are a derived concept. The exact connection between contexts in $\overline{\lambda}\mu\tilde{\mu}$ and $\lambda\mu$let, which justifies the choice of notation, will be established later, after the isomorphism between the two systems is proved.

Since there is an intended interpretation of the signature (the algebra $\mathbb{E}$), each $\mathcal{E}$ is associated with a unique context. Since $\mathbb{E}$ generates the set of contexts, any context is denoted by some $\mathcal{E}$. So, we can *identify* contextuals with contexts (as we can identify numbers with numerals once the usual interpretation of 0 and s is fixed). For instance, hole filling $\mathcal{E}[H]$ can now be defined by recursion:

$$a[H] = a(H)$$
$$(\tilde{\mu}x.S)[H] = \text{let } x = H \text{ in } S \qquad (3)$$
$$(N :: \mathcal{E})[H] = \mathcal{E}[HN]$$

In addition to meta-substitution for variables, there are three operations of meta-substitution for co-variables $[\mathcal{E}/a]M$, $[\mathcal{E}/a]H$, and $[\mathcal{E}/a]S$, defined by a simultaneous recursion, all of whose clauses are homomorphic, but the crucial one:

$$[\mathcal{E}/a](a(H)) = \mathcal{E}[H'] \qquad \text{where } H' = [\mathcal{E}/a]H.$$

For instance: (i) $[N :: \mathcal{E}/a](a(\mathsf{h}(M))) = \mathcal{E}[\mathsf{h}(M')N]$, with $M' = [N :: \mathcal{E}/a]M$; so, $[N :: \mathcal{E}/a]_-$ is a form of "structural substitution" as found in $\lambda\mu$. (ii) $[b/a](a(H)) = b([b/a]H)$; $[b/a]_-$ is a renaming operation, also found in $\lambda\mu$. [7]

Reduction rules. Some of the reduction rules of $\underline{\lambda}\mu$let will act on the head of statements. We use contexts as a device for bringing to surface such heads, which normally are buried under a sequence of arguments. For instance, if S is $\text{let } x = \mathsf{h}(M)N_1 \cdots N_m \text{ in } S'$, then $S = \mathcal{E}[\mathsf{h}(M)]$, where $\mathcal{E} = N_1 :: \cdots N_m :: \tilde{\mu}x.S'$.

The reduction rules of $\underline{\lambda}\mu$let are as follows:

(β) $\mathcal{E}[\mathsf{h}(\lambda x.M)N] \rightarrow \langle N/x \rangle \mathcal{E}[\mathsf{h}(M)]$
(σ) $\langle N/x \rangle S \rightarrow [N/x]S$ (η_μ) $\mu a.a(\mathsf{h}(M)) \rightarrow M,\ a \notin M$
(π) $\mathcal{E}[\mathsf{h}(\mu a.S)] \rightarrow [\mathcal{E}/a]S$ (η_let) $\text{let } x = H \text{ in } \mathcal{E}[\mathsf{h}(x)] \rightarrow \mathcal{E}[H],\ x \notin \mathcal{E}$

By *normalisation* we mean $\beta\pi\sigma$-reduction.

Rule β generates a substitution, which is executed *implicitly* by a separate rule (σ). So, it would be perhaps more appropriate to call $\langle N/x \rangle S$ a "delayed" substitution. Rule π plays in $\underline{\lambda}\mu$let a role similar to the role played by rules μ and ρ in $\lambda\mu$, being the union of two rules:

$$b((\mathsf{h}(\mu a.s)N)) \rightarrow [N :: b/a]S \qquad (4)$$
$$\text{let } x = \mathsf{h}(\mu a.S)N \text{ in } S' \rightarrow [N :: \tilde{\mu}x.S'/a]S\ , \qquad (5)$$

with N of length $m \geq 0$. If $m = 0$ in (4), then we have a version of the "renaming" rule ρ. If $m > 0$ in (5), then a subexpression of the form $\mathsf{h}(\mu a.S)N$ exists, but, in contrast to rule μ of $\lambda\mu$, the whole statement of which $\mathsf{h}(\mu a.S)$ is the head is transformed in a single π-step. Rule η_μ is similar to the rule with

---

[7] Informally, the connection with "structural substitution" is as follows (N of length $m \geq 0$):

$$[N :: b/a]_- = [b(\bullet N)/a\bullet]_-$$
$$[N :: \tilde{\mu}x.S/a]_- = [\text{let } x = \bullet N \text{ in } S/a\bullet]_-$$

$$[\mu a.S/x]S' \xleftarrow{\quad\sigma\quad} \mathsf{let}\, x = \mathsf{h}(\mu a.S) \,\mathsf{in}\, S' \xrightarrow{\quad\pi\quad} [\tilde{\mu}x.S'/a]S$$

Fig. 3. CBN/CBV dilemma in $\underline{\lambda}\mu\mathsf{let}$

same name in $\lambda\mu$. Rule η_{let} has no counterpart in $\lambda\mu$ because the latter has no let-expressions.

Properties. Strong normalisation of typable expressions of $\underline{\lambda}\mu\mathsf{let}$ will be a consequence of isomorphism with $\overline{\lambda}\mu\tilde{\mu}$, to be proved in the next section.

If we take $\boldsymbol{N}$ of length 0 in (5), the redex is also a σ-redex. Hence, like $\overline{\lambda}\mu\tilde{\mu}$, $\underline{\lambda}\mu\mathsf{let}$ has a critical pair between π and σ that breaks confluence: see Fig. 3. Later (see Section 5) we will discuss fragments of $\underline{\lambda}\mu\mathsf{let}$ that are isomorphic to confluent fragments of $\overline{\lambda}\mu\tilde{\mu}$, and therefore confluent themselves.

The $\beta\pi\sigma$-normal forms are given by:

$$\begin{aligned}
M_{nf}, N_{nf} &::= x \mid \lambda x.M_{nf} \mid \mu a.S_{nf} \\
H_{nf} &::= \mathsf{h}(x) \mid H_{nf}N_{nf} \\
S_{nf} &::= a(\mathsf{h}(\lambda x.M_{nf})) \\
&\mid\; a(H_{nf}) \mid \mathsf{let}\, x = H_{nf}N_{nf} \,\mathsf{in}\, S_{nf}
\end{aligned}$$

At the level of derivations, the *normality criterion* is:

– The left premiss of every substitution is the conclusion of an elimination;
– The premiss of a coercion is never the conclusion of an activation; moreover if a coercion is the main premiss of an elimination, then its premiss is an assumption.

Theorem 1 (Subformula property). *In a derivation of $\Gamma \vdash M_{nf} : A|\Delta$, all formulas are subformulas of Γ, A, or Δ.*[8]

Proof. Similar claims for S_{nf} and H_{nf} are proved by simultaneous induction; but, crucially, the claim for H_{nf} is stronger: the type A is a subformula of Γ. □

Discussion. At first sight, $\underline{\lambda}\mu\mathsf{let}$ is a complex system. For instance, contexts are derived syntax, but the expressions that are filled in the hole of contexts are primitive. However, we seek, not what we would like natural deduction to be, but what natural deduction is, if it is to be isomorphic to $\overline{\lambda}\mu\tilde{\mu}$. Consider another example: reduction rules of $\underline{\lambda}\mu\mathsf{let}$. We might regret their complex formulation, with manipulation of contexts $\mathcal{E}$. But isn't $\underline{\lambda}\mu\mathsf{let}$ supposed to be a control calculus? The rule π is particularly revealing: it should express the features of μ-abstraction as a control operator; but, in $\overline{\lambda}\mu\tilde{\mu}$, π is *prima facie* a substitution execution rule; only its isomorphic counterpart in $\underline{\lambda}\mu\mathsf{let}$ reveals the control operation.

---

[8] We say that A is a subformula of Γ (resp. Δ) if A is subformula of some formula in Γ (resp. Δ).

$\underline{\lambda}\mu$let is a "coercion calculus". Simplifying matters, there is a coercion calculus in [2,6], whose syntax has the typical separation into several classes

$$M, N, P ::= x \mid \lambda x.M \mid \{H\} \qquad H ::= \mathsf{h}(M) \mid HN \ ,$$

reflecting in natural deduction a fragment of intuitionistic sequent calculus. In addition to $\mathsf{h}(M)$, there is a backward coercion $\{H\}$, which had to be developed in [7] to a substitution construction $\{H/x\}P$, in order to reflect full intuitionistic sequent calculus. $\underline{\lambda}\mu$let represents a further elaboration of the same construction, capable of capturing full classical sequent calculus.[9]

Regarding the proof of the subformula property, in $\underline{\lambda}\mu$let inspection of inference rules falls short[10], but nevertheless a proof by induction on normal forms is possible and straightforward. Prawitz [20] proves only a "slightly weakened subformula property" [25], that requires a preliminary analysis of the structure of normal derivations, by which "branches" are shown to have elimination and introduction parts. A similar structure is *built in* every derivation of $\underline{\lambda}\mu$let, as a consequence of its organization as a coercion calculus.

4   Isomorphism

In this section mappings $\Theta : \overline{\lambda}\mu\tilde{\mu} \rightarrow \underline{\lambda}\mu$let and $\Psi : \underline{\lambda}\mu$let $\rightarrow \overline{\lambda}\mu\tilde{\mu}$ are defined and analised. In particular, they establish $\overline{\lambda}\mu\tilde{\mu} \cong \underline{\lambda}\mu$let. As a corollary, strong normalisation for $\underline{\lambda}\mu$let follows. Next we show why Θ is a semantics of $\overline{\lambda}\mu\tilde{\mu}$, and explain the proof-theory of let-expressions and named expressions.

Mappings Ψ and Θ. Let $\Psi(M) = t$, $\Psi(N_i) = u_i$ and $\Psi(S) = c$. The idea behind $\Psi : \underline{\lambda}\mu$let $\longrightarrow \overline{\lambda}\mu\tilde{\mu}$ is to map statements as follows:

$$\mathsf{let}\, x = \mathsf{h}(M)N_1 \cdots N_m \,\mathsf{in}\, S \mapsto \langle t | u_1 :: \cdots :: u_m :: \tilde{\mu}x.c \rangle \qquad (6)$$

$$a((\mathsf{h}(M)N_1 \cdots N_m)) \mapsto \langle t | u_1 :: \cdots :: u_m :: a \rangle \qquad (7)$$

The idea behind $\Theta : \overline{\lambda}\mu\tilde{\mu} \longrightarrow \underline{\lambda}\mu$let is the translation of commands obtained by reverting these mappings, with $\Theta(t) = M$, $\Theta(u_i) = N_i$ and $\Theta(c) = S$. See Fig. 4. Observe that, in (6) and (7), each occurrence of application H_iN_i is replaced by an occurrence of left introduction $u_i :: e_i$. Conversely for Θ. Soundness of Θ and Ψ is routine. As a consequence, Θ and Ψ preserve typability.

Theorem 2 (Isomorphism). *Mappings Ψ and Θ are mutually inverse bijections between the set of $\overline{\lambda}\mu\tilde{\mu}$-terms and the set of $\underline{\lambda}\mu$let-terms. Moreover, for $R = \beta$ (resp. $R = \sigma, \pi, \eta_\mu, \eta_{\tilde{\mu}}$), and $R' = \beta$ (resp. $R' = \sigma, \pi, \eta_\mu, \eta_{\mathsf{let}}$):*

1. $t \rightarrow_R t'$ in $\overline{\lambda}\mu\tilde{\mu}$ iff $\Theta t \rightarrow_{R'} \Theta t'$ in $\underline{\lambda}\mu$let.
2. $M \rightarrow_{R'} M'$ in $\underline{\lambda}\mu$let iff $\Psi M \rightarrow_R \Psi M'$ in $\overline{\lambda}\mu\tilde{\mu}$.

---

[9] Observe the progression: $\{H\} := \{H/x\}x$ and $\{H/x\}P := \mu a.\mathsf{let}\, x = H \,\mathsf{in}\, a(\mathsf{h}(P))$.
[10] Inspection of inference rules is also insufficient for establishing the subformula property for $\overline{\lambda}\mu\tilde{\mu}$, because some instances of *Cut* are not eliminable.

$\Psi(x) = x$	$\Theta(x) = x$
$\Psi(\lambda x.M) = \lambda x.\Psi M$	$\Theta(\lambda x.t) = \lambda x.\Theta t$
$\Psi(\mu a.S) = \mu a.\Psi S$	$\Theta(\mu a.c) = \mu a.\Theta c$
$\Psi(a(H)) = \Psi(H, a)$	$\Theta\langle t|e\rangle = \Theta(\mathsf{h}(\Theta t), e)$
$\Psi(\text{let } x = H \text{ in } S) = \Psi(H, \tilde{\mu}x.\Psi S)$	$\Theta(H, a) = a(H)$
$\Psi(\mathsf{h}(M), e) = \langle \Psi M|e\rangle$	$\Theta(H, \tilde{\mu}x.c) = \text{let } x = H \text{ in } \Theta c$
$\Psi(HN, e) = \Psi(H, \Psi N :: e)$	$\Theta(H, u :: e) = \Theta(H\Theta u, e)$

Fig. 4. Mappings $\Psi : \underline{\lambda}\mu\text{let} \to \overline{\lambda}\mu\tilde{\mu}$ and $\Theta : \overline{\lambda}\mu\tilde{\mu} \to \underline{\lambda}\mu\text{let}$

Corollary 1 (SN). *Every typable expression of $\underline{\lambda}\mu\text{let}$ is $\beta\sigma\pi\eta_\mu\eta_{\text{let}}$-SN.*

Proof. SN holds of $\overline{\lambda}\mu\tilde{\mu}$ [19], Θ and Ψ preserve typability, and $\overline{\lambda}\mu\tilde{\mu} \cong \underline{\lambda}\mu\text{let}$. □

Semantics of $\overline{\lambda}\mu\tilde{\mu}$. The choice of notation for contexts in $\underline{\lambda}\mu\text{let}$ imposes the following trivial extensions of Ψ and Θ to contexts and co-terms:

$$\begin{aligned}
\Psi a &= a & \Theta a &= a \\
\Psi(\tilde{\mu}x.S) &= \tilde{\mu}x.\Psi S & \Theta(\tilde{\mu}x.c) &= \tilde{\mu}x.\Theta c \\
\Psi(N :: \mathcal{E}) &= \Psi N :: \Psi\mathcal{E} & \Theta(u :: e) &= \Theta u :: \Theta e
\end{aligned} \tag{8}$$

We can identify each context $\mathcal{E}$ of $\underline{\lambda}\mu\text{let}$ with a function of type $\underline{\lambda}\mu\text{let} - HoleExpressions \to \underline{\lambda}\mu\text{let} - Statements$; it is the function that sends H to $\mathcal{E}[H]$ (hence $\mathcal{E}(H) = \mathcal{E}[H]$). Now let e be a co-term of $\overline{\lambda}\mu\tilde{\mu}$ and consider $\Theta(\_, e) :$ $\underline{\lambda}\mu\text{let} - HoleExpressions \to \underline{\lambda}\mu\text{let} - Statements$. By induction on e one proves (simply by unfolding the definitions of $\Theta(H, e)$ in Fig. 4 and $\mathcal{E}[H]$ in (3)) that

$$\Theta(c)[H] = \Theta(H, e) . \tag{9}$$

Hence, $\Theta(\_, e)$ and Θe are the same function.

So, $\Theta(\_, a)$ and the $\underline{\lambda}\mu\text{let}$-context denoted a are the same function; if $S = \Theta c$, then $\Theta(\_, \tilde{\mu}x.c)$ and the $\underline{\lambda}\mu\text{let}$-context denoted $\tilde{\mu}x.S$ are the same function; finally, if $\Theta u = N$ and $\Theta e = \mathcal{E}$, then $\Theta(\_, u :: e)$ and the $\underline{\lambda}\mu\text{let}$-context denoted $N :: \mathcal{E}$ are the same function. This justifies the choice of notation for contexts in $\underline{\lambda}\mu\text{let}$.

The formalization of the intuitive *semantics* of $\overline{\lambda}\mu\tilde{\mu}$, offered by $\underline{\lambda}\mu\text{let}$, is the mapping $\theta : \overline{\lambda}\mu\tilde{\mu} \to \underline{\lambda}\mu\text{let}$ defined homomorphically on terms, like Θ; that sends co-terms to contexts homomorphically, as in (8); and defined by $\theta\langle t|e\rangle = \theta(e)[\mathsf{h}(\theta t)]$ on commands. The whole action of θ is concentrated on the translation of $\langle t|e\rangle$, that reads "fill $\mathsf{h}(\theta t)$ in the hole of the context θe".

Corollary 2 (Semantics of $\overline{\lambda}\mu\tilde{\mu}$). $\theta t = \Theta t$ and $\theta e = \Theta e$ and $\theta c = \Theta c$.

Proof. Trivial induction on t, e, and c. The case $c = \langle t|e\rangle$ follows from (9). □

So, the proof-theoretical mapping Θ, that replaces left-introductions by eliminations, is the semantics θ; and the latter is an isomorphism by Theorem 2.

Proof-theory of let-expressions and named expressions. Recall the typing systems of $\overline{\lambda}\mu\tilde{\mu}$ and $\underline{\lambda}\mu\text{let}$ (Figs. 1 and 2). We explain the difference between cut in $\overline{\lambda}\mu\tilde{\mu}$ and primitive substitution in $\lambda\mu$let, thereby clarifying the proof-theoretical status of let-expressions. We also argue that explicit substitutions and Parigot's named terms are, in some sense, neutral w.r.t. the sequent calculus/natural deduction difference.[11]

We say, for the sake of this discussion, that a cut $\langle t|e\rangle$ is of type I (resp. II) if it has the shape of the r.h.s. of (6) (resp. (7)). Through Θ, cuts of type I correspond to let-expressions/primitive substitutions $\mathsf{let}\, x = H \,\mathsf{in}\, S$, whereas cuts of type II correspond to the naming construction $a(H)$.[12]

In contrast to the right premiss e of the cut of type I $\langle t|e\rangle$, the right premiss S of the primitive substitution $\mathsf{let}\, x = H \,\mathsf{in}\, S$ can never be the conclusion of left-introduction (similar remark already made by Negri and von Plato [15], page 172). But, as a compensation, the left premiss H is not limited to be morally a term $\mathsf{h}(M)$ (as is the left premiss t in $\langle t|e\rangle$), it can be a sequence of eliminations (as already remarked in [7] for the intuitionistic case). So, cuts of type I (in sequent calculus) are more general on the right premiss, while substitutions (in natural deduction) are more general on the left premiss. But there is a kind of common case, when $e = \tilde{\mu}x.c$ (so e is not a left introduction), and $H = \mathsf{h}(M)$ (so H is not an elimination). Then the cut of type I has the form $\langle t/x\rangle c = \langle t|\tilde{\mu}x.c\rangle$ and the primitive substitution has the form $\langle N/x\rangle S = \mathsf{let}\, x = N \,\mathsf{in}\, S$, the form of an explicit substitution.

Similarly, Parigot's named terms can be seen as the common case of cuts of type II and the construction $a(H)$: such case reads $a(t) = \langle t|a\rangle$ ($e = a$ is not a left introduction) and $a(M) = a(\mathsf{h}(M))$ ($H = \mathsf{h}(M)$ is not an elimination).

5   Call-by-Name and Call-by-Value

In this section we analyse CBN and CBV in $\lambda\mu$let. We do "read-back" [3,12] in a systematic fashion, reflecting into $\lambda\mu$let, through Θ, the definitions of CBN and CBV reductions and fragments of $\overline{\lambda}\mu\tilde{\mu}$. Finally, we analyse the largest CBV fragment of $\lambda\mu$let obtained.

CBN and CBV reduction. In $\overline{\lambda}\mu\tilde{\mu}$, CBN and CBV reduction is defined by giving priority to either σ or π, respectively, in the CBN/CBV dilemma. Recall the CBN-CBV dilemma of $\lambda\mu$let (Fig. 3). In $\lambda\mu$let we define:

CBV reduction: σ is restricted to the case $\mathsf{let}\, x = \mathsf{h}(V) \,\mathsf{in}\, S' \to [V/x]S'$.

CBN reduction: π is restricted to the case $\mathcal{E}_n[\mathsf{h}(\mu a.S)] \to [\mathcal{E}_n/a]S$, where *CBN contexts* are given by: $\mathcal{E}_n ::= a \mid N :: \mathcal{E}_n$.

With the first restriction, the σ-reduction in Fig. 3 becomes forbidden; with the second, it is the π-reduction in Fig. 3 which becomes blocked.

CBN and CBV fragments. $\overline{\lambda}\mu\tilde{\mu}$ contains a CBN fragment $\overline{\lambda}\mu\tilde{\mu}_{\mathsf{T}}$ and a CBV fragment $\overline{\lambda}\mu\tilde{\mu}_{\mathsf{Q}}$, closed for CBN and CBV reduction, respectively. In addition, $\overline{\lambda}\mu\tilde{\mu}_{\mathsf{T}}$ contains itself a fragment $\overline{\lambda}\mu$ close to $\lambda\mu$, whereas $\overline{\lambda}\mu\tilde{\mu}_{\mathsf{Q}}$ contains itself

---

[11] Recall the particular cases $\langle M/x\rangle S \mapsto \langle t/x\rangle c$ and $a(M) \mapsto a(t)$ of (6) and (7), resp.

[12] In intuitionistic logic [7], cuts correspond only to primitive substitution.

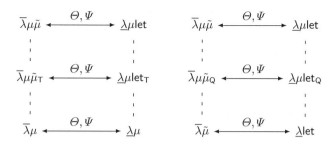

Fig. 5. CBN and CBV fragments

a fragment $\overline{\lambda}\tilde{\mu}$ which can be "read-back" as a CBV λ-calculus. All this comes from [3].

The following result can only be given here through a diagramatic summary. The proof is by suitable adaptations of Theorem 2.

Theorem 3 (Read-back). *There are CBN fragments $\underline{\lambda}\mu\mathsf{let}_\mathsf{T}$, $\underline{\lambda}\mu$, and CBV fragments $\underline{\lambda}\mu\mathsf{let}_\mathsf{Q}$, $\underline{\lambda}\mathsf{let}$ of $\underline{\lambda}\mu\mathsf{let}$ such that appropriate restrictions of Θ, Ψ establish the isomorphisms illustrated in Fig. 5.* [13]

In $\overline{\lambda}\mu\tilde{\mu}$ the T (resp. Q) subsystem is defined by requiring the right (resp. left) premiss of the left-introduction rule to be a co-value (resp. value). This is remarkably elegant. In $\underline{\lambda}\mu\mathsf{let}$ we have:

  T subsystem: obtained by restricting let-expressions to explicit substitutions.
  Q subsystem: obtained by restricting HN to HV.

These characterisations of the largest CBN and CBV fragments do not exhibit so clearly the duality of CBN/CBV [3], but nevertheless are either familiar (CBV case [18,24]) or insightful (CBN case). In fact, the collapse of let-expressions into explicit substitutions becomes an explanation for the fact that traditional natural deduction is CBN.[14]

CBV λ-calculus. The read-back results depicted in Fig. 5 cannot be found in [3,11]: in *op. cit* they were either not attempted, or not formalized, or not successful. The case of CBV is surprising. There were a number of recent attempts to obtain a CBV λ-calculus (in natural deduction syntax) with a formulation validated by a good correspondence with $\overline{\lambda}\mu\tilde{\mu}$ [22,11,12].[15] And yet, nothing like the natural deduction fragment $\underline{\lambda}\mu\mathsf{let}_\mathsf{Q}$ that corresponds to $\overline{\lambda}\mu\tilde{\mu}_\mathsf{Q}$ was obtained. $\underline{\lambda}\mu\mathsf{let}_\mathsf{Q}$ is given in Fig. 6, where *CBV contexts* are: $\mathcal{E}_v ::= a \mid \tilde{\mu}x.S \mid V :: \mathcal{E}_v$.

---

[13] The naming of systems is as follows. Symbols μ, T, and Q are invariant, when moving between sequent calculus and natural deduction. The remaining symbols obey the correspondence $\overline{\lambda}/\underline{\lambda}$ and $\tilde{\mu}/\mathsf{let}$.

[14] Traditional natural deduction goes even further, by allowing only implicit (*i.e.* meta) substitution.

[15] Such proof-theoretical approach contrasts with the development from [14] to [24], that put forward the computational λ-calculus as the paradigmatic CBV λ-calculus.

| $V ::= x \mid \lambda x.M$
$M, N ::= V \mid \mu a.S$
$H ::= \mathsf{h}(M) \mid HV$
$S ::= a(H) \mid \mathsf{let}\, x = H \,\mathsf{in}\, S$ | (β) $\mathcal{E}_v[\mathsf{h}(\lambda x.M)V] \to \langle V/x\rangle \mathcal{E}_v[\mathsf{h}(M)]$
(σ) $\langle V/x\rangle S \to [V/x]S$
(π) $\mathcal{E}_v[\mathsf{h}(\mu a.S)] \to [\mathcal{E}_v/a]S$
(η_μ) $\mu a.a(\mathsf{h}(M)) \to M,\ a \notin M$
(η_{let}) $\mathsf{let}\, x = H \,\mathsf{in}\, \mathcal{E}_v[\mathsf{h}(x)] \to \mathcal{E}_v[H],\ x \notin \mathcal{E}_v$ |

Fig. 6. $\lambda\mu\mathsf{let}_{\mathsf{Q}}$: a CBV fragment of $\lambda\mu\mathsf{let}$

Rocheteau's definition of CBV [22] does not agree with Ong-Stewart's [16][16]. The attempt to obtain the counterpart of $\overline{\lambda}\mu\tilde{\mu}_{\mathsf{Q}}$ in [11] admittedly failed [17]. Finally, the system in [12] places applications and let-expressions in the class of terms. As a result, there is a set of "structural" reduction rules in this system devoted to eliminate expressions which in $\lambda\mu\mathsf{let}$ (and therefore in $\overline{\lambda}\mu\tilde{\mu}$) are already ruled out by the organization of the syntactic classes. For instance, one such rule is the "associativity" of let-expressions, that reduces a let whose actual parameter is another let. Such expression does not exist in $\lambda\mu\mathsf{let}$.

6   Final Remarks

Summary. The system $\lambda\mu\mathsf{let}$ is not claimed to be as elegant as $\overline{\lambda}\mu\tilde{\mu}$, but its study is rich and fruitful, summarized in the following high-level lessons:

1. The syntax of natural deduction is non-trivial. Issues: the correct separation between what is primitive and what is derived; the correct organization into syntactic categories of the primitive syntax; only then let-expressions can be added.
2. There is a correspondence between cut in sequent calculus and primitive substitution in natural deduction; let-expressions and primitive substitution are in Curry-Howard correspondence; let-expressions generalize explicit substitutions, and are not exclusive of CBV.
3. It is the amalgamation of let-expressions and explicit substitutions that makes a natural deduction system CBN.
4. The isomorphism $\Theta : \overline{\lambda}\mu\tilde{\mu} \to \lambda\mu\mathsf{let}$ is a semantics that makes precise why co-terms and commands of $\overline{\lambda}\mu\tilde{\mu}$ are "contexts" and "hole-filling" instructions.
5. The isomorphism $\Theta : \overline{\lambda}\mu\tilde{\mu} \to \lambda\mu\mathsf{let}$ is a formal recipe for the "read-back" into natural deduction; in particular, is a recipe for the systematic generation of CBV λ-calculi in natural deduction style.

Related work. In the body of the paper detailed comparison was made between the proposed system $\lambda\mu\mathsf{let}$ and both $\lambda\mu$ and $\overline{\lambda}\mu\tilde{\mu}$ [17,3], as well as between the CBV fragments of $\lambda\mu\mathsf{let}$ and other proposals for CBV λ-calculi recently appeared in the literature [22,11,12].

---

[16] Let $M = (\mu b.S')(\mu a.S)$ and N be the CBV reduct of M. According to Rocheteau, N is $\mu a.[a((\mu b.S')\bullet)/a(\bullet)]S$, whereas, according to Ong-Stewart, N (as well as the CBN reduct of M) is $\mu b.[b(\bullet(\mu a.S))/b(\bullet)]S'$.

[17] It is the calculus called $\lambda^\eta_{\mu_{let}} - \eta^{let-app}_\mu$ in [11].

In the recent studies about the correspondence between sequent calculus and natural deduction, one approach is to identify fragments of sequent calculus isomorphic to natural deduction. The initial result is $\lambda_H \cong \lambda$ of [5]. Other contributions of this kind are in [3,13], although no isomorphism is claimed. The present paper belongs to another approach [26,7], which pursues extensions of natural deduction isomorphic to full sequent calculus. The isomorphism $\overline{\lambda}\mu\tilde{\mu} \cong \lambda\mu$let extends to classical logic the intuitionistic $\lambda^{\mathsf{Gtz}} \cong \lambda_{\mathsf{Nat}}$ of [7].

Dyckhoff and Lengrand [4] prove an equational correspondence [23] between LJQ (the Q subsystem of intuitionistic sequent calculus) and Moggi's computational λ-calculus [14]. An isomorphism is to be expected between LJQ and the intuitionistic, Q subsystem of $\lambda\mu$let.

Moggi [14] explained the difference between substitution and let-expressions as the difference between the *composition principles* of two different but related categories: some category with a monad and the corresponding Kleisli category. In the present paper we explain that cut and let are composition principles of two different but related proof-systems: sequent calculus and natural deduction.

Future work. This paper did not aim to contribute to the theory of CBV, but instead to produce, through a proof-theoretical analysis, new calculi for the future investigation of that theory. In spite of differing from other CBV λ-calculi in the literature, the new calculus $\lambda\mu$let$_{\mathsf{Q}}$, being isomorphic to $\overline{\lambda}\mu\tilde{\mu}_{\mathsf{Q}}$, validates the usual cps semantics [3]. The difference may be telling, however, if we consider reductions instead of equations, and operational aspects like standardization and abstract machines.

Acknowledgments. The author is supported by FCT, through Centro de Matemática, Universidade do Minho. Paul Taylor's macros were used for typesetting diagrams.

References

1. Abadi, M., Cardelli, L., Curien, P.-L., Lévy, J.-J.: Explicit substitutions. Journal of Functional Programming 1(4), 375–416 (1991)
2. Cervesato, I., Pfenning, F.: A linear spine calculus. Journal of Logic and Computation 13(5), 639–688 (2003)
3. Curien, P.-L., Herbelin, H.: The duality of computation. In: Proceedings of the Fifth ACM SIGPLAN International Conference on Functional Programming (ICFP 2000), Montreal, Canada, September 18-21. SIGPLAN Notices, vol. 35(9), pp. 233–243. ACM, New York (2000)
4. Dyckhoff, R., Lengrand, S.: Call-by-value lambda calculus and LJQ. Journal of Logic and Computation 17, 1109–1134 (2007)
5. Espírito Santo, J.: Revisiting the correspondence between cut-elimination and normalisation. In: Welzl, E., Montanari, U., Rolim, J.D.P. (eds.) ICALP 2000. LNCS, vol. 1853, pp. 600–611. Springer, Heidelberg (2000)
6. Espírito Santo, J.: An isomorphism between a fragment of sequent calculus and an extension of natural deduction. In: Baaz, M., Voronkov, A. (eds.) LPAR 2002. LNCS (LNAI), vol. 2514, pp. 354–366. Springer, Heidelberg (2002)

7. Espírito Santo, J.: The λ-calculus and the unity of structural proof theory. Theory of Computing Systems 45, 963–994 (2009)
8. Felleisen, M., Friedman, D., Kohlbecker, E., Duba, B.: Reasoning with continuations. In: 1st Symposium on Logic and Computer Science. IEEE, Los Alamitos (1986)
9. Gentzen, G.: Investigations into logical deduction. In: Szabo, M.E. (ed.) The collected papers of Gerhard Gentzen, pp. 68–131. North Holland, Amsterdam (1969)
10. Griffin, T.: A formulae-as-types notion of control. In: ACM Conf. Principles of Programming Languages. ACM Press, New York (1990)
11. Herbelin, H.: C'est maintenant qu'on calcule, Habilitation Thesis (2005)
12. Herbelin, H., Zimmermann, S.: An operational account of call-by-value minimal and classical lambda-calculus in "natural deduction" form. In: Curien, P.-L. (ed.) TLCA 2009. LNCS, vol. 5608, pp. 142–156. Springer, Heidelberg (2009)
13. Kikuchi, K.: Call-by-name reduction and cut-elimination in classical logic. Annals of Pure and Applied Logic 153, 38–65 (2008)
14. Moggi, E.: Computational lambda-calculus and monads. Technical Report ECS-LFCS-88-86, University of Edinburgh (1988)
15. Negri, S., von Plato, J.: Structural Proof Theory, Cambridge (2001)
16. Ong, C.-H.L., Stewart, C.A.: A Curry-Howard foundation for functional computation with control. In: Proc. of Symposium on Principles of Programming Languages (POPL 1997), pp. 215–217. ACM Press, New York (1997)
17. Parigot, M.: λμ-calculus: an algorithmic interpretation of classic natural deduction. In: Voronkov, A. (ed.) LPAR 1992. LNCS, vol. 624, pp. 190–201. Springer, Heidelberg (1992)
18. Plotkin, G.: Call-by-name, call-by-value and the λ-calculus. Theoretical Computer Science 1, 125–159 (1975)
19. Polonovski, E.: Strong normalization of lambda-mu-mu-tilde with explicit substitutions. In: Walukiewicz, I. (ed.) FOSSACS 2004. LNCS, vol. 2987, pp. 423–437. Springer, Heidelberg (2004)
20. Prawitz, D.: Natural Deduction. A Proof-Theoretical Study. Almquist and Wiksell, Stockholm (1965)
21. Rehof, N., Sorensen, M.: The λΔ-calculus. In: Hagiya, M., Mitchell, J.C. (eds.) TACS 1994. LNCS, vol. 789. Springer, Heidelberg (1994)
22. Rocheteau, J.: λμ-calculus and duality: call-by-name and call-by-value. In: Giesl, J. (ed.) RTA 2005. LNCS, vol. 3467, pp. 204–218. Springer, Heidelberg (2005)
23. Sabry, A., Felleisen, M.: Reasoning about programms in continuation-passing-style. LISP and Symbolic Computation 6(3/4), 289–360 (1993)
24. Sabry, A., Wadler, P.: A reflection on call-by-value. ACM Transactions on Programming Languages and Systems 19(6), 916–941 (1997)
25. Troelstra, A., Schwitchtenberg, H.: Basic Proof Theory, 2nd edn. Cambridge University Press, Cambridge (2000)
26. von Plato, J.: Natural deduction with general elimination rules. Annals of Mathematical Logic 40(7), 541–567 (2001)

Coordination Logic*

Bernd Finkbeiner[1] and Sven Schewe[2]

[1] Universität des Saarlandes
[2] University of Liverpool

Abstract. We introduce Coordination Logic (CL), a new temporal logic
that reasons about the interplay between behavior and informedness in
distributed systems. CL provides a logical representation for the distributed realizability problem and extends the game-based temporal logics, including the alternating-time temporal logics, strategy logic, and
game logic, with quantification over strategies under incomplete information. We show that the structure in CL that results from the nesting
of the quantifiers is sufficient to guarantee the decidability of the logic
and at the same time general enough to subsume and extend all previously known decidable cases of the distributed realizability problem.

1 Introduction

An intriguing aspect of the design of a distributed system is the interplay between
behavior and informedness: the *behavior* of a distributed system is determined
by the combination of local decisions, made by processes that only have *partial
information* about the system state. To ensure that the behavior of the full
system is correct, the processes must carefully coordinate so that each process
obtains the information needed for the right decision.

Historically, specification languages for distributed systems, in particular the
temporal logics, have focused on specifying the acceptable behavior and ignored
the question which level of informedness is needed to implement it. This is not
surprising, because the main application of these logics has been verification,
where one proves that the behavior of a complete system, with all implementation decisions already made, is correct. More recently, however, a lot of attention
has shifted towards analyzing distributed systems at early design stages, where
one has requirements but not yet a complete implementation [1,2,3,4,5,6,7,8,9].
At such a point in the design process, one is interested in *realizability* [6,7,8,9] (is
there an implementation that satisfies the requirements?) and other *game-based*
properties [1,2,3,4,5], such as: can a given coalition of processes accomplish a
certain goal against all possible actions of the other processes?

In the game-based setting, the connection between behavior and information becomes crucially important, because the strategic capabilities of a process
strongly depend on its informedness. Realizability and other game-based properties have therefore been investigated with respect to specific *system architectures*, that is, graphs of the communication topology, where the nodes represent

---

* This work was supported by DFG TR AVACS and by EPSRC grant EP/H046623/1.

A. Dawar and H. Veith (Eds.): CSL 2010, LNCS 6247, pp. 305–319, 2010.
© Springer-Verlag Berlin Heidelberg 2010

processes and edges represent communication links. Unfortunately, very few system architectures can be analyzed algorithmically: even for simple architectures, like the two-process architecture of a distributed arbiter, the realizability problem for the standard temporal logics LTL, CTL, and CTL*, as well as the model checking problems for the game-based extensions, including the alternating-time temporal logics [1,4], strategy logic [2], and game logic [1], are undecidable. Most practical approaches therefore concentrate on the simple but unrealistic special case where all processes have complete information.

In this paper, we re-investigate the interplay of behavior and informedness from a logical perspective. We introduce *Coordination Logic (CL)*, the first specification language that defines behavior and informedness *within* the logic instead of by referring to an external system architecture. CL uses two types of variables. *Coordination variables* represent knowledge, directly observed from the external environment or obtained through coordination with other system processes. *Strategy variables* encode the result of strategic choices that are made based on the values of the coordination variables. Either type of information can be hidden from other processes by quantification. As we will see, CL is a decidable logic that is not only sufficiently expressive to encode all queries over system architectures for which the game-based logics are decidable, but can additionally, because behavior and informedness are represented in the same logical framework, answer many queries over systems with otherwise undecidable architectures.

We motivate CL with a simple example. Consider the "statement" functionality of an automated banking terminal, where the user can choose to either show the statement on the screen or get a printout. We model this system with three coordination variables, a for account number, s for screen, p for printout, and two strategy variables, d for data, modeling the content of the statement sent from a central server to the terminal, and o for output, modeling the terminal's output. CL includes linear-time temporal logic (LTL) as a sublogic for the specification of behavioral requirements, so let us assume that the functionality of the terminal has been specified by an LTL formula φ. The CL specification now precisely identifies what information is visible to the terminal and what information is visible to the server. For example, the formula $\exists a, s, p \exists d, o\, \varphi$ specifies that the functionality specified in φ can be realized by communicating the full information to the server: the existential quantification $\exists d, o$ over the strategy variables d and o expresses the existence of a strategy for the server and the terminal; the existential quantification $\exists a, s, p$ over the coordination variables a, s, and p introduces the information on which the decisions on d and o are based. Clearly, however, full information is not needed in this example: the server does not need to know whether the client wants the statement on the screen or on the printer. This is expressed by the alternative specification $\exists a \exists d \exists s, p \exists o\, \varphi$, which hides the coordination variables s and p from the strategy variable d. The example can easily be extended to systems with multiple terminals, resulting in the conjunction $\bigwedge_{i=1,\ldots,n} \exists a_i \exists d_i \exists s_i, p_i \exists o_i\, \varphi_i$. The resulting star topology (many terminals communicate with a single server) is an example of a system architecture where game-based properties are in general undecidable [9]; the representation as a CL formula reveals, however, that this particular query is in fact decidable.

The remainder of the paper is structured as follows. After reviewing some basic notation on trees and tree automata in Section 2, we formally define CL in Section 3. Section 4 is devoted to a thorough study of the expressiveness of CL: we show that CL subsumes the usual linear and branching-time logics LTL, CTL, and CTL*, as well as the game-based logics ATL and ATL* [1], strategy logic [2], and game logic [1]. We furthermore show that the *distributed realizability problem* [6,7,8,9] can be encoded in CL for all system architectures where the problem is decidable. In fact, we show that CL makes it easier to identify decidable cases. For example, in the special case of local specifications, where the LTL specification consists of a separate conjunct for each process, the doubly flanked pipeline architecture, in which the otherwise least informed process has an additional input, is also decidable [10]. We give a new, simple proof of the decidability of doubly-flanked pipelines and local specifications by encoding the realizability problem as a CL formula.

Related work. There is a rich literature on game-based extensions of temporal logic, including the alternating-time temporal logics [1,4], strategy logic [2], and game logic [1]. Model checking algorithms for these logics typically assume that all processes are fully informed; however, versions with incomplete information have been defined, in particular for the alternating-time temporal logics [1,11]. Unlike CL, none of these logics combine the specification of behavior and informedness in the same formula.

There are several variations of the alternating-time temporal logics that are orthogonal to our study of the interplay of behavior and informedness. Alternating-time temporal epistemic logic [12] extends strategic properties with knowledge modalities. Hence, while CL specifies the existence of strategies that are *based* on incomplete information, this logic specifies the existence of strategies to *obtain* certain knowledge. Since the strategies itself are based on full information, actions that require certain knowledge must be restricted individually with explicit knowledge preconditions. Other notable variations of the alternating-time temporal logics include the extension to strategy contexts [13,5] and the restriction to bounded resources [3,5].

Our decision procedure for CL builds on standard automata constructions used in synthesis algorithms for distributed systems, in particular for pipeline and, more generally, weakly-ordered system architectures [6,7,8,9]. Since distributed realizability can be encoded in CL, our decision procedure subsumes the decidable realizability problems. Moreover, since we study behavior and informedness in a common logical representation, new cases can be identified as decidable simply by encoding the queries in CL.

2   Preliminaries

Trees. We use trees as a representation for strategies and computations. As usual, a (full) *tree* is given as the set Υ^* of all finite words over a given set of directions Υ. For given finite sets Σ and Υ, a Σ-*labeled* Υ-*tree* is a pair $\langle \Upsilon^*, l \rangle$ with a labeling function (or strategy) $l : \Upsilon^* \to \Sigma$ that maps every node of Υ^* to a letter of Σ. For a set $\Xi \times \Upsilon$ of directions and a node $x \in (\Xi \times \Upsilon)^*$, $hide_\Upsilon(x)$ denotes the node in Ξ^* obtained by replacing (ξ, υ) by ξ in each letter of x.

For a $\Sigma \times \Xi$-labeled Υ-tree $\langle \Upsilon^*, l \rangle$ we define the Ξ-projection of $\langle \Upsilon^*, l \rangle$, denoted by $proj_\Xi(\langle \Upsilon^*, l \rangle)$, as the Σ-labeled Υ-tree $\langle \Upsilon^*, \mathrm{pr}_1 \circ l \rangle$. That is, $proj_\Xi(\langle \Upsilon^*, l \rangle)$ is obtained from $\langle \Upsilon^*, l \rangle$ by projecting away the Ξ-part from the label in every node of Υ^*.

For a Σ-labeled Ξ-tree $\langle \Xi^*, l \rangle$ we define the Υ-widening of $\langle \Xi^*, l \rangle$, denoted by $wide_\Upsilon(\langle \Xi^*, l \rangle)$, as the Σ-labeled $\Xi \times \Upsilon$-tree $\langle (\Xi \times \Upsilon)^*, l' \rangle$ with $l'(x) = l(hide_\Upsilon(x))$. By abuse of notation, we use $wide_\Upsilon(l)$ for l'. In $wide_\Upsilon(\langle \Xi^*, l \rangle)$, nodes that are indistinguishable for someone who cannot observe Υ—that is, nodes x, y with $hide_\Upsilon(x) = hide_\Upsilon(y)$—have the same label.

If $\Xi = 2^X$ and $\Upsilon = 2^Y$ are power-sets of disjoint sets X and Y, we identify $\Xi \times \Upsilon$ with $2^{X \dot\cup Y}$, and use the widening operator $wide_\Upsilon$ accordingly. Let X and Y be sets with $Z = X \cup Y$, and let M and N be disjoint set. Then we denote with $\langle (2^Z)^*, l_M : (2^Z)^* \to 2^M \rangle \dot\cup \langle (2^Z)^*, l_N : (2^Z)^* \to 2^N \rangle$ the $2^{M \dot\cup N}$-labeled tree $\langle (2^Z)^*, l \rangle$ with $l(x) = l_M(x) \dot\cup l_N(x)$, and use $\langle (2^X)^*, l \rangle \oplus \langle (2^Y)^*, l' \rangle = wide_{2^Z \smallsetminus X}(\langle (2^X)^*, l \rangle) \dot\cup wide_{2^Z \smallsetminus Y}(\langle (2^Y)^*, l' \rangle)$.

For a Σ-labeled Υ-tree $\langle \Upsilon^*, l \rangle$ and a word $x \in \Upsilon^*$, we denote with $\langle \Upsilon^*, l \rangle | x$ the sub-tree rooted in x, that is, the tree $\langle \Upsilon^*, l' \rangle$ with $l'(y) = l(x \cdot y)$.

Automata. An (alternating parity) automaton $\mathcal{A} = (\Sigma, Q, q_0, \delta, \alpha)$ runs on Σ-labeled Υ-trees (for a predefined finite set Υ of directions). Q denotes a finite set of states, $q_0 \in Q$ denotes a designated initial state, δ denotes a transition function $\delta : Q \times \Sigma \to \mathbb{B}^+(Q \times \Upsilon_\varepsilon)$ for $\Upsilon_\varepsilon = \Upsilon \dot\cup \{\varepsilon\}$, and $\alpha : Q \to C$ is a function that maps the states of $\mathcal{A}$ to a finite set of colors $C \subset \mathbb{N}$. If $C = \{0, 1\}$, we call $\mathcal{A}$ a co-Büchi automaton.

A run tree on a given Σ-labeled Υ-tree $\langle \Upsilon^*, l \rangle$ is a $Q \times \Upsilon^*$-labeled tree where the root is labeled with (q_0, ε) and where for a node n with a label (q, x) and a set of children $child(n)$, the labels of these children have the following properties:

- for all $m \in child(n)$: the label of m is $(q_m, x \cdot \upsilon_m)$, $q_m \in Q, \upsilon_m \in \Upsilon_\varepsilon$ such that (q_m, υ_m) is an atom of $\delta(q, l(x))$, and
- the set of atoms defined by the children of n satisfies $\delta(q, l(x))$.

A path is accepted if the highest color appearing infinitely often is even. A run tree is *accepting* if all its paths are accepted, and a Σ-labeled Υ-tree is accepted by $\mathcal{A}$ if it has an accepting run tree. The set of trees accepted by an automaton $\mathcal{A}$ is called its *language* $\mathcal{L}(\mathcal{A})$.

The acceptance of a tree can also be viewed as the outcome of a game, where player *accept* chooses, for every pair $(q, x) \in Q \times \Upsilon^*$, a set of atoms that satisfy $\delta(q, l(x))$, and player *reject* chooses one of these atoms, which is executed. The input tree is accepted iff player *accept* has a strategy to enforce a path that satisfies the parity condition.

Theorem 1 (narrowing). *[14] For an automaton $\mathcal{A} = (\Sigma, Q, q_0, \delta, \alpha)$ over $\Xi \times \Upsilon$-trees, we can build an automaton $\mathcal{A}_n = (\Sigma, Q, q_0, \delta', \alpha)$ that accepts a Σ-labeled tree $\langle \Upsilon^*, l \rangle$ iff $wide_\Xi(\langle \Upsilon^*, l \rangle)$ is accepted by $\mathcal{A}$.* ◻

Theorem 2 (projection). *[15] For an automaton $\mathcal{A} = (\Sigma \times \Xi, Q, q_0, \delta, \alpha)$ over Υ-trees, we can build (1) an automaton $\mathcal{A}_w^b = (\Sigma, Q', q_0, \delta', \alpha')$ that accepts a Σ-labeled tree $\langle \Upsilon^*, l \rangle$ iff some $\Sigma \times \Xi$-labeled tree $\langle \Upsilon^*, l' \rangle$ that satisfies $\langle \Upsilon^*, l \rangle = proj_\Xi(\langle \Upsilon^*, l' \rangle)$ is accepted by $\mathcal{A}$, and (2) an automaton $\mathcal{A}_s^b = (\Sigma, Q', q_0, \delta', \alpha')$ that accepts a Σ-labeled tree $\langle \Upsilon^*, l \rangle$ iff all $\Sigma \times \Xi$-labeled trees $\langle \Upsilon^*, l' \rangle$ that satisfy $\langle \Upsilon^*, l \rangle = proj_\Xi(\langle \Upsilon^*, l' \rangle)$ are accepted by $\mathcal{A}$.* ◻

Note that, for technical convenience in the upcoming proofs, we assume that the initial state of $\mathcal{A}$ and the initial state of the respective transformed automaton are the same.

We call an automaton a *word automaton* if the set of directions is singleton, and *universal* if δ consists only of conjunctions. By abuse of notation, we interpret $\delta(q)$ as the set of its conjuncts for universal word automata.

3 Coordination Logic

Syntax. CL formulas are defined over two types of variables: coordination variables $\mathcal{C}$, and strategy variables $\mathcal{S}$. The operators of CL consist of the usual LTL operators Next $\bigcirc$, Until $\mathcal{U}$, and the dual Until $\overline{\mathcal{U}}$, as well as the new *subtree quantifiers* $\exists C \exists s.\varphi \mid \exists C \forall s.\varphi$. The syntax of CL is given by the grammar

$$\varphi ::= x \mid \neg x \mid \varphi \vee \varphi \mid \varphi \wedge \varphi \mid \bigcirc \varphi \mid \varphi \, \mathcal{U} \, \varphi \mid \varphi \, \overline{\mathcal{U}} \, \varphi \mid \exists C \exists s.\varphi \mid \exists C \forall s.\varphi,$$

where $x \in \mathcal{C} \dot\cup \mathcal{S}$, $C \subseteq \mathcal{C}$, and $s \in \mathcal{S}$.

We call a formula *well-formed* if the sets of coordination variables that occur under different $\exists$-operators are pairwise disjoint, and the same strategy variable is not introduced more than once. In the following we assume that all formulas are well-formed. (Well-formedness can be ensured by a suitable renaming.)

Note that we combine, for technical convenience and to emphasize the close connection between coordination and strategy variables, the introduction of both types of variables into a single subtree quantifier. We use $\forall s.\ \varphi$ and $\exists s.\ \varphi$ as abbreviations for $\exists \emptyset \forall s.\ \varphi$ and $\exists \emptyset \exists s.\ \varphi$, respectively, and $\exists C.\ \varphi$ as an abbreviation for $\exists C \forall s.\ \varphi$ (or, likewise, $\exists C \exists s.\ \varphi$), where s is a fresh strategy variable (which in particular does not occur in φ). We also use the standard abbreviations $true \equiv x \vee \neg x$, $false \equiv x \wedge \neg x$, $\diamondsuit \varphi \equiv true \, \mathcal{U} \, \varphi$, and $\square \varphi \equiv false \, \overline{\mathcal{U}} \, \varphi$.

Semantics. Coordination variables provide strategy variables with the information required for their decisions. Following the structure of a formula, a bound coordination variable c is *visible* to a bound strategy variable s, if s is in the scope of the subtree quantifier that introduced c. We denote the set of bound coordination variables that are visible to s by $scope(s)$. The free strategy variables, also called *atomic propositions*, are denoted by Π. For all atomic propositions $p \in \Pi$ it holds that $scope(p) = \emptyset$.

The set of free coordination variables is denoted by $\mathcal{F}$. Free coordination variables are visible to all strategy variables. We call the set of coordination variables visible to a strategy variable s the *scope* of s, denoted $Scope(s) = scope(s)\dot{\cup}\mathcal{F}$. By abuse of notation, we use $Scope(S) = \bigcup_{s \in S} scope(s)$ and $Scope(S) = \bigcup_{s \in S} Scope(s)$ for a set $S \subseteq \mathcal{S}$ of strategy variables, and $Scope(\lrcorner CQs.\varphi) = Scope(s)$, for $Q \in \{\exists, \forall\}$.

The meaning of a strategy variable s is a *strategy* $f_s : (2^{Scope(s)})^* \rightarrow 2^{\{s\}}$, i.e., a mapping from the information available to s, which consists of the history of the valuations of the coordination variables in the scope of s, to a (Boolean) valuation of s.

For a subset $S \subseteq \mathcal{S}$ of the strategy variables, we call the tree $\mathcal{T} = \bigoplus_{s \in S}\langle (2^{Scope(s)})^*, f_s\rangle$ defined by their joint valuation a *frame* over S. CL formulas are interpreted over frames $\mathcal{T} = \bigoplus_{p \in \Pi}\langle(2^{\mathcal{F}})^*, f_p\rangle$ over the atomic propositions, called *computation trees*.

As usual, a path in the tree $\mathcal{T}$ is an ω-word $\sigma = \sigma_0\sigma_1\sigma_2\ldots \in (2^{\mathcal{F}})^{\omega}$, and we denote the related labeled path by $\sigma^{\mathcal{T}} = (l(\varepsilon) \cup \sigma_0)(l(\sigma_0) \cup \sigma_1)(l(\sigma_0\sigma_1) \cup \sigma_2)(l(\sigma_0\sigma_1\sigma_2) \cup \sigma_3)\ldots \in (2^{\mathcal{F} \cup \Pi})^{\omega}$.

A tree $\mathcal{T}$ satisfies a CL formula φ, denoted by $\mathcal{T} \vDash \varphi$, iff all paths satisfy φ, i.e., $\forall\sigma \in (2^{\mathcal{F}})^{\omega}$. $\sigma, 0 \vDash^{\mathcal{T}} \varphi$, where the satisfaction of a CL formula φ on a path σ at position $i \geq 0$, denoted by $\sigma, i \vDash^{\mathcal{T}} \varphi$, is defined inductively as follows:

– for the strategy and coordination variables $x \in S\dot{\cup}\mathcal{C}$,
  - $\sigma, i \vDash^{\mathcal{T}} x :\Leftrightarrow x \in \sigma^{\mathcal{T}}(i)$, and
    $\sigma, i \vDash^{\mathcal{T}} \neg x :\Leftrightarrow x \notin \sigma^{\mathcal{T}}(i)$ for all $x \in \mathcal{S} \cup \mathcal{C}$;
– for the boolean connectives, where φ and ψ are CL formulas,
  - $\sigma, i \vDash^{\mathcal{T}} \varphi \vee \psi :\Leftrightarrow \sigma, i \vDash^{\mathcal{T}} \varphi$ or $\sigma, i \vDash^{\mathcal{T}} \psi$, and
  - $\sigma, i \vDash^{\mathcal{T}} \varphi \wedge \psi :\Leftrightarrow \sigma, i \vDash^{\mathcal{T}} \varphi$ and $\sigma, i \vDash^{\mathcal{T}} \psi$;
– for the temporal path operators, where φ and ψ are CL formulas,
  - $\sigma, i \vDash^{\mathcal{T}} \bigcirc \varphi :\Leftrightarrow \sigma, i+1 \vDash^{\mathcal{T}} \varphi$,
  - $\sigma, i \vDash^{\mathcal{T}} \varphi \mathcal{U} \psi :\Leftrightarrow \exists n \geq i. \ \sigma, n \vDash^{\mathcal{T}} \psi$ and $\forall m \in \{i, \ldots, n-1\}. \ \sigma, m \vDash^{\mathcal{T}} \varphi$,
  - $\sigma, i \vDash^{\mathcal{T}} \varphi \overline{\mathcal{U}} \psi :\Leftrightarrow \forall n \geq i. \ \sigma, n \vDash^{\mathcal{T}} \psi$ or
    $\exists n \geq i. \ \sigma, n \vDash^{\mathcal{T}} \varphi$ and $\forall m \in \{i, \ldots, n\}. \ \sigma, m \vDash^{\mathcal{T}} \psi$;
– for the subtree quantifiers, where $C \subseteq \mathcal{C}, s \in \mathcal{S}$, and φ is a CL formula,
  - $\sigma, i \vDash^{\mathcal{T}} \lrcorner C\exists s.\varphi :\Leftrightarrow \exists f : (2^{Scope(s)})^* \rightarrow 2^{\{s\}}. \ (\mathcal{T}|\sigma_i)\oplus\langle(2^{Scope(s)})^*, f\rangle \vDash \varphi$, where σ_i is the initial sequence of length i of σ,
  - $\sigma, i \vDash^{\mathcal{T}} \lrcorner C\forall s.\varphi :\Leftrightarrow \forall f : (2^{Scope(s)})^* \rightarrow 2^{\{s\}}. \ (\mathcal{T}|\sigma_i)\oplus\langle(2^{Scope(s)})^*, f\rangle \vDash \varphi$.

4 Expressive Power of Coordination Logic

Coordination logic is sufficiently expressive to subsume the model-checking problem for all other popular temporal logics, in particular for LTL, CTL, CTL*, ATL, ATL*, and strategy logic. Moreover, it can also express the satisfiability of these logics, as long as the branching degree of the models is fixed and can therefore be encoded using a finite set of variables. For logics like ATL*, where models of fixed branching degree are known to be sufficient [16], the satisfiability problem can thus be expressed in CL.

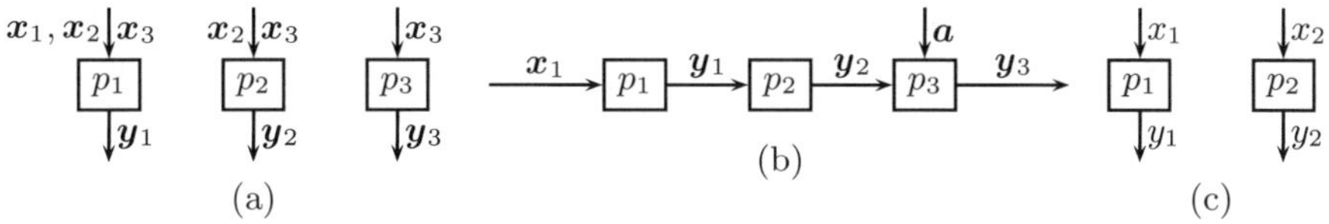

Fig. 1. Distributed architectures

Proposition 1. *The decision problem for strategy logic, game logic, and ATL** *and its sub-logics over models with a fixed branching degree can be encoded in CL.*

The distributed realizability problem is defined with respect to a system architecture, which is a directed finite graph whose nodes correspond to processes and whose edges are labeled with sets of variables: each process can read the variables on incoming edges and write to variables on the outgoing edges. There is a distinguished process, called the *environment process*, that provides the input to the system. Given such a system architecture, the *distributed realizability problem* [6,7,8,9] checks for the existence of a set of strategies, one for each process, such that the combination of these strategies satisfies the specification. We now describe an encoding of the realizability problem in CL for the two known decidable cases, the weakly-ordered architectures and the doubly-flanked pipelines. We begin with a simple special case of the weakly-ordered architectures, the linear architectures (cf. Figure 1a).

Realizability in linear architectures. In a *linear* architecture, each process reads only inputs from the external environment, not any outputs of other processes. Furthermore, we assume that the sets of variables visible to the processes are pairwise comparable (cf. Figure 1a) and, hence, define a linear 'informedness' pre-order on the output variables.

In the following, we will reuse the variables from the architecture as coordination and strategy variables in CL, denoting a vector $x_1, x_2, \ldots, x_i$ of variables by a single symbol $\boldsymbol{x}$. The realizability of an LTL formula φ in a linear architecture can be encoded as the CL formula $\exists \boldsymbol{x}_n \exists \boldsymbol{y}_n \ldots \exists \boldsymbol{x}_2 \exists \boldsymbol{y}_2 \exists \boldsymbol{x}_1 \exists \boldsymbol{y}_1 \varphi$, where the strategy variables $\boldsymbol{y}_i$ represent the output of the i-th best informed processes, and the coordination variables $\boldsymbol{x}_i$ represent the inputs from the environment that are available to the ith best informed processes, but not the $i + 1$st best informed processes.

Realizability in weakly-ordered architectures. Weakly-ordered architectures generalize linear architectures by allowing the processes to also read the output of other processes, while still requiring that ordering the processes according to their informedness results in a linear pre-order on the output variables. The realizability of temporal specifications in weakly-ordered architectures is decidable. In fact, the class of weakly-ordered architectures consists exactly of those architectures for which the realizability problem is decidable [9].

In a weakly-ordered architecture, we can assume w.l.o.g. that each process reads all inputs of less-informed processes directly as its own input [9]. In our encoding, we introduce additional coordination variables that simulate the input for the processes and then restrict the LTL formula to those paths where the true input and the mock input we introduced coincide. We obtain the CL formula $\exists x_n \exists y_n \ldots \exists x_2 \exists y_2 \exists x_1 \exists y_1 (\Box\, x^{mock} = y^{real}) \rightarrow \varphi$, where x_i are the (mock) input variables, and $\Box\, x^{mock} = y^{real}$ is the restriction to the paths in which the mock input corresponds to the true input.

Proposition 2. *The realizability problem for weakly-ordered architectures can be encoded in CL.*

This encoding also demonstrates the conciseness of CL: The encoding consists only of the LTL specification from the distributed realizability problem, and at most four copies of each variables. Deciding CL is thus at least as expensive as the realizability problem for weakly-ordered architectures, which is non-elementary [7].

Proposition 3. *The decision and model checking problem of CL are non-elementary.*

Since CL is decidable (cf. Corollary 1 in Section 5), it is clear that the realizability problem of undecidable architectures cannot be encoded in CL, but this does by no means imply that CL is restricted to encoding problems for decidable architectures. An interesting example are doubly-flanked pipeline architectures, for which the realizability of local LTL specifications is decidable.

Local specifications and doubly-flanked pipelines. A specification is called *local* if it only reasons about the variables of a single process, and a doubly flanked pipelines is, as shown in Figure 1b, a pipelines in which the otherwise least informed process has an additional input. The realizability of local LTL specifications in doubly-flanked pipelines is decidable [10]. In our encoding, we divide the realizability problem into two parts: one for the pipeline (minus process p_n) and one for p_n, and then couple these problems logically. This can be done by extending both pipelines (the one of length $n-1$ and the one of length 1) by a shadow process p_e which controls a Boolean variable e and reads a mock input x_n reflecting y_{n-1} (which is regarded as a true environment input for the short pipeline from the right); if ψ is the local specification for the rightmost process, and φ the conjunction over the specifications of the remaining processes, then we can simply strengthen φ to $\varphi \wedge \Box\, e$, forcing e to be true on all possible runs of y_{n-1}, and weaken ψ to $\Box\, e \rightarrow \psi$, which restricts ψ to paths marked as existing. Now, both of these sub-specifications start with $\exists x_n \exists e$, and it is easy to see that applying a conjunction after this operator provides the right level of light entanglement between the two sub-specifications.

In case of the example architecture from Figure 1b, this specification reads $\exists x_3 \exists e (\exists x_2 \exists y_2 \exists x_1 \exists y_1 (\Box\, x_2 = y_1 \wedge x_3 = y_2) \rightarrow (\varphi \wedge \Box\, e)) \wedge \exists a \exists y_3 (\Box\, e \rightarrow \psi)$.

Proposition 4. *The distributed realizability problem for doubly flanked pipelines can be encoded in CL.*

In fact, this encoding can easily be generalized to larger classes of specifications. In the full version of this paper [17] we describe such an extension.

5   Automata-Based Decision Procedure

Our decision procedure for coordination logic draws from the rich tool box of ω-automata transformations available in the literature for satisfiability checking and synthesis. As a preparation for the development of the decision procedure, we first rephrase the semantics for coordination logic as a model-checking game, which checks the correctness of $\mathcal{T} \vDash \varphi$.

Model-Checking Game.   For a CL formula φ, we denote with $dqsf(\varphi)$ the set of direct quantified sub-formulas defined by $dqsf(\exists CQs.\varphi) = \widehat{dqsf}(\varphi)$ for $\widehat{dqsf}(x) = \widehat{dqsf}(\neg x) = \emptyset$ for $x \in \mathcal{C} \cup \mathcal{S}$, $\widehat{dqsf}(\varphi \circ \psi) = \widehat{dqsf}(\varphi) \cup \widehat{dqsf}(\psi)$ for $\circ \in \{\wedge, \vee, \mathcal{U}, \overline{\mathcal{U}}\}$, $\widehat{dqsf}(\bigcirc \varphi) = \widehat{dqsf}(\varphi)$, and $\widehat{dqsf}(\exists CQs.\varphi) = \{\exists CQs.\varphi\}$.

With $\widehat{\psi}$, we denote the formula derived from ψ by replacing its direct quantified sub-formulas $dqsf(\varphi)$ by variables that reflect their correctness.

A model-checking game can, starting with the candidate $\mathcal{T}$ under consideration, expand $\mathcal{T}$ along the specification. Acceptance is determined by a game between two players, *accept* and *reject*. For unquantified formulas, the model-checking for $\mathcal{T} \vDash \varphi$ starts in a state $(\mathcal{T}, \varphi)$ and proceeds as follows:

1. player *accept* guesses the correctness of the state formulas $dqsf(\varphi)$, expanding the labeling function of $\mathcal{T}$ to $\mathcal{T}_1$,
2. player *reject* either (a) chooses an infinite path σ in $\mathcal{T}_1$ and test if it satisfies $\widehat{\varphi}$ and stop the game, or she (b) chooses a finite path π in $\mathcal{T}_1$ and a formula $\exists CQs.\psi \in \widehat{\varphi}$ that is marked valid in this position in $\mathcal{T}_1$, and proceeds in $\mathcal{T}_2 = \mathcal{T}_1|\pi$,
3. $\mathcal{T}_2$ is widened by 2^C to $\mathcal{T}_3 = wide_{2^C}(\mathcal{T}_2)$
4. for a formula $\exists C\exists s.\psi$ player accept, and for a formula $\exists C\forall s.\psi$ player reject extends the labeling of $\mathcal{T}_3$ by a valuation of s to $\mathcal{T}_4$, and the game proceeds in (1) from state $(\mathcal{T}_4, \psi)$.

For quantified formulas $\varphi = \exists CQs.\psi$, we choose initially $\mathcal{T}_3 = \mathcal{T}$ and start in Step (3).

Player *accept* wins if the path evaluated at the end of the game in Step (2) satisfies $\widehat{\varphi}$, while player reject wins otherwise. (Note that the game goes down in the formula tree in each round, and player *reject* must eventually choose to validate a path.)

Proposition 5. *The model-checking game is won by player accept iff $\mathcal{T} \vDash \varphi$.*

Proof. The game simply follows the structural definition of the semantics.

'$\Rightarrow$': Let $\mathcal{T} \vDash \varphi$. For the choices in Step (1), we can assume that player accept uses a perfect oracle, whose choice can be challenged by player reject. By the perfect choices of the oracle, player accept won the valuation of any path player reject chose in Step (2a), which might leave player reject with choosing a sub-formula that is claimed to be valid—and is therefore valid as the oracle is perfect—in Step (2b). By the definition of validity, this means that any (for a universally quantified sub-formula $\exists C \forall s.\psi$) or some (for an existentially quanti-fied sub-formula $\exists C \exists s.\psi$) extension of the proper widening of the tree contains only paths that satisfy ψ, which is reflected by Steps (3) and (4). This argument can then be repeated with the chosen sub-formula, until the a sub-formula φ with an empty set $dqsf(\varphi) = \emptyset$ of direct quantified sub-formulas is reached.

'$\Leftarrow$': Let $\mathcal{T} \nvDash \varphi$. For the choices player *accept* makes in Step (1), player *reject* uses a perfect oracle to find a position and direct quantified sub-formula, such that the sub-formula is claimed to be true. If no such position exists, there must be a trace that contradicts φ by our assumption, and player *reject* wins. (Note that claiming that a satisfied direct quantified sub-formula does not hold cannot help the acceptance of a path, because our specification is in positive form.) If such a position exists, the choice of the perfect oracle shows that some (for a sub-formula $\exists C \forall s.\psi$) or all (for a sub-formula $\exists C \forall s.\psi$) extensions of the proper widening of the tree is contains a path that does not satisfy ψ. This argument can again be repeated with the chosen sub-formula, until a sub-formula ψ with an empty set $dqsf(\varphi) = \emptyset$ of direct quantified sub-formulas is reached.

To bridge the remaining gap between this game and working with trees, we can obviously change the second step of the game to checking all paths and, for each direct quantified sub-formula and each position in the tree, constructing a copy of the tree. For each position in the tree, the respective proof obligation is handed down to the copies spawned for the direct quantified sub-formulas that are marked valid (but not for those marked invalid), and the procedure is continued for each copy as if it was chosen in the game described above.

This adjustment indicates the relation of the CL model-checking problem with current synthesis procedures [6,7,8,9] and outlines the required changes. In distributed synthesis, causal bound variables are usually existentially quantified and occur in a prenex. For such prenex quantifiers, the truth of sub-formulas is only relevant in the root ε, and the set of direct quantified sub-formulas is singleton or empty. Hence, while we need to expand the tree by copying the respective sub-tree and perform widening operations on all copies individually for CL, it suffices for current synthesis procedures to cope with widening operations for the complete tree.

Our automata-based decision procedure performs the inverse to the functions occurring in the adjusted acceptance game: narrowing [14] as the inverse of widening (Step 3 of the adjusted game), friendly and hostile projection [15] of a strategy as the inverse of friendly and hostile causal choice (Step 1 and 4), and re-routing the test-automaton for correctness of a direct quantified sub-formula from the copy to its blueprint (Step 2b). We therefore have to introduce a more intricate tree structure, to reason about sub-trees instead of full trees, and to re-route intermediate test-automata.

Down-trees. Our construction is based on *down-trees* (cf. Figure 2), which follow the structure of a CL specification. Down-trees are trees of trees that refer to a quantified sub-formula. Down-trees can be viewed as the outcome of the model checking game, where the operations are applied in all places at the same time, and serve as a structure to run an automata based technique that

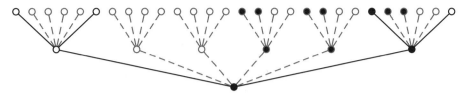

Fig. 2. Example down-tree: In a down tree, we start out with a slim tree that only branches by the valuations of the free communication variables, like the tree in black (full lines). This tree is labeled by the free strategy variables. An operator $\exists c \exists s$ spawns a new wider sub-tree (dashed lines) with a richer labeling function that additionally includes truth values of the bound strategy variable s. After projecting the new strategy variable s away, the new sub-tree is a *widening* of the sub-tree rooted in the respective node. That is, when restricted to the free strategy variables, the labeling of every path that is indistinguishable by the free coordination variables in the resulting tree is similar, as indicated by the blue-green-black path in the initial tree and its many copies of its ending sequences in the newly spawned sub-trees.

step-wise undoes the decisions in such a game. Viewed as a concurrent version of the game, the black (full) basic tree spawns siblings in each node, which are first widened, and whose label is then extended, using a friendly guess in case of existential quantifier, and a hostile guess in case of a universal quantifier. The automata-based construction introduced below puts a weak projection against the friendly guess, a strong projection against the hostile guess, and a narrowing operation against the widening.

Let Φ be the set of quantified sub-formulas of φ plus φ itself. We call a subset $\Psi \subseteq \Phi$ of Φ *sub-formula closed* if (1) $\psi' \in \Psi$ and $\psi \in dqsf(\psi') \cap \Phi$ imply $\psi \in \Psi$, and if (2) $\Psi \neq \emptyset$ implies $\varphi \subset \Psi$. A formula $\psi \subset \Psi$ is called *minimal* if none of its sub-formulas is in Ψ ($dqsf(\psi) \cap \Psi = \emptyset$).

For each formula $\psi \in \Psi$, we introduce a set $D_\psi = \{\psi\} \times 2^{Scope(\psi)}$ of directions, and denote their union by $D_\Psi = \bigcup_{\psi \in \Psi} D_\psi$. We call a sequence $d = \delta_0 \delta_1 \ldots \delta_n \in D_\Psi^*$ *falling* if, for all $i \geq 0$, $\delta_i \in D_\psi$ and $\delta_{i+1} \in D_{\psi'}$ implies that ψ' is a (not necessarily true) sub-formula of ψ. We call the set $\downarrow D_\Psi \subset D_\Psi^*$ of falling sequences in D_Ψ a *down-tree*, and denote, for a $\psi' \in \Psi$ and a $\psi \in dqsf(\psi') \cap \Psi$ that has no sub-formulas in Ψ ($dqsf(\psi) \cap \Psi = \emptyset$), with $\downarrow D_\Psi^\psi$ the down-tree obtained when using $D_\psi = \{\psi\} \times 2^{Scope(\psi')}$ (that is, we intuitively hide the fresh information from the variable bound by the leading quantifier of ψ).

We call the formula ψ from the first projection of the last letter $\delta_n = (\psi, V)$ of $d = \delta_0 \delta_1 \ldots \delta_n$ the *head* of a node d, and define φ to be the head of the empty word ε.

According to our demands, the labeling function for our down-trees has an amorphous co-domain that depends on the head of the node. A node with head ψ is labeled by a validity claim for all quantified super- and sub-formulas of ψ in Ψ (including ψ itself), the decisions of all bound strategy variables that are bound by a leading quantifier of these super- and sub-formulas, and the atomic propositions. We call down-trees with this amorphous co-domain Σ_Ψ-labeled down-trees. For the co-domain obtained by removing, for a minimal formula

$\exists CQs.\vartheta \in \Psi$, the $2^{\{s\}}$ part from the amorphous co-domain, we refer to Σ_ψ^s-labeled trees.

For $\varphi \neq \psi$ and a down-tree $\downarrow D_\Phi$, we call a sub-trees $\mathfrak{D} = d \cdot D_\psi^* \subseteq \downarrow D_\Phi$, for which ψ is a true sub-formula of the head of $d \in D_\Phi$, a ψ-tree in $\downarrow D_\Phi$. We call $\mathfrak{D}$ in $\downarrow D_\Phi$ reachable if, for all $d' \cdot \delta \in \mathfrak{D}$, the following holds: for the head φ' of d' and the head ψ' of $d' \cdot \delta$, all quantified true sub-formulas of φ' that contain ψ' as their sub-formula are marked as valid in $l(d')$. D_φ^* is the only φ-tree, and always reachable.

For a reachable ψ-tree $\mathfrak{D} = d \cdot D_\psi^* \subseteq \downarrow D_\Phi$ of a labeled down-tree $\langle \downarrow D_\Phi, l \rangle$, a path in $\mathfrak{D}$ is an ω-word $d, d \cdot (\psi, v_1), d \cdot (\psi, v_1) \cdot (\psi, v_2), \ldots$, and its trace is the ω-word $(l(d) \dot\cup v_1), (l(d) \dot\cup v_2), \ldots$. The reachable ψ-trees directly relate to the trees constructed in the adjusted model-checking game:

Observation 3. *For a given 2^Π-labeled $2^{\mathcal{F}}$-tree $\mathcal{T}$ and a given formula φ, the outcome of the adjusted acceptance game is a labeled down-tree intersected with the reachable trees.*

Player accept wins if, for all $\psi \in \Phi$, the trace of every labeled path of every reachable ψ-tree satisfies ψ.

We call a labeled down-tree where, for all $\psi \in \Phi$, the trace of every labeled path of every reachable ψ-tree satisfies ψ, *path accepting*.

Automata-Based Decision Procedure. Building on the above observation, we construct an automaton that accepts a labeled down-tree iff it is path accepting.

The simple path acceptance condition can be encoded in a universal co-Büchi automaton over labeled down-trees.

Lemma 1. *We can build a universal co-Büchi automaton that accepts a labeled down-tree iff it is path accepting.*

Construction: We first build, for every formula $\psi \in \Phi$, a universal co-Büchi automaton $\mathcal{U}_\psi = (\Sigma, Q_\psi, q_\psi, \delta_\psi, \alpha_\psi)$ for the claim-formula $\widehat{\psi}$ of ψ, using the standard translation for LTL. (The valuation of variables not in the language of $\mathcal{U}_\psi$ do not affect δ.) Using these automata as building blocks, we then build the universal automaton $\mathcal{U}^\varphi = (\Sigma, Q, \overline{\varphi}, \delta, \alpha)$, where Q consists of the disjoint union of the states of the individual $\mathcal{U}_\psi$, a fresh initial state $\overline{\varphi}$, and two fresh states, $\widetilde{\psi}$ and $\overline{\psi}$, for all other formulas $\psi \neq \varphi$ in Φ. All fresh states have color 0, while each other state $q \in Q_\psi$ keeps its color $\alpha(q) = \alpha_\psi(q)$.

The transition function δ is defined by

- $\delta(\overline{\psi}, \sigma) = (q_\psi, \varepsilon) \wedge \bigwedge_{\psi' \sigma \cap dqsf(\psi)} \delta(\widetilde{\psi'}, \varepsilon)$,
- $\delta(\widetilde{\psi}, \sigma) = \bigwedge_{d \in D_\vartheta}(\widetilde{\psi}, d)$ for $\psi \in dqsf(\vartheta)$ if $\psi \notin \sigma$ and
  $\delta(\widetilde{\psi}, \sigma) = \bigwedge_{d \in D_\vartheta}(\widetilde{\psi}, d) \wedge (\overline{\psi}, \varepsilon)$ otherwise, and
- $\delta(q, \sigma) = \bigwedge_{(\psi, v) \in D_\psi} \bigwedge_{q' \in \delta_\psi(q, \sigma \dot\cup v)} (q', (\psi, v))$ for all $q \in Q_\psi$. $\quad\square$

The role of the fresh states is to ensure that checking is initiated at the root of exactly the reachable ψ-trees, and the transition functions from the last line ensure that the correct paths are checked for the correct properties from there.

We call the states in Q_ψ of $\mathcal{U}^\varphi$ ψ-*states*, the respective state q_ψ the *initial ψ-state*, and $\overline{\psi}$ and $\widetilde{\psi}$ *fresh states*.

Using this automaton as a starting point, we can construct an alternating automaton that accepts the models of a specification by successively applying the inverse operations of widening and guessing operations from the adjusted acceptance game.

The widening and projection operation for standard trees naturally extend to down-trees. For a Σ-labeled down-tree $\langle \downarrow D_\Psi, l \rangle$, $proj_\Xi(\langle \downarrow D_\Psi, l \rangle)$ denotes the Σ'-labeled down-tree $\langle \downarrow D_\Psi, l' \rangle$ that results from node-wise projecting Ξ, provided the co-domain for the node is $\Xi' \times \Xi$ for some Ξ'.

For a minimal formula $\psi = \exists CQs.\vartheta'$ of Ψ, a Σ_ψ^s-labeled down-tree $\mathcal{T} = \langle \downarrow D_\Psi, l \rangle$ is the ψ-*widening* of a $\Sigma_{\tilde{\psi}}^s$-labeled down-tree $\mathcal{T}' = \langle \downarrow D_{\tilde{\psi}}^\psi, l' \rangle$, denoted $wide_{2^C,\psi}^{D_\psi}(\mathcal{T}') = \mathcal{T}$, iff $l(d \cdot d') = l'(d \cdot d'')$ holds for all $d \in \downarrow D_{\tilde{\psi}}^\psi \cap \downarrow D_\Psi$, $d' \in (\{\psi\} \times 2^{Scope(\psi)\setminus C})^*$, $d'' \in D_{\tilde{\psi}}^*$, and $d' = hide_{2^C}(d'')$.

Let $\psi = \exists CQs.\vartheta'$ be a minimal formula of Ψ and a direct quantified sub-formula of $\vartheta \in \Psi$, $\Psi' = \Psi \setminus \{\psi\}$, and $\langle \downarrow D_{\Psi'}, l \rangle$ a $\Sigma_{\tilde{\psi}}^s$-labeled down-tree. Then we denote with $copy_\psi \langle \downarrow D_{\Psi'}, l \rangle$ the Σ_Ψ^s-labeled down-tree $\langle \downarrow D_\Psi^\psi, l' \rangle$ with $l'(x_\psi) = l(x_\vartheta)$, where x_ϑ is derived from x_ψ by changing every letter (ψ, V) to (ϑ, V).

Theorem 4. *For a given CL specification φ, we can build an alternating automaton that accepts a 2^Π-labeled $2^\mathcal{F}$-tree iff it is a model of φ.*

Construction: The starting point of our construction is the automaton $\mathcal{A}_\Phi^1 = \mathcal{U}^\varphi$ from Lemma 1 that accepts a Σ_Φ-labeled down-tree $\langle \downarrow D_\Phi, l \rangle$ iff it is path accepting. Following the reverse of the structure of the adjusted acceptance game, we stepwise transform $\mathcal{A}_\Phi^1$ into an automaton $\mathcal{A}_\emptyset^3$ (for quantified) or $\mathcal{A}_{\{\varphi\}}^1$ (for unquantified formulas φ) that recognizes the models of φ.

For a non-empty subset $\Psi \subseteq \Phi$ of Φ, we first choose a sub-formula $\psi \in \Psi$ such that no true sub-formula of ψ is in Ψ ($dqsf(\psi) \cap \Psi = \emptyset$), and set $\Psi' = \Psi \setminus \{\psi\}$.

Let $\psi = \exists CQs.\psi'$. Note that s occurs only in the labels of ψ-trees, and only influences their acceptance, because they are only interpreted by the automaton A_ψ^1, iff it is in a ψ-state.

The **first transformation** refers to the $\forall s.$ or $\exists s.$ part of the specification, or to the fourth step of the adjusted acceptance game. Using Theorem 2, we construct an automaton $\mathcal{A}_{\Psi'}^4$ that accepts a Σ_Ψ^s-labeled down-tree $\langle \downarrow D_\Psi, l \rangle$ iff

- all Σ_Ψ-labeled down-trees $\langle \downarrow D_\Psi, l' \rangle$ with $proj_{2^{\{s\}}}(\langle \downarrow D_\Psi, l' \rangle) = \langle \downarrow D_\Psi, l \rangle$ are accepted by $\mathcal{A}_\Psi^1$ (for $Q = \forall$)), or
- some Σ_Ψ-labeled down-tree $\langle \downarrow D_\Psi, l' \rangle$ with $proj_{2^{\{s\}}}(\langle \downarrow D_\Psi, l' \rangle) = \langle \downarrow D_\Psi, l \rangle$ are accepted by $\mathcal{A}_\Psi^1$ (for $Q = \exists$)), respectively,

by applying the respective projection to the standard tree automaton that results from restricting $\mathcal{A}_\Psi^1$ to the ψ-states, with the initial ψ-state as initial state, and then replacing the old ψ-states (and transitions from there) by the new ones.

The **second transformation** refers to the $\exists C$ part of the specification, or to the third step of the adjusted model-checking game. We build an automaton $\mathcal{A}_{\Psi'}^3$

that accepts a Σ_ψ^s-labeled down-tree $\langle \downarrow D_\psi^\psi, l \rangle$ iff its widening $wide_{2^C,\psi}^{D_\psi}(\langle \downarrow D_\psi^\psi, l \rangle)$ is accepted by $\mathcal{A}_{\psi'}^4$. This transformation is the narrowing from Theorem 1 applied to the standard tree automaton that results from restricting $\mathcal{A}_\psi^4$ to the ψ-states. It only affects the transitions from the ψ-states.

The **third transformation** refers to **binding the extension to the labeled sub-tree**, or to copying the current sub-tree in the second step of the adjusted model-checking game. In the first step of this transformation, we construct the automaton $\mathcal{A}_{\psi'}^2{}' = (\Sigma_\psi^s, Q_\psi, \overline{\varphi}, \delta_\psi, \alpha_\psi)$ with the same states as $\mathcal{A}_{\psi'}^3$, that accepts a Σ_ψ^s-labeled down-tree $\langle \downarrow D_{\Psi'}, l \rangle$ if $copy_\psi \langle \downarrow D_{\Psi'}, l \rangle$ is accepted by $\mathcal{A}_{\psi'}^3$ by simply replacing every direction (ψ, V) by (ϑ, V), where ϑ is the formula in Ψ for which $\psi \in dqsf(\vartheta)$ holds: It obviously makes no difference if we continue in the blueprint or the copy. In a second step, we apply a minor change to $\mathcal{A}_{\psi'}^2{}'$ to properly turn the ψ-states into ϑ-states. For this change, we consider that the initial ϑ-state q_0^ϑ and $\widetilde{\psi}$ are only called from the state $\overline{\vartheta}$ in the transition $\delta(\overline{\vartheta}, \sigma) = (q_0^\vartheta, \varepsilon) \wedge \bigwedge_{\psi' \sigma \cap dqsf(\vartheta) \cap \Psi} \delta(\widetilde{\psi}', \varepsilon)$. We can therefore introduce a new initial ϑ-state $\widetilde{q_0^\vartheta}$ and call both states, q_0^ϑ and $\widetilde{\vartheta}$, through $\widetilde{q_0^\vartheta}$ by adjusting $\delta(\overline{\vartheta}, \sigma)$ to $(\widetilde{q_0^\vartheta}, \varepsilon) \wedge \bigwedge_{\psi' \sigma \cap dqsf(\vartheta) \cap \Psi'} \delta(\widetilde{\psi}', \varepsilon)$, and choosing $\delta(\widetilde{q_0^\vartheta}, \sigma) = (q_0^\vartheta, \varepsilon) \wedge (\widetilde{\psi}, \varepsilon)$. Transforming the winning strategy for either player is trivial for both steps, and $\widetilde{\psi}$, $\overline{\psi}$, and the former ψ-states become ϑ-states.

The **fourth transformation** refers to **guessing the correctness** of ψ, or to simulating the perfect oracle of the first step of the model-checking game. We build an automaton $\mathcal{A}_{\psi'}^1$ that accepts a $\Sigma_{\Psi'}$-labeled down-tree $\langle \downarrow D_{\Psi'}, l \rangle$ iff some Σ_ψ^s-labeled down-tree $\langle \downarrow D_\Psi, l' \rangle$ with $proj_{2^{\{\psi\}}}(\langle \downarrow D_\Psi, l' \rangle) = \langle \downarrow D_\Psi, l \rangle$ is accepted by $\mathcal{A}_{\psi'}^2$ by a transformation similar to the transformation from $\mathcal{A}_\psi^1$ to $\mathcal{A}_{\psi'}^4$.

These transformations are repeated until we have constructed $\mathcal{A}_\emptyset^3$ if φ is quantified, and $\mathcal{A}_{\{\varphi\}}^1$ otherwise.   □

Corollary 1. *The validity, satisfiability, and model-checking problems for CL are decidable.*   □

The proposed decision procedure is non-elementary, and Proposition 3 shows that this is unavoidable: The complexity of the easily encodable distributed synthesis problem [6,7,8,9] implies this for the restricted class of specifications with only existential (or only universal) quantification. However, a similar effect can be observed if we concentrate on the sub-logic without coordination variables; Disallowing coordination variables leaves us with QPTL, and hence with a tower of exponents linear in the number of quantifier alternations [18].

Beyond Coordination Logic. The power of fragments of Coordination Logic raises the question if there are natural decidable extensions. The first natural extension of CL would be to allow for an arbitrary assignment of information to strategy variables. This can, for example, be done by replacing the quantifiers $\exists CQs$ of the logic by more general quantifiers $QC \triangleright s$ that assign a set of coordination variables to s. This extension would allow to introduce information in a non-ordered fashion, for example, by introducing the same information multiple times or by withdrawing information. We call the resulting logic Extended Coordination Logic. While the semantics of CL naturally extends to Extended

CL—it suffices to change the quantifiers in the last two bullet points—Extended CL is undecidable, because we can encode the realizability problem for the undecidable architecture [6,7] of Figure 1c by $\exists\{x_1\} \triangleright y_1.\exists\{x_2\} \triangleright y_2.\varphi$ for every system specification φ.

Proposition 6. *The fragment of Extended Coordination Logic with two strategy variables and only prenex existential (or universal) quantification is undecidable.*

References

1. Alur, R., Henzinger, T.A., Kupferman, O.: Alternating-time temporal logic. J. ACM 49, 672–713 (2002)
2. Chatterjee, K., Henzinger, T.A., Piterman, N.: Strategy logic. In: Caires, L., Vasconcelos, V.T. (eds.) CONCUR 2007. LNCS, vol. 4703, pp. 59–73. Springer, Heidelberg (2007)
3. Schobbens, P.Y.: Alternating-time logic with imperfect recall. In: Proc. of LCMAS 2003. Electronic Notes in Theoretical Computer Science, vol. 85, pp. 82–93 (2004)
4. Pinchinat, S.: A generic constructive solution for concurrent games with expressive constraints on strategies. In: Namjoshi, K.S., Yoneda, T., Higashino, T., Okamura, Y. (eds.) ATVA 2007. LNCS, vol. 4762, pp. 253–267. Springer, Heidelberg (2007)
5. Brihaye, T., Lopes, A.D.C., Laroussinie, F., Markey, N.: ATL with strategy contexts and bounded memory. In: Artemov, S., Nerode, A. (eds.) LFCS 2009. LNCS, vol. 5407, pp. 92–106. Springer, Heidelberg (2008)
6. Pnueli, A., Rosner, R.: Distributed reactive systems are hard to synthesize. In: Proc. of FOCS, pp. 746–757 (1990)
7. Rosner, R.: Modular Synthesis of Reactive Systems. PhD thesis, Weizmann Institute of Science, Rehovot, Israel (1992)
8. Kupferman, O., Vardi, M.Y.: Synthesizing distributed systems. In: Proc. of LICS, pp. 389–398 (2001)
9. Finkbeiner, B., Schewe, S.: Uniform distributed synthesis. In: Proc. of LICS, pp. 321–330 (2005)
10. Madhusudan, P., Thiagarajan, P.S.: Distributed controller synthesis for local specifications. In: Orejas, F., Spirakis, P.G., van Leeuwen, J. (eds.) ICALP 2001. LNCS, vol. 2076, pp. 396–407. Springer, Heidelberg (2001)
11. Pinchinat, S., Riedweg, S.: A decidable class of problems for control under partial observation. Information Processing Letters 95, 454–460 (2005)
12. van der Hoek, W., Wooldridge, M.: Cooperation, knowledge, and time: Alternating-time temporal epistemic logic and its applications. Studia Logica 75, 125–157 (2003)
13. Ågotnes, T., Goranko, V., Jamroga, W.: Alternating-time temporal logics with irrevocable strategies. In: Proc. of TARK, pp. 15–24 (2007)
14. Kupferman, O., Vardi, M.Y.: Synthesis with incomplete informatio. In: Proc. of ICTL (1997)
15. Schewe, S., Finkbeiner, B.: Semi-automatic distributed synthesis. International Journal of Foundations of Computer Science 18, 113–138 (2007)
16. Schewe, S., Finkbeiner, B.: Satisfiability and finite model property for the alternating-time μ-calculus. In: Ésik, Z. (ed.) CSL 2006. LNCS, vol. 4207, pp. 591–605. Springer, Heidelberg (2006)
17. Finkbeiner, B., Schewe, S.: Coordination logic. Reports of SFB/TR 14 AVACS 63. SFB/TR 14 AVACS (2010), http://www.avacs.org, ISSN: 1860-9821
18. Sistla, A.P., Vardi, M.Y., Wolper, P.: The complementation problem for Büchi automata with applications to temporal logic. Theoretical Computer Science 49, 217–237 (1987)

Second-Order Equational Logic
(Extended Abstract)

Marcelo Fiore[1] and Chung-Kil Hur[2],[*]

[1] Computer Laboratory, University of Cambridge
[2] Laboratoire PPS, Université Paris 7

Abstract. We extend universal algebra and its equational logic from first to second order as follows.

1. We consider second-order equational presentations as specified by identities between second-order terms, with both variables and parameterised metavariables over signatures of variable-binding operators.
2. We develop an algebraic model theory for second-order equational presentations, generalising the semantics of (first-order) algebraic theories and of (untyped and simply-typed) lambda calculi.
3. We introduce a deductive system, *Second-Order Equational Logic*, for reasoning about the equality of second-order terms. Our development is novel in that this equational logic is synthesised from the model theory. Hence it is necessarily sound.
4. *Second-Order Equational Logic* is shown to be a conservative extension of Birkhoff's *(First-Order) Equational Logic*.
5. Two completeness results are established: the semantic completeness of equational derivability, and the derivability completeness of (bidirectional) *Second-Order Term Rewriting*.

1 Introduction

The notion of algebraic structure has solid mathematical foundations. In the traditional, first order, case our understanding of the subject is complete; allowing us to look at it from three different perspectives: universal algebra, equational logic, and categorical algebra. Of direct concern to us in this paper is the relationship between the first two.

Universal algebra provides a model theory for algebraic structure and equational logic a formal deductive system for reasoning about it. These are related by Birkhoff's theorem [4] establishing the semantic soundness and completeness of equational deduction (see Goguen and Meseguer [16] for the many-sorted case). The theory of computation also plays a role here: (bidirectional) term rewriting provides a sound and complete computational method for establishing equational derivability (see *e.g.* [3]).

We are interested in this paper in extending the above fundamental theory from first to second order, *i.e.* to languages with variable binding. Such formalisms arise in a wide range of subjects: category theory (*e.g.* ends), logic (*e.g.*

---
[*] Supported by Digiteo/Ile-de-France project COLLODI (2009-28HD).

A. Dawar and H. Veith (Eds.): CSL 2010, LNCS 6247, pp. 320–335, 2010.
© Springer-Verlag Berlin Heidelberg 2010

quantifiers), mathematics (*e.g.* integration), process calculi (*e.g.* restriction), programming languages (*e.g.* local scope), type theory (*e.g.* lambda calculi).

A central theme of our development is thus to set up the algebraic model theory and the formal deductive system that underlie higher-order equational theories. As in the first-order case, the model theory should provide general algebraic semantics from which syntactic models are to arise as free algebras. In addition, the deductive system should elucidate higher-order equational reasoning. This requirement rules out any system based on a higher-order metalanguage.

Syntactically, the passage from first to second order involves extending the language with both variable-binding operators and parameterised metavariables. These two concepts are orthogonal to each other, but it is with both of them in place that the language attains the required expressiveness. Variable-binding operators may bind a list of variables in each of their arguments and thereby lead to syntax up to alpha equivalence. Parameterised metavariables are, in effect, second-order variables for which substitution also involves instantiation. As far as we are aware, such second-order syntax was first put forward by Aczel [1]. (A variation of it incorporating abstractions features in the *CRSs* of Klop [21].)

A mathematical theory of second-order syntax was developed by Fiore [11], building on work of Fiore, Plotkin and Turi [15] and of Hamana [18]. In it, second-order syntax is abstractly characterised by free algebras of a term monad on a suitable semantic universe. This provides initial-algebra semantics, induction principles, and structural recursion. Moreover, the crucial result that term monads are strong provides a second-order substitution calculus, see [11, Part I].

Term monads for second-order syntax (being strong with respect to a biclosed action) fit into the mathematical framework of Fiore and Hur [13, 7, 19] for synthesising equational logics. This framework provides a canonical algebraic model theory for categorical equational presentations (in the form of sets of parallel pairs of Kleisli maps) together with a sound categorical equational metalogic for reasoning about them.

The gist of the work in this paper is then to instantiate our framework and apply the supporting methodology to: (*i*) derive a universal algebra for second-order equational presentations; (*ii*) synthesise a sound equational logic for reasoning about them; and (*iii*) relate the two by means of a completeness theorem.

Our work initiates thus the development of *Second-Order Universal Algebra*, which generalises the model theory of (first-order) algebraic theories and of (untyped and simply-typed) lambda calculi. The associated *Second-Order Equational Logic* is distilled from a categorical *Equational Metalogic*, but thereafter can be understood completely independent of it. Besides the rules for axioms and equivalence, it consists of just one additional rule stating that the operation of metavariable substitution in extended variable contexts is a congruence. At the level of equational derivability, the relationship between universal algebra and our second-order extension translates as a conservative-extension result. We further establish the semantic completeness of equational derivability, and the derivability completeness of (bidirectional) *Second-Order Term Rewriting*. These results firmly establish *Second-Order Universal Algebra*, *Second-Order*

Equational Logic, and *Second-Order Term Rewriting* as the model theory, proof theory, and rewriting theory of higher-order equational theories. (In particular, we provide model-theoretic foundations for *CRSs*; finally answering question (f) in [22, Section 15].)

In addition, we note that the perspective to first-order algebraic structure offered by Lawvere theories [23] has also been extended to second-order by Fiore and Mahmoud, see the companion paper [14].

Concerning related work, equational deductive systems for reasoning about algebraic structure with binding have already been considered in the literature. The systems closest to ours are the *Equational Logic for Binding Algebras* of Sun [27, 28] and the *Multi-Sorted Binding Equational Logic* of Plotkin [26]. These somehow sit in between our *Second-Order Equational Logic* and our bidirectional *Second-Order Term Rewriting*. The core of Sun's system consists of a substitution rule for variables and metavariables, and congruence rules for metavariables and operators. A major difference appears in the model theory, which Sun restricts to functional models (as in Aczel's *Frege Structures* [2]) that do not support free constructions and lead to a restricted completeness result. On the other hand, the system outlined by Plotkin shares the same syntax with ours, but it is also set up with congruence rules for metavariables and operators, and cut rules for variables and metavariables. Plotkin also considers general abstract models that axiomatise the algebraic structure of functional concrete models and are able to encompass initial syntactic models.

Another early system is the *Abstract Variable Binding Calculus* of Pigozzi and Salibra [25]. A strong point of departure between this system and ours is that in it metavariables are treated informally in the metalanguage. This results in the deductive system not being a true equational theory. More recently, there have been the *Equational Logic for Binding Terms (ELBT)* of Hamana [17], the *Nominal Algebra* of Gabbay and Mathijssen [24], and the *Nominal Equational Logic* of Clouston and Pitts [6]. The nominal systems have been shown to correspond to the *Synthetic Nominal Equational Logic (SNEL)* of Fiore and Hur [13] with metavariables that can be solely parameterised by names. The only essential difference between *SNEL* and *ELBT* is that the latter lacks a rule for atom elimination.

2   Syntactic Theory

The syntactic theory underlying *Second-Order Equational Logic* is introduced. The development comprises second-order signatures on top of which second-order terms in context are defined. For these the needed two-level substitution calculus is presented.

Signatures. A (second-order) *signature* $\Sigma = (T, O, |-|)$ is specified by a set of types T, a set of operators O, and an arity function $|-| : O \longrightarrow (T^* \times T)^* \times T$. This definition is a typed version of the binding signatures of Aczel [1] (see also [22, 15]).

Notation. We let $|\vec{\sigma}|$ be the length of a sequence $\vec{\sigma}$. For $1 \leq i \leq |\vec{\sigma}|$, we let σ_i be the ith element of $\vec{\sigma}$; so that $\vec{\sigma} = \sigma_1, \ldots, \sigma_{|\vec{\sigma}|}$.

For an operator $o \in O$, we typically write $o : (\vec{\sigma_1})\tau_1, \ldots, (\vec{\sigma_n})\tau_n \longrightarrow \tau$ whenever $|o| = \big((\vec{\sigma_1}, \tau_1) \ldots (\vec{\sigma_n}, \tau_n), \tau\big)$. The intended meaning here is that o is an operator of type τ taking n arguments each of which binds $n_i = |\vec{\sigma_i}|$ variables of types $\sigma_{i,1}, \ldots, \sigma_{i,n_i}$ in a term of type τ_i.

The second-order signature of the λ-calculus [1] is given below. Further examples already spelled out in the literature are the primitive recursion operator [1], the quantifiers [2], the fixpoint operator [22], and the list iterator [29]. In fact, any language with variable binding fits the formalism.

Example 1. The signature of the *typed λ-calculus* over a set of base types B has set of types $B^{\Rightarrow}$ given by

$$\frac{\beta \in B}{\beta \in B^{\Rightarrow}} \qquad\qquad \frac{\sigma, \tau \in B^{\Rightarrow}}{\sigma \Rightarrow \tau \in B^{\Rightarrow}}$$

and, for $\sigma, \tau \in B^{\Rightarrow}$, operators $\mathsf{abs}^{\sigma,\tau} : (\sigma)\tau \longrightarrow \sigma \Rightarrow \tau$ and $\mathsf{app}^{\sigma,\tau} : \sigma \Rightarrow \tau, \sigma \longrightarrow \tau$.

The signature of the *untyped λ-calculus* is as above when only one type, say D, is available. Hence, it has operators $\mathsf{abs} : (\mathsf{D})\mathsf{D} \longrightarrow \mathsf{D}$ and $\mathsf{app} : \mathsf{D}, \mathsf{D} \longrightarrow \mathsf{D}$.

Contexts. We will consider terms in typing contexts. Typing contexts have two zones, each respectively typing variables and metavariables. Variable typings are types. Metavariable typings are parameterised types: a metavariable of type $[\sigma_1, \ldots, \sigma_n]\tau$, when parameterised by terms of type $\sigma_1, \ldots, \sigma_n$, will yield a term of type τ. In accordance, we use the following representation for typing contexts: $\mathrm{M}_1 : [\vec{\sigma_1}]\tau_1, \ldots, \mathrm{M}_k : [\vec{\sigma_k}]\tau_k \triangleright x_1 : \sigma'_1, \ldots, x_\ell : \sigma'_\ell$, where all metavariables and all variables are assumed distinct.

Terms. Signatures give rise to terms. These are built up by means of operators from both variables and metavariables, and hence referred to as second-order.

Terms are considered up the α-equivalence relation induced by stipulating that, for every operator o, in the term $o\big(\ldots, (\vec{x_i})t_i, \ldots\big)$ the $\vec{x_i}$ are bound in t_i. This may be formalised in a variety of ways, but it is not necessary for us to do so here.

The judgement for *terms* in context $\Theta \triangleright \Gamma \vdash - : \tau$ is defined by the rules below. This definition is a typed version of the second-order syntax of Aczel [1].

(Variables) For $(x : \tau) \in \Gamma$,

$$\frac{}{\Theta \triangleright \Gamma \vdash x : \tau} \tag{1}$$

(Metavariables) For $(\mathrm{M} : [\tau_1, \ldots, \tau_n]\tau) \in \Theta$,

$$\frac{\Theta \triangleright \Gamma \vdash t_i : \tau_i \ (1 \le i \le n)}{\Theta \triangleright \Gamma \vdash \mathrm{M}[t_1, \ldots, t_n] : \tau} \tag{2}$$

(Operators) For $o : (\vec{\sigma_1})\tau_1, \ldots, (\vec{\sigma_n})\tau_n \longrightarrow \tau$,

$$\frac{\Theta \triangleright \Gamma, \vec{x_i} : \vec{\sigma_i} \vdash t_i : \tau_i \ (1 \le i \le n)}{\Theta \triangleright \Gamma \vdash o\big((\vec{x_1})\, t_1, \ldots, (\vec{x_n})\, t_n\big) : \tau} \tag{3}$$

where $\vec{x} : \vec{\sigma}$ stands for $x_1 : \sigma_1, \ldots, x_k : \sigma_k$.

Example 2. Two sample terms for the signature of the typed λ-calculus follow:

$$\mathrm{M} : [\sigma]\tau, \mathrm{N} : \sigma \rhd \cdot \vdash \mathsf{app}\big(\mathsf{abs}((x)\mathrm{M}[x]), \mathrm{N}[]\big) : \tau \ ,$$

$$\mathrm{M} : [\sigma]\tau, \mathrm{N} : \sigma \rhd \cdot \vdash \mathrm{M}[\mathrm{N}[]] : \tau \ .$$

Substitution calculus. The second-order nature of the syntax requires a two-level substitution calculus [1, 22, 29, 11]. Each level respectively accounts for the substitution of variables and metavariables, with the latter operation depending on the former.

The operation of *capture-avoiding simultaneous substitution* of terms for variables maps

$$\Theta \rhd x_1 : \sigma_1, \ldots, x_n : \sigma_n \vdash t : \tau \quad \text{and} \quad \Theta \rhd \Gamma \vdash t_i : \sigma_i \ (1 \leq i \leq n)$$

to

$$\Theta \rhd \Gamma \vdash t[t_i/x_i]_{1 \leq i \leq n} : \tau$$

according to the following definition:

- $x_j[t_i/x_i]_{1 \leq i \leq n} = t_j$
- $\big(\mathrm{M}[\ldots, s, \ldots]\big)[t_i/x_i]_{1 \leq i \leq n} = \mathrm{M}\big[\ldots, s[t_i/x_i]_{1 \leq i \leq n}, \ldots\big]$
- $\big(\mathrm{o}(\ldots, (y_1, \ldots, y_k)s, \ldots)\big)[t_i/x_i]_{1 \leq i \leq n}$
  $= \mathrm{o}\big(\ldots, (z_1, \ldots, z_k)s[t_i/x_i, z_j/y_j]_{1 \leq i \leq n, 1 \leq j \leq k}, \ldots\big)$
  with $z_j \notin \mathrm{dom}(\Gamma)$ for all $1 \leq j \leq k$

The operation of *metasubstitution* of abstracted terms for metavariables maps

$$\mathrm{M}_1 : [\vec{\sigma_1}]\tau_1, \ldots, \mathrm{M}_k : [\vec{\sigma_k}]\tau_k \rhd \Gamma \vdash t : \tau \text{ and } \Theta \rhd \Gamma, \vec{x_i} : \vec{\sigma_i} \vdash t_i : \tau_i \ (1 \leq i \leq k)$$

to

$$\Theta \rhd \Gamma \vdash t\{\mathrm{M}_i := (\vec{x_i})t_i\}_{1 \leq i \leq k} : \tau$$

according to the following definition:

- $x\{\mathrm{M}_i := (\vec{x_i})t_i\}_{1 \leq i \leq k} = x$
- $\big(\mathrm{M}_\ell[s_1, \ldots, s_m]\big)\{\mathrm{M}_i := (\vec{x_i})t_i\}_{1 \leq i \leq k} = t_\ell[s'_j/x_{i,j}]_{1 \leq j \leq m}$
  where, for $1 \leq j \leq m$, $s'_j = s_j\{\mathrm{M}_i := (\vec{x_i})t_i\}_{1 \leq i \leq k}$
- $\big(\mathrm{o}(\ldots, (\vec{x})s, \ldots)\big)\{\mathrm{M}_i := (\vec{x_i})t_i\}_{1 \leq i \leq k} = \mathrm{o}\big(\ldots, (\vec{x})s\{\mathrm{M}_i := (\vec{x_i})t_i\}_{1 \leq i \leq k}, \ldots\big)$

The syntactic theory can be completely justified on model-theoretic grounds, see [11]. We turn to this next.

3   Abstract Syntactic Theory

Having developed the second-order syntactic theory, our purpose in this section is to show how it arises from a model theory. This is important for several reasons: it provides an abstract characterisation of syntax by free constructions and thereby supports initial-algebra semantics and definitions by structural recursion; it encompasses and guarantees all the necessary properties of the substitution calculus; and it opens up the development of an algebraic model theory for second-order equational presentations together with an associated equational logic.

We now introduce the semantic universe and, within it, constructions for modelling substitution and algebraic structure. These lead to a canonical notion of model for second-order signatures [15, 10]. The syntactic nature of free models is then explained.

Notation. For a sequence $\vec{\sigma}$, we let $[\vec{\sigma}] = \{1, \ldots, |\vec{\sigma}|\}$.

Semantic universe. For a set T, we write $\mathbb{F}[T]$ for the free cocartesian category on T. Explicitly, it has set of objects T^* and morphisms $\vec{\sigma} \longrightarrow \vec{\tau}$ given by functions $\rho : [\vec{\sigma}] \longrightarrow [\vec{\tau}]$ such that $\sigma_i = \tau_{\rho i}$ for all $i \in [\vec{\sigma}]$.

For a set of types T, we will work within and over the semantic universe $\left(\boldsymbol{Set}^{\mathbb{F}[T]}\right)^T$ of T-sorted sets in T-typed contexts [8]. We write $\boldsymbol{y}$ for the Yoneda embedding $\mathbb{F}[T]^{\mathrm{op}} \hookrightarrow \boldsymbol{Set}^{\mathbb{F}[T]}$.

Substitution. We recall the *substitution monoidal structure* in semantic universes [9]. It has tensor unit and tensor product respectively given by $V_\tau = \boldsymbol{y}(\tau)$ and $(X \bullet Y)_\tau = X_\tau \odot Y$ where $P \odot Y = \int^{\vec{\sigma} \in \mathbb{F}[T]} P(\vec{\sigma}) \times \prod_{i \in [\vec{\sigma}]} Y_{\sigma_i}$.

A monoid $V \longrightarrow A \longleftarrow A \bullet A$ for the substitution monoidal structure equips A with substitution structure. In particular, the components $\boldsymbol{y}(\gamma) \longrightarrow A_\gamma$ of the unit induce the embedding

$$\left(A_\tau{}^{\boldsymbol{y}(\vec{\sigma})} \times \prod_{i \in [\vec{\sigma}]} A_{\sigma_i}\right)(\vec{\gamma}) \longrightarrow A_\tau(\vec{\gamma}, \vec{\sigma}) \times \prod_{j \in [\vec{\gamma}]} A_{\gamma_j}(\vec{\gamma}) \times \prod_{i \in [\vec{\sigma}]} A_{\sigma_i}(\vec{\gamma}) \longrightarrow (A_\tau \odot A)(\vec{\gamma})$$

which together with the component $A_\tau \odot A \longrightarrow A_\tau$ of the multiplication yield a *substitution operation*

$$\varsigma_{\vec{\sigma}, \tau} : A_\tau{}^{\boldsymbol{y}(\vec{\sigma})} \times \prod_{i \in [\vec{\sigma}]} A_{\sigma_i} \longrightarrow A_\tau \ .$$

These substitution operations provide the interpretation of metavariables.

The category of monoids for the substitution tensor product is isomorphic to that of T-sorted Lawvere theories and maps. The Lawvere theory $\mathbb{L}_A$ associated to A has objects T^* and hom-sets $\mathbb{L}_A(\vec{\sigma}, \vec{\tau}) = \prod_{i \in [\vec{\tau}]} A_{\tau_i}(\vec{\sigma})$, with identities and composition provided by the monoid structure. On the other hand, for every cartesian category $\mathscr{C}$ and assignment $C \in \mathscr{C}^T$ consider the functor

$$\langle C, - \rangle : \mathscr{C}^T \longrightarrow \left(\boldsymbol{Set}^{\mathbb{F}[T]}\right)^T \tag{4}$$

defined as $\langle C, D \rangle_\tau = \langle\!\langle C, D_\tau \rangle\!\rangle$ with $\langle\!\langle C, d \rangle\!\rangle(\vec{\sigma}) = \mathscr{C}\left(\prod_{1 \leq i \leq |\vec{\sigma}|} C_{\sigma_i}, d\right)$. Then, $\langle C, C \rangle$ has a canonical monoid structure given by projections and composition.

Algebras. Every signature Σ over a set of types T induces a *signature endofunctor* on $(\boldsymbol{Set}^{\mathbb{F}[T]})^T$ given by $(\Sigma X)_\tau = \coprod_{o:(\vec{\sigma_1})\tau_1, \ldots, (\vec{\sigma_n})\tau_n \to \tau} \prod_{1 \leq i \leq n} X_{\tau_i}{}^{\boldsymbol{y}(\vec{\sigma_i})}$. Σ-algebras provide interpretations for the operators of Σ.

We note that there are canonical natural isomorphisms

$$\coprod_{i \in I}(X_i \bullet Y) \cong \left(\coprod_{i \in I} X_i\right) \bullet Y$$

$$\left(\prod_{1 \leq i \leq n} X_i\right) \bullet Y \cong \prod_{1 \leq i \leq n}(X_i \bullet Y)$$

and, for all points $\nu : V \longrightarrow Y$, a natural extension map

$$\nu^\# : P^{\boldsymbol{y}(\vec{\sigma})} \odot Y \longrightarrow (P \odot Y)^{\boldsymbol{y}(\vec{\sigma})} \ .$$

These constructions equip every signature endofunctor with a *pointed strength*

$$\varpi_{X,V\to Y} : \underline{\Sigma}(X) \bullet Y \longrightarrow \underline{\Sigma}(X \bullet Y) \ .$$

(See [11] for details.)

Models. The models that we are interested in (referred to as Σ-*monoids* in [15, 11]) are algebras equipped with a compatible substitution structure.

For a signature Σ over a set of types T, we let Σ-Mod be the category of Σ-*models* with objects $A \in (\boldsymbol{Set}^{\mathbb{F}[T]})^T$ equipped with a $\underline{\Sigma}$-algebra structure $\underline{\Sigma}A \to A$ and a monoid structure $V \to A \leftarrow A \bullet A$ that are compatible in the sense that the diagram

$$
\begin{array}{ccc}
\underline{\Sigma}(A) \bullet A & \xrightarrow{\varpi_{A,V \to A}} \underline{\Sigma}(A \bullet A) \longrightarrow & \underline{\Sigma}(A) \\
\downarrow & & \downarrow \\
A \bullet A & \longrightarrow & A
\end{array}
$$

commutes. Morphisms are maps that are both $\underline{\Sigma}$-algebra and monoid homomorphims.

Term monad. The forgetful functor Σ-Mod $\to (\boldsymbol{Set}^{\mathbb{F}[T]})^T$ is monadic [11, 12]. Hence, writing $\mathcal{M}$ for the induced monad and $\mathcal{M}$-Alg for its category of Eilenberg-Moore algebras, we have a canonical isomorphism Σ-Mod $\cong \mathcal{M}$-Alg.

Carriers of free models can be explicitly described as initial algebras:

$$\mathcal{M}(X) = \mu Z. \, V + X \bullet Z + \underline{\Sigma}Z \ .$$

Free models on objects arising from metavariable contexts have a syntactic description [18, 11]. Indeed, for $\Theta = \big(M_1 : [\vec{\sigma_1}]\tau_1, \ldots, M_k : [\vec{\sigma_k}]\tau_k\big)$ a metavariable context, let $\underline{\Theta} = \coprod_{1 \le i \le k} \boldsymbol{y}(\vec{\sigma_i})_{@\tau_i}$ in $(\boldsymbol{Set}^{\mathbb{F}[T]})^T$, where $(P_{@\tau})_\alpha$ is P for $\alpha = \tau$ and 0 otherwise. Then, using that

$$\underline{\Theta} \bullet Z \cong \coprod_{1 \le i \le k} \big(\prod_{1 \le j \le |\vec{\sigma_i}|} Z_{\sigma_{i,j}}\big)_{@\tau_i} \ ,$$

the initial algebra structure

$$V + \underline{\Theta} \bullet \mathcal{M}\Theta + \underline{\Sigma}\mathcal{M}\Theta \overset{\cong}{\longrightarrow} \mathcal{M}\Theta$$

corresponds to the rules in (1–3), and we have the following syntactic characterisation

$$(\mathcal{M}\Theta)_\tau(\vec{\sigma}) \cong \{\, t \mid \Theta \rhd \vec{x} : \vec{\sigma} \vdash t : \tau \,\} \ . \tag{5}$$

We thus refer to $\mathcal{M}$ as the *term monad*.

The two-level substitution calculus arises as follows. The monoid multiplication $\mathcal{M}(\Theta) \bullet \mathcal{M}(\Theta) \to \mathcal{M}(\Theta)$, for Θ a metavariable context, amounts to the operation of capture-avoiding simultaneous substitution. On the other hand, the term monad comes equipped with a strength $\mathcal{M}(X) \otimes P \to \mathcal{M}(X \otimes P)$ where $(X \otimes P)_\tau = X_\tau \times P$. Thereby, every model $\mathcal{M}A \to A$ admits an interpretation map $\mathcal{M}(X) \otimes [X, A] \to \mathcal{M}\big(X \otimes [X, A]\big) \to \mathcal{M}(A) \to A$ where $[X, Y] = \prod_{\tau \in T} Y_\tau^{X_\tau}$. In particular, for metavariable contexts Θ and Ξ, the interpretation map $\mathcal{M}(\Theta) \otimes [\Theta, \mathcal{M}(\Xi)] \to \mathcal{M}(\Xi)$ amounts to the operation of metasubstitution. (See [11] for details.)

4   Equational Metalogic

Our aim now is to use the above monadic model theory for second-order syntax to synthesise a *Second-Order Equational Logic*. This development, which is presented in Section 5, depends on a general theory and methodology of the authors [13, 7, 19]. For the sake of completeness, an outline of the framework follows.

To every strong monad T with respect to a biclosed action [20] we associate an *Equational Metalogic*. This is a deductive system for reasoning about the equality of the interpretation of Kleisli maps $X \longrightarrow TY$ in Eilenberg-Moore algebras $TA \longrightarrow A$ as captured by the following satisfaction relation:

$$A \models f \equiv g : X \longrightarrow TY \text{ iff } \llbracket f \rrbracket = \llbracket g \rrbracket : X \otimes [Y, A] \longrightarrow A$$

where

$$\llbracket h \rrbracket = \left(X \otimes [Y, A] \xrightarrow{h \otimes \mathrm{id}} T(Y) \otimes [Y, A] \longrightarrow A \right) . \tag{6}$$

Equational metalogic is parameterised by a set of axioms E given by parallel pairs of Kleisli maps. The rules assert the derivability of judgements of the form $E \vdash f \equiv g : X \longrightarrow TY$ and are given in Figure 1.

(Axiom)

$$\frac{(f, g : X \longrightarrow TY) \in E}{E \vdash f \equiv g : X \longrightarrow TY}$$

(Equivalence)

$$\frac{f : X \longrightarrow TY}{E \vdash f = f : X \longrightarrow TY} \qquad \frac{E \vdash f \equiv g : X \longrightarrow TY}{E \vdash g = f : X \longrightarrow TY} \qquad \frac{\begin{array}{c} E \vdash f \equiv g : X \longrightarrow TY \\ E \vdash g \equiv h : X \longrightarrow TY \end{array}}{E \vdash f \equiv h : X \longrightarrow TY}$$

(Composition)

$$\frac{E \vdash f_1 \equiv g_1 : X \longrightarrow TY \qquad E \vdash f_2 \equiv g_2 : Y \longrightarrow TZ}{E \vdash f_1[f_2] \equiv g_1[g_2] : X \longrightarrow TZ}$$

where, for $f : X \longrightarrow TY$ and $g : Y \longrightarrow TZ$, $f[g]$ is the Kleisli composite
$X \xrightarrow{f} TY \xrightarrow{Tg} TTY \longrightarrow TY$

(Parameterisation)

$$\frac{E \vdash f \equiv g : X \longrightarrow TY}{E \vdash f\langle P \rangle \equiv g\langle P \rangle : X \otimes P \longrightarrow T(Y \otimes P)}$$

where, for $h : X \longrightarrow TY$, $h\langle P \rangle = \left(X \otimes P \xrightarrow{h \otimes \mathrm{id}} T(Y) \otimes P \longrightarrow T(Y \otimes P) \right)$

(Local character)

$$\frac{E \vdash f \, e_i \equiv g \, e_i : X_i \longrightarrow TY \quad (i \in I)}{E \vdash f \equiv g : X \longrightarrow TY} \quad (\{e_i : X_i \longrightarrow X\}_{i \in I} \text{ jointly epi})$$

Fig. 1. Equational Metalogic

Remark. In the presence of coproducts, the rule

(Local parameterised composition)

$$\frac{E \vdash f \equiv g : X \longrightarrow T\left(\coprod_{i \in I} Y_i\right) \qquad E \vdash f_i \equiv g_i : Y_i \otimes P \longrightarrow TZ \quad (i \in I)}{E \vdash f\langle P\rangle\big[\,[f_i]_{i \in I}\,\big] \equiv g\langle P\rangle\big[\,[g_i]_{i \in I}\,\big] : X \otimes P \longrightarrow T(Z)}$$

is derivable, and may be used instead of the (Composition) and (Parameterisation) rules.

The category (T, E)-**Alg** of (T, E)-*algebras* is defined as the full subcategory of the category T-**Alg** of Eilenberg-Moore algebras that satisfy the axioms E. We have the following two important results.

(Soundness) If $E \vdash f \equiv g$ then $A \models f \equiv g$ for all (T, E)-algebras A.

(Internal completeness) If every object Z admits a free (T, E)-algebra $T_E(Z)$,
  then we have a quotient map $q : T \longrightarrow T_E$ and the following are equivalent:
  (1) $A \models f \equiv g : X \longrightarrow TY$ for all (T, E)-algebras A
  (2) $T_E(Y) \models f \equiv g : X \longrightarrow TY$
  (3) $q_Y\, f = q_Y\, g : X \longrightarrow T_E(Y)$

5   Second-Order Equational Logic

Second-Order Equational Logic is now synthesised from *Equational Metalogic*. This is done by: (i) considering the term monad $\mathcal{M}$; (ii) restricting attention to Kleisli maps of the form $\boldsymbol{y}(\vec{\sigma})_{@\tau} \longrightarrow \mathcal{M}(\Theta)$, which by (5) amount to second-order terms of type τ in context $\Theta \rhd \vec{x} : \vec{\sigma}$; and ($iii$) rendering the rules in syntactic form.

Presentations. An *equational presentation* is a set of axioms each of which is a pair of terms in context.

Example 3. The equational presentation of the typed λ-calculus follows.

$$(\beta)\ \text{M} : [\sigma]\tau, \text{N} : [\,]\sigma \rhd \cdot \vdash \mathsf{app}\big(\mathsf{abs}(\,(x)\text{M}[x]\,), \text{N}[\,]\big) \equiv \text{M}\big[\text{N}[\,]\big] : \tau$$

$$(\eta)\ \text{F} : [\,](\sigma \Rightarrow \tau) \rhd \cdot \vdash \mathsf{abs}\big(\,(x)\mathsf{app}(\text{F}[\,], x)\,\big) \equiv \text{F}[\,] : \sigma \Rightarrow \tau$$

On top of the second-order equational presentation of the typed λ-calculus, one can then formalise any higher-order equational theory (like, for instance, equational axiomatisations of Church's *Simple Theory of Types* [5]) as an extended second-order equational presentation. We emphasise, however, that the expressiveness of our formalism does not rely on that of lambda calculi. For instance, one can directly axiomatise primitive recursion [1], predicate logic [26], and integration [25] as second-order equational presentations.

Logic. The rules of *Second-Order Equational Logic* are given in Figure 2. The (Extended metasubstitution) rule is a syntactic rendering of the (Local parameterised composition) rule. The syntactic counterpart of the (Local character) rule is derivable and hence omitted.

   We illustrate the expressive power of the system by giving two sample derivable rules.

(Axiom)

$$\frac{(\Theta \rhd \Gamma \vdash s \equiv t : \tau) \in E}{\Theta \rhd \Gamma \vdash s \equiv t : \tau}$$

(Equivalence)

$$\frac{\Theta \rhd \Gamma \vdash t : \tau}{\Theta \rhd \Gamma \vdash t \equiv t : \tau} \qquad \frac{\Theta \rhd \Gamma \vdash s \equiv t : \tau}{\Theta \rhd \Gamma \vdash t \equiv s : \tau} \qquad \frac{\Theta \rhd \Gamma \vdash s \equiv t : \tau \quad \Theta \rhd \Gamma \vdash t \equiv u : \tau}{\Theta \rhd \Gamma \vdash s \equiv u : \tau}$$

(Extended metasubstitution)

$$\frac{\begin{array}{c} \mathrm{M}_1 : [\vec{\sigma_1}]\tau_1, \ldots, \mathrm{M}_k : [\vec{\sigma_k}]\tau_k \rhd \Gamma \vdash s \equiv t : \tau \\ \Theta \rhd \Delta, \vec{x}_i : \vec{\sigma}_i \vdash s_i \equiv t_i : \tau_i \quad (1 \le i \le k) \end{array}}{\Theta \rhd \Gamma, \Delta \vdash s\{\mathrm{M}_i := (\vec{x}_i)s_i\}_{1 \le i \le k} \equiv t\{\mathrm{M}_i := (\vec{x}_i)t_i\}_{1 \le i \le k} : \tau}$$

Fig. 2. Second-Order Equational Logic

(Substitution)

$$\frac{\Theta \rhd x_1 : \sigma_1, \ldots, x_n : \sigma_n \vdash s \equiv t : \tau \qquad \Theta \rhd \Gamma \vdash s_i \equiv t_i : \sigma_i \quad (1 \le i \le n)}{\Theta \rhd \Gamma \vdash s[s_i/x_i]_{1 \le i \le n} \equiv t[t_i/x_i]_{1 \le i \le n} : \tau}$$

(Extension)

$$\frac{\mathrm{M}_1 : [\vec{\sigma_1}]\tau_1, \ldots, \mathrm{M}_k : [\vec{\sigma_k}]\tau_k \rhd \Gamma \vdash s \equiv t : \tau}{\mathrm{M}_1 : [\vec{\sigma_1}, \vec{\sigma}]\tau_1, \ldots, \mathrm{M}_k : [\vec{\sigma_k}, \vec{\sigma}]\tau_k \rhd \Gamma, \vec{x} : \vec{\sigma} \vdash s^\# \equiv t^\# : \tau}$$

where $u^\# - u\{\mathrm{M}_i := (\vec{x}_i)\mathrm{M}_i[\vec{x}_i, \vec{x}]\}_{1 \le i \le k}$

Parameterisation. Every term $\Theta \rhd \Gamma \vdash t : \tau$ can be *parameterised* to yield a term $\Theta, \widehat{\Gamma} \rhd \cdot \vdash \widehat{t} : \tau$ where, for $\Gamma = (x_1 : \tau_1, \ldots, x_n : \tau_n)$,

$$\widehat{\Gamma} = (\mathrm{X}_1 : []\tau_1, \ldots, \mathrm{X}_n : []\tau_n) \quad \text{and} \quad \widehat{t} = t[\mathrm{X}_1[]/x_1, \ldots, \mathrm{X}_n[]/x_n] \ .$$

Performing the operation on a set of equations E to obtain a set of parameterised equations $\widehat{E}$, we have that the following are equivalent:

$$\Theta \rhd \Gamma \vdash_E s \equiv t : \tau \ , \qquad \Theta, \widehat{\Gamma} \rhd \cdot \vdash_E \widehat{s} \equiv \widehat{t} : \tau \ ,$$

$$\Theta \rhd \Gamma \vdash_{\widehat{E}} s \equiv t : \tau \ , \qquad \Theta, \widehat{\Gamma} \rhd \cdot \vdash_{\widehat{E}} \widehat{s} \equiv \widehat{t} : \tau \ .$$

Thus, without loss of generality, one may restrict to axioms containing an empty variable context as in the *CRSs* of Klop [22]. However, there is no need for us to do so here.

6 Model Theory

The model theory of *Second-Order Equational Logic* is presented and exemplified. The soundness of deduction is a by-product of our methodology. In the next section, the model theory is used to establish a conservative-extension result.

Semantics. The interpretation of a term $\Theta \rhd \vec{x} : \vec{\sigma} \vdash t : \tau$ in a model A is that of its associated Kleisli map $\boldsymbol{y}(\vec{\sigma})_{@\tau} \rightarrow \mathcal{M}(\underline{\Theta})$ (see (5)) according to the general definition (6). Explicitly, for $\Theta = (\mathrm{M}_1 : [\vec{\alpha_1}]\beta_1, \ldots, \mathrm{M}_k : [\vec{\alpha_k}]\beta_k)$ and $\Gamma = (\vec{x} : \vec{\sigma})$, we have that the interpretation

$$[\![\Theta \rhd \Gamma \vdash t : \tau]\!]_A : [\![\Theta \rhd \Gamma]\!]_A \rightarrow A_\tau \ ,$$

where $[\![\Theta \rhd \Gamma]\!]_A = \prod_{1 \leq i \leq k} A_{\beta_i}{}^{\boldsymbol{y}(\vec{\alpha_i})} \times \boldsymbol{y}(\vec{\sigma})$, is given inductively on the structure of terms as follows.

- $[\![\Theta \rhd \Gamma \vdash x_j : \sigma_j]\!]_A$ is the composite $[\![\Theta \rhd \Gamma]\!]_A \xrightarrow{\pi_2} \boldsymbol{y}(\vec{\sigma}) \rightarrow \boldsymbol{y}(\sigma_j) \rightarrow A_{\sigma_j}$.

- $[\![\Theta \rhd \Gamma \vdash \mathrm{M}_i[t_1, \ldots, t_{m_i}] : \beta_i]\!]_A$ is the composite

$$[\![\Theta \rhd \Gamma]\!]_A \xrightarrow{\langle \pi_i \pi_1, f \rangle} A_{\beta_i}{}^{\boldsymbol{y}(\vec{\alpha_i})} \times \prod_{1 \leq j \leq m_i} A_{\alpha_{i,j}} \xrightarrow{\varsigma} A_{\beta_i}$$

  where $f = \big\langle [\![\Theta \rhd \Gamma \vdash t_j : \alpha_{i,j}]\!]_A \big\rangle_{1 \leq j \leq m_i}$.

- For $\mathsf{o} : (\vec{\gamma_1})\tau_1, \ldots, (\vec{\gamma_n})\tau_n \rightarrow \tau$,

$$[\![\Theta \rhd \Gamma \vdash \mathsf{o}\big((\vec{y_1})t_1, \ldots, (\vec{y_n})t_n\big) : \tau]\!]$$

  is the composite $[\![\Theta \rhd \Gamma]\!]_A \xrightarrow{\langle f_j \rangle_{1 \leq j \leq n}} \prod_{1 \leq j \leq n} A_{\tau_j}{}^{\boldsymbol{y}(\vec{\gamma_j})} \rightarrow A_\tau$ where f_j is the exponential transpose of

$$\prod_{1 \leq i \leq k} A_{\beta_i}{}^{\boldsymbol{y}(\vec{\alpha_i})} \times \boldsymbol{y}(\vec{\sigma}) \times \boldsymbol{y}(\vec{\gamma_j})$$
$$\cong \prod_{1 \leq i \leq k} A_{\beta_i}{}^{\boldsymbol{y}(\vec{\alpha_i})} \times \boldsymbol{y}(\vec{\sigma}, \vec{\gamma_j}) \xrightarrow{[\![\Theta \rhd \Gamma, \vec{y_j}:\vec{\gamma_j} \vdash t_j:\tau_j]\!]_A} A_{\tau_j} \ .$$

Models. A model A *satisfies* $\Theta \rhd \Gamma \vdash s \equiv t : \tau$, written $A \models (\Theta \rhd \Gamma \vdash s \equiv t : \tau)$, iff $[\![\Theta \rhd \Gamma \vdash s : \tau]\!]_A = [\![\Theta \rhd \Gamma \vdash t : \tau]\!]_A$.

For an equational presentation E over a signature Σ, we write (Σ, E)-Mod for the full subcategory of Σ-Mod consisting of the Σ-models A that satisfy the axioms E. Thus, (Σ, E)-Mod $\cong (\mathcal{M}, \underline{E})$-Alg where $\underline{E}$ is the set of parallel pairs of Kleisli maps corresponding to the pairs of terms in E.

Example 4. For the signature of the typed λ-calculus over a set of base types B (Example 1), a model

$$A_\tau{}^{\boldsymbol{y}(\sigma)} \xrightarrow{\mathsf{abs}} A_{\sigma \Rightarrow \tau} \ , \qquad A_{\sigma \Rightarrow \tau} \times A_\sigma \xrightarrow{\mathsf{app}} A_\tau$$
$$\boldsymbol{y}(\tau) \xrightarrow{\nu} A_\tau \leftarrow A_\tau \odot A$$

satisfies the (β) and (η) axioms (Example 3) iff the following diagrams commute.

The Lawvere theory $\mathbb{L}$ associated to such a model is a $B^{\Rightarrow}$-sorted Lawvere theory equipped with cartesian closed structure $\mathbb{L}(\vec{\gamma} \cdot \sigma, \tau) \cong \mathbb{L}(\vec{\gamma}, \sigma \Rightarrow \tau)$.

On the other hand, for every cartesian closed category $\mathscr{C}$, an assignment $C : B \to \mathscr{C}$ extends to an assignment $C^{\#} : B^{\Rightarrow} \to \mathscr{C}$ $\left(\text{with } C^{\#}(\beta) = C_{\beta} \text{ for } \beta \in B, \text{ and } C^{\#}(\sigma \Rightarrow \tau) = C^{\#}(\sigma) \Rightarrow C^{\#}(\tau)\right)$ and canonically gives rise to a model on $\langle C^{\#}, C^{\#} \rangle$ that satisfies the (β) and (η) axioms.

Soundness. The soundness of *Second-Order Equational Logic* follows as a direct consequence of that of *Equational Metalogic*.

(Soundness) For an equational presentation E over a signature Σ, if the judgement $\Theta \rhd \Gamma \vdash s \equiv t : \tau$ is derivable from E then $A \models (\Theta \rhd \Gamma \vdash s \equiv t : \tau)$ for all (Σ, E)-models A.

7 Conservativity

Every first-order signature can be regarded as a second-order signature, and every first-order term $\Gamma \vdash t : \tau$ as the second-order term $\cdot \rhd \Gamma \vdash t : \tau$. It follows that, for a set of first-order equations,

$$\text{if } \Gamma \vdash s \equiv t : \tau \text{ is derivable in (first-order) equational logic, then} \atop \cdot \rhd \Gamma \vdash s \equiv t : \tau \text{ is derivable in second-order equational logic.} \tag{7}$$

We now proceed to establish the converse.

Let Ω be a first-order signature over a set of types T. For $\mathscr{C}$ cartesian and $C \in \mathscr{C}^{T}$, since $\langle C, - \rangle : \mathscr{C}^{T} \to (\mathbf{Set}^{\mathbb{F}[T]})^{T}$ preserves limits, it follows that an Ω-algebra structure

$$\prod_{1 \le i \le n} C_{\tau_i} \to C_{\tau} \qquad (\tau_1, \ldots, \tau_n \to \tau \text{ in } \Omega)$$

on C yields the Ω-algebra structure

$$\prod_{1 \le i \le n} \langle\!\langle C, C_{\tau_i} \rangle\!\rangle \cong \langle\!\langle C, \prod_{1 \le i \le n} C_{\tau_i} \rangle\!\rangle \to \langle\!\langle C, C_{\tau} \rangle\!\rangle \qquad (\tau_1, \ldots, \tau_n \to \tau \text{ in } \Omega)$$

on $\langle C, C \rangle$. This Ω-algebra structure is compatible with the canonical monoid structure, and we thus obtain an $\underline{\Omega}$-model on $\langle C, C \rangle$.

The interpretations of first-order terms are related as follows:

$$\prod_{1 \le i \le n} \langle\!\langle C, C_{\tau_i} \rangle\!\rangle \xrightarrow{\;\cong\;} \langle\!\langle C, \prod_{1 \le i \le n} C_{\tau_i} \rangle\!\rangle$$

$$[\![\widehat{\Gamma} \rhd \cdot \vdash \widehat{t} : \tau]\!]_{\langle C,C \rangle} \searrow \qquad \swarrow \langle\!\langle C, [\![\Gamma \vdash t : \tau]\!]_{C} \rangle\!\rangle$$

$$\langle\!\langle C, C_{\tau} \rangle\!\rangle$$

and we have that $C \models (\Gamma \vdash s \equiv t : \tau)$ iff $\langle C, C \rangle \models (\widehat{\Gamma} \rhd \cdot \vdash \widehat{s} \equiv \widehat{t} : \tau)$. Consequently, if $A \models (\widehat{\Gamma} \rhd \cdot \vdash \widehat{s} \equiv \widehat{t} : \tau)$ for all $(\underline{\Omega}, \widehat{E})$-models $A \in (\mathbf{Set}^{\mathbb{F}[T]})^{T}$ then $C \models (\Gamma \vdash s \equiv t : \tau)$ for all (Ω, E)-algebras $C \in \mathscr{C}^{T}$. Thus, the converse of (7) holds, and we have established the following result.

(Conservativity) *Second-Order Equational Logic* is a conservative extension of *(First-Order) Equational Logic*.

8   Completeness

We finally outline the semantic completeness of equational derivability and the derivability completeness of (bidirectional) *Second-Order Term Rewriting*.

Free algebras. It follows from our theory of free constructions [12, 13] that the forgetful functor $(\Sigma, E)\text{-Mod} \to (\mathbf{Set}^{\mathbb{F}[T]})^T$ is monadic. Hence, writing $\mathcal{M}_E$ for the induced monad, we have a quotient map $q : \mathcal{M} \to \mathcal{M}_E$.

In fact, since $\mathcal{M}$ is finitary and preserves epimorphisms, we have the following construction of free algebras, see [12, 13].

(A) For $E = \{\Theta_i \rhd \Gamma_i \vdash l_i \equiv r_i : \tau_i\}_{i \in I}$ we take the joint coequaliser

$$(\llbracket \Theta_i \rhd \Gamma_i \rrbracket_{\mathcal{M}\Theta})_{@\tau_i} \underset{\llbracket \Theta_i \rhd \Gamma_i \vdash r_i : \tau_i \rrbracket_{@\tau_i}}{\overset{\llbracket \Theta_i \rhd \Gamma_i \vdash l_i : \tau_i \rrbracket_{@\tau_i}}{\rightrightarrows}} \mathcal{M}\Theta \overset{q_1}{\underset{\mathrm{coed}}{\twoheadrightarrow}} (\mathcal{M}\Theta)_1 \qquad\qquad (i \in I)$$

(B) We perform the following inductive construction setting $(\mathcal{M}\Theta)_0 = \mathcal{M}\Theta$.

$$\mathcal{M}\mathcal{M}\Theta \qquad\qquad \mathcal{M}(\mathcal{M}\Theta)_n \overset{\mathcal{M}q_{n+1}}{\longrightarrow} \mathcal{M}(\mathcal{M}\Theta)_{n+1}$$

with μ_Θ, μ_1, μ_{n+1}, pushout, μ_{n+2} morphisms to

$$\mathcal{M}\Theta \overset{q_1}{\twoheadrightarrow} (\mathcal{M}\Theta)_1 \qquad\qquad (\mathcal{M}\Theta)_{n+1} \overset{q_{n+2}}{\longrightarrow} (\mathcal{M}\Theta)_{n+2}$$

(C) We obtain $\mathcal{M}_E\Theta$ as the colimit of

$$\mathcal{M}\Theta \overset{q_1}{\twoheadrightarrow} (\mathcal{M}\Theta)_1 \twoheadrightarrow \cdots \longrightarrow (\mathcal{M}\Theta)_n \overset{q_n}{\twoheadrightarrow} \cdots$$

Hence we have an epimorphic quotient map

$$q_\Theta : \mathcal{M}\Theta \twoheadrightarrow \mathcal{M}_E\Theta \ . \tag{8}$$

In the light of the (Internal completeness) result, our method for establishing completeness is to show that, for $\Theta \rhd \vec{x} : \vec{\sigma} \vdash s : \tau$ and $\Theta \rhd \vec{x} : \vec{\sigma} \vdash t : \tau$, if $q_{\Theta,\tau,\vec{\sigma}}(s) = q_{\Theta,\tau,\vec{\sigma}}(t)$ then $\Theta \rhd \vec{x} : \vec{\sigma} \vdash s \equiv t : \tau$ is derivable from E.

Syntactic model. A concrete analysis of the constructions (A–C) yields a characterisation of the quotient (8) as induced by the equivalence relation $\approx$ on $\mathcal{M}\Theta$ given by the rules in Figure 3. Consequently, since derivability in this deductive system can be mimicked in *Second-Order Equational Logic*, we have:

(Completeness)   For an equational presentation E over a signature Σ, if $A \models (\Theta \rhd \Gamma \vdash s \equiv t : \tau)$ for all (Σ, E)-models A then $\Theta \rhd \Gamma \vdash s \equiv t : \tau$ is derivable from E.

Moreover, since $\approx$ can be characterised as the equivalence relation generated by the *Second-Order Term Rewriting* relation $\to$ given in Figure 4, we also have:

(Completeness of *Second-Order Term Rewriting*)   For every equational presentation, $\Theta \rhd \Gamma \vdash s \equiv t : \tau$ iff $\Theta \rhd \Gamma \vdash s \overset{*}{\leftrightarrow} t : \tau$.

$$(\mathrm{M}_1 : [\vec{\sigma_1}]\tau_1, \ldots, \mathrm{M}_k : [\vec{\sigma_k}]\tau_k \rhd \vec{x} : \vec{\alpha} \vdash l \equiv r : \tau) \in E$$
$$\rho : \vec{\alpha} \longrightarrow \vec{\beta} \ , \quad \Theta \rhd \vec{y} : \vec{\beta}, \vec{x_j} : \vec{\sigma_j} \vdash t_j : \tau_j \ \ (1 \leq j \leq k)$$
$$\overline{\Theta \rhd \vec{y} : \vec{\beta} \vdash l[y_{\rho_i}/x_i]_{1 \leq i \leq |\vec{\alpha}|}\{\mathrm{M}_j := (\vec{x_j})t_j\}_{1 \leq j \leq k} \approx r[y_{\rho_i}/x_i]_{1 \leq i \leq |\vec{\alpha}|}\{\mathrm{M}_j := (\vec{x_j})t_j\}_{1 \leq j \leq k} : \tau}$$

$$\frac{\Theta \rhd \vec{x} : \vec{\sigma} \vdash s \approx t : \tau \qquad \Theta \rhd \Gamma \vdash s_i \approx t_i : \sigma_i \ (1 \leq i \leq |\vec{\sigma}|)}{\Theta \rhd \Gamma \vdash s[s_i/x_i]_{1 \leq i \leq |\vec{\sigma}|} \approx t[t_i/x_i]_{1 \leq i \leq |\vec{\sigma}|} : \tau}$$

$$\frac{\Theta \rhd \Gamma, \vec{x_i} : \vec{\sigma_i} \vdash s_i \approx t_i : \tau_i \quad (1 \leq i \leq k)}{\Theta \rhd \Gamma \vdash \mathsf{o}((\vec{x_1})s_1, \ldots, (\vec{x_k})s_k) \approx \mathsf{o}((\vec{x_1})t_1, \ldots, (\vec{x_k})t_k) : \tau} \ \left(\mathsf{o} : (\vec{\sigma_1})\tau_1, \ldots, (\vec{\sigma_k})\tau_k \longrightarrow \tau\right)$$

Fig. 3. Rules of $\approx$ (omitting those of equivalence)

$$(\mathrm{M}_1 : [\vec{\sigma_1}]\tau_1, \ldots, \mathrm{M}_k : [\vec{\sigma_k}]\tau_k \rhd \vec{x} : \vec{\alpha} \vdash l \equiv r : \tau) \in E$$
$$\rho : \vec{\alpha} \longrightarrow \vec{\beta} \ , \qquad \Theta \rhd \vec{y} : \vec{\beta}, \vec{x_j} : \vec{\sigma_j} \vdash t_j : \tau_j \ \ (1 \leq j \leq k)$$
$$\Theta \rhd \Gamma \vdash s_\ell : \beta_\ell \quad (1 \leq \ell \leq |\vec{\beta}|)$$
$$\overline{\Theta \rhd \Gamma \vdash l' \to r' : \tau}$$
$$\text{where } u' = u[y_{\rho_i}/x_i]_{1 \leq i \leq |\vec{\alpha}|}\{\mathrm{M}_j := (\vec{x_j})t_j\}_{1 \leq j \leq k}[s_\ell/y_\ell]_{1 \leq \ell \leq |\vec{\beta}|}$$

$$\frac{\Theta \rhd \Gamma \vdash s_i \to t_i : \sigma_i}{\Theta \rhd \Gamma \vdash \mathrm{M}[\ldots, s_i, \ldots] \to \mathrm{M}[\ldots, t_i, \ldots] : \tau} \ \left(1 \leq i \leq n \ , \ (\mathrm{M} : [\sigma_1, \ldots, \sigma_n]\tau) \in \Theta\right)$$

$$\frac{\Theta \rhd \Gamma, \vec{x_i} : \vec{\sigma_i} \vdash s_i \to t_i : \tau_i}{\Theta \rhd \Gamma \vdash \mathsf{o}(\ldots, (\vec{x_i})s_i, \ldots) \to \mathsf{o}(\ldots, (\vec{x_i})t_i, \ldots) : \tau} \ \left(\begin{array}{c} \mathsf{o} : (\vec{\sigma_1})\tau_1, \ldots, (\vec{\sigma_k})\tau_k \longrightarrow \tau \ , \\ 1 \leq i \leq k \end{array}\right)$$

Fig. 4. Second-Order Term Rewriting

9   Conclusion

We have introduced *Second-Order Equational Logic*: a logical framework for specifying and reasoning about simply-typed equational theories over algebraic signatures with variable-binding operators. The conceptual part of our development consisted in the synthesis of the equational deductive system from a canonical algebraic model theory that forms the basis of *Second-Order Universal Algebra*; the technical part established the soundness and completeness of the logic. We have also provided logical and semantic foundations for higher-order term rewriting, specifically *CRSs*, by exhibiting *Second-Order Term Rewriting* as a sound and complete computational method for establishing equality.

Acknowledgement. We are most grateful to Pierre-Louis Curien for detailed comments on a preliminary version of the paper.

References

[1] Aczel, P.: A general Church-Rosser theorem. Typescript (1978)
[2] Aczel, P.: Frege structures and the notion of proposition, truth and set. In: The Kleene Symposium, pp. 31–59 (1980)
[3] Baader, F., Nipkow, T.: Term Rewriting and All That. CUP (1998)
[4] Birkhoff, G.: On the structure of abstract algebras. P. Camb. Philos. Soc. 31, 433–454 (1935)
[5] Church, A.: A formulation of the simple theory of types. J. Symbolic Logic 5, 56–68 (1940)
[6] Clouston, R., Pitts, A.: Nominal equational logic. ENTCS 172, 223–257 (2007)
[7] Fiore, M.: Algebraic meta-theories and synthesis of equational logics. Research Programme (2009)
[8] Fiore, M.: Semantic analysis of normalisation by evaluation for typed lambda calculus. In: PPDP 2002, pp. 26–37 (2002)
[9] Fiore, M.: Mathematical models of computational and combinatorial structures. In: Sassone, V. (ed.) FOSSACS 2005. LNCS, vol. 3441, pp. 25–46. Springer, Heidelberg (2005)
[10] Fiore, M.: A mathematical theory of substitution and its applications to syntax and semantics. In: Invited tutorial for the Workshop on Mathematical Theories of Abstraction, Substitution and Naming in Computer Science, ICMS (2007)
[11] Fiore, M.: Second-order and dependently-sorted abstract syntax. In: LICS 2008, pp. 57–68 (2008)
[12] Fiore, M., Hur, C.-K.: On the construction of free algebras for equational systems. Theor. Comput. Sci. 410, 1704–1729 (2008)
[13] Fiore, M., Hur, C.-K.: Term equational systems and logics. In: MFPS XXIV. ENTCS, vol. 218, pp. 171–192 (2008)
[14] Fiore, M., Mahmoud, O.: Second-order algebraic theories. In: MFCS 2010. LNCS 6281, pp. 368–380 (2010)
[15] Fiore, M., Plotkin, G., Turi, D.: Abstract syntax and variable binding. In: LICS 1999, pp. 193–202 (1999)
[16] Goguen, J., Meseguer, J.: Completeness of many-sorted equational logic. Houston J. Math. 11, 307–334 (1985)
[17] Hamana, M.: Term rewriting with variable binding: An initial algebra approach. In: PPDP 2003, pp. 148–159 (2003)
[18] Hamana, M.: Free Σ-monoids: A higher-order syntax with metavariables. In: Chin, W.-N. (ed.) APLAS 2004. LNCS, vol. 3302, pp. 348–363. Springer, Heidelberg (2004)
[19] Hur, C.-K.: Categorical Equational Systems: Algebraic Models and Equational Reasoning. PhD thesis, Computer Laboratory, University of Cambridge (2010)
[20] Janelidze, G., Kelly, G.: A note on actions of a monoidal category. TAC 9(4), 61–91 (2001)
[21] Klop, J.: Combinatory Reduction Systems. PhD thesis, Mathematical Centre Tracts 127, CWI, Amsterdam (1980)
[22] Klop, J., van Oostrom, V., van Raamsdonk, F.: Combinatory reduction systems: introduction and survey. Theor. Comput. Sci. 121, 279–308 (1993)
[23] Lawvere, F.: Functorial semantics of algebraic theories. Republished in: Reprints in TAC (5), 1–121 (2004)
[24] Gabbay, M.J., Mathijssen, A.: Nominal (universal) algebra: Equational logic with names and binding. J. Logic Computation 19(6), 1455–1508 (2009)

[25] Pigozzi, D., Salibra, A.: The abstract variable-binding calculus. Studia Logica 55, 129–179 (1995)

[26] Plotkin, G.: Binding algebras: A step from universal algebra to type theory. Invited talk at RTA 1998 (1998)

[27] Sun, Y.: A Framework for Binding Operators. PhD thesis, LFCS, The University of Edinburgh (1992)

[28] Sun, Y.: An algebraic generalization of Frege structures — binding algebras. Theor. Comput. Sci. 211, 189–232 (1999)

[29] van Raamsdonk, F.: Higher-order rewriting. In: Term Rewriting Systems. Cambridge Tracts in Theoretical Computer Science, vol. 55, pp. 588–667 (2003)

Fibrational Induction Rules for Initial Algebras⋆

Neil Ghani, Patricia Johann, and Clément Fumex

University of Strathclyde, Glasgow G1 1XH, UK
{neil.ghani,patricia.johann,clement.fumex}@cis.strath.ac.uk

Abstract. This paper provides an induction rule that can be used to prove properties of data structures whose types are inductive, i.e., are carriers of initial algebras of functors. Our results are semantic in nature and are inspired by Hermida and Jacobs' elegant algebraic formulation of induction for polynomial data types. Our contribution is to derive, under slightly different assumptions, an induction rule that is generic over *all* inductive types, polynomial or not. Our induction rule is generic over the kinds of properties to be proved as well: like Hermida and Jacobs, we work in a general fibrational setting and so can accommodate very general notions of properties on inductive types rather than just those of particular syntactic forms. We establish the correctness of our generic induction rule by reducing induction to iteration. We show how our rule can be instantiated to give induction rules for the data types of rose trees, finite hereditary sets, and hyperfunctions. The former lies outside the scope of Hermida and Jacobs' work because it is not polynomial; as far as we are aware, no induction rules have been known to exist for the latter two in a general fibrational framework. Our instantiation for hyperfunctions underscores the value of working in the general fibrational setting since this data type cannot be interpreted as a set.

1 Introduction

Iteration operators provide a uniform way to express common and naturally occurring patterns of recursion over inductive data types. Expressing recursion via iteration operators makes code easier to read, write, and understand; facilitates code reuse; guarantees properties of programs such as totality and termination; and supports optimising program transformations such as `fold` fusion and short cut fusion. Categorically, iteration operators arise from initial algebra semantics of data types, in which each data type is regarded as the carrier of the initial algebra of a functor F. Lambek's Lemma ensures that this carrier is the least fixed point μF of F, and initiality ensures that, given any F-algebra $h : FA \to A$, there is a unique F-algebra homomorphism, denoted $fold\,h$, from the initial algebra $in : F(\mu F) \to \mu F$ to that algebra. For each functor F, the map $fold : (FA \to A) \to \mu F \to A$ is the iteration operator for the data type μF. Initial algebra semantics thus provides a well-developed theory of iteration which is i) *principled*, and so helps ensure that programs have rigorous mathematical

---

⋆ This research is partially supported by EPSRC grant EP/C0608917/1.

A. Dawar and H. Veith (Eds.): CSL 2010, LNCS 6247, pp. 336–350, 2010.
© Springer-Verlag Berlin Heidelberg 2010

foundations that can be used to ascertain their meaning and correctness; ii) *expressive*, and so is applicable to all inductive types, rather than just syntactically defined classes of data types such as polynomial data types; and iii) *correct*, and so is valid in any model — set-theoretic, domain-theoretic, realisability, etc. — in which data types are interpreted as carriers of initial algebras.

Because induction and iteration are closely linked we may reasonably expect that initial algebra semantics can be used to derive a principled, expressive, and correct theory of induction for data types as well. In most treatments of induction, given a functor F together with a property P to be proved about data of type μF, the premises of the induction rule for μF constitute an F-algebra with carrier $\Sigma x : \mu F. Px$. The conclusion of the rule is obtained by supplying such an F-algebra as input to the *fold* for μF. This yields a function from μF to $\Sigma x : \mu F. Px$ from which function of type $\forall x : \mu F. Px$ can be obtained. It has not, however, been possible to characterise F-algebras with carrier $\Sigma x : \mu F. Px$ without additional assumptions on F. Induction rules are thus typically derived under the assumption that the functors involved have a certain structure, e.g., that they are polynomial. Moreover, taking the carriers of the algebras to be Σ-types assumes that properties are represented as type-valued functions. So while induction rules derived as described are both principled and correct, their expressiveness is limited along two dimensions: with respect to the data types for which they can be derived and the nature of the properties they can verify.

One principled and correct approach to induction is given by Hermida and Jacobs [6]. They lift each functor F on a base category of types to a functor $\hat{F}$ on a category of properties over those types, and take the premises of the induction rule for the type μF to be an $\hat{F}$-algebra. Hermida and Jacobs work in a fibrational setting and the notion of property they consider is, accordingly, very general. Indeed, they accommodate any notion of property that can be fibred over the category of types, and so overcome one of the two limitations mentioned above. On the other hand, their approach is only applicable to polynomial data types, so the limitation on the class of data types treated remains in their work.

This paper shows how to remove the restriction on the class of data types treated. *Our main result is a derivation of a generic induction rule that can be instantiated to* every *inductive type* — i.e., to *every* type which is the carrier of the initial algebra of a functor — regardless of whether it is polynomial. We take Hermida and Jacobs' approach as our point of departure and show that, under slightly different assumptions on the fibration involved, we can lift *any* functor on its base category that has an initial algebra to a functor on its properties. This is clearly an important theoretical result, but it also has practical consequences:

- We show in Example 2 how our generic induction rule can be instantiated to the codomain fibration to derive the rule for rose trees that one would intuitively expect. The data type of rose trees lies outside the scope of Hermida and Jacobs' results because it is not polynomial. On the other hand, an induction rule for rose trees is available in the proof assistant Coq, although it is neither the one we intuitively expect nor expressive enough to prove properties that ought to be amenable to inductive proof. The rule we derive for rose trees is indeed the expected one, which suggests that our derivation may enable automatic generation of more useful induction rules in Coq, rather than requiring the user to hand code them as is currently necessary.

- We further show in Example 3 how our generic induction rule can be instantiated, again to the codomain fibration, to derive a rule for the data type of finite hereditary sets. This data type is defined in terms of quotients and so lies outside current theories of induction.

- Finally, we show in Example 4 how our generic induction rule can be instantiated to the subobject fibration over ωcpo to derive a rule for the data type of hyperfunctions. Because this data type cannot be interpreted as a set, a fibration other than the codomain fibration over Set is required; in this case, use of the subobject fibration allows us to derive an induction rule for admissible subsets of hyperfunctions. Moreover, the functor underlying the data type of hyperfunctions is not strictly positive, and this fact again underscores the advantage of being able to handle a very general class of functors. As far as we know, induction rules for finite hereditary sets and hyperfunctions have not previously existed in the general fibrational framework.

Although our theory of induction is applicable to all functors having initial algebras, including higher-order ones, our examples show that working in the general fibrational setting is beneficial even if attention is restricted to first-order functors. Note also that our induction rules coincide with those of Hermida and Jacobs when specialised to polynomial functors in the codomain fibration. But the structure we require of fibrations generally is slightly different from that required by Hermida and Jacobs, so while our theory is in essence a generalisation of theirs, the two are, strictly speaking, incomparable. The structure we require is, however, still minimal and certainly present in all standard fibrational models of type theory (see Section 4). Like Hermida and Jacobs, we prove our generic induction rule correct by reducing induction to iteration.

We take a purely categorical approach to induction in this paper, and derive our generic induction rule from only the initial algebra semantics of data types. As a result, our work is inherently extensional. While translating our constructions into intensional settings may therefore require additional effort, we expect the guidance offered by the categorical viewpoint to support the derivation of induction rules for functors that are not treatable at present. Since we do not use any form of impredicativity in our constructions, and instead use only the weaker assumption that initial algebras exist, this guidance will be widely applicable.

The remainder of this paper is structured as follows. To make our results as accessible as possible, we illustrate them in Section 2 with a categorical derivation of the familiar induction rule for the natural numbers. In Section 3 we derive an induction rule for the special case of the codomain fibration over Set, i.e., for functors on the category of sets and properties representable as set-valued predicates. We also show how this rule can be instantiated to derive the one from Section 2, and the ones for rose trees and finite hereditary sets mentioned above. Then, in Section 4 we sketch the general fibrational form of our derivation (space constraints prevent a full treatment) and illustrate the resulting generic induction rule with the aforementioned application to hyperfunctions. Section 5 concludes and offers some additional directions for future research.

When convenient, we identify isomorphic objects of a category and write $=$ rather than $\simeq$. We write 1 for the canonical singleton set and denote its single element by $\cdot$. In Sections 2 and 3 we assume that types are interpreted as objects in the category Set of sets, and so 1 also denotes the unit type in those sections.

2   A Familiar Induction Rule

Consider the inductive data type Nat, which defines the natural numbers and can be specified in a programming language with Haskell-like syntax by

$$data\ Nat\ =\ Zero \mid Succ\ Nat$$

The observation that Nat is the least fixed point of the functor N on Set defined by $NX\ =\ 1\ +\ X$ can be used to define the following iteration operator for it:

$$
\begin{aligned}
foldNat &= X \to (X \to X) \to Nat \to X \\
foldNat\ z\ s\ Zero &= z \\
foldNat\ z\ s\ (Succ\ n) &= s\ (foldNat\ z\ s\ n)
\end{aligned}
$$

Categorically, iteration operators such as $foldNat$ arise from the initial algebra semantics of data types. If $\mathcal{B}$ is a category and F is a functor on $\mathcal{B}$, then an F-algebra is a morphism $h : FX \to X$ for some object X of $\mathcal{B}$. We call X the carrier of h. For any functor F, the collection of F-algebras itself forms a category Alg_F which we call the category of F-algebras. In Alg_F, an F-algebra morphism between F-algebras $h : FX \to X$ and $g : FY \to Y$ is a map $f : X \to Y$ such that $f \circ h = g \circ Ff$. When it exists, the initial F-algebra $in : F(\mu F) \to \mu F$ is unique up to isomorphism and has the least fixed point μF of F as its carrier. Initiality ensures that there is a unique F-algebra morphism $fold\ h : \mu F \to X$ from in to any other F-algebra $h : FX \to X$. This gives rise to the following iteration operator $fold$ for F or, equivalently, for the inductive type μF:

$$
\begin{aligned}
fold &: (FX \to X) \to \mu F \to X \\
fold\ h\ (in\ t) &= h\ (F\ (fold\ h)\ t)
\end{aligned}
$$

Since $fold$ is derived from initial algebra semantics it is principled and correct. It is also expressive, since it can be defined for $every$ inductive type. In fact, $fold$ is a single iteration operator parameterised over inductive types rather than a family of iteration operators, one for each such type, and the iteration operator $foldNat$ above is the instantiation to Nat of the generic iteration operator $fold$.

The iteration operator $foldNat$ can be used to derive the standard induction rule for Nat. This rule says that if a property P holds for 0, and if P holds for $n+1$ whenever it holds for a natural number n, then P holds for all natural numbers. Representing each property of natural numbers as a predicate $P : Nat \to$ Set mapping each $n : Nat$ to the set of proofs that P holds for n, we wish to represent this rule at the object level as a function $indNat$ with type

$$\forall(P : Nat \to \mathsf{Set}).\ P\ Zero \to (\forall n : Nat.\ P\ n \to P\ (Succ\ n)) \to (\forall n : Nat.\ P\ n)$$

Code fragments such as the above, which involve quantification over sets, properties, or functors, are to be treated as "categorically inspired" within this paper. This is because quantification over such higher-kinded objects cannot be interpreted in Set. In order to give a formal interpretation to code fragments like the one above, we would need to work in a category such as that of modest sets. The ability to work with functors over categories other than Set is one of the motivations for working in the general fibrational setting of Section 4. Of course, the use of category theory to suggest computational constructions has long been accepted within the functional programming community (see, e.g., [1,2,13]).

A function *indNat* with the above type takes as input the property P to be proved, a proof ϕ that P holds for *Zero*, and a function ψ mapping each $n : Nat$ and each proof that P holds for n to a proof that P holds for *Succ n*, and returns a function mapping each $n : Nat$ to a proof that P holds for n. We can write *indNat* in terms of *foldNat* — and thus reduce induction for *Nat* to iteration for *Nat* — as follows. First note that *indNat* cannot be obtained by instantiating the type X in the type of *foldNat* to a type of the form Pn for a specific n because *indNat* returns elements of the types $P n$ for different values n and these types are, in general, distinct from one another. We therefore need a type containing all of the elements of $P n$ for every n. Such a type can be formally given by the dependent type $\Sigma n : Nat. P n$ comprising pairs (n, p) where $n : Nat$ and $p : P n$.

The standard approach to defining *indNat* is thus to apply *foldNat* to an N-algebra with carrier $\Sigma n : Nat. P n$. Such an algebra has components $\alpha : \Sigma n : Nat. P n$ and $\beta : \Sigma n : Nat. P n \rightarrow \Sigma n : Nat. P n$. Given $\phi : P \, Zero$ and $\psi : \forall n. P n \rightarrow P(Succ \, n)$, we choose $\alpha = (Zero, \phi)$ and $\beta(n, p) = (Succ \, n, \psi \, n \, p)$ and note that $foldNat \, \alpha \, \beta : Nat \rightarrow \Sigma n : Nat. P n$. We tentatively take *indNat* $P \, \phi \, \psi \, n$ to be p, where $foldNat \, \alpha \, \beta \, n = (m, p)$. But in order to know that p actually gives a proof for n itself, we must show that $m = n$. Fortunately, this follows easily from the uniqueness of $foldNat \, \alpha \, \beta$. Letting π'_P be the second projection on dependent pairs, the induction rule for *Nat* is

$$indNat \; : \; \forall(P : Nat \rightarrow \mathsf{Set}). \, P \, Zero \rightarrow (\forall n : Nat. \, P \, n \rightarrow P(Succ \, n))$$
$$\rightarrow (\forall n : Nat. \, P \, n)$$
$$indNat \; P \, \phi \, \psi \; = \; \pi'_P \circ (foldNat \; (Zero, \phi) \; (\lambda(n, p). \, (Succ \, n, \psi \, n \, p)))$$

The use of dependent types is fundamental to this formalization of the induction rule for *Nat*, but this is only possible because properties are taken to be set-valued functions. The remainder of this paper uses fibrations to generalise the above treatment of induction to arbitrary functors which have initial algebras and arbitrary properties which are fibred over the category whose objects interpret types. In the general fibrational setting, properties are given axiomatically via the fibrational structure rather than assumed to be (set-valued) functions.

3   Induction Rules over Set

The main result of this paper is the derivation of an induction rule that is generic over inductive types and can be used to verify any notion of property that is fibred over the category whose objects interpret types. In the remainder of the paper we restrict attention to functors that have initial algebras. In this section we further assume that types are modelled by sets, so the functors we consider are on Set and the properties we consider are functions mapping data to sets of proofs that these properties hold for them. We make these assumptions to present our derivation in the simplest setting possible. But they are not always valid, so we derive a more general induction rule which relaxes them in Section 4. It should be more easily digestible once the derivation in this section is understood.

The derivation for *Nat* in Section 2 suggests that an induction rule for an inductive data type μF should, in general, look something like this:

$$ind \ : \ \forall P : \mu F \rightarrow \mathsf{Set}. \ ??? \ \rightarrow \ \forall x : \mu F. P\, x$$

But what should the premises — denoted ??? here — of the generic induction rule *ind* be? Since we want to construct, for any term $x : \mu F$, a proof term of type $P\, x$ from proof terms for x's substructures, and since the functionality of the *fold* operator for μF is precisely to compute a value for $x : \mu F$ from the values for x's substructures, it is natural to try to equip P with an F-algebra structure that can be input to *fold* to yield a mapping of each $x : \mu F$ to an element of $P\, x$. But this approach quickly hits a snag. Since the codomain of every predicate $P : \mu F \rightarrow \mathsf{Set}$ is Set itself, rather than an object of Set, F cannot be applied to P as is needed to equip P with an F-algebra structure. Moreover, an induction rule for μF cannot be obtained by applying *fold* to an F-algebra with carrier $P\, x$ for any specific x.

Such considerations led Hermida and Jacobs [6] to define a category of predicates $\mathcal{P}$ and a lifting $\hat{F}$ for every polynomial functor F on Set to a functor $\hat{F}$ on $\mathcal{P}$ that respects the structure of F. They then constructed $\hat{F}$-algebras with carrier P to serve as the premises of their induction rules. Their construction is very general: they consider functors on bicartesian categories rather than just on Set, and represent properties by bicartesian fibrations over such categories instead of using the specific notion of predicate from Definition 2 below. On the other hand, they define liftings for polynomial functors only. In this section we focus exclusively on functors on Set and a particular category of predicates, and show how to define a lifting for all functors on Set, including non-polynomial ones. In this setting our results properly extend those of Hermida and Jacobs, thus catering for a variety of data types that they cannot treat.

Definition 1. *Let X be a set. A* predicate *on X is a pair (X, P) where $P : X \rightarrow \mathsf{Set}$ maps each $x \in X$ to a set $P\, x$. We call X the* domain *of the predicate (X, P).*

Definition 2. *The* category of predicates $\mathcal{P}$ *has predicates as its objects. A* morphism *from a predicate (X, P) to a predicate (X', P') is a pair $(f, f^\sim) : (X, P) \rightarrow (X', P')$ of functions, where $f : X \rightarrow X'$ and $f^\sim : \forall x : X. P\, x \rightarrow P'(f\, x)$.*

The notion of a morphism from (X, P) to (X', P') does not require the sets of proofs $P\, x$ and $P'(f\, x)$, for any $x \in X$, to be *equal*. Instead, it requires only the existence of a function $f^\sim$ which maps, for each x, each proof in $P\,x$ to a proof in $P'\,(f\,x)$. We denote by $U : \mathcal{P} \to \mathsf{Set}$ the *forgetful functor* mapping each predicate (X, P) to its domain X and each predicate morphism $(f, f^\sim)$ to f.

An alternative to Definition 2 would take the category of predicates to be the arrow category over Set, but the natural lifting in this setting does not generalise to arbitrary fibrations. Indeed, if properties are modelled as functions, then every functor can be applied to a property, and hence every functor can be its own lifting. In the general fibrational setting, properties are not necessarily modelled by functions, so a functor cannot, in general, be its own lifting. The decision not to use arrow categories to model properties is thus dictated by our desire to lift functors in such a way that it can be extended to the general fibrational setting.

Definition 3. *Let F be a functor on Set. A* lifting *of F from Set to $\mathcal{P}$ is a functor $\hat{F}$ on $\mathcal{P}$ such that $FU = U\hat{F}$.*

Note that if P is a predicate on X, then $\hat{F}P$ is a predicate on FX. We can now derive the standard induction rule from Section 2 for *Nat* as follows.

Example 1. *The data type of natural numbers is μN where N is the functor on Set defined by $N\,X = 1+X$. If P is a predicate on X, then a lifting $\hat{N}P : 1+X \to \mathsf{Set}$ of N from Set to $\mathcal{P}$ is given by $\hat{N}P\,(inl\,\cdot) = 1$ and $\hat{N}P\,(inr\,n) = P\,n$. An $\hat{N}$-algebra with carrier $P : Nat \to \mathsf{Set}$ can be given by $in : 1 + Nat \to Nat$ and $in^\sim : \forall t : 1+Nat.\ \hat{N}P\,t \to P(in\,t)$. Since $in\,(inl\,\cdot) = 0$ and $in\,(inr\,n) = n+1$, we see that $in^\sim$ is an element $h_1 : P\,0$ and a function $h_2 : \forall n : Nat.\ P\,n \to P\,(n+1)$. Thus, the second component $in^\sim$ of the $\hat{N}$-algebra with carrier $P : Nat \to \mathsf{Set}$ and first component in gives the premises of the familiar induction rule in Example 1.*

The notion of predicate comprehension is a key ingredient of our lifting.

Definition 4. *Let P be a predicate on X. The* comprehension *of P, denoted $\{P\}$, is the type $\Sigma x : X.\,P\,x$ comprising pairs (x, p) where $x : X$ and $p : Px$. The map taking each predicate P to $\{P\}$, and taking each predicate morphism $(f, f^\sim) : P \to P'$ to $\{(f, f^\sim)\} : \{P\} \to \{P'\}$ defined by $\{(f, f^\sim)\}(x, p) = (fx, f^\sim x\,p)$, defines the* comprehension functor $\{-\}$ *from $\mathcal{P}$ to Set.*

Definition 5. *If F is a functor on Set, then the lifting $\hat{F}$ is the functor on $\mathcal{P}$ given as follows. For every predicate P on X, $\hat{F}P : FX \to \mathsf{Set}$ is defined by $\hat{F}P = (F\,\pi_P)^{-1}$, where the natural transformation $\pi : \{-\} \to U$ is given by $\pi_P\,(x, p) = x$. For every predicate morphism $f : P \to P'$, $\hat{F}f = (k, k^\sim)$ where $k = F(Uf)$, and $k^\sim : \forall y : FX.\hat{F}P\,y \to \hat{F}P'\,(k\,y)$ is given by $k^\sim\,y\,z = F\{f\}z$.*

The inverse image f^{-1} of $f : X \to Y$ is a predicate $P : Y \to \mathsf{Set}$. Thus if P is a predicate on X, then $\hat{F}P$ is a predicate on FX, so $\hat{F}$ is a lifting of F from Set to $\mathcal{P}$. The lifting $\hat{F}$ captures an "all" modality generalising Haskell's $\mathtt{all}$ function on lists to arbitrary data types. A similar modality is given in [12] for indexed containers.

The lifting in Example 1 is the instantiation of the construction in Definition 5 to $NX = 1+X$ on Set. Indeed, if P is any predicate, then $\hat{N}\,P = (N\,\pi_P)^{-1}$, i.e., $\hat{N}\,P = (id + \pi_P)^{-1}$, by Definition 5. Since the inverse image of the coproduct of functions is the coproduct of their inverse images, since $id^{-1}1 = 1$, and since $\pi_P^{-1}n = \{(n, p) \mid p : Pn\}$ for all n, we have $\hat{N}\,P\,(inl\,\cdot) = 1$ and $\hat{N}\,P\,(inr\,n) = P\,n$.

The rest of this section shows that F-algebras with carrier $\{P\}$ are inter-derivable with $\hat{F}$-algebras with carrier P, and then uses this result to derive our induction rule.

Definition 6. *The functor* K_1 : Set $\rightarrow \mathcal{P}$ *maps each set* X *to the predicate* $K_1 X = \lambda x : X. 1$ *and each* $f : X \rightarrow Y$ *to the predicate morphism* $(f, \lambda x : X. id)$.

The predicate $K_1 X$ is called the *truth predicate on* X. For every $x : X$, the set $K_1 X x$ of proofs that $K_1 X$ holds for x is a singleton, and thus is non-empty. For any functor F, the lifting $\hat{F}$ maps the truth predicate on a set X to that on FX.

Lemma 1. *For any functor* F *on* Set *and any* X : Set, $\hat{F}(K_1 X) = K_1(FX)$.

Proof. By Definition 5, $\hat{F}(K_1 X) = (F\pi_{K_1 X})^{-1}$. We have that $\pi_{K_1 X}$ is a iso-morphism since there is only one proof of $K_1 X$ for each $x : X$, and thus that $F\pi_{K_1 X}$ is an isomorphism as well. As a result, $(F\pi_{K_1 X})^{-1}$ maps every $y : FX$ to a singleton set, and therefore $\hat{F}(K_1 X) = (F\pi_{K_1 X})^{-1} = \lambda y : FX. 1 = K_1(FX)$.

The fact that $K_1 \dashv \{-\}$ is critical to the constructions below. This is proved in [6]; we include its proof here for completeness and to establish notation. The descrip-tion of comprehension as a right adjoint can be traced back to Lawvere [10].

Lemma 2. K_1 *is left adjoint to* $\{-\}$.

Proof. We must show that, for any predicate P and any set Y, the set $\mathcal{P}(K_1 Y, P)$ of morphisms from $K_1 Y$ to P in $\mathcal{P}$ is in bijective correspondence with the set Set$(Y, \{P\})$ of morphisms from Y to $\{P\}$. Define maps $(-)^{\dagger}$: Set$(Y, \{P\}) \rightarrow \mathcal{P}(K_1 Y, P)$ and $(-)^{\#}$: $\mathcal{P}(K_1 Y, P) \rightarrow$ Set$(Y, \{P\})$ by $h^{\dagger} = (h_1, h_2)$ where $hy = (v, p)$, $h_1 y = v$ and $h_2 y = p$, and $(k, k^{\sim})^{\#} = \lambda(y : Y). (ky, k^{\sim}y)$. These give a natural isomorphism between Set$(Y, \{P\})$ and $\mathcal{P}(K_1 Y, P)$.

Naturality of $(-)^{\dagger}$ ensures that $(g \circ f)^{\dagger} = g^{\dagger} \circ K_1 f$ for all $f : Y' \rightarrow Y$ and $g : Y \rightarrow \{P\}$. Similarly for $(-)^{\#}$. Moreover, $id^{\dagger}$ is the counit of the adjunction between K_1 and $\{-\}$. These observations are used in the proof of Lemma 4.

Lemma 3. *There is a functor* $\Phi : Alg_F \rightarrow Alg_{\hat{F}}$ *such that if* $k : FX \rightarrow X$, *then* $\Phi k : \hat{F}(K_1 X) \rightarrow K_1 X$.

Proof. For an F-algebra $k : FX \rightarrow X$ define $\Phi k = K_1 k$, and for two F-algebras $k : FX \rightarrow X$ and $k' : FX' \rightarrow X'$ and an F-algebra morphism $h : X \rightarrow X'$ between them define the $\hat{F}$-algebra morphism $\Phi h : \Phi k \rightarrow \Phi k'$ by $\Phi h = K_1 h$. Then $K_1(FX) = \hat{F}(K_1 X)$ by Lemma 1, so that Φk is an $\hat{F}$-algebra and $K_1 h$ is an $\hat{F}$-algebra morphism. It is easy to see that Φ preserves identities and composition.

Lemma 4. *The functor* Φ *has a right adjoint* Ψ *such that if* $j : \hat{F}P \rightarrow P$, *then* $\Psi j : F\{P\} \rightarrow \{P\}$.

Proof. We construct $\Psi : Alg_{\hat{F}} \rightarrow Alg_F$ as follows. Given an $\hat{F}$-algebra $j : \hat{F}P \rightarrow P$, we use the fact that $\hat{F}(K_1\{P\}) = K_1(F\{P\})$ by Lemma 1 to define $\Psi j : F\{P\} \rightarrow \{P\}$ by $\Psi j = (j \circ \hat{F} id^{\dagger})^{\dagger}$. To specify the action of Ψ on an $\hat{F}$-algebra morphism h, define $\Psi h = \{h\}$. Clearly Ψ preserves identity and composition.

Next we show $\Phi \dashv \Psi$, i.e., for every F-algebra $k : FX \to X$ and $\hat{F}$-algebra $j : \hat{F}P \to P$ with P a predicate on X, there is a natural isomorphism between F-algebra morphisms from k to Ψj and $\hat{F}$-algebra morphisms from Φk to j. First observe that an F-algebra morphism from k to Ψj is a map from X to $\{P\}$, and an $\hat{F}$-algebra morphism from Φk to j is a map from $K_1 X$ to P. An isomorphism between such maps is given by the adjunction $K_1 \dashv \{-\}$ from Lemma 2, and so is natural. We must check that $f : X \to \{P\}$ is an F-algebra morphism from k to Ψj iff $f^\dagger : K_1 X \to P$ is an $\hat{F}$-algebra morphism from Φk to j.

So assume $f : X \to \{P\}$ is an F-algebra morphism from k to Ψj, i.e., $f \circ k = \Psi j \circ Ff$. We must prove that $f^\dagger \circ \Phi k = j \circ \hat{F} f^\dagger$. By the definition of Φ in Lemma 3, thus amounts to showing $f^\dagger \circ K_1 k = j \circ \hat{F} f^\dagger$. Since $(-)^\dagger$ is an isomorphism, f is an F-algebra morphism iff $(f \circ k)^\dagger = (\Psi j \circ Ff)^\dagger$. Naturality of $(-)^\dagger$ ensures that $(f \circ k)^\dagger = f^\dagger \circ K_1 k$ and that $(\Psi j \circ Ff)^\dagger = (\Psi j)^\dagger \circ K_1(Ff)$, so the previous equality holds iff $f^\dagger \circ K_1 k = (\Psi j)^\dagger \circ K_1(Ff)$. But

$$
\begin{aligned}
&j \circ \hat{F} f^\dagger \\
&= j \circ \hat{F}(id^\dagger \circ K_1 f) &&\text{by naturality of } (-)^\dagger \text{ and } f = id \circ f \\
&= (j \circ \hat{F} id^\dagger) \circ \hat{F}(K_1 f) &&\text{by the functoriality of } \hat{F} \\
&= (\Psi j)^\dagger \circ K_1(Ff) &&\text{by the definition of } \Psi, \text{ the fact that } (-)^\dagger \text{ and } (-)^\# \\
&&&\text{are inverses, and Lemma 1} \\
&= f^* \circ K_1 k &&\text{by the observation immediately preceding this proof} \\
&= f^\dagger \circ \Phi k &&\text{by the definition of } \Phi
\end{aligned}
$$

So $f^\dagger \circ K_1 k = (\Psi j)^\dagger \circ K_1(Ff)$, and $f^\dagger$ is an $\hat{F}$-algebra morphism from Φk to j.

Lemma 4 ensures that F-algebras with carrier $\{P\}$ are interderivable with $\hat{F}$-algebras with carrier P. For example, the N-algebra $[\alpha, \beta]$ with carrier $\{P\}$ from Section 2 can be derived from the $\hat{N}$-algebra with carrier P given in Example 1. Since we define a lifting $\hat{F}$ for any functor F, Lemma 4 thus shows how to construct F-algebras with carrier $\Sigma x : \mu F. Px$ for any F.

We can now derive our generic induction rule. For every predicate P on X and every $\hat{F}$-algebra $(k, k^\sim) : \hat{F}P \to P$, Lemma 4 ensures that Ψ constructs from $(k, k^\sim)$ an F-algebra with carrier $\{P\}$. Thus, $fold\ (\Psi\ (k, k^\sim)) : \mu F \to \{P\}$ and this map decomposes into two parts: $\phi = \pi_P \circ fold\ (\Psi\ (k, k^\sim)) : \mu F \to X$ and $\psi : \forall(t : \mu F). P(\phi t)$. Initiality of in ensures $\phi = fold\ k$. This gives the following generic induction rule for the type X, which reduces induction to iteration:

$genind \quad : \quad \forall\,(F : \mathsf{Set} \to \mathsf{Set})\,(P : X \to \mathsf{Set})\,((k, k^\sim) : (\hat{F}P \to P))\,(x : \mu F).$
$\qquad\qquad\qquad P\,(fold\ k\ x)$
$genind\ F\ P \;=\; \pi'_P \circ fold \circ \Psi$

When $X = \mu F$ and $k = in$, initiality of in further ensures that $\phi = fold\ in = id$, and thus that $genind$ specialises to the expected induction rule for an inductive data type μF:

$ind \quad : \quad \forall\,(F : \mathsf{Set} \to \mathsf{Set})\,(P : \mu F \to \mathsf{Set})\,((k, k^\sim) : (\hat{F}P \to P)).$
$\qquad\qquad\quad (k = in) \to \forall(x : \mu F).\ P\,x$
$ind\ F\ P \;=\; \pi'_P \circ fold \circ \Psi$

This rule can be instantiated to familiar rules for polynomial data types, as well as to ones we would expect for data types such as rose trees and finite hereditary sets, both of which lie outside the scope of standard methods.

Example 2. *The data type of rose trees is given in Haskell-like syntax by*

$$data\ Rose = Node(Int, List\ Rose)$$

The functor underlying Rose is $FX = Int \times List\ X$ *and its induction rule is*

$$
\begin{aligned}
indRose &\quad:\quad \forall\,(P: Rose \to \mathsf{Set})\,((k, k^\sim): (\hat{F}P \to P)). \\
&\qquad (k = in) \to \forall(x: Rose).\,P\,x \\
indRose\ F\ P &\ =\ \pi'_P \circ fold \circ \Psi
\end{aligned}
$$

Calculating $\hat{F}P = (F\pi_P)^{-1} : F\,Rose \to \mathsf{Set}$, *and writing* $xs\,!!\,k$ *for the* k^{th} *component of a list* xs, *we have that*

$$
\begin{aligned}
&\hat{F}\,P\,(i, rs) \\
&= \{z: F\{P\} \mid F\pi_p z = (i, rs)\} \\
&= \{(j, cps): Int \times List\,\{P\} \mid F\pi_P(j, cps) = (i, rs)\} \\
&= \{(j, cps): Int \times List\,\{P\} \mid (id \times List\,\pi_P)(j, cps) = (i, rs)\} \\
&= \{(j, cps): Int \times List\,\{P\} \mid j = i \text{ and } List\,\pi_P\,cps = rs\} \\
&= \{(j, cps): Int \times List\,\{P\} \mid j = i \text{ and } \forall k < length\,cps.\,\pi_P\,(cps\,!!\,k) = rs\,!!\,k\}
\end{aligned}
$$

An $\hat{F}$*-algebra whose underlying F-algebra is in : F Rose* $\to$ *Rose is thus a pair of functions* $(in, k^\sim)$, *where* $k^\sim$ *has type*

$$
\begin{aligned}
&\forall i: Int.\ \forall rs: List\ Rose. \\
&\quad \{(j, cps): Int \times List\,\{P\} \mid j = i \text{ and } \forall k < length\,cps.\,\pi_P\,(cps\,!!\,k) = rs\,!!\,k\} \\
&\qquad \to P(Node\,(i, rs)) \\
&= \forall i: Int.\ \forall rs: List\ Rose. \\
&\quad \{cps: List\,\{P\} \mid \forall k < length\,cps.\,\pi_P\,(cps\,!!\,k) = rs\,!!\,k\} \ \to\ P\,(Node\,(i, rs)) \\
&= \forall i: Int.\ \forall rs: List\ Rose.\ (\forall k < length\,rs.\,P\,(rs\,!!\,k)) \to P(Node\,(i, rs))
\end{aligned}
$$

The last equality is due to surjective pairing for dependent products and the fact that $length\,cps = length\,rs$. *The type of* $k^\sim$ *gives the hypotheses of the induction rule for rose trees.*

Example 3. *Hereditary sets are sets whose elements are themselves sets, and so are the core data structures within set theory. The data type* HS *of finite hereditary sets is* μP_f *for the finite powerset functor* P_f. *If* $P: X \to \mathsf{Set}$, *then* $P_f\pi_P: P_f(\Sigma x: X.Px) \to P_f X$ *maps each set* $\{(x_1, p_1), \dots, (x_n, p_n)\}$ *to the set* $\{x_1, \dots, x_n\}$, *so that* $(P_f\pi_P)^{-1}$ *maps a set* $\{x_1, \dots, x_n\}$ *to the set* $Px_1 \times \dots \times Px_n$. *A* $\hat{P}_f$*-algebra with carrier* $P: HS \to \mathsf{Set}$ *and first component in therefore has as its second component a function of type*

$$\forall(\{s_1, \dots, s_n\}: P_f(HS)).\,Ps_1 \times \dots \times Ps_n \to P(in\{s_1, \dots, s_n\})$$

The induction rule for finite hereditary sets is thus

$$
\begin{aligned}
indHS :: &\ (\forall(\{s_1, \dots, s_n\}: P_f(HS)).\,Ps_1 \times \dots \times Ps_n \to P(in\{s_1, \dots, s_n\})) \\
&\to \forall(s: HS).P\,s
\end{aligned}
$$

4   Induction Rules in the Fibrational Setting

We can treat a more general notion of predicate using fibrations. We motivate the move from the codomain fibration to arbitrary fibrations by observing that i) the semantics of data types in languages involving recursion and other effects usually involves categories other than Set; ii) in such circumstances, the notion of a predicate can no longer be taken as a function with codomain Set; iii) even when working in Set there are reasonable notions of "predicate" other than that in Section 3 (for example, a predicate on a set X could be a subobject of X); and iv) when, in future work, we come to consider induction rules for data types such as nested types, GADTs, indexed containers, and dependent types (see Section 5), we will want to appropriately instantiate a general theory of induction rather than having to invent a new one. Thus, although we could develop an *ad hoc* theory for each choice of category, functor, and predicate, it is far preferable to develop a uniform, axiomatic approach that is widely applicable.

Fibrations support precisely this kind of axiomatic approach, so this section generalises the constructions of the previous one to the general fibrational setting. The standard model of type theory based on locally cartesian closed categories does arise as a specific fibration — namely, the codomain fibration — but the general fibrational setting is far more flexible. In locally cartesian closed models of type theory, predicates and types coexist in the same category, so a functor can be taken to be its own lifting. In the general setting, predicates are not simply functions or morphisms, properties and types do not coexist in the same category, and a functor cannot be taken to be its own lifting. There is no choice but to construct a lifting. Details about fibrations can be found in standard references such as [8,14].

Working in the general fibrational setting also facilitates a direct comparison of our work with that of Hermida and Jacobs [6]. The main difference is that they use fibred products and coproducts in defining their liftings, whereas we use left adjoints to reindexing functors instead. The codomain fibration over Set has both, so their derivation gives exactly the same induction rule as ours in the setting of Section 3.

Let $U : \mathcal{E} \to \mathcal{B}$ be a fibration. Objects of the total category $\mathcal{E}$ can be thought of as properties, objects of the base category $\mathcal{B}$ can be thought of as types, and U can be thought of as mapping each property E in $\mathcal{E}$ to the type UE of which E is a property. One fibration U can capture many different properties of the same type, so U is not injective on objects. For any object B of $\mathcal{B}$, we write $\mathcal{E}_B$ for the *fibre above* B, i.e., for the subcategory of $\mathcal{E}$ consisting of objects E such that $UE = B$ and morphisms k between objects of $\mathcal{E}_B$ such that $Uk = id_B$. Let $f_E^\S$ be the cartesian morphism determined by f and E. Then $f_E^\S$ is unique up to isomorphism for every choice of object E and morphism f with codomain UE. If $f : B \to B'$ is a morphism in $\mathcal{B}$, then the *reindexing functor induced by* f is the functor $f^* : \mathcal{E}_{B'} \to \mathcal{E}_B$ defined on objects by $f^*E = dom(f_E^\S)$ and, for a morphism $k : E \to E'$ in $\mathcal{E}_{B'}$, f^*k is the morphism such that $k \circ f_E^\S = f_{E'}^\S \circ f^*k$. The universal property of $f_{E'}^\S$ ensures the existence and uniqueness of f^*k.

Proceeding by analogy with the situation for Set-based predicates — where Set plays the role of $\mathcal{B}$ and $\mathcal{P}$ plays the role of $\mathcal{E}$ — we now define, for every functor F on $\mathcal{B}$, a lifting $\hat{F}$ of F to $\mathcal{E}$ such that $U\hat{F} = FU$. We construct $\hat{F}$ by generalising each aspect of the construction of Section 3 to the general setting.

- *The Truth Functor.* To construct the truth functor in the general setting, we assume $\mathcal{B}$ and $\mathcal{E}$ have terminal objects $1_\mathcal{B}$ and $1_\mathcal{E}$, respectively, such that $U(1_\mathcal{E}) = 1_\mathcal{B}$. Writing $!_B$ for the unique map from an object B of $\mathcal{B}$ to $1_\mathcal{B}$, we define $K_1 : \mathcal{B} \to \mathcal{E}$ by setting $K_1 B = (!_B)^* 1_\mathcal{E}$ and, for a morphism $k : B \to B'$, taking $K_1 k$ to be the unique morphism guaranteed to exist by the universal property of $k^\S$. Then, for every B in $\mathcal{B}$, $K_1 B$ is the terminal object of $\mathcal{E}_B$, so $U(K_1 B) = B$. In fact, $U \dashv K_1$, and the unit of this adjunction is id, so $U K_1 = id$.

- *Comprehension.* Recall from Lemma 2 that the comprehension functor of Section 3 is right adjoint to the truth functor. Since right adjoints are defined up to isomorphism, in the general fibrational setting we can define the comprehension functor $\{-\}$ to be the right adjoint to the truth functor K_1. A fibration $U : \mathcal{E} \to \mathcal{B}$ which has a right adjoint K_1 which itself has a right adjoint $\{-\}$ is called a *comprehension category* [8]. We henceforth restrict attention to comprehension categories. We write ϵ for the counit of the adjunction $\{-\} \vdash K_1$ and so, for any object E of $\mathcal{E}$, we have that $\epsilon_E : K_1\{E\} \to E$.

- *Projection.* Recall from Section 3 that the first step of the construction of our lifting is to define the projection π_P mapping the comprehension of a predicate P to P's domain UP. As in Section 3, we also want comprehension to be a natural transformation, so we actually seek to construct $\pi : \{-\} \to U$ for an arbitrary comprehension category. Since $\epsilon_E : K_1\{E\} \to E$ for every object E of $\mathcal{E}$, we have that $U\epsilon_E : UK_1\{E\} \to UE$. Because $UK_1 = id$, defining $U\epsilon$ by $(U\epsilon)_E = U\epsilon_E$ gives a natural transformation from $\{-\}$ to U. We may therefore define the projection in an arbitrary comprehension category by $\pi = U\epsilon$.

- *Inverses.* The final step in defining $\hat{F}$ is to turn each component $F\pi_E$ of the natural transformation $F\pi : F\{-\} \to FU$ defined by $(F\pi)_E = F\pi_E$ into a predicate over FUE. In Section 3, this was done via an inverse image construction. To generalise it, first note that we can construct a predicate $invf$ in $\mathcal{E}_{B'}$ for any map $f : B \to B'$ in $\mathcal{B}$ if we assume a small amount of additional standard fibrational structure, namely that for each such f the functor $f^* : \mathcal{E}_{B'} \to \mathcal{E}_B$ has a left adjoint. As in [6], no Beck-Chevalley condition is required on this adjoint, which we denote $\Sigma_f : \mathcal{E}_B \to \mathcal{E}_{B'}$. We define $invf$ to be $\Sigma_f(K_1 B)$.

- *The Lifting.* Putting this all together, we now define the lifting $\hat{F} : \mathcal{E} \to \mathcal{E}$ by $\hat{F}E = \Sigma_{F\pi_E}(K_1(F\{E\}))$ for every object E of $\mathcal{E}$. For completeness we also give the action of $\hat{F}$ on morphisms. For each $k : E \to E'$, define $\hat{F}k = (FUk)^\S \alpha_{K_1 F\{E'\}} \Sigma_{F\pi_E} \gamma(K_1 F\{E\})$. Here, i) $\alpha_{K_1 F\{E'\}} : \Sigma_{F\pi_E}(F\{k\})^* K_1 F\{E'\} \to (FU\{k\})^* \Sigma_{F\pi_{E'}} K_1 F\{E'\}$ is the component for $K_1 F\{E'\}$ of the natural transformation from $\Sigma_{F\pi_E}(F\{k\})^*$ to $(FU\{k\})^* \Sigma_{F\pi_{E'}}$ arising from the facts that $\Sigma_{F\pi_E}$ is the left adjoint of $(F\pi_E)^*$ and that $F\pi$ is a natural transformation, and ii) $\gamma : \Sigma_{F\pi_E} K_1 F\{E\} \to \Sigma_{F\pi_E}(F\{k\})^* K_1 F\{E'\}$ is the isomorphism arising from the fact that $(F\{k\})^*$ is a right adjoint by the existence of $\Sigma_{F\{k\}}$ and hence preserves terminal objects. It is trivial to check that $\hat{F}$ is indeed a lifting.

- *Generalising Lemma 1.* As in Section 3, we ultimately want to show that F-algebras with carrier $\{P\}$ are interderivable with $\hat{F}$-algebras with carrier P. We first show that, as in Lemma 1, $\hat{F}(K_1B) = K_1(FB)$ for any functor F on $\mathcal{B}$ and B in $\mathcal{B}$. Recall that $UK_1 = id$ and define $\pi K_1 : \{-\}K_1 \to Id$ to be the natural transformation with components $(\pi K_1)_B = \pi_{K_1B}$. Note that $((\pi K_1)_B)^{-1} = UK_1\eta_B$, where $\eta : Id \to \{-\}K_1$ is the unit of the adjunction $\{-\} \vdash K_1$, so that πK_1 is a natural isomorphism. If we further define $F\pi K_1 : F\{-\}K_1 \to FUK_1$ to be the natural transformation with components $(F\pi K_1)_B = F((\pi K_1)_B)$, then $F\pi K_1$ is also a natural isomorphism. We will use this observation below to show that, for every object B of $\mathcal{B}$, $\Sigma_{(F\pi K_1)_B}$ is not only left adjoint by definition, but also right adjoint, to $((F\pi K_1)_B)^*$. Then, observing that right adjoints preserve terminal objects and that $K_1(FB)$ is the terminal object of $\mathcal{E}_{FB}$ (since K_1B is the terminal object of $\mathcal{E}_B$ for any B), we will have shown that $\hat{F}(K_1B)$ — i.e., $\Sigma_{(F\pi K_1)_B}(K_1(F\{K_1B\}))$ — must be the terminal object of $\mathcal{E}_{FU(K_1B)}$, i.e., of $\mathcal{E}_{FB}$. In other words, we will have shown that $\hat{F}(K_1B) = K_1(FB)$.

So, fix an object B of $\mathcal{B}$. To see that $\Sigma_{(F\pi K_1)_B} \vdash ((F\pi K_1)_B)^*$, first note that, for any isomorphism $f : B \to B'$ in $\mathcal{B}$, f^* and $(f^{-1})^*$ both exist and both $f^* \vdash (f^{-1})^*$ and $(f^{-1})^* \vdash f^*$ hold. Then, since $f^* \vdash \Sigma_f$ by definition, we have Σ_f is $(f^{-1})^*$, and thus that $\Sigma_f \vdash f^*$. Instantiating f to $(F\pi K_1)_B$ and recalling that $(F\pi K_1)_B$ is an isomorphism, we have that $\Sigma_{(F\pi K_1)_B} \vdash ((F\pi K_1)_B)^*$.

- *A Generic Fibrational Induction Rule.* Analogues of Lemma 3 and Lemma 4 hold in the general fibrational setting provided all occurrences of Set are replaced by $\mathcal{B}$ and all occurrences of $\mathcal{P}$ are replaced by $\mathcal{E}$ and, in the analogue of Lemma 2, $(-)^\dagger : \mathcal{B}(B, \{E\}) \to \mathcal{E}(K_1B, E)$ and $(-)^\# : \mathcal{E}(K_1B, E) \to \mathcal{B}(B, \{E\})$ are defined by the adjunction $\{-\} \vdash K_1$.

The above construction thus yields the following generalised induction rule:

$$\begin{aligned}
genfibind \quad &: \quad \forall\, (F : \mathcal{B} \to \mathcal{B})\,(E : \mathcal{E}_X)\,(k : \hat{F}E \to E).\, \mu F \to \{E\} \\
genfibind\, F\, E &= \; fold \circ \Psi
\end{aligned}$$

This induction rule looks slightly different from the one for set-valued predicates. In Section 3, we were able to use the specific structure of comprehensions for set-valued predicates to extract proofs for particular data elements from them. But in the general fibrational setting, predicates, and hence comprehensions, are left abstract, so we take the return type of the general induction scheme *genfibind* to be a comprehension. We expect that, when *genfibind* is instantiated to a fibration of interest, we should be able to use knowledge about that fibration to extract from the comprehension it constructs further proof information relevant to the application at hand. This expectation is justified, as in [6], by $\{-\} \vdash K_1$.

We now give an induction rule for a data type and properties that cannot be modelled in Set.

Example 4. *The fixed point $Hyp = \mu F$ of the functor $FX = (X \to Int) \to Int$ is the data type of hyperfunctions. Since F has no fixed point in* Set*, we interpret it in the category $\omega CPO_\perp$ of ω-cpos with $\perp$ and strict continuous monotone functions. In this setting, a property of an object X of $\omega CPO_\perp$ is an admissible sub-$\omega CPO_\perp$ A of X. Admissibility means that the bottom element of X is in*

A and A is closed under the least upper bounds of X. This structure forms a Lawvere category [7,8]. The truth functor maps X to X, and comprehension maps a sub-$\omega CPO_\perp$ A of X to A. The lifting $\hat{F}$ maps a sub-$\omega CPO_\perp$ A of X to the sub-$\omega CPO_\perp$ FA of FX. Finally, the derived induction rule states that if A is an admissible sub-$\omega CPO_\perp$ of Hyp, and if $\hat{F}(A) \subseteq A$, then A = Hyp.

5   Conclusion and Future Work

We give an induction rule that can be used to prove properties of data structures of inductive types. Like Hermida and Jacobs, we give a fibrational account of induction, but we derive, under slightly different assumptions on fibrations, a generic induction rule that can be instantiated to *any* inductive type rather than just to polynomial ones. This rule is based on initial algebra semantics of data types, and is parameterised over both the data types and the properties involved. It is also principled, expressive, and correct. Our derivation yields the same induction rules as Hermida and Jacobs' when specialised to polynomial functors in the codomain fibration, but it also gives induction rules for non-polynomial data types such as rose trees, and for data types such as finite hereditary sets and hyperfunctions, for which no induction rules have previously been known.

There are several directions for future work. The most immediate is to instantiate our theory to give induction rules for nested types. These are exemplified by the data type of perfect trees given in Haskell-like syntax as follows:

$$data\ PTree\ a : \mathsf{Set}\ where$$
$$PLeaf : a \rightarrow PTree\ a$$
$$PNode : PTree\ (a,a) \rightarrow PTree\ a$$

Nested types arise as least fixed points of rank-2 functors; for example, the type of perfect trees is μH for the functor H given by $H F = \lambda X.\ X + F(X \times X)$. An appropriate fibration for induction rules for nested types thus takes $\mathcal{B}$ to be the category of functors on Set, $\mathcal{E}$ to be the category of functors from Set to $\mathcal{P}$, and U to be postcomposition with the forgetful functor from Section 3. A lifting $\hat{H}$ of H is given by $\hat{H}\ P\ X\ (inl\ a) = 1$ and $\hat{H}\ P\ X\ (inr\ n) = P\ (X \times X)\ n$. Taking the premise to be an $\hat{H}$-algebra gives the following induction rule for perfect trees:

$$indPTree : \forall\ (P : \mathsf{Set} \rightarrow \mathcal{P}).$$
$$(UP = PTree) \rightarrow (\forall(X : \mathsf{Set})(x : X).\ PX\ (PLeaf\ x)) \rightarrow$$
$$(\forall(X : \mathsf{Set})(t : PTree\ (X \times X).\ P\ (X \times X)\ t \rightarrow PX\ (PNode\ t))) \rightarrow$$
$$\forall(X : \mathsf{Set})(t : PTree\ X).\ P\ X\ t$$

This rule can be used to show, for example, that *PTree* is a functor.

Extending the above instantiation for the codomain fibration to "truly nested types" and fibrations is current work. We expect to be able to instantiate our theory for truly nested types, GADTs, indexed containers, and dependent types, but initial investigations show care is needed. We must ascertain which fibrations can model predicates on such types, since the codomain fibration may not give useful induction rules, as well as how to translate the rules to which these fibrations give rise to an intensional setting.

Matthes [11] gives induction rules for nested types (including truly nested ones) in an intensional type theory. He handles only rank-2 functors that underlie nested types (while we handle any functor of any rank with an initial algebra), but his insights may help guide choices of fibrations for truly nested types. These may in turn inform choices for GADTs, indexed containers, and dependent types.

Induction rules can automatically be generated in many type theories. Within the Calculus of Constructions [3] an induction rule for a data type can be generated solely from the inductive structure of that type. Such generation is also a key idea in the Coq proof assistant [4]. But as far as we know, generation can currently be done only for syntactic classes of functors rather than for all functors with initial algebras. In some type theories induction schemes are added as axioms rather than generated. For example, attempts to generate induction schemes based on Church encodings in the Calculus of Constructions proved unsuccessful and so initiality was added to the system, thus giving the Calculus of Inductive Constructions. Whereas Matthes' work is based on concepts such as impredicativity and induction recursion rather than initial algebras, ours reduces induction to initiality, and may therefore help lay the groundwork for extending implementations of induction to more sophisticated data types.

References

1. Bird, R.S., De Moor, O.: Algebra of Programming. International Series in Computing Science, vol. 100. Prentice-Hall, Englewood Cliffs (1997)
2. Bird, R., Meertens, L.: Nested Datatypes. In: Jeuring, J. (ed.) MPC 1998. LNCS, vol. 1422, pp. 52–67. Springer, Heidelberg (1998)
3. Coquand, T., Huet, G.: The Calculus of Constructions. Information and Computation 76(2-3), 95–120 (1988)
4. The Coq Proof Assistant, coq.inria.fr
5. Ghani, N., Johann, P.: Foundations for Structured Programming with GADTs. In: Proceedings, Principles of Programming Languages, pp. 297–308 (2008)
6. Hermida, C., Jacobs, B.: Structural Induction and Coinduction in a Fibrational Setting. Information and Computation 145(2), 107–152 (1998)
7. Jacobs, B.: Comprehension Categories and the Semantics of Type Dependency. Theoretical Computer Science 107, 169–207 (1993)
8. Jacobs, B.: Categorical Logic and Type Theory. North Holland, Amsterdam (1999)
9. Johann, P., Ghani, N.: Initial Algebra Semantics is Enough! Proceedings, Typed Lambda Calculus and Applications, pp. 207–222 (2007)
10. Lawvere, F.W.: Equality in Hyperdoctrines and Comprehension Scheme as an Adjoint Functor. Applications of Categorical Algebra, 1–14 (1970)
11. Matthes, R.: An Induction Principle for Nested Datatypes in Intensional Type Theory. Journal of Functional Programming 19(3&4), 439–468 (2009)
12. Morris, P.: Constructing Universes for Generic Programming. Dissertation, University of Nottingham (2007)
13. Moggi, E.: Notations of Computation and Monads. Information and Computation 93(1), 55–92 (1991)
14. Pavlovic, D.: Predicates and Fibrations. Dissertation, University of Utrecht (1990)

A Sequent Calculus with Implicit Term Representation

Stefan Hetzl

Laboratoire Preuves, Programmes et Systèmes (PPS)
Université Paris Diderot
175 Rue du Chevaleret, 75013 Paris, France

Abstract. We investigate a modification of the sequent calculus which separates a first-order proof into its abstract deductive structure and a unifier which renders this structure a valid proof. We define a cut-elimination procedure for this calculus and show that it produces the same cut-free proofs as the standard calculus, but, due to the implicit representation of terms, it provides exponentially shorter normal forms. This modified calculus is applied as a tool for theoretical analyses of the standard calculus and as a mechanism for a more efficient implementation of cut-elimination.

1 Introduction

It is a fundamental observation, made independently by several researchers, that a formal proof can be subdivided into its abstract deductive structure, often called skeleton, and a way of instantiating it with formulas which renders it a valid proof. For proof-search, the separation of these two layers is a principle whose importance can hardly be overemphasised. It is already visible in the original resolution rule [24] but even more apparent in the extension [18] of resolution to type theory. It is central for matings [1] and has applications in logic programming where proof-search provides an operational semantics for Prolog-like languages [21]. From a proof-theoretic point of view, the relation between these two levels has been investigated in [22]. Such questions give rise naturally to unification problems [20,10]: filling up a skeleton for a cut-free first-order proof can be done by solving a first-order unification problem, the case with cuts corresponds to second-order unification, which is undecidable [15].

In the present paper this separation is investigated *from the point of view of cut-elimination*. We introduce the calculus $\mathbf{LK^s}$, for first-order classical logic, which makes these two levels explicit: a proof contains formulas with free variables whose instantiation is specified independently. We define a cut-elimination procedure for $\mathbf{LK^s}$ and show that it has the same set of normal forms as the standard sequent calculus. We describe two applications of this calculus: on the one hand we obtain an exponential compression of the size of normal forms which makes $\mathbf{LK^s}$ a powerful mechanism for the implementation of $\mathbf{LK}$. On the other hand the implicit representation of terms is used to give a considerably

A. Dawar and H. Veith (Eds.): CSL 2010, LNCS 6247, pp. 351–365, 2010.

simplified proof of a characterisation of the form of witness terms obtainable by
cut-elimination in terms of a regular tree grammar.

From an implementational perspective, we investigate the role of sharing in
the context of first-order proofs from a novel point of view. Previous work on
proof normalisation with sharing treated the level of the proof, respectively the
term calculus associated to it via a Curry-Howard correspondence: for example
the work on optimal reduction for the lambda calculus, see [2] for a survey, or
deduction graphs [12,13] which treat natural deduction directly. The present paper provides a complementary study of redundancy in the formulas of a proof, in
particular the exponential compression described in Section 5 cannot be obtained
by the above-mentioned sharing mechanisms.

2   The Calculus LK^s

In order to introduce the calculus **LK^s** we first need some preliminary notions
and results about first-order substitutions. We assume two disjoint countably
infinite sets of variables at our disposal: one for free variables and one for bound
variables; the letters $\alpha, \beta, \gamma, \ldots$ will only be used for free variables, the letters
$x, y, z, \ldots$ will be used for both free and bound variables, substitutions may
contain free and bound variables. The variables in some expression e will be
denoted by $V(e)$. A substitution σ is a function mapping variables to terms s.t.
its domain $\mathrm{dom}(\sigma) := \{x \mid x \neq x\sigma\}$ is finite. The variable-range is $\mathrm{vrge}(\sigma) :=$
$V(\{x\sigma \mid x \in \mathrm{dom}(\sigma)\})$. For a set S of substitutions, $\mathrm{dom}(S) := \bigcup_{\sigma \in S} \mathrm{dom}(\sigma)$
and $\mathrm{vrge}(S) := \bigcup_{\sigma \in S} \mathrm{vrge}(\sigma)$. For σ and θ being substitutions call σ *right-
independent of* θ if $\mathrm{dom}(\sigma) \cap \mathrm{dom}(\theta) = \emptyset$ and $\mathrm{vrge}(\sigma) \cap \mathrm{dom}(\theta) = \emptyset$; σ and θ
are called *independent* if σ is right-independent of θ and θ is right-independent
of σ. The (right-)independence of substitutions is a useful technical property
for carrying out rearrangements of substitution sequences which will be used
throughout this paper.

Lemma 1. *If σ is right-independent of $\theta = [x_1\backslash t_1, \ldots, x_n\backslash t_n]$, then $\theta\sigma =$
$\sigma[x_1\backslash t_1\sigma, \ldots, x_n\backslash t_n\sigma]$. If σ and θ are independent, then $\theta\sigma = \sigma\theta$.*

A substitution σ is called *base substitution* if $|\mathrm{dom}(\sigma)| = 1$. A set S of base
substitutions is called *functional* if for all $\sigma_1, \sigma_2 \in S$: $\mathrm{dom}(\sigma_1) = \mathrm{dom}(\sigma_2) \Rightarrow$
$\sigma_1 = \sigma_2$. For substitutions σ, θ write $\sigma <^1 \theta$ if $\mathrm{vrge}(\sigma) \cap \mathrm{dom}(\theta) \neq \emptyset$. A set S
of substitutions is called *acyclic* if the directed graph $(S, <^1)$ does not contain
a directed cycle. For a set S of substitutions write $\sigma <_S \theta$ if there is a directed
path from σ to θ in $(S \cup \{\sigma, \theta\}, <^1)$ and $\leq_S$ for its reflexive closure. This ordering
of substitutions will play an important role, it is convenient to extend it also to
other objects as follows: For variables x, y write $x \leq_S y$ if $x = y$ or there are
$\sigma, \theta \in S$ s.t. $\sigma \leq_S \theta$ and $x \in \mathrm{dom}(\sigma)$ and $y \in \mathrm{vrge}(\theta)$. For a set V of variables
write $V \leq_S y$ if there is an $x \in V$ s.t. $x \leq_S y$, for a term t write $t \leq_S y$ if t
contains a variable x s.t. $x \leq_S y$ and for a formula F write $F \leq_S y$ if F contains
a free variable α s.t. $\alpha \leq_S y$.

Definition 1. *Let S be a finite, acyclic, functional set of base substitutions. A list $\sigma_1, \ldots, \sigma_n$ is called* linearisation *of S if for every $\sigma \in S$ there is exactly one $i \in \{1, \ldots, n\}$ s.t. $\sigma_i = \sigma$ and whenever $\sigma_i <_S \sigma_j$, then $i < j$.*

Lemma 2. *Let S be a finite, acyclic, functional set of base substitutions. Let $\sigma_{i_1}, \ldots, \sigma_{i_n}$ and $\sigma_{j_1}, \ldots, \sigma_{j_n}$ be linearisations of S. Then $\sigma_{i_1} \cdots \sigma_{i_n} = \sigma_{j_1} \cdots \sigma_{j_n}$.*

Proof. By induction on n.

Therefore, each finite, acyclic, functional set S of base substitutions induces a unique substitution $\sigma_1 \cdots \sigma_n$ for $\sigma_1, \ldots, \sigma_n$ being any linearisation of S. We denote this substitution by S°. This description of a substitution is particularly natural in the context of cut-elimination because a global substitution is computed successively by composing base substitutions. This point of view is the design principle behind **LK^s**.

Definition 2. *A sequent is a pair of multisets of formulas. An **LK^s**-proof is a pair (π, S) s.t. S is a finite, acyclic, functional set of base substitutions containing free variables only and π is built up from the following axioms and rules:*

$$A_1 \to A_2 \quad \text{if } A_1 S^\circ = A_2 S^\circ$$

$$\frac{\Gamma \to \Delta, A \quad \Pi \to \Lambda, B}{\Gamma, \Pi \to \Delta, \Lambda, A \wedge B} \wedge_r \qquad \frac{A, \Gamma \to \Delta \quad B, \Pi \to \Lambda}{A \vee B, \Gamma, \Pi \to \Delta, \Lambda} \vee_l$$

$$\frac{A, B, \Gamma \to \Delta}{A \wedge B, \Gamma \to \Delta} \wedge_l \qquad \frac{\Gamma \to \Delta, A, B}{\Gamma \to \Delta, A \vee B} \vee_r \qquad \frac{\Gamma \to \Delta, A}{\neg A, \Gamma \to \Delta} \neg_l \qquad \frac{A, \Gamma \to \Delta}{\Gamma \to \Delta, \neg A} \neg_r$$

$$\frac{A[x\backslash t], \Gamma \to \Delta}{\forall x\, A, \Gamma \to \Delta} \forall_l \qquad \frac{\Gamma \to \Delta, A[x\backslash \alpha]}{\Gamma \to \Delta, \forall x\, A} \forall_r \qquad \frac{A[x\backslash \alpha], \Gamma \to \Delta}{\exists x\, A, \Gamma \to \Delta} \exists_l \qquad \frac{\Gamma \to \Delta, A[x\backslash t]}{\Gamma \to \Delta, \exists x\, A} \exists_r$$

where $\alpha \notin \mathrm{dom}(S)$ and t does not contain a variable that is bound in A

$$\frac{A, A, \Gamma \to \Delta}{A, \Gamma \to \Delta} c_l \qquad \frac{\Gamma \to \Delta, A, A}{\Gamma \to \Delta, A} c_r \qquad \frac{\Gamma \to \Delta}{A, \Gamma \to \Delta} w_l \qquad \frac{\Gamma \to \Delta}{\Gamma \to \Delta, A} w_r$$

$$\frac{\Gamma \to \Delta, A_1 \quad A_2, \Pi \to \Lambda}{\Gamma, \Pi \to \Delta, \Lambda} cut \quad \text{if } A_1 S^\circ = A_2 S^\circ$$

Furthermore, the following global variable condition *must be fulfilled: For every $\forall_r$- and $\exists_l$-inference ι with an eigenvariable α and every $\beta \leq_S \alpha$: β occurs in π only above ι.*

We have thus relaxed the usual identity constraints on axioms and cuts and replaced it by the weaker constraint of *unifiability* by S°. An even more liberal calculus could be used instead where also the identity constraints on contractions and even on the context of rules are replaced by unifiability. However, our aim here is the analysis of cut-elimination in **LK** and the above calculus **LK^s** is sufficiently flexible for that purpose. This calculus also bears some resemblance to deduction modulo [8,9] in relaxing identity constraints, its focus however is rather different as proofs modulo are typically considered w.r.t some fixed background theory, in **LK^s** however we will rather start from $S = \emptyset$ and fill S by cut-elimination.

Example 1. Let $\pi =$

$$
\cfrac{
\cfrac{
\cfrac{P(f(\alpha),g(\alpha)) \to P(f(\alpha),g(\alpha))}{P(f(\alpha),g(\alpha)) \to \exists x\, P(f(\alpha),g(x))} \exists_r
\quad
\cfrac{
\cfrac{
\cfrac{P(\beta,g(\gamma)) \to P(\beta,\delta)}{P(\beta,g(\gamma)) \to \exists y\, P(\beta,y)} \exists_r
}{P(\beta,g(\gamma)) \to \exists x \exists y\, P(x,y)} \exists_r
}{\exists x\, P(\beta,g(x)) \to \exists x \exists y\, P(x,y)} \exists_l
}{P(f(\alpha),g(\alpha)) \to \exists x \exists y\, P(x,y)} \text{cut}
}{\exists x\, P(f(x),g(x)) \to \exists x \exists y\, P(x,y)} \exists_l
$$

and $S = \{[\beta\backslash f(\alpha)], [\delta\backslash g(\gamma)]\}$. Then (π, S) is an **LK^s**-proof.

It should be noted that this transition from a calculus **K** to a calculus **K^s** where syntactic identity is replaced by unifiability is conceivable in a very broad setting: it depends neither on **K** being a sequent calculus nor on working in first-order classical logic. The analysis carried out in this paper is therefore also extendable to other proof systems with quantifiers, e.g. to sequent calculi or natural deduction systems for intuitionistic or higher-order logic.

An **LK**-proof is called regular if different strong quantifier inferences (i.e. $\forall_r$- and $\exists_l$-inferences) have different eigenvariables. **LK^s** is complete as every regular **LK**-proof π can be regarded as an **LK^s**-proof $(\pi, \emptyset)$. For soundness we need the following

Proposition 1. *If (π, S) is an **LK^s**-proof, then πS° is a regular **LK**-proof.*

Proof. The rules remain correct under substitution, the eigenvariable condition of πS° being implied by the global variable condition of (π, S). For regularity, suppose there are strong quantifier inferences ι_1 and ι_2 with the same eigenvariable. By the global variable condition applied to ι_1 and ι_2, ι_1 must be above ι_2 and ι_2 must be above ι_1 and thus $\iota_1 = \iota_2$, so πS° is regular.

3   Cut-Elimination

In this section, we describe cut-elimination for **LK^s**. The proof reduction steps will be based on those of **LK**. There are however two crucial differences: upon reduction of a quantifier, the substitution will *not* be applied to the proof but rather be stored in S and secondly variable renamings have to be carried out in S as well. The basic idea behind this procedure, namely to not carry out all substitutions immediately, bears some resemblance to calculi of explicit substitutions, see e.g. [19] for a recent survey. However, **LK^s** differs from calculi of explicit substitutions as it does not consider substitutions as part of the object level and does not extend the standard proof reductions by reductions that deal with substitutions.

For the reader's convenience we first recall the reduction of a universal quantifier in **LK**. Let π be an **LK**-proof. If it contains a subproof of the form

$$\psi \quad = \quad \dfrac{\dfrac{(\psi_1)}{\Gamma \to \Delta, A[x\backslash\alpha]}\ \forall_r \quad \dfrac{(\psi_2)}{A[x\backslash t], \Pi \to \Lambda}\ \forall_l}{\dfrac{\forall x A, \Pi \to \Lambda}{\Gamma, \Pi \to \Delta, \Lambda}}\ ,$$
$$\text{cut}$$

we denote this by $\pi = \pi[\psi]$ and define

$$\psi' \quad := \quad \dfrac{(\psi_1[\alpha\backslash t]) \qquad (\psi_2)}{\Gamma \to \Delta, A[x\backslash t] \quad A[x\backslash t], \Pi \to \Lambda}{\Gamma, \Pi \to \Delta, \Lambda}\ \text{cut}$$

and $\pi[\psi] \to \pi[\psi']$ where $\pi[\psi']$ denotes the proof π where the subproof ψ has been replaced by ψ'. This reduction is adapted to $\mathbf{LK^s}$ in the following sense.

Lemma 3. *Let (π, S) be an $\mathbf{LK^s}$-proof where π contains a subproof*

$$\psi = \dfrac{\dfrac{(\psi_1)}{\Gamma \to \Delta, A_1[x\backslash\alpha]}\ \forall_r \quad \dfrac{(\psi_2)}{A_2[x\backslash t], \Pi \to \Lambda}\ \forall_l}{\dfrac{\forall x A_2, \Pi \to \Lambda}{\Gamma, \Pi \to \Delta, \Lambda}}\ \text{cut}$$

and let

$$\psi' := \dfrac{(\psi_1) \qquad\qquad (\psi_2)}{\Gamma \to \Delta, A_1[x\backslash\alpha] \quad A_2[x\backslash t], \Pi \to \Lambda}{\Gamma, \Pi \to \Delta, \Lambda}\ \text{cut}\ .$$

Then there is an S' s.t. $(\pi[\psi'], S')$ is an $\mathbf{LK^s}$-proof.

Proof. If x does not appear in A_1, then it also does not appear in A_2 since $A_1 S^\circ = A_2 S^\circ$ and S contains only free variables. In this case, let $S' = S$ and observe that $(\pi[\psi'], S')$ is an $\mathbf{LK^s}$-proof. If x does appear in A_1, let $S' = S \cup \{[\alpha\backslash t]\}$. S' is obviously finite; it is also functional as the $\forall_r$-side condition ensures that $\alpha \notin \text{dom}(S)$. Suppose S' is cyclic, then the cycle in S' must contain $[\alpha\backslash t]$ and thus $t \leq_S \alpha$ which, as t occurs outside of ψ_1 contradicts the global variable assumption of (π, S).

Let $[\alpha_1\backslash t_1], \ldots, [\alpha_n\backslash t_n]$ be a linearisation of S. Then there is a $k \in \{0, \ldots, n\}$ s.t. $S'^\circ = \sigma_l[\alpha\backslash t]\sigma_r$ for $\sigma_l = [\alpha_1\backslash t_1]\cdots[\alpha_k\backslash t_k]$ and $\sigma_r = [\alpha_{k+1}\backslash t_{k+1}]\cdots[\alpha_n\backslash t_n]$. Then

$$A_1[x\backslash\alpha]S'^\circ = A_1\sigma_l\sigma_r[x\backslash t\sigma_r, \alpha\backslash t\sigma_r] = A_2\sigma_l\sigma_r[x\backslash t\sigma_r, \alpha\backslash t\sigma_r] = A_2[x\backslash t]S'^\circ.$$

Let ι be a $\forall_r$- or $\exists_l$-inference in $\pi[\psi']$ with eigenvariable β and let γ be a variable with $\gamma \leq_{S'} \beta$. If $[\alpha\backslash t]$ does not appear in the substitution path $\gamma \leq_{S'} \beta$, then $\gamma \leq_S \beta$ and the global variable condition of $(\pi[\psi'], S')$ follows from that of $(\pi[\psi], S)$. If $[\alpha\backslash t]$ does appear, it does so exactly once for suppose it would appear twice, then $t \leq_S \alpha$ contradicting acyclicity of S, hence $\gamma \leq_S \alpha$ and $t \leq_S \beta$. By $\gamma \leq_S \alpha$, γ occurs only in ψ_1 and by $t \leq_S \beta$, ι is below the reduced cut and thus γ appears only above ι.

Finally, the remaining identity constraints in $(\pi[\psi'], S')$ are satisfied as they are closed under substitution and the side conditions of the quantifier rules are fulfilled too.

A technical aspect of cut-elimination is to keep track of the names of eigenvariables. The traditional solution of this problem is to work on regular proofs. An alternative would be to use additional constructs for local binding of these variables. In order to keep the object-level formalism as simple as possible, we opted for the first solution. The elimination of a contraction is the only reduction rule where this aspect has to be dealt with. Let V be a set of variables. A substitution ρ is called *fresh-variable renaming for V* if $\rho = [\alpha_i \backslash \alpha_i']_{i=1}^n$, ρ is injective and none of the α_i' occurs in V. We say that ρ is a fresh-variable renaming for an expression e if it is one for $V(e)$. If an **LK**-proof π contains a subproof of the form

$$\psi \quad = \quad \cfrac{\cfrac{\cfrac{(\psi_1)}{\Gamma \rightarrow \Delta, A, A}}{\Gamma \rightarrow \Delta, A}\ c_r \qquad \cfrac{(\psi_2)}{A, \Pi \rightarrow \Lambda}}{\Gamma, \Pi \rightarrow \Delta, \Lambda}\ \text{cut} \quad ,$$

define $\psi' :=$

$$\cfrac{\cfrac{\cfrac{(\psi_1)}{\Gamma \rightarrow \Delta, A, A} \quad \cfrac{(\psi_2\rho')}{A, \Pi \rightarrow \Lambda}}{\Gamma, \Pi \rightarrow \Delta, \Lambda, A}\ \text{cut} \quad \cfrac{(\psi_2\rho'')}{A, \Pi \rightarrow \Lambda}}{\cfrac{\Gamma, \Pi, \Pi \rightarrow \Delta, \Delta, \Lambda}{\Gamma, \Pi \rightarrow \Delta, \Lambda}\ c^*}\ \text{cut}$$

where $\{\alpha_1, \ldots, \alpha_k\}$ are the eigenvariables of ψ_2 and $\rho' := [\alpha_i \backslash \alpha_i']_{i=1}^k$, $\rho'' := [\alpha_i \backslash \alpha_i'']_{i=1}^k$ are fresh-variable renamings for π. Define $\pi[\psi] \rightarrow \pi[\psi']$. For simplifying the comparison with **LK^s** we assume that the above variables α_i' and α_i'' have been chosen in such a way that they are not only fresh for the proof currently under consideration but also for the whole cut-elimination sequence up to the current proof. Given a substitution $\sigma = [\beta_j \backslash s_j]_{j=1}^m$, ρ is a fresh-variable renaming for σ if it is one for $V = \text{dom}(\sigma) \cup \text{vrge}(\sigma)$. In this case, define $\sigma^\rho := [\beta_j \rho \backslash s_j \rho]_{j=1}^m$. Given a set S of substitutions, ρ is a fresh-variable renaming for S if it is one for all $\sigma \in S$; in this case, define $S^\rho := \{\sigma^\rho \mid \sigma \in S\}$. For the reduction of a contraction in **LK^s** we have to extend the renaming to all variables which depend on eigenvariables of the duplicated proof.

Lemma 4. *Let (π, S) be an **LK^s**-proof where π contains a subproof*

$$\psi \quad = \quad \cfrac{\cfrac{\cfrac{(\psi_1)}{\Gamma \rightarrow \Delta, A_1, A_1}}{\Gamma \rightarrow \Delta, A_1}\ c_r \qquad \cfrac{(\psi_2)}{A_2, \Pi \rightarrow \Lambda}}{\Gamma, \Pi \rightarrow \Delta, \Lambda}\ \text{cut} \quad .$$

Let $\alpha_1, \ldots, \alpha_k$ be the eigenvariables of ψ_2 and let $\{\alpha_1, \ldots, \alpha_n\} = \{\alpha \mid \alpha \leq_S \alpha_i$ for an $i \in \{1, \ldots, k\}\}$. Let $\alpha_1', \alpha_1'', \ldots, \alpha_n', \alpha_n''$ be distinct variables s.t. $\rho' :=$

$[\alpha_i \backslash \alpha_i']_{i=1}^n$ and $\rho'' := [\alpha_i \backslash \alpha_i'']_{i=1}^n$ are fresh-variable renamings for π and S. Then, by the global variable condition, $\psi_2 \rho'$ and $\psi_2 \rho''$ end with $A_2, \Pi \to \Lambda$. Let $\psi' :=$

$$
\cfrac{
  \cfrac{
    \begin{array}{cc} (\psi_1) & (\psi_2 \rho') \\ \Gamma \to \Delta, A_1, A_1 & A_2, \Pi \to \Lambda \end{array}
  }{\Gamma, \Pi \to \Delta, \Lambda, A_1} \; \text{cut} \qquad \cfrac{(\psi_2 \rho'')}{A_2, \Pi \to \Lambda}
}{
  \cfrac{\Gamma, \Pi, \Pi \to \Delta, \Lambda, \Lambda}{\Gamma, \Pi \to \Delta, \Lambda} \; c^*
} \; \text{cut}
$$

and $S' := S^{\rho'} \cup S^{\rho''}$, then $(\pi[\psi'], S')$ is an $\mathbf{LK^s}$-proof.

Having established the reductions of quantifiers and contractions above we have a cut-elimination relation for $\mathbf{LK^s}$.

Definition 3. We will write $(\pi, S) \to (\pi', S')$ if π, S, π', S' are as in Lemma 3 or in Lemma 4 above (including the symmetric variants for $\exists$ and contraction-left). Furthermore we also write $(\pi, S) \to (\pi', S)$ if π reduces to π' by a standard $\mathbf{LK}$-reduction of a propositional connective, a weakening, an axiom or the rank of a cut-formula. The reader interested in technical details is invited to consult [16] for a comprehensive list of all reduction rules for this calculus. For $\mathbf{LK}$-proofs π, π' we write $\pi \to \pi'$ for the standard reduction. We will also use $\to$ to denote a sequence of the above reduction steps for both $\mathbf{LK}$ and $\mathbf{LK^s}$.

Note that we do not impose any restriction on the strategy that can be applied. Therefore this set of reduction rules is not confluent, see [4] for a strongly non-confluent example. It is also not strongly normalising by allowing the double-contraction example found e.g. in [7] and in a similar form in [25]. It is however weakly normalising which follows from known results about $\mathbf{LK}$. The rationale for considering this liberal cut-elimination relation lies in the fact that each restriction by a strategy limits the obtainable normal forms. From the point of view of obtaining a confluent calculus, see e.g. [7,23], to be used as a programming language this effect is intended. However, from the foundational point of view that asks for the constructive content of a mathematical proof in classical logic it has the unfortunate consequence of strongly reducing the degree of generality in which the original proof is considered, see [4].

4   Relation to LK

We can now reduce an $\mathbf{LK}$-proof π using either the standard $\mathbf{LK}$-reductions to obtain a cut-free $\mathbf{LK}$-proof π^* or the $\mathbf{LK^s}$-reductions to obtain a proof (ψ, S) where ψ is cut-free. For a regular $\mathbf{LK}$-proof π we define

$$\mathrm{NF}_{\mathrm{LK}}(\pi) := \{\pi^* \mid \pi \to \pi^*, \pi^* \text{ cut-free}\} \quad \text{and}$$
$$\mathrm{NF}_{\mathrm{LK^s}}(\pi) := \{(\psi, S) \mid (\pi, \emptyset) \to (\psi, S), \psi \text{ cut-free}\}.$$

In this section we will show that $\mathbf{LK}$ and $\mathbf{LK^s}$ have the same normal forms. In order to compare the normal forms of $\mathbf{LK^s}$ with those of $\mathbf{LK}$ we consider the set $(\mathrm{NF}_{\mathrm{LK^s}}(\pi))^\circ$ where, for a set P of $\mathbf{LK^s}$-proofs, we define $P^\circ := \{\psi S^\circ \mid (\psi, S) \in P\}$. First we need some auxiliary commutation properties.

Lemma 5. *Let V be a set of variables, ρ be a fresh-variable renaming for V and σ a substitution with $\mathrm{dom}(\sigma) \subseteq V$ and $\mathrm{vrge}(\sigma) \subseteq V$. Then $(\sigma\rho)|_V = (\rho\sigma^\rho)|_V$.*

Lemma 6. *Let S be a finite, acyclic, functional set of base substitutions and let ρ be a fresh-variable renaming for S. Then $(S^\rho)^\circ = (S^\circ)^\rho$.*

Proposition 2. *Let $\pi \to \pi^*$ be a cut-elimination sequence in $\mathbf{LK}$. Then there is a cut-elimination sequence $(\pi, \emptyset) \to (\psi, S)$ in $\mathbf{LK^s}$ s.t. $\psi S^\circ = \pi^*$.*

Proof. By induction on the length of $\pi \to \pi^*$; the case of the empty sequence is trivial. So assume given a sequence $\pi \to \pi' \to \pi^*$ where $\pi' \to \pi^*$ consists of exactly one reduction. By induction hypothesis there is an $\mathbf{LK^s}$-proof (ψ', S') s.t. $\psi' S'^\circ = \pi'$. Note that the inferences in π' are in 1-1 correspondence with those in ψ', so the cut-reduction step $\pi' \to \pi^*$ uniquely induces one in (ψ', S') which we use to define (ψ^*, S^*). It remains to prove $\psi^* S^{*\circ} = \pi^*$. This is easy for the reduction of axioms, propositional connectives, weakening and the rank reductions as $S' = S^*$ in these cases.

For the reduction of a quantifier, let $[\alpha \backslash t]$ be the substitution and π_1 be the subproof of π' to which the substitution is applied in the reduction step $\pi' \to \pi^*$. Then, for some term s we have $S^* = S' \cup \{[\alpha \backslash s]\}$ where, as $\psi' S'^\circ = \pi'$, also $sS'^\circ = t$. Let $[\alpha_1 \backslash t_1], \ldots, [\alpha_k \backslash t_k], [\alpha \backslash s], [\alpha_{k+1} \backslash t_{k+1}], \ldots, [\alpha_n \backslash t_n]$ be a linearisation of S', then $[\alpha_1 \backslash t_1], \ldots, [\alpha_n \backslash t_n]$ is a linearisation of S. Abbreviating $\sigma_l = [\alpha_1 \backslash t_1] \cdots [\alpha_k \backslash t_k]$ and $\sigma_r = [\alpha_{k+1} \backslash t_{k+1}] \cdots [\alpha_n \backslash t_n]$ we thus have $t = s\sigma_r$. Letting ψ_1 be the subproof of ψ' that corresponds to π_1 we have $\pi_1 [\alpha \backslash t] = \psi_1 \sigma_l \sigma_r [\alpha \backslash s\sigma_r]$. But now, for $i \in \{k+1, \ldots, n\}$, $\alpha \notin V(t_i)$ by the linearisation property and $\alpha \neq \alpha_i$ by the $\forall_r$-side condition in ψ, so σ_r is right-independent of $[\alpha \backslash s]$ and thus by Lemma 1: $\pi_1 [\alpha \backslash t] = \psi_1 S^{*\circ}$. If F is a formula in ψ^* outside of ψ_1, then $FS'^\circ = FS^{*\circ}$ because $F \not\leq_S \alpha$ by the global variable condition of ψ' and therefore $\psi^* S^{*\circ} = \pi^*$.

For the reduction of contraction, let $\alpha_1, \ldots, \alpha_k$ be the eigenvariables of the subproof π_2 of π' that is duplicated in the reduction $\pi' \to \pi^*$. Then $\alpha_1, \ldots, \alpha_k$ are also the eigenvariables of the subproof ψ_2 of ψ' corresponding to π_2. Let $\{\alpha_1, \ldots, \alpha_n\} = \{\alpha \mid \alpha \leq_{S'} \alpha_i \text{ for an } i \in \{1, \ldots, k\}\}$, then the variables $\alpha'_1, \alpha''_1, \ldots, \alpha'_k, \alpha''_k$ are fresh for ψ' and S' because they are fresh for $\pi \to \pi'$. For the $\mathbf{LK^s}$-step, they are extended to $\alpha'_1, \alpha''_1, \ldots, \alpha'_n, \alpha''_n$ which are also fresh for ψ' and S'. Define $\rho = [\alpha_i \backslash \alpha'_i]_{i=1}^n$, $\hat{\rho} = [\alpha_i \backslash \alpha''_i]_{i=1}^k$, $\sigma = [\alpha_i \backslash \alpha'_i]_{i=1}^n$ and $\hat{\sigma} = [\alpha_i \backslash \alpha''_i]_{i=1}^k$. As $\psi_2 \rho$ does not contain any α''_i we have $\psi_2 \rho S^{*\circ} = \psi_2 \rho(S'^\rho)^\circ$. By Lemma 6: $\psi_2 \rho(S'^\rho)^\circ = \psi_2 \rho(S'^\circ)^\rho$. Letting $V := \mathrm{dom}(S') \cup \mathrm{vrge}(S') \cup V(\psi_2)$ and observing that ρ is fresh for V, apply Lemma 5 to obtain $\psi_2 \rho(S'^\circ)^\rho = \psi_2 S'^\circ \rho$. Now by induction hypothesis $\psi_2 S'^\circ = \pi_2$ and as $\alpha_{k+1}, \ldots, \alpha_n$ do not appear in π_2, we have $\pi_2 \rho = \pi_2 \hat{\rho}$ and thus $\psi_2 \rho S^{*\circ} = \pi_2 \hat{\rho}$. Analogously we obtain $\psi_2 \sigma S^{*\circ} = \pi_2 \hat{\sigma}$. If F is a formula in ψ^* outside of $\psi_2 \rho$ and $\psi_2 \sigma$, then for all $i \in \{1, \ldots, n\}$: $F \not\leq_{S'} \alpha_i$ by the global variable condition, so $FS'^\circ = FS^{*\circ}$ and therefore $\psi^* S^{*\circ} = \pi^*$.

Theorem 1. *Let π be a regular $\mathbf{LK}$-proof, then $\mathrm{NF}_{\mathbf{LK}}(\pi) = (\mathrm{NF}_{\mathbf{LK^s}}(\pi))^\circ$.*

Proof. The direction $\subseteq$ follows from the above Proposition 2, the direction $\supseteq$ from Proposition 1 and the observation that for $(\psi, S) \to (\psi', S')$ being an $\mathbf{LK^s}$-step, $\psi S^\circ \to \psi' S'^\circ$ is an $\mathbf{LK}$-step.

So **LK**^{s} is equivalent to **LK** from an extensional point of view. It is however different from an intensional point of view, a property that will be exploited in the next two sections to demonstrate that **LK**^{s} is an advantageous mechanism for implementing cut-elimination and a useful tool for carrying out a more fine-grained analysis of **LK**.

5   Implementation and Complexity

It is a well-known observation going back to Kreisel that proof-theoretic methods for consistency-proofs like Gentzen's cut-elimination, Hilbert's ε-calculus or Gödel's Dialectica-interpretation can be applied to concrete mathematical proofs in order to extract constructive information, e.g. bounds or programs, from them. An example for this kind of mathematical application of cut-elimination is Girard's analysis of the Fürstenberg-Weiss proof of van der Waerden's theorem on arithmetic progressions [14, annex 4.A]. A central motivation for implementing cut-elimination thus lies in, at least partially, automating such analyses. The ceres-system[1] is an implementation of the cut-elimination method [6] based on resolution and has been applied to concrete proof analyses, see e.g. [5]. In this section we will argue that **LK**^{s} is a useful mechanism for the implementation of the standard cut-elimination as the implicit term representation allows for exponentially shorter normal forms.

The *size* of a term, formula or **LK**-proof is the number of symbols it contains, the size of a set S of substitutions is $\sum_{\sigma \in S} \text{size}(\sigma)$, the size of an **LK**^{s}-proof (ψ, S) is $\text{size}(\psi) + \text{size}(S)$. We consider a language containing the constant symbol 0, the function symbols $s(\cdot), +, 2^\cdot$ and the binary predicate symbol $=$ with $\mathbb{N}$ as intended interpretation. A numeral is a term of the form $s^n(0)$ for some $n \in \mathbb{N}$; for ease of notation we identify a numeral with the number it denotes. Furthermore the language contains a constant symbol a and a binary function symbol f formalising a data-structure, e.g. binary trees as well as a unary function symbol $|\cdot|$ whose intended interpretation is the number of leaves in a tree built up by f and a. Accordingly, we define the following set $\mathcal{A}$ of axioms, some of which are assigned abbreviations:

$$1 = 2^0$$
$$P \equiv \forall x\, 2^x + 2^x = 2^{s(x)}$$
$$|a| = 1$$
$$S \equiv \forall x \forall y\, |f(x,y)| = |x| + |y|$$
$$T \equiv \forall x \forall y \forall z\, (x = y \supset y = z \supset x = z)$$
$$C \equiv \forall x \forall y \forall y' \forall z \forall z'\, (x = y + z \supset y = y' \supset z = z' \supset x = y' + z')$$

where the implication $F \supset G$ is an abbreviation for $\neg F \vee G$ and is right-associative. The sequences of proofs we are going to consider will prove $\exists x\, |x| = 2^n$ from $\mathcal{A}$. When writing down proofs, a list of rule names next to an inference

---

[1] http://www.logic.at/ceres/

line denotes the application of this list in bottom-up order. We also use the above letters P, S, T, C for denoting a macro-inference which consists of an application of the respective axiom, i.e. one contraction to make a working copy of the axiom, instantiating all quantifiers and removing all implications by axioms on the left so that only the head atom remains. Let

$$\pi_0 \quad := \quad \cfrac{\cfrac{|a| = 2^0 \to |a| = 2^0}{|a| = 2^0 \to \exists x\,|x| = 2^0}\ \exists_r}{\mathcal{A} \to \exists x\,|x| = 2^0}\ T, w^*$$

which, in expanded form, is

$$\cfrac{\cfrac{1 = 2^0 \to 1 = 2^0 \quad \cfrac{\cfrac{|a| = 2^0 \to |a| = 2^0}{|a| = 2^0 \to \exists x\,|x| = 2^0}\ \exists_r}{P, S, |a| = 2^0, T, C \to \exists x\,|x| = 2^0}\ w^*}{\cfrac{|a| = 1 \to |a| = 1 \quad 1 = 2^0, P, S, 1 = 2^0 \supset |a| = 2^0, T, C \to \exists x\,|x| = 2^0}{\cfrac{1 = 2^0, P, |a| = 1, S, |a| = 1 \supset 1 = 2^0 \supset |a| = 2^0, T, C \to \exists x\,|x| = 2^0}{\cfrac{1 = 2^0, P, |a| = 1, S, T, T, C \to \exists x\,|x| = 2^0}{1 = 2^0, P, |a| = 1, S, T, C \to \exists x\,|x| = 2^0}\ c_l}\ \forall_{l(3\times)}}\ \supset_l}\ \supset_l}$$

Let furthermore $\pi_{n+1} :=$

$$\cfrac{\cfrac{(\pi_n)}{\mathcal{A} \to \exists x\,|x| = 2^n} \quad \cfrac{\cfrac{(\xi_n)}{|\alpha_n| = 2^n, \mathcal{A} \to \exists x\,|x| = 2^{s(n)}}}{\exists x\,|x| = 2^n, \mathcal{A} \to \exists x\,|x| = 2^{s(n)}}\ \exists_l}{\cfrac{\mathcal{A}, \mathcal{A} \to \exists x\,|x| = 2^{s(n)}}{\mathcal{A} \to \exists x\,|x| = 2^{s(n)}}\ c^*}\ \text{cut}$$

Let $t_0 := a$, $t_{n+1} := f(\alpha_n, \alpha_n)$ and define $\xi_n :=$

$$\cfrac{\cfrac{\cfrac{\cfrac{|t_{n+1}| = 2^{s(n)} \to |t_{n+1}| = 2^{s(n)}}{|t_{n+1}| = 2^{s(n)} \to \exists x\,|x| = 2^{s(n)}}\ \exists_r}{|t_{n+1}| = 2^n + 2^n, \mathcal{A} \to \exists x\,|x| = 2^{s(n)}}\ P, T, w^*}{|t_{n+1}| = |\alpha_n| + |\alpha_n|, |\alpha_n| = 2^n, \mathcal{A} \to \exists x\,|x| = 2^{s(n)}}\ c_l, C}{|\alpha_n| = 2^n, \mathcal{A} \to \exists x\,|x| = 2^{s(n)}}\ S$$

Now, due to the numerals, $\text{size}(\xi_n) = O(n)$ and $\text{size}(\pi_{n+1}) = \text{size}(\pi_n) + \text{size}(\xi_n) + O(n)$ hence $\text{size}(\pi_n) = O(n^2)$. For describing the cut-elimination of π_n we define the following additional proofs. Let $S_n := \{[\alpha_1 \backslash t_1], \ldots, [\alpha_n \backslash t_n]\}$. Write $\mathcal{A}^n$ for n copies of $\mathcal{A}$. For all $n \geq 0$, define a derivation

$$\cfrac{|a| = 2^0, \mathcal{A}^n \to \exists x\,|x| = 2^n}{\mathcal{A}^{n+1} \to \exists x\,|x| = 2^n}\ (\chi_n^0)$$

by the succession T, w^* as used in π_0. For $1 \leq k \leq n$, define a derivation

$$\frac{|t_k| = 2^k, \mathcal{A}^{n-k} \to \exists x \, |x| = 2^n}{|t_{k-1}| = 2^{k-1}, \mathcal{A}^{n-(k-1)} \to \exists x \, |x| = 2^n} \ (\chi_n^k)$$

by the succession $S, c_1, C, P, T, \mathrm{w}^*$ as used in ξ_n and for $n \geq 0$, define the proof

$$\psi_n \quad := \quad \frac{\dfrac{\dfrac{\dfrac{\dfrac{|t_n| = 2^n \to |t_n| = 2^n}{|t_n| = 2^n \to \exists x \, |x| = 2^n} \ \exists_{\mathrm{r}}}{(\chi_n^n)}}{\vdots}}{\dfrac{(\chi_n^0)}{\mathcal{A}^{n+1} \to \exists x \, |x| = 2^n}}}{\mathcal{A} \to \exists x \, |x| = 2^n} \ c^*$$

We have $\mathrm{size}(\chi_n^k) = O(n)$ hence $\mathrm{size}(\psi_n) = c + \sum_{k=0}^{n} \mathrm{size}(\chi_n^k) = O(n^2)$ and as $\mathrm{size}(S_n) = O(n)$ finally $\mathrm{size}(\psi_n, S_n) = O(n^2)$.

Theorem 2. *There is a sequence $(\pi_n)_{n \geq 0}$ of regular **LK**-proofs with $\mathrm{size}(\pi_n) = O(n^2)$ s.t.*

1. *every sequence $(\pi_n^*)_{n \geq 0}$ of **LK**-normal forms has $\mathrm{size}(\pi_n^*) = \Omega(2^n)$ and*
2. *there is a sequence $(\psi_n, S_n)_{n \geq 0}$ of **LK^{s}**-normal forms with $\mathrm{size}(\psi_n, S_n) = O(n^2)$. Furthermore, the reduction sequences $(\pi_n, \emptyset) \to (\psi_n, S_n)$ have length $O(n^2)$ and contain only proofs of size $O(n^2)$.*

Proof. Let π_n, ψ_n and S_n be as above. For 1 note that the intended interpretation of our language shows that every cut-free proof of $\mathcal{A} \to \exists x \, |x| = 2^n$ must contain a witness term for x that has 2^n occurrences of a.

For 2 we have to show that $(\pi_n, \emptyset) \to (\psi_n, S_n)$. We proceed by induction on n: the base case $n = 0$ is fulfilled by the empty reduction sequence. To treat the case $n + 1$, first apply the induction hypothesis which costs $O(n^2)$ reductions steps, then apply $O(n)$ rank reductions to transform $(\pi_{n+1}, \emptyset)$ to the proof

$$\frac{\dfrac{\dfrac{\dfrac{|t_n| = 2^n \to |t_n| = 2^n}{|t_n| = 2^n \to \exists x \, |x| = 2^n} \ \exists_{\mathrm{r}} \qquad \dfrac{(\xi_n)}{\dfrac{|\alpha_n| = 2^n, \mathcal{A} \to \exists x \, |x| = 2^{s(n)}}{\exists x \, |x| = 2^n, \mathcal{A} \to \exists x \, |x| = 2^{s(n)}} \ \exists_{\mathrm{l}}}}{|t_n| = 2^n, \mathcal{A} \to \exists x \, |x| = 2^{s(n)}} \ \mathrm{cut}}{\dfrac{(\chi_{n+1}^n)}{\vdots}}}{\dfrac{\dfrac{(\chi_{n+1}^0)}{\mathcal{A}^{n+2} \to \exists x \, |x| = 2^{s(n)}}}{\mathcal{A} \to \exists x \, |x| = 2^{s(n)}} \ c^*}$$

with S_n as set of substitutions. This **LK^{s}**-proof in turn reduces to (ψ_{n+1}, S_{n+1}) in a constant number of reduction steps.

In total, this sums up to $O(n^2)$ reduction steps for $(\pi_n, \emptyset) \rightarrow (\psi_n, S_n)$. All proofs in the reduction sequence have size $O(n^2)$ as rank reductions do not change the size and the quantifier reductions only add $[\alpha_1 \backslash t_1], \ldots, [\alpha_n \backslash t_n]$ to the set of base substitutions.

Note that the length of the reduction sequence to $\psi_n S_n^\circ$ in **LK** is also $O(n^2)$ so the above result is an improvement w.r.t. proof size. The above compression cannot be obtained by sharing mechanisms that work on the level of the proof because the redundancy lies at the formula level. Also note that this result is reminiscent of the situation known from first-order unification that, while the unifiability problem is decidable in linear time, the size of the most general unifier is exponential [3].

The above result shows that **LK^s** is an advantageous mechanism for implementing cut-elimination because it avoids to unfold terms as long as possible. In addition, it should be noted that due to the simplicity of the used data structure – a set – implementing **LK^s** does not require more effort than implementing **LK**. The global substitution which is explicitly computed by **LK^s** represents the full cut-elimination in a concise way and can also be applied to structures derived from the original proof π with cuts: for example to a short tautology [17] read off from π to obtain a Herbrand-disjunction or to the characteristic clause set [6] to obtain a propositionally refutable clause set.

6   LK^s as Tool for Analysing LK

Carrying out the above analysis of sharing mechanisms on the proof-theoretic instead of on the implementational level has the benefit that it can be used for theoretical analyses as well. An investigation of the form of witness terms obtainable by cut-elimination has been carried out in [16] by different means. One of the central results obtained there is a characterisation of the form of terms obtainable by cut-elimination by regular tree grammars. In this section we will provide a simple proof of this result by observing that it is a corollary of cut-elimination in **LK^s**.

A *regular tree grammar* [11] is a quadruple $G = (\alpha, N, F, R)$ composed of an axiom α, a set N of non-terminal symbols with $\alpha \in N$, a set F of terminal symbols with $F \cap N = \emptyset$ and a set R of production rules of the form $\beta \rightarrow t$ where $\beta \in N$ and t is a term built from $F \cup N$. Given a regular tree grammar $G = (\alpha, N, F, R)$, the derivation relation $\rightarrow_G$ associated to G is defined as $s \rightarrow_G t$ if there is a production rule $\beta \rightarrow u$ and a context $r[]$ s.t. $s = r[\beta]$ and $t = r[u]$. Furthermore, $\twoheadrightarrow_G$ is the reflexive and transitive closure of $\rightarrow_G$. The language $L(G)$ generated by G is the set of all terms containing only symbols from F which can be reached by a derivation path from α.

For the sake of comparability with Section 5, we describe a slightly more general setting than in [16] by working on proofs of Σ_1-sentences in a unversial theory T. For a proof π of a Σ_1-sentence $F = \exists x_1 \ldots \exists x_n A$ with A quantifier-free from axioms of T, let $H(\pi)$ be the set of auxiliary formulas of $\exists_r$-inferences introducing $\exists x_n$ in π. Note that $H(\pi)$ is quantifier-free, that T proves the existential closure of $\bigvee H(\pi)$, if π is cut-free, then T proves $\bigvee H(\pi)$ and if, in addition, T is the empty theory, then $\bigvee H(\pi)$ is a tautology, the Herbrand-disjunction induced by π.

Let π be a proof and Q be a quantifier occurrence in π. Define a set of terms $t(Q)$ associated with Q as follows: if Q occurs in the main formula of a weakening, then $t(Q) := \emptyset$. If Q is introduced by a quantifier inference from a term t or a variable x, then $t(Q) := \{t\}$ or $t(Q) := \{x\}$ respectively. If Q occurs in the main formula of a contraction and Q_1, Q_2 are the two corresponding quantifiers in the auxiliary formulas of the contraction, then $t(Q) := t(Q_1) \cup t(Q_2)$. In all other cases Q has exactly one immediate ancestor Q' and $t(Q) := t(Q')$.

Let π be a proof, c be a cut in π. Write $\mathrm{Q}(c)$ for the set of pairs (Q, Q') of quantifier occurrences where Q is a strong occurrence in one cut-formula of c and Q' the corresponding weak occurrence on the other side of the cut. Define the set of base substitutions of c as $\mathrm{B}(c) := \bigcup_{(Q,Q') \in \mathrm{Q}(c)} \{[x \backslash t] \mid x \in t(Q), t \in t(Q')\}$. For $c_1, \ldots, c_n$ being the cuts in π define the base substitutions of π as $\mathrm{B}(\pi) := \bigcup_{i=1}^{n} \mathrm{B}(c_i)$. A proof then induces a grammar as follows.

Definition 4. *The grammar* $\mathrm{G}(\pi) = (\varphi, N, F, R)$ *is defined by setting* $N = \{\varphi, \alpha_1, \ldots, \alpha_n\}$ *where* $\{\alpha_1, \ldots, \alpha_n\}$ *are the eigenvariables of* π, φ *is a new symbol,* F *is the signature of* π *plus the propositional connectives* $\neg, \vee, \wedge$ *and*

$$R = \{\varphi \to F \mid F \in H(\pi)\} \cup \{\alpha \to t \mid [\alpha \backslash t] \in \mathrm{B}(\pi)\}.$$

Example 2. For the proofs π_n of Section 5 we obtain $\mathrm{G}(\pi_n) = (\varphi, N, F, R)$ where

$$N = \{\varphi, \alpha_0, \ldots, \alpha_{n-1}\},$$
$$F = \{\neg, \vee, \wedge, 0, s, +, 2^{\cdot}, =, a, f, |\cdot|\}, \text{ and}$$
$$R = \{\varphi \to |f(\alpha_{n-1}, \alpha_{n-1})| = 2^{s^n(0)},$$
$$\alpha_{n-1} \to f(\alpha_{n-2}, \alpha_{n-2}), \ldots, \alpha_1 \to f(\alpha_0, \alpha_0), \alpha_0 \to a\}.$$

One of the central results of [16] is

Theorem 3. *Let* π *be an* **LK***-proof of a* Σ_1*-sentence from universal axioms, then there is a regular tree grammar* $\mathrm{G}(\pi)$ *s.t. for every cut-free* π^* *with* $\pi \to \pi^*$: $H(\pi^*) \subseteq L(\mathrm{G}(\pi))$.

The importance of this result lies in the fact that the grammar provides a characterisation of all possibly obtainable witness terms that depends only on the original proof π and not on the chosen cut-elimination strategy. In [16] this result has been obtained by considering structured terms which use an additional tree structure for representing substitutions applied to terms. We can now give a simple proof based on cut-elimination in $\mathbf{LK^s}$.

Proof. By Proposition 2 there is a cut-elimination sequence $(\pi, \emptyset) \to (\psi, S)$ in $\mathbf{LK^s}$ s.t. $\psi S^{\circ} = \pi^*$. Given a variable α in (ψ, S) we write $\iota(\alpha)$ for the unique variable in π that has been renamed to α. The function ι is extended to terms and formulas in the obvious way. By induction on the length of the cut-elimination sequence, it is then straighforward to show (i) $\iota(H(\psi)) \subseteq H(\pi)$ and (ii) $\iota(S) \subseteq$

$B(\pi)$ where ι is needed for contraction- and $\subseteq$ for weakening-reduction. As $\psi S^\circ = \pi^*$ also $H(\pi^*) = H(\psi)S^\circ$ and as π^* is a cut-free proof of a Σ_1-sentence from universal axioms, $H(\pi^*) = \iota(H(\pi^*))$. Let now $H \in H(\psi)$ and $\sigma_1, \ldots, \sigma_n$ be a linearisation of S. We will show $\varphi \twoheadrightarrow_{G(\pi)} \iota(HS^\circ)$ by induction on n. For $n = 0$, $\varphi \twoheadrightarrow_{G(\pi)} \iota(H)$ by (i). For $n > 0$ let $\sigma_n = [\alpha\backslash t]$, then by (ii) $[\iota(\alpha)\backslash\iota(t)] \in B(\pi)$ and by applying the production rule $\iota(\alpha) \rightarrow \iota(t)$ to all positions of α in $H\sigma_1 \cdots \sigma_{n-1}$ we obtain $\iota(H\sigma_1 \cdots \sigma_{n-1}) \twoheadrightarrow_{G(\pi)} \iota(H\sigma_1 \cdots \sigma_n)$.

The author is convinced that **LK^s** will be a useful tool for obtaining stronger results of the above kind which is left to future work.

7   Conclusion

We have introduced the calculus **LK^s** which differs from standard sequent calculus by presenting a proof in a two-layered form: its abstract deductive structure on the one hand and a unifier which renders this structure a proof on the other hand. It has been shown that cut-elimination in **LK^s** is equivalent to **LK** in the sense that the same set of normal forms is produced. The implicit term representation provided by **LK^s** can be used for an implementation that provides an exponential compression of normal forms as well as for a fine-grained theoretical analysis of **LK**.

Acknowledgements. The author would like to thank Delia Kesner, Alexander Leitsch, Dale Miller, Daniel Weller and the anonymous referees for useful comments on this work.

This research was supported by INRIA and by a Marie Curie Intra European Fellowship within the 7th European Community Framework Programme.

References

1. Andrews, P.B.: Theorem Proving via General Matings. Journal of the ACM 28(2), 193–214 (1981)
2. Asperti, A., Guerrini, S.: The Optimal Implementation of Functional Programming Languages. Cambridge Tracts in Theoretical Computer Science, vol. 45. Cambridge University Press, Cambridge (1998)
3. Baader, F., Snyder, W.: Unification Theory. In: Robinson, A., Voronkov, A. (eds.) Handbook of Automated Reasoning, pp. 445–533. Elsevier, Amsterdam (2001)
4. Baaz, M., Hetzl, S.: On the non-confluence of cut-elimination. To appear in the Journal of Symbolic Logic (preprint), http://www.logic.at/people/hetzl/
5. Baaz, M., Hetzl, S., Leitsch, A., Richter, C., Spohr, H.: CERES: An Analysis of Fürstenberg's Proof of the Infinity of Primes. Theoretical Computer Science 403(2-3), 160–175 (2008)
6. Baaz, M., Leitsch, A.: Cut-elimination and Redundancy-elimination by Resolution. Journal of Symbolic Computation 29(2), 149–176 (2000)
7. Danos, V., Joinet, J.B., Schellinx, H.: A New Deconstructive Logic: Linear Logic. Journal of Symbolic Logic 62(3), 755–807 (1997)

8. Dowek, G., Hardin, T., Kirchner, C.: Theorem proving modulo. Journal of Automated Reasoning 31, 33–72 (2003)
9. Dowek, G., Werner, B.: Proof normalization modulo. The Journal of Symbolic Logic 68(4), 1289–1316 (2003)
10. Farmer, W.M.: A unification-theoretic method for investigating the k-provability problem. Annals of Pure and Applied Logic 51, 173–214 (1991)
11. Gécseg, F., Steinby, M.: Tree Languages. In: Rozenberg, G., Salomaa, A. (eds.) Handbook of Formal Languages. Beyond Words, vol. 3, pp. 1–68. Springer, Heidelberg (1997)
12. Geuvers, H., Loeb, I.: Natural Deduction via Graphs: Formal Definition and Computation Rules. Mathematical Structures in Computer Science 17(3), 485–526 (2007)
13. Geuvers, H., Loeb, I.: Deduction Graphs with Universal Quantification. Electronic Notes in Theoretical Computer Science 203(1), 93–108 (2008)
14. Girard, J.Y.: Proof Theory and Logical Complexity. Elsevier, Amsterdam (1987)
15. Goldfarb, W.D.: The undecidability of the second-order unification problem. Theoretical Computer Science 13(2), 225–230 (1981)
16. Hetzl, S.: On the form of witness terms. Archive for Mathematical Logic 49(5), 529–554 (2010)
17. Hetzl, S.: Describing proofs by short tautologies. Annals of Pure and Applied Logic 159(1-2), 129–145 (2009)
18. Huet, G.: A Mechanization of Type Theory. In: Third Interational Joint Conference on Articifical Intelligence (IJCAI), pp. 139–146 (1973)
19. Kesner, D.: A Theory of Explicit Substitutions with Safe and Full Composition. Logical Methods in Computer Science 5(3:1), 1–29 (2009)
20. Krajíček, J., Pudlák, P.: The Number of Proof Lines and the Size of Proofs in First Order Logic. Archive for Mathematical Logic 27, 69–84 (1988)
21. Miller, D., Nadathur, G., Pfenning, F., Scedrov, A.: Uniform proofs as a foundation for logic programming. Annals of Pure and Applied Logic 51(1-2), 125–157 (1991)
22. Orevkov, V.: Reconstruction of a proof by its analysis (russian). Doklady Akademii Nauk 293(3), 313–316 (1987)
23. Parigot, M.: $\lambda\mu$-Calculus: An Algorithmic Interpretation of Classical Natural Deduction. In: Voronkov, A. (ed.) LPAR 1992. LNCS, vol. 624, pp. 190–201. Springer, Heidelberg (1992)
24. Robinson, J.A.: A Machine-Oriented Logic Based on the Resolution Principle. Journal of the ACM 12(1), 23–41 (1965)
25. Zucker, J.: The Correspondence Between Cut-Elimination and Normalization. Annals of Mathematical Logic 7, 1–112 (1974)

New Algorithm for Weak Monadic Second-Order Logic on Inductive Structures

Tobias Ganzow and Łukasz Kaiser

Mathematische Grundlagen der Informatik, RWTH Aachen University, Germany
{ganzow,kaiser}@logic.rwth-aachen.de

Abstract. We present a new algorithm for model-checking weak monadic second-order logic on inductive structures, a class of structures of bounded clique width. Our algorithm directly manipulates formulas and checks them on the structure of interest, thus avoiding both the use of automata and the need to interpret the structure in the binary tree. In addition to the algorithm, we give a new proof of decidability of weak MSO on inductive structures which follows Shelah's composition method. Generalizing this proof technique, we obtain decidability of weak MSO extended with the unbounding quantifier on the binary tree, which was open before.

1 Introduction

Monadic second-order logic (MSO) is an extension of first-order logic in which quantification over subsets of the universe is allowed. Using the connection to automata, it was shown by Büchi that MSO is decidable on $(\omega, <)$ [1], and by Rabin [2] that it is decidable on the infinite binary tree. Using interpretations, this result has been extended from the binary tree to all structures of bounded clique-width [3], showing that MSO is decidable on a large class of structures.

In practical applications such as verification of software systems or hardware, the domain of interest is often finite but not a priori bounded in size, and thus many verification problems can be naturally formalized in *weak* MSO, a fragment of MSO which allows only quantification over *finite* subsets of the universe. The best known tool for model-checking WMSO, MONA, has been used to verify hardware [4] and pointer manipulating programs [5], and is part of software verification systems, e.g. [6]. To use MONA for program verification it is necessary to interpret the structure of interest in the binary tree, which is often a cause of inefficiency. Moreover, since MONA is based on automata, it is challenging to use it for verifying properties which mix terms from different theories.

These problems motivated us to devise an algorithm for weak MSO model-checking, together with a proof of its correctness, that exploits logical tools and structural aspects of the models rather than being based on automata. Our algorithm works on the general class of inductive structures which comprise classical structures such as $(\omega, <)$ and the binary tree as well as practically relevant structures such as doubly-linked lists or lists of lists. Inductive structures can in fact be encoded in the binary tree, but we avoid this both because it

A. Dawar and H. Veith (Eds.): CSL 2010, LNCS 6247, pp. 366–380, 2010.

is a source of inefficiency and because our algorithm can be easily formulated directly for arbitrary inductive structures. Moreover, our algorithm is not based on automata and in each step only manipulates a set of formulas. This makes it well-suited to be a part of a larger verification system or SMT solver, since it is amenable to Nelson-Oppen style combination with other theories.

In addition to the algorithm, we present a new proof of decidability of weak MSO on inductive structures. Our proof follows the *composition method*, which was used by Shelah [7] (see also [8]) to show decidability of unrestricted MSO on $(\omega, <)$ and other countable linear orders, as well as by Läuchli [9] in his proof of the decidability of the weak MSO theory of linear orders. Both proofs are based on the enumeration of all types of a certain quantifier rank, and can therefore not be used as a basis for an algorithm. As yet, the composition method has not been generalized to unrestricted MSO on the binary tree, and the question about a composition-based proof of decidability of MSO on the binary tree is, in fact, considered a major open problem, because of its close relationship to the challenge of understanding the algebraic structure of regular tree languages.

A thorough overview of applications of the composition method for obtaining decidability results for MSO on various classes of structures is given in [10]. Furthermore, see [11] for an account on the evolution of the field.

We exploit that, in contrast to $(\omega, <)$, the weak MSO theory of the binary tree is simpler than its unrestricted MSO theory, and show, using decompositions of weak MSO formulas, that the model-checking problem for weak MSO on inductively defined structures can be reduced to determining the winner of a finite reachability game. However, the worst-case complexity of checking weak MSO sentences on $(\omega, <)$ is already non-elementary. Therefore the decompositions of the checked formula, and hence the game graph, can be huge. As the bound is tight, this cannot be avoided in general, but a preliminary implementation of the algorithm shows that the approach works on basic examples.

We also show that more general quantifiers can be integrated in our approach by proving that WMSO with the unbounding quantifier, a logic which has recently been shown to be decidable on labelings of $(\omega, <)$ [12], is also decidable on inductive structures, in particular on the binary tree.

2 Preliminaries

A relational structure $\mathfrak{A} = (A, R_1^{\mathfrak{A}}, \ldots, R_K^{\mathfrak{A}})$ over the signature $\tau = \{R_1, \ldots, R_K\}$ (where each R_i has an associated arity r_i) consists of the universe A and relations $R_i^{\mathfrak{A}} \subseteq A^{r_i}$. We say that $\mathfrak{A} \subseteq \mathfrak{B}$ if the universe $A \subseteq B$ and each $R_i^{\mathfrak{A}} \subseteq R_i^{\mathfrak{B}}$. For a subset $B \subseteq A$ we define $\mathfrak{A} \cap B$ as the structure with universe B and relations $R_i^{\mathfrak{A}} \cap B^{r_i}$. Two structures $\mathfrak{A}$ and $\mathfrak{B}$ are isomorphic if there exists a bijection $\pi : A \to B$ between their universes such that $(a_1, \ldots, a_{r_i}) \in R_i^{\mathfrak{A}} \iff (\pi(a_1), \ldots, \pi(a_{r_i})) \in R_i^{\mathfrak{B}}$. We write $[k]$ for the set $\{1, \ldots, k\}$, and, for a given set A, we write A^* for the set of all finite sequences of elements of A.

Weak monadic second-order logic (WMSO) extends first-order logic by quantification over *finite subsets* of the universe. In WMSO, first-order variables

$x, y, \ldots$ are interpreted as elements, and set variables $X, Y, \ldots$ as *finite* subsets of the universe. Set variables are capitalized to distinguish them from first-order variables. The atomic formulas are $R_i(\bar{x})$, $x = y$, $x \in X$, and $\bot$ for *false* and $\top$ for *true*. All other formulas are built from atomic ones by applying Boolean connectives and universal and existential quantifiers for both kinds of variables.

2.1   Inductive Structures

We investigate weak monadic second-order logic on *inductive structures*. One way to characterize such structures is using the notion of bounded clique-width decomposition: inductive structures admit a bounded clique-width decomposition with regular labels. However, to remain self-contained and due to the way our algorithms work, we give another definition using a system of equations, similar to the definition of vertex replacement (VR) graphs but strictly monotone.

In the following, we will frequently speak of *indexed structures* and *indexed elements*. The latter are elements paired with a finite word (called index) over a specific alphabet Σ. An indexed structure consists of a universe of indexed elements. We usually identify a plain structure with the indexed structure in which all elements are indexed by ε (i.e. the empty word).

Definition 1. *Given, for each $R_i \in \tau$, a function $f_i : \{1, \ldots, k\}^{r_i} \to \{\bot, \top\}$, and indexed structures $\mathfrak{A}_1, \ldots, \mathfrak{A}_k$ over $\Sigma \supseteq [k]$, we define the* (k-ary) disjoint sum with connections $\mathfrak{B} = (B, R_1^{\mathfrak{B}}, \ldots, R_k^{\mathfrak{B}})$, *denoted $\bigoplus_{\bar{f}}(\mathfrak{A}_1, \ldots, \mathfrak{A}_k)$, by:*

- $B := \{(a, jw) : (a, w) \in A_j, \ j \in [k]\}$ *and*

- $((b_1, j_1 w_1), \ldots, (b_{r_i}, j_{r_i} w_{r_i})) \in R_i^{\mathfrak{B}}$ *if*
    - $|\{j_1, \ldots, j_{r_i}\}| = 1$ *and* $(b_1, \ldots, b_{r_i}) \in R_i^{\mathfrak{A}_{j_1}}$ *or*
    - $|\{j_1, \ldots, j_{r_i}\}| > 1$ *and* $f_i(j_1, \ldots, j_{r_i}) = \top$.

That is, $\mathfrak{B}$ is constructed by taking the disjoint union of the structures $\mathfrak{A}_j$, and adding tuples spanning multiple components according to the given functions f_i. It is implicit in the definition that unary relations are only inherited from the components, whereas only at least binary relations are augmented with additional tuples. Intuitively, the indices keep track of the origin of elements. We let $\mathfrak{B}[j] := \mathfrak{B} \cap \{(b, w) \in B : w = jw'\}$ denote the *j-th component* of the disjoint sum. Note that, as expected, $\mathfrak{B}[j]$ is isomorphic to $\mathfrak{A}_j$ via $\pi_j : (b, jw') \mapsto (b, w')$. Furthermore, defining $\mathfrak{B}[\varepsilon] := \mathfrak{B}$, the notation naturally extends to $\mathfrak{B}[wj] := (\mathfrak{B}[w])[j] = \mathfrak{B} \cap \{(b, v) \in B : v = wjw'\}$.

Example 2. Given $f(1,2) = \top$ and $f(i,j) = \bot$ otherwise, $\uparrow \oplus_f \downarrow = $.

Definition 3. *A system of* structure equations $\mathcal{D}$ *over τ has the form*

$$\mathcal{D} = \begin{cases} \Lambda^1 = \mathfrak{A}_1^1 \oplus \mathfrak{A}_2^1 \oplus \ldots \oplus \mathfrak{A}_{k_1}^1 & \text{with } f_1^1, \ldots, f_K^1 \\ \vdots \qquad\qquad \vdots \qquad\qquad\qquad \vdots \\ \Lambda^n = \mathfrak{A}_1^n \oplus \mathfrak{A}_2^n \oplus \ldots \oplus \mathfrak{A}_{k_n}^n & \text{with } f_1^n, \ldots, f_K^n \end{cases}$$

where each $\mathfrak{A}^i_j$ is either a finite *structure* or one of the formal variables $\Lambda^1, \ldots, \Lambda^n$ and each f^i_j is a function $\{1, \ldots, k_i\}^{r_j} \rightarrow \{\bot, \top\}$. We write $\lambda(i, j) = m$ if $\mathfrak{A}^i_j = \Lambda^m$ and $\lambda(i, j) = Fin$ otherwise. Let $\overline{\mathfrak{B}} = (\mathfrak{B}_1, \ldots, \mathfrak{B}_n)$ be relational structures to substitute for variables on the right-hand side of $\mathcal{D}$. Then, we define the new left-hand side structures $(\mathfrak{C}_1, \ldots, \mathfrak{C}_n) = \mathcal{D}(\overline{\mathfrak{B}})$ by:

$$\mathfrak{C}_i = \bigoplus_{\overline{f}^i} (\mathfrak{D}_1, \ldots, \mathfrak{D}_{k_i}) \ where \ \mathfrak{D}_j = \begin{cases} \mathfrak{A}^i_j & if \ \lambda(i, j) = Fin, \\ \mathfrak{B}_k & if \ \lambda(i, j) = k \,. \end{cases}$$

We say that a tuple $\overline{\mathfrak{B}}$ of structures *satisfies* $\mathcal{D}$ if $\mathcal{D}(\overline{\mathfrak{B}}) = \overline{\mathfrak{B}}$. Observe that the operator $\overline{\mathfrak{B}} \mapsto \mathcal{D}(\overline{\mathfrak{B}})$, mapping n-tuples of structures to new n-tuples of structures as defined above, is monotone since it only adds elements to the universe and tuples to relations. Hence, it has a unique least fixed-point $(\mathfrak{A}_1, \ldots, \mathfrak{A}_n)$, i.e. a minimal tuple of structures that satisfies $\mathcal{D}$ and which we refer to by $\mathcal{S}(\mathcal{D})$. We denote the i-th structure of the fixed-point by $\mathcal{S}_i(\mathcal{D})$, and we call a structure $\mathfrak{A}$ *inductive* if and only if there exists a system of equations $\mathcal{D}$ such that $\mathfrak{A}$ is isomorphic to some $\mathcal{S}_i(\mathcal{D})$.

Let $\mathcal{S}(\mathcal{D}) = (\mathfrak{A}_1, \ldots, \mathfrak{A}_n)$. By definition, each $\mathfrak{A}_m$ is an indexed structure over $\Sigma = [\max(k_1, \ldots, k_n)]$ obtained as a (k_m-ary) disjoint sum $\bigoplus_{\overline{f}^m} (\mathfrak{D}_j)_{j \in [k_m]}$ with additional tuples spanning components according to $\mathcal{D}$, and hence, for each $j = 1, \ldots, k_m$, the component $\mathfrak{A}_m[j]$ is either isomorphic to the finite structure $\mathfrak{A}^m_j$ given in $\mathcal{D}$ if $\lambda(m, j) = Fin$ or to $\mathfrak{A}_{\lambda(m,j)}$ otherwise. For easier referencing, we will partition the sets of indices into $Fin_i = \{j : \lambda(i, j) = Fin\}$, and $\Delta_i = \{j : \lambda(i, j) \neq Fin\}$. Furthermore, for an indexed element $(a, w) \in A_i$, the *depth* of $(a, w) \in A_i$ is defined as $\mathrm{dp}_i(a, w) = |w|$, and the depth of a set is the maximal depth of its elements, $\mathrm{dp}_i(S) = \max\{\mathrm{dp}_i(s) : s \in S\}$.

Example 4. The system defining the infinite binary tree $\mathfrak{T}_2$ with prefix ordering and unary predicates S_0 and S_1 for the left and right successor is:

$$\Lambda^1 = \big(\{\bullet\}, S_0 = \emptyset, S_1 = \emptyset, < \ = \emptyset\big) \quad \oplus \Lambda^2 \oplus \Lambda^3 \ with \ f_<$$
$$\Lambda^2 = \big(\{\bullet\}, S_0 = \{\bullet\}, S_1 = \emptyset, < \ = \emptyset\big) \oplus \Lambda^2 \oplus \Lambda^3 \ with \ f_<$$
$$\Lambda^3 = \big(\{\bullet\}, S_0 = \emptyset, S_1 = \{\bullet\}, < \ = \emptyset\big) \oplus \Lambda^2 \oplus \Lambda^3 \ with \ f_<$$

where $f_<(i, j) = \top$ if $i = 1$ and $j \in \{2, 3\}$ and $\bot$ in all other cases. Note that, by definition, the functions must be given only for tuples where at least two arguments differ. Therefore we give no functions for S_0 and S_1—predicates are determined solely by the right-hand side structures, as depicted in Figure 1.

As another example, we give a system defining a list of lists with two order relations, S on the primary list and L on the other lists, as depicted in Figure 2.

$$\Lambda^1 = \big(\{\bullet\}, R_L = \emptyset, R_S = \emptyset\big) \oplus \Lambda^1 \oplus \Lambda^2 \ with \ f^1_L, f^1_S$$
$$\Lambda^2 = \big(\{\bullet\}, R_L = \emptyset, R_S = \emptyset\big) \oplus \Lambda^2 \qquad with \ f^2_L, f^2_S$$

where $f^1_L(1, 2) = f^1_S(1, 3) = \top$ and $f^2_L(1, 2) = \top$, and $f^k_r(i, j) = \bot$ in other cases.

Observe that in both examples above a direct successor relation is definable in WMSO from the constructed orderings.

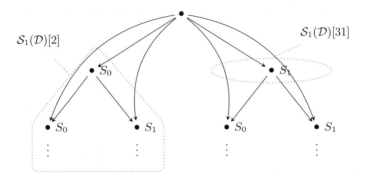

Fig. 1. Inductive definition of the binary tree $\mathfrak{T}_2 \cong \mathcal{S}_1(\mathcal{D})$

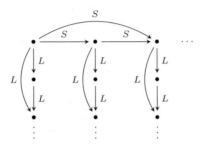

Fig. 2. Inductive definition of the infinite list of lists

2.2   Formulas with Restricted Variables

Intuitively, inductive structures are disjoint sums of other inductive structures with added relation tuples, and thus naturally decompose into *components*. When writing formulas over such structures, it is often convenient to restrict specific variables to specific components of the universe. Here we introduce related notions and a procedure to split variables so as to convert a formula into one that only contains variables restricted to disjoint parts of the universe.

Formulas with restricted variables of k kinds are defined in the same way as WMSO formulas, but in addition to the standard first- and second-order variables $x_1, x_2, \ldots$ and $X_1, X_2, \ldots$ we allow to write restricted variables $x_1^i, x_2^i, \ldots$ and $X_1^i, X_2^i, \ldots$ for $i = 1, \ldots, k$. (We use superscripts to distinguish restricted variables.) Given a structure $\mathfrak{A}$, a partition of the universe $A = A^1 \cup \cdots \cup A^k$ into k pairwise disjoint sets $A^1, \ldots, A^k$ gives rise to the so-called *partitioned structure* $\mathfrak{A}_{\langle A^1, \ldots, A^k \rangle}$. We interpret formulas with restricted variables on such partitioned structures, and intuitively x^i and X^i are understood as referring only to the i-th component A^i. More formally, we define the semantics of formulas with restricted variables on structures with partitioned universe in the standard way, with the additional rule that $\mathfrak{A}_{\langle A^1, \ldots, A^k \rangle} \models \exists X^i \varphi(X^i)$ if and only if there exists a $U \subseteq A^i$ (instead of a $U \subseteq A$) for which $\mathfrak{A}_{\langle A^1, \ldots, A^k \rangle} \models \varphi(U)$. The definition for $\forall X^i$ and first-order quantification is analogous. The interpretation of free restricted variables follows the same intuition, however, for the sake of clarity, we only allow free second-order variables.

Quantifier rank of formulas plays an important role in our proofs, and we extend this notion to formulas with restricted variables. Classically, the quantifier rank of a formula φ, $\mathrm{qr}(\varphi)$, is defined to be 0 if φ is an atomic formula, the maximum of the quantifier ranks of the conjuncts if φ is a Boolean combination and the rank of the quantified formula plus 1 if φ starts with a quantifier. We extend this notion to a formula φ with restricted variables so that $\mathrm{qr}^i(\varphi)$ counts only the nesting of quantified variables restricted to i:

- $\mathrm{qr}^i(\varphi) = 0$ if φ is an atomic formula,
- $\mathrm{qr}^i(\neg\varphi) = \mathrm{qr}^i(\varphi)$,
- $\mathrm{qr}^i(\varphi) = \max(\mathrm{qr}^i(\psi), \mathrm{qr}^i(\vartheta))$ if $\varphi = \psi \wedge \vartheta$ or $\varphi = \psi \wedge \vartheta$,
- $\mathrm{qr}^i(\exists X^j \varphi) = \mathrm{qr}^i(\exists x^j \varphi) = \mathrm{qr}^i(\forall X^j \varphi) = \mathrm{qr}^i(\forall x^j \varphi) = \begin{cases} \mathrm{qr}^i(\varphi) + 1 & \text{if } j = i \\ \mathrm{qr}^i(\varphi) & \text{otherwise.} \end{cases}$

Finally, the *restricted quantifier rank* $\mathrm{qr}^*(\varphi)$ is defined as the maximum over quantifier ranks restricted to the components: $\mathrm{qr}^*(\psi) = \max\{\mathrm{qr}^i(\psi) : 1 \le i \le k\}$.

2.3   Splitting Variables

Each formula of monadic second-order logic (with free second-order variables only) can be transformed into an equivalent formula in which all variables are restricted. The procedure $\mathtt{split}_k$ below computes, for a formula φ with variables $\overline{X}, \overline{x}$ and a fixed k, a formula ψ with variables $\overline{X}^i, \overline{x}^i$, $i = 1, \ldots, k$ such that $\mathfrak{A}, \overline{V} \models \varphi$ if and only if $\mathfrak{A}_{\langle A^1, \ldots, A^k\rangle}, \overline{V} \models \psi$ for any partition $A^1, \ldots, A^k$ of the universe of $\mathfrak{A}$ and any interpretation of the free second-order variables by sets $\overline{V}$; if a free variable X is assigned the set V, then the corresponding restricted variables X^i are assigned the sets $V \cap A^i$. In the notation used in procedure $\mathtt{split}_k$, we allow to substitute a sum, e.g. $X \cup Y$ for a second-order variable Z. This should be understood as replacing each atom $z \in Z$ by $z \in X \vee z \in Y$ (and $Z \leftarrow \emptyset$ means substituting $z \in Z$ by $\bot$).

By induction on the structure of the formulas and using the above definition of $\mathtt{split}_k(\varphi)$, we directly obtain the following lemma.

Lemma 5. *For every weak MSO formula φ with free monadic second-order variables only, every structure $\mathfrak{A}$, every partition $(A^1, \ldots, A^k)$ of the universe of $\mathfrak{A}$, and every assignment of sets $\overline{V}$ to the free second-order variables of φ, we have $(\mathfrak{A}, \overline{V}) \models \varphi$ if and only if $(\mathfrak{A}_{\langle A^1, \ldots, A^k\rangle}, \overline{V}) \models \mathtt{split}_k(\varphi)$. Moreover, $\mathrm{qr}^*(\mathtt{split}_k(\varphi)) \le \mathrm{qr}(\varphi)$.*

3   Decomposing Formulas

Given a system of equations which defines an inductive structure, we can decompose a WMSO formula into a Boolean combination of formulas to be checked on the constituent structures.

Procedure. $\mathtt{split}_k(\varphi)$

---

case φ *contains a free (unrestricted) variable* X **return** $\mathtt{split}_k(\varphi[X \leftarrow \bigcup_i X^i])$;

case φ *is an atom* **return** φ;

case $\varphi = \neg\psi$ **return** $\neg\mathtt{split}_k(\psi)$;

case $\varphi = \varphi_1 \vee \varphi_2$ **return** $\mathtt{split}_k(\varphi_1) \vee \mathtt{split}_k(\varphi_2)$;

case $\varphi = \varphi_1 \wedge \varphi_2$ **return** $\mathtt{split}_k(\varphi_1) \wedge \mathtt{split}_k(\varphi_2)$;

case $\varphi = \exists x\psi$ **return** $\bigvee_{i=1,\dots,k} \exists x^i \mathtt{split}_k(\psi)[x \leftarrow x^i]$;

case $\varphi = \forall x\psi$ **return** $\bigwedge_{i=1,\dots,k} \forall x^i \mathtt{split}_k(\psi)[x \leftarrow x^i]$;

case $\varphi = \exists X\psi$ **return** $\exists X^1 \dots X^k \mathtt{split}_k(\psi)[X \leftarrow \bigcup_i X^i]$;

case $\varphi = \forall X\psi$ **return** $\forall X^1 \dots X^k \mathtt{split}_k(\psi)[X \leftarrow \bigcup_i X^i]$;

Definition 6. *Let $\mathcal{D}$ be a system of n structure equations such that k_i structures appear on the right-hand side of the i-th equation. Let $\mathcal{S}(\mathcal{D}) = (\mathfrak{A}_1, \dots, \mathfrak{A}_n)$ and let φ be a WMSO formula with free variables $X_1, \dots, X_r$ (note that it has no free first-order variables). For each $m \in [n]$, a $\mathcal{D}_m$-decomposition of φ is a sequence of k-tuples ($k = k_m$) of formulas $(\psi_1^1, \dots, \psi_k^1), \dots, (\psi_1^l, \dots, \psi_k^l)$ such that the free variables of each ψ_j^i are included in $X_1, \dots, X_r$, $\mathrm{qr}(\psi_j^i) \leq \mathrm{qr}(\varphi)$, and*

$$\mathfrak{A}_m, \overline{V} \models \varphi \iff \text{ for some } i \in [l] \text{ and each } j \in [k] \quad \mathfrak{A}_m[j], \overline{V} \cap \mathfrak{A}_m[j] \models \psi_j^i.$$

The following theorem is the main result used to prove the correctness of our algorithm. Let us remark that it can be obtained from more general composition theorems of Shelah [7], but those theorems do not yield a practical algorithm.

Theorem 7. *For every WMSO formula φ, system of n structure equations $\mathcal{D}$, and $m \in [n]$, there exists an effectively computable $\mathcal{D}_m$-decomposition of φ.*

Note that our notion of $\mathcal{D}_m$-decompositions corresponds to reduction sequences introduced by Feferman and Vaught for FO. An example of how to compute these for MSO in a special case was described in [11]. The rest of this section is devoted to a proof of the above theorem in a more general setting which yields a basic building block for the model-checking algorithm. Towards this, we introduce a new normal form of WMSO formulas, which we call TNF, the *type normal form*. TNF is in a sense a converse of the prenex normal form since quantifiers are pushed as deep inside the formulas as possible.

3.1   Type Normal Form

For a set of formulas Φ we denote by $\mathcal{B}^+(\Phi)$ all positive Boolean combinations of formulas from Φ, i.e. formulas given by $\mathcal{B}^+(\Phi) = \Phi \mid \mathcal{B}^+(\Phi) \vee \mathcal{B}^+(\Phi) \mid \mathcal{B}^+(\Phi) \wedge \mathcal{B}^+(\Phi)$. A formula is in TNF if and only if it is a positive Boolean combination of formulas of the following form

$$\tau = R_i(\overline{x}) \mid \neg R_i(\overline{x}) \mid x = y \mid x \neq y \mid x \in X \mid x \notin X$$
$$\mid \exists x\mathcal{B}^+(\tau) \mid \exists X\mathcal{B}^+(\tau) \mid \forall x\mathcal{B}^+(\tau) \mid \forall X\mathcal{B}^+(\tau)$$

satisfying the following crucial constraint: in $\exists x \mathcal{B}^+(\tau_i)$, $\exists X \mathcal{B}^+(\tau_i)$, $\forall x \mathcal{B}^+(\tau_i)$, and $\forall X \mathcal{B}^+(\tau_i)$ the free variables of *each* τ_i appearing in the Boolean combination *must contain* x, or respectively X.

We claim that for each formula φ there exists an equivalent formula ψ in TNF such that $\mathrm{qr}(\psi) \leq \mathrm{qr}(\varphi)$ (and $\mathrm{qr}^*(\psi) \leq \mathrm{qr}^*(\varphi)$ for formulas with restricted variables) and the set of atoms of ψ is a subset of the atoms of φ. The procedure $\mathtt{TNF}(\varphi)$ computes such a formula ψ given a formula φ in negation normal form. Note that it uses sub-procedures $\mathtt{DNF}$ and $\mathtt{CNF}$ which, given a Boolean combination of formulas, convert it to disjunctive or conjunctive normal form. As an example, consider $\varphi = \exists x (P(x) \wedge (Q(y) \vee R(x)))$; $\mathtt{TNF}(\varphi) = (Q(y) \wedge \exists x P(x)) \vee \exists x (P(x) \wedge R(x))$.

Theorem 8. *The formula $\psi = TNF(\varphi)$ is in TNF, equivalent to φ, its atoms and free variables are included in the ones of φ and $\mathrm{qr}(\psi) \leq \mathrm{qr}(\varphi)$. If φ contains restricted variables, then $\mathrm{qr}^*(\psi) \leq \mathrm{qr}^*(\varphi)$.*

Proof. We proceed inductively on the structure of φ. For literals all the claims are trivial since TNF is an identity. For Boolean combinations of formulas, the procedure TNF only calls itself recursively, thus all claims of the theorem follow inductively as well.

Consider the case when $\varphi = \exists x \psi$ and $\mathtt{DNF}(\mathtt{TNF}(\psi)) = \bigvee_i (\bigwedge_j \psi_j^i)$. We convert $\mathtt{TNF}(\psi)$ to disjunctive normal form in this case since the existential quantifier is distributive over disjunction, and thus $\mathtt{TNF}(\varphi) \equiv \bigvee_i (\exists x \bigwedge_j (\psi_j^i))$. Since quantifiers are also distributive over formulas which do not contain the quantified variable, we get that the result, $\bigvee_i \left(\bigwedge_{j \in J_i} \psi_j^i \wedge \exists x (\bigwedge_{j \notin J_i} \psi_j^i) \right)$, is equivalent to $\exists x \mathtt{TNF}(\psi)$, and thus by inductive hypothesis also to φ. Since each formula ψ_j^i is, by inductive hypothesis, in the form τ, to show that the result is in TNF we only need to check that $\exists x (\bigwedge_{j \in J_i} \psi_j^i)$ is in the form τ. Syntactically this is trivial, and the constraint on variables in the TNF is indeed satisfied by the choice of J_i. The set of atoms does not increase by inductive hypothesis, and no new free variables appear by the choice of J_i. Furthermore, neither the quantifier rank nor the rank over any restricted variable increases. The case of universal quantification is analogous, modulo conversions between disjunctive and conjunctive normal forms (we assume that CNF and DNF do not create new atoms). □

We will use the following important property of formulas in TNF.

Procedure. $\mathtt{TNF}(\varphi)$

---

case φ *is a literal* **return** φ;
case $\varphi = \varphi_1 \vee \varphi_2$ **return** $\mathtt{TNF}(\varphi_1) \vee \mathtt{TNF}(\varphi_2)$;
case $\varphi = \varphi_1 \wedge \varphi_2$ **return** $\mathtt{TNF}(\varphi_1) \wedge \mathtt{TNF}(\varphi_2)$;
case $\varphi = \exists x \psi$ *(or $\exists X \psi$) and* $\mathtt{DNF}(\mathtt{TNF}(\psi)) = \bigvee_i (\bigwedge_j \psi_j^i)$
   Let $J_i = \{j \mid x \in \mathrm{free}(\psi_j^i)\}$; **return** $\bigvee_i \left(\bigwedge_{j \notin J_i} \psi_j^i \wedge \exists x (\bigwedge_{j \in J_i} \psi_j^i) \right)$;
case $\varphi = \forall x \psi$ *(or $\forall X \psi$) and* $\mathtt{CNF}(\mathtt{TNF}(\psi)) = \bigwedge_i (\bigvee_j \psi_j^i)$
   Let $J_i = \{j \mid x \in \mathrm{free}(\psi_j^i)\}$; **return** $\bigwedge_i \left(\bigvee_{j \notin J_i} \psi_j^i \vee \forall x (\bigvee_{j \in J_i} \psi_j^i) \right)$;

Lemma 9. *Let φ be a formula in TNF and $V_1, \ldots, V_n$ pairwise disjoint sets of variables such that if two variables appear in the same atom in φ, these variables belong to the same V_i. Then φ is a Boolean combination of formulas τ such that each τ contains only atoms with variables from one of the sets V_i.*

Proof. By contradiction, assume that there exists a formula φ in TNF which does not satisfy the above condition. Take such formula with smallest size (measured simply as the number of symbols). Then φ consists of only a single τ, since from a Boolean combination of more τ's one could choose a single one with atoms from different sets. Additionally, each sub-formula of φ satisfies the above lemma.

By assumption, $\varphi = \tau$ is not an atom, thus it is of the form $\exists X \mathcal{B}^+(\tau_i)$ or $\forall X \mathcal{B}^+(\tau_i)$ (or of the same form for first-order quantification). Each τ_i contains atoms only from a single set V_{j_i}, since otherwise it would be a smaller counter-example to the lemma and we have chosen τ as the smallest one. But, by the constraint on TNF, we know that X is contained in the free variables of each τ_i, and thus in each V_{j_i}. Since the sets V_i are pairwise disjoint, all j_i must be the same. This contradicts the assumption that τ contains atoms with variables from different sets V_i. $\qquad\square$

3.2   Formula Decomposition Algorithm

Let φ be a formula with only second-order free variables $X_1, \ldots, X_s$ and let $\mathcal{D}$ be a system of n structure equations

$$
\mathcal{D} = \begin{cases}
\Lambda^1 = \mathfrak{A}^1_1 \oplus \mathfrak{A}^1_2 \oplus \ldots \oplus \mathfrak{A}^1_{k_1} & \text{with } f^1_1, \ldots, f^1_K \\
\ \ \vdots \qquad \qquad \vdots \qquad \qquad \qquad \vdots \\
\Lambda^n = \mathfrak{A}^n_1 \oplus \mathfrak{A}^n_2 \oplus \ldots \oplus \mathfrak{A}^n_{k_n} & \text{with } f^n_1, \ldots, f^n_K
\end{cases}
$$

with $\mathcal{S}(\mathcal{D}) = (\mathfrak{A}_1, \ldots, \mathfrak{A}_n)$. For each $m \in [n]$, the $\mathcal{D}_m$-decomposition of φ can be computed by performing the following steps:

(1) compute $\psi_m = \texttt{split}_{k_m}(\varphi)$;
(2) compute ϑ_m from ψ_m by replacing each atom $x^j \in X^k$ or $x^j = x^k$ with $\bot$ if $j \neq k$ and each atom $R_i(x_1^{j_1}, \ldots, x_{r_i}^{j_{r_i}})$ such that not all j_l are equal with $f_i^m(j_1, \ldots, j_{r_i})$;
(3) compute $\texttt{DNF}(\texttt{TNF}(\vartheta_m)) = \bigvee_i \bigwedge_j \tau_{i,j}$.

We show that these steps indeed yield a $\mathcal{D}_m$-decomposition. By Lemma 5 and the definition of WMSO semantics we get that $\mathfrak{A}_m, \overline{P} \models \varphi \iff \mathfrak{A}_m, \overline{P^j} \models \psi_m$, where $P_i^j = P_i \cap \mathfrak{A}_m[j]$. Considering Step 2 of the algorithm, by the semantics of WMSO with restricted variables and the definition of $\mathcal{S}(\mathcal{D})$ we further get that $\mathfrak{A}_m, \overline{P^j} \models \psi_m \iff \mathfrak{A}_m, \overline{P^j} \models \vartheta_m$.

After this simplification step, all variables occurring in the same atomic sub-formula in ϑ_m are restricted to the same component, and by Lemma 9, each subformula $\tau_{i,j}$ in $\texttt{DNF}(\texttt{TNF}(\vartheta_m)) = \bigvee_i \bigwedge_j \tau_{i,j}$ contains only atoms (and thus also quantifiers) with variables restricted to a single component. Let ψ_k^i be the conjunction of all $\tau_{i,j}$ containing variables restricted to the component $k \in [k_l]$, or $\top$ if no such $\tau_{i,j}$ occurs. Clearly $\mathrm{TNF}(\vartheta_m)$ is equivalent to $\bigvee_i (\bigwedge_k \psi_k^i)$, and combining this with the previous equivalences we get that

$$\mathfrak{A}_m, \overline{P} \models \varphi \iff \mathfrak{A}_m, \overline{P}^j \models \bigvee_i (\bigwedge_k \psi_k^i).$$

To show that ψ_k^i with restricted variables X^k, x^k replaced by the standard ones X, x is a $\mathcal{D}_m$-decomposition of φ, it only remains to prove that $\mathrm{qr}(\tau_{i,j}) \leq \mathrm{qr}(\varphi)$ for all i, j. Observe that, by Lemma 5, we have $\mathrm{qr}^*(\psi_m) \leq \mathrm{qr}(\varphi)$. Replacing atoms does not change the quantifier rank, and by Theorem 8 we get that $\mathrm{qr}^*(\mathrm{TNF}(\vartheta_m)) \leq \mathrm{qr}^*(\psi_m)$. But since each $\tau_{i,j}$ contains only quantification over variables from one component, we obtain that $\mathrm{qr}^*(\mathrm{TNF}(\vartheta_m)) = \max_{i,j} \mathrm{qr}(\tau_{i,j}) \leq \mathrm{qr}(\varphi)$. This finally concludes the proof of Theorem 7.

4   Model Checking Algorithm

Our algorithm for model checking weak MSO sentences (i.e. formulas without free variables) on $\mathcal{S}_m(\mathcal{D})$ operates as follows.

- The only atomic sentences $\top$ and $\bot$ are verified trivially.
- Boolean combinations are verified by checking the subformulas and combining the results accordingly.
- Formulas of the form $\exists X \varphi(X)$ or $\exists x \varphi(x)$ are checked on $\mathcal{S}_m(\mathcal{D})$ by determining the winner of the finite reachability game $\mathcal{G}^\exists(\varphi, m)$ presented below.
- For formulas of the form $\forall X \varphi(X)$ or $\forall x \varphi(x)$ we check the equivalent formula $\neg \exists X \neg \varphi(X)$ or $\neg \exists x \neg \varphi(x)$, respectively, instead by determining the *loser* of the game $\mathcal{G}^\exists(\neg\varphi, m)$.

The main part of our model checking algorithm consists of establishing the winner of the following finite reachability game, which is based on the idea of decomposing formulas and on Theorem 7.

Definition 10. *Let $\exists X \varphi(X)$ be a sentence, $\Phi = \{\psi \mid \mathrm{qr}(\psi) \leq \mathrm{qr}(\varphi), \mathrm{free}(\psi) \subseteq \{X\}\}$, and let $\mathcal{D}$ be a system of n structure equations. The two-player game $\mathcal{G}^\exists(\varphi, m)$ is played by the Verifier, who tries to show that $\mathcal{S}_m(\mathcal{D}) \models \exists X \varphi(X)$, against the Falsifier, who tries to disprove this. $\mathcal{G}^\exists(\varphi, m)$ is defined as follows.*

- *Positions of Verifier: $\{[\psi, i] \mid \psi \in \Phi, i \in [n]\}$.*
- *Positions of Falsifier: $\{[(\psi_1, \ldots, \psi_{k_i}), S, i] \mid \psi_j \in \Phi, S \subseteq \bigcup_{j \in Fin_i} \mathfrak{A}_i[j]\}$.*
- *Initial position: $[\varphi, i]$.*
- *Terminal positions:*

$$\{[\mathfrak{A}_j^i, \psi_j, S, i] \mid \lambda(i, j) = Fin, \psi_j \in \Phi\} \text{ and } \{[\varphi[X \leftarrow \emptyset], i] \mid \varphi \in \Phi, i \in [n]\}$$

- *Moves:* $[\varphi, i] \xrightarrow{V} [\varphi[X \leftarrow \emptyset], i],$

$$[\varphi, i] \xrightarrow{V} [(\psi_1, \ldots, \psi_{k_i}), S, i], \text{ for each tuple } (\psi_1, \ldots, \psi_{k_i}) \text{ in}$$
$$\text{the } \mathcal{D}_i\text{-decomposition of } \varphi, \text{ and}$$

$$[(\psi_1, \ldots, \psi_{k_i}), S, i] \xrightarrow{F} \begin{cases} [\mathfrak{A}_j^i, \psi_j, S, i] & \text{if } \lambda(i, j) = Fin \\ [\psi_j, \ell] & \text{if } \lambda(i, j) = \ell. \end{cases}$$

– *Winning condition: Verifier wins at a terminal position* $[\mathfrak{A}_j^i, \psi_j, S, i]$ *if and only if* $(\mathcal{S}_i(\mathcal{D})[j], S \cap \mathcal{S}_i(\mathcal{D})[j]) \models \psi_j(X)$. *At a position* $[\varphi[X \leftarrow \emptyset], i]$ *the Verifier wins if and only if* $\mathcal{S}_i(\mathcal{D}) \models \varphi[X \leftarrow \emptyset]$. *Falsifier wins infinite plays.*

Since the quantifier rank of the formulas in the decomposition tuples is bounded by the quantifier rank of φ and there are only finitely many non-equivalent formulas with fixed quantifier rank, Φ is finite. Furthermore, the size of the sets chosen by Verifier is bounded by the size of the structures in $\mathcal{D}$, and hence the arena of $\mathcal{G}^\exists(\varphi, m)$ is finite.

Theorem 11. *Verifier wins the game* $\mathcal{G}^\exists(\varphi, m)$ *if and only if* $\mathcal{S}_m(\mathcal{D}) \models \exists X \varphi(X)$.

Proof. We prove that there is a direct correspondence between winning strategies for Verifier and finite sets satisfying formulas.

($\Leftarrow$) Let $(\mathfrak{A}_1, \ldots, \mathfrak{A}_n) = \mathcal{S}(\mathcal{D})$ and assume that $\mathfrak{A}_m \models \exists X \varphi(X)$. Let S be a finite set such that $\mathfrak{A}_m, S \models \varphi$. We prove the existence of a winning strategy for Verifier by induction on the depth of S.

Let $dp(S) = 1$, i.e. $S \subseteq \bigcup_{j \in \text{Fin}_m} \mathfrak{A}_m[j]$. By Theorem 7 there exists a $\mathcal{D}_m$-decomposition $(\psi_1^1, \ldots, \psi_{k_m}^1), \ldots, (\psi_1^r, \ldots, \psi_{k_m}^r)$ of φ and an index $\ell \in [r]$ such that $(\mathfrak{A}_m[j], S \cap \mathfrak{A}_m[j]) \models \psi_j^\ell$ for all $j \in [k_m]$. Since $dp(S) = 1$, all elements in S are from the finite components of $\mathfrak{A}_m$, i.e. $S \cap \bigcup_{j \in \Delta_m} \mathfrak{A}_m[j] = \emptyset$, and $\mathfrak{A}_{\lambda(m,j)}, \emptyset \models \psi_j$ for all $j \in \Delta_m$. Hence, Verifier wins by moving to $[(\psi_1^\ell, \ldots, \psi_{k_m}^\ell), S, m]$: Falsifier cannot win by moving to a position $[\mathfrak{A}_m[j], \psi_j^\ell, S, m]$, for $j \in \text{Fin}_m$, and from any position $[\psi_j^\ell]$, for $j \in \Delta_m$, Verifier can move to $[\psi_j^\ell[X \leftarrow \emptyset], \lambda(m,j)]$ and win.

Let $dp(S) > 1$ and let $(\psi_1^1, \ldots, \psi_{k_m}^1), \ldots, (\psi_1^r, \ldots, \psi_{k_m}^r)$ be the $\mathcal{D}_m$-decomposition of φ. Choose $\ell \in [r]$ such that $(\mathfrak{A}_m[j], S \cap \mathfrak{A}_m[j]) \models \psi_j^\ell$ for all $j \in [k_m]$. Let $S_0 = S \cap \bigcup_{j \in \text{Fin}_m} \mathfrak{A}_m[j]$. We show that Verifier wins from $[(\psi_1^\ell, \ldots, \psi_{k_m}^\ell), S_0, m]$. If Falsifier chooses $j \in \text{Fin}_m$ and moves to $[\mathfrak{A}_m[j], \psi_j^\ell, S_0, m]$, then Verifier wins because $(\mathfrak{A}_m[j], S \cap \mathfrak{A}_m[j]) \models \psi_j^\ell$. If Falsifiers chooses $j \in \Delta_m$, then we have that $dp_j(\pi_j((S \setminus S_0) \cap \mathfrak{A}_m[j])) < dp_j(S)$ (where $\pi_j : (s, jw) \mapsto (s, w)$), i.e. the depth of the remaining elements decreases upon descending into the j-th component. Since $(\mathfrak{A}_m[j], S_0 \cap \mathfrak{A}_m[j]) \models \psi_j^\ell$, applying the inductive hypothesis to positions $[\psi_j^\ell, \lambda(m,j)]$ for each $j \in \Delta_m$ we get that Verifier wins again.

($\Rightarrow$) Assume that Verifier has a strategy to win the game from the initial position $[\varphi(X), m]$. Since all plays won by Verifier are finite, unraveling the game graph and removing branches that do not correspond to moves taken by Verifier's winning strategy, we obtain a finite tree representing all possible plays of Falsifier against the fixed winning strategy of Verifier. The leaves of this tree are positions of the form $[\mathfrak{A}_j^i, \psi_j, S, i]$ or $[\psi[X \leftarrow \emptyset], i]$. We label the edges of the tree as follows: Edges representing Verifier's moves are labeled with ε; edges representing Falsifier's moves are labeled with letters from $\{1, \ldots, k_i\}$ corresponding to which part of the tuple Falsifier chooses, i.e. $[(\psi_1, \ldots, \psi_{k_i}), S, i] \xrightarrow{j} [\mathfrak{A}_i[j], \psi_j, S]$ or $[(\psi_1, \ldots, \psi_{k_i}), S, i] \xrightarrow{j} [\psi_j, \lambda(i,j)]$.

For each of Verifier's positions $p = [\psi, i]$ in the tree, we define the set $S(p)$ as the unique set which satisfies

$$S(p) \cap \mathfrak{A}_i[w] = S' \iff \text{a leaf } [\mathfrak{A}_w, \cdot, S', \cdot] \text{ is reachable from } p \text{ via labels } w$$

(note that the structure $\mathfrak{A}_w$ in the leaf, being one of the finite structures in $\mathcal{D}$, is actually isomorphic to $\mathfrak{A}_i[w]$). Intuitively, this set is obtained by combining all structures in reachable leaves after appropriately indexing their elements by the path w leading to them. We prove by induction on the *height* of positions in the tree that $\mathfrak{A}_i, S([\varphi, i]) \models \varphi$ holds for each position $[\varphi, i]$.

Let $h([\varphi, i]) = 0$. Then the only successor is the leaf $[\varphi[X \leftarrow \emptyset], i]$, therefore $S([\varphi, i]) = \emptyset$ and by definition $(\mathfrak{A}_i, \emptyset) \models \varphi$.

Let $h([\varphi, i]) > 0$. Then the only successor position $[(\psi_1, \ldots, \psi_{k_i}), S, i]$ has successors $[\mathfrak{A}_i[j], \psi_j, S'_j, i]$ (leaves), and $[\psi_j, \lambda(i, j)]$ with $h([\psi_j, \lambda(i, j)]) < h([\varphi, i])$. By induction hypothesis, $(\mathfrak{A}_{\lambda(i,j)}, S([\psi_j, \lambda(i, j)])) \models \psi_j$ for all $j \in \Delta_i$, and since we assume that Verifier plays a winning strategy, $(\mathfrak{A}_i[j], S'_j) \models \psi_j$ for $j \in \mathrm{Fin}_i$. Due to Theorem 7 we conclude that $(\mathfrak{A}_i, S([\varphi, i])) \models \varphi$. Considering the initial position $[\varphi, m]$ we obtain $(\mathfrak{A}_m, S([\varphi, m])) \models \varphi$, and hence $\mathfrak{A}_m \models \exists X \varphi(X)$. □

As presented, the model checking algorithm works in a top-down fashion and relies on solving finite reachability games. To establish the winner at positions of the form $[\psi[X \leftarrow \emptyset], j]$ in $\mathcal{G}^\exists(\varphi, i)$, we have to solve the model checking problem for the formula $\psi[X \leftarrow \emptyset]$, but note that $\psi[X \leftarrow \emptyset]$ has less variables and a smaller quantifier rank than $\exists X \varphi(X)$. Hence, the algorithm actually terminates.

Concerning the handling of existential first-order quantifiers there are two feasible approaches. By introducing a few special predicates for the subset relation and for expressing that a set is a singleton, one can avoid the use of first-order variables in the first place. On the other hand, the game can be easily modified to capture first-order quantification: Intuitively, instead of sets S, Verifier chooses either an element from one of the finite structures or announces in which of the inductively defined components the element is to be found.

5   Unbounding and Generalized Quantifiers

Many standard quantifiers, such as "there exists exactly one", do not increase the expressive power of MSO. One interesting exception is the unbounding quantifier: $UX\varphi$ expresses that the size of finite sets X satisfying φ is unbounded, i.e.

$$UX\varphi(X) \equiv \text{for all } n \in \mathbb{N} \; \exists X \varphi(X) \text{ with } X \text{ finite and } |X| \geq n.$$

First introduced in [13], MSO with this quantifier was proven to be decidable on trees only with very restricted quantification patterns. Recently, only a technical analysis of max-automata allowed to show that satisfiability of WMSO with the unbounding quantifier is decidable on the class of all labelings of $(\omega, <)$ [12]. We prove that WMSO+U is decidable on all inductive structures, which is a more general result as far as the class of structures is concerned, but it is less general as we allow only finite labelings of the structures. For our proof, we only need to extend the algorithm presented above. Again, we fix a system $\mathcal{D}$ of n equations and let $\mathcal{S}(\mathcal{D}) = (\mathfrak{A}_1, \ldots, \mathfrak{A}_n)$.

Definition 12. *A family* $\mathcal{U} = \{S_i \mid i \in \mathbb{N}\}$ *of finite sets is called* unbounded *in a component* $\mathfrak{A}_m[j]$ *if* $\{i \mid \mathfrak{A}_m[j] \cap S_i \neq \emptyset\}$ *is infinite.*

The following lemma is a consequence of the fact that our equations contain only a bounded number of structures.

Lemma 13. *Let* $\mathcal{U} = \{S_i \mid (\mathfrak{A}_m, S_i) \models \varphi(X), |S_i| \geq i\}$ *be a family of sets witnessing that* $\mathfrak{A}_m \models UX\varphi(X)$. *Then* $\mathcal{U}$ *is unbounded in some component* $\mathfrak{A}_m[j]$.

The above lemma, applied to k components, justifies the following extension of the $\texttt{split}_k$ procedure to the case $\varphi = UX\psi$ ($\overline{X}_{-j}$ denotes $\overline{X}$ without X^j):

$$\texttt{split}_k(\varphi) = \bigvee_{j=1,\ldots,k} \exists \overline{X^i}_{-j} UX^j \texttt{split}_k(\psi)[X \leftarrow \bigcup_i X^i].$$

The unbounding quantifier distributes over disjunctions, and the definition of TNF and the conversion procedure for U is the same as for $\exists$. Thus, the theorem about $\mathcal{D}$-decompositions holds for WMSO+U as well.

To check WMSO+U, we proceed as for WMSO and instead of asking whether there exists a winning strategy, we impose different conditions on the set of all winning strategies of Verifier in the game.

Definition 14. *The game* $\mathcal{G}^U(\varphi, m)$ *is defined as* $\mathcal{G}^\exists(\varphi, m)$ *with only one addition: Falsifier's positions* $[(\psi_1, \ldots, \psi_n), S, i]$ *with* $S \neq \emptyset$ *are considered to be* marked.

By $\mathcal{T}_\sigma(\varphi, i)$ we denote the unraveling of the game graph from position $[\varphi, i]$ where all branches that are not chosen by Verifier's strategy σ are pruned.

Theorem 15. $\mathfrak{A}_m \models UX\varphi(X)$ *if and only if for each* $n \in \mathbb{N}$, *Verifier has a winning strategy* σ_n *such that* $\mathcal{T}_{\sigma_n}(\varphi, m)$ *contains at least* n *marked positions.*

Proof. ($\Rightarrow$) Let M be the maximum number of elements in the universe of all finite structures appearing in $\mathcal{D}$ and assume that $\mathfrak{A}_m \models UX\varphi(X)$. Thus, for each $n \in \mathbb{N}$ there is a set S_n with $|S_n| \geq n$ such that $\mathfrak{A}_m, S_n \models \varphi(X)$. Following the same arguments as in the proof of Theorem 11, each S_n gives rise to a winning strategy σ_n for Verifier, namely "choose the upcoming elements of S_n." Consider the strategy $\sigma_{n \cdot M}$. Since $\sigma_{n \cdot M}$ chooses elements from $S_{n \cdot M}$, and at each marked position at most M of those, it follows from $|S_{n \cdot M}| \geq n \cdot M$ that there are at least n marked positions in $\mathcal{T}_{\sigma_{n \cdot M}}(\varphi, m)$.

($\Leftarrow$) Given a winning strategy σ, we construct, as in the proof of Theorem 11, a set S_σ satisfying φ. Consider a strategy σ_n with at least n marked positions in $\mathcal{T}_{\sigma_n}(\varphi, m)$. Since each marked position corresponds to a choice of a non-empty subset, and these subsets are disjoint, $|S_{\sigma_n}| \geq n$. Hence, $\mathfrak{A}_m \models UX\varphi(X)$ as we have assumed the existence of a winning strategy for each $n \in \mathbb{N}$. $\qquad \square$

For a reachability game with a finite arena, the above condition, i.e. the existence of winning strategies which result in game trees containing arbitrarily many marked positions, can be verified by a basic graph algorithm. Including any such procedure into our model checking algorithm, we obtain a procedure for model checking WMSO+U formulas on arbitrary inductive structures.

6   Implementation

We implemented a prototype in OCaml interfacing to MiniSat for performing CNF $\leftrightarrow$ DNF conversions following the idea described in [14]. The implementation[1] is functional but still leaves much room for improvement and optimization.

For a comparison with Mona we ran two tests—checking simple formulas of Presburger arithmetic taken from the examples shipped with Mona, and artificially constructed Horn formulas of the form

$$\varphi_n := \exists X \forall x_1 \ldots \forall x_n \big((x_1 \in X \to x_2 \in X) \wedge \cdots \wedge (x_{n-1} \in X \to x_n \in X)\big).$$

The results in Table 1 show that Presburger arithmetic presents no problem for Mona since an automaton recognizing addition is fairly small and easy to construct. For the prototype, the result depends on whether the constants are encoded in the input formula (A) or in the structure equations (B). On the other hand, the Horn formulas could be easily decomposed by our algorithm whereas Mona soon reaches its limits, being only able to handle formulas up to φ_{15}. This supports our claim that there are verification problems that might be better suited for a treatment on a logical level while there are others for which automata theoretic approaches are adequate.

However, due to the lack of example formulas, not to mention a benchmark suite, and the evident need for further optimization of our prototype, it is hard to carry out a meaningful comparison.

Table 1. Comparison of the running times measured in seconds

	Prototype A	B	Mona		Prototype	Mona
$\exists x(2x = 9)$	0.5	0.1	0.1	φ_{14}	0.1	7
$\exists x(2x = 16)$	3	0.6	0.1	φ_{15}	0.1	17
$\exists x(2x = 24)$	8	0.6	0.1	φ_{100}	0.3	–
$\exists x(2x = 25)$	7	0.1	0.1	φ_{500}	12	–

7   Future Work

Unlike advances in complementation and minimization techniques for automata, which usually do not provide any new intuitions about the logical aspects of the model-checking procedure, we think that, in addition to the pure algorithmic

---

[1] Available from `toss.sourceforge.net`, SVN revision 1049, in Solver/

value, our method can provide new insights into the composition method and might help to understand the algebraic structure of tree languages definable in weak MSO. Moreover, we aim at extending our method to further logics. Similar to the presented modification of the game that yields a decision procedure for WMSO+U, the game might be extended to capture other quantifiers. Additionally, we hope that our method can at least partially be extended to richer fragments of MSO and, as a long term goal, give an insight into the structure of tree languages definable in various fragments of MSO.

References

1. Büchi, J.R.: On a decision method in restricted second order arithmetic. In: International Congress on Logic, Methodology and Philosophy of Science, pp. 1–11. Stanford University Press, Standford (1962)
2. Rabin, M.O.: Decidability of second-order theories and automata on infinite trees. Transactions of the American Mathematical Society 141, 1–35 (1969)
3. Courcelle, B.: The monadic second order logic of graphs, II: Infinite graphs of bounded width. Mathematical System Theory 21, 187–222 (1989)
4. Basin, D.A., Klarlund, N.: Hardware verification using monadic second-order logic. In: Wolper, P. (ed.) CAV 1995. LNCS, vol. 939, pp. 31–41. Springer, Heidelberg (1995)
5. Jensen, J.L., Jørgensen, M.E., Klarlund, N., Schwartzbach, M.I.: Automatic verification of pointer programs using monadic second-order logic. In: Proceedings of PLDI 1997, pp. 226–236 (1997)
6. Zee, K., Kuncak, V., Rinard, M.C.: An integrated proof language for imperative programs. In: PLDI, pp. 338–351 (2009)
7. Shelah, S.: The monadic second order theory of order. Annals of Mathematics 102, 379–419 (1975)
8. Thomas, W.: Ehrenfeucht games, the composition method, and the monadic theory of ordinal words. In: Mycielski, J., Rozenberg, G., Salomaa, A. (eds.) Structures in Logic and Computer Science. LNCS, vol. 1261, pp. 118–143. Springer, Heidelberg (1997)
9. Läuchli, H.: A decision procedure for the weak second order theory of linear order. In: Arnold, H., Schmidt, K.S., Thiele, H.J. (eds.) Proceedings of the Logic Colloquium 1966, vol. 50, pp. 189–197. Elsevier, Amsterdam (1968)
10. Blumensath, A., Colcombet, T., Löding, C.: Logical theories and compatible operations. In: Flum, J., Grädel, E., Wilke, T. (eds.) Logic and automata: History and Perspectives, pp. 72–106. Amsterdam University Press, Amsterdam (2007)
11. Makowsky, J.A.: Algorithmic uses of the Feferman-Vaught theorem. Annals of Pure and Applied Logic 126(1-3), 159–213 (2004)
12. Bojanczyk, M.: Weak MSO with the unbounding quantifier. In: Proceedings of STACS 2009, Schloss Dagstuhl (IBFI). LIPIcs, vol. 09001, pp. 159–170 (2009)
13. Bojanczyk, M.: A bounding quantifier. In: Marcinkowski, J., Tarlecki, A. (eds.) CSL 2004. LNCS, vol. 3210, pp. 41–55. Springer, Heidelberg (2004)
14. McMillan, K.L.: Applying sat methods in unbounded symbolic model checking. In: Brinksma, E., Larsen, K.G. (eds.) CAV 2002. LNCS, vol. 2404, pp. 250–264. Springer, Heidelberg (2002)

The Structural λ-Calculus

Beniamino Accattoli and Delia Kesner

PPS (CNRS and Université Paris Diderot)

Abstract. Inspired by a recent graphical formalism for λ-calculus based
on Linear Logic technology, we introduce an untyped structural λ-calculus,
called λj, which combines action at a distance with exponential rules decomposing the substitution by means of weakening, contraction and dereliction. Firstly, we prove fundamental properties such as confluence and
preservation of β-strong normalisation. Secondly, we use λj to describe
known notions of developments and superdevelopments, and introduce a
more general one called XL-development. Then we show how to reformulate Regnier's σ-equivalence in λj so that it becomes a strong bisimulation.
Finally, we prove that explicit composition or de-composition of substitutions can be added to λj while still preserving β-strong normalisation.

1 Introduction

Computer science has been greatly influenced by Linear Logic [9], especially
because it provides a mechanism to explicitly control the use of resources by
limiting the liberal use of the *structural rules* of weakening and contraction.
Erasure and duplication are restricted to formulas marked with an *exponential*
modality?, and can only act on non-linear proofs marked with a bang modality !.
Intuitionistic and Classical Logic can thus be encoded by a fragment containing
such modalities, notably Multiplicative Exponential Linear Logic (MELL).

MELL proofs can be represented by sequent trees, but MELL Proof-Nets [9]
provide a better-suited geometrical representation of proofs that eliminates irrelevant syntactical details. They have been extensively used to develop different
encodings of intuitionistic logic/λ-calculus, giving rise to the geometry of interaction [10].

Normalisation of proofs (*i.e. cut elimination*) in MELL Proof-Nets is performed using three groups of rules, *multiplicative*, *exponential* and *commutative*.
Non-linear proofs are distinguished by surrounding *boxes* which are handled by
exponential rules: erasure, duplication and linear use correspond respectively to
a cut elimination step involving a box and either a *weakening*, a *contraction* or
a *dereliction*. The commutative rule allows to *compose* non-linear resources.

Different cut elimination systems [7,15,13], called *explicit substitution* (ES)
calculi, were explained in terms of, or inspired by, the notion of reduction of
MELL Proof-Nets. All of them use the idea that the content of a substitution/cut
is a non-linear resource, *i.e.* a box that can be composed with another one by
means of commutative rules. They also have in common an operational semantics
defined in terms of a *propagation system* in which a substitution traverses a term
to reach the variable occurrences.

A. Dawar and H. Veith (Eds.): CSL 2010, LNCS 6247, pp. 381–395, 2010.

A graph formalism for λ-terms inspired by Intuitionistic MELL has recently been proposed [1]. It avoids boxes by representing them through additional edges called *jumps*, and has no commutative reduction rule. This paper studies the term formalism, called λj-calculus, resulting from the reading back of the graphs λj-dags (and their reductions) by means of their sequentialisation theorem [1].

No rule of λj propagates cuts, as the constructors in a term interact *at a distance*, *i.e.* they work modulo positions of cuts. Action at a distance is not a complete novelty [21,5,22], but none of the previous approaches faithfully reflect resource control as suggested by Linear Logic. We propose to recognise such behaviour as a new paradigm, more primitive than ES, particularly because propagations can be added on top of action at a distance (as we shall show). Despite the absence of commutative rules in λj, cuts can be composed, but in a different (more natural) way.

Similarly to formalisms [16] inspired by Proof-Nets, cut elimination is defined in terms of the number of free occurrences of variables in a term, here called *multiplicities*. More precisely, the weakening-box rule (resp. dereliction-box and contraction-box) applies to terms that are of the form $t[x/u]$ when $|t|_x = 0$ (resp. $|t|_x = 1$ and $|t|_x > 1$). The computation is, however, performed without propagating $[x/u]$, which we call a *jump* to stress that such action at a distance is really different from propagation in ES calculi. The rules of λj therefore combine action at a distance, due to the tight correspondance with a graphical formalism, with exponential rules, due to the strong affinity with Linear Logic. Because of the weakening and contraction rules we call our language the *structural* λ-calculus.

Some calculi using either distance or multiplicities already exist, but without combining the two: only together those concepts unleash their full expressive power. Indeed, [5,22] use distance rules to refine β-reduction, but add ES to the syntax without distinguishing between dereliction and contraction. This causes the formalism to be less expressive than λj as discussed in Sections 4 and 6. Milner defines a λ-calculus with ES inspired by another graphical formalism, Bigraphs [21], where cuts also act at a distance. Again, he neither distinguishes between dereliction and contraction, nor does his β-rule exploit distance. The same goes for [28,23].

This paper studies the λj-calculus focusing on four different aspects:

- **Basic properties:** Section 2 presents the calculus while Section 3 shows full composition, simulation of one-step β-reduction, confluence, and preservation of β-strong normalisation (PSN). Particularly, we prove PSN using a modular technique [14], which results in an extremely short formal argument thanks to the absence of propagations.
- **Developments:** The λj-calculus is a powerful, elegant and concise tool for studying β-reduction. As an example, in Section 4 we analyse the redex creation mechanism of λ-calculus, using normal forms of certain subsystems of λj to characterise the result of full developments [12] and full superdevelopments [17]. By adding *more distance* to the previous subsystems, we characterise the result of a new, more powerful notion of development, which we call XL-development.
- **Operational equivalence:** Section 5 studies an operational equivalence $\equiv_o$ which equates λj-terms behaving the same way but differing only in

the positioning of their jumps. The relation $\equiv_o$ includes a reformulation of Regnier's σ-equivalence [26], but also contains commutation for independent jumps. We show that $\equiv_o$ is a strong bisimulation on λj-terms. Interestingly, this result holds only because of distance.

- **(De)composition of jumps:** In Section 6 we consider two further extensions of the system devised in Section 5, including, respectively, explicit composition and decomposition of jumps. We prove both new reduction relations to be confluent modulo $\equiv_o$ and to enjoy PSN. The two systems, reintroducing some propagation rules, bridge the gap with traditional ES calculi and implementations. The PSN proofs in this section are the more technically demanding proofs of this paper, and a non-trivial contribution to the theory of termination proofs of ES calculi.

A technical report including detailed proofs can be found in [2].

2   The Calculus

The set $\mathcal{T}$ of **terms** is defined by the following grammar:

$$t ::= x \text{ (variable)} \mid \lambda x.t \text{ (abstraction)} \mid t\, t \text{ (application)} \mid \mid t[x/t] \text{ (closure)}$$

The object $[x/t]$, which is not a term itself, is called a **jump**. A term without jumps is a λ-**term**. We use the notation $\overline{v}_n^1$ for a list of terms $v_1 \ldots v_n$, $t\, \overline{v}_n^1$ for $(\ldots(t\, v_1)\ldots v_n)$ and $t[x_i/u_i]_n^1$ for $t[x_1/u_1]\ldots[x_n/u_n]$ $(n \geq 0)$.

Free and **bound** variables of t, respectively written $\mathtt{fv}(t)$ and $\mathtt{bv}(t)$, are defined as usual. The constructors $\lambda x.u$ and $u[x/v]$ bind the free occurrences of x in u. The congruence generated by renaming of bound variables is called α-**conversion**. Thus for example $(\lambda y.x)[x/y] =_\alpha (\lambda y'.x')[x'/y]$.

The **multiplicity of the variable** x **in the term** t is defined as the number of free occurrences of x in t, written $|t|_x$. We use $|t|_\Gamma$ for $\Sigma_{x\in\Gamma}|t|_x$. When $|t|_x = n \geq 2$, we write $t_{[y]_x}$ for the **non-deterministic replacement** of i $(1 \leq i \leq n-1)$ occurrences of x in t by a *fresh* variable y. Thus, $(x\, z)[z/x]_{[y]_x}$ may denote either $(y\, z)[z/x]$ or $(x\, z)[z/y]$ but not $(y\, z)[z/y]$.

Λ **(meta-level) substitution** is a finite function from variables to terms. **Substitution** is defined, as usual, modulo α-conversion so that the capture of variables is avoided. We use $t\sigma$ to denote the **application** of the **meta-level substitution** σ to the term t. Thus for example $(\lambda y.x)\{x/y\} = \lambda z.y$. Moreover, $t\{x/u\} = t$ if $x \notin \mathtt{fv}(t)$. We use juxtaposition of substitutions to denote composition so that $\tau\sigma$ is the substitution given by $x(\tau\sigma) := (x\tau)\sigma$. Besides α-conversion, we consider the following rewriting rules:

$$
\begin{array}{llll}
(\mathtt{dB}) & (\lambda x.t)\mathtt{L}\, u \to t[x/u]\mathtt{L} & \\
(\mathtt{w}) & t[x/u] \to t & \text{if } |t|_x = 0 \\
(\mathtt{d}) & t[x/u] \to t\{x/u\} & \text{if } |t|_x = 1 \\
(\mathtt{c}) & t[x/u] \to t_{[y]_x}[x/u][y/u] & \text{if } |t|_x \geq 2
\end{array}
$$

where we use the (meta)notation $\mathtt{L}$ for a list $[x_i/u_i]_n^1$ with $n \geq 0$.

Note that dB reformulates the classical B-rule of ES calculi as a *distance* rule which skips the jumps affecting the abstraction of the redex. This same rule notably appears in weak ES calculi [19] to avoid the the β-redexes that are hidden by blocked substitutions. Here, the dB-rule is the natural term counterpart of a graphical and *local* rule in proof-nets and λj-dags. Section 4 puts the expressiveness of this concept in evidence. The rules w, d and c are to be understood as the weakening, dereliction and contraction rules in λj-dags.

It is worth noting that λj allows to *compose* jumps, as for example reduction from $t = y[x/zy][y/v]$ computes the (simultaneous) jumps in $y[x/zv][y/v]$. Usually, the so-called *composition* of the two jumps of t rather yields $y[y/v][x/zy[y/v]]$. We will study this more structural notion in Section 6.

The **rewriting relation** $\to_{\lambda j}$ (resp. $\to_j$) is generated by all (resp. all expect dB) the previous rewriting rules modulo α-conversion. The j-rewriting rules are based on global side conditions, which may seem difficult to implement. However, if implementation is done via graphical formalisms (such as proof-nets, bigraphs, λj-dags), these conditions become local and completely harmless.

Now consider any reduction relation $\mathcal{R}$. A term t is said to be in $\mathcal{R}$-**normal form**, written $\mathcal{R}$-nf, if there is no u so that $t \to_{\mathcal{R}} u$. We use $\mathcal{R}(t)$ to denote the *unique* $\mathcal{R}$-nf of t, when it exists. A term t is $\mathcal{R}$-**strongly normalising** or $\mathcal{R}$-**terminating**, written $t \in \mathcal{SN}_{\mathcal{R}}$, if there is no infinite $\mathcal{R}$-reduction sequence starting at t, in which case $\eta_{\mathcal{R}}(t)$ denotes the **maximal length of a $\mathcal{R}$-reduction sequence starting at** t. The relation $\mathcal{R}$ is called **complete** if it is strongly normalising and confluent.

3   Main Properties

In this section we prove some sanity properties of the calculus: full composition, simulation of one-step β-reduction, confluence and PSN. Since the first three can easily be shown using standard rewriting technology, we concentrate on proving PSN, which usually is tricky, but turns out to be surprisingly simple in our case. By induction on $|t|_x$ (and not on t!) we get the following lemma:

Lemma 1 (Full Composition (FC)). *Let* $t, u \in \mathcal{T}$. *Then* $t[x/u] \to_j^+ t\{x/u\}$.

Corollary 1 (Simulation). *Let* $t \in \lambda$*-term. If* $t \to_\beta t'$, *then* $t \to_{\lambda j}^+ t'$.

The following notion, which counts the maximal number of free occurrences of a variable x that may appear during a j-reduction sequence from a term t, will be useful for various proofs. The **potential multiplicity** of the variable x in the term t, written $M_x(t)$, is defined for α-equivalence classes as follows: if $x \notin \mathtt{fv}(t)$, then $M_x(t) := 0$; otherwise:

$$M_x(x) \quad := 1 \qquad\qquad M_x(u\,v) \quad := M_x(u) + M_x(v)$$
$$M_x(\lambda y.u) := M_x(u) \qquad M_x(u[y/v]) := M_x(u) + \mathtt{max}(1, M_y(u)) \cdot M_x(v)$$

Lemma 2. *The* j-*reduction relation is complete.*

Proof. For each $t \in \mathcal{T}$ define a finite multiset of natural numbers $\mathtt{jm}(t)$ given by:

$$\mathtt{jm}(x) \quad := [\,] \qquad\qquad \mathtt{jm}(tu) \quad := \mathtt{jm}(t) \sqcup \mathtt{jm}(u)$$
$$\mathtt{jm}(\lambda x.t) := \mathtt{jm}(t) \qquad \mathtt{jm}(t[x/u]) := [M_x(t)] \sqcup \mathtt{jm}(t) \sqcup \mathtt{max}(1, M_x(t)) \cdot \mathtt{jm}(u)$$

where $\sqcup$ is multiset union and $n \cdot [a_1, \ldots, a_n] := [n \cdot a_1, \ldots, n \cdot a_n]$. Then show that $\to_j$ strictly decreases $\mathtt{jm}(\_)$ and thus conclude termination. Local confluence (straightforward) and termination imply confluence by Newman's Lemma.

This is used to prove confluence of $\rightarrow^*_{\lambda j}$, by means of the Tait and Martin-Löf technique (details in [2]):

Theorem 1 (Confluence). *For all* $t, u_1, u_2 \in \mathcal{T}$, *if* $t \rightarrow^*_{\lambda j} u_i$ $(i = 1, 2)$, *then* $\exists v$ *s.t.* $u_i \rightarrow^*_{\lambda j} v$ $(i = 1, 2)$.

We now discuss PSN. A reduction system $\mathcal{R}$ is said to enjoy the **PSN property** w.r.t. another system $\mathcal{S}$ iff every term which is $\mathcal{S}$-strongly normalising is also $\mathcal{R}$-strongly normalising. Here PSN will mean PSN w.r.t. β-reduction.

The proof of PSN can be stated in terms of the **IE** property which relates termination of **I**mplicit substitution to termination of **E**xplicit substitution. A reduction system $\mathcal{R}$ enjoys the **IE property** iff for $n \geq 0$ and for all $t, u, \overline{v}^1_n \in \lambda$-terms: $u \in \mathcal{SN}_{\mathcal{R}}$ and $t\{x/u\}\overline{v}^1_n \in \mathcal{SN}_{\mathcal{R}}$ imply $t[x/u]\overline{v}^1_n \in \mathcal{SN}_{\mathcal{R}}$.

Theorem 2 (IE implies PSN). *A reduction relation* $\mathcal{R}$ *enjoys PSN if* $\mathcal{R}$ *verifies the **IE**-property and the following:*

(F0) *If* $\overline{t}^1_n \in \lambda$-*terms in* $\mathcal{SN}_{\mathcal{R}}$, *then* $x\overline{t}^1_n \in \mathcal{SN}_{\mathcal{R}}$.
(F1) *If* $u \in \lambda$-*term in* $\mathcal{SN}_{\mathcal{R}}$, *then* $\lambda x.u \in \mathcal{SN}_{\mathcal{R}}$.
(F2) *The only* $\mathcal{R}$-*reducts of a* λ-*term* $(\lambda x.u)v\overline{t}^1_n$ *are* $u[x/v]\overline{t}^1_n$ *and those coming from internal reduction on* $u, v, \overline{t}^1_n$.

Intuitively, the first two requirements (F0) and (F1) mean that head-normal forms are stable under $\mathcal{R}$. The last requirement (F2) means that the head-redex can only be refined by $\mathcal{R}$, but nothing else.

Proof. We show $t \in \mathcal{SN}_{\mathcal{R}}$ by induction on the definition of $t \in \mathcal{SN}_{\beta}$ (as in [29]):

 - If $t = x\overline{t}^1_n$ with $t_i \in \mathcal{SN}_{\beta}$, then (i.h.) $t_i \in \mathcal{SN}_{\mathcal{R}}$ and thus **(F0)** $x\overline{t}^1_n \in \mathcal{SN}_{\mathcal{R}}$.
 - If $t = \lambda x.u$ with $u \in \mathcal{SN}_{\beta}$, then (i.h.) $u \in \mathcal{SN}_{\mathcal{R}}$ and thus **(F1)** $\lambda x.u \in \mathcal{SN}_{\mathcal{R}}$.
 - If $t = (\lambda x.u)v\overline{t}^1_n$, with $u\{x/v\}\overline{t}^1_n \in \mathcal{SN}_{\beta}$ and $v \in \mathcal{SN}_{\beta}$, then (i.h.) both terms are in $\mathcal{SN}_{\mathcal{R}}$, **IE** gives $U = u[x/v]\overline{t}^1_n \in \mathcal{SN}_{\mathcal{R}}$, so in particular $u, v, \overline{t}^1_n \in \mathcal{SN}_{\mathcal{R}}$. We show $t \in \mathcal{SN}_{\mathcal{R}}$ by induction on $\eta_{\mathcal{R}}(u) + \eta_{\mathcal{R}}(v) + \Sigma_i \; \eta_{\mathcal{R}}(t_i)$. For that, we show that every $\mathcal{R}$-reduct of t is in $\mathcal{SN}_{\mathcal{R}}$.

     Now, if $t \rightarrow_{\mathcal{R}} t'$ is an internal reduction, apply the i.h. Otherwise, **F2** gives $t \twoheadrightarrow_{\mathcal{R}} u[x/v]t_1 \ldots t_n = U$ which is in $\mathcal{SN}_{\mathcal{R}}$.

Theorem 3 (IE for λj). *λj enjoys the **IE** property.*

Proof. We show the following more general statement. For all terms $t, \overline{u}^1_m$ $(m \geq 1), \overline{v}^1_n$ $(n \geq 0)$, if $\overline{u}^1_m \in \mathcal{SN}_{\lambda j}$ & $t\{x_i/u_i\}^1_m \overline{v}^1_n \in \mathcal{SN}_{\lambda j}$, then $t[x_i/u_i]^1_m \overline{v}^1_n \in \mathcal{SN}_{\lambda j}$, where $x_i \neq x_j$ for $i, j = 1 \ldots m$ and $x_i \notin \mathtt{fv}(u_j)$ for $i, j = 1 \ldots m$. The **IE** property holds by taking $m = 1$. Now, we prove $t[x_i/u_i]^1_m \overline{v}^1_n \in \mathcal{SN}_{\lambda j}$, by induction on the 3-tuple $\langle \eta_{\lambda j}(t\{x_i/u_i\}^1_m \overline{v}^1_n), \mathsf{o}_{\overline{x}^1_m}(t), \eta_{\lambda j}(\overline{u}^1_m) \rangle$ where $\mathsf{o}_{x_i}(t) = 3^{|t|_{x_i}}$ and $\mathsf{o}_{\overline{x}^1_m}(t) = \Sigma_i \; \mathsf{o}_{x_i}(t)$. Details in [2].

In contrast to known PSN proofs for calculi with ES and composition of substitutions [4,13,15], we get a very concise and simple proof of the **IE** property, and thus of PSN, due to the fact that λj has no propagation rule. Indeed, since λj-reduction enjoys the **IE**-property and **F0**, **F1** and **F2** in Theorem 2 are straightforward for the λj-calculus, we get:

Corollary 2 (PSN for λj). *Let* $t \in \lambda$-*term. If* $t \in \mathcal{SN}_{\beta}$, *then* $t \in \mathcal{SN}_{\lambda j}$.

4   Developments and All That

In λ-calculus creation of redexes can be classified in three types [18]:

(Type 1) $((\lambda x.\lambda y.t)\ u)\ v \to_\beta (\lambda y.t\{x/u\})\ v.$
(Type 2) $(\lambda x.x)\ (\lambda y.t)\ u \to_\beta (\lambda y.t)\ u.$
(Type 3) $(\lambda x.C[x\ v])\ (\lambda y.u) \to_\beta C\{x/\lambda y.u\}[(\lambda y.u)\ v]$

When λ-terms are considered as trees, the first and second type create a redex *upward*, while the third creates it *downward*, which is the dangerous kind of creation since it may lead to divergence.

According to the previous classification, different ways to compute a term can be defined. A reduction sequence starting at t is a **development** [12] (resp. a **full development**) if only (resp. all the) residuals of redexes (resp. all the redexes) of t are contracted. A more liberal notion, called **L-development** here, and known as superdevelopment [17], allows to also reduce created redexes of type 1 and 2. A major result states that all developments (resp. L-developments) of a λ-term are finite, and that the results of all full developments (resp. full L-developments) coincide.

Note that reductions of type 1 and 2 are acceptable because the created redex is *hidden* in the initial term, so that non-termination only happens when creating redexes of type 3. However, *linear creations* of type 3 - *i.e.* creations which do not involve duplications - are also safe, and infinite reductions only happen if redexes created after duplication are reduced - we call such cases *non-linear creations* of type 3. As an example, consider $\Omega = (\lambda x.x\ x)\ (\lambda x.x\ x)$ whose infinite reduction involves only non-linear creations of the third type. These observations suggest that banning the third type of creation is excessive: it is sufficient to avoid non-linear ones. This extended form of L-development needs a language capable of distinguishing the linear/erasing/duplicating nature of redexes. This section extends the notion of L-development to that of **XL-development**, which also reduces linearly created redexes of type 3, and provides a finiteness result.

The following table summarises the behaviour of each computational notion studied in this section on the λ-term $u_0 = (I\ I)\ ((\lambda z.z\ y)\ I)$, where $I = \lambda x.x$.

$$
\begin{array}{ll}
\text{full development of } u_0 & = I\ (I\ y) \\
\text{full L-development of } u_0 & = I\ y \\
\text{full XL-development of } u_0 & = y
\end{array}
\tag{1}
$$

The specification of all the reduction subsystems used in this section exploits the idea of *multiplicity*. Thus, the λj-calculus provides a uniform and expressive framework to reason about creation of redexes in λ-calculus.

A **development** (resp. full development) of a term t is a reduction sequence in which only (resp. all the) residuals of redex occurrences (resp. all the redex occurrences) that already exist in t are contracted. There are many proofs of finiteness of developments, like [12,29]. The **result of a full development** of a λ-term is unique and can simply be defined by induction on the structure of terms as follows:

$$
\begin{array}{llll}
x^\circ & := x & ((\lambda x.t)\ u)^\circ := t^\circ\{x/u^\circ\} & \\
(\lambda x.t)^\circ & := \lambda x.t^\circ & (t\ u)^\circ \quad := t^\circ\ u^\circ & \text{if } t \neq \lambda
\end{array}
$$

But in $\lambda\mathsf{j}$ it can also be characterised in a more operational way. Let B be the rewriting rule $(\lambda x.t)u \rightarrow_\mathsf{B} t[x/u]$, which is the restriction of our dB-rule to a *proximity* action. This relation is trivially *complete* so that we use $\mathsf{B}(t)$ for the (unique) B-nf of the term t. By induction on t we get the following corollary:

Corollary 3. *Let $t \in \lambda$-term. Then $t^\circ = \mathsf{j}(\mathsf{B}(t))$.*

Developments can be extended to **L-developments** which also reduce created redexes of type 1 and 2 and are always finite. The **result of a full L-development** of a λ-term is unique and admits the following inductive definition [17]:

$$
\begin{aligned}
x^{\circ\circ} &:= x & (t\ u)^{\circ\circ} &:= t^{\circ\circ}\ u^{\circ\circ} & &\text{if } t^{\circ\circ} \neq \lambda \\
(\lambda x.t)^{\circ\circ} &:= \lambda x.t^{\circ\circ} & (t\ u)^{\circ\circ} &:= t_1\{x/u^{\circ\circ}\} & &\text{if } t^{\circ\circ} = \lambda x.t_1
\end{aligned}
$$

Remark that $t^{\circ\circ} \neq \lambda$ implies $t \neq \lambda$.

Let us recover $t^{\circ\circ}$ by means of our language $\lambda\mathsf{j}$. The key to operationally describe the first type of creation is the *distance* dB-rule, whose (unique) nf will be noted $\mathsf{dB}(t)$. Replacing our definition of development $\mathsf{j}(\mathsf{B}(t))$ with $\mathsf{j}(\mathsf{dB}(t))$ gives:

$$\mathsf{dB}(((\lambda x.\lambda y.t)\ u)\ v) = \mathsf{dB}(t)[y/\mathsf{dB}(v)][x/\mathsf{dB}(u)] = M$$

Then, computing jumps, we get:

$$\mathsf{j}(M) = \mathsf{j}(\mathsf{dB}(t))\{x/\mathsf{j}(\mathsf{dB}(u))\}\{y/\mathsf{j}(\mathsf{dB}(v))\}$$

And we are done. Now, to specify L-developments within our language $\lambda\mathsf{j}$ we also need to capture the second type of creation. We would therefore need to use $\mathsf{dB} \cup \mathsf{d} \cup \mathsf{w}$ instead of dB, but our (distance) d-rule turns out to be too powerful since created redexes of type 3 would also be captured as shown by the term $(\lambda x.x\ t)(\lambda y.u)$, where $x \notin \mathtt{fv}(t)$. Thus, the reduction d is restricted to act only on variables, written md (for *minimal dereliction*), so that $\rightarrow_\mathsf{md}$ is the context closure of the rule $x[x/u] \rightarrow u$. We then let A be the relation $\mathsf{dB} \cup \mathsf{md} \cup \mathsf{w}$.

Lemma 3. *The reduction relation $\rightarrow_\mathsf{A}$ is complete.*

Proof. Termination of A is straightforward. Confluence follows from local confluence (straightforward by case-analysis) and Newman's Lemma.

Interestingly, $\rightarrow_\mathsf{A}$ cannot be weakened to $\rightarrow_{\mathsf{dB}\cup\mathsf{md}}$ as illustrated by the term $s = ((\lambda x.((\lambda y.x)\ t))\ \lambda z.z)\ u$. Due to lack of space the proof of the following proposition has been omitted (details in [2]):

Proposition 1. *Let t be a λ-term. Then $t^{\circ\circ} = \mathsf{j}(\mathsf{A}(t))$.*

It is now natural to relax the previous relation A from $\mathsf{dB} \cup \mathsf{md} \cup \mathsf{w}$ to $\mathsf{dB} \cup \mathsf{d} \cup \mathsf{w}$, in other words, to also allow unrestricted d-steps. Thus L-developments are extended to **XL-developments**, which also allow linear creations of type 3. Completeness of this extended notion is stated by the following lemma, proved similarly to Lemma 3.

Lemma 4. *The reduction relation $\rightarrow_{\mathsf{dB}\cup\mathsf{d}\cup\mathsf{w}}$ is complete.*

The result of a **full XL-development** of a λ-term t, noted $t^{\circ\circ\circ}$, is defined by $\mathtt{j}((\mathtt{dB} \cup \mathtt{d} \cup \mathtt{w})(t))$ where $(\mathtt{dB} \cup \mathtt{d} \cup \mathtt{w})(t)$ denotes the (unique) $(\mathtt{dB} \cup \mathtt{d} \cup \mathtt{w})$-nf of t. This notion extends L-developments in a deterministic way, *i.e.* provides a complete reduction relation for λ-terms, more liberal than L-developments.

It is well known that every **affine** λ-term t (*i.e.* a term where no variable has more than one occurrence in t) is β-strongly normalising (the number of constructors strictly diminishes with each step). Moreover, β-reduction of affine terms can be performed in $\lambda\mathtt{j}$ using only $\mathtt{dB} \cup \mathtt{d} \cup \mathtt{w}$, *i.e.* β-nf$(t) = (\mathtt{dB} \cup \mathtt{d} \cup \mathtt{w})(t)$. Thus:

Corollary 4. *Let t be an affine λ-term. Then $t^{\circ\circ\circ} = \beta$-nf$(t)$.*

We hope that our extended notion of XL-development can be applied to obtain more expressive solutions for higher-order matching problems, which arise for example in higher-order logic programming, logical frameworks, program transformations, etc. Indeed, the approach of higher-order matching in *untyped* frameworks [8,6], which currently uses L-developments, may be improved using XL-developments, as suggested by example (1) at the beginning of this section.

5   Bisimilar Terms

The simplicity of the $\lambda\mathtt{j}$-calculus naturally suggests the study of some operational equivalence which should equate terms that differ only concerning the positioning of their jumps but *behave identically*. For instance, if $y \notin \mathtt{fv}(u)$, then $\lambda y.t[x/u]$ and $(\lambda y.t)[x/u]$ behave equivalently: there is a bijection between their redexes and their reducts, *i.e.* they are *bisimilar*. This idea is reminiscent of Regnier's equivalence on λ-terms [25], here written σ^R:

$$(\lambda x.\lambda y.t)\ u \equiv_{\sigma_1^R} \lambda y.((\lambda x.t)\ u) \quad \text{if } y \notin \mathtt{fv}(u)$$
$$(\lambda x.t\ v)\ u \ \equiv_{\sigma_2^R} (\lambda x.t)\ u\ v \quad \text{if } x \notin \mathtt{fv}(v)$$

Reduction of the $\mathtt{dB}$-redexes in the previous equations yields the following σ-equivalence notion, now on $\lambda\mathtt{j}$-terms:

$$(\lambda y.t)[x/u] \equiv_{\sigma_1} \lambda y.t[x/u] \text{ if } y \notin \mathtt{fv}(u)$$
$$(t\ v)[x/u] \ \equiv_{\sigma_2} t[x/u]\ v \ \text{ if } x \notin \mathtt{fv}(v)$$

This is not very surprising since σ^R-equivalence was introduced by noting that the two terms of each equation represent the *same* MELL proof-net modulo multiplicative redexes, which correspond exactly to the $\mathtt{dB}$-redexes of the $\lambda\mathtt{j}$-calculus. Regnier proved that σ^R-equivalent terms have the same maximal β-reduction length. However, this does not imply that σ^R-equivalence is a strong bisimilarity on λ-terms. Indeed, take λ-terms $t_0 = ((\lambda x.\lambda y.y)\ z)\ w \equiv_{\sigma_1^R} (\lambda y.((\lambda x.y)\ z))\ w = t_1$. Both share the same β-normal form w and $\eta_\beta(t_0) = \eta_\beta(t_1)$. Nevertheless, t_0 has one redex, while t_1 has two redexes, and the redex of t_1 involving w has no corresponding redex in t_0. They also differ in terms of creation of redexes: the result of the full development of t_0 has a *created* redex, while the result of the full development of t_1 is the normal form of the term. Our reformulation of σ^R, however, equates two $\lambda\mathtt{j}$-terms t_0' and t_1' which are strongly bisimilar:

$$t_0 \to_{\mathtt{dB}} t_0' = (\lambda y.y)[x/z]\ w \quad \equiv_{\sigma_1} \quad (\lambda y.y[z/x])\ w = t_1'\ {}_{\mathtt{dB}}\!\!\leftarrow t_1 \qquad (2)$$

Actually, bisimulation holds also for permutation of *independent* jumps [13]:

$$t[x/u][y/v] \equiv_{\mathsf{CS}} t[y/v][x/u] \qquad \text{if } y \notin \mathtt{fv}(u) \ \& \ x \notin \mathtt{fv}(v)$$

While CS should naturally remain an equivalence, σ has often been restricted to being considered a *reduction* relation [26], for no good reason. Here, we add CS and σ to $\lambda\mathtt{j}$ without any trouble, in particular without loosing the PSN property (Corollary 8). The **operational equivalence** relation generated by $\mathsf{o} = \{\alpha, \mathsf{CS}, \sigma_1, \sigma_2\}$ realises a strong bisimulation, proved by induction on $\equiv_{\mathsf{o}}$:

Proposition 2 (Strong Bisimulation). *For all* $t, u, u' \in \mathcal{T}$ *s.t.* $t \equiv_{\mathsf{o}} u \to_{\lambda\mathtt{j}} u'$ $\exists t'$ *s.t.* $t \to_{\lambda\mathtt{j}} t' \equiv_{\mathsf{o}} u'$.

Such bisimulation implies that two o-equivalent terms share the same maximal reduction length. Moreover, the strong bisimulation would not hold without distance rules. Indeed, the two σ_1-equivalent terms t'_0 and t'_1 in (2) do not have the same B-redexes but the same dB-redexes.

6   (De)composing Substitutions

Explicit substitution (ES) calculi may or may not include rewriting rules to *explicitly* compose substitutions. One often adds them to recover confluence on terms with metavariables. However, naïve rules may break the PSN property, so that *safe* composition rules are needed to recover both PSN and confluence on terms with metavariables [13]. The $\lambda\mathtt{j}$-calculus is peculiar as it allows to compose substitutions, but only *implicitly*. Indeed, a term $t[x/u][y/v]$ s.t. $y \in \mathtt{fv}(u) \ \& \ y \in \mathtt{fv}(t)$ reduces in various steps to $t[x/u\{y/v\}][y/v]$, but not to the explicit composition $t[x/u[y/v]][y/v]$. One of the aims of this section is adding *explicit composition* to $\lambda\mathtt{j}$ keeping PSN and confluence.

The second aim of this section concerns *explicit decomposition*. Indeed, some calculi [24,20,27,11] explicitly *decompose* substitutions, *i.e.* reduce $t[x/u[y/v]]$ to $t[x/u][y/v]$. We show that even in such a case PSN and confluence still hold.

Composition (boxing) and decomposition (unboxing) are dual systems:

The **Boxing** system b
if $x \notin \mathtt{fv}(t) \ \& \ x \in \mathtt{fv}(v)$:
$(t \ v)[x/u] \quad \to_{\mathsf{ab}} t \ v[x/u]$
$t[y/v][x/u] \to_{\mathsf{sb}} t[y/v[x/u]]$

The **Unboxing** system u
if $x \notin \mathtt{fv}(t) \ \& \ x \in \mathtt{fv}(v)$:
$t \ v[x/u] \quad \to_{\mathsf{au}} (t \ v)[x/u]$
$t[y/v[x/u]] \to_{\mathsf{su}} t[y/v][x/u]$

The boxing system reflects the commutative box-box rule of Linear Logic, the unboxing system is obtained by reversing its rules. Moreover, we consider the system modulo the o-equivalence. Choosing a particular orientation for σ_1 and σ_2 leads to a full set of propagating rules, that is, something closer to traditional ES calculi. We prefer, however, to work modulo an equivalence to obtain a more general result. Remark that the constraint $x \notin \mathtt{fv}(t)$ for the unboxing rules does not limit their applicability, as it can always be satisfied through α-equivalence.

Digression. It is natural to wonder if one could also work modulo (de)composition, *i.e.* adding two more general axioms:

$$(t\ v)[x/u]\ \equiv_{\sigma_3}\ t\ v[x/u]\qquad \text{if } x \notin \mathtt{fv}(t)$$
$$t[y/v][x/u] \equiv_{\sigma_4} t[y/v[x/u]] \text{ if } x \notin \mathtt{fv}(t)$$

The answer is no, as these last two congruences break the PSN property, if naïvely added. For example: let $u = (z\ z)[z/y]$, then

$$t = u[x/u] = (z\ z)[z/y][x/u] \equiv_{\sigma_4} (z\ z)[z/y[x/u]] \ \rightarrow_{\mathsf{c}}$$
$$(z_1\ z_2)[z_1/y[x/u]][z_2/y[x/u]] \rightarrow_{\mathsf{d}}^{+} y[x/u]\ (y[x/u]) \ \equiv_{\sigma_2,\sigma_3,\alpha}$$
$$(y\ y)[x_1/u][x/u] \qquad\qquad\qquad\quad \equiv_{\sigma_4} (y\ y)[x_1/u[x/u]]$$

i.e. t reduces to a term containing t. Now, take $(\lambda x.((\lambda z.zz)y))\ ((\lambda z.zz)y) \in \mathcal{SN}_\beta$ which reduces to t, so that it is no longer strongly normalising in the $\lambda\mathtt{j}$-calculus extended by the five previous equations $\{\mathsf{CS}, \sigma_1, \sigma_2, \sigma_3, \sigma_4\}$.

Such a counter-example can be avoided imposing the constraint "$x \in \mathtt{fv}(v)$" to σ_3 and σ_4 (note that such constraint is also found in the definition of the boxing system). Nevertheless, $\lambda\mathtt{j}$-reduction modulo the *constrained* equivalences $\{\mathsf{CS}, \sigma_1, \sigma_2, \sigma_3, \sigma_4\}$ is an incredibly subtle and complex relation. For instance, w-steps cannot be postponed, nor can the use of equivalences. Two natural canonical representations of the equivalence classes are obtained by pushing jumps towards the variables, or as far away from them as possible. None of them is stable by reduction, so working with equivalence classes is impossible. The PSN property for this calculus, if it holds, is very challenging.

One of the difficulties is that the equivalence $\{\mathsf{CS}, \sigma_1, \sigma_2, \sigma_3, \sigma_4\}$ is not a bisimulation: the reducts $(xx_1)[x/y[y/z]][x_1/y[y/z]]$ of $t_2 = (xx)[x/y[y/z]]$ and $(xx_1)[x/y][x_1/y][y/z]$ of $t_3 = (xx)[x/y][y/z]$ are no longer equivalent. Nevertheless, t_2 and t_3 share the same normal form, and thus are still operationally equivalent, but in a weaker sense.

From here on we use the letter p to denote a **parameter** which represents any of the propagation systems $\{\mathsf{b}, \mathsf{u}\}$. For every $\mathsf{p} \in \{\mathsf{b}, \mathsf{u}\}$ we consider its associated **structural reduction system** $\lambda\mathtt{j}_\mathsf{p}/\mathsf{o}$, written $\lambda\mathtt{j}_\mathsf{b}/\mathsf{o}$ and $\lambda\mathtt{j}_\mathsf{u}/\mathsf{o}$ respectively, defined by the reduction relation $\mathsf{dB} \cup \mathtt{j} \cup \mathsf{p}$ modulo the equivalence relation o, a relation which is denoted by $(\mathsf{dB} \cup \mathtt{j} \cup \mathsf{p})/\mathsf{o}$. Both structural systems have good properties. By interpreting t into $\mathtt{j}(t)$ and using Theorem 1 we get:

Theorem 4 (Confluence Modulo). *For all $t_1, t_2 \in \mathcal{T}$, if $t_1 \equiv_\mathsf{o} t_2$ and $t_i \rightarrow^*_{\lambda\mathtt{j}_\mathsf{p}/\mathsf{o}}$ u_i $(i = 1, 2)$, then $\exists v_i$ $(i = 1, 2)$ s.t. $u_i \rightarrow^*_{\lambda\mathtt{j}} v_i$ $(i = 1, 2)$ and $v_1 \equiv_\mathsf{o} v_2$.*

To prove PSN for $\lambda\mathtt{j}_\mathsf{b}/\mathsf{o}$ and $\lambda\mathtt{j}_\mathsf{u}/\mathsf{o}$ it is sufficient, according to Theorem 2, to show the **IE** property. However, a simple inductive argument like the one used for $\lambda\mathtt{j}$-reduction relation does no longer work. Therefore we shall show the **IE** property by adapting the technique in [13]. This has proven a challenging venture, so that this section presents the perhaps most important technical achievement in this paper. We split the proof into the following steps:

1. Define a labelling to mark some $\lambda\mathtt{j}_\mathsf{p}/\mathsf{o}$-strongly normalising terms used within jumps. Thus for example $t[\![x/u]\!]$ means that $u \in \mathcal{T}$ and $u \in \mathcal{SN}_{\lambda\mathtt{j}_\mathsf{p}/\mathsf{o}}$.

2. Enrich the original $\lambda\mathtt{j}_\mathtt{p}/\mathtt{o}$-reduction system with a relation used only to propagate terminating labelled jumps. Let $\mathcal{J}_\mathtt{p}/\mathtt{O}$ be the resulting calculus.
3. Show that $u \in \mathcal{SN}_{\lambda\mathtt{j}_\mathtt{p}/\mathtt{o}}$ and $t\{x/u\}\overline{v}^1_n \in \mathcal{SN}_{\lambda\mathtt{j}_\mathtt{p}/\mathtt{o}}$ imply $t[\![x/u]\!]\overline{v}^1_n \in \mathcal{SN}_{\mathcal{J}_\mathtt{p}/\mathtt{O}}$.
4. Show that $t[\![x/u]\!]\overline{v}^1_n \in \mathcal{SN}_{\mathcal{J}_\mathtt{p}/\mathtt{O}}$ implies $t[x/u]\overline{v}^1_n \in \mathcal{SN}_{\lambda\mathtt{j}_\mathtt{p}/\mathtt{o}}$.

In Sections 6.1 and 6.2 points 1 and 2 are developed, while Section 6.3 deals with points 3 and 4.

6.1 The Labelled Systems

Each labelled system is defined by a set of labelled terms together with a set of reduction rules and axioms.

Definition 1 (Labelled Terms). *Let* $\mathtt{p} \in \{\mathtt{b}, \mathtt{u}\}$. *The set* $\mathbb{T}_\mathtt{p}$ *of* **labelled p-terms** *is generated using the following grammar:*

$$t ::= x \mid tt \mid \lambda x.t \mid t[x/t] \mid t[\![x/v]\!] \;\; (v \in \mathcal{T} \cap \mathcal{SN}_{\lambda\mathtt{j}_\mathtt{p}/\mathtt{o}})$$

Now consider the following reduction subsystems:

The **Labelled Equations** $\underline{\mathtt{CS}}$

if $y \notin \mathtt{fv}(u)$ & $x \notin \mathtt{fv}(v)$:

$$t[\![x/u]\!][y/v] \equiv_{\underline{\mathtt{CS}}_1} t[y/v][\![x/u]\!]$$
$$t[\![x/u]\!][\![y/v]\!] \equiv_{\underline{\mathtt{CS}}_2} t[\![y/v]\!][\![x/u]\!]$$

The **Labelled Unboxing** system $\underline{\mathtt{u}}$

if $x \notin \mathtt{fv}(t)$ & $x \in \mathtt{fv}(v)$:

$$tv[\![x/u]\!] \to_{\underline{\mathtt{au}}} (tv)[\![x/u]\!]$$
$$t[y/v[\![x/u]\!]] \to_{\underline{\mathtt{su}}_1} t[y/v][\![x/u]\!]$$
$$t[\![y/v[x/u]]\!] \to_{\underline{\mathtt{su}}_2} t[\![y/v]\!][\![x/u]\!]$$

The **Generalised** $\mathtt{dB}$ **rule**

$$(\lambda x.t)\mathbb{L}u \to_{\mathtt{gdB}} t[x/u]\mathbb{L}$$

The **Labelled Equations** $\underline{\sigma}$

$$(\lambda y.t)[\![x/u]\!] \equiv_{\underline{\sigma}_1} \lambda y.t[\![x/u]\!] \quad \text{if } y \notin \mathtt{fv}(u)$$
$$(tv)[\![x/u]\!] \equiv_{\underline{\sigma}_2} t[\![x/u]\!]v \quad \text{if } x \notin \mathtt{fv}(v)$$

The **Labelled Boxing** system $\underline{\mathtt{b}}$

if $x \in \mathtt{fv}(v)$:

$$(tv)[\![x/u]\!] \to_{\underline{\mathtt{ab}}} tv[\![x/u]\!]$$
$$t[y/v][\![x/u]\!] \to_{\underline{\mathtt{sb}}} t[y/v[\![x/u]\!]]$$

The **Labelled Jumping** system $\underline{\mathtt{j}}$

$$t[\![x/u]\!] \to_{\underline{\mathtt{w}}} t \quad \text{if } |t|_x = 0$$
$$t[\![x/u]\!] \to_{\underline{\mathtt{d}}} t\{x/u\} \quad \text{if } |t|_x = 1$$
$$t[\![x/u]\!] \to_{\underline{\mathtt{c}}} t_{[y]_x}[\![x/u]\!][\![y/u]\!] \quad \text{if } |t|_x \geq 2$$

where $\mathbb{L}$ is a list of jumps, some of which, potentially all, may be labelled. Note that $\mathtt{dB}$-reduction on the set $\mathcal{T}$ just is a particular case of $\mathtt{gdB}$-reduction on $\mathbb{T}_\mathtt{p}$. The **equivalence relation** $\underline{\alpha}$ (resp. $\underline{\mathtt{o}}$) is generated by axiom α (resp. $\{\underline{\alpha}, \underline{\mathtt{CS}}, \underline{\sigma}\}$) on labelled terms. The **equivalence relation** $\mathtt{O}$ is generated by $\mathtt{o} \cup \underline{\mathtt{o}}$. The **reduction relation** $\mathcal{J}_\mathtt{p}$ (resp. $\mathcal{J}_\mathtt{p}/\mathtt{O}$) is generated by $(\mathtt{gdB} \cup \mathtt{j} \cup \underline{\mathtt{j}} \cup \mathtt{p} \cup \underline{\mathtt{p}})$ (resp. $\mathtt{gdB} \cup \mathtt{j} \cup \underline{\mathtt{j}} \cup \mathtt{p} \cup \underline{\mathtt{p}}$ modulo $\mathtt{O}$). The relation $\mathcal{J}_\mathtt{p}$ can be understood as the union of two disjoint reduction relations, respectively called forgettable and persistent. Forgettable reductions do not create persistent redexes, and they are strongly normalising (Lemma 6). These two facts imply that termination of $\mathcal{J}_\mathtt{p}$ does not depend on its forgettable subsystem.

The **forgettable** reduction relation $\to_{\mathtt{Fp}}$:

- If $t \to_{\underline{\mathtt{j}},\underline{\mathtt{p}}} t'$, then $t \to_{\mathtt{Fp}} t'$.
- If $v \to_{\lambda\mathtt{j}_\mathtt{p}/\mathtt{o}} v'$, then $u[\![x/v]\!] \to_{\mathtt{Fp}} u[\![x/v']\!]$.
- If $t \to_{\mathtt{Fp}} t'$, then $tu \to_{\mathtt{Fp}} t'u$, $ut \to_{\mathtt{Fp}} ut'$, $\lambda x.t \to_{\mathtt{Fp}} \lambda x.t'$, $t[x/u] \to_{\mathtt{Fp}} t'[x/u]$, $u[x/t] \to_{\mathtt{Fp}} u[x/t']$ and $t[\![x/u]\!] \to_{\mathtt{Fp}} t'[\![x/u]\!]$.

The **persistent** reduction relation $\to_{\mathsf{Pp}}$:

- If $t \mapsto_{\mathsf{gdB},\mathsf{j},\mathsf{p}} t'$ (where $\mapsto$ denotes root reduction), then $t \to_{\mathsf{Pp}} t'$.
- If $t \to_{\mathsf{Pp}} t'$, then $tu \to_{\mathsf{Pp}} t'u$, $ut \to_{\mathsf{Pp}} ut'$, $\lambda x.t \to_{\mathsf{Pp}} \lambda x.t'$, $t[x/u] \to_{\mathsf{Pp}} t'[x/u]$, $u[x/t] \to_{\mathsf{Pp}} u[x/t']$ and $t[\![x/u]\!] \to_{\mathsf{Pp}} t'[\![x/u]\!]$.

6.2   Well-Formed Labelled Terms

In order to prove that the $\lambda\mathsf{j}_{\mathsf{p}}/\mathsf{o}$-calculus enjoys PSN, according to Theorem 2 it is sufficient to show the **IE**-property. The reasoning for that is splitted in two steps: we first show that $u \in \mathcal{SN}_{\lambda\mathsf{j}_{\mathsf{p}}/\mathsf{o}}$ and $t\{x/u\}\overline{v}_n^1 \in \mathcal{SN}_{\lambda\mathsf{j}_{\mathsf{p}}/\mathsf{o}}$ imply $t[\![x/u]\!]\overline{v}_n^1 \in \mathcal{SN}_{\mathcal{J}_{\mathsf{p}}/\mathsf{o}}$ (Corollary 6), thereafter we prove that $t[\![x/u]\!]\overline{v}_n^1 \in \mathcal{SN}_{\mathcal{J}_{\mathsf{p}}/\mathsf{o}}$ implies $t[x/u]\overline{v}_n^1 \in \mathcal{SN}_{\lambda\mathsf{j}_{\mathsf{p}}/\mathsf{o}}$ (Corollary 7).

The first implication is much more difficult to prove, particularly because termination of the forgettable subsystem F_{p}, proved using a strictly decreasing measure on labelled terms, is required. This measure is based on the assumption that all terms inside labelled jumps are $\lambda\mathsf{j}_{\mathsf{p}}/\mathsf{o}$-strongly normalising w.r.t. the environment in which they are evaluated. Moreover, this property of labelled jumps needs to be preserved by reduction and equivalence. We concretely formalise this using the following key notions.

The set of **labelled free variables** of $t \in \mathbb{T}_{\mathsf{p}}$ is given by:

$$
\begin{aligned}
&\mathbb{L}\mathtt{fv}(x) && := [\,] && \mathbb{L}\mathtt{fv}(u[x/v]) := (\mathbb{L}\mathtt{fv}(u) \setminus \{x\}) \cup \mathbb{L}\mathtt{fv}(v) \\
&\mathbb{L}\mathtt{fv}(uv) && := \mathbb{L}\mathtt{fv}(u) \cup \mathbb{L}\mathtt{fv}(v) && \mathbb{L}\mathtt{fv}(u[\![x/v]\!]) := (\mathbb{L}\mathtt{fv}(u) \setminus \{x\}) \cup \mathtt{fv}(v) \\
&\mathbb{L}\mathtt{fv}(\lambda x.u) := \mathbb{L}\mathtt{fv}(u) \setminus \{x\}
\end{aligned}
$$

Note that $u \in \mathcal{T}$ implies $\mathbb{L}\mathtt{fv}(u) = [\,]$ and also $\mathbb{L}\mathtt{fv}(t) \subseteq \mathtt{fv}(t)$. Moreover, if $t \equiv_0 u$ then $\mathbb{L}\mathtt{fv}(t) = \mathbb{L}\mathtt{fv}(u)$, and if $t \to_{\mathcal{J}_{\mathsf{p}}} u$ then $\mathbb{L}\mathtt{fv}(t) \supseteq \mathbb{L}\mathtt{fv}(u)$.

A labelled term $t \in \mathbb{T}_{\mathsf{p}}$ is SN-**labelled** for a substitution γ iff $\mathtt{SNL}_{\mathsf{p}}(t, \gamma)$ holds:

$$
\begin{aligned}
&\mathtt{SNL}_{\mathsf{p}}(x, \gamma) && := \mathtt{true} && \mathtt{SNL}_{\mathsf{p}}(tu, \gamma) && := \mathtt{SNL}_{\mathsf{p}}(t, \gamma) \;\&\; \mathtt{SNL}_{\mathsf{p}}(u, \gamma) \\
&\mathtt{SNL}_{\mathsf{p}}(\lambda x.t, \gamma) := \mathtt{SNL}_{\mathsf{p}}(t, \gamma) && \mathtt{SNL}_{\mathsf{p}}(t[x/u], \gamma) && := \mathtt{SNL}_{\mathsf{p}}(t, \gamma) \;\&\; \mathtt{SNL}_{\mathsf{p}}(u, \gamma) \\
& && \mathtt{SNL}_{\mathsf{p}}(t[\![x/u]\!], \gamma) && := \mathtt{SNL}_{\mathsf{p}}(t, \{x/u\}\gamma) \;\&\; u\gamma \in \mathcal{SN}_{\lambda\mathsf{j}_{\mathsf{p}}/\mathsf{o}}
\end{aligned}
$$

A p-labelled term t is **p-well-formed**, written $t \in \mathbb{WF}_{\mathsf{p}}$, iff **(1)** $\mathtt{SNL}_{\mathsf{p}}(t, [\,])$ **(2)** every subterm $u[y/v]$ or $\lambda y.u$ in t verifies $y \notin \mathbb{L}\mathtt{fv}(u)$ **(3)** $\mathsf{p} = \mathsf{b}$ implies subterms $u[\![y/v]\!] \in t$ verify $y \notin \mathbb{L}\mathtt{fv}(u)$. Thus for example $t_0 = (xx)[\![x/y]\!][\![y/z]\!]$ is not b-well-formed since y is not a labelled free variable of t_0, whereas t_0 is u-well-formed since $z \in \mathcal{SN}_{\lambda\mathsf{j}_{\mathsf{u}}/\mathsf{o}}$. Also, $t_1 = y[y/x][x/\lambda z.zz]$ is b and u well-formed but $t_2 = y[\![y/xx]\!][x/\lambda z.zz]$ is not. More precisely, x is a labelled free variable of $y[\![y/xx]\!]$ so that t_2 is not b-well-formed, and $\mathtt{SNL}_{\mathsf{u}}(t_2, \emptyset)$ does not hold (since $(\lambda z.zz)(\lambda z.zz) \notin \mathcal{SN}_{\lambda\mathsf{j}_{\mathsf{u}}/\mathsf{o}}$) hence t_2 is not u-well-formed.

SN-labelled (and well-formed) terms are stable by equivalence and reduction.

Lemma 5. *Let* $\mathtt{SNL}_{\mathsf{p}}(t_0, \gamma)$. *If* $t_0 \equiv_0 t_1$ *or* $t_0 \to_{\mathcal{J}_{\mathsf{p}}} t_1$, *then* $\mathtt{SNL}_{\mathsf{p}}(t_1, \gamma)$.

Corollary 5. *Let* $t \in \mathbb{WF}_{\mathsf{p}}$. *If* $t \equiv_0 t'$ *or* $t \to_{\mathcal{J}_{\mathsf{p}}} t'$, *then* $t' \in \mathbb{WF}_{\mathsf{p}}$.

The given corollary is essential in developing the termination proofs for the forgettable relations $\mathsf{F}_{\mathsf{b}}/\mathsf{O}$ and $\mathsf{F}_{\mathsf{u}}/\mathsf{O}$. More precisely, for each forgettable reduction $\mathsf{F}_{\mathsf{p}}/\mathsf{O}$, with $\mathsf{p} \in \{\mathsf{b}, \mathsf{u}\}$, we define a measure on p-well-formed labelled terms which strictly decreases by $\mathsf{F}_{\mathsf{p}}/\mathsf{O}$-reduction. For lack of space we relegate the proof to [2].

Lemma 6. *The relation* $\to_{\mathrm{F_b}/\mathrm{O}}$ *(resp.* $\to_{\mathrm{F_u}/\mathrm{O}}$*) is terminating on* $\mathrm{WF_b}$ *(resp.* $\mathrm{WF_u}$*).*

6.3   From Implicit to Explicit through Labelled

To show our first point, namely, that $u \in \mathcal{SN}_{\lambda \mathrm{j_p}/\mathrm{o}}$ and $t\{x/u\}\overline{v}_n^1 \in \mathcal{SN}_{\lambda \mathrm{j_p}/\mathrm{o}}$ imply $t[\![x/u]\!]\overline{v}_n^1 \in \mathcal{SN}_{\mathcal{J_p}/\mathrm{O}}$, we now consider the following projection function $\mathbb{P}(\_)$ from labelled terms to terms, which also projects $\mathcal{J_p}/\mathrm{O}$ into the reduction $\lambda \mathrm{j_p}/\mathrm{o}$:

$$\mathbb{P}(x) := x \qquad \begin{aligned} \mathbb{P}(\lambda x.t) &:= \lambda x.\mathbb{P}(t) \\ \mathbb{P}(tu) &:= \mathbb{P}(t)\mathbb{P}(u) \end{aligned} \qquad \begin{aligned} \mathbb{P}(t[x/u]) &:= \mathbb{P}(t)[x/\mathbb{P}(u)] \\ \mathbb{P}(t[\![x/u]\!]) &:= \mathbb{P}(t)\{x/u\} \end{aligned}$$

Note that $u \in \mathcal{T}$ implies $\mathbb{P}(u) = u$.

Lemma 7. *Let* $t_0 \in \mathbb{T_p}$*. Then,*

1. $t_0 \equiv_0 t_1$ *implies* $\mathbb{P}(t_0) \equiv_0 \mathbb{P}(t_1)$.
2. $t_0 \to_{\mathrm{F_p}} t_1$ *implies* $\mathbb{P}(t_0) \to_{\lambda \mathrm{j_p}/\mathrm{o}}^* \mathbb{P}(t_1)$.
3. $t_0 \to_{\mathrm{P_p}} t_1$ *implies* $\mathbb{P}(t_0) \to_{\lambda \mathrm{j_p}/\mathrm{o}}^+ \mathbb{P}(t_1)$.

Proof. By induction on labelled terms. The case $t_0 \to_{\underline{\mathrm{su}}_2} t_1$ uses Lemma 1.

Lemma 8. *Let* $t \in \mathrm{WF_p}$*. If* $\mathbb{P}(t) \in \mathcal{SN}_{\lambda \mathrm{j_p}/\mathrm{o}}$*, then* $t \in \mathcal{SN}_{\mathcal{J_p}/\mathrm{o}}$*.*

Proof. Since $\to_{\mathcal{J_p}} = \to_{\mathrm{F_p}} \cup \to_{\mathrm{P_p}}$ we show that $t \in \mathcal{SN}_{\mathrm{F_p} \cup \mathrm{P_p}/\mathrm{o}}$ by using Lemma 7 and termination of the forgettable relations (Lemma 6).

Now let $\mathrm{p} \in \{\mathrm{b}, \mathrm{u}\}$ and consider $t, u, \overline{v}_n^1 \in \mathcal{T}$ s.t. $u \in \mathcal{SN}_{\lambda \mathrm{j_p}/\mathrm{o}}$. We immediately get $t[\![x/u]\!]\overline{v}_n^1 \in \mathrm{WF_p}$. Using $\mathbb{P}(t[\![x/u]\!]\overline{v}_n^1) = t\{x/u\}\overline{v}_n^1$ we thus conclude:

Corollary 6. *Let* $t, u, \overline{v}_n^1 \in \mathcal{T}$*. If* $u \in \mathcal{SN}_{\lambda \mathrm{j_p}/\mathrm{o}}$ & $t\{x/u\}\overline{v}_n^1 \in \mathcal{SN}_{\lambda \mathrm{j_p}/\mathrm{o}}$*, then* $t[\![x/u]\!]\overline{v}_n^1 \in \mathcal{SN}_{\mathcal{J_p}/\mathrm{O}}$*.*

The last point of our proof is to show that $t[\![x/u]\!]\overline{v}_n^1 \in \mathcal{SN}_{\mathcal{J_p}/\mathrm{O}}$ implies $t[x/u]\overline{v}_n^1 \in \mathcal{SN}_{\lambda \mathrm{j_p}/\mathrm{o}}$ by relating labelled terms and reductions to unlabelled terms and reductions. To do that, let us introduce an **unlabelling function on labelled terms**:

$$\mathrm{U}(x) := x \qquad \begin{aligned} \mathrm{U}(\lambda x.t) &:= \lambda x.\mathrm{U}(t) \\ \mathrm{U}(tu) &:= \mathrm{U}(t)\mathrm{U}(u) \end{aligned} \qquad \begin{aligned} \mathrm{U}(t[x/u]) &:= \mathrm{U}(t)[x/\mathrm{U}(u)] \\ \mathrm{U}(t[\![x/u]\!]) &:= \mathrm{U}(t)[x/u] \end{aligned}$$

There is a one-to-one correspondence between labelled and unlabelled reduction. Moreover, well-formed labelled terms are essential here to get the following:

Lemma 9. *Let* $t \in \mathrm{WF_p}$*. If* $t \in \mathcal{SN}_{\mathcal{J_p}/\mathrm{O}}$*, then* $\mathrm{U}(t) \in \mathcal{SN}_{\lambda \mathrm{j_p}/\mathrm{o}}$*.*

Proof. We prove $\mathrm{U}(t) \in \mathcal{SN}_{\lambda \mathrm{j_p}/\mathrm{o}}$ by induction on $\eta_{\mathcal{J_p}/\mathrm{O}}(t)$. This is done by considering all the $\lambda \mathrm{j_p}/\mathrm{o}$-reducts of $\mathrm{U}(t)$ and using the following: if $t \in \mathrm{WF_p}$ and $\mathrm{U}(t) \to_{\lambda \mathrm{j_p}/\mathrm{o}} u$, then $\exists\, v \in \mathrm{WF_p}$ s.t. $t \to_{\mathcal{J_p}/\mathrm{O}} v$ and $\mathrm{U}(v) = u$.

394   B. Accattoli and D. Kesner

Now let $p \in \{b, u\}$ and consider $t, u, \overline{v}_n^1 \in \mathcal{T}$ s.t. $u \in \mathcal{SN}_{\lambda j_p/o}$. We immediately get $t[\![x/u]\!]\overline{v}_n^1 \in \mathbb{WF}_p$. Using $\mathbb{U}(t[\![x/u]\!]\overline{v}_n^1) = t[x/u]\overline{v}_n^1$ we thus conclude:

Corollary 7. *Let $t, u, \overline{v}_n^1 \in \mathcal{T}$. If $t[\![x/u]\!]\overline{v}_n^1 \in \mathbb{WF}_p \cap \mathcal{SN}_{\mathcal{J}_p/0}$, then $t[x/u]\overline{v}_n^1 \in \mathcal{SN}_{\lambda j_p/o}$.*

From Corollaries 6 and 7 we get:

Lemma 10 (IE for $\lambda j_p/o$). *For $p \in \{b, u\}$, $\lambda j_p/o$ enjoys the* **IE** *property.*

Theorem 2 thus allows us to conclude with the main result of this section:

Corollary 8 (PSN for $\lambda j_p/o$). *For $p \in \{b, u\}$, $\lambda j_p/o$ enjoys PSN.*

7 Conclusions

We have introduced the structural λj-calculus, a concise but expressive λ-calculus with jumps. No prior knowledge of Linear Logic is necessary to understand λj, despite their strong connection. We have established many different sanity properties for λj such as confluence and PSN. We have used λj as an operational framework to elaborate new characterisations of the well-known notions of full developments and L-developments, and to obtain the new, more powerful notion of XL-development. Finally, we have modularly added commutation of independent jumps, σ-equivalence and two kinds of propagations of jumps, while showing that PSN still holds.

As noted in Section 6, PSN for the λj-calculus plus the constrained equivalences $\{CS, \sigma_1, \sigma_2, \sigma_3, \sigma_4\}$ is - at present - a challenging conjecture. Indeed, the merging of the two similar, yet different uses of $\{\sigma_3, \sigma_4\}$ that we study in this paper presents several non-trivial difficulties. A further in-depth re-elaboration of the labelling technique would be necessary, perhaps even the use of a completely different technique dealing with reduction modulo a set of equations.

An interesting research direction is the study of linear head reduction [3] for λ-calculus - which is closely connected to game semantics and abstract machines - whose formulation is not a strategy in the usual sense. Indeed, jumps and distance permit to reformulate linear head reduction as a strategy of λj.

It would also be interesting to exploit distance and multiplicities in other frameworks for example when dealing with pattern matching, continuations or differential features.

References

1. Accattoli, B., Guerrini, S.: Jumping boxes. representing lambda-calculus boxes by jumps. In: Grädel, E., Kahle, R. (eds.) CSL 2009. LNCS, vol. 5771, pp. 55–70. Springer, Heidelberg (2009)
2. Accattoli, B., Kesner, D.: The structural calculus λj. Technical report, PPS, CNRS and University Paris-Diderot (2010)
3. Danos, V., Regnier, L.: Reversible, irreversible and optimal lambda-machines. TCS 227(1), 79–97 (1999)
4. David, R., Guillaume, B.: A λ-calculus with explicit weakening and explicit substitution. MSCS 11, 169–206 (2001)

5. de Bruijn, N.G.: Generalizing Automath by Means of a Lambda-Typed Lambda Calculus. In: Mathematical Logic and Theoretical Computer Science. Lecture Notes in Pure and Applied Mathematics, vol. 106, pp. 71–92. Marcel Dekker, New York (1987)
6. de Moor, O., Sittampalam, G.: Higher-order matching for program transformation. TCS 269(1-2), 135–162 (2001)
7. Di Cosmo, R., Kesner, D., Polonovski, E.: Proof nets and explicit substitutions. MSCS 13(3), 409–450 (2003)
8. Faure, G.: Matching modulo superdevelopments application to second-order matching. In: Hermann, M., Voronkov, A. (eds.) LPAR 2006. LNCS (LNAI), vol. 4246, pp. 60–74. Springer, Heidelberg (2006)
9. Girard, J.-Y.: Linear logic. TCS 50 (1987)
10. Girard, J.-Y.: Geometry of interaction i: an interpretation of system f. In: Proc. of the Logic Colloquim, vol. 88, pp. 221–260 (1989)
11. Herbelin, H., Zimmermann, S.: An operational account of call-by-value minimal and classical lambda-calculus in "natural deduction" form. In: Curien, P.-L. (ed.) TLCA 2009. LNCS, vol. 5608, pp. 142–156. Springer, Heidelberg (2009)
12. Hindley, J.R.: Reductions of residuals are finite. Transactions of the American Mathematical Society 240, 345–361 (1978)
13. Kesner, D.: The theory of calculi with explicit substitutions revisited. In: Duparc, J., Henzinger, T.A. (eds.) CSL 2007. LNCS, vol. 4646, pp. 238–252. Springer, Heidelberg (2007)
14. Kesner, D.: A theory of explicit substitutions with safe and full composition. LMCS 5(3:1), 1–29 (2009)
15. Kesner, D., Lengrand, S.: Resource operators for lambda-calculus. I & C 205(4), 419–473 (2007)
16. Kesner, D., Renaud, F.: The prismoid of resources. In: Královič, R., Niwiński, D. (eds.) MFCS 2009. LNCS, vol. 5734, pp. 464–476. Springer, Heidelberg (2009)
17. Klop, J.-W., van Oostrom, V., van Raamsdonk, F.: Combinatory reduction systems: introduction and survey. TCS 121(1/2), 279–308 (1993)
18. Lévy, J.-J.: Réductions correctes et optimales dans le lambda-calcul. PhD thesis, Univ. Paris VII, France (1978)
19. Lévy, J.-J., Maranget, L.: Explicit substitutions and programming languages. In: Pandu Rangan, C., Raman, V., Sarukkai, S. (eds.) FSTTCS 1999. LNCS, vol. 1738, pp. 181–200. Springer, Heidelberg (1999)
20. Maraist, J., Odersky, M., Turner, D.N., Wadler, P.: Call-by-name, call-by-value, call-by-need and the linear lambda calculus. TCS 228(1-2), 175–210 (1999)
21. Milner, R.: Local bigraphs and confluence: two conjectures. In: Proc. of 13th EXPRESS. ENTCS, vol. 175. Elsevier, Amsterdam (2006)
22. Nederpelt, R.P.: The fine-structure of lambda calculus. Technical Report CSN 92/07, Eindhoven Univ. of Technology (1992)
23. Ó Conchúir, S.: Proving PSN by simulating non-local substitutions with local substitution. In: Proceedings of the 3rd HOR, August 2006, pp. 37–42 (2006)
24. Ohta, Y., Hasegawa, M.: A terminating and confluent linear lambda calculus. In: Pfenning, F. (ed.) RTA 2006. LNCS, vol. 4098, pp. 166–180. Springer, Heidelberg (2006)
25. Regnier, L.: Lambda-calcul et réseaux. Thèse de doctorat, Univ. Paris VII (1992)
26. Regnier, L.: Une équivalence sur les lambda-termes. TCS 2(126), 281–292 (1994)
27. Schwichtenberg, H.: Termination of permutative conversions in intuitionistic Gentzen calculi. TCS 212(1-2), 247–260 (1999)
28. Severi, P., Poll, E.: Pure type systems with definitions. In: Matiyasevich, Y.V., Nerode, A. (eds.) LFCS 1994. LNCS, vol. 813, pp. 316–328. Springer, Heidelberg (1994)
29. van Raamsdonk, F.: Confluence and Normalization for Higher-Order Rewriting. PhD thesis, Amsterdam Univ., Netherlands (1996)

The Isomorphism Problem for ω-Automatic Trees

Dietrich Kuske[1], Jiamou Liu[2], and Markus Lohrey[2,*]

[1] Laboratoire Bordelais de Recherche en Informatique (LaBRI), CNRS and Université
Bordeaux I, Bordeaux, France
[2] Universität Leipzig, Institut für Informatik, Germany
kuske@labri.fr, liujiamou@gmail.com,
lohrey@informatik.uni-leipzig.de

Abstract. The main result of this paper is that the isomorphism problem for ω-automatic trees of finite height is at least as hard as second-order arithmetic and therefore not analytical. This strengthens a recent result by Hjorth, Khoussainov, Montalbán, and Nies [9] showing that the isomorphism problem for ω-automatic structures is not Σ_2^1. Moreover, assuming the continuum hypothesis **CH**, we can show that the isomorphism problem for ω-automatic trees of finite height is recursively equivalent with second-order arithmetic. On the way to our main results, we show lower and upper bounds for the isomorphism problem for ω-automatic trees of every finite height: (i) It is decidable (Π_1^0-complete, resp.) for height 1 (2, resp.), (ii) Π_1^1-hard and in Π_2^1 for height 3, and (iii) Π_{n-3}^1- and Σ_{n-3}^1-hard and in Π_{2n-4}^1 (assuming **CH**) for all $n \geq 4$. All proofs are elementary and do not rely on theorems from set theory. Complete proofs can be found in [18].

1 Introduction

A graph is computable if its domain is a computable set of natural numbers and the edge relation is computable as well. Hence, one can compute effectively in the graph. On the other hand, practically all other properties are undecidable for computable graphs (e.g., reachability, connectedness, and even the existence of isolated nodes). In particular, the isomorphism problem is highly undecidable in the sense that it is complete for Σ_1^1 (the first existential level of the analytical hierarchy [21, Chapter IV.2]); see e.g. [3, 8] for further investigations of the isomorphism problem for computable structures. These algorithmic deficiencies have motivated in computer science the study of more restricted classes of finitely presented infinite graphs. For instance, pushdown graphs, equational graphs, and prefix recognizable graphs have a decidable monadic second-order theory and for the former two the isomorphism problem is known to be decidable [5] (for prefix recognizable graphs the status of the isomorphism problem seems to be open).

Automatic graphs [13] are between prefix recognizable and computable graphs. In essence, a graph is automatic if the elements of the universe can be represented as strings from a regular language and the edge relation can be recognized by a finite state automaton with several heads that proceed synchronously. Automatic graphs (and more general, automatic structures) received increasing interest over the last years [2, 10, 14, 15, 24]. One of the main motivations for investigating automatic graphs is

---

* The second and third author are supported by the DFG research project GELO.

A. Dawar and H. Veith (Eds.): CSL 2010, LNCS 6247, pp. 396–410, 2010.
© Springer-Verlag Berlin Heidelberg 2010

that their first-order theories can be decided uniformly (i.e., the input is an automatic presentation and a first-order sentence). On the other hand, the isomorphism problem for automatic graphs is Σ_1^1-complete [14] and hence as complex as for computable graphs.

In our recent paper [17], we studied the isomorphism problem for restricted classes of automatic graphs. Among other results, we proved that (i) the isomorphism problem for automatic trees of height at most $n \geq 2$ is complete for the level Π_{2n-3}^0 of the arithmetical hierarchy and (ii) that the isomorphism problem for automatic trees of finite height is recursively equivalent to true arithmetic. In this paper, we extend our techniques from [17] to ω-*automatic trees*. The class of ω-automatic structures was introduced in [1]. It generalizes automatic structures by replacing ordinary finite automata by Büchi automata on ω-words. In this way, uncountable graphs can be specified. Some recent results on ω-automatic structures can be found in [19,9,11,16]. On the logical side, many of the positive results for automatic structures carry over to ω-automatic structures [1, 11]. On the other hand, the isomorphism problem of ω-automatic structures is more complicated than that of automatic structures (which is Σ_1^1-complete). Hjorth et al. [9] constructed two ω-automatic structures for which the existence of an isomorphism depends on the axioms of set theory. Using Shoenfield's absoluteness theorem, they infer that isomorphism of ω-automatic structures does not belong to Σ_2^1. Also using Shoenfield's absoluteness theorem, Finkel and Todorčević [7] recently showed that the isomorphism problems of ω-tree-automatic[1] partial orders, Boolean algebras, rings, and non-commutative groups are not in the class Σ_2^1.

The extension of our elementary techniques from [17] to ω-automatic trees allows us to show directly (without a "detour" through set theory) that the isomorphism problem for ω-automatic trees of finite height is not analytical (i.e., does not belong to any of the levels Σ_n^1). For this, we prove that the isomorphism problem for ω-automatic trees of height $n \geq 4$ is hard for both levels Σ_{n-3}^1 and Π_{n-3}^1 of the analytical hierarchy (our proof is uniform in n). A more precise analysis reveals at which height the complexity jump for ω-automatic trees occurs: For automatic as well as for ω-automatic trees of height 2, the isomorphism problem is Π_1^0-complete and hence arithmetical. But the isomorphism problem for ω-automatic trees of height 3 is hard for Π_1^1 (and therefore outside of the arithmetical hierarchy) while the isomorphism problem for automatic trees of height 3 is Π_3^0-complete [17].

We prove our results by reductions from monadic second-order (fragments of) number theory. The first step in the proof is a normal form for analytical predicates. The basic idea of the reduction then is that a subset $X \subseteq \mathbb{N}$ can be encoded by an ω-word w_X over $\{0, 1\}$, where the ith symbol is 1 if and only if $i \in X$. The combination of this basic observation with our techniques from [17] allows us to encode monadic second-order formulas over $(\mathbb{N}, +, \times)$ by ω-automatic trees of finite height. This yields the lower bounds mentioned above. We also give an upper bound for the isomorphism problem: for ω-automatic trees of height n, the isomorphism problem belongs to Π_{2n-4}^1. While the lower bound holds in the usual system **ZFC** of set theory, we can prove the upper bound only assuming in addition the continuum hypothesis. The precise recursion

---

[1] An ω-tree-automatic structure is a structure whose elements are coded as infinite trees and whose universe and relations are accepted by Muller or Rabin tree automata.

theoretic complexity of the isomorphism problem for ω-automatic trees remains open, it might depend on the underlying axioms for set theory.

Related work. Results on isomorphism problems for various subclasses of automatic structures can be found in [7, 14, 15, 17, 23]. Some completeness results for low levels of the analytical hierarchy for decision problems on infinitary rational relations were shown in [6].

2   Preliminaries

Let $\mathbb{N}_+ = \{1, 2, 3, \ldots\}$. With $\bar{x}$ we denote a tuple $(x_1, \ldots, x_m)$ of variables, whose length m does not matter.

The arithmetical and analytical hierarchy: In this paper we follow the definitions of the arithmetical and analytical hierarchy from [21, Chapter IV.1 and IV.2]. In order to avoid some technical complications, it is useful to exclude 0 in the following, i.e., to consider subsets of $\mathbb{N}_+$. In the following, f_i ranges over unary functions on $\mathbb{N}_+$, X_i over subsets of $\mathbb{N}_+$, and $u, x, y, z, x_i, \ldots$ over elements of $\mathbb{N}_+$. The class $\Sigma_n^0 \subseteq 2^{\mathbb{N}_+}$ is the collection of all sets $A \subseteq \mathbb{N}_+$ of the form

$$A = \{x \in \mathbb{N}_+ \mid (\mathbb{N}, +, \times) \models \exists y_1 \, \forall y_2 \cdots Q y_n : \varphi(x, y_1, \ldots, y_n)\},$$

where $Q = \forall$ (resp. $Q = \exists$) if n is even (resp. odd) and φ is a quantifier-free formula over the signature containing $+$ and $\times$. The class Π_n^0 is the class of all complements of Σ_n^0 sets. The classes Σ_n^0, Π_n^0 ($n \geq 1$) make up the *arithmetical hierarchy*.

The analytical hierarchy extends the arithmetical hierarchy and is defined analogously using function quantifiers: The class $\Sigma_n^1 \subseteq 2^{\mathbb{N}_+}$ is the collection of all sets $A \subseteq \mathbb{N}_+$ of the form

$$A = \{x \in \mathbb{N}_+ \mid (\mathbb{N}, +, \times) \models \exists f_1 \, \forall f_2 \cdots Q f_n : \varphi(x, f_1, \ldots, f_n)\},$$

where $Q = \forall$ (resp. $Q = \exists$) if n is even (resp. odd) and φ is a first-order formula over the signature containing $+$, $\times$, and the functions $f_1, \ldots, f_n$. The class Π_n^1 is the class of all complements of Σ_n^1 sets. The classes Σ_n^1, Π_n^1 ($n \geq 1$) make up the *analytical hierarchy*. The class of *analytical sets*[2] is exactly $\bigcup_{n \geq 1} \Sigma_n^1 \cup \Pi_n^1$.

As usual in computability theory, a Gödel numbering of all finite objects of interest allows to quantify over, say, finite automata as well. We will always assume such a numbering without mentioning it explicitly.

Büchi automata: For details on Büchi automata, see [22, 25]. Let Γ be a finite alphabet. With Γ^* we denote the set of all finite words over the alphabet Γ. The set of all nonempty finite words is Γ^+. An ω-word over Γ is an infinite sequence $w = a_1 a_2 a_3 \cdots$ with $a_i \in \Gamma$. We set $w[i] = a_i$ for $i \in \mathbb{N}_+$. The set of all ω-words over Γ is denoted by Γ^ω.

---

[2] Here the notion of *analytical sets* is defined for sets of natural numbers and is not to be confused with the *analytic sets* studied in descriptive set theory [12].

A (nondeterministic) Büchi automaton is a tuple $M = (Q, \Gamma, \Delta, I, F)$, where Q is a finite set of states, $I, F \subseteq Q$ are resp. the sets of initial and final states, and $\Delta \subseteq Q \times \Gamma \times Q$ is the transition relation. If $\Gamma = \Sigma^n$ for some alphabet Σ, then we refer to M as an n-*dimensional Büchi automaton over* Σ. A *run* of M on an ω-word $w = a_1 a_2 a_3 \cdots$ is an ω-word $r = (q_1, a_1, q_2)(q_2, a_2, q_3)(q_3, a_3, q_4) \cdots \in \Delta^\omega$ such that $q_1 \in I$. The run r is *accepting* if there exists a final state from F that occurs infinitely often in r. The language $L(M) \subseteq \Gamma^\omega$ defined by M is the set of all ω-words for which there exists an accepting run. An ω-language $L \subseteq \Gamma^\omega$ is *regular* if there exists a Büchi automaton M with $L(M) = L$. The class of all regular ω-languages is effectively closed under Boolean operations and projections.

For ω-words $w_1, \ldots, w_n \in \Gamma^\omega$, the *convolution* $w_1 \otimes w_2 \otimes \cdots \otimes w_n \in (\Gamma^n)^\omega$ is defined by

$$w_1 \otimes w_2 \otimes \cdots \otimes w_n = (w_1[1], \ldots, w_n[1])(w_1[2], \ldots, w_n[2])(w_1[3], \ldots, w_n[3]) \cdots .$$

For $\overline{w} = (w_1, \ldots, w_n)$, we write $\otimes(\overline{w})$ for $w_1 \otimes \cdots \otimes w_n$.

An n-ary relation $R \subseteq (\Gamma^\omega)^n$ is called ω-*automatic* if $\otimes R = \{\otimes(\overline{w}) \mid \overline{w} \in R\}$ is a regular ω-language, i.e., it is accepted by some n-dimensional Büchi automaton. We denote with $R(M) \subseteq (\Gamma^\omega)^n$ the relation defined by the n-dimensional Büchi automaton M over the alphabet Γ.

To also define the convolution of finite words (and of finite words with infinite words), we identify a finite word $u \in \Gamma^*$ with the ω-word $u\diamond^\omega$, where $\diamond$ is a new symbol. Then, for $u, v \in \Gamma^*, w \in \Gamma^\omega$, we write $u \otimes v$ for the ω-word $u\diamond^\omega \otimes v\diamond^\omega$ and $u \otimes w$ (resp. $w \otimes u$) for $u\diamond^\omega \otimes w$ (resp. $w \otimes u\diamond^\omega$).

ω-**automatic structures:** A *signature* is a finite set τ of relational symbols together with an arity $n_S \in \mathbb{N}_+$ for every relational symbol $S \in \tau$. A τ-*structure* is a tuple $\mathcal{A} = (A, (S^\mathcal{A})_{S\in\tau})$, where A is a set (the *universe* of $\mathcal{A}$) and $S^\mathcal{A} \subseteq A^{n_S}$. When the context is clear, we simply denote $S^\mathcal{A}$ by S, and we write $a \in \mathcal{A}$ for $a \in A$. Let $E \subseteq A^2$ be an equivalence relation on A. Then E is a *congruence* on $\mathcal{A}$ if $(u_1, v_1), \ldots, (u_{n_S}, v_{n_S}) \in E$ and $(u_1, \ldots, u_{n_S}) \in S$ imply $(v_1, \ldots, v_{n_S}) \in S$ for all $S \in \tau$. Then the *quotient structure* $\mathcal{A}/E$ can be defined:

- The universe of $\mathcal{A}/E$ is the set of all E-equivalence classes $[u]$ for $u \in A$.
- The interpretation of $S \in \tau$ is the relation $\{([u_1], \ldots, [u_{n_S}]) \mid (u_1, \ldots, u_{n_S}) \in S\}$.

Definition 2.1. *An ω-automatic presentation over the signature τ is a tuple*

$$P = (\Gamma, M, M_\equiv, (M_S)_{S\in\tau})$$

with the following properties:

- Γ *is a finite alphabet*
- M *is a Büchi automaton over the alphabet Γ.*
- *For every $S \in \tau$, M_S is an n_S-dimensional Büchi automaton over the alphabet Γ such that $R(M_S) \subseteq L(M)^{n_S}$.*
- $M_\equiv$ *is a 2-dimensional Büchi automaton over the alphabet Γ such that $R(M_\equiv)$ is a congruence relation on $(L(M), (R(M_S))_{S\in\tau})$.*

The τ-structure defined by the ω-automatic presentation P is the quotient structure

$$\mathcal{S}(P) = (L(M), (R(M_S))_{S\in\tau})/R(M_{\equiv}).$$

If $R(M_{\equiv})$ is the identity relation on $L(M)$, then P is called *injective*. A structure $\mathcal{A}$ is *(injectively) ω-automatic* if there is an (injectively) ω-automatic presentation P with $\mathcal{A} \cong \mathcal{S}(P)$. There exist ω-automatic structures that are not injectively ω-automatic [9]. We simplify our statements by saying "given/compute an (injectively) ω-automatic structure $\mathcal{A}$" for "given/compute an (injectively) ω-automatic presentation P of a structure $\mathcal{S}(P) \cong \mathcal{A}$". *Automatic structures* [13] are defined analogously to ω-automatic structures, but instead of Büchi automata ordinary finite automata over finite words are used. For this, one has to pad shorter strings with the padding symbol $\diamond$ when defining the convolution of finite strings. More details on ω-automatic structures can be found in [2, 9, 11].

Let $\mathsf{FO}[\exists^{\aleph_0}, \exists^{2^{\aleph_0}}]$ be first-order logic extended by the quantifiers $\exists^{\kappa}x \ldots$ ($\kappa \in \{\aleph_0, 2^{\aleph_0}\}$) saying that there exist exactly κ many x satisfying .... The following theorem lays out the main motivation for investigating ω-automatic structures.

Theorem 2.2 ([1,11]). *From an ω-automatic presentation $P = (\Gamma, M, M_{\equiv}, (M_S)_{S\in\tau})$ and a formula $\varphi(\overline{x}) \in \mathsf{FO}[\exists^{\aleph_0}, \exists^{2^{\aleph_0}}]$ in the signature τ with n free variables, one can compute a Büchi automaton for the relation*

$$\{\overline{a} \in L(M)^n \mid \mathcal{S}(P) \models \varphi([a_1], [a_2], \ldots, [a_n])\}.$$

In particular, the $\mathsf{FO}[\exists^{\aleph_0}, \exists^{2^{\aleph_0}}]$ theory of any ω-automatic structure $\mathcal{A}$ is (uniformly) decidable.

Definition 2.3. *Let $\mathcal{K}$ be a class of ω-automatic presentations. The* isomorphism problem $\mathsf{Iso}(\mathcal{K})$ *is the set of pairs $(P_1, P_2) \in \mathcal{K}^2$ of ω-automatic presentations from $\mathcal{K}$ with $\mathcal{S}(P_1) \cong \mathcal{S}(P_2)$.*

If $\mathcal{A}_1$ and $\mathcal{A}_2$ are two structures over the same signature, we write $\mathcal{A}_1 \uplus \mathcal{A}_2$ for the disjoint union of the two structures. We use $\mathcal{A}^{\kappa}$ to denote the disjoint union of κ many copies of the structure $\mathcal{A}$ (where κ is any cardinal).

Trees and dags: A *forest* is a partial order $F = (V, \leq)$ such that for every $x \in V$, the set $\{y \mid y \leq x\}$ of ancestors of x is finite and linearly ordered by $\leq$. The *level* of a node $x \in V$ is $|\{y \mid y < x\}| \in \mathbb{N}$. The *height* of F is the supremum of the levels of all nodes in V; it may be infinite, but this paper deals with forests of finite height only. For all $u \in V$, $F(u)$ denotes the restriction of F to the set $\{v \in V \mid u \leq v\}$ of successors of u. We will speak of the *subtree rooted at u*. A *tree* is a forest that has a minimal element, called the *root*. For a forest F and r not belonging to the domain of F, we denote with $r \circ F$ the tree that results from adding r to F as a new root. The *edge relation E* of the forest F is the set of pairs $(u, v) \in V^2$ such that u is the largest element in $\{x \mid x < v\}$. For any node $u \in V$, we use $E(u)$ to denote the set of children (or immediate successors) of u.

We use $\mathcal{T}_n$ (resp. $\mathcal{T}_n^i$) to denote the class of (injectively) ω-automatic presentations of trees of height at most n. Note that it is decidable whether a given ω-automatic presentation P belongs to $\mathcal{T}_n$ and $\mathcal{T}_n^i$, resp. (since the class of trees of height at most n can be axiomatized in first-order logic).

3 ω-Automatic Trees of Height 1 and 2

Two trees of height 1 are isomorphic if and only if they have the same size. Since the size of an ω-automatic structure is computable from any presentation [11], the isomorphism problem for ω-automatic trees of height 1 is decidable.

For ω-automatic trees of height 2 we need the following result:

Theorem 3.1 ([11]). *Let $\mathcal{A}$ be an ω-automatic structure and let $\varphi(x_1,\ldots,x_n,y)$ be a formula of $\mathsf{FO}[\exists^{\aleph_0}, \exists^{2^{\aleph_0}}]$. Then, for all $a_1,\ldots,a_n \in \mathcal{A}$, the cardinality of the set $\{b \in \mathcal{A} \mid \mathcal{A} \models \varphi(a_1,\ldots,a_n,b)\}$ belongs to $\mathbb{N} \cup \{\aleph_0, 2^{\aleph_0}\}$.*

Now, let us take two trees T_1 and T_2 of height 2 and let E_i be the edge relation of T_i and r_i its root. For $i \in \{1,2\}$ and a cardinal λ let $\kappa_{\lambda,i}$ be the cardinality of the set of all $u \in E_i(r_i)$ such that $|E_i(u)| = \lambda$. Then $T_1 \cong T_2$ if and only if $\kappa_{\lambda,1} = \kappa_{\lambda,2}$ for any cardinal λ. Now assume that T_1 and T_2 are both ω-automatic. By Theorem 3.1, for all $i \in \{1,2\}$ and every $u \in E_i(r_i)$ we have $|E_i(u)| \in \mathbb{N} \cup \{\aleph_0, 2^{\aleph_0}\}$. Moreover, again by Theorem 3.1, every cardinal $\kappa_{\lambda,i}$ ($\lambda \in \mathbb{N} \cup \{\aleph_0, 2^{\aleph_0}\}$) belongs to $\mathbb{N} \cup \{\aleph_0, 2^{\aleph_0}\}$ as well. Hence, $T_1 \cong T_2$ if and only if: $\forall \lambda, \kappa \in \mathbb{N} \cup \{\aleph_0, 2^{\aleph_0}\} : \kappa_{\lambda,1} = \kappa \Leftrightarrow \kappa_{\lambda,2} = \kappa$. By Theorem 2.2, the statement $\kappa_{\lambda,1} = \kappa \Leftrightarrow \kappa_{\lambda,2} = \kappa$ is decidable, so the whole statement belongs to Π_1^0. Hardness for Π_1^0 follows from the corresponding result on automatic trees of height 2 [17].

Theorem 3.2. *The following holds:*

- *The isomorphism problem $\mathsf{Iso}(\mathcal{T}_1)$ for ω-automatic trees of height 1 is decidable.*
- *There exists a tree U such that $\{P \in \mathcal{T}_2^i \mid \mathcal{S}(P) \cong U\}$ is Π_1^0-hard. The isomorphism problems $\mathsf{Iso}(\mathcal{T}_2)$ and $\mathsf{Iso}(\mathcal{T}_2^i)$ for (injectively) ω-automatic trees of height 2 are Π_1^0-complete.*

4 A Normal Form for Analytical Sets

To prove our lower bound for the isomorphism problem of ω-automatic trees of height $n \geq 3$, we will use the following normal form of analytical sets. A formula of the form $x \in X$ or $x \notin X$ is called a *set constraint*.

Proposition 4.1. *For every odd (resp. even) $n \in \mathbb{N}_+$ and every Π_n^1 (resp. Σ_n^1) relation $A \subseteq \mathbb{N}_+^r$, there exist polynomials $p_i, q_i \in \mathbb{N}[\overline{x}, y, \overline{z}]$ and disjunctions ψ_i ($1 \leq i \leq \ell$) of set constraints (on the set variables $X_1,\ldots,X_n$ and individual variables $\overline{x}, y, \overline{z}$) such that $\overline{x} \in A$ if and only if*

$$Q_1 X_1 \, Q_2 X_2 \cdots Q_n X_n \, \exists y \, \forall \overline{z} : \bigwedge_{i=1}^{\ell} p_i(\overline{x}, y, \overline{z}) \neq q_i(\overline{x}, y, \overline{z}) \vee \psi_i(\overline{x}, y, \overline{z}, X_1,\ldots,X_n)$$

where $Q_1, Q_2,\ldots,Q_n$ are alternating quantifiers with $Q_n = \forall$.

The proof of this proposition uses standard arguments and Matiyasevich's theorem on the equivalence of recursively enumerable and Diophantine sets [20], but we could not find it stated in precisely this form anywhere in the literature. It is known that the first-order quantifier block $\exists y \forall \overline{z}$ in Proposition 4.1 cannot be replaced by a block with only one type of first-order quantifiers, see e.g. [21, p. 379].

5 ω-Automatic Trees of Height at Least 4

We prove the following theorem for injectively ω-automatic trees of height at least 4.

Theorem 5.1. *Let $n \geq 1$ and $\Theta \in \{\Sigma, \Pi\}$. There exists a tree $U_{n,\Theta}$ of height $n+3$ such that $\{P \in \mathcal{T}_{n+3}^i \mid \mathcal{S}(P) \cong U_{n,\Theta}\}$ is hard for Θ_n^1. Hence,*

- *the isomorphism problem $\mathsf{Iso}(\mathcal{T}_{n+3}^i)$ for the class of injectively ω-automatic trees of height $n+3$ is hard for both the classes Π_n^1 and Σ_n^1,*
- *and the isomorphism problem $\mathsf{Iso}(\mathcal{T}^i)$ for the class of injectively ω-automatic trees of finite height is not analytical.*

Theorem 5.1 will be derived from the following proposition whose proof occupies Sections 5.1 and 5.2.

Proposition 5.2. *Let $n \geq 1$. There are trees $U[0]$ and $U[1]$ of height $n+3$ such that for any set A that is Π_n^1 if n is odd and Σ_n^1 if n is even, one can compute from $x \in \mathbb{N}_+$ an injectively ω-automatic tree $T[x]$ of height $n+3$ with $T[x] \cong U[0]$ if and only if $x \in A$ and $T[x] \cong U[1]$ otherwise.*

Note that this implies in particular that $U[0]$ and $U[1]$ are injectively ω-automatic.

Let $n \geq 1$ and set $U_{n,\Sigma} = U[n \bmod 2]$ and $U_{n,\Pi} = U[(n+1) \bmod 2]$. Then Proposition 5.2 implies the first statement of Theorem 5.1. The remaining statements are consequences of this first statement.

The construction of the trees $T[x]$, $U[0]$, and $U[1]$ is uniform in n and the formula defining A. Hence the second-order theory of $(\mathbb{N}, +, \times)$ can be reduced to $\bigcup_{n \in \mathbb{N}_+} \{n\} \times \mathsf{Iso}(\mathcal{T}_n^i)$ and therefore to the isomorphism problem $\mathsf{Iso}(\bigcup_{n \in \mathbb{N}_+} \mathcal{T}_n^i)$. This proves:

Corollary 5.3. *The second-order theory of $(\mathbb{N}, +, \times)$ can be reduced to the isomorphism problem $\mathsf{Iso}(\bigcup_{n \in \mathbb{N}_+} \mathcal{T}_n^i)$ for the class of all injectively ω-automatic trees of finite height.*

We now start to prove Proposition 5.2. Let A be a set that is Π_n^1 if n is odd and Σ_n^1 otherwise. By Proposition 4.1 it can be written in the form

$$A = \{x \in \mathbb{N}_+ \mid Q_1 X_1 \cdots Q_n X_n \exists y \, \forall \bar{z} : \bigwedge_{i=1}^{\ell} p_i(x, y, \bar{z}) \neq q_i(x, y, \bar{z}) \vee \psi_i(x, y, \bar{z}, \overline{X})\}$$

where

- $Q_1, Q_2, \ldots, Q_n$ are alternating quantifiers with $Q_n = \forall$,
- p_i, q_i $(1 \leq i \leq \ell)$ are polynomials in $\mathbb{N}[x, y, \bar{z}]$ where $\bar{z}$ has length k, and
- every ψ_i is a disjunction of set constraints on the set variables $X_1, \ldots, X_n$ and the individual variables $x, y, \bar{z}$.

For $0 \leq m \leq n$, we will consider the formula $\varphi_m(x, X_1, \ldots, X_{n-m})$ defined by

$$Q_{n+1-m} X_{n+1-m} \cdots Q_n X_n \, \exists y \, \forall \bar{z} : \bigwedge_{i=1}^{\ell} p_i(x, y, \bar{z}) \neq q_i(x, y, \bar{z}) \vee \psi_i(x, y, \bar{z}, \overline{X})$$

such that $\varphi_0(x, X_1, \ldots, X_n)$ is a first-order formula and $\varphi_n(x)$ holds if and only if $x \in A$. In addition, let $\varphi_{-1}(x, y, X_1, \ldots, X_n)$ be the subformula starting with $\forall \overline{z}$.

To prove Proposition 5.2, we construct by induction on $0 \leq m \leq n$ height-$(m+3)$ trees $T_m[X_1, \ldots, X_{n-m}, x]$ and $U_m[i]$ where $X_1, \ldots, X_{n-m} \subseteq \mathbb{N}_+$, $x \in \mathbb{N}_+$, and $i \in \{0, 1\}$ such that the following holds:

$$\forall \overline{X} \in (2^{\mathbb{N}_+})^{n-m} \; \forall x \in \mathbb{N}_+ : T_m[\overline{X}, x] \cong \begin{cases} U_m[0] & \text{if } \varphi_m(x, \overline{X}) \text{ holds} \\ U_m[1] & \text{otherwise} \end{cases} \tag{1}$$

Setting $T[x] = T_n[x]$, $U[0] = U_n[0]$, and $U[1] = U_n[1]$ and constructing from x an injectively ω-automatic presentation of $T[x]$ then proves Proposition 5.2.

5.1 Construction of Trees

Note that $C : \mathbb{N}_+^2 \to \mathbb{N}_+$ with $C(x, y) = (x + y)^2 + 3x + y$ is an injective polynomial function $(C(x, y)/2$ is the position of $(x + y, x)$ in the lexicographic enumeration of $\mathbb{N}^2$). For two numbers $x, y \in \mathbb{N}_+$, let $S[x, y]$ denote the height-1 tree with $C(x, y)$ many leaves.

The trees are constructed by induction on m, $m = 0$ being the base case: For all $\overline{X} \in (2^{\mathbb{N}_+})^n, \overline{z} \in \mathbb{N}_+^k, x, y, z_{k+1} \in \mathbb{N}_+, 1 \leq i \leq \ell$, and $\kappa \in \mathbb{N}_+ \cup \{\omega\}$ define the trees[3]

$$T'[\overline{X}, x, y, \overline{z}, z_{k+1}, i] = \begin{cases} S[1, 2] & \text{if } \psi_i(x, y, \overline{z}, \overline{X}) \\ S[p_i(x, y, \overline{z}) + z_{k+1}, q_i(x, y, \overline{z}) + z_{k+1}] & \text{otherwise} \end{cases}$$

and

$$T''[\overline{X}, x, y] = r \circ \left(\biguplus \{S[e_1, e_2] \mid e_1 \neq e_2\} \uplus \biguplus \{T'[\overline{X}, x, y, \overline{z}, z_{k+1}, i] \mid \overline{z} \in \mathbb{N}_+^k, z_{k+1} \in \mathbb{N}_+, 1 \leq i \leq \ell\} \right)^{\aleph_0}$$

$$U''[\kappa] = r \circ \left(\biguplus \{S[e_1, e_2] \mid e_1 \neq e_2\} \uplus \biguplus \{S[e, e] \mid \kappa \leq e < \omega\} \right)^{\aleph_0}.$$

Note that all the trees $T''[\overline{X}, x, y]$ and $U''[\kappa]$ are build from trees of the form $S[e_1, e_2]$. Furthermore, if $S[e, e]$ appears as a building block, then $S[e + a, e + a]$ also appears as one for all $a \in \mathbb{N}$. In addition, any building block $S[e_1, e_2]$ appears either infinitely often or not at all. These observations allow to prove the following:

(a) $T''[\overline{X}, x, y] \cong U''[\kappa]$ for some $\kappa \in \mathbb{N}_+ \cup \{\omega\}$
(b) $T''[\overline{X}, x, y] \cong U''[\omega]$ if and only if $\varphi_{-1}(x, y, \overline{X})$ holds

In a next step, we collect the trees $T''[\overline{X}, x, y]$ and $U''[\kappa]$ into the trees $T_0[\overline{X}, x]$, $U_0[0]$, and $U_0[1]$ as follows:

$$T_0[\overline{X}, x] = r \circ \left(\biguplus \{U''[m] \mid m \in \mathbb{N}_+\} \uplus \biguplus \{T''[\overline{X}, x, y] \mid y \in \mathbb{N}_+\} \right)^{\aleph_0}$$

$$U_0[0] = r \circ \left(\biguplus \{U''[m] \mid m \in \mathbb{N}_+ \cup \{\omega\}\} \right)^{\aleph_0}$$

$$U_0[1] = r \circ \left(\biguplus \{U''[m] \mid m \in \mathbb{N}_+\} \right)^{\aleph_0}$$

---

[3] The choice of $S[1, 2]$ in the definition of $T'[\overline{X}, x, y, \overline{z}, z_{k+1}, i]$ is arbitrary. Any $S[a, b]$ with $a \neq b$ would be acceptable.

By (a), these trees are build from copies of the trees $U''[\kappa]$ (and are therefore of height 3), each appearing infinitely often or not at all. Hence $T_0[\overline{X}, x]$ is isomorphic to $U_0[0]$ or to $U_0[1]$ (and these two trees are not isomorphic). Note that $T_0[\overline{X}, x] \cong U_0[0]$ if and only if there exists some $y \in \mathbb{N}_+$ with $T''[\overline{X}, x, y] \cong U''[\omega]$. By (b) and the definition of $\varphi_0(\overline{X}, x)$, this is the case if and only if $\varphi_0(\overline{X}, x)$ holds. Hence (1) holds for $m = 0$.

Suppose for some number $0 \le m < n$ we have trees $T_m[X_1, \ldots, X_{n-m}, x]$, $U_m[0]$ and $U_m[1]$ satisfying (1). Let $\overline{X}$ stand for $(X_1, \ldots, X_{n-m-1})$ and let $\alpha = m \bmod 2$. We define the following height-$(m+4)$ trees:

$$T_{m+1}[\overline{X}, x] = r \circ \left(U_m[\alpha] \uplus \biguplus \{ T_m[\overline{X}, X_{n-m}, x] \mid X_{n-m} \subseteq \mathbb{N}_+ \} \right)^{2^{\aleph_0}}$$

$$U_{m+1}[i] = r \circ (U_m[\alpha] \uplus U_m[i])^{2^{\aleph_0}} \quad \text{for } i \in \{0, 1\}$$

Note that the trees $T_{m+1}[\overline{X}, x]$, $U_{m+1}[0]$, and $U_{m+1}[1]$ consist of $2^{\aleph_0}$ many copies of $U_m[\alpha]$ and possibly $2^{\aleph_0}$ many copies of $U_m[1 - \alpha]$. Hence $T_{m+1}[\overline{X}, x]$ is isomorphic to one of the trees $U_{m+1}[0]$ or $U_{m+1}[1]$. We show that $T_{m+1}[\overline{X}, x] \cong U_{m+1}[0]$ if and only if $\varphi_{m+1}(x, \overline{X})$ for the case that m even, i.e., $\alpha = 0$ (the case m odd is similar): The two trees are isomorphic if and only if $T_m[\overline{X}, X_{n-m}, x] \cong U_m[0]$ for all sets $X_{n-m} \subseteq \mathbb{N}_+$. By the induction hypothesis, this is equivalent to saying that the formula $\varphi_m(x, \overline{X}, X_{n-m})$ holds for all sets $X_{n-m} \subseteq \mathbb{N}_+$. But since m is even, the formula $\varphi_{m+1}(x, \overline{X})$ equals $\forall X_{n-m} : \varphi_m(x, \overline{X}, X_{n-m})$.

This finishes the construction of the trees $T_m[\overline{X}, x]$, $U_m[0]$, and $U_m[1]$ as well as the verification of (1). For $m = n$ we get:

Lemma 5.4. *For all $x \in \mathbb{N}_+$, we have $T_n[x] \cong U_n[0]$ if $x \in A$ and $T_n[x] \cong U_n[1]$ otherwise.*

5.2 Injective ω-Automaticity

Injectively ω-automatic presentations of the trees $T_m[\overline{X}, x]$, $U_m[0]$, and $U_m[1]$ will be constructed inductively. Note that the construction of $T_{m+1}[\overline{X}, x]$ involves all the trees $T_m[\overline{X}, X_{n-m}, x]$ for $X_{n-m} \subseteq \mathbb{N}_+$. Hence we need *one single injectively ω-automatic presentation* for the forest consisting of all these trees. Therefore, we will deal with forests. To move from one forest to the next, we will always proceed as follows: add a set of new roots and connect them to some of the old roots *which results in a directed acyclic graph* (or dag) and not necessarily in a forest. The next forest will then be the unfolding of this dag.

The *height* of a dag D is the length (number of edges) of a longest directed path in D. We only consider dags of finite height. A *root* of a dag is a node without incoming edges. A dag $D = (V, E)$ can be unfold into a forest $\text{unfold}(D)$ in the usual way: Nodes of $\text{unfold}(D)$ are directed paths in D that start in a root and the order relation is the prefix relation between these paths. For a root $v \in V$ of D, we define the tree $\text{unfold}(D, v)$ as the restriction of $\text{unfold}(D)$ to those paths that start in v. We will make use of the following lemma whose proof is based on the immediate observation that the set of convolutions of paths in D is again a regular language.

Lemma 5.5. *From a given $k \in \mathbb{N}$ and an injectively ω-automatic presentation for a dag D of height at most k, one can construct effectively an injectively ω-automatic presentation for* $\mathrm{unfold}(D)$ *such that the roots of* $\mathrm{unfold}(D)$ *coincide with the roots of D and* $\mathrm{unfold}(D, r) = (\mathrm{unfold}(D))(r)$ *for any root r.*

For a symbol a and a tuple $\bar{e} = (e_1, \ldots, e_k) \in \mathbb{N}_+^k$, we write $a^{\bar{e}}$ for the ω-word

$$a^{e_1} \otimes a^{e_2} \otimes \cdots \otimes a^{e_k} = (a^{e_1} \diamond^\omega) \otimes (a^{e_2} \diamond^\omega) \otimes \cdots \otimes (a^{e_k} \diamond^\omega).$$

For an ω-language L, we write $\otimes_k(L)$ for $\otimes(L^k)$. For $X \subseteq \mathbb{N}_+$, let $w_X \in \{0, 1\}^*$ be the characteristic word (i.e., $w_X[i] = 1$ if and only if $i \in X$) and, for $\overline{X} = (X_1, \ldots, X_n) \in (2^{\mathbb{N}_+})^n$, write $w_{\overline{X}}$ for the convolution of the words w_{X_i}. The following lemma is the key to the construction of ω-automatic presentations for $T_n[x]$, $U_n[0]$, and $U_n[1]$. We refer to the definition of the set A from Section 5.

Lemma 5.6. *For $1 \leq i \leq \ell$, there exists a Büchi automaton $\mathcal{A}_i$ with the following property: For all $\overline{X} \in (2^{\mathbb{N}_+})^n$, $\bar{z} \in \mathbb{N}_+^k$, and $x, y, z_{k+1} \in \mathbb{N}_+$, the number of accepting runs of $\mathcal{A}_i$ on the word $w_{\overline{X}} \otimes a^{(x,y,\bar{z},z_{k+1})}$ equals $C(1, 2)$ if $\psi_i(x, y, \bar{z}, X_1, \ldots, X_n)$ holds and $C(p_i(x, y, \bar{z}) + z_{k+1}, q_i(x, y, \bar{z}) + z_{k+1})$ otherwise.*

Proof sketch. One first builds a Büchi automaton that, on the ω-word $a^{(x,y,\bar{z},z_{k+1})}$, has precisely $C(p_i(x, y, \bar{z}) + z_{k+1}, q_i(x, y, \bar{z}) + z_{k+1})$ many accepting runs. This is possible using disjoint union of automata and the flag construction (cf. [4, 22, 25]) for addition and multiplication of polynomials since $C(p_i(x, y, \bar{z}) + z_{k+1}, q_i(x, y, \bar{z}) + z_{k+1})$ is a polynomial over $\mathbb{N}$. Secondly, one builds deterministic Büchi automata accepting a word $w_{\overline{X}} \otimes a^{(x,y,\bar{z},z_{k+1})}$ if and only if the disjunction $\psi_i(x, y, \bar{z}, \overline{X})$ of set constraints is satisfied (not satisfied, resp.) A straightforward combination of (several copies of) the automata obtained in this way has the desired properties. $\qquad\square$

For a Büchi automaton $\mathcal{A}$, let $\mathrm{Run}_{\mathcal{A}}$ denote the set of accepting runs. Note that this set is a regular ω-language over the alphabet of transitions of $\mathcal{A}$.

We now build a first injectively ω-automatic forest $\mathcal{H}' = (L', E')$: its underlying ω-language is (every $1 \leq i < \ell$ is a new symbol in L')

$$L' = \bigcup_{1 \leq i \leq \ell} i \otimes (L(\mathcal{A}_i) \cup \mathrm{Run}_{\mathcal{A}_i})$$

and $(i \otimes v, j \otimes w)$ forms an edge if and only if $i = j$ and w is an accepting run of $\mathcal{A}_i$ on v. Then $\mathcal{H}'$ is a forest of height 1, the roots of $\mathcal{H}'$ are the words from $\{1, \ldots, \ell\} \otimes (\otimes_n(\{0, 1\}^\omega)) \otimes (\otimes_{k+3}(a^+))$, and for any root $r = i \otimes w_{\overline{X}} \otimes a^{(x,y,\bar{z},z_{k+1})}$, we have $\mathcal{H}'(r) \cong T'[\overline{X}, x, y, \bar{z}, z_{k+1}, i]$ by Lemma 5.6.

In a similar way, one can build an injectively ω-automatic forest $\mathcal{F} = (L_{\mathcal{F}}, E_{\mathcal{F}})$ whose roots are the words from $b^+ \otimes b^+$ such that $\mathcal{F}(b^{(e_1, e_2)}) \cong S[e_1, e_2]$. From $\mathcal{H}'$ and $\mathcal{F}$, we build an injectively ω-automatic dag $\mathcal{D}$ as follows:

- The domain of $\mathcal{D}$ is the set $(\otimes_n(\{0, 1\}^\omega) \otimes a^+ \otimes a^+) \cup b^* \cup (\$^* \otimes (L' \cup L_{\mathcal{F}}))$.
- For $u, v \in L' \cup L_{\mathcal{F}}$, the words $\$^i \otimes u$ and $\$^j \otimes v$ are connected if and only if $i = j$ and $(u, v) \in E' \cup E_{\mathcal{F}}$. In other words, the restriction of $\mathcal{D}$ to $\$^* \otimes (L' \cup L_{\mathcal{F}})$ is isomorphic to $(\mathcal{H}' \uplus \mathcal{F})^{\aleph_0}$.

– For all $\overline{X} \in (2_+^{\mathbb{N}})^n$, $x, y \in \mathbb{N}_+$, the new root $w_{\overline{X}} \otimes a^{(x,y)}$ is connected to all nodes in

$$\$^* \otimes \left((\{1, \ldots, \ell\} \otimes w_{\overline{X}} \otimes a^{(x,y)} \otimes (\otimes_{k+1}(a^+))) \cup \{b^{(e_1,e_2)} \mid e_1 \neq e_2\} \right) .$$

– The new root ε is connected to all nodes in $\$^* \otimes \{b^{(e_1,e_2)} \mid e_1 \neq e_2\}$.
– For all $m \in \mathbb{N}_+$, the new root b^m is connected to all nodes in

$$\$^* \otimes \{b^{(e_1,e_2)} \mid e_1 \neq e_2 \vee e_1 = e_2 \geq m\}.$$

It is easily seen that $\mathcal{D}$ is an injectively ω-automatic dag. Setting $\mathcal{H}'' = \text{unfold}(\mathcal{D})$, one can then verify $\mathcal{H}''(w_X \otimes a^{(x,y)}) \cong T''[\overline{X}, x, y]$, $\mathcal{H}''(\varepsilon) \cong U''[\omega]$, and $\mathcal{H}''(b^m) \cong U''[m]$ for all $m \in \mathbb{N}_+$. Note that also $\mathcal{H}''$ is injectively ω-automatic by Lemma 5.5.

We now construct a new forest $\mathcal{H}_0$ from $\$^* \otimes \mathcal{H}''$ by adding new roots:

– For $\overline{X} \in (2^{\mathbb{N}_+})^n$, $x \in \mathbb{N}_+$, connect a new root $w_{\overline{X}} \otimes a^x$ to all nodes in

$$\$^* \otimes \left(w_{\overline{X}} \otimes a^x \otimes a^+ \cup b^+ \right).$$

– Connect a new root ε to all nodes in $\$^* \otimes b^*$.
– Connect a new root b to all nodes in $\$^* \otimes b^+$.

The result is an injectively ω-automatic dag of height 3 whose unfolding we denote by $\mathcal{H}_0$. This forest $\mathcal{H}_0$ is actually the base case of the following lemma. The induction is done similarly: one adds to $\{\$_1\$_2\}^\omega \otimes \mathcal{H}_m$ new roots $w_{\overline{X}} \otimes a^x$ for $x \in \mathbb{N}_+$ and $\overline{X} \in (2^{\mathbb{N}_+})^{n-m-1}$, ε, and b and one connects them to the appropriate words $u \otimes v$ with $u \in \{\$_1, \$_2\}^\omega$ and $v \in \mathcal{H}_m$ (cf. the definition of the trees $T_{m+1}[\overline{X}, x]$ and $U_{m+1}[i]$ for $i \in \{0, 1\}$).

Lemma 5.7. *From each $0 \leq m \leq n$, one can effectively construct an injectively ω-automatic forest $\mathcal{H}_m$ such that*

– *the set of roots of $\mathcal{H}_m$ is $\left(\otimes_{n-m}(\{0,1\}^\omega) \otimes a^+ \right) \cup \{\varepsilon, b\}$,*
– *$\mathcal{H}_m(w_{\overline{X}} \otimes a^x) \cong T_m[\overline{X}, x]$ for all $\overline{X} \in (2^{\mathbb{N}_+})^{n-m}$ and $x \in \mathbb{N}_+$,*
– *$\mathcal{H}_m(\varepsilon) \cong U_m[0]$, and*
– *$\mathcal{H}_m(b) \cong U_m[1]$.*

Note that $T_n[x]$ is the tree in $\mathcal{H}_n$ rooted at a^x. Hence $T_n[x]$ is (effectively) an injectively ω-automatic tree. Now Lemma 5.4 finishes the proof of Proposition 5.2 and therefore of Theorem 5.1.

6 ω-Automatic Trees of Height 3

Recall that the isomorphism problem $\mathsf{Iso}(\mathcal{T}_2)$ is arithmetical by Theorem 3.2 and that $\mathsf{Iso}(\mathcal{T}_4^i)$ is not by Theorem 5.1. In this section, we modify the proof of Theorem 5.1 in order to show:

Theorem 6.1. *There exists a tree U such that $\{P \in T_3^i \mid S(P) \cong U\}$ is Π_1^1-hard. Hence the isomorphism problem $\mathsf{Iso}(T_3^i)$ for injectively ω-automatic trees of height 3 is Π_1^1-hard.*

So let $A \subseteq \mathbb{N}_+$ be some set from Π_1^1. By Proposition 4.1, it can be written as

$$A = \{x \in \mathbb{N}_+ : \forall X\ \exists y\ \forall \bar{z} : \bigwedge_{i=1}^{\ell} p_i(x, y, \bar{z}) \neq q_i(x, y, \bar{z}) \vee \psi_i(x, y, \bar{z}, X)\},$$

where p_i and q_i are polynomials with coefficients in $\mathbb{N}$ and ψ_i is a disjunction of set constraints. As in Section 5, let $\varphi_0(x, X)$ denote the first-order kernel of this formula (starting with $\exists y$) and let $\varphi_{-1}(x, y, X)$ denote the subformula starting with $\forall \bar{z}$. We reuse the trees $T'[X, x, y, \bar{z}, z_{k+1}, i]$ of height 1. Recall that they are all of the form $S[e_1, e_2]$ and therefore have an even number of leaves (since the range of the polynomial $C : \mathbb{N}^2 \to \mathbb{N}$ consists of even numbers). For $e \in \mathbb{N}_+$, let $S[e]$ denote the height-1 tree with $2e + 1$ leaves.

Recall that the tree $T''[X, x, y]$ encodes the set of pairs $(e_1, e_2) \in \mathbb{N}_+^2$ such that $e_1 \neq e_2$ or there exist $\bar{z}, z_{k+1}$, and i with $e_1 = p_i(x, y, \bar{z}) + z_{k+1}$ and $e_2 = q_i(x, y, \bar{z}) + z_{k+1}$. We now modify the construction of this tree such that, in addition, it also encodes the set $X \subseteq \mathbb{N}_+$:

$$\widehat{T}[X, x, y] = r \circ \left(\begin{array}{l} \biguplus\{S[e] \mid e \in X\} \uplus \biguplus\{S[e_1, e_2] \mid e_1 \neq e_2\} \uplus \\ \biguplus\{T'[\overline{X}, x, y, \bar{z}, z_{k+1}i] \mid \bar{z} \in \mathbb{N}_+^k, z_{k+1} \in \mathbb{N}_+, 1 \leq i \leq \ell\} \end{array} \right)^{\aleph_0}$$

In a similar spirit, we define $\widehat{U}[\kappa, X]$ for $X \subseteq \mathbb{N}_+$ and $\kappa \in \mathbb{N}_+ \cup \{\omega\}$:

$$\widehat{U}[\kappa, X] = r \circ \left(\begin{array}{l} \biguplus\{S[e] \mid e \in X\} \uplus \biguplus\{S[e_1, e_2] \mid e_1 \neq e_2\} \uplus \\ \biguplus\{S[e, e] \mid \kappa \leq e < \omega\} \end{array} \right)^{\aleph_0}$$

Then $\widehat{T}[X, x, y] \cong \widehat{U}[\omega, Y]$ if and only if $X = Y$ and $T''[X, x, y] \cong U''[\omega]$, i.e., (by (b) from Section 5.1) if and only if $X = Y$ and $\varphi_{-1}(x, y, X)$ holds. Finally, we set

$$T[x] = r \circ \left(\begin{array}{l} \biguplus\{\widehat{U}[\kappa, X] \mid X \subseteq \mathbb{N}_+, \kappa \in \mathbb{N}_+\} \uplus \\ \biguplus\{\widehat{T}[X, x, y] \mid X \subseteq \mathbb{N}_+, y \in \mathbb{N}_+\} \end{array} \right)^{\aleph_0}$$

$$U = r \circ \left(\biguplus\{\widehat{U}[\kappa, X] \mid X \subseteq \mathbb{N}_+, \kappa \in \mathbb{N}_+ \cup \{\omega\}\} \right)^{\aleph_0}.$$

Assume first that $T[x] \cong U$. Thus, both trees have the same height-2 subtrees. The crucial point is that, for any $X \subseteq \mathbb{N}_+$, $\widehat{U}[X, \omega]$ appears in U, i.e., there must be some $Y \subseteq \mathbb{N}_+$ and $y \in \mathbb{N}_+$ such that $\widehat{T}[Y, x, y] \cong \widehat{U}[\omega, X]$ (implying $X = Y$) and therefore $T''[X, x, y] \cong U''[\omega]$. But this is equivalent to saying that $\varphi_{-1}(x, y, X)$ holds. Since $X \subseteq \mathbb{N}_+$ is arbitrary, we showed $x \in A$. The other implication can be shown similarly. Injective ω-automaticity can be shown similar to Section 5.2. This finishes our proof sketch of Theorem 6.1.

7 Upper Bounds Assuming CH

We denote with **CH** the continuum hypothesis: Every infinite subset of $2^{\mathbb{N}}$ has either cardinality $\aleph_0$ or cardinality $2^{\aleph_0}$. By the seminal work of Cohen and Gödel, **CH** is independent of the axiom system **ZFC**.

An ω-word $w \in \Gamma^{\omega}$ can be identified with the function $w : \mathbb{N}_+ \to \Gamma$ (and hence with a second-order object) where $w(i) = w[i]$. We need the following lemma:

Lemma 7.1. *From a given Büchi automaton M over an alphabet Γ one can construct an arithmetical predicate $\mathrm{acc}_M(u)$ (where $u : \mathbb{N}_+ \to \Gamma$) such that $u \in L(M)$ if and only if $\mathrm{acc}_M(u)$ holds.*

Proof sketch. The idea is to transform M into an equivalent (deterministic and complete) Muller automaton. Determinism then allows to express acceptance using the arithmetical predicate "the prefix of length n results in state q".   □

Theorem 7.2. *Assuming **CH**, the isomorphism problem $\mathrm{Iso}(\mathcal{T}_n)$ belongs to Π^1_{2n-4} for $n \geq 3$.*

Proof sketch. Consider trees $T_i = \mathcal{S}(P_i)$ for $P_1, P_2 \in \mathcal{T}_n$. Define the forest $F = (V, \leq)$ as $F = T_1 \uplus T_2$. Let us fix an ω-automatic presentation $P = (\Sigma, M, M_{\equiv}, M_{\leq})$ for F where $M_{\leq}$ recognizes the order relation $\leq$. In the following, for $u \in L(M)$ we write $F(u)$ for the subtree $F([u])$ rooted in the F-node $[u] = [u]_{R(M_{\equiv})}$ represented by the ω-word u. Similarly, we write $E(u)$ for the set of children of $[u]$. We will define a $\Pi^1_{2n-2k-4}$-predicate $\mathrm{iso}_k(u_1, u_2)$, where $u_1, u_2 \in L(M)$ are on level k in F. This predicate expresses that $F(u_1) \cong F(u_2)$.

As induction base, let $k = n-2$. Then the trees $F(u_1)$ and $F(u_2)$ have height at most 2. Then $F(u_1) \cong F(u_2)$ if and only if the following holds for all $\kappa, \lambda \in \mathbb{N} \cup \{\aleph_0, 2^{\aleph_0}\}$ (see Section 3):

$$F \models \left(\exists^{\kappa} x \in V : (([u_1], x) \in E \wedge \exists^{\lambda} y \in V : (x, y) \in E) \right) \leftrightarrow$$
$$\left(\exists^{\kappa} x \in V : (([u_2], x) \in E \wedge \exists^{\lambda} y \in V : (x, y) \in E) \right).$$

Note that by Theorem 2.2, one can compute from $\kappa, \lambda \in \mathbb{N} \cup \{\aleph_0, 2^{\aleph_0}\}$ a Büchi automaton $M_{\kappa,\lambda}$ accepting the set of convolutions of pairs of ω-words (u_1, u_2) satisfying the above formula. Hence $F(u_1) \cong F(u_2)$ if and only if the following arithmetical predicate holds: $\forall \kappa, \lambda \in \mathbb{N} \cup \{\aleph_0, 2^{\aleph_0}\} : \mathrm{acc}_{M_{\kappa,\lambda}}(u_1, u_2)$.

Now let $0 \leq k < n - 2$. For a set A, let $\mathrm{count}(A)$ denote the set of all countable (possibly finite) subsets of A. On an abstract level, the formula $\mathrm{iso}_k(u_1, u_2)$ is:

$$\left(\forall x \in E(u_1) \exists y \in E(u_2) : \mathrm{iso}_{k+1}(x, y) \right) \wedge \left(\forall x \in E(u_2) \exists y \in E(u_1) : \mathrm{iso}_{k+1}(x, y) \right)$$
$$\wedge \; \forall X_1 \in \mathrm{count}(E(u_1)) \, \forall X_2 \in \mathrm{count}(E(u_2)) :$$
$$|X_1| = |X_2| \; \vee \; (\exists x, y \in X_1 \cup X_2 : \neg\mathrm{iso}_{k+1}(x, y)) \; \vee$$
$$(\exists x \in X_1 \cup X_2 \; \exists y \in (E(u_1) \cup E(u_2)) \setminus (X_1 \cup X_2) : \mathrm{iso}_{k+1}(x, y))$$

The first line expresses that the children of u_1 and u_2 realize the same isomorphism types of trees of height $n - k - 1$. The rest of the formula expresses that if a certain isomorphism type τ of height-$(n - k - 1)$ trees appears countably many times below u_1 then it appears with the same multiplicity below u_2 and vice versa. Assuming **CH** and the correctness of iso_{k+1}, one gets $\text{iso}_k(u_1, u_2)$ if and only if $F(u_1) \cong F(u_2)$.

The sets X_i in the above formula can be coded as mappings $f_i : \mathbb{N}_+^2 \to \Sigma$. Then the elements of X_i correspond to natural numbers j coding the word $k \mapsto f_i(j, k)$. But the ω-word $y \notin X_1 \cup X_2$ is another second-order object. This results in two additional second-order quantifier blocks in iso_k. Hence the formula iso_0 belongs to Π^1_{2n-4}. In order to express that e.g. $x \in E(u_i)$ we use Lemma 7.1 with the automaton $M_{\leq}$. $\square$

Corollary 5.3 and Theorem 7.2 imply:

Corollary 7.3. *Assuming **CH**, the isomorphism problem for (injectively) ω-automatic trees of finite height is recursively equivalent to the second-order theory of $(\mathbb{N}, +, \times)$.*

Remark 7.4. For the case $n = 3$ we can avoid the use of **CH** in Theorem 7.2: Let us consider the proof of Theorem 7.2 for $n = 3$. Then, the binary relation iso_1 (which holds between two ω-words u, v in F if and only if $[u]$ and $[v]$ are on level 1 and $F(u) \cong F(v)$) is a Π^0_1-predicate. It follows that this relation is Borel (see e.g. [12] for background on Borel sets). Now let u be an ω-word on level 1 in F. It follows that the set of all ω-words v on level 1 with $\text{iso}_1(u, v)$ is again Borel. Now, every uncountable Borel set has cardinality $2^{\aleph_0}$ (this holds even for analytic sets [12]). It follows that the definition of iso_0 in the proof of Theorem 7.2 is correct even without assuming **CH**. Hence, $\text{Iso}(\mathcal{T}_3)$ belongs to Π^1_2 (recall that we proved Π^1_1-hardness for this problem in Section 6), this can be shown in **ZFC**.

8   Open Problems

The main open problem concerns upper bounds in case we assume the negation of the continuum hypothesis. Assuming $\neg$**CH**, is the isomorphism problem for (injectively) ω-automatic trees of height n still analytical? In our paper [17] we also proved that the isomorphism problem for automatic linear orders is not arithmetical. This leads to the question whether our techniques for ω-automatic trees can be also used for proving lower bounds on the isomorphism problem for ω-automatic linear orders. More specifically, one might ask whether the isomorphism problem for ω-automatic linear orders is analytical. A more general question asks for the complexity of the isomorphism problem for ω-automatic structures in general. On the face of it, it is an existential third-order property (since any isomorphism has to map second-order objects to second-order objects). But it is not clear whether it is complete for this class.

References

1. Blumensath, A.: Automatic structures. Diploma thesis, RWTH Aachen (1999)
2. Blumensath, A., Grädel, E.: Finite presentations of infinite structures: Automata and interpretations. Theory of Computing Systems 37(6), 641–674 (2004)

3. Calvert, W., Knight, J.F.: Classification from a computable viewpoint. Bulletin of Symbolic Logic 12(2), 191–218 (2006)
4. Choueka, Y.: Theories of automata on ω-tapes: a simplified approach. Journal of Computer and System Sciences 8, 117–141 (1974)
5. Courcelle, B.: The definability of equational graphs in monadic second-order logic. In: Ronchi Della Rocca, S., Ausiello, G., Dezani-Ciancaglini, M. (eds.) ICALP 1989. LNCS, vol. 372, pp. 207–221. Springer, Heidelberg (1989)
6. Finkel, O.: Highly undecidable problems for infinite computations. R.A.I.R.O. — Informatique Théorique et Applications 43(2), 339–364 (2009)
7. Finkel, O., Todorčević, S.: The isomorphism relation between tree-autoamtic structures. Central European Journal of Mathematics 8(2), 299–313 (2010)
8. Goncharov, S.S., Knight, J.F.: Computable structure and antistructure theorems. Algebra Logika 41(6), 639–681 (2002)
9. Hjorth, G., Khoussainov, B., Montalbán, A., Nies, A.: From automatic structures to Borel structures. In: Proc. LICS 2008, pp. 431–441. IEEE Computer Society, Los Alamitos (2008)
10. Ishihara, H., Khoussainov, B., Rubin, S.: Some results on automatic structures. In: Proc. LICS 2002, pp. 235–244. IEEE Computer Society, Los Alamitos (2002)
11. Kaiser, L., Rubin, S., Bárány, V.: Cardinality and counting quantifiers on omega-automatic structures. In: Proc. STACS 2008. LIPIcs, vol. 1, pp. 385–396. Schloss Dagstuhl–Leibniz-Zentrum für Informatik (2010)
12. Kechris, A.: Classical Descriptive Set Theory. Springer, Heidelberg (1995)
13. Khoussainov, B., Nerode, A.: Automatic presentations of structures. In: Leivant, D. (ed.) LCC 1994. LNCS, vol. 960, pp. 367–392. Springer, Heidelberg (1995)
14. Khoussainov, B., Nies, A., Rubin, S., Stephan, F.: Automatic structures: richness and limitations. Logical Methods in Computer Science 3(2):2:2, 18 (electronic) (2007)
15. Khoussainov, B., Rubin, S., Stephan, F.: Automatic linear orders and trees. ACM Transactions on Computational Logic 6(4), 675–700 (2005)
16. Kuske, D.: Is Ramsey's theorem ω-automatic? In: Proc. STACS 2010. LIPIcs, vol. 5, pp. 537–548. Schloss Dagstuhl–Leibniz-Zentrum für Informatik (2010)
17. Kuske, D., Liu, J., Lohrey, M.: The isomorphism problem on classes of automatic structures. In: Proc. LICS 2010. IEEE Computer Society, Los Alamitos (2010) (accepted for publication)
18. Kuske, D., Liu, J., Lohrey, M.: The isomorphism problem for ω-automatic trees, http://arxiv.org/abs/1004.0610
19. Kuske, D., Lohrey, M.: First-order and counting theories of omega-automatic structures. Journal of Symbolic Logic 73, 129–150 (2008)
20. Matiyasevich, Y.V.: Hilbert's Tenth Problem. MIT Press, Cambridge (1993)
21. Odifreddi, P.: Classical recursion theory. Studies in Logic and the Foundations of Mathematics, vol. 125. North-Holland Publishing Co., Amsterdam (1989)
22. Perrin, D., Pin, J.-E.: Infinite Words. In: Pure and Applied Mathematics, vol. 141. Elsevier, Amsterdam (2004)
23. Rubin, S.: Automatic Structures. PhD thesis, University of Auckland (2004)
24. Rubin, S.: Automata presenting structures: A survey of the finite string case. Bulletin of Symbolic Logic 14, 169–209 (2008)
25. Thomas, W.: Automata on infinite objects. In: van Leeuwen, J. (ed.) Handbook of Theoretical Computer Science, ch. 4, pp. 133–191. Elsevier Science Publishers B. V., Amsterdam (1990)

Complexity Results for Modal Dependence Logic

Peter Lohmann* and Heribert Vollmer**

Institut für Theoretische Informatik
Leibniz Universität Hannover
Appelstr. 4, 30167 Hannover, Germany
{lohmann,vollmer}@thi.uni-hannover.de

Abstract. Modal dependence logic was introduced very recently by Väänänen. It enhances the basic modal language by an operator dep. For propositional variables $p_1, \ldots, p_n$, $\mathrm{dep}(p_1, \ldots, p_{n-1}; p_n)$ intuitively states that the value of p_n only depends on those of $p_1, \ldots, p_{n-1}$. Sevenster (J. Logic and Computation, 2009) showed that satisfiability for modal dependence logic is complete for nondeterministic exponential time.

In this paper we consider fragments of modal dependence logic obtained by restricting the set of allowed propositional connectives. We show that satisfibility for *poor man's dependence logic*, the language consisting of formulas built from literals and dependence atoms using $\wedge, \Box, \Diamond$ (i. e., disallowing disjunction), remains NEXPTIME-complete. If we only allow monotone formulas (without negation, but with disjunction), the complexity drops to PSPACE-completeness. We also extend Väänänen's language by allowing classical disjunction besides dependence disjunction and show that the satisfiability problem remains NEXPTIME-complete. If we then disallow both negation and dependence disjunction, satistiability is complete for the second level of the polynomial hierarchy.

In this way we completely classifiy the computational complexity of the satisfiability problem for all restrictions of propositional and dependence operators considered by Väänänen and Sevenster.

Keywords: dependence logic, satisfiability problem, computational complexity, poor man's logic.

1   Introduction

The concept of extending first-order logic with partially ordered quantifiers, and hence expressing some form of independence between variables, was first introduced by Henkin [8]. Later, Hintikka and Sandu developed independence friendly logic [9] which can be viewed as a generalization of Henkin's logic. Recently, Jouko Väänänen introduced the dual notion of functional dependence into the language of first-order logic [16]. In the case of first-order logic, the independence and the dependence variants are expressively equivalent.

Dependence among values of variables occurs everywhere in computer science (databases, software engineering, knowledge representation, AI) but also

* Supported by the NTH Focused Research School for IT Ecosystems.
** Supported in part by DFG VO 630/6-1.

A. Dawar and H. Veith (Eds.): CSL 2010, LNCS 6247, pp. 411–425, 2010.

the social sciences (human history, stock markets, etc.), and thus dependence logic is nowadays a much discussed formalism in the area called *logic for interaction*. Functional dependence of the value of a variable p_n from the values of the variables $p_1, \ldots, p_{n-1}$ states that there is a function, say f, such that $p_n = f(p_1, \ldots, p_{n-1})$, i. e., the value of p_n only depends on those of $p_1, \ldots, p_{n-1}$. We will denote this in this paper by $\mathrm{dep}(p_1, \ldots, p_{n-1}; p_n)$.

Of course, dependence does not manifest itself in a single world, play, event or observation. Important for such a dependence to make sense is a collection of such worlds, plays, events or observations. These collections are called *teams*. They are the basic objects in the definition of semantics of dependence logic. A team can be a set of plays in a game. Then $\mathrm{dep}(p_1, \ldots, p_{n-1}; p_n)$ intuitively states that in each play, move p_n is determined by moves $p_1, \ldots, p_{n-1}$. A team can be a database. Then $\mathrm{dep}(p_1, \ldots, p_{n-1}; p_n)$ intuitively states that in each line, the value of attribute p_n is determined by the values of attributes $p_1, \ldots, p_{n-1}$, i. e., that p_n is functionally dependent on $p_1, \ldots, p_{n-1}$. In first-order logic, a team formally is a set of assignments; and $\mathrm{dep}(p_1, \ldots, p_{n-1}; p_n)$ states that in each assignment, the value of p_n is determined by the values of $p_1, \ldots, p_{n-1}$. Most important for this paper, in modal logic, a team is a set of worlds in a Kripke structure; and $\mathrm{dep}(p_1, \ldots, p_{n-1}; p_n)$ states that in each of these worlds, the value of the propositional variable p_n is determined by the values of $p_1, \ldots, p_{n-1}$.

Dependence logic is defined by simply adding these dependence atoms to usual first-order logic [16]. Modal dependence logic (MDL) is defined by introducing these dependence atoms to modal logic [17,15]. The semantics of MDL is defined with respect to sets T of worlds in a frame (Kripke structure) W, for example $W, T \models \mathrm{dep}(p_1, \ldots, p_{n-1}; p_n)$ if for all worlds $s, t \in T$, if $p_1, \ldots, p_{n-1}$ have the same values in both s and t, then p_n has the same value in s and t, and a formula

$$\Box\mathrm{dep}(p_1, \ldots, p_{n-1}; p_n)$$

is satisfied in a world w in a Kripke structure W, if in the team T consisting of all successor worlds of w, $W, T \models \mathrm{dep}(p_1, \ldots, p_{n-1}; p_n)$.

MDL was introduced in [17]. Väänänen introduced besides the usual inductive semantics an equivalent game-theoretic semantics. Sevenster [15] considered the expressibility of MDL and proved, that on singleton teams T, there is a translation from MDL to usual modal logic, while on arbitrary sets of teams there is no such translation. Sevenster also initiated a complexity-theoretic study of modal dependence logic by proving that the satisfiability problem for MDL is complete for the class NEXPTIME of all problems decidable nondeterministically in exponential time.

In this paper, we continue the work of Sevenster by presenting a more thorough study on complexity questions related to modal dependence logic. A line of research going back to Lewis [11] and recently taken up in a number of papers [14,5,3,12] has considered fragments of different propositional logics by restricting the propositional and temporal operators allowed in the language. The rationale behind this approach is that by systematically restricting the language, one might find a fragment with efficient algorithms but still high enough expressibility in order to be interesting for applications. This in turn might lead to better tools for model checking, verification, etc. On the other hand, it is worthwhile to identify the sources of hardness: What exactly makes satisfiability, model checking, or other problems so hard for certain languages?

We follow the same approach here. We consider all subsets of modal operators $\Box, \Diamond$ and propositional operators $\wedge$, $\vee$, $^-$ (atomic negation), $\top, \bot$ (the Boolean constants true and false), i. e., we study exactly those operators considered by Väänänen [17], and examine the satisfiability problem for MDL restricted to the fragment given by these operators. In each case we exactly determine the computational complexity in terms of completeness for a complexity class such as NEXPTIME, PSPACE, coNP, etc., or by showing that the satisfiability problem admits an efficient (polynomial-time) solution. We also extend the logical language of [17] by adding classical disjunction (denoted here by Ⓥ) besides the dependence disjunction. Connective Ⓥ was already considered by Sevenster (he denoted it by •), but not from a complexity point of view. In this way, we obtain a complexity analysis of the satisfiability problem for MDL for all subsets of operators studied by Väänänen and Sevenster.

Our results are summarized in Table 1, where + denotes presence and − denotes absence of an operator, and ∗ states that the complexity does not depend on the operator. One of our main and technically most involved contributions addresses a fragment that has been called *Poor Man's Logic* in the literature on modal logic [5], i. e., the language without disjunction ∨. We show that for

Table 1. Complete classification of complexity for fragments of MDL-SAT All results are completeness results except for the P cases

□	◊	∧	∨	⁻	⊤	⊥	dep	Ⓥ	Complexity	Reference
+	+	+	∗	+	∗	∗	+	∗	NEXPTIME	Theorem 5
+	+	+	+	+	∗	∗	−	∗	PSPACE	Corollary 3a
+	+	+	+	−	∗	+	∗	∗	PSPACE	Corollary 3b
+	+	+	−	+	∗	∗	−	+	Σ_2^p	Theorem 4
+	+	+	−	−	∗	+	∗	+	Σ_2^p	Theorem 4
+	+	+	−	+	∗	∗	−	−	coNP	[10], [4]
+	+	+	−	−	∗	+	∗	−	coNP	Corollary 3c
+	−	+	+	+	∗	∗	∗	∗	NP	Corollary 7a
−	+	+	+	+	∗	∗	∗	∗	NP	Corollary 7a
+	−	+	−	+	∗	∗	∗	+	NP	Corollary 7a
−	+	+	−	+	∗	∗	∗	+	NP	Corollary 7a
+	−	+	−	+	∗	∗	∗	−	P	Corollary 7b
−	+	+	−	+	∗	∗	∗	−	P	Corollary 7b
+	−	+	∗	−	∗	∗	∗	∗	P	Corollary 7c
−	+	+	∗	−	∗	∗	∗	∗	P	Corollary 7c
∗	∗	−	∗	∗	∗	∗	∗	∗	P	Corollary 7d
∗	∗	∗	∗	−	∗	−	∗	∗	trivial	Corollary 3d
−	−	∗	∗	∗	∗	∗	∗	∗	ordinary propositional logic ((Ⓥ≡ ∨, dep(·;·) ≡ ⊤))	

+ : operator present   − : operator absent   ∗ : complexity independent of operator dependence logic we still have full complexity (Theorem 5, first line of the table), i. e., we show that Poor Man's Dependence Logic is NEXPTIME-complete. If we also forbid negation, then the complexity drops down to $\Sigma_2^p(=$ NP$^{\text{NP}})$; i. e., Monotone Poor Man's Dependence Logic is Σ_2^p-complete (Theorem 4, but note that we need $\bigvee$ here).

2 Modal Dependence Logic

We will only briefly introduce the syntax and semantics of modal dependence logic here. For a more profound overview consult Väänänen's introduction [17] or Sevenster's analysis [15] which includes a self-contained introduction to MDL.

2.1 Syntax

The formulas of *modal dependence logic* (MDL) are built from a set AP of *atomic propositions* and the MDL *operators* $\Box$, $\Diamond$, $\wedge$, $\vee$, $\dot{\neg}$ (also denoted $\neg$), $\top$, $\bot$, dep and $\bigvee$.

The set of MDL *formulas* is defined by the following grammar

$$\varphi ::= \top \mid \bot \mid p \mid \neg p \mid \text{dep}(p_1,\ldots,p_{n-1};p_n) \mid \neg\text{dep}(p_1,\ldots,p_{n-1};p_n) \mid$$
$$\varphi \wedge \varphi \mid \varphi \vee \varphi \mid \varphi \bigvee \varphi \mid \Box\varphi \mid \Diamond\varphi,$$

where $n \geq 1$.

All formulas in the first row will sometimes be denoted as *atomic* formulas and formulas of the form $\text{dep}(p_1,\ldots,p_{n-1};p_n)$ as *dependence atoms*. We sometimes write ∇^k for $\underbrace{\nabla\ldots\nabla}_{k \text{ times}}$ (with $\nabla \in \{\Box,\Diamond\}$, $k \in \mathbb{N}$).

2.2 Semantics

A *frame* (or *Kripke structure*) is a tuple $W = (S, R, \pi)$ where S is a non-empty set of *worlds*, $R \subseteq S \times S$ is the *accessibility relation* and $\pi : S \to \mathcal{P}(AP)$ is the *labeling function*.

In contrast to usual modal logic, truth of a MDL formula is not defined with respect to a single world of a frame but with respect to a set of worlds, as already pointed out in the introduction. The *truth* of a MDL formula φ in an *evaluation set* T of worlds of a frame $W = (S, R, \pi)$ is denoted by $W, T \models \varphi$ and is defined as follows:

$$
\begin{array}{lll}
W, T \models \top & & \text{always holds} \\
W, T \models \bot & \text{iff} & T = \emptyset \\
W, T \models p & \text{iff} & p \in \pi(s) \text{ for all } s \in T \\
W, T \models \neg p & \text{iff} & p \notin \pi(s) \text{ for all } s \in T \\
W, T \models \text{dep}(p_1,\ldots,p_{n-1};p_n) & \text{iff} & \text{for all } s_1, s_2 \in T \text{ with}
\end{array}
$$
$$\pi(s_1) \cap \{p_1,\ldots,p_{n-1}\} = \pi(s_2) \cap \{p_1,\ldots,p_{n-1}\}:$$
$$p_n \in \pi(s_1) \quad \text{iff} \quad p_n \in \pi(s_2)$$

$$
\begin{aligned}
W,T &\models \neg\mathrm{dep}(p_1,\dots,p_{n-1};p_n) &&\text{iff} && T = \emptyset \\
W,T &\models \varphi \wedge \psi &&\text{iff} && W,T \models \varphi \text{ and } W,T \models \psi \\
W,T &\models \varphi \vee \psi &&\text{iff} && \text{there are sets } T_1,T_2 \text{ with } T = T_1 \cup T_2, \\
& && && W,T_1 \models \varphi \text{ and } W,T_2 \models \psi \\
W,T &\models \varphi \,\mbox{\footnotesize$\bigvee$}\, \psi &&\text{iff} && W,T \models \varphi \text{ or } W,T \models \psi \\
W,T &\models \Box\varphi &&\text{iff} && W,\{s' \mid \exists s \in T \text{ with } (s,s') \in R\} \models \varphi \\
W,T &\models \Diamond\varphi &&\text{iff} && \text{there is a set } T' \subseteq S \text{ such that } W,T' \models \varphi \\
& && && \text{and for all } s \in T \text{ there is a } s' \in T' \text{ with} \\
& && && (s,s') \in R
\end{aligned}
$$

By $\vee$ we denote dependence disjunction instead of classical disjunction because the semantics of dependence disjunction is an extension of the semantics of usual modal logic disjunction and thus we preserve downward compatibility of our notation in this way. However, we still call the $\bigvee$ operator "classical" because in a higher level context – where our sets of states are viewed as single objects themselves – it is indeed the usual disjunction, cf. [1]. Note that rationales for the seemingly rather strange definitions of the truth of $\varphi \vee \psi$ as well as $\neg\mathrm{dep}(p_1,\dots,p_{n-1};p_n)$ were given by Väänänen [17,16].

For each $M \subseteq \{\Box,\Diamond,\wedge,\vee,\bar{\cdot},\top,\bot,\mathrm{dep},\bigvee\}$ define the set of $\mathsf{MDL}(M)$ formulas to be the set of MDL formulas which are built from atomic propositions using only operators and constants from M.

We are interested in the parameterized decision problem **MDL-SAT(M)**:

Given: A $\mathsf{MDL}(M)$ formula φ.
Question: Is there a frame W and a non-empty set T of worlds in W such that $W,T \models \varphi$?

Note that, as Väänänen already pointed out [17, Lemma 4.2.1], the semantics of MDL satisfies the *downward closure property*, i.e., if $W,T \models \varphi$, then $W,T' \models \varphi$ for all $T' \subseteq T$. Hence, to check satisfiability of a formula φ it is enough to check whether there is a frame W and a single world w in W such that $W,\{w\} \models \varphi$.

3   Complexity Results

To state the first lemma we need the following complexity operator. If $\mathcal{C}$ is an arbitrary complexity class then $\exists \cdot \mathcal{C}$ denotes the class of all sets A for which there is a set $B \in \mathcal{C}$ and a polynomial p such that for all x,

$$x \in A \text{ iff there is a } y \text{ with } |y| \leq p(|x|) \text{ and } \langle x,y \rangle \in B.$$

Note that for every class $\mathcal{C}$, $\exists \cdot \mathcal{C} \subseteq \mathrm{NP}^{\mathcal{C}}$. However, the converse does not hold in general. We will only need the following facts: $\exists \cdot \mathrm{coNP} = \Sigma_2^p$, $\exists \cdot \mathrm{PSPACE} = \mathrm{PSPACE}$ and $\exists \cdot \mathrm{NEXPTIME} = \mathrm{NEXPTIME}$.

Our first lemma concerns sets of operators including classical disjunction.

Lemma 1. *Let M be a set of* MDL *operators. Then it holds:*

a) *Every* $\mathsf{MDL}(M \cup \{\varovee\})$ *formula φ is equivalent to a formula $\bigvarovee_{i=1}^{2^{|\varphi|}} \psi_i$ with $\psi_i \in \mathsf{MDL}(M)$ for all $i \in \{1, \ldots, 2^{|\varphi|}\}$.*

b) *If $\mathcal{C}$ is an arbitrary complexity class with $\mathrm{P} \subseteq \mathcal{C}$ and $\mathsf{MDL\text{-}SAT}(M) \in \mathcal{C}$ then $\mathsf{MDL\text{-}SAT}(M \cup \{\varovee\}) \in \exists \cdot \mathcal{C}$.*

Proof. a) follows from the distributivity of $\varovee$ with all other operators. More specifically $\varphi \star (\psi \varovee \sigma) \equiv (\varphi \star \psi) \varovee (\varphi \star \sigma)$ for $\star \in \{\wedge, \vee\}$ and $\nabla(\varphi \varovee \psi) \equiv (\nabla\varphi) \varovee (\nabla\varphi)$ for $\nabla \in \{\Diamond, \Box\}$.[1] b) follows from a) with the observation that $\bigvarovee_{i=1}^{2^{|\varphi|}} \psi_i$ is satisfiable if and only if there is an $i \in \{1, \ldots, 2^{|\varphi|}\}$ such that ψ_i is satisfiable. Note that given $i \in \{1, \ldots, 2^{|\varphi|}\}$ the formula ψ_i can be computed from the original formula φ in polynomial time by choosing (for all $j \in \{1, \ldots, |\varphi|\}$) from the jth subformula of the form $\psi \varovee \sigma$ the formula ψ if the jth bit of i is 0 and σ if it is 1.   □

We need the following simple property of monotone MDL formulas.

Lemma 2. *Let M be a set of* MDL *operators with $\dot{\neg} \notin M$. Then an arbitrary* $\mathsf{MDL}(M)$ *formula φ is satisfiable iff the formula generated from φ by replacing every dependence atom and every atomic proposition with the same atomic proposition t is satisfiable.*

Proof. If a frame W is a model for φ, so is the frame generated from W by setting all atomic propositions in all worlds to true.   □

We are now able to classify some cases that can be easily reduced to known results.

Corollary 3. a) *If* $\{\Box, \Diamond, \wedge, \vee, \dot{\neg}\} \subseteq M \subseteq \{\Box, \Diamond, \wedge, \vee, \dot{\neg}, \top, \bot, \varovee\}$ *then* MDL-SAT(M) *is* PSPACE-*complete.*

b) *If* $\{\Box, \Diamond, \wedge, \vee, \bot\} \subseteq M \subseteq \{\Box, \Diamond, \wedge, \vee, \top, \bot, \mathrm{dep}, \varovee\}$ *then* MDL-SAT(M) *is* PSPACE-*complete.*

c) *If* $\{\Box, \Diamond, \wedge, \bot\} \subseteq M \subseteq \{\Box, \Diamond, \wedge, \top, \bot, \mathrm{dep}\}$ *then* MDL-SAT(M) *is* coNP-*complete.*

d) *If* $M \subseteq \{\Box, \Diamond, \wedge, \vee, \top, \mathrm{dep}, \varovee\}$ *then every* $\mathsf{MDL}(M)$ *formula is satisfiable.*

Proof. a) follows immediately from Ladner's proof for the case of ordinary modal logic [10], Lemma 1 and $\exists \cdot \mathrm{PSPACE} = \mathrm{PSPACE}$. The lower bound for b) was shown by Hemaspaandra [5, Theorem 6.5] and the upper bound follows from a) together with Lemma 2. The lower bound for c) was shown by Donini et al. [4] and the upper bound follows from Ladner's algorithm [10] together with Lemma 2. d) follows from Lemma 2 together with the fact that every MDL formula with t as the only atomic subformula is satisfied in the transitive singleton, i.e. the frame consisting of only one state which has itself as successor, in which t is true.   □

---

[1] Interestingly, but not of relevance for our work, $\varphi \varovee (\psi \vee \sigma) \not\equiv (\varphi \varovee \psi) \vee (\varphi \varovee \sigma)$.

3.1 Poor Man's Dependence Logic

We now turn to the Σ_2^p-complete cases. These include monotone poor man's logic, with and without dependence atoms.

Theorem 4. *If* $\{\Box, \Diamond, \wedge, \overline{}, \textcircled{\vee}\} \subseteq M \subseteq \{\Box, \Diamond, \wedge, \overline{}, \top, \bot, \textcircled{\vee}\}$ *or* $\{\Box, \Diamond, \wedge, \bot, \textcircled{\vee}\} \subseteq M \subseteq \{\Box, \Diamond, \wedge, \top, \bot, \text{dep}, \textcircled{\vee}\}$ *then* MDL-SAT(M) *is* Σ_2^p-*complete.*

Proof. Proving the upper bound for the second case reduces to proving the upper bound for the first case by Lemma 2. For the first case it holds with Lemma 1 that MDL-SAT$(\Box, \Diamond, \wedge, \overline{}, \top, \bot, \textcircled{\vee}) \in \exists \cdot \text{coNP} = \Sigma_2^p$ since MDL-SAT$(\Box, \Diamond, \wedge, \overline{}, \top, \bot) \in \text{coNP}$, which follows directly from Ladner's AP-algorithm for modal logic satisfiability [10].

For the lower bound we consider the quantified constraint satisfaction problem QCSP$_2(\text{R}_{1/3})$ shown to be Π_2^p-complete by Bauland et al. [2]. This problem can be reduced to the complement of MDL-SAT$(\Box, \Diamond, \wedge, \overline{}/\bot, \textcircled{\vee})$ in polynomial time.

An instance of QCSP$_2(\text{R}_{1/3})$ consists of universally quantified Boolean variables $p_1, \ldots, p_k$, existentially quantified Boolean variables $p_{k+1}, \ldots, p_n$ and a set of clauses each consisting of exactly three of those variables. QCSP$_2(\text{R}_{1/3})$ is the set of all those instances for which for every truth assignment for $p_1, \ldots, p_k$ there is a truth assignment for $p_{k+1}, \ldots, p_n$ such that in each clause exactly one variable evaluates to true.[2]

For the reduction from QCSP$_2(\text{R}_{1/3})$ to the complement of MDL-SAT$(\Box, \Diamond, \wedge, \overline{}/\bot, \textcircled{\vee})$ we extend a technique from the coNP-hardness proof for MDL-SAT$(\Box, \Diamond, \wedge, \bot)$ by Donini et al. [4, Theorem 3.3]. Let $p_1, \ldots, p_k$ be the universally quantified and $p_{k+1}, \ldots, p_n$ the existentially quantified variables of a QCSP$_2(\text{R}_{1/3})$ instance and let $C_1, \ldots, C_m$ be its clauses (we assume w.l.o.g. that each variable occurs in at least one clause). Then the corresponding MDL$(\Box, \Diamond, \wedge, \bot, \textcircled{\vee})$ formula is

$$
\begin{aligned}
\varphi := \bigwedge_{i=1}^{k} \big(\quad &\nabla_{i1} \ldots \nabla_{im}\, \nabla_{i1} \ldots \nabla_{im}\, \Box^{i-1}\Diamond\Box^{k-i}\, p \\
&\textcircled{\vee}\Box^m \qquad\quad \Box^m \qquad\quad \Box^{i-1}\Diamond\Box^{k-i}\, p\,\big) \\
\wedge \bigwedge_{i=k+1}^{n} \quad &\nabla_{i1} \ldots \nabla_{im}\, \nabla_{i1} \ldots \nabla_{im}\, \Box^{k} \qquad\qquad p \\
\wedge \quad &\Box^m \qquad\qquad \Box^m \qquad\quad \Box^{k} \qquad\qquad \bot
\end{aligned}
$$

where p is an arbitrary atomic proposition and $\nabla_{ij} := \begin{cases} \Diamond & \text{if } p_i \in C_j \\ \Box & \text{else} \end{cases}$.

For the corresponding MDL$(\Box, \Diamond, \wedge, \overline{}, \textcircled{\vee})$ formula replace every $\bot$ with $\neg p$.

To prove the correctness of our reduction we will need two claims.

Claim 1. For $r, s \geq 0$ a MDL$(\Box, \Diamond, \wedge, \overline{}, \top, \bot)$ formula $\Diamond\varphi_1 \wedge \cdots \wedge \Diamond\varphi_r \wedge \Box\psi_1 \wedge \cdots \wedge \Box\psi_s$ is unsatisfiable iff there is an $i \in \{1, \ldots, r\}$ such that $\varphi_i \wedge \psi_1 \wedge \cdots \wedge \psi_s$ is unsatisfiable.

---

[2] For our reduction it is necessary that in each clause the variables are pairwise different whereas in QCSP$_2(\text{R}_{1/3})$ this need not be the case. However, the Π_2^p-hardness proof can easily be adapted to account for this.

Proof of Claim 1. "⇐": If $\varphi_i \wedge \psi_1 \wedge \cdots \wedge \psi_s$ is unsatisfiable, so is $\Diamond\varphi_i \wedge \Box\psi_1 \wedge \cdots \wedge \Box\psi_s$ and even more $\Diamond\varphi_1 \wedge \cdots \wedge \Diamond\varphi_r \wedge \Box\psi_1 \wedge \cdots \wedge \Box\psi_s$.

"⇒: Suppose that $\varphi_i \wedge \psi_1 \wedge \cdots \wedge \psi_s$ is satisfiable for all $i \in \{1,\ldots,r\}$. Then $\Diamond\varphi_1 \wedge \cdots \wedge \Diamond\varphi_r \wedge \Box\psi_1 \wedge \cdots \wedge \Box\psi_s$ is satisfiable in a frame that consists of a root state and for each $i \in \{1,\ldots,r\}$ a separate branch, reachable from the root in one step, which satisfies $\varphi_i \wedge \psi_1 \wedge \cdots \wedge \psi_s$. $<<$

Note that $\Diamond\varphi_1 \wedge \cdots \wedge \Diamond\varphi_r \wedge \Box\psi_1 \wedge \cdots \wedge \Box\psi_s$ is always satisfiable if $r = 0$.

Definition. Let $v : \{p_1,\ldots,p_k\} \to \{0,1\}$ be a valuation of $\{p_1,\ldots,p_k\}$. Then φ_v denotes the $\mathsf{MDL}(\Box,\Diamond,\wedge,\overline{}/\bot)$ formula

$$
\begin{array}{llll}
\bigwedge_{\substack{i\in\{1,\ldots,k\},\\ v(p_i)=1}} & \nabla_{i1}\ldots\nabla_{im}\,\nabla_{i1}\ldots\nabla_{im}\,\Box^{i-1}\Diamond\Box^{k-i} & p \\[2.5em]
\wedge \quad \bigwedge_{\substack{i\in\{1,\ldots,k\},\\ v(p_i)=0}} & \Box^m \qquad\qquad \Box^m \qquad\qquad \Box^{i-1}\Diamond\Box^{k-i} & p \\[2.5em]
\wedge \quad \bigwedge_{i=k+1}^{n} & \nabla_{i1}\ldots\nabla_{im}\,\nabla_{i1}\ldots\nabla_{im}\,\Box^k & p \\[2em]
\wedge & \Box^m \qquad\qquad \Box^m \qquad\qquad \Box^k & \neg p\,/\bot
\end{array}
$$

Claim 2. Let $v : \{p_1,\ldots,p_k\} \to \{0,1\}$ be a valuation. Then φ_v is unsatisfiable iff v can be continued to a valuation $v' : \{p_1,\ldots,p_n\} \to \{0,1\}$ such that in each of the clauses $\{C_1,\ldots,C_m\}$ exactly one variable evaluates to true under v'.

Proof of Claim 2. By iterated use of Claim 1, φ_v is unsatisfiable iff there are $i_1,\ldots,i_{2m}$ with

$$
\begin{aligned}
i_j \in\ & \{i \in \{1,\ldots,n\} \mid \nabla_{ij'} = \Diamond\} \setminus \{i \in \{1,\ldots,k\} \mid v(p_i) = 0\} \\
=\ & \{i \in \{1,\ldots,n\} \mid p_i \in C_{j'}\} \setminus \{i \in \{1,\ldots,k\} \mid v(p_i) = 0\},
\end{aligned}
$$

where $j' := \begin{cases} j & \text{if } j \le m \\ j - m & \text{else} \end{cases}$,   such that

$$
\begin{array}{lll}
\varphi_v(i_1,\ldots,i_{2m}) := & \bigwedge_{\substack{i\in\{1,\ldots,k\},\\ i\in\{i_1,\ldots,i_{2m}\},\\ v(p_i)=1}} \Box^{i-1}\Diamond\Box^{k-i} & p \\[2.5em]
\wedge & \bigwedge_{\substack{i\in\{1,\ldots,k\},\\ v(p_i)=0}} \Box^{i-1}\Diamond\Box^{k-i} & p \\[2.5em]
\wedge & \bigwedge_{\substack{i\in\{k+1,\ldots,n\},\\ i\in\{i_1,\ldots,i_{2m}\}}} \Box^k & p \\[2.5em]
\wedge & \Box^k & \neg p\,/\bot
\end{array}
$$

is unsatisfiable (*i*) and such that there are no $a,b \in \{1,\ldots,2m\}$ with $a < b$, $\nabla_{i_b a'} = \nabla_{i_b b'} = \Diamond$ (this is the case iff $p_{i_b} \in C_{a'}$ and $p_{i_b} \in C_{b'}$) and $i_a \ne i_b$ (*ii*). The latter condition is already implied by Claim 1 as it simply ensures that no subformula is selected after it has already been discarded in an earlier step. Note that $\varphi_v(i_1,\ldots,i_{2m})$ is unsatisfiable iff for all $i \in \{1,\ldots,k\}$: $v(p_i) = 1$ and $i \in \{i_1,\ldots,i_{2m}\}$ or $v(p_i) = 0$ (and $i \notin \{i_1,\ldots,i_{2m}\}$) (*i'*).

We are now able to prove the claim.

"$\Leftarrow$": For $j = 1, \ldots, 2m$ choose $i_j \in \{1, \ldots, n\}$ such that $p_{i_j} \in C_{j'}$ and $v'(p_{i_j}) = 1$. By assumption, all i_j exist and are uniquely determined. Hence, for all $i \in \{1, \ldots, k\}$ we have that $v(p_i) = 0$ (and then $i \notin \{i_1, \ldots, i_{2m}\}$) or $v(p_i) = 1$ and there is a j such that $i_j = i$ (because each variable occurs in at least one clause). Therefore condition (i') is satisfied. Now suppose there are $a < b$ that violate condition (ii). By definition of i_b it holds that $p_{i_b} \in C_{b'}$ and $v'(p_{i_b}) = 1$. Analogously, $p_{i_a} \in C_{a'}$ and $v'(p_{i_a}) = 1$. By the supposition $p_{i_b} \in C_{a'}$ and $p_{i_a} \neq p_{i_b}$. But since $v'(p_{i_a}) = v'(p_{i_b}) = 1$, that is a contradiction to the fact that in clause $C_{a'}$ only one variable evaluates to true.

"$\Rightarrow$": If φ_v is unsatisfiable, there are $i_1, \ldots, i_{2m}$ such that (i') and (ii) hold. Let the valuation $v' : \{p_1, \ldots, p_n\} \to \{0, 1\}$ be defined by

$$v'(p_i) := \begin{cases} 1 \text{ if } i \in \{i_1, \ldots, i_{2m}\} \\ 0 \text{ else} \end{cases}.$$

Note that v' is a continuation of v because (i') holds.

We will now prove that in each of the clauses $C_1, \ldots, C_m$ exactly one variable evaluates to true under v'. Therefore let $j \in \{1, \ldots, m\}$ be arbitrarily chosen.

By choice of i_j it holds that $p_{i_j} \in C_j$. It follows by definition of v' that $v'(p_{i_j}) = 1$. Hence, there is at least one variable in C_j that evaluates to true.

Now suppose that besides p_{i_j} another variable in C_j evaluates to true. Then by definition of v' it follows that there is a $\ell \in \{1, \ldots, 2m\}, \ell \neq j$, such that this other variable is p_{i_ℓ}. We now consider two cases.

Case $j < \ell$: This is a contradiction to (ii) since, by definition of ℓ, p_{i_ℓ} is in $C_{j'}$ as well as, by definition of i_ℓ, in $C_{\ell'}$ and $i_j \neq i_\ell$.

Case $\ell < j$: Since $j \in \{1, \ldots, m\}$ it follows that $\ell \leq m$. Since $C_{\ell'} = C_{(\ell+m)'}$ it holds that $p_{i_{\ell+m}} \in C_{\ell'}$ and $p_{i_{\ell+m}} \in C_{(\ell+m)'}$. Furthermore $\ell < \ell + m$ and thus, by condition (ii), it must hold that $i_\ell = i_{\ell+m}$. Therefore $p_{i_{\ell+m}} \in C_j$ and $v'(p_{i_{\ell+m}}) = 1$. Because $j < \ell + m$ this is a contradiction to condition (ii) as in the first case. $<<$

The correctness of the reduction now follows with the observation that φ is

equivalent to $\displaystyle\bigvee_{v : \{p_1, \ldots, p_k\} \to \{0,1\}} \varphi_v$ and that φ is unsatisfiable iff φ_v is unsatisfiable

for all valuations $v : \{p_1, \ldots, p_k\} \to \{0, 1\}$.

The QCSP$_2$(R$_{1/3}$) instance is true iff every valuation $v : \{p_1, \ldots, p_k\} \to \{0, 1\}$ can be continued to a valuation $v' : \{p_1, \ldots, p_n\} \to \{0, 1\}$ such that in each of the clauses $\{C_1, \ldots, C_m\}$ exactly one variable evaluates to true under v' iff, by Claim 2, φ_v is unsatisfiable for all $v : \{p_1, \ldots, p_k\} \to \{0, 1\}$ iff, by the above observation, φ is unsatisfiable. $\square$

Next we turn to (non-monotone) poor man's logic.

Theorem 5. *If* $\{\Box, \Diamond, \wedge, \overline{}, \text{dep}\} \subseteq M$ *then* MDL-SAT(M) *is* NEXPTIME-*complete.*

Proof. Sevenster showed that the problem is in NEXPTIME in the case of $\Diamond \notin M$ [15, Lemma 14]. Together with Lemma 1 and the fact that $\exists \cdot$ NEXPTIME $=$ NEXPTIME the upper bound applies.

For the lower bound we reduce 3CNF-DQBF, which was shown to be NEXP-TIME-hard by Peterson et al. [13, Lemma 5.2.2][3], to our problem.

An instance of 3CNF-DQBF consists of universally quantified Boolean variables $p_1, \ldots, p_k$, existentially quantified Boolean variables $p_{k+1}, \ldots, p_n$, dependence constraints $P_{k+1}, \ldots, P_n \subseteq \{p_1, \ldots, p_k\}$ and a set of clauses each consisting of three (not necessarily distinct) literals. Here, P_i intuitively states that the value of p_i only depends on the values of the variables in P_i. Now, 3CNF-DQBF is the set of all those instances for which there is a collection of functions $f_{k+1}, \ldots, f_n$ with $f_i : \{0,1\}^{P_i} \to \{0,1\}$ such that for every valuation $v : \{p_1, \ldots, p_k\} \to \{0,1\}$ there is at least one literal in each clause that evaluates to true under the valuation $v' : \{p_1, \ldots, p_n\} \to \{0,1\}$ defined by

$$v'(p_i) := \begin{cases} v(p_i) & \text{if } i \in \{1, \ldots, k\} \\ f_i(v \upharpoonright P_i) & \text{if } i \in \{k+1, \ldots, n\} \end{cases} .$$

The functions $f_{k+1}, \ldots, f_n$ act as restricted existential quantifiers, i.e., for an $i \in \{k+1, \ldots, n\}$ the variable p_i can be assumed to be existentially quantified dependent on all universally quantified variables in P_i (and, more importantly, independent of all universally quantified variables not in P_i). Dependencies are thus explicitly specified through the dependence constraints and can contain – but are not limited to – the traditional sequential dependencies, e.g. the quantifier sequence $\forall p_1 \exists p_2 \forall p_3 \exists p_4$ can be modeled by the dependence constraints $P_2 = \{p_1\}$ and $P_4 = \{p_1, p_3\}$.

For the reduction from 3CNF-DQBF to MDL-SAT$(\Box, \Diamond, \wedge, \bar{\cdot}, \mathrm{dep})$ we use an idea from the PSPACE-hardness proof of MDL-SAT$(\Box, \Diamond, \wedge, \bar{\cdot})$ over a restricted frame class by Hemaspaandra [5, Theorem 4.2]. Let $p_1, \ldots, p_k$ be the universally quantified and $p_{k+1}, \ldots, p_n$ the existentially quantified variables of a 3CNF-DQBF instance φ and let $P_{k+1}, \ldots, P_n$ be its dependence constraints and $\{l_{11}, l_{12}, l_{13}\}, \ldots, \{l_{m1}, l_{m2}, l_{m3}\}$ its clauses. Then the corresponding MDL$(\Box, \Diamond, \wedge, \bar{\cdot}, \mathrm{dep})$ formula is

$$g(\varphi) := \bigwedge_{i=1}^{n} \Box^{i-1}(\Diamond\Box^{n-i}p_i \wedge \Diamond\Box^{n-i}\overline{p_i}) \qquad (i)$$

$$\wedge \bigwedge_{i=1}^{m} \Diamond^n(\overline{l_{i1}} \wedge \overline{l_{i2}} \wedge \overline{l_{i3}} \wedge f_i) \qquad (ii)$$

$$\wedge \bigwedge_{i=1}^{m} \Box^n \mathrm{dep}(l'_{i1}, l'_{i2}, l'_{i3}; f_i) \qquad (iii)$$

$$\wedge \Box^k \Diamond^{n-k} \left(\overline{f_1} \wedge \cdots \wedge \overline{f_m} \wedge \bigwedge_{i=k+1}^{n} \mathrm{dep}(P_i; p_i) \right) \qquad (iv)$$

where $p_1, \ldots, p_n, f_1, \ldots, f_m$ are atomic propositions and $l'_{ij} := \begin{cases} p & \text{if } l_{ij} = p \\ p & \text{if } l_{ij} = \overline{p} \end{cases} .$

Now if φ is valid, consider the frame which consists of a complete binary tree with n levels (not counting the root) and where each of the 2^n possible labelings

[3] Peterson et al. showed NEXPTIME-hardness for DQBF without the restriction that the formulae must be in 3CNF. However, the restriction does not lower the complexity since every propositional formula is satisfiability-equivalent to a formula in 3CNF whose size is bounded by a polynomial in the size of the original formula.

of the atomic propositions $p_1, \ldots, p_n$ occurs in exactly one leaf. Additionally, for each $i \in \{1, \ldots, m\}$ f_i is labeled in exactly those leaves in which $l_{i1} \vee l_{i2} \vee l_{i3}$ is false. This frame obviously satisfies (i), (ii) and (iii). And since the modalities in (iv) model the quantors of φ, $\overline{f_i}$ is true exactly in the leaves in which $l_{i1} \vee l_{i2} \vee l_{i3}$ is true and the dep atoms in (iv) model the dependence constraints of φ, (iv) is also true and therefore $g(\varphi)$ is satisfied in the root of the tree.

As an example see Fig. 1 for a frame satisfying $g(\varphi)$ if the first clause in φ is $\{\overline{p_1}, p_n\}$.

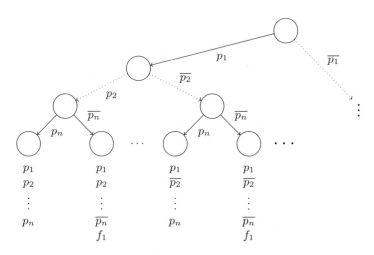

Fig. 1. Frame satisfying $g(\varphi)$

If, on the other hand, $g(\varphi)$ is satisfiable, let W be a frame and t a world in W such that $W, \{t\} \models g(\varphi)$. Now (i) enforces W to contain a complete binary tree T with root t such that each labeling of $p_1, \ldots, p_n$ occurs in a leaf of T.

We can further assume w.l.o.g. that W itself is a tree since in MDL different worlds with identical proposition labelings are indistinguishable and therefore every frame can simply be unwinded to become a tree. Since the modal depth of $g(\varphi)$ is n we can assume that the depth of W is at most n. And since (i) enforces that every path in W from t to a leaf has a length of at least n, all leaves of W lie at levels greater or equal to n. Altogether we can assume that W is a tree, that all its leaves lie at level n and that it has the same root as T. The only difference is that the degree of W may be greater than that of T.

But we can nonetheless assume that up to level k the degree of W is 2 $(*)$. This is the case because if any world up to level $k - 1$ had more successors than the two lying in T, the additional successors could be omitted and (i), (ii), (iii) and (iv) would still be fulfilled. For (i), (ii) and (iii) this is clear and for (iv) it holds because (iv) begins with $\square^k$.

We will now show that, although T may be a proper subframe of W, T is already sufficient to fulfill $g(\varphi)$. From this the validity of φ will follow immediately.

Claim. $T, \{t\} \models g(\varphi)$.

Proof of Claim. We consider sets of leaves of W that satisfy $\overline{f_1} \wedge \cdots \wedge \overline{f_m} \wedge \bigwedge_{i=k+1}^{n} \text{dep}(P_i; p_i)$ and that can be reached from the set $\{t\}$ by the modality sequence $\Box^k \Diamond^{n-k}$. Let S be such a set and let S be chosen so that there is no other such set that contains less worlds outside of T than S does. Assume there is a $s \in S$ that does not lie in T.

Let $i \in \{1, \ldots, m\}$ and let s' be the leaf in T that agrees with s on the labeling of $p_1, \ldots, p_n$. Then, with $W, \{s\} \models \overline{f_i}$ and (iii), it follows that $W, \{s'\} \models \overline{f_i}$.

Let $S' := (S \setminus \{s\}) \cup \{s'\}$. Then it follows by the previous paragraph that $W, S' \models \overline{f_1} \wedge \cdots \wedge \overline{f_m}$. Since $W, S \models \bigwedge_{i=k+1}^{n} \text{dep}(P_i; p_i)$ and s' agrees with s on the propositions $p_1, \ldots, p_n$ it follows that $W, S' \models \bigwedge_{i=k+1}^{n} \text{dep}(P_i; p_i)$. Hence, S' satisfies $\overline{f_1} \wedge \cdots \wedge \overline{f_m} \wedge \bigwedge_{i=k+1}^{n} \text{dep}(P_i; p_i)$ and as it only differs from S by replacing s with s' it can be reached from $\{t\}$ by $\Box^k \Diamond^{n-k}$ because s and s' agree on $p_1, \ldots, p_k$ and, by $(*)$, W does not differ from T up to level k. But this is a contradiction to the assumption since S' contains one world less than S outside of T. Thus, there is no $s \in S$ that does not lie in T and therefore (iv) is fulfilled in T. Since (i), (ii) and (iii) are obviously also fulfilled in T, it follows that $T, \{t\} \models g(\varphi)$. $<<$

(ii) ensures that for all $i \in \{1, \ldots, m\}$ there is a leaf in W in which $\neg(l_{i1} \vee l_{i2} \vee l_{i3}) \wedge f_i$ is true. This leaf can lie outside of T. However, (iii) ensures that all leaves that agree on the labeling of l_{i1}, l_{i2} and l_{i3} also agree on the labeling of f_i. And since there is a leaf where $\neg(l_{i1} \vee l_{i2} \vee l_{i3}) \wedge f_i$ is true, it follows that in all leaves, in which $\neg(l_{i1} \vee l_{i2} \vee l_{i3})$ is true, f_i is true. Conversely, if $\overline{f_i}$ is true in an arbitrary leaf of W then so is $l_{i1} \vee l_{i2} \vee l_{i3}$ $(**)$.

The modality sequence $\Box^k \Diamond^{n-k}$ models the quantors of φ and $\bigwedge_{i=k+1}^{n} \text{dep}(P_i; p_i)$ models its dependence constraints. And so there is a bijective correspondence between sets of worlds reachable in T by $\Box^k \Diamond^{n-k}$ from $\{t\}$ and that satisfy $\bigwedge_{i=k+1}^{n} \text{dep}(P_i; p_i)$ on the one hand and truth assignments to $p_1, \ldots, p_n$ generated by the quantors of φ and satisfying its dependence constraints on the other hand. Additionally, by $(**)$ follows that $\overline{f_1} \wedge \cdots \wedge \overline{f_m}$ implies $\bigwedge_{i=1}^{m}(l_{i1} \vee l_{i2} \vee l_{i3})$ and since $T, \{t\} \models g(\varphi)$, φ is valid. $\Box$

3.2   Cases with Only One Modality

We finally examine formulas with only one modality.

Theorem 6. *Let* $M \subseteq \{\Box, \Diamond, \wedge, \vee, {}^-, \top, \bot, \text{\textcircled{V}}\}$ *with* $\Box \notin M$ *or* $\Diamond \notin M$. *Then the following hold:*

a) $\text{MDL-SAT}(M \cup \{\text{dep}\}) \leq_m^p \text{MDL-SAT}(M \cup \{\top, \bot\})$, *i.e., adding the dep operator does not increase the complexity if we only have one modality.*

b) *For every* $\text{MDL}(M \cup \{\text{dep}\})$ *formula* φ *it holds that* $\text{\textcircled{V}}$ *is equivalent to* $\vee$, *i.e.,* φ *is equivalent to every formula that is generated from* φ *by replacing some or all occurrences of* $\text{\textcircled{V}}$ *by* $\vee$ *and vice versa.*

Proof. Every negation ¬dep of a dependence atom is by definition always equivalent to ⊥ and can thus be replaced by the latter. For positive dep atoms and the ⊙ operator we consider two cases.

Case ◊ ∉ M. If an arbitrary MDL(□, ∧, ∨, ⁻, ⊤, ⊥, dep, ⊙) formula φ is satisfiable then it is so in an intransitive singleton frame, i.e. a frame that only contains one world which does not have a successor, because there every subformula that begins with a □ is automatically satisfied. In a singleton frame all dep atoms obviously hold and ⊙ is equivalent to ∨. Therefore the (un-)satisfiability of φ is preserved when substituting every dep atom in φ with ⊤ and every ⊙ with ∨ (or vice versa).

Case □ ∉ M. If an arbitrary MDL(◊, ∧, ∨, ⁻, ⊤, ⊥, dep, ⊙) formula φ is satisfiable then, by the downward closure property, there is a frame W with a world s such that $W, \{s\} \models \varphi$. Since there is no □ in φ, every subformula of φ is also evaluated in a singleton set (because a ◊ can never increase the cardinality of the evaluation set). And as in the former case we can replace every dep atom with ⊤ and every ⊙ with ∨ (or vice versa).   □

Thus we obtain the following consequences – note that with the preceding results this takes care of all cases in Table 1.

Corollary 7. *a) If $\{\wedge, ^{-}\} \subseteq M \subseteq \{\Box, \Diamond, \wedge, \vee, ^{-}, \top, \bot, \text{dep}, \textcircled{\vee}\}$, $M \cap \{\vee, \textcircled{\vee}\} \neq \emptyset$ and $|M \cap \{\Box, \Diamond\}| = 1$ then MDL-SAT(M) is NP-complete.*
b) If $\{\wedge, ^{-}\} \subseteq M \subseteq \{\Box, \Diamond, \wedge, ^{-}, \top, \bot, \text{dep}\}$ and $|M \cap \{\Box, \Diamond\}| = 1$ then MDL-SAT(M) ∈ P.
c) If $\{\wedge\} \subseteq M \subseteq \{\Box, \Diamond, \wedge, \vee, \top, \bot, \text{dep}, \textcircled{\vee}\}$ and $|M \cap \{\Box, \Diamond\}| = 1$ then MDL-SAT(M) ∈ P.
d) If $\wedge \notin M$ then MDL-SAT(M) ∈ P.

Proof. a) follows from [5, Theorem 6.2(2)] and Theorem 6a,b. b) follows from [5, Theorem 6.4(c,d)] and Theorem 6a. c) follows from [5, Theorem 6.4(e,f)] and Theorem 6a,b.

For d) the proof of [5, Theorem 6.4(b)] can be adapted as follows. Let φ be an arbitrary MDL(M) formula. By the same argument as in the proof of Theorem 6b we can replace all top-level (i.e. not lying inside a modality) occurrences of ⊙ in φ with ∨ to get the equivalent formula φ'. φ' is of the form $\Box\psi_1 \vee \cdots \vee \Box\psi_k \vee \Diamond\sigma_1 \vee \cdots \vee \Diamond\sigma_m \vee a_1 \vee \cdots \vee a_s$ where every ψ_i and σ_i is a MDL(M) formula and every a_i is an atomic formula. If $k > 0$ or any a_i is a literal, ⊤ or a dependence atom then φ' is satisfiable. Otherwise it is satisfiable iff one of the σ_i is satisfiable and this can be checked recursively in polynomial time.   □

4 Conclusion

In this paper we completely classified the complexity of the satisfiability problem for modal dependence logic for all fragments of the language defined by restricting the modal and propositional operators to a subset of those considered by Väänänen and Sevenster. Interestingly, our results show a dichotomy for the dep operator; either the complexity jumps to NEXPTIME-completeness when introducing dep or it does not increase at all – and in the latter case the dep operator does not increase the expressiveness of the logic.

In a number of precursor papers, e. g., [11] on propositional logic or [3] on modal logic, not only subsets of the classical operators $\{\Box, \Diamond, \wedge, \vee, \overline{\cdot}\}$ were considered but also propositional connectives given by arbitrary Boolean functions. The main result of Lewis, e. g., can be succinctly summarized as follows: Propositional satisfiability is NP-complete if and only if in the input formulas the connective $\varphi \wedge \neg\psi$ is allowed (or can be "implemented" with the allowed connectives).

We consider it interesting to initiate such a more general study for modal dependence logic and determine the computational complexity of satisfiability if the allowed connectives are taken from a fixed class in Post's lattice. Contrary to propositional or modal logic, however, the semantics of such generalized formulas is not clear a priori – for instance, how should exclusive-or be defined in dependence logic? Even for simple implication, there seem to be several reasonable definitions, cf. [1].

A further possibly interesting restriction of dependence logic might be to restrict the type of functional dependency. Right now, dependence just means that there is some function whatsoever that determines the value of a variable from the given values of certain other variables. Also here it might be interesting to restrict the function to be taken from a fixed class in Post's lattice, e. g., to be monotone or self-dual.

Related is the more general problem of finding interesting fragments of modal dependence logic where adding the dep operator does not let the complexity of satisfiability testing jump up to NEXPTIME but still increases the expressiveness of the logic.

Finally, it seems advisable to study the expressiveness of MDL further – especially of the classical disjunction $\oslash$ and other extensions, e. g., implication. Also, the relation between MDL and first-order dependence logic seems to be an interesting field as there is no canonical embedding of MDL into first-order dependence logic.

References

1. Abramsky, S., Väänänen, J.: From IF to BI. Synthese 167(2), 207–230 (2009)
2. Bauland, M., Böhler, E., Creignou, N., Reith, S., Schnoor, H., Vollmer, H.: The complexity of problems for quantified constraints. Theory of Computing Systems (to appear), http://dx.doi.org/10.1007/s00224-009-9194-6
3. Bauland, M., Hemaspaandra, E., Schnoor, H., Schnoor, I.: Generalized modal satisfiability. In: Durand, B., Thomas, W. (eds.) STACS 2006. LNCS, vol. 3884, pp. 500–511. Springer, Heidelberg (2006), revised version: [7]
4. Donini, F.M., Lenzerini, M., Nardi, D., Hollunder, B., Nutt, W., Marchetti-Spaccamela, A.: The complexity of existential quantification in concept languages. Artif. Intell. 53(2-3), 309–327 (1992)
5. Hemaspaandra, E.: The complexity of poor man's logic. Journal of Logic and Computation 11(4), 609–622 (2001); corrected version: [6]

6. Hemaspaandra, E.: The complexity of poor man's logic. CoRR cs.LO/9911014v2 (2005), http://arxiv.org/abs/cs/9911014v2
7. Hemaspaandra, E., Schnoor, H., Schnoor, I.: Generalized modal satisability. CoRR abs/0804.2729 (2008), http://arxiv.org/abs/0804.2729
8. Henkin, L.: Some remarks on infinitely long formulas. In: Proceedings Symposium Foundations of Mathematics, Infinitistic Methods, pp. 167–183. Pergamon, Warsaw (1961)
9. Hintikka, J., Sandu, G.: Informational independence as a semantical phenomenon. In: Fenstad, J.E., Frolov, I.T., Hilpinen, R. (eds.) Logic, Methodology and Philosophy of Science, vol. 8, pp. 571–589. Elsevier, Amsterdam (1989)
10. Ladner, R.E.: The computational complexity of provability in systems of modal propositional logic. SIAM Journal on Computing 6(3), 467–480 (1977)
11. Lewis, H.: Satisfiability problems for propositional calculi. Mathematical Systems Theory 13, 45–53 (1979)
12. Meier, A., Mundhenk, M., Thomas, M., Vollmer, H.: The complexity of satisfiability for fragments of CTL and CTL*. Electronic Notes in Theoretical Computer Science, vol. 223, pp. 201–213 (2008), http://www.sciencedirect.com/science/article/B75H1-4V74F2X-H/2/c7a568c03e20ed2064b112167445414d; Proceedings of the Second Workshop on Reachability Problems in Computational Models (RP 2008)
13. Peterson, G., Reif, J., Azhar, S.: Lower bounds for multiplayer noncooperative games of incomplete information. Computers & Mathematics with Applications 41(7-8), 957–992 (2001), http://www.sciencedirect.com/science/article/B6TYJ-43P387P-19/2/cd72ba7ccb5f3c2a2b65eb3c45aa2ca7
14. Reith, S., Wagner, K.W.: The complexity of problems defined by boolean circuits. In: Proceedings International Conference Mathematical Foundation of Informatics (MFI 1999), pp. 25–28. World Science Publishing (2000)
15. Sevenster, M.: Model-theoretic and computational properties of modal dependence logic. Journal of Logic and Computation 19(6), 1157–1173 (2009), http://logcom.oxfordjournals.org/cgi/content/abstract/exn102v1
16. Väänänen, J.: Dependence logic: A new approach to independence friendly logic. London Mathematical Society student texts, vol. 70. Cambridge University Press, Cambridge (2007)
17. Väänänen, J.: Modal dependence logic. In: Apt, K.R., van Rooij, R. (eds.) New Perspectives on Games and Interaction, Texts in Logic and Games, vol. 4, pp. 237–254. Amsterdam University Press, Amsterdam (2008)

The Complexity of Positive First-Order Logic without Equality II: The Four-Element Case

Barnaby Martin[1,*] and Jos Martin[2]

[1] School of Engineering and Computing Sciences, Durham University,
Science Site, South Road, Durham DH1 3LE, U.K.
[2] The MathWorks, Matrix House, Cambridge, CB4 0HH, U.K.

Abstract. We study the complexity of evaluating positive equality-free sentences of first-order logic over fixed, finite structures $\mathcal{B}$. This may be seen as a natural generalisation of the non-uniform quantified constraint satisfaction problem QCSP($\mathcal{B}$). Extending the algebraic methods of a previous paper, we derive a complete complexity classification for these problems as $\mathcal{B}$ ranges over structures of domain size 4. Specifically, each problem is either in L, is NP-complete, is co-NP-complete or is Pspace-complete.

1 Introduction

We continue the study of the evaluation problem for positive equality-free first-order logic, on a fixed finite structure $\mathcal{B}$, denoted $\{\exists, \forall, \wedge, \vee\}$-FO($\mathcal{B}$), started in [5]. This problem is a close relative of the *constraint satisfaction problem*, CSP($\mathcal{B}$), and an even closer relative of the *quantified CSP*, QCSP($\mathcal{B}$). In fact, it is noted in [5] that among a wide family of problems, the only interesting case, other than the CSP and QCSP, is the one addressed in the present paper (the other cases fail to manifest complexity-theoretic richness). The bulk of the theoretical research into CSPs concerns the so-called *dichotomy conjecture*: that the complexity of the problem of evaluating a primitive positive sentence on a fixed finite $\mathcal{B}$, CSP($\mathcal{B}$), is either in P or is NP-complete. This was solved for structures with two-element domains in [9] and improved to encompass structures with three-element domains in [2]. The most successful approach to date, and the method used in [2], has been the so-called algebraic method, in which the problem of classification reverts to classes of functions under which the relevant relational systems are invariant. A similar algebraic approach has been successful in the study of the evaluation problem for positive Horn sentences, QCSP($\mathcal{B}$), and, while no formal trichotomy has there been conjectured, the only known attainable complexities are P, NP-complete and Pspace-complete.

The problem $\{\exists, \forall, \wedge, \vee\}$-FO($\mathcal{B}$) may be seen as a generalisation of CSP($\mathcal{B}$) (which becomes in our notation $\{\exists, \wedge, =\}$-FO($\mathcal{B}$)) and QCSP($\mathcal{B}$) ($\{\exists, \forall, \wedge, =\}$-FO($\mathcal{B}$)) despite the forbidding of equality – as in instances of CSP and QCSP,

---
* The first author is supported by EPSRC grant EP/G020604/1.

A. Dawar and H. Veith (Eds.): CSL 2010, LNCS 6247, pp. 426–438, 2010.

equalities may be propagated out in all but trivial cases. In contrast, the forbidding of equality from $\{\exists, \forall, \wedge, \vee =\}$-FO($\mathcal{B}$) becomes very significant, as these problems with equality have a straightforward complexity classification [7] (note that equalities may no longer be propagated out). In [5], the complexity of $\{\exists, \forall, \wedge, \vee\}$-FO($\mathcal{B}$) is studied through an analogous algebraic method to that used for CSP($\mathcal{B}$). The paper culminates in a full classification – a tetrachotomy – as $\mathcal{B}$ ranges over structures with three-element domains. Specifically, the problems $\{\exists, \forall, \wedge, \vee\}$-FO($\mathcal{B}$) are either Pspace-complete, NP-complete, co-NP-complete or in L. In this paper we extend this work to deriving a similar tetrachotomy for structures with a four-element domain. This is the largest domain size for which a comparable result is known. However, our task is somewhat easier since our lattices are finite for all finite domain sizes, while the clone lattice even for three-element domains – that is used for the study of CSP($\mathcal{B}$) – is not only infinite, but actually uncountable.

We derive our result by studying sets of surjective hyper-operations (shops) under which our relational $\mathcal{B}$ may be invariant. These sets, always containing the identity and closed under composition and sub-shops, are known as down shop-monoids (DSMs). For membership of L, NP and co-NP, it turns out that it is sufficient to have certain special shops as surjective hyper-endomorphisms (shes). In the four-element case, we are able to prove that these are necessary, too. We do this by isolating certain maximal DSMs and proving the relevant properties of them. Many of our proofs contain parts where the case-verification is undertaken by computer. There are 41503 shops on a four element domain, so the number of DSMs is bound by 2^{41503}. This is far too large a search space to simply be scanned, therefore we have come up with a novel, computational, inductive way to demonstrate that certain small collections of DSMs are exactly those that are in some sense "maximal". A trade-off between size of search space and number of putative solutions ensures that our computational procedures are not of too high complexity.

Having isolated the maximal DSMs, we find that we can use the methods of [5] to classify most of them, but there is one completely new class in the four-element case that is unlike anything in the three-element case. For this class, a separate proof of Pspace-hardness is required.

The paper is organised as follows. In Section 2, we detail the necessary preliminaries and necessary results of [5]. In Section 3, we prove the completeness of our Pspace-complete classes. Section 4, we prove the completeness of the NP-complete classes; Section 5 does likewise with the co-NP-complete classes. In Section 6, we conclude with the *coup de grâce* and some final remarks. The code used for the computational verification procedures is available at http://www.mathworks.com/matlabcentral/fileexchange/26264.

2   Preliminaries

Throughout, let $\mathcal{B}$ be a finite structure, with domain B, over the finite relational signature σ. Let $\{\exists, \forall, \wedge, \vee\}$-FO be the positive fragment of first-order (FO) logic without equality. An *extensional* relation is one that appears in the signature σ. We will usually denote extensional relations of $\mathcal{B}$ by R and other relations by S (or by some formula that defines them). In $\{\exists, \forall, \wedge, \vee\}$-FO the atomic formulae are exactly substitution instances of extensional relations. The problem $\{\exists, \forall, \wedge, \vee\}$-FO$(\mathcal{B})$ has:

- Input: a sentence $\varphi \in \{\exists, \forall, \wedge, \vee\}$-FO.
- Question: does $\mathcal{B} \models \varphi$?

When $\mathcal{B}$ is of size one, the evaluation of any FO sentence may be accomplished in L (essentially, the quantifiers are irrelevant and the problem amounts to the *boolean sentence value problem*, see [4]). In this case, it follows that $\{\exists, \forall, \wedge, \vee\}$-FO$(\mathcal{B})$ is in L. Furthermore, by inward evaluation of the quantifiers, $\{\exists, \forall, \wedge, \vee\}$-FO$(\mathcal{B})$ is readily seen to always be in Pspace.

Consider the set B and its power set $\mathfrak{P}(B)$. A *hyper-operation* on B is a function $f : B \to \mathfrak{P}(B) \setminus \{\emptyset\}$ (that the image may not be the empty set corresponds to the hyper-operation being *total*, in the parlance of [1]). If the hyper-operation f has the additional property that

- for all $y \in B$, there exists $x \in B$ such that $y \in f(x)$,

then we designate (somewhat abusing terminology) f *surjective*. A surjective hyper-operation (shop) in which each element is mapped to a singleton set is identified with a *permutation* (bijection). A *surjective hyper-endomorphism* (she) of $\mathcal{B}$ is a shop f on B that satisfies, for all extensional relations R of $\mathcal{B}$,

- if $\mathcal{B} \models R(x_1, \ldots, x_i)$ then, for all $y_1 \in f(x_1), \ldots, y_i \in f(x_i)$, $\mathcal{B} \models R(y_1, \ldots, y_i)$.

A she may be identified with a *surjective endomorphism* if each element is mapped to a singleton set. On finite structures surjective endomorphisms are necessarily automorphisms.

2.1   Galois Connections

For a set F of shops on the finite domain B, let $\mathsf{Inv}(F)$ be the set of relations on B of which each $f \in F$ is a she (when these relations are viewed as a structure over B). We say that $S \in \mathsf{Inv}(F)$ is invariant or *preserved* by (the shops in) F. Let $\mathsf{shE}(\mathcal{B})$ be the set of shes of $\mathcal{B}$. Let $\langle \mathcal{B} \rangle_{\{\exists, \forall, \wedge, \vee\}\text{-FO}}$ be the set of relations that may be defined on $\mathcal{B}$ in $\{\exists, \forall, \wedge, \vee\}$-FO. We recall the following results from [5], where $\leq_\mathsf{L}$ indicates logspace many-to-one reduction.

Theorem 1 ([5]). *For a finite structure $\mathcal{B}$ we have*

(i) $\langle \mathcal{B} \rangle_{\{\exists, \forall, \wedge, \vee\}\text{-FO}} = \mathsf{Inv}(\mathsf{shE}(\mathcal{B}))$, *and*
(ii) *If* $\mathsf{shE}(\mathcal{B}) \subseteq \mathsf{shE}(\mathcal{B}')$ *then* $\{\exists, \forall, \wedge, \vee\}$-FO$(\mathcal{B}') \leq_\mathsf{L} \{\exists, \forall, \wedge, \vee\}$-FO$(\mathcal{B})$.

2.2   Down-She-Monoids

Consider a finite domain B. The *identity* shop id_B is defined by $x \mapsto \{x\}$. Given shops f and g, define the *composition* $g \circ f$ by $x \mapsto \{z : \exists y\ z \in g(y) \wedge y \in f(x)\}$. Finally, a shop f is a *sub-shop* of g – denoted $f \subseteq g$ – if $f(x) \subseteq g(x)$, for all x. A set of shops on a finite set B is a *down-shop-monoid* (DSM), if it contains id_B, and is closed under composition and sub-shops (of course, not all sub-hyper-operations of a shop are surjective – we are only concerned with those that are). id_B is a she of all structures, and, if f and g are shes of $\mathcal{B}$, then so is $g \circ f$. Further, if g is a she of $\mathcal{B}$, then so is f for all (surjective) $f \subseteq g$. It follows that $\mathsf{shE}(\mathcal{B})$ is always a DSM. The DSMs of B form a lattice under (set-theoretic) inclusion and, as per the Galois connection of Theorem 1, classify the complexities of $\{\exists, \forall, \wedge, \vee\}$-$\mathsf{FO}(\mathcal{B})$. If F is a set of shops on B, then let $\langle F \rangle$ denote the minimal DSM containing the shops of F. If F is the singleton $\{f\}$, then, by abuse of notation, we write $\langle f \rangle$ instead of $\langle \{f\} \rangle$

Lemma 1 ([5]). *Let $\mathcal{B}$, with $|B| \geq 2$, be a structure s.t. $\mathsf{shE}(\mathcal{B})$ is a permutation subgroup. Then $\{\exists, \forall, \wedge, \vee\}$-$\mathsf{FO}(\mathcal{B})$ is Pspace-hard.*

Proof. Let $\mathcal{B}_{NAE}$ be the structure on B with a single ternary relation $R_{NAE} := B^3 \setminus \{(b,b,b) : b \in B\}$. $\{\exists, \forall, \wedge, \vee\}$-$\mathsf{FO}(\mathcal{B}_{NAE})$ is a generalisation of the problem $\mathsf{QCSP}(\mathcal{B}_{NAE})$, well-known to be Pspace-complete (in the case $|B| = 2$, this is *quantified not-all-equal 3-satisfiability*, see, e.g., [8]). $\mathsf{shE}(\mathcal{B}_{NAE})$ is the symmetric group $S_{|B|}$. The statement of the theorem now follows from Theorem 1, since $\mathsf{shE}(\mathcal{B}) \subseteq \mathsf{shE}(\mathcal{B}_{NAE})$.

The following is a generalisation of Lemma 1.

Lemma 2 ([5]). *Let $\mathcal{B}$ be a structure whose universe admits the partition $B_1, \ldots, B_l$ ($l \geq 2$). If all shes of $\mathcal{B}$ are sub-shops of some f of the form $f(x) := B_i$ iff $x \in B_{\pi(i)}$, for π a permutation on the set $\{1, \ldots, l\}$, then $\{\exists, \forall, \wedge, \vee\}$-$\mathsf{FO}(\mathcal{B})$ is Pspace-hard.*

Proof. Let $\mathcal{K}_{|B_1|,\ldots,|B_l|}$ be the complete l-partite graph with partitions of size $|B_1|, \ldots, |B_l|$. It may easily be verified that $\mathsf{shE}(\mathcal{B}) \subseteq \mathsf{shE}(\mathcal{K}_{|B_1|,\ldots,|B_l|})$. Furthermore, $\mathcal{K}_{|B_1|,\ldots,|B_l|}$ agrees with the antireflexive l-clique $\mathcal{K}_l$ on all sentences of equality-free FO logic (for more detail on why this is, see, e.g., the Homomorphism Theorem of [3]), and certainly $\{\exists, \forall, \wedge, \vee\}$-$\mathsf{FO}$. Pspace-hardness of $\{\exists, \forall, \wedge, \vee\}$-$\mathsf{FO}(\mathcal{K}_l)$ follows from the Lemma 1, and so Pspace-hardness of $\{\exists, \forall, \wedge, \vee\}$-$\mathsf{FO}(\mathcal{K}_{|B_1|,\ldots,|B_l|})$ follows a fortiori. Finally, Pspace-hardness of $\{\exists, \forall, \wedge, \vee\}$-$\mathsf{FO}(\mathcal{B})$ now follows from Theorem 1.

Call a shop $f : B \to \mathfrak{P}(B) \setminus \{\emptyset\}$ an A-*shop* if there exists $b \in B$ s.t. $f(b) = B$. Call f an E-*shop* if there exists $b \in B$ s.t. $b \in f(x)$, for all $x \in B$. The following is a generalisation of a result from [5] that appears in the journal version of that paper, [6].

Theorem 2. *If $\mathcal{B}$ has an A-shop as a she then $\{\exists, \forall, \wedge, \vee\}$-FO($\mathcal{B}$) is in* NP. *If $\mathcal{B}$ has an E-shop as a she then $\{\exists, \forall, \wedge, \vee\}$-FO($\mathcal{B}$) is in* co-NP. *If $\mathcal{B}$ has both an A-shop and an E-shop as a she then $\{\exists, \forall, \wedge, \vee\}$-FO($\mathcal{B}$) is in* L.[1]

The following is the main result of [5].

Theorem 3 (Tetrachotomy [5]). *Let $\mathcal{B}$ be s.t. $|\mathcal{B}| \leq 3$.*

  I. *If* shE($\mathcal{B}$) *contains both an A-shop and an E-shop, then $\{\exists, \forall, \wedge, \vee\}$-FO($\mathcal{B}$) is in* L.
  II. *If* shE($\mathcal{B}$) *contains an A-shop but no E-shop, then $\{\exists, \forall, \wedge, \vee\}$-FO($\mathcal{B}$) is* NP-*complete.*
  III. *If* shE($\mathcal{B}$) *contains an E-shop but no A-shop, then $\{\exists, \forall, \wedge, \vee\}$-FO($\mathcal{B}$) is* co-NP-*complete.*
  IV. *If* shE($\mathcal{B}$) *contains neither an A-shop nor an E-shop, then $\{\exists, \forall, \wedge, \vee\}$-FO($\mathcal{B}$) is* Pspace-*complete.*

3   The Pspace-case

This section will progress in the pursuit of the following.

Proposition 1. *If* shE($\mathcal{B}$), *where $|\mathcal{B}| = 4$, contains neither an A-shop nor an E-shop, then $\{\exists, \forall, \wedge, \vee\}$-FO($\mathcal{B}$) is* Pspace-*complete.*

This will follow from the classification of all maximal DSMs which contain neither an A-shop nor an E-shop. Call a DSM M *maximally* Pspace-*hard* if M contains neither an A-shop nor an E-shop, but for any shop $f \notin M$, $\langle M \cup \{f\}\rangle$ contains either an A-shop or an E-shop. In the case of the three-element domain there are four maximally Pspace-hard DSMs, $\left\langle \begin{smallmatrix} 0|12 \\ 1|0 \\ 2|0 \end{smallmatrix} \right\rangle$, $\left\langle \begin{smallmatrix} 0|1 \\ 1|02 \\ 2|1 \end{smallmatrix} \right\rangle$, $\left\langle \begin{smallmatrix} 0|2 \\ 1|2 \\ 2|01 \end{smallmatrix} \right\rangle$ and $\left\langle \begin{smallmatrix} 0|1 \\ 1|0 \\ 2|2 \end{smallmatrix}, \begin{smallmatrix} 0|0 \\ 1|2 \\ 2|1 \end{smallmatrix} \right\rangle$, in two classes [5]. The first class involves three DSMs that are copies of the symmetric group S_2 obtained from a three-element domain by blurring two elements to one, and the second class involves the single DSM S_3. In the case of a four-element domain, it follows from Lemma 6, below, that there are twenty maximally Pspace-hard DSMs, in five classes.

Class V contains only S_4. Class IV contains variants of S_3 formed by blurring two elements to one. Classes III and II are each variants of S_2, in III there are three elements blurred to one, while in IV there are twice two elements blurred to one. Class I, however, is of a different form altogether. It is not based on a symmetric group, and provides sport in the four-element case that was absent from the three-element case – where all maximally Pspace-hard DSMs were variants of S_2 or S_3. We know from [5] how to classify the complexity for Classes II – V, but we will need a new proof for Class I. Let $M_1, \ldots, M_{20}$

---

[1] In this last case, $\{\exists, \forall, \wedge, \vee\}$-FO($\mathcal{B}$) can be seen to be in *alternating logarithmic time* – like the boolean sentence value problem of which it is essentially an instance. It follows that the L membership results of this paper are unlikely to be concurrently L-complete.

enumerate the DSMs of Classes I – V. We note that, although one may verify that the single DSM of Class V is maximally Pspace-hard, the union of the DSMs of Classes I-IV in fact equals the union of the DSMs of Classes I-V.

Class I	Class II	Class III	Class IV	Class V

Class I:

$$\left\langle \begin{smallmatrix}0&1\\1&0\\2&012\\3&013\end{smallmatrix}, \begin{smallmatrix}0&0\\1&1\\2&013\\3&012\end{smallmatrix}\right\rangle \quad \left\langle \begin{smallmatrix}0&2\\1&012\\2&0\\3&023\end{smallmatrix}, \begin{smallmatrix}0&0\\1&023\\2&2\\3&012\end{smallmatrix}\right\rangle \quad \left\langle \begin{smallmatrix}0&3\\1&013\\2&023\\3&0\end{smallmatrix}, \begin{smallmatrix}0&0\\1&023\\2&013\\3&3\end{smallmatrix}\right\rangle$$

$$\left\langle \begin{smallmatrix}0&012\\1&2\\2&1\\3&123\end{smallmatrix}, \begin{smallmatrix}0&123\\1&1\\2&2\\3&012\end{smallmatrix}\right\rangle \quad \left\langle \begin{smallmatrix}0&013\\1&3\\2&123\\3&1\end{smallmatrix}, \begin{smallmatrix}0&123\\1&1\\2&013\\3&3\end{smallmatrix}\right\rangle \quad \left\langle \begin{smallmatrix}0&023\\1&123\\2&3\\3&2\end{smallmatrix}, \begin{smallmatrix}0&123\\1&023\\2&2\\3&3\end{smallmatrix}\right\rangle$$

Class II:

$$\left\langle \begin{smallmatrix}0&23\\1&23\\2&01\\3&01\end{smallmatrix}\right\rangle \quad \left\langle \begin{smallmatrix}0&13\\1&02\\2&13\\3&02\end{smallmatrix}\right\rangle \quad \left\langle \begin{smallmatrix}0&03\\1&03\\2&03\\3&12\end{smallmatrix}\right\rangle$$

Class III:

$$\left\langle \begin{smallmatrix}0&3\\1&3\\2&3\\3&012\end{smallmatrix}\right\rangle \quad \left\langle \begin{smallmatrix}0&2\\1&2\\2&013\\3&2\end{smallmatrix}\right\rangle \quad \left\langle \begin{smallmatrix}0&1\\1&023\\2&1\\3&1\end{smallmatrix}\right\rangle \quad \left\langle \begin{smallmatrix}0&123\\1&0\\2&0\\3&0\end{smallmatrix}\right\rangle$$

Class IV:

$$\left\langle \begin{smallmatrix}0&2\\1&2\\2&01\\3&3\end{smallmatrix}, \begin{smallmatrix}0&01\\1&01\\2&3\\3&2\end{smallmatrix}\right\rangle \quad \left\langle \begin{smallmatrix}0&1\\1&02\\2&1\\3&3\end{smallmatrix}, \begin{smallmatrix}0&02\\1&3\\2&02\\3&1\end{smallmatrix}\right\rangle$$

$$\left\langle \begin{smallmatrix}0&1\\1&03\\2&2\\3&1\end{smallmatrix}, \begin{smallmatrix}0&03\\1&2\\2&1\\3&03\end{smallmatrix}\right\rangle \quad \left\langle \begin{smallmatrix}0&12\\1&0\\2&0\\3&3\end{smallmatrix}, \begin{smallmatrix}0&3\\1&12\\2&12\\3&0\end{smallmatrix}\right\rangle$$

$$\left\langle \begin{smallmatrix}0&13\\1&0\\2&2\\3&0\end{smallmatrix}, \begin{smallmatrix}0&2\\1&13\\2&0\\3&13\end{smallmatrix}\right\rangle \quad \left\langle \begin{smallmatrix}0&23\\1&1\\2&0\\3&0\end{smallmatrix}, \begin{smallmatrix}0&1\\1&0\\2&23\\3&23\end{smallmatrix}\right\rangle$$

Class V:

$$\left\langle \begin{smallmatrix}0&1\\1&0\\2&2\\3&3\end{smallmatrix}, \begin{smallmatrix}0&0\\1&2\\2&1\\3&3\end{smallmatrix}, \begin{smallmatrix}0&0\\1&1\\2&3\\3&2\end{smallmatrix}\right\rangle$$

Lemma 3. *Let* shE($\mathcal{B}$) *be any of the DSMs in Classes II – V. Then* $\{\exists, \forall, \wedge, \vee\}$-FO($\mathcal{B}$) *is* Pspace-*hard*.

Proof. A canonical representative $\mathcal{B}$ for each of the Classes II – V is drawn in Figure 1 (a canonical representative of a DSM here becomes an exact representative under a certain labelling of the vertices by $\{0, 1, 2, 3\}$). That is, a $\mathcal{B}$ is drawn s.t. shE($\mathcal{B}$) ranges over the DSMs of Classes II – V. The result follows from Lemmas 1 and 2.

Lemma 4. *Let* shE($\mathcal{B}$) *be any of the the DSMs in Class I. Then* $\{\exists, \forall, \wedge, \vee\}$-FO($\mathcal{B}$) *is* Pspace-*hard*.

Proof. Let us begin by introducing the following graph $\mathcal{H}$. Note that shE($\mathcal{H}$) is in fact $\left\langle \begin{smallmatrix}0&123\\1&2\\2&1\\3&012\end{smallmatrix}\right\rangle \subset \left\langle \begin{smallmatrix}0&123\\1&1\\2&2\\3&012\end{smallmatrix}, \begin{smallmatrix}0&012\\1&2\\2&1\\3&123\end{smallmatrix}\right\rangle$.

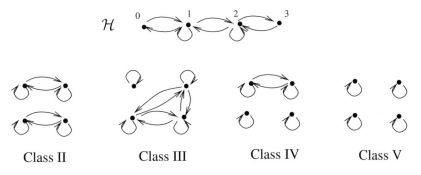

Fig. 1. Canonical representatives

We will first prove that $\{\exists, \forall, \wedge, \vee\}$-$\mathsf{FO}(\mathcal{H})$ is Pspace-hard, by reduction from $\mathrm{QCSP}(\mathcal{B}_{NAE})$ (introduced in the proof of Lemma 1). Define $\Theta(x, v^\top, v^\perp, y)$ to be

$$E(x, v^\top) \wedge E(v^\top, v^\top) \wedge E(v^\top, v^\perp) \wedge E(v^\perp, v^\perp) \wedge E(v^\perp, y).$$

From an instance of $\mathrm{QCSP}(\mathcal{B}_{NAE})$, we build an instance of $\{\exists, \forall, \wedge, \vee\}$-$\mathsf{FO}(\mathcal{H})$. In the following, when we talk of adding to the body we mean adding conjunctively. Firstly,

– for each clause $C_j := (v_\alpha \vee v_\beta \vee v_\gamma)$ we introduce to the body $\forall s_j, t_j$

$$(\exists r_j E(s_j, r_j) \wedge E(r_j, t_j)) \vee \Theta(s_j, v_\alpha^\top, v_\alpha^\perp, t_j) \vee \Theta(s_j, v_\beta^\top, v_\beta^\perp, t_j) \vee \Theta(s_j, v_\gamma^\top, v_\gamma^\perp, t_j).$$

Note that the first disjunct is satisfiable whenever s_j, t_j are *not* evaluated at opposite ends of $\mathcal{H}$, i.e. not to 0, 3 or 3, 0. Therefore we need only consider the Θ disjunctions when s_j, t_j is 0, 3 or 3, 0. Thereafter, and following the prefix order of the instance of $\mathrm{QCSP}(\mathcal{B}_{NAE})$,

– for each existentially quantified variable v_i, we add $\exists v_i^\top, v_i^\perp \forall x_i, y_i$ to the quantifier prefix and to the body

$$(\exists w_i E(x_i, w_i) \wedge E(w_i, y_i)) \vee \Theta(x_i, v_i^\top, v_i^\perp, y_i) \vee \Theta(x_i, v_i^\perp, v_i^\top, y_i)$$

– For each universally quantified variable v_i, we add $\forall z_i \exists v_i^\top, v_i^\perp \forall x_i, y_i$ to the quantifier prefix and to the body

$$(\exists w_i E(x_i, w_i) \wedge E(w_i, y_i)) \vee \left(E(z_i, v_i^\top) \wedge (\Theta(x_i, v_i^\top, v_i^\perp, y_i) \vee \Theta(x_i, v_i^\perp, v_i^\top, y_i))\right)$$

Suppose we have a yes-instance $\mathrm{QCSP}(\mathcal{B}_{NAE})$. No matter how the z_i are evaluated, there is the possibility of placing each $(v_i^\top, v_i^\perp)$ on one of $(1, 2)$ or $(2, 1)$, corresponding to the variable v_i being true or false, respectively. Finally, we check with the clause variables s_j and t_j that the assignment to each clause is not-all-equal. It follows that we have a yes-instance of $\{\exists, \forall, \wedge, \vee\}$-$\mathsf{FO}(\mathcal{H})$. Conversely, a yes-instance of $\{\exists, \forall, \wedge, \vee\}$-$\mathsf{FO}(\mathcal{H})$ verifies all mappings to the universal variables v_i, through the choice of z_i, since each $(v_i^\top, v_i^\perp)$ is forced to map to one of $(1, 2)$ or $(2, 1)$. A valuation for the variables of $\mathrm{QCSP}(\mathcal{B}_{NAE})$ may be read from this.

Let Σ be the set of pairs of the edge set of $\mathcal{H}$, i.e. $\{(0, 1), (1, 0), (1, 1), (1, 2), (2, 1), (2, 2), (2, 3), (3, 2)\}$. Let

$$\Sigma' := \{(0, 2), (2, 0), (2, 2), (2, 1), (1, 2), (1, 1), (1, 3), (3, 1)\}.$$

Note that the digraph given by Σ' is isomorphic to $\mathcal{H}$. We now introduce the structure $\mathcal{H}'$, on domain $\{0, 1, 2, 3\}$, with a single 4-ary relation R given by the union of

$$\begin{array}{ll} (1, 3) \times \Sigma & \qquad (1, 0) \times \Sigma' \\ (2, 0) \times \Sigma & \qquad (2, 3) \times \Sigma' \\ (1, 1) \times \Sigma & \qquad (2, 1) \times \Sigma' \\ (1, 2) \times \Sigma & \qquad (2, 2) \times \Sigma' \end{array}$$

where, e.g., $(1,3) \times \Sigma$ is the set of quadruples $\{(1,3,0,1),(1,3,1,0),(1,3,1,1),$
$(1,3,1,2),(1,3,2,1),(1,3,2,2),(1,3,2,3),(1,3,3,2)\}$. Now, $\mathsf{shE}(\mathcal{H}')$ is $\langle \begin{smallmatrix} 0 & 123 \\ 1 & 1 \\ 2 & 2 \\ 3 & 012 \end{smallmatrix}, \begin{smallmatrix} 0 & 012 \\ 1 & 2 \\ 2 & 1 \\ 3 & 123 \end{smallmatrix} \rangle$.
Further, we can prove $\{\exists, \forall, \wedge, \vee\}$-$\mathsf{FO}(\mathcal{H}')$ is Pspace-hard exacly as we did $\{\exists, \forall, \wedge, \vee\}$-$\mathsf{FO}(\mathcal{H})$, by adding $\forall q \exists p\, R(p,q,p,p)$ to the sentence and turning all instances of $E(u,v)$ to $R(p,q,u,v)$. The non-trivial cases then arise when $q \in \{0,3\}$, and a choice for $p \in \{1,2\}$ selects either Σ or Σ' to be the copy in which the remainder of the sentence is evaluated.

It remains for us to demonstrate that all DSMs that contain neither an A-shop nor an E-shop are sub-DSMs of one of the twenty maximally Pspace-hard DSMs of Classes I-V.

Lemma 5. *The shops f s.t. $\langle f \rangle$ contains neither an A-shop nor an E-shop number 1478 and are exactly those from the twenty DSMs in Classes I-V.*

Proof. Verification by computer. For any shop f, if none of f, f^2, f^4, f^8 is an A-shop or E-shop then check that f is in one of the DSMs $M_1, \ldots, M_{20}$.[2]

It follows that DSMs which contain neither an A-shop nor an E-shop must draw their members exclusively from among $M_1, \ldots, M_{20}$.

Lemma 6. *The maximally Pspace-hard DSMs are precisely those of $M_1, \ldots, M_{20}$.*

Proof. That for no $i, j \in \{1, \ldots, 20\}$ is $M_i \subseteq M_j$ may readily be seen. We will prove that there is no further maximally Pspace-hard DSM.

Let M be a maximally Pspace-hard DSM that is not among $M_1, \ldots, M_{20}$. We will aim for a contradiction which will follow immediately from this claim.

(*) if M contains some k elements other than the identity, then these k elements must all be within one of $M_1, \ldots, M_{20}$.

Proof of claim, by induction. It is true for $k = 1$ by Lemma 5. Suppose it is true for k. Consider a set of shops $\{f_1, \ldots, f_{k+1}\} \subseteq M$. If $\{f_1, \ldots, f_{k+1}\}$ is not already contained in one of $M_1, \ldots, M_{20}$, then by closure and inductive hypothesis, each of the $k+1$ sets $S_i := \{f_1, \ldots, f_{k+1}\} \setminus \{f_i\}$ must be contained within a *different* DSM among $M_1, \ldots, M_{20}$. That is, there exist pairwise distinct $a_1, \ldots, a_{k+1}$ s.t. $S_i \subseteq M_{a_i}$. But then we may verify that, either $\langle \{f_1, \ldots, f_{k+1}\} \rangle$ contains an A-shop or an E-shop, or $\langle \{f_1, \ldots, f_{k+1}\} \rangle$ is contained in one of $M_1, \ldots, M_{20}$. The step of verification is accomplished by computer. In the case of $k < 5$, this verification is done by considering all $k+1$-tuples such that every sub-k-tuple is drawn from a distinct DSM among $M_1, \ldots, M_{20}$. Either the $k+1$-tuple is shown to generate an A-shop or an E-shop, or to be contained in one among $M_1, \ldots, M_{20}$. The key idea is that the number of cases to verify is maintained low by the combinatorial stipulation that the shops come from different DSMs. The cases $k \geq 5$ turn out to be trivial, as there are not k distinct DSMs containing any shop other than the identity.

---

[2] It is not clear a priori that it is sufficient to check powers of f that are themselves powers of 2, up to 8. Rather we know this a posteriori from our computation.

Proof (of Proposition 1). Membership in Pspace has already been discussed. Hardness follows from Lemmas 6, 3 and 4, in light of Theorem 1.

4   The NP-case

This section will culminate in a proof of the following.

Proposition 2. *If* shE($\mathcal{B}$), *where* $|B| = 4$, *contains an* A-*shop but no* E-*shop, then* $\{\exists, \forall, \wedge, \vee\}$-FO($\mathcal{B}$) *is* NP-*complete*.

This will ultimately follow from the classification of all (maximal) DSMs which contain no A-shop. Call a DSM M *maximally* NP-*hard* if M contains no E-shop, but for any shop $f \notin M$, $\langle M \cup \{f\} \rangle$ contains an E-shop. Of course, the maximally Pspace-hard DSMs are such; in the three-element domain case there are three additional DSMs, all of the same class, $\langle \begin{smallmatrix} 0 & 012 \\ 1 & 2 \\ 2 & 1 \end{smallmatrix} \rangle$, $\langle \begin{smallmatrix} 0 & 2 \\ 1 & 012 \\ 2 & 0 \end{smallmatrix} \rangle$ and $\langle \begin{smallmatrix} 0 & 1 \\ 1 & 0 \\ 2 & 012 \end{smallmatrix} \rangle$ [5]. In the four-element domain case, it follows from Lemma 9, below, that there are thirty-four more DSMs, in four further classes.

Class VI	Class VII	Class VIII	Class IX
$\langle \begin{smallmatrix} 0 & 0123 \\ 1 & 2 \\ 2 & 1 \\ 3 & 3 \end{smallmatrix}, \begin{smallmatrix} 0 & 0123 \\ 1 & 1 \\ 2 & 3 \\ 3 & 2 \end{smallmatrix} \rangle$	$\langle \begin{smallmatrix} 0 & 0123 \\ 1 & 0123 \\ 2 & 3 \\ 3 & 2 \end{smallmatrix} \rangle$	$\langle \begin{smallmatrix} 0 & 0123 \\ 1 & 3 \\ 2 & 3 \\ 3 & 12 \end{smallmatrix} \rangle$	$\langle \begin{smallmatrix} 0 & 0123 \\ 1 & 2 \\ 2 & 1 \\ 3 & 12 \end{smallmatrix} \rangle$
+ 3 others	+ 5 others	+ 11 others	+ 11 others

The DSMs not explicitly listed may be derived from those given by permutations of $\{0, 1, 2, 3\}$. Let $N_1, \ldots, N_{32}$ enumerate the DSMs of Classes VI – IX.

Lemma 7. *Let* shE($\mathcal{B}$) *be any of the DSMs in Classes VI – IX. Then* $\{\exists, \forall, \wedge, \vee\}$-FO($\mathcal{B}$) *is* NP-*hard*.

Proof. Consider the structures depicted for each of these classes in Figure 2. When $\mathcal{B}$ is any of these structures we must demonstrate that $\{\exists, \forall, \wedge, \vee\}$-FO($\mathcal{B}$) is NP-hard. Let $\mathcal{B}_9^E$ be the restriction of $\mathcal{B}_9$ to the binary relation depicted as a solid line. Our first observation is that $\{\exists, \forall, \wedge, \vee\}$-FO($\mathcal{B}_7$) = $\{\exists, \forall, \wedge, \vee\}$-FO($\mathcal{B}_8$) = $\{\exists, \forall, \wedge, \vee\}$-FO ($\mathcal{B}_9^E$) = $\{\exists, \forall, \wedge, \vee\}$-FO($\mathcal{K}_2 \uplus \mathcal{K}_1$), where $\mathcal{K}_2 \uplus \mathcal{K}_1$ is the digraph on vertices $\{0, 1, 2\}$ with edge set $\{(1, 2), (2, 1)\}$. This is because $\mathcal{B}_7$, $\mathcal{B}_8$, $\mathcal{B}_7^E$

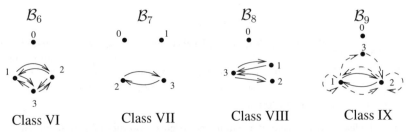

Fig. 2. Canonical representatives. The dotted lines in $\mathcal{B}_9$ are a second binary relation.

and $\mathcal{K}_2 \uplus \mathcal{K}_1$ agree on all equality-free FO sentences. Note that $\mathcal{B}_6 := \mathcal{K}_3 \uplus \mathcal{K}_1$. The problem of evaluating primitive positive ($\{\exists, \wedge\}$-) sentences on $\mathcal{K}_3 \uplus \mathcal{K}_1$ is equivalent to that of evaluating primitive positive sentences on $\mathcal{K}_3$, and this is equivalent to the well-known NP-complete problem of graph 3-colourability. It follows that $\{\exists, \forall, \wedge, \vee\}$-FO($\mathcal{B}_6$) is NP-hard. Similarly, the problem of evaluating existential positive ($\{\exists, \wedge, \vee\}$-) sentences on $\mathcal{K}_2 \uplus \mathcal{K}_1$) is equivalent to that of evaluating existential positive sentences on $\mathcal{K}_2$, and this gives an easy encoding of the NP-complete not-all-equal 3-colourability (encode $R_{NAE}(x, y, z) := E(x, y) \vee E(y, z) \vee E(x, z)$ – see [5]). It follows that $\{\exists, \forall, \wedge, \vee\}$-FO($\mathcal{K}_2 \uplus \mathcal{K}_1$)) is NP-hard, and, consequently, so are $\{\exists, \forall, \wedge, \vee\}$-FO($\mathcal{B}_7$), $\{\exists, \forall, \wedge, \vee\}$-FO($\mathcal{B}_8$) and $\{\exists, \forall, \wedge, \vee\}$-FO($\mathcal{B}_9$).

It remains for us to demonstrate that all DSMs that contain no E-shops are among the twenty plus thirty-two (NP-hard) DSMs of Classes I-IX.

Lemma 8. *The shops f s.t. $\langle f \rangle$ contains no E-shop number 2678 and are exactly those from $M_1, \ldots, M_{20}, N_1, \ldots, N_{32}$.*

Proof. Verification by computer. For any shop f, if none of f, f^2, f^4, f^8 is an E-shop then check that f is in one of the DSMs $M_1, \ldots, M_{20}, N_1, \ldots, N_{32}$.

It follows that DSMs which contain no E-shop must draw their members exclusively from $M_1, \ldots, M_{20}, M_1', \ldots, M_{32}'$.

Lemma 9. *The maximally NP-hard DSMs are precisely those of $M_1, \ldots, M_{20}$, $N_1, \ldots, N_{32}$.*

Proof. That for no distinct $M, M' \in \{M_1, \ldots, M_{20}, N_1, \ldots, N_{32}\}$ is $M \subseteq M'$ may readily be seen. We will prove that there is no further NP-hard DSM.

Let M be a maximally NP-hard DSM that is not among $M_1, \ldots, M_{20}, N_1, \ldots, N_{32}$. We will aim for a contradiction which will follow immediately from this claim.

(*) if M contains some k elements other than the identity, then these k elements must all be within one of $M_1, \ldots, M_{20}, N_1, \ldots, N_{32}$.

Proof of claim, by induction. It is true for $k = 1$ by Lemma 8. Suppose it is true for k. Consider a set of shops $\{f_1, \ldots, f_{k+1}\} \subseteq M$. If $\{f_1, \ldots, f_{k+1}\}$ is not already contained in one of $M_1, \ldots, M_{20}, N_1, \ldots, N_{32}$, then by closure and inductive hypothesis, each of the $k + 1$ sets $S_i := \{f_1, \ldots, f_{k+1}\} \setminus \{f_i\}$ must be contained within a *different* DSM among $M_1, \ldots, M_{20}$. But then we may verify that, either $\langle \{f_1, \ldots, f_{k+1}\} \rangle$ contains an E-shop, or $\langle \{f_1, \ldots, f_{k+1}\} \rangle$ is contained in one of $M_1, \ldots, M_{20}, N_1, \ldots, N_{32}$. The step of verification is accomplished by computer. In the case of $k < 8$, this verification is done by considering all $k+1$-tuples such that every sub-k-tuple is drawn from a distinct DSM among $M_1, \ldots, M_{20}, N_1, \ldots, N_{32}$. Either the $k+1$-tuple is shown to generate an E-shop, or to be contained in one among $M_1, \ldots, M_{20}, N_1, \ldots, N_{32}$. The cases $k \geq 8$ turn out to be trivial, as there are not k distinct DSMs containing any shop other than the identity.

Proof (of Proposition 2). Membership in NP follows from Theorem 2. NP-hardness follows from Lemmas 9, 7, in light of Theorem 1.

5   The co-NP-case

This case is perfectly dual to the NP-case. We state the results nonetheless.[3]

Proposition 3. *If* $\mathsf{shE}(\mathcal{B})$*, where* $|B| = 4$*, contains an* E*-shop but no* A*-shop, then* $\{\exists, \forall, \wedge, \vee\}$-$\mathsf{FO}(\mathcal{B})$ *is* co-NP*-complete.*

This will ultimately follow from the classification of all (maximal) DSMs which contain no E-shop. Call a DSM M *maximally* co-NP-*hard* if M contains no A-shop, but for any shop $f \notin M$, $\langle M \cup \{f\}\rangle$ contains an A-shop. In the three-element domain case there are three additional DSMs, all of the same class, $\langle \frac{\frac{0|0}{1|01}}{2|02} \rangle$, $\langle \frac{\frac{0|01}{1|1}}{2|12} \rangle$ and $\langle \frac{\frac{0|02}{1|12}}{2|2} \rangle$ [5]. In the four-element domain case, it follows from Lemma 12, below, that there are thirty-four more DSMs, in four further classes.

Class VI'   Class VII'   Class VIII'   Class IX'

$\langle \frac{\frac{0|0}{1|02}}{\frac{2|01}{3|03}}, \frac{\frac{0|0}{1|01}}{\frac{2|03}{3|02}} \rangle$ $\langle \frac{\frac{0|0}{1|01}}{\frac{2|013}{3|012}} \rangle$ $\langle \frac{\frac{0|0}{1|03}}{\frac{2|03}{3|012}} \rangle$ $\langle \frac{\frac{0|0}{1|02}}{\frac{2|01}{3|0}} \rangle$

+ 3 others   + 5 others   + 11 others   + 11 others

Let $N'_1, \ldots, N'_{32}$ enumerate the DSMs of Classes VI – IX.

Lemma 10. *Let* $\mathsf{shE}(\mathcal{B})$ *be any of the DSMs in Classes VI' – IX'. Then* $\{\exists, \forall, \wedge, \vee\}$-$\mathsf{FO}(\mathcal{B})$ *is* co-NP-*hard.*

Proof. If $\mathcal{B}$ is a structure, then let $\overline{\mathcal{B}}$ be the complement structure, over the same domain but with i-ary relations $R^{\overline{\mathcal{B}}} = B^i \setminus R^{\mathcal{B}}$. It is not hard to see that $\{\exists, \forall, \wedge, \vee\}$-$\mathsf{FO}(\overline{\mathcal{B}})$ is co-NP-hard iff $\{\exists, \forall, \wedge, \vee\}$-$\mathsf{FO}(\mathcal{B})$ is NP-hard (see [7]). It follows we may use the complements of the structures depicted in Figure 2 for hardness.

It remains for us to demonstrate that all DSMs that contain no A-shops are among the twenty plus thirty-two (co-NP-hard) DSMs of Classes I-V and VI'-IX'.

Lemma 11. *The shops* f *s.t.* $\langle f \rangle$ *contains no* E*-shop number 2678 and are exactly those from* $M_1, \ldots, M_{20}, N'_1, \ldots, N'_{32}$.

Lemma 12. *The maximally* co-NP-*hard DSMs are precisely those of* $M_1, \ldots, M_{20}$, $N'_1, \ldots, N'_{32}$.

Proof (Proof of Proposition 3). Membership in co-NP follows from Theorem 2. co-NP-hardness follws from Lemmas 12, 10, in light of Theorem 1.

---

[3] As we also undertook the respective computations, by way of a checksum.

6   Final Remarks

We have now derived the following.

Theorem 4 (Tetrachotomy [5]). *Let $\mathcal{B}$ be s.t. $|B| \leq 4$.*

I. *If* shE($\mathcal{B}$) *contains both an* A-*shop and an* E-*shop, then* $\{\exists, \forall, \wedge, \vee\}$-FO($\mathcal{B}$) *is in* L.

II. *If* shE($\mathcal{B}$) *contains an* A-*shop but no* E-*shop, then* $\{\exists, \forall, \wedge, \vee\}$-FO($\mathcal{B}$) *is* NP-*complete.*

III. *If* shE($\mathcal{B}$) *contains an* E-*shop but no* A-*shop, then* $\{\exists, \forall, \wedge, \vee\}$-FO($\mathcal{B}$) *is* co-NP-*complete.*

IV. *If* shE($\mathcal{B}$) *contains neither an* A-*shop nor an* E-*shop, then* $\{\exists, \forall, \wedge, \vee\}$-FO($\mathcal{B}$) *is* Pspace-*complete.*

Proof. The case $|B| \leq 3$ was taken care of in Theorem 3. The case $|B| = 4$ follows from Propositions 1, 2 and 3.

There are two reasons why our work is a substantial addition to that which appeared in [5]. Firstly, we have encountered cases of a distinctly different nature. This is especially true for the DSMs of Class I, analogs of which do not appear in the case of three-element domains, and whose associated structures needed a fundamentally new proof for Pspace-hardness. Secondly, the search space of DSMs is too large for four-element domains to simply compute it or its significant components. Therefore, an intelligent computational procedure was required to prove that the requisite DSMs were indeed exactly those that are maximal. On a Core Duo machine, the time taken for the verification of Lemma 6 coded in Matlab was 5 hours, improved to 5 minutes when coded in C. The time for the verification of Lemmas 9 and 12 coded in Matlab was about a day each, improved to 10 minutes when coded in C. It is not clear that these methods even extend to five-element domains (at least on modest computers – we have even been trying unsuccessfully on a Core 2 Quad CPU Q6600 2.40 GHz 6 GB memory, with some parallelisation). In the five-element domain case, it appears as though there are 161 maximally Pspace-hard DSMs in eleven classes (this is not yet verified). Certainly we can not use these methods to settle the conjecture of [5] here reiterated.

Conjecture 1. For any finite $\mathcal{B}$.

I. If shE($\mathcal{B}$) contains both an A-shop and an E-shop, then $\{\exists, \forall, \wedge, \vee\}$-FO($\mathcal{B}$) is in L.

II. If shE($\mathcal{B}$) contains an A-shop but no E-shop, then $\{\exists, \forall, \wedge, \vee\}$-FO($\mathcal{B}$) is NP-complete.

III. If shE($\mathcal{B}$) contains an E-shop but no A-shop, then $\{\exists, \forall, \wedge, \vee\}$-FO($\mathcal{B}$) is co-NP-complete.

IV. If shE($\mathcal{B}$) contains neither an A-shop nor an E-shop, then $\{\exists, \forall, \wedge, \vee\}$-FO($\mathcal{B}$) is Pspace-complete.

It seems as if the resolution of this conjecture will require different methods, and perhaps a greater algebraic understanding of the properties of DSMs on arbitrary finite domains. Some hope for this is provided if the conjectured 161 maximally Pspace-hard DSMs in the five-element case are correct, as there appears to be nothing particularly new in the five-element case that was not present in the four-element case.

References

1. Börner, F.: Total multifunctions and relations. In: AAA60: Workshop on General Algebra, Dresden, Germany (2000)
2. Bulatov, A.A.: A dichotomy theorem for constraint satisfaction problems on a 3-element set. J. ACM 53(1), 66–120 (2006)
3. Enderton, H.B.: A Mathematical Introduction to Logic. Academic Press, London (1972)
4. Lynch, N.: Log space recognition and translation of parenthesis languages. J. ACM 24, 583–590 (1977)
5. Madelaine, F., Martin, B.: The complexity of positive first-order logic without equality. In: Symposium on Logic in Computer Science, pp. 429–438 (2009)
6. Madelaine, F., Martin, B.: The complexity of positive first-order logic without equality. CoRR abs/1003.0802 (2010) (submitted to ACM TOCL)
7. MARTIN, B.: First order model checking problems parameterized by the model. In: Beckmann, A., Dimitracopoulos, C., Löwe, B. (eds.) CiE 2008. LNCS, vol. 5028, pp. 417–427. Springer, Heidelberg (2008)
8. PAPADIMITRIOU, C.: Computational Complexity. Addison-Wesley, Reading (1994)
9. SCHAEFER, T.: The complexity of satisfiability problems. In: STOC (1978)

On the Computability of Region-Based Euclidean Logics

Yavor Nenov and Ian Pratt-Hartmann

School of Computer Science, University of Manchester, UK
{nenovy,ipratt}@cs.man.ac.uk

Abstract. By a *Euclidean logic*, we understand a formal language whose variables range over subsets of Euclidean space, of some fixed dimension, and whose non-logical primitives have fixed meanings as geometrical properties, relations and operations involving those sets. In this paper, we consider first-order Euclidean logics with primitives for the properties of *connectedness* and *convexity*, the binary relation of *contact* and the ternary relation of *being closer-than*. We investigate the computational properties of the corresponding first-order theories when variables are taken to range over various collections of subsets of 1-, 2- and 3-dimensional space. We show that the theories based on Euclidean spaces of dimension greater than 1 can all encode either first- or second-order arithmetic, and hence are undecidable. We show that, for logics able to express the *closer-than* relation, the theories of structures based on 1-dimensional Euclidean space have the same complexities as their higher-dimensional counterparts. By contrast, in the absence of the *closer-than* predicate, all of the theories based on 1-dimensional Euclidean space considered here are decidable, but non-elementary.

1 Introduction

By a *Euclidean logic*, we understand a formal language whose variables range over subsets of $\mathbb{R}^n$ for some fixed n, and whose non-logical primitives have fixed meanings as geometrical properties, relations and operations. The motivation for studying such languages comes primarily from the field of Artificial Intelligence—the idea being that an agent's qualitative knowledge of the space it inhabits can be understood as its access to the validities of such a logic.

Euclidean logics trace their ancestry back to the region-based spatial theories developed by Whitehead [23] and de Laguna [14], later taken up within AI by Randall, Cui and Cohn [19], Egenhoffer [7] and others. The fundamental idea behind such logics is that the the natural domain of quantification for theories representing an agent's spatial knowledge is the collection of *regions* potentially occupied by physical objects, rather than the set of points constituting the space in question. Conformably, the non-logical primitives should take such regions, not points, as their relata. Whitehead, for instance, built his logic on a single spatial primitive which he referred to as *extensive connection*, where, intuitively, two regions stand in this relation if they either overlap or touch at their boundaries. Latterly, such logics have been subject to a more rigorous, model-theoretic

A. Dawar and H. Veith (Eds.): CSL 2010, LNCS 6247, pp. 439–453, 2010.

reconstruction, in which the spatial regions in question are identified with certain subsets of some standard model of the space under investigation, and the primitive non-logical relations and operations interpreted accordingly. Thus, for example, it is now customary to reconstruct Whitehead's relation of extensive connection between regions simply as the set-theoretic relation of having a non-empty intersection. We remark that this relation is nowadays generally referred to as *contact*, to avoid confusion with the separate notion of *connectedness* encountered in topology.

One of the first issues to resolve in the context of these logics is *which* subsets of the space in question their variables should range over. By far the most popular choice in the literature is the collection of *regular closed* sets—that is, those sets which are equal to the topological closures of their *interiors*. Taking variables to range only over the regular closed sets provides a convenient way of finessing the issue of whether spatial regions are open, closed or semi-open; at the same time, since the regular closed sets of a topological space always form a Boolean algebra under inclusion, such 'regions' can be combined in a natural way. The logics obtained by interpreting Whitehead's language over (dense subalgebras of) the regular closed algebras of various classes of topological spaces were investigated by Roeper [20], Düntsch and Winter [6] and Dimov and Vakarelov [4]. In each case, the authors provided a complete axiomatization of the theory corresponding to a particular class of topological spaces. We remark that some of these results can be found in the earlier work of de Vries [3], which was motivated by purely mathematical considerations.

However, the regular closed subsets of $\mathbb{R}^2$ or $\mathbb{R}^3$ still include many pathological sets, and thus are arguably poor candidates to represent the regions of space occupied by physical objects (Pratt-Hartmann [17] , Kontchakov et al. [11]). To avoid such 'abnormal' regions, it has been proposed that Euclidean logics should instead restrict themselves to collections of "tame" regular closed sets. Candidates include: $RCS(\mathbb{R}^n)$—the regular closed *semi-algebraic* sets; $RCP(\mathbb{R}^n)$—the regular closed *semi-linear* sets (*polytopes*); $RCP_{\mathbb{A}}(\mathbb{R}^n)$—the *algebraic polytopes* (i.e. polytopes whose vertices have algebraic coordinates); and $RCP_{\mathbb{Q}}(\mathbb{R}^n)$—the *rational polytopes* (i.e. polytopes whose vertices have rational coordinates). One natural question that arises in this context is whether, for a fixed set of non-logical primitives, such restrictions actually make a difference to the resulting logics (see, e.g. Kontchakov *et al.* [12]).

Logics interpreted over Euclidean spaces may employ primitives representing non-topological notions, of course. For example, Tarski [22] considers second-order logic with variables ranging over subsets of $\mathbb{R}^3$ and predicates expressing the parthood relation and the property of being *spherical*. More recently, there has been some interest within AI in logics featuring a primitive expressing the property of *convexity* (Davis [2]) and the ternary relation of being *closer than* (Sheremet *et al.* [21]). Thus, given any combination of non-logical primitives expressing *contact*, *convexity* and *relative closeness*, and any of the domains of quantification $RCS(\mathbb{R}^n)$, $RCP(\mathbb{R}^n)$, $RCP_{\mathbb{A}}(\mathbb{R}^n)$ and $RCP_{\mathbb{Q}}(\mathbb{R}^n)$, we obtain a particular first-order theory. The aim of this paper is to establish the complexity of these theories.

One of the earliest results of this kind was proved by Grzegorczyk [8]. Taking $\mathcal{L}_C$ to be the first-order language whose only non-logical primitive is the binary predicate C, interpreted as the *contact* relation, Grzegorczyk showed that the $\mathcal{L}_C$-theories of the regular closed sets of a large class of topological spaces can encode *first-order arithmetic*, and thus are *undecidable*. In [5], Dornheim showed that the $\mathcal{L}_C$-theory of $RCP(\mathbb{R}^2)$ is *r.e.-hard*. In [2], Davis considered the Euclidean logics $\mathcal{L}_{closer}$ and $\mathcal{L}_{conv}$ with primitives expressing the relation of being *closer-than* and the property of being *convex*, respectively. He showed that the $\mathcal{L}_{closer}$-theories and the $\mathcal{L}_{conv}$-theories of $RCP_{\mathbb{Q}}(\mathbb{R}^n)$ and $RCP_{\mathbb{A}}(\mathbb{R}^n)$ can encode first-order arithmetic, and that the $\mathcal{L}_{closer}$-theories and the $\mathcal{L}_{conv}$-theories of $RCP(\mathbb{R}^n)$, $RCS(\mathbb{R}^n)$ and $RC(\mathbb{R}^n)$ can encode second-order arithmetic.

In this paper, we provide a systematic overview of results of this kind, filling in some of the gaps left by the literature. We show that, for $n = 1$, the $\mathcal{L}_C$-theories of $RC(\mathbb{R}^n)$, $RCS(\mathbb{R}^n)$, $RCP(\mathbb{R}^n)$, $RCP_{\mathbb{A}}(\mathbb{R}^n)$ and $RCP_{\mathbb{Q}}(\mathbb{R}^n)$ are decidable but not *elementary*. For $n > 1$, we show that, the corresponding $\mathcal{L}_C$-theories can encode first-order arithmetic, and that the $\mathcal{L}_C$-theory of $RC(\mathbb{R}^n)$ can encode second-order arithmetic. For $n > 0$, we establish upper complexity bounds for the $\mathcal{L}_C$-theories, the $\mathcal{L}_{closer}$-theories and the $\mathcal{L}_{conv}$-theories of $RC(\mathbb{R}^n)$, $RCS(\mathbb{R}^n)$, $RCP(\mathbb{R}^n)$, $RCP_{\mathbb{A}}(\mathbb{R}^n)$ and $RCP_{\mathbb{Q}}(\mathbb{R}^n)$. These results are summarized in Table 1.

Table 1. A complexity map of the first-order region-based Euclidean spatial logics

	Signatures		
	$\langle C\rangle, \langle C,\leq\rangle, \langle c,\leq\rangle$	$\langle conv,\leq\rangle, \langle C,conv\rangle$	$\langle closer\rangle$
$RC(\mathbb{R})$	Decidable, NONELEMENTARY		Δ^1_ω-complete
$RCS(\mathbb{R})$			Δ^1_ω-complete
$RCP(\mathbb{R})$	Decidable, NONELEMENTARY		Δ^1_ω-complete
$RCP_{\mathbb{A}}(\mathbb{R})$			Δ^0_ω-complete
$RCP_{\mathbb{Q}}(\mathbb{R})$			Δ^0_ω-complete
$RC(\mathbb{R}^n), n>1$	Δ^1_ω-complete	Δ^1_ω-complete	Δ^1_ω-complete
$RCS(\mathbb{R}^n), n>1$	Δ^0_ω-hard	Δ^1_ω-complete	Δ^1_ω-complete
$RCP(\mathbb{R}^n), n>1$	Δ^0_ω-hard	Δ^1_ω-complete	Δ^1_ω-complete
$RCP_{\mathbb{A}}(\mathbb{R}^n), n>1$	Δ^0_ω-complete	Δ^0_ω-complete	Δ^0_ω-complete
$RCP_{\mathbb{Q}}(\mathbb{R}^n), n>1$	Δ^0_ω-complete	Δ^0_ω-complete	Δ^0_ω-complete

(Domains)

We obtain a surprising model-theoretic result from the established complexity bounds. Pratt [16] observed that the $\mathcal{L}_{conv}$-theories of $RCP(\mathbb{R}^2)$ and $RCP_{\mathbb{Q}}(\mathbb{R}^2)$ are different. The observation is based on a simple geometrical figure allowing the construction, in $RCP(\mathbb{R}^2)$, of square roots of arbitrary lengths. Because all real numbers constructable in this way are algebraic, one might be tempted to think that the $\mathcal{L}_{conv}$-theories of $RCP_{\mathbb{A}}(\mathbb{R}^2)$ and $RCP(\mathbb{R}^2)$ are the same. This, however, turns out to be false, because the two theories are shown to have different complexities.

2 Preliminaries

For basic model theoretic definitions and results, we refer to [10] ([10, p. 212] for the definition of *interpretation*). Let σ be a signature, $\mathcal{M}$ a σ-structure and $\psi(x_1, \ldots, x_n)$ a σ-formula. We define $\psi(\mathcal{M}) := \{\langle a_1, \ldots, a_n \rangle \in M \mid \mathcal{M} \models \psi[a_1, \ldots, a_n]\}$. Let σ and τ be signatures and $\mathcal{A}$ and $\mathcal{B}$ be two structures over these signatures. An *interpretation* Γ of $\mathcal{A}$ in $\mathcal{B}$ consists of:

1. for each sort i in $\mathcal{A}$, τ-formulas $\psi_{s_i}(\bar{x})$ and $\psi_{s_i \sim}(\bar{x}, \bar{y})$;
2. for each unnested atomic σ-formula $\phi(x_1^{i_1}, \ldots, x_k^{i_k})$, a τ-formula $\phi_\Gamma(\bar{x}_1, \ldots, \bar{x}_k)$;
3. a surjective mapping $f_\Gamma^i : \psi_{s_i}(\mathcal{B}) \to A_i$ for each sort i in $\mathcal{A}$, where A_i is the ith universe of $\mathcal{A}$,

such that for each unnested atomic σ-formula $\phi(x_1^{i_1}, \ldots, x_k^{i_k})$, $j = 1, \ldots, k$ and every $a_j^{i_j} \in \psi_{s_j}(\mathcal{B})$, $\mathcal{B} \models \phi_\Gamma[a_1^{i_1}, \ldots, a_k^{i_k}]$ iff $\mathcal{A} \models \phi[f_\Gamma^{i_1}(a_1^{i_1}), \ldots, f_\Gamma^{i_k}(a_k^{i_k})]$. If there exists an interpretation Γ of $\mathcal{A}$ in $\mathcal{B}$ such that $\phi \mapsto \phi_\Gamma$ is computable in polynomial time, then the theory of $\mathcal{A}$ is *polynomial-time many-one reducible* to the theory of $\mathcal{B}$ (see [10, pp. 214-215]). In this case we write $\mathcal{A} \leq_m^p \mathcal{B}$, and if in addition $\mathcal{B} \leq_m^p \mathcal{A}$, we write $\mathcal{A} \equiv_m^p \mathcal{B}$.

Let $\mathcal{X} = \langle X, \tau \rangle$ be a topological space with $\cdot^-$ and $\cdot^\circ$ the closure and interior operations in $\mathcal{X}$. A subset A of X is called *regular closed* in $\mathcal{X}$, if it equals the closure of its interior, i.e. $A = A^{\circ-}$. The set of all regular closed sets in $\mathcal{X}$ is denoted by $RC(\mathcal{X})$. $\langle RC(\mathcal{X}), +, -, \cdot, 0, 1, \leq \rangle$ is a Boolean algebra (see e.g. [13, pp. 25-28]), where, for $a, b \in RC(\mathcal{X})$, $a + b := a \cup b$, $a \cdot b := (a \cap b)^{\circ-}$, $-a := (X \setminus a)^-$ and $a \leq b$ iff $a \subseteq b$. A Boolean sub-algebra M of $RC(\mathcal{X})$ is called a *mereotopology* over $\mathcal{X}$ iff the domain of M is a closed basis for $\mathcal{X}$ (see [17, Definition 2.5]). A mereotopology over a Euclidean topological space is called a *Euclidean mereotopology*. We refer to the elements of a mereotopology as *regions*. The maximal connected subsets of $A \subseteq X$ are called *connected components* of A. A mereotopology M over $\mathcal{X}$ *respects components* iff the connected components of every $a \in M$ are also in M. M is *finitely decomposable* iff every $a \in M$ has only finitely many connected components.

In this paper, for a given Euclidean topological space, we consider different Euclidean mereotopologies. Recall that a real number is *algebraic* if it is a root of a non-zero polynomial in one variable with rational coefficients. The collection of algebraic numbers is denoted by $\mathbb{A}$. A subset of $\mathbb{R}^n$, for $n > 0$, which can be obtained by a Boolean combination of a finite number of polynomial equations and inequalities is called a *semi-algebraic* set (see e.g. [1]). If the polynomial equations and inequalities are linear, then the semi-algebraic set is called *semi-linear* or a *polytope*. A polytope whose polynomial equations and inequalities are with algebraic coefficients is called an *algebraic polytope*. Similarly, a polytope whose polynomial equations and inequalities are with rational coefficients is called a *rational polytope*. For $n > 0$, we denote by $RCS(\mathbb{R}^n)$, $RCP(\mathbb{R}^n)$, $RCP_\mathbb{A}(\mathbb{R}^n)$ and $RCP_\mathbb{Q}(\mathbb{R}^n)$ the regular closed semi-algebraic sets, the regular closed polytopes, the regular closed algebraic polytopes and the regular closed rational polytopes. It is easy to see that $RCS(\mathbb{R}^n)$, $RCP(\mathbb{R}^n)$, $RCP_\mathbb{A}(\mathbb{R}^n)$ and $RCP_\mathbb{Q}(\mathbb{R}^n)$ are all dense Boolean subalgebras of $RC(\mathbb{R}^n)$.

For a Euclidean mereotopology M we are interested in languages able to express the property of being *connected* (denoted by c), the binary *contact* relation (denoted by C), the property of being *convex* (denoted by *conv*) and the ternary relation *closer-than* (denoted by *closer*). For $n > 0$, denote the Euclidean distance between the points $p, q \in \mathbb{R}^n$ by $d(p, q)$ and define:

$$c := \{a \in M \mid a \text{ is connected}\}; \qquad closer := \{\langle a, b, c \rangle \in M^3 \mid$$
$$C := \{\langle a, b \rangle \in M^2 \mid a \cap b \neq \emptyset\}; \qquad glb(\{d(p, q) \mid p \in a, q \in b\}) \leq$$
$$conv := \{a \in M \mid a \text{ is convex}\}; \qquad glb(\{d(p, q) \mid p \in a, q \in c\})\}.$$

The following lemma characterizes the relative complexity of these properties and relations.

Lemma 1. *Let $n > 0$ and M any of $RC(\mathbb{R}^n)$, $RCS(\mathbb{R}^n)$, $RCP(\mathbb{R}^n)$, $RCP_{\mathbb{A}}(\mathbb{R}^n)$ and $RCP_{\mathbb{Q}}(\mathbb{R}^n)$. Then:*

$$\langle M, \leq, C \rangle \equiv_m^p \langle M, C \rangle; \qquad \langle M, \leq, closer \rangle \equiv_m^p \langle M, closer \rangle;$$
$$\langle M, \leq, c \rangle \equiv_m^p \langle M, C \rangle \leq_m^p \langle M, \leq, conv \rangle \leq_m^p \langle M, closer \rangle.$$

Dimov and Vakarelov [4] showed that the relation $\leq$ is definable in terms of the relation C; Davis [2] showed that the property *conv* is definable in terms of the relation *closer*; and Pratt-Hartmann [16] showed that, if M is finitely decomposable, the relation C is definable in terms of *conv* and $\leq$. It is not hard to show that the other statements also hold.

As we see in the following lemma, the regions in every Euclidean mereotopology M are determined by the rational points which they contain.

Lemma 2. *For $a, b, c \in RC(\mathbb{R}^n)$,*

1) $\qquad a \leq b$ *iff* $a \cap \mathbb{Q}^n \subseteq b \cap \mathbb{Q}^n$; $a = b$ *iff* $a \cap \mathbb{Q}^n = b \cap \mathbb{Q}^n$;
2) $closer(a, b, c)$ *iff* $glb(\{d(p, q) \mid p \in a^\circ \cap \mathbb{Q}^n, q \in b^\circ \cap \mathbb{Q}^n\}) \leq$
$$glb(\{d(p, q) \mid p \in a^\circ \cap \mathbb{Q}^n, q \in c^\circ \cap \mathbb{Q}^n\}).$$

The *first-order arithmetic* (FOA) and the *second-order arithmetic* (SOA) are the first- and second-order languages of the signature $\upsilon = \langle \leq, +, \cdot, 0, 1 \rangle$. The *arithmetical* hierarchy Δ_ω^0 and the *analytical* hierarchy Δ_ω^1 comprise the sets of natural numbers which are definable in $\langle \mathbb{N}, \upsilon \rangle$ using FOA and SOA, respectively ([9]). Let T be a theory. T is in Δ_ω^0 if it is many-one reducible to FOA of $\langle \mathbb{N}, \upsilon \rangle$; T is Δ_ω^0-hard if FOA of $\langle \mathbb{N}, \upsilon \rangle$ is many-one reducible to T; and T is Δ_ω^0-complete if it is in Δ_ω^0 and it is Δ_ω^0-hard. The same notions are defined for Δ_ω^1.

It is a standard result that using FOA one can interpret $\langle \mathbb{Z}, \upsilon \rangle$ and $\langle \mathbb{Q}, \upsilon \rangle$ in $\langle \mathbb{N}, \upsilon \rangle$. The same can be shown for $\langle \mathbb{A}, \upsilon \rangle$. Consider the signature $\tau = \langle \leq, +, \cdot, 0, 1, \pi, [\,], N \rangle$. Let the structures $\langle \mathbb{Q}, \tau \rangle$, $\langle \mathbb{A}, \tau \rangle$ and $\langle \mathbb{R}, \tau \rangle$ be such that, $N := \mathbb{N}$; and the predicate $\pi(x)$ and the function $x[y]$ are means of encoding finite sequences of numbers. I.e. if $\pi(q)$ holds, $q[0]$ is the length of the sequence encoded by q and for every natural $1 \leq n \leq q[0]$, $q[n]$ is the nth element of the sequence encoded by q. It is not hard to see that:

Lemma 3

1. *The first-order theory of* $\langle \mathbb{N}, +, \cdot \rangle$ *is* Δ^0_ω-*complete. The first-order theory of the two-sorted structure* $\langle \mathbb{N}, \wp(\mathbb{N}); +, \cdot, \in \rangle$ *is* Δ^1_ω-*complete.*
2. *The first-order theories of* $\langle \mathbb{Q}, \tau \rangle$ *and* $\langle \mathbb{A}, \tau \rangle$ *are* Δ^0_ω-*complete.*
3. *The first-order theory of* $\langle \mathbb{R}, \tau \rangle$ *is* Δ^1_ω-*complete.*

3 Decidable Theories

We now show that the structures $\langle RC(\mathbb{R}), \sigma \rangle$, $\langle RCS(\mathbb{R}), \sigma \rangle$, $\langle RCP(\mathbb{R}), \sigma \rangle$, $\langle RCP_\mathbb{A}(\mathbb{R}), \sigma \rangle$ and $\langle RCP_\mathbb{Q}(\mathbb{R}), \sigma \rangle$, with σ being either $\langle C \rangle$ or $\langle conv, \leq \rangle$, have decidable theories which are not elementary. Note that a non-empty regular closed set $a \in RC(\mathbb{R})$ is convex iff it is connected. So WLOG we fix $\sigma = \langle C \rangle$.

We write $\mathcal{A} \preceq \mathcal{B}$ when $\mathcal{A}$ is an elementary substructure of $\mathcal{B}$. We have that:

$$\langle RCP_\mathbb{Q}(\mathbb{R}), \sigma \rangle \prec \langle RCP_\mathbb{A}(\mathbb{R}), \sigma \rangle \prec \langle RCP(\mathbb{R}), \sigma \rangle = \langle RCS(\mathbb{R}), \sigma \rangle \leq^p_m \langle RC(\mathbb{R}), \sigma \rangle.$$

To see that the structure $\langle RCP(\mathbb{R}), \sigma \rangle$ can be interpreted in $\langle RC(\mathbb{R}), \sigma \rangle$, we only need to provide a formula $\psi_{RCP}(x)$ for which $\psi_{RCP}(RC(\mathbb{R})) = RCP(\mathbb{R})$. A regular closed set a is in $RCP(\mathbb{R})$ exactly when it has finitely many frontier points. In other words, $a \in RCP(\mathbb{R})$ just in case the set of endpoints of its connected components lie in a bounded interval, and have no accumulation points. We identify a point in $r \in \mathbb{R}$ with the unbounded connected $a \in RC(\mathbb{R})$ whose single endpoint is r. Let the formula $\psi_{cc}(x,y)$ define the pairs $\langle a, b \rangle \in RC(\mathbb{R})^2$ for which a is a connected component of b; the formula $\psi_\perp(x)$ define the regular closed sets encoding the points in $\mathbb{R}$; and the formula $\psi_\odot(x,y)$ define the pairs $\langle a, b \rangle \in RC(\mathbb{R})^2$ for which a represents a real number which is in the interior of the connected b. Then the formula $\psi_{EP}(l,x) := \psi_\perp(l) \wedge \exists y (\psi_{cc}(y,x) \wedge C(y,l) \wedge C(y,-l) \wedge (y \leq l \vee y \leq -l))$ defines the pairs $\langle a, b \rangle \in RC(\mathbb{R})^2$ for which a represents an endpoint of b. The formula $\psi_{Iso}(x) := \forall l (\psi_\perp(l) \to \exists u (\psi_\odot(l,u) \wedge \forall t (\psi_{EP}(t,x) \wedge \psi_\odot(t,u) \to l = t \vee l = -t)))$ is satisfied by those $a \in RC(\mathbb{R})$ whose endpoints lack accumulation points. And the formula $\psi_{Bnd}(x) := \exists u (c(u) \wedge \neg c(-u) \wedge \forall l (\psi_{EP}(l,x) \to \psi_\odot(l,u)))$ is satisfied by those $a \in RC(\mathbb{R})$ whose endpoints are bounded. Finally, the formula $\psi_{RCP}(x) := \psi_{Iso}(x) \wedge \psi_{Bnd}(x)$ is satisfied by those $a \in RC(\mathbb{R})$ which are in $RCP(\mathbb{R})$. We have thus shown the following.

Lemma 4. $\langle RCP(\mathbb{R}), \sigma \rangle \leq^p_m \langle RC(\mathbb{R}), \sigma \rangle$

We now show that $\langle RCP_\mathbb{Q}(\mathbb{R}), \sigma \rangle \prec \langle RCP_\mathbb{A}(\mathbb{R}), \sigma \rangle \prec \langle RCP(\mathbb{R}), \sigma \rangle$. For a function $f : A \to B$ denote by $f^+ : \wp(A) \to \wp(B)$ the function defined by $f^+(a) = \{f(x) \mid x \in a\}$. Let $\mathcal{X} = \langle X, \tau \rangle$ be a topological space. Two n-tuples $\bar{a}$ and $\bar{b}$ of subsets of $\mathcal{X}$ are *similarly situated*, denoted by $\bar{a} \sim \bar{b}$, iff there is a homeomorphism $f : \mathcal{X} \to \mathcal{X}$ such that $f^+ : \bar{a} \mapsto \bar{b}$. One can easily check that for every homeomorphism $f : \mathbb{R} \to \mathbb{R}$, the function f^+ is an automorphism for the structure $\langle RCP(\mathbb{R}), C \rangle$. For every $F \subseteq \mathbb{R}$, denote by $RCP_F(\mathbb{R})$ the set of all elements in $RCP(\mathbb{R})$ with endpoints in F.

Lemma 5. *Let F be a dense subset of $\mathbb{R}$, $b \in RCP(\mathbb{R})$ and $\bar{a}$ be an n-tuple of elements in $RCP_F(\mathbb{R})$. Then there is an $a \in RCP_F(\mathbb{R})$ such that $\bar{a}a \sim \bar{a}b$.*

Corollary 1. *Let F be a dense subset of $\mathbb{R}$, $\psi(x, \bar{y})$ be a $\langle C \rangle$-formula, $\bar{a} \in RCP_F(\mathbb{R})^n$ and $b \in RCP(\mathbb{R})$. Then $RCP(\mathbb{R}) \models \psi[b, \bar{a}]$ iff there exists $a \in RCP_F(\mathbb{R})$ such that $RCP(\mathbb{R}) \models \psi[a, \bar{a}]$.*

Lemma 6. *[Tarski-Vaught Test] Let $\mathcal{A}$ be a substructure of $\mathcal{B}$. Then $\mathcal{A} \prec \mathcal{B}$ iff for every formula $\phi(x, \bar{y})$ and $\bar{a} \in A$, if there is $b \in B$ such that $\mathcal{B} \models \phi[b, \bar{a}]$ then there is $a \in A$ such that $\mathcal{B} \models \phi[a, \bar{a}]$. (See e.g. [10, Theorem 2.5.1, p. 55].)*

Corollary 2. $\langle RCP_{\mathbb{Q}}(\mathbb{R}), C \rangle \prec \langle RCP_{\mathbb{A}}(\mathbb{R}), C \rangle \prec \langle RCP(\mathbb{R}), C \rangle$.

3.1   Upper Bounds

We now show that the first-order theory of $\langle RC(\mathbb{R}), C \rangle$ is decidable. We provide an interpretation of $\langle RC(\mathbb{R}), C \rangle$ in the monadic second-order theory of $\langle \mathbb{Q}, < \rangle$, which Rabin showed decidable in [18]. In the monadic second-order theory of $\langle \mathbb{Q}, < \rangle$, we may evidently define the constants $\emptyset$ and $\mathbb{Q}$, the relation $\subseteq$ and the operations $\cup$ and $\cap$.

Denote by $\tau_{\mathbb{R}}$ the set of open sets in $\mathbb{R}$ and by $\beta_{\mathbb{R}}$ the set of open connected sets in $\mathbb{R}$. Let the mapping $f : \wp(\mathbb{R}) \to \wp(\mathbb{Q})$ be defined by $f(a) = a \cap \mathbb{Q}$. We identify every region $a \in RC(\mathbb{R})$ with the set of rational points that it contains, i.e. with $f(a)$. By Lemma 2 $f \restriction RC(\mathbb{R})$ has an inverse. Note that a set $A \subseteq \mathbb{Q}$ is an f-image of some $a \in RC(\mathbb{R})$ iff A consists of exactly those $q \in \mathbb{Q}$ which are dense in A (i.e. not isolated from A).

The formula $\psi_i(X) := \forall x \forall y(X(x) \wedge X(y) \wedge x < y \to \forall z(x < z \wedge z < y \to X(z)))$ defines the f-images of *intervals*, and the formula $\psi_o = \psi_i(X) \wedge \forall x(X(x) \to \exists y \exists z(X(y) \wedge X(z) \wedge y < x \wedge x < z))$ defines the f-images of *open intervals*. The pairs $\langle q, A \rangle \in \mathbb{Q} \times \wp(\mathbb{Q})$ with q being isolated from A are defined by $\psi_{iso}(x, X) := \exists Y_1(Y_1(x) \wedge \psi_o(Y_1) \wedge \forall Y_2(\psi_o(Y_2) \wedge Y_2 \subseteq X \to Y_1 \cap Y_2 = \emptyset))$. As a result, the formula $\psi_{RC}(X) := \forall x(X(x) \leftrightarrow \neg \psi_{iso}(x, X))$ defines the set of f-images of regular closed sets in $\mathbb{R}$ (see Lemma 7).

To define the contact relation, we encode a real number r by the pair $\langle L, R \rangle \in \wp(\mathbb{Q})^2$, where $L = \{q \in \mathbb{Q} \mid q \leq r\}$ and $R = \{q \in \mathbb{Q} \mid q \geq r\}$. Clearly, a pair $\langle L, R \rangle \in \wp(\mathbb{Q})^2$ encodes a real number iff it satisfies the formula $\psi_{\mathbb{R}}(L, R) := L \cup R = \mathbb{Q} \wedge L \neq \emptyset \wedge R \neq \emptyset \wedge \forall x \forall y(L(x) \wedge R(y) \to x \leq y)$. The formula $\psi_{\odot}(L, R, X) := \psi_{\mathbb{R}}(L, R) \wedge \psi_o(X) \wedge L \cap X \neq \emptyset \wedge R \cap X \neq \emptyset$ defines the tuples $\langle A, B, D \rangle \in \wp(\mathbb{Q})^3$, such that $\langle A, B \rangle$ represent a some $r \in \mathbb{R}$ and D represents a connected open neighborhood of r. The tuples $\langle A, B, D \rangle \in \wp(\mathbb{Q})^3$ such that $\langle A, B \rangle$ represents some $r \in \mathbb{R}$ that is in the closure of D are defined by the formula $\psi_{\in}(L, R, X) := \psi_{\mathbb{R}}(L, R) \wedge \forall N(\psi_{\odot}(L, R, N) \to N \cap X \neq \emptyset)$. Finally, two regular closed sets are in contact iff their f-images satisfy the formula $\psi_C(X, Y) := \exists L \exists R(\psi_{\in}(L, R, X) \wedge \psi_{\in}(L, R, Y))$.

Lemma 7. *For $t, u \subseteq \mathbb{Q}$ we have that:*

(i) $\mathbb{Q} \models \psi_{RC}[t]$ *iff there is some $a \in RC(\mathbb{R})$, such that $f(a) = t$;*
(ii) if $\mathbb{Q} \models \psi_{RC}[t] \wedge \psi_{RC}[u]$, *then* $\mathbb{Q} \models \psi_C[t, u]$ *iff* $f^{-1}(t)Cf^{-1}(u)$.

Lemma 8. Γ *is an interpretation of* $\langle RC(\mathbb{R}), C\rangle$ *in the monadic second-order theory of* $\langle \mathbb{Q}, <\rangle$*, where* Γ *consists of:*

1. $\psi_{RC}(X)$ *as a formula defining the domain;*
2. *the inverse function of* $f \upharpoonright RC(\mathbb{R})$*;*
3. $\psi_C(X, Y)$ *as the formula defining the contact relation.*

Theorem 1. *[18] The monadic second-order theory of* $\langle \mathbb{Q}, <\rangle$ *is decidable.*

Corollary 3. *For* $M \in \{RC(\mathbb{R}), RCS(\mathbb{R}), RCP(\mathbb{R}), RCP_{\mathbb{A}}(\mathbb{R}), RCP_{\mathbb{Q}}(\mathbb{R})\}$*, the theories of* $\langle M, C\rangle$ *and* $\langle M, conv, \leq\rangle$ *are decidable.*

3.2   Lower Bounds

We show that the theory of $\langle RCP(\mathbb{R}), \sigma\rangle$ is not elementary by introducing a polynomial reduction from the weak monadic second-order theory of one successor, denoted by $WS1S$, to the the theory of $\langle RCP(\mathbb{R}), \sigma\rangle$. Denote by $\mathcal{L}_{S1S}^{Mon}$ the monadic second-order language of the structure $\langle \mathbb{N}, S\rangle$, where $S = \{\langle n, n+1\rangle \mid n \in \mathbb{N}\}$. $WS1S$ is shown to be non-elementary by Meyer [15].

For the rest of the section, we abbreviate $M := RCP(\mathbb{R})$ and $\mathcal{M} := \langle M, \sigma\rangle$. For $n \in \mathbb{N}$, we encode the initial segment $\{0, \ldots, n\}$ of $\mathbb{N}$ by the pairs of disconnected regions $\langle a, b\rangle \in M^2$ (later defined by the formula $\psi_\vdash(x, y)$) such that the connected components of $a + b$ are bounded, a is non-empty and all the connected components of b are on the same side of a. A natural number $k \leq n$ is represented by the $(k+1)$st connected component of b closest to a. A set $A \subseteq \{0, \ldots, n\}$ is represented by the sum (in $\mathcal{M}$) of the representatives of its members.

Let $\psi_{cc}(x, y)$ define the pairs $\langle a, b\rangle \in M^2$ such that a is a connected component of b. The formula

$$\psi_{ord}(x, y, z) := c(x) \wedge c(y) \wedge c(z) \wedge \neg C(y, x+z) \wedge \forall t(c(t) \wedge x + z \leq t \rightarrow y \leq t),$$

defines the tuples $\langle a, b, c\rangle \in M^3$ of connected regions such that the endpoints of b are between all of the endpoints of a and all of the endpoints of c. The formula $\psi_\subseteq(x, y) := \forall x'(\psi_{cc}(x', x) \rightarrow \psi_{cc}(x', y))$ defines the pairs $\langle a, b\rangle \in M^2$ such that every connected component of a is a connected component of b. The formula

$$\psi_\vdash(x, y) := c(x) \wedge \neg c(-x) \wedge \neg C(x, y) \wedge \forall z(\psi_{cc}(z, y) \rightarrow \neg c(-z)) \wedge$$
$$\forall z \forall t(\psi_{cc}(z, y) \wedge \psi_{cc}(t, y) \rightarrow \neg \psi_{ord}(z, x, t))$$

defines the pairs $\langle a, b\rangle \in M^2$ encoding an initial segment of natural numbers. The formula

$$\psi_\leq(x, y, z) := \psi_\vdash(x, y) \wedge \psi_\vdash(x, z) \wedge \psi_\subseteq(y, z) \wedge$$
$$\forall c \forall d(\psi_{cc}(c, y) \wedge \psi_{cc}(d, z) \wedge \psi_{ord}(x, d, c) \rightarrow \psi_{cc}(d, y))$$

defines the tuples $\langle a, b, c\rangle \in M^3$ such that $\langle a, b\rangle$ and $\langle a, c\rangle$ encode initial segments of $\mathbb{N}$, say $\{0, \ldots, n\}$ and $\{0, \ldots, m\}$, with $n \leq m$, and $\langle a, b\rangle$ and $\langle a, c\rangle$ are compatible in the sense that every $k \in \{0, \ldots, n\}$ is represented by the same region in M with respect to $\langle a, b \rangle$ and $\langle a, c \rangle$.

Let the pair $\langle a, b \rangle \in M^2$ encode an initial segment $\{0, \ldots, n\}$ of $\mathbb{N}$. Let $c, d \in M$ represent numbers $k, l \in \{0, \ldots, n\}$ and $e \in M$ represent a finite $A \subseteq \{0, \ldots, n\}$ all with respect to $\langle a, b \rangle$. Then $k \in A$ iff $\langle c, e \rangle$ satisfies the formula $\psi_\in(x, y) := \psi_{cc}(x, y)$, and $k + 1 = l$ iff $\langle c, d, a, b \rangle$ satisfies the formula

$$\psi_S(x, y; x_0, x_1) := \psi_{cc}(x, x_1) \wedge \psi_{cc}(y, x_1) \wedge \psi_{ord}(x_0, x, y) \wedge x \neq y \wedge$$
$$\forall z (\psi_{cc}(z, x_1) \wedge \psi_{ord}(x_0, z, y) \wedge z \neq y \rightarrow \psi_{ord}(x_0, z, x)).$$

For every $\phi \in \mathcal{L}^{Mon}_{S1S}$, denote by $\delta(\phi)$ the *quantifier depth* of ϕ.

Definition 1. *We now define a translation* $(\cdot)_\Gamma : \mathcal{L}^{PMon}_{S1S} \rightarrow \mathcal{L}_\sigma$, *where* $\mathcal{L}^{PMon}_{S1S}$ *is the set of all formulas in the language* $\mathcal{L}^{Mon}_{S1S}$ *that are in prenex normal form. We use the special variables* $r, s_0, \ldots, s_{\delta(\phi)}$.

$$(x_n = x_m)_\Gamma := p_n = p_m; \ (X_n = X_m)_\Gamma := q_n = q_m;$$
$$(S(x_n, x_m))_\Gamma := \psi_S(p_n, p_m; r, s_0); (x_n \in X_m)_\Gamma := \psi_\in(p_n, q_m);$$
$$(\neg\psi)_\Gamma := \neg\psi_\Gamma; \ (\psi' \wedge \psi'')_\Gamma := \psi'_\Gamma \wedge \psi''_\Gamma;$$
$$(\exists x_n \psi)_\Gamma := \exists p_n \exists s_{\delta(\psi)} \big(\psi_\leq (r, s_{\delta(\psi)+1}, s_{\delta(\psi)}) \wedge \psi_{cc}(p_n, s_{\delta(\psi)}) \wedge \psi_\Gamma \big),$$
$$(\forall x_n \psi)_\Gamma := \forall p_n \forall s_{\delta(\psi)} \big(\psi_\leq (r, s_{\delta(\psi)+1}, s_{\delta(\psi)}) \wedge \psi_{cc}(p_n, s_{\delta(\psi)}) \rightarrow \psi_\Gamma \big),$$
$$(\exists X_n \psi)_\Gamma := \exists q_n \exists s_{\delta(\psi)} \big(\psi_\leq (r, s_{\delta(\psi)+1}, s_{\delta(\psi)}) \wedge \psi_\subseteq (q_n, s_{\delta(\psi)}) \wedge \psi_\Gamma \big),$$
$$(\forall X_n \psi)_\Gamma := \forall q_n \forall s_{\delta(\psi)} \big(\psi_\leq (r, s_{\delta(\psi)+1}, s_{\delta(\psi)}) \wedge \psi_\subseteq (q_n, s_{\delta(\psi)}) \rightarrow \psi_\Gamma \big).$$

Lemma 9. *For every* $\phi \in \mathcal{L}^{PMon}_{S1S}$, $\mathbb{N} \models \phi$ *iff* $\mathcal{M} \models \forall r \forall s_{\delta(\phi)} \psi_\vdash (r, s_{\delta(\phi)}) \rightarrow \psi_\Gamma$.

Theorem 2. *[15] WS1S is not elementary.*

Corollary 4. *The first-order theory of* $\langle RCP(\mathbb{R}), C \rangle$ *is not elementary.*

4   Undecidable Theories

In this section we establish upper and lower bounds on the complexities of some undecidable region-based theories of space. In particular, we show that the theory of $\langle RC(\mathbb{R}^n), \sigma \rangle$ with $n > 1$ and σ any of $\langle C \rangle$, $\langle conv, \leq \rangle$ and $\langle closer \rangle$ is Δ^1_ω-complete. Further, the theories of $RCP_\mathbb{A}(\mathbb{R}^n)$ and $RCP_\mathbb{Q}(\mathbb{R}^n)$, with the same non-logical primitives, are all Δ^0_ω-complete. Although we show that the theories of $\langle RCS(\mathbb{R}^n), \sigma \rangle$ and $\langle RCP(\mathbb{R}^n), \sigma \rangle$ are Δ^0_ω-hard, their precise complexity remains open. In contrast to the decidable one-dimensional region-based theories of space considered in Section 3, we shall show that the theories of $\langle RC(\mathbb{R}), closer \rangle$, $\langle RCS(\mathbb{R}), closer \rangle$ and $\langle RCP(\mathbb{R}), closer \rangle$ are Δ^1_ω-complete and that the theories of $\langle RCP_\mathbb{A}(\mathbb{R}), closer \rangle$ and $\langle RCP_\mathbb{Q}(\mathbb{R}), closer \rangle$ are Δ^0_ω-complete.

4.1   Lower Bounds

Combining ideas from [2] and [8], we show that, for $\sigma = \langle C, c, +, \cdot, -, \leq \rangle$ and $n > 1$, the theory of every extension of $\langle RCP_{\mathbb{Q}}(\mathbb{R}^n), \sigma \rangle$ is Δ_ω^0-hard, and that the theory of $\langle RC(\mathbb{R}^n), \sigma \rangle$ is Δ_ω^1-hard.

Fix an extension $\mathcal{M} = \langle M, \sigma \rangle$ of $\langle RCP_{\mathbb{Q}}(\mathbb{R}^n), \sigma \rangle$, for some $n > 1$. For every $a \in M$, denote by $|a|$ the number of connected components of a. We interpret the structure $\langle \mathbb{N}, +, \cdot \rangle$ in $\mathcal{M}$, by encoding any natural number k as a region $a \in M$ having k connected components, i.e. with $|a| = k$.

The first step is to provide a formula $\psi_\sim(x, y)$ which is satisfied by the pairs $\langle a, b \rangle \in M$ having the same number of connected components. Let the formula $\psi_{cc}(x, y)$ define the pairs of regions $\langle a, b \rangle \in M^2$, with a being a connected component of b. For $a, b \in M$, we say that a is a *shrinking* of b if and only if every connected component of a is contained in a connected component of b and every connected component of b contains exactly one connected component of a. The formula $\psi_{shrink}(x, y) := x \leq y \wedge \forall y'(\psi_{cc}(y', y) \rightarrow \psi_{cc}(x \cdot y', x))$ defines the pairs of regions $\langle a, b \rangle \in M^2$ such that a is a shrinking of b.

For $a, b, c \in M$ we say that c is a *wrapping* of a and b if and only if $a + b \leq c$ and every connected component of c contains one connected component of a and b. The formula

$$\psi_{d\sim}(x, y) := \exists z(x + y \leq z \wedge \forall z'(\psi_{cc}(z', z) \rightarrow \psi_{cc}(x \cdot z', x) \wedge \psi_{cc}(y \cdot z', y))$$

defines the pairs of regions $\langle a, b \rangle \in M^2$ for which there exists a wrapping $c \in M$.

Lemma 10. *Let $a, b \in M$. Then $|a| = |b|$ if and only if there exist $a', b', c \in M$ such that a' and b' are shrinkings of a and b and c is a wrapping of a' and b'.*

So, the formula $\psi_\sim(x, y) := \exists x' \exists y'(\psi_{shrink}(x', x) \wedge \psi_{shrink}(y', y) \wedge \psi_{d\sim}(x', y'))$ defines the pairs $\langle a, b \rangle \in M^2$ such that $|a| = |b|$. The formula $\psi_S(x, y) := \exists x'(\psi_{cc}(x', x) \wedge \psi_\sim(x \cdot -x', y))$ defines the pairs of regions $\langle a, b \rangle \in M^2$ with $|a| = |b| + 1$ (taking $\aleph_0 + 1 = \aleph_0$), and the formula $\psi_{fin}(x) := \neg \psi_S(x, x)$ defines the regions having finitely many components. Clearly,

Lemma 11. *The function $f_\Gamma : \psi_{fin}(\mathcal{M}) \rightarrow \mathbb{N}$ defined by $f_\Gamma(a) = |a|$ is surjective.*

The following formulas define the arithmetical operations on numbers:

$$\psi_+(x, y, z) := \exists x' \exists y'(\psi_\sim(x, x') \wedge \psi_\sim(y, y') \wedge \neg C(x', y') \wedge x' + y' = z) \text{ and}$$
$$\psi_\times(x, y, z) := \exists u \exists v [\psi_{shrink}(u, z) \wedge u \leq v \wedge \psi_\sim(v, y) \wedge \forall t(\psi_{cc}(t, v) \rightarrow \psi_\sim(t \cdot u, x))].$$

Lemma 12. *Γ is an interpretation of $\langle \mathbb{N}, +, \cdot \rangle$ in $\mathcal{M}$, where Γ consists of:*

1. *the σ-formulas $\psi_{fin}(x)$ and $\psi_\sim(x, y)$;*
2. *the σ-formulas $\psi_+(x, y, z)$ and $\psi_\times(x, y, z)$;*
3. *the surjective map: f_Γ.*

Corollary 5. *Let τ be any of $\langle C \rangle$, $\langle conv, \leq \rangle$ and $\langle closer \rangle$, $n > 1$ and M be any of $RC(\mathbb{R}^n)$, $RCS(\mathbb{R}^n)$, $RCP(\mathbb{R}^n)$, $RCP_\mathbb{A}(\mathbb{R}^n)$ and $RCP_\mathbb{Q}(\mathbb{R}^n)$. Then the theory of $\langle M, \tau \rangle$ is Δ_ω^0-hard.*

We now show that when $M = RC(\mathbb{R}^n)$, $\langle M, \sigma \rangle$ can interpret $\langle \mathbb{N}, \wp(\mathbb{N}); +, \cdot, \in \rangle$. We identify every set $A \subseteq \mathbb{N}$ with a pair of regions $\langle a, b \rangle \in M^2$ such that, for every $k \in \mathbb{N}$, $k \in A$ if and only if there exists a connected component a' of a with $|a' \cdot b| = k$. The collection of pairs $\langle a, b \rangle \in M^2$ that represent a set of natural numbers is thus defined by the formula $\psi_{set}(x, y) := \forall x'(\psi_{cc}(x', x) \to \psi_{fin}(x' \cdot y))$. The formula $\psi_\in(z; x, y) := \exists x'(\psi_{cc}(x', x) \wedge \psi_\sim(z, x' \cdot y))$ likewise defines a set of triples $\langle a, b, c \rangle \in M^3$ such that, if a represents the natural number k and $\langle b, c \rangle$ represents a set of natural numbers A, then $k \in A$.

Lemma 13. *The function $f'_\Gamma : \psi_{set}(M) \to \wp(\mathbb{N})$ is surjective, where $f'_\Gamma(a, b) = \{|a' \cdot b| : a'$ a connected component of $a\}$.*

Lemma 14. *Let $a, b, c \in M$. If $M \models \psi_{fin}[a]$ and $M \models \psi_{set}[b, c]$ then $M \models \psi_\in[a, b, c]$ iff $f_\Gamma(a) \in f'_\Gamma(b, c)$.*

Lemma 15. *Γ is an interpretation of $\langle \mathbb{N}, \wp(\mathbb{N}); +, \cdot, \in \rangle$ in M, where Γ consists of:*

1. *the formulas $\psi_{fin}(x)$, $\psi_{set}(x, y)$, $\psi_\sim(x, y)$ and $\psi_{set\sim}(x, y, x', y')$;*
2. *the formulas $\psi_+(x, y, z)$, $\psi_\times(x, y, z)$ and $\psi_\in(x, y, z)$;*
3. *the surjective maps: f_Γ, f'_Γ.*

Corollary 6. *Let σ be any of $\langle C \rangle$, $\langle covn, \leq \rangle$ and $\langle closer \rangle$ and $n > 1$. Then the theory of $\langle RC(\mathbb{R}^n), \sigma \rangle$ is Δ_ω^1-hard.*

Some of the theories from Corollary 5 and Corollary 6 are known to have even higher computational complexities. In particular:

Lemma 16. *[2] Let σ be any of $\langle conv, \leq \rangle$ and $\langle closer \rangle$, and let $n \geq 1$. Then*

- *$\langle RC(\mathbb{R}), closer \rangle$, $\langle RCS(\mathbb{R}), closer \rangle$ and $\langle RCP(\mathbb{R}), closer \rangle$ are Δ_ω^1-hard;*
- *$\langle RCP_\mathbb{A}(\mathbb{R}), closer \rangle$ and $\langle RCP_\mathbb{Q}(\mathbb{R}), closer \rangle$ are Δ_ω^0-hard;*
- *$\langle RCS(\mathbb{R}^n), \sigma \rangle$ and $\langle RCP(\mathbb{R}^n), \sigma \rangle$ are Δ_ω^1-hard*

4.2 Upper Bounds

We now show that for $n > 0$ the theories of the structures $\langle RCP(\mathbb{R}^n), closer \rangle$, $\langle RCP_\mathbb{A}(\mathbb{R}^n), closer \rangle$ and $\langle RCP_\mathbb{Q}(\mathbb{R}^n), closer \rangle$ are interpretable in the structures $\langle \mathbb{R}, \tau \rangle$, $\langle \mathbb{A}, \tau \rangle$ and $\langle \mathbb{Q}, \tau \rangle$, respectively, where $\tau = \langle \leq, +, \cdot, 0, 1, \pi, [\,], N \rangle$. In the sequel, we take R to range over the fields $\mathbb{R}$, $\mathbb{A}$ and $\mathbb{Q}$, writing $RCP(\mathbb{R}^n)$ alternatively as $RCP_R(\mathbb{R}^n)$. We denote the structure $\langle R, \tau \rangle$ by $\mathcal{R}$. Note that the regions in $RCP_R(\mathbb{R}^n)$ are exactly the sums of finitely many products of finitely many half-spaces whose boundaries are $(n-1)$-dimensional hyperplanes definable by degree 1 polynomials in $R[X_1, \ldots, X_n]$. So, for every sequence of sequences $s = \langle \langle a_{11}, \ldots, a_{1m_1} \rangle, \ldots, \langle a_{m1}, \ldots, a_{mm_m} \rangle \rangle$ of half-spaces in $RCP_R(\mathbb{R}^n)$, there is an unique region $a \in RCP_R(\mathbb{R}^n)$ such that $a = \sum_{i=1}^{m} \prod_{j=1}^{m_i} a_{ij}$. And conversely, every region $a \in RCP_R(\mathbb{R}^n)$ is represented by some (in fact infinitely many) sequences of that form. Thus, we may encode elements of $RCP_R(\mathbb{R}^n)$ using sequences of sequences of half-spaces. Further, since each half-space is defined by a linear equation, we may encode it as the sequence of its coefficients, so that elements of $RCP_R(\mathbb{R}^n)$ may be encoded as sequences of sequences of sequences of real numbers. Of course, we may represent points in R^n by the sequence of real numbers in the obvious way. Let $\psi_\bullet(x)$, $\psi_{PT}(x)$, $\psi_{\in PT}(x, y)$ and $\psi_{\in PT^\circ}(x, y)$ be τ-formulas such that: $\psi_\bullet(x)$ defines those $r \in R$ that encode points in R^n; $\psi_{PT}(x)$ defines those $r \in R$ that encode regions in $RCP_R(\mathbb{R}^n)$; $\psi_{\in PT}(x, y)$ defines the pairs $\langle r, s \rangle \in R$ such that r encodes a point in the region encoded by s; and $\psi_{\in PT^\circ}(x, y)$ defines the pairs $\langle r, s \rangle$ such that r encodes a point in R^n in the interior of the region in $RCP_R(\mathbb{R}^n)$ encoded by s.

By Lemma 2, we get that the τ-formula $\psi_\leq(x, y) := \forall z(\psi_\bullet(z) \wedge \psi_{\in PT}(z, x) \rightarrow \psi_{\in PT}(z, y))$ defines the part-of relation, and that the τ-formula $\psi_{closer}(x, y, z)$ defines the relation closer-than, where:

$$\psi_{closer}(x, y, z) := \forall p \forall q \big(\psi_{\in PT^\circ}(p, x) \wedge \psi_{\in PT^\circ}(q, z) \rightarrow \exists r \exists s \big(\psi_{\in PT^\circ}(r, x) \wedge$$
$$\psi_{\in PT^\circ}(s, y) \wedge \sum_{i=1}^{n}(r[i] - s[i])^2 \leq \sum_{i=1}^{n}(p[i] - q[i])^2 \big) \big).$$

Lemma 17. *For $n > 0$, Γ is an interpretation of $\langle RCP_R(\mathbb{R}^n), closer \rangle$ in $\mathcal{R}$, where Γ consists of:*

1. *the formulas $\psi_{PT}(x)$ and $\psi_{PT\sim}(x, y) := \psi_\leq(x, y) \wedge \psi_\leq(y, x)$;*
2. *the formula $\psi_{closer}(x, y, z)$ corresponding to the closer relation;*
3. *the surjective map $f : \psi_{PT}(\mathcal{R}) \rightarrow RCP_R(\mathbb{R}^n)$ defined by:*

$$f(a) = \sum_{i=1}^{a[0]} \prod_{j=1}^{a[i][0]} \big\{ \langle x_1, \ldots, x_n \rangle \in \mathbb{R}^n \big| \sum_{k=1}^{n} a[i][j][k] \cdot x_k + a[i][j][n+1] \leq 0 \big\}.$$

Corollary 7. *Let $n > 0$ and σ be any of the signatures $\langle C \rangle$, $\langle conv, \leq \rangle$ and $\langle closer \rangle$. Then $\langle RCP_\mathbb{Q}(\mathbb{R}^n), \sigma \rangle$ and $\langle RCP_\mathbb{A}(\mathbb{R}^n), \sigma \rangle$ are in Δ_ω^0 and $\langle RCP(\mathbb{R}^n), \sigma \rangle$ is in Δ_ω^1.*

Now, as we promised in the introduction, for $n > 1$ and $\sigma = \langle conv, \leq \rangle$, we obtain from the computational properties of $\langle RCP(\mathbb{R}^n), \sigma \rangle$ and $\langle RCP_\mathbb{A}(\mathbb{R}^n), \sigma \rangle$ a very interesting and surprising model-theoretic result.

Corollary 8. *The structure $\langle RCP_\mathbb{A}(\mathbb{R}), conv, \leq \rangle$ is not an elementary substructure of the structure $\langle RCP(\mathbb{R}), conv, \leq \rangle$.*

We now show that the structures $\langle RCS(\mathbb{R}^n), closer \rangle$, for $n > 0$, are definable in the structure $\mathcal{R} = \langle \mathbb{R}, \tau \rangle$. Fix a positive $n \in \mathbb{N}$. Recall that a subset of $\mathbb{R}^n$ is semi-algebraic if it is definable by a Boolean combination of finite number of polynomial equations and inequalities. Following essentially the same procedure as for semi-linear sets, it is routine to encode semi-algebraic sets as real numbers.

All that then remains to do is to show that we can write a formula defining the real numbers that encode semi-algebraic sets which are also *regular closed*.

Let the formula $\psi_\bullet(x)$ define the real numbers encoding points in $\mathbb{R}^n$; let the formula $\psi_{SA}(x)$ define the set of real numbers encoding semi-algebraic sets in $\mathbb{R}^n$; and let the formula $\psi_{\in SA}(x, y)$ define the pair $\langle r, s \rangle \in \mathbb{R}^2$ such that r encodes a point in $\mathbb{R}^n$ which is in a semi-algebraic set encoded by s. We use n-balls to determine if a semi-algebraic sets is regular closed. We identify each n-ball with the $n + 1$ coefficients of its inequality. A real number encodes an n-ball iff it satisfies the formula $\psi_\bigcirc(x) := \pi(x) \wedge x[0] = n+1$, and a point, encoded by some $p \in \mathbb{R}$, lies in the interior of an n-ball, encoded by some $o \in \mathbb{R}$, iff the pair $\langle p, o \rangle$ satisfies the formula $\psi_{\in\bigcirc}(x, y) := \sum_{i=1}^{n}(x[i] - y[i])^2 < x[n + 1]$.

A point, encoded by $p \in \mathbb{R}$, is isolated from a semi-algebraic set, encoded by $o \in \mathbb{R}$, iff $\langle p, o \rangle$ satisfies the formula:

$$\psi_\odot(x, y) := \exists z(\psi_\bigcirc(z) \wedge \psi_{\in\bigcirc}(x, z) \wedge \forall t(\psi_\bullet(t) \wedge \psi_{\in\bigcirc}(t, z) \rightarrow \neg\psi_{\in SA}(t, y))).$$

A set $A \subseteq \mathbb{R}^n$ is regular closed iff it contains exactly the points that are dense in it. So the formula $\psi_{RCS}(x) := \psi_{SA}(x) \wedge \forall y(\psi_{\in\bigcirc}(y, x) \leftrightarrow \neg\psi_\odot(y, x))$ defines exactly the codes of the regular closed semi-algebraic sets. Two numbers encode the same regular closed semi-algebraic sets if they satisfy the formula: $\psi_{RCS\sim}(x, y) := \forall t(\psi_\bullet(t) \rightarrow (\psi_{\in SAS}(t, x) \leftrightarrow \psi_{\in SA}(t, y)))$. One can easily write a formula $\psi_{closer}(x, y, z)$ defining the relation closer-than.

Lemma 18. *For $n > 0$, Γ is an interpretation of $\langle RCS(\mathbb{R}^n), closer \rangle$ in $\mathcal{R}$, where Γ consists of:*

1. *the formulas $\psi_{RCS}(x)$ and $\psi_{RCS\sim}(x, y)$;*
2. *the formula $\psi_{closer}(x, y, z)$;*
3. *the surjective map $f : \psi_{RCS}(\mathcal{R}) \rightarrow RCS(\mathbb{R}^n)$ defined by:*

$$f(a) = \{\langle k[1], \ldots, k[n] \rangle \mid \mathcal{R} \models \psi_\bullet[k], \mathcal{R} \models \psi_{\bullet\in SAS}[k, a]\}.$$

Corollary 9. *Let $n > 0$ and σ be any of the signatures $\langle C \rangle$, $\langle conv, \leq \rangle$ and $\langle closer \rangle$. Then the theory of $\langle RCS(\mathbb{R}^n), \sigma \rangle$ is in Δ^1_ω.*

We now show that, for $n > 0$, the structures $\langle RC(\mathbb{R}^n), closer \rangle$ can be interpreted in the second-order theory of $\mathcal{Q} = \langle \mathbb{Q}, \tau \rangle$. We identify every region in $RC(\mathbb{R}^n)$ with the set of rational points that it contains, and we make use of the fact that a subset of $\mathbb{R}^n$ is regular closed iff it contains exactly the points that are dense in it. A point $p \in \mathbb{R}^n$ is dense in $A \subseteq \mathbb{R}^n$ iff every open neighborhood of p intersects A. Define $f^n : \wp(\mathbb{R}^n) \rightarrow \wp(\mathbb{Q}^n)$ by $f^n(a) := a \cap \mathbb{Q}^n$.

Let $\psi_\bullet(x)$, $\psi_\bigcirc(x)$ and $\psi_{\in\bigcirc}(x, y)$ be as in the case of semi-algebraic sets. The formula $\psi_\odot(x, X) := \exists z(\psi_\bigcirc(z) \wedge \psi_{\in\bigcirc}(x, z) \wedge \forall t(\neg(\psi_{\in\bigcirc}(t, z) \wedge t \in X)))$ defines the pairs $\langle q, A \rangle \in \mathbb{Q} \times \wp(\mathbb{Q})$ such that q encodes a point which is isolated from the set of points encoded by the members of A.

A set A of rational points is an f^n-image of a regular closed set iff it contains exactly the rational points that are dense in it iff A satisfies

$$\psi_{RC}(X) := \forall x(x \in X \rightarrow \psi_\bullet(x)) \wedge \forall x(x \in X \leftrightarrow \neg\psi_\odot(x, X)).$$

One can easily find a formula $\psi_{closer}(X, Y, Z)$ defining the relation closer-than.

Lemma 19. *For $n > 0$, Γ is an interpretation of $\langle RC(\mathbb{R}^n), closer \rangle$ in $\mathcal{Q}$, where Γ consists of:*

1. *the formulas $\psi_{RC}(X)$ and $\psi_{RC\sim}(X, Y) := \forall x(x \in X \leftrightarrow x \in Y)$;*
2. *the formula $\psi_{closer}(X, Y, Z)$ corresponding to the closer relation;*
3. *the inverse of f^n as a surjective map.*

Corollary 10. *Let σ be any of $\langle C \rangle$, $\langle conv, \leq \rangle$ and $\langle closer \rangle$. Then the theory of $\langle RC(\mathbb{R}^n), \sigma \rangle$ is in Δ_ω^1.*

5   Conclusions

In this paper we examined the complexity of the first-order theories of some region-based Euclidean spatial logics. We showed that the spatial logic for expressing the *contact* relation is decidable but not elementary, when interpreted over $\mathbb{R}$. We showed that the same logic interpreted over $\mathbb{R}^n$, for $n > 1$, can encode first-order arithmetic, and when regions with infinitely many components are allowed, second-order arithmetic as well. These lower complexity bounds also hold for more expressive logics such as those able to express the property of *convexity* or the relation *closer-than*. It was shown in [2] that when polytopes with vertices having transcendental coordinates are allowed, these logics have complexities no less than that of second-order arithmetic. It also follows from [2] that, the complexities of the spatial logics which are able to express the *closer-than* relation are not influenced by the dimension of the space over which they are interpreted.

We showed that all structures with countable domains are definable in first-order arithmetic and that all others are definable in second-order arithmetic. This yields precise complexity bounds for all our structures but $\langle RCS(\mathbb{R}^n), C \rangle$ and $\langle RCP(\mathbb{R}^n), C \rangle$, where $n > 1$. For $n = 2$, the theories of these structures are the same as the theory of $\langle RCP_{\mathbb{Q}}(\mathbb{R}^2), C \rangle$ (see [17]), which makes them complete with respect to first-order arithmetic. However, for $n > 2$, the precise complexity the theories of $\langle RCS(\mathbb{R}^n), C \rangle$ and $\langle RCP(\mathbb{R}^n), C \rangle$ remains open.

From the established complexity bounds we obtain an interesting and surprising model-theoretic result — namely that $\langle RCP_{\mathbb{A}}(\mathbb{R}^2), conv, \leq \rangle$ is not an elementary substructure of $\langle RCP(\mathbb{R}^2), conv, \leq \rangle$.

Acknowledgements. The work on this paper was supported by the UK EPSRC research grants EP/P504724/1 and EP/E035248/1.

References

1. Bochnak, J., Coste, M., Roy, M.F.: Real algebraic geometry. Springer, Heidelberg (1998)
2. Davis, E.: The expressivity of quantifying over regions. Journal of Logic and Computation 16(6), 891–916 (2006)
3. de Vries, H.: Compact Spaces and Compactifications: an algebraic approach. Van Gorcum, Assen (1962)

4. Dimov, G., Vakarelov, D.: Contact algebras and region-based theory of space: Proximity approach - I. Fundamenta Mathematicae 74(2,3), 209–249 (2006)
5. Dornheim, C.: Undecidability of plane polygonal mereotopology. In: Principles of Knowledge Representation and Reasoning: Proceedings of the Sixth International Conference, pp. 342–355 (1998)
6. Düntsch, I., Winter, M.: A representation theorem for boolean contact algebras. Theor. Comput. Sci. 347(3), 498–512 (2005)
7. Egenhofer, M.J.: Reasoning about binary topological relations. In: Günther, O., Schek, H.-J. (eds.) SSD 1991. LNCS, vol. 525, pp. 143–160. Springer, Heidelberg (1991)
8. Grzegorczyk, A.: Undecidability of some topological theories. Fundamenta Mathematicae 38, 137–152 (1951)
9. Hinman, P.G., Frontmatter, M.: Recursion-theoretic hierarchies, New York (1978)
10. Hodges, W.: Model theory. Cambridge Univ. Pr., Cambridge (1993)
11. Kontchakov, R., Pratt-Hartmann, I., Wolter, F., Zakharyaschev, M.: On the computational complexity of spatial logics with connectedness constraints. In: Cervesato, I., Veith, H., Voronkov, A. (eds.) LPAR 2008. LNCS (LNAI), vol. 5330, pp. 574–589. Springer, Heidelberg (2008)
12. Kontchakov, R., Pratt-Hartmann, I., Zakharyaschev, M.: Interpreting topological logics over Euclidean spaces. In: Proc. of the 12th International Conference on Principles of Knowledge Representation and Reasoning, pp. 534–544. AAAI Press, Menlo Park (2010)
13. Koppelberg, S., Bonnet, R., Monk, J.D.: Handbook of Boolean Algebras, vol. 1. Elsevier, Amsterdam (1989)
14. de Laguna, T.: Point, line, and surface, as sets of solids. The Journal of Philosophy 19(17), 449–461 (1922)
15. Meyer, A.R.: Weak monadic second order theory of succesor is not elementary-recursive. In: Logic Colloquium. Lecture Notes in Mathematics, vol. 453, pp. 132–154. Springer, Heidelberg (1975)
16. Pratt, I.: First-order qualitative spatial representation languages with convexity. Spatial Cognition and Computation 1(2), 181–204 (1999)
17. Pratt-Hartmann, I.: First-order mereotopology. In: Handbook of Spatial Logics, pp. 13–97. Springer, Netherlands (2007)
18. Rabin, M.O.: Decidability of second-order theories and automata on infinite trees. Transactions of the American Mathematical Society 141(1-35), 4 (1969)
19. Randell, D., Cui, Z., Cohn, A.: A spatial logic based on regions and connection. In: Nebel, B., Rich, C., Swartout, W. (eds.) Proc. 3rd International Conference on Principles of Knowledge Representation and Reasoning, pp. 165–176. Morgan Kaufmann, San Francisco (1992)
20. Roeper, P.: Region-Based Topology. Journal of Philosophical Logic 26(3), 251–309 (1997)
21. Sheremet, M., Tishkovsky, D., Wolter, F., Zakharyaschev, M.: From topology to metric: modal logic and quantification in metric spaces. In: Hodkinson, I., Venema, Y. (eds.) Advances in Modal Logic, vol. 6, pp. 429–448. College Publications, London (2006)
22. Tarski, A.: Foundations of the geometry of solids. Logic, semantics, metamathematics, 24–29 (1956)
23. Whitehead, A.N.: Process and reality: an essay in cosmology. Cambridge University Press, Cambridge (1929)

Inductive-Inductive Definitions

Fredrik Nordvall Forsberg[*] and Anton Setzer[*]

Swansea University
{csfnf,a.g.setzer}@swansea.ac.uk

Abstract. We present a principle for introducing new types in type theory which generalises strictly positive indexed inductive data types. In this new principle a set A is defined inductively simultaneously with an A-indexed set B, which is also defined inductively. Compared to indexed inductive definitions, the novelty is that the index set A is generated inductively simultaneously with B. In other words, we mutually define two inductive sets, of which one depends on the other.

Instances of this principle have previously been used in order to formalise type theory inside type theory. However the consistency of the framework used (the theorem prover Agda) is not so clear, as it allows the definition of a universe containing a code for itself. We give an axiomatisation of the new principle in such a way that the resulting type theory is consistent, which we prove by constructing a set-theoretic model.

1 Introduction

Martin-Löf Type Theory [12] is a foundational framework for constructive mathematics, where induction plays a major part in the construction of sets. Martin-Löf's formulation [12] includes inductive definitions of for example Cartesian products, disjoint unions, the identity set, finite sets, the natural numbers, well-orderings and lists. External schemas for general inductive sets and inductive families have been given by Backhouse et. al. [2] and Dybjer [6] respectively. Indexed inductive definitions have also been used for generic programming in dependent type theory [3,13].

Another induction principle is *induction-recursion*, where a set U is constructed inductively simultaneously with a recursively defined function $T : U \to D$ for some possibly large type D. The constructor for U may depend negatively on T applied to elements of U. The main example is Martin-Löf's universe à la Tarski [15]. Dybjer [8] gave a schema for such inductive-recursive definitions, and this has been internalised by Dybjer and Setzer [9,10,11].

In this article, we present another induction principle, which we, in reference to induction-recursion, call *induction-induction*. A set A is inductively defined simultaneously with an A-indexed set B, which is also inductively defined, and

---

[*] Supported by EPSRC grant EP/G033374/1, Theory and applications of induction-recursion.

A. Dawar and H. Veith (Eds.): CSL 2010, LNCS 6247, pp. 454–468, 2010.
© Springer-Verlag Berlin Heidelberg 2010

the introduction rules for A may also refer to B. So we have formation rules $A : \mathrm{Set}$, $B : A \to \mathrm{Set}$ and typical introduction rules might take the form

$$\frac{a : A \quad b : B(a) \quad \ldots}{\mathrm{intro}_A(a, b, \ldots) : A} \qquad \frac{a_0 : A \quad b : B(a_0) \quad a_1 : A \quad \ldots}{\mathrm{intro}_B(a_0, b, a_1, \ldots) : B(a_1)}$$

This is not a simple mutual inductive definition of two sets, as B is indexed by A. It is not an ordinary inductive family, as A may refer to B. Finally, it is not an instance of induction-recursion, as B is constructed inductively, not recursively.

Let us consider a first example, which will serve as a running example to illustrate the formal rules. We simultaneously define a set of platforms together with buildings constructed on these platforms. The ground is a platform, and if we have a building, we can always construct a new platform from it by building an extension. We can always build a building on top of any platform, and if we have an extension, we can also construct a building hanging from it. See the extended version [14] of this article for an illustration.) This gives rise to the following inductive-inductive definition of Platform : Set, Building : Platform $\to$ Set (where p : Platform means that p is a platform and b : Building(p) means that b is a building constructed on the platform p)[1] with constructors

> ground : Platform ,
>
> extension : $((p : \mathrm{Platform}) \times \mathrm{Building}(p)) \to \mathrm{Platform}$,
>
> onTop : $(p : \mathrm{Platform}) \to \mathrm{Building}(p)$,
>
> hangingUnder : $((p : \mathrm{Platform}) \times (b : \mathrm{Building}(p))) \to \mathrm{Building}(\mathrm{extension}(\langle p, b \rangle))$.

Note that the index of the codomain of hangingUnder is extension($\langle p, b \rangle$), i.e. hangingUnder($\langle p, b \rangle$) : Building(extension($\langle p, b \rangle$)). In other words, it is not possible to have a building hanging under the ground.

Inductive-inductive definitions have been used by Dybjer [7], Danielsson [5] and Chapman [4] to internalise the syntax and semantics of type theory. Slightly simplified, they define a set Ctxt of contexts, a family Ty : Ctxt $\to$ Set of types in a given context, and a family Term : $(\Gamma : \mathrm{Ctxt}) \to \mathrm{Ty}(\Gamma) \to \mathrm{Set}$ of terms of a given type. Let us for simplicity only consider contexts and types. The set Ctxt of contexts has two constructors

> ε : Ctxt ,
>
> cons : $((\Gamma : \mathrm{Ctxt}) \times \mathrm{Ty}(\Gamma)) \to \mathrm{Ctxt}$,

corresponding to the empty context and extending a context Γ with a new type. In our simplified setting, Ty : Ctxt $\to$ Set has the following constructors

> 'set' : $(\Gamma : \mathrm{Ctxt}) \to \mathrm{Ty}(\Gamma)$,
>
> Π : $((\Gamma : \mathrm{Ctxt}) \times (A : \mathrm{Ty}(\Gamma)) \times \mathrm{Ty}(\mathrm{cons}(\langle \Gamma, A \rangle))) \to \mathrm{Ty}(\Gamma)$.

---

[1] The collection of small types in Martin-Löf type theory is called Set for historic reasons, whereas Type is reserved for the collection of large types. The judgement Building : Platform $\to$ Set means that for every p : Platform, Building(p) : Set. The type theoretic notation will be further explained in Section 2.

The first constructor states that 'set' is a type in any context. The second constructor Π is the constructor for the Π-type: If we have a type A in a context Γ, and another type B in Γ extended by A (corresponding to abstracting a variable of type A), then $\Pi(A, B)$ is also a type in Γ.

Note how the constructor cons for Ctxt has an argument of type $\mathrm{Ty}(\Gamma)$, even though Ty is indexed by Ctxt. It is also worth noting that Π has an argument of type $\mathrm{Ty}(\mathrm{cons}(\langle \Gamma, A \rangle))$, i.e. we are using the constructor for Ctxt in the index of Ty. In general, we could of course imagine an argument of type $\mathrm{Ty}(\mathrm{cons}(\langle \mathrm{cons}(\langle \Gamma, A \rangle), A' \rangle))$ etc.

Both Danielsson [5] and Chapman [4] have used the proof assistant Agda [17] as a framework for their formalisation. Agda supports inductive-inductive (and inductive-recursive) definitions via the `mutual` keyword. However, the theory behind Agda is unclear, especially in relation to mutual definitions. For example, Agda allows the definition of a universe U à la Tarski, with a code $u : U$ for itself, i.e. $T(u) = U$. This does not necessarily mean that Agda is inconsistent by Girard's paradox, as, if we also demand closure under Π or Σ, the positivity checker rejects the code. However the consistency of Agda is by no means clear.

Nevertheless, Agda is an excellent tool for trying out ideas. We have formalised our theory in Agda, and this formalisation can be found on the authors' home pages, together with an extended version of this article [14], containing proofs and details that have been omitted due to space constraints.

2   Type Theoretic Preliminaries

We work in a type theory with at least two universes Set and Type, with Set : Type and if A : Set then A : Type. Both Set and Type are closed under dependent function types, written $(x : A) \to B$ (sometimes denoted $(\Pi x : A)B$), where B is a set or type depending on $x : A$. Abstraction is written as $\lambda x : A.e$, where $e : B$ depending on $x : A$, and application as $f(x)$. Repeated abstraction and application are written as $\lambda x_1 : A_1 \ldots x_k : A_k.e$ and $f(x_1, \ldots, x_k)$. If the type of x can be inferred, we simply write $\lambda x.e$ as an abbreviation. Furthermore, both Set and Type are closed under dependent sums, written $(x : A) \times B$ (sometimes denoted $(\Sigma x : A)B$), where B is a set or type depending on $x : A$, with pairs $\langle a, b \rangle$, where $a : A$ and $b : B[x := a]$. We also have β- and η-rules for both dependent function types and sums.

We need an empty type $\mathbf{0}$: Set, with elimination $!_A : (x : \mathbf{0}) \to A$ for every $A : \mathbf{0} \to$ Set. We need a unit type $\mathbf{1}$: Set, with unique element $\star : \mathbf{1}$. We include an η-rule stating that if $x : \mathbf{1}$, then $x = \star : \mathbf{1}$. Moreover, we include a two element set $\mathbf{2}$: Set, with elements tt : $\mathbf{2}$, ff : $\mathbf{2}$ and elimination constant if $\cdot$ then $\cdot$ else $\cdot$: $(a : \mathbf{2}) \to A(\mathrm{tt}) \to A(\mathrm{ff}) \to A(a)$ where $A(i)$: Type for $i : \mathbf{2}$.

With if $\cdot$ then $\cdot$ else $\cdot$ and dependent products, we can now define the disjoint union of two sets $A + B := (x : \mathbf{2}) \times ($if x then A else $B)$ with constructors inl = $\lambda a : A.\langle \mathrm{tt}, a \rangle$ and inr = $\lambda b : B.\langle \mathrm{ff}, b \rangle$, and prove the usual formation, introduction, elimination and equality rules. We write $A_0 + A_1 + \ldots + A_n$ for $A_0 + (A_1 + (\ldots + A_n)\cdots)$ and $\mathrm{in}_k(a)$ for the kth injection $\mathrm{inl}(\mathrm{inr}^k(a))$ (with special case $\mathrm{in}_n(a) = \mathrm{inr}^n(a)$).

Using (the derived) elimination rules for +, we can, for A, B : Set, $C : A + B \to$ Type and $f : (a : A) \to C(\mathrm{inl}(a))$, $g : (b : B) \to C(\mathrm{inr}(b))$, define the case distinction $f \sqcup g : (c : A + B) \to C(c)$ with equality rules

$$(f \sqcup g)(\mathrm{inl}(a)) = f(a) \; ,$$
$$(f \sqcup g)(\mathrm{inr}(b)) = g(b) \; .$$

We will use the same notation even when C does not depend on $c : A + B$, and we will write $f \parallel g : A + B \to C + D$, where $f : A \to C$, $g : B \to D$, for $(\mathrm{inl} \circ f) \sqcup (\mathrm{inr} \circ g)$.

Intensional type theory in Martin-Löf's logical framework extended with dependent products and **0**, **1** and **2** has all the features we need. Thus, our development could, if one so wishes, be seen as an extension of the logical framework.

3   From Inductive to Inductive-Inductive Definitions

Let us first, before we move on to inductive-inductive definitions, informally consider how to formalise a simultaneous (generalised) inductive definition of two sets A and B, given by constructors

$$\mathrm{intro_A} : \Phi_A(A, B) \to A \quad \mathrm{intro_B} : \Phi_B(A, B) \to B$$

where Φ_A and Φ_B are strictly positive in the following sense:

- The constant $\Phi(A, B) = \mathbf{1}$ is strictly positive. It corresponds to an introduction rule with no arguments (or more precisely, the trivial argument $x : \mathbf{1}$).
- If K is a set and Ψ_x is strictly positive, depending on $x : K$, then $\Phi(A, B) = (x : K) \times \Psi_x(A, B)$, corresponding to the addition of a non-inductive premise, is strictly positive. So intro_A has one non-inductive argument $x : K$, followed by the arguments given by $\Psi_x(A, B)$.
- If K is a set and Ψ is strictly positive, then $\Phi(A, B) = (K \to A) \times \Psi(A, B)$ is strictly positive. This corresponds to the addition of a premise inductive in A, where K corresponds to the hypothesis of this premise in a generalised inductive definition. So intro_A has one inductive argument $f : K \to A$, followed by the arguments given by $\Psi(A, B)$.
- Likewise, if K is a set and Ψ is strictly positive, then $\Phi(A, B) = (K \to B) \times \Psi(A, B)$ is strictly positive. This is similar to the previous case.

In an inductive-inductive definition, B is indexed by A, so the constructor for B is replaced by

$$\mathrm{intro_B} : (a : \Phi_B(A, B)) \to B(i_{A,B}(a))$$

for some index $i_{A,B}(a) : A$ which might depend on $a : \Phi_B(A, B)$. Furthermore, we must modify the inductive case for B to specify an index as well. This index can (and usually does) depend on earlier inductive arguments, so that the new inductive cases become

- If K is a set, and Ψ_f is strictly positive, depending[2] on $f : K \to A$ only in indices for B, then $\Phi(A,B) = (f : K \to A) \times \Psi_f(A,B)$ is strictly positive.
- If K is a set, $i_{A,B} : K \to A$ is a function and Ψ_f is strictly positive, depending on $f : (x : K) \to B(i_{A,B}(x))$ only in indices for B, then $\Phi(A,B) = (f : ((x : K) \to B(i_{A,B}(x)))) \times \Psi_f(A,B)$ is strictly positive.

In what way can the index depend on f? Before we know the constructor for A, we do not know any functions with codomain A, so the index can only depend directly on f (e.g. $B(f(x))$). When we define the constructor for B, the situation is similar, but now we know one function into A, namely $\mathrm{intro}_A : \Phi_A(A,B) \to A$, so that the index could be e.g. $\mathrm{intro}_A(f(x),b)$. (Our approach could also be straightforwardly extended to allow several constructors for A, where later constructors make use of earlier ones.)

4   An Axiomatisation

We proceed as in Dybjer and Setzer [9] and introduce a datatype of codes for constructors. In other words, we define a type SP (for strictly positive) whose elements represent the inductively defined sets, together with a way to construct the real sets from the representing codes. However, as we have two sets A and B with different roles, we need two types SP_A and SP_B of codes.

What do we need to know in order to reconstruct the inductively defined sets? A moment's thought shows that all we need is the domain of the constructors, and in the case of B, we also need the index of the codomain of the constructor. From this, we can write down the introduction rules, and the elimination rules should be determined by these (see e.g. [6]). Thus, the codes in SP_A and SP_B will be codes for the domain of the constructors, and we will have functions Arg_A, Arg_B that map the code to the domain it represents. For B, there will also be a function Index_B that gives the index (in A) of the codomain of the constructor.

We will have special codes A-ind, B-ind for arguments that are inductive in A and B respectively. In the case of B-ind, we also need to specify an index, which might depend on earlier arguments. For instance, the index p of the type of the second argument for the extension constructor

$$\mathrm{extension} : ((p : \mathrm{Platform}) \times \mathrm{Building}(p)) \to \mathrm{Platform}$$

depends on the first argument. How can we specify this index in the code? We cannot make use of the sets A and B themselves, since they are to be defined, but we can refer to their existence. We will introduce parameters A_{ref}, B_{ref} that get updated during the construction of the code. A_{ref} determines the elements of A that we can refer to, and B_{ref} determines the elements b of B, together with the index a such that $b : B(a)$. At the beginning, we cannot refer to any arguments, and so $A_{\mathrm{ref}} = B_{\mathrm{ref}} = \mathbf{0}$. For example, after having written down the first argument $p : \mathrm{Platform}$, A_{ref} would be extended to include also an element representing p, which we use when writing down the type of the second argument, $\mathrm{Building}(p)$.

---

[2] The somewhat vague and informal phrase "depending on f only in indices for B" will be given an exact meaning in the formalisation in the next section.

4.1 SP$_A$ and Arg$_A$

The above discussion leads us to the following formation rule for SP$_A$:

$$\frac{A_{\mathrm{ref}} : \mathrm{Set} \quad B_{\mathrm{ref}} : \mathrm{Set}}{\mathrm{SP}_A(A_{\mathrm{ref}}, B_{\mathrm{ref}}) : \mathrm{Type}}$$

A_{ref} and B_{ref} can be any sets. The codes for inductive-inductive definitions will however be elements from $\mathrm{SP}'_A \coloneqq \mathrm{SP}_A(\mathbf{0}, \mathbf{0})$, i.e. codes that do not refer to any elements to start with.

The introduction rules for SP$_A$ reflect the rules for strict positivity in Section 3. The rules are as follows (we suppress the global premise $A_{\mathrm{ref}}, B_{\mathrm{ref}} : \mathrm{Set}$):

$$\frac{}{\mathrm{nil}_A : \mathrm{SP}_A(A_{\mathrm{ref}}, B_{\mathrm{ref}})} \qquad \frac{K : \mathrm{Set} \quad \gamma : K \to \mathrm{SP}_A(A_{\mathrm{ref}}, B_{\mathrm{ref}})}{\mathrm{nonind}(K, \gamma) : \mathrm{SP}_A(A_{\mathrm{ref}}, B_{\mathrm{ref}})}$$

$$\frac{K : \mathrm{Set} \quad \gamma : \mathrm{SP}_A(A_{\mathrm{ref}} + K, B_{\mathrm{ref}})}{\text{A-ind}(K, \gamma) : \mathrm{SP}_A(A_{\mathrm{ref}}, B_{\mathrm{ref}})} \qquad \frac{K : \mathrm{Set} \quad h_{\mathrm{index}} : K \to A_{\mathrm{ref}} \quad \gamma : \mathrm{SP}_A(A_{\mathrm{ref}}, B_{\mathrm{ref}} + K)}{\text{B-ind}(K, h_{\mathrm{index}}, \gamma) : \mathrm{SP}_A(A_{\mathrm{ref}}, B_{\mathrm{ref}})}$$

The code nil_A represents a trivial constructor (the base case). The code $\mathrm{nonind}(K, \gamma)$ is meant to represent a noninductive argument $x : K$, with the rest of the arguments given by $\gamma(x)$. The code A-ind(K, γ) is meant to represent a (generalised) inductive argument of type $K \to A$, with the rest of the arguments given by γ. Finally, the code B-ind$(K, h_{\mathrm{index}}, \gamma)$ represents an inductive argument of type $(x : K) \to B(i(x))$, where the index $i(x)$ is determined by h_{index}, and the rest of the arguments are given by γ. For instance, a constructor

$$c : ((x : \mathbf{2}) \times (\mathbb{N} \to A)) \to A$$

has the code $\gamma_c = \mathrm{nonind}(\mathbf{2}, \lambda x.\text{A-ind}(\mathbb{N}, \mathrm{nil}_A))$. Note how $\mathbf{2}$ and $\mathbb{N}$ appear in the code. We will see an example of the slightly more complicated constructor B-ind later.

We will now define Arg$_A$, which maps a code to the domain of the constructor it represents. Arg$_A$ will need to take arbitrary $A : \mathrm{Set}$ and $B : A \to \mathrm{Set}$ as parameters to use as A and B in the inductive arguments, since we need Arg$_A$ to define the A and B we want. We will then have axioms stating that for every code $\gamma : \mathrm{SP}'_A$, there are sets A_γ, B_γ closed under Arg$_A$, i.e. there is a constructor $\mathrm{intro}_A : \mathrm{Arg}_A(\gamma, A_\gamma, B_\gamma) \to A_\gamma$. Arg$_A$ has formation rule

$$\frac{\begin{array}{c} A_{\mathrm{ref}}, B_{\mathrm{ref}} : \mathrm{Set} \\ \gamma : \mathrm{SP}_A(A_{\mathrm{ref}}, B_{\mathrm{ref}}) \end{array} \quad \begin{array}{c} A : \mathrm{Set} \\ B : A \to \mathrm{Set} \end{array} \quad \begin{array}{c} \mathrm{rep}_A : A_{\mathrm{ref}} \to A \\ \mathrm{rep}_{\mathrm{index}} : B_{\mathrm{ref}} \to A \\ \mathrm{rep}_B : (x : B_{\mathrm{ref}}) \to B(\mathrm{rep}_{\mathrm{index}}(x)) \end{array}}{\mathrm{Arg}_A(A_{\mathrm{ref}}, B_{\mathrm{ref}}, \gamma, A, B, \mathrm{rep}_A, \mathrm{rep}_{\mathrm{index}}, \mathrm{rep}_B) : \mathrm{Set}}$$

The function rep_A translates elements in A_{ref} into the real elements they represent in A. Elements in B_{ref} represent elements b from B, but also elements from A, as we also need to store the index a such that $b : B(a)$. This index is given by $\mathrm{rep}_{\mathrm{index}}$, and rep_B gives the real element in $B(\mathrm{rep}_{\mathrm{index}}(y))$ an element $y : B_{\mathrm{ref}}$ represents.

We are actually only interested in $\mathrm{Arg_A}$ for codes $\gamma : \mathrm{SP}'_A$ for inductive-inductive definitions (i.e. with $A_{\mathrm{ref}} = B_{\mathrm{ref}} = \mathbf{0}$), but we need to consider arbitrary A_{ref}, B_{ref} for the intermediate codes. For $\gamma : \mathrm{SP}'_A$, we can define a simplified version $\mathrm{Arg}'_A : \mathrm{SP}'_A \to (A : \mathrm{Set}) \to (B : A \to \mathrm{Set}) \to \mathrm{Set}$ by $\mathrm{Arg}'_A(\gamma, A, B) :$ $= \mathrm{Arg_A}(\mathbf{0}, \mathbf{0}, \gamma, A, B, !_A, !_A, !_{B \circ !_A})$. (Recall that $!_X : (x : \mathbf{0}) \to X$ is the function given by ex falso quodlibet.)

The definition of $\mathrm{Arg_A}$ also follows the rules for strict positivity in Section 3. We will, for readability, write "_" for arguments which are simply passed on in the recursive call.

The code $\mathrm{nil_A}$ represents the constructor with no argument (i.e. a trivial argument of type $\mathbf{1}$):

$$\mathrm{Arg_A}(A_{\mathrm{ref}}, B_{\mathrm{ref}}, \mathrm{nil_A}, A, B, \mathrm{rep_A}, \mathrm{rep_{index}}, \mathrm{rep_B}) = \mathbf{1}$$

The code $\mathrm{nonind}(K, \gamma)$ represents one non-inductive argument $k : K$, with the rest of the arguments given by the code γ (depending on $k : K$):

$$\mathrm{Arg_A}(A_{\mathrm{ref}}, B_{\mathrm{ref}}, \mathrm{nonind}(K, \gamma), A, B, \mathrm{rep_A}, \mathrm{rep_{index}}, \mathrm{rep_B}) =$$
$$\big(k : K\big) \times \mathrm{Arg_A}(\text{-}, \text{-}, \gamma(k), \text{-}, \text{-}, \text{-}, \text{-}, \text{-})$$

The code $\mathrm{A\text{-}ind}(K, \gamma)$ represents one generalised inductive argument $j : K \to A$, with the rest of the arguments given by the code γ. In the following arguments, A_{ref} has now been updated to $A_{\mathrm{ref}} + K$, where elements in the old A_{ref} are mapped to A by the old $\mathrm{rep_A}$, and elements in K are mapped to A by j. In effect, this means that we can refer to $j(k)$ for $k : K$ in the following arguments.

$$\mathrm{Arg_A}(A_{\mathrm{ref}}, B_{\mathrm{ref}}, \mathrm{A\text{-}ind}(K, \gamma), A, B, \mathrm{rep_A}, \mathrm{rep_{index}}, \mathrm{rep_B}) =$$
$$\big(j : K \to A\big) \times \mathrm{Arg_A}(A_{\mathrm{ref}} + K, \text{-}, \gamma, \text{-}, \text{-}, \mathrm{rep_A} \sqcup j, \text{-}, \text{-})$$

Finally, the code $\mathrm{B\text{-}ind}(K, h_{\mathrm{index}}, \gamma)$ represents one generalised inductive argument $j : (x : K) \to B((\mathrm{rep_A} \circ h_{\mathrm{index}})(x))$, where $\mathrm{rep_A} \circ h_{\mathrm{index}}$ picks out the index of the type of $j(x)$. This time, we can refer to more elements in B afterwards, namely those given by j (and indices given by $\mathrm{rep_A} \circ h_{\mathrm{index}}$):

$$\mathrm{Arg_A}(A_{\mathrm{ref}}, B_{\mathrm{ref}}, \mathrm{B\text{-}ind}(K, h_{\mathrm{index}}, \gamma), A, B, \mathrm{rep_A}, \mathrm{rep_{index}}, \mathrm{rep_B}) =$$
$$\big(j : (k : K) \to B((\mathrm{rep_A} \circ h_{\mathrm{index}})(k))\big) \times$$
$$\mathrm{Arg_A}(\text{-}, B_{\mathrm{ref}} + K, \gamma, \text{-}, \text{-}, \text{-}, \mathrm{rep_{index}} \sqcup (\mathrm{rep_A} \circ h_{\mathrm{index}}), \mathrm{rep_B} \sqcup j)$$

Let us take a look at the constructor

$$\mathrm{extension} : ((p : \mathrm{Platform}) \times \mathrm{Building}(p)) \to \mathrm{Platform}$$

again. It would have the code $\gamma_{\mathrm{ext}} = \mathrm{A\text{-}ind}(\mathbf{1}, \mathrm{B\text{-}ind}(\mathbf{1}, \lambda \star . \hat{p}, \mathrm{nil_A})) : \mathrm{SP}'_A$ where $\hat{p} = \mathrm{inr}(\star)$ is the element in $A_{\mathrm{ref}} = \mathbf{0} + \mathbf{1}$ representing the element introduced by $\mathrm{A\text{-}ind}$. We have

$$\mathrm{Arg}'_A(\gamma_{\mathrm{ext}}, \mathrm{Platform}, \mathrm{Building}) = (p : \mathbf{1} \to \mathrm{Platform}) \times (\mathbf{1} \to \mathrm{Building}(p(\star))) \times \mathbf{1}$$

which is isomorphic to the domain of extension thanks to the η-rules for $\mathbf{1}$ (i.e. $X \cong \mathbf{1} \to X$ and $X \cong X \times \mathbf{1}$).

4.2   Towards SP$_B$

If we did not want to use constructors for A as indices for B, like for example Building(extension($\langle p,b\rangle$)), we could construct SP$_B$ in more or less the same way as SP$_A$ (this corresponds to choosing $k = 0$ below). However, in general we do want to use constructors as indices, hence we have some more work to do. What do we need to know for such a constructor index? We need to know that we want to use a constructor, but that can be encoded in the code. We also need a way to specify the arguments to the constructor, i.e. we need to represent an element of $\mathrm{Arg}'_A(\gamma, A, B)$! If we want to use nested constructors (e.g. extension($\langle\mathrm{extension}(\langle p,b\rangle), b'\rangle$)), we also need to be able to represent elements in $\mathrm{Arg}'_A(\gamma, \mathrm{Arg}'_A(\gamma, A, B_0), B_1)$ etc.

The idea is to represent elements in $\mathrm{Arg}'_A(\gamma, A, B)$ by corresponding elements in "$\mathrm{Arg}'_A(\gamma, A_{\mathrm{ref}}, B_{\mathrm{ref}})$". However, we must first reconstruct the structure of A_{ref}, B_{ref} as a family, i.e. we will construct $\overline{A_{\mathrm{ref}}}$: Set, $\overline{B_{\mathrm{ref}}} : \overline{A_{\mathrm{ref}}} \to$ Set, together with functions $\overline{\mathrm{rep}_A} : \overline{A_{\mathrm{ref}}} \to A$ and $\overline{\mathrm{rep}_B} : (x : \overline{A_{\mathrm{ref}}}) \to \overline{B_{\mathrm{ref}}}(x) \to B(\overline{\mathrm{rep}_A}(x))$. Then, we will show that $\overline{\mathrm{rep}_A}$ and $\overline{\mathrm{rep}_B}$ can be lifted to a map $\mathrm{lift}'(\overline{\mathrm{rep}_A},\overline{\mathrm{rep}_B})$: $\mathrm{Arg}'_A(\gamma, \overline{A_{\mathrm{ref}}}, \overline{B_{\mathrm{ref}}}) \to \mathrm{Arg}'_A(\gamma, A, B)$, so that elements in $\mathrm{Arg}'_A(\gamma, \overline{A_{\mathrm{ref}}}, \overline{B_{\mathrm{ref}}})$ indeed can represent elements in $\mathrm{Arg}'_A(\gamma, A, B)$. The process can then be iterated to represent elements in $\mathrm{Arg}'_A(\gamma, \mathrm{Arg}'_A(\gamma, A, B_0), B_1)$ etc.

$\overline{A_{\mathrm{ref}}}$ should consist of representatives $\overline{a}$ for elements a in A, and $\overline{B_{\mathrm{ref}}}(\overline{a})$ should consist of representatives for elements in $B(a)$. The representative $\overline{a}$ could either be from A_{ref} (with $a = \mathrm{rep}_A(\overline{a})$), in which case we do not know any elements in $B(a)$, or from B_{ref} (with $a = \mathrm{rep}_{\mathrm{index}}(\overline{a})$), in which case we know a single element in $B(a)$, namely $\mathrm{rep}_B(\overline{a})$. Therefore, for $A_{\mathrm{ref}}, B_{\mathrm{ref}}$: Set, we define

$$\overline{A_{\mathrm{ref}}} := A_{\mathrm{ref}} + B_{\mathrm{ref}} , \qquad \overline{B_{\mathrm{ref}}} := (\lambda x.\mathbf{0}) \sqcup (\lambda x.\mathbf{1}) ,$$

i.e. $\overline{B_{\mathrm{ref}}}(\mathrm{inl}(a)) = \mathbf{0}$ and $\overline{B_{\mathrm{ref}}}(\mathrm{inr}(b)) = \mathbf{1}$.

Mapping representatives in $\overline{A_{\mathrm{ref}}}$ to the elements they represent in A is now easy: we map $\mathrm{inl}(\overline{a}) : \overline{A_{\mathrm{ref}}}$ to $\mathrm{rep}_A(\overline{a})$ and $\mathrm{inr}(\overline{a})$ to $\mathrm{rep}_{\mathrm{index}}(\overline{a})$. For $\overline{B_{\mathrm{ref}}}$, we want to map representatives in $\overline{B_{\mathrm{ref}}}(\overline{a})$ to the elements they represent in $B(a)$. However, we only have to consider $\overline{B_{\mathrm{ref}}}(\mathrm{inr}(x)) = \mathbf{1}$, as there are no elements in $\overline{B_{\mathrm{ref}}}(\mathrm{inl}(x)) = \mathbf{0}$. We map $\star : \overline{B_{\mathrm{ref}}}(\mathrm{inr}(\overline{a}))$ to $\mathrm{rep}_B(\overline{a})$. To sum up, we can define maps $\overline{\mathrm{rep}_A} : \overline{A_{\mathrm{ref}}} \to A$, $\overline{\mathrm{rep}_B} : (x : \overline{A_{\mathrm{ref}}}) \to \overline{B_{\mathrm{ref}}}(x) \to B(\overline{\mathrm{rep}_A}(x))$ by $\overline{\mathrm{rep}_A} := \mathrm{rep}_A \sqcup \mathrm{rep}_{\mathrm{index}}$ and $\overline{\mathrm{rep}_B} := (\lambda x.!_{B\circ!_A}) \sqcup (\lambda x \star .\mathrm{rep}_B(x))$.

We now want to lift these maps to a map $\mathrm{rep}_{A,1} : \mathrm{Arg}'_A(\gamma, \overline{A_{\mathrm{ref}}}, \overline{B_{\mathrm{ref}}}) \to \mathrm{Arg}'_A(\gamma, A, B)$. This is made possible by the following more general result for arbitrary families A, B, A^*, B^* with respective representing functions rep_A, rep_A^* etc. Assume we have maps $g : A \to A^*$, $g' : (x : A) \to B(x) \to B^*(g(x))$ that respect the translations rep_A and rep_A^*, i.e. we have a proof p that $g(\mathrm{rep}_A(x)) = \mathrm{rep}_A^*(x)$ for all $x : A_{\mathrm{ref}}$. Then we can lift g to a map

$$\mathrm{lift}(g,g',p) : \mathrm{Arg}_A(A_{\mathrm{ref}}, B_{\mathrm{ref}}, \gamma, A, B, \mathrm{rep}_A, \mathrm{rep}_{\mathrm{index}}, \mathrm{rep}_B) \to$$
$$\mathrm{Arg}_A(A_{\mathrm{ref}}, B_{\mathrm{ref}}, \gamma, A^*, B^*, \mathrm{rep}_A^*, \mathrm{rep}_{\mathrm{index}}^*, \mathrm{rep}_B^*) .$$

This can be done component-wise by using the translation functions g, g', and using the proof that $g(\mathrm{rep}_A(x)) = \mathrm{rep}_A^*(x)$ to go from $B^*(g(\mathrm{rep}_A(x)))$

to $B^*(\text{rep}_A^*(x))$ in the B-ind case. (It might be worth pointing out that this also works in intensional type theory, as we only need that $g \circ \text{rep}_A$ and rep_A^* are pointwise equal.) We will omit the definition here for lack of space (see [14] for details). Instead, recall the code γ_{ext} for the constructor

$$\text{extension} : ((p : \text{Platform}) \times \text{Building}(p)) \to \text{Platform} .$$

An element from $\text{Arg}_A'(\gamma_{\text{ext}}, \text{Platform}, \text{Building})$ is of the form[3] $z = \langle p, b, \star \rangle$ where $p : \text{Platform}$ and $b : \text{Building}(p)$. Given functions $g : \text{Platform} \to A^*$ and $g' : (x : \text{Platform}) \to \text{Building}(x) \to B^*(g(x))$ for some other A^*, B^*, then z would be mapped to

$$\text{lift}(g, g', \text{triv})(z) = \langle g(p), g'(p, b), \star \rangle : \text{Arg}_A'(\gamma_{\text{ext}}, A^*, B^*) .$$

Here, triv is a trivial proof that $g(\text{rep}_A(x)) = \text{rep}_A^*(x)$ for every $x : \mathbf{0}$. This will be a valid proof for every $\gamma : \text{SP}_A'$, so once again we define a simplified version

$$\text{lift}'(g, g') : \text{Arg}_A'(\gamma, A, B) \to \text{Arg}_A'(\gamma, A^*, B^*)$$

by $\text{lift}'(g, g') \coloneqq \text{lift}(g, g', \text{triv})$.

In our specific case, let for $\gamma : \text{SP}_A'$, $A_{\text{ref}}, B_{\text{ref}} : \text{Set}$ and $\text{rep}_A : A_{\text{ref}} \to A$, $\text{rep}_{\text{index}} : B_{\text{ref}} \to A$, $\text{rep}_B : (b : B_{\text{ref}}) \to B(\text{rep}_{\text{index}}(b))$

$$\overline{\text{arg}_A}(\gamma, A_{\text{ref}}, B_{\text{ref}}) \coloneqq \text{Arg}_A'(\gamma, \overline{A_{\text{ref}}}, \overline{B_{\text{ref}}}) ,$$

$$\overline{\text{lift}}(\text{rep}_A, \text{rep}_{\text{index}}, \text{rep}_B) \coloneqq \text{lift}'(\overline{\text{rep}_A}, \overline{\text{rep}_B}) : \overline{\text{arg}_A}(\gamma, A_{\text{ref}}, B_{\text{ref}}) \to \text{Arg}_A'(\gamma, A, B).$$

We can now represent elements in $\text{Arg}_A'(\gamma, A, B)$ by elements in $\overline{\text{arg}_A}(\gamma, A_{\text{ref}}, B_{\text{ref}})$ via $\text{rep}_{A,1} \coloneqq \overline{\text{lift}}(\text{rep}_A, \text{rep}_{\text{index}}, \text{rep}_B)$. For example, consider γ_{ext} once again. Suppose that we want to specify an element of $\text{Arg}_A'(\gamma_{\text{ext}}, \text{Platform}, \text{Building})$, i.e. an argument to the extension constructor, and we have $A_{\text{ref}} = B_{\text{ref}} = \mathbf{0} + \mathbf{1}$. A_{ref} then consists of two elements, namely $\hat{p} = \text{inl}(\text{inr}(\star))$ and $\widehat{pb} = \text{inr}(\text{inr}(\star))$. We have that $\overline{B_{\text{ref}}}(\hat{p}) = \mathbf{0}$ and $\overline{B_{\text{ref}}}(\widehat{pb}) = \mathbf{1}$. In other words, there is only one element $\langle \widehat{pb} \rangle = \langle \widehat{pb}, \star, \star \rangle$ of $\text{Arg}_A'(\gamma_{\text{ext}}, \overline{A_{\text{ref}}}, \overline{B_{\text{ref}}})$, and $\text{rep}_{A,1}(\langle \widehat{pb} \rangle) = \langle \text{rep}_{\text{index}}(\widehat{pb}), \text{rep}_B(\widehat{pb}), \star \rangle = \langle p, b, \star \rangle$ where $\text{rep}_{\text{index}}(\widehat{pb}) = p : \text{Platform}$, $\text{rep}_B(\widehat{pb}) = b : \text{Building}(p)$.

Let us now generalise this to multiple nestings of constructors. Given a sequence $\vec{B}_{\text{ref}(n)} = B_{\text{ref}, 0}, B_{\text{ref}, 1}, \ldots, B_{\text{ref}, n-1}$ of sets, we iterate $\overline{\text{arg}_A}$ by defining

$$\text{arg}_A^0(\gamma, A_{\text{ref}}, \vec{B}_{\text{ref}(0)}) = A_{\text{ref}} ,$$

$$\text{arg}_A^{n+1}(\gamma, A_{\text{ref}}, \vec{B}_{\text{ref}(n+1)}) = \overline{\text{arg}_A}(\gamma, \overset{n}{\underset{i=0}{+}} \text{arg}_A^i(\gamma, A_{\text{ref}}, \vec{B}_{\text{ref}(i)}), B_{\text{ref}, n}) .$$

arg_A^k should represent k nested constructors. The corresponding iteration of Arg_A' justifying this, is

$$\text{Arg}_A^0(\gamma, A, \vec{B}_{(0)}) = A ,$$

$$\text{Arg}_A^{n+1}(\gamma, A, \vec{B}_{(n+1)}) = \text{Arg}_A'(\gamma, \overset{n}{\underset{i=0}{+}} \text{Arg}_A^i(\gamma, A, \vec{B}_{(i)}), \overset{n}{\underset{i=0}{\bigsqcup}} B_i) ,$$

---

[3] We identify $\mathbf{1} \to X$ and X for the sake of readability. If not, p would be $\lambda \star .p$ and so on.

where $\vec{B}_{(n)}$ is a sequence $B_0, B_1, \ldots, B_{n-1}$ of families $B_i : \mathrm{Arg}_A^i(\gamma_A, A, \vec{B}_{(i-1)}) \to$ Set.

Now assume that we have a sequence $\vec{B}_{\mathrm{ref}(n)}$ of sets and a sequence $\vec{B}_{(n)}$ of families of sets as above. If we now in addition to $\mathrm{rep}_A : A_{\mathrm{ref}} \to A$, also have functions $\mathrm{rep}_{\mathrm{index},i} : B_{\mathrm{ref},\,i} \to \mathrm{Arg}_A^i(\gamma, A, \vec{B})$, and $\mathrm{rep}_{B,i} : (x : B_{\mathrm{ref},\,i}) \to B_i(\mathrm{rep}_{\mathrm{index},i}(x))$ (we will assume all this when working with SP_B), we can now construct functions $\mathrm{rep}_{A,n} : \mathrm{arg}_A^n(\gamma, A_{\mathrm{ref}}, \vec{B}_{\mathrm{ref}}) \to \mathrm{Arg}_A^n(\gamma, A, \vec{B})$ with the help of lift' by defining

$$\mathrm{rep}_{A,0} = \mathrm{rep}_A \; ,$$
$$\mathrm{rep}_{A,n+1} = \overline{\mathrm{lift}}(\coprod_{i=0}^{n} \mathrm{rep}_{A,i}, \mathrm{in}_n \circ \mathrm{rep}_{\mathrm{index},n}, \mathrm{rep}_{B,n}) \; .$$

Note that $\mathrm{rep}_{A,1}$ as defined earlier is an instance of this definition.

4.3 SP_B, Arg_B and Index_B

The datatype SP_B of codes for constructors for B is just as SP_A, but with two differences: first, we can refer to constructors of A (so we will need a code $\gamma_A : \mathrm{SP}_A'$ to know their form, and sets $B_{\mathrm{ref},\,0}, B_{\mathrm{ref},\,1}, \ldots B_{\mathrm{ref},\,i}, \ldots$ to represent elements in B indexed by i nested constructors). Second, we also need to specify an index for the codomain of the constructor (so we will store this index in the nil_B code).

All constructions from now on will be parameterised on the maximum number k of nested constructors for A that we are using, so we are really introducing $\mathrm{SP}_{B,k}$, $\mathrm{Arg}_{B,k}$ etc. However, we will work with an arbitrary k but suppress it as a premise. With this in mind, we have formation rule

$$\frac{\gamma_A : \mathrm{SP}_A' \quad A_{\mathrm{ref}} : \mathrm{Set} \quad B_{\mathrm{ref},\,0}, B_{\mathrm{ref},\,1}, \ldots, B_{\mathrm{ref},\,k} : \mathrm{Set}}{\mathrm{SP}_B(\gamma_A, A_{\mathrm{ref}}, B_{\mathrm{ref},\,0}, B_{\mathrm{ref},\,1}, \ldots, B_{\mathrm{ref},\,k}) : \mathrm{Type}}$$

Let $\mathrm{SP}_B'(\gamma_A) := \mathrm{SP}_B(\gamma_A, \mathbf{0}, \mathbf{0}, \ldots, \mathbf{0})$ for $\gamma_A : \mathrm{SP}_A'$ be the code of inductive-inductive definitions.

The introduction rules for SP_B are very similar to the rules for SP_A, but now we specify an index in nil_B, and we have $k+1$ rules B_0-ind$, \ldots, \mathrm{B}_k$-ind corresponding to how many nested constructors for A we want to use:

$$\frac{a_{\mathrm{index}} : +_{i=0}^{k} \mathrm{arg}_A^i(\gamma_A, A_{\mathrm{ref}}, \vec{B}_{\mathrm{ref}})}{\mathrm{nil}_B(a_{\mathrm{index}}) : \mathrm{SP}_B(\gamma_A, A_{\mathrm{ref}}, B_{\mathrm{ref},\,0}, \ldots, B_{\mathrm{ref},\,k})}$$

$$\frac{K : \mathrm{Set} \quad \gamma : K \to \mathrm{SP}_B(\gamma_A, A_{\mathrm{ref}}, B_{\mathrm{ref},\,0}, \ldots, B_{\mathrm{ref},\,k})}{\mathrm{nonind}(K, \gamma) : \mathrm{SP}_B(\gamma_A, A_{\mathrm{ref}}, B_{\mathrm{ref},\,0}, \ldots, B_{\mathrm{ref},\,k})}$$

$$\frac{K : \mathrm{Set} \quad \gamma : \mathrm{SP}_B(\gamma_A, A_{\mathrm{ref}} + K, B_{\mathrm{ref},\,0}, \ldots, B_{\mathrm{ref},\,k})}{\mathrm{A\text{-}ind}(K, \gamma) : \mathrm{SP}_B(\gamma_A, A_{\mathrm{ref}}, B_{\mathrm{ref},\,0}, \ldots, B_{\mathrm{ref},\,k})}$$

$$\frac{h_{\mathrm{index}} : K \to \mathrm{arg}_A^\ell(\gamma_A, A_{\mathrm{ref}}, \vec{B}_{\mathrm{ref}})}{\mathrm{B}_\ell\text{-}ind(K, h_{\mathrm{index}}, \gamma) : \mathrm{SP}_B(\gamma_A, A_{\mathrm{ref}}, B_{\mathrm{ref},\,0}, \ldots, B_{\mathrm{ref},\,\ell + K}, \ldots, B_{\mathrm{ref},\,k})}{K : \mathrm{Set} \quad \gamma : \mathrm{SP}_B(\gamma_A, A_{\mathrm{ref}}, B_{\mathrm{ref},\,0}, \ldots, B_{\mathrm{ref},\,\ell + K}, \ldots, B_{\mathrm{ref},\,k})}$$

The rules $\mathrm{nil_B}$, nonind and A-ind have the same meaning as before, but B-ind has been split up into several rules. The code $\mathrm{B}_\ell\text{-ind}(K, h_{\mathrm{index}}, \gamma)$ represents an inductive argument of type $(x : K) \to B(i_\ell(x))$ with the index $i_\ell(x)$, using ℓ nested constructors for A, given by h_{index}. Hence h_{index} has codomain $\mathrm{arg}_A^\ell(\gamma_A, A_{\mathrm{ref}}, \vec{B}_{\mathrm{ref}})$. For this to work, we will need $k + 1$ families $B_i : \mathrm{Arg}_A^i(\gamma_A, A, \vec{B}_{(i-1)}) \to \mathrm{Set}$ to interpret these nested constructor indices, together with functions $\mathrm{rep}_{\mathrm{index},i} : B_{\mathrm{ref},\,i} \to \mathrm{Arg}_A^i(\gamma, A, \vec{B}_{(i-1)})$ and $\mathrm{rep}_{\mathrm{B},i} : (x : B_{\mathrm{ref},\,i}) \to B_i(\mathrm{rep}_{\mathrm{index},i}(x))$ to map elements to the real elements they represent. Recall that from this and $\mathrm{rep}_A : A_{\mathrm{ref}} \to A$, we can construct functions $\mathrm{rep}_{A,\ell} : \mathrm{arg}_A^\ell(\gamma, A_{\mathrm{ref}}, \vec{B}_{\mathrm{ref}}) \to \mathrm{Arg}_A^\ell(\gamma, A, \vec{B})$.

Every case of $\mathrm{Arg_B}$ is the same as the corresponding case for $\mathrm{Arg_A}$, except for B_ℓ-ind, where B has been replaced by B_ℓ and rep_A by $\mathrm{rep}_{A,\ell}$ (we write "$\_$" for passed on arguments and "$\_\_$" for passed on sequents of arguments in the recursive call):

$$\mathrm{Arg_B}(\gamma_A, A_{\mathrm{ref}}, \vec{B}_{\mathrm{ref}}, \mathrm{nil_B}(a_{\mathrm{index}}), A, \vec{B}, \mathrm{rep}_A, \vec{\mathrm{rep}}_{\mathrm{index}}, \vec{\mathrm{rep}}_B) = \mathbf{1}$$

$$\mathrm{Arg_B}(\gamma_A, A_{\mathrm{ref}}, \vec{B}_{\mathrm{ref}}, \mathrm{nonind}(K, \gamma), A, \vec{B}, \mathrm{rep}_A, \vec{\mathrm{rep}}_{\mathrm{index}}, \vec{\mathrm{rep}}_B) =$$
$$\big(k : K\big) \times \mathrm{Arg_B}(\_, \_, \_\_, \gamma(k), \_, \_\_, \_, \_\_, \_\_)$$

$$\mathrm{Arg_B}(\gamma_A, A_{\mathrm{ref}}, \vec{B}_{\mathrm{ref}}, \mathrm{A\text{-}ind}(K, \gamma), A, \vec{B}, \mathrm{rep}_A, \vec{\mathrm{rep}}_{\mathrm{index}}, \vec{\mathrm{rep}}_B) =$$
$$\big(j : K \to A\big) \times \mathrm{Arg_B}(\_, A_{\mathrm{ref}} + K, \_\_, \gamma, \_, \_\_, \mathrm{rep}_A \sqcup j, \_\_, \_\_)$$

$$\mathrm{Arg_B}(\gamma_A, A_{\mathrm{ref}}, \vec{B}_{\mathrm{ref}}, \mathrm{B}_\ell\text{-ind}(K, h_{\mathrm{index}}, \gamma), A, \vec{B}, \mathrm{rep}_A, \vec{\mathrm{rep}}_{\mathrm{index}}, \vec{\mathrm{rep}}_B) =$$
$$\big(j : (k : K) \to B_\ell((\mathrm{rep}_{A,\ell} \circ h_{\mathrm{index}})(k))\big) \times$$
$$\mathrm{Arg_B}(\_, \_, \_\_, B_{\mathrm{ref}}, \ell + K, \_\_, \gamma, \_, \_, \_\_, \_, \_\_, \mathrm{rep}_{\mathrm{index},\ell} \sqcup (\mathrm{rep}_{A,\ell} \circ h_{\mathrm{index}}), \_\_, \_\_, \mathrm{rep}_{\mathrm{B},\ell} \sqcup j, \_\_)$$

The last missing piece is now $\mathrm{Index_B}$, which to each $b : \mathrm{Arg}'_B(\gamma_A, \gamma_B, A, \vec{B})$ assigns the index a such that the element constructed from b is in $B(a)$. With γ_A, A_{ref}, $B_{\mathrm{ref},\,i}$ etc as above, $\mathrm{Index_B}$ has formation rule

$$\mathrm{Index_B}(\gamma_A, A_{\mathrm{ref}}, \vec{B}_{\mathrm{ref}}, \gamma_B, A, \vec{B}, \mathrm{rep}_A, \vec{\mathrm{rep}}_{\mathrm{index}}, \vec{\mathrm{rep}}_B) :$$
$$\mathrm{Arg_B}(\gamma_A, A_{\mathrm{ref}}, \vec{B}_{\mathrm{ref}}, \gamma_B, A, \vec{B}, \mathrm{rep}_A, \vec{\mathrm{rep}}_{\mathrm{index}}, \vec{\mathrm{rep}}_B) \to \overset{k}{\underset{i=0}{+}} \mathrm{Arg}_A^i(\gamma_A, A, \vec{B}).$$

$\mathrm{Index_B}$ will take $a_{\mathrm{index}} : +_{i=0}^k \mathrm{arg}_A^i(\gamma_A, A_{\mathrm{ref}}, \vec{B}_{\mathrm{ref}})$ which is stored in $\mathrm{nil_B}$ and map it to the index element it represents in $+_{i=0}^k \mathrm{Arg}_A^i(\gamma_A, A, \vec{B})$. For other codes, it will follow exactly the same pattern as $\mathrm{Arg_B}$, so we omit the rules for them here.

$$\mathrm{Index_B}(\gamma_A, A_{\mathrm{ref}}, \vec{B}_{\mathrm{ref}}, \mathrm{nil_B}(a_{\mathrm{index}}), A, \vec{B}, \mathrm{rep}_A, \vec{\mathrm{rep}}_{\mathrm{index}}, \vec{\mathrm{rep}}_B, \star) = (\overset{k}{\underset{i=0}{\|}} \mathrm{rep}_{A,i})(a_{\mathrm{index}})$$

$$\mathrm{Index_B}(\gamma_A, A_{\mathrm{ref}}, \vec{B}_{\mathrm{ref}}, \mathrm{nonind}(K, \gamma), A, \vec{B}, \mathrm{rep}_A, \vec{\mathrm{rep}}_{\mathrm{index}}, \vec{\mathrm{rep}}_B, \langle k, y \rangle) =$$
$$\mathrm{Index_B}(\_, \_, \_\_, \gamma(k), \_, \_\_, \_, \_\_, \_\_, y)$$

$$\vdots$$

For codes $\gamma_B : \mathrm{SP}'_B(\gamma_A)$ for inductive-inductive definitions, let

$$\mathrm{Arg}'_B(\gamma_A,\gamma_B,A,\vec{B}) := \mathrm{Arg}_B(\gamma_A,\mathbf{0},\vec{\mathbf{0}},\gamma_B,A,\vec{B},!_A,!_{\mathrm{Arg}_A},!_{\vec{B0!}})\ ,$$
$$\mathrm{Index}'_B(\gamma_A,\gamma_B,A,\vec{B}) := \mathrm{Index}_B(\gamma_A,\mathbf{0},\vec{\mathbf{0}},\gamma_B,A,\vec{B},!_A,!_{\mathrm{Arg}_A},!_{B0!})\ .$$

As an illustration, let us consider the constructor

hangingUnder $: ((p:\mathrm{Platform})\times(b:\mathrm{Building}(p))) \to \mathrm{Building}(\mathrm{extension}(\langle p,b\rangle))$.

Here it is interesting to see that the index of the codomain of the constructor uses the constructor extension, so it will be represented by an element from $\overline{\mathrm{arg}_A}(\gamma_{\mathrm{ext}},A_{\mathrm{ref}},B_{\mathrm{ref}})$. We end up with the code $\gamma_{\mathrm{hu}} = \mathrm{A\text{-}ind}(\mathbf{1},\mathrm{B_0\text{-}ind}(\mathbf{1},\lambda\star.\hat{p},$ $\mathrm{nil}_B(\mathrm{in}_1(\widehat{\langle pb\rangle}))))$, where $\hat{p}=\mathrm{inr}(\star)$ and $\widehat{\langle pb\rangle}=\langle\mathrm{inr}(\mathrm{inr}(\star)),\star,\star\rangle$. (The reader is invited to check that $\widehat{\langle pb\rangle}:\overline{\mathrm{arg}_A}(\gamma_{\mathrm{ext}},A_{\mathrm{ref}},B_{\mathrm{ref}})$ at that point in the construction of γ_{hu}.) We get

$$\mathrm{Arg}'_B(\gamma_{\mathrm{ext}},\gamma_{\mathrm{hu}},P,B) = (p:\mathbf{1}\to P)\times(b:\mathbf{1}\to B(p(\star)))\times\mathbf{1}$$

and $\mathrm{Index}'_B(\gamma_{\mathrm{ext}},\gamma_{\mathrm{hu}},P,B,\langle p,b,\star\rangle) = \mathrm{in}_1(\langle p,b,\star\rangle)$.

4.4 Formation and Introduction Rules

We are now ready to give the formal formation and introduction rules for A and B. They all have the common premises $\gamma_A : \mathrm{SP}'_A$ and $\gamma_B : \mathrm{SP}'_B(\gamma_A)$, which will be omitted.

Formation rules:

$$A_{\gamma_A,\gamma_B}:\mathrm{Set}\ ,\qquad B_{\gamma_A,\gamma_B}:A_{\gamma_A,\gamma_B}\to\mathrm{Set}\ .$$

Introduction rule for A_{γ_A,γ_B}:

$$\frac{a:\mathrm{Arg}'_A(\gamma_A,A_{\gamma_A,\gamma_B},B_{\gamma_A,\gamma_B})}{\mathrm{intro}_A(a):A_{\gamma_A,\gamma_B}}$$

For the introduction rule for B_{γ_A,γ_B}, we need some preliminary definitions. We have $B_{\gamma_A,\gamma_B}:A_{\gamma_A,\gamma_B}\to\mathrm{Set}$, but need $B_i:\mathrm{Arg}^i_A(\gamma_A,A_{\gamma_A,\gamma_B},\vec{B}_{(i-1)})\to\mathrm{Set}$ for $0\le i\le k$ to give to Arg'_B. We can assemble such B_i's from B_{γ_A,γ_B}, intro_A and lift'. To do so, define in a step by step manner

$$\mathrm{intro}_n:\mathrm{Arg}^n_A(\gamma_A,A_{\gamma_A,\gamma_B},B_0,\dots,B_{n-1})\to A_{\gamma_A,\gamma_B}$$
$$B_n:\mathrm{Arg}^n_A(\gamma_A,A_{\gamma_A,\gamma_B},B_0,\dots,B_{n-1})\to\mathrm{Set}$$

(i.e. introduce first intro_0, B_0, then intro_1, B_1 and so on) by

$$\mathrm{intro}_0=\mathrm{id}$$
$$\mathrm{intro}_{n+1}=\mathrm{intro}_A\circ\mathrm{lift}'(\bigsqcup_{i=0}^n\mathrm{intro}_i,\bigsqcup_{i=0}^n(\lambda a.\mathrm{id}))$$
$$B_i(x)=B_{\gamma_A,\gamma_B}(\mathrm{intro}_i(x))$$

Hence the introduction rule for B_{γ_A,γ_B} can be given as:

$$\frac{b : \mathrm{Arg}'_B(\gamma_A, A_{\gamma_A,\gamma_B}, B_{\gamma_A,\gamma_B}, B_1, \ldots, B_k)}{\mathrm{intro}_B(b) : B_{\gamma_A,\gamma_B}(\overline{\mathrm{index}}(b))}$$

where $\overline{\mathrm{index}}$ takes the index in $+_{i=1}^k \mathrm{Arg}_A^i(\gamma_A, A_{\gamma_A,\gamma_B}, \vec{B})$ returned by Index'_B and applies the right intro_i to it, i.e.

$$\overline{\mathrm{index}} = (\bigsqcup_{i=0}^k \mathrm{intro}_i) \circ \mathrm{Index}'_B(\gamma_A, \gamma_B, A_{\gamma_A,\gamma_B}, B_0, \ldots, B_k) \ .$$

Elimination rules similar to the rules for indexed inductive definitions can also be formulated, but we here omit them due to lack of space (see [14] for full details).

4.5   Contexts and Types Again

As a final example, let us construct Ctxt and Ty from Section 1. With the abbreviation $\gamma_0 +_{SP} \gamma_1 := \mathrm{nonind}(\mathbf{2}, \lambda x.\mathbf{if}\ x\ \mathbf{then}\ \gamma_0\ \mathbf{else}\ \gamma_1)$, we can encode several constructors into one. The codes for the contexts and types are

$\gamma_{\mathrm{Ctxt}} = \mathrm{nil}_A +_{SP} \mathrm{A\text{-}ind}(\mathbf{1}, \mathrm{B\text{-}ind}(\mathbf{1}, \lambda \star .\mathrm{inr}(\star), \mathrm{nil}_A)) : \mathrm{SP}'_A$

$\gamma_{\text{'set'}} = \mathrm{A\text{-}ind}(\mathbf{1}, \mathrm{nil}_B(\mathrm{inl}(\mathrm{inr}(\star))))$

$\gamma_\Pi = \mathrm{A\text{-}ind}(\mathbf{1}, \mathrm{B}_0\text{-}\mathrm{ind}(\mathbf{1}, \lambda \star .\mathrm{inr}(\star), \mathrm{B}_1\text{-}\mathrm{ind}(\mathbf{1}, \lambda \star .\langle\mathrm{ff}, \langle\lambda \star .\mathrm{inr}(\mathrm{inr}(\star)),$

$\qquad\qquad \langle\lambda \star .\star, \star\rangle\rangle\rangle, \mathrm{nil}_B(\mathrm{inl}(\mathrm{inr}(\star))))))))$

$\gamma_{\mathrm{Ty}} = \gamma_{\text{'set'}} +_{SP} \gamma_\Pi : \mathrm{SP}'_B(\gamma_{\mathrm{Ctxt}})\ .$

We have $\mathrm{Ctxt} = A_{\gamma_{\mathrm{Ctxt}},\gamma_{\mathrm{Ty}}}$ and $\mathrm{Ty} = B_{\gamma_{\mathrm{Ctxt}},\gamma_{\mathrm{Ty}}}$ and we can define the usual constructors by

$\varepsilon : \mathrm{Ctxt}$ 'set' $: (\varGamma : \mathrm{Ctxt}) \to \mathrm{Ty}(\varGamma)$

$\varepsilon = \mathrm{intro}_A\langle\mathrm{tt}, \star\rangle\ ,$ 'set'$(\varGamma) = \mathrm{intro}_B\langle\mathrm{tt}, \langle(\lambda \star .\varGamma), \star\rangle\rangle\ ,$

$\mathrm{cons} : (\varGamma : \mathrm{Ctxt}) \to \mathrm{Ty}(\varGamma) \to \mathrm{Ctxt}$

$\mathrm{cons}(\varGamma, b) = \mathrm{intro}_A(\langle\mathrm{ff}, \langle(\lambda \star .\varGamma), \langle(\lambda \star .b), \star\rangle\rangle\rangle)\ ,$

$\Pi : (\varGamma : \mathrm{Ctxt}) \to (A : \mathrm{Ty}(\varGamma)) \to \mathrm{Ty}(\mathrm{cons}(\varGamma, A)) \to \mathrm{Ty}(\varGamma)$

$\Pi(\varGamma, A, B) = \mathrm{intro}_B(\langle\mathrm{ff}, \langle(\lambda \star .\varGamma), \langle(\lambda \star .A), \langle(\lambda \star .B), \star\rangle\rangle\rangle\rangle)\ .$

5   A Set-Theoretic Model

Even though SP_A and SP_B are straightforward (large) inductive definitions, this axiomatisation does not reduce inductive-inductive definitions to indexed inductive definitions, since the formation and introduction rules are not instances of ordinary indexed inductive definitions. (However, we do believe that induction-induction *can* be reduced to indexed induction with a bit of more work, and plan to publish an article about this in the future.) To make sure that our theory is consistent, it is thus neccessary to construct a model.

A model of our theory can be constructed in ZFC set theory, extended by two strongly inaccessible cardinals $i_0 < i_1$ in order to interpret Set and Type.

Our model will be a simpler version of the models developed in [9,11]. Here we present the main ideas; more details can be found in [14]. See Aczel [1] for a more detailed treatment of interpreting type theory in set theory.

For every expression A of our type theory, we will give an interpretation $[\![A]\!]_\rho$, which might be undefined. Open terms will be interpreted relative to an environment ρ, i.e. a function mapping variables to terms, and contexts will be interpreted as sets of environments.

We interpret the logical framework exactly as in [9]; Each type is interpreted as a set, $a : A$ is interpreted as $a \in A$, $(x : A) \to B$ as the set-theoretic Cartesian product $\Pi_{x \in A} B$ etc. Set is interpreted as V_{i_0} and Type as V_{i_1}.

SP_A can be interpreted as the least set $[\![\mathrm{SP}_A]\!](D, D')$ such that

$$[\![\mathrm{SP}_A]\!](D, D') = 1 + \sum_{K \in [\![\mathrm{Set}]\!]} (K \to [\![\mathrm{SP}_A]\!](D, D')) + \sum_{K \in [\![\mathrm{Set}]\!]} [\![\mathrm{SP}_A]\!](D + K, D')$$
$$+ \sum_{K \in [\![\mathrm{Set}]\!]} \sum_{h : K \to D} [\![\mathrm{SP}_A]\!](D, D' + K) \ ,$$

which must be an element of $[\![\mathrm{Type}]\!] = V_{i_1}$ by the inaccessibility of i_1. We define

$$[\![\mathrm{nil}_A]\!] :\simeq \langle 0, 0 \rangle \ , \qquad\qquad [\![\text{A-ind}(K, \gamma)]\!] :\simeq \langle 2, \langle K, \gamma \rangle \rangle \ ,$$
$$[\![\mathrm{nonind}(K, \gamma)]\!] := \langle 1, \langle K, \gamma \rangle \rangle \ , \qquad [\![\text{B-ind}(K, h, \gamma)]\!] :\simeq \langle 3, \langle K, \langle h, \gamma \rangle \rangle \rangle \ .$$

$[\![\mathrm{SP}_B]\!]$ and $[\![\mathrm{nil}_B]\!]$, $[\![\mathrm{B}_\ell\text{-ind}]\!]$ are defined analogously. $[\![\mathrm{Arg}_A]\!]$. $[\![\mathrm{Arg}_B]\!]$, and $[\![\mathrm{Index}_B]\!]$ are defined according to their equations.

Finally, we have to interpret A_{γ_A, γ_B}, B_{γ_A, γ_B}, intro_A and intro_B. Let

$$[\![A_{\gamma_A, \gamma_B}]\!] :\simeq A^{i_0} \ , \quad [\![B_{\gamma_A, \gamma_B}]\!](a) :\simeq B^{i_0}(a) \ , \quad [\![\mathrm{intro}_A]\!](a) :\simeq a \ , \quad [\![\mathrm{intro}_B]\!](b) :\simeq b \ ,$$

where A^α and B^α are simultaneously defined by recursion on α as

$$A^\alpha := [\![\mathrm{Arg}'_A]\!](\gamma_A, A^{<\alpha}, B^{<\alpha}) \ ,$$
$$B^\alpha(a) := \{b \mid b \in [\![\mathrm{Arg}'_B]\!](\gamma_A, \gamma_B, A^{<\alpha}, \vec{B}^{<\alpha}) \wedge [\![\mathrm{Index}'_B]\!](\gamma_A, \gamma_B, A^{<\alpha}, \vec{B}^{<\alpha}, b) = a\} \ .$$

Theorem 1 (Soundness)

(i) If $\vdash \Gamma\,context$, then $[\![\Gamma]\!] \downarrow$.

(ii) If $\Gamma \vdash A : E$, then $[\![\Gamma]\!] \downarrow$, and for all $\rho \in [\![\Gamma]\!]$, $[\![A]\!]_\rho \in [\![E]\!]_\rho$, and also $[\![E]\!]_\rho \in [\![\mathrm{Type}]\!]$ if $E \not\equiv Type$.

(iii) If $\Gamma \vdash A = B : E$, then $[\![\Gamma]\!] \downarrow$, and for all $\rho \in [\![\Gamma]\!]$, $[\![A]\!]_\rho = [\![B]\!]_\rho$, $[\![A]\!]_\rho \in [\![E]\!]_\rho$ and also $[\![E]\!]_\rho \in [\![\mathrm{Type}]\!]$ if $E \not\equiv Type$.

(iv) $\not\vdash a : \mathbf{0}$. $\Box$

6   Conclusions and Future Work

We have introduced and formalised a new principle, namely induction-induction, for defining sets in Martin-Löf type theory. The principle allows us to simultaneously introduce $A : \mathrm{Set}$ and $B : A \to \mathrm{Set}$, both defined inductively. This principle is used in recent formulations of the meta-theory of type theory in type theory [5,4].

In the future, the relationship between the principle presented here and what is implemented in Agda will be investigated further. Agda implements arbitrary number of levels, i.e. we can have A : Set, $B : A \to$ Set, $C : (a : A) \to B(a) \to$ Set etc., and induction-induction can be used in conjunction with induction-recursion (with the side effect of a self-referring universe). Apart from this, we speculate that our theory covers what can be defined in Agda. However, just as for ordinary induction, we do not expect dependent pattern matching to follow from our elimination rules without the addition of Streicher's Axiom K [16].

On the theoretical side, work is underway to show that inductive-inductive definitions can be reduced to indexed inductive definitions. This would show that the proof theoretical strength does not increase compared to ordinary induction. Normalisation, decidability of type checking and a categorical semantics similar to initial algebra semantics for ordinary inductive types are other topics left for future work.

Acknowledgements. We wish to thank Phillip James and the anonoymous referees of this and previous versions of this article for their helpful comments.

References

1. Aczel, P.: On relating type theories and set theories. In: Altenkirch, T., Naraschewski, W., Reus, B. (eds.) TYPES 1998. LNCS, vol. 1657, pp. 1–18. Springer, Heidelberg (1999)
2. Backhouse, R., Chisholm, P., Malcolm, G., Saaman, E.: Do-it-yourself type theory. Formal Aspects of Computing 1(1), 19–84 (1989)
3. Benke, M., Dybjer, P., Jansson, P.: Universes for generic programs and proofs in dependent type theory. Nordic Journal of Computing 10, 265–269 (2003)
4. Chapman, J.: Type theory should eat itself. Electronic Notes in Theoretical Computer Science 228, 21–36 (2009)
5. Danielsson, N.: A formalisation of a dependently typed language as an inductive-recursive family. In: Altenkirch, T., McBride, C. (eds.) TYPES 2006. LNCS, vol. 4502, pp. 93–109. Springer, Heidelberg (2007)
6. Dybjer, P.: Inductive families. Formal aspects of computing 6(4), 440–465 (1994)
7. Dybjer, P.: Internal type theory. In: Berardi, S., Coppo, M. (eds.) TYPES 1995. LNCS, vol. 1158, pp. 120–134. Springer, Heidelberg (1996)
8. Dybjer, P.: A general formulation of simultaneous inductive-recursive definitions in type theory. Journal of Symbolic Logic 65(2), 525–549 (2000)
9. Dybjer, P., Setzer, A.: A finite axiomatization of inductive-recursive definitions. In: Girard, J. (ed.) TLCA 1999. LNCS, vol. 1581, pp. 129–146. Springer, Heidelberg (1999)
10. Dybjer, P., Setzer, A.: Induction–recursion and initial algebras. Annals of Pure and Applied Logic 124(1-3), 1–47 (2003)
11. Dybjer, P., Setzer, A.: Indexed induction–recursion. Journal of logic and algebraic programming 66(1), 1–49 (2006)
12. Martin-Löf, P.: Intuitionistic type theory. Bibliopolis Naples (1984)
13. Morris, P.: Constructing Universes for Generic Programming. Ph.D. thesis, University of Nottingham (2007)
14. Nordvall Forsberg, F., Setzer, A.: Induction-induction: Agda development and extended version (2010), http://cs.swan.ac.uk/~csfnf/induction-induction/
15. Palmgren, E.: On universes in type theory. In: Sambin, G., Smith, J. (eds.) Twenty five years of constructive type theory, pp. 191–204. Oxford University Press, Oxford (1998)
16. Streicher, T.: Investigations into intensional type theory. Habilitiation Thesis (1993)
17. The Agda Team: The Agda wiki (2010), http://wiki.portal.chalmers.se/agda/

Quantified Differential Dynamic Logic
for Distributed Hybrid Systems[*]

André Platzer

Carnegie Mellon University, Computer Science Department, Pittsburgh, PA, USA
aplatzer@cs.cmu.edu

Abstract. We address a fundamental mismatch between the combinations of dynamics that occur in complex physical systems and the limited kinds of dynamics supported in analysis. Modern applications combine communication, computation, and control. They may even form dynamic networks, where neither structure nor dimension stay the same while the system follows mixed discrete and continuous dynamics.

We provide the logical foundations for closing this analytic gap. We develop a system model for distributed hybrid systems that combines quantified differential equations with quantified assignments and dynamic dimensionality-changes. We introduce a dynamic logic for verifying distributed hybrid systems and present a proof calculus for it. We prove that this calculus is a sound and complete axiomatization of the behavior of distributed hybrid systems relative to quantified differential equations. In our calculus we have proven collision freedom in distributed car control even when new cars may appear dynamically on the road.

1 Introduction

Many safety-critical computers are embedded in cyber-physical systems like cars [1] or aircraft [2]. How do we know that their designs will work as intended? Ensuring correct functioning of cyber-physical systems is among the most challenging and most important problems in computer science, mathematics, and engineering. But the ability to analyze and understand global system behavior is the key to designing smart and reliable control.

Today, there is a fundamental mismatch between the actual combinations of dynamics that occur in applications and the restricted kinds of dynamics supported in analysis. Safety-critical systems in automotive, aviation, railway, and power grids combine *communication, computation, and control*. Combining computation and control leads to *hybrid systems* [3], whose behavior involves both discrete and continuous dynamics originating, e.g., from discrete control decisions and differential equations of movement. Combining communication and computation leads to *distributed systems* [4], whose dynamics are discrete transitions of system parts that communicate with each other. They may form *dynamic*

---

[*] This material is based upon work supported by the National Science Foundation under Grant Nos. CNS-0926181 and CNS-0931985, by the NASA grant NNG-05GF84H, and by the ONR award N00014-10-1-0188.

A. Dawar and H. Veith (Eds.): CSL 2010, LNCS 6247, pp. 469–483, 2010.

distributed systems, where the structure of the system is not fixed but evolves over time and agents may appear or disappear during the system evolution.

Combinations of all three aspects (communication, computation, and control) are used in sophisticated applications, e.g., cooperative distributed car control [1]. Neither structure nor dimension stay the same, because new cars can appear on the street or leave it; see Fig. 1. These systems are

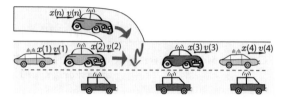

Fig. 1. Distributed car control

(dynamic) distributed hybrid systems. They cannot be considered just as a distributed system (because, e.g., the continuous evolution of positions and velocities matters for collision freedom in car control) nor just as a hybrid system (because the evolving system structure and appearance of new agents can make an otherwise collision-free system unsafe). It is generally impossible to split the analysis of distributed hybrid systems soundly into an analysis of a distributed system (without continuous movement) and an analysis of a hybrid system (without structural changes or appearance), because all kinds of dynamics interact. Just like hybrid systems that generally cannot be analyzed from a purely discrete or a purely continuous perspective [3,5].

Distributed hybrid systems have been considered to varying degrees in modeling languages [6,7,8,9]. In order to build these systems, however, scientists and engineers also need analytic tools to understand and predict their behavior. But formal verification and proof techniques do not yet support the required combination of dynamical effects—which is not surprising given the numerous sources of undecidability for distributed hybrid systems verification.

In this paper, we provide the logical foundations to close this fundamental analytic gap. We develop *quantified hybrid programs* (QHPs) as a model for distributed hybrid systems, which combine dynamical effects from multiple sources: *discrete transitions, continuous evolution, dimension changes, and structural dynamics*. In order to account for changes in the dimension and for co-evolution of an unbounded and evolving number of participants, we generalize the notion of states from assignments for primitive system variables to full first-order structures. Function term $x(i)$ may denote the position of car i of type C, $f(i)$ could be the car registered by communication as the car following car i, and the term $d(i, f(i))$ could denote the minimum safety distance negotiated between car i and its follower. The values of all these terms may evolve *for all i* as time progresses according to interacting laws of discrete and continuous dynamics. They are also affected by changing the system dimension as new cars appear, disappear, or by reconfiguring the system structure dynamically. The defining characteristic of QHPs is that they allow *quantified hybrid dynamics* in which variables like i that occur in function arguments of the system dynamics are quantified over, such that the system co-evolves, e.g., *for all cars i of type C*.

There is a crucial difference between a primitive system variable x and a first-order function term $x(i)$, where i is quantified over. Hybrid dynamics of primitive system variables can model, say, 5 cars (putting scalability issues aside), but not n cars and not systems with a varying number of cars. With first-order function symbols $x(i)$ and hybrid dynamics quantifying over all cars i, a QHP can represent *any* number of cars at once and even (dis)appearance of cars.

Verification of distributed hybrid systems is challenging, because they have three independent sources of undecidability: discrete dynamics, continuous dynamics, and structural/dimensional dynamics. As an analysis tool for distributed hybrid systems, we introduce a specification and verification logic for QHPs that we call *quantified differential dynamic logic* (Qd$\mathcal{L}$). Qd$\mathcal{L}$ provides dynamic logic [10] modal operators $[\alpha]$ and $\langle\alpha\rangle$ that refer to the states reachable by QHP α and can be placed in front of any formula. Formula $[\alpha]\phi$ expresses that all states reachable by system α satisfy formula ϕ, while $\langle\alpha\rangle\phi$ expresses that there is at least one reachable state satisfying ϕ. These modalities can express necessary or possible properties of the transition behavior of α. With its ability to verify (dynamic) distributed hybrid systems and quantified dynamics, Qd$\mathcal{L}$ is a major extension of prior work for static hybrid systems [5,11] or programs [12,13].

Our primary contributions are:

- We introduce a *system model and semantics* that succinctly captures the logical quintessence of (dynamic) distributed hybrid systems with joint discrete, continuous, structural, and dimension-changing dynamics.
- We introduce a *specification/verification logic* for distributed hybrid systems.
- We present a *proof calculus* for this logic, which, to the best of our knowledge, is the *first verification approach* that can handle distributed hybrid systems with their hybrid dynamics and unbounded (and evolving) dimensions.
- We prove that this compositional calculus is a *sound and complete axiomatization* relative to differential equations.
- We have used our proof calculus to verify *collision freedom in a distributed car control system*, where new cars may appear dynamically on the road.

This work constitutes the logical foundation for analysis of distributed hybrid systems. Since distributed hybrid control is the key to control numerous advanced systems, analytic approaches have significant potential for applications.

Our verification approach for distributed hybrid systems is a fundamental extension compared to previous approaches. In much the same way as first-order logic increases the expressive power over propositional logic (quantifiers and function symbols are required to express properties of unbounded structures), Qd$\mathcal{L}$ increases the expressive power over its predecessors (because first-order functions and quantifiers in the dynamics of QHPs are required to characterize systems with unbounded and changing dimensions).

2 Related Work

Multi-party distributed control has been suggested for car control [1] and air traffic control [2]. Due to limits in verification technology, no formal analysis of the distributed hybrid dynamics has been possible for these systems yet. Analysis results include discrete message handling [1] or collision avoidance for two participants [2]. In distributed car control and air traffic control systems, appearance of new participants is a major unsolved challenge for formal verification.

The importance of understanding dynamic / reconfigurable distributed hybrid systems was recognized in modeling languages SHIFT [6] and R-Charon [8]. They focused on simulation / compilation [6] or the development of a semantics [8], so that no verification is possible yet. For stochastic simulation see [9], where soundness has not been proven, because ensuring coverage is difficult.

For distributed hybrid systems, even giving a formal semantics is very challenging [14,7,8,15]! Zhou et al. [14] gave a semantics for a hybrid version of CSP in the Extended Duration Calculus. Rounds [7] gave a semantics in a rich set theory for a spatial logic for a hybrid version of the π-calculus. In the hybrid π-calculus, processes interact with a continuously changing environment, but cannot themselves evolve continuously, which would be crucial to capture the physical movement of traffic agents. From the semantics alone, no verification is possible in these approaches, except perhaps by manual semantic reasoning.

Other process-algebraic approaches, like χ [15], have been developed for modeling and simulation. Verification is still limited to small fragments that can be translated directly to other verification tools like PHAVer or UPPAAL, which have fixed dimensions and restricted dynamics (no distributed hybrid systems).

Our approach is completely different. It is based on first-order structures and dynamic logic. We focus on developing a logic that supports distributed hybrid dynamics and is amenable to automated theorem proving in the logic itself.

Our previous work and other verification approaches for static hybrid systems cannot verify distributed hybrid systems. Distributed hybrid systems may have an unbounded and changing number of components/participants, which cannot be represented with any fixed number of dimensions of the state space. In distributed car control, for instance, there is no prior limit on the number of cars on the street. Even when there is a limit, explicit replication of the system, say, 100 times, does not yield a scalable verification approach.

Approaches for distributed systems [4] do not cover hybrid systems, because the addition of differential equations to distributed systems is even more challenging than the addition of differential equations to discrete dynamics.

3   Syntax of Qd$\mathcal{L}$

As a formal logic for specifying and verifying correctness properties of distributed hybrid systems, we introduce *quantified differential dynamic logic* (Qd$\mathcal{L}$). Qd$\mathcal{L}$ combines dynamic logic for reasoning about system runs [10] with many-sorted first-order logic for reasoning about all ($\forall i : C \ \phi$) or some ($\exists i : C \ \phi$) objects of a sort C, e.g., the sort of all cars. The most important defining characteristic of Qd$\mathcal{L}$ is that its system model of *quantified hybrid programs* (QHP) supports quantified operations that affect *all* objects of a sort C at once. If C is the sort of cars, QHP $\forall i : C \ a(i) := a(i) + 1$ increases the respective accelerations $a(i)$ of

all cars i at once. QHP $\forall i : C\ v(i)' = a(i)$ represents a continuous evolution of
the respective velocities $v(i)$ of *all cars* at once according to their acceleration.
Quantified assignments and quantified differential equation systems are crucial
for representing distributed hybrid systems where an unbounded number of objects co-evolve simultaneously. Note that we use the same quantifier notation
$\forall i : C$ for quantified operations in programs and for logical formulas.

We model the appearance of new participants in the distributed hybrid system, e.g., new cars entering the road, by a program $n := \mathsf{new}\, C$. It creates a
new object of type C, thereby extending the range of subsequent quantified assignments or differential equations ranging over created objects of type C. With
quantifiers and function terms, new can be handled in a modular way (Section 5).

3.1   Quantified Differential Dynamic Logic

Sorts. Qd$\mathcal{L}$ supports a (finite) number of object sorts, e.g., the sort of all cars.
For continuous quantities of distributed hybrid systems like positions or velocities, we add the sort $\mathbb{R}$ for real numbers. See previous work [12] for subtyping
of sorts.

Terms. Qd$\mathcal{L}$ terms are built from a set of (sorted) function/variable symbols
as in many-sorted first-order logic. Unlike in first-order logic, the interpretation
of function symbols can change by running QHPs. Even objects may appear
or disappear while running QHPs. We use function symbol $\mathsf{E}(\cdot)$ to distinguish
between objects i that actually exist and those that have not been created yet,
depending on the value of $\mathsf{E}(i)$, which may change its interpretation. We use
$0, 1, +, -, \cdot$ with the usual notation and fixed semantics for real arithmetic. For
$n \geq 0$ we abbreviate $f(s_1, \ldots, s_n)$ by $f(\boldsymbol{s})$ using vectorial notation and we use
$\boldsymbol{s} = \boldsymbol{t}$ for element-wise equality.

Formulas. The formulas of Qd$\mathcal{L}$ are defined as in first-order dynamic logic plus
many-sorted first-order logic by the following grammar (ϕ, ψ are formulas, θ_1, θ_2
are terms of the same sort, i is a variable of sort C, and α is a QHP):

$$\phi, \psi ::= \theta_1 = \theta_2 \mid \theta_1 \geq \theta_2 \mid \neg\phi \mid \phi \wedge \psi \mid \forall i : C\ \phi \mid \exists i : C\ \phi \mid [\alpha]\phi \mid \langle\alpha\rangle\phi$$

We use standard abbreviations to define $\leq, >, <, \vee, \rightarrow$. Sorts $C \neq \mathbb{R}$ have no
ordering and only $\theta_1 = \theta_2$ is allowed. For sort $\mathbb{R}$, we abbreviate $\forall x : \mathbb{R}\ \phi$ by $\forall x\ \phi$.
In the following, all formulas and terms have to be well-typed. Qd$\mathcal{L}$ formula $[\alpha]\phi$
expresses that *all states* reachable by QHP α satisfy formula ϕ. Likewise, $\langle\alpha\rangle\phi$
expresses that *there is at least one state* reachable by α for which ϕ holds.

For short notation, we allow conditional terms of the form if ϕ then θ_1 else θ_2 fi
(where θ_1 and θ_2 have the same sort). This term evaluates to θ_1 if the formula
ϕ is true and to θ_2 otherwise. We consider formulas with conditional terms as
abbreviations, e.g., $\psi(\text{if } \phi \text{ then } \theta_1 \text{ else } \theta_2 \text{ fi})$ for $(\phi \rightarrow \psi(\theta_1)) \wedge (\neg\phi \rightarrow \psi(\theta_2))$.

Example. A major challenge in distributed car control systems [1] is that they
do not follow fixed, static setups. Instead, new situations can arise dynamically

that change structure and dimension of the system whenever new cars appear on the road from on-ramps or leave it; see Fig. 1. As a running example, we model a *distributed car control system DCCS*. First, we consider Qd$\mathcal{L}$ properties.

If i is a term of type C (for cars), let $x(i)$ denote the position of car i, $v(i)$ its current velocity, and $a(i)$ its current acceleration. A state is collision-free if all cars are at different positions, i.e., $\forall i \neq j : C\ x(i) \neq x(j)$. The following Qd$\mathcal{L}$ formula expresses that the system $DCCS$ controls cars collision-free:

$$(\forall i, j : C\ \mathcal{M}(i,j)) \rightarrow [DCCS]\ \forall i \neq j : C\ x(i) \neq x(j) \tag{1}$$

It says that $DCCS$ controlled cars are always in a collision-free state (postcondition), provided that $DCCS$ starts in a state satisfying $\mathcal{M}(i,j)$ for all cars i, j (precondition). Formula $\mathcal{M}(i,j)$ characterizes a simple compatibility condition: for different cars $i \neq j$, the car that is further down the road (i.e., with greater position) neither moves slower nor accelerates slower than the other car, i.e.:

$$\mathcal{M}(i,j) \equiv i \neq j \rightarrow \big((x(i) < x(j) \wedge v(i) \leq v(j) \wedge a(i) \leq a(j))$$
$$\vee\ (x(i) > x(j) \wedge v(i) \geq v(j) \wedge a(i) \geq a(j))\big) \tag{2}$$

3.2   Quantified Hybrid Programs

As a system model for distributed hybrid systems, we introduce *quantified hybrid programs* (QHP). These are regular programs from dynamic logic [10] to which we add quantified assignments and quantified differential equation systems for *distributed* hybrid dynamics. From these, QHPs are built like a Kleene algebra with tests [16]. QHPs are defined by the following grammar (α, β are QHPs, θ a term, i a variable of sort C, f is a function symbol, $\boldsymbol{s}$ is a vector of terms with sorts compatible to f, and χ is a formula of first-order logic):

$$\alpha, \beta\ ::=\ \forall i : C\ f(\boldsymbol{s}) := \theta \mid \forall i : C\ f(\boldsymbol{s})' = \theta\ \&\ \chi \mid ?\chi \mid \alpha \cup \beta \mid \alpha; \beta \mid \alpha^*$$

Quantified State Change. The effect of *quantified assignment* $\forall i : C\ f(\boldsymbol{s}) := \theta$ is an instantaneous discrete jump assigning θ to $f(\boldsymbol{s})$ simultaneously for all objects i of sort C. The effect of *quantified differential equation* $\forall i : C\ f(\boldsymbol{s})' = \theta\ \&\ \chi$ is a continuous evolution where, for all objects i of sort C, all differential equations $f(\boldsymbol{s})' = \theta$ hold and formula χ holds throughout the evolution (the state remains in the region described by χ). The dynamics of QHPs changes the interpretation of terms over time: $f(\boldsymbol{s})'$ is intended to denote the derivative of the interpretation of the term $f(\boldsymbol{s})$ over time during continuous evolution, not the derivative of $f(\boldsymbol{s})$ by its argument $\boldsymbol{s}$. For $f(\boldsymbol{s})'$ to be defined, we assume f is an $\mathbb{R}$-valued function symbol. For simplicity, we assume that f does not occur in $\boldsymbol{s}$. In most quantified assignments/differential equations $\boldsymbol{s}$ is just i. Time itself is implicit. If a clock variable t is needed in a QHP, it can be axiomatized by $t' = 1$, which is equivalent to $\forall i : C\ t' = 1$ where i does not occur in t. For such *vacuous quantification* (i does not occur anywhere), we may omit $\forall i : C$ from assignments and differential equations. Similarly, we may omit vectors $\boldsymbol{s}$ of length 0.

Regular Programs. The effect of *test* $?\chi$ is a *skip* (i.e., no change) if formula χ is true in the current state and *abort* (blocking the system run by a failed assertion), otherwise. *Nondeterministic choice* $\alpha \cup \beta$ is for alternatives in the behavior of the distributed hybrid system. In the *sequential composition* $\alpha; \beta$, QHP β starts after α finishes (β never starts if α continues indefinitely). *Nondeterministic repetition* α^* repeats α an arbitrary number of times, possibly zero times.

QHPs (with their semantics and our proof rules) can be extended to systems of quantified differential equations, simultaneous assignments to multiple functions f, g, or statements with multiple quantifiers ($\forall i : C \ \forall j : D \ \ldots$). To simplify notation, we do not focus on these cases, which are vectorial extensions [5,12].

Example. Continuous movement of position $x(i)$ of car i with acceleration $a(i)$ is expressed by differential equation $x(i)'' = a(i)$, which corresponds to the first-order differential equation system $x(i)' = v(i), v(i)' = a(i)$ with velocity $v(i)$. Simultaneous movement of all cars with their respective accelerations $a(i)$ is expressed by the QHP $\forall i : C \ (x(i)'' = a(i))$ where quantifier $\forall i : C$ ranges over all cars, such that all cars co-evolve at the same time.

In addition to continuous dynamics, cars have discrete control. In the following QHP, discrete and continuous dynamics interact (repeatedly by the *):

$$\bigl(\forall i : C \ (a(i) := \text{if } \forall j : C \ far(i,j) \text{ then } a \text{ else } -b \text{ fi}); \ \ \forall i : C \ (x(i)'' = a(i)))\bigr)^*$$

First, all cars i control their acceleration $a(i)$. Each car i chooses maximum acceleration $a \geq 0$ for $a(i)$ if its distance to all other cars j is far enough (some condition $far(i,j)$). Otherwise, i chooses full braking $-b < 0$. After all accelerations have been set, all cars move continuously along $\forall i : C \ (x(i)'' - a(i))$. Accelerations may change repeatedly, because the repetition operator * can repeat the QHP when the continuous evolution stops at any time.

4 Semantics of Qd$\mathcal{L}$

The Qd$\mathcal{L}$ semantics is a *constant domain Kripke semantics [17] with first-order structures as states* that associate total functions of appropriate type with function symbols. In constant domain, all states share the same domain for quantifiers. In particular, we choose to represent object creation not by changing the domain of states, but by changing the interpretation of the createdness flag $\mathsf{E}(i)$ of the object denoted by i. With $\mathsf{E}(i)$, object creation is definable (Section 5).

States. A *state* σ associates an infinite set $\sigma(C)$ of objects with each sort C, and it associates a function $\sigma(f)$ of appropriate type with each function symbol f, including $\mathsf{E}(\cdot)$. For simplicity, σ also associates a value $\sigma(i)$ of appropriate type with each variable i. The domain of $\mathbb{R}$ and the interpretation of $0, 1, +, -, \cdot$ is that of real arithmetic. We assume constant domain for each sort C: all states σ, τ share the same infinite domains $\sigma(C) = \tau(C)$. Sorts $C \neq D$ are disjoint: $\sigma(C) \cap \sigma(D) = \emptyset$. The set of all states is denoted by $\mathcal{S}$. The state σ_i^e agrees with σ except for the interpretation of variable i, which is changed to e.

Formulas. We use $\sigma[\![\theta]\!]$ to denote the value of term θ at state σ. Especially, $\sigma_i^e[\![\theta]\!]$ denotes the value of θ in state σ_i^e, i.e., in state σ with i interpreted as e. Further, $\rho(\alpha)$ denotes the state transition relation of QHP α as defined below. The *interpretation* $\sigma \models \phi$ of QdℒL formula ϕ with respect to state σ is defined as:

1. $\sigma \models (\theta_1 = \theta_2)$ iff $\sigma[\![\theta_1]\!] = \sigma[\![\theta_2]\!]$; accordingly for $\geq$.
2. $\sigma \models \phi \wedge \psi$ iff $\sigma \models \phi$ and $\sigma \models \psi$; accordingly for $\neg$.
3. $\sigma \models \forall i : C\ \phi$ iff $\sigma_i^e \models \phi$ for all objects $e \in \sigma(C)$.
4. $\sigma \models \exists i : C\ \phi$ iff $\sigma_i^e \models \phi$ for some object $e \in \sigma(C)$.
5. $\sigma \models [\alpha]\phi$ iff $\tau \models \phi$ for all states τ with $(\sigma, \tau) \in \rho(\alpha)$.
6. $\sigma \models \langle\alpha\rangle\phi$ iff $\tau \models \phi$ for some τ with $(\sigma, \tau) \in \rho(\alpha)$.

Programs. The *transition relation*, $\rho(\alpha) \subseteq \mathcal{S} \times \mathcal{S}$, of QHP α specifies which state $\tau \in \mathcal{S}$ is reachable from $\sigma \in \mathcal{S}$ by running QHP α. It is defined inductively:

1. $(\sigma, \tau) \in \rho(\forall i : C\ f(\boldsymbol{s}) := \theta)$ iff state τ is identical to σ except that at each position $\boldsymbol{o}$ of f: if $\sigma_i^e[\![\boldsymbol{s}]\!] = \boldsymbol{o}$ for some object $e \in \sigma(C)$, then $\tau(f)(\sigma_i^e[\![\boldsymbol{s}]\!]) = \sigma_i^e[\![\theta]\!]$. If there are multiple objects e giving the same position $\sigma_i^e[\![\boldsymbol{s}]\!] = \boldsymbol{o}$, then all of the resulting states τ are reachable.
2. $(\sigma, \tau) \in \rho(\forall i : C\ f(\boldsymbol{s})' = \theta\ \&\ \chi)$ iff, there is a function $\varphi : [0, r] \to \mathcal{S}$ for some $r \geq 0$ with $\varphi(0) = \sigma$ and $\varphi(r) = \tau$ satisfying the following conditions. At each time $t \in [0, r]$, state $\varphi(t)$ is identical to σ, except that at each position $\boldsymbol{o}$ of f: if $\sigma_i^e[\![\boldsymbol{s}]\!] = \boldsymbol{o}$ for some object $e \in \sigma(C)$, then, at each time $\zeta \in [0, r]$:
   - The differential equations hold and derivatives exist (trivial for $r = 0$):

   $$\frac{\mathrm{d}\left(\varphi(t)_i^e[\![f(\boldsymbol{s})]\!]\right)}{\mathrm{d}t}(\zeta) = (\varphi(\zeta)_i^e[\![\theta]\!])$$

   - The evolution domain is respected: $\varphi(\zeta)_i^e \models \chi$.
   If there are multiple objects e giving the same position $\sigma_i^e[\![\boldsymbol{s}]\!] = \boldsymbol{o}$, then all of the resulting states τ are reachable.
3. $\rho(?\chi) = \{(\sigma, \sigma)\ :\ \sigma \models \chi\}$
4. $\rho(\alpha \cup \beta) = \rho(\alpha) \cup \rho(\beta)$
5. $\rho(\alpha; \beta) = \{(\sigma, \tau)\ :\ (\sigma, z) \in \rho(\alpha)$ and $(z, \tau) \in \rho(\beta)$ for a state $z\}$
6. $(\sigma, \tau) \in \rho(\alpha^*)$ iff there is an $n \in \mathbb{N}$ with $n \geq 0$ and there are states $\sigma = \sigma_0, \ldots, \sigma_n = \tau$ such that $(\sigma_i, \sigma_{i+1}) \in \rho(\alpha)$ for all $0 \leq i < n$.

The semantics is *explicit change*: nothing changes unless an assignment or differential equation specifies how. In cases 1–2, only f changes and only at positions of the form $\sigma_i^e[\![\boldsymbol{s}]\!]$ for some interpretation $e \in \sigma(C)$ of i. If there are multiple such e that affect the same position $\boldsymbol{o}$, any of those changes can take effect by a non-deterministic choice. QHP $\forall i : C\ x := a(i)$ may change x to *any* $a(i)$. Hence, $[\forall i : C\ x := a(i)]\phi(x) \equiv \forall i : C\ \phi(a(i))$ and $\langle\forall i : C\ x := a(i)\rangle\phi(x) \equiv \exists i : C\ \phi(a(i))$. Similarly, x can evolve along $\forall i : C\ x' = a(i)$ with any of the slopes $a(i)$. But evolutions cannot start with slope $a(c)$ and then switch to a different slope $a(d)$ later. Any choice for i is possible but i remains unchanged during each evolution.

We call a quantified assignment $\forall i : C\ f(\boldsymbol{s}) := \theta$ or a quantified differential equation $\forall i : C\ f(\boldsymbol{s})' = \theta\ \&\ \chi$ *injective* iff there is at most one e satisfying cases 1–2. We call quantified assignments and quantified differential equations *schematic* iff s is i (thus injective) and the only arguments to function symbols in θ are i. Schematic quantified differential equations like $\forall i : C\ f(i)' = a(i)\ \&\ \chi$ are very common, because distributed hybrid systems often have a family of similar differential equations replicated for multiple participants i. Their synchronization typically comes from discrete communication on top of their continuous dynamics, less often from complicated, physically coupled differential equations.

5 Actual Existence and Object Creation

Actual Existence. For the Qd$\mathcal{L}$ semantics, we chose constant domain semantics, i.e., all states share the same domains. Thus quantifiers range over all possible objects (*possibilist quantification*) not just over active existing objects (*actualist quantification* in varying domains) [17]. In order to distinguish between *actual objects* that exist in a state, because they have already been created and can now actively take part in its evolution, versus *possible objects* that still passively await creation, we use function symbol $\mathsf{E}(\cdot)$. Symbol $\mathsf{E}(\cdot)$ is similar to existence predicates in first-order modal logic [17], but its value can be assigned to in QHPs.

Object Creation. For term i of type $C \neq \mathbb{R}$, $\mathsf{E}(i) = 1$ represents that the object denoted by i has been created and actually exists. We use $\mathsf{E}(i) = 0$ to represent that i has not been created. Object creation amounts to changing the interpretation of $\mathsf{E}(i)$. For an object denoted by i that has not been created ($\mathsf{E}(i) = 0$), object creation corresponds to the state change caused by assignment $\mathsf{E}(i) := 1$. With quantified assignments and function symbols, *object creation* is definable:

$$n := \mathsf{new}\ C \equiv (\forall j : C\ n := j);\ ?(\mathsf{E}(n) = 0);\ \mathsf{E}(n) := 1$$

It assigns an arbitrary j of type C to n that did not exist before ($\mathsf{E}(n) = 0$) and adjusts existence ($\mathsf{E}(n) := 1$). *Disappearance* of object i corresponds to $\mathsf{E}(i) := 0$. Our choice avoids semantic subtleties of varying domains about the meaning of free variables denoting non-existent objects as in free logics [17]. Denotation is standard. Terms may just denote objects that have not been activated yet. This is useful to initialize new objects (e.g., $x(n) := 8$) before activation ($\mathsf{E}(n) := 1$).

Actualist Quantifiers. We define abbreviations for *actualist quantifiers* in formulas / quantified assignments / quantified differential equations that range only over previously *created objects*, similar to relativization in modal logic [17]:

$$\forall i : C!\ \phi \equiv \forall i : C\ (\mathsf{E}(i) = 1 \to \phi)$$
$$\exists i : C!\ \phi \equiv \exists i : C\ (\mathsf{E}(i) = 1 \land \phi)$$
$$\forall i : C!\ f(s) := \theta \equiv \forall i : C\ f(s) := (\mathsf{if}\,\mathsf{E}(i) = 1\,\mathsf{then}\,\theta\,\mathsf{else}\,f(s)\,\mathsf{fi})$$
$$\forall i : C!\ f(s)' = \theta \equiv \forall i : C\ f(s)' = (\mathsf{if}\,\mathsf{E}(i) = 1\,\mathsf{then}\,\theta\,\mathsf{else}\,0\,\mathsf{fi}) \equiv \forall i : C\ f(s)' = \mathsf{E}(i)\theta$$

The last 2 cases define quantified state change for actually existing objects using conditional terms that choose effect θ if $\mathsf{E}(i) = 1$ and choose no effect (retaining the old value $f(s)$ or evolving with slope 0) if $\mathsf{E}(i) = 0$. Notation $C!$ signifies that the quantifier domain is restricted to actually existing objects of type C.

We generally assume that QHPs involve only quantified assignments / differential equations that are restricted to created objects, because real systems only affect objects that are physically present, not those that will be created later. We still treat actualist quantification over $C!$ as a defined notion, in order to simplify the semantics and proof calculus by separating object creation from quantified state change rules in a modular way. If only finitely many objects have been created in the initial state (say 0), then it is easy to see that only finitely many new objects will be created with finitely many such QHP transitions, because each quantified state change for $C!$ only ranges over a finite domain then. We thus assume $\mathsf{E}(\cdot)$ to have *(unbounded but) finite support*, i.e., each state only has a finite number of positions i at which $\mathsf{E}(i) = 1$. This makes sense in practice, because there is a varying but still finite numbers of participants (e.g., cars).

Example. In order to restrict the dynamics and properties in the car control examples of Section 3 to created and physically present cars, we simply replace each occurrence of $\forall i : C$ with $\forall i : C!$. A challenging feature of distributed car control, however, is that new cars may appear dynamically from on-ramps (Fig. 1) changing the set of active objects. To model this, we consider the following QHP:

$$DCCS \equiv (n := \mathsf{new}\, C;\ (?\forall i : C!\ \mathcal{M}(i, n));\ \forall i : C!\ (x(i)'' = a(i)))^* \qquad (3)$$

It creates a new car n at an arbitrary position $x(n)$ satisfying compatibility condition $\mathcal{M}(i, n)$ with respect to all other created cars i. Hence $DCCS$ allows new cars to appear, but not drop right out of the sky in front of a fast car or run at Mach 8 only 10ft away. When cars appear into the horizon from on-ramps, this condition captures that a car is only allowed to join the lane ("appear" into the model world) if it cannot cause a crash with other existing cars (Fig. 1). Unboundedly many cars may appear during the operation of $DCCS$ and change the system dimension arbitrarily, because of the repetition operator *.

$DCCS$ is simple but shows how properties of distributed hybrid systems can be expressed in QdℒC. Structural dynamics corresponds to assignments to function terms. Say, $f(i)$ is the car registered by communication as the car following car i. Then a term $d(i, f(i))$, which denotes the minimum safety distance negotiated between car i and its follower, is a crucial part of the system dynamics. Restructuring the system in response to lane change corresponds to assigning a new value to $f(i)$, which impacts the value of $d(i, f(i))$ in the system dynamics.

6   Proof Calculus

In Fig. 2, we present a proof calculus for QdℒC formulas. We use the sequent notation informally for a systematic proof structure. With finite sets of formulas for the *antecedent* Γ and *succedent* Δ, sequent $\Gamma \rightarrow \Delta$ is an abbreviation for the formula $\bigwedge_{\phi \in \Gamma} \phi \rightarrow \bigvee_{\psi \in \Delta} \psi$. The calculus uses standard proof rules for propositional logic with cut rule (not shown). The proof rules are used backwards from the *conclusion* (goal below horizontal bar) to the *premisses* (subgoals above bar).

In the calculus, we use substitutions that take effect within formulas and programs (defined as usual). Only admissible substitutions are applicable, which is crucial for soundness. An application of a substitution σ is *admissible* if no replaced term θ occurs in the scope of a quantifier or modality binding a symbol in θ or in its replacement $\sigma\theta$. A modality *binds* a symbol f iff it contains an assignment to f (like $\forall i : C\ f(s) := \theta$) or a differential equation containing a $f(s)'$ (like $\forall i : C\ f(s)' = \theta$). The substitutions in Fig. 2 that insert a term θ into $\phi(\theta)$ also have to be admissible for the proof rules to be applicable.

Regular Rules. The next proof rules axiomatize sequential composition ($[;],\langle;\rangle$), nondeterministic choice ($[\cup],\langle\cup\rangle$), and test ($[?],\langle?\rangle$) of regular programs as in dynamic logic [10]. Like other rules in Fig. 2, these rules do not contain sequent symbol $\rightarrow$, i.e., they can be applied to any subformula. These rules represent (directed) equivalences: conclusion and premiss are equivalent.

Quantified Differential Equations. Rules $['],\langle'\rangle$ handle continuous evolutions for quantified differential equations with first-order definable solutions. Given a solution for the quantified differential equation system with symbolic initial values $f(s)$, continuous evolution along differential equations can be replaced with a quantified assignment $\forall i : C\ \mathcal{S}(t)$ corresponding to the solution (footnote 1 in Fig. 2), and an additional quantifier for evolution time t. In $[']$, postcondition ϕ needs to hold *for all* evolution durations t. In $\langle'\rangle$, it needs to hold after *some* duration t. The constraint on χ restricts the continuous evolution to remain in the evolution domain region χ at all intermediate times $\tilde{t} \leq t$.

For schematic cases like $\forall i : C\ f(i)' = a(i)$, first-order definable solutions can be obtained by adding argument i to first-order definable solutions of the de-parametrized version $f' = a$. We only present proof rules for first-order definable solutions of quantified differential equations here. See [11] for other proof rules.

Quantified Assignments. Rules $[:=],\langle:=\rangle$ handle quantified assignments (both are equivalent for the injective case, i.e., a match for at most one i). Their effect depends on whether the quantified assignment $\forall i : C\ f(s) := \theta$ *matches* $f(u)$, i.e., there is a choice for i such that $f(u)$ is affected by the assignment, because u is of the form s for some i. If it matches, the premiss uses the term θ assigned to $f(s)$ instead of $f(u)$, either for all possible $i : C$ that match $f(u)$ in case of $[:=]$, or for some of those $i : C$ in case of $\langle:=\rangle$. Otherwise, the occurrence of f in $\phi(f(u))$ will be left unchanged. Rules $[:=],\langle:=\rangle$ make a case distinction on matching by if-then-else. In all cases, the original quantified assignment $\forall i : C\ f(s) := \theta$, which we abbreviate by $\mathcal{A}$, will be applied to u in the premiss, because the value of argument u may also be affected by $\mathcal{A}$, recursively. Rule *skip* characterizes that quantified assignments to f have no effect on all other operators $\Upsilon \neq f$ (including other function symbols, $\wedge$, if then else fi), so that only argument u is affected by prefixing $\mathcal{A}$ but Υ remains unchanged.

Rules $[:=],\langle:=\rangle,skip$ also apply for assignments without quantifiers, which correspond to vacuous quantification $\forall i : C$ where i does not occur anywhere. Rules $[:*],\langle:*\rangle$ reduce nondeterministic assignments to universal or existential quantification. For nondeterministic differential equations, see [11].

$$([;]) \quad \frac{[\alpha][\beta]\phi}{[\alpha;\beta]\phi} \qquad ([\cup]) \quad \frac{[\alpha]\phi \wedge [\beta]\phi}{[\alpha \cup \beta]\phi} \qquad ([?]) \quad \frac{\chi \to \psi}{[?\chi]\psi}$$

$$(\langle;\rangle) \quad \frac{\langle\alpha\rangle\langle\beta\rangle\phi}{\langle\alpha;\beta\rangle\phi} \qquad (\langle\cup\rangle) \quad \frac{\langle\alpha\rangle\phi \vee \langle\beta\rangle\phi}{\langle\alpha \cup \beta\rangle\phi} \qquad (\langle?\rangle) \quad \frac{\chi \wedge \psi}{\langle?\chi\rangle\psi}$$

$$(['])\quad \frac{\forall t\geq 0\,\left((\forall 0\leq \tilde{t}\leq t\,[\forall i:C\ \mathcal{S}(\tilde{t})]\chi) \to [\forall i:C\ \mathcal{S}(t)]\phi\right)}{[\forall i:C\ f(s)' = \theta\,\&\,\chi]\phi}\ {}_1$$

$$(\langle'\rangle)\quad \frac{\exists t\geq 0\,\left((\forall 0\leq \tilde{t}\leq t\,\langle\forall i:C\ \mathcal{S}(\tilde{t})\rangle\chi) \wedge \langle\forall i:C\ \mathcal{S}(t)\rangle\phi\right)}{\langle\forall i:C\ f(s)' = \theta\,\&\,\chi\rangle\phi}\ {}_1$$

$$([:=])\quad \frac{\text{if }\exists i:C\ s = [\mathcal{A}]u \text{ then } \forall i:C\ (s = [\mathcal{A}]u \to \phi(\theta)) \text{ else } \phi(f([\mathcal{A}]u))\text{ fi}}{\phi([\forall i:C\ f(s):=\theta]f(u))}\ {}_2$$

$$(\langle:=\rangle)\quad \frac{\text{if }\exists i:C\ s = \langle\mathcal{A}\rangle u \text{ then } \exists i:C\ (s = \langle\mathcal{A}\rangle u \wedge \phi(\theta)) \text{ else } \phi(f(\langle\mathcal{A}\rangle u))\text{ fi}}{\phi(\langle\forall i:C\ f(s):=\theta\rangle f(u))}\ {}_2$$

$$(skip)\quad \frac{\Upsilon([\forall i:C\ f(s):=\theta]u)}{[\forall i:C\ f(s):=\theta]\Upsilon(u)}\ {}_3 \qquad ([:*])\quad \frac{\forall j:C\ \phi(\theta)}{[\forall j:C\ n:=\theta]\phi(n)} \qquad (\langle:*\rangle)\quad \frac{\exists j:C\ \phi(\theta)}{\langle\forall j:C\ n:=\theta\rangle\phi(n)}$$

$$(ex)\quad \frac{true}{\exists n:C\ \mathsf{E}(n) = 0}$$

$$(\exists r)\quad \frac{\Gamma \to \phi(\theta), \exists x\,\phi(x), \Delta}{\Gamma \to \exists x\,\phi(x), \Delta}\ {}_4 \qquad (\forall r)\quad \frac{\Gamma \to \phi(f(X_1,\dots,X_n)), \Delta}{\Gamma \to \forall x\,\phi(x), \Delta}\ {}_5$$

$$(\forall l)\quad \frac{\Gamma, \phi(\theta), \forall x\,\phi(x) \to \Delta}{\Gamma, \forall x\,\phi(x) \to \Delta}\ {}_4 \qquad (\exists l)\quad \frac{\Gamma, \phi(f(X_1,\dots,X_n)) \to \Delta}{\Gamma, \exists x\,\phi(x) \to \Delta}\ {}_5$$

$$(i\forall)\quad \frac{\mathrm{QE}(\forall X, Y\,(\text{if } s = t \text{ then } \Phi(X) \to \Psi(X) \text{ else } \Phi(X) \to \Psi(Y)\,\text{fi}))}{\Phi(f(s)) \to \Psi(f(t))}\ {}_6$$

$$(i\exists)\quad \frac{\mathrm{QE}(\exists X\,\bigwedge_i(\Phi_i \to \Psi_i))}{\Phi_1 \to \Psi_1 \quad \dots \quad \Phi_n \to \Psi_n}\ {}_7$$

$$([]gen)\quad \frac{\phi \to \psi}{\Gamma, [\alpha]\phi \to [\alpha]\psi, \Delta} \qquad (\langle\rangle gen)\quad \frac{\phi \to \psi}{\Gamma, \langle\alpha\rangle\phi \to \langle\alpha\rangle\psi, \Delta} \qquad (ind)\quad \frac{\phi \to [\alpha]\phi}{\Gamma, \phi \to [\alpha^*]\phi, \Delta}$$

$$(con)\quad \frac{v > 0 \wedge \varphi(v) \to \langle\alpha\rangle\varphi(v-1)}{\Gamma, \exists v\,\varphi(v) \to \langle\alpha^*\rangle\exists v\leq 0\,\varphi(v), \Delta}\ {}_8$$

---

[1] $t, \tilde{t}$ are new variables, $\forall i:C\ \mathcal{S}(t)$ is the quantified assignment $\forall i:C\ f(s):=y_s(t)$ with solutions $y_s(t)$ of the (injective) differential equations and $f(s)$ as initial values.

[2] Occurrence $f(u)$ in $\phi(f(u))$ is not in scope of a modality (admissible substitution) and we abbreviate assignment $\forall i:C\ f(s):=\theta$ by $\mathcal{A}$, which is assumed to be injective.

[3] $f \neq \Upsilon$ and the quantified assignment $\forall i:C\ f(s):=\theta$ is injective. The same rule applies for $\langle\forall i:C\ f(s):=\theta\rangle$ instead of $[\forall i:C\ f(s):=\theta]$.

[4] θ is an arbitrary term, often a new logical variable.

[5] f is a new (Skolem) function and $X_1,\dots,X_n$ are all free logical variables of $\forall x\,\phi(x)$.

[6] X, Y are new variables of sort $\mathbb{R}$. QE needs to be applicable in the premiss.

[7] Among all open branches, the free (existential) logical variable X of sort $\mathbb{R}$ only occurs in the branches $\Phi_i \to \Psi_i$. QE needs to be defined for the formula in the premiss, especially, no Skolem dependencies on X occur.

[8] logical variable v does not occur in α.

Fig. 2. Rule schemata of the proof calculus for quantified differential dynamic logic

Object Creation. Given our definition of new C as a QHP from Section 5, object creation can be proven by the other proof rules in Fig. 2. In addition, axiom ex expresses that, for sort $C \neq \mathbb{R}$, there always is a new object n that has not been created yet ($\mathsf{E}(n) = 0$), because domains are infinite.

Quantifiers. For quantifiers, we cannot just use standard rules [18], because these are for uninterpreted first-order logic and work by instantiating quantifiers, eagerly as in ground tableaux or lazily by unification as in free variable tableaux [18]. Qdℒ is based on first-order logic interpreted over the reals [19]. A formula like $\exists a : \mathbb{R} \, \forall x : \mathbb{R} \, (x^2 + a > 0)$ cannot be proven by instantiating quantifiers but is still valid for reals. Unfortunately, the decision procedure for real arithmetic, *quantifier elimination* (QE) in the theory of real-closed fields [19], cannot be applied to formulas with modalities either, because these are quantified reachability statements. Even in discrete dynamic logic, quantifiers plus modalities make validity Π_1^1-complete [10]. Also QE cannot handle sorts $C \neq \mathbb{R}$.

Instead, our Qdℒ proof rules combine quantifier handling of many-sorted logic based on instantiation with theory reasoning by QE for the theory of reals. Figure 2 shows rules for quantifiers that combine with decision procedures for real-closed fields. Classical instantiation is sound for sort $\mathbb{R}$, just incomplete.

Rules $\exists$r and $\forall$l instantiate with arbitrary terms θ, including a new free variable X, where $\exists$r and $\forall$l become the usual γ-rules [18,17]. Rules $\forall$r and $\exists$l correspond to the δ-rule [18]. As in our previous work [5], rules i$\forall$ and i$\exists$ reintroduce and eliminate quantifiers over $\mathbb{R}$ once QE is applicable, as the remaining constraints are first-order in the respective variables. Unlike in previous work, however, functions and different argument vectors can occur in QdℒL. If the argument vectors s and t in i$\forall$ have the same value, the same variable X can be reintroduced for $f(s)$ and $f(t)$, otherwise different variables $X \neq Y$ have to be used. Rule i$\exists$ merges all proof branches containing (existential) variable X, because X has to satisfy all branches simultaneously. It thus has multiple conclusions. See [5] for merging and for lifting QE to the presence of function symbols, including formulas that result from the base theory by substitution.

Global Rules. The rules in the last block depend on the truth of their premisses in all states reachable by α, thus the context Γ, Δ cannot be used in the premiss. Rules $[]gen, \langle\rangle gen$ are Gödel generalization rules and *ind* is an induction schema for loops with *inductive invariant* ϕ [10]. Similarly, *con* generalizes Harel's convergence rule [10] to the hybrid case with decreasing *variant* φ [5].

7   Soundness and Completeness

The verification problem for distributed hybrid systems has *three independent sources* of undecidability. Thus, no verification technique can be effective. Hence, QdℒL cannot be effectively axiomatizable. Both its discrete and its continuous fragments alone are subject to Gödel's incompleteness theorem [5]. The fragment with only structural and dimension-changing dynamics is not effective either, because it can encode two-counter machines. The standard way to show adequacy of proof calculi for problems that are not effective is to prove completeness relative to an oracle for handling a fragment of the logic. Unlike in Cook/Harel relative completeness for discrete programs [10], however, QdℒC cannot be complete relative to the fragment of the data logic ($\mathbb{R}$), because real arithmetic is decidable. Instead, we prove that our QdℒC calculus is a complete axiomatization relative to an oracle for the fragment of QdℒC that has only quantified differential equations in modalities. We replace rules $['], \langle'\rangle$ with an oracle and show that the QdℒC calculus would be complete if only we had complete replacements for $['], \langle'\rangle$. The calculus completely lifts *any* approximation of this oracle to the full QdℒC!

Theorem 1 (Axiomatization). *The calculus in Fig. 2 is a sound and complete axiomatization of* QdℒC *relative to quantified differential equations; see [20].*

This shows that properties of distributed hybrid systems can be proven to exactly the same extent to which properties of quantified differential equations can be proven. Proof-theoretically, the QdℒC calculus completely lifts verification techniques for quantified continuous dynamics to distributed hybrid dynamics.

8   Distributed Car Control Verification

With the QdℒC calculus and the compatibility condition $\mathcal{M}(i,j)$ from eqn. (2), we can easily prove collision freedom in the distributed car control system (3):

$$(\forall i, j : C!\ \mathcal{M}(i,j)) \rightarrow$$
$$[(n := \mathsf{new}\,C;\,?\forall i : C!\ \mathcal{M}(i,n); \forall i : C!\ (x(i)'' = a(i)))^*]\ \forall i \neq j : C!\ x(i) \neq x(j)$$

See [20] for a formal QdℒC proof of this QdℒC formula, which proves collision freedom despite dynamic appearance of new cars, following the pattern of (1).

9   Conclusions

We have introduced a system model and semantics for dynamic distributed hybrid systems together with a compositional verification logic and proof calculus. We believe this is the *first formal verification approach for distributed hybrid dynamics*, where structure and dimension of the system can evolve jointly with the discrete and continuous dynamics. We have proven our calculus to be a *sound and complete axiomatization* relative to quantified differential equations. Our calculus proves collision avoidance in distributed car control with dynamic appearance of new cars on the road, which is out of scope for other approaches.

Future work includes modular concurrency in distributed hybrid systems, which is already challenging in discrete programs.

Acknowledgments. I want to thank Frank Pfenning for his helpful comments.

References

1. Hsu, A., Eskafi, F., Sachs, S., Varaiya, P.: Design of platoon maneuver protocols for IVHS. PATH Research Report UCB-ITS-PRR-91-6, UC Berkeley (1991)
2. Dowek, G., Muñoz, C., Carreño, V.A.: Provably safe coordinated strategy for distributed conflict resolution. In: AIAA Proceedings, AIAA-2005-6047 (2005)
3. Henzinger, T.A.: The theory of hybrid automata. In: LICS, pp. 278–292. IEEE, Los Alamitos (1996)
4. Attie, P.C., Lynch, N.A.: Dynamic input/output automata: A formal model for dynamic systems. In: Larsen, K.G., Nielsen, M. (eds.) CONCUR 2001. LNCS, vol. 2154, pp. 137–151. Springer, Heidelberg (2001)
5. Platzer, A.: Differential dynamic logic for hybrid systems. J. Autom. Reas. 41(2), 143–189 (2008)
6. Deshpande, A., Göllü, A., Varaiya, P.: SHIFT: A formalism and a programming language for dynamic networks of hybrid automata. In: Antsaklis, P.J., Kohn, W., Nerode, A., Sastry, S.S. (eds.) HS 1996. LNCS, vol. 1273, pp. 113–133. Springer, Heidelberg (1997)
7. Rounds, W.C.: A spatial logic for the hybrid π-calculus. In: Alur, R., Pappas, G.J. (eds.) HSCC 2004. LNCS, vol. 2993, pp. 508–522. Springer, Heidelberg (2004)
8. Kratz, F., Sokolsky, O., Pappas, G.J., Lee, I.: R-Charon, a modeling language for reconfigurable hybrid systems. In: [21], pp. 392–406
9. Meseguer, J., Sharykin, R.: Specification and analysis of distributed object-based stochastic hybrid systems. In: [21], pp. 460–475
10. Harel, D., Kozen, D., Tiuryn, J.: Dynamic logic. MIT Press, Cambridge (2000)
11. Platzer, A.: Differential-algebraic dynamic logic for differential-algebraic programs. J. Log. Comput. 20(1), 309–352 (2010)
12. Beckert, B., Platzer, A.: Dynamic logic with non-rigid functions: A basis for object-oriented program verification. In: Furbach, U., Shankar, N. (eds.) IJCAR 2006. LNCS (LNAI), vol. 4130, pp. 266–280. Springer, Heidelberg (2006)
13. Rümmer, P.: Sequential, parallel, and quantified updates of first-order structures. In: Hermann, M., Voronkov, A. (eds.) LPAR 2006. LNCS (LNAI), vol. 4246, pp. 422–436. Springer, Heidelberg (2006)
14. Chaochen, Z., Ji, W., Ravn, A.P.: A formal description of hybrid systems. In: Alur, R., Sontag, E.D., Henzinger, T.A. (eds.) HS 1995. LNCS, vol. 1066, pp. 511–530. Springer, Heidelberg (1996)
15. van Beek, D.A., Man, K.L., Reniers, M.A., Rooda, J.E., Schiffelers, R.R.H.: Syntax and consistent equation semantics of hybrid. Chi. J. Log. Algebr. Program. 68(1-2), 129–210 (2006)
16. Kozen, D.: Kleene algebra with tests. ACM TOPLAS 19(3), 427–443 (1997)
17. Fitting, M., Mendelsohn, R.L.: First-Order Modal Logic. Kluwer, Dordrecht (1999)
18. Fitting, M.: First-Order Logic and Automated Theorem Proving. Springer, Heidelberg (1996)
19. Collins, G.E., Hong, H.: Partial cylindrical algebraic decomposition for quantifier elimination. J. Symb. Comput. 12(3), 299–328 (1991)
20. Platzer, A.: Quantified differential dynamic logic for distributed hybrid systems. Technical Report CMU-CS-10-126, SCS, Carnegie Mellon University (2010)
21. Hespanha, J.P., Tiwari, A. (eds.): HSCC 2006. LNCS, vol. 3927. Springer, Heidelberg (2006)

Untyping Typed Algebraic Structures and Colouring Proof Nets of Cyclic Linear Logic

Damien Pous*

CNRS (LIG, UMR 5217)

Abstract. We prove "untyping" theorems: in some typed theories (semi-rings, Kleene algebras, residuated lattices, involutive residuated lattices), typed equations can be derived from the underlying untyped equations. As a consequence, the corresponding untyped decision procedures can be extended for free to the typed settings. Some of these theorems are obtained via a detour through fragments of cyclic linear logic, and give rise to a substantial optimisation of standard proof search algorithms.

1 Introduction

Motivations. The literature contains many decidability or complexity results for various algebraic structures. Some of these structures (rings, Kleene algebras [19], residuated lattices [27]) can be generalised to *typed* structures, where the elements come with a domain and a codomain, and where operations are defined only when these domains and codomains agree according to some simple rules. Although such typed structures are frequently encountered in practice (e.g., rectangular matrices, heterogeneous binary relations, or more generally, categories), there are apparently no proper tools to easily reason about these.

This is notably problematic in proof assistants, where powerful decision procedures are required to let the user focus on difficult reasoning steps by leaving administrative details to the computer. Indeed, although some important theories that can be decided automatically in Coq or HOL (e.g., Presburger arithmetic [25], elementary real algebra [14], rings [13]), there are no high-level tools to reason about heterogeneous relations or rectangular matrices.

In this paper, we show how to extend the standard decision procedures from the untyped structures to the corresponding typed structures. In particular, we make it possible to use standard tools to reason about rectangular matrices or heterogeneous relations, without bothering about types (i.e., matrix dimensions or domain/codomain information). The approach we propose is depicted below: we study "untyping" theorems that allow one to prove typed equations as follows: 1) erase type informations, 2) prove the equation using standard, untyped, decision procedures, and 3) derive a typed proof from the untyped one.

$$
\begin{array}{c}
\text{untyped setting:} \quad \widehat{a} \overset{\text{decide}}{=\!=\!=\!=} \widehat{b} \\
\text{erase types} \Big\uparrow \qquad \Big\downarrow \text{rebuild types} \\
\text{typed setting:} \quad a = ? = b
\end{array}
$$

* Work partially funded by the French project "Choco", ANR-07-BLAN-0324.

A. Dawar and H. Veith (Eds.): CSL 2010, LNCS 6247, pp. 484–498, 2010.

Besides the theoretical aspects, an important motivation behind this work comes from a Coq library [4] in which we developed efficient tactics for partial axiomatisations of relations: the ideas presented here were used and integrated in this library to extend our tactics to typed structures, for free.

Overview. We shall mainly focus on the two algebraic structures we mentioned above, since they raise different problems and illustrate several aspects of these untyping theorems: Kleene algebras [18] and residuated lattices [16].

- The case of Kleene algebras is the simplest one. The main difficulty comes from the annihilating element (0): its polymorphic typing rule requires us to show that equational proofs can be factorised so as to use the annihilation laws at first, and then reason using the other axioms.
- The case of residuated structures is more involved: due to the particular form of axioms about residuals, we cannot rely on standard equational axiomatisations of these structures. Instead, we need to exploit an equivalent cut-free sequent proof system (first proposed by Ono and Komori [27]), and to notice that this proof system corresponds to the intuitionistic fragment of cyclic linear logic [33]. The latter logic is much more concise and the corresponding proof nets are easier to reason about, so that we obtain the untyping theorem in this setting. We finally port the result back to residuated lattices by standard means.

The above sequent proof systems have the sub-formula property, so that they yield decision procedures, using proof search algorithms. As an unexpected application, we show that the untyping theorem makes it possible to improve these algorithms by reducing the set of proofs that have to be explored.

Outline. We introduce our notations and make the notion of typed structure precise in §2. We study Kleene algebras and residuated lattices in §3 and §4, respectively. We conclude with applications, related work, and directions for future work in §5.

2 Notation, Typed Structures

Let $\mathcal{X}$ be an arbitrary set of *variables*, ranged over using letters x, y. Given a signature Σ, we let a, b, c range over the set $T(\Sigma + \mathcal{X})$ of *terms with variables*. Given a set $\mathcal{T}$ of *objects* (ranged over using letters n, m, p, q), a *type* is a pair (n, m) of objects (which we denote by $n \to m$, following categorical notation), a *type environment* $\Gamma : \mathcal{X} \to \mathcal{T}^2$ is a function from variables to types, and we will define *type judgements* of the form $\Gamma \vdash a : n \to m$, to be read "in environment Γ, term a has type $n \to m$, or, equivalently, a is a morphism from n to m". By $\Gamma \vdash a, b : n \to m$, we mean that both a and b have type $n \to m$; type judgements will include the following rule for variables:

$$\frac{\Gamma(x) = (n, m)}{\Gamma \vdash x : n \to m} \text{ Tv}$$

Similarly, we will define *typed equality* judgements of the form $\Gamma \vdash a = b : n \to m$: "in environment Γ, terms a and b are equal, at type $n \to m$". Equality judgements will generally include the following rules, so as to obtain an equivalence relation at each type:

$$\frac{\Gamma(x) = (n, m)}{\Gamma \vdash x = x : n \to m} \text{ V} \qquad \frac{\begin{array}{c}\Gamma \vdash a = b : n \to m \\ \Gamma \vdash b = c : n \to m\end{array}}{\Gamma \vdash a = c : n \to m} \text{ T} \qquad \frac{\Gamma \vdash a = b : n \to m}{\Gamma \vdash b = a : n \to m} \text{ S}$$

By taking the singleton set as set of objects ($\mathcal{T} = \{\emptyset\}$), we recover standard, untyped structures: the only typing environment is $\widehat{\emptyset} : x \mapsto (\emptyset, \emptyset)$, and types become uninformative (this corresponds to working in a one-object category; all operations are total functions). To alleviate notations, since the typing environment will always be either $\widehat{\emptyset}$ or an abstract constant value Γ, we shall leave it implicit in type and equality judgements, by relying on the absence or the presence of types to indicate which one to use. For example, we shall write $\vdash a = b : n \to m$ for $\Gamma \vdash a = b : n \to m$, while $\vdash a = b$ will denote the judgement $\widehat{\emptyset} \vdash a = b : \emptyset \to \emptyset$.

The question we study in this paper is the following one: given a signature and a set of inference rules defining a type judgement and an equality judgement, does the implication below hold, for all a, b, n, m such that $\vdash a, b : n \to m$?

$$\vdash a = b \quad \textit{entails} \quad \vdash a = b : n \to m \ .$$

In other words, in order to prove an equality in a typed structure, is it safe to remove all type annotations, so as to work in the untyped underlying structure?

3   Kleene Algebras

We study the case of residuated lattices in §4; here we focus on Kleene algebras. In order to illustrate our methodology, we actually give the proof in three steps, by considering two intermediate algebraic structures: monoids and semirings. The former admit a rather simple and direct proof, while the latter are sufficient to expose concisely the main difficulty in handling Kleene algebras.

3.1   Monoids

Definition 1. *Typed monoids* are defined by the signature $\{\cdot_2, 1_0\}$, together with the following inference rules, in addition to the rules from §2.

$$\frac{}{\vdash 1 : n \to n} \text{ To} \qquad \frac{\vdash a : n \to m \qquad \vdash b : m \to p}{\vdash a \cdot b : n \to p} \text{ TD} \qquad \frac{}{\vdash 1 = 1 : n \to n} \text{ O}$$

$$\frac{\vdash a = a' : n \to m \qquad \vdash b = b' : m \to p}{\vdash a \cdot b = a' \cdot b' : n \to p} \text{ D} \qquad \frac{\vdash a : n \to m}{\vdash 1 \cdot a = a : n \to m} \text{ OD}$$

$$\frac{\vdash a : n \to m \qquad \vdash b : m \to p \qquad \vdash c : p \to q}{\vdash (a \cdot b) \cdot c = a \cdot (b \cdot c) : n \to q} \text{ DA} \qquad \frac{\vdash a : n \to m}{\vdash a \cdot 1 = a : n \to m} \text{ DO}$$

In other words, typed monoids are just categories: 1 and $\cdot$ correspond to identities and composition. Rules (O) and (D) ensure that equality is reflexive at each type (point (i) below) and preserved by composition. As expected, equalities relate correctly typed terms only (ii):

Lemma 2. *(i) If $\vdash a : n \to m$, then $\vdash a = a : n \to m$.*
(ii) If $\vdash a = b : n \to m$, then $\vdash a, b : n \to m$.

Moreover, in this setting, type judgements enjoy some form of injectivity (types are not uniquely determined due to 1, which is typed in a polymorphic way):

Lemma 3. *If $\vdash a : n \to m$ and $\vdash a : n' \to m'$, then we have $n = n'$ iff $m = m'$.*

We need another lemma to obtain the untyping theorem: all terms related by the untyped equality admit the same type derivations.

Lemma 4. *If $\vdash a = b$; then for all n, m, we have $\vdash a : n \to m$ iff $\vdash b : n \to m$.*

Theorem 5. *If $\vdash a = b$ and $\vdash a, b : n \to m$, then $\vdash a = b : n \to m$.*

Proof. We reason by induction on the derivation $\vdash a = b$; the interesting cases are the following ones:

- the last rule used is the transitivity rule (T): we have $\vdash a = b$, $\vdash b = c$, $\vdash a, c : n \to m$, and we need to show that $\vdash a = c : n \to m$. By Lemma 4, we have $\vdash b : n \to m$, so that by the induction hypotheses, we get $\vdash a = b : n \to m$ and $\vdash b = c : n \to m$, and we can apply rule (T).
- the last rule used is the compatibility of $\cdot$ (D): we have $\vdash a = a'$, $\vdash b = b'$, $\vdash a \cdot b, a' \cdot b' : n \to m$, and we need to show that $\vdash a \cdot b = a' \cdot b' : n \to m$. By case analysis on the typing judgements, we deduce that $\vdash a : n \to p$, $\vdash b : p \to m$, $\vdash a' : n \to q$, $\vdash b' : q \to m$, for some p, q. Thanks to Lemmas 3 and 4, we have $p = q$, so that we can conclude using the induction hypotheses ($\vdash a = a' : n \to p$ and $\vdash b = b' : p \to m$), and rule (D). ∎

Note that the converse of Theorem 5 ($\vdash a = b : n \to m$ entails $\vdash a = b$) is straightforward, so that we actually have an equivalence.

3.2 Non-commutative Semirings

Definition 6. *Typed semirings* are defined by the signature $\{\cdot_2, +_2, 1_0, 0_0\}$, together with the following rules, in addition to the rules from Def. 1 and §2.

$$\frac{}{\vdash 0 : n \to m}\ \text{Tz} \qquad \frac{\vdash a, b : n \to m}{\vdash a + b : n \to m}\ \text{TP} \qquad \frac{\vdash a = a' : n \to m \qquad \vdash b = b' : n \to m}{\vdash a + b = a' + b' : n \to m}\ \text{P}$$

$$\frac{}{\vdash 0 = 0 : n \to m}\ \text{Z} \qquad \frac{\vdash a : n \to m}{\vdash a + 0 = a : n \to m}\ \text{PZ} \qquad \frac{\vdash a, b : n \to m}{\vdash a + b = b + a : n \to m}\ \text{PC}$$

$$\frac{\vdash a, b, c : n \to m}{\vdash (a + b) + c = a + (b + c) : n \to m}\ \text{PA} \qquad \frac{\vdash a : n \to m \qquad \vdash b, c : m \to p}{\vdash a \cdot (b + c) = a \cdot b + a \cdot c : n \to p}\ \text{DP}$$

$$\frac{\vdash a : n \to m}{\vdash a \cdot 0 = 0 : n \to p}\ \text{DZ} \qquad \frac{\vdash a : n \to m}{\vdash 0 \cdot a = 0 : p \to m}\ \text{ZD} \qquad \frac{\vdash a : n \to m \qquad \vdash b, c : p \to n}{\vdash (b + c) \cdot a = b \cdot a + c \cdot a : p \to m}\ \text{PD}$$

In other words, typed semiring are categories enriched over a commutative monoid: each homset is equipped with a commutative monoid structure, and composition distributes over these monoid structures.

Lemma 2 is also valid in this setting: equality is reflexive and relates correctly typed terms only. However, due to the presence of the annihilator element (0), Lemmas 3 and 4 no longer hold: 0 has any type, and we have $\vdash x \cdot 0 \cdot x = 0$ while $x \cdot 0 \cdot x$ only admits $\Gamma(x)$ as a valid type. Moreover, some valid proofs cannot be typed just by adding decorations: for example, $0 = 0 \cdot a \cdot a = 0$ is a valid untyped proof of $0 = 0$; however, this proof cannot be typed if a has a non-square type. Therefore, we have to adopt another strategy: we reduce the problem to the annihilator-free case, by showing that equality proofs can be factorised so as to use rules (PZ), (DZ), and (ZD) at first, as oriented rewriting rules.

Definition 7. Let a be a term; we denote by $a_\downarrow$ the *normal form of a*, obtained with the following convergent rewriting system:

$$a + 0 \to a \qquad 0 + a \to a \qquad 0 \cdot a \to 0 \qquad a \cdot 0 \to 0$$

We say that a is *strict* if $a_\downarrow \neq 0$. We let $\_ \vdash^+ \_ = \_ : \_ \to \_$ denote the *strict equality* judgement obtained by removing rules (DZ) and (ZD), and requiring a to be strict in rules (DP) and (PD).

On strict terms, we recover the injectivity property of types we had for monoids. Then, using the same methodology as previously, one easily obtain the untyping theorem for strict equality judgements.

Lemma 8. *For all strict terms a such that $\vdash a : n \to m$ and $\vdash a : n' \to m'$, we have $n = n'$ iff $m = m'$.*

Proposition 9. *If $\vdash^+ a = b$ and $\vdash a, b : n \to m$, then $\vdash^+ a = b : n \to m$.*

Note that the patched rules for distributivity, (DP$^+$) and (PD$^+$) are required in order to obtain the counterpart of Lemma 4: if a was not required to be strict, we would have $\vdash^+ 0 \cdot (x + y) = 0 \cdot x + 0 \cdot y$, and the right-hand side can be typed in environment $\Gamma = \{x \mapsto (3, 2),\ y \mapsto (4, 2)\}$ while the left-hand side cannot.

We now have to show that any equality proof can be factorised, so as to obtain a strict equality proof relating the corresponding normal forms:

Proposition 10. *If $\vdash a = b$, then we have $\vdash^+ a_\downarrow = b_\downarrow$.*

Proof of Prop. 10. We first show by induction that whenever $\vdash a = b$, a is strict iff b is strict (†). Then we proceed by induction on the derivation $\vdash a = b$, we detail only some cases:

(D) we have $\vdash^+ a_\downarrow = a'_\downarrow$ and $\vdash^+ b_\downarrow = b'_\downarrow$ by induction; we need to show that $\vdash^+ (a \cdot b)_\downarrow = (a' \cdot b')_\downarrow$. If one of a, a', b, b' is not strict, then $(a \cdot b)_\downarrow = (a' \cdot b')_\downarrow = 0$, thanks to (†), so that we are done; otherwise, $(a \cdot b)_\downarrow = a_\downarrow \cdot b_\downarrow$, and $(a' \cdot b')_\downarrow = a'_\downarrow \cdot b'_\downarrow$, so that we can apply rule (D).

(DP) we need to show that $\vdash^+ (a \cdot (b+c))_\downarrow = (a \cdot b + a \cdot c)_\downarrow$; if one of a, b, c is not strict, both sides reduce to the same term, so that we can apply Lemma 2(i) (which holds in this setting); otherwise we have $(a \cdot (b+c))_\downarrow = a_\downarrow \cdot (b_\downarrow + c_\downarrow)$ and $(a \cdot b + a \cdot c)_\downarrow = a_\downarrow \cdot b_\downarrow + a_\downarrow \cdot c_\downarrow$, so that we can apply rule (DP$^+$) ($a_\downarrow$ is obviously strict). ∎

Since the normalisation procedure preserves types and respects equalities, we finally obtain the untyping theorem.

Lemma 11. *If $\vdash a : n \to m$, then $\vdash a_\downarrow : n \to m$ and $\vdash a = a_\downarrow : n \to m$.*

Theorem 12. *In semirings, for all a, b, n, m such that $\vdash a, b : n \to m$, we have $\vdash a = b$ iff $\vdash a = b : n \to m$.*

3.3   Kleene Algebras

Kleene algebras are idempotent semirings equipped with a star operation [18]; they admit several important models, among which binary relations and *regular languages* (the latter is complete [22,19]; since equality of regular languages is decidable, so is the equational theory of Kleene algebras). Like previously, we type Kleene algebras in a natural way, where star operates on "square" types: types of the form $n \to n$, i.e., square matrices or homogeneous binary relations.

Definition 13. We define *typed Kleene algebras* by the signature $\{\cdot_2, +_2, \star_1, 1_0, 0_0\}$, together with the following rules, in addition that from Defs. 1 and 6, and §2), and where $\vdash a \le b : n \to m$ is an abbreviation for $\vdash a + b = b : n \to m$.

$$\frac{\vdash a : n \to n}{\vdash a^\star : n \to n}\ \text{Ts} \qquad \frac{\vdash a = b : n \to n}{\vdash a^\star = b^\star : n \to n}\ \text{S} \qquad \frac{\vdash a : n \to m}{\vdash a + a = a : n \to m}\ \text{PI}$$

$$\frac{\vdash a : n \to n}{\vdash 1 + a \cdot a^\star = a^\star : n \to n}\ \text{SP} \qquad \frac{\vdash a \cdot b \le b : n \to m}{\vdash a^\star \cdot b \le b : n \to m}\ \text{SL} \qquad \frac{\vdash b \cdot a \le b : n \to m}{\vdash b \cdot a^\star \le b : n \to m}\ \text{SR}$$

The untyped version of this axiomatisation is that from Kozen [19]: axiom (PI) corresponds to idempotence of $+$, the three other rules define the star operation (we omitted the mirror image of axiom (SP), which is derivable from the other ones [4]). The proofs from the previous section extend without unexpected difficulties: we add the rule $0^\star \to 1$ to the rewriting system used for normalising terms, and we require b to be strict in the strict versions of rules (SL) and (SR). We do not give details here: complete proofs are available as Coq scripts [29].

Theorem 14. *In Kleene algebras, for all a, b, n, m such that $\vdash a, b : n \to m$, we have $\vdash a = b$ iff $\vdash a = b : n \to m$.*

4   Residuated Lattices

We now move to our second example, *residuated lattices*. These structures also admit binary relations as models; they are of special interest to reason algebraically about well-founded relations. For example, residuation is used to prove Newman's Lemma in relation algebras [9]. We start with a simpler structure.

A *residuated monoid* is a tuple $(X, \leq, \cdot, 1, \backslash, /)$, such that $(X, \leq)$ is a partial order, $(X, \cdot, 1)$ is a monoid whose product is monotonic ($a \leq a'$ and $b \leq b'$ entail $a \cdot b \leq a' \cdot b'$), and $\backslash, /$ are binary operations, respectively called *left* and *right divisions*, characterised by the following equivalences:

$$a \cdot b \leq c \quad \Leftrightarrow \quad b \leq a \backslash c \quad \Leftrightarrow \quad a \leq c/b$$

Accordingly, divisions can be typed in a natural way using following rules:

$$\frac{\vdash c : n \to m \qquad \vdash a : n \to p}{\vdash a \backslash c : p \to m} \; \text{TL} \qquad\qquad \frac{\vdash c : n \to m \qquad \vdash b : p \to m}{\vdash c/b : n \to p} \; \text{TR}$$

Although we can easily define a set of axioms to capture equalities provable in residuated monoids [16], the transitivity rule (T) becomes problematic in this setting (there is no counterpart to Lemma 4). Instead, we exploit a characterisation due to Ono and Komori [27], based on a Gentzen proof system for the full Lambek calculus [23]. Indeed, the "cut" rule corresponding to this system, which plays the role of the transitivity rule, can be eliminated. Therefore, this characterisation allows us to avoid the problems we encountered with standard equational proof systems. In some sense, moving to cut-free proofs corresponds to using a factorisation system, like we did in the previous section (Prop. 10).

4.1   Gentzen Proof System for Residuated Monoids

Let l, k, h range over lists of terms, let $l; k$ denote the concatenation of l and k, and let ϵ be the empty list. The Gentzen proof system is presented below; it relates lists of terms to terms. It is quite standard [16]: there is an axiom rule (V), and, for each operator, an introduction and an elimination rule.

$$\frac{}{x \vdash x} \; \text{V} \qquad \frac{}{\epsilon \vdash 1} \; \text{Io} \qquad \frac{l \vdash a \qquad l' \vdash a'}{l; l' \vdash a \cdot a'} \; \text{ID} \qquad \frac{l; b \vdash a}{l \vdash a/b} \; \text{IR} \qquad \frac{b; l \vdash a}{l \vdash b \backslash a} \; \text{IL}$$

$$\frac{l; l' \vdash a}{l; 1; l' \vdash a} \; \text{Eo} \qquad \frac{l; b; c; l' \vdash a}{l; b \cdot c; l' \vdash a} \; \text{ED} \qquad \frac{k \vdash b \qquad l; c; l' \vdash a}{l; c/b; k; l' \vdash a} \; \text{ER} \qquad \frac{k \vdash b \qquad l; c; l' \vdash a}{l; k; b \backslash c; l' \vdash a} \; \text{EL}$$

The axiom rule can be generalised to terms (*i*), the cut rule is admissible (*ii*), and the proof system is correct and complete w.r.t. residuated monoids (*iii*).

Proposition 15.   (*i*) *For all a, we have $a \vdash a$.*
(*ii*) *For all l, k, k', a, b such that $l \vdash a$ and $k; a; k' \vdash b$, we have $k; l; k' \vdash b$.*
(*iii*) *For all a, b, we have $a \vdash b$ iff $a \leq b$ holds in all residuated monoids.*

Proof. Point (*i*) is easy; see [27,26,16] for cut admissibility and completeness. ■

Type decorations can be added to the proof system rather easily [29]. However, using this proof system, we were able to prove the untyping theorem only for the unit-free fragment: we needed to assume that terms have at most one type, which is not true in presence of 1. This proof was rather involved, so that we did not manage to circumvent this difficulty in a nice and direct way. Instead, as hinted in the introduction, we move to the following more symmetrical setting.

4.2 Cyclic MLL

The sequent proof system for residuated monoids actually corresponds to a non-commutative version of intuitionistic multiplicative linear logic (IMLL) [12]: the product $(\cdot)$ is a non-commutative tensor $(\otimes)$, and left and right divisions $(\backslash, /)$ are the corresponding left and right linear implications $(\multimap, \circ\!\!-)$. Moreover, it happens that this system is just the intuitionistic fragment of cyclic multiplicative linear logic (MLL) [33]. The untyping theorem turned out to be easier to prove in this setting, which we describe below.

We assume a copy $\mathcal{X}^{\perp}$ of the set of variables $(\mathcal{X})$, and we denote by $x^{\perp}$ the corresponding elements which we call *dual variables*. From now on, we shall consider terms with both kinds of variables: $T(\Sigma + X + X^{\perp})$. We keep an algebraic terminology to remain consistent with the previous sections; notice that using terminology from logic, a term is a formula and a variable is an atomic formula.

Definition 16. *Typed MLL terms* are defined by the signature $\{\otimes_2, \mathcal{R}_2, 1_0, \perp_0\}$, together with the following typing rules:

$$\dfrac{\Gamma(x) = (n,m)}{\vdash x : n \to m} \; \text{Tv} \qquad \dfrac{}{\vdash 1 : n \to n} \; \text{T}_1 \qquad \dfrac{\vdash a : n \to m \qquad \vdash b : m \to p}{\vdash a \otimes b : n \to p} \; \text{T}_\otimes$$

$$\dfrac{\Gamma(x) = (n,m)}{\vdash x^{\perp} : m \to n} \; \text{Tv}^{\perp} \qquad \dfrac{}{\vdash \perp : n \to n} \; \text{T}_\perp \qquad \dfrac{\vdash a : n \to m \qquad \vdash b : m \to p}{\vdash a \,\mathcal{R}\, b : n \to p} \; \text{T}_\mathcal{R}$$

Tensor $(\otimes)$ and par $(\mathcal{R})$ are typed like the previous dot operation; bottom $(\perp)$ is typed like the unit (1); dual variables are typed by mirroring the types of the corresponding variables. We extend type judgements to lists of terms as follows:

$$\dfrac{}{\vdash \epsilon : n \to n} \; \text{T}_\text{E} \qquad \dfrac{\vdash a : n \to m \qquad \vdash l : m \to p}{\vdash a; l : n \to p} \; \text{T}_\text{C}$$

(be careful not to confuse $\vdash a, b : n \to m$, which indicates that both a and b have type $n \to m$, with $\vdash a; b : n \to m$, which indicates that the list $a; b$ has type $n \to m$). *Linear negation* is defined over terms and lists of terms as follows:

$$(x)^{\perp} \triangleq x^{\perp} \qquad 1^{\perp} \triangleq \perp \qquad (a \otimes b)^{\perp} \triangleq b^{\perp} \,\mathcal{R}\, a^{\perp} \qquad (a; l)^{\perp} \triangleq l^{\perp}; a^{\perp}$$

$$(x^{\perp})^{\perp} \triangleq x \qquad \perp^{\perp} \triangleq 1 \qquad (a \,\mathcal{R}\, b)^{\perp} \triangleq b^{\perp} \otimes a^{\perp} \qquad \epsilon^{\perp} \triangleq \epsilon$$

Note that since we are in a non-commutative setting, negation has to reverse the arguments of tensors and pars, as well as lists. Negation is involutive and mirrors type judgements:

Lemma 17. *For all l, $l^{\perp\perp} = l$; for all l, n, m, $\vdash l : n \to m$ iff $\vdash l^{\perp} : m \to n$.*

If we were using a two-sided presentation of MLL, judgements would be of the form $l \vdash k : m \to n$, intuitively meaning "$l \vdash k$ is derivable in cyclic MLL, and lists l and k have type $m \to n$". Instead, we work with one-sided sequents to benefit from the symmetrical nature of MLL. At the untyped level, this means that we replace $l \vdash k$ with $\vdash l^{\perp}; k$. According to the previous intuitions, the list $l^{\perp}; k$ has a square type $n \to n$: object m is hidden in the concatenation, so that it suffices to record the outer object (n). Judgements finally take the form $\vdash l : n$, meaning "the one-sided MLL sequent $\vdash l$ is derivable at type $n \to n$".

$$\frac{\Gamma(x) = (n, m)}{\vdash x^{\perp}; x : m} \; A \qquad \frac{}{\vdash 1 : n} \; 1 \qquad \frac{\vdash l : n}{\vdash \perp; l : n} \; \perp \qquad \frac{\vdash l; a : n \qquad \vdash b; k : n}{\vdash l; a \otimes b; k : n} \; \otimes$$

$$\frac{\vdash a; b; l : n}{\vdash a \,\gimel\, b; l : n} \;\gimel \qquad \frac{\vdash a : n \to m \qquad \vdash l; a : m}{\vdash a; l : n} \; E$$

Fig. 1. Typed Sequents for Cyclic MLL

Definition 18. *Typed cyclic MLL* is defined by the sequent calculus from Fig. 1.

Except for type decorations, the system is standard: the five first rules are the logical rules of MLL [12]. Rule (E) is the only structural rule, this is a restricted form of the exchange rule, yielding cyclic permutations: sequents have to be thought of as rings [33]. As before, we added type decorations in a minimal way, so as to ensure that derivable sequents have square types, as explained above:

Lemma 19. *For all l, n, if $\vdash l : n$ then $\vdash l : n \to n$.*

We now give a graphical interpretation of the untyping theorem, using proof nets. Since provability is preserved by cyclic permutations, one can draw proof structures by putting the terms of a sequent on a circle [33]. For example, a proof π of a sequent $\vdash l_0, \ldots, l_i$ will be represented by a proof net whose interface is given by the left drawing below.

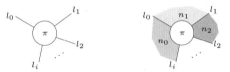

Suppose now that the corresponding list admits a square type: $\vdash l : n \to n$, i.e., $\forall j \leq i$, $\vdash l_j : n_j \to n_{j+1}$, for some $n_0, \ldots, n_{i+1}$ with $n = n_0 = n_{i+1}$. One can add these type decorations as background colours, in the areas delimited by terms, as we did on the right-hand side.

The logical rules of the proof system (Fig. 1) can then be represented by the proof net constructions below (thanks to this sequent representation, the exchange rule (E) is implicit). Since these constructions preserve planarity, all proof nets are planar [2], and the idea of background colours makes sense. Moreover, they can be coloured in a consistent way, so that typed derivations correspond to proof nets that can be entirely and consistently coloured.

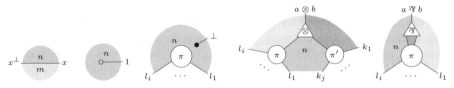

Therefore, one way to prove the untyping theorem consists in showing that any proof net whose outer interface can be coloured can be coloured entirely. As an example, we give an untyped derivation below, together with the corresponding proof net. Assuming that $\Gamma(x) = n \to m$ and $\Gamma(y) = m \to p$, the conclusion has type $p \to p$, and the outer interface of the proof net can be coloured (here, with colours p and n). The untyping theorem will ensure that there exists a typed proof; indeed, the whole proof net can be coloured in a consistent way.

$$
\dfrac{
\dfrac{
\dfrac{
\dfrac{
\dfrac{\quad}{\vdash x^{\perp}; x}\ \text{A} \qquad \dfrac{\quad}{\vdash y; y^{\perp}}\ \text{E,A}
}{\vdash x^{\perp}; (x \otimes y); y^{\perp}}\ \otimes
}{
\dfrac{\vdash x^{\perp}; (x \otimes y) \,\mathbin{⅋}\, y^{\perp} \qquad \dfrac{\quad}{\vdash y; y^{\perp}}\ \text{E,A}}{}\ \mathbin{⅋}
}{
\vdash x^{\perp}; ((x \otimes y) \,\mathbin{⅋}\, y^{\perp}) \otimes y; y^{\perp}
}\ \otimes
}{\vdash \perp; x^{\perp}; ((x \otimes y) \,\mathbin{⅋}\, y^{\perp}) \otimes y; y^{\perp}}\ \perp
}{
\dfrac{\vdash y^{\perp}; \perp; x^{\perp}; ((x \otimes y) \,\mathbin{⅋}\, y^{\perp}) \otimes y}{\vdash y^{\perp} \,\mathbin{⅋}\, \perp \,\mathbin{⅋}\, x^{\perp}; ((x \otimes y) \,\mathbin{⅋}\, y^{\perp}) \otimes y}\ \mathbin{⅋}
}\ \text{E}
$$

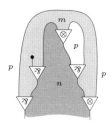

We now embark in the proof of the untyping theorem for cyclic MLL; the key property is that the types of derivable sequents are all squares:

Proposition 20. *If* $\vdash l$ *and* $\vdash l : n \to m$, *then* $n = m$.

Proof. We proceed by induction on the untyped derivation $\vdash l$, but we prove a stronger property: "the potential types of all cyclic permutations of l are squares", i.e., for all h,k such that $l = h; k$, for all n, m such that $\vdash k; h : n \to m$, $n = m$. The most involved case is that of the tensor rule. Using symmetry arguments, we can assume that the cutting point belongs to the left premise: the conclusion of the tensor rule is $\vdash l; l'; a \otimes b; k$, we suppose that the induction hypothesis holds for $l; l'; a$ and $b; k$, and knowing that $\vdash l'; a \otimes b; k; l : n \to m$, we have to show $n = m$. Clearly, we have $\vdash l'; a : n \to p$, $\vdash b; k : p \to q$, and $\vdash l : q \to m$ for some p, q. By induction on the second premise, we have $p = q$, so that $\vdash l'; a; l : n \to m$. Since the latter list is a cyclic permutation of $l; l'; a$, we can conclude with the induction hypothesis on the first premise. ∎

Theorem 21. *In cyclic MLL, if* $\vdash l : n \to n$, *then we have* $\vdash l$ *iff* $\vdash l : n$.

Proof. The right-to-left implication is straightforward; for the direct implication, we proceed by induction on the untyped derivation. The previous proposition is required in the case of the tensor rule: we know that $\vdash l; a$, $\vdash b; k$, and $\vdash l; a \otimes b; k : n \to n$, and we have to show that $\vdash l; a \otimes b; k : n$. Necessarily, there is some m such that $\vdash l; a : n \to m$ and $\vdash b; k : m \to n$; moreover, by Prop. 20, $n = m$. Therefore, we can apply the induction hypotheses (so that $\vdash l; a : n$ and $\vdash b; k : n$) and we conclude with the typed tensor rule. ∎

4.3   Intuitionistic Fragment

To deduce that the untyping theorem holds in residuated monoids, it suffices to show that the typed version of the proof system from §4.1 corresponds to the intuitionistic fragment of the proof system from Fig. 1. This is well-known for the untyped case, and type decorations do not add particular difficulties. Therefore, we just give a brief overview of the extended proof.

The idea is to define the following families of *input* and *output* terms (Danos-Regnier polarities [31,3]), and to work with sequents composed of exactly one output term and an arbitrary number of input terms.

$$i ::= x^\perp \mid \perp \mid i \,\mathfrak{N}\, i \mid i \otimes o \mid o \otimes i$$
$$o ::= x \mid 1 \mid o \otimes o \mid i \,\mathfrak{N}\, o \mid o \,\mathfrak{N}\, i$$

Negation $(-^\perp)$ establishes a bijection between input and output terms. Terms of residuated monoids (IMLL formulae) are encoded into output terms as follows.

$$\lfloor a \cdot b \rfloor \triangleq \lfloor a \rfloor \otimes \lfloor b \rfloor \qquad \lfloor a/b \rfloor \triangleq \lfloor a \rfloor \,\mathfrak{N}\, \lfloor b \rfloor^\perp \qquad \lfloor x \rfloor \triangleq x$$
$$\lfloor 1 \rfloor \triangleq 1 \qquad \lfloor a \backslash b \rfloor \triangleq \lfloor a \rfloor^\perp \,\mathfrak{N}\, \lfloor b \rfloor$$

This encoding is a bijection between IMLL terms and output MLL terms; it preserves typing judgements:

Lemma 22. *For all a, n, m, we have $\vdash a : n \to m$ iff $\vdash \lfloor a \rfloor : n \to m$.*

(Note that we heavily rely on overloading to keep notation simple.) The next proposition shows that we actually obtained a fragment of typed cyclic MLL; it requires the lemma below: input-only lists are not derivable. The untyping theorem for residuated monoids follows using Thm. 21.

Lemma 23. *If $\vdash l$, then l contains at least one output term.*

Proposition 24. *If $\vdash l, a : n \to m$, then $l \vdash a : n \to m$ iff $\vdash \lfloor l \rfloor^\perp ; \lfloor a \rfloor : m$.*

Corollary 25. *In residuated monoids, if $\vdash l, a : n \to m$, then we have $l \vdash a$ iff $l \vdash a : n \to m$.*

4.4 Residuated Lattices: Additives

The Gentzen proof system we presented for residuated monoids was actually designed for residuated *lattices* [27], obtained by further requiring the partial order $(X, \leq)$ to be a lattice $(X, \vee, \wedge)$. Binary relations fall into this family, by considering set-theoretic unions and intersections. The previous proofs scale without major difficulty: on the logical side, this amounts to considering the additive binary connectives $(\oplus, \&)$. By working in multiplicative additive linear logic (MALL) without additive constants, we get an untyping theorem for *involutive residuated lattices* [32]; we deduce the untyping theorem for residuated lattices by considering the corresponding intuitionistic fragment (see [29] for proofs).

On the contrary, and rather surprisingly, the theorem breaks if we include additive constants $(0, \top)$, or equivalently, if we consider *bounded* residuated lattices. The corresponding typing rules are given below, together with the logical rule for top (there is no rule for zero).

$$\frac{}{\vdash 0 : n \to m} \; \top_0 \qquad \frac{}{\vdash \top : n \to m} \; \top_\top \qquad \frac{\vdash l : m \to n}{\vdash \top ; l : n} \; \top$$

The sequent $x^\perp \otimes \top ; y^\perp ; \top \otimes x$ gives a counter-example. This sequent basically admits the two following untyped proofs:

$$\dfrac{\dfrac{\dfrac{\overline{\vdash x; x^{\bot}}\ \text{E,A}\quad \overline{\vdash \top}\ \top}{\vdash x; x^{\bot} \otimes \top}\ \otimes}{\vdash y^{\bot}; \top \otimes x; x^{\bot} \otimes \top}\ \text{E,}\top \quad}{\vdash x^{\bot} \otimes \top; y^{\bot}; \top \otimes x}\ \text{E}$$

$$\dfrac{\dfrac{\overline{\vdash \top}\ \top \quad \dfrac{\overline{\vdash x; x^{\bot}}\ \text{E,A}\quad \overline{\vdash \top; y^{\bot}}\ \top}{\vdash x; x^{\bot} \otimes \top; y^{\bot}}\ \otimes}{\vdash \top \otimes x; x^{\bot} \otimes \top; y^{\bot}}\ \otimes}{\vdash x^{\bot} \otimes \top; y^{\bot}; \top \otimes x}\ \text{E,E}$$

However, this sequent admits the square type $m \to m$ whenever $\Gamma(x) = (n, m)$ and $\Gamma(y) = (p, q)$, while the above proofs cannot be typed unless $n = q$ or $n = p$, respectively. Graphically, these proofs correspond to the proof nets below (where the proof net construction for rule $(\top)$ is depicted on the left-hand side); these proof nets cannot be coloured unless $n = q$ or $n = p$.

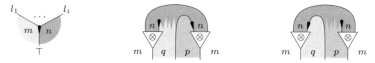

This counter-example for MALL also gives a counter-example for IMALL: the above proofs translate to intuitionistic proofs of $y \cdot (\top \backslash x) \vdash \top \cdot x$, which is also not derivable in the typed setting, unless $n = q$ or $n = p$. The problem is actually even stronger: while $S \cdot (\top \backslash R) \subseteq \top \cdot R$ holds for all homogeneous binary relations R, S (by the above proofs, for example), this law does not hold for arbitrary heterogeneous relations (take, e.g., the empty relation from the empty set to $\{\emptyset\}$ for R, and an arbitrary non-empty relation for S). This shows that we cannot always reduce the analysis of typed structures to that of the underlying untyped structures. Here, the equational theory of heterogeneous binary relations does not reduce to the equational theory of homogeneous binary relations.

5 Conclusions and Directions for Future Work

We proved untyping theorems for several standard structures, allowing us to extend decidability results to the typed settings. All results have been formally checked [29] with the Coq proof assistant. We conclude by discussing applications, related work, and directions for future work.

5.1 Applications

Improving proof search for residuated structures. The sequent proof systems we mentioned in this paper have the sub-formula property, so that provability is decidable in each case, using a simple proof search algorithm [26]. Surprisingly, the concept of types can be used to cut off useless branches. Indeed, recall Prop. 20: "the types of any derivable sequent are squares". By contrapositive, given an untyped sequent l, one can easily compute an abstract 'most general type and environment' $(n \to m, \Gamma)$, such that $\Gamma \vdash l : n \to m$ holds (taking $\mathbb{N}$ as the set of objects, for example); if $n \neq m$, then the sequent is not derivable, and proof search can fail immediately on this sequent.

We did some experiments with a simple prototype [29]: we implemented focused [1] proof search for cyclic MALL, i.e., a recursive algorithm composed of an *asynchronous* phase which is deterministic and a *synchronous* phase, where branching occurs (e.g., when applying rule ($\otimes$)). The optimisation consists in checking that the most general type of the sequent is square before entering the synchronous phase. The overall complexity remains exponential (provability is NP-complete [28]—PSPACE-complete with additives [17]) but we get an exponential speed-up: we can abort proof search immediately on approximately two sequents over three. Even on small examples, we gain an order of magnitude [29].

Decision of typed Kleene algebras in Coq. The untyping theorem for typed Kleene algebras is quite important in the ATBR Coq library [4]: it allows one to use our tactic for Kleene algebras [5] in typed settings, and, in particular, with heterogeneous binary relations. The underlying decision procedure being quite involved, we can hardly imagine proving its soundness w.r.t. typed settings. Even writing a type-preserving version of the algorithm seems challenging.

At another level, we used the untyping theorem for semirings in order to formalise Kozen's completeness proof [19] for Kleene algebras (which we had to formalise to reach all models). Indeed, this proof heavily relies on matrix constructions, so that having adequate lemmas and tactics for working with possibly rectangular matrices was a big plus: this allowed us to avoid the ad-hoc constructions Kozen used to inject rectangular matrices into square ones.

5.2   References and Related Work

The relationship between residuated lattices and substructural logics is due to Ono and Komori [27]; see [11] for a thorough introduction. Cyclic linear logic was suggested by Girard and studied by Yetter [33]. To the best of our knowledge, the idea of adding types to the above structures is new. The axiomatisation of Kleene algebras is due to Kozen [19].

Our typed structures can be seen as very special cases of *partial* algebras [6], where the domain of partial operations is defined by typing judgements. Several encodings from partial algebras to total ones were proposed in the literature [24,7]. Although they are quite general, these results do not apply here: these encodings do not preserve the considered theory since they need to introduce new symbols and equations; as a consequence, ordinary untyped decision procedures can no longer be used after the translation. Dojer has shown that under some conditions, convergent term rewriting systems for total algebras can be used to prove existence equations in partial algebras [8]. While it seems applicable to semirings, this approach does not scale to Kleene algebras or residuated lattices, for which decidability does not arise from a term rewriting system.

Closer to our work is that from Kozen, who first proposed the idea of untyping typed Kleene algebras, in order to avoid the aforementioned matrix constructions [21]. He provided a different answer, however: using model-theoretic arguments, he proved an untyping theorem for the Horn theory of "1-free Kleene algebras". The restriction to 1-free expressions is required, as shown by the following counter-example: $\vdash 0 = 1 \Rightarrow a = b$ is a theorem of semirings, although there are non trivial typed semirings where $0 = 1$ holds at some types (e.g., empty matrices), while $a = b$ is not universally true at other types.

5.3 Handling Other Structures

Action algebras [30,15] are a natural extension of the structures we studied in this paper: they combine the ingredients from residuated lattices and Kleene algebras. Although we do not know whether the untyping theorem holds in this case, we can think of two strategies to tackle this problem: 1) find a cut-free extension of the Gentzen proof system for residuated lattices and adapt our current proof—such an extension is left as an open question in [15], it would entail decidability of the equational theory of action algebras; 2) find a "direct" proof of the untyping theorem for residuated monoids, without using a Gentzen proof system, so that the methodology we used for Kleene algebras can be extended.

Kleene algebras with tests [20] are another extension of Kleene algebras, which is useful in program verification. Their equational theory is decidable, and the untyping theorem is likely to hold for these structures: a possible difficulty could appear with the complement operation from the Boolean algebra of tests, but tests are inherently homogeneous.

Our proofs about semirings can be adapted to handle the cases of *allegories* and *distributive allegories* [10] (see [29] for proofs); however, the case of *division allegories*, where left and right divisions are added, remains open.

5.4 Towards a Generic Theory

The typed structures we focused on can be described in terms of enriched categories, and the untyping theorems can be rephrased as asserting the existence of faithful functors to one-object categories. It would therefore be interesting to find out whether category theory may help to define a reasonable class of structures for which the untyping theorem holds. In particular, how could we exclude the counter-example with additive constants in MALL?

For structures that are varieties, another approach would consist in using term rewriting theory to obtain generic factorisation theorems (Lemma 10, which we used to handle the annihilating element in semirings, would become a particular case). This seems rather difficult, however, since these kind of properties are quite sensitive to the whole set of operations and axioms that are considered.

Acknowledgements. We warmly thank Olivier Laurent, Tom Hirschowitz and the Choco band for the highly stimulating discussions we had about this work.

References

1. Andreoli, J.-M.: Logic programming with focusing proofs in linear logic. Journal of Logic and Computation 2(3), 297–347 (1992)
2. Bellin, G., Fleury, A.: Planar and braided proof-nets for MLL with mix. Archive for Mathematical Logic 37, 309–325 (1998)
3. Bellin, G., Scott, P.: On the π-calculus and linear logic. TCS 135, 11–65 (1994)
4. Braibant, T., Pous, D.: Coq library: ATBR, algebraic tools for binary relations (May 2009), http://sardes.inrialpes.fr/~braibant/atbr/
5. Braibant, T., Pous, D.: An efficient coq tactic for deciding Kleene algebras. In: Kaufmann, M., Paulson, L.C. (eds.) Interactive Theorem Proving. LNCS, vol. 6172, pp. 163–178. Springer, Heidelberg (2010)

6. Burmeister, P.: Partial Algebra. In: Algebras and Orders. Kluwer Pub., Dordrecht (1993)
7. Diaconescu, R.: An encoding of partial algebras as total algebras. Information Processing Letters 109(23-24), 1245–1251 (2009)
8. Dojer, N.: Applying term rewriting to partial algebra theory. Fundamenta Informaticae 63(4), 375–384 (2004)
9. Doornbos, H., Backhouse, R., van der Woude, J.: A calculational approach to mathematical induction. TCS 179(1-2), 103–135 (1997)
10. Freyd, P., Scedrov, A.: Categories, Allegories. North-Holland, Amsterdam (1990)
11. Galatos, N., Jipsen, P., Kowalski, T., Ono, H.: Residuated lattices: an algebraic glimpse at substructural logics. Stud. in Log. and Found. of Math. 151, 532 (2007)
12. Girard, J.-Y.: Linear logic. TCS 50, 1–102 (1987)
13. Grégoire, B., Mahboubi, A.: Proving equalities in a commutative ring done right in Coq. In: Hurd, J., Melham, T. (eds.) TPHOLs 2005. LNCS, vol. 3603, pp. 98–113. Springer, Heidelberg (2005)
14. Harrison, J.: A HOL decision procedure for elementary real algebra. In: Joyce, J.J., Seger, C.-J.H. (eds.) HUG 1993. LNCS, vol. 780, pp. 426–435. Springer, Heidelberg (1994)
15. Jipsen, P.: Semirings to residuated Kleene lattices. Stud. Log. 76(2), 291–303 (2004)
16. Jipsen, P., Tsinakis, C.: A survey of residuated lattices. Ord. Alg. Struct. (2002)
17. Kanovich, M.: The complexity of neutrals in linear logic. In: Proc. LICS, pp. 486–495. IEEE, Los Alamitos (1995)
18. Kleene, S.C.: Representation of events in nerve nets and finite automata. In: Automata Studies, pp. 3–41. Princeton University Press, Princeton (1956)
19. Kozen, D.: A completeness theorem for Kleene algebras and the algebra of regular events. Information and Computation 110(2), 366–390 (1994)
20. Kozen, D.: Kleene algebra with tests. Trans. PLS 19(3), 427–443 (1997)
21. Kozen, D.: Typed Kleene algebra. Technical Report 98-1669, Cornell Univ. (1998)
22. Krob, D.: Complete systems of B-rational identities. TCS 89(2), 207–343 (1991)
23. Lambek, J.: The mathematics of sentence structure. American Mathematical Monthly 65, 154–170 (1958)
24. Mossakowski, T.: Relating CASL with other specification languages: the institution level. TCS 286(2), 367–475 (2002)
25. Norrish, M.: Complete integer decision procedures as derived rules in HOL. In: Basin, D., Wolff, B. (eds.) TPHOLs 2003. LNCS, vol. 2758, pp. 71–86. Springer, Heidelberg (2003)
26. Okada, M., Terui, K.: The finite model property for various fragments of intuitionistic linear logic. Journal of Symbolic Logic 64(2), 790–802 (1999)
27. Ono, H., Komori, Y.: Logics without the contraction rule. Journal of Symbolic Logic 50(1), 169–201 (1985)
28. Pentus, M.: Lambek calculus is NP-complete. TCS 357(1-3), 186–201 (2006)
29. Pous, D.: Web appendix of this paper, http://sardes.inrialpes.fr/~pous/utas
30. Pratt, V.R.: Action logic and pure induction. In: van Eijck, J. (ed.) JELIA 1990. LNCS, vol. 478, pp. 97–120. Springer, Heidelberg (1991)
31. Regnier, L.: Lambda-calcul et réseaux. Thèse de doctorat, Univ. Paris VII (1992)
32. Wille, A.: A Gentzen system for involutive residuated lattices. Algebra Universalis 54, 449–463 (2005)
33. Yetter, D.: Quantales and (noncommutative) linear logic. Journal of Symbolic Logic 55(1), 41–64 (1990)

Two-Variable Logic with Two Order Relations*
(Extended Abstract)

Thomas Schwentick and Thomas Zeume

TU Dortmund University

Abstract. The finite satisfiability problem for two-variable logic over structures with unary relations and two order relations is investigated. Firstly, decidability is shown for structures with one total preorder relation and one linear order relation. More specifically, we show that this problem is complete for EXPSPACE. As a consequence, the same upper bound applies to the case of two linear orders. Secondly, we prove undecidability for structures with two total preorder relations as well as for structures with one total preorder and two linear order relations. Further, we point out connections to other logics. Decidability is shown for two-variable logic on data words with orders on both positions and data values, but without a successor relation. We also study "partial models" of compass and interval temporal logic and prove decidability for some of their fragments.

1 Introduction

First-order logic restricted to two-variables (*two-variable logic* or FO^2 in the following) is generally known to be reasonably expressive for many purposes and to behave moderately with respect to the possibility of testing satisfiability. As opposed to full first-order logic, its satisfiability and its finite satisfiability problem are decidable [Mor75], in fact they are NEXPTIME-complete [GKV97]. However, there are some simple properties like transitivity of a binary relation that cannot be expressed in FO^2. As a consequence, if one is interested in models with particular properties it might be the case that these properties cannot be described in an FO^2 formula and thus one is interested in the question whether a formula has a model with these additional properties. Two particular examples are the inability to express that a binary relation is a linear order or that it is an equivalence relation, both are actually due to the inability to axiomatize transitivity.

In [Ott01] it is shown that it is decidable in NEXPTIME whether a given FO^2 sentence has a model (or whether it has a finite model) in which a particular relation symbol is interpreted by a linear order. On the other hand, in the

* We acknowledge the financial support of the Future and Emerging Technologies (FET) programme within the Seventh Framework Programme for Research of the European Commission, under the FET-Open grant agreement FOX, number FP7-ICT-233599. We further acknowledge the financial support by the German DFG under grant SCHW 678/4-1.

A. Dawar and H. Veith (Eds.): CSL 2010, LNCS 6247, pp. 499–513, 2010.

presence of eight binary symbols that have to be interpreted as linear orders it is undecidable. Note that in these results the formulas might use further relation symbols for which the possible interpretations are unrestricted. In [KO05] it is shown[1] that finite satisfiability is NEXPTIME-complete over structures with one equivalence relation and undecidable over structures with three equivalence relations. In [KT09] it is shown that over structures with two equivalence classes the problem is decidable in triply exponential nondeterministic time.

In this paper we study two-variable logic over structures with linear orders and total preorders. A total preorder $\precsim$ is basically an equivalence relation $\sim$ whose equivalence classes are ordered by $\prec$. Total preorders can therefore encode equivalence relations as well as linear orders and in this sense they generalize both these kinds of relations. It should be stressed that in our results, formulas can refer to an arbitrary number of additional unary relations but they are *not* allowed to refer to arbitrary non-unary relations besides the orders that are explicitly mentioned.

Our motivation stems from the context of so-called data words. A *data word* is a word, that is, a finite sequence of symbols from a finite alphabet, but besides a symbol, every position also carries a value from a possibly infinite domain. The interest in data words and data trees comes on one hand from applications in database theory, where XML documents can be modeled by data trees in which the symbols correspond to the tags and the data values to text or number values. On the other hand, (infinite) data words can also be considered as traces of a computation in a distributed environment, where symbols correspond to states of processes and the data values encode process numbers. Recently many logics and automata models have been considered for data words and data trees (see [Seg06] for a gentle introduction).

First-order logic on data words is undecidable in general (with a linear order on positions and equality on data values), even for formulas with three variables [BMS+06]. Whether two-variable logics is decidable depends on the way the order of positions in the word is represented and on the ability to compare data values. In [BMS+06] it is shown that finite satisfiability of FO^2 over data words is NEXPTIME-complete if only a linear order on the positions is given and data values can only be compared with respect to equality. The attentive reader might have noticed that this is just the setting of structures with one linear order and one equivalence relation (and some unary relations). If the successor relation (+1) on the positions is also available the problem remains decidable but the complexity is unknown (but basically equivalent to the open complexity of Petri net reachability). The same paper shows that if furthermore data values can be compared with respect to a linear order (by a binary relation stating that "the value at position x is smaller than the value at y") the logic immediately becomes undecidable. The latter case draws a link between data words and structures with linear orders and total preorders. As already mentioned, the representation of words usually involves a linear order on the positions. A linear order on data

---

[1] As this paper only deals with finite structures we henceforth only mention results on finite satisfiability.

values induces a total preorder on the positions. Two positions can carry the same data value and therefore are considered "equivalent" with respect to their data value or one can carry a smaller data value than the other. It is exactly this setting which triggered our study of structures with a linear order, a total preorder and a number of unary relations.

Results. We show that finite satisfiability of two-variable logic over structures with a linear order, a total preorder and unary relations is EXPSPACE-complete. Thus, finite satisfiability of FO^2 over data words with a linear order on the positions (but no successor relation) and a linear order on the data values can also be decided in exponential space. As it can be expressed in FO^2 that a total preorder is a linear order, the corresponding problem with two linear orders (and no total preorder) is solvable in EXPSPACE, thus the gap left in the work of Otto [Ott01] is narrowed. In contrast, finite satisfiability of FO^2 over structures[2] with two total preorders and over structures with two linear orders and a total preorder is undecidable.

The upper bound in the case of a linear order and a total preorder is by a reduction to finite satisfiability of *semi-positive* FO^2 sentences over sets of labeled points in the plane, where points can be compared by their relative position with respect to the directions $\nwarrow, \nearrow, \swarrow, \searrow, \leftarrow, \rightarrow$. In semi-positive formulas, negated binary atoms are not allowed in the "immediate scope" of an existential quantifier. This satisfiability problem in turn is reduced to a constraint problem for labeled points in the plane. The lower bound is by a reduction from exponential width corridor tiling.

Furthermore, we use the result on semi-positive two-variable logics over labeled point sets to obtain complexity bounds for the problem to decide the existence of partial models for some fragments of compass logic and interval logic.

Organization. After some basic definitions in Section 2 we show the main results on ordered structures in Section 3 and discuss the applications for data words, compass logics and interval logics in Section 4. We conclude with Section 5. Due to space restrictions, some proof details are deferred to the full version of the paper.

Related work. As mentioned before, also other logics for data words besides FO^2 have been studied. As an example we mention the "freeze"-extension of LTL studied, e.g. in [DL09] and [FS09]. The latter paper is more closely related to our work as it considers a restriction of LTL without the X-operator. We are aware that Amaldev Manuel has recently proved decidability and undecidability results for FO^2-logic over structures with orders [Man10]. However, as in his results structures always contain at least one successor relation neither results nor techniques translate from his work to ours nor vice versa. Besides the relations to compass logic and interval logic discussed above we conjecture that there are connections to spatial reasoning such as it is done in the context of Geographical Information Systems (for a survey, see [CH01]). Related work on compass and interval logic is mentioned in Section 4.

---

[2] Additional unary relations are again allowed.

2 Preliminaries

We consider two kinds of two-variable logics: over ordered structures and over labeled point sets in the plane. We first fix our notation concerning order relations. A *total preorder* $\precsim$ is a transitive, total relation, i.e. $u \precsim v$ and $v \precsim w$ implies $u \precsim w$ and for every two elements u, v of a structure $u \precsim v$ or $v \precsim u$ holds. A *linear order* $\leq$ is a total preorder which is antisymmetric, i.e. if $u \leq v$ and $v \leq u$ then $u = v$. Thus, the essential difference between a total preorder and a linear order is that the former allows that two distinct elements u, v are equivalent with respect to $\precsim$, that is, both $u \precsim v$ and $v \precsim u$ hold. Thus, a total preorder can also be viewed as an equivalence relation $\sim$ whose equivalence classes are strictly and linearly ordered by $\prec$. Clearly, every linear order is a total preorder.

We use binary relation symbols $\precsim, \precsim_1, \precsim_2, \ldots$ that are always interpreted by total preorders as well as binary relation symbols $\leq, \leq_1, \leq_2, \ldots$ that are always interpreted as linear orders.

In this paper, an *ordered structure* is a finite structure with non-empty universe and some linear orders, some total preorders and some unary relations. We always allow an unlimited number of unary relations and specify the numbers of allowed linear orders and total preorders explicitly. For example, by $FO^2(\leq_1, \precsim_1, \precsim_2)$ we denote the set of two-variable sentences over structures with one linear order, two total preorders and arbitrarily many unary relations. Furthermore, all two-variable formulas in this paper can refer to the equality relation $=$.

As mentioned before, we also consider formulas that express properties of sets of labeled points. Let $\mathcal{P} = \{e_1, \ldots, e_k\}$ be a set of propositions. A $\mathcal{P}$-*labeled point* p is a point in $\mathbb{Q}^2$ in which propositions $e_1, \ldots, e_k$ may or may not hold. We refer to the x-coordinate, the y-coordinate of a point p by $p.x$ and $p.y$, respectively, and write $p.e_i = 1$, if proposition e_i holds in p. We simply say *point* if $\mathcal{P}$ is understood from the context.

We write $p \nearrow q$ if $p.x < q.x$ and $p.y < q.y$, we write $p \nwarrow q$ if $p.x > q.x$ and $p.y < q.y$. Analogously for $p \searrow q$ and $p \swarrow q$. We write $p \rightarrow q$ if $p.y = q.y$ and $p.x < q.x$ and likewise $p \leftarrow q$. Analogously for $\uparrow$ and $\downarrow$. Let $\mathcal{D} = \{\nwarrow, \nearrow, \swarrow, \searrow, \leftarrow, \rightarrow, \uparrow, \downarrow\}$ denote the set of *directions*. We denote the set $\{\nwarrow, \nearrow, \swarrow, \searrow, \leftarrow, \rightarrow\}$) by $\mathcal{D}_-$.

A set $\mathcal{O} \subseteq \mathcal{D}$ is *symmetric* if it contains, for each direction also the opposite direction, e.g., if it contains $\nearrow$ then also $\swarrow$. We will only consider symmetric sets of directions. For a symmetric set $\mathcal{O} \subseteq \mathcal{D}$, $FO^2(\mathcal{O})$ denotes two-variable logic sentences with binary atoms using directions from $\mathcal{O}$. Such a sentence is *semi-positive* if it is in negation normal form (NNF) and fulfils the following condition: whenever a negated binary atom $\neg(x \circ_d y)$ with $\circ_d \in \mathcal{O}$ occurs in the scope of an $\exists$-quantifier, there is a $\forall$-quantifier in the scope of this quantifier and the atom in turn is in the scope of this $\forall$-quantifier. In this sense, no negated binary atom is in the "immediate scope" of an $\exists$-quantifier. Negated atoms of the form $x \neq y$ are allowed in the immediate scope of $\exists$-quantifiers.

We interpret $FO^2(\mathcal{O})$ sentences over non-empty sets of $\mathcal{P}$-points in $\mathbb{Q}^2$, where $\mathcal{P}$ has a proposition e_i, for every unary relation symbol U_i.

3 Two-Variable Logic with a Total Preorder and a Linear Order

In this section we show the main result of the paper.

Theorem 1. *Finite satisfiability of* $\mathrm{FO}^2(\leq, \precsim)$ *is* EXPSPACE-*complete.*

The upper bound of Theorem 1 is shown in three steps. First, we reduce finite satisfiability of $\mathrm{FO}^2(\leq, \precsim)$-sentences in polynomial time to finite satisfiability of semi-positive $\mathrm{FO}^2(\mathcal{D}_-)$-sentences. Next, we reduce finite satisfiability for semi-positive $\mathrm{FO}^2(\mathcal{O})$, for every symmetric set $\mathcal{O}$ of directions, in exponential time to the two-dimensional labeled point problem (2LPP($\mathcal{O}$)) which is defined below. Finally, we show that 2LPP($\mathcal{D}_-$) can be solved in polynomial space. The lower bound is by a reduction from exponential width corridor tiling. As a FO^2-formula can express that a total preorder is actually a linear order, we get the following.

Corollary 2. *Finite satisfiability of* $\mathrm{FO}^2(\leq_1, \leq_2)$ *is in* EXPSPACE.

3.1 From Ordered Structures to Point Sets

Proposition 3. *For each* $\mathrm{FO}^2(\leq, \precsim)$-*sentence* φ *a semi-positive* $\mathrm{FO}^2(\mathcal{D}_-)$-*sentence* φ' *can be computed in polynomial time that is equivalent with respect to finite satisfiability.*

Proof. We first explain, how finite point sets and structures with a linear order $\leq$ and a total preorder $\precsim$ can be translated into each other.

With every finite ordered structure S with domain D and relations $\leq$ and $\precsim$ and some unary relations one can associate a finite point set P in the plane and a bijection π such that

- $u < v$ in S if and only if $\pi(u) \nearrow \pi(v)$ or $\pi(u) \to \pi(v)$ or $\pi(u) \searrow \pi(v)$,
- $u \prec v$ in S if and only if $\pi(u) \searrow \pi(v)$ or $\pi(u) \nearrow \pi(v)$, and
- $u \sim v$ in S if and only if $\pi(u) \leftarrow \pi(v)$ or $\pi(u) \to \pi(v)$.

To this end, one can first assign to each element of D an x-value in increasing fashion with respect to $<$. Second, each element gets a y-value in accordance with $\precsim$. It is easy to see that in P there are no two points with the same x-value. Thus, our reduction has to guarantee that φ' only has models with this additional property. The translation in the other direction is analogous.

For the actual reduction, first of all, φ' has a conjunct χ that ensures that no two points are on the same vertical line. This can be easily expressed by $\forall x \forall y \bigvee_{\circ_d \in \mathcal{D}_-} x \circ_d y$. As we can assume that φ is given in NNF it suffices to explain how the possible negated or positive binary atoms of φ are translated. The translation is as follows.

φ	φ'
$x \leq y$	$x = y \lor x \nearrow y \lor x \to y \lor x \searrow y$
$\neg(x \leq y)$	$x \searrow y \lor x \leftarrow y \lor x \nearrow y$
$x \precsim y$	$x = y \lor x \to y \lor x \leftarrow y \lor x \nearrow y \lor x \searrow y$
$\neg(x \precsim y)$	$x \searrow y \lor x \nearrow y$

The correctness of this translation relies on the fact that χ ensures that no two points are on the same vertical line.   □

Theorem 1 follows from Proposition 3 and the following result, the main technical contribution of this paper, which will be shown in the next two subsections.

Theorem 4. *Whether a semi-positive* $\mathrm{FO}^2(\mathcal{D}_-)$*-formula has a finite model, can be decided in exponential space.*

3.2   From Two-Variable Logic to Two-Dimensional Constraints

We next define 2LPP($\mathcal{O}$). For an alphabet Σ, a Σ-*labeled point* p is an element from $\mathbb{Q}^2 \times \Sigma$. The only difference between Σ-labeled points and $\mathcal{P}$-labeled points is that the former are labeled by one symbol from a finite alphabet whereas the latter carry several propositions.

An *existential constraint* (∃-*constraint*) is a pair (σ, E) where $\sigma \in \Sigma$ and E is a possibly empty set of pairs $(\circ_d, \tau)$ with $\circ_d \in \mathcal{O} \cup \{*, \neq\}$ and $\tau \in \Sigma$. A *universal constraint* (∀-*constraint*) is a tuple (σ, τ, O_1, O_2) where $\sigma, \tau \in \Sigma$, $O_1 \subseteq \mathcal{O} \cup \{=\}$ and $O_2 \subseteq \mathcal{O}$. A set M of Σ-labeled points *satisfies* an ∃-constraint (σ, E) if, for every $p \in M$ with $p.l = \sigma$ there is $q \in M$ such that, for some $(\circ_d, \tau)$ in E, $q.l = \tau$ and $p \circ_d q$. Here, $p * q$ is true for all p, q. It *satisfies* a ∀-constraint (σ, τ, O_1, O_2) if for all points $p, q \in M$ with $p.l = \sigma$, $q.l = \tau$ it holds $p \circ_d q$ for some $\circ_d \in O_1$ or $\circ_d \notin O_2$.

An input $L = (\Sigma, C_\exists, C_\forall)$ to the *two-dimensional labeled point problem* (*2LPP($\mathcal{O}$)*) consists of an alphabet Σ, a set $C_\exists$ of existential constraints and a set $C_\forall$ of universal constraints and all constraints only use directions from $\mathcal{O}$. A non-empty finite set $M \subseteq \mathbb{Q}^2 \times \Sigma$ is a *solution* of L if M satisfies all constraints from $C_\exists$ and $C_\forall$.

Proposition 5. *Let* $\mathcal{O} \subseteq \mathcal{D}$ *be a symmetric set of directions. From every semi-positive* $\mathrm{FO}^2(\mathcal{O})$*-sentence* φ *an instance* L *of 2LPP($\mathcal{O}$) can be computed in exponential time such that* φ *has a finite model if and only if* L *has a solution.*

Proof. Let $\mathcal{O} \subseteq \mathcal{D}$ and φ be an $\mathrm{FO}^2(\mathcal{O})$-sentence.

First, φ can be translated into a formula φ' in Scott normal form (SNF)

$$\forall x \forall y \, \psi(x, y) \wedge \bigwedge_{i=1}^m \forall x \exists y \, \psi_i(x, y),$$

that has a finite model if and only if φ has a finite model. The translation can be done in a way that ensures that

(1) ψ and all ψ_i are quantifier-free formulas,
(2) φ' is of linear size in the size of φ,
(3) negated binary atoms only occur in ψ.

In general, φ' uses more unary relation symbols than φ.

The translation is basically done as described in [GO99, Section 2.1]. However, some care is needed to guarantee condition (3). In the translation into SNF given in [GO99], for every quantified sub-formula $\psi(x)$ of the form $\exists y\ \psi_0$ or $\forall y\ \psi_0$ a unary relation P_ψ is introduced with the intention that every element a in a structure should obey $P_\psi(a) \Leftrightarrow \psi(a)$. The addition of such formulas would introduce a negation of ψ and therefore destroy condition (3). Fortunately, as we only consider formulas in NNF, it is sufficient that every element respects $P_\psi(a) \Rightarrow \psi(a)$ and therefore the introduction of negation can be avoided. To see that this suffices let us assume without loss of generality that φ is of the form $\exists x \chi$. If A is a model of φ then the relations P_ψ can be chosen such that $P_\psi(a) \Leftrightarrow \psi(a)$ holds, for every a and every subformula ψ of χ. On the other hand, by induction it can be shown that $P_\psi(a)$ only holds if $\psi(a)$ holds, thus the outermost formula $\exists x P_\chi(x)$ becomes true only if φ is true. Semi-positivity of φ ensures that no atoms $\neg(x \circ_d y)$ occur in any ψ_i.

In order to continue the translation into an 2LPP-instance, let ψ' be a disjunctive normal form of ψ. We can ensure that each disjunct of ψ' is the conjunction of a full atomic type σ for x, a full atomic type τ for y, and some (negated or positive) binary atoms. As the binary relations interpreting the directions in $\mathcal{O}$ are pairwise disjoint, we can assume that there is either (1) one positive binary atom or (2) a set of negated binary atoms of the form $x \circ_d y$ with $\circ_d \in \mathcal{O}$. For two positive atoms with different directions would evaluate to false and likewise negative atoms (with other directions) are redundant in the presence of a positive atom. Thus, by combining all clauses with the same σ and τ we get a set O_1 of "allowed directions" and a set O_2' of sets of forbidden directions. The set O_2' can be combined into one set O_2 of forbidden directions. It should be noted that O_2 could be the empty set. Altogether, we obtain a set $C_\forall$ of universal constraints equivalent to ψ. Clearly, the size of $C_\forall$ is at most exponential in φ.

By transforming the ψ_i into DNF and some additional simple steps, the second conjunct, $\bigwedge_{j=1}^{m} \forall x \exists y\ \psi_i(x,y)$, of φ' can be rewritten as

$$\forall x \bigwedge_{i=1}^{K} \left(\sigma_i(x) \Rightarrow \bigwedge_{j=1}^{m} \exists y \bigvee_{\ell=1}^{M} \psi_{ij\ell}\right),$$

where the σ_i describe pairwise distinct full atomic types and every $\psi_{ij\ell}$ is the conjunction of a full atomic type for y and (1) an atom $x \circ_d y$ with $\circ_d \in \mathcal{O} \cup \{\neq\}$ or (2) no further literals. The numbers K and M are at most exponential in $|\varphi|$. The semantics of this formula can be easily expressed by a set $C_\exists$ of $\exists$-constraints. For each $i \leq K$ and every $j \leq m$, the formulas $\psi_{ij\ell}$ can be combined into one $\exists$-constraint. Thus, $L = (\Sigma, C_\exists, C_\forall)$ is an instance of 2LPP($\mathcal{O}$) and a Σ-labeled point set is a solution to L if and only if the corresponding labeled point set $\mathcal{P}$ is a model of φ. Therefore L has a solution if and only if φ has a finite model. Furthermore, the size of L is at most exponential in $|\varphi|$ and the construction of L from φ can be done in exponential time.   □

3.3   2LPP($\mathcal{D}_-$) Is in PSPACE

Proposition 6. *Whether an instance L of 2LPP($\mathcal{D}_-$) has a solution can be decided in polynomial space.*

We basically show that every satisfiable formula has a model of exponential size and polynomial width.

To this end, we assume that every solution M of a labeled point problem comes with a partial *witness function* $w : M \times C_\exists \to M$ such that, for every point $p \in M$ and every $\exists$-constraint $c = (\sigma, E)$ with $p.l = \sigma$

- $w(p, c)$ exists, and
- there is some $(\circ_d, \tau)$ in E such that $p \circ_d w(p, c)$, and $w(p, c).l = \tau$.

We call the point $w(p, c)$ *witness* of p wrt c. A *horizontal line* $H(r)$ is a non-empty set of points $p \in M$ with $p.y = r$.

Lemma 7. *If M is a model for an instance of 2LPP($\mathcal{D}_-$) with alphabet Σ then every horizontal line of M contains at most $2|\Sigma|$ points.*

The proof uses the simple observation that if a horizontal line contains three points with the same label, only the two outermost points are needed as witnesses for other points.

Lemma 8. *Let L be an instance of 2LPP($\mathcal{D}_-$) and M a minimal solution to L. Then the number of horizontal lines that contain points from M is bounded by $(6|\Sigma| + 1)!2^{6|\Sigma|}$.*

Proof. For $r \in \mathbb{Q}$, we define the set $A(r)$ of **available witness points** for r containing $H(r)$ and, for each $\sigma \in \Sigma$, σ-points with minimum and maximum x-value above $H(r)$ and σ-points with minimum and maximum x-value below $H(r)$. Note that $A(r)$ contains at most six points with a given σ and thus $|A(r)| \leq 6|\Sigma|$.

The *profile* Pro(r) is obtained from $A(r)$ as follows. First, for each point $p \in A(r)$ we construct a pair $(p.l, p.f)$, where $p.f =\uparrow$ if $p.y > r$, $p.f = \cdot$ if $p.y = r$ and $p.f =\downarrow$ if $p.y < r$. We partition this set into maximal sets of pairs resulting from points with the same x-value and order the partition by these x-values. We refer to Figure 1 for two example profiles. Singleton sets in profiles are written without braces. Thus, a profile is an ordered partition of a multiset of size $\leq 6|\Sigma|$. It is easy to see that there are less than $N =_{\text{def}} (6|\Sigma| + 1)!2^{6|\Sigma|}$ different profiles. Thus, if M has more than N horizontal lines two of them must have the same profile.

Let us thus assume, towards a contradiction, that there exist $r < s$ such that there are points p, q in M with $p.y = r$ and $q.y = s$ and Pro(r) = Pro(s). We let $S_{<r} =_{\text{def}} \{q \in \mathbb{Q}^2 \mid q.y < r\}$, $S_{=r} =_{\text{def}} \{q \in \mathbb{Q}^2 \mid q.y = r\}$, and $S_{>r} =_{\text{def}} \{q \in \mathbb{Q}^2 \mid q.y > r\}$.

We construct M' as follows (Figure 2 illustrates the construction).

- All points p from $M \cap S_{\geq s}$ are in M'.
- No point p from M with $r \leq p.y < s$ is in M'.

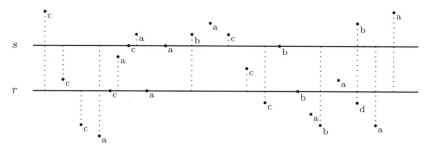

Fig. 1. Two horizontal lines with the same profile $(c, \uparrow)(c, \downarrow)(a, \downarrow)(c, \cdot)(a, \uparrow)(a, \cdot)(b, \uparrow)(c, \uparrow)(c, \downarrow)(b, \cdot)(b, \downarrow)\{(b, \uparrow), (d, \downarrow)\}(a, \downarrow)(a, \uparrow)$. Dotted lines indicate points contributing to the profiles.

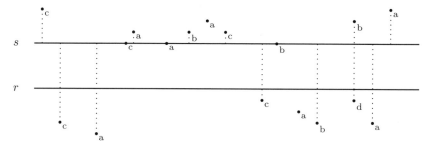

Fig. 2. Contraction of Figure 1. It should be noted that the lower a-point not in $A(r)$ is slightly shifted to the left and is now in the exact middle between the b-point on the upper horizontal line and the lower b-point.

- Informally, the vertical stripe between p_i and p_{i+1} and below r is scaled proportionally and shifted to the vertical stripe between q_i and q_{i+1}. More precisely, let k be the number of points in $A(r)$ (and $A(s)$) and let $p_1, \ldots, p_k$ and $q_1, \ldots, q_k$ be the points from $A(r)$ and $A(s)$, respectively, sorted with respect to their x-coordinate (and thus in the same way as in $\mathrm{Pro}(r)$ and $\mathrm{Pro}(s)$, respectively). Let $p \in M \cap S_{<r}$ and let $i \in \{1, \ldots, k\}$ be such that $p_i.x \le p.x < p_{i+1}.x$. It should be noted that there is no point p with $p.x < p_1.x$ or $p.x > p_k.x$. Then M' contains the point p' defined by
  - $p'.l = p.l$,
  - $p'.y = p.y$, and
  - $p'.x = q_i.x + \frac{p.x - p_i.x}{p_{i+1}.x - p_i.x}(q_{i+1}.x - q_i.x)$.

  We call p the source of p'.

  It could happen that a point below r has the same x-value as some point above r. To avoid that a point $p \notin A(r)$ below r has the same x-value as some point $s \notin A(s)$ above s, we finally shift every point $p \notin A(r)$ below r by ϵ in eastern direction, where ϵ is smaller than the minimal non-zero vertical distance of any two points. This final step ensures that in M' there are no two points with the same x-value if in M there were no such two points.

Clearly, $|M'| < |M|$ as we removed (at least) the points of the horizontal line with y-coordinate r. Thus, to obtain a contradiction it is sufficient to show that M' is a solution to L.

To show that all $\forall$-constraints are satisfied it is sufficient to observe that if there are points p', q' in M' with $p' \circ_d q'$ for any $\circ_d \in \mathcal{D}$ then there are points p and q in M such that $p.l = p'.l$, $q.l = q'.l$ and $p \circ_d q$. This is clear for all pairs $p'q'$ of points above or on s as M and M' are identical here. It is also true for all pairs below r as the points in this area were moved in a way that preserved the relative positions. Let us therefore assume that p' is below r and q' is on or above s. If p' is in $A(r)$ then the statement holds as p' was moved to the same vertical line which contained the corresponding point from $A(s)$ of M. Thus, there is a point $p \in A(r)$ with the desired relative position to q'. If $p' \notin A(r)$ and $\circ_d \in \{\nwarrow, \nearrow\}$ then the statement holds as p' was moved to a vertical stripe that has the same available upper witnesses in both directions as the stripe of q' had in M. It should be stressed here that the final ϵ-shift does not introduce new relationships between nodes in the same vertical stripe as for points that are not available witness points there are always available witness points in eastern *and* western direction. Finally, there can be no points $p' \notin A(r)$ and q' above s with $p' \uparrow q'$ by the final shift in the construction.

To show that all $\exists$-constraints are satisfied in M', we consider the witness function w of M. We say that a point p from M below r has a *remote witness with respect to a constraint c* if $w(p, c)$ is not below r, otherwise $w(p, c)$ is a *local witness*. Let p' be a point from M' below r, p its original point in M and $c \in C_\exists$. If $q = w(p, c)$ is a local witness then its corresponding point q' in M' is a witness for p'. If q is a remote witness we can assume without loss of generality that $q \in A(r)$. As the vertical stripe of p with respect to $A(r)$ is moved into the corresponding stripe with respect to $A(s)$, p' has a corresponding remote witness in $A(s)$.

The argument for witnesses to points above or on s is analogous.   □

Now we are ready to complete the proof of Proposition 6.

Proof. [of Proposition 6] Let $L = (\Sigma, C_\exists, C_\forall)$ be an instance of 2LPP($\mathcal{D}_-$). From Lemmas 7 and 8 we can infer that if L has a solution then it has one with at most $N =_{\text{def}} (6|\Sigma| + 1)! 2^{6|\Sigma|}$ lines each of which contains at most $M =_{\text{def}} 2|\Sigma|$ points. Thus, altogether a possible minimal solution has at most $K =_{\text{def}} MN$ points. Hence, if there is a solution there is one with points from $G =_{\text{def}} \{1, \ldots, K\} \times \{1, \ldots, N\}$. However, such a set cannot be represented in polynomial at once.

To achieve the polynomial space bound, the algorithm follows the plane sweep paradigm. It sweeps over G from south to north and guesses, for each $r \in \{1, \ldots, N\}$, a profile A_r. To this end, in round $r + 1$, the algorithm guesses a profile A_{r+1} and checks that A_r and A_{r+1} are *consistent* with the semantics of profiles and that A_{r+1} is *valid* with respect to L.

More details can be found in the full version of the paper.   □

3.4   A Lower Bound for $FO^2(\leq, \precsim)$

The following result shows that the upper bound of Theorem 1 is sharp.

Theorem 9. *Finite satisfiability for $FO^2(\leq, \precsim)$ is* EXPSPACE-*hard.*

Proof. We reduce from a tiling problem. A *tile* is a square with colored edges. A *valid tiling* of an $m \times n$ grid with tiles from a tile-set T is a mapping $t : m \times n \to T$ such that adjacent edges have the same color, i.e., for example, the northern edge of $t(i,j)$ and the southern edge of $t(i, j+1)$ are colored equally.

The following tiling problem is EXPSPACE-hard [Boa97]:

> *Problem:* EXPCORRIDORTILING
> *Input:* Tiles $T_1, \ldots, T_k$ over a set of colors $\{c_1, \ldots, c_m\}$, and
>   a string 1^n.
> *Question:* Is there a tiling of size $2^n \times l$ for $l \in \mathbb{N}$, such that the
>   south of the bottom row as well as the north of the
>   top row are colored c_1?

We reduce EXPCORRIDORTILING to $FO^2(\leq, \precsim)$. The rough idea is as follows. For a given tiling instance, we build an $FO^2(\leq, \precsim)$ formula φ such that positions of a valid tiling correspond to points in a model of φ. For encoding the column number of a tile we use unary relations $C_1, \ldots, C_n$, i.e. two tiles are in the same column iff they fulfill the same relations $C_1, \ldots, C_n$. For encoding rows of a tiling, we use equivalence classes of $\precsim$. In particular, two positions of a tiling are in the same row, if they are in the same equivalence class of $\precsim$. That is why we call equivalence classes of $\precsim$ rows, too.

The complete construction is given in the full paper.   □

3.5   Undeciable Extensions

Theorem 10. *Finite satisfiability for $FO^2(\precsim_1, \precsim_2)$ is undecidable.*

Proof. We reduce from the Post Correspondence Problem:

> *Problem:* PCP
> *Input:* $(u_1, v_1), \ldots, (u_k, v_k) \in \Sigma^* \times \Sigma^*$
> *Question:* Is there a non-empty sequence $i_1, \ldots, i_m$ such that
> $u_{i_1} \ldots u_{i_m} = v_{i_1} \ldots v_{i_m}$?

Let $(u_1, v_1), \ldots, (u_k, v_k)$ be an instance of the PCP over alphabet Σ. Firstly, we explain how an intended model, that is to say a valid sequence, shall be represented. Consider a valid sequence $(u_{i_1}, v_{i_1}), \ldots, (u_{i_m}, v_{i_m})$, i.e. a sequence such that $u := u_{i_1} \ldots u_{i_m} = v_{i_1} \ldots v_{i_m} =: v$. The intended model has one element, for every letter in the valid sequence, in particular, the size of the model is $2|u|$. The elements corresponding to the letters of a pair (u_{i_j}, v_{i_j}) are in one equivalence class E_{i_j} of $\precsim_1$. The equivalence classes of $\precsim_1$ are ordered as the pairs in the valid sequence, i.e. if $x \in E_{i_j}$, $y \in E_{i_k}$ and $j < k$ then $x \precsim_1 y$. All equivalence classes of $\precsim_2$ are of size 2 and contain exactly one element representing a letter

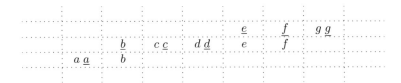

Fig. 3. How the valid sequences $u := ab|cdef|g$ and $v := a|bcd|efg$ are represented in a model for the $FO^2(\precsim_1, \precsim_2)$-formula φ. Rows represent equivalence classes of $\precsim_1$ and columns represent equivalence classes of $\precsim_2$. Letters from v are underlined.

of the u-sequence and its corresponding element for the v-sequence (and they should carry the same symbol). The equivalence classes of $\precsim_2$ are ordered as the sequences u and v. Figure 3 illustrates the construction for a simple example. The details of the proof can be found in the full version. □

Remark 11. In the above proof two elements p_1, p_2 can be equivalent with respect to both, $\precsim_1$ and $\precsim_2$. The proof can easily be extended for cases where no two points can be in the same equivalence class of both total preorders, for example in subsets of $\mathbb{Z} \times \mathbb{Z}$ with total preorders induced by the usual linear orders on x- and y-axis. Note, that in the above proof at most two elements can be in the same equivalence class of $\precsim_1$ and $\precsim_2$, and that one of them is labeled with U and the other one with V. An extended model can combine two such elements by allowing elements to carry both U and V labels at once. Then it has to be ensured that positions carrying both types of symbols are alone in their $\precsim_2$ equivalence class.

As the following result shows two linear orders and one total preorder yield undecidability as well..

Theorem 12. *Finite satisfiability for $FO^2(\leq_1, \leq_2, \precsim)$ is undecidable.*

4   Applications

In this section we outline how our result interacts with other well-known logics. We start with an informal discussion.

Data words extend conventional words by assigning data values to every position. Logics on data words then allow to use the usual relations for words as well as relations for the data values. We consider sets of data values with an order. It is known, that allowing the successor and order relations on positions of the word, as well as the order relation on data values, leads to an undecidable finite satisfiability problem. We prove that the finite satisfiability problem becomes decidable, when only the order relation on positions and order relation on data values are allowed.

Compass logic is a two-dimensional temporal logic, whose operators allow for moving north, south, east and west along a grid [Ven90]. Satisfiability for compass logic is known to be undecidable [MR97]. We extend compass logic in two directions. Upto now, only complete grids have been considered as underlying structure. We consider also partial grids as underlying structures, i.e. grids where not all crossings need to exist. Furthermore, we extend the model with the operators northeast, northwest, southeast and southwest. With these extensions, compass logic becomes decidable when only the operators northwest, northeast, southwest, southeast, west and east are used.

Interval temporal logic is a logic that can reason about intervals of time using operators as for example 'after', 'during', 'begins' etc. Expressions such as 'Immediately after we finnished writing the paper, we will go to the beach' can be captured. Therefore propositions, as for example "writing the paper" or "go to the beach", are assigned to time intervals. In conventional interval temporal logic, all intervals are part of a structure, i.e. reasoning always considers all intervals. We consider structures that are subsets of the set of all intervals and prove that satisfiability for reasoning with the operators 'ends', 'later' and 'during' as well as their duals, is decidable.

In both cases, compass logic and interval temporal logic, we show that the problems with more liberal semantics are at most as hard as the original problem.

4.1   Data Words

A *data word* is a finite sequence, in which every element (position) is labeled by a symbol from an alphabet Σ and a "data value" from some possibly infinite domain. For simplicity, we can assume that the domain consists of the set $\mathbb{N}$ of natural numbers. By $\mathrm{FO}^2(\Sigma, \leq, \preceq)$ we denote two-variable first-order logic with the binary relation symbols $\leq$, $\preceq$ and $a(x)$, for every $a \in \Sigma$. Data words can be seen as models for this logic. $a(x)$ is interpreted as 'there is an a at position x', $x < y$ is interpreted as 'x occurs before y' and $x \preceq y$ is interpreted as 'the data value of x is at most the data value of y'. We note that the same data value can appear more than once, whereas positions in the word are unique. We note further that data words can also be viewed as a set of points in the two-dimensional plane that are labeled with letters from Σ. Then the order on positions becomes a linear order on the x-axis and the order on the data values becomes a total preorder on the y-axis. Thus, the only difference between $FO^2(\leq, \preceq)$ and $\mathrm{FO}^2(\Sigma, \leq, \preceq)$ is, that in the latter the unary relations are always required to be a partition of the universe.

Given this connection, the following theorem follows readily from Theorem 1.

Theorem 13. *Finite satisfiability for* $\mathrm{FO}^2(\Sigma, \leq, \preceq)$ *is in* EXPSPACE.

However, the lower bound does not follow from Theorem 9 as the translation from $FO^2(\leq, \preceq)$ to $\mathrm{FO}^2(\Sigma, \leq, \preceq)$ might require an exponential size alphabet Σ. Thus, there remains a gap between this result and the NEXPTIME lower bound from [BMS⁺06].

Open question 1. *What is the exact complexity of finite satisfiability for* $\mathrm{FO}^2(\Sigma, \leq, \preceq)$?

4.2   Compass Logic

Due to lack of space we only state the main results on compass logic. The precise definitions and proofs can be found in the full paper.

Usually, compass logics is interpreted over grids $\langle \mathbb{D}_1 \times \mathbb{D}_2, \leq_1, \leq_2 \rangle$ that are the product of two linear orders $\langle \mathbb{D}_1, \leq_1 \rangle$ and $\langle \mathbb{D}_2, \leq_2 \rangle$. In this paper, we also consider *partial grids*, that is, subsets of grids. We show the following results.

Proposition 14. *Let $\mathcal{O}$ be a set of directional operators. If finite satisfiability of $CL(\mathcal{O})$ is decidable on labeled grids, then it is decidable on labeled partial grids as well.*

Open question 2. *Is there a set $\mathcal{O}$ of operators, such that $CL(\mathcal{O})$ on partial grids is decidable, but $CL(\mathcal{O})$ on grids is undecidable?*

Theorem 15. *Finite satisfiability for $CL(\langle \rightarrow \rangle, \langle \leftarrow \rangle, \langle \nearrow \rangle, \langle \searrow \rangle, \langle \swarrow \rangle, \langle \nwarrow \rangle)$ over partial grids is in* EXPSPACE.

4.3   Interval Temporal Logic

Similarly, as for compass logic, we consider interval logics over *partial interval structures*, that is subsets of the set of intervals over some linearly ordered set $\langle \mathbb{D}, \leq \rangle$. Detailed definitions and proofs are given in the full paper. We prove the following results.

Proposition 16. *Let $\mathcal{O}$ be a set of interval operators. If $HS(\mathcal{O})$ is decidable over interval models, then $HS(\mathcal{O})$ is decidable over partial interval models as well.*

Open question 3. *Is there a set $\mathcal{O}$ of operators, such that $HS(\mathcal{O})$ on partial interval models is decidable, but $HS(\mathcal{O})$ on interval models is undecidable?*

Theorem 17. *Finite satisfiability for $HS(\langle E \rangle, \langle \bar{E} \rangle, \langle L \rangle, \langle \bar{L} \rangle, \langle D \rangle, \langle \bar{D} \rangle)$ over partial grid structures is in* EXPSPACE.

5   Conclusion

The context of our results was already discussed in the introduction and some open questions were stated in the body of the text. We mention some further open questions and possible lines of research.

- In the context of verification it would be interesting to generalize our results from data words to data ω-words
- There is still a gap between the "eight orders" undecidability result of [Ott01] and the decidability for FO^2 with two linear orders in this paper.
- We believe that partial models for compass and interval logic deserve some further investigations.

Acknowledgements. We thank Jan van den Bussche for fruitful discussions and Amaldev Manuel for sharing his results with us.

References

[BMS⁺06] Bojanczyk, M., Muscholl, A., Schwentick, T., Segoufin, L., David, C.: Two-variable logic on words with data. In: LICS, pp. 7–16 (2006)

[Boa97] Van Emde Boas, P.: The convenience of tilings. In: Complexity, Logic, and Recursion Theory, pp. 331–363. Marcel Dekker Inc., New York (1997)

[CH01] Cohn, A.G., Hazarika, S.M.: Qualitative spatial representation and reasoning: An overview. Fundam. Inform. 46(1-2), 1–29 (2001)

[DL09] Demri, S., Lazic, R.: Ltl with the freeze quantifier and register automata. ACM Trans. Comput. Log. 10(3), 16:1–16:30 (2009)

[FS09] Figueira, D., Segoufin, L.: Future-looking logics on data words and trees. In: Královič, R., Niwiński, D. (eds.) MFCS 2009. LNCS, vol. 5734, pp. 331–343. Springer, Heidelberg (2009)

[GKV97] Grädel, E., Kolaitis, P.G., Vardi, M.Y.: On the decision problem for two-variable first-order logic. Bulletin of Symbolic Logic 3(1), 53–69 (1997)

[GO99] Grädel, E., Otto, M.: On logics with two variables. Theor. Comput. Sci. 224(1-2), 73–113 (1999)

[KO05] Kieronski, E., Otto, M.: Small substructures and decidability issues for first-order logic with two variables. In: LICS, pp. 448–457 (2005)

[KT09] Kieronski, E., Tendera, L.: On finite satisfiability of two-variable first-order logic with equivalence relations. In: LICS, pp. 123–132 (2009)

[Man10] Manuel, A.: Personal communication (2010)

[Mor75] Mortimer, M.: On languages with two variables. Zeitschr. f. math. Logik u. Grundlagen d. Math. 21, 135–140 (1975)

[MR97] Marx, M., Reynolds, M.: Undecidability of compass logic. Journal of Logic and Computation 9, 897–941 (1997)

[Ott01] Otto, M.: Two variable first-order logic over ordered domains. J. Symb. Log. 66(2), 685–702 (2001)

[Seg06] Segoufin, L.: Automata and logics for words and trees over an infinite alphabet. In: Ésik, Z. (ed.) CSL 2006. LNCS, vol. 4207, pp. 41–57. Springer, Heidelberg (2006)

[Ven90] Venema, Y.: Expressiveness and completeness of an interval tense logic. Notre Dame Journal of Formal Logic 31(4), 529–547 (1990)

Signature Extensions Preserve Termination
An Alternative Proof via Dependency Pairs

Christian Sternagel* and René Thiemann

University of Innsbruck
{christian.sternagel,rene.thiemann}@uibk.ac.at

Abstract. We give the first mechanized proof of the fact that for showing termination of a term rewrite system, we may restrict to well-formed
terms using just the function symbols actually occurring in the rules
of the system. Or equivalently, termination of a term rewrite system is
preserved under signature extensions. We did not directly formalize the
existing proofs for this well-known result, but developed a new and more
elegant proof by reusing facts about dependency pairs.

We also investigate signature extensions for termination proofs that
use dependency pairs. Here, we were able to develop counterexamples
which demonstrate that signature extensions are unsound in general. We
further give two conditions where signature extensions are still possible.

1 Introduction

Our main objective is to formally show that the termination behavior of (first-
order) term rewrite systems (TRSs) [2] does not change under signature extensions. This is an important part of a bigger development inside IsaFoR (an
Isabelle **Fo**rmalization of **R**ewriting) which is used to generate CeTA (a tool
for **Ce**rtified **T**ermination **A**nalysis) [10].[1] All our results have been formalized
and machine-checked in the interactive proof assistant Isabelle/HOL [6]. In the
following, whenever we speak about *formalizing* something, we mean a machine-
checked formalization using Isabelle/HOL.

In the literature, termination of $\mathcal{R}$ (denoted by $\mathsf{SN}(\mathcal{R})$), is usually only defined
for terms that do exclusively incorporate function symbols from the *signature*
$\mathcal{F}$ of $\mathcal{R}$. Often, it is implicitly assumed that this is equivalent to termination
for terms over arbitrary extensions $\mathcal{F}' \supseteq \mathcal{F}$. This is legitimate, since it has
been shown that termination is modular under certain conditions (see [5,7] for
details) and signature extensions satisfy these conditions. A property P is called
modular, whenever $P\ \mathcal{R}$ and $P\ \mathcal{S}$, for TRSs $\mathcal{R}$ and $\mathcal{S}$ over disjoint signatures $\mathcal{F}$
and $\mathcal{G}$, implies $P\ (\mathcal{R} \cup \mathcal{S})$. (Note that $P\ x$ is Isabelle/HOL's way of writing a
function or predicate P applied to an argument x.) Now, to use modularity of
termination to achieve $\mathsf{SN}(\mathcal{R})$ over the signature $\mathcal{F}' \supseteq \mathcal{F}$, we choose $\mathcal{S} = \varnothing$ and
$\mathcal{G} = \mathcal{F}' - \mathcal{F}$. Then, the above mentioned conditions are trivially satisfied and we

---

* This research is supported by FWF (Austrian Science Fund) project P18763.
[1] http://cl-informatik.uibk.ac.at/software/ceta

A. Dawar and H. Veith (Eds.): CSL 2010, LNCS 6247, pp. 514–528, 2010.
© Springer-Verlag Berlin Heidelberg 2010

obtain $\mathsf{SN}(\mathcal{R}) \Longrightarrow \mathsf{SN}(\mathcal{R} \cup \mathcal{S})$, where the latter system has the same rules as $\mathcal{R}$, but the signature $\mathcal{F}'$.

In this way, the two aforementioned proofs (which both use rather similar proof techniques), can be used to obtain termination preservation under signature extensions. However, the first proof [5] is quite long and complicated even on paper (10 pages, neglecting preliminaries). Concerning the second proof [7]—although short on paper—there are two reasons for not going that way:

1. This proof would require to formalize concepts that are currently not available in our library but are assumed as preliminaries in the paper proof (which is the only reason that the proof is short). This includes, e.g., multi-hole contexts, and functions like *rank*, *top*, etc. Furthermore, some of those concepts seem bulky to formalize, e.g., multi-hole contexts would require that a context having n holes is always applied to exactly n terms. This cannot be guaranteed on the type level without having dependent types and would lead to side-conditions that had to be added to all proofs using multi-hole contexts.
2. We do already have a formalization of many term rewriting related concepts. Thus, it seems only natural to build on top of those available results.

Hence, we take a different road (that may seem as a detour in the beginning). We use $\mathcal{F}(\mathcal{R})$ to denote the signature just containing function symbols that do actually occur in some rule of $\mathcal{R}$. By $\Rrightarrow_{\mathcal{R}}$ we denote the rewrite relation induced by $\mathcal{R}$ just using terms over $\mathcal{F}(\mathcal{R})$ and by $\rightarrow_{\mathcal{R}}$ the same relation but for terms over arbitrary extensions of $\mathcal{F}(\mathcal{R})$ (i.e., $\Rrightarrow_{\mathcal{R}}$ is a restriction of $\rightarrow_{\mathcal{R}}$). Hence, our first main result can be written as

Theorem 1. $\mathsf{SN}(\Rrightarrow_{\mathcal{R}}) \longleftrightarrow \mathsf{SN}(\rightarrow_{\mathcal{R}})$

In the proof, we concentrate on the direction from left to right, since the converse trivially holds. Before we give our general proof idea, we want to show why "the direct approach" is difficult. By "direct" we mean:

> Assume that there is an infinite sequence in $\rightarrow_{\mathcal{R}}$ and construct an infinite sequence in $\Rrightarrow_{\mathcal{R}}$ out of it.

For this purpose we would have to provide a function f such that $f\,s \Rrightarrow_{\mathcal{R}} f\,t$ is implied by $s \rightarrow_{\mathcal{R}} t$ for arbitrary terms s and t. This requires that f somehow removes all function symbols that are not in $\mathcal{F}(\mathcal{R})$ from its argument but still preserves any redexes (i.e., subterms where rules are applicable). For example the simple idea to *clean* terms by replacing all subterms $f(\ldots)$ where $f \notin \mathcal{F}(\mathcal{R})$ by the same variable, does not work. The reason is that a given infinite $\rightarrow_{\mathcal{R}}$-derivation might take place strictly below a symbol $f \notin \mathcal{F}(\mathcal{R})$ and then, after turning $f(\ldots)$ into a variable, those reductions can no longer be simulated. To cut a long story short, we stopped at some point to investigate this direction further, since all our approaches became awfully complicated (especially for mechanizing the proof).

Our salvation appeared in the form of *dependency pairs* (DPs). By redirecting the course of our proof into the DP setting [1] and back again, we were able to give a short and (in our opinion) elegant proof of Theorem 1, using the simple technique of cleaning. The reason is that by using DPs we obtain a derivation which contains infinitely many reductions at the root position. And all these root reductions are still possible after cleaning. Note that this also shows that signature extensions are sound for termination problems in the DP setting (Lemma 8)—our second main result.

However, after trying to extend our proof to the DP setting with *minimal chains*, we discovered a counterexample demonstrating that signature extensions are unsound for non-left-linear TRSs. A small modification of this counterexample also shows that the technique of root-labeling [8] in the DP setting with minimal chains—which relies on signature extensions—is also only sound for left-linear TRSs. This refutes the corresponding result in [8] which does not demand left-linearity. (As the modularity results of [5,7] do not consider minimal chains, these results are not affected by our counterexample.)

In total, in this paper we show that signature extensions are possible for termination of TRSs and that they can be used in the DP setting for left-linear TRSs or for non-minimal chains. We also show that the soundness proofs of root-labeling can be repaired by additionally demanding left-linearity.

The structure of our discourse is as follows: In Section 2 we recall some necessary definitions of term rewriting (as used in our formalization). Afterwards, in Section 3, we give some results on DPs. Two of our main results are given in Section 4, where we also formally prove completeness of DPs. Then, in Section 5 we show some applications—including root-labeling—and limitations of our results. Here, we also discuss the problem of signature extensions in combination with minimal chains and show that there is no problem in the left-linear case. We finally conclude in Section 6.

Since all facts we are using have been machine-checked, we do not give any proofs for results from Sections 2 and 3 and refer the interested reader to the IsaFoR sources (freely available from its website). Our formalization of Theorem 1 can be found under the name SN_wfrstep_SN_rstep_conv in the theory DpFramework. Also in Section 4 we try to skip technical details and give a high-level overview of our proofs.

2   Preliminaries

In IsaFoR we are concerned with first-order *terms* defined by the data type:

$$\textbf{datatype } (\alpha,\ \beta)\ term\ =\ Var\ \beta\ |\ Fun\ \alpha\ ((\alpha,\ \beta)\ term\ list)$$

Hence, a term is either a *variable*, or a *function symbol* applied to a list of argument terms. Note that this definition does not incorporate any well-formedness conditions. In particular, there is no signature that terms are restricted to. We identify a function symbol by its representation together with its arity. Hence, the function symbol f in the term $Fun\ f\ []$ is different from the function symbol f in the term $Fun\ f\ [Var\ x]$ (the former has arity 0 and the latter arity 1). To increase readability we write terms like the previous two as f (a constant without arguments) and $f(x)$, respectively. A *(rewrite) rule* is a pair of terms and a *TRS* is a set of rules. A TRS is *well-formed* iff all left-hand sides of rules are non-variable terms and for each rule every variable occurring in the right-hand side also occurs in the left-hand side. We write wf_trs $\mathcal{R}$ to indicate that the TRS $\mathcal{R}$ is well-formed.

Example 2. The TRS { add(0, y) $\to$ y, add(s(x), y) $\to$ s(add(x, y)) }, encoding addition on Peano numbers, is well-formed.

The *rewrite relation induced by a TRS* $\mathcal{R}$ is obtained by closing $\mathcal{R}$ under substitutions and contexts, i.e., $\to_{\mathcal{R}}$ is defined inductively by the rules:

$$\frac{(l,\ r) \in \mathcal{R}}{l \to_{\mathcal{R}} r} \qquad \frac{s \to_{\mathcal{R}} t}{s\sigma \to_{\mathcal{R}} t\sigma} \qquad \frac{s \to_{\mathcal{R}} t}{C[s] \to_{\mathcal{R}} C[t]}$$

Here, $t\sigma$ denotes the application of a substitution σ to a term t and $C[t]$ denotes substituting the hole in the context C by the term t. Whenever $s \to_{\mathcal{R}} t$, we say that s rewrites (in one step) to t.

A TRS is *terminating/strongly normalizing* iff the rewrite relation $\to_{\mathcal{R}}$ induced by $\mathcal{R}$ is well-founded—denoted by $\mathsf{SN}(\to_{\mathcal{R}})$. (We sometimes write $\mathsf{SN}(\mathcal{R})$ instead of $\mathsf{SN}(\to_{\mathcal{R}})$ to stress that termination is a property depending merely on $\mathcal{R}$.) Termination of a specific term is written as $\mathsf{SN}_{\mathcal{R}}(t)$, i.e., there is no infinite $\to_{\mathcal{R}}$-derivation starting from t.

Using the definition of $\to_{\mathcal{R}}$, termination is formalized as $\mathsf{SN}(\to_{\mathcal{R}}) \equiv \nexists \mathbf{t}.\ \forall i.$ $\mathbf{t}_i \to_{\mathcal{R}} \mathbf{t}_{i+1}$. Here, we use functions from natural numbers to some type τ, to encode infinite sequences over elements of type τ, which are written by $\mathbf{t}$ in contrast to terms t. We use subscripts to indicate positions in such infinite sequences, i.e., we write $\mathbf{t}_i$ to denote the i-th element in the infinite sequence $\mathbf{t}$.

Remember that by $\mathcal{F}(\mathcal{R})$ we denote the signature of function symbols actually occurring in some rule of $\mathcal{R}$. Using the function

$$\begin{aligned} \mathcal{F}(x) &= \varnothing, \\ \mathcal{F}(f(\vec{ts})) &= \{(f, |\vec{ts}|)\} \cup \bigcup \{\mathcal{F}(t) \mid t \in \vec{ts}\}. \end{aligned}$$

$\mathcal{F}(\mathcal{R})$ is obtained by extending $\mathcal{F}(\cdot)$ to TRSs in the obvious way.

Example 3. The signature of the TRS from Example 2 is $\{(\mathsf{add}, 2), (\mathsf{s}, 1), (0, 0)\}$.

3   Dependency Pairs

To get hold of the *(recursive) function calls* in a TRS, the so called *dependency pairs* are used [1,3].

Definition 4. *The DPs of a TRS $\mathcal{R}$ are defined by*

$$\mathsf{DP}(\mathcal{R}) = \{(l^\sharp, f^\sharp(\vec{ts})) \mid \exists r.\ (l,\ r) \in \mathcal{R} \land f \in \mathcal{D}(\mathcal{R}) \land r \trianglerighteq f(\vec{ts}) \land l \ntrianglerighteq f(\vec{ts})\}$$

where $(\triangleright) \trianglerighteq$ denotes the (proper) subterm relation on terms and $\mathcal{D}(\mathcal{R})$ is the set of defined function symbols in $\mathcal{R}$.[2] By $\cdot^\sharp$ we denote the operation of marking the root symbol of a term with the special marker $\sharp$. In examples we use capitalization and hence write F instead of $f^\sharp$.

---

[2] A function symbol is defined in a TRS, if it occurs as the root of a left-hand side.

Example 5. Since the TRS of Example 2 contains just one "recursive call," we get the single DP $\mathsf{ADD}(\mathsf{s}(x), y) \to \mathsf{ADD}(x, y)$.

Note how DPs get rid of context information. This is exactly what makes them so useful in our proof.

Having DPs, we can use an alternative characterization of nontermination using DP problems and chains. A *DP problem* $(\mathcal{P}, \mathcal{R})$ just consists of two TRSs $\mathcal{P}$ and $\mathcal{R}$. Then a $(\mathcal{P}, \mathcal{R})$-*chain* is an infinite sequence of the following shape:

$$\forall\, i.\ (\mathbf{s}_i, \mathbf{t}_i) \in \mathcal{P} \wedge \mathbf{t}_i \sigma_i \to_\mathcal{R}^* \mathbf{s}_{i+1} \sigma_{i+1}.$$

We use the abbreviation ichain $(\mathcal{P},\ \mathcal{R})\ \mathbf{s}\ \mathbf{t}\ \sigma$ for such a sequence. The soundness result of DPs then states that a (well-formed) TRS $\mathcal{R}$ is terminating if there is no infinite $(\mathsf{DP}(\mathcal{R}), \mathcal{R})$-chain where the formalization was described in [10].

Lemma 6. $\mathsf{wf\_trs}\ \mathcal{R} \implies \neg\ \mathsf{SN}(\to_\mathcal{R}) \implies \exists\, \mathbf{s}\ \mathbf{t}\ \sigma.\ \mathsf{ichain}\ (\mathsf{DP}(\mathcal{R}),\ \mathcal{R})\ \mathbf{s}\ \mathbf{t}\ \sigma$ □

Sometimes, we are interested in *minimal* $(\mathcal{P}, \mathcal{R})$-chains. The only difference between $\mathsf{min\_ichain}\ (\mathcal{P},\ \mathcal{R})\ \mathbf{s}\ \mathbf{t}\ \sigma$ and ichain $(\mathcal{P},\ \mathcal{R})\ \mathbf{s}\ \mathbf{t}\ \sigma$, is the additional requirement in minimal chains that $\mathsf{SN}_\mathcal{R}(\mathbf{t}_i \sigma_i)$ for all i.

4 Main Results

Since our term data type does not take care of building only terms corresponding to a specific signature, by default any rewrite relation $\to_\mathcal{R}$ in our formalization is defined over terms containing arbitrary function symbols. Our first goal is to show that once we have shown termination for terms using only function symbols from $\mathcal{F}(\mathcal{R})$, this implies that $\to_\mathcal{R}$ does terminate for arbitrary terms. Before doing that, we need means to identify well-formed terms. To this end we use the inductively defined set $\mathcal{T}(\mathcal{F})$, containing all terms that are well-formed with respect to the signature $\mathcal{F}$.

Definition 7 (Well-Formed Terms)

$$\frac{}{x \in \mathcal{T}(\mathcal{F})} \qquad \frac{(f, |\vec{ts}|) \in \mathcal{F} \quad \forall\, t \in \vec{ts}.\ t \in \mathcal{T}(\mathcal{F})}{f(\vec{ts}) \in \mathcal{T}(\mathcal{F})}$$

Using this definition we can define the well-formed rewrite relation induced by a TRS $\mathcal{R}$:

$$\Rightarrow_\mathcal{R} \equiv \{(s, t) \mid s \to_\mathcal{R} t \wedge s \in \mathcal{T}(\mathcal{F}(\mathcal{R})) \wedge t \in \mathcal{T}(\mathcal{F}(\mathcal{R}))\}.$$

Further, let $\mathcal{C}(\mathcal{F})$ denote the set of well-formed contexts with respect to the signature $\mathcal{F}$. What we want to show is $\mathsf{SN}(\Rightarrow_\mathcal{R}) \implies \mathsf{SN}(\to_\mathcal{R})$. For the proof we need a way to remove unwanted function symbols from terms. This is the purpose of the following *cleaning* function:

$$\begin{aligned} [\![y]\!]_\mathcal{F} &= y \\ [\![f(\vec{ts})]\!]_\mathcal{F} &= \textit{if}\ (f, |\vec{ts}|) \in \mathcal{F}\ \textit{then}\ f(\textit{map}\ [\![\cdot]\!]_\mathcal{F}\ \vec{ts})\ \textit{else}\ z \end{aligned}$$

where z denotes an arbitrary but fixed variable. Intuitively, every subterm of a term whose root is not in the given signature, is replaced by z. Having this, the proof of $\mathsf{SN}(\Rrightarrow_\mathcal{R}) \implies \mathsf{SN}(\to_\mathcal{R})$ (actually we prove its contrapositive) is done in three stages:

1. First, we assume $\neg\,\mathsf{SN}(\to_\mathcal{R})$. Then by the soundness of DPs (Lemma 6) we obtain an infinite $(\mathsf{DP}(\mathcal{R}),\ \mathcal{R})$-chain.
2. Next, we show that every infinite chain can be transformed into an infinite *clean* chain.
3. And finally, we show completeness of the DP-transformation for well-formed terms, i.e., that an infinite clean $(\mathsf{DP}(\mathcal{R}),\ \mathcal{R})$-chain can be transformed into an infinite derivation w.r.t. $\Rrightarrow_\mathcal{R}$. Hence, $\neg\,\mathsf{SN}(\Rrightarrow_\mathcal{R})$, concluding the proof.

In total we get $\mathsf{wf\_trs}\ \mathcal{R} \implies \mathsf{SN}(\Rrightarrow_\mathcal{R}) \implies \mathsf{SN}(\to_\mathcal{R})$ and since every non-well-formed TRS is nonterminating, we finally have a proof of Theorem 1. Note that the second step also shows the second main result: signature extensions are valid when performing termination proofs using DPs (without minimality).

It remains to prove the following two lemmas:

Lemma 8 (Signature Restrictions for Chains)
$$\mathcal{F}(\mathcal{P},\ \mathcal{R}) \subseteq \mathcal{F} \implies \text{ichain } (\mathcal{P},\ \mathcal{R})\ \mathbf{s\ t}\ \sigma \implies \text{ichain } (\mathcal{P},\ \mathcal{R})\ \mathbf{s\ t}\ [\![\sigma]\!]_\mathcal{F}$$

Lemma 9 (Completeness of DPs for $\Rrightarrow_\mathcal{R}$)
$$\text{ichain } (\mathsf{DP}(\mathcal{R}),\ \mathcal{R})\ \mathbf{s\ t}\ [\![\sigma]\!]_{\sharp(\mathcal{R})} \implies \neg\,\mathsf{SN}(\Rrightarrow_\mathcal{R})$$

where we use the abbreviations $\mathcal{F}(\mathcal{P},\ \mathcal{R}) \equiv \mathcal{F}(\mathcal{P}) \cup \mathcal{F}(\mathcal{R})$ and $\sharp(\mathcal{R}) \equiv \mathcal{F}(\mathcal{R}) \cup \mathcal{F}^\sharp(\mathcal{R})$ with $\mathcal{F}^\sharp(\mathcal{R}) \equiv \{(f^\sharp,\ n)\ |\ (f,\ n) \in \mathcal{F}(\mathcal{R})\}$, and the cleaning function is extended to sequences of substitutions in the obvious way.

Note that by applying first Lemma 8 and then Lemma 9, we also obtain the classical completeness result of DPs.

Lemma 10 (Completeness of DPs). ichain $(\mathsf{DP}(\mathcal{R}),\ \mathcal{R})\ \mathbf{s\ t}\ \sigma \implies \neg\,\mathsf{SN}(\to_\mathcal{R})$

Proof. Obviously, we have $\mathcal{F}(\mathsf{DP}(\mathcal{R}),\ \mathcal{R}) \subseteq \sharp(\mathcal{R})$. Together with the assumption ichain $(\mathsf{DP}(\mathcal{R}),\ \mathcal{R})\ \mathbf{s\ t}\ \sigma$, this yields ichain $(\mathsf{DP}(\mathcal{R}),\ \mathcal{R})\ \mathbf{s\ t}\ [\![\sigma]\!]_{\sharp(\mathcal{R})}$, using Lemma 8. Then, from Lemma 9, we obtain $\neg\,\mathsf{SN}(\Rrightarrow_\mathcal{R})$ and thus $\neg\,\mathsf{SN}(\to_\mathcal{R})$. □

Proof (of Lemma 8). From the assumptions of Lemma 8 we obtain

$$\forall i.\,\mathbf{s}_i \in \mathcal{T}(\mathcal{F}) \wedge \mathbf{t}_i \in \mathcal{T}(\mathcal{F}), \tag{1}$$

$$\forall i.\,\mathbf{t}_i\boldsymbol{\sigma}_i \to_\mathcal{R}^* \mathbf{s}_{i+1}\boldsymbol{\sigma}_{i+1}, \tag{2}$$

$$\forall i.\,(\mathbf{s}_i, \mathbf{t}_i) \in \mathcal{P}. \tag{3}$$

Further note that whenever there is an $\mathcal{R}$-step from s to t, then either this step is also possible in the cleaned versions of s and t, or the cleaned versions are equal, i.e.,

$$s \to_\mathcal{R} t \implies [\![s]\!]_{\mathcal{F}(\mathcal{R})} \to_\mathcal{R}^= [\![t]\!]_{\mathcal{F}(\mathcal{R})}.$$

From this and (2) we may conclude

$$\forall i.\ [\![\mathbf{t}_i\boldsymbol{\sigma}_i]\!]_{\mathcal{F}} \to_{\mathcal{R}}^* [\![\mathbf{s}_{i+1}\boldsymbol{\sigma}_{i+1}]\!]_{\mathcal{F}}$$

by induction over the length of the rewrite sequence (remember that $\mathcal{F}(\mathcal{R}) \subseteq \mathcal{F}$). Using (1) we may push the applications of the clean function inside, resulting in

$$\forall i.\ [\![\mathbf{t}_i]\!]_{\mathcal{F}}[\![\boldsymbol{\sigma}_i]\!]_{\mathcal{F}} \to_{\mathcal{R}}^* [\![\mathbf{s}_{i+1}]\!]_{\mathcal{F}}[\![\boldsymbol{\sigma}_{i+1}]\!]_{\mathcal{F}}.$$

Together with (3) we obtain the desired clean infinite chain as (1) shows $[\![\mathbf{s}_i]\!]_{\mathcal{F}} = \mathbf{s}_i$ and $[\![\mathbf{t}_i]\!]_{\mathcal{F}} = \mathbf{t}_i$ for all i.   □

Proof (of Lemma 9). Again, we show the lemma in its contrapositive form. Thus, we assume $\mathsf{SN}(\Rightarrow_{\mathcal{R}})$. Now, let $\mathcal{F}$ denote the signature of $\mathcal{R}$ and $\mathsf{u}(\cdot)$ the operation of 'unsharping,' i.e., removing ♯s from terms:

$$\mathsf{u}(t) = \begin{cases} f(\textit{map } \mathsf{u}(\cdot)\ \vec{ts}) & \text{if } t = f^{\sharp}(\vec{ts}) \text{ or } t = f(\vec{ts}), \text{ and} \\ t & \text{otherwise.} \end{cases}$$

The extension of u to substitutions is defined as $\mathsf{u}(\sigma)(x) = \mathsf{u}(\sigma(x))$. For the sake of a contradiction, assume that there is an infinite $(\mathsf{DP}(\mathcal{R}), \mathcal{R})$-chain over $\mathbf{s}$, $\mathbf{t}$, and $[\![\boldsymbol{\sigma}]\!]_{\sharp(\mathcal{R})}$. Since cleaning does not affect $\mathbf{s}$ and $\mathbf{t}$, this implies an infinite $(\mathsf{DP}(\mathcal{R}), \mathcal{R})$-chain over $[\![\mathbf{s}]\!]_{\sharp(\mathcal{R})}$, $[\![\mathbf{t}]\!]_{\sharp(\mathcal{R})}$, and $[\![\boldsymbol{\sigma}]\!]_{\sharp(\mathcal{R})}$, i.e.,

$$\forall i.\ ([\![\mathbf{s}_i]\!]_{\sharp(\mathcal{R})}, [\![\mathbf{t}_i]\!]_{\sharp(\mathcal{R})}) \in \mathsf{DP}(\mathcal{R}) \tag{4}$$

$$\forall i.\ [\![\mathbf{t}_i]\!]_{\sharp(\mathcal{R})}[\![\boldsymbol{\sigma}_i]\!]_{\sharp(\mathcal{R})} \to_{\mathcal{R}}^* [\![\mathbf{s}_{i+1}]\!]_{\sharp(\mathcal{R})}[\![\boldsymbol{\sigma}_{i+1}]\!]_{\sharp(\mathcal{R})} \tag{5}$$

Then from (4) we obtain

$$\forall i.\ \exists C.\ C \in \mathcal{C}(\mathcal{F}) \wedge [\![\mathsf{u}(\mathbf{s}_i)]\!]_{\mathcal{F}} \to_{\mathcal{R}} C[[\![\mathsf{u}(\mathbf{t}_i)]\!]_{\mathcal{F}}]$$

by construction of $\mathsf{DP}(\mathcal{R})$. Using the *Axiom of Choice* we hence obtain a sequence of contexts $\mathbf{C}$, such that $\mathbf{C}_i$ is the context employed in the i-th step of (4), i.e.,

$$\forall i.\ \mathbf{C}_i \in \mathcal{C}(\mathcal{F}) \wedge [\![\mathsf{u}(\mathbf{s}_i)]\!]_{\mathcal{F}} \to_{\mathcal{R}} \mathbf{C}_i[[\![\mathsf{u}(\mathbf{t}_i)]\!]_{\mathcal{F}}] \tag{6}$$

Let $\mathbf{D}$ denote the following sequence:

$$\mathbf{D}_i = \begin{cases} \square & \text{if } i = 0, \\ \mathbf{D}_{i-1} \circ (\mathbf{C}_i[\![\mathsf{u}(\sigma_i)]\!]_{\mathcal{F}}) & \text{otherwise.} \end{cases}$$

Where $\circ$ denotes the composition of contexts, i.e., the right context replaces the hole of the left one. This function gives for the i-th DP-step in the infinite chain, all the contexts that have been lost due to using $\mathsf{DP}(\mathcal{R})$ instead of $\mathcal{R}$ and additionally applies all the necessary substitutions. For the sake of brevity we define:

$$\mathbf{s}_i' = \mathbf{D}_i[[\![\mathsf{u}(\mathbf{s}_i)]\!]_{\mathcal{F}}[\![\mathsf{u}(\sigma_i)]\!]_{\mathcal{F}}]$$
$$\mathbf{t}_i' = \mathbf{D}_{i+1}[[\![\mathsf{u}(\mathbf{t}_i)]\!]_{\mathcal{F}}[\![\mathsf{u}(\sigma_i)]\!]_{\mathcal{F}}]$$

Then by (6) we have $\mathbf{s}'_i \to_{\mathcal{R}} \mathbf{t}'_i$, since rewriting is closed under contexts and substitutions. From (5) we conclude $[\![u(\mathbf{t}_i)]\!]_{\mathcal{F}}[\![u(\boldsymbol{\sigma}_i)]\!]_{\mathcal{F}} \to^*_{\mathcal{R}} [\![u(\mathbf{s}_{i+1})]\!]_{\mathcal{F}}[\![u(\boldsymbol{\sigma}_{i+1})]\!]_{\mathcal{F}}$, since removing $\sharp$s does not destroy any redexes of $\mathcal{R}$. By wrapping this derivation in the context $\mathbf{D}_{i+1}$ we obtain $\mathbf{t}'_i \to^*_{\mathcal{R}} \mathbf{s}'_{i+1}$. Combining this with $\mathbf{s}'_i \to_{\mathcal{R}} \mathbf{t}'_i$ yields

$$\mathbf{s}'_i \to^+_{\mathcal{R}} \mathbf{s}'_{i+1}$$

From our assumption $\mathsf{SN}(\Rrightarrow_{\mathcal{R}})$ we conclude that $\mathcal{R}$ is well-formed. Moreover, it is apparent from the definitions of $[\![\cdot]\!]_{\mathcal{F}}$ and $\mathbf{D}_i$, together with (6) that all the $\mathbf{s}'_i$s are well-formed, i.e., $\mathbf{s}'_i \in \mathcal{T}(\mathcal{F})$. Together with the well-formedness of $\mathcal{R}$ one can prove that also all intermediate terms in all derivations $\mathbf{s}'_i \to^+_{\mathcal{R}} \mathbf{s}'_{i+1}$ are in $\mathcal{T}(\mathcal{F})$. Thus we have an infinite $\Rrightarrow_{\mathcal{R}}$-sequence which contradicts our assumption $\mathsf{SN}(\Rrightarrow_{\mathcal{R}})$.   □

5   Applications

In most termination tools, termination techniques are freely combined within a complex termination proof. For example, it is a standard procedure to first remove some rules from $\mathcal{R}$, resulting in $\mathcal{R}'$, and then prove $\mathsf{SN}(\mathcal{R}')$ without caring about any changes in the signature. I.e., proving termination of $\mathsf{SN}(\mathcal{R}')$ is performed as if the signature were $\mathcal{F}(\mathcal{R}')$ and not the original signature $\mathcal{F}(\mathcal{R})$. The soundness of this approach relies upon Theorem 1.

At first view, Theorem 1 might not seem important, as there are several termination techniques which do not rely upon the signature. For example, when using polynomial interpretations, it always suffices to give the interpretations for the function symbols occurring in the TRS, no matter if the signature contains other symbols. The reason is that the interpretation of any other symbol has no impact when computing the polynomials for the left-hand sides and right-hand sides of the rules. Similar situations occur for other reduction orders and other termination techniques, like semantic labeling [11].

However, we are aware of at least two termination techniques where the signature is essential.

String Reversal. If we restrict terms in rewriting to employ only unary function symbols, we are in the setting of *string rewriting*. For notational convenience we write abc instead of $a(b(c(x)))$, where the variable x is implicit. There are several termination techniques that work only/better for strings. One of them is string reversal. This technique uses the fact that a string rewrite system (SRS) $\mathcal{S}$ is terminating iff $\mathsf{rev}(\mathcal{S})$ is terminating. Here, $\mathsf{rev}(\mathcal{S})$ denotes the mapping of the function

$$\mathsf{rev}(t) = \begin{cases} \mathsf{rev}(t')a & \text{if } t = at', \\ t & \text{otherwise,} \end{cases}$$

over all left-hand sides and right-hand sides of $\mathcal{S}$. In practice, this often helps to automatically find a termination proof.

Example 11. Consider the following TRS

$$a(b(b(x))) \rightarrow a(b(a(a(a(a(a(x)))))))$$
$$f(x,y) \rightarrow x$$

which is not an SRS. One can remove the second rule by a polynomial order which maps $a(x)$ and $b(x)$ to x, and $f(x,y)$ to $x + y + 1$. Then the SRS

$$abb \rightarrow abaaaa$$

remains, where the signature still contains the binary symbol f. As string reversal is only defined for unary symbols, the presence of f forbids the application of string reversal. But after applying the signature restriction to a and b we are allowed to forget about f and apply string reversal to obtain the following SRS:

$$bba \rightarrow aaaaba$$

Note that in this reversed SRS there are no dependency pairs as ba is a proper subterm of bba. Therefore, termination is now trivially proven.

Root-Labeling. Root-labeling [8] is a special version of semantic labeling [11]. We start with a short description of semantic labeling. We interpret a TRS $\mathcal{R}$ by an $\mathcal{F}$-algebra $\mathcal{M} = (M, \{f_{\mathcal{M}}\}_{f \in \mathcal{F}})$. That is, we interpret every function symbol f of arity n, by a function $f_{\mathcal{M}} \colon M^n \rightarrow M$, over the carrier M. Then, the interpretation of a term with respect to a given variable assignment μ, is given by: $[\mu]_{\mathcal{M}}(x) = \mu(x)$ and $[\mu]_{\mathcal{M}}(f(t_1, \ldots, t_n)) = f_{\mathcal{M}}([\mu]_{\mathcal{M}}(t_1), \ldots, [\mu]_{\mathcal{M}}(t_n))$. We say that $\mathcal{M}$ is a *model* of $\mathcal{R}$ iff for all assignments μ and all rules $l \rightarrow r \in \mathcal{R}$, we have $[\mu]_{\mathcal{M}}(l) = [\mu]_{\mathcal{M}}(r)$.

Now, we can label the function symbols of $\mathcal{R}$ according to the interpretation of their arguments. For every n-ary function symbol f, we choose a set of labels $L_f \neq \varnothing$ in combination with a mapping $\pi_f \colon M^n \rightarrow L_f$. The labeling is extended to terms as follows: $\mathsf{lab}_\mu(x) = x$ and $\mathsf{lab}_\mu(f(t_1, \ldots, t_n)) = f_m(\mathsf{lab}_\mu(t_1), \ldots, \mathsf{lab}_\mu(t_n))$ with $m = \pi_f([\mu]_{\mathcal{M}}(t_1), \ldots, [\mu]_{\mathcal{M}}(t_n))$. Then, the labeled TRS $\mathcal{R}_{\mathsf{lab}}$ consists of the rules $\mathsf{lab}_\mu(l) \rightarrow \mathsf{lab}_\mu(r)$ for all $l \rightarrow r \in \mathcal{R}$ and assignments μ. Zantema [11] has shown that for every model of $\mathcal{R}$, the TRS $\mathcal{R}$ is terminating iff the TRS $\mathcal{R}_{\mathsf{lab}}$ is terminating.

The difficult part of applying semantic labeling for proving termination, is to find a proper model. This is solved in the special case of root-labeling by fixing the interpretation. Every function symbol is interpreted by itself (i.e., $f_{\mathcal{M}}(x_1, \ldots, x_n) = f$) and the labeling is fixed to tuples of function symbols (i.e., $\pi_f(x_1, \ldots, x_n) = (x_1, \ldots, x_n)$). Now, to satisfy the necessary *model condition*, we close the rules of a TRS under the so called *flat contexts* before labeling. This makes sure that for every resulting rule $l \rightarrow r$, the root symbol of l is the same as the root symbol of r and thus, $[\mu]_{\mathcal{M}}(l) = [\mu]_{\mathcal{M}}(r)$ for every assignment μ. Here, the flat contexts are determined solely by the signature. Again, Theorem 1 shows that one can reduce the possibly infinite set of flat contexts (if the signature $\mathcal{F}$ is infinite) to a finite set of flat contexts (if $\mathcal{F}(\mathcal{R})$ is finite).

Example 12. Consider the TRS $\{a(b(x)) \rightarrow b(a(a(x)))\}$. This yields the set of flat contexts $\{a(\Box), b(\Box)\}$. After closing the TRS under flat contexts we obtain the two rules $\{a(a(b(x))) \rightarrow a(b(a(a(x)))), b(a(b(x))) \rightarrow b(b(a(a(x))))\}$.[3] Now, root-labeling results in the following labeled TRS:

$$a_a(a_b(b_a(x))) \rightarrow a_b(b_a(a_a(a_a(x))))$$
$$a_a(a_b(b_b(x))) \rightarrow a_b(b_a(a_a(a_b(x))))$$
$$b_a(a_b(b_a(x))) \rightarrow b_b(b_a(a_a(a_a(x))))$$
$$b_a(a_b(b_b(x))) \rightarrow b_b(b_a(a_a(a_b(x))))$$

The advantage of root-labeling or semantic labeling is that afterwards one can distinguish different occurrences of symbols as they might have different labels. For example, the last but one symbols of the left- and right-hand sides are a_b and a_a, respectively, whereas in the original TRS these symbols were just a and could not be distinguished. That such a distinction can be helpful is demonstrated in several examples [8,11].

Note that root-labeling is also applied in the DP setting. Here, Lemma 8 can be used to show that it suffices to build the flat contexts w.r.t. the signature of the given DP problem.

However, many termination tools base their termination analysis on DPs where always minimal chains are considered. The reason to work with minimal chains is that many powerful termination techniques are only sound when regarding minimal chains [4,9].

Unfortunately, when trying to lift Lemma 8 to minimal chains, we figured out that this is impossible. It is easy to show that cleaning terms might introduce nontermination if non-left-linear rules are present. For example if a and b are not in the signature and there is a rule $f(x, x) \rightarrow f(x, x)$, then this rule cannot be applied on $f(a, b)$. However, it is applicable on the cleaned term $f(z, z)$.

Moreover, we even found a counter-example where there is an infinite minimal $(\mathcal{P}, \mathcal{R})$-chain, but no infinite minimal $(\mathcal{P}, \mathcal{R})$-chain if only terms over $\mathcal{F}(\mathcal{P} \cup \mathcal{R})$ may be used. Hence, there cannot be any function that transforms an infinite minimal $(\mathcal{P}, \mathcal{R})$-chain over an arbitrary signature into an infinite minimal chain which only contains terms over $\mathcal{F}(\mathcal{P} \cup \mathcal{R})$. In other words, Lemma 8 does not hold if one would replace infinite chains by minimal infinite chains.

Example 13 (Restricting the signature to $\mathcal{F}(\mathcal{P} \cup \mathcal{R})$ is unsound for minimal chains). To present a counter-example we give a "termination proof" for a non-terminating TRS where the only unsound step is the signature restriction to the signature of the current DP problem. Here, we make use of the DP-framework [4] in which one proves termination by simplifying the initial DP problems by termination techniques until one obtains a DP problem that does not admit an

---

[3] If the signature would be larger, e.g., if there would be an additional ternary symbol c, then the flat contexts would include $\{c(\Box, x_2, x_3), c(x_1, \Box, x_3), c(x_1, x_2, \Box)\}$ and for each of these contexts one would get another rule. Hence, the signature restriction is essential to get few flat contexts and therefore small systems.

infinite minimal chain. For soundness it is only required that whenever $(\mathcal{P}, \mathcal{R})$ is simplified to $(\mathcal{P}', \mathcal{R}')$ then an infinite minimal $(\mathcal{P}, \mathcal{R})$-chain must imply the existence of an infinite minimal $(\mathcal{P}', \mathcal{R}')$-chain.

So, let $\mathcal{R}$ be the following nonterminating TRS.

$$g(f(x, y, x', z, z, u)) \rightarrow g(f(x, y, x, x, y, h(y, x')))$$
$$a \rightarrow b$$
$$a \rightarrow c$$
$$h(x, x) \rightarrow h(x, x)$$
$$h(a, x) \rightarrow h(x, x)$$
$$h(b, x) \rightarrow h(x, x)$$
$$h(c, x) \rightarrow h(x, x)$$
$$h(h(x_1, x_2), x) \rightarrow h(x, x)$$
$$h(f(x_1, \ldots, x_6), x) \rightarrow h(x, x)$$

The initial DP problem $(\mathsf{DP}(\mathcal{R}), \mathcal{R})$ can be simplified to $(\mathcal{P}, \mathcal{R})$ where $\mathcal{P} = \{G(f(x, y, x', z, z, u)) \rightarrow G(f(x, y, x, x, y, h(y, x')))\}$. The reason is that there is a minimal infinite $(\mathcal{P}, \mathcal{R})$-chain: choose every s_i and t_i to be the left-hand side and right-hand side of the only rule in $\mathcal{P}$, respectively. Further, choose $\sigma_i = \sigma$ for $\sigma(x) = g(a)$, $\sigma(y) = \sigma(z) = g(b)$, $\sigma(x') = g(c)$, and $\sigma(u) = h(g(b), g(c))$.

Note that this chain is also a minimal $(\mathcal{P}, \mathcal{R}')$-chain where $\mathcal{R}'$ is like $\mathcal{R}$ but without the $g(\ldots) \rightarrow g(\ldots)$-rule. Thus, $(\mathcal{P}, \mathcal{R})$ can be simplified to $(\mathcal{P}, \mathcal{R}')$.

Using the argument filter processor [9, Theorem 4.37], it is shown that there also is an infinite minimal chain when collapsing G to its first argument. Hence, the same substitution σ can be used to obtain an infinite minimal chain for the DP problem $(\mathcal{P}', \mathcal{R}')$ where $\mathcal{P}' = \{f(x, y, x', z, z, u) \rightarrow f(x, y, x, x, y, h(y, x'))\}$.

Now, if it would be sound to restrict the signature of $(\mathcal{P}', \mathcal{R}')$ to $\mathcal{F}(\mathcal{P}' \cup \mathcal{R}') = \{a, b, c, f, h\}$ then we can conclude termination. The reason is that over this signature there are no infinite minimal $(\mathcal{P}', \mathcal{R}')$-chains anymore.

We prove this last statement by contradiction. Suppose there is an infinite minimal $(\mathcal{P}', \mathcal{R}')$-chain over s, t, and δ, where δ_i instantiates all variables by terms over $\mathcal{F}(\mathcal{P}' \cup \mathcal{R}')$, $s_i = f(x, y, x', z, z, u)$, and $t_i = f(x, y, x, x, y, h(y, x'))$, for all i. δ_i. Then all $t_i \delta_i$ are terminating w.r.t. $\mathcal{R}'$. Hence, $\delta_1(y)$ must be a variable (otherwise, $h(y, x')\delta_1$ would not be terminating due to the six h-rules of $\mathcal{R}'$). Moreover, by using that $\delta_1(y)$ is a variable, the derivation $t_1\delta_1 \rightarrow_{\mathcal{R}'}^* s_2\delta_2$ shows that $\delta_1(y) = \delta_2(y)$ and $\delta_1(y) = \delta_2(z)$. Note that since $\mathcal{R}'$ is not collapsing, whenever a term rewrites to a variable then the term must be identical to the variable. Hence, since $\delta_2(z)$ is a variable and $\delta_1(x) \rightarrow_{\mathcal{R}'}^* \delta_2(z)$ we obtain $\delta_1(x) = \delta_2(z)$ and for a similar reason we obtain $\delta_1(x) = \delta_2(x')$. In total, we can conclude $\delta_2(y) = \delta_2(x')$. This finally yields a contradiction as there is the nonterminating subterm $h(y, x')\delta_2 = h(\delta_2(y), \delta_2(y))$.

The consequences are severe: termination proofs relying upon techniques that require minimal chains and also use signature restrictions are unsound without further restrictions.

And indeed, for the technique of root-labeling—which performs a signature restriction within the soundness proof—we were able to construct a counter-example which refutes the main theorem for root-labeling with DPs.

Example 14 (Root-labeling is unsound for minimal chains). We use a similar TRS as in Example 13 to show the problem of root-labeling with minimal chains. Let $\mathcal{R}$ consist of the following rules.

$$g(f(x,y,x',z,z,u)) \rightarrow g(f(x,y,x,x,y,h(y,x')))$$
$$a \rightarrow b$$
$$a \rightarrow c$$
$$h(x,x) \rightarrow h(x,x)$$
$$h(a,x) \rightarrow h(x,x)$$
$$h(x,a) \rightarrow h(x,x)$$
$$f(x_1,\ldots,a,\ldots,x_5) \rightarrow f(x_1,\ldots,a,\ldots,x_5)$$

Here, the last rule represents 6 rules where the a can be at any position.

We again can simplify the initial DP-problem $(DP(\mathcal{R}),\mathcal{R})$ to $(\mathcal{P},\mathcal{R})$ for the same $\mathcal{P} = \{G(f(x,y,x',z,z,u)) \rightarrow G(f(x,y,x,x,y,h(y,x')))\}$ that we had in the previous example. The reason is again that there is an infinite minimal chain by choosing $\sigma_i = \sigma$ for $\sigma(x) = g(a)$, $\sigma(y) = \sigma(z) = g(b)$, $\sigma(x') = g(c)$, and $\sigma(u) = h(g(b),g(c))$.

Note that by using this substitution we also get an infinite minimal $(\mathcal{P},\mathcal{R}')$-chain where $\mathcal{R}' = \mathcal{R} \setminus \{g(\ldots) \rightarrow g(\ldots)\}$. Hence, it is sound to simplify $(\mathcal{P},\mathcal{R})$ to $(\mathcal{P},\mathcal{R}')$.

Now, in [8, proofs of Lemmas 13 and 17] it is wrongly stated[4] that for this example, *w.l.o.g. one can restrict to substitutions over the signature* $\{a,b,c,f,h\}$: With a similar reasoning as in Example 13 one can prove that there is no infinite minimal $(\mathcal{P},\mathcal{R}')$-chain using this restricted class of substitutions. We further show in detail that Lemma 17 of [8] itself is wrong, not only its proof.

The result of Lemma 17 states that if there is an infinite minimal $(\mathcal{P},\mathcal{R}')$-chain then there also is an infinite minimal chain for the DP problem $(\mathcal{P}',\mathcal{R}'')$ that is obtained by the flat context closure. In our example we obtain $\mathcal{P}' = \mathcal{P} \cup \{G(a) \rightarrow G(b), G(a) \rightarrow G(c)\}$ and $\mathcal{R}'' = (\mathcal{R}' \setminus \{a \rightarrow b, a \rightarrow c\}) \cup \mathcal{R}'''$ where $\mathcal{R}'''$ consists of the following rules:

$$h(a,x) \rightarrow h(b,x)$$
$$h(a,x) \rightarrow h(c,x)$$
$$h(x,a) \rightarrow h(x,b)$$
$$h(x,a) \rightarrow h(x,c)$$
$$f(x_1,\ldots,a,\ldots,x_5) \rightarrow f(x_1,\ldots,b,\ldots,x_5)$$
$$f(x_1,\ldots,a,\ldots,x_5) \rightarrow f(x_1,\ldots,c,\ldots,x_5)$$

---

[4] In detail, in [8] our upcoming Lemma 17 is used without the requirement of left-linearity.

We show that for this DP problem $(\mathcal{P}', \mathcal{R}'')$ there are no infinite minimal chains anymore. So, if Lemma 17 of [8] would be sound, we could wrongly "prove" termination of $\mathcal{R}$. Again, we assume there is an infinite minimal $(\mathcal{P}', \mathcal{R}'')$-chain where δ_i are the corresponding substitutions and where we do not even restrict the signature of any δ_i. Obviously, all $(\mathbf{s}_i, \mathbf{t}_i)$ are taken from $\mathcal{P}$ and not from one of the additional rules in $\mathcal{P}'$. Since every left-hand side of $\mathcal{R}''$ also is a left-hand side of a nonterminating rule in $\mathcal{R}''$, we know that every terminating term w.r.t. $\mathcal{R}''$ is also a normal form w.r.t. $\mathcal{R}''$. Hence, from $\mathbf{t}_1\delta_1 \to_{\mathcal{R}''}^* \mathbf{s}_2\delta_2$ we conclude $\mathbf{t}_1\delta_1 = \mathbf{s}_2\delta_2$. Thus, $\delta_2(x') = \delta_1(x) = \delta_2(z) = \delta_1(y) = \delta_2(y)$. Therefore, we obtain the nonterminating subterm $\mathsf{h}(y, x')\delta_2 = \mathsf{h}(\delta_2(y), \delta_2(y))$ which is a contradiction to the minimality of the chain.

To conclude, the current applications of root-labeling in termination tools which rely upon DPs with minimal chains are wrong for two reasons: first, one cannot restrict the signature to the implicit signature of the given DP-problem, and second, root-labeling is unsound in the DP setting with minimal chains.

However, for signature restrictions in combination with minimal chains we were able to prove soundness, provided that the TRS $\mathcal{R}$ of a DP problem $(\mathcal{P}, \mathcal{R})$ is left-linear.

Lemma 15 (Signature Restrictions for Minimal Chains)
left_linear $\mathcal{R} \implies$
  $\mathcal{F}(\mathcal{P}, \mathcal{R}) \subseteq \mathcal{F} \implies$ min_ichain $(\mathcal{P}, \mathcal{R})$ **s t** $\sigma \implies$ min_ichain $(\mathcal{P}, \mathcal{R})$ **s t** $[\![\sigma]\!]_{\mathcal{F}}$

The proof of Lemma 15 is similar to the proof of Lemma 8. The only missing step is to prove that left-linearity ensures that cleaning does not introduce nontermination.

Lemma 16 (Cleaning of Left-Linear TRSs Preservers SN)

1. left_linear $\mathcal{R} \implies \mathcal{F}(\mathcal{R}) \subseteq \mathcal{F} \implies \mathsf{SN}_{\mathcal{R}}(s) \implies [\![s]\!]_{\mathcal{F}} \to_{\mathcal{R}} t \implies \exists u. \ [\![u]\!]_{\mathcal{F}} = t$
   $\wedge \ s \to_{\mathcal{R}} u$
2. left_linear $\mathcal{R} \implies \mathcal{F}(\mathcal{R}) \subseteq \mathcal{F} \implies \mathsf{SN}_{\mathcal{R}}(s) \implies \mathsf{SN}_{\mathcal{R}}([\![s]\!]_{\mathcal{F}})$

Proof. 1. We prove this fact via induction over s. In the base case, s is a variable. Then we have the rewrite step $s \to_{\mathcal{R}} t$, since cleaning does not change variables. But then, there is a variable left-hand side, implying that $\mathcal{R}$ is not terminating and thus contradicting $\mathsf{SN}_{\mathcal{R}}(s)$.

In the step case we have $s = f(\vec{ss})$. Now, we proceed by a case distinction. If $(f, |\vec{ss}|) \notin \mathcal{F}$ then cleaning will transform s into the variable z. Again, there would be a variable left-hand side, contradicting strong normalization of s. Thus, $(f, |\vec{ss}|) \in \mathcal{F}$. Hence, $f(map \ [\![\cdot]\!]_{\mathcal{F}} \ \vec{ss}) \to_{\mathcal{R}} t$. If this is a non-root step, the result follows from the induction hypothesis. Otherwise, this is a root rewrite step. Thus we obtain a rule $(l, r) \in \mathcal{R}$ and a substitution σ, such that, $[\![f(\vec{ss})]\!]_{\mathcal{F}} = l\sigma$ and $r\sigma = t$. Additionally, we know that this rule is left-linear and that its left-hand side is well-formed. It can be shown that this implies the existence of a substitution τ, such that, $[\![\tau_{\mathsf{Var}(l)}]\!]_{\mathcal{F}} = \sigma|_{\mathsf{Var}(l)}$ and $f(\vec{ss}) = l\tau$ (we omit the rather technical proof). Here, $\sigma|_V$ denotes the restriction of a substitution σ to a set of variables V, i.e., all variables that are not in V, are no longer modified by the restricted substitution. Then $[\![r\tau]\!]_\mathcal{F} = [\![r]\!]_\mathcal{F} [\![\tau]\!]_\mathcal{F} = r[\![\tau_{\mathcal{V}\mathrm{ar}(l)}]\!]_\mathcal{F} = r\sigma|_{\mathcal{V}\mathrm{ar}(l)} = r\sigma = t$ and $s = f(\vec{s}\vec{s}) = l\tau \to_\mathcal{R} r\tau$. Here, we needed to use the property $\mathcal{V}\mathrm{ar}(r) \subseteq \mathcal{V}\mathrm{ar}(l)$, which must be valid since otherwise $\mathsf{SN}_\mathcal{R}(s)$ does not hold.

2. Assume that $[\![s]\!]_\mathcal{F}$ is not terminating. Thus, there is an infinite sequence of $\mathcal{R}$-steps, starting from $[\![s]\!]_\mathcal{F}$. By iteratively applying the previous result, we obtain an infinite $\mathcal{R}$-sequence starting at s. □

We were also able to formally show that the signature restriction that is done in root-labeling (which is exactly the upcoming Lemma 17 without the requirement of left-linearity) is sound for minimal chains with the requirement of left-linearity. Hence, with the following lemma one can repair the paper proofs of [8, Lemmas 13 and 17] by demanding left-linearity. Essentially, the lemma states that one can restrict to the symbols that occur below the root in $\mathcal{P}$ ($\mathcal{F}_{>\epsilon}(\mathcal{P})$), together with the symbols of $\mathcal{R}$, under the additional assumption that neither left-hand sides nor right-hand sides of $\mathcal{P}$ are variables and the roots of $\mathcal{P}$ are not defined in $\mathcal{R}$.

Lemma 17 (Signature Restrictions Ignoring Roots)

left_linear $\mathcal{R} \Longrightarrow$

$\qquad \mathcal{F}_{>\epsilon}(\mathcal{P}) \cup \mathcal{F}(\mathcal{R}) \subseteq \mathcal{F} \Longrightarrow$

$\qquad \forall s\, t.\ (s,\, t) \in \mathcal{P} \longrightarrow s \notin \mathcal{V}\mathrm{ar} \wedge t \notin \mathcal{V}\mathrm{ar} \wedge \neg\ \mathrm{root}(t) \in \mathcal{D}(\mathcal{R}) \Longrightarrow$

$\qquad$ min_ichain $(\mathcal{P},\, \mathcal{R})$ s t $\sigma \Longrightarrow$ min_ichain $(\mathcal{P},\, \mathcal{R})$ s t $[\![\sigma]\!]_\mathcal{F}$

The lemma is proven in the same way as Lemma 15, except that one only applies cleaning strictly below the root. By cleaning below the root one can also proof a variant of Lemma 17 where minimal chains are replaced by arbitrary chains, and where left-linearity is no longer required.[5]

Using Lemma 17 and the original proofs of [8] it is shown that root-labeling is sound in combination with minimal chains if we restrict to left-linear $\mathcal{R}$-components. Hence, the main example of [8, Touzet's SRS] is still working, since it applies root-labeling on a DP problem with left-linear $\mathcal{R}$.

6   Conclusion

We presented an alternative, and more importantly, the first mechanized proof of the fact that termination is preserved under signature extensions. We have also shown that signature extensions are possible when using DPs, but only if one considers arbitrary chains or left-linear TRSs. For minimal chains we have given a counterexample which shows that for non-left-linear TRSs one cannot restrict to the signature of the current DP problem.

We believe these results to be interesting in their own. However, we developed these results with a certain goal in mind. In the end we want to apply our

---

[5] However, one needs the additional requirement that left-hand sides of $\mathcal{R}$ are not variables, which in Lemma 17 follows from the minimality of the chain.

main positive results to be able to certify termination proofs which rely upon techniques where the signature is essential: string reversal and root-labeling. If one applies these techniques directly on a TRS, then both techniques can now be certified in the way they are used in current termination tools. For root-labeling in the DP setting with minimal chains, we have shown that it is unsound for arbitrary DP problems. We have further shown how to repair the existing proofs by demanding left-linearity. It remains as future work, to also formalize the remaining proof for root-labeling in the DP setting.

References

1. Arts, T., Giesl, J.: Termination of term rewriting using dependency pairs. Theoretical Computer Science 236, 133–178 (2000)
2. Baader, F., Nipkow, T.: Term Rewriting and All That. Cambridge University Press, Cambridge (1998)
3. Dershowitz, N.: Termination dependencies. In: Proc. WST 2003, pp. 27–30 (2003)
4. Giesl, J., Thiemann, R., Schneider-Kamp, P., Falke, S.: Mechanizing and improving dependency pairs. Journal of Automated Reasoning 37(3), 155–203 (2006)
5. Middeldorp, A.: Modular Properties of Term Rewriting Systems. PhD thesis, Vrije Universiteit, Amsterdam (1990)
6. Nipkow, T., Paulson, L., Wenzel, M.: Isabelle/HOL. LNCS, vol. 2283. Springer, Heidelberg (2002)
7. Ohlebusch, E.: A simple proof of sufficient conditions for the termination of the disjoint union of term rewriting systems. Bulletin of the EATCS 50, 223–228 (1993)
8. Sternagel, C., Middeldorp, A.: Root-Labeling. In: Voronkov, A. (ed.) RTA 2008. LNCS, vol. 5117, pp. 336–350. Springer, Heidelberg (2008)
9. Thiemann, R.: The DP Framework for Proving Termination of Term Rewriting. PhD thesis, RWTH Aachen University (2007), Available as Technical Report AIB-2007-17, http://aib.informatik.rwth-aachen.de/2007/2007-17.pdf
10. Thiemann, R., Sternagel, C.: Certification of termination proofs using CeTA. In: Berghofer, S., Nipkow, T., Urban, C., Wenzel, M. (eds.) TPHOLs 2009. LNCS, vol. 5674, pp. 452–468. Springer, Heidelberg (2009)
11. Zantema, H.: Termination of term rewriting by semantic labelling. Fundamenta Informaticae 24(1/2), 89–105 (1995)

Coq Modulo Theory*

Pierre-Yves Strub

INRIA - Tsinghua University
Offices 3-604, FIT Building, Tsinghua University
Haidian District, Beijing, 100084, China

Abstract. Coq Modulo Theory (CoqMT) is an extension of the
Coq proof assistant incorporating, in its computational mechanism,
validity entailment for user-defined first-order equational theories. Such a
mechanism strictly enriches the system (more terms are typable), eases
the use of dependent types and provides more automation during the
development of proofs.

CoqMT improves over the Calculus of Congruent Inductive
Constructions by getting rid of various restrictions and simplifying
the type-checking algorithm and the integration of first-order decision
procedures.

We present here CoqMT, and outline its meta-theoretical study. We
also give a brief description of our CoqMT implementation.

1 Introduction

Theorem provers like Coq [1] based on the Curry-Howard isomorphism enjoy
a mechanism which incorporates computations within deductions. This allows
replacing the proof of a proposition by the proof of an equivalent proposition
obtained from the former thanks to possibly complex computations. Adding
more power to this mechanism leads to a calculus which is more expressive (more
terms are typable), which provides more automation (more deduction steps are
hidden in computations) and eases the use of dependent data types in proof
development.

Coq was initially based on the Calculus of Constructions (CC) of Coquand
and Huet [2], which is an impredicative type theory incorporating polymorphism,
dependent types and type constructors. At that time, computations were
restricted to β-reduction: other forms of computations were encoded as
deductions.

The Calculus of Inductive Constructions of Coquand and Paulin [3,4,5]
introduced inductive types and their associated elimination rules. CIC allows for
example the definition of Peano natural numbers based on the two constructors
0 and S along with the ability to define addition by induction: $x + 0 \rightarrow x$
and $x + S(y) \rightarrow S(x + y)$. This mechanism allows the system to identify the
expressions $x + S(S(y))$ and $S(x + y) + S(0)$, but fails in identifying $x + S(y)$ and
$S(x) + y$. This forbids users to easily define functions on dependent data-types

---

* This work was partly supported by the ANR ANR-08-BLAN-0326-01.

A. Dawar and H. Veith (Eds.): CSL 2010, LNCS 6247, pp. 529–543, 2010.

(like the **reverse** function on lists) as the types **list**$(n + 1)$ and **list**$(1 + n)$ will not be convertible either.

In the 90's, new attempts to incorporate user-defined computations as rewrite rules were carried out. This resulted in the definition of the Calculus of Algebraic Constructions [6]. By introducing the correct rewriting rules, the calculus is able to identify terms like $x + S(y)$ and $S(x) + y$. Although quite powerful (CAC captures CIC [7]), this paradigm does not yet fulfill all needs, as it fails to identify open terms like $x + y$ and $y + x$.

Further steps in the direction of integrating first-order theories into the Calculus of Constructions are Stehr's Open Calculus of Constructions (OCC) [8] and Oury's Extensional Calculus of Constructions (ECC) [9]. OCC allows the use of an arbitrary equational theory in conversion. ECC can be seen as a particular case of OCC in which all provable equalities can be used in conversion, which can also be achieved by adding the extensionality and Streicher's axiom [10] to CIC, hence the name of this calculus. Unfortunately, strong normalization and decidability of type checking are lost in ECC and OCC.

In a preliminary work, we designed a new, rather restrictive framework, the Calculus of Congruent Constructions, which incorporates the congruence closure algorithm [11] in CC's conversion, while preserving the good properties of the calculus. We then defined the Calculus of Inductive Congruence Constructions (CCIC [12,13]), which was our first answer to the problem of incorporating validity entailment of an equational first-order theory $\mathcal{T}$ in the computation mechanism of the Calculus of Inductive Constructions. This calculus partially solved the problem but contained too many ad-hoc restrictions to be implementable in practice. In particular, the procedure could not be invoked to solve goals occurring below eliminators.

Problem. The main question investigated in this paper is the incorporation of a general mechanism invoking a decision procedure for solving conversion-goals of the form $\Gamma \Rightarrow U = V$ in the Calculus of Inductive Constructions which uses the relevant information available from the current context Γ of the proof. This mechanism should be simple enough to be implementable in practice.

Theoretical contribution. Our theoretical contribution is the definition and the meta-theoretical study of a new version of the Calculus of Congruent Inductive Constructions (called CoqMT). Not only is the new formulation much simpler, but we succeeded in addition to remove most ad-hoc restrictions of CCIC. In particular, conversion now contains the entire equational theory $\mathcal{T}$. We show that we keep all the desired properties of such a calculus: subject reduction, strong normalization of reduction, logical consistency and decidability of type-checking.

Practical contribution. We implemented CoqMT, a new version of Coq based on the Calculus of Inductive Congruent Constructions. We also formally defined our calculus in Coq, and started its formal meta-theoretical study.[1]

---

[1] This development is available at http://strub.nu/research/coqmt/

We assume the reader familiar with typed λ-calculus [14] and rewriting [15]. *Due to the lack of space, we restrict our presentation to the Calculus of Constructions with two inductive types, natural numbers and lists depending on their size. The only embedded theory is the theory of Presburger arithmetic. This version captures all technical and theoretical problems encountered in the development of the full version of the calculus.*

From now on, $\mathcal{T}$ designates the first-order theory of Presburger arithmetic, built from the function symbols 0, S and $+$ and on the equality predicate $=$. By extension, we write $\mathcal{T}$ for the set of first-order terms belonging to the theory $\mathcal{T}$. If $\mathcal{E} = \{t_1 = u_1, \ldots, t_n = u_n\}$ is a finite set of equations in $\mathcal{T}$ (or $\mathcal{T}$-equations) and $t = u$ is a $\mathcal{T}$-equation, we write $\mathcal{T}, \mathcal{E} \vDash t = u$ if $t_1 = u_1 \wedge \cdots \wedge t_n = u_n \Rightarrow t = u$ is a valid formula in $\mathcal{T}$.

1.1   Syntax and Notations

Definition 1 (Terms). *The set of* CoQMT *pseudo-terms is defined by:*

$$t, u, T, U, \ldots ::= s \in \{\star, \square\} \mid x \in \mathcal{X} \mid f \in \Sigma \mid \bullet[t :^e T].\, u \mid u\, v$$
$$\mid \lambda[x :^{e?} U].\, v \mid \forall(x :^{e?} U).\, V \mid \mathrm{Elim}(t : Q)\{f_0, f_S\} \mid \doteq \mid \mathrm{refl}_T(t)$$

where $\Sigma = \{\mathbf{0}, \mathbf{S}, +, \mathbf{nil}, \mathbf{cons}, \mathbf{nat}, \mathbf{list}\}$, *e denotes an* extracted equation, *a notion to be explained later. The notation* e? *denotes either an extracted equation* e *or the symbol* $\bot$. *To ease the reading, we allow us to omit the* $\bot$ *symbol.*

Pseudo-terms of CoQMT are made of the usual terms of the Calculus of Constructions: *variables*, *sorts*, *abstraction* $\lambda[x : U].\, v$, *dependent product* $\forall(x : U).\, V$. Binders can be optionally decorated with an *extracted equation* e. For dealing with equalities and natural numbers, the following symbols are added: **nat** is the type of natural numbers, whereas $\mathbf{0}$, $\mathbf{S}$ and $+$ are resp. the *zero*, *successor* and *addition* symbols. Similarly, $\doteq$ is the (dependent) equality predicate ($\doteq T\, t_1\, t_2$ or $t_1 \doteq_T t_2$ denotes that t_1 and t_2 are two equal terms of type T), while $\mathrm{refl}_T(t)$ denotes the proof by reflexivity of $t \doteq_T t$. Also, to illustrate the use of integrating Presburger arithmetic in CoQMT, we add symbols for dealing with dependent lists: **list** is the type of dependent lists, whereas **nil** and **cons** are its constructors. The construction $\mathrm{Elim}(t : Q)\{f_0, f_S\}$ denotes the usual recursor for natural numbers. Its semantic is detailed later when defining the reduction relation of our calculus.

A major novelty of CoQMT is the new symbol $\bullet[t :^e T].\, u$, called *extracted equation marker* or simply *equation marker*. It aims at carrying the equation e available for conversion - the terms t and T being present for typing purposes. Definitions to come ensure that this construction does not interfere with reduction: if substituting u in a term creates redexes, substituting $\bullet[t :^e T].\, u$ in the same term should create the same *kind* of redexes at the same positions.

We still need to clarify what is an *extracted equation*. As our calculus will incorporate the validity entailment of $\mathcal{T}$ in its conversion along with $\mathcal{T}$-equations extracted from the environment, we first need a process to convert CoQMT terms into $\mathcal{T}$ terms: this is called *algebraisation*. For CoQMT terms containing only symbols relative to **nat** and variables, algebraisation is simply the process of currying symbols: from $\mathbf{S}\,x + \mathbf{0}$, we can extract the $\mathcal{T}$-term $S(x) + 0$ - note the font change. Unfortunately, due to substitution occurring in β-reduction, extracting only this kind of terms is not sufficient. Indeed, when substituting x by a arbitrary term t in the previous example, we first abstract t in the expression $\mathbf{S}\,t + \mathbf{0}$ by a fresh *variable* (say y), and then do the algebraisation. Here, we obtain the $\mathcal{T}$-term $S(y) + 0$ with y abstracting t.

Definition 2 (Algebraic context). *A context is said* algebraic *if it is of the form* $C_{\mathcal{A}} ::= \mathbf{0} \mid \mathbf{S}\,C_{\mathcal{A}} \mid \bullet_n + \bullet_p \mid \bullet_n$, *and not reduced to* $\bullet_n$, *where* $\bullet_n$ *denotes a hole with index* $n \in \mathbb{N}$. *By convention, two different holes in a context cannot have the same index.*

If $C_{\mathcal{A}}$ is an algebraic context whose maximal holes index is n, we write $C_{\mathcal{A}}[1 \leftarrow t_1, \ldots, n \leftarrow t_n]$ the term obtained by replacing the ith hole of $C_{\mathcal{A}}$ by t_i. We call *context instantiation* the construct $[1 \leftarrow t_1, \ldots, n \leftarrow t_n]$, and denote by the letters $\mathcal{I}, \mathcal{J}$ *instantiation variables*. A *pre-algebraic* term is simply a term which can be obtained by instantiation of an algebraic context.

Definition 3 (Pre-algebraic term). *A pseudo-term* t *is* pre-algebraic *if it is of the form* $C_{\mathcal{A}}[1 \leftarrow t_1, \ldots, n \leftarrow t_n]$. *If none of the* t_i's *are pre-algebraic, we say that* $C_{\mathcal{A}}$ *is the* maximal algebraic cap *of* t *and* $\{t_1, \ldots, t_n\}$ *are the* aliens *of* t.

For example, the term $(\mathbf{S}\,t) + u$ is pre-algebraic. We can take $\bullet_1 + \bullet_2$ as algebraic context with the instantiation $[1 \leftarrow \mathbf{S}\,t, 2 \leftarrow u]$. This context is not maximal. Assuming t and u not headed by a symbol of $\mathcal{T}$ (and hence not being pre-algebraic), $(\mathbf{S}\,\bullet_1) + \bullet_2$ is the maximal algebraic cap of $(\mathbf{S}\,t) + u$, and t, u are its two aliens. One can remark that a pseudo-term has exactly one maximal algebraic cap and the set of aliens is uniquely defined. Note that we consider the variables of a CoQMT term as aliens.

Definition 4 (Algebraisation). *For any term* t, *an* algebraisation *of* t *is a pair* $(C, \mathcal{I})$ *s.t.* $t = C[\mathcal{I}]$. *If* C *is the maximal algebraic cap of* t, *we say that* $(C, \mathcal{I})$ *is the* maximal algebraisation *of* t.

Definition 5 (Extracted equation). *An* extracted equation *is a 4-tuple* $(C_1, C_2, \mathcal{I}_1, \mathcal{I}_2)$ *(written* $(C_1 = C_2, \mathcal{I}_1, \mathcal{I}_2)$*) s.t.* C_1 *and* C_2 *are algebraic context and* $\mathcal{I}_1$, $\mathcal{I}_2$ *are context instantiations.*

For example, $(\bullet_1 + \bullet_2 = \mathbf{0}, [1 \leftarrow t, 2 \leftarrow u], [])$ is an extracted equation. By replacing holes with fresh variables and currying, we obtain the $\mathcal{T}$-equation $x + y = 0$ which can be used in a conversion check. Context instantiations allows us to related the extracted equations to CoQMT types: the extracted equation $(\bullet_1 + \bullet_2 = \mathbf{0}, [1 \leftarrow t, 2 \leftarrow u], [])$ will be extractable from a CoQMT term T if and only if T is of the form $(\bullet_1 + \bullet_2)[1 \leftarrow t, 2 \leftarrow u] \doteq \mathbf{0}[]$ i.e. of the form $t + u \doteq \mathbf{0}$.

When extracted equations are *pure*, i.e. the instantiations fill holes with variables only, we simplify our notations by giving the instantiated extracted equations instead of the 4-tuple. For example, we write $x + \mathbf{0} = \mathbf{S}\,\mathbf{0}$ for the extracted equation $(\bullet_1 + \mathbf{0} = \mathbf{S}\,\mathbf{0}, [1 \leftarrow x], [\,])$.

Definition 6 (Substitution). *We denote by $t\theta$ with $\theta = \{x \leftarrow w\}$ the term obtained by substituting in t all free occurrences of x by w - including the term appearing in the extracted equations:*

$$
\begin{aligned}
& f\theta = f \quad s\theta = f \quad (\doteq \theta) = (\doteq) \qquad\quad x\theta = w \quad y\theta = y \text{ when } x \neq y \\
& (\bullet[t :^e T].\,u)\theta = \bullet[t\theta :^{e\theta} T\theta].\,u\theta \qquad (u\,v)\theta = (u\theta)\,(v\theta) \\
& (\lambda[x :^{e?} U].\,v)\theta = \lambda[x :^{e?\theta} U\theta].\,v\theta \qquad (\forall(x :^{e?} U).\,v)\theta = \forall(x :^{e?\theta} U\theta).\,v\theta \\
& (\mathrm{Elim}(t : Q)\{f_0, f_S\})\theta = \qquad\qquad (\mathrm{refl}_T(t))\theta = \mathrm{refl}_{T\theta}(t\theta) \\
& \qquad\quad \mathrm{Elim}(t\theta : Q\theta)\{f_0\theta, f_S\theta\} \\
& (C_1 = C_2, \mathcal{I}, \mathcal{J})\theta = (C_1 = C_2, \mathcal{I}\theta, \mathcal{J}\theta) \quad \perp\theta = \perp \quad [i \leftarrow t_i]\theta = [i \leftarrow t_i\theta]
\end{aligned}
$$

Regarding variables capture, we here assume the Barendregt convention.

Notation 1. By $\{\overrightarrow{t_i}\}_{1 \leq i \leq n}$, or simply $\overrightarrow{t}$, we denote the terms $t_1\, t_2 \cdots t_n$. We write $T \rightarrow^{e?} U$ for $\forall(x :^{e?} T).\,U$ when x is not free in T. When using sequences, we write ϵ for the empty sequence and $x :: xs$ for the cons operation. The notation $[x_1, x_2, \ldots, x_n]$ denotes $x_1 :: x_2 :: \cdots :: \epsilon$.

1.2 Converting Terms

Our conversion relation is split in two parts. The first part is a rewriting relation $\rightarrow_{\beta\iota\mathcal{T}}$, which includes β-reduction and the Martin-Löf recursor reduction for natural numbers, so called ι-reduction. Our reduction $\rightarrow_{\beta\iota\mathcal{T}}$ differs from the standard $\rightarrow_{\beta\iota}$ by its ability to operate modulo the theory $\mathcal{T}$. For example, the term $\mathrm{Elim}((x + (\mathbf{S}\,\mathbf{0})) + y : Q)\{f_0, f_S\}$, which is head-normal for $\rightarrow_{\beta\iota}$, is head-reducible for $\rightarrow_{\beta\iota\mathcal{T}}$. Actually, our definition of $\rightarrow_{\beta\iota\mathcal{T}}$ is such that $\mathrm{Elim}((x + (\mathbf{S}\,\mathbf{0})) + y : Q)\{f_0, f_S\}$ (resp. $\mathrm{Elim}(\mathbf{S}\,(x + y) : Q)\{f_0, f_S\}$) $\rightarrow_{\beta\iota\mathcal{T}}$-head-reduces (resp. $\rightarrow_{\beta\iota}$-head-reduces) to the same term $f_S\,(x + y)\,\mathrm{Elim}(x + y : Q)\{f_0, f_S\}$. The second part of our conversion relation is the extension of the validity entailment of $\mathcal{T}, E$ to the set of CoQMT pseudo-terms, where E is a set of extracted equations. We call this the $\mathcal{T}$-*congruence relation*. This $\mathcal{T}$-congruence will be parametrized by its ability to use the equations in E or not. We write $\equiv_E^\top$ for the $\mathcal{T}$-congruence having the ability to use the equations of E, and $\equiv_E^\perp$ for the other one. For example, if from E we can use the equation $x = (\mathbf{S}\,\mathbf{0})$, $\equiv_E^\top$ will be such that $x + x \equiv_E^\top (\mathbf{S}\,(\mathbf{S}\,\mathbf{0}))$, whereas $x + x$ and $\mathbf{S}\,(\mathbf{S}\,\mathbf{0})$ will not be convertible using $\equiv_E^\perp$.

We start with the definition of the reduction relation $\rightarrow_{\beta\iota\mathcal{T}}$. (From now on, for ease of notations, we write $\rightarrow$ for $\rightarrow_{\beta\iota\mathcal{T}}$) We achieve the reduction modulo by applying a normalization function to terms being in deconstruction position [16,17]. For that, we introduce a function $\mathrm{norm}_\mathcal{T}$ normalizing first-order $\mathcal{T}$-terms as found in Shostak's method for combining decision procedures [18]:

1. $\mathcal{T} \vDash t = \mathrm{norm}_\mathcal{T}(t)$,   2. the variables of $\mathrm{norm}_\mathcal{T}(t)$ appear in t,
3. $\mathrm{norm}_\mathcal{T}$ is involutive,   4. sub-terms of a normalized term are normalized.

We lift the norm$_\mathcal{T}$ function to pre-algebraic terms as follows:

Definition 7 ($\mathcal{T}$-normalization). *Let $t = C[\mathcal{I}]$ a CoQMT term with maximal algebraic context C, and $\mathcal{I} = [1 \leftarrow t_1, \ldots, n \leftarrow t_n]$. Let $\mathcal{J} = [1 \leftarrow x_1, \ldots, n \leftarrow x_n]$ where all the x_i's are pairwise different, and not free in the t_i's. The $\mathcal{T}$-normalization of t, written $\mathbf{norm}(t)$, is defined as:*

$$\mathbf{norm}(t) = \mathrm{norm}_\mathcal{T}(t[\mathcal{J}])\{x_1 \rightarrow t_1\} \cdots \{x_n \rightarrow t_n\}.$$

For example, assuming $\mathrm{norm}((x+S(0))+y) = S(x+y)$, then $\mathbf{norm}((u + (\mathbf{S}\,0)) + u') = \mathbf{S}\,(u + u')$. We could have defined a stronger normalization function in which sub-expressions are abstracted by the same variable when they are in the same equivalence class of the conversion relation of the calculus. This would have lead to a mutual definition of normalization, rewriting and conversion, a possibility explored in an unpublished work with a heavy price. We now have all the ingredients for defining our reduction relation:

Definition 8 (Reduction). *The rewriting relation $\rightarrow$ is the smallest relation stable by context and substitution s.t.:*

(β) $(\bullet[\overrightarrow{w :^e W}].\, \lambda[x : U].\, v)\, u$
$\qquad \rightarrow \bullet[\overrightarrow{w :^e W}].\, v\{x \leftarrow u\}$

(β-$\mathcal{E}$) $(\bullet[\overrightarrow{w :^e W}].\, \lambda[x :^{e'} U].\, v)\, u$
$\qquad \rightarrow \bullet[\overrightarrow{w :^e W}].\, \bullet[u :^{e'} U].\, v\{x \leftarrow u\}$

(ι_0) $\mathrm{Elim}(t : Q)\{f_0, f_S\} \rightarrow f_0$
$\qquad$ *if t is pre-algebraic, and*
$\qquad\quad \mathbf{norm}(t) = \mathbf{0}$

(ι_S) $\quad \mathrm{Elim}(t : Q)\{f_0, f_S\}$
$\qquad \rightarrow f_S\, v\, \mathrm{Elim}(v : Q)\{f_0, f_S\}$
$\qquad$ *if t is pre-algebraic, and $\mathbf{norm}(t){=}\mathbf{S}\,v$*

Rule (β) (resp. ($\beta - \mathcal{E}$) could have been split in two more basic actions:

$$(\bullet[\overrightarrow{w :^e W}].\, \lambda[x : U].\, v)\, u \qquad \rightarrow_\bullet \bullet[\overrightarrow{w :^e W}].\, ((\lambda[x : U].\, v)\, u) \tag{1}$$
$$\rightarrow_\beta \bullet[\overrightarrow{w :^e W}].\, v\{x \leftarrow u\} \tag{2}$$

where reduction (1) is the action of moving the bullet expression hiding the β-redex, whereas reduction (2) is the standard β-reduction. This remark applies to (β-$\mathcal{E}$) also.

Rule (β-$\mathcal{E}$) has an additional role: the introduction of an equation marker as is clear for its instance $(\lambda[x :^e U].\, v)\, u \rightarrow \bullet[u :^e U].\, v\{x \leftarrow u\}$. Equation markers are essential for the subject reduction property: consider for example the term $(\lambda[p :^{x=\mathbf{0}} T].\, \mathrm{refl}(x))\, t$. Being a proof of reflexivity, $\mathrm{refl}(x)$ has type $x \doteq x$. Using the extracted equation $x = \mathbf{0}$, our conversion rule should allow us to derive $[x : \mathbf{nat}][p :^{x=\mathbf{0}} T] \vdash \mathrm{refl}(x) : x \doteq \mathbf{0}$, and hence $[x : \mathbf{nat}] \vdash (\lambda[x :^{x=\mathbf{0}} T].\, \mathrm{refl}(x))\, t : x \doteq \mathbf{0}$ as well. Without the introduction of equation markers, β-reduction would yield $(\lambda[x :^{x=\mathbf{0}} T].\, \mathrm{refl}(x))\, t \rightarrow_\beta \mathrm{refl}(x)$ of type $x \doteq x$ which is not convertible to $x \doteq \mathbf{0}$ anymore since the equation $x = \mathbf{0}$ has been lost. Adding the equation marker $(\bullet[t :^{x=\mathbf{0}} T].\, \_)$ at root position solves the problem by reintroducing the extracted equation $x = \mathbf{0}$.

This problem already appeared in [13], and was solved by forbidding the application of annotated λ-abstractions to other terms. At that time, we thought the problem could be by-passed by locking such problematic β-redexes. Although our calculus is more general than a calculus where problematic β-redexes are locked (the latter can be easily encoded in the former), its study is much easier: locking β-redexes leads to normal terms containing β-redexes, and hence the standard proof of consistency based on cut elimination does not apply anymore.

The two last rules deal with reduction of Martin-Löf like recursors. Usual reduction rules for elimination of **nat** are:

$$\mathrm{Elim}(\mathbf{0} : Q)\{f_0, f_S\} \rightarrow f_0$$
$$\mathrm{Elim}(\mathbf{S}\, t : Q)\{f_0, f_S\} \rightarrow f_S\, t\ \mathrm{Elim}(t : Q)\{f_0, f_S\}$$

As said, reduction is done modulo the theory $\mathcal{T}$ through the use of **norm**. For example, the term $\mathrm{Elim}((x + (\mathbf{S}\,\mathbf{0})) + y : Q)\{f_0, f_S\}$ which is normal for the standard ι-reduction will reduce to f_0 using ι_0, as $\mathbf{norm}((x + (\mathbf{S}\,\mathbf{0})) + y) = \mathbf{S}(x + y)$. Reduction also contains the recursor rules for lists which are identical to the corresponding ones in the Calculus of Inductive Constructions, and do not play any critical role in our definition.

Notation 2. We write $\overset{\leq}{\rightarrow}$, $\overset{*}{\rightarrow}$, $\overset{*}{\longleftrightarrow}$ for resp. the reflexive, reflexive-transitive and equivalence closure of $\rightarrow$. We write $t \rightarrow_\downarrow u$ if t has a unique normal form equal to u.

We move now to the definition of our conversion relation. We start explaining how $\mathcal{T}$-validity entailment makes use of pre-algebraic terms and extracted equations, via the notion of $(\mathcal{T}, E)$-consequence. Let us assume the following two extracted equations of E: i) $(\bullet_1 + \bullet_2 = \mathbf{S}\,\mathbf{0}, [1 \leftarrow \iota, 2 \leftarrow u], [])$, and ii) $(\mathbf{S}\,\bullet_1 = \mathbf{S}\,\mathbf{0}, [1 \leftarrow t'], [])$; with $t \overset{*}{\longleftrightarrow} t'$. Then, for any u' s.t. $u \overset{*}{\longleftrightarrow} u'$, we say that $x + u' \doteq \mathbf{S}\,x$ is a $(\mathcal{T}, E)$-consequence modulo $\overset{*}{\longleftrightarrow}$ as the entailment $\mathcal{T}, z_1 + z_2 = 1, S(z_3) = 1, \mathcal{V} \vDash x + z_4 = S(x)$ holds, taking $\mathcal{V} = \{z_1 = z_3, z_2 = z_4\}$:

- $z_1 + z_2 = 1$ and $S(z_3) = 1$ are the two extracted equations of E where holes are replaced by pairwise disjoint fresh variables. Hence, z_1 (resp. z_2 and z_3) abstracts t (resp. u and t'),
- from $t \overset{*}{\longleftrightarrow} t'$ (resp. $u \overset{*}{\longleftrightarrow} u'$), we add the equation $z_1 = z_3$ (resp. $z_2 = z_4$) to the set of available equations, via the set $\mathcal{V}$.
- $x + z_4 = S(x)$ (the conclusion of the $\mathcal{T}$-entailment) is the algebraisation of $x + u' = \mathbf{S}\,x$.

We now describe formally the notion of $(\mathcal{T}, E)$-consequence.

Definition 9. *Let $\{C_i\}_{1 \leq i \leq n}$ a set of pre-algebraic contexts, $\{\mathcal{I}_i\}_{1 \leq i \leq n}$ a set of context instantiations and $\mathcal{R}$ a binary relation on CoqMT terms. For any $i \in \{1..n\}$, k, let $t_{i,k}$ the term associated to the kth hole by $\mathcal{I}_i$.*

Let $\{\mathcal{J}_i\}_{1 \leq i \leq n}$ be a set of instantiations and $\mathcal{V}$ a set of equations between variables. We say that $\{\mathcal{J}_i\}_i$ abstracts $\{(C_i, \mathcal{I}_i)\}_i$ accordingly to $\mathcal{V}$ and $\mathcal{R}$ if:

1. *for any $i \in \{1..n\}$, k, $\mathcal{J}_i$ associates a fresh variable $x_{i,k}$ to the kth hole of C_i,*
2. *$(x_{i,p} = x_{j,q}) \in \mathcal{V}$ implies $t_{i,p} \, \mathcal{R} \, t_{j,q}$.*

Definition 10 ($(\mathcal{T}, E)$-consequence). *Let $E = [(C_i^l = C_i^r, \mathcal{I}_i^l, \mathcal{I}_i^r) \mid 1 \le i \le n]$ be a sequence of extracted equations, and t, u two COQMT terms of the form $C_0^l[\mathcal{I}_0^l]$ and $C_0^r[\mathcal{I}_0^r]$ respectively. Let $\mathcal{R}$ be any binary relation on COQMT terms.*

We say that $(t = u)$ is a $(\mathcal{T}, E)$-consequence modulo $\mathcal{R}$ if there exists a set $\{\mathcal{J}_i^\alpha\}_{i,\alpha}$ of context instantiations and a set $\mathcal{V}$ of equations between variables s.t.

1. *$\mathcal{T}, \{C_i^l[\mathcal{J}_i^l] = C_i^r[\mathcal{J}_i^r]\}, \mathcal{V} \models C_0^l[\mathcal{J}_0^l] = C_0^r[\mathcal{J}_0^r]$,*
2. *$\{\mathcal{J}_i^\alpha\}_{i,\alpha}$ abstracts $\{(C_i^\alpha, \mathcal{I}_i^\alpha)\}_{i,\alpha}$ accordingly to $\mathcal{V}$ and $\mathcal{R}$.*

We introduce two variants of conversion: a *strong* one which can use the equations of E, and a *weak* one which cannot. Doing this is crucial for the logical consistency proof of our calculus in the presence of strong recursors (i.e. construction of types by induction). Assume the function $f(n) := \mathrm{Elim}(n :$

$$Q)\{\mathbf{nat}, \lambda[\_\mathbf{nat}]. \lambda[T : \star]. T \to \mathbf{nat}\}, \text{ i.e. a function s.t. } f(n) = \overbrace{\mathbf{nat} \to \cdots \to \mathbf{nat}}^{n \text{ times}}.$$

If we allow the use of any equation in the conversion of n of $f(n)$, for example the equation $\mathbf{0} \doteq \mathbf{S}\,\mathbf{0}$, then $f(0)$ would be convertible to $f(1)$ which respectively $\to$-reduce to $\mathbf{nat}$ and $\mathbf{nat} \to \mathbf{nat}$. Having $\mathbf{nat}$ convertible to $\mathbf{nat} \to \mathbf{nat}$ would then allows us to type-check the term $(\lambda[x : \mathbf{nat}].\, x\, x)\, (\lambda[x : \mathbf{nat}].\, x\, x)$, which is not strongly-normalizing.

Restricting conversion under recursors is not enough: let $A = (\lambda[x : \mathbf{nat}].\, f(x))\, t$, in which f is defined as above. If we allow t to be convertible to $\mathbf{0}$ and $\mathbf{S}\,\mathbf{0}$, since $A \to_\beta f(t)$, we are back to the previous example. We called *strong* such problematic terms. Of course, we want a syntactic characterization of non-strong terms. The following lemma gives one which is convenient for its use in the context of dependent data types:

Lemma 1. *Terms headed by constructor and inductive symbols (hence $\mathbf{0}$, $\mathbf{S}$, $\mathbf{nil}$, $\mathbf{cons}$, $\mathbf{list}$) are non-strong. We call them* weak.

We now define the $\mathcal{T}$-congruence $\equiv_E^b$:

Definition 11. *The $\mathcal{T}$-congruence $\equiv_E^b$, $b \in \{\top, \bot\}$ is given in Figure 1.*

The $\mathcal{T}$-congruence is defined as follows. First, our notion of $(\mathcal{T}, E)$-consequence is included through the [DED] rules. In the case of a weak conversion, the [DED$_\bot$] rule does not use extracted equations, and uses the empty relation for aliens comparison. The rules [•], [LAM], [ELIM] and [PROD] are congruence rules. Of course, when crossing a binder annotated with an extracted equation, the set of available equations must be updated (this was already the case in [13]). Note also that in the definition of conversion for recursors, the term in deconstructing position can only be converted using weak conversion. There are two rules for application. As explained, applications headed with a weak term can be

$$[\textsc{Refl}]\ \frac{}{t \equiv^b_E t} \qquad\qquad [\textsc{Trans}]\ \frac{t_1 \equiv^b_E t_2 \quad t_2 \equiv^b_E t_3}{t_1 \equiv^b_E t_3}$$

$$[\textsc{App}_\mathcal{W}]\ \frac{t,u\ \text{are weak terms}}{}\ \frac{t \equiv^\top_E u \quad \forall i, t_i \equiv^\top_E u_i}{t\,t_1\cdots t_n \equiv^\top_E u\,u_1\cdots u_n} \qquad [\textsc{App}_\mathcal{S}]\ \frac{\forall i, t_i \equiv^\perp_E u_i}{t_1\cdots t_n \equiv^b_E u_1\cdots u_n}$$

$$[\textsc{Lam}]\ \frac{U \equiv^b_E U' \quad v \equiv^b_E v'}{\lambda[x:U].v \equiv^b_E \lambda[x:U'].v'} \qquad [\textsc{Prod}]\ \frac{U \equiv^b_E U' \quad v \equiv^b_E v'}{\forall(x:U).v \equiv^b_E \forall(x:U').v'}$$

$$[\textsc{Lam-}\mathcal{E}]\ \frac{U \equiv^b_E U' \quad v \equiv^b_{e::E} v' \quad e \equiv^b_E e'}{\lambda[x:^e U].v \equiv^b_E \lambda[x:^{e'} U'].v'} \quad [\textsc{Prod-}\mathcal{E}]\ \frac{U \equiv^b_E U' \quad v \equiv^b_{e::E} v' \quad e \equiv^b_E e'}{\forall(x:^e U).v \equiv^b_E \forall(x:^{e'} U').v'}$$

$$[\bullet]\ \frac{t \equiv^b_E t' \quad T \equiv^b_E T' \quad U \equiv^b_{e::E} U' \quad e \equiv^b_E e'}{\bullet[t:^e T].U \equiv^b_E \bullet[t':^{e'} T'].U'}$$

$$[\textsc{Eq}]\ \frac{\forall i, t_i \equiv^b_E u_i \quad \forall i, t'_i \equiv^b_E u'_i \quad e_1 = (C=C',[i\leftarrow t_i],[i\leftarrow t'_i]) \quad e_2 = (C=C',[i\leftarrow u_i],[i\leftarrow u'_i])}{e_1 \equiv^b_E e_2}$$

$$[\textsc{Ded}_\top]\ \frac{t=u\ \text{is a}\ (\mathcal{T},E)\text{-consequence modulo}\ \xleftrightarrow{*}\cdot\equiv^b_E\cdot\xleftrightarrow{*}}{t \equiv^\top_E u} \qquad [\textsc{Ded}_\perp]\ \frac{t=u\ \text{is a}\ (\mathcal{T},\emptyset)\text{-consequence modulo the empty relation}}{t \equiv^\perp_E u}$$

$$[\textsc{Elim}]\ \frac{t \equiv^\perp_E t' \quad Q \equiv^b_E Q' \quad f_0 \equiv^b_E f'_0 \quad f_S \equiv^b_E f'_S}{\mathrm{Elim}(t:Q)\{\vec{f}\} \equiv^b_E \mathrm{Elim}(t':Q')\{\vec{f'}\}}$$

Fig. 1. CoqMT $\mathcal{T}$-congruence relation

converted using strong conversion. Otherwise, weak conversion must be used. Finally, the rule [EQ] is used to convert extracted equations: two extracted equations are convertible if they contain the same algebraic cap and have pairwise convertible aliens.

The conversion $\sim_E$ of CoqMT, w.r.t. a set E of extracted equations, is simply defined as $(\xleftrightarrow{*} \cdot \equiv^\top_E \cdot \xleftrightarrow{*})$.

1.3 CoqMT Typing

Contrary to our previous calculus [13], extracted equations are now directly accessible via annotations. Although this greatly simplifies the definition of the calculus by removing the CCIC complex notion of extraction, one must verify some consistency properties between the extracted equations and the terms which are annotated with. For example, from the term $x \doteq \mathbf{S}\,t$, one wants $x = \mathbf{S}\,y$ to be a valid extractable equation (with y abstracting t), but not $x = \mathbf{0}$. Allowing the extraction of $x = \mathbf{0}$ from $x \doteq \mathbf{S}\,t$ would allow users to prove $x \doteq \mathbf{S}\,t$ and $x \doteq \mathbf{0}$ without the use of any assumptions, thus leading to a non-consistent system.

Definition 12 (E-extractability). *Let $(C_1 = C_2, \mathcal{I}, \mathcal{J})$ be an extracted equation and T a term. We say that e is extractable from T if T is convertible, using $\sim_E$, to $C_1[\mathcal{I}] \doteq C_2[\mathcal{J}]$.*

Before defining our typing judgment, we are left to define our typing environments. As usual, typing environments bind variables to types, but with two modifications. First, as for λ-expressions and dependent products, bindings can be optionally annotated with extracted equations. Second, typing environments will also contain equation markers.

Definition 13 (Typing environment). *The set of typing environments is defined by $\Gamma, \Delta ::= \epsilon \mid \Gamma, [x :^{e?} T] \mid \Gamma, \bullet[t :^{e?} T]$.*

Definition 14 (Typing judgement). *For any environment Γ, let $\sim_\Gamma$ defined as $\sim_E$ where E is the set of all extractable equations appearing in Γ. Typing rules of COQMT are given in Figure 2.*

The rules for $\doteq$ and **nat** symbols are identical to the ones of CIC - for lack of space, we omit the rules for lists. Several modifications are made to the pure Calculus of Constructions rules. First, when adding to a typing environment Γ a new binding annotated by an extracted equation e (rules [WEAK], [WEAK-•] and [VAR]), we check that e is indeed extractable, hence making sure that we do not extract inconsistent equations from a consistent typing environment.

Moreover, the rule for application has been duplicated, as for β-reduction. For the two rules, we allow the left hand-side to have a product type modulo the presence of equation markers. This is for the non-interference of reduction as discussed before and is very similar to the equation markers we found in the (β) and $(\beta\text{-}\mathcal{E})$ in the definition of $\rightarrow$ rules. The second one, [APP-$\mathcal{E}$], handles the case where a term annotated by an equation is applied. As for the $(\beta\text{-}\mathcal{E})$ rule which handles the case where an extracted equation annotating a λ-abstraction has disappeared, [APP-$\mathcal{E}$] handles the case of for dependent products with the very same technique.

We also add two rules for typing equation markers. One is a weakening style rule and allows the user to add extracted equations to the environment. The second allows markers to be moved from terms and types to the environment.

The conversion rule is of course updated to use the relation $\sim_\Gamma$.

2   Meta-theoretical Properties

The meta-theory of our calculus is carried out in a similar way as that of CC or CIC. As usual, the logical consistency is proved in three steps. First, we prove the *subject reduction* property stating that the reduction relation is correct w.r.t. typing: if $\Gamma \vdash t : T$ and $t \rightarrow t'$, then $\Gamma \vdash t' : T$. In the second step, we prove that the reduction relation is strongly normalizing for well-typed terms. In the last step, we prove that there exists a term which is non-typable in the empty environment.

$$[\textsc{Sort}] \ \frac{}{\vdash \star : \Box}$$

$$[\textsc{Var}] \ \frac{\Gamma \vdash T : s \qquad x \notin \mathrm{dom}(\Gamma) \qquad e? \text{ is extractable from } T}{\Gamma, [x :^{e?} T] \vdash x : T}$$

$$[\textsc{Weak}] \ \frac{\begin{array}{c} x \notin \mathrm{dom}(\Gamma) \\ e? \text{ is extractable from } V \\ \Gamma \vdash t : T \qquad \Gamma \vdash V : s \end{array}}{\Gamma, [x :^{e?} V] \vdash t : T}$$

$$[\textsc{Weak-}\bullet] \ \frac{\begin{array}{c} x \notin \mathrm{dom}(\Gamma) \\ e \text{ is extractable from } T \\ \Gamma \vdash t : T \qquad \Gamma \vdash u : U \end{array}}{\Gamma, \bullet[t :^{e} T] \vdash u : U}$$

$$[\textsc{App}] \ \frac{\Gamma \vdash u : U \qquad \Gamma \vdash t : \bullet \overrightarrow{[t :^{e} T]}. \forall (x : U).\, V}{\Gamma \vdash t\, u : \bullet \overrightarrow{[t :^{e} T]}.\, V\{x \leftarrow u\}}$$

$$[\textsc{App-}\mathcal{E}] \ \frac{\Gamma \vdash u : U \qquad \Gamma \vdash t : \bullet \overrightarrow{[t :^{e} T]}. \forall (x :^{e} U).\, V}{\Gamma \vdash t\, u : \bullet \overrightarrow{[t :^{e} T]}. \bullet [u :^{e} U].\, V\{x \leftarrow u\}}$$

$$[\textsc{Lam}] \ \frac{\begin{array}{c} \Gamma, [x :^{e?} U] \vdash v : V \\ \Gamma \vdash \forall (x :^{e?} U).\, V : s \end{array}}{\Gamma \vdash \lambda[x :^{e?} U].\, v : \forall (x :^{e?} U).\, V}$$

$$[\textsc{Prod}] \ \frac{\Gamma \vdash U : s_1 \qquad \Gamma, [x :^{e?} U] \vdash V : s_2}{\Gamma \vdash \forall (x :^{e?} U).\, V : s_2}$$

$$[\bullet] \ \frac{\begin{array}{c} e \text{ is extractable from } T \\ \Gamma, \bullet[t :^{e} T] \vdash u : U \qquad \Gamma \vdash t : T \end{array}}{\Gamma \vdash \bullet[t :^{e} T].\, u : \bullet[t :^{e} T].\, U}$$

$$[\textsc{Conv}] \ \frac{\Gamma \vdash t : T \qquad \Gamma \vdash U : s \qquad T \sim_{\Gamma} U}{\Gamma \vdash t : U}$$

$$[\mathbf{0}] \ \frac{}{\mathbf{0} : \mathbf{nat}} \qquad [\mathbf{S}] \ \frac{}{\mathbf{S} : \mathbf{nat} \to \mathbf{nat}} \qquad [+] \ \frac{}{+: \mathbf{nat} \to \mathbf{nat} \to \mathbf{nat}} \qquad [\mathbf{nat}] \ \frac{}{\mathbf{nat} : \star}$$

$$[\textsc{Refl}] \ \frac{\Gamma \vdash t : T}{\Gamma \vdash \mathrm{refl}_T(t) : t \dot{=}_T t} \qquad [\textsc{Eq}] \ \frac{}{\Gamma \vdash \dot{=}: \forall (T : \star).\, T \to T \to \star}$$

$$[\textsc{Elim}] \ \frac{\Gamma \vdash t : \mathbf{nat} \qquad \Gamma, [x : \mathbf{nat}] \vdash Q : s \qquad \Gamma \vdash f_0 : Q\{x \leftarrow \mathbf{0}\} \qquad \Gamma \vdash f_S : \forall (y : \mathbf{nat}).\, Q\{x \leftarrow y\} \to Q\{x \leftarrow \mathbf{S}\, y\}}{\mathrm{Elim}(t : \lambda[x : \mathbf{nat}].\, Q)\{f_0, f_S\} : Q\{x \leftarrow t\}}$$

Fig. 2. CoqMT typing relation

2.1 Subject Reduction

The subject reduction proof requires the following property:

$$\forall (x :^{e} U).\, V \sim_E \forall (x :^{e'} U').\, V' \Rightarrow U \sim_E U' \wedge V \sim_{e::E} \wedge e \sim_E e'$$

called *product compatibility* [19]. Usually, conversion coincides with the closure by equivalence of reduction, and product compatibility is then an immediate consequence of the confluence property of reduction. In CCIC, product compatibility was obtained via a complex sequence of definitions and lemmas. It is much simpler here. The proof is structured as follows.

We first prove confluence of $\to$. The proof follows the method of Tait for β-reduction [20]: we define a parallel reduction $\Rightarrow$ s.t. $(\to^*) = (\Rightarrow^*)$, and prove its confluence as in Tait's proof. Let us give the definition for the case of (ι_0) reduction: $\mathrm{Elim}(t : Q)\{f_0, f_S\} \Rightarrow f_0'$ if $t \Rightarrow t'$, $f_0 \Rightarrow f_0'$ and $\mathbf{norm}(t') = \mathbf{0}$. We then prove the key property of $\mathcal{T}$-congruence, called *coherence* in [21]:

Lemma 2. *For any terms t, u, and set of extracted equation E, if $t \equiv^b_E u$ and $t \to t'$, then there exists a term u' s.t. $u \overset{\leq}{\to} u'$ and $t' \equiv^b_E u'$.*

Such a property is crucially based on the fact that our reduction is done modulo the theory. For example, the term $\mathrm{Elim}((x + (\mathbf{S}\,\mathbf{0})) + y : Q)\{f_0, f_S\}$ is convertible to $\mathrm{Elim}(\mathbf{S}\,(x + y) : Q)\{f_0, f_S\}$ and reducible using the (ι_S) rule. Thanks to the use of the **norm** function, we can conclude that $\sim_E$ is equal to $\overset{*}{\to} \cdot \equiv^\top_E \cdot \overset{*}{\leftarrow}$ (See Figure 3a), and then that $\sim_E$ is transitive (i.e. $\overset{*}{\to} \cdot \equiv^\top_E \cdot \overset{*}{\leftarrow}$ is transitive - see Figure 3b). Product compatibility for $\sim^*_E$ is then reduced to the product compatibility of $\sim_E$, which itself is reduced to the product compatibility of $\to$ and $\equiv^b_E$, two properties which are immediate.

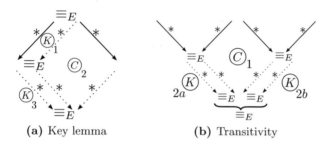

(a) Key lemma   (b) Transitivity

Fig. 3. Transitivity of $\to$ - (C) is application of confluence, and (K) of our key lemma

2.2   Strong Normalization

In [13], we prove strong normalization of CCIC by an embedding into a variation of the Calculus of Algebraic Constructions [6,7]. Due to the use of reduction modulo, this is no more possible. Proof of strong normalization of $\to$ is now obtained by adapting the proof for CIC to our calculus, which is based on Coquand and Gallier's extension to the Calculus of Constructions of Tait and Girard's computability predicate technique. The idea is to define an interpretation for each type and to prove that each well-typed term belongs to the interpretation of its type. The main difficulty is to define the interpretation for type constructed by induction. For the case of natural number, the CIC interpretation of $\mathrm{Elim}(t : Q)\{f_0, f_S\}$ is

> the one of f_0 if $t \to_\downarrow \mathbf{0}$
> the one of $f_S\, u\, \mathrm{Elim}(u : Q)\{f0, f_S\}$ if $t \to_\downarrow \mathbf{S}\, u$
> an arbitrary value otherwise

We simply adapt this definition by modifying the condition $t \to_\downarrow \mathbf{0}$ (resp. $t \to_\downarrow \mathbf{S}\, u$) by $t \to_\downarrow u$ with **norm**$(u) = \mathbf{0}$ (resp. $t \to_\downarrow v$ with **norm**$(v) = \mathbf{S}\, u$). The rest of the proof is the same. The interpretation of the equation marker $\bullet[t :^e T].\, U$ is that of U. From strong normalization, we then deduce consistency as usual, by proving that there is no normal proof of false in the empty environment:

Theorem 1. *If $\Gamma \vdash t : T$, then t is strongly normalizable. Hence, there is no proof of $\mathbf{0} \doteq \mathbf{S\,0}$ in the empty environment.*

Here, the choice of $\mathbf{0} \doteq \mathbf{S\,0}$ follows from the fact that $\neg(\mathbf{0} \sim_\epsilon \mathbf{S\,0})$. (Remember that ϵ is the empty sequence).

2.3 Decidability

Decidability is split in two parts. First, assuming decidability of the conversion relation, we shows decidability of the typing judgement. We define a syntax oriented (hence decidable) relation $\Gamma \vdash_i t : T$ s.t. if $\Gamma \vdash t : T$ then $\Gamma \vdash_i t : T'$ with $T \sim_\Gamma^* T'$. The definition of $\vdash_i$ is usually done by removing the conversion rule from [CONV] and integrating it in the rules for application (See Figure 4). All this is routine.

$$[\text{APP}]\ \frac{\Gamma \vdash u : U' \qquad U \sim_\Gamma U'}{\Gamma \vdash t : \bullet[\overrightarrow{t :^e T}].\forall(x : U).V}{\Gamma \vdash t\,u : \bullet[\overrightarrow{t :^e T}].V\{x \leftarrow u\}} \qquad [\text{APP-}\mathcal{E}]\ \frac{\Gamma \vdash u : U' \qquad U \sim_\Gamma U'}{\Gamma \vdash t : \bullet[\overrightarrow{t :^e T}].\forall(x :^e U).V}{\Gamma \vdash t\,u : \bullet[\overrightarrow{t :^e T}].\bullet[u :^e U].V\{x \leftarrow u\}}$$

Fig. 4. Application rule for $\vdash_i$

Second, we consider convertibility of well-formed (hence strongly normalizing) terms. We first slightly modify the $\mathcal{T}$-congruence by i) requiring maximal algebraic cap in rule [DED$_b$], and ii) restrict the [APP] rules to non pre-algebraic terms. This does not change the obtained relation, but allows us to remove [TRANS], hence obtaining a syntax directed definition. (On the other hand, our initial formulation eased the meta-theoretical study) Finally, using again the key lemma used for subject reduction, we can prove that COQMT conversion can be decomposed in a reduction phase followed by a $\mathcal{T}$-congruence phase:

Lemma 3. *Let t and u be two strongly normalized terms and E a set of extracted equations composed only of strongly normalized terms. Then $t \sim_E u$ if and only if $t_\downarrow \equiv_{E_\downarrow}^b u_\downarrow$ - where $w_\downarrow$ is the normal form of w.*

Theorem 2. *The conversion $\sim$ is decidable on strongly normalizing terms.*

3 Implementation

A new version of COQ based on this work, called COQMT, is available on the author's website[2]. COQMT allows a user to dynamically load any decision procedure for a first-order theory in the conversion of the system. It does not implement yet the mechanism of equations extraction. Full commented examples can be found in the source release of COQMT (*/test-suite/dp/**).

---

[2] http://pierre-yves.strub.nu/research/coqmt/

4   Conclusions and Future Work

We have defined a new version of the Calculus of Congruent Inductive Constructions, called CoqMT, allowing the use of decision procedures in its conversion rule.

We drastically simplified the definition of CCIC, notably by removing almost all ad-hoc restrictions introduced in [13]. In particular, based on this, a formal proof of CoqMT in Coq is in development. As of today, an implementation of CoqMT allowing the use of decision procedures in the conversion rule is available. The implementation of the extraction mechanism is to be released soon. More details, along with all sources, can be found on the author's page. We now discuss interesting extension of this work.

We expect to remove the presence of equation markers in types by the use of sub-typing. In our work, non-interference of equation markers has only be addressed, in an ad-hoc manner, for β-reduction and typing of application. Extending this ad-hoc method to all constructions of the calculus would lead to an over-complicated definition. Introducing sub-typing s.t. $\bullet[t :^e T]. A$ is a sub-type of A could lead to a calculus where a term of type $\forall(x : A). B$ is applicable to a term of type $\bullet[t :^e T]. A$ for free.

Reduction modulo theory $\mathcal{T}$ does not use any extracted equation so that inconsistencies at the extracted equations level do not break logical consistency. A work-around would be to only use, during reduction, a subset of extracted equations which is consistent by construction. Although the idea is quite straightforward, due to the high dependency between weak and strong conversion, reduction modulo and consistency of extracted equation, we have not yet succeeded to obtain a workable definition. We hope solving this problem in a near future.

The link between first order theories and Coq symbols is a one-to-one mapping: each first-order symbol is mapped to a Coq constructor. We want to add a notion of view to break this restriction. This would allow e.g. to map Presburger arithmetic to a Coq binary representation of natural numbers. This could be extended to view dependent data-types as first order data-types with constraints. For example, assuming we embed the first-order theories of lists along with Presburger arithmetic in CoqMT, Coq dependent lists could be viewed by the theories as standard lists plus arithmetical constraints on their lengths.

Finally, we want to extend the extraction from equations to arbitrary first-order propositions (like ordering on natural numbers), or even add the ability to extract first-order formulas.

Acknowledgment. We thank Gilles Barthe and Jean-Pierre Jouannaud for useful discussions.

References

1. Coq-Development-Team: The Coq Proof Assistant Reference Manual - Version 8.2. INRIA, INRIA Rocquencourt, France (2009), http://coq.inria.fr/
2. Coquand, T., Huet, G.: The Calculus of Constructions. Information and Computation 76(2-3), 95–120 (1988)

3. Coquand, T., Paulin-Mohring, C.: Inductively defined types. In: Martin-Löf, P., Mints, G. (eds.) COLOG 1988. LNCS, vol. 417, pp. 50–66. Springer, Heidelberg (1990)

4. Werner, B.: Une Théorie des Constructions Inductives. PhD thesis, University of Paris VII (1994)

5. Giménez, E.: Structural recursive definitions in type theory. In: Larsen, K.G., Skyum, S., Winskel, G. (eds.) ICALP 1998. LNCS, vol. 1443, pp. 397–408. Springer, Heidelberg (1998)

6. Blanqui, F.: Definitions by rewriting in the calculus of constructions. Mathematical Structures in Computer Science 15(1), 37–92 (2005); Journal version of LICS 2001

7. Blanqui, F.: Inductive types in the calculus of algebraic constructions. Fundamenta Informaticae 65(1-2), 61–86 (2005); Journal version of TLCA 2003

8. Stehr, M.: The Open Calculus of Constructions: An equational type theory with dependent types for programming, specification, and interactive theorem proving (part I and II). Fundamenta Informaticae 68 (2005)

9. Oury, N.: Extensionality in the calculus of constructions. In: Hurd, J., Melham, T. (eds.) TPHOLs 2005. LNCS, vol. 3603, pp. 278–293. Springer, Heidelberg (2005)

10. Hofmann, M., Streicher, T.: The groupoid model refutes uniqueness of identity proofs. In: LICS, pp. 208–212. IEEE Computer Society, Los Alamitos (1994)

11. Nelson, G., Oppen, D.C.: Fast decision procedures based on congruence closure. J. ACM 27(2), 356–364 (1980)

12. Blanqui, F., Jouannaud, J., Strub, P.: Building decision procedures in the calculus of inductive constructions. In: Duparc, J., Henzinger, T.A. (eds.) CSL 2007. LNCS, vol. 4646, pp. 328–342. Springer, Heidelberg (2007)

13. Strub, P.Y.: Type Theory and Decision Procedures. PhD thesis, École Polytechnique (2008)

14. Barendregt, H.P.: Lambda calculi with types, pp. 117–309 (1992)

15. Dershowitz, N., Jouannaud, J.P.: Rewrite systems. In: Handbook of Theoretical Computer Science. Formal Models and Sematics (B), vol. B, pp. 243–320 (1990)

16. Courtieu, P.: Normalized types. In: Fribourg, L. (ed.) CSL 2001 and EACSL 2001. LNCS, vol. 2142, pp. 554–569. Springer, Heidelberg (2001)

17. Petcher, A., Stump, A.: Deciding joinability modulo ground equations in operational type theory. In: Proof Search in Type Theories, PSTT (2009)

18. Shostak, R.E.: An efficient decision procedure for arithmetic with function symbols. J. of the Association for Computing Machinery 26(2), 351–360 (1979)

19. Barbanera, F., Fernández, M., Geuvers, H.: Modularity of strong normalization and confluence in the algebraic-lambda-cube. In: LICS, pp. 406–415. IEEE Computer Society, Los Alamitos (1994)

20. Barendregt, H.P.: The Lambda Calculus. Its Syntax and Semantics. North-Holland, Amsterdam (1984) (revised edition)

21. Jouannaud, J.P., Kirchner, H.: Completion of a set of rules modulo a set of equations. SIAM J. Comput. 15(4), 1155–1194 (1986)

The Ackermann Award 2010

Johann A. Makowsky and Damian Niwinski

Members of EACSL Jury for the Ackermann Award

The sixth **Ackermann Award** was to be presented at this CSL'10, held in Brno, Czech Republic. This is the fourth year the EACSL Ackermann Award is generously sponsored. Our sponsor for the period of 2010-2012 is the Kurt Gödel Society (KGS). Besides its financial support of the Ackermann Award the KGS also commited itself to inviting the receiver of the Award for a special lecture to be given in Vienna.

Eligible for the 2010 **Ackermann Award** were PhD dissertations in topics specified by the EACSL and LICS conferences, which were formally accepted as Ph.D. theses at a university or an equivalent institution between 1.1. 2008 and 31.12. 2009. The Jury received 5 nominations for the **Ackermann Award 2010**. The candidates came from 5 different countries in Europe, South America and Asia and received their degrees in 5 different countries in Europe, South America and Israel.

The topics covered the full range of Logic and Computer Science as represented by the LICS and CSL Conferences. All the submissions were of very high standard and contained outstanding results in their particular domain. In the past, the Jury always reached a consensus to give one or more than one award.

Decision of the Jury

In spite of the extremely high quality of the nominated theses, the Jury finally, and almost unanimously, decided

not to give an Ackermann Award in 2010.

Nevertheless, the Jury wishes to congratulate all the nominated candidates for their outstanding work. The Jury encourages them to continue their scientific careers, and hopes to see more of their work in the future.

A few words are in order the explain the Jury's decision. Since the creation of the Ackermann Award in 2004, the Jury consisted of 7-10 members chosen among the board members of EACSL, LICS and among eminent researchers of the Logic in Computer Science community. After the first two years, every year some of the Jury members were replaced by new ones. Our intention was to gradually renew the Jury, and at the same time we wanted to maintain the high standards of the evaluation process. All Jury members had access to the records of the decision-making process of the previous years. In these six years of the existence of the Ackermann Award over 60 theses have been nominated and discussed by the Jury. Out of these, 10 theses were chosen for the Ackermann Award. It would

A. Dawar and H. Veith (Eds.): CSL 2010, LNCS 6247, pp. 544–546, 2010.

be unreasonable to expect that theses marking exceptional breakthroughs could be produced every year. This year the Jury decided that it was more important to maintain the established high standards of the Ackermann Award than to just choose one or more of the nominated theses as the winner/s of the Ackermann Award. We would like to emphasize that this decision does not imply that the nominations this year were weaker than in the past. Most of the nominations this year were at the same level as many of the shortlisted nominations in the previous years. Yet none of them had the additional extra quality required for the Ackermann Award.

The Ackermann Award

The EACSL Board decided in November 2004 to launch the EACSL Outstanding Dissertation Award for Logic in Computer Science, the **Ackermann Award**, The award[1]. is named after the eminent logician Wilhelm Ackermann (1896-1962), mostly known for the Ackermann function, a landmark contribution in early complexity theory and the study of the rate of growth of recursive functions, and for his coauthorship with D. Hilbert of the classic *Grundzüge der Theoretischen Logik*, first published in 1928. Translated early into several languages, this monograph was the most influential book in the formative years of mathematical logic. In fact, Gödel's completeness theorem proves the completeness of the system presented and proved sound by Hilbert and Ackermann. As one of the pioneers of logic, W. Ackermann left his mark in shaping logic and the theory of computation.

The **Ackermann Award** is presented to the recipients at the annual conference of the EACSL. The Jury is entitled to give more than one award per year. The award consists of a diploma, an invitation to present the thesis at the CSL conference, the publication of the abstract of the thesis and the citation in the CSL proceedings, and travel support to attend the conference.

The Jury

The Jury for the **Ackermann Award 2010** consisted of ten members, three of them ex officio, namely the president and the vice-president of EACSL, and one member of the LICS organizing committee.

The members of the Jury were A. Atserias (Barcelona, Spain) R. Alur (Philadelphia, USA) J. van Benthem (Amsterdam, The Netherlands), T. Coquand (Gothenburg, Sweden) P.-L. Curien (Paris, France) A. Dawar (Cambridge, U.K., Vice-president of EACSL) A. Durand (Paris, France) J.A. Makowsky (Haifa, Israel, Chair of the Jury and Member of the EACSL Board), D. Niwinski (Warsaw, Poland, President of EACSL) and G. Plotkin (Edinburgh, U.K., LICS Organizing Committee).

---

[1] Details concerning the Ackermann Award and a biographic sketch of W. Ackermann was published in the CSL'05 proceedings and can also be found at http://www.eacsl.org/award.html.

Previous winners of the Ackermann Award

2005, Oxford:
Mikołaj Bojańczyk from Poland,
Konstantin Korovin from Russia, and
Nathan Segerlind from the USA.

2006, Szeged:
Balder ten Cate from The Netherlands, and
Stefan Milius from Germany.

2007, Lausanne
Dietmar Berwanger from Germany and Romania,
Stéphane Lengrand from France, and
Ting Zhang from the People's Republic of China.

2008, Bertinoro:
Krishnendu Chatterjee from India.

2009, Coimbra:
Jakob Nordström from Sweden.

Detailed reports on their work appeared in the CSL'05, CSL'06, CSL'07, CSL'08
and CSL'09 proceedings, and are also available via the EACSL homepage.

Author Index

Accattoli, Beniamino 381
Alenda, Régis 52

Baaz, Matthias 67
Bagan, Guillaume 80
Barthwal, Aditi 95
Basin, David 1
Benedikt, Michael 110
Bianco, Alessandro 125
Blass, Andreas 140
Burel, Guillaume 155

Carraro, Alberto 170
Chaudhuri, Kaustuv 185
Chen, Yijia 200
Churchill, Martin 215
Coecke, Bob 230
Cook, Stephen 245
Cremers, Cas 1

Degorre, Aldric 260
Dershowitz, Nachum 140
Doyen, Laurent 260
Durand, Arnaud 80

Ehrhard, Thomas 170
Eickmeyer, Kord 275
Espírito Santo, José 290

Fermüller, Christian G. 67
Filiot, Emmanuel 80
Finkbeiner, Bernd 305
Fiore, Marcelo 320
Flum, Jörg 200
Fontes, Lila 245
Fumex, Clément 336

Ganzow, Tobias 366
Gauwin, Olivier 80
Gentilini, Raffaella 260
Ghani, Neil 336
Grädel, Erich 19
Grohe, Martin 275
Gurevich, Yuri 140

Hetzl, Stefan 351
Hur, Chung-Kil 320

Johann, Patricia 336

Kaiser, Łukasz 366
Kesner, Delia 381
Krajíček, Jan 22
Krokhin, Andrei 32
Kuncak, Viktor 34
Kuske, Dietrich 396

Laird, James 215
Ley, Clemens 110
Liu, Jiamou 396
Lohmann, Peter 411
Lohrey, Markus 396

Makowsky, Johann A. 544
Martin, Barnaby 426
Martin, Jos 426
Mogavero, Fabio 125
Murano, Aniello 125

Nenov, Yavor 439
Niwinski, Damian 544
Nordvall Forsberg, Fredrik 454
Norrish, Michael 95

O'Hearn, Peter W. 49
Olivetti, Nicola 52

Perdrix, Simon 230
Piskac, Ruzica 34
Platzer, André 469
Pous, Damien 484
Pratt-Hartmann, Ian 439
Puppis, Gabriele 110

Raskin, Jean-François 260
Rybalchenko, Andrey 51

Salibra, Antonino   170
Schewe, Sven   305
Schwentick, Thomas   499
Schwind, Camilla   52
Setzer, Anton   454
Sternagel, Christian   514
Strub, Pierre-Yves   529
Suter, Philippe   34

Thiemann, René   514
Tishkovsky, Dmitry   52
Toruńczyk, Szymon   260

Vollmer, Heribert   411

Zeume, Thomas   499

Printing: Mercedes-Druck, Berlin
Binding: Stein+Lehmann, Berlin